Wine Spectator's

CALIFORNIA WINE

by James Laube

A COMPREHENSIVE GUIDE TO THE WINERIES,

WINES, VINTAGES AND VINEYARDS, WITH RATINGS

AND TASTING NOTES FOR **5000** WINES

WINE SPECTATOR PRESS • NEW YORK

©1999 by Wine Spectator Press/M. Shanken Communications, Inc.

Second Edition. First Edition published in 1995.

All rights reserved under the Pan-American and International Copyright Conventions

Printed in the United States of America

9 8 7 6 5 4 3 2 1
Digit on the right indicates the number of this printing

ISBN 1-881659-56-9

Published by M. Shanken Communications, Inc.
387 Park Avenue South
New York, NY 10016

Illustrations by Dorothy Reinhardt
Maps by Richard L. Thompson

For subscriptions to *Wine Spectator*, please call: (800) 752-7799 in the U.S. and Canada,
or write:
PO Box 37367
Boone, IA 50037-0367

Visit our Web site at: www.winespectator.com

Distributed by Running Press Book Publishers
125 South Twenty-second Street
Philadelphia, PA 19103-4399

FOR WINE LOVERS EVERYWHERE.

FOREWORD

◆

When the first edition of this book was published in 1995, I was so confident of its success that I predicted it would quickly become the Webster's of California wine. At the risk of sounding boastful, my confidence was well founded. *California Wine* did become a classic in its field and one of the best-selling wine books of all time.

Now, James Laube has updated this classic to keep pace with the fast-changing world of California wine. This new edition is fully revised, with new tasting notes, new vintage ratings, 100 new wineries described and a host of other improvements. One especially helpful addition is a directory of winery phone numbers, fax numbers, addresses, email addresses and Web sites. It's an all-around guide that you can trust when deciding which wines to buy.

The value of *California Wine* derives directly from the integrity and knowledge of its author. As a journalist for *Wine Spectator* magazine, full-time since 1983, James Laube has earned the respect of millions of wine lovers throughout the world. Laube is *Wine Spectator's* leading critic on California wine. His authoritative views are grounded in experience; he blind-tastes more than 5,000 bottles of California wine per year. This book draws on his comprehensive understanding of wine and makes this complicated subject easy to comprehend.

I wish this book had been available when I started drinking and collecting California wine 25 years ago. It would have saved me from a lot of false starts and frustrations. Today, many more books are available, but none of them provides the combination of expert opinion, comprehensive information and easy readability that *California Wine* does.

Laube tells the stories of more than 700 wineries and wine brands. Then he makes waves by rating the wineries and more than 5,000 individual wines. This book provides blanket coverage of California Cabernet Sauvignon and Chardonnay, but it doesn't stop there. Who makes the best Pinot Noir from year to year? How should you store your wine? What are the best older vintages?

For all the details that the serious student of wine will find invaluable, this book is not for snobs. It is written in a deliberately accessible style to help you learn as much as possible about California wine. Maps show where the wineries and key vineyards are located. Introductory chapters help you understand what the various types of wine taste like, how wine is made and how to build an intelligent wine collection, among other topics.

I know of no writer other than James Laube, and no organization other than *Wine Spectator*, that could have done this book right. I am proud to present this new edition of *California Wine*.

MARVIN R. SHANKEN
Editor and Publisher, *Wine Spectator*

v

DISCOVERING CALIFORNIA WINE

❖

After 21 years of writing about wine, I am as amazed as everyone else by the accelerated growth in production and popularity of California wine. There are hundreds of wineries and thousands of brands that are multiplying at a staggering pace. Each year, there are perhaps 6,000 new wines released to the market. New wineries are being built, while only a few actually close, and even these end up being reopened by a new owner. Vineyards are constantly being bought, sold, planted and replanted at a breakneck pace. Winemakers are continually rethinking their vineyards—what they have planted and why—and how they can make better wines by fine-tuning their techniques. New vintages are being released, other vintages are maturing, and still others are fading. All of this adds up to an Internet-paced business that provides us with an astonishing array of different wine choices.

My purpose in writing this book is to provide a comprehensive guide to California wine as I see it. In one sense, *California Wine* is a diary of notes, observations, recollections, analysis, opinion and conjecture. It presents the results of 21 years of research, 50,000 tasting notes, thousands of interviews and discussions with winemakers, and many miles of travel throughout the Golden State's vineyards. This edition is completely revised and updated, with lots of new facts, figures, tasting notes and ratings.

This book is built around the information I find most interesting and relevant. It reflects my belief that our desire to learn more about wine is driven by our wine-drinking experiences. That is, when we find a wine that excites our taste buds, it stimulates a greater curiosity

about why this wine tastes so good. The process of discovery often begins at a very simple level: the mere enjoyment of a delicious wine and whatever taste sensations it provides.

Your palate, and your palate alone, is the final judge of a wine's quality, for no one knows your tastes better than you. Even at the most basic level, a wine is good or it isn't. It pleases or it doesn't. When it pleases, then you're on to something. When it doesn't, it can easily be replaced by another. When a wine excites, then the questions arise and your curiosity is stimulated. What is the grape type, and where was it grown? How was it made? Why is it different from other red or white wines? Should I drink it now or cellar it? How long will it age?

Once begun, this process of discovery leads to an almost endless succession of steps backward. Even after you have tracked a wine back to its most specific origins, to the very plot of land where its grapes were grown, to the year they were picked and vinified and the climatic circumstances of that year, further mysteries remain. Exactly what is it that makes one wine so different from the next, or one vintage so different from another, even when the grapes are grown in seemingly identical sites under seemingly identical circumstances. Why does one grape variety grow so well in one appellation or climate, yet so poorly in another? Why do some wines age so gloriously and others so miserably?

Fortunately, no one can answer all of these questions all the time, or much of the mystery of wine would be gone. Professionals who have studied wine their entire lives still seek answers to these intricate puzzles and how they interact with and relate to each other. A wine's character is the result of a complex set of circumstances involving grape type, soil, climate and vinification technique. Researching these details should be fun. It's like detective work, gathering evidence and piecing together clues about a wine's origins and style and then trying to define what it is that makes that wine unique. It is this kind of wine discovery that drives our curiosity to learn more.

As your curiosity takes hold, you'll find that wine encompasses many subjects. It involves sensory evaluation, using sight, smell and taste to critique wine. It involves geography, geology, chemistry, marketing, even complex laws regarding labeling. The most fascinating part of discovering wine for me is crisscrossing the state and learning about geography and climate and how it influences wine style and quality. You observe that it's cool and foggy—even chilly—in Russian River at midday in the summer, yet scorching hot as you drive inland to Alexander Valley, only 20 miles away. You discover the proximity of sandy soils to river beds, the clay flats and gusty winds of Carneros or Monterey County, or the low-lying fog that clings to the floor of the twisting Santa Ynez Valley. You notice the steep hillsides and rocky terrain of the mountains and later learn that hillside vines yield more austere wines because the vines are naturally stressed, there's good drainage and the elevation helps protect against the threat of spring frosts. And as you descend to the valley below, you discover that it is cooler on the mountain top than on the valley floor. You experience the changes in temperature as you shed your sweatshirt in he morning, find your shorts and T-shirt for the afternoon, then wish you'd brought a jacket as you dine outdoors in the evening and the cool night air blows off the chilly waters of the churning Pacific Ocean.

This detective work, this process of discovery, has led to the growth in popularity of California wine and contributed to its rise in quality. As a fast-growing, well-educated, upwardly mobile and financially able generation of wine lovers emerged in the 1960s, 1970s, 1980s and 1990s, it has created synergies between supply and demand, creativity and innovation, curiosity and education. At times there are imbalances, as nature intervenes to influence supply, making one year's crop larger or better than the next or previous year's. In much the same way, the economy seems to stretch or shrink the consumer's buying power from year to year.

Today's California wine drinker is already well informed, educated, sophisticated and opinionated. Still, good advice always comes in handy. This book is written for wine lovers—whether young and inexperienced, seeking guidance on what can be a complex and intriguing subject, or older and wiser, with great wine collections and knowledge to match. Throughout this book I have tried to focus on what is most likely to interest you, specifically the best wines and producers. This book contains chapters and discussions on different grape and wine types, appellations where different grapes are grown, vintages, how wine is made and the thought process involved, along with my thoughts on how California's fine wine industry emerged and evolved into what it is today. I offer general overviews of these subjects, simply as a way to stimulate further thought, since there are several well written books that deal with them in far greater detail. I've also offered my advice on making the most of your wine collection, whether you're new to wine or you're already an expert but would like to read one writers diary of tasting notes.

You won't find in this book a tasting note on every wine ever produced in California—that would be impossible—or a reference to every single winery or wine brand that's out there. Nor is this an attempt to tell all the stories behind the wineries and winemakers, or to analyze why and how the soils in Anderson Valley differ from those in Temecula. Nor will you find much discussion about wine chemistry, pHs, or trellising systems. What you will find here are a lot of useful reviews, ratings, comparisons and discussions about California wine. It is my hope that this book will make you a wiser and better-informed wine drinker—that it will give you greater insight and perspective when you're drinking or thinking about California wine.

James Laube
Napa, California

ACKNOWLEDGMENTS

❖

California Wine is completely revised and updated, but it is more than just that. We completely overhauled and retooled this book, down to the finest details. Authors get most of the credit for such a project, but no book of this magnitude could be organized, edited and completed without a great support team, which I had.

At the top of the list I'd like to thank my editor and publisher at *Wine Spectator*, Marvin R. Shanken. Marvin's been one of California wine's biggest fans and boosters, and were it not for him *California Wine* might not exist. I am grateful to him for all his enthusiasm and support.

Ann Berkhausen, Tom Garrett, Mary Ann Worobiec and Jennifer Groseclos were on the front lines from the start, working on improvements and revisions from the first edition, organizing the collection of data and the analyses of wineries, wines, appellations and vintages.

Ann worked on virtually every editing phase and detail and literally every word in the book. I appreciate having her trusted eyes—and her trusted staff, Amy Lyons, Steffanie Diamond Brown and Alan Richtmyer—always on the lookout for a misspelled word or crooked sentence, and for all of their time, energy and contributions to this new edition.

For Tom and MaryAnn, this—their first book—was an eye-opener, and they came through with flying colors. I'm sure they had no idea of what they were getting into

when they signed on for this project. As they now know, there's a lot of thinking and planning that goes into a book of this size and scope. They have both become better writers, editors and critics as a result. Jennifer's experience in book projects moved mountains of information, facts and figures, and made all of us look a little better.

When you work on a project such as *California Wine*, you are constantly thinking about each and every aspect of the book; it's an all-encompassing, time-consuming, thought-absorbing process in which you eat, sleep, drink and think about wine. Many of my colleagues at *Wine Spectator* contribute to this process and I'd like to thank them, too. Among those who deserve a special mention are Niki Singer and Jim Gordon. I'd also like to thank my good friend Greg Walter, who helped me create the first edition of *California Wine* and offered suggestions that made this edition even better.

On top of that, there are countless winemakers, growers, retailers, restaurateurs and consumers who have contributed to this book by sharing their knowledge (and sometimes their wines), and giving me ideas on how they view wine.

Last and never least, thanks to Cheryl, for all her loving support, and to our children, Dwight and Margaux. They all hung in there through some squeaky-tight deadlines, and for that I am grateful.

TABLE OF CONTENTS

HOW TO USE
THIS BOOK

❖

This is a tremendously exciting era in the history of California wine. At no time has California wine been better, the wine industry faster-paced or our wine-buying options greater. Yet greater choice in the marketplace can often mean greater confusion for the buyer, who may easily feel overwhelmed. No single source can give you all the information you need about wine, but a good reference book can point you in the right direction. This book is my effort to provide such a reference.

Wine reviews form the heart of this book. More than 5,000 individual tasting notes are included, and each reviewed wine is given a numerical rating on a scale of 50 to 100 points. Many of the wines reviewed in this book are still available, but some may be hard to find. (Once a vintage's best wines are identified—usually soon after their release—by critics or alert wine merchants, they sell rather quickly.) You'll come across them at auctions, at fine wine stores and on the best restaurant wine lists. Still others are stored away in collectors' wine cellars. How are they aging? Are they still worth collecting or drinking? Or are they old and tired, headed over the hill? In researching this book over the past 10 years, I've tracked virtually all the major wines produced in California, from Alicante to Zinfandel, compiling detailed vertical tasting notes on the most important wines and on some very rare ones too.

This book is not a buyer's guide, but rather a broad analysis of wineries, wines and the appellations they come from. Even as the book ages and the wines listed here get harder to find, I think you'll find it useful. The tasting notes will help when you need to look up an older

wine. Information about the vintages and which grapes grow best in which appellations will continue to be valuable, as will the maps. In time, vineyards will be replanted, often to different grape varieties, so things will both change and remain the same. New appellations will emerge and prominent vineyards will be sold to new owners. Despite that, the profiles found here will remain pertinent because vineyards like Martha's Vineyard in Napa Valley, Rochioli Vineyard in the Russian River Valley or Sanford & Benedict Vineyard in Santa Ynez Valley will still be talked about years from now, regardless of who owns them.

This book covers hundreds of wineries and wine brands, from the largest, which produce millions of cases, to the smallest family-owned ones, which put out just a few hundred cases. Each winery or brand entry identifies the owner, when the winery was founded, where it is located, whether it owns its own vineyards (and if so, which grapes it grows) or buys grapes, where the grapes are grown and who makes the wine. It also provides an overall winery performance rating of one to five stars. For details on the winery star ratings, see the section below entitled "Rating the Producers."

RESEARCH, TASTING NOTES AND RATINGS

Statistical information about the wineries was obtained from the wineries themselves. Most wineries are willing to provide detailed information about such things as vineyard acres owned, the types of grapes they have planted or where they buy their grapes. But some wineries consider this information top secret. Many wineries closely guard their production figures, often because they want you to think they make far less wine than they do. A winery that makes 100,000 or 1 million cases a year may fear being thought of as merely a wine factory. (For the purposes of this book, a winery that makes between 1,000 and 25,000 cases of wine a year is considered a small winery. Wineries that make 25,000 to 250,000 cases are mid-sized and wineries that make more than 250,000 cases are large.) It is important to understand that size has little to do with quality. There are many large wineries capable of producing hundreds of thousands of cases of wine that also make excellent wines, usually in limited quantities. Conversely, there are plenty of small wineries that make very ordinary wines. The quality of the vineyard is more important to overall wine quality than is the size of the winery, as we will see later.

Analyses of vintages, wine styles and appellations are based on my research as well as on interviews with winery owners, winemakers, grape growers and members of the wine trade. The boundaries and grape acreage statistics for the American Viticultural Areas come from the state and federal agencies that monitor them. Specific vineyard acreage figures change every year.

Most of the wine research comes from my 21 years of covering the California wine industry and from some 50,000 tasting notes compiled during the past decade; virtually all of the notes are based on tastings conducted in the past five years. There's no perfect way to taste wine. Most of the tasting analysis, notes and ratings come from blind tastings, in which objectivity is preserved because the identity of the wine is not known. I try to taste each wine as many times as possible so as to form the most accurate profile of the wine. Virtually every wine reviewed in this book has been tasted at least twice; many have been tasted three or four times. Others may have been tasted more than a dozen times. I also taste wines at wineries, with winemakers and owners present; this can be an instructive forum to learn specific details about a wine, vineyard, blend or style. I also taste wine just for fun, in totally informal, relaxed settings. Drinking a wine at dinner with friends can often provide insights and perspectives that add to my appreciation of it.

In general, when giving a wine a score, I give the wine the best review it has earned. I also try to retaste wines that have been inconsistent in tastings. Young

wines are more consistent that older wines; as wines age, bottle variation becomes a factor, and every bottle becomes in effect a singular and unique wine. I try to taste the major red wines—Cabernet Sauvignon, Merlot, Pinot Noir and Zinfandel—of the major producers from the barrel as well as from the bottle. This gives me an early look at the wines and the vintage, which helps shape and reinforce later impressions. However, none of the tasting notes in this book are based on barrel samples of unbottled wine. I typically taste 40 to 60 wines in a single day, two to three times a week—an average of 5,000 wines a year, give or take a few hundred, for the past 10 years.

For blind tastings, the wines are wrapped with paper to conceal their labels and identities. Price, appellation, producer, vintage and wine type are not factors in evaluating the wines. Price is only a factor in determining whether a wine is a good or poor value. White wines and sparkling wines are chilled before tasting to an appropriate level, 50 to 55 degrees Fahrenheit. Red wines are served at cool room temperature, usually 60 to 65 degrees.

ABOUT THE SCORING SYSTEM

After tasting a wine several times (and spitting it out into a bucket), I write a description of it and rate it from 50 to 100 points. I find the scale useful, simply because it clarifies how much (or how little) I liked the wine. I prefer the 100-point scale because it offers a wider range of scoring possibilities than a system of one to five stars. The latter might be adequate if there were only a few hundred wines to rate each year. But to successfully distinguish between several thousand wines each year, the 100-point scale is the better choice. I've come to think of the 100-point system as a pleasure scale, with the higher numbers representing the most pleasurable wines. However, no rating system is perfect.

A number can't tell you everything you need to know. You will also want to study a wine's description, which will specify its style, its flavors, its degree of balance or perhaps a unique feature. But when sorting through thousands of wines, sometimes remembering a number helps, just as it helps to remember a producer's name or the best vintages for different wines. Another way of looking at the 100-point scale is to say that a wine that gets 90 to 100 points earns an A grade, 80 to 89 a B,

70 to 79 a C, and 60 to 69 a D. Below 60 is failing.

Wines that score between 95 and 100 points I consider classics. These are wines that display uncommon richness, depth and complexity and rank among the very finest wines in the world. Wines that rate 90 to 94 I consider excellent, wines you would be more than happy to drink every day. Wines that rate 85 to 89 I consider very good. These are well-crafted wines that offer ripe, rich, complex flavors, true varietal character and often the potential to be outstanding. They also can represent very good value, but a few are high-priced, so beware. Wines that rate 80 to 84 I consider good everyday wines. They may not be as fruity or complex as more highly rated wines and they may have one or more minor flaws. They might be somewhat too tannic, or have strong earthy flavors mingling with the fruit, but they're not sufficiently off-putting to warrant a lower score.

Wines that rate 70 to 79 I consider fair, ordinary wines that may have noticeable flaws, such as too much tannin or a sour edge, or they may taste watery or diluted from lack of concentration. They may also be older wines that have started to decline in quality; it's important to remember this when looking at ratings for older wines. (In fact, rating older wines was one of the trickiest aspects of preparing this book. It is impossible to constantly retaste old wines; many are simply next to impossible to find. So for some older wines, I've kept my notes and rating, even though they may be dated. An older review is better than none.) Wines that rate 60 to 69 are flawed or really old wines that are best avoided. These wines are marked by serious defects, such as moldiness, excessively high acidity (or volatile acidity), gamy flavors, sulfur or spoilage defects. No winery would remain in business if it routinely produces wines that score in the 60s; even those that consistently rate in the 70s are in danger of losing their audience. Below 60, forget it.

There are plenty of ordinary wines being produced in California, but few truly awful ones reach mainstream markets. This is an indication that producers have the proper quality control mechanisms in place to isolate and eliminate wines with obvious defects before they reach the market. For this revised and updated edition, I've deliberately dropped many of the poorer wines, and have not closely tracked wines of ordinary quality. Instead, I've focused on the best wineries, wines and vineyards, believing that this will best serve your wine-buying interests.

RATING THE WINES; THE WINE LISTINGS

For each major bottling produced by a winery, I've assigned an overall rating of between one and five stars, with five stars being outstanding, four stars excellent, three stars very good, two stars fair or mildly satisfying and one star poor. I consider the individual wine star ratings the most important ratings in this book; they are my measure of overall quality and consistency.

The star ratings for a winery's major wines are listed near the top of that winery's entry in Chapter 7. Immediately below each major wine, you will find the approximate number of cases produced (as provided by the winery, or, in rare cases, as estimated by us), as well as an approximate current release price per bottle for that wine (again, usually the producer's estimated retail price). But *please note* that wine prices vary widely across the country, from state to state and from store to store; we provide prices for comparative purposes only. In some cases you will see the word "Discontinued" under a wine name instead of case and price figures. This indicates that the wine was no longer in production at press time—but recent vintages may still be available, and were recently a significant enough part of a winery's product line that a star rating seems justified.

Below the major wines and their ratings you will sometimes find another listing entitled "Also Produced." These wines either are too new to rate, or are produced in such tiny quantities (and will therefore have such limited availability) that a star rating seems irrelevant, or are wines for which I have no recent notes on which to base an informed opinion or honest advice.

Within the past five years, the sheer explosive growth in the number of both vineyard-designated and broader California appellation wines requires that some sort of differentiation be made between them. I have deliberately focused on the finest wines. Most of my time and emphasis has been directed specifically to vineyard-designated and estate-bottled wines, since these comprise most of the best wines and are the most likely to have the kind of track record that will indicate how well they might age and their potential for ultimate greatness. Wines that earn ★★ or ★★★ ratings do not rank among the best; I have included my impressions of these, including recent notes where applicable, but have not tried to track them with extended or vertical notes.

The five-star (★★★★★) wines are the ones I consider the finest California has to offer. If you were to build a dream cellar, these are the wines you'd want to focus on. In general, wines that have earned this highest designation

• have long, consistent track records for style and excellence (and the reds, such as Cabernet, Merlot, Pinot Noir, Syrah or Zinfandel, may be ageworthy as well);

• come from vineyards with long, consistent track records for distinctive styles and excellent quality;

• are from winemakers who have long and distinguished track records for excellence.

Four-star (★★★★) and three-star (★★★) wines are also well above average and are excellent choices. They too should be on your list of wines to look for. Four-star wines are often wines that are improving and reaching higher quality levels, and they may have just missed earning five stars. Many wines in this book fall into that category. In some instances these are wines that have been great in the past, but may have recently declined in quality. The same is true with three-star wines, which are, in general, good to very good. Bear in mind, that with many varietals such as Chenin Blanc, Gewürztraminer, Riesling and Sauvignon Blanc, a three-star entry may be the best available. These wines may also be less consistent than more highly rated ones, with a few lesser vintages mixed in among otherwise superb wines. In this category you may also find some higher-priced wines with inflated reputations; their quality does not justify their expense.

Two-star (★★) wines are considered fair, average, serviceable wines that are pleasant enough, but lack the extra dimensions and distinctive qualities to merit a higher rating. Here too, you may encounter some higher-priced wines that don't measure up in quality. One-star (★) wines are best avoided, not so much because they're necessarily awful, but because you have far better options available. These are wines of last resort. If you read this book carefully, you'll buy the right wines and dodge the dreary.

Rating the Producers

For each winery, I've studied the overall quality of its wines and given it a one- to five-star rating, or a sliding rating indicating a range of quality, using the same criteria outlined above. (When you're starting out, you need advice about which wineries consistently produce the highest-quality wines across the board.) For this edition, I've modified the producer star ratings to indicate a winery that rates in between, or one whose wines vary considerably in quality. For example, a winery designated ★★★★–★★★★★ merits an excellent to outstanding rating. A winery with ★★–★★★★ makes some wines which are fair, some which are good, and others which are outstanding. The winery analysis is based on my tasting research, as discussed above.

What to Look for in a Wine

The simple answer is pleasure. That's what wine is all about. For me, the world's great wines have several things in common. They are ripe, intense, well focused, richly flavored, deeply concentrated and impeccably balanced, and are either true expressions of the grape variety, or when blended, represent a distinctive style. These wines also have a sense of harmony, finesse and grace. Finally, they have long, lingering, complex aftertastes that keep reminding you of how great and well defined their flavors are. These factors apply to wines that are young, middle-aged or old. If you can find four or five of these qualities in any given wine, you'll find pleasure. What should you avoid in a wine? The absence of these qualities—which is sometimes a challenge to define. It is often easier to idenfify what you find and like in a wine than to describe what is missing. With experience, you'll learn to identify significant flaws: when a wine lacks ripe fruit flavors or concentration or is out of balance; when one characteristic, such as tannin, acidity or oak, dominates a wine to its detriment; when a wine is too woody or too chewy from tannins, giving it a coarse texture; or when its flavors simply don't appeal to you.

How the Book Is Organized

California Wine includes the following chapters:

• *Chapter 1: California Wine: Yesterday and Today.* This is an overview of the evolution of winegrowing in California. It presents the origins and early growth of California's wine culture, and the development of the commercial wine industry, leading to the current quest to make the finest wines in the world.

• *Chapter 2: Grapes and Wine Styles.* This chapter examines the different grape varieties, their characteristics, where they excel, how much of each is grown in California, and the wine styles that have emerged. Particular emphasis is placed on the main varieties— Cabernet, Chardonnay, Merlot, Pinot Noir and Zinfandel—but Sauvignon Blanc, Syrah and Petite Sirah are discussed, as are their various styles; recommendations about which producers make the best of each wine are provided as well. This chapter also discusses which appellations are best for different grapes.

• *Chapter 3: Appellations and Vineyards.* This chapter focuses on the main winegrowing appellations, how climate and soil influence the grapes and wine styles, and which grapes grow best (and worst) in each area. Included are vineyard acreage statistics and maps showing the wineries and vineyards within each appellation.

• *Chapter 4: How Wine Is Made.* This is a general discussion of how red, white, dessert and sparkling wines are made, and how appellation, varietal, barrel type and stylistic considerations combine to give a wine its unique personality.

• *Chapter 5: A Summary of the Vintages: 1933 to 1998.* Here I present a year-by-year analysis of the vintages for most major varietals, using a five-star rating system. This discussion addresses the growing season and harvest conditions as they affect the overall quality of wines. The main focus is on Cabernet, Chardonnay, Merlot, Pinot Noir and Zinfandel.

• *Chapter 6: Building Your Wine Collection.* This chapter talks about what you need to start a wine collection or cellar, offering some specific advice you'll want to consider, whether you're just starting out or already have a cellar full of wines.

• *Chapter 7: Winery Profiles and Tasting Notes.* This chapter forms the heart of the book. It lists alphabetically all the major and many of the minor wineries and brands, providing facts about each winery: who owns it, when it was founded, its acreage and the wines it produces, plus its overall ratings. Individual wine ratings, as well as a summary description of each wine and its style, are also found here, along with tasting notes and the 50- to 100-point ratings.

CHAPTER 1

CALIFORNIA WINE:
YESTERDAY AND TODAY

I t is easy to view California wine as a new and fast-paced industry that has arisen out of nowhere. We see in this business an amazing proliferation of new wines and wineries, new labels and appellations, new winemakers, new technology, new vintages—all a whirlwind of change. And while it is true that California wine today is indeed evolving at a brisk pace, its roots date back more than 200 years, to the time when the first European settlers arrived. Modern California wine retains some fascinating links to both the successes and failures of its past.

WINE AND CULTURE

The early settlers, led by Spanish missionaries, planted Mission grapes as they built a chain of missions on the California coast along what is now Highway 1 and part of Highway 101. As important as the Mission grape was to these pioneers, its origins remain a mystery. Like the settlers, it probably came from Spain. It proved a productive vine, better suited for sweet wines than dry, but still versatile; with its red skin, it was capable of producing both red and white wines. Later it was used for fortified wines and also distilled into brandy. Although the Mission grape is still grown in California, its acreage has

declined to 928 and it no longer plays an important role.

The first known vineyard was planted at Mission San Juan Capistrano near the coast mid-way between Los Angeles and San Diego in 1779, and it yielded its first wine—a sweet, fortified beverage—in 1782. After that, small vineyards were planted with increasing regularity at missions and on larger ranches. Father Junipero Serra, whose vision guided the formation of the mission system, moved back and forth along the coast and inland, reaching as far north as Sonoma. As he established missions, vineyards often followed, but apparently not always fast enough to suit him. Historian Thomas Pinney, in his excellent book, *A History of Wine in America* (1989), recounts that Serra "regularly complained of the difficulty of obtaining a supply of wine for the celebration of mass"; indeed, the Catholic Church was one of the first markets for wine in California. On the other hand, "Plenty of good wine during supper," remarked a member of explorer Jedediah Smith's party while in San Gabriel in 1826. One can only imagine how satisfying a glass or two of wine must have tasted after spending days or weeks on foot or horseback, trekking throughout the wilderness.

Mission San Gabriel, east of Los Angeles, grew into the largest and most prosperous of the missions and was

6

also the largest winemaking operation, but, as Pinney notes, California winemaking at that time could not be described as any larger than a cottage industry. After the Spanish missionary period ended around 1833, wine-growing continued to be centered in the greater Los Angeles area, and Southern California dominated California wine for the next 50 years. A prophetic observation was made by General Mariano Vallejo, a leader of the Spanish territory: that the wine from Sonoma—the northernmost of the missions—which used Sonoma-grown grapes, "was considered by the Padres the best wine raised in California."

As the Spanish were setting up missions, a wave of immigrants, among them French, German, Italian and Hungarian, began to arrive in California. These new arrivals often came from countries where wine was an integral part of everyday living. For them, planting grapes, even a small vineyard, and making wines, even a few barrels, provided a direct link to their European heritage. Wine for these settlers had always been the meal-time beverage, drunk at lunch and dinner, after long days of hard work. Wine had also been part of festivals, parties, weddings and other celebrations, and of religious ceremonies. Even in a new land, one needed to make enough wine for family and friends to last a year—until the next harvest.

COMMERCIAL WINE

Jean Louis Vignes, a Frenchman whose family hailed from Bordeaux, is credited with introducing fine wine to California and raising wine from a domestic craft to a commercial enterprise. The well-named Vignes (*vines* in French) imported Cabernet Sauvignon vines from Bordeaux and planted them in what is now the heart of Los Angeles in the 1830s, and may have produced his first Cabernet around 1837, for in 1857 he advertised some of his wine as being 20 years old.

By the 1850s another prominent Frenchman, Charles LeFranc, had begun planting Cabernet and other varieties in the Santa Clara Valley, using Château Margaux, the famous estate in Bordeaux, as a model. The Bordeaux model, a blend in which Cabernet or Merlot dominates and the wines are uncommonly long-lived, influenced many of the pioneering vintners of the mid- to late-1800s, both in their desire to create magnificent

wines and also in their willingness to blend different grapes, à la Bordeaux.

Southern California continued to be the place where most of California's wine was grown, and San Francisco, especially after the Gold Rush, was where most of it was sold and drunk. Nevertheless, many winegrowing advances were being made farther north. Pinney makes references to wine in Santa Clara in 1824 and General Vallejo's mission vineyard in Sonoma in 1835. In 1838 George Yount planted the first vineyard in Napa Valley near what is now the town of Yountville, employing grapevine cuttings from Vallejo in Sonoma.

In 1846 a vineyard was planted at the foot of Mount Diablo in Contra Costa County by Dr. John Marsh. Winegrowing spread slowly throughout California, but when gold was discovered at Sutter's Mill in 1848, leading to the Gold Rush of 1849, the state changed forever, becoming the destination of many more thousands of immigrants who came to pan for gold, work in mines and otherwise carve out a living for themselves and their families. They too planted vines for wine.

In 1857 the remarkable Count Agoston Harazsthy of Hungary, a leading importer of grapevine cuttings, founded Buena Vista Winery in the town of Sonoma. Two years later, the wine industry was large enough to be recognized by the state legislature, which passed an act that exempted new grapevines from taxation until they were four years old. Harazsthy, among others, observed that the California wine industry would never reach its potential as long as the Mission grape was the standard. Better grapes were needed to make superior wines. Vintners would have to rethink wine from theory to practice and learn how the great wines of Europe were made. They would also eventually learn how the great wines of the world were sold, but that would come much later.

THE NOTION OF FINE WINE

According to Pinney, the most ambitious and sustained application of California's early wealth and devotion to wine came from railroad baron Leland Stanford. In 1869 he bought land already planted to grapevines in what is now Alameda, across the bay to the east from San Francisco, and was making wine by 1871. In 1881, following a visit to the great châteaux of Bordeaux, he began to buy large quantities of land along the

Sacramento River in Tehama and Butte counties, between Red Bluff and Chico, with the aim of growing wines that would rival the great wines of France. In one year, 1,000 acres of vines were planted using an elaborate plan for irrigation and drainage. Among the many grapes rooted at Stanford's Vina Ranch were Burger, Charbono and Zinfandel. By the time Stanford died, his ranch had 3,500 acres in vines and a wine cellar that could hold 2 million gallons. Unfortunately, despite Stanford's ambition, his vineyards and his wine had little impact on the industry as a whole, according to Pinney. A vineyard he planted near Palo Alto is today the site of Stanford University.

Elsewhere more important progress was being made and better grapes planted. In 1861 Charles Krug founded a small winery in St. Helena (in Napa Valley), and in 1862 Jacob Schram started his winery—now home of Schramsberg—in the hills northwest of Krug and St. Helena. Many more wineries were founded in the 1870s that still exist today. Beringer Vineyards in St. Helena dates to 1876. Gustav Niebaum, a Finnish fur trader, founded the grand Inglenook chateau in Rutherford in 1879; it is now the Niebaum-Coppola Estate, owned by filmmaker Francis Ford Coppola and his wife. The Christian Brothers founded a winery in 1882, as did whaling tycoon Alfred Tubbs, who built the handsome stone Chateau Montelena winery north of Calistoga. Still others planted their vineyards on the hills and mountains: Mayacamas was founded in 1889 on Mount Veeder, and Rossini, founded in 1885 on Howell Mountain, is now Burgess Cellars. Though difficult to plant and farm, mountain vineyards—where days are cooler but nights are warmer—were above frost lines; dangerous spring frosts could wipe out a grape crop if it hit when the young buds were unprotected. Best of all, the generally cooler mountain vineyards yielded wines with dark colors and intense flavors, a plus in the minds of many vintners.

In northern Sonoma County, all kinds of farm and agricultural endeavors were unfolding. Many European immigrants planted small vineyards to make their own wine. One Italian settlement named its community Asti after the city in Piedmont, Italy, and began making wine around 1882, calling itself Italian Swiss Colony. A year later, one of the largest vineyard estates, Fountain Grove, was planted, eventually expanding to 400 acres of vines and a winery capacity of 600,000 gallons. The Simi brothers were making wine in Healdsburg by 1881.

There were many more. The original Ridge Vineyards winery in the Santa Cruz Mountains was built in 1885, high atop this coastal range at elevations reaching 2,600 feet. Actress Lillie Langtry pursued fine wine in Lake County, north of Napa Valley, from 1886 to 1906, the year of the great San Francisco earthquake and fire. Today her former property is known as Guenoc for its winery and appellation of the same name. Nichelini Winery in Chiles Valley, an eastern offshoot of Napa Valley, was founded in 1890, as was Deer Park Winery on Howell Mountain.

The wineries of this era were small-scale, unspecialized and individually owned, according to Pinney. Charles Wetmore, the state's chief executive viticultural officer, says that "not a single bearing vineyard" was planted systematically with the types of grapes to produce the kinds of great wines being made in Bordeaux, Burgundy, Sauternes or Hermitage, or to make Port or Sherry. There was Cabernet Sauvignon, but mostly in small experimental vineyards. There was Pinot Noir too, apparently, but also in very small quantities. Chardonnay appears not to have been well known until the 1930s (nor widely planted until the 1970s), though Sémillon was. As these grape vines began to be imported from Europe, California wineries named their wines after the appellations where they excelled, calling their wines Chambertin, Hermitage, Burgundy, even Chateau Yquem—named after, though spelled differently than, the famous Château d'Yquem.

Scores more wineries were built and abandoned in the quarter-century between 1890 and 1915. (Many were later to be rediscovered by a new wave of wine enthusiasts in the 1960s to 1990s, who bought land for a weekend retreat only to find an old overgrown vineyard with stumpy vines, or a weathered stone winery or cave burrowed into a hillside.) These old wineries typically produced a variety of wines of ordinary quality, using whatever grapes they could obtain. As vintners, especially those familiar with the wines of Europe, began to focus on higher-quality wines, they sought better grape varieties, those considered the classics, such as Cabernet, and looked for the right soils and the best climates to grow them in. They also worked to improve their techniques, though for the most part winemaking remained rustic and truly old-world.

Many of these pioneers made intelligent decisions about where to begin. Early vineyards planted to Cabernet in Rutherford, Oakville and St. Helena in Napa Valley are still prime wine real estate, as are parts of Livermore Valley, Russian River Valley, Alexander Valley and mountaintop areas from Santa Cruz to Mendocino. This is compelling evidence that vintners were aware of the role of soil and climate in seeking to create finer wines. Areas such as Santa Clara that later fell victim to urban sprawl were once choice locations for world-class wine grapes. Evidence of the quality of those early wines is not abundant today, but many of them were highly regarded at the time and won medals in world competitions. Inglenook's "California Claret" and "Medoc-Type" Cabernets of the late 1800s aged well—often amazingly well—for 100 years. The failure to develop a market for wine outside California hurt the industry most of all, according to Pinney, "for it destroyed all incentive to take the trouble and run the risks required to grow the best varieties and to make the highest standard of wine."

In 1900 Frenchman Georges de Latour seized upon a largely unfilled market niche when he founded Beaulieu Vineyard in Rutherford, creating an elaborate home estate, vineyard and winery. The early wines at Beaulieu were not unlike those made elsewhere in California, a mixture of different grapes and styles, mostly sweet but many dry. But increasingly de Latour focused on Bordeaux as a wine style and Cabernet as his primary grape, eventually growing several hundred acres. Nearby in Rutherford, the handsome stone Inglenook chateau would rival Beaulieu, also relying on Cabernet for its finest wines.

TROUBLED TIMES

As the notion of fine wine began to take shape in the minds of California vintners, two disasters struck. Phylloxera, a louse that attacks the root system of grapevines, appeared in the late 1800s, and the infestation extended into the next century, eventually wiping out most of California's vineyards. According to one estimate, in Napa Valley alone 10,000 acres of vineyard were destroyed between 1889 and 1892; by 1900 there were only 2,000 acres of vineyard left there. Efforts to replant the vineyards were hampered not only by the costs, but also by the absence of phylloxera-resistant rootstock. By 1915, 250,000 acres of vineyard statewide had been ruined by phylloxera. According to Pinney,

> The symbolic high point of California wine-growing before Prohibition overwhelmed it came, as all well-made dramas, only shortly before the fall. In 1915, when the shadow of Prohibition was already moving rapidly over the country, California seized on the opportunity provided by the nearly opened Panama Canal to promote its climate, its industries, and its future through the great Panama-Pacific International Exposition in San Francisco; it was also a dramatic way for San Francisco to show the world how it had risen, phoenix-like, from the ashes of [the] 1906 [earthquake and fire]. California's wine men, now pretty well seasoned in the business of international exhibitions, were ready to make the most of their chance to show the best on their own ground.

By the time the Panama-Pacific Exposition opened, though, much of Europe was embroiled in World War I, and there was little reason to pay attention to California wine; its chances for international publicity vanished. When the official history of the Exposition was published, in five large and pretentious volumes, it gave California wine the briefest of descriptions.

Wrote Pinney: "This is history—closed by the Eighteenth Amendment." Prohibition was instituted with the passage of this Constitutional amendment in 1919. It outlawed the manufacture, transportation, sale and possession of alcoholic beverages (although not the consumption thereof) from 1920 to 1933—and forced most of California's several hundred wineries to close permanently. Their vineyards were left untended and susceptible to disease, or were replanted to other cash-generating crops or used to graze cattle or sheep.

Not everyone quit, though. Californians could still make wine for their own consumption, and did. A few wineries, including Beaulieu, survived by producing altar wines for the church. In 1919, on the eve of Prohibition, a Frenchman named Tam founded what is now Chalone Vineyard in the Gavilan Mountains, planting Chenin Blanc vines, perhaps believing he was rooting Chardonnay. Nevertheless, at the very moment when a broader, better organized and more sophisticated wine industry seemed poised to emerge from California—ready to take on a broader U.S. and perhaps even international market—it nearly vanished completely.

It's difficult to predict what might have happened if Prohibition had not become law. Phylloxera and World War I had already affected the California wine industry negatively. It is likely that the industry would have continued to grow and improve the quality of its wines, however slowly and unsurely. But clearly the industry would have faced arduous economic times. It might have flourished during the Roaring '20s, only to face the collapse of the stock market in 1929, the Great Depression of the 1930s and the global devastation of World War II. (Certainly Europe's great wine estates suffered from the ravages of the wars and depressed economies.) In all likelihood, whatever progress California wine might have made in this era would have been offset by domestic and global turmoil. But a healthy wine industry would have given California a real advantage immediately after WW II, when there was little European competition and thousands of American military personnel were coming home after being exposed to wine during their stay in Europe.

AFTER REPEAL

For many reasons, some quite obvious, Prohibition proved unpopular. Wine, although illegal everywhere, was nevertheless also available everywhere. Although bars and saloons were closed, alcohol was being smuggled into the country. Moreover, Americans continued to make wine for personal use. Those who viewed wine as part of their culture and heritage kept on nourishing their vines and making wine. Wine grapes continued to be shipped east in refrigerated railroad cars, where Americans of European descent would buy them and crush and ferment them into their own homemade wines. Enforcement of Prohibitionist laws proved difficult. When the Depression hit and people needed jobs, California's wine industry began to revive itself ever so slowly.

By 1932, indications were that Prohibition would be repealed in time for the 1933 vintage. Many would-be vintners anxiously prepared for the rebirth of the wine industry. Upon Repeal, Inglenook made a brilliant 1933 Cabernet, still uncommonly dark and intense 60 years

after its release. That same year Louis M. Martini readied his new winery in St. Helena, and the great wine dynasty of Ernest and Julio Gallo was born in a small warehouse in Modesto. Shipping grapes east for home winemakers remained a viable industry, but it became apparent that the California wine industry needed to reestablish its credentials, make better wines and serve broader markets. It was obvious to some, including the Gallos, that one way to penetrate and capture Midwestern and Eastern markets was to provide palatable wines at affordable prices, serving markets where European immigrants lived and drank wine daily. As long as immigrants could make homemade wine that was better than anything they could afford to buy, the demand for California wine would be minimal.

In 1937 Alfred Fromm, a native German, came to California and visited several wineries, finding the Christian Brothers' Mont La Salle facility on Mount Veeder in Napa Valley most attractive. The Christian Brothers Winery was on the verge of bankruptcy but had lots of good wine in storage, and Fromm, a marketing visionary, struck a deal to sell the wine, correctly figuring that if he put the Christian Brothers name on the bottle he could inspire a sense of confidence in the buyer through the wine's connection with a religious order. It worked, and Christian Brothers became one of the most popular and successful brands in history.

In the aftermath of Repeal, California's wineries were in sad shape, having been largely neglected for years. According to Professor Harold Winkler of the University of California at Davis, Napa's wineries were in no better condition in 1934 than in 1880. Many of the wines produced in the 1930s, 1940s and 1950s had serious bacterial defects. They had been made in vessels contaminated with mold and other microorganisms, which led to undesirable aromas and flavors. Sweet wines were more popular than dry wines, as their defects could easily be masked. The wine industry had to make the best of the grapes, vineyards and facilities it had before it could invest in the new equipment and technology that would raise quality. The University of California at Davis played a major role in this transition. The work done there was instrumental in defining the climatic zones for growing fine-wine grapes—identifying five regions and rating them from coolest to warmest—and in cleaning up California's wines, establishing strict sanitation guidelines for winery operations and for wine stability.

In the past decade, Davis has been criticized by many for its doctrine of sterile, filtered, highly processed, squeaky-clean wines, and many winemakers who studied there followed that doctrine carefully—perhaps to a fault. Davis was correct in identifying many of the stability and bacterial problems facing both California and European wines, and as a result, its professors and graduates tended to approach wine as something that could be manipulated or corrected from within the cellar—more a laboratory product than an agricultural one. They knew that the best wines came from the best grapes and vineyards, but they also recognized how many wines—both domestic and European—suffered from serious and obvious defects. The fact that scores of Europe's great winemakers, including Christian Moueix of Château Petrus, attended Davis and benefited from it is proof of the school's importance in technical matters. While it may be easy to criticize Davis now, it played a significant role in the transition years when the California wine industry needed to focus on cleanliness and stability.

In the period from 1940 to the 1960s, those at Davis and elsewhere recognized the need for a viable wine economy to serve the new American consumer—who had learned to love wine while in Europe during and after World War II—as well as wine drinkers who expected quality and consistency. Tools of mass production led to many commercial successes, perhaps none of them greater than Gallo Hearty Burgundy, a perfectly consistent, highly reliable, technically faultless, mass-produced wine that carried no vintage date or specific grape variety, could be found virtually everywhere and could be relied on to taste the same year after year.

By the 1950s, California vintners recognized the need to develop markets throughout the country. Producers such as the Gallos, the Sebastianis, Fromm and later Robert Mondavi studied the market more and more carefully. Some serviced it with ordinary table wines. Others looked ahead to greater possibilities.

THE NEW VISION

In 1937 Georges de Latour traveled to Europe to find a classically trained French winemaker. He hired a Russian-born, French-educated enologist named André Tchelistcheff, a brilliant perfectionist who loved vineyards, wine and teaching. He immediately helped Beaulieu Vineyard improve its wines. The more California wine he tasted, the more impressed he was, even though the industry faced serious hurdles. When de Latour died in 1940, the 1936 vintage of BV Cabernet was still in small oak barrels. As a tribute to de Latour, Tchelistcheff suggested naming the wine Georges de Latour Private Reserve, and a new standard for the finest wine California had to offer was set. At the time there were fewer than 100 acres of Cabernet in Napa Valley; BV Private Reserve 1936 sold for $1.50 a bottle, and commanded the same price 15 years later. Vineyards were infested with diseases such as red leaf virus, which made for pretty red and orange grape leaves in the fall, but were in reality a sign that the vines were seriously ill. Hope and expectations for the future outpaced the reality that revitalizing the vineyards and crafting fine wines would take time.

In 1938 Inglenook's John Daniel, wine writer Frank Schoonmaker and their good friend John Gantner began their quest for the perfect Pinot Noir vineyard in Napa Valley, with the vision of making a wine from the same grape that the great red Burgundies are made of. They finally settled on Spring Mountain, where they planted a vineyard and started producing experimental wines in the 1940s, eventually choosing the name School House for their brand. In 1941 Jack and Mary Taylor revived Mayacamas on Mount Veeder, and in the early 1940s Martin Ray left Paul Masson Vineyards to start his own winery in the Santa Cruz Mountains. In 1943 Frank Bartholomew, a famous newspaperman and war correspondent for UPI, revived the crumbling Buena Vista winery in Sonoma, and Lee Stewart was making wine in an old winery at the base of Howell Mountain that he called Souverain. In 1952 James Zellerbach, a one-time U.S. ambassador to Italy, began planting Chardonnay and later Pinot Noir in the hills above Sonoma for his Hanzell Vineyards, where he hoped to one day create wines that were the equals of fine red and white Burgundies.

Fred and Eleanor McCrea bought property on Spring Mountain in the 1940s and planted Stony Hill Vineyard to Chardonnay, Riesling and several other varieties, from which they began making small lots of wine in 1952. In 1959, the once-abandoned Ridge Vineyards in the Santa Cruz Mountains was rejuvenated by a trio of Stanford Research Institute engineers who used the estate Cabernet vineyard, Monte Bello, as an anchor before branching out to explore and tap into the many excellent Zinfandel vineyards spread throughout the state. Slowly but surely, the quest for fine wine began to move forward, pushed by tiny vineyard and winery operations that aimed for high-quality wines.

THE PACE QUICKENS

In the 1960s the California wine industry began to lay the foundation for a wine boom in the 1970s. In 1961 Joe and Alice Heitz founded Heitz Wine Cellar on Highway 29 and in 1966 Heitz bottled his first single-vineyard Cabernet from Tom and Martha May's Martha's Vineyard in Oakville. That same year, Robert Mondavi, who had encouraged his family to move from the Central Valley and buy the Charles Krug Winery in 1943, and who believed that Napa Valley wine had a great future, built his own winery in Oakville, Napa's first new winery since Prohibition. In the Gavilan Mountains, east of Monterey, Richard Graff convinced his mother to buy an old run-down vineyard and winery called Chalone Vineyard; in 1966, the winery made its first Pinot Noir, followed by Chardonnay, Chenin Blanc and Pinot Blanc, some of the wine coming from vines planted more than 30 years earlier. A group of old-time Napa Valley farmers headed by Chuck Carpy opened Freemark Abbey north of St. Helena.

As the wine industry began to stir, consumer tastes began to change; dry wines with varietal names such as Cabernet Sauvignon and Zinfandel became increasingly popular, gradually replacing sweeter wines such as Riesling. Wine drinkers who knew fine Bordeaux or Rhône reds appreciated the distinctive qualities of dry table wines. At the time, many critics expected red wine to capture the imagination of consumers, and it did for a while. But what surprised everyone was that white wine quickly grew in popularity, soon taking over the lead. Perhaps that should not have been such a surprise; Americans drank ice-cold soft drinks and martinis, so chilled wine found an easy niche. All of a sudden, white wine was popular and it seemed that wineries couldn't produce enough of it to meet consumer demand.

Most of the white wine being drunk in the 1970s was still generic table wine, but at the same time, more wineries began to turn their attention to the fine-wine varietals. Without a model for growing Chardonnay or Sauvignon Blanc, though, wineries planted those grapes where they knew they would ripen—often right next to their Cabernet or Zinfandel vines. Only later would they learn that cooler climates were better suited for growing white wine grapes. And without a model for vinifying white wines, winemakers employed the same vinification used for reds; here too, winemakers found that they needed to employ different vinification techniques if they were to make better wines.

Studies conducted in the 1970s suggested that Americans were becoming more curious about wine. In hindsight, one wonders whether these studies had any real foundation in fact or whether they were inspired by someone's hope that wine might catch on in America. Articles in newspapers and magazines often painted a pretty picture of the future of California wine and there were many predictions of a wine boom. Americans weren't great wine consumers then or now, but logic held that if average consumption doubled or tripled, to several gallons a year, there would be a tremendous demand for wine. If America ever became like France or Italy, where per capita wine consumption exceeded 20 gallons a year at that time, California wine would enjoy a bonanza. This potential caught people's attention. In 1977, Coca-Cola bought Sterling Vineyards in Napa Valley while launching a media blitz promoting its Taylor California Cellars brand, a mix of rather dull, bland wines. Schlitz, the brewer, owned Geyser Peak in Sonoma. Nestlé, the food giant, bought into Beringer Vineyards. Many signs, it seemed, pointed to a promising future for California wine.

FINE WINE AS ART AND LIFESTYLE

The late 1960s and early 1970s spawned new interest in country living. The rural lifestyle had an allure for many businessmen and professionals who had succeeded in one career but were looking for new challenges or something more fulfilling. Owning a vineyard or winery became a not only a dream but a status symbol for many of them. Tom Jordan, the multimillionaire Colorado oilman, built a luxurious chateau in Alexander Valley in 1972, producing his first wine in 1976. In the Santa Ynez Valley, an heir to the Firestone tire company founded a winery, while other business executives pooled their money to build Zaca Mesa. In Napa Valley, big money poured in like never before. Multimillionaire nurseryman Gil Nickel revived a historic stone winery in Oakville, renaming it Far Niente, Italian for "without a care." Money was no obstacle to the pursuit of fine wine. The prospect of Americans drinking wine as Europeans did, combined with the romantic lure of lush green vineyards, country living and working the land led to a wave of new wineries opening up in the 1970s and 1980s, many of whose owners aspired to make the world's greatest wines. And the evolution of fine dining and imaginative new restaurants only added to the excitement of fine wines.

In 1976, when a Franco-Californian tasting was held in Paris to commemorate the United States Bicentennial, two upstart wineries from Napa Valley finished in first place, winning in both the red and white wine categories, with French critics serving as judges. The results were stunning to the French and uplifting to Americans. It was the tasting heard around the world. Stag's Leap Wine Cellars 1973 Cabernet, the winery's second vintage, placed first ahead of Château Mouton-Rothschild 1970, Château Haut-Brion 1970 and Château Montrose 1970. In fifth place was Ridge Monte Bello 1971, followed by Château Leoville-Las Cases 1971, Mayacamas Cabernet Napa Valley 1971, Clos Du Val Cabernet Napa Valley 1972, Heitz Martha's Vineyard Cabernet Napa Valley 1970 and Freemark Abbey Cabernet Napa Valley 1969. In the white-wine category, Chateau Montelena Chardonnay 1973, a blend of Alexander Valley and Napa Valley grapes, placed first ahead of a group of highly regarded white Burgundies. The tasting triggered an avalanche of global publicity for California wine, as newspapers and magazines around the world heralded the story.

The allure of California wine so captured the world's imagination that the greatest French winemaker of the 20th century, Baron Philippe de Rothschild, owner of the great Mouton-Rothschild estate in Pauillac, decided to invest in California, forging a partnership in Napa Valley with Robert Mondavi. In 1979 they announced their joint venture. Their wine, later named Opus One, would be a marriage of French and California winemaking know-how applied to Napa Valley Cabernet. A decade later they built a spectacular winery in Oakville, close to Mondavi's own winery. Rothschild's arrival in California signaled the beginning of a new era. During

the next decade, several dozen foreign wine companies, led by several esteemed French Champagne houses, purchased land, planted vineyards and built wineries in California, still anticipating a wine boom. Money flowed from Germany, Belgium, Switzerland and Japan, with Sonoma's crown jewel, Chateau St. Jean, being purchased by Suntory. Christian Moueix, a former student at Davis, liked California wine and its possibilities enough to follow Baron Philippe's lead and become a partner in a historic Napa vineyard with John Daniel's two daughters. Napanook, which Daniel planted in the 1930s, became home to Dominus Estate, and by 1994, Moueix was sole proprietor.

By the late 1970s and through the 1990s, several other important trends emerged and further shaped the market. Many of the assumptions about which grapes grew best in which areas proved true, while others did not. Cabernet was perfect for Oakville, Rutherford and the Stags Leap District in Napa, along with sites on Howell Mountain, Mount Veeder and along the eastern hills of Napa Valley. Cabernet also fared well in pockets of Sonoma Valley and Alexander Valley and a few sites in Russian River Valley and Dry Creek Valley. Chardonnay and Pinot Noir, once thought ideal for the heart of Napa Valley, were better suited for the cooler climates of Carneros, Russian River Valley, Monterey County and Santa Barbara County. Finicky Merlot was widely planted throughout the state, but it only excels in certain specific sites and by the end of the century there were precious few spots where it proved a natural match.

Monterey Cabernet, widely planted in the 1970s and early 1980s, proved a colossal failure in most cases. The sites chosen were far too cool to ripen the grapes, leaving them marked by pungent vegetal flavors. A new admiration for Zinfandel and century-old vines emerged following a curious sensation, white Zinfandel—a sweet tasting, pink-colored wine made from Zinfandel grapes. Purists cringed, but many consumers loved it and sales soared. Many companies reaped huge profits from this otherwise simple, fruity, often innocuous wine. Those gnarly old Zin vines planted around 1900 in Dry Creek Valley, Sonoma Valley, Alexander Valley and Amador County proved that the farmers who planted them understood where fine-wine grapes would excel and fully ripen. The move toward cooler climates for appropriate grapes proved as important as the recognition that controlling crop yields, using natural winemaking techniques and fermenting wines in toasty oak barrels would lead to finer, more complex wines.

Many of the earlier assumptions about grape growing and winemaking in California had come under full review by the late 1980s and early 1990s, and innovations and refinements continued. Foremost among the changes was the emphasis on the French concept of *terroir*: planting the ripe grapes in the right soil and microclimate. For the most part, grapes such as Chardonnay and Pinot Noir were planted in cooler climates, with the right rootstock and clones to survive and prosper. Red varieties such as Cabernet, Merlot and Syrah were planted in warmer areas, including the Paso Robles area. Closer attention was paid to farming techniques—how tightly grape vines were spaced and the preferred overall crop size. The best vineyards were tightly pruned to limit the number of grape clusters. Growers focused on grape canopies as well, rejecting early theories that a full umbrella-like covering protected the grapes from severe heat. Instead, grapevines were trimmed back and grape clusters were exposed to direct sunlight early on, in the belief that the grapes would ripen more evenly and fully if directly exposed than they would if shaded.

Winemakers started taking more chances with their wines in hopes of crafting even finer, more complex, concentrated and detailed wines. They used natural yeasts that developed on grape clusters to ferment many wines, instead of inoculating grape musts with laboratory yeasts. They left Chardonnay in new French oak barrels for up to two years. They used minimal filtering, if any at all, with the intention of making wines as naturally as possible.

At the same time, vintners continued to seek out unique sites for their vineyards and winemakers experimented—with mixed results—with grapes such as Sangiovese, Syrah, Viognier and Pinot Blanc. Many of the tiniest wine companies (with names such as Screaming Eagle, Harlan Estate, Talley and Flowers) found isolated pieces of land and then zeroed in on very specific grape varieties—much in the way Stony Hill, Hanzell, Ridge and Heitz had done with vineyards decades earlier. Still others further explored the oldest fine-wine grape—Zinfandel—with wineries such as Turley Wine Cellars and Rosenblum making up to 17 different bottlings in 1997.

Even the biggest wineries saw the changes in the market and sought to capitalize on them. The Gallo brothers, after decades of mass-producing modestly flavored wines, moved into northern Sonoma and began to make the highest-quality wines possible. Under the early direction of legendary winemaker Julio Gallo, the Gallos planted thousands of acres to new vines and both the quality and volume of wines grew. Their Chardonnay was planted in prime Russian River Valley soil, their Cabernet and Zinfandel rooted in the hills of Dry Creek Valley; hundreds more acres were planted in Alexander Valley. Gallo's investment in the production of fine wine demonstrated—if further proof were still needed—that this was the future for California wine. Meanwhile, newcomers such as Jess Jackson proved you could build a huge and diversified wine company in a comparatively short period of time. Starting out in 1982, with a sweet-tasting Chardonnay, Jackson built Kendall-Jackson into a multi-million case brand that eventually added nearly a dozen brands, chief among them Stonestreet in Alexander Valley, Hartford Court in Russian River Valley, Cambria in Santa Maria Valley and Cardinale in Napa Valley.

Demand for California wine grew into a global market and the bullish U.S. economy of the 1990s propelled brisk sales. As a small but keenly interested wine culture, closely allied with new trends in fine cuisine and restaurants, solidified in the United States, California's largest fine-wine producers—Robert Mondavi, Beringer, Gallo and Kendall-Jackson—spread their interests throughout the state, buying land, planting vineyards and building new wineries. Smaller wineries expanded as well: Caymus, based in Napa, bought vineyard land and built a small winery in Monterey for Chardonnay, then considered planting Pinot Noir on the Sonoma Coast. Even the smallest vintners found niches in the market, hiring a winemaker, buying grapes, making their wine in a rented space and selling it by direct mail to consumers, often at very high prices.

Still more money flowed into California wine. In 1995 William Jarvis completed a $20-million subterranean winery in Napa Valley to produce 5,000 cases of wine. Restaurateur Pat Kuleto spent millions, too, developing a rugged hillside vineyard in the hills east of Napa Valley. Clos du Bois and Stonestreet built huge new wineries and Mondavi began to remodel its Oakville facility and talked of building a new winery in Monterey.

California wine continued to attract small artisans as well, whose passion for and love of fine wine inspired even greater quality. When the money didn't flow, wineries such as Mondavi and Beringer went public, raising millions to retire debt and expand business. Even smaller wineries opted to go public: an example is Ravenswood, which decided to sell part of its business in a 1999 limited public offering.

In keeping with the maxim that history repeats itself, phylloxera returned to Napa Valley in the 1980s, as well as to many other parts of the state. Its arrival forced a $3 billion replanting of vineyards—including $1 billion in Napa Valley alone—most of which was completed by 1999. Optimists claimed this would hasten the matching of the right grape varieties to the proper soils and climates, the first and most important step toward even greater quality.

Anti-alcohol sentiments reappeared, leading to warning labels on wine and higher taxes, but also to a healthy debate about the benefits of moderate wine consumption. By the end of the 1990s, the tide had clearly turned in wine's favor, as its benefits were touted in one study after another.

As the century ends, fierce competition prevails in the wine industry; only the fittest and finest are poised to survive. As long as the economy flourishes, American wine lovers are willing to pay for the best California wines available—the strongest endorsement possible for the state's producers, some of whom are making the kinds of wine that rival and often surpass the great wines of the world. At the turn of the century, after more than 200 years of winemaking, California is making its best wines ever, with seemingly unlimited possibilities in many areas. Its successes appear to be a solid foundation for even grander things to come.

CHAPTER 2

GRAPES AND WINE STYLES

In order to appreciate wine, it's essential to understand the characteristics different grapes offer and how those characteristics should be expressed in wines. Cabernet, Merlot and Zinfandel are all red grapes, but as wines, their personalities are quite different. Even when grown in different appellations and vinified using different techniques, a varietal wine displays qualities that are inherent to its personality. Muscat should always be spicy, Sauvignon Blanc a touch herbal. Zinfandel is zesty, with pepper and wild berry flavors. Cabernet is marked by plum, currant and black cherry flavors and firm tannins. Understanding what a grape should be as a wine is fundamental, and knowing what a grape can achieve at its greatest is the essence of fine-wine appreciation.

This chapter focuses on the major grape varieties and varietal wines in California. It discusses each grape's varietal character, how well it succeeds or fails as wine, where it grows best and how styles differ based on appellation, whether the wine is suited for blending or best on its own, when it reaches maturity and how it ages. There is also a statistical overview of where the grapes are planted and charts showing how the state's grape acreage has changed in the past few decades. These charts are divided by county (not appellation) and show the favored spots for the major varietals, as well as which grapes are gaining favor and which are declining in popularity. Grapes and wine styles are also discussed in Chapter 3:

"Appellations and Vineyards," as is the question of which grapes perform best in the key growing areas.

In Europe, the finest wines are known primarily by geographic appellation (although this is changing; witness the occasional French and Italian use of varietal names). In California, however, despite a greater recognition of the influence of *terroir*, most wines are still labeled by their varietal names. To a large extent, this is because Americans were first introduced to California fine wine by varietal name, and also because in California the process of sorting out which grapes grow best in which appellations is ongoing.

Europe has a longer history for matching grape types to soil and climate, and the evidence is more conclusive. Chardonnay and Pinot Noir, for instance, are the major grapes of Burgundy; hardly any other grapes matter. Cabernet Sauvignon, Merlot, Cabernet Franc, Malbec and Petit Verdot are the red grapes of Bordeaux; Zinfandel isn't allowed to be grown there. In Pauillac, a commune in Bordeaux, Cabernet is favored, while in Pomerol and St-Emilion, Merlot is the preferred grape. Syrah dominates Rhône reds, while Marsanne and Roussanne are used for Rhône whites. Barolo and Barbaresco are both made from the Nebbiolo grape, but those two different appellations produce markedly different styles of wine. In Tuscany, Sangiovese provides the backbone of Chianti, but it's just one grape in a blend. A different clone of Sangiovese is used for wines made in the area known as Brunello di Montalcino.

California's appellation system is slowly evolving in the direction of Europe's—though I doubt there will ever be laws prohibiting certain grapes from being planted in certain areas. Already appellations such as Carneros and Santa Maria Valley are becoming synonymous with Chardonnay and Pinot Noir, while Rutherford, Oakville and the Stags Leap District are associated with Cabernet-based red table wines. Wineries with vested financial interests in these appellations and the marketing clout to emphasize the distinctive features of the wines grown in these areas will determine how the appellation system evolves and whether specific wine styles emerge. The appellations themselves will also determine which grapes excel and deserve special recognition.

This chapter also discusses when wines are at their peak for drinking and, in general, how they age. It's my view that virtually all California wines, regardless of their color, varietal character or history, are best consumed in their youth. Specifically, all whites and virtually all reds reach maturity and should be consumed within one to three years of their vintage dates. Wines with a 1998 vintage date should therefore be at or near their peak from 1999 to 2001. I know there are exceptions to this and that some California wines do age well. But I also think most wines, regardless of where they're grown, don't benefit significantly from aging. I know that some wines do need to age and others have reputations for improving with age. But the simple fact is that most do not.

Moreover, the trend among winemakers throughout the world is to make wines that are more accessible earlier. Even in areas such as Bordeaux, Burgundy and the Rhône, where there's a history of long-lived wines, the vast majority of wines are not meant to be cellared for long periods. Vintners understand that most wines are consumed early on—usually within hours of purchase—and are styling their wines for more immediate pleasure. This doesn't mean that there aren't exceptions or that you should never cellar wines or should drink all your wines young. Clearly wines grown at the great estates in great vintages are capable of aging and improving. These wines may need several years of cellaring, but given today's wine styles, most are very appealing much earlier than consumers often realize. To protect yourself from buying wines and aging them only to find they've lost their fruit or charm, it's wise to drink them earlier. Unless you're

sure you know what you're doing, don't stockpile cases of wines for indefinite periods—unless you want to set yourself up for disappointment.

A second crucial element in deciding when to drink a given wine is your own taste. If you buy a wine, drink it and think it's delicious now, there's little reason to age it for several more years unless you strongly believe it's going to improve (or are simply curious to see what will happen to it with age). If a wine tastes wonderful to you now, the odds are it will lose some or most of its fruit (and charm) and be less pleasing in four or five years. Moreover, the odds are that your tastes will change a little too; that the wines you think are great today may not always have the same appeal to you. If, however, you know your tastes and like older, more mature-tasting wines, then you're aware of the risks, consequences and potential pleasure of drinking them. If you're new to wine and want to age wines and experience drinking older wines, there are several options. You can easily buy older wines at retail, at auctions, or in a fine restaurant. You can also cellar a few bottles and taste how they evolve. But buying a case or two of expensive Cabernet or Pinot Noir and then not tasting it for 10 or 15 years is, in my view, taking a huge risk. The most ageworthy wines I can recommend are the four- and five-star wines, but it's best to follow your own taste preferences and remember that wine is a living thing that can spoil.

I have tasted literally thousands of older wines—and I still recommend that you drink your wines young, when they are at their freshest, most vibrant and fruitiest, and that you age wines with great caution and care. There are collectors who say that money is no object in building their wine cellars, who buy as much fine wine as they can each year. They may impress their spouses or friends with a wonderful wine collection. But what happens when they begin to open up those bottles and realize the wines they paid large sums of money for have faded and lost their charm? These wine connoisseurs look much less savvy when they're stuck with several cases of expensive wine that have faded and turned earthy and dull.

The remainder of this chapter looks at major the grape varieties and styles of wine they yield. In some instances I've recommended specific wines, but for the major wine categories, such as Cabernet, Chardonnay, Merlot, etc., see the "Reference Wines" in Chapter 3: "Appellations & Vineyards" for my recommendations. In the grape variety charts, I've tracked the major counties—"other" includes those not specified.

ALICANTE BOUSCHET

Alicante Bouschet is used primarily in blending, for its dark color and intense flavors. A few wineries still produce it as a wine, but it fails to excite. Acreage is now 1,451 and falling, having steadily declined from some 30,000 acres after Prohibition.

BARBERA

Plantings of this once popular grape have declined sharply, dropping from 19,267 acres in 1980 to 11,137 in 1997, with most of that grown in the Central Valley. A few wineries never stopped producing it as a varietal wine, though, and a few more have recently begun. Its main attribute as a blending wine is its ability to maintain a naturally high acidity even in hot climates. As a stand-alone wine, it features crisp acidity, and wild blackberry flavors that tend to be lean rather than deep or plush. Louis M. Martini made excellent, even ageworthy Barberas for years. I think the wine has more potential than is currently realized, with its bright, crisp berry flavors, and I suspect it has a more promising future as Italian-style wines gain popularity. A few favorites: Boeger, Ca del Solo (in Monterey), Renwood (in Amador County), Sebastiani and Seghesio.

BURGER

Wildly popular in California's jug-wine era, this white vinifera grape outnumbered all other white varietals for years. It's known for its ability to produce a large crop, but its quality is ordinary, ideal for jug wines. Acreage now stands at 1,895.

CABERNET FRANC

Increasingly popular as both a stand-alone varietal and a blending grape, Cabernet Franc is used primarily for blending in Bordeaux—although it can rise to great heights of quality, as seen in the grand wine Cheval Blanc, a mix of Franc and Merlot. As a varietal wine, it usually benefits from small amounts of Cabernet and Merlot, and can be as intense and full-bodied as either of those wines, but it often strays from currant and berry notes into stalky green flavors that become more pronounced with age. In France, it's also made into a lighter wine called Chinon, but only a few wineries in California take it seriously. Given its newness to California, it may just be a matter of time before Cabernet Franc gets more attention and rises in quality. Acreage is now 2,245. Look for Benziger Alexander Valley, Justin San Luis Obispo, La Jota, Lang & Reed, Ravenswood, Niebaum-Coppola Napa Valley and Steele Lake County.

CABERNET SAUVIGNON

The undisputed king of red wines, Cabernet Sauvignon has a long and distinguished history in California dating to the late 1800s. It is a remarkably steady and consistent performer throughout much of the state. In specific appellations, it is capable of rendering wines of uncommon depth, richness, concentration and longevity. While it grows well in many appellations, this

CABERNET SAUVIGNON ACREAGE BY COUNTY

County	1970	1980	1990	1997	Percent Change 1970-1980	Percent Change 1980-1990	Percent Change 1990-1997
Napa	2,398	5,569	9,131	10,618	132%	64%	16%
Sonoma	1,201	4,480	6,468	7,529	273%	44%	16%
Mendocino	313	925	1,314	1,463	196%	42%	11%
Monterey	880	4,489	3,763	3,757	410%	(-16%)	(-.002%)
San Luis Obispo	37	942	2,451	3,657	245%	160%	49%
Santa Barbara	85	1,092	902	554	118%	(-17%)	(-39%)
Other	1,169	5,314	9,177	17,729	355%	73%	93%
State Total	**6,083**	**22,811**	**33,206**	**45,307**	**275%**	**46%**	**36%**

grape rises to its greatest heights in Napa Valley and the appellations within, such as Calistoga, Oakville, Rutherford and the Stags Leap District. It also performs exceptionally well in the mountains on both sides of the valley and in select vineyards in Alexander Valley, Dry Creek Valley, Sonoma Valley, Sonoma Mountain and Paso Robles. Beyond that, it grows well in pockets here and there, such as Ridge's Monte Bello Vineyard in the Santa Cruz Mountains and at Santa Cruz Mountain Vineyards. Even as Cabernet's popularity as a wine grows, it's unlikely any appellation will surpass Napa Valley's high-quality Cabernets and Cabernet blends. Year after year, the sheer number of excellent Cabernets produced in Napa dominates the market.

At its best, Cabernet produces wines of great intensity and depth of flavor. Its classic flavors are currant, plum, black cherry and spice. It can also be marked by herb, olive (green and black), mint, tobacco, cedar, sage and anise flavors. Ripe, jammy notes are also often evident in some wines, and occasionally wild berry and raspberry flavors are present. In warmer areas, Cabernet can be supple and elegant. In cooler areas, such as Monterey or Carneros, it can be marked by pronounced vegetal, bell pepper, oregano and tar flavors. It can also be very tannic if that is a feature the winemaker finds desirable. These days, most wineries are cognizant of the market—which enjoys young, robust wines—and employ techniques to make their wines less astringent.

The best Cabernets start out dark purple-ruby in color, with firm acidity, a full body, great intensity, concentrated flavors and firm, sometimes thick tannins. Cabernet has an affinity for oak and usually spends 15 to 30 months in new or used French or American barrels, a process that, when properly executed, imparts a woody, toasty, cedar or vanilla flavor to the wine while slowly oxidizing it and softening its tannins. Through most of their history in California, the best Cabernets have been 100 percent Cabernet. A few still are, notably Caymus Special Selection and Heitz Martha's Vineyard. But since the late 1970s, many vintners have turned to the Bordeaux model and blended smaller portions of Merlot, Cabernet Franc, Malbec and Petit Verdot into their Cabernets.

The case for blending is still under review. Clearly there are successes, particularly as winemakers find the best sites to plant those grapes and learn how to work with them in the vineyard and in the winery. Increasingly

there are fewer 100 percent Cabernets, with some wineries adding just a touch—three to five percent—of Cabernet Franc or Merlot for texture and depth. The Bordeaux model is built around not only the desire to craft complex wines, but also the need to give a wine color, tannin or backbone. Many other producers are shifting back to higher percentages of Cabernet, however, having found that blending doesn't add complexity and that Cabernet on its own has a stronger character.

Within Napa Valley, microclimates are a major factor in the weight and intensity of the Cabernets. (Winemakers also influence the style, as they can extract high levels of tannin and oak their wines heavily.) Rutherford-grown Cabernets, for instance, are marked by deep, complex currant, plum and cherry flavors and firm but fine tannins. Oakville wines share a similar weight and intensity, but are also often marked by more herb, mint and cedar flavors. In Yountville, the coolest area, the wines sometimes have substantial tannins. Stags Leap District Cabernets tend to be more supple, with black cherry, herb and olive notes and polished tannins. In St. Helena, a small area, the wines are remarkably well focused, with dark currant and black cherry flavors and firm but fine tannins. Many Calistoga vineyards yield bold, intense, deeply flavored wines, while those on Diamond Mountain produce wines that share an earthy austerity and firm tannins. On Howell Mountain the wines are quite dense and tannic, with an earthy edge.

Sonoma Valley Cabernets are often quite hard and tannic, with a green herb and olive edge to the flavors. In Dry Creek Valley they are lighter, less concentrated and less intense than in Napa Valley, although when grown in the hills, the wines generally show more depth and richness. In the cool Russian River Valley, certain vineyards can produce Cabernets of sufficient ripeness, but usually the wines are not as heavy and dense as they are in Napa Valley, and there is often a green, hard, tannic edge to their raspberry flavors. In the Santa Cruz Mountains, another cool appellation, the Cabernets are often marked by hard, intense, gritty tannins and mushroom flavors. In Paso Robles the wines are medium-bodied, with supple textures and elegant fruit flavors. (Further discussions of Cabernet as it relates to different appellations appear in Chapter 3).

With 45,307 acres in vines, Cabernet is second only to Zinfandel in red grape acreage. Napa County, with 10,618 acres in vines, and Sonoma County, with 7,529 acres spread out among its districts, are the most popular sites. Mendocino (1,463 acres), Monterey (3,757), Sacramento (1,681), San Joaquin (7,359) and San Luis Obispo (3,657) also have significant Cabernet plantings. It's worth noting that Napa and Sonoma both enjoyed a 16 percent increase in plantings between 1990 and 1997. Santa Barbara, where it's mostly too cool for Cabernet, declined in acreage by 39 percent during the same period. The fastest-growing area is the Central Valley, where Madera County's plantings increased 884 percent (from a negligible 115 acres) and San Joaquin County posted a 133 percent increase between 1990 and 1997. Most of these grapes will go into California-appellation wines.

CARIGNANE

Once a major blending grape for jug wines, Carignane's popularity has diminished, and plantings have dropped from 25,293 acres in 1980 to 7,839 in 1997. It still appears in some blends, and old vineyards are sought after for the intensity of their grapes. But the likelihood is that other grapes with even more intensity and flavor will replace it in the future. If you're looking for a worthy example, check out Cline Contra Costa County or Rosenblum Napa Valley Kenefick Ranch.

CHARBONO

This grape has dwindled in acreage. Its stature as a wine was supported mainly by the now defunct Inglenook-Napa Valley winery, which bottled a Charbono on a regular basis. Occasionally it made for interesting drinking and it aged well. But more often it was lean and tannic, a better story than bottle of wine. A few wineries still produce it, but only Parducci and Ca' del Solo with any success.

CHARDONNAY

As Cabernet is the king of reds, so is Chardonnay the king of white wines, for it makes the state's most consistently excellent, rich and complex white. This is an amazingly versatile grape that grows well in a variety of locations up and down the state's coastal areas. Compared to Cabernet, which dates to the 1800s, Chardonnay is much newer to California, introduced in the 1930s but not popular until the 1970s. In the 1950s to 1970s, most of the state's Chardonnay was planted in areas now considered far too warm for it to reach its full potential. Warmer areas in Napa Valley, for instance, have been abandoned, while areas such as Anderson Valley, Carneros, Monterey, Russian River Valley, Santa Barbara and Santa Maria Valley, all closer to cooler maritime influences, are now producing wines far superior to those made a decade ago.

When well made, Chardonnay offers bold, ripe, rich and intense fruit flavors of apple, fig, melon, pear, peach, pineapple, lemon and grapefruit, along with spice, honey, butter, butterscotch and hazelnut flavors. Winemakers build more complexity into this easy-to-manipulate wine using common vinification techniques: barrel fermentation, *sur lie* aging (during which the wine is left on its natural sediment), and malolactic fermentation (a process which converts tart malic acid to softer lactic acid). No

CHARDONNAY ACREAGE BY COUNTY

County	1970	1980	1990	1997	Percent Change 1970-1980	Percent Change 1980-1990	Percent Change 1990-1997
Napa	664	4,269	9,639	9,333	543%	126%	(-3%)
Sonoma	449	4,504	11,276	13,277	903%	150%	18%
Mendocino	130	901	3,435	4,567	593%	281%	33%
Monterey	317	3,140	8,469	15,058	890%	170%	78%
San Luis Obispo	10	506	2,412	3,597	496%	377%	49%
Santa Barbara	14	1,514	5,135	6,931	1,071%	239%	35%
Other	1,157	2,199	11,791	35,754	90%	436%	203%
State Total	**2,741**	**17,033**	**52,157**	**88,517**	**521%**	**206%**	**70%**

other white table wine benefits as much from oak aging or barrel fermentation. Chardonnay grapes have a fairly neutral flavor, and because they are usually crushed or pressed and not fermented with their skins the way red wines are, whatever flavors emerge from the grape are extracted almost instantly after crushing. Red wines that soak with their skins for days or weeks through fermentation extract their flavors quite differently.

Because Chardonnay is also a prolific producer that can easily yield 4 to 5 tons of high-quality grapes per acre, it is a cash cow for producers. Many Chardonnays are very showy, well oaked and appealing on release, but they lack the richness, depth and concentration to age and in fact evolve quickly, often losing their intensity and concentration within a year or two. Many vintners, having studied and recognized this, are now sharply reducing crop yields, holding tonnage down to 2 to 3 tons per acre in the belief that this will lead to greater concentration. The major downside to this strategy is that lower crop loads lead to significantly less wine to sell, and therefore higher prices. A new tier of high-quality Chardonnays from California's coolest appellations is now emerging, showing even greater depth, richness and concentration, but they will probably be made in much smaller case lots and sell for higher prices. Consumers appear willing to finance this trend, which is likely to affect all the major varietal wines in California.

Chardonnay's popularity has also led to a huge market of ordinary wines, so there's a broad range of quality to choose from in this varietal. There are a substantial number of California-appellation Chardonnays, which can range from simple and off-dry to more complex and sophisticated. The producer's name on the wine, and often its price, are indicators of the level of quality.

Sonoma County, with its vast Chardonnay plantings in Alexander Valley, Russian River Valley, Sonoma Valley and the Sonoma portion of Carneros, once led in plantings with 13,277 acres, but now Monterey County, with 15,058 acres has the largest acreage. Following Sonoma County are Napa County (9,333 acres, including Carneros), Santa Barbara County (6,931), San Joaquin (11,051), Mendocino (4,567) and San Luis Obispo (3,597). Total state plantings of Chardonnay have reached 88,517 acres, making it the most widely planted wine grape in the state.

CHENIN BLANC

Currently used primarily as a blending grape for generic table wines, Chenin Blanc should perform better in California, and someday it may. In 1980 it trailed only French Colombard in total acres, but now it's in third place behind Chardonnay and French Colombard. It can yield a pleasant wine, with subtle melon, peach, spice and citrus notes. Chalone and Chappellet have both made excellent wines from this grape, though not in the crisp, flinty, complex style found in the best Loire Valley whites. Most of the 21,647 total acres planted are in the Central Valley. Acreage declined by 34 percent during the 1990's.

FRENCH COLOMBARD

The king of jug wine white grapes, French Colombard is the second most widely planted in the state. Virtually all of it goes into jug wines; its value is that it produces an abundant crop, averaging 11 tons per acre, and makes clean and simple wines with firm acidity. There are now 46,076 acres of this grape in the state, a drop of 22 percent from 1990 to 1997.

GAMAY

Fading in popularity, and the subject of some debate as to its real identity, Gamay in California is really a grape called Valdigue, which produces a simple, ordinary, somewhat fruity wine. It is used primarily for blending. Plantings are fewer than 1,135 acres and dropping.

GAMAY BEAUJOLAIS

This grape is a high-yield clone of Pinot Noir that makes undistinguished wines in most places where it's grown. Used primarily for blending, it now covers 800 acres and is declining, as those serious about Pinot Noir are using superior clones and planting in cooler areas. There are some good ones left, though—try Beringer or Preston.

GEWÜRZTRAMINER

Gewürztraminer can yield magnificent wines, as is best demonstrated in Alsace, France, where it is made into a variety of styles from dry to off-dry to sweet. In California this wine has always been an afterthought, although the late-harvest version can be excellent and among the very best sweet wines in the world. The grape needs a cool climate that allows it to get ripe; areas such as Anderson Valley and Russian River Valley appear well suited to it. It's a temperamental grape to grow and vinify, as its potent spiciness can be overbearing when unchecked; it can also have a bitter edge, which is often offset by a touch of residual sugar. At its best, it produces a floral and refreshing wine with crisp acidity that pairs well with spicy dishes. When left for late harvest, it's uncommonly rich and complex, a tremendous dessert wine. Acreage stands at 1,715 acres. Navarro, Fetzer, Handley, Edmeades, Martinelli, Cosentino and Louis M. Martini are reliable sources.

GRENACHE

The second most widely planted grape in the world, Grenache is a workhorse blending grape, with 11,699 acres in vines in California, mostly in the Central Valley, where it yields a fruity, spicy, medium-bodied wine with supple tannins. Occasionally an old vineyard is found and its grapes made into a varietal wine, which at its best can be quite good. Grenache may make a comeback as Rhône enthusiasts seek cooler areas and an appropriate blending grape. Certainly the success at Alban with Edna Valley Grenache is heartening. Jaffurs is another stylish effort.

GRIGNOLINO

This grape, which can yield a pleasant rosé wine, has all but vanished from the landscape, with current state figures indicating an insignificant 78 acres. Heitz is a true believer in Grignolino.

JOHANNISBERG RIESLING

In California this grape is also known simply as Riesling or, occasionally, White Riesling. It has been declining in acreage the past few years and quality rarely

rises above the good category. As a dessert wine, though, it can be exceptional, with characteristic floral, spice and grapey pear flavors and ultra-rich texture. Arrowood, Navarro, Joseph Phelps and Chateau St. Jean are among its leading producers. Riesling grows best in cool coastal areas that allow the grapes to ripen slowly. There are now 2,522 acres statewide.

MALBEC

Malbec is considered by most to be a blending grape only, and an insignificant one at that with only 232 acres, but a few wineries use it as part of the Bordeaux-blend recipe. Arrowood makes the best single-varietal version.

MARSANNE

A few California wineries are experimenting with this white grape, which is popular in the Rhône (along with Roussanne and Viognier), but so far the acreage is minimal. At its best, Marsanne can be a full-bodied, moderately intense wine with spice, pear and citrus notes. But it is not likely to be a major stand-alone varietal, even as Rhône-style wines gain popularity. Karly in Amador County makes a very good one, and so does Preston. Domaine de la Terre Rouge in the Sierra Foothills, though, comes the closest to summing up the character of this hard-to-define grape in the name of its Marsanne Blend: "Enigma."

MERLOT

Merlot is the red-wine success of the 1990s: its popularity has soared along with its acreage. It now totals 38,522 acres in vines, a 418 percent increase from its 1990 acreage, and it seems wine lovers can't drink enough of it. Despite its popularity, its quality ranges only from good to very good most of the time, though there are a few stellar producers—Beringer Bancroft Vineyard, St. Francis, Duckhorn and Matanzas Creek, for instance.

Several styles have emerged. One is a Cabernet-style Merlot, which includes a high percentage (up to 25 percent) of Cabernet, similar currant and cherry flavors and firm tannins. A second style is less reliant on Cabernet, softer, more supple, medium-weight and less tannic, and features more herb, cherry and chocolate fla-

MERLOT ACREAGE BY COUNTY

County	1970	1980	1990	1997	Percent Change 1970-1980	Percent Change 1980-1990	Percent Change 1990-1997
Napa	159	693	2,148	5,891	336%	210%	174%
Sonoma	52	517	1,907	5,526	894%	269%	190%
Mendocino	0	102	266	1,361	100%	161%	412%
Monterey	36	632	674	3,159	1,656%	7%	369%
San Luis Obispo	0	166	201	1,946	100%	21%	868%
Santa Barbara	0	275	262	525	100%	(-5%)	100%
Other	21	282	1,977	20,115	1,609%	115%	935%
State Total	**268**	**2,667**	**7,435**	**38,522**	**895%**	**179%**	**418%**

vors. A third style is a very light and simple wine, almost vapid in flavor; this type's sales are fueling Merlot's overall growth.

Like Cabernet, Merlot can benefit from some blending, as Cabernet can give it backbone, color and tannic strength. It also marries well with oak. It's important to remember that Merlot is relatively new in California, dating only to the early 1970s. It is also a difficult grape to grow, as it sets and ripens unevenly. Still, progress is being made as vintners determine which areas are best suited to this grape variety.

As a wine, Merlot's aging potential is above average to good. I think it's better in its youth than with four or five years' cellaring, but there are some Merlots that surprise by aging well. The wine may become softer with age, but often the fruit flavors fade and the herbal flavors dominate. In the Central Valley overall, nearly 20,000 acres are planted. Napa County, with 5,891 acres, has the second-largest plantings, followed closely by Sonoma County at 5,526 acres, and Monterey with 3,159 acres. For specific recommendations, see the Reference Wines for Napa, Sonoma, Mendocino, Monterey and San Luis Obispo.

MOURVÈDRE

This grape is also known as Mataro, and with some 398 acres it's a minor factor now, pursued only by a few wineries that specialize in Rhône-style wines. The wine can be pleasing, with medium-weight, spicy cherry and berry flavors and mild tannins. Check out Bonny Doon, Cline, Ridge, Rosenblum, Jade Mountain or Jaffurs.

MUSCAT

Known as Muscat, Muscat Blanc and Muscat Canelli, this grape's acreage now totals 1,333. As a wine it is marked by strong spice and floral notes. It can be used in blending.

NEBBIOLO

The great grape of Northern Italy, which excels there in Barolo and Barbaresco, Nebbiolo now has a small foothold in California, with about 200 acres. So far the wines are light and uncomplicated, bearing no resemblance to the Italian types. But given the grape's potential for complex and ageworthy wines, and California's multitude of microclimates, it is worth a try.

PETITE SIRAH

Long favored as a blending grape, giving otherwise simple, light-colored wines more color, depth, intensity and tannin, Petite Sirah covered 2,692 acres in 1997, down from 11,254 in 1980. The grape produces dense, inky wines with ripe berry flavors and crisp, chewy tannins. It initially showed promise as a stand-alone varietal, but most of the wines failed to improve with age, only becoming more tannic and earthy. Stags' Leap Winery continues to excel with a Petite Sirah made from very old vines. In the mid-1990s, several other wineries successfully revived this variety. Among the leaders: David Bruce Paso Robles Shell Creek and Central Coast, Turley Napa Valley Hayne, Markham Napa Valley, Rosenblum, Fife, Beaulieu, La Jota and Ridge.

PINOT BLANC

Once referred to as a poor man's Chardonnay because of its similar flavor and texture profile, Pinot Blanc measures 1,026 acres in California and can make a terrific wine, as it does in the Chalone, Chateau St. Jean and Steele bottlings. When well made, it is intense, concentrated and complex, with ripe pear, peach, nectarine, spice, citrus and honey notes. It can age well, but is best early on while its fruit shines through. Also worth looking for are Au Bon Climat, Paraiso Springs, Villa Mt. Eden and Benziger.

PINOT GRIGIO

This is another grape widely-planted in Italy that is getting a tryout in California on a very small scale. Also known as Pinot Gris, at its best it yields a light, clean, crisp and refreshing wine, with a slight nutty or almond-like aroma and flavor. Among those worth trying are Long, Robert Mondavi, Chalk Hill, Steele and Joseph Swan.

PINOT NOIR

Pinot Noir, the great grape of red Burgundy, began to excel in California in the late 1980s and seems poised for further progress. Once producers stopped vinifying it as if it were Cabernet, planted vineyards in cooler climates and paid closer attention to tonnage, quality increased substantially, particularly in areas such as Carneros, Russian River Valley and Santa Barbara County. It's clear that California is producing world-class Pinot Noir. The best examples offer the classic black cherry, plum, spice, raspberry and currant flavors, and an aroma that can resemble wilted roses, along with earth, tar, herb and cola notes. It can also be rather ordinary, light, simple, herbal, vegetal and occasionally weedy. It can even be downright funky, with pungent barnyard aromas (though these negative descriptors fit few of the wines made today).

Pinot Noir is the most fickle of all grapes to grow: it reacts strongly to environmental changes such as heat and cold spells, and is notoriously fussy to work with once picked, since its thin skins are easily bruised and broken, setting the juice free in the vineyard before it's at the crush pad. Even after fermentation, Pinot Noir can hide its weaknesses and strengths, making it a most difficult wine to evaluate out of barrel. In the bottle, too, it is often a chameleon, showing poorly one day, brilliantly the next.

The current emphasis on cooler climates coincides with more rigorous clonal selection; those clones suited for sparkling wine, which have even thinner skins, are begin eliminated. These days there is also a greater understanding of, and appreciation for, different styles of Pinot Noir wine, even if there is little agreement about those styles. Should it be rich, concentrated and loaded with flavor, or a wine of elegance, finesse and delicacy? Or can it, in classic Pinot Noir sense, be both? Even varietal character remains subject to debate. Pinot Noir can certainly be tannic, especially when it is fermented with some of its stems, a practice that many vintners around the world believe contributes to the wine's backbone and

PINOT NOIR ACREAGE BY COUNTY

County	1970	1980	1990	1997	Percent Change 1970-1980	Percent Change 1980-1990	Percent Change 1990-1997
Napa	957	2,393	2,719	2,360	150%	14%	(-13%)
Sonoma	626	2,839	3,130	4,128	354%	10%	32%
Mendocino	109	323	690	670	196%	114%	(-3%)
Monterey	333	1,971	1,616	1,751	492%	(-18%)	8%
San Luis Obispo	58	96	180	410	66%	88%	128%
Santa Barbara	0	724	821	1,182	100%	13%	44%
Other	1,076	1,056	393	657	0	(-46%)	90%
State Total	**3,159**	**9,402**	**9,549**	**11,158**	**198%**	**2%**	**17%**

longevity. Pinot Noir can also be long-lived, but predicting with any precision which wines or vintages will age is often the ultimate challenge in forecasting.

In the 1980s Carneros, which covers the southern portions of Napa and Sonoma, experienced tremendous growth in plantings. The grapes were to be used both for table wine and for sparkling wine, and the best cuvées of the latter became highly reliant on Pinot Noir. This caused some concern, as the well-financed sparkling wine houses snapped up Pinot Noir wherever they could find it. In the process, many vineyards that might have yielded superb table wines were lost and prices for the grapes escalated.

Carneros Pinot Noirs are spicy, with red cherry and earthy nuances, with many showing extra dimensions of richness and depth. Moreover, for all their early appeal, they mature rather quickly. Still, Carneros Pinot Noirs have finally come into their own, with Carneros Creek, Robert Mondavi, Acacia, Truchard and Saintsbury, among others, occasionally producing brilliant wines.

Sharing the spotlight for Pinot Noir appellations are Russian River Valley and, to a lesser extent, Santa Barbara County. Russian River wineries have less money and marketing clout than those in Carneros, but the quality of Pinot Noir from Rochioli, Williams & Selyem (via the Rochioli and Allen vineyards), Gary Farrell and Dehlinger, among others, has quickly risen. The wines feature bold, ripe, bright black cherry, raspberry and spice flavors, and they're a shade more delicate and floral, even while maintaining their intensity and finesse.

Pinot Noirs from Santa Barbara and the Central Coast can offer distinctive vegetal and herbaceous flavors, but when things go right and the grapes fully ripen, cola, cherry, spice and earthy nuances rise above the vegetal notes and can render wines of tremendous depth, intensity, focus and finesse. Coolness alone is not always a virtue, as it can lead to grapes with thick skins and firm if not chewy tannins. The best offerings come from Sanford, Au Bon Climat, Byron, Cambria, Talley in Arroyo Grande Valley and others. Monterey's progress with Chardonnay should be a good harbinger of Pinot Noir's future here. In this area, both Chalone and Calera have made excellent wines, and since the best soil and exposure sites have been identified, there's every reason to believe quality will continue to rise.

Sonoma County has the largest plantings, with 4,128 acres in vines, followed by Napa (2,360), Santa Barbara (1,182) and Monterey (1,751). Carneros, which has roughly 1,440 acres in Pinot Noir, is not broken out as a district by the state.

SANGIOVESE

Despite a first decade marked by uneven quality wines, this grape appears to have a future in California, both as a stand-alone varietal and for use in blends with Cabernet, Merlot and maybe even Zinfandel. Sangiovese is best known for providing the backbone for many superb Italian red wines from Tuscany, such as Chianti, Brunello di Montalcino and the so-called Super Tuscan blends. It is somewhat surprising that Sangiovese wasn't more popular in California given the strong role Italian immigrants have played in the state's winemaking heritage. Until the mid-1980s, acreage was minimal, but there has been a recent surge in plantings, and there are now 2,498 bearing acres. Atlas Peak Vineyards in Napa Valley made an early commitment to this grape; its initial wines showed modest varietal character. Also among the early entries: Seghesio, with its Chianti Station red; Robert Pepi, under the Colline di Sassi label; Ferrari-Carano, with both a Sangiovese and a blend called Siena that includes Cabernet and Merlot; Swanson; and Flora Springs.

Sangiovese is distinctive for its supple texture and medium- to full-bodied spice, raspberry, cherry and anise flavors. When blended with a grape such as Cabernet, Sangiovese gives the wine a smoother texture and lightens up the tannins. In that regard, Ferrari-Carano's Siena is the current trendsetter, but stylistic changes are emerging as winemakers learn more about how the grape performs in different locales as well as how it marries with different grapes. Worth watching: Altamura, Flora Springs, Rabbit Ridge and Beaulieu Vineyard.

SAUVIGNON BLANC

Among varietal white wines, Sauvignon Blanc, or Fumé Blanc as it's often labeled, comes in second behind Chardonnay in terms of quality and popularity, by a good distance. The fundamental taste difference between the two is that leading Chardonnays rely on rich fruit—pear, apple, fig and grapefruit—and Sauvignon Blanc relies more on a spectrum of herbal and grassy flavors. Robert Mondavi rescued the variety by labeling it Fumé Blanc in the 1970s and he and others have made complex wines. The key to its success seems to be in taming its overt varietal intensity, which at its extreme leads to pungent grassy, vegetal and herbaceous flavors.

Many winemakers treat it like Chardonnay, employing barrel fermentation, *sur lie* aging and malolactic fermentation. The result is a sort of poor man's Chardonnay, which in some instances works well. But its popularity for growers and winemakers comes as well from the fact that it is a prodigious producer and a highly profitable wine to sell. It is also versatile at the table; often crisp and refreshing, it matches well with foods. It costs less to produce and grow than Chardonnay and sells for less. It also gets less respect from vintners than perhaps it should. Its popularity ebbs and flows, at times appearing to challenge Chardonnay and at other times appearing to be a cash-flow afterthought. But even at its best, it does not achieve the kind of richness, depth or complexity Chardonnay does, and in the end that alone may be the defining difference.

With 11,312 acres in vines—compared to 88,517 acres of Chardonnay—Sauvignon Blanc is still a distant second in plantings (among grapes used primarily in varietal wines). To its credit, it grows well in a variety of appellations, ranging from Lake and Mendocino Counties to Sonoma and Napa and farther south in Santa Barbara. It marries well with oak and Sémillon, and many vintners are adding a touch of Chardonnay for extra body. Sauvignon Blanc drinks best in its youth, but sometimes will benefit from short-term cellaring. As a late-harvest dessert wine, it's often fantastic, capable of yielding amazingly complex and richly flavored wines.

SÉMILLON

Sémillon, which enjoys modest success as a varietal wine, continues to lose ground in acreage, dropping to 1,381 acres statewide. It can make a wonderful late-harvest dessert wine, and those wineries that do focus on it can make well balanced wines with complex fig, pear, tobacco and honey notes. When blended into Sauvignon Blanc, it adds body, flavor and texture. When Sauvignon Blanc is added to Sémillon, the latter gains grassy herbal notes. Clos du Val, Cosentino and Preston produce it as a varietal wine.

SYMPHONY

A new grape variety that crosses Muscat of Alexandria and Grenache Gris, Symphony can be vinified in a wide variety of styles, from dry to dessert. Its signature is its spiciness; it gains additional peach, honey and apricot flavors when fermented as a dessert wine.

SAUVIGNON BLANC ACREAGE BY COUNTY

County	1970	1980	1990	1997	Percent Change 1970-1980	Percent Change 1980-1990	Percent Change 1990-1997
Napa	390	1,721	2,873	1,893	341%	23%	(-34%)
Sonoma	306	919	1,627	1,699	200%	77%	4%
Mendocino	44	462	880	647	950%	90%	(-26%)
Monterey	128	1,212	1,489	1,088	847%	23%	(-27%)
San Luis Obispo	0	522	702	621	100%	34%	(-12%)
Santa Barbara	17	261	443	279	1435%	70%	(-37%)
Other	477	2,172	5,419	5,288	355%	149%	(-2%)
State Total	**1,362**	**7,269**	**13,433**	**11,312**	**356%**	**85%**	**(-16%)**

Before it closed its doors in the late 1990's, Chateau de Baun pursued this grape enthusiastically in a variety of styles from dry to dessert, with mixed results.

SYRAH

The emergence of Syrah is one of the most exciting new developments in California wine. Already its rise in quality is most impressive, as the grape seems to grow well in a number of areas and is capable of rendering rich, complex and distinctive wines, with pronounced pepper, spice, black cherry, tar, meat, leather and roasted nut flavors, a smooth, supple texture and round tannins. Syrah has the early-drinking appeal of Pinot Noir and Zinfandel and few of the eccentricities of Merlot, and it may well prove far easier to grow and vinify than any other red wine aside from Cabernet. It can also be quite dense, firm and tannic, with a much more powerful personality than Zinfandel. Plantings have grown steadily to 4,277 acres, most in ideal locations along coastal valleys, so their future should be bright. The proliferation of fine wines makes this a challenging wine to follow. Among the names to look for: Swanson, Arrowood, Dehlinger, Foxen, Joseph Phelps under his Vin du Mistral label, Beaulieu Vineyard, Ojai, Qupe, Truchard, Alban, Araujo, Neyers, Cline, Edmunds St. John and Zaca Mesa.

VIOGNIER

Viognier was an early-1990s darling of Rhône lovers, but with only a little more than 100 acres, there wasn't much to taste. Acreage has grown ten-fold since 1990 and totals 1,117 acres. Viognier is one of the most difficult grapes to grow, as it struggles to produce grape clusters. Fans of the floral, spicy wine are thrilled by its prospects, and as winemakers gain experience, some Viogniers have moved beyond the one-dimensional and are offering complexity, depth and finesse. Names to look for: Arrowood, Calera, Beaulieu Vineyard, Beringer, Foxen, La Jota, Gregory Graham and Joseph Phelps' Vin du Mistral label.

ZINFANDEL

This tremendously versatile and popular grape is still tops in acreage for red grapes, with 50,498 acres of vines statewide, showing a steady gain in plantings. Much of Zinfandel is grown in the state's San Joaquin Valley, where it's vinified into white Zinfandel, a light pink-colored, slightly sweet wine. Real Zinfandel, the red wine, is the quintessential California wine. Its roots are not known for certain, although it is thought to have originated in Southern Italy as a cousin of Primitivo. In California it has served many masters. It has been used for blending with other grapes, including Cabernet and Petite Sirah. It has been made in a claret style, with berry and cherry flavors, mild tannins and pretty oak shadings. It has been made into a full-bodied, ultra-ripe, intensely flavored and firmly tannic wine designed to age. And it has been made into late-harvest and Port-style wines that feature very ripe, raisiny flavors, alcohol above 15 percent and chewy tannins.

Zinfandel's popularity among consumers fluctuates, though there is a steady hard-core base of fans. By the

SYRAH ACREAGE BY COUNTY

County	1970	1980	1990	1997	Percent Change 1970-1980	Percent Change 1980-1990	Percent Change 1990-1997
Napa	0	35	25	161	100%	(-29%)	544%
Sonoma	0	6	66	411	100%	1,000%	523%
Mendocino	0	0	112	234	0%	100%	109%
Monterey	0	4	2	189	100%	(-50%)	9,350%
San Luis Obispo	0	34	37	389	100%	9%	951%
Santa Barbara	0	0	32	187	0%	100%	484%
Other	0	2	70	2,706	100%	97%	3,766%
State Total	**0**	**81**	**344**	**4,277**	**100%**	**325%**	**1,143%**

ZINFANDEL ACREAGE BY COUNTY

County	1970	1980	1990	1997	Percent Change 1970-1980	Percent Change 1980-1990	Percent Change 1990-1997
Napa	778	2,136	1,993	1,970	175%	(-7%)	(-1%)
Sonoma	3,780	4,664	4,130	4,259	23%	(-11%)	3%
Mendocino	702	1,336	1,849	1,889	90%	38%	2%
Monterey	128	2,415	1,878	1,310	1,787%	(-22%)	(-30%)
San Luis Obispo	410	1,008	1,367	1,737	146%	36%	27%
Santa Barbara	0	75	31	18	100%	(-59%)	(-42)
Other	14,486	17,514	22,915	39,315	21%	31%	72%
State Total	**20,284**	**29,148**	**34,163**	**50,498**	**44%**	**17%**	**48%**

early 1990s Zinfandel was enjoying another ground swell of popularity, as winemakers took renewed interest, focusing on higher-quality vineyards in areas well suited to Zinfandel. Styles aimed more for the mainstream and less for extremes, emphasizing the grape's zesty, spicy pepper, raspberry, cherry, wild berry and plum flavors, and its complex range of tar, earth and leather notes. Zinfandel lends itself to blending. Many of the best are so-called field blends from vineyards planted years ago along with small amounts of Alicante, Petite Sirah and Carignane. One classic style is Ridge Vineyards' Geyserville bottling, a field blend which doesn't indicate a varietal on the label. (It is about 60 percent Zinfandel, less than the 75 percent required for varietal labeling.)

Zinfandel is a challenging grape to grow: its berry size varies significantly within a bunch, which can lead to uneven ripening. Because of that, the grape often needs to hang on the vine longer to ripen as many berries as possible. Closer attention to viticulture and an appreciation for older vines, which tend to produce smaller crops of uniformly higher quality, account for better-balanced and riper-flavored wines. Zinfandel fares well in a variety of appellations, but seems to have an edge as it moves closer to the coast in warm valleys such as Dry Creek Valley. It also performs well in the hills and mountains of Napa Valley, Sonoma and Mendocino, as well as farther south in Paso Robles. One huge advantage to growing Zinfandel: it is a very healthy, disease-resistant grapevine, which explains why for some vines are more than 100 years old and still producing. The oldest vines, planted by immigrants seeking gold, date to around 1856 and are rooted in the Sierra Foothills.

RED VARIETALS ACREAGE BY GRAPE

GRAPE (1997 Rank)	1970	1980	1990	1997	Percent Change 1970-1980	Percent Change 1980-1990	Percent Change 1990-1997
Zinfandel	20,284	29,148	34,163	50,498	44%	17%	48%
Cabernet Sauvignon	6,083	22,811	33,206	45,307	275%	46%	36%
Merlot	268	2,667	7,435	38,522	895%	179%	418%
Grenache	12,684	17,560	13,644	11,699	38%	(-22%)	(-14%)
Pinot Noir	3,159	9,402	9,549	11,158	198%	2%	17%
Barbera	3,304	19,305	10,666	11,137	484%	-45%	4%
Syrah	0	81	344	4,277	100%	325%	1,143%
Petite Sirah	4,088	11,254	3,072	2,692	175%	(-78%)	(-12%)
Sangiovese	109	0	186	2,498	(-100%)	100%	1,243%
Cabernet Franc	156	156	1,620	2,245	0%	938%	39%
Petit Verdot	0	0	97	315	0%	100%	224%
Malbec	22	57	122	232	159%	114%	90%
Nebbiolo	76	500	0	199	558%	(-100%)	100%
Other	60,794	86,253	36,702	36,206	42%	(-57%)	(-1%)
Total Acres	**111,027**	**199,194**	**150,806**	**216,984**	**79%**	**(-28%)**	**44%**

WHITE VARIETALS ACREAGE BY GRAPE

GRAPE (1997 Rank)	1970	1980	1990	1997	Percent Change 1970-1980	Percent Change 1980-1990	Percent Change 1990-1997
Chardonnay	2,741	17,033	52,157	88,517	521%	206%	70%
French Colombard	13,643	44,252	58,888	46,076	224%	33%	(-22%)
Chenin Blanc	5,276	32,279	32,957	21,647	512%	2%	(-34%)
Sauvignon Blanc	1,362	7,269	13,433	11,312	434%	85%	(-16%)
White Riesling	1,617	10,186	4,979	2,522	530%	(-51%)	(-49%)
Gewürztraminer	650	3,645	1,858	1,715	461%	(-49%)	(-8%)
Sémillon	1,245	2,848	2,229	1,381	129%	(-22%)	(-38%)
Viognier	0	0	50	1,117	0	100%	2,134%
Pinot Blanc	724	1,930	1,839	1,026	167%	(-5%)	(-44%)
Roussanne	0	0	12	81	0	100%	575%
Other	14,725	18,205	11,148	14,854	24%	(-39%)	33%
Total Acres	**41,983**	**137,647**	**179,550**	**190,247**	**228%**	**87%**	**6%**

APPELLATIONS AND VINEYARDS

Where a wine's grapes are grown ultimately determines its style, character and personality. As we will see in the next chapter, "How Wine Is Made," the decisions that are *most* crucial to a wine's quality and style concern which grapes to grow and where to plant them. Cabernet needs a steady supply of warm to hot weather for its flavors to fully ripen and develop. When it's planted in too cool a climate, it doesn't ripen and will be astringent, with green, tealike tannins. Conversely, Pinot Noir grown in too warm a climate overripens and is robbed of its varietal character and delicacy; it needs a cooler climate for success. Some grapes, such as Chardonnay and Sauvignon Blanc, perform well in a variety of soils and climates. Chardonnay in particular thrives in cooler areas all along the California coast, from Mendocino to Santa Barbara. Other grapes, such as Merlot, Cabernet Franc, Riesling and Syrah, are much more challenging to match with the right soil and climate, which are key reasons why these grapes have not yet experienced the same levels of success. Correctly matching grapes to soil and climate is a precise exercise that is nevertheless often carried out by trial and error.

Many vintners are successful right from the start in planting the proper grapes in the proper place. If you owned land in Rutherford or the Stags Leap District areas of Napa Valley, you would immediately think of planting Cabernet. If your vineyard was in Carneros,

Santa Barbara or Russian River Valley, Chardonnay and Pinot Noir would be wise choices. Some vineyards are unique in that they provide enough different microclimates, soils and exposures for several different varieties to triumph. Still, many vintners try to force their will on nature; they want to plant Pinot Noir where it's too hot, or Zinfandel where it's too cool, choices that usually result in less successful wines. Planting many acres of vines which will only produce ordinary wines for years can be a costly lesson. For many vintners, discovering which combinations work and which don't can be expensive, even painful. In California, many thousands of acres have been planted to the wrong varieties. Even today, with precise analysis of soil, grape type and climate available, mistakes are still sometimes made.

In Europe, after several hundred years of matching grapes to soil and climate, a disciplined system of appellations has evolved. In California, vintners are still learning, although since the late 1970s there has been tremendous progress in identifying which appellations best accommodate which grape types. As early as the late 1800s, vintners in Napa Valley and other parts of the state began to pinpoint areas well suited for Cabernet. In Napa—home to Inglenook and Beaulieu Vineyard—Rutherford emerged as a favored site. In Sonoma County, vintners found that Dry Creek Valley produced wonderful Zinfandel and Petite Sirah. During the 1940s, Pinot

Noir's potential in Carneros became evident in Beaulieu Vineyard's brilliant Pinots, though it was another 40 years before that potential was realized by other wineries. The pace today is much quicker, and our knowledge about which match-ups work is much greater, but there is still more to be learned. For instance, Santa Maria Valley has now been recognized as natural for Chardonnay, and it is also proving to be ideal for Sangiovese and Syrah. Monterey County has been a testing ground for grapes since the 1970s; now, after 20-some years of research, many grapes are grown there successfully. The evolution of appellations—and the vineyards within them—is fascinating to study, as they are continually changing with the addition of new areas and sites.

When you buy a bottle of wine, the producer's name, grape variety and vintage date can help you assess its style and quality. A wine's appellation should also be a clue, though, as you learn which grapes and appellations show an affinity for each other: Cabernet for Rutherford, Oakville and Stags Leap; Pinot Noir for Russian River Valley, Carneros and Santa Barbara County; Sauvignon Blanc for Lake County and Napa Valley; and Chardonnay for Carneros, Napa Valley, Russian River and Santa Barbara.

Great wines are distinctive; they convey a sense of the place where they're grown. The French call this *terroir*; it's the way in which soil and climate influence the biology of the vine stock and grape. *Terroir* is the interaction of an infinite number of variables that include temperatures by day and night, rainfall distribution by season and year, exposure, soil acidity, soil depth and so on. In short, it's anything natural that influences the growth of a vine.

Distinctive wines are not always consensus wines; they can polarize consumers. A wine with too strong a personality—an ultra-grassy Sauvignon Blanc or a richly herbal Cabernet, for example—may seem overbearing to some, yet may be a perfect example of a wine from a given appellation, a true reflection of its *terroir*. The best examples of *terroir* are seen when a wine's grapes are sourced from a very specific site. A vineyard might be 30 or 40 acres large, but within that area one or two spots will yield wines of superior quality. Often, the greatest wines are made in limited quantities from these most-specific sites. This is more true of Pinot Noir, Syrah and Zinfandel than of Cabernet and Chardonnay, which per-

form well in more diverse areas. When wines are distinctive, of high quality and limited in supply, they are usually expensive. This scenario is a classic example of supply and demand dictating prices.

Unlike Europe, in California, there are no restrictions that limit which grapes can be grown in an appellation. But common sense, experience and economics influence choices. A vintner who owns expensive hillside property in Napa Valley where Cabernet excels won't grow Gewürztraminer there for two reasons: Gewürztraminer likes cooler weather than Cabernet, and it sells for far less. The dual forces of *terroir* and economics combine to influence where grapes are grown.

U.S. APPELLATION SYSTEM

In the United States, appellations have been formalized as American Viticultural Areas (AVAs), which determine the wording that is permitted on a wine label. In order for a wine to carry an AVA, 85 percent of it must come from that appellation. In the case of varietal wines, 75 percent of the named variety must be from that appellation. If a vineyard name is used, 95 percent of that wine must come from that source. To use the term "estate bottled," both the winery and vineyard or vineyards must fall within the AVA used on the label, and the producing winery must own or control, through a long-term lease, all vineyards used in the wine.

The AVAs are mostly new, and generally useful, but far from perfect. AVAs are requested by petitioners, usually vintners and growers who own land in or buy grapes from an area they believe is distinctive and merits greater recognition. They apply to the U.S. Bureau of Alcohol, Tobacco and Firearms, which holds hearings where evidence is introduced to support or oppose an appellation, usually on the basis of boundary (but sometimes based on the name too, as in the case of Stags Leap and Dry Creek). The basic outline for an AVA includes not only specific geographic features such as soil, but also climate, temperature, elevation and rainfall, as well as whether the area is known locally or nationally (there are many Dry Creeks). The boundaries must also be readily identifiable on a U.S. Geologic Survey Map. Historic and geographic evidence of a name (Rutherford, Howell Mountain) weighs in as a factor, as do distinctive geographic boundaries and features (such as mountains, ridges and elevations), and to some extent winegrowing history, however brief.

AVAs do not follow political boundaries, such as county lines, except where the political boundary follows a natural one, such as a river, a bay or a ridge line. The boundaries are usually drawn to include the largest area under consideration rather than the smallest. For example, Napa Valley is a narrow valley through which the Napa River flows, bordered on the west and east by two mountain ranges. Yet the Napa Valley AVA covers most of Napa County, extending far beyond the real valley and well into northern and eastern valleys that really are separate. This is because growers in outlying areas historically sold grapes to prominent Napa wineries for bottling of "Napa Valley" wines. Depriving them of the right to sell their grapes as "Napa Valley" Cabernet, they claimed, would have caused them financial hardship. Conversely, wineries buying grapes from vineyards outside a narrower Napa Valley appellation might have been forced to change their labels to Napa County—a less prestigious name. The way things stand, they can claim their wine is from Napa Valley—and capitalize on the market clout of the Napa Valley name—even if it's of a different or lesser quality than the typical Napa product.

There are obvious differences between Calistoga in the north and Yountville, or even Carneros, farther south. Clearly, these areas have different soils and climates. How does the AVA system distinguish between them? Part of the answer lies in the smaller appellations within Napa Valley. Rutherford, Oakville, Yountville, Chiles Valley and the Stags Leap District are now appellations that designate wines with distinctive styles. Spring Mountain, Mount Veeder and Howell Mountain are also AVAs, and soon St. Helena and Calistoga will join them. It's also likely that Diamond Mountain and Coombsville will eventually be AVAs, as will the Oak Knoll area, which lies south of Yountville and north of Napa. Single vineyards or estate vineyards further define specific sites within an appellation.

Sonoma County, too, has its share of problems with multiple overlapping AVAs. A vineyard in Windsor (in northern Sonoma County, off U.S. Highway 101) could label its wine any number of ways, from California, the broadest possible appellation, to North Coast, Sonoma County, Northern Sonoma, Sonoma Coast, Russian River

Valley or Chalk Hill, and still comply with the spirit of the appellation system.

Glamour and marketing prestige have a lot to do with which appellations are used. California has more appeal than San Joaquin Valley. Growers in Pope Valley, northeast of Napa Valley, could have their own AVA (and probably will someday), but Napa Valley has a far greater national and international reputation. It would take years to establish any similar renown for the name Pope Valley. This is one of the most important lessons about appellations: Many vintners who make ordinary Napa Valley wines benefit from the use of the name, in effect riding on the coat tails of the region's great wines. In fact, I've seen one study of American consumers who thought most wine in California came from Napa Valley—as if it were a gigantic area—when in fact Napa is rather small, accounting for only about 4 percent of the state's total wine output. AVAs are no guarantee of quality—style, perhaps, but not quality. Names and reputations do, however, help sell wine.

THE INFLUENCE OF CLIMATE AND SOIL

The single greatest influence on California's climate is the Pacific Ocean. Were it not for the cooling effect of the ocean, most of the coastal valleys that form the state's finest winegrowing areas would simply be too warm for producing fine wine. Each of the key coastal appellations—from Anderson Valley to Temecula—owes its moderate temperatures to the ocean (in the case of Carneros and Livermore Valley, the San Pablo and San Francisco Bays play a major role, too). The regular occurrence of coastal fog, especially during the summer months, and its movement inland in the late afternoon and evening, creates California's natural air conditioning system. The most dramatic presentation of this phenomenon can be experienced while standing on the Golden Gate Bridge on a summer afternoon when the cold fog whips in under and over the famous bridge via gusting winds of 20 to 40 miles per hour. It is in this way that the Pacific Ocean shapes and defines the climate in the coastal valleys, most of which run north-south. Each of these valleys is different in size and faces the ocean at a slightly different angle. Some have higher mountains and elevations than others. All of these and other factors contribute to the unique features of the appellation.

Soil is the other major factor influencing how a grapevine grows. Compared to Europe's, California's soils are "young," rich in minerals and fertile—sometimes to a fault. California's soils also vary greatly, from the sandy benches that line rivers to the limestone beneath Calera or Chalone. A walk through Rutherford in August will leave your boots caked with a very fine dust. Even within a vineyard, soils can vary significantly. There is skill involved in matching grapevine rootstock to soil type, as certain stocks perform better in rich soils and others are better suited to sparse or shallow ones. Clay soils hold water better and longer than stony vineyards that were once river bottom, and drain easily. An iron-rich red soil will hold the day's heat longer than a chalky white soil. Mountain vineyards are mostly rocky and well drained.

The major North Coast valleys—such as Napa and Sonoma—are complex geographic entities, fascinating to study on their own. The alluvial fans along both sides of both valleys are highly regarded for their rich soils, sun exposure and drainage. It has taken centuries for them to form as the mountains shifted and crumbled. While there is no one soil that is best suited for all grapes, some sites are clearly better, as reflected by their expression of *terroir* and the quality of the wines they yield. When you taste a great wine, you can be assured that if you trace its evolution, it will lead to a specific site that's ideally suited to the grape's success.

Here, alphabetically, are the major appellations, including AVAs and counties. I have also listed what I call "Reference Wines" for the major appellations. These are wines that year in and year out display the best regional character that each appellation has to offer. One way to measure an appellation's importance for wine buying purposes is to examine the number and diversity of the Reference Wines

ALEXANDER VALLEY
AVA 1984, 66,000 acres, 11,000 acres in vines

This northern Sonoma County appellation straddles the upper reaches of the Russian River, from Healdsburg north to Cloverdale. Cabernet and Chardonnay are its leading wines. It is home to many wineries; among the better known are Simi, Jordan, Clos du Bois, Alexander Valley Vineyards, Chateau Souverain and Geyser Peak.

Curiously, Silver Oak, based in Napa Valley, helped build this appellation's Cabernet credentials as much as Simi, Clos du Bois' Marlstone and Briarcrest, Rodney Strong's Alexander's Crown or Jordan did. Despite its proximity to the Pacific Ocean, Alexander Valley is a warm appellation, with the valley floor a mix of gravely loam soils. Grapes grow well here—sometimes too well, as excess vine vigor has been an issue. One of the area's real stars is Robert Young Vineyard, known for the superb Chardonnays it yields for Chateau St. Jean, and for its dessert-style wines. This vineyard can easily produce five to six tons of Chardonnay per acre without sacrificing quality.

Alexander Valley Cabernets are supple and elegant, often marked by herb and bell pepper notes mixed in with currant, plum and cherry flavors. They are less tannic and structured than those grown in Napa Valley. Replanting vineyards with new rootstock and clones and the use of new trellising systems have changed the wine styles, giving many of the best Cabernets greater concentration and depth of flavor. Chardonnays tend to be ripe and full-blown, with juicy tropical, apple and pear-laced fruit flavors, but they can also be lean and one-dimensional. Clearly it's a diversified appellation, with wineries such as Marcassin using Gauer Ranch grapes for its "Upper Barn" bottling of Chardonnay, and Ridge relying on Geyserville at the northernmost edge of the appellation for its Zinfandel-based table wine. Clos du Bois' Briarcrest and Marlstone add to the diversity. Briarcrest is 100 percent Cabernet, and is dark and concentrated; Marlstone, located nearby, is a Bordeaux field blend, with Merlot and Cabernet Franc playing ever more equal roles with Cabernet. Perhaps the most dramatic addition this past decade is Gallo of Sonoma, which has planted nearly 1,000 acres in and around Asti to a variety of reds, including Zinfandel, Syrah and Sangiovese. Of note: the Northern Sonoma appellation was drawn, at Gallo's request, to encompass its 2,000 acres in vines reaching from Russian River (for Chardonnay) to Asti, and including its Frei Ranch in Dry Creek Valley.

REFERENCE WINES

Cabernet Sauvignon: Chateau Souverain Winemaker's Reserve, Clos du Bois Marlstone and Briarcrest, Estancia Meritage, Geyser Peak Reserve Alexandre and Geyser Peak Reserve, Jordan, Silver Oak, Simi Reserve,

Stonestreet Legacy.
Chardonnay: Chateau St. Jean Belle Terre and Robert Young Vineyards, Ferrari-Carano, Marcassin Gauer Ranch Upper Barn
Merlot: Alexander Valley Vineyards, Chateau Souverain, Stonestreet
Zinfandel: Ridge Geyserville, Rosenblum Harris-Kratka, Sausal, Scherrer, Turley 101 Vineyard

AMADOR COUNTY

Not an AVA, but significant for its Zinfandel, which occupies two-thirds of its Sierra Foothills acreage. The vineyards are found at elevations of 1,500 to 2,500 feet. This area was made popular by Sutter Home, the white (and red) Zinfandel producer, which has some 1,800 acres here. More than half of it is Zinfandel, which produces a hearty if rustic and earthy wine with wild berry flavors and often substantial tannins. Progress with quality has been slow, but often good values emerge. Both the Fiddletown (310 acres in vine) and Shenandoah Valley (1,200 acres) AVAs are within Amador County, although a portion of the latter stretches into El Dorado County.

REFERENCE WINES

Barbera: Renwood
Syrah: Domaine de la Terre Rouge
Zinfandel: Karly, Renwood

ANDERSON VALLEY
AVA 1983, 57,000 acres, 1,400 acres in vines

This slender valley in Mendocino County stretches inland from close to the Pacific Ocean and is home to both mainstream and offbeat wine styles. Chardonnay, Pinot Noir and Zinfandel are often excellent, but it's the Gewürztraminers and Rieslings—dry, off-dry and dessert-style—and sparkling wines that add excitement and dimension to the mix. Moreover, in some spots along the mountaintop ridges Cabernet does well (The Villa Mt. Eden Signature Series Cabernet 1992 from Greenwood Ridge Vineyard proved uncommonly rich and concentrated); Merlot might have a promising future there too. Riesling and Gewürztraminer plantings are more than 100 acres each, not much in size, but the quality is often excellent, led by Navarro's bottlings.

Chardonnay tends to be crisp, with apple and spice notes. Again, it's Navarro, with its Premiere Reserve Chardonnay, that often gets the most flavor from this grape, while Jed Steele shows his touch with various vineyard-designated wines at Steele Wines. Pinot Noir continues to improve, adding depth and richness to both table wines and Roederer Estate's and Pacific Echo's (formerly Scharffenberger's) sparkling wines. The best Pinot Noir is Williams & Selyem's Ferrington Vineyard, which made its debut in 1992.

REFERENCE WINES

Cabernet Sauvignon: Greenwood Ridge, Steele
Chardonnay: Edmeades, Navarro, Steele Dennison
Pinot Noir: Edmeades, Greenwood Ridge, Navarro, Steele DuPratt Vineyard, Williams & Selyem Ferrington Vineyard
Zinfandel: Edmeades Ciapusci and Zeni Vineyards. Navarro, Greenwood Ridge, Edmeades
Sparkling: Pacific Echo, Roederer L'Ermitage
Riesling: Navarro
Gewürztraminer: Edmeades, Handley, Navarro
Late Harvest Riesling and Gewürztraminer: Navarro

ARROYO GRANDE
AVA 1990, 42,880 acres, 420 acres in vines

This relatively new AVA in southern San Luis Obispo County is home to Talley Vineyards, Saucelito Canyon and Laetitia (formerly Maison Deutz) wineries, and has a climate similar to its neighbor to the north, Edna Valley. So far Chardonnay and Pinot Noir are the early leaders, and there are high hopes for the Talley Vineyards Pinot Noir. Saucelito Canyon's Zinfandels, grown at the eastern edge of the appellation, have been impressive.

REFERENCE WINES

Chardonnay: Talley Rincon Vineyard and Talley Rosemary's Vineyard, Au Bon Climat Talley Reserve, Laetitia, Nichols Talley Vineyards, Ojai Talley Vineyard
Pinot Noir: Talley Rosemary's and Rincon Vineyards
Zinfandel: Saucelito Canyon

ARROYO SECO
AVA 1983, 18,240 acres, 8,400 acres in vines

Jekel and Ventana are the two main wineries in this Monterey County appellation which rests on the eastern side of the coastal range and is best known for Chardonnay and Riesling. Jekel's Sanctuary Vineyard is the only notable one rooted to red grapes here, while Kendall-Jackson made impressive Chardonnays from its Paradise Vineyard. This appellation is of little importance so far, but that could change, as acreage has nearly quadrupled from 2,200 acres in 1995.

REFERENCE WINE

Chardonnay: Kendall-Jackson Paradise Vineyard

ATLAS PEAK
AVA 1992, 11,400 acres, 900 acres in vines

High above the Stags Leap outcropping in the Napa Valley is Foss Valley, which sits like a shallow bowl surrounded by hills and Atlas Peak. William Hill bought the property and planted the first vines, believing it ideally suited for Cabernet. He eventually sold it to a group headed by Tuscany's Piero Antinori that also included Bollinger and Whitbread. Today Atlas Peak Vineyards (see listing) is part of the Wine Alliance family of wineries, and is best known for its efforts with Sangiovese. The wines, including a varietal Cabernet, have been inconsistent, ranging from fair to good. Chardonnay also is untested. The bottom line is that this AVA has yet to prove itself.

REFERENCE WINES

Cabernet Sauvignon: Atlas Peak Consenso and Elan

CALAVERAS COUNTY

This county lies southeast of Sacramento in the Sierra Foothills. It's not an AVA, but it is home to some 200 acres in vines, including Chardonnay, Sauvignon Blanc and Zinfandel. It's of little importance as a viticultural area.

CALIFORNIA

This is the all-encompassing statewide appellation. Any grape grown within its boundaries can carry the name. California has more than 407,231 acres in vines and produces 85 percent of the country's wine. On wine labels, California usually means the grapes have come from a variety of appellations, rather than one specific AVA, region or county. The California appellation is used on a wide range of products including expensive wines such as Martin Ray Chardonnay, but mostly on inexpensive wines. Depending on the producer, "California" can represent good quality and value. But as more wineries focus on Coastal-grown grapes, the gap in quality between specific, narrow appellations and the broad California one should widen. Wineries can make great-California appellation wines merely by blending grapes and/or wines from excellent sources. But most wineries that can tap into such superior quality sources choose to keep them separate and more sharply defined by AVA or vineyard.

CALIFORNIA SHENANDOAH VALLEY
AVA 1983, 10,000 acres, 1,200 acres in vines

There are two Shenandoah Valleys in the U.S.—Virginia has the other, hence the use of California in the name of this Sierra Foothills appellation. Zinfandel is the major grape, with many decades-old vines that yield ripe, intense wines featuring firm tannins, earthy berry and tar flavors and a rustic edge. Rhône- and Italian-style reds are also joining the mix.

REFERENCE WINES

Syrah: Sobon
Zinfandel: Amador Foothill, Easton, Renwood Grandpère, Sobon

CALISTOGA

Not an AVA, but sure to be one eventually as Napa Valley is further subdivided. This northernmost city in the valley is warm and excels with many grapes, but Cabernet is the star, and Sauvignon Blanc is also favored. A number of important wineries are based here, among them Araujo Estate, Chateau Montelena, Sterling Vineyard, Clos Pegase and Cuvaison.

REFERENCE WINES

Cabernet Sauvignon: Araujo Estate Eisele Vineyard, Chateau Montelena, Robert Pecota Kara's Vineyard
Merlot: Duckhorn Three Palms Vineyard, Robert Pecota Steven André Vineyard
Syrah: Araujo Estate Eisele Vineyard

CARMEL VALLEY
AVA 1983, 19,200 acres, 150 acres in vines

Southeast of the famous town of Carmel, this Monterey County appellation rises up from sea level and gets substantial rainfall. It is home to Bernardus, Durney, Galante, Chateau Julien and Georis. Durney's Cabernets can be good, but more often are hard and tannic and even with age they fail to impress. Bernardus has emerged as the quality leader with its Marinus Cabernet. Galante's Cabernet and Merlot are also well made. Georis Merlot is distinctive, but quite tannic.

REFERENCE WINES

Cabernet Sauvignon: Bernardus Marinus, Galante Blackjack Pasture and Red Rose Hill
Merlot: Galante, Georis

CARNEROS
AVA 1983, 36,900 acres, 6,200 acres in vines

This AVA straddles the southernmost portions of Napa and Sonoma Valleys and is synonymous with consistently high-quality Chardonnays and Pinot Noirs. Its soils vary, but in general are thin (usually less than 3 to 4 feet deep), especially when compared with the rich, loamy soils in the heart of Napa Valley. Nor is the soil very fertile, since it was once part of the bottom of San Pablo Bay, a mix of clay and loamy deposits. Rainfall is sparse, the growing season long and the climate shaped by the bay and whipping winds that blow through the area almost daily. Because it is cooler than the Napa and Sonoma Valleys proper, and because vintners here could use the valuable names Napa Valley or Sonoma Valley if they chose, it emerged as Napa and Sonoma vintners' best choice for Chardonnay and Pinot Noir. Both of these grapes have had successes here. The Chardonnays are bright and lively, with earthy apple, pineapple and crisp lemon flavors. Pinot Noir is marked by spicy cherry and berry flavors and is crisp and tight in structure, much like the Chardonnay. In the best vintages, both wines age well for four to six and up to ten years. *Méthode champenoise* sparkling wine is the other major product of Carneros' Chardonnay and Pinot Noir plantings, led by Codorniu Napa, Domaine Carneros, Domaine Chandon and Gloria Ferrer.

Cabernet, which once fared well at Buena Vista with its excellent Special Selection and Private Reserve bottlings, has faltered of late, with wines that increasingly display an herbal, weedy edge and lack tart cherry and berry notes. Merlot, however, shows potential; Cuvaison's is first-class, as is Truchard's. The Syrah from Truchard, grown at the northernmost edge of Carneros-Napa, is so rich and authentic, with classic toasty cherry and berry flavors, that it too may be a strong presence in the future. Syrah and other red varieties may prove a good match for the dark, warm soils of Carneros.

REFERENCE WINES

Cabernet Sauvignon: Buena Vista, Paul Hobbs Hyde Vineyard, Truchard
Chardonnay: Acacia, Gloria Ferrer, Grgich Hills Carneros, Kistler Hyde Vineyard, Robert Mondavi, Ravenswood Sangiacomo Vineyard, Saintsbury, David Ramey, Robert Sinskey, Patz & Hall Hyde Vineyard, Truchard
Merlot: Buena Vista, Cuvaison, Havens, Robert Sinskey, Truchard, Ravenswood
Pinot Noir: Acacia, Carneros Creek, El Molino, Etude, Robert Mondavi, Saintsbury, Patz & Hall Hyde, Truchard
Syrah: Havens, Kongsgaard, Truchard

CENTRAL COAST

This giant appellation covers coastal counties from the San Francisco Bay Area in the north to Santa Barbara County in the south. It includes the following AVAs: Arroyo Grande, Arroyo Seco, Carmel Valley, Chalone, Edna Valley, Livermore Valley, Mount Harlan, Paso Robles, San Lucas, San Ysidro, Santa Cruz Mountains, Santa Lucia Highlands, Santa Maria Valley, Santa Ynez Valley and York Mountain.

CHALK HILL
AVA 1983, 21,100 acres, 1,000 acres in vines

Chalk Hill covers the easternmost portion of Russian River Valley in northern Sonoma, taking its name from the area's chalky, volcanic dust soils. Chardonnay is the predominant grape grown here, with Rodney Strong's Chalk Hill Chardonnay and Chalk Hill Winery carrying the name to market. Chalk Hill Winery, with nearly 300 acres in vines, does well with Chardonnay and Sauvignon Blanc. Its Cabernet and Merlot, once highly variable, have been better of late, bordering on excellent.

CHALONE
AVA 1982, 8,640 acres, 300 acres in vines

This single-winery appellation in the Gavilan Mountains straddles the Monterey and San Benito county borders, near Pinnacles National Monument. These mountains rise up from the Salinas Valley, and the vineyard is 1,800 feet above sea level in rugged, parched, windswept terrain. The area has been home to Chalone's excellent Chardonnays, Chenin Blancs, Pinot Blancs and Pinot Noirs for nearly four decades. Some of the vines date to the 1940s. All four of the main wines are excellent and long-lived, marked by a youthful austerity and a capacity to develop complex nuances, often with flinty mineral flavors. The Chardonnay is the most consistently excellent performer, capable of rendering uncommonly complex and long-lived wines. Pinot Noir also fares well here, but as a grape it's more variable; through the 1980s it produced a leaner, more tannic, less interesting wine than it did the decade before, while the vintages of the 1990s showed more finesse but remained tannic and austere overall. The Pinot Blanc is simply California's finest, at times sharing the focus, intensity and discipline of the Chardonnay. The Chenin Blanc, too, merits special attention, as it often renders a remarkably complex and enduring wine.

REFERENCE WINES

Chardonnay: Chalone, Testarossa
Pinot Blanc: Chalone, Testarossa
Pinot Noir: Chalone, David Bruce

CHILES VALLEY
AVA 1999, 6,000 acres, 1,000 acres in vines

Located within the Napa Valley AVA, this brand-new appellation is a separate valley east of Rutherford. It's at a slightly higher elevation and has a cooler climate than Rutherford and the Napa Valley floor. Chiles Valley is home to Green & Red, Volker Eisele, Nichelini and Rustridge wineries. So far the Green & Red Chiles Mill Vineyard Zinfandel is the best wine from this area.

REFERENCE WINES:

Cabernet Sauvignon: Volker Eisele
Zinfandel: Green & Red Chiles Mill Vineyard

CLARKSBURG
AVA 1984, 65,000 acres, 8,000 acres in vines

Best known for its Chenin Blanc, this appellation is home only to Bogle Vineyards. There are no other wineries here. Chardonnay, Merlot, Petite Sirah and Cabernet are also grown in this area just outside of Sacramento.

CLEAR LAKE
AVA 1984, 168,900 acres, 3,200 acres in vines

Years ago most grapes gave way to pears in this Lake County AVA, but Sauvignon Blanc still excels and Cabernet, Chardonnay and Zinfandel can make very appealing, lighter wines. Steele's Catfish Vineyard Zinfandel carries this appellation.

DIAMOND MOUNTAIN

This region of northwestern Napa is not an AVA, but is likely to become one. The most famous property here is Diamond Creek Vineyards (see listing), which bottles three (and sometimes four) separate vineyard-designated Cabernets from its 20 acres in vines. These are uncommonly complex and long-lived wines, from as distinctive a vineyard as exists in California. Others, including Sterling Vineyards' Diamond Mountain Ranch, have had less success with both Cabernet and Chardonnay, while von Strasser appears to have found a groove with its Cabernets. Cabernet and certain other Bordeaux-style reds will likely dominate; Merlot is more challenging to grow here.

REFERENCE WINES

Cabernet Sauvignon: Diamond Creek Gravelly Meadow, Lake, Red Rock Terrace and Volcanic Hill vineyards; Constant Diamond Mountain Vineyard, Martin Ray, Sterling Diamond Mountain Ranch, von Strasser

DRY CREEK VALLEY
AVA 1983, 80,000 acres, 5,500 acres in vines

This narrow valley in Northern Sonoma is home to many first-class Zinfandels; the varietal seems to excel in this area which, during the growing season, starts with cool mornings and warms sufficiently in the afternoons to give the tricky Zinfandel grape the right amount of heat without overdoing it. Ridge Lytton Springs, Rafanelli, Quivira, Ferrari-Carano, Nalle, Preston, Dry Creek Vineyards and Gallo of Sonoma are all crafting superb Zinfandels marked by spicy raspberry and black cherry flavors. Cabernet is slowly making inroads and seems to perform best in the hills—witness the excellent Gallo Northern Sonoma, which is estate-bottled, and Rafanelli—but it can be lighter and lacking the richness, depth and concentration of the best from Napa Valley. Among whites, Sauvignon Blanc leads in acreage and can yield good wines marked by grassy, herbal notes. Clos du Bois' Flintwood Chardonnay, grown farther south, is the best known of that variety.

REFERENCE WINES

Cabernet Sauvignon: Dry Creek Vineyard Meritage, Gallo Northern Sonoma, Pezzi King, Rafanelli
Chardonnay: Alderbrook Dorothy's Vineyard, Clos du Bois Flintwood, Gallo of Sonoma Stefani Vineyard
Merlot: Dry Creek Vineyard, Mazzocco, McCray Ridge Two Moon Vineyard
Sauvignon Blanc: Dry Creek Vineyard Reserve Fumé, Preston, Quivira
Zinfandel: David Coffaro, Chateau Souverain, Dry Creek Vineyard, Ferrari-Carano, Gallo Frei Ranch, Meeker, Nalle, Quivira, Pezzi King, Preston, Rabbit Ridge, Rafanelli, Ridge, Turley Grist Vineyard

DUNNIGAN HILLS
AVA 1993, 89,000 acres, 1,500 acres in vines

A series of low, rolling hills in the Sacramento Valley in Yolo County rising to about 400 feet in elevation comprise this AVA. This appellation is home to R.H. Phillips, which owns the majority of acreage planted here. Generally well made, the Phillips wines offer good value.

EDNA VALLEY
AVA 1982, 22,400 acres, 1,700 acres in vines

Edna Valley is best known for its intensely flavored Chardonnays, led by Edna Valley Vineyard, Meridian and Mount Eden. This South Central Coast AVA is close to the ocean and is quite cool and breezy, so much so that Edna Valley Vineyards' Pinot Noirs, which failed to ripen in too many years and frequently led to pungently vegetal wines, have largely faded. In warm years, the Edna Valley Chardonnay is bold, rich and intensely flavored. Alban has carved a niche with estate-grown Rhône-inspired reds and whites that are increasingly noteworthy, demonstrating that in the right areas, grapes other than Chardonnay have a promising future.

REFERENCE WINES

Chardonnay: Au Bon Climat Alban Vineyard, Edna Valley Vineyards, Meridian Reserve, Mount Eden MacGregor Vineyard, Nichols Edna Ranch Vineyard, Seven Peaks Reserve, Stephen Ross Edna Ranch, Talley Oliver's Vineyard
Grenache: Alban
Pinot Noir: Nichols Paragon Vineyard, Stephen Ross Edna Ranch
Roussanne: Alban
Syrah: Alban
Viognier: Alban

EL DORADO
AVA 1983, 414,000 acres, 1,000 acres in vines

The few vineyards in this Sierra Foothills appellation northeast of Sacramento rise to between 2,200 and 3,000 feet of elevation. Most of the major varieties are grown here, with Zinfandel the leader among reds and Chardonnay the leader among whites. The Zinfandels

CALIFORNIA WINE REGION MAPS

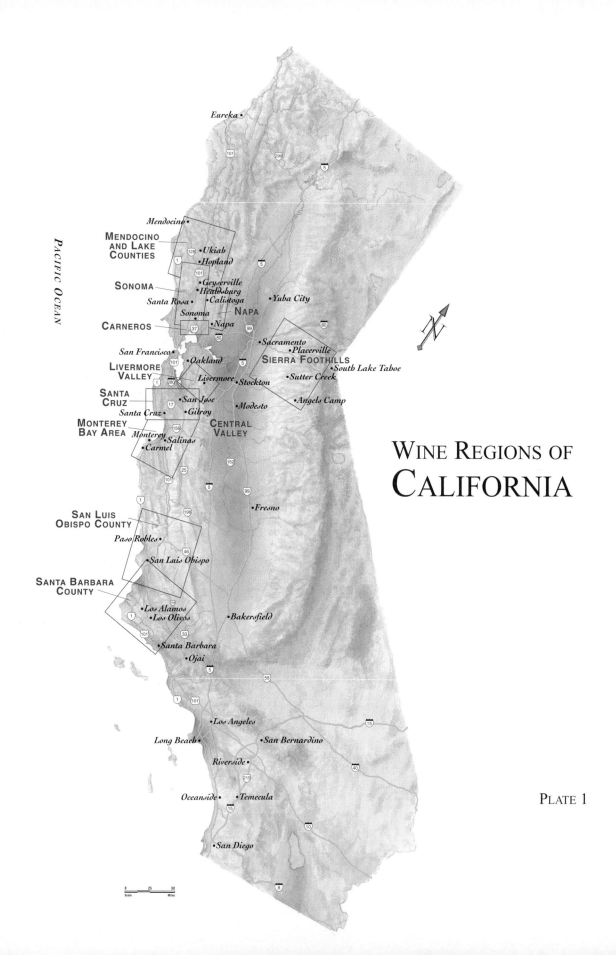

Eureka •

PACIFIC OCEAN

Mendocino •

**MENDOCINO
AND LAKE
COUNTIES**

128 • Ukiah
1 • Hopland
101

SONOMA
• Geyserville
• Healdsburg
Santa Rosa • • Calistoga
Sonoma **NAPA**
37 • Napa
CARNEROS
80

San Francisco •
**LIVERMORE
VALLEY**
101 • Oakland
Livermore •
1 280
**SANTA
CRUZ**
17 • San Jose
Santa Cruz • • Gilroy
**MONTEREY
BAY AREA** Monterey • 156
• Salinas
• Carmel
25

101

1

**SAN LUIS
OBISPO COUNTY**

Paso Robles •
46
• San Luis Obispo

198

5

**SANTA BARBARA
COUNTY**

1 • Los Alamos
• Los Olivos
101 33
• Santa Barbara
• Ojai
5

• Yuba City
80
99
• Sacramento
• Placerville
SIERRA FOOTHILLS
5 • South Lake Tahoe
• Stockton • Sutter Creek
• Modesto
• Angels Camp
**CENTRAL
VALLEY**
152

5
99

• Fresno

• Bakersfield

58

1 101

• Los Angeles
Long Beach • • San Bernardino
Riverside •
215
Oceanside • • Temecula
15
10
• San Diego

N

WINE REGIONS OF
CALIFORNIA

PLATE 1

0 25 50
Scale Miles

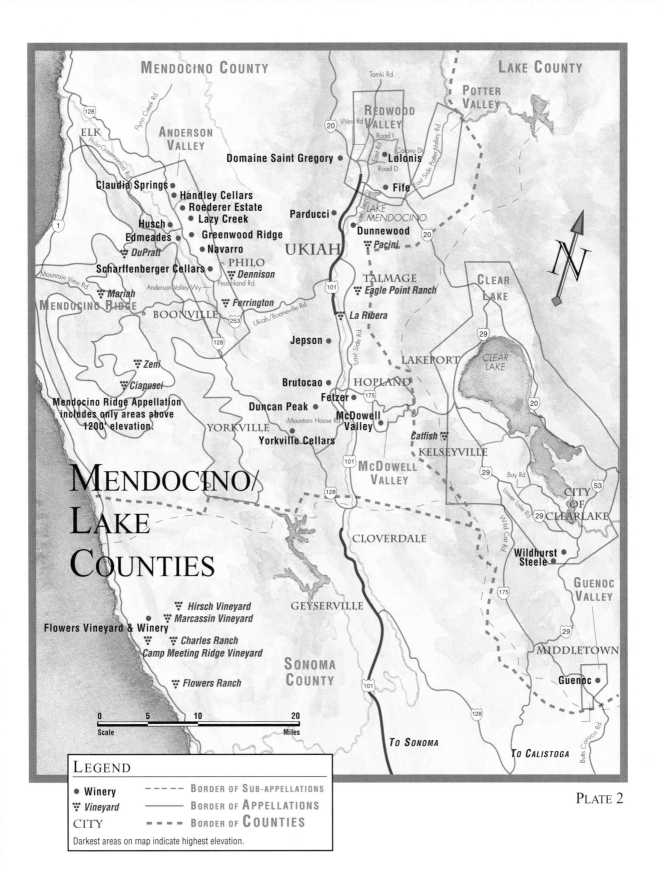

MENDOCINO COUNTY   LAKE COUNTY

Tomki Rd.

POTTER
VALLEY

REDWOOD
VALLEY

West Rd.

Road 1

● Domaine Saint Gregory   ● Lolonis

Road D

ELK

ANDERSON
VALLEY

Claudia Springs ●
● Handley Cellars
● Roederer Estate
● Lazy Creek
Husch ●   ● Fife
Edmeades ●
🌱 DuPratt   ● Greenwood Ridge

Parducci ●

LAKE
MENDOCINO

● Dunnewood

🌱 Pacini

● Navarro

UKIAH

CLEAR
LAKE

Scharffenberger Cellars ●

PHILO
🌱 Dennison

TALMAGE
🌱 Eagle Point Ranch

Peachland Rd.

Anderson Valley Wy.

🌱 Mariah

MENDOCINO RIDGE

BOONVILLE ●

🌱 Ferrington

Ukiah/Booneville Rd.

● La Ribera

CLEAR
LAKE

Jepson ●

LAKEPORT

🌱 Zeni

🌱 Ciapusci

Mendocino Ridge Appellation
includes only areas above
1200' elevation.

YORKVILLE

Brutocao ●

Duncan Peak ●

Fetzer ●

HOPLAND

McDowell
Valley ●

Catfish ●

Mountain House Rd.

Yorkville Cellars ●

KELSEYVILLE

MENDOCINO/
LAKE
COUNTIES

McDOWELL
VALLEY

Bay Rd.

CITY
OF
CLEARLAKE

CLOVERDALE

Wildhurst ●
Steele ●

GUENOC
VALLEY

Hirsch Vineyard 🌱
Marcassin Vineyard 🌱

Flowers Vineyard & Winery ●

🌱 Charles Ranch

Camp Meeting Ridge Vineyard

GEYSERVILLE

MIDDLETOWN

Guenoc ●

🌱 Flowers Ranch

SONOMA
COUNTY

TO SONOMA

TO CALISTOGA

Butts Canyon Rd.

0   5   10   20

Scale   Miles

N

PLATE 2

LEGEND

● Winery   - - - - BORDER OF SUB-APPELLATIONS
🌱 Vineyard   ——— BORDER OF APPELLATIONS
CITY   - - - - BORDER OF COUNTIES

Darkest areas on map indicate highest elevation.

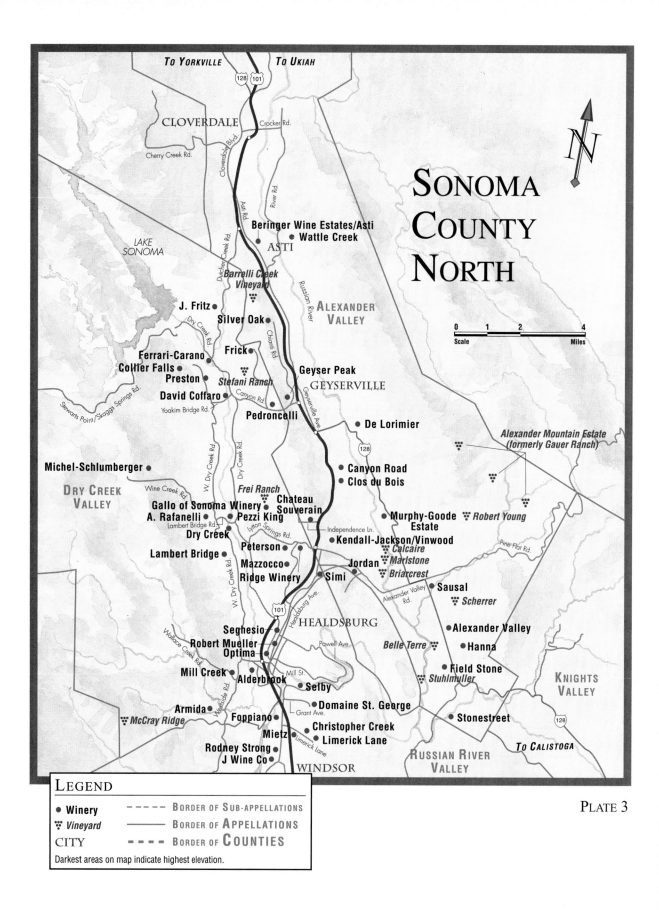

TO YORKVILLE TO UKIAH
128 101

CLOVERDALE Crocker Rd.

Cherry Creek Rd.

LAKE
SONOMA

River Rd.

Beringer Wine Estates/Asti
Wattle Creek
ASTI

Barrelli Creek
Vineyard

Russian River

ALEXANDER
VALLEY

J. Fritz
Silver Oak

Frick

Ferrari-Carano
Collier Falls
Preston
David Coffaro

Stefani Ranch

Geyser Peak
GEYSERVILLE

Pedroncelli

De Lorimier

128

Alexander Mountain Estate
(formerly Gauer Ranch)

Michel-Schlumberger

DRY CREEK
VALLEY

Wine Creek Rd.

Frei Ranch

Canyon Road
Clos du Bois

Gallo of Sonoma Winery
A. Rafanelli
Pezzi King
Dry Creek
Peterson
Lambert Bridge
Mazzocco
Ridge Winery

Chateau
Souverain

Lytton Springs Rd.
Independence Ln.

Simi

Murphy-Goode
Estate

Robert Young

Kendall-Jackson/Vinwood
Calcaire
Marlstone
Jordan
Briarcrest

Sausal
Scherrer

Seghesio
Robert Mueller
Optima

Mill Creek
Alderbrook

Armida
McCray Ridge

Foppiano

Mietz

Rodney Strong
J Wine Co

HEALDSBURG

Powell Ave.

Selby

Domaine St. George
Grant Ave.

Christopher Creek
Limerick Lane

WINDSOR

Belle Terre

Alexander Valley
Hanna

Field Stone
Stuhlmuller

Stonestreet

KNIGHTS
VALLEY

128

TO CALISTOGA

RUSSIAN RIVER
VALLEY

SONOMA
COUNTY
NORTH

N

0 1 2 4
Scale   Miles

LEGEND

● Winery   - - - - BORDER OF SUB-APPELLATIONS
🍇 Vineyard   ——— BORDER OF APPELLATIONS
CITY   - - - - BORDER OF COUNTIES

Darkest areas on map indicate highest elevation.

PLATE 3

SONOMA COUNTY CENTRAL

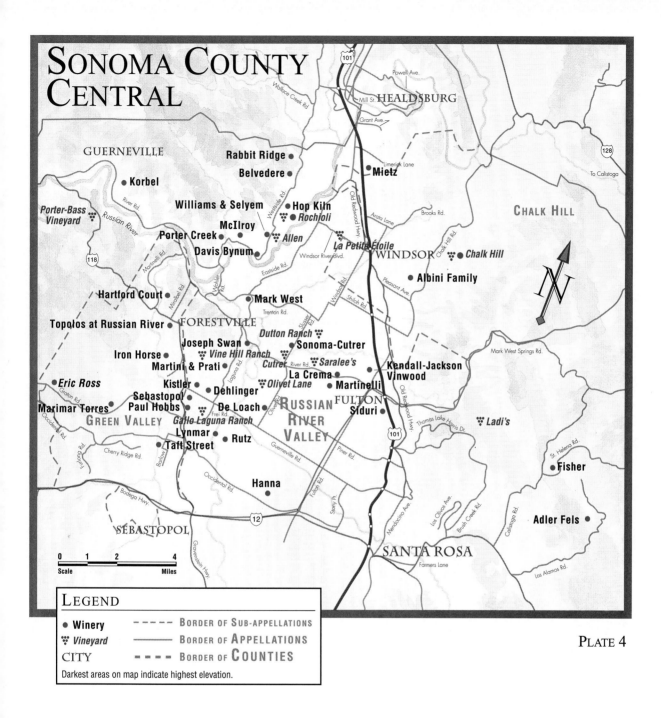

GUERNEVILLE

Porter-Bass Vineyard

Korbel

Russian River

Rabbit Ridge
Belvedere

Mietz

Williams & Selyem

Hop Kiln
Rochioli

McIlroy

Allen

Porter Creek

Davis Bynum

La Petite Étoile

WINDSOR

Chalk Hill

CHALK HILL

Albini Family

Hartford Court

Mark West

Topolos at Russian River

FORESTVILLE

Dutton Ranch

Joseph Swan

Sonoma-Cutrer

Vine Hill Ranch

Iron Horse

Martini & Prati

Cutrer

Saralee's

Kendall-Jackson
Vinwood

Eric Ross

Kistler

Dehlinger

La Crema
Olivet Lane

Martinelli

Marimar Torres

Sebastopol

Paul Hobbs

De Loach

RUSSIAN
RIVER
VALLEY

FULTON

Ladi's

GREEN VALLEY

Gallo Laguna Ranch

Siduri

Lynmar

Rutz

Taft Street

Fisher

Hanna

Adler Fels

SEBASTOPOL

SANTA ROSA

HEALDSBURG

```
0   1   2        4
Scale           Miles
```

LEGEND

● Winery
❦ Vineyard
CITY

- - - - BORDER OF SUB-APPELLATIONS
──── BORDER OF APPELLATIONS
- - - - BORDER OF COUNTIES

Darkest areas on map indicate highest elevation.

PLATE 4

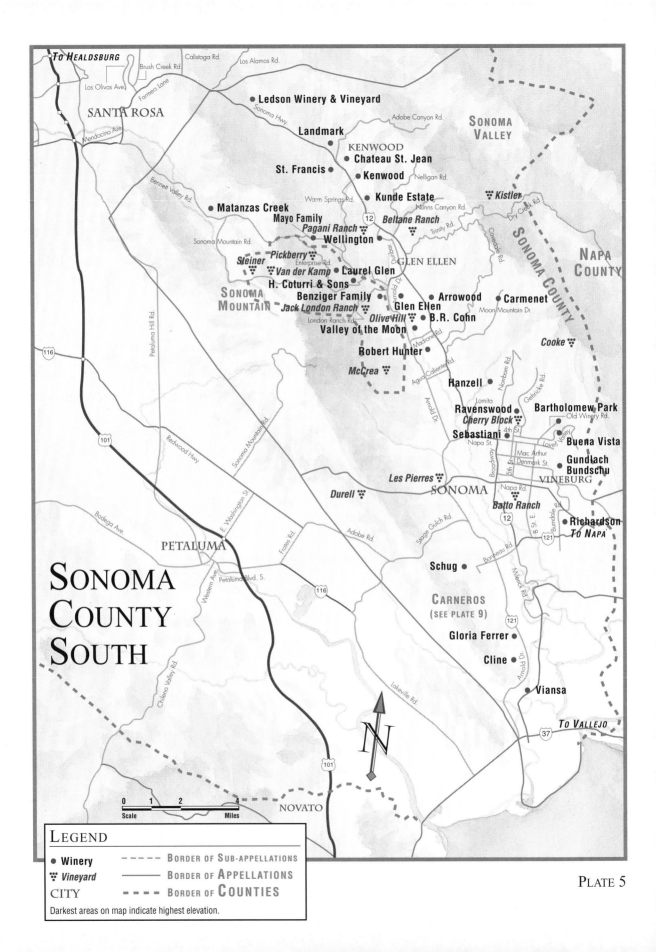

To Healdsburg

Calistoga Rd.
Brush Creek Rd.
Los Alamos Rd.
Los Olivos Ave.
Farmers Lane
SANTA ROSA
Mendocino Ave.

● Ledson Winery & Vineyard
Sonoma Hwy.
Adobe Canyon Rd.

● Landmark
KENWOOD
● Chateau St. Jean
SONOMA VALLEY

● St. Francis
● Kenwood
Nelligan Rd.

Bennett Valley Rd.
Warm Springs Rd.
● Kunde Estate
Nunns Canyon Rd.
🍇 Kistler

● Matanzas Creek
Mayo Family 🍇
Pagani Ranch 🍇
● Wellington
Dunbar Rd.
🍇 Beltane Ranch
Trinity Rd.
Dry Creek Rd.

Sonoma Mountain Rd.
Pickberry 🍇
Steiner 🍇 Van der Kamp
● Laurel Glen
Enterprise Rd.
GLEN ELLEN
NAPA COUNTY

SONOMA COUNTY

H. Coturri & Sons
SONOMA MOUNTAIN
Benziger Family
Jack London Ranch 🍇
● Arrowood
● Carmenet
Coneable Rd.

London Ranch Rd.
Olive Hill 🍇
Glen Ellen
● B.R. Cohn
Moon/Mountain Dr.

● Valley of the Moon
Madrone Rd.

● Robert Hunter
🍇 Cooke

🍇 McCrea
Agua Caliente Rd.
● Hanzell
Norrbom Rd.

Arnold Dr.
Lomita
Gehricke Rd.
● Ravenswood
● Bartholomew Park
Old Winery Rd.
Cherry Block 🍇
Lovell Valley Rd.
4th St.
● Buena Vista
● Sebastiani
Napa St.
● Gundlach Bundschu

Petaluma Hill Rd.
Redwood Hwy.
Sonoma Mountain Rd.
● Les Pierres 🍇
SONOMA
Broadway
Mac Arthur
Denmark St.
5th St. E.
VINEBURG

Durell 🍇
Napa Rd.
12
Batto Ranch 🍇
8th St. E.
Burndale Rd.
● Richardson
To Napa
121

Bodega Ave.
E. Washington St.
Frates Rd.
Adobe Rd.
Stage Gulch Rd.
Bonneau Rd.

PETALUMA
● Schug
Milerick Rd.

116
CARNEROS
(SEE PLATE 9)
121

SONOMA COUNTY SOUTH

Western Ave.
Petaluma Blvd. S.
116
● Gloria Ferrer

Chileno Valley Rd.
● Cline
Arnold Dr.

Lakeville Rd.
● Viansa
N
37
To Vallejo

0 1 2 4
Scale   Miles
NOVATO

101

PLATE 5

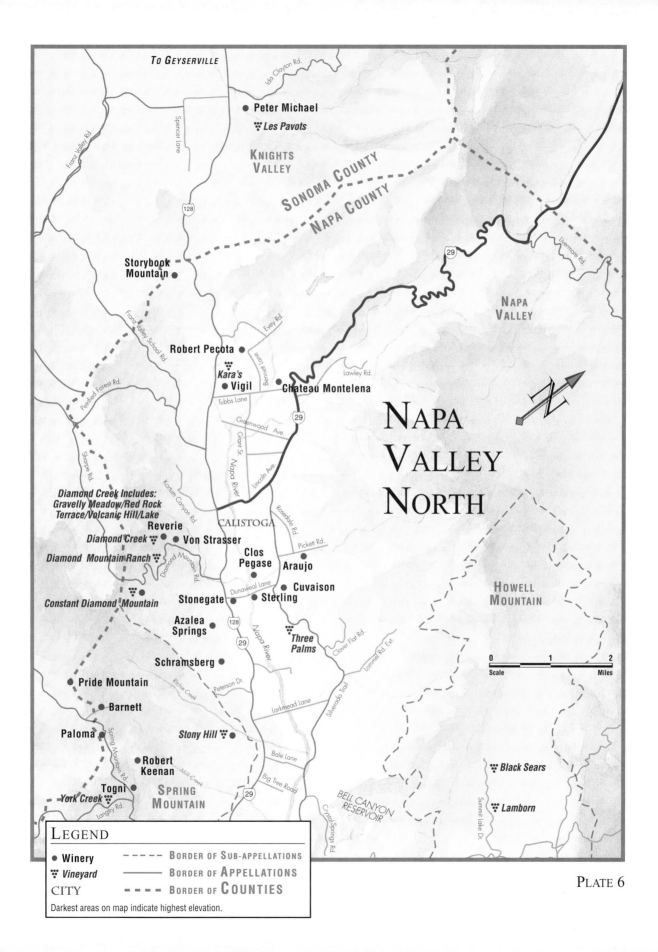

To Geyserville

Ida Clayton Rd.

● Peter Michael

🍇 Les Pavots

Spencer Lane

KNIGHTS
VALLEY

SONOMA COUNTY

NAPA COUNTY

Livermore Rd.

29

Franz Valley Rd.

128

NAPA
VALLEY

Storybook
Mountain ●

Evey Rd.

Franz Valley School Rd.

Petrified Forest Rd.

Robert Pecota ●

🍇 Kara's
● Vigil

Benneh Lane

Lawley Rd.

Chateau Montelena

29

Tubbs Lane

Greenwood Ave.

Sharpe Rd.

Grant St.

Lincoln Ave.

Napa River

NAPA
VALLEY
NORTH

Karum Canyon Rd.

Rosedale Rd.

Diamond Creek Includes:
Gravelly Meadow/Red Rock
Terrace/Volcanic Hill/Lake

Reverie ●
Diamond Creek 🍇 ● Von Strasser
Diamond Mountain Ranch 🍇

CALISTOGA

Clos
Pegase ●
● Araujo

Pickett Rd.

HOWELL
MOUNTAIN

Diamond Mountain Rd.

Cuvaison

🍇 Constant Diamond Mountain

Stonegate ●

Dunaweal Lane

● Sterling

Azalea
Springs ●

128

29

Napa River

🍇 Three
Palms

Clover Flat Rd.

Lommel Rd. Ext.

0   1   2
Scale   Miles

Schramsberg ●

Richie Creek

Peterson Dr.

Larkmead Lane

Silverado Trail

● Pride Mountain

● Barnett

Paloma ●

Spring Mountain Rd.

Stony Hill 🍇

Bale Lane

● Robert
Keenan

Mill Creek

Big Tree Road

SPRING
MOUNTAIN

🍇 Black Sears

● Togni
🍇 York Creek

Langtry Rd.

29

BELL CANYON
RESERVOIR

Crystal Springs Rd.

Summit Lake Dr.

🍇 Lamborn

LEGEND

● Winery
🍇 Vineyard
CITY

- - - - BORDER OF SUB-APPELLATIONS
——— BORDER OF APPELLATIONS
▬ ▬ ▬ ▬ BORDER OF COUNTIES

Darkest areas on map indicate highest elevation.

PLATE 6

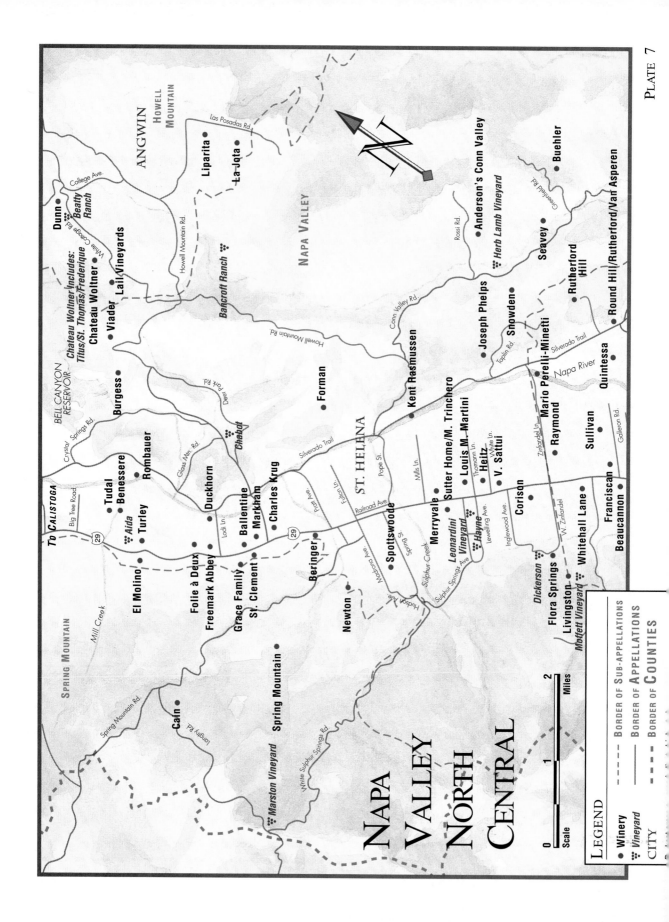

PLATE 7

NAPA VALLEY NORTH CENTRAL

HOWELL MOUNTAIN

ANGWIN

NAPA VALLEY

Las Posadas Rd.

Liparita

La Jota

College Ave.

Dunn

Beatty Ranch

White College Rd.

Chateau Woltner Includes:
Titus/St. Thomas/Frederique

Chateau Woltner

Viader

Lail Vineyards

Howell Mountain Rd.

Bancroft Ranch

Anderson's Conn Valley

Herb Lamb Vineyard

Greenfield Rd.

Buehler

Seavey

Rossi Rd.

Rutherford Hill

Round Hill/Rutherford/Van Asperen

Conn Valley Rd.

Joseph Phelps

Snowden

BELL CANYON RESERVOIR

Crystal Springs Rd.

Burgess

Deer Park Rd.

Howell Mountain Rd.

Forman

Kent Rasmussen

Taplin Rd.

Silverado Trail

Mario Perelli-Minetti

Napa River

Quintessa

SPRING MOUNTAIN

Mill Creek

To CALISTOGA

Big Tree Road

Tudal

Benessere

Aida

Turley

Rombauer

Glass Mtn. Rd.

Chabot

Duckhorn

Lodi Ln.

Ballentine

Markham

Charles Krug

Silverado Trail

Pope St.

Pratt Ave.

Railroad Ave.

Fulton Ln.

Mills Ln.

ST. HELENA

Sutter Home/M. Trinchero

Louis M. Martini

Thomann Ln.

Heitz

White Ln.

V. Sattui

Lewelling Ave.

Corison

Inglewood Ave.

Zinfandel Ln.

Raymond

Sullivan

Galleron Rd.

Franciscan

Beaucannon

Spring Mountain Rd.

Longhry Rd.

Cain

El Molino

Folie à Deux

Freemark Abbey

Grace Family

St. Clement

Spring Mountain

Newton

29

Beringer

Madrona Ave.

Spottswoode

Spring St.

Sulphur Creek

Merryvale

Leonardini

Vineyard

Hayne

Sulphur Springs Ave.

Hudson Ave.

W. Zinfandel

Whitehall Lane

Dickerson

Flora Springs

Livingston

Moffett Vineyard

White Sulphur Springs Rd.

Marston Vineyard

NAPA VALLEY NORTH CENTRAL

0   1   2

Scale   Miles

LEGEND

• Winery

❋ Vineyard

CITY

BORDER OF SUB-APPELLATIONS

BORDER OF APPELLATIONS

BORDER OF COUNTIES

29

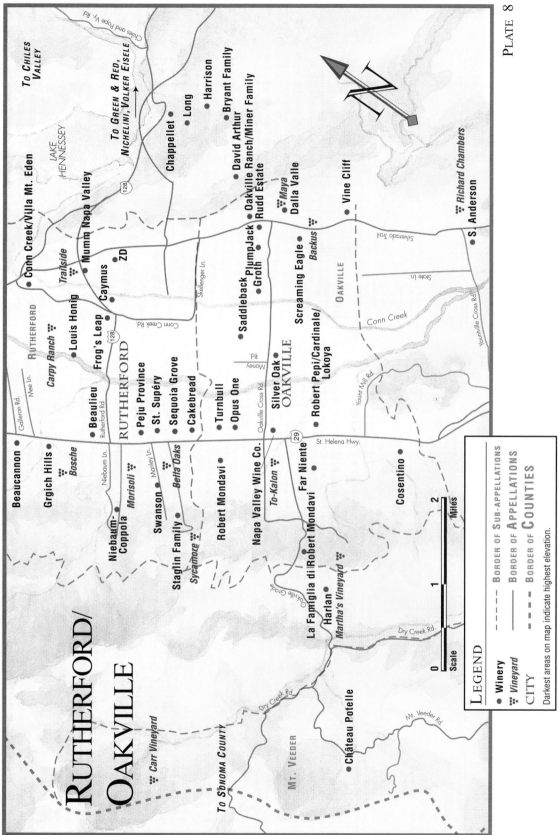

RUTHERFORD/ OAKVILLE

PLATE 8

To CHILES VALLEY

LAKE HENNESSEY

To GREEN & RED, NICHELINI, VOLKER EISELE

Chiles and Pope Vy. Rd.

Conn Creek/Villa Mt. Eden

Mumm Napa Valley

Trailside

Caymus

ZD

Louis Honig

Frog's Leap

Carpy Ranch

RUTHERFORD

Mee Ln.

Galleron Rd.

Beaucannon

Grgich Hills

Bosche

Niebaum-Coppola

Swanson

Morisoli

Staglin Family

Sycamore

Manley Ln.

Bella Oaks

Beaulieu

Rutherford Rd.

RUTHERFORD

Peju Province

St. Supéry

Sequoia Grove

Cakebread

Turnbull

Opus One

Skellenger Ln.

Conn Creek Rd.

Money Rd.

Oakville Cross Rd.

Robert Mondavi

To-Kalon

Napa Valley Wine Co.

Far Niente

Silver Oak

OAKVILLE

Robert Pepi/Cardinale/ Lokoya

Screaming Eagle

Saddleback

Groth

PlumpJack

Oakville Ranch/Miner Family

Rudd Estate

Maya

Dalla Valle

Backus

Vine Cliff

OAKVILLE

Conn Creek

State Ln.

Silverado Trail

Yountville Cross Rd.

Richard Chambers

S. Anderson

Chappellet

Long

Harrison

Bryant Family

David Arthur

128

128

29

St. Helena Hwy.

La Famiglia di Robert Mondavi

Harlan

Martha's Vineyard

Oakville Grade

Cosentino

Yount Mill Rd.

Dry Creek Rd.

Château Potelle

Mt. Veeder Rd.

MT. VEEDER

To SONOMA COUNTY

Carr Vineyard

Dry Creek Rd.

LEGEND

● Winery	--- BORDER OF SUB-APPELLATIONS
⁞ Vineyard	— BORDER OF APPELLATIONS
CITY	- - - BORDER OF COUNTIES

Darkest areas on map indicate highest elevation.

Scale

0   1   2

Miles

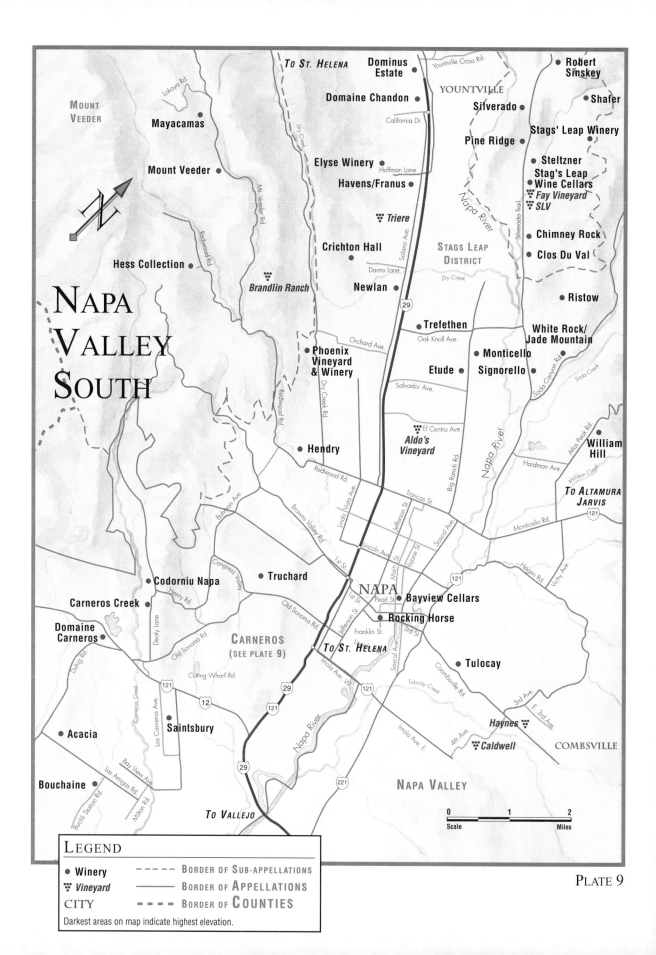

To St. Helena

Dominus
Estate

Domaine Chandon

YOUNTVILLE

Robert
Sinskey

Silverado

Shafer

Mayacamas

Stags' Leap Winery

Pine Ridge

MOUNT
VEEDER

Mount Veeder

Elyse Winery

Steltzner

Stag's Leap
Wine Cellars

Havens/Franus

Fay Vineyard
SLV

Triere

Hess Collection

Brandlin Ranch

Crichton Hall

STAGS LEAP
DISTRICT

Chimney Rock

Clos Du Val

Newlan

NAPA
VALLEY
SOUTH

Ristow

Trefethen

White Rock/
Jade Mountain

Phoenix
Vineyard
& Winery

Etude

Monticello

Signorello

Hendry

Aldo's
Vineyard

William
Hill

To Altamura
Jarvis

Codorniu Napa

Truchard

Carneros Creek

NAPA

Bayview Cellars

Domaine
Carneros

Rocking Horse

CARNEROS
(SEE PLATE 9)

To St. Helena

Tulocay

Saintsbury

Acacia

Haynes

Caldwell

COMBSVILLE

Bouchaine

NAPA VALLEY

To Vallejo

0   1   2
Scale   Miles

PLATE 9

LEGEND

● Winery   - - - - - BORDER OF SUB-APPELLATIONS

❦ Vineyard   ———— BORDER OF APPELLATIONS

CITY   - - - - BORDER OF COUNTIES

Darkest areas on map indicate highest elevation.

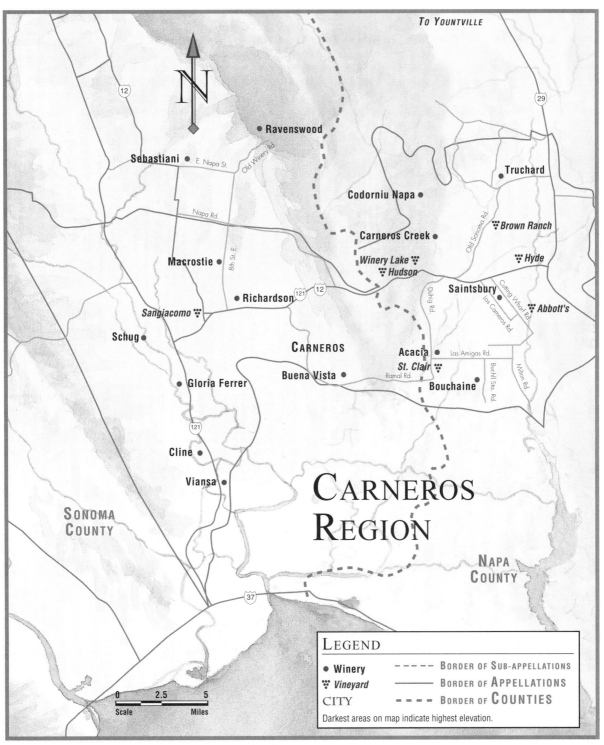

TO YOUNTVILLE

12

29

N

• Ravenswood

Sebastiani • E. Napa St.

Old Winery Rd.

• Truchard

Codorniu Napa •

Old Sonoma Rd.

🍇 Brown Ranch

Napa Rd.

Carneros Creek •

🍇 Hyde

Winery Lake 🍇
🍇 Hudson

8th St. E.

Macrostie •

Saintsbury •

Cutting Wharf Rd.

Los Carneros Rd.

🍇 Abbott's

• Richardson

121 12

Duhig Rd.

Sangiacomo 🍇

CARNEROS

Schug •

Acacia •   Las Amigas Rd.

St. Clair 🍇

Buchli Sta. Rd.

Milton Rd.

Buena Vista •

Ramal Rd.

• Gloria Ferrer

Bouchaine •

121

Cline •

Viansa •

CARNEROS REGION

SONOMA COUNTY

NAPA COUNTY

| 0 | 2.5 | 5 |
Scale   Miles

37

LEGEND

• Winery   – – – – BORDER OF SUB-APPELLATIONS

🍇 Vineyard   ——— BORDER OF APPELLATIONS

CITY   ▬ ▬ ▬ BORDER OF COUNTIES

Darkest areas on map indicate highest elevation.

PLATE 10

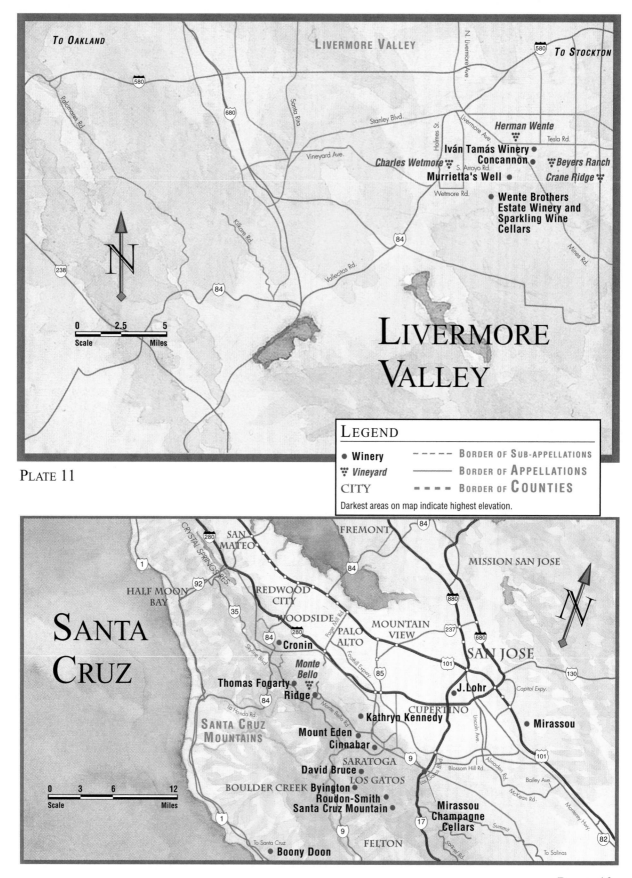

TO OAKLAND

LIVERMORE VALLEY

TO STOCKTON

580

Palomares Rd.

580

680

Santa Rita

Stanley Blvd.

Holmes St.

Livermore Ave.

N. Livermore Ave.

Tesla Rd.

Herman Wente

Vineyard Ave.

Iván Tamás Winery
Concannon

Beyers Ranch

Charles Wetmore

S. Arroyo Rd.

Crane Ridge

Murrietta's Well

Killore Rd.

Wetmore Rd.

Wente Brothers
Estate Winery and
Sparkling Wine
Cellars

Mines Rd.

84

238

N

Vallecitos Rd.

84

84

LIVERMORE
VALLEY

0   2.5   5
Scale   Miles

PLATE 11

LEGEND

- **Winery**
- *Vineyard*
- CITY

- - - - - BORDER OF SUB-APPELLATIONS
───── BORDER OF APPELLATIONS
─ ─ ─ BORDER OF COUNTIES

Darkest areas on map indicate highest elevation.

84

CRYSTAL SPRINGS RES.

280

SAN
MATEO

FREMONT

84

1

92

MISSION SAN JOSE

HALF MOON
BAY

35

REDWOOD
CITY

880

N

WOODSIDE

84

280

Page Mill Rd.

PALO
ALTO

MOUNTAIN
VIEW

237

680

SAN JOSE

SANTA

Cronin

Skyline Blvd.

*Monte
Bello*

Foothill Expwy.

85

101

130

CRUZ

Thomas Fogarty

Ridge

la Honda Rd.

J. Lohr

Capitol Expy.

84

Monte Bello Rd.

Kathryn Kennedy

CUPERTINO

Mirassou

SANTA CRUZ
MOUNTAINS

Mount Eden

Cinnabar

Lincoln Ave.

101

David Bruce

SARATOGA

9

Blossom Hill Rd.

Almaden Rd.

Bailey Ave.

McKean Rd.

BOULDER CREEK Byington

LOS GATOS

Roudon-Smith
Santa Cruz Mountain

0   3   6   12
Scale   Miles

1

9

Mirassou
Champagne
Cellars

17

Summit

Monterey Hwy.

82

To Santa Cruz

Boony Doon

FELTON

Soquel Rd.

To Salinas

PLATE 12

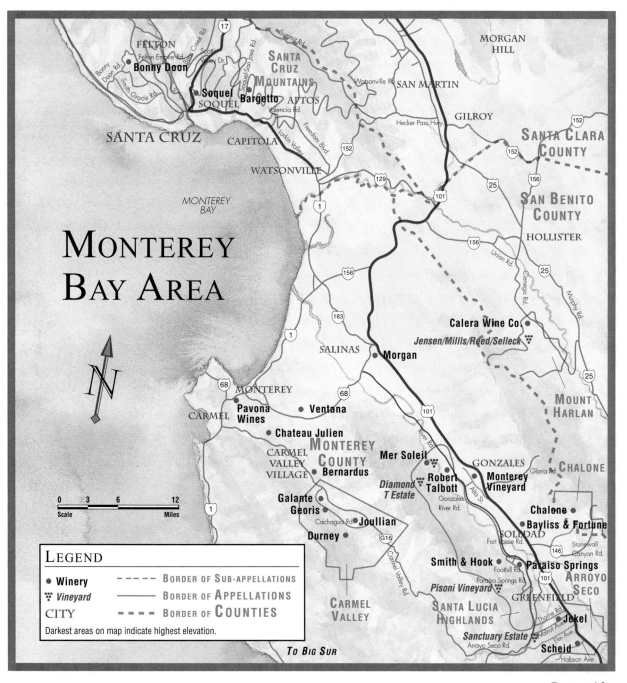

MONTEREY BAY AREA

FELTON

Bonny Doon

SANTA CRUZ MOUNTAINS

Soquel
SOQUEL
Bargetto
APTOS

SANTA CRUZ

CAPITOLA

WATSONVILLE

MONTEREY BAY

SUMMIT RD.

SAN MARTIN

MORGAN HILL

GILROY

SANTA CLARA COUNTY

SAN BENITO COUNTY

HOLLISTER

Calera Wine Co.
Jensen/Mills/Reed/Selleck

SALINAS

Morgan

MONTEREY

Pavona Wines

Ventana

CARMEL

Chateau Julien

CARMEL VALLEY VILLAGE

MONTEREY COUNTY

Bernardus

Mer Soleil

Diamond T Estate

Robert Talbott

GONZALES

Monterey Vineyard

MOUNT HARLAN

CHALONE

Galante
Georis

Joullian

Durney

Chalone

Bayliss & Fortune

SOLEDAD

Smith & Hook

Paraiso Springs

ARROYO SECO

Pisoni Vineyard

GREENFIELD

CARMEL VALLEY

SANTA LUCIA HIGHLANDS

Jekel

Sanctuary Estate

Scheid

TO BIG SUR

Scale
0   3   6   12
Miles

LEGEND

● Winery
❦ Vineyard
CITY

– – – BORDER OF SUB-APPELLATIONS
——— BORDER OF APPELLATIONS
– ▪ – BORDER OF COUNTIES

Darkest areas on map indicate highest elevation.

PLATE 13

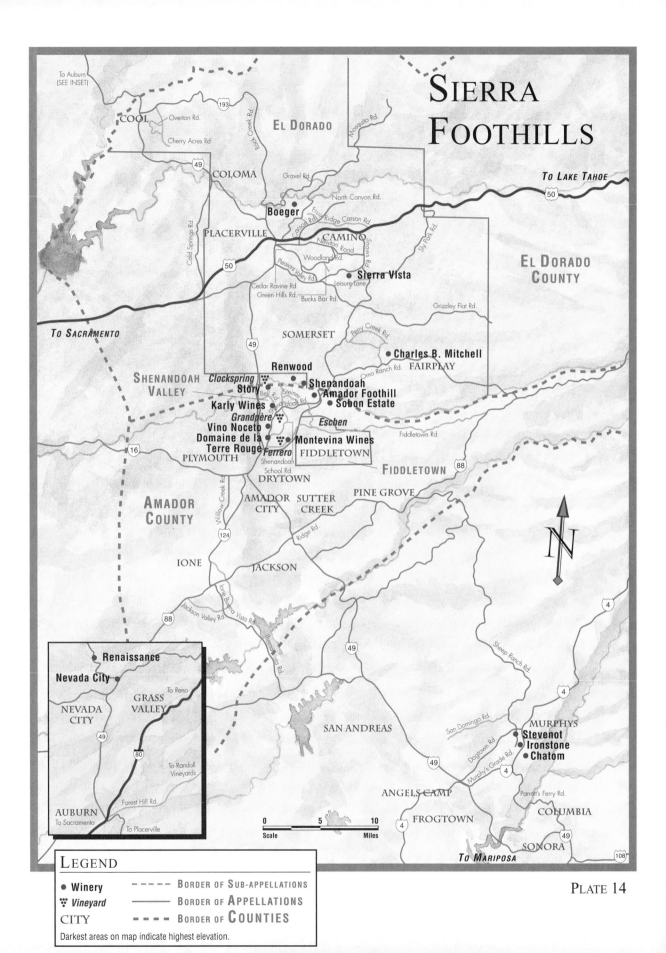

SIERRA FOOTHILLS

To Auburn (SEE INSET)

COOL

Overton Rd.

Cherry Acres Rd.

193

EL DORADO

49

COLOMA

Gravel Rd.

Rock Creek Rd.

TO LAKE TAHOE

50

North Canyon Rd.

Boeger

PLACERVILLE

Carson Rd.

Fruit Ridge Rd.

CAMINO

Carson Rd.

Newton Road

50

Woodland Rd.

Snows Rd.

Sly Park Rd.

EL DORADO COUNTY

Pleasant Valley Rd.

Sierra Vista

Leisure Lane

Cedar Ravine Rd.

Green Hills Rd.

Bucks Bar Rd.

Grizzley Flat Rd.

TO SACRAMENTO

SOMERSET

49

Perry Creek Rd.

● **Charles B. Mitchell**

FAIRPLAY

Renwood

Clockspring ☙

SHENANDOAH VALLEY

Story

Bell Rd.

Steiner Rd.

● **Shenandoah**

Shenandoah Rd.

● **Amador Foothill**

Karly Wines ●

Omo Ranch Rd.

● **Sobon Estate**

Grandpère ☙

Eschen

Vino Noceto ●

Fiddletown Rd.

Domaine de la ☙

Terre Rouge **Ferrero**

● **Montevina Wines**

PLYMOUTH

Shenandoah School Rd.

FIDDLETOWN

FIDDLETOWN

88

16

DRYTOWN

PINE GROVE

AMADOR COUNTY

AMADOR CITY

SUTTER CREEK

Willow Creek Rd.

124

Ridge Rd.

N

IONE

JACKSON

Jackson Valley Rd.

Buena Vista Rd.

Sheep Ranch Rd.

88

49

4

4

Renaissance ●

To Reno

Nevada City ●

GRASS VALLEY

NEVADA CITY

49

To Randall Vineyards

80

SAN ANDREAS

San Domingo Rd.

MURPHYS

Dogtown Rd.

● **Stevenot**

● **Ironstone**

● **Chatom**

AUBURN

To Sacramento

Forest Hill Rd.

To Placerville

49

Murphy's Grade Rd.

4

ANGELS CAMP

Parrott's Ferry Rd.

COLUMBIA

0   5   10

Scale   Miles

4

FROGTOWN

49

TO MARIPOSA

SONORA

108

LEGEND

● **Winery**   - - - - - BORDER OF SUB-APPELLATIONS

☙ *Vineyard*   ———— BORDER OF APPELLATIONS

CITY   ■ ■ ■ ■ BORDER OF COUNTIES

Darkest areas on map indicate highest elevation.

PLATE 14

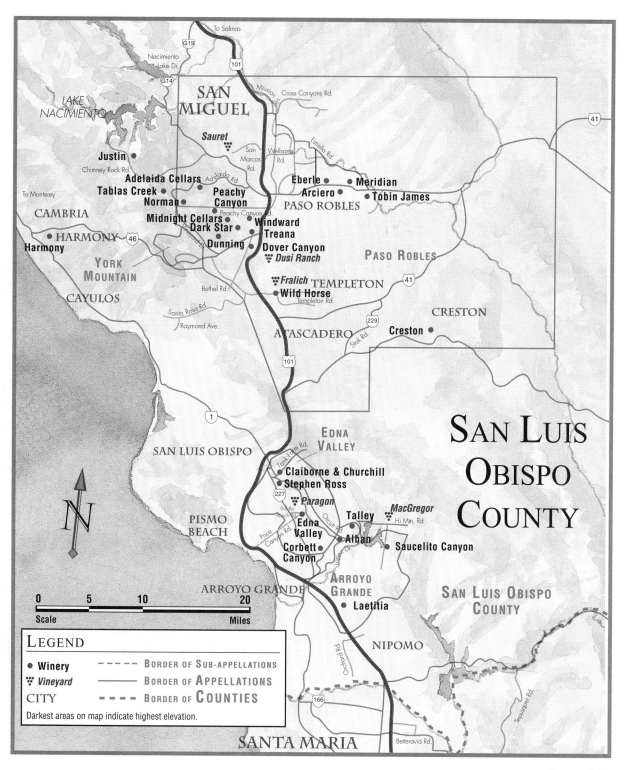

Legend

- ● Winery
- ❦ *Vineyard*
- CITY

- - - - BORDER OF SUB-APPELLATIONS
———— BORDER OF APPELLATIONS
- - - - BORDER OF COUNTIES

Darkest areas on map indicate highest elevation.

0   5   10   20

Scale   Miles

SAN LUIS OBISPO COUNTY

PLATE 15

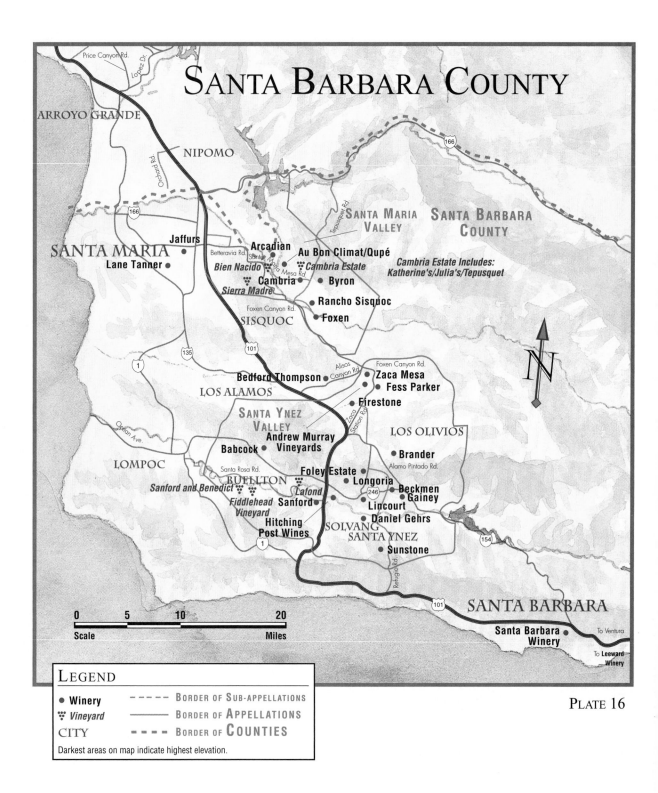

SANTA BARBARA COUNTY

ARROYO GRANDE

NIPOMO

Price Canyon Rd.

Lopez Dr.

Orchard Rd.

166

Tepusquet Rd.

SANTA MARIA VALLEY

SANTA BARBARA COUNTY

Jaffurs

SANTA MARIA

Lane Tanner

Betteravia Rd.

Santa Maria Mesa Rd.

Arcadian

Au Bon Climat/Qupé

Bien Nacido

Cambria Estate

Cambria Estate Includes: Katherine's/Julia's/Tepusquet

Cambria

Byron

Sierra Madre

Foxen Canyon Rd.

SISQUOC

Rancho Sisquoc

Foxen

135

1

101

Alisos Canyon Rd.

Foxen Canyon Rd.

Bedford Thompson

Zaca Mesa

Fess Parker

LOS ALAMOS

SANTA YNEZ VALLEY

Firestone

Zaca Station Rd.

Ocean Ave.

Andrew Murray Vineyards

LOS OLIVIOS

Babcock

Brander

LOMPOC

Alamo Pintado Rd.

Santa Rosa Rd.

Foley Estate

BUELLTON

Longoria

Beckmen

Sanford and Benedict

Lafond

Gainey

Fiddlehead Vineyard

Sanford

246

Lincourt

Hitching Post Wines

Daniel Gehrs

SOLVANG

SANTA YNEZ

1

Sunstone

154

Refugio Rd.

101

SANTA BARBARA

0   5   10   20

Scale   Miles

Santa Barbara Winery

To Ventura

To Leeward Winery

LEGEND

- ● Winery
- 🍇 Vineyard
- CITY

----- BORDER OF SUB-APPELLATIONS

——— BORDER OF APPELLATIONS

==== BORDER OF COUNTIES

Darkest areas on map indicate highest elevation.

PLATE 16

have a distinctive presence, often marked by very ripe berry and tar flavors, with firm, chewy tannins that give them a rustic edge.

REFERENCE WINES

Zinfandel: Boeger Walker Vineyard

FIDDLETOWN
AVA 1983, 11,500 acres, 310 acres in vines

Fiddletown borders the Shenandoah Valley in the Sierra Foothills and its Zinfandel, the main grape grown, shows a style similar to Shenandoah's: very ripe, sometimes raisiny flavors and an earthy, tarry edge.

GREEN VALLEY-SONOMA COUNTY
AVA 1983, 32,000 acres, 1,000 acres in vines

In the southwest corner of the Russian River Valley appellation, Green Valley-Sonoma County is closer to the ocean and therefore even cooler. It's best suited for cool-climate grapes such as Chardonnay and Pinot Noir and the sparkling wines made from them. Iron Horse excels with both grapes, yet often has a struggle to fully ripen the Pinot Noir. Marimar Torres Estate produces both wines too, building more richness and depth into the Chardonnay and a bit more flavor and finesse into the Pinot, which is often marked by herb, tea and cherry notes. Kistler's Dutton Ranch bottling remains the benchmark for quality, yet carries the broader Russian River Valley appellation.

REFERENCE WINES

Chardonnay: Iron Horse, Marimar Torres
Pinot Noir: Iron Horse, Marimar Torres

GUENOC VALLEY
AVA 1981, 3,000 acres, 400 acres in vines

This is a single-winery appellation in Lake County that bears the name of its only winery, Guenoc (see listing), which is succeeding with many varieties. Cabernet and Chardonnay (Genevieve Magoon Vineyard) are the early quality leaders; Zinfandel, Sauvignon Blanc and Petite Sirah show promise.

HOWELL MOUNTAIN
AVA 1984, 14,080 acres, 198 acres in vines

Howell Mountain, in the northeastern portion of Napa Valley, is an old winegrowing area with vineyards and wineries dating to the late 1800s. But it was Randy Dunn and his Dunn Cabernets that established its credentials, with enormously rich, complex and earthy wines that have quickly established themselves among California's elite. Other vineyards—namely La Jota, Bancroft Ranch (for stunning Merlot made by Beringer), Park-Muscadine (now owned by Dunn, but long a source of Zinfandel for Ridge) and Black Sears (Zinfandel from Turley)—have also focused on red grapes, with styles that reflect the earthy austerity of the appellation. Still others, most notably Chateau Woltner, have gone in the opposite direction, favoring Chardonnay. Wineries at the base of the mountain (Burgess, Forman) don't meet elevation qualifications for inclusion in the appellation. Ironically, Angwin, the only town on the mountain, is a hamlet founded by Seventh Day Adventists, who are tee-totalers.

REFERENCE WINES

Cabernet Sauvignon: Cornerstone, Robert Craig, Duckhorn Vineyards, Dunn Vineyards, La Jota, Liparita, Lokoya, White Cottage Ranch
Chardonnay: Chateau Woltner, Liparita, Peter Michael
Merlot: Beringer Bancroft Ranch, Duckhorn, Liparita
Zinfandel: Howell Mountain Vineyard, Rocking Horse Lamborn Family Vineyard, Turley Black Sears

KNIGHTS VALLEY
AVA 1983, 36,240 acres, 1,500 acres in vines

Beringer Vineyards is the major landowner and pacesetter in this northeastern Sonoma AVA, with two varieties: Cabernet, which dates to 1976, and Sauvignon Blanc. Peter Michael Winery is the lone winery at the south end of Knights Valley near Napa Valley, and is making tremendous wines. Beringer's Cabernet and red Meritage (called Alluvium) are medium-bodied, moderately tannic and very flavorful wines that reach a pleasant drinking plateau early on. But if you want full-throttle Cabernet, try Peter Michael.

REFERENCE WINES

Cabernet: Beringer Alluvium Red, Peter Michael Les Pavots
White Table Wine: Beringer Alluvium White

LAKE COUNTY

Not an AVA, but a political boundary used occasionally in wine labeling. With nearly 3,500 acres in vines, it is part of the North Coast appellation, even though, like Napa Valley, it doesn't touch the coast. Includes both the Clear Lake and Guenoc AVAs.

REFERENCE WINES

Cabernet Sauvignon: Guenoc Langtry
Sauvignon Blanc: Buena Vista, Lakewood
Zinfandel: Steele Catfish Vineyard

LIVERMORE VALLEY
AVA 1982, 96,000 acres, 3.000 acres in vines

Historically important as the home of Wente Bros. and Concannon, this appellation east of San Francisco is marked by lean, stony soils and encroaching suburbs. Its best wines are Sauvignon Blanc, Sémillon (and blends thereof), Chardonnay and Cabernet, even if the latter two don't show the depth and complexities of the state's best. Concannon's Petite Sirah, among the first bottled as a varietal wine, can be complex, with dried fruit and spice flavors and chewy tannins.

REFERENCE WINES

Chardonnay: Wente
Petite Sirah: Concannon
Sauvignon Blanc: Concannon, Wente

LODI
AVA 1986, 458,000 acres, 70,000 acres in vines

Lodi is home to Guild, Robert Mondavi's Woodbridge winery and Sebastiani's California-appellation wines. This Central Valley AVA south of Sacramento can make good table wines, but most of the grapes are used in blends that end up carrying the larger and higher-profile California appellation.

REFERENCE WINES

Zinfandel: Franus, Ravenswood, Turley Spenker Ranch

MALIBU-NEWTON CANYON
AVA 1996, 850 acres, 21 acres in vines

Located in the Malibu area of Los Angeles County, this new AVA is home to George Rosenthal's 21-acre vineyard, Rosenthal-Malibu Estate, which produces an excellent Bordeaux-inspired Cabernet blend.

REFERENCE WINE

Cabernet Sauvignon: Rosenthal-Malibu Estate

McDOWELL VALLEY
AVA 1983, 2,300 acres, 700 acres in vine

This is a single-winery appellation in Mendocino County east of Hopland. McDowell Valley Vineyards has followed the varietal trends of the era, focusing first on Cabernet and Chardonnay with modest success and producing many wines of uneven quality. Since redirecting its attention to Rhône-style wines, the winery's success ratio has risen significantly, with appealing Syrah and Grenache among the noteworthy bottlings.

MENDOCINO COUNTY

Not an AVA, but a political boundary that takes in the northernmost appellations of the North Coast and includes the AVAs Anderson Valley, McDowell Valley, Mendocino Ridge and Potter Valley. Long dedicated to Colombard and Carignane for use as blending grapes in jug wines, Parducci, and later Fetzer, pioneered varietal wines here through trial-and-error winemaking. They determined that grapes such as Sauvignon Blanc and Zinfandel thrived best inland in warmer areas and that Chardonnay, Pinot Noir and Riesling were better suited to the cooler climate of Anderson Valley which lies to the west of the county's major city, Ukiah. Today, some 15,000 acres are planted to vines, and winegrowing is important (as is logging in the densely forested areas), but it's still considered the county's number-two cash crop; number one, according to the county's agricultural commissioner is the harvest from the well-tended, well-protected and highly clandestine marijuana gardens.

MENDOCINO COUNTY ACREAGE BY GRAPE

Varietal	1970	1980	1990	1997	Percent Change 1970-1980	Percent Change 1980-1990	Percent Change 1990-1997
Cabernet Sauvignon	313	925	1,314	1,463	196%	42%	11%
Chardonnay	130	901	3,435	4,567	593%	281%	33%
Merlot	0	102	266	1,361	100%	161%	412%
Pinot Noir	109	323	690	670	196%	114%	(-3%)
Zinfandel	702	1,336	1,849	1,889	90%	38%	2%
Sauvignon Blanc	44	462	880	647	950%	90%	(-26%)
Syrah	0	0	112	234	0%	100%	109%
Other	5,146	6,248	3,800	2,692	21%	(-39%)	(-29%)
Total	**6,444**	**10,297**	**12,346**	**13,522**	**60%**	**20%**	**10%**

Many of the best wines still carry the broader Mendocino County appellation rather than a more specific one, notably Edmeades' Ciapusci and Zeni Vineyard Zinfandels, and Villa Mt. Eden's Signature Series Cabernet Sauvignon, which comes from Greenwood Ridge Vineyard in Anderson Valley. In the Reference Wines, I've listed such wines under the specific appellations within which they lie, even though their labels indicate the broader county area.

REFERENCE WINES

Cabernet Sauvignon: Duncan Peak, Husch La Ribera Vineyard
Chardonnay: Fetzer, Hidden Cellars, Lolonis, Steele Lolonis Vineyard, Navarro
Pinot Noir: Greenwood Ridge, Navarro
Sauvignon Blanc: Fetzer, Hidden Cellars, Navarro Cuvée 128, Yorkville, Parducci
Petite Sirah: Hidden Cellars Eagle Point Ranch, JC Cellars Eagle Point Ranch
Syrah: Bonterra, Hidden Cellars, Lonetree
Zinfandel: Fife, Gabrielli, Hidden Cellars, Lonetree, Lolonis, Parducci, Steele Pacini

MENDOCINO RIDGE

AVA 1998, 88,000 acres, 75 acres in vines

This AVA is first of its kind in California, a non-contiguous appellation based on elevation. Stretching over a large portion of Mendocino County, about 410 square miles altogether, it includes only land at the 1,200 foot elevation or higher. Currently just six vineyards measuring some 75 planted acres are within the boundary, but among them are some are well-known vineyards, including the estate vineyards of Greenwood Ridge; the DuPratt, Zeni, and Ciapusci vineyards; and the less well-known Mariah vineyard.

REFERENCE WINES

Cabernet Sauvignon: Greenwood Ridge
Zinfandel: Edmeades Ciapusci and Zeni vineyards, Steele DuPratt, Mariah Vineyard

MONTEREY COUNTY

Monterey County is not an AVA, but a political boundary used when a wine fails to meet more specific appellation requirements. Arroyo Seco, Santa Lucia Highlands, Chalone, San Lucas and Carmel Valley are AVAs within the county. Many wineries use the broader Monterey appellation with excellent results.

REFERENCE WINES

Cabernet Sauvignon: Durney, Lockwood, Mirassou
Chardonnay: Bernardus, Chalone, Cronin Ventana Vineyard, Estancia, J. Lohr Riverstone Vineyard, Lockwood, Mer Soleil, Mirassou, Morgan, Talbott
Merlot: Chateau Julian, Galante, Georis, Lockwood
Pinot Noir: Chalone, Estancia Pinnacles Vineyard, Morgan
Sauvignon Blanc: Bernardus, Cain, Lockwood

MONTEREY COUNTY ACREAGE BY GRAPE

Varietal	1970	1980	1990	1997	Percent Change 1970-1980	Percent Change 1980-1990	Percent Change 1990-1997
Cabernet Sauvignon	880	4,489	3,763	3,757	410%	(-16%)	(-.002%)
Chardonnay	317	3,140	8,469	15,058	890%	170%	78%
Merlot	36	632	674	3,159	1,656%	7%	369%
Pinot Noir	333	1,971	1,616	1,751	492%	(-18%)	8%
Zinfandel	128	2,415	1,878	1,310	1,787%	(-22%)	(-30%)
Sauvignon Blanc	128	1,212	1,489	1,088	847%	23%	(-27%)
Syrah	0	4	2	189	100%	(-50%)	9350%
Other	1,934	18,347	10,605	6,286	849%	(-42%)	(-41%)
Total	**3,756**	**32,237**	**28,496**	**32,598**	**758%**	**(-11%)**	**14%**

MOUNT HARLAN

AVA 1990, 7,440 acres, 74 acres in vines

This single-winery appellation features Calera's vineyards, nestled in lime-rich soils 2,000 feet above sea level in the Gavilan range east of Salinas. Calera bottles four separate vineyard-designated Pinot Noirs—Jensen, Mills, Reed and Selleck—all marked by ultra-ripe, very complex flavors. Small vineyards of Chardonnay and Viognier are also rooted.

MOUNT VEEDER

AVA 1990, 15,000 acres, 1,000 acres in vines

For years, the venerable Mayacamas Vineyards carried the torch for this rugged mountain appellation in southwestern Napa County, producing distinctive and ageworthy Cabernets and Chardonnays. Mount Veeder Winery was founded later; the old Christian Brothers Mont La Salle winery—now home to The Hess Collection—dates back years. Red wines dominate, with Cabernets that are characteristically earthy, concentrated, tannic and chewy. Hess manages to polish the edges a bit more than Mayacamas, whose wines have been lighter and more herbal of late. Mount Veeder Winery blends in grapes from the valley floor to soften its Cabernets. Zinfandel is the other big wine, with wineries such as Chateau Potelle, Franus and Sky making impressive wines. Chardonnay is austere, with a tight, flinty edge to it. Jade Mountain likes Syrah grown near the peak. The appellation rises up to 2,500 feet and gets drenched with rain; nearly double the city of Napa's 24 inches per year.

REFERENCE WINES

Cabernet Sauvignon: Robert Craig, Chateau Potelle, The Hess Collection, Lokoya, Mayacamas
Chardonnay: Chateau Potelle, The Hess Collection, Mayacamas, Patz & Hall Carr Vineyard
Zinfandel: Chateau Potelle, Franus Brandlin Vineyard, Sky

NAPA VALLEY

AVA 1983, 300,000 acres, 36,100 acres in vines

Napa Valley is far and away California's most famous winegrowing district. It owes much of its reputation to pioneers who settled in the Rutherford area and established such important winery estates as Beaulieu Vineyard and Inglenook. Those two wineries created many fine wines, but it was always Cabernet Sauvignon that led in quality—much as it still does today. By the late 1940s and early 1950s, BV and Inglenook were joined by Charles Krug and Louis M. Martini to form the Big Four Cabernet producers, which slowly carried Napa's high-quality Cabernet message to the broader domestic market. The list of leading Cabernet and Meritage producers is still long and impressive. By the 1960s Heitz Cellar, Robert Mondavi, Freemark Abbey, Mayacamas and Sterling Vineyards were crafting excellent Cabernets. In the 1970s, Caymus, Diamond Creek,

NAPA COUNTY ACREAGE BY GRAPE

Varietal	1970	1980	1990	1997	Percent Change 1970-1980	Percent Change 1980-1990	Percent Change 1990-1997
Cabernet Sauvignon	2,398	5,569	9,131	10,618	132%	64%	16%
Chardonnay	664	4,269	9,639	9,333	543%	126%	(-3%)
Merlot	159	693	2,148	5,891	336%	210%	174%
Pinot Noir	957	2,393	2,719	2,360	150%	14%	(-13%)
Zinfandel	778	2,136	1,993	1,970	175%	(-7%)	(-1%)
Sauvignon Blanc	390	1,721	2,873	1,893	341%	23%	(-34%)
Syrah	0	35	25	161	100%	(-29%)	544%
Other	9,058	9,502	4,666	3,889	5%	(-51%)	(-17%)
Total	**14,404**	**26,318**	**33,194**	**36,115**	**83%**	**26%**	**9%**

Clos Du Val, Stag's Leap Wine Cellars, Joseph Phelps and Chateau Montelena joined the group.

From the 1960s through the 1980s, the valley gradually shifted to more site-specific wines with the realization that the places where Cabernet flourished, in rich soil with warm temperatures, were not ideal for other varieties. This led to the steady march of Chardonnay and Pinot Noir to Carneros, to the uprooting of less popular Petite Sirah and Gamay, among others, and to the planting of more Merlot and Sauvignon Blanc.

During the 1980s, the valley began to be divided into smaller appellations. Areas such as Carneros, the Stags Leap District, Oakville, Rutherford, Mount Veeder, Howell Mountain, Yountville and Spring Mountain are now all AVAs (they are covered elsewhere in this chapter in more specific detail), and there are plans to add St. Helena, Calistoga, Diamond Mountain, Coombsville (east of Napa) and Oak Knoll, an area between Napa and Yountville well regarded for Chardonnay, to the list. The trend toward smaller appellations will help define which grapes excel in different areas. It will also help clean up the overly large Napa Valley appellation, which should be limited to the Napa River watershed, but for historical and commercial reasons includes remote areas such as Pope Valley, Chiles Valley and Wooden Valley—virtually the entire county. By the late 1990s nearly two-thirds of Napa Valley was planted to Cabernet and Chardonnay, with smaller amounts of Zinfandel, Merlot and Pinot Noir, the latter mostly in Carneros.

A number of varieties grow well in this appellation, but clearly Cabernet is king of Napa's reds. Economics helps explain why: Cabernet or Cabernet blends that sell for $30, $40, $50 or more a bottle provide a greater profit potential than Zinfandel or Syrah at half or a third of the price. Merlot is off to a good start in many areas, but is more site-specific than any red grape other than Pinot Noir. Stags' Leap Winery Petite Syrah remains one of the state's finest. Sangiovese plantings, still at just a few hundred acres, occasionally show promise.

REFERENCE WINES

Cabernet Sauvignon: Beringer Private Reserve, Cafaro, Caymus, Duckhorn, Forman, Robert Mondavi, Sequoia Grove, Silver Oak, Sterling Reserve, St. Clement and St. Clement Oroppas

Chardonnay: Beringer Vineyards Private Reserve, Chateau Montelena, Far Niente, Flora Springs Barrel Fermented, Franciscan, Forman, Grgich Hills, Long, Merryvale, Patz & Hall, Silverado, Stag's Leap Wine Cellars

Merlot: Duckhorn, Markham, Robert Mondavi, Newton, Shafer, St. Clement, Sterling Vineyards, Swanson

Pinot Noir: Robert Mondavi and Robert Mondavi Reserve, Monticello

Syrah: Jade Mountain, Phelps Vin du Mistral, Swanson

Zinfandel: Beaulieu, Robert Biale Aldo's Vineyard, Dickerson Vineyard, Robert Mondavi, Ravenswood Dickerson Vineyard, Storybook Mountain, The Terraces; Turley Wine Cellars Aïda, Hayne and Moore Vineyards

Others: Beringer (Nightingale dessert wine), Far Niente (Dolce), Stags' Leap Winery (Petite Syrah)

NORTH YUBA
AVA 1985, 17,500 acres, 365 acres in vines

Renaissance Winery is the lone winery here, with a full assortment of the major varieties planted in these hills above the Sacramento Valley. While the winery has its fans, no one wine has yet to emerge as a star. Still, the vineyard is young, and there is considerable enthusiasm about its potential.

NORTHERN SONOMA
AVA 1985, no official record of acres in vines

Drawn at the request of Gallo to include all of its Sonoma County vineyards, it includes portions of Dry Creek Valley, Alexander Valley, Russian River Valley and Knights Valley.

OAKVILLE
AVA 1994, 5,800 acres, 5,000 acres in vines

As in Rutherford, Cabernet rules in this Napa Valley district, although here it offers more diversity; the area is also more diverse in its grape planting. The names of the wines and vineyards tell the story: Robert Mondavi Reserve, Opus One, Heitz Martha's Vineyard, Groth Reserve Harlan Estate, Screaming Eagle and Far Niente are all here. Oakville Cabernets share with Rutherford's the right to be called rich and complex wines. They are also similar in structure, intensity and weight. The most marked difference is that Oakville Cabernets, from grapes grown in a slightly cooler area, are often marked by mint, herb, and sage notes. Representing the extremes are Heitz Martha's Vineyard, famous for its minty currant notes, and Groth Reserve, which often features coffee, sage and tobacco notes commingled with cherry and currant flavors. Proximity to the Napa River accounts for the vines' vigorous growth and need for a long growing season to ripen fully; Groth's is often among the last—if not the last—Cabernet vineyard harvested on the valley floor. Chardonnay, Sauvignon Blanc and Zinfandel also do well in pockets; Beringer is reliant upon the Gamble Ranch vineyards for its excellent Private Reserve Chardonnay. The district extends into the foothills and includes about half of Dalla Valle Vineyards to the east. It stops short of Napanook Vineyard, home to Dominus Estate, to the south, but includes Harlan Estate and Oakford Vineyards, both located on the western boundary.

REFERENCE WINES

Cabernet Sauvignon: Dalla Valle and Dalla Valle Maya, Far Niente, Franciscan Oakville Estate, Groth and Groth Reserve, Harlan Estate, Heitz Martha's Vineyard, Robert Mondavi To-Kalon, Oakville Ranch, Oakford, Opus One, Paradigm, Miner Family, PlumpJack, Screaming Eagle, Vine Cliff
Chardonnay: Miner Family, Oakville Ranch
Merlot: Cosentino, Paradigm
Sauvignon Blanc: Robert Mondavi To-Kalon Vineyard
Zinfandel: Paradigm

PASO ROBLES
AVA 1983, 614,000 acres, 6,300 acres in vines

This area is gaining a reputation for a number of red varieties, with Syrah, Zinfandel and Cabernet the leaders. Most of the vineyards are planted east of Highway 101. The major wineries are Meridian, Arciero, J. Lohr, Wild Horse and Eberle. Cabernets from Meridian and Eberle are medium- to full-bodied and mature early, with good depth and flavor, but lack the richness and concentration found in Napa Valley's best. Zinfandel is bright and intense, with Peachy Canyon a leader. Syrah from Meridian can be spicy and complex. Wild Horse excels with Chardonnay, Pinot Noir and Merlot. The Perrin family (owners of Chateau de Beaucastel in France), in partnership with wine importer Robert Haas, make red and white Rhône-style blends from the estate vineyards at Tablas Creek, their winery in the eastern portion of the AVA. The best wines lie ahead.

REFERENCE WINES

Cabernet Sauvignon: Adelaida, Eberle, Justin, J. Lohr Seven Oaks, Meridian, Peachy Canyon, Wild Horse
Chardonnay: Justin Reserve, Wild Horse
Petite Sirah: David Bruce
Pinot Noir: Adelaida, Wild Horse Cheval Sauvage
Syrah: Eberle Fralich Vineyard, Tobin James, Meridian
Zinfandel: Adelaida, Eberle, Peachy Canyon, Norman The Monster, Ridge, Rosenblum, Wild Horse

POPE VALLEY

Part of the broad Napa Valley AVA, Pope Valley is in reality a separate and distinct area northeast of Napa Valley, with several thousand acres in vines. Early indications are that it's a very good area for Sauvignon Blanc, Cabernet, Chardonnay and Merlot. In time, it will probably become an AVA that can carry both the Pope Valley and the Napa Valley names.

POTTER VALLEY
AVA 1983, 27,500 acres, 1,000 acres in vines

Located in northeastern Mendocino County, Potter Valley is insignificant as appellations go. Sauvignon Blanc appears to be the favored grape at this stage, although some Chardonnay is grown there, as it likes the cool climate.

REDWOOD VALLEY
AVA 1996, 22,400 acres, 2,500 acres in vines

This Mendocino County AVA lies north of Ukiah and northwest of Potter Valley. It is home to a number of wineries, including Fetzer, Lolonis and Fife. Planted primarily to red varietals, it is best known for its Zinfandel and Petite Sirah.

REFERENCE WINES
Zinfandel: Fife Redhead Vineyard, Lolonis Private Reserve, Rosenblum Rhodes Vineyard, JC Cellars Rhodes Vineyard
Petite Sirah: Fife Redhead Vineyard

RUSSIAN RIVER VALLEY
AVA 1983, 96,000 acres, 8,375 acres in vines

Because of its proximity to the ocean and its cool, damp climate, this central Sonoma County appellation has been slow to develop, but now it ranks among the best in the state. Early Italian settlers planted red grape varieties farther inland, but as the Chardonnay boom took hold, more vintners focused on this area, realizing its potential for both Chardonnay and Pinot Noir. In terms of acreage, Chardonnay rules supreme, with names such as DeLoach, Rochioli, Kistler, Sonoma-Cutrer, Gallo (Estate-Bottled Chardonnay), Dehlinger and dozens

more that buy grapes from here and blend them with Chardonnay grown elsewhere. Meanwhile, Pinot Noir is gaining by leaps and bounds. Led by J. Rochioli Reserve, Gary Farrell, Williams & Selyem (Rochioli, Allen, Olivet Lane and a generic Russian River Valley bottling), Kistler and Dehlinger, Pinot Noir can be bright, rich, lush and complex, combining delicacy and finesse with intensity and concentration. Several other varieties, namely Zinfandel, Sauvignon Blanc, Gewürztraminer and Merlot, also shine in warmer areas. The next decade should better define the appellation, but figure on Chardonnay and Pinot Noir as major players either way.

REFERENCE WINES
Cabernet Sauvignon: Dehlinger Bordeaux Blend, De Loach O.F.S.
Chardonnay: Dehlinger, De Loach O.F.S., Gary Farrell Allen Vineyard, Iron Horse, Kistler Dutton Ranch and Vine Hill Vineyards, Landmark Lorenzo, Marimar Torres Estate, Martinelli Gold Ridge, Mueller, Patz & Hall, Sebastiani Dutton Ranch, Rochioli Allen Vineyard, Rochioli River Block and South River Vineyard, Williams & Selyem Allen Vineyard
Merlot: De Loach O.F.S.
Pinot Noir: Dehlinger, Gary Farrell Allen Vineyard, Williams & Selyem Allen and J. Rochioli Vineyard, Kistler Cuvée Catherine and Kistler Vineyard, Rochioli, Rochioli West Block, Rochioli Little Hill Block, Rochioli Three Corner Vineyard, Joseph Swan Estate
Sauvignon Blanc: Chateau St. Jean La Petite Étoile, De Loach, J. Rochioli and J. Rochioli Reserve
Syrah: Arrowood Saralee's Vineyard, Dehlinger, Hamel
Zinfandel: De Loach O.F.S. and Barbieri Ranch and Papera Ranch and Pelletti Ranch, Gary Farrell Collins Ranch, Hartford Court Hartford Vineyard, Hop Kiln, Limerick Lane, Martinelli, Joseph Swan Frati Ranch and V.H.S.R Vineyard, Rochioli Sodini Vineyard, Williams & Selyem

RUTHERFORD
AVA 1994, 6,500 acres, 5,000 acres in vines

Pioneers Beaulieu and Inglenook set the pace here early on with Cabernet, and it is still the finest varietal from this appellation in the heart of Napa Valley. The names alone tell the story: BV Private Reserve, Caymus

Special Selection, Flora Springs Reserve, Freemark Abbey Bosché, Niebaum-Coppola Estate Rubicon, Livingston Moffett Vineyard and Heitz Bella Oaks, to name the important wines. Rutherford's rich and loamy soils are largely alluvial fans that have been formed from the mountains that line both sides of the valley. Cabernet performs exceptionally well here, as there is an ideal mixture of cool mornings and evenings and warm, sunny days, usually ripening the grapes fully and quite easily; the result is an abundance of rich currant, plum and cherry flavors, with herb, mint and spice notes and fine but substantial tannins. Because of those supple tannins most Rutherford wines are showy early on. But they often have the richness, depth and concentration to age well for 15 to 30 years, sometimes even longer. Zinfandel is a minor player here, but Niebaum-Coppola's estate-bottled Edizione Pennino, and the Elyse Zinfandel from Morisoli Vineyard are lovely wines.

It would not surprise me if at some future date an effort is made to claim a Rutherford Bench appellation that would focus on the western vineyards. Many believe this modern term best describes the gentle slope from the western foothills.

REFERENCE WINES

Cabernet Sauvignon: Beaulieu Private Reserve, Caymus Special Selection, Flora Springs Hillside Reserve, Freemark Abbey Bosché Vineyard, Livingston Moffett, Lokoya, Niebaum-Coppola Rubicon, Staglin, Whitehall Lane Morisoli Vineyard
Chardonnay: El Molino
Merlot: Niebaum-Coppola, Whitehall Lane
Sauvignon Blanc: Voss
Zinfandel: Niebaum-Coppola Edizione Pennino, Elyse Morisoli Vineyard

SAN FRANCISCO BAY
AVA 1999, 1,566,720 acres, 5,800 acres in vines.

Wente Winery in Livermore spearheaded the drive for this large and unwieldy AVA which wraps itself around the San Francisco Bay and is included within the Central Coast AVA. While not including any shoreline, this AVA is spread throughout seven different counties—San Francisco, San Mateo, Santa Clara, Alameda, Contra Costa, Santa Cruz and San Benito—encompassing 2,448 square miles and 39 wineries. Soil and climatic conditions are diverse within the region, but the cooling influence of the San Francisco Bay is what distinguishes this area from other parts of the Central Coast. San Francisco is included even though there are no commercial wine grapes grown there. Because of its size, it is doubtful this appellation will have much significance, but it may be used to distinguish wines grown here from those carrying the California, Central Coast or North Coast appellations.

ST. HELENA

St. Helena's AVA application is still pending with federal officials. Once the AVA has been established, this Napa Valley district will likely extend from the northern boundary of Rutherford at Zinfandel Lane to the southern boundary of Calistoga. St. Helena is a famous and beautiful city and home to many wineries, including Beringer, Charles Krug, Markham, Merryvale and Louis M. Martini. It is an excellent area for Cabernet Sauvignon, notably from Spottswoode, Grace Family Vineyard and Abreu Vineyard, using Madrona Ranch grapes. Petite Sirah (Markham) and Zinfandel are also favored grapes.

REFERENCE WINES

Cabernet Sauvignon: Abreu Madrona Ranch, Grace Family Vineyard, Spottswoode
Petite Sirah: Markham
Syrah: Sean Thackery Orion

SAN BENITO COUNTY
AVA 1987, 45,000 acres, 1,800 acres in vines

This county east of Monterey is rarely used as an AVA, but Calera occasionally uses it for its vineyard-designated Pinot Noirs from Mount Harlan (see AVA)—all of which are excellent, ultra-ripe and juicy—and its Chardonnay and Viognier.

REFERENCE WINES

Chardonnay: Calera
Pinot Noir: Calera: Mills and Reed and Jensen

SAN LUIS OBISPO COUNTY ACREAGE BY GRAPE

Varietal	1970	1980	1990	1997	Percent Change 1970-1980	Percent Change 1980-1990	Percent Change 1990-1997
Cabernet Sauvignon	37	942	2,451	3,657	245%	160%	49%
Chardonnay	10	506	2,412	3,597	496%	377%	49%
Merlot	0	166	201	1,946	100%	21%	868%
Pinot Noir	58	96	180	410	66%	88%	128%
Zinfandel	410	1,008	1,367	1,737	146%	36%	27%
Sauvignon Blanc	0	522	702	621	100%	34%	(-12%)
Syrah	0	34	37	389	100%	9%	951%
Other	149	1,435	993	1,120	863%	(-31%)	(13%)
Total	**664**	**4,709**	**8,343**	**13,476**	**609%**	**77%**	**62%**

SAN LUCAS

AVA 1987, 32,000 acres, 13,900 acres in vines

Rarely used on labels, since many of the grapes grown in this southernmost Monterey County district go into wines that carry the California appellation. Grapes grown include Cabernet, Chardonnay and Sauvignon Blanc. Lockwood is the lone winery.

SAN LUIS OBISPO COUNTY

This county is not an AVA, but a South Central Coast political boundary that includes the Paso Robles, York Mountain, Edna Valley and Arroyo Grande AVAs.

REFERENCE WINES

Cabernet Sauvignon: Adelaida, Justin, Wild Horse
Chardonnay: Adelaida, Laetitia, Wild Horse
Merlot: Tobin James
Pinot Noir: Laetitia
Zinfandel: Santa Barbara Winery

SANTA BARBARA COUNTY

Not an AVA, but a political boundary that includes the Santa Ynez Valley and Santa Maria Valley appellations within. Santa Barbara enjoys a generally cool, coastal climate; thus, many of the Chardonnays and Pinot Noirs blended from the different vineyards here are excellent.

SANTA BARBARA COUNTY ACREAGE BY GRAPE

Varietal	1970	1980	1990	1997	Percent Change 1970-1980	Percent Change 1980-1990	Percent Change 1990-1997
Cabernet Sauvignon	85	1,092	902	554	118%	(-17%)	(-39%)
Chardonnay	14	1,514	5,135	6,931	1,071%	239%	35%
Merlot	0	275	262	525	100%	(-5%)	100%
Pinot Noir	0	724	821	1,182	100%	13%	44%
Zinfandel	0	75	31	18	100%	(-59%)	(-42)
Sauvignon Blanc	17	261	443	279	1,435%	70%	(-37%)
Syrah	0	0	32	187	0	100%	484%
Other	55	3,078	1,676	1,293	5,496%	(-46%)	(-23%)
Total	**171**	**7,019**	**9,302**	**10,969**	**4,005%**	**33%**	**18%**

REFERENCE WINES

Cabernet Sauvignon: Foxen, Gainey Limited Selection
Chardonnay: Au Bon Climat, Babcock, Byron and Byron Reserve, Camelot, Cottonwood Canyon Barrel Select, Gainey Limited Selection, Meridian Limited Release, Nichols, Qupé Bien Nacido Sanford Barrel Select, Steele Bien Nacido, Testarossa Bien Nacido, Steele Goodchild Vineyard
Merlot: Foxen
Pinot Noir: Au Bon Climat, Babcock, Byron, Foxen, Hitching Post, Longoria, Meridian, Sanford, Steele Bien Nacido, Lane Tanner, Wild Horse, Whitcraft
Syrah: Beckmen, Bedford Thompson, Jaffurs, Fess Parker, Ojai Bien Nacido, Qupé, Zaca Mesa

SANTA CRUZ MOUNTAINS
AVA 1982, 110,000 acres, 700 acres in vines

Small in vineyard acreage, rugged and mountainous in physical geography, but rich in distinctive wines, the Santa Cruz Mountains AVA is home to Ridge Vineyards (and its Monte Bello vineyard), David Bruce and Bonny Doon and their eccentric wines, Santa Cruz Mountain Vineyards, Mount Eden, and Cronin Vineyards. Because of the area's various microclimates, Cabernet, Chardonnay, Pinot Noir and Zinfandel all achieve both successes and failures. The generally cool climate can make it ideal for Chardonnay or Pinot Noir but tough on Cabernet one year, and vice versa when it's hotter. Clearly Monte Bello, at an elevation of 2,000 feet, is a great site for Cabernet. Bruce's Pinot Noirs once strayed all over the course, but the past few vintages have yielded exceptional wines, deep and complex. Bruce and Ridge also regularly hit the mark with Chardonnay. Ken Burnap's Santa Cruz Mountain Vineyards produces ultra-ripe and deeply concentrated Cabernets and Pinot Noirs. Kathryn Kennedy's Cabernets are also well crafted.

REFERENCE WINES

Cabernet Sauvignon: Cinnabar, Cronin, Kathryn Kennedy, Mount Eden Old Vine Reserve, Ridge Monte Bello, Santa Cruz Mountain Vineyards Bates Ranch
Chardonnay: Clos LaChance, David Bruce, Byington, Cinnabar, Cronin, Mount Eden Estate, Thomas Fogarty, Ridge, Storrs
Merlot: Ridge Monte Bello

Pinot Noir: David Bruce, Mount Eden, Sarah's Vineyard, Santa Cruz Mountain Vineyards
Syrah: Katherine Kennedy Maridon Vineyard

SANTA LUCIA HIGHLANDS
AVA 1992, 22,000 acres, 2,000 acres in vines

Smith & Hook and Paraiso Springs are the major proponents of this slender appellation in central Monterey County and use it for their Cabernet, but Talbott's estate vineyard, planted to Chardonnay, is also here. So far, Chardonnay, as evidenced by Talbott's fine offerings, is the quality leader. Cabernet, Merlot and Pinot Noir are promising.

SANTA MARIA VALLEY
AVA 1981, 82,180 acres, 13,000 in vines

Increasingly important for its high-quality Chardonnays and Pinot Noirs, Santa Maria Valley, in northern Santa Barbara County, is home to Au Bon Climat, Byron, Cambria, Foxen Vineyard and Rancho Sisquoc, along with the independently owned Bien Nacido Vineyard. Santa Maria's popularity as a winegrowing area was fueled by the success of the former Tepusquet Vineyard, which supplied Chardonnay to dozens of wineries, many from Napa and Sonoma. Tepusquet was sold, and divided between Kendall-Jackson and Robert Mondavi Winery, the former founding Cambria and the latter buying Byron. Nestlé's Wine World, owner of Beringer and Meridian, is the other major landholder; it owns Riverbench Vineyard near Byron. The stars of this AVA are Chardonnay, which is bright, rich and intensely flavored, and Pinot Noir, which is marked by rich cherry and cola flavors and herb and spice notes. Syrah, from Qupé and Cambria, is also excellent.

REFERENCE WINES

Cabernet Sauvignon: Rancho Sisquoc
Chardonnay: Au Bon Climat, Byron, Cambria, Foxen, Testarossa Bien Nacido, Villa Mt. Eden Signature Series Bien Nacido, Whitcraft
Pinot Noir: Au Bon Climat, Byron and Byron Reserve, Foxen Julia's Vineyard, Hitching Post Bien Nacido, Whitcraft Bien Nacido, Villa Mt. Eden Bien Nacido, Wild Horse

SANTA YNEZ VALLEY

AVA 1983, 154,000 acres, 3,000 acres in vines

This narrow valley in Santa Barbara County stretches eastward from near the Pacific Ocean to farther inland, where it's considerably warmer. A debate has arisen as to whether the appellation is better suited for cooler-climate varieties such as Chardonnay and Pinot Noir or warm-weather grapes such as Cabernet and Merlot. Sanford & Benedict Vineyard in the western portion is the best known, and is the source for some of Sanford's Chardonnays and Pinot Noirs. To the east lie Zaca Mesa, Fess Parker, Firestone, The Gainey Vineyard and Buttonwood Farm. Firestone, with 227 acres in vines, is the largest vineyard. Syrah, Gewürztraminer and Riesling fare well in some parts, while Cabernet, Merlot and Sauvignon Blanc are often marked by strong vegetal flavors.

REFERENCE WINES

Cabernet Sauvignon: Santa Barbara Winery
Chardonnay: Au Bon Climat Sanford & Benedict, Babcock Grand Cuvée, Gainey Limited Selection, Firestone, Longoria Santa Rita Cuvée, Santa Barbara Winery Lafond and Santa Barbara Reserve, Sanford Winery Sanford & Benedict, Sanford Estate
Pinot Noir: Au Bon Climat, Babcock Grand Cuvée Foxen, Gainey Limited Selection, Hitching Post Sanford & Benedict, Sanford Winery Sanford & Benedict, Lane Tanner
Sauvignon Blanc: Babcock Eleven Oaks, Brander Au-Naturel, Brander Cuvée Nicolas, Gainey Limited Selection
Syrah: Foxen Morehouse
Others: Firestone (Merlot, Gewürztraminer, Riesling)

SIERRA FOOTHILLS

AVA 1987, 3,800 acres in vines

An umbrella AVA that covers Amador, Calaveras, El Dorado, Mariposa, Nevada, Placer, Tuolomne and Yuba counties. Several wineries use this designation, and Zinfandel is the quality leader.

SONOMA COAST

AVA 1987, 480,000 acres, 11,400 acres in vines.

This is an unwieldy AVA formed primarily to suit Sonoma-Cutrer's desire to include all of its major Chardonnay districts within one boundary for use in its "estate-bottled" label, in much the same way Northern Sonoma was created to encompass the Gallo vineyards. It stretches from north of the Green Valley-Russian River area to Carneros, and includes small pockets of vineyards north of Jenner at the 1,000 foot elevation. Among the more exciting wineries are Flowers, Marcassin, Peter Michael and Hirsch. A narrower Sonoma Coast AVA along the coast would be useful.

REFERENCE WINES

Chardonnay: Kistler, Flowers Camp Meeting Ridge, Littorai Occidental, Marcassin, Martinelli Charles Ranch, Patz & Hall
Pinot Noir: Kistler, Flowers Camp Meeting Ridge, Littorai Hirsch; Siduri Hirsch, Williams Selyem: Hirsch, Sonoma Coast, Summa

SONOMA COUNTY

The Sonoma County designation is not an AVA but is a reflection of the political boundary. It's commonly used as a catch-all for many excellent wines hailing from areas that do not qualify for a more specific appellation, or that are blends of wines from more than one area within the county. Sonoma's diverse winegrowing appellations encompass several prominent AVAs; among the most important are Alexander Valley, Dry Creek Valley, Russian River Valley and Sonoma Valley. Sonoma County is also home to many smaller AVAs, including Chalk Hill, Green Valley-Sonoma County, Knights Valley, Sonoma Mountain and Sonoma Coast. Carneros, which lies partly within Sonoma County, is usually treated as a separate appellation.

As a general rule, the most westerly areas are too cool for wine grapes to ripen, but vines are being planted within several miles of the ocean on south-facing hills protected from the winds. Moving eastward and inland, the temperatures get increasingly warm and then hot. The soils in each of the areas can also vary significantly, from rocky volcanic ones to the sandy loam soils found, for example, along the Russian River.

SONOMA COUNTY ACREAGE BY GRAPE

Varietal	1970	1980	1990	1997	Percent Change 1970-1980	Percent Change 1980-1990	Percent Change 1990-1997
Cabernet Sauvignon	1,201	4,480	6,468	7,529	273%	44%	16%
Chardonnay	449	4,504	11,276	13,277	903%	150%	18%
Merlot	52	517	1,907	5,526	894%	269%	190%
Pinot Noir	626	2,839	3,130	4,128	354%	10%	32%
Zinfandel	3,780	4,664	4,130	4,259	23%	(-11%)	3%
Sauvignon Blanc	306	919	1,627	1,699	200%	77%	4%
Syrah	0	6	66	411	100%	1,000%	523%
Other	7,638	9,893	4,713	3,680	30%	(-52%)	(-22%)
Total	**14,052**	**27,822**	**33,317**	**40,510**	**98%**	**20%**	**22%**

Clear patterns are developing regarding the best matches between grapes and appellations, each of which is discussed under the specific AVA, but Zinfandel in Dry Creek, Cabernet in Alexander Valley and Chardonnay and Pinot Noir in Russian River Valley are working best. Indeed, Russian River Chardonnays and Pinot Noirs are among the best in the state. This county's Cabernet, while often excellent in Alexander Valley and Sonoma Valley, lags well behind Napa Valley's. Zinfandel rises to its greatest heights in Sonoma County's Dry Creek and Sonoma valleys. Sauvignon Blanc, Merlot and sparkling wines also excel here.

REFERENCE WINES

Cabernet Sauvignon: Arrowood, Chateau St. Jean, Ferrari-Carano Trésor, St. Francis Reserve, Simi Reserve
Chardonnay: Arrowood, Chateau Souverain, Fisher Coach Insignia, Landmark, Peter Michael, Rabbit Ridge Winemaker's Grand Reserve, Simi Reserve, Sonoma-Loeb, Stonestreet
Merlot: Arrowood, Chateau St. Jean Reserve, Gary Farrell Ladi's Vineyard, St. Francis, Stonestreet
Pinot Noir: Williams Selyem
Zinfandel: Alderbrook, Dry Creek, Greenwood Ridge, Grgich Hills, Mazzocco, Rabbit Ridge, Ravenswood, Ridge, Rosenblum, St. Francis Old Vines, Seghesio

SONOMA MOUNTAIN
AVA 1985, 5,000 acres, 633 acres in vines

Laurel Glen's superb Cabernet is the star of this mountain appellation. Owner Patrick Campbell's excellent vineyard typically yields dark, intense and complex wines from a sloping, eastward-facing vineyard. Also of note are Benziger's estate vineyard; Jack London Ranch, a source of Cabernet, Merlot, Pinot Noir and Zinfandel for Kenwood; McCrea Vineyard and Steiner Vineyard.

REFERENCE WINES

Cabernet Sauvignon: Benziger Estate Tribute, Laurel Glen, Ravenswood Pickberry Vineyards
Chardonnay: Paul Hobbs Richard Dinner Vineyard, Kistler McCrea Vineyard
Pinot Noir: Landmark Grand Detour Van der Kamp, Siduri Van der Kamp, Joseph Swan Steiner Vineyard

SONOMA VALLEY
AVA 1982, 103,200 acres, 13,300 acres in vines

Sonoma County's oldest winegrowing area is one mountain range west of Napa Valley and has a similar—but much smaller—narrow north-south shape. Buena Vista and the old Bundschu winery (now Gundlach Bundschu) date to the 1800s, but this appellation has yet to define itself by a single wine—not that that's bad. So far, Cabernet from Laurel Glen (on Sonoma Mountain), Kenwood Artist Series, B.R. Cohn Olive Hill Vineyard, Carmenet, Gundlach Bundschu Rhinefarm and Louis M.

Martini's Monte Rosso hold an edge among reds. Zinfandel also does well in several vineyard-designated wines but isn't widely planted. Chardonnay, led by Hanzell, Sonoma-Cutrer's Les Pierres, McCrea Vineyard, Kistler Estate and Durell Vineyard, fares well in the southern part of the valley where it borders on Carneros. Pinot Noir, after a glorious run at Hanzell from the 1960s through the 1970s, fares less well in warmer areas but does better when it hits Carneros. St. Francis is producing excellent Merlot, which represents a most intriguing possibility for the future.

Gundlach Bundschu's Rhinefarm Vineyard at the southernmost part of the appellation challenges all the rules: it is a mixture of all the major varieties—Cabernet, Chardonnay, Gewürztraminer, Merlot, Pinot Noir and Zinfandel—most of them capable of yielding fine wines. Kunde, long the major source of Sonoma Valley grapes for Sebastiani but now a winery of its own, is the biggest vineyard, covering several hundred acres with a wide variety of grapes.

REFERENCE WINES

Cabernet Sauvignon: Carmenet, B.R. Cohn Olivė Hill Vineyard, Kenwood Artist Series, Kenwood Jack London Vineyard, Kistler Estate, Louis M. Martini Monte Rosso, Ravenswood Rancho Salina Vineyard, Sebastiani Cherry Block, St. Francis Reserve
Chardonnay: Hanzell, Kistler Estate and Durell Vineyard, Matanzas Creek, St. Francis Reserve, Steele Parmalee-Hill Vineyard
Merlot: B.R. Cohn, Kenwood Jack London Vineyard, Matanzas Creek, St. Francis Reserve, Sebastiani Town
Pinot Noir: Hanzell
Syrah: Edmunds St. John Durell Vineyard, Kendall-Jackson Durell Vineyard
Zinfandel: Robert Biale Monte Rosso Vineyard, Gundlach Bundschu Rhinefarm Vineyards, Haywood Chamisal Vineyard; Ravenswood: Cooke, Old Hill and Monte Rosso vineyards; Ridge Pagani Vineyard, Rosenblum Samsel Vineyard Maggie's Reserve, St. Francis Pagani Vineyard Reserve

SPRING MOUNTAIN DISTRICT
AVA 1993, 8,600 acres, 900 acres in vines

This is an old winegrowing area in the hills west of St. Helena, rising up to nearly 2,500 feet. Grapes have been grown here for more than a century. Higher up, Cain, with its excellent Cain Five, merits attention; Keenan and Smith-Madrone have done well on occasion, but are uneven in quality. Philip Togni's Cabernet has been consistently dark and flavorful. The best winery by a stretch is Pride Mountain Vineyards.

REFERENCE WINES

Cabernet Sauvignon: Barnett, Cain Five, Pride Mountain, Spring Mountain, Togni
Merlot: Paloma, Pride Mountain

STAGS LEAP DISTRICT
AVA 1989, 2,700 acres, 1,300 acres in vines

Best known for its supple Cabernets and its many excellent wineries, the Stags Leap District is proof of how the appellation system works for consumers in defining styles and as a marketing tool. Because it won AVA approval ahead of Oakville and Rutherford, it had a head start in marketing. The Cabernets in particular impress, led by Stag's Leap Wine Cellars with its Cask 23, Fay and SLV bottlings; Silverado Vineyards with its estate and Limited Reserve; Shafer Hillside Select, Clos Du Val Reserve, Pine Ridge and its Stags Leap Vineyard, Steltzner, S. Anderson with its Richard Chambers Vineyard and Chimney Rock with its Elevage and Reserve bottlings. Each of these wineries produces very fine wines across the board, from Merlot to Chardonnay, although in the end the reds are best. Many of the whites, while appearing to come from this area, are in fact made from grapes grown elsewhere, so reading the label carefully is important.

Nathan Fay planted the area's first Cabernet vines in the Stags Leap area in the 1960s, realizing that at the time there were only a few hundred acres of Cabernet in Napa and many wineries wanted it. Vintners Warren Winiarski of Stag's Leap Wine Cellars and Bernard Portet of Clos Du Val both decided Stags Leap was slightly cooler than the upper valley and therefore conducive to planting Cabernet. It is also an absolutely beautiful area, with its huge rock outcropping. In 1972 both wineries produced their first Cabernets and in 1976 Winiarski's 1973 vintage won the Paris Tasting. Portet's 1972, while from a lesser year, also made an impression in that tasting.

The district may be cooler than Rutherford, St. Helena or Calistoga, but it is warm enough to ripen Cabernet, and these wines are typically marked by smooth, polished textures and soft tannins. The range of flavors includes black cherry, olive, herb, tobacco and currant, but the winemaker's hand greatly influences the style—witness the difference between Cask 23 and Silverado Limited Reserve. Despite being showy and appealing early on, the Cabernets can age exceptionally well—Stag's Leap Wine Cellars Cask 23 1974 was amazingly complex and vibrant on its 20th anniversary.

REFERENCE WINES

Cabernet Sauvignon: S. Anderson Richard Chambers Vineyard, Chimney Rock Reserve, Clos Du Val Reserve, Hartwell, Pine Ridge, Shafer and Shafer Hillside Select, Silverado Vineyards and Silverado Vineyards Limited Reserve, Stag's Leap Wine Cellars Cask 23, Fay and SLV vineyards
Chardonnay: Hartwell, Pine Ridge
Merlot: S. Anderson Reserve, Clos Du Val, Shafer, Silverado, Robert Sinskey

TEMECULA
AVA 1984, 100,000 acres, 2,800 acres in vines

This appellation, near the border of Riverside and San Diego counties, is built around the fortunes of Callaway Vineyard & Winery. Early experiments with standards such as Cabernet, Petite Sirah and Chardonnay drew mixed results, and today many early assumptions are under reconsideration. Whites, led by Sauvignon Blanc, Chardonnay and some Viognier, have an edge over the reds, but that may change as winemakers study Rhône varietals. The area is inland and warm, but the Rainbow Gap lets through the afternoon breezes which cool things off by late afternoon and evening.

YORK MOUNTAIN
AVA 1983, 5,200 acres, 30 acres in vines

A single-winery appellation that lies west of Paso Robles in a cool area. York Mountain, the single winery, fails to inspire across the board.

YOUNTVILLE
AVA 1999, 3,500 acres, 2,200 in vines

Yountville is a new AVA, bordered by Mill Road and Oakville to the north, the Stags Leap District to the east, Mount Veeder below the 400 to 500 foot elevation to the west, and Ragatz Road and Dry Creek to the south. Eventually the southern border will bump up against Oak Knoll, a pending AVA. Dominus Estate, the best-known vineyard, was once known as Napanook—the source of many great Inglenook Cask Cabernets. Charles Krug Winery's Slinsen Vineyard and the Grgich Hills Yountville Vineyard are also in the area, which is dominated by Cabernet and Chardonnay plantings. Domaine Chandon is the largest winery within the AVA.

REFERENCE WINES

Cabernet Sauvignon: Dominus, Grgich Hills Yountville

CHAPTER 4

HOW WINE IS MADE

Wine is simply fermented grape juice. You could make wine in your hand if you could hold squeezed grape juice long enough. The natural yeasts on the grape skins would convert the sugar in the juice to alcohol, giving you wine. As your appreciation for wine grows, so may your curiosity about the winemaking process. The basic chemistry is simple, but making fine, complex wines is far more involved, and there are significant differences in how wines are made when different styles are the goal. These involve such basics as the ripeness of the grapes when harvested, whether the wine undergoes a secondary fermentation, called malolactic fermentation (ML), and whether it's aged in new or used oak barrels and for how long—or whether it's aged in oak at all. This chapter will highlight some of the important winemaking steps involved in making great wine.

THE ROOTS OF GREAT WINES

The notion of fine wine begins with the most basic decisions: what kind of grapes to grow and where to plant them. A wine's potential quality is determined by where and how it's grown; great wines start in the vineyard.

Factors that influence a vine's health include the soil's texture, drainage, depth and color. Areas that receive lots of rainfall benefit from rocky soils that drain easily. Cool areas benefit from soils that collect and hold heat. Exposures influence how much or how little sun a vine receives; a north-facing vineyard receives less sunlight than a south-facing vineyard. Yet, grapevines are amazingly hardy plants that actually grow well in most soils. This is why there are often many different grape varieties planted in one area—why you'll find a Chardonnay or Pinot Noir vineyard flourishing in an area considered perfect for Cabernet or Zinfandel. So any given area may in fact be well suited for a variety of grapes. In the Russian River Valley, for instance, you can find Chardonnay, Merlot, Pinot Noir, Syrah and Zinfandel vineyards planted in close proximity to each other, with each variety yielding successful wines.

While some grape varieties will flourish in a wide variety of soils and climates, the finest wine grapes need fairly specific soils and climatic conditions to excel. When grape and soil are properly matched, the resulting wines reflect the place where they're grown, what the French call *terroir*. As discussed in Chapter 3, *terroir* expresses the interaction of many factors with the grapevines: temperatures by day and night, rainfall distribution by season and year, exposure, soil acidity, soil depth and so on; in short, anything natural that influences the growth of a vine.

This is perhaps the most important trend in winegrowing today—matching the right grape to the right soil and climate, or microclimate—a vineyard's immediate surroundings. Thus, many vintners are currently seeking cooler coastal climates, such as Carneros, Monterey, Russian River Valley, Santa Barbara and Santa Maria for grapes such as Chardonnay and Pinot Noir. The jury is still out on varietals such as Merlot and Syrah, but in the next decade vintners will have more experience and, hopefully, a better understanding about where these grapes have the best chances for success. There's a far better awareness of why Cabernet ripens so well in areas such as Oakville, Rutherford and the Stags Leap District and Zinfandel blossoms in Dry Creek and Sonoma Valleys. Chapter 3, "Appellations and Vineyards," and Chapter 2, "Grapes and Wine Styles," touch on this subject.

There are also important if not vital economic considerations that determine where grapes are grown and what kinds of wines they produce. For example, even though the Gamay grape might grow very well in Napa Valley, planting Gamay there would make little sense. Napa is small, and great vineyards there are expensive. Moreover, there aren't any great Gamays, and even the finest bottlings command only modest prices. Cabernet, however, which in many parts of Napa Valley has flourished for nearly a century, commands prices—in the $30 to $100 a bottle range for the best ones—high enough to produce profits. For parallel reasons, growing Cabernet in cool areas of Monterey County, as was tried in the 1970s, proved disastrous. Many of those vineyards were planted as investments by large agribusiness concerns more interested in growing grapes for profit than in making quality wines. Looking at the prices commanded by Napa Valley Cabernets, those investors believed that planting Cabernet anywhere would bring them the highest monetary return. But the original Monterey Cabernets were marked by strong vegetal flavors because the grapes didn't fully ripen even in hot years. The result was a steady stream of mediocre wines that hurt the reputation of Monterey winegrowing more than it helped. In recent years, though, winemakers have found areas in Monterey better suited to red grapes, including Merlot.

ROOTSTOCK AND CLONES

Having decided what kinds of grapes to grow and where to grow them, vintners can choose from a variety of rootstocks, grape clones and vine trellising systems, all of which contribute to the vine's health and ultimately to the wine's quality. Vigorous rootstock can lead to vines that are very productive—productive enough for areas where five to ten tons of fruit per acre is the desired yield and ordinary table wines are the end result. Conversely, devigorating rootstock leads to less vigorous vines, and is preferred by vintners seeking a smaller crop and superior quality. Different grape clones can produce berries of varying sizes which will ripen at different times. Their flavor profiles may differ as well; a winery might use two or three different clones of Pinot Noir or Chardonnay in a vineyard in hopes of creating wines with more complex flavors. If those clones ripen at different stages, it can be a real challenge to harvest all the grapes at optimum maturity. Trellising systems influence how vigorous a grapevine becomes and how much sun exposure it receives, factors which in turn influence how grape berries and clusters ripen.

The basic fact to keep in mind is this: crop yield is crucial to a wine's quality. The lower the grape yield per acre, the more concentrated the juice will be and the more complex and intensely flavored the resulting wine. A vine tries to ripen all its berries. If it's carrying many clusters, it has to work harder and longer to supply the nutrients to ripen all the berries. If the vine is overcropped—i.e., is bearing too many grapes—often it will stop short of full maturation, resulting in wines that have a green, unripe flavor. That's why there's such an emphasis today on reducing or limiting crop loads, and why growers thin large crops once the grape clusters have formed.

Where a vine is grown will also help determine its ability to produce. Mountain-grown vines are notorious for their meager crops. Getting two to three tons per acre off a mountainside vineyard is an achievement. But those berries may be smaller and have a lower juice-to-skin ratio, and thus be more intensely flavored (and tannic) than berries from vines grown in more hospitable soils. Valley-floor vines rooted in rich soils can produce a much larger crop and in fact don't self-limit their crops as well as mountain-grown vines do. It's instructive to taste mountain-grown wines and compare them with valley-floor grapes, especially with varieties such as Cabernet, Pinot Noir and Zinfandel.

Again, economics plays a role in determining crop yields. Large-scale wineries need enough grapes to produce the thousands of cases of wine they sell each year.

They want vineyards and grapevines that yield sufficiently large crops on a consistent basis. A vineyard that typically yields five or six tons of Chardonnay grapes a year may be ideal for a winery producing a good Chardonnay that sells for $15 a bottle. Cutting that vineyard's yield in half might produce a richer, more concentrated wine, but it would also cut production in half, driving the wine's price tag up as well, and the winery might not be able to sell as many $30 bottles of wine as $15 bottles of wine. Large-volume wines in particular have price ceilings, and a winery that needs to sell 50,000 or 100,000 cases of Chardonnay or Cabernet to meet marketing goals simply can't afford to have its production cut in half. High-quality, small-production wines, however, can often charge what the market will bear. Pricing is directly related to quality, supply, demand and image.

GROWING, PICKING AND CRUSHING GRAPES

Climatic conditions and weather patterns—rain, hail, frosts, droughts, windstorms and cold—influence how a grape cluster forms and ripens and what kind of quality it will produce. When grape clusters bloom in spring, the number of berries a cluster will produce is determined. Heavy winds at bloom can affect flowering. If there's frost at the wrong time, young berries can be damaged. California has experienced a series of droughts in the past 20 years, but for the most part established vines with deep roots survive droughts just fine, though they may yield smaller crops. Younger, developing vines, however, are likely to be affected, as they require more water.

Vintners prefer years when there is plenty of rain in the fall after harvest and during the winter months—but not enough to flood or seriously erode vineyards. They prefer mild springs, so their grapes set healthy grape clusters. They prefer mild-to-warm summers, which favor even ripening patterns, over heat waves or cold spells. They prefer their grapes to ripen fully and to be harvested when they have optimum flavor. No vintner likes rain at harvest. While some rain at harvest is usual and won't necessarily harm the grapes, persistent rain can break the ripening pattern, temporarily lower sugar levels, and lead to mold, grape shatter and mildew, particularly among grapes that are literally thin-skinned, such as Pinot Noir. The rain will have less impact on the grapes if the weather turns dry and warm immediately thereafter, rather than remaining cool.

Vintners must determine, as best they can, the optimal time to harvest their grapes. Often the decision is influenced by the weather, the size of the crop, the number of days it might take to harvest, and the threat of rain or prolonged heat or a cooling pattern. Once harvest approaches, a vintage is on the line—and so is the winery's economic livelihood. Picking dates can make or break an entire year, directly influencing a wine's flavor and shaping its style, character and aging potential. Young, immature grapes yield wines with less depth, richness and flavor in both reds and whites. Immature white wines are marked by crisp acidity and flinty or lemony flavors. In some styles of Sauvignon Blanc or Chenin Blanc this can be desirable. With reds, immature grapes lead to light colors and green herb and tea flavors. Overripe grapes, both red and white, often make wine with jammy flavors, thicker textures and higher alcohol levels. The trend today among fine-wine producers is to pick the grapes based on flavor rather than on statistical measurements such as sugar level or acidity. In order to justify high prices, vintners need the ultimate in quality, and that usually means letting the grapes hang on the vine even in the face of a late harvest, unseasonable rain, or the remote prospect of a crop failure.

Once picked, the grapes are sorted—to remove rotted, unripened or overripened clusters and matter other than grapes (leaves, bugs, stems)—crushed and fermented. Red and white wines go through different fermentation processes, so we will discuss them separately.

FERMENTATION OF RED WINES

Because they get their flavor from the grape skins, most red wines—Cabernet, Merlot, Pinot Noir, Syrah and Zinfandel—are fermented with natural yeasts that grow on the grape skins or with yeasts that work especially well with the grape variety and desired wine style. The crushed grapes ferment or soak with their skins, often at varying temperatures, until the fermentation is complete and the yeasts have converted the sugar to alcohol. Occasionally, a small number of stems are left in with varieties such as Pinot Noir or Syrah grapes during fermentation for added tannin—at the risk of adding unwanted astringency—but this practice has diminished in recent years. Sometimes a fermentation is trickier than expected; the winemaker may face a "stuck" or incom-

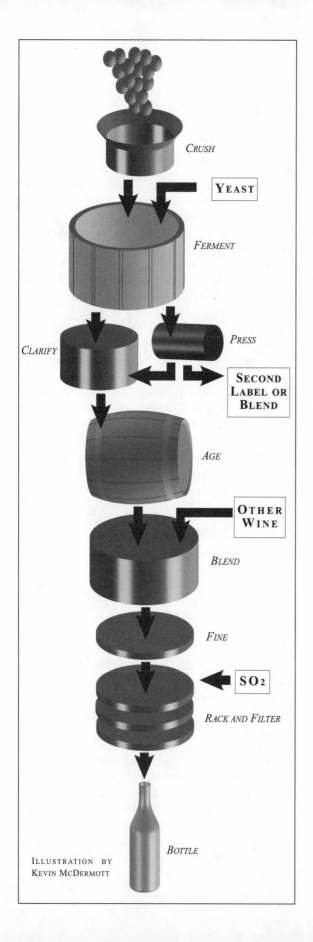

CRUSH

YEAST

FERMENT

CLARIFY

PRESS

SECOND
LABEL OR
BLEND

AGE

OTHER
WINE

BLEND

FINE

SO₂

RACK AND FILTER

BOTTLE

ILLUSTRATION BY
KEVIN McDERMOTT

MAKING RED WINES

This chart shows the more common steps and methods used for making Cabernet, Merlot, Pinot Noir, Sangiovese, Syrah and Zinfandel. The options and individual style permutations are too numerous to cover here, although I have indicated the more common differences below.

1. Harvest: Ripe grapes are harvested at between 22 and 27 degrees Brix, leading to wines of 12 to 14 percent alcohol. To get an approximate alcohol conversion level, multiply the stated Brix by .55.

2. Crush: Grapes are crushed and destemmed. The resulting unfermented juice, known as "must," remains in contact with skins and sometimes stems. The juice is inoculated with yeast or begins fermentation with natural (wild) yeasts living on grape skins. Red wines can spend from five to 25 days or longer fermenting on the skins, depending on the winemaker's desired style. During this phase, the must is "pumped over" the floating grape skins or otherwise manipulated to extract color and flavor and allow in sufficient air for fermentation. Fermentation usually continues until it is complete and all the sugar has been converted to alcohol, leaving the wine "dry".

3. Press and Clarify: "Free run" wine is separated from the must and allowed to settle, often going directly into barrel. The remaining grape skins are then pressed, which squeezes out the remaining wine and leaves the pomace.

4. Aging and Blending: Most red wines are aged in oak barrels for 10 to 36 months. With the exception of Pinot Noir (which is rarely blended with other grapes), they may or may not be blended. Some winemakers prefer to make their blends early on; others choose to wait longer to evaluate the wines which will go into the possible blends.

5. Racking and Clarification: For most reds, the wines are moved from barrel to barrel, a process called "racking," which aerates and clarifies the wine. During this process, a small amount of lees, or sediment, may remain at the bottom of the barrel or tank. Several rackings usually leave the wine clear. Occasionally fining or filtration is required to remove unwanted sediment or bacteria. Many wines are unfined and unfiltered. At some point after fermentation and prior to bottling, a small amount of sulfur dioxide is added.

6. Bottling: After the wines have aged in oak and have been racked and clarified, they are ready to be bottled. Depending on the wine, the finished bottle is either ready to be sold or aged at the winery for one to three years.

plete fermentation and need to add nutrients to the juice to restart the process.

The wine is usually "worked" or manipulated to maximize or minimize color and flavor extraction during fermentation. One technique is "pumping over". Wine is pumped from the bottom of the tank to the top with hoses. This not only aerates the wine but mixes the juice and skins. Another technique is known as "punching the cap." The grape cap, which is formed when crushed grape skins riding carbon dioxide bubbles float to the top of the vat, is punched down into the juice, either by foot (in the old days) or by plunger, in effect mixing the grape skins with the juice. Large wineries use huge rotary tank fermentors that turn like a cement mixer, continually mixing the grape skins and must back into the juice. Either way, the grape skin cap is periodically broken up to encourage flavor extraction, allow more air in and encourage the yeasts to complete the fermentation.

Certain grapes, such as Pinot Noir, are often fermented by a process called carbonic maceration, or whole-berry fermentation: the grapes are poured into a closed, carbon dioxide-filled vat and ferment on their natural yeasts until their skins soften and eventually break, freeing the juice, which is then gently squeezed out. Some Pinot Noir producers will set aside a portion of their grapes for this technique, because it captures bright, fresh fruit flavors and gives the wine a healthy red berry color.

After fermentation, the free-run juice is separated from the grape solids. Most fine red wines are aged short-term either in upright tanks (made sometimes of wood but usually of temperature-controlled stainless steel) or put directly into a combination of American and French, new and used, small oak barrels. The remaining grape juice is pressed out of the grape solids, and a portion of this "press juice" is sometimes added back to the main wine depending on the grape variety and wine style. The press juice is usually more tannic, and sometimes a touch bitter.

At some point, either before or after going into barrel, virtually all red wines undergo a secondary fermentation called malolactic (ML), which converts crisp malic acid into softer lactic acid. Occasionally a red wine will have a difficult time sustaining ML or may not go through it at all. The resulting wine will be crisper and slightly higher in malic acid than usual and may require more barrel aging to soften it. The greater danger is that the wine might undergo ML in the bottle—a rare disaster that can lead to a spritzy wine or even push the cork out of a bottle.

BARRELS

Aging wine in small oak barrels accomplishes several things. It allows a tiny amount of oxygen through the barrel staves to slowly oxidize the wine slightly and soften the tannins. It also imparts certain flavors, which vary with the type and age of the wood. Oak can impart strong aromas and flavors of toasty, smoky, charred wood or vanilla. If mishandled or not kept clean, barrels can impart a dirty, dank, earthy or musty edge and spoil a wine's flavor. The major reds that receive oak aging include Cabernet, Cabernet blends, Merlot, Pinot Noir, Sangiovese, Syrah and Zinfandel. Depending on the wine's weight and intensity, it will spend from ten months to three years in oak. Lighter reds such as Pinot Noir spend less time in oak than full-bodied Cabernets. A good range for most reds is one to two years in oak.

There are many different kinds of oak and many different ways to treat them. Some oaks are selected and treated specifically for Cabernet and others for Pinot Noir or Zinfandel. The decision is influenced by two factors: a desired oak flavor (or lack thereof) and wine style, and the cost of the barrels. In 1999 the best French oak barrels cost about $700 each, with American oak costing about half that. One barrel holds enough wine for about 25 cases. Well-treated barrels can be used several times, especially for white wines, and are often passed on for use with heavier reds. In barrel, reds are periodically racked, or moved from one barrel to another; this is done by using a hose to transfer the wine from one vessel to another. Racking exposes the wine to oxygen and helps clean it up by separating it from tiny solids remaining from fermentation. After several rackings a wine should be sufficiently clear for bottling.

FINING AND FILTRATION

The trend today is for the finest wines to go into bottled unfined and unfiltered. These wines often have a hazy edge to their color, but they also can have more richness, complexity and flavor, because nothing's been removed from them by filtration. Unfiltered wines can look unappealing—like cloudy water—to those unac-

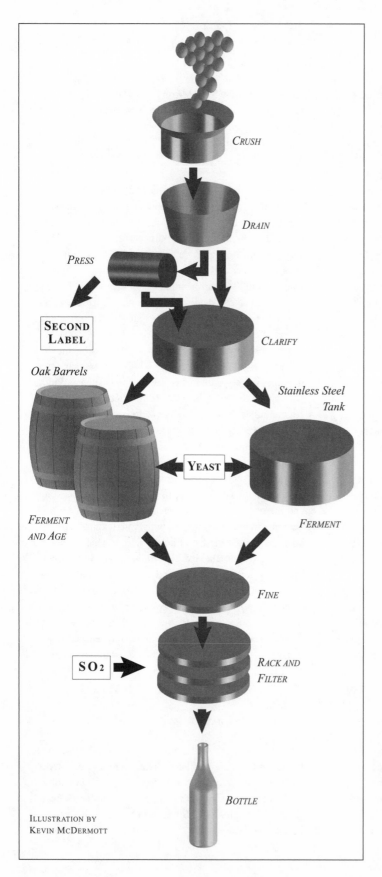

CRUSH

DRAIN

PRESS

SECOND
LABEL

Oak Barrels

CLARIFY

*Stainless Steel
Tank*

YEAST

FERMENT
AND AGE

FERMENT

FINE

SO₂

RACK AND
FILTER

BOTTLE

ILLUSTRATION BY
KEVIN MCDERMOTT

MAKING WHITE WINES

This chart shows common steps and methods used for making the major white wines of California. The options and style permutations vary greatly. Chardonnay and Sauvignon Blanc are often either fermented in or aged in oak barrels. Chenin Blanc, Gewürztraminer and Riesling most often age in stainless steel to preserve their freshness; they are very rarely aged in oak, except when made as a dessert-style wine.

1. Harvest: Ripe grapes are harvested at between 21 and 25 degrees Brix, leading to wines of 11.5 to 14 percent alcohol. Dessert-style wines can be picked at up to 25 to 40 degrees Brix, but are not fermented dry.

2. Crush, Press and Clarify: Grapes are crushed and destemmed; the resulting unfermented grape juice is known as must. The free run juice is quickly drained away from grape skins (to minimize contact) into either oak or stainless steel for fermentation, and is chilled. The remaining material is then gently pressed; the additional must is either added back to the free run juice or used in other wines, such as second labels. Wines are clarified by letting solids settle at the bottom of the tank or barrel.

3. Fermentation and Aging: Juice is inoculated with yeast or allowed to ferment with its own natural yeasts. Fermentation converts sugar to alcohol; many whites have a trace of residual sugar after fermentation. Chardonnay and Sauvignon Blanc then age for six to 14 months in oak barrels, often on the lees (i.e. with the sediment that results from fermentation left in); Chenin Blanc, Gewürztraminer and Riesling age in stainless steel tanks. Malolactic fermentation for all or a part of the wine is an option.

4 Blending: Chenin Blanc, Gewürztraminer and Riesling are aged briefly and released for sale while they are young and fresh; they are rarely blended. Sauvignon Blanc and/or Sémillon are often blended with each other. Chardonnay is rarely blended.

5. Fining and Cold Stabilization (optional)**:** Most whites are fined by adding bentonite, a powdery clay, which removes excess proteins and clarifies the wine. Cold stabilization at 30 degrees Fahrenheit removes excess potassium bitartrate.

6. Racking and Filtration: In racking, the wine is clarified by being pumped off its lees. Sulfur dioxide is generally added at this point, but it can be added at most stages of winemaking. Filtration (optional) can range from a very fine polish filter to a coarser one. Many Chardonnays are unfined and unfiltered.

7. Bottling: Most white wines are bottled and go directly to market within six months to a year.

customed to natural wine. Unfined and unfiltered wines also run the risk of bacterial growth occurring in the bottle, which can ruin the taste of the wine. Most red wines are fined, usually by adding whipped egg whites, gelatin, isinglass (fish glue) or other coagulants that combine with the sediment particles and then settle out in the barrel; others are separated in centrifuges. The purpose of the process is to give the wine clarity and brilliance, to remove any unnecessary particles that are too light to sink to the bottom, and to eliminate spoilage bacteria. *Brettanomyces*, one of the worst of these, is a yeast bacterium that when left unchecked can induce a strong, dry, horsy, leathery flavor in wines.

Filtration is used in many wines for the aformentioned reasons, but when overdone it can rob a wine of its character. It can not only strip away the aroma, textural nuances and body, but occasionally impart a sterile, filter-pad flavor. The whole issue of filtration is controversial. Clearly the best wines are those that are "made" in the vineyard through precision farming techniques, and handled as little as possible thereafter—filtration is significant handling. Many winemakers, however, believe a fine, or polish, filtration is an insurance policy against having a wine go bad in the bottle, which not only destroys the wine but has an immeasurable long-term negative impact on their businesses. If a high-profile winery that specializes in small case lots of several wines loses one lot of wine to spoilage, consumers might be forgiving. If a winery loses 20,000 cases of a nationally distributed brand it could be fatal. I believe in the minimalist or non-interventionist school of winemaking, where as little as possible is done to the wine in shepherding it from the vine to the bottle. But if a winemaker discovers a bacterial problem, fining or filtering to remove that problem is essential to the wine's quality and to the vintner's financial well-being.

BLENDING

Wines such as Cabernet, Merlot, Zinfandel and Sangiovese often benefit from blending. Pinot Noir, because its flavors are so delicate and easily influenced by even a tiny amount of another wine, is seldom blended. Cabernet and Merlot are well suited for each other and are often paired with Malbec, Petite Verdot and Cabernet Franc in what is known as a classic Bordeaux-style blend; Merlot can soften Cabernet's tannic or astringent tendencies, while Cabernet can add flavor and tannin to Merlot. Zinfandel is occasionally blended with small portions of Petite Sirah, Carignane and Sangiovese to give it color or texture. Sangiovese often blends well with Cabernet, as either the dominant or the secondary flavor. Ten or 15 years ago, there were many 100 percent Cabernets, but today almost all the great wines include at least a small percentage of blended wine. Deciding when to blend is another stylistic choice. Some winemakers like to marry their blends right after fermentation; others prefer to wait and taste how the wines have developed before blending them together.

FERMENTATION OF WHITE WINES

White-wine production differs from red-wine production beginning at the time the grapes are crushed. (Until then, the same principles regarding ripeness and clean grapes apply.) White wines are crushed and separated from their skins almost immediately. Often the "crush" is a gentle squeeze—just enough pressure to break open the skins and let the juice run free without smashing the skins. Then the grapes are pressed—again, more gently than red grapes. The press juice may be added back to the wine, or it may be used for a lower-priced or different-style wine. At this stage, control of oxidation is crucial to the freshness and vitality of the unfermented grape juice. Many wineries chill the juice to preserve freshness prior to fermentation. Those that prefer to barrel-ferment their Chardonnay or Sauvignon Blanc may pump it directly into barrels.

This process differs markedly from the techniques used in the 1960s through 1980s, when white wines were made more like reds. They were often allowed one to two days of skin contact to extract flavor and were fermented in vats or stainless-steel tanks. At that time, also, there was widespread avoidance of malolactic fermentation for whites. Because the Chardonnays of the era were often grown in warm areas, they were harvested at lower acidity levels than today. Putting a wine through ML would have reduced the acid level even further. It was also common then to add acidity to wines as needed. Putting a wine through ML and then adding acidity back in created two contradictory and seemingly unnecessary steps.

Winemaker-controlled cold fermentation was considered revolutionary in winemaking circles. In Burgundy, a Chardonnay can be barrel-fermented in a naturally cool cellar. In California, winemakers battled with warm cellar temperatures for years. The introduction of temperature-controlled stainless steel tanks was a welcome solution to this problem. For whites such as Gewürztraminer or Riesling, neither of which is normally aged in oak, temperature-controlled stainless steel helps preserve the freshness and vitality of the young wine—and these wines are best when they are at their fruitiest.

A wine's style is also affected by whether its fermentation is allowed to finish, leaving a dry wine, or stopped early, leaving an off-dry wine with a trace of residual sugar. Both styles are common in wines such as Gewürztraminer and Riesling. A touch of sweetness is appealing to many wine drinkers, and it can take the edge off a wine such as Gewürztraminer, which by nature may have a slight bitter taste. Many wineries deliberately leave a trace of residual sugar in even their Chardonnays for flavor, sweetness and body. Most of the finest Chardonnays are fermented until dry, then aged in contact with their lees (the sediment from dead yeast cells expired after fermentation), a process called *sur lie* aging. The lees continue to interact with the wine while it ages, usually for eight months to a year or more.

After fermentation, either in barrel or stainless steel, the wine is allowed to settle and clarify. While in barrel, the wine may be racked off its sediment, or lees, into a different barrel or it may be left in its original barrel until time for bottling. As with reds, a white wine is either left unfined and unfiltered, or is lightly filtered in one or more of these ways: with a centrifuge, with a powdery clay called bentonite or with filter pads. Many whites are then cold stabilized, in a process that eliminates all or most of the tartaric acid crystals which are created when tartaric acid combines with potassium or calcium. The crystals are not harmful, but they can be an annoyance to consumers, just as sediment or a cloudy haze may raise questions about a wine's cleanliness or stability.

Most white wines are not blended. Chardonnay, Gewürztraminer, Riesling and Viognier, for example, are usually left 100 percent varietal. However, Sauvignon Blanc and Sémillon are often blended with each other in different proportions to achieve a desired style and flavor profile.

SPARKLING WINES

Legally, California sparkling wines can be called Champagne, a name that the French Champagne trade would prefer was restricted to only those wines produced in the Champagne region. The French Champagne houses who make many of the leading sparkling wines in California honor the name and don't use it. Several California wineries, however, do call their wines Champagne, including Schramsberg.

The finest sparkling wines are made by the process known as *méthode champenoise*, a labor-intensive process that turns the still wine into a bubbly or sparkling one. The essence of *méthode champenoise* is that the wine undergoes a secondary fermentation inside the bottle. In general, California sparkling wines employ Chardonnay, Pinot Noir, Pinot Meunier and blends thereof. These grapes are generally harvested at slightly lower sugar and ripeness levels than those used for table wines. This is changing slightly, however, as vintners re-examine their earlier efforts, many of which were overly crisp and tart. Sparkling-wine producers want to begin with a fairly neutral-flavored wine that is naturally high in acidity, because sparkling wine is highly manipulated. The *méthode champenoise* builds complexity into the wine.

After the primary fermentation, (which can occur in stainless steel or oak barrels), and sometimes after malolactic fermentation as well, the cuvée is either kept separate for a vintage-dated wine (rare in both California and Champagne) or used for blending with several vintages. The cuvée is then bottled with a little fresh yeast and a precise amount of sugar that will re-ferment in the bottle, adding about 1 percent alcohol and producing a gas pressure of six atmospheres.

The second fermentation takes a few months, during which time the yeast adds other flavor dimensions to the cuvée. When the wine has aged the desired time, the yeast must be removed. To concentrate the yeast cells in the neck of the bottle for easy removal, the bottles are stored in racks facing downward at an angle and rotated periodically, a process called riddling. When all the sediment is resting in the neck of the bottle, the bottle necks are placed in an icy solution that freezes the sediment. The bottle cap (or cork) is then removed, allowing the pressure to "pop out" the solid sediment—a process called disgorgement. Next the wine is immediately topped up with more wine (called dosage; this may include a trace more sugar or a dash of brandy), recorked and wrapped with a wire cage to hold the cork in place. Finally, the wine may be aged further, depending on the winery's desired style.

Most sparkling wines and Champagnes are non-vintage—the goal being a consistent house style year after year. In exceptional years, vintage-dated wines are made; usually these should benefit from aging. Rosés are created by adding a small percentage of Pinot Noir to the cuvée to give it color and flavor. Blanc de blancs are made with Chardonnay. Blanc de noirs are made from Pinot Noir grapes and can have a slightly pink hue, but are often indistinguishable in color from other sparklers. Cremant is a lighter, less pressurized, less gassy style that's often more elegant and creamier in texture.

DESSERT WINES

California makes wonderful dessert wines from Riesling, Gewürztraminer, Sauvignon Blanc and Sémillon grapes. With these white dessert wines, the most common production method is a natural—and curious—one, employing *botrytis cinerea* mold, the "noble rot" that forms on grape clusters under certain autumn weather conditions. When misty mornings and sunny afternoons lead to the spread of botrytis, the clusters of mature grapes shrivel, concentrating both sugar and acid. As the rot spreads, the berries shrink and their juice evaporates. When harvested, the berries are very gently squeezed, and the resulting juice is intensely sweet, rich and honeyed. Fermentation must be warm, often takes place in barrels, and lasts for several weeks, until the yeasts stop working—leaving behind alcohol, sugar, and honey, pear, nectarine and apricot flavors. Often these dessert wines carry the words "selected late harvest," which indicates the grapes were picked especially late, making a wine that's even sweeter than a "late harvest"— a term that can apply to white or red wines, as in late-harvest Zinfandel.

Port is a sweet, fortified, usually red wine that is made with modest success in several styles, often with Zinfandel and Petite Sirah. The wine's fermentation is stopped at about 6 percent alcohol, leaving plenty of residual sugar, at which time brandy is added. The Port is then aged in barrels for two to three years, with an alcohol level of about 16 to 20 percent. Several wineries are beginning to experiment with the grape varieties used in Portugal for genuine Port—Tinta Madeira, Touriga, Tinta Cão and Souzão, among others. But for now, California Port remains mostly a curiosity, with a few good, and no great, examples.

CHAPTER 5

A SUMMARY OF THE VINTAGES: 1933 TO 1998

A vintage date is like a snapshot. It reflects the year's growing conditions in a given appellation and is often an important indicator of a wine's quality. Growing conditions include many factors—whether the weather was warm, hot, cool or rainy, when those climatic conditions occurred and how they might have affected the quality of the grape crop and subsequent wines. In analyzing a vintage we also take into account such factors as the size of the harvest.

Is there such a thing as a perfect vintage? In theory, yes. It would go something like this: normal rainfall from late fall through winter, no frost and light (if any) rain in spring, an average to slightly below average-sized grape crop, mild, dry weather in the spring through summer months followed by a steady warming pattern in September—allowing a well balanced grape crop to ripen fully without the hindrance of rain.

A vintage date becomes a more precise quality indicator when it is combined with a producer's name, a grape or wine style and an appellation. When all this information is presented together, it provides a solid basis for making buying decisions and anticipating the wine's quality and style.

This chapter offers a general assessment of

California's vintages and how they have been expressed in the major wine types. The wines covered are Cabernet, Chardonnay, Merlot, Pinot Noir and Zinfandel; the primary vintages covered are 1980 through 1998. A one- to five-star rating is provided for each year overall, as well as a similar rating for each of the major varietals. The vintages before 1980 are discussed in more general terms, focusing primarily on Napa Valley Cabernet and tracing the years back to 1933.

Chapters 2 and 3, "Grapes and Wine Styles," and "Appellations and Vineyards," discuss which grapes and wines tend to excel in different appellations. This chapter summarizes how each grape did in the major areas in any given year. But clearly there are important distinctions to be made within most vintages on the basis of appellation and wine style. In the case of Cabernet, the vintage rating is weighted heavily toward Napa Valley, which produces more than triple the number of superb Cabernets than the entire rest of the state combined. However, when they're of note, Alexander Valley, Sonoma Valley and Dry Creek Valley Cabernets are also discussed. For Chardonnay the major areas are Napa Valley, Carneros, Russian River Valley, Monterey County and the South Central Coast appellations of

Santa Barbara County and Santa Maria Valley. For Merlot, the major areas considered are Napa Valley, Carneros, Sonoma Valley, Alexander Valley and Sonoma County. For Pinot Noir, Carneros, Russian River Valley and the Santa Maria Valley-Santa Barbara County areas are considered. For Zinfandel, it's Napa and Sonoma Counties and the appellations within them. Note also that the vintage ratings are weighted toward the most important wines, and to wineries that specialize in the finest wines. They are not weighted toward California-appellation wines, which are blends of wines and/or grapes from several appellations.

Five stars (★★★★★) indicate an outstanding vintage, with many classic wines. These are vintages that give you the best odds of buying great and ageworthy wines. In California, Cabernet has the best and longest track record for excellence, followed very closely by Chardonnay. These two wines have higher ratings than either Merlot, Pinot Noir or Zinfandel, which are more difficult grapes to grow and which make more temperamental and variable wines.

Four stars (★★★★) indicate a very good to excellent year that falls just short of outstanding, and may well have many outstanding wines. This rating could also indicate a particularly outstanding year in just one appellation.

Three stars (★★★) indicate an above-average to good vintage which may include a few outstanding wines, but will be more variable in quality.

Two stars (★★) indicate a fair to average year. In these vintages, there will be few truly outstanding wines.

One star (★) indicates a poor vintage that is best avoided. California's vintages vary significantly, especially given the diversity of the state's appellations. On the other hand it rarely has disastrous vintages, as Europe does; there, it's not uncommon for an entire appellation to have an off year.

To assess the more recent vintages, I have monitored climatic patterns and growing seasons and interviewed dozens of winemakers during and immediately after harvest. There are years when rain at harvest does not affect the wines. Other times a little rain can cause significant damage. Thus, a vintage can't be judged by weather records alone. The best way to judge a vintage is simply to taste the wines on a regular basis. I often taste the major wines four to six months after harvest, which gives an early indication of quality. The character of a

vintage may well be readily apparent at harvest time, but other times it can take years for its personality to be fully revealed.

When using the following vintage information to aid in your purchasing decisions, bear in mind that most wines are usually at their best early in their lives. Most of the best Cabernets reach a mature and appealing drinking age five to seven years after the vintage, and are surely ready to drink at eight to ten years. Many can age and continue to improve much longer, especially if stored properly (see Chapter 6: "Building Your Wine Collection"). There are also ageworthy Chardonnays, Merlots, Pinot Noirs, Syrahs and Zinfandels (see Chapter 2: Grapes and Wine Styles). The key to deciding when to drink the wines lies in your own taste. Once you decide whether you like young, fruity, fresh and vibrant wines, or more mature wines with softer textures and perhaps more complex flavors, you'll make the most of your buying decisions. The point is that if you age your wines, you're accepting the risk that the wine might change and lose its appeal, or that your tastes might change and you'll find yourself less enthused by wines you once liked.

See Appendix 4 for a chart summarizing the following discussion of vintages:

1998	★★★–★★★★★
Cabernet Sauvignon	★★★★
Chardonnay	★★★★
Merlot	★★★
Pinot Noir	★★★
Zinfandel	★★★

This is an early assessment of a vintage that came perilously close to crop failure along the North Coast, with one of the latest harvests on record. Blame or credit El Niño for unseasonably wet spring weather and a very cool summer that prolonged harvest well into September for the whites and into October and November for many reds. What may have saved the North Coast harvest was severe thinning of grape clusters and the fact that rain didn't douse the late harvest. Along the Central and South Coasts, temperatures were moderate, and the harvest was neither as small or as late. Expect some very good Cabernets, Chardonnays and Pinot Noirs, but also expect the small size to impact case volume. In short, there was less wine made and depending on winery selections—what is sold under the wineries' primary labels—quality and availability will vary.

1997	★★★★★
Cabernet Sauvignon	★★★★★
Chardonnay	★★★★★
Merlot	★★★
Pinot Noir	★★★
Zinfandel	★★★★★

A blockbuster year that combined a huge crop—in some instances 30 percent above normal—with exceptionally high quality. The growing season was long, mild and warm to hot; not overdone in any respect. The resulting wines are very ripe, rich, complex, balanced and complete, with particularly strong showings from Cabernet, Chardonnay and Zinfandel. The Cabernets and Chardonnays rival the best vintages ever; the former will challenge 1994 for top honors. For Merlot, it was a merely good year. Zinfandels were very ripe and high in alcohol, with overall quality very high. Pinot Noirs were a touch lighter and firmer than in 1994 or 1995, two standout vintages with richer, more complex wines, but still quite impressive. All of the wines should age well from 2000 to 2006 and beyond.

1996	★★★
Cabernet Sauvignon	★★★★
Chardonnay	★★★★★
Merlot	★★★
Pinot Noir	★★★
Zinfandel	★★★

A small crop of generally very good quality wines came after a warm winter and some very hot summer temperatures. There was some uneven ripening in Merlot, Pinot Noir and Zinfandel vineyards, resulting in less color, extract and concentration. In short, many wines were ripe in sugar but less flavorful, making this a year to shop selectively. Cabernet and Chardonnay are again the steady stars, outperforming the rest of the field. The top Cabernets are very dark, ripe, rich and complex—not as opulent as 1994 or 1997, but quite exciting on their own terms. Chardonnays, too, were ripe and concentrated, with dozens of great wines.

1995	★★★★★
Cabernet Sauvignon	★★★★★
Chardonnay	★★★★★
Merlot	★★★
Pinot Noir	★★★★★
Zinfandel	★★★★★

Another small crop of impressive wines, the 1995s were a shade less rich and concentrated than the 1994s, but there were plenty of success stories. Cabernets were full-bodied, if a shade sleeker than in 1994; Chardonnays were ripe and elegant, rich in body and flavor. Pinot Noirs were generally quite impressive, too—not as dark and deep as in 1994, but showing fine balance and lots of flavor and finesse. Zinfandel, too, surprised, with ripe, appealing flavors and slightly lower alcohol. Merlot suffered a bit from too much heat and many were marked by green flavors and tealike tannins.

1994	★★★★★
Cabernet Sauvignon	★★★★★
Chardonnay	★★★★★
Merlot	★★★★
Pinot Noir	★★★★★
Zinfandel	★★★★★

As of 1999, this ranks as the best overall vintage of the decade. A small grape crop benefited from a long, moderate growing season throughout the state. Though the North Coast harvest was interrupted by several heavy rainstorms, the wet weather did not adversely affect the grapes; throughout most of the state, harvest weather conditions were excellent. This was an outstanding year for Cabernet, Chardonnay, Pinot Noir and Zinfandel, and a very good one for Merlot. The Cabernets and Pinot Noirs were very ripe and opulent, with rich flavors and polished tannins; in fact, 1994 was the best Pinot Noir vintage ever. The Zinfandels, while high in alcohol, were brimming with zesty flavors and were deeply concentrated. Chardonnay once again came through with scores of rich, concentrated wines.

1993	★★★
Cabernet Sauvignon	★★★★
Chardonnay	★★★★
Merlot	★★
Pinot Noir	★★★
Zinfandel	★★★

Across the board, this vintage produced light-colored, medium-bodied and in some instances thin wines in several of the major varieties, but it was surprisingly excellent for Cabernet and Chardonnay. Vintners reported generally good climatic conditions throughout the year, but noted uneven ripening patterns with red wines, which led to variable quality. Though several major Cabernet wineries failed to release 1993s, the vintage yielded many sturdy, concentrated wines with ample tannins for mid-range cellaring. Zinfandel proved a sleeper, with many well balanced and appealing wines that were lower in alcohol than the 1990 through 1992 vintages. Pinot Noir in Santa Barbara and Santa Maria was very good as well, but typically light, though well balanced in both Carneros and Russian River Valley. It was a decent year for Merlot as well, though many of the wines were marked by hollowness.

1992	★★★★
Cabernet Sauvignon	★★★★★
Chardonnay	★★★★★
Merlot	★★★★
Pinot Noir	★★★★
Zinfandel	★★★★

This vintage was excellent to outstanding for the major varieties, in part because the growing season came off without the interference of rain. Cabernets from Napa Valley and the North Coast were ripe, complex and well balanced, not quite as deep and complex as either the 1990s or 1991s, but supple and appealing, drinking well early on. Chardonnay was first-rate in all the major districts, with rich, full-bodied and very complex wines. Merlot was very good to excellent, and Pinot Noir was most impressive in Russian River and Santa Barbara. Zinfandel yielded very ripe and full-bodied wines.

1991	★★★★★
Cabernet Sauvignon	★★★★★
Chardonnay	★★★★★
Merlot	★★★★
Pinot Noir	★★★★
Zinfandel	★★★★★

This is a first-class vintage across the board for all the major varieties except Merlot, which was nevertheless well above average and not far off the pace. There was a very long growing season throughout most of the state, and also a large crop, which led to some wines having green tannins and slightly unripe flavors. But quality was still very high. Cabernets from Napa Valley in particular were intense, tannic and well balanced, a shade less opulent than the 1990 vintage, but with the potential for long lives. Chardonnays were ripe, rich, intense and flavorful, with scores of top-flight wines. Pinot Noirs from Russian River, Carneros, Santa Barbara and Santa Maria were intense and complex, well above average and well structured for cellaring. Zinfandel hung on the vines a long time, producing an excellent crop of wines.

1990	★★★★★
Cabernet Sauvignon	★★★★★
Chardonnay	★★★★★
Merlot	★★★★
Pinot Noir	★★★★★
Zinfandel	★★★★★

An outstanding vintage all around, 1990 has been among the best of the 1990s decade. This drought year produced a smaller-than-normal crop, and each of the major varieties was impressive in each of the key growing areas. Cabernet experienced the best vintage since its star run of 1985, 1986 and 1987, with the 1990 vintage most closely resembling 1985 for its ripe, opulent flavors and supple, fleshy textures. These wines were appealing to drink early on, and have the intensity, depth and concentration to age well for 10 to 15 years—and in some instances much longer. Chardonnays, too, were ripe, full-bodied, complex and concentrated—delicious to drink. Merlot also came through in fine fashion, showing a style similar to the Cabernets, with ripe, fleshy flavors and good concentration. A small crop and warm weather combined to render this Pinot Noir vintage the best since 1986, as the best producers made ripe, full-bodied and enormously complex wines that are still developing quite well. Low yields played to Zinfandel's favor as well, allowing the grapes to ripen to their fullest, making this the best vintage since 1985 for most wines and the best since 1987 for many others.

1989	★★
Cabernet Sauvignon	★★★
Chardonnay	★★★
Merlot	★★★
Pinot Noir	★★
Zinfandel	★★

This year was dubbed "the vintage from hell" by many vintners, as rain wreaked havoc at harvest time, especially in the North Coast growing areas, with all major varietals showing the effects. The 1989 crop was also larger than normal, which meant that the grapevines had to struggle to ripen all their grapes. When rain fell it led to botrytis in the white wines and earthy, diluted flavors in many of the reds. Hillside vineyards planted to red varieties fared the best. Cabernet, Pinot Noir and Zinfandel tended to be lean and austere, with modest flavors and a hollowness at mid-palate, showing more crisp, earthy tannins than needed. Chardonnays too were highly variable, with a few impressive wines picked before the rains, but many more with earthy, diluted flavors and a lack of concentration. Merlot fared better, with many very good and well-balanced wines. It was a better year all around south of San Francisco, as the South Central Coast Pinot Noirs in particular were ripe and full-bodied.

1988	★★
Cabernet Sauvignon	★★
Chardonnay	★★★★
Merlot	★★
Pinot Noir	★★
Zinfandel	★★

In this drought year with a smaller than average crop, Chardonnay fared better than the reds, which were crisp and lean with modest depth. A heat wave in May led to significant berry shatter and uneven ripening. While the growing season was otherwise good, some rain in October affected late-ripening vineyards. Most of the wines were medium-bodied, with modest fruit intensity, lacking richness and concentration. Chardonnay, howev-er, produced a good crop of ripe and delicately flavored. Merlot, Pinot Noir and Zinfandel all had spots of success but overall quality was below normal.

1987	★★★★
Cabernet Sauvignon	★★★★★
Chardonnay	★★★★
Merlot	★★★★
Pinot Noir	★★
Zinfandel	★★★★

A drought year with a much smaller than average crop, 1987 had a growing season that ranged from warm to hot, which worked well for Cabernet, Chardonnay, Merlot and Zinfandel, but less well for Pinot Noir. Chardonnays tended to be tight and concentrated, and turned out very well, while Pinot Noirs were light- to medium-bodied, with modest color and depth. Cabernet was clearly the star, especially in Napa Valley, followed closely by Merlot in Napa and Sonoma counties, helped perhaps by the fact the crop was off by 30 to 40 percent. Both Cabernet and Merlot matured early and showed ripe, plush and complex flavors with excellent depth and fine balance. Zinfandel had its crop severely reduced, but that can often be a good thing for heavy-bearing vines, as it ensures all the berries will ripen—a key to the grape's success.

1986	★★★★
Cabernet Sauvignon	★★★★★
Chardonnay	★★★★★
Merlot	★★★
Pinot Noir	★★★★
Zinfandel	★★★★

This was an excellent vintage across the board despite an unusually large crop. Cabernet followed its superb 1985 vintage with many ripe, intense and firmly tannic wines that were well structured. There were also a large number of rich, intense and well focused Chardonnays made in the major growing areas. Merlot fared less well, with the large crop experiencing variable quality, while Zinfandel enjoyed another above-average year, although many wines were enormously tannic. Carneros- and Russian River-grown Pinot Noirs were superb and ageworthy—the best of the decade.

1985	★★★★★
Cabernet Sauvignon	★★★★★
Chardonnay	★★★★★
Merlot	★★★★
Pinot Noir	★★★★
Zinfandel	★★★★★

Largely due to the success of the Cabernet Sauvignon crop, which yielded a broad range of supple, complex and impeccably well balanced wines, 1985 is generally considered the best of the many fine vintages of the decade. A long, mild growing season and slightly below average crop size contributed to the wines' fine balance. At harvest the temperatures remained mild without heat waves, which allowed the grapes to reach ideal maturity. The red wines, for example, were uniform in their excellent colors, rich fruit flavors and very fine, gentle tannins. Chardonnay too was very complex and concentrated, perhaps the best vintage since 1975. Merlot, Pinot Noir and Zinfandel were also well above average, with many finely balanced, seductive and appealing wines. Few wineries missed capturing the excellence of the year and all of the wines are now mature. The Cabernets have generally aged very well, perhaps not as well as some of the early forecasts, but one of the appealing factors of the vintage was the wines' early-drinking allure. Many collectors waited too long on these wines; most peaked some time ago, and the number of truly outstanding wines has begun to dwindle.

1984	★★★★
Cabernet Sauvignon	★★★★★
Chardonnay	★★★★
Merlot	★★★
Pinot Noir	★★★★
Zinfandel	★★★★

A very warm to hot and relatively compact growing season in 1984 yielded an unusually high number of ripe, plump and showy red wines. Cabernet led the way with its best vintage since 1978, and were it not for the excellent 1985 and 1986 vintages, it would receive even higher acclaim. While these were enormously complex and effusively fruity wines, their tannins were soft and fleshy. Most of the 1984 Cabernets reached an early plateau and many are now declining. Chardonnays were ripe and intense too, with early-drinking allure. Pinot Noirs and

Zinfandels were also excellent, especially in the North Coast, with Merlot just off the pace.

1983	★★
Cabernet Sauvignon	★★
Chardonnay	★★
Merlot	★★★★
Pinot Noir	★★
Zinfandel	★★★

A troubled vintage, 1983 saw a huge crop, uneven weather patterns, heat waves that dehydrated grapes and rain at harvest. It all added up to an assortment of clumsy, unbalanced and often unappealing wines. The saving grace was Merlot, which beat the odds; it tops Cabernet in only about one year out of five. Cabernets were intense, but marked by earthy, diluted flavors and harsh tannins that left them dry and uninteresting by age ten. Chardonnays lacked finesse and harmony; many were crisp and austere, made from grapes that were not ripe. Others showed evidence of botrytis. Zinfandel fared slightly better than Cabernet—vintners whose grapes ripened early made balanced wines, while many others were crisp and tannic. Pinot Noir fared well given the odd weather.

1982	★★
Cabernet Sauvignon	★★
Chardonnay	★★
Merlot	★★★
Pinot Noir	★★
Zinfandel	★★★

This was a difficult year, with a large crop, uneven weather patterns and rain at harvest all contributing to a curious mix of wines. Early on, the Cabernets tasted fine, but with each passing year they showed more earthy, diluted flavors. Chardonnay, too, rendered a few appealing wines, but many showed earthy botrytis flavors, especially in cool areas of Sonoma. The small amount of Merlot that was made fared well. Pinot Noir was good but variable, and Zinfandel was slightly above average, but in this transitional year its popularity as a red table wine dropped in the face of rising white Zinfandel production.

1981	★★★
Cabernet Sauvignon	★★★
Chardonnay	★★★★
Merlot	★★★
Pinot Noir	★★★
Zinfandel	★★

A drought year with a short, warm-to-hot growing season and no rain at harvest, 1981 yielded a crop of supple, well-balanced wines that were showy early on. Cabernets were ripe and balanced, medium-bodied and very pleasing to drink in their youth; they aged fairly well. Chardonnay was very fruity and well balanced, with many excellent offerings. The Merlots were supple and forward, with soft tannins. Pinot Noir, especially from Carneros, was excellent. Zinfandel was average.

1980	★★
Cabernet Sauvignon	★★
Chardonnay	★★★
Merlot	★★
Pinot Noir	★★★
Zinfandel	★★

This was a warm to hot year with many heat waves and a very large crop, yielding wines of average quality, with many reds marked by very ripe and earthy flavors but modest concentration. Cabernet proved especially variable, with the best being bold, ripe and fruity, with supple tannins. Chardonnay was above average, with many good wines. Merlot was good, with several appealing wines, but from a small sampling. Pinot Noir was above average, from a small sampling. Heat played havoc with Zinfandel's ripening patterns.

1979	★★★★

This vintage was very good to excellent for Cabernet, Chardonnay, Merlot and Pinot Noir, but less so for Zinfandel. It was also markedly different from 1978, which offered very ripe and rich wines; the 1979s were more austere and elegant, but well structured. The top Cabernets aged well, and a few are still holding.

1978	★★★★★

This was a watershed year for Cabernet, with many ripe, rich and full-bodied wines produced in the wake of the breakthrough 1974 vintage and the famous Paris Tasting of 1976. The vintage was first class for Chardonnay, Merlot and Zinfandel, but a shade too hot for Pinot Noir, which was grown in far warmer areas than today. The 1978 Cabernets have aged very well, although by now most have peaked or declined. A dozen or so from Napa Valley should make it to thirty years.

1977	★★★

The second year of a two-year drought, 1977 produced a very small crop of pleasantly balanced wines. Especially successful for Cabernet and Chardonnay, both of which were early-maturing. A few stars remain.

1976	★★

This was the first of two drought years and it yielded a very small crop of intensely flavored wines, with many reds that dried out because the berries were shriveled at harvest.

1975	★★★★

Coming after the monumental 1974 vintage, 1975 lived in its shadow. But this was a very good year for Cabernet and Chardonnay, both of which were elegant and well balanced.

1974	★★★★★

A big crop of bold, ripe and complex wines were made in 1974, especially by many of the new Napa Cabernet producers. The Paris Tasting of 1976 focused global attention on California Cabernet and Chardonnay, which outperformed expensive French wines from Bordeaux and Burgundy; when these wines came to market in 1977 and 1978 they were a huge hit. The Cabernets in particular were intense and full-blown. They aged well, but most are now past their prime.

1973	★★★

This was a very good year all around, with a clean, well-balanced grape crop and generally elegant, subtle, well-proportioned and harmonious Cabernets and Chardonnays. This vintage was generally underrated; it immediately preceded the 1974 vintage, which won most of the headlines.

1972	★

One of the few vintages to be hurt by harvest rains, the 1972 vintage was notable mainly for the number of new producers who went on to make an impact. Among the newcomers that year were Caymus, Chateau Montelena, Diamond Creek, Dry Creek Vineyards, Silver Oak, Clos Du Val, Stag's Leap Wine Cellars and Burgess. The wines are now well past their primes.

1971	★

Another wet harvest, remarkably back to back with 1972, 1971 left a crop of largely uninspiring wines with earthy, diluted flavors.

1970	★★★★★

Severe spring frosts reduced the crop size by nearly half in 1970, but the wines, Cabernet in particular, were spectacular and among the longest-lived in the past 30 years. The top wines, such Beaulieu Private Reserve, Ridge Monte Bello, Mayacamas and Heitz Martha's Vineyard, remain in superb condition. This is the last in a string of great vintages starting with 1968.

1969	★★★★

Considered the least of the 1968 through 1970 vintages, 1969 nonetheless provided its share of great wines, led again by Heitz Martha's Vineyard, Mayacamas, Beaulieu Private Reserve, Ridge Monte Bello and Robert Mondavi Unfined Cabernets. Supple, harmonious and elegant, they aged exceptionally well and still provide fine drinking moments. Hanzell Pinot Noir remains excellent as well.

1968	★★★★★

This was a great vintage of ripe, complex and age-worthy wines, the best of which—the Beaulieu Private Reserve, Heitz Martha's Vineyard, Mayacamas, Ridge Monte Bello and Robert Mondavi Cabernets are still in amazingly good condition. Hanzell's Pinot Noir was brilliant.

1967	★★

Considered good, with early-maturing wines, but 1967 is nowhere near the class of 1966 or 1968.

1966	★★★★

This vintage was first-class for ripe, supple and complex Cabernets, with Heitz Martha's Vineyard, Mondavi and Beaulieu Private Reserve the best bets.

1965	★★★

A good vintage of early-drinking wines, but 1965 is nothing memorable now.

1964	★★★★

This year's crop was extremely short, having been reduced by spring frosts, but so good that all 24,000 cases of Beaulieu Cabernet were bottled under the Private Reserve label—the only time in history that this occurred.

1963	★

Another vintage hard hit by spring frosts, 1963's quality is considered only fair.

1962	★

Spring frosts took their toll again in 1962, a vintage of poor to ordinary quality.

1961	★★

Springs frosts were a factor in reducing the 1961 crop size by 50 to 75 percent, but the wines were ordinary to good.

1960	★★★

The wines from this vintage were widely admired by winemakers of the era, with Charles Krug and Inglenook the leaders.

1959	★★★

In a year well-regarded by winemakers, the Inglenook and Beaulieu Vineyard Private Reserve bottlings were particularly excellent.

1958	★★★★★

This has long been considered a great vintage, with impressive Cabernets from Beaulieu Vineyard, Charles Krug, Inglenook and Louis M. Martini, all of which aged exceptionally well.

1957	★★

Considered a fair to good vintage, but the Louis M. Martini Cabernet was extraordinary for years.

1956	★★★

Considered good by vintners of the era.

1955	★★★

This year got high marks from vintners of the era, and many of its wines aged well.

1954	★★★

A year viewed as very good by vintners of the era.

1953	★

Remembered for the "Freeze of '53," spring frosts that wiped out most of the year's crop, but the first windmill—windmills prevent freezing by keeping the air moving—was installed near Calistoga, saving one vineyard.

1952	★★★

Hard hit by spring frosts and record-breaking cold weather, but the Louis M. Martini and Charles Krug Cabernets were superb.

1951	★★★★★

Along with 1958, 1951 is considered the best vintage of the decade, with mild weather and a good crop of fully ripened grapes. Beaulieu Vineyard Private Reserve, Charles Krug and Louis M. Martini Cabernets were all excellent into the 1990s.

1950	★★★★

Considered an excellent year by vintners of the era.

1949	★★★

Heavy frosts cut 1949's crop size, but the Cabernets were well structured and aged well.

1948	★

Plagued by adversity, 1948 included a drought into March followed by 14 days of rain in Napa Valley, which delayed development of the vines. Grapes were harvested under cool conditions and the wines were considered only fair.

1947	★★★

Frosts were again a factor in reducing 1947's grape crop, but warm weather led to a ripe and well-balanced group of Cabernets.

1946	★★★★

Viewed as a great vintage at harvest time and for several years thereafter, although its quality was later debated.

1945	★★★★

Heavy rains led to a potentially large crop, but spring frosts cut its size.

1944	★★

Heavy frosts cut 1944's crop size. Vintners of the era rated the vintage as good.

1943	★★

Winemakers of the era considered 1943 only good.

1942	★★★

Few wines were produced, but vintners rated the 1942 vintage very good.

1941	★★★★

Memorable for the magnificent Inglenook Cabernet, a profoundly complex and amazingly long-lived wine that I've rated a perfect 100 on several occasions.

1940	★★★★

Winemakers of the era thought 1940 an excellent year. Few notes.

1939	★★★

Rated as good by winemakers.

1938	★★

I have no notes on the 1938 vintage; a few winemakers liked it.

1937	★★★

Considered very good by winemakers of the time.

1936	★★★★

Memorably, this vintage produced the first Beaulieu Vineyard Private Reserve bottling, which aged exceptionally well for 40-plus years.

1935	★★

Simi's 1935 Cabernet was memorable for its vitality into the 1980s.

1934	★★★

Collectors and winemakers recall this as an excellent year.

1933	★★★

The year of Repeal boasted an Inglenook Cabernet that remained amazingly dark, rich and complex in 1989.

CHAPTER 6

BUILDING YOUR WINE COLLECTION

What is a wine collection? It can be as simple as a case or two stashed in an unused corner for daily consumption. Or it can constitute a serious hobby—an enjoyable obsession, for some. This chapter is written to help you make the most of your wine-buying dollars, whatever level of wine interest you might have.

As you get started, it's best to let your curiosity and tastes lead you to discoveries. You've probably already tasted a great many wines; you've read the reviews others have given them, you've followed the producers, styles and vintages. You're already following the market and know which wines you like and drink the most often. The next step is stocking your cellar.

Once you catch the wine bug and start buying wine, you'll want to consider building or buying a cellar. In this book, "wine cellar" means nothing more than a place to store your wine. The most important considerations are that it be cool (ideally no warmer than 65°F), dark and vibration-free. "Wine cellars" come in all shapes and sizes, from a few bottles in a rack above the refrigerator (the kitchen, however, is not a great place to store wine) to elaborate, barn-sized underground cellars that can cost more than most new homes.

I've seen spectacular cellars that look like shrines to Bacchus and I've seen stacks of cardboard wine boxes wedged in a hallway closet. One of California's greatest winemakers, André Tchelistcheff, used to keep his modest wine collection under his bed. Ingenuity has a way of creating a cellar that works. The best cellars I've seen are the ones that are well thought out, organized, easy to use and used on a regular basis. They're not mausoleums, filled with dead or dying trophy wines, owned by someone who has no idea what he has or when he will ever drink it. If money is no object in building your collection, that's fine. But if you stockpile your cellar with the most expensive and sought-after California wines and let them age too long, you've wasted your money. Opening up rare, old and dead wines won't impress your closest friends any more than will burning money in your fireplace to keep warm, or serving three-day-old leftovers for that special occasion dinner. Buying fine wines and not drinking them before they fade is a waste of money and wine. Above all, the wines you collect or cellar should reflect your personal tastes and the kinds of wines you like to drink or serve to friends.

THE BASICS

Because wine has become so popular, many new and clever ideas have cropped up about how to build a cellar. Several companies sell temperature-controlled wine cellars that plug into electrical outlets and can store hundreds of bottles. These cellars are excellent for storing wines. You can buy books on build-it-yourself cellars that include details on insulation, air conditioning and building bins to store single bottles or cases of wine. You can also rent wine cellar space. Wine stores often have lockers where you can keep your wine. (The only drawbacks are that your access is limited to store hours and you may have to travel a significant distance.)

Since wine is a living thing, it is constantly changing. Wine reacts most adversely to heat and direct light, which is why traditional cellars are cool and dark. A cellar does need to be dark. It needs to be moderately cool, ideally between 55° and 65°, and must maintain an even temperature that doesn't rise or fall dramatically within a few hours or days. If your cellar is 55° from November to March, and gradually warms to 65° in June or July, your wine won't be adversely affected. Many European winemakers I've interviewed say it is healthy for a wine cellar to undergo modest temperature changes with the seasons, as they believe it helps ageworthy wines develop.

If your cellar area stays above 65°, your wines will mature more quickly. Whites and lighter reds, such as Pinot Noir, are particularly susceptible to heat. Heartier reds will also mature faster—which isn't always such a bad thing, depending on your age. If the temperature stays above 70° to 75° for weeks and months, your wine may well get cooked. Excessive heat all but eliminates a wine's fruity flavors and can leave it tasting flat and dull. Humidity isn't a factor in home wine cellars. Humidity is desirable inside a winery's barrel-aging room because it minimizes the amount of wine that can evaporate from a barrel. But once wine is in a bottle, sealed with a cork and, usually, a tin foil capsule around the neck, the humidity level shouldn't affect it.

Above all, if you're going to age wines, you need an appropriate cellar. If you don't take care of your wines, you're liable to be disappointed by how they taste.

WHAT TO BUY

Once you've settled on storage conditions, the focus turns to what, and how much, to collect. Again, your personal tastes in wine should guide you. I've dwelled on personal taste throughout this book, because it's the essence of enjoying fine wine. No one knows your taste preferences better than you and the sooner you become comfortable knowing which wines you like, when you like to drink them and how much money you're willing to spend, the sooner you will feel comfortable with your cellar.

I like to drink most of my wines when they are very young, rich, fruity, complex and concentrated, and I think this is true of many wine critics. I taste more than 5,000 new releases each year, the vast majority being young wines (and some barrel samples). My palate is attuned to young wines. I drink most whites—Chardonnays, Sauvignon Blancs, Rieslings and Gewürztraminers—within a year of their release. I drink most Pinot Noirs and Zinfandels within a year or two of release, Merlots and Syrahs within two to four years of release, Cabernets at five to seven year after release. I also taste hundreds and hundreds of older wines, both for pleasure and research. And while mature, complex wines are often fascinating to experience and analyze, many other times older wines are merely older wines—and not all that much fun to drink.

As a general rule, I'd rather drink a wine a year or two too early than one week too late. I age a few wines, ones I think will develop with additional bottle time or that have a track record for improving with age. But I'm often disappointed with older wines—sometimes because I really liked the wine when it was young, and it has merely changed with aging, other times because the wine has not improved with age, or worse, it has deteriorated. I've spent a lot of money on certain wines that I've aged too long. Since coming to this realization, I've bought wines more carefully. I often buy three or four bottles of a wine I like instead of a case. I drink the wines whenever I (or my friends) feel like it and I'm not worried when my supplies dwindle. I hate to see the last bottle of my favorite Pinot Noir sitting there empty. But it's a much worse feeling to open an expensive wine I've aged for 10 years and find that it's no longer delicious, but merely an old wine whose time has come and gone—and I'm there to administer its last rites.

Coming to grips with when you like to drink your wines will be an important factor in determining the size and scope of your collection. If you like to age and drink more mature wines and are good at picking the right ones and keeping them properly stored, then you'll need to make accommodations to store those wines. If you drink them earlier, your turnover will be faster and you'll need less cellar space.

If you're new to wine, I would encourage you to age a few wines to see how they develop. Or spend a few dollars ordering old wine off a restaurant wine list. Once you get into wine you'll find plenty of people with wine collections and most will be happy to share some of their older wines so you can see what happens to wines with age. This process will help you decide whether you do or don't like older wines, or to what degree you want to commit your finances and cellar space. One easy taste test is to buy a case each of a very good or outstanding Chardonnay, Pinot Noir, Merlot, Zinfandel and Cabernet. Drink a few bottles within the first few months and then try a bottle every four to six months, saving a few bottles for further aging. Make sure you make notes—written or mental—about how well you liked the wine. It's also a good idea to mix and match the different wines. That way you'll learn about how tannins are different in Pinot Noir and Zinfandel. And you'll learn about different wines and their textures. If, after your research, you find that you still like the wines at four or five years, that's fine. If they seem young and intense, then cellar them longer. Try and keep one or two bottles for six to eight or ten years, and see how you like them then. Reds will age longer most of the time, so if you find the Cabernet is still tough and chewy at age five or six, it will probably make it to year ten or twelve in good shape. But if you open the Chardonnay in a year and find it's less appealing than it was the day you bought it, then you've learned a valuable lesson. Drink up the rest. Wines go through developmental phases, so it's not uncommon for a wine to hit what's called a "dumb" phase where it tastes closed or awkward. Once a wine loses its fruit, though, it's not going to regain it at some later date.

Bear in mind that bottles can vary in quality, so don't be surprised if you open two bottles from the same case and find one's more pleasing than the next. It happens. I'd also recommend you buy a few very expensive wines and put them in a blind tasting against some lower-priced wines. Cover all the bottles with paper and taste the wines. Then try them with dinner. See which you like the best. See which bottles empty the fastest. Then take the paper off. If you liked the least expensive wines, you've learned another good lesson: High prices don't always guarantee quality. They're more often a result of supply and demand factors. If you like less expensive

wines, you'll save lots of money over the years. There are indeed rewards to being a value shopper.

WHOSE ADVICE SHOULD YOU TRUST?

How you obtain wine buying advice is another important link to a successful cellar. I hope you'll read *Wine Spectator's* coverage of California wine, which is comprehensive, timely and more thorough than that of any other publication I know. In addition to the magazine, our Web site **Wine Spectator Online** at **www.winespectator.com** has lots of information about new wineries and wines, along with a database of reviews. You can also tap other resources: critics, wine merchants, books and friends. And don't forget the most important critic of all—you.

You'll get your most objective advice from independent critics and friends as they can easily tell you what they like with no strings attached. You'll get highly biased advice from the wineries and winemakers, as they're keenly interested in selling their wine. This is why you often hear a winery or winemaker claim that their current release—the wine they're selling right now—is the best wine they've ever made. The truth is no one hits a home run every time. Winemakers may be trying to be honest and objective when they say this wine is their best wine ever, but most of the time, they're too close to their work to be very objective. Besides, they have a lot riding on a wine's sales success. Your wine merchants should also be good sources of information. Knowledgeable wine merchants can help steer you to the wine styles you like and can afford. But sometimes merchants overbuy a wine, find it's not as good as they thought (or as the winemaker or critics said) and then start looking for ways to unload it. After all, making and selling wine is a business. My advice is to get to know your merchants and put them to work for you. Tell them the kinds of wines you like and the kinds of prices you're willing to pay for wine. Then see how well they fulfill your requests.

What about wine critics? There are many out there. Most take wine seriously. Some take wine (and themselves) too seriously. Some aren't serious enough. A good critic should be someone you trust, whose tastes usually coincide with yours. Good critics should be able to describe which wines please them the most and why, as well as which ones disappoint the most, and why—and say so in terms you can comprehend. They should have several years' experience (the more the better) with the wines they're recommending. They should taste all or most of the major wines released each year, and most importantly, they should be consistent; that is, if they like a wine or wine style one time, they should still like it the next time they critique it. On the other hand, I wouldn't expect a critic to be "right" all the time and I certainly wouldn't want a critic to ignore a wine's flaws simply because that winery or wine has earned praise in the past.

How often are critics "correct" in their advice? How often is anyone right about anything? How often do you agree with your friends about movies, books, music or the new restaurant in town? In my view, if a critic is correct 75 percent of the time, that's a pretty good average. (If your stockbroker beat the stock market by that average, you'd be ecstatic.) In this case being correct means that the critic's view of the wine is borne out by your own impressions. If you rarely agree with a critic, or don't like his style of writing, descriptions, or rating system, then seek different advice. I'd be especially cautious (no, downright suspicious) of critics who think they're always right and everyone else is always wrong, or who assume everyone's tastes should be identical to theirs. Even when I taste with my colleagues at *Wine Spectator*—when six or seven of us taste a number of wines and critique them—there are often real differences about which ones are the best and which have flaws. Critics who can admit their mistakes—when they have misjudged a wine or vintage or style—and point out where they went wrong, are credible and in tune with reality. They can generally be counted on to give you a straight answer.

Be suspicious of critics who:

• Are reluctant to take stands or defend their descriptions of wines they like or dislike.

• Claim (or think) they're always right and that other critics are always wrong.

• Think they're experts on all wines from all over the world all the time.

• Never visit the appellations or countries they profess to know so well.

• Overgeneralize (or wing it) when finding fault with a style they don't like (or perhaps don't understand).

• Are unwilling to admit they might have been wrong and unwilling to change their minds.

• Only taste the high-profile wines. Real depth of tasting experience—that is, knowledge of modest and inexpensive wines as well as famous and high-end ones—is essential in forming a broad market view.

• Boast they taste hundreds of wines a day. We each have different capacities to taste and comprehend what we're tasting. I can remember when tasting 12 wines seemed like a lot. I've also been in situations where I've tasted more than 100 wines in a day (and usually regretted it). It is possible to taste that many wines. But at some point you lose your ability to concentrate and the margin for error increases. Even when spitting, you absorb some alcohol and it affects your ability to concentrate. Simple fatigue takes its toll.

• Routinely only taste a wine once and pronounce judgment. I try to taste a wine two to three times, especially wines I give high ratings to or wines that have excellent reputations for high standards.

• Never go out on a limb for wines they feel strongly about.

• Don't taste blind—that is, without knowing a wine's identity. Blind tasting isn't the only way to judge wines, but it is the most objective.

• Rate wines out of barrel and don't tell you. I've seen this trend increase of late as critics scramble to be the first in print with a review. Critics who rate barrel samples and then write reviews implying it was a bottled wine are deceiving their readers. I've visited wineries shortly after reading glowing reviews of a wine, only to discover the wine reviewed was a barrel sample and is still several weeks (or months) away from bottling.

• Decry wines of elegance, grace, finesse, delicacy or wines that are "too fruity." Or, conversely, those who describe wines that are pickley, gamy, dirty, leathery, horsey or have fecal aromas as complex. (Sorry, but you've got to draw the line somewhere.)

• Have a conflict of interest, either as a part-owner of, investor in or as a consultant to wineries they write about. A critic who has a financial interest in a winery may refrain from writing directly about his wine, but still promote his own interests through criticism of the competition.

• Identify with the wine trade rather than with you, the consumer.

• Appear to like all wines and dislike none.

Put more faith in critics who:

• Have experience: at least five and preferably ten years covering the topic they're writing about. As the California wine industry has grown to thousands of brands—with thousands of new wines released each year—it's increasingly more complex to cover than it was in the 1970s and 1980s, when there were one-fifth or one-quarter as many wineries as well as a fraction of the number of wines.

• Have an open mind about wines and are willing to rethink their views.

• Taste often and cover the whole spectrum of wines.

• Reexamine older vintages in the same serious manner as they review new releases.

• Admit they haven't tried every wine and don't know everything there is to know about wine.

• Speak a language you can understand and offer advice you find useful.

Making Your Buying Decisions

Even after you've determined your wine tastes and needs, assembling a wine collection still presents challenges. Wine can be expensive, and many of the best wines are difficult to obtain as well. Cabernet and Chardonnay are popular because they not only have strong personalities, but are usually made in large quantities, which makes them available to a broad audience.

In this book I've reviewed and rated over 5,000 individual wines. I've also rated each winery's overall performance on a one- to five-star scale, and many of their wines on the same one- to five-star scale. The four- and five-star wines are the ones I think are the best. In building a wine collection, that's where I'd start. (For more about the 100-point and star ratings see the Introduction, "How To Use This Book").

With Cabernet and Chardonnay, you'll have the broadest choice of outstanding wines. California winemakers have more experience and success with these two varieties and in a great year it's not unusual to find dozens of outstanding wines to choose from. It's much harder on a year-to-year basis to find outstanding Pinot Noir, Zinfandel and Merlot, and even harder to find great Sangiovese or Syrah. A great year for Pinot Noir might yield 15 or 20 stellar wines, most of which have fewer than 500 cases for the world. That's changing slowly, as more fine wines of these types are made. But you'll often have to work harder at finding these wines. As a bottom line, I'd recommend focusing on the wines California excels at, which are the primary focus of this book: Cabernet and Cabernet blends, Chardonnay, Merlot, Pinot Noir, Sangiovese, Sauvignon Blanc, Syrah and Zinfandel. Within these types, I'd diversify; concentrate on what you like to drink most often. Be sure not to ignore other kinds of wine, however, as you may find your tastes change with time.

Investing in Wine

I'm amazed by how many people associate (or confuse) collecting wine with investing in it. Even neophytes who've just bought their first few cases of Cabernet from a great vintage start talking about their "investment" in wine and how much more the wine will be worth in 10 years. I suppose part of this is rationalization. It sounds much better to tell your spouse that the $5,000 or $10,000 you just spent on wine for your cellar (that you'll drink in five to ten years) represents a great investment. But you shouldn't confuse collecting with investing. You collect wines to drink, enjoy and study. You invest in wines to earn a profit.

Great wines from great producers in great vintages do appreciate in value, but the market is highly unpredictable. Often a wine's value is greatly distorted by the sale of one bottle of wine at a charity auction for an astronomical price. In general, I don't recommend using wine as an investment tool. If you're looking to earn a return on your capital, to make money, there are better ways to do it. Put your $5,000 or $10,000 in growth-oriented mutual funds and watch it grow. I certainly wouldn't forgo your IRA contribution or stop funding your 401(k) plan and put that money into wine instead.

If, however, you have diversified investments already and decide you'd like to invest in wine as well, here are some guidelines.

• Make sure you have a cool, dark cellar and a written inventory of its contents. (Keeping records of which wines you own is a good idea anyway, even for a collector's cellar).

• Make sure you have a specific insurance policy in case of fire, theft or earthquake.

• Focus on wines that have the greatest chance for price appreciation and wines that will be in demand in five to ten years—or even later. This is where it gets tricky, because a wine that sells for $50 or $100 a bottle today may be in great demand. But it may not appreciate in value as fast as a $25 or $35 bottle of wine.

• Buy low and sell high as often as possible. Reread the general rules for investing and recognize that when a wine you paid $25 for starts selling for $50 or $75, it's a good time to sell. Why? You've doubled or tripled your money. If there are buyers willing to pay, be prepared to sell. That same wine may appear in a tasting and get panned. What's it worth then? Maybe far less.

• Pay close attention to the market. I don't know many wine investors. I know many people who claim they invest in wine, but I've never seen their financial books, so I can't say whether they're making a profit or wise investment. My guess is that if they are right 60 to 70 percent of the time—picking the right wine and selling it at a good profit—then they're happy. But I expect many collectors make bad investments in wine, occasionally (or often) sustaining losses, and that others end up drinking their investments, realizing that that was the real reason they bought the wine in the first place.

• Remember that wine really isn't a liquid investment if you need cash in a hurry. It can take months to sell 50 or 100 cases of wine. And what if you have to move? Transporting a thousand bottles of wine is expensive and risky, especially during the summer months.

• Remember that despite a cozy black market in which wines are sold and traded without paperwork, any profits you earn are taxable.

• Focus on the best vintages. In years such as 1984, 1985, 1986 and 1987, there were many excellent Cabernets produced, but the one year that sticks out in collectors' minds is 1985. The other vintages may be just as good for certain wines, but 1985 has the cachet.

• Consider oversized bottles, such as magnums or double magnums. They're rarer and are sometimes prized by other collectors.

• Keep an eye out for the new stars. Often, new producers' wines sell at lower prices than the competition. Once discovered, they will become more expensive.

• Consider buying futures in great years, as you will pay a discounted price in advance of the wine's release.

• If there is one blue-chip wine to invest in, it is estate-grown or vineyard-designated Cabernet from Napa Valley and its subappellations.

When investing in wine, the two most important considerations are trying to imagine who will be interested in

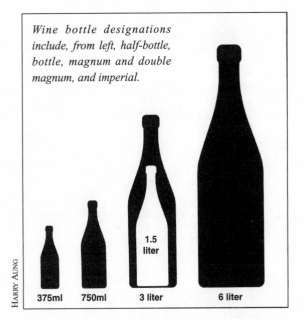

Wine bottle designations include, from left, half-bottle, bottle, magnum and double magnum, and imperial.

HARRY AUNG

375ml   750ml   3 liter   6 liter

buying your wine when you sell it, and then being ready to sell when price appreciates. If no one is willing to buy your wine at a future date for a profit, then you're in trouble. If you're not willing to sell your wine when the price rises and there are buyers, then you're really not an investor.

Wine Futures

Collecting or investing in wine futures involves buying a wine, at a discounted price, prior to its release—usually a year or two in advance. This option has its risks: the wine may not live up to its advance billing; the winery or retailer who took your money may go out of business. Also, since so often you cannot taste a wine before buying futures in it, how can you know for sure whether it's a wine you'll like? I'd have the most confidence in the wines of an established producer who has a track record for excellence.

Unfortunately, because many of the best wines are in limited supply and sell quickly, we have to buy some wines without tasting them—or we don't get a crack at them at all. Also, if you live in an area where it's difficult to obtain certain wines, buying futures can be helpful. Another good reason to consider futures is you can often ask a winery to set aside several magnums or double magnums of the wine you want.

CHAPTER 7

WINERY PROFILES AND TASTING NOTES

In this chapter, the wineries chosen for this book are profiled and tasting notes are provided for their noteworthy wines. Use this section as a guide for your wine-buying strategy, or as a reference guide to check up on the wines in your cellar.

Wineries are listed alphabetically. Note that a winery named for a person will be alphabetized under the person's last name. Example: Robert Mondavi Winery is alphabetized under M.

The typical listing has the following features:

• The winery name is listed, followed by the winery's location (the city and/or appellation), ownership and winemaker information.

• Overall Rating: This rating on the five-star scale denotes the winery's overall quality.

• Wine Ratings: These ratings on the five-star scale indicate the quality of each of the winery's featured wines.

• Winery Data: This section contains data on case production, vineyards' holdings and grape purchases.

• Winery Profile: This is a brief description of the winery with an evaluation of its overall strengths, weaknesses and notable features.

• Tasting Notes: These are presented for selected wines. In many cases, a wine summary will precede the actual tasting notes. This summary gives you a general look at the wine's style and other characteristics common to the wine regardless of vintage. The individual tasting notes focus on each vintage of that wine and what makes it distinct.

For detailed explanations of the 100-point and five-star rating scales, please see the Introduction, "How To Use This Book."

ABREU VINEYARDS (★★★★★)
St. Helena, Napa Valley
Founded: 1987. **Owner:** Dave Abreu. **Winemaker:** Ric Forman.

WINE RATINGS
Cabernet Sauvignon Napa Valley
  Madrona Ranch
  ($80, 400)   ★★★★★

WINERY DATA
Case Production: 400. **Vineyard Designations**: Madrona Ranch. **Varietals Purchased:** Cabernet Sauvignon (Napa Valley).

Dave Abreu operates a highly respected vineyard management firm in Napa Valley, overseeing the farming and vineyard operations of many wineries, including Araujo, Staglin and Spottswoode. In 1987 he began producing wine from Madrona Vineyard in St. Helena near Spottswoode. Long-time friend Ric Forman serves as winemaker, in addition to making his own wines at Forman Winery. Most of Abreu's 400 cases are sold through a mailing list.

TASTING NOTES

CABERNET SAUVIGNON NAPA VALLEY MADRONA RANCH (★★★★★): Consistently rich, complex and enormously concentrated, with spicy currant, earth and mineral flavors supported by thick, chewy tannins. Ages well.
1994: Massive, rich and deeply flavored, packed with complex currant, mineral, spice, sage and cedary oak flavors and chewy but polished tannins. This one will require some patience. **96**
1992: Dense, tight and concentrated, with intense tannins and lots of rich chocolate, black cherry and wild berry fruit. **93**
1991: Shows enormous concentration and complexity; smooth, ripe, rich and polished, with dense currant, black cherry, anise, cedar and mineral flavors. **95**
1989: Mature, supple, dark and complex, with a range of earthy currant, blackberry, mineral, sage, mushroom and spicy notes. **91**
1987: Complex, with rich currant, spice, mineral and anise notes, finishing with plush tannins. **89**

ACACIA WINERY (★★★–★★★★)
Carneros
Founded: 1979. **Owner:** Chalone Wine Group Ltd. **Winemaker:** Michael Richmond.

MAJOR WINES: PRICE, CASES, RATING
Chardonnay Carneros
  ($20, 36,000)   ★★★
Chardonnay Carneros Reserve
  ($30, 2,500)   ★★★★
Pinot Noir Carneros
  ($23, 20,000)   ★★★
Pinot Noir Carneros Beckstoffer
  Vineyard Reserve
  ($45, 500)   ★★★★
Pinot Noir Carneros Reserve
  ($30, 1,200)   ★★★
Pinot Noir Carneros St. Clair
  Vineyard Reserve
  ($45, 300)   ★★★

ALSO PRODUCED
Pinot Noir Carneros DeSoto Vineyard Reserve ($45, 500); Pinot Noir Carneros Lee Vineyard Reserve ($45, 500); Vintage Brut Carneros ($30, 900); Vintage Brut Carneros RD ($45, 150); Viognier Carneros Estate ($25, 200).

WINERY DATA
Case Production: 60,000. **Acres Owned:** 91 acres in Carneros. **Varietals by Acre:** Chardonnay (39 acres), Pinot Noir (51), Viognier (1). **Vineyard Designations:** Beckstoffer (Pinot Noir), DeSoto (Pinot Noir), Lee (Pinot Noir), St. Clair (Pinot Noir). **Varietals Purchased:** Chardonnay (Carneros), Pinot Noir (Carneros).

A pioneer of Carneros-grown, vineyard-designated Chardonnays and Pinot Noirs, Acacia had early success with these two varietals, sparking interest in the Carneros appellation and demonstrating the unique personalities of different vineyard microclimates. At one point in the 1980s, Acacia offered six different Pinot Noirs: one from Carneros grapes and five vineyard-designated bottlings from Iund, Lee, Madonna, St. Clair and Winery Lake vineyards, along with Chardonnays from Marina Vineyard, Winery Lake Vineyard, Napa Valley and Carneros. While Chardonnay was always made in larger quantities, Acacia's single-vineyard Pinot Noirs captured the imagination of Burgundy lovers.

In 1984 the managing partners attempted to branch into Bordeaux-style wines in an ill-fated venture with Joe Cafaro. Acacia-Cafaro produced one vintage of a Cabernet, a Merlot and a Sauvignon Blanc. Acacia was acquired by the Chalone Wine Group in 1986.

In the early 1990s, the winery narrowed its focus and dropped many of the vineyard-designated wines, only to abandon that strategy and refocus on some vineyard-designated Pinot Noirs.

Founder Mike Richmond returned as winemaker in 1998, and Acacia appears to be retooling itself and making better wines.

TASTING NOTES

CHARDONNAY CARNEROS (★★★): Captures the essence of Carneros with its crisp, bright pear, apple, pineapple and citrus flavors. Oak adds another dimension but never dominates. The 1994 (90 points) and 1995 (90) were both impressive.

CHARDONNAY CARNEROS RESERVE (★★★★): The Reserve is a shade richer and more complex.
1995: Shows off ripe pear, earth and buttery flavors that are well focused and long on the finish. **90**
1994: Ripe and juicy, with a peachy edge to the pear, spice and pineapple flavors, turning smooth and creamy. **91**

PINOT NOIR CARNEROS (★★★): Typically elegant, with ripe, spicy cherry and raspberry flavors and firm tannins. Best to drink on release.
1996: Crisp and snappy, with a grapey edge to the cherry and berry notes. **87**
1995: Smooth and polished, with a supple core of cola and black cherry flavors, finishing with a spicy edge. **88**
1994: A supple, harmonious young red sporting ripe cherry, cedar, spice and plum flavors. **89**

PINOT NOIR CARNEROS BECKSTOFFER VINEYARD RESERVE (★★★★): New to the lineup. Made from 40-year-old vines; dense and richly flavored. Worth watching, once again.
1995: Ripe, with juicy, spicy black cherry, wild berry, plum and cedary notes; intense, concentrated, rich and complex. **91**

PINOT NOIR CARNEROS RESERVE (★★★)
1995: Openly fruity, with complex plum, cherry and spice flavors that are supple and polished. **90**

1993: Firm and well focused, with pretty cherry, spice, cedar and green tea flavors. **86**

PINOT NOIR CARNEROS ST. CLAIR VINEYARD RESERVE (★★★): The St. Clair Vineyard usually provides richness, intensity and depth, with distinctive berry and mineral flavors, but most recent vintages have not been as complex as the best from the 1980s.
1994: Mature for its age, with earthy plum and berry flavors and herb and tar notes. **88**
1991: Lean and tannic, with a green tea edge to the tart cherry and berry flavors. **85**
1990: Firm and ripe, with a tight core of plum and cherry flavors. **88**
1986: Deep, ripe, rich and intense, packed with dense chewy, earthy currant and cherry flavors. Finishes with pepper notes. **91**

ADELAIDA CELLARS (★★)
Paso Robles, San Luis Obispo County
Founded: 1981. **Owner:** van Steenwyh Family. **Winemaker:** John Munch.

MAJOR WINES: PRICE, CASES, RATING
Cabernet Sauvignon Paso Robles ($21, 2000)	★★★
Calitage Red Paso Robles ($26, 300)	★★★
Chardonnay San Luis Obispo County ($20, 1500)	★★
Chenin Blanc Paso Robles Pavanne ($15, 700)	★★
Pinot Noir Paso Robles HMR Vineyard ($27, 1000)	★★
Sangiovese Paso Robles ($22, 200)	★★
Syrah Paso Robles ($24, 100)	★★
Zinfandel Paso Robles ($19, 2000)	★★

WINERY DATA
Case Production: 10,000. **Acres Owned:** 75 acres in Paso Robles. **Varietals by Acre:** Cabernet Sauvignon (30 acres), Chardonnay (14), Pinot Noir (26), Syrah (5). **Vineyard Designations:** HMR Vineyard (Pinot Noir). **Varietals Purchased:** Cabernet Sauvignon (San Luis Obispo County), Chardonnay (San Luis Obispo County), Chenin Blanc (Paso Robles), Sangiovese (Paso Robles), Zinfandel (Paso Robles).

Adelaida Cellars, under John Munch's direction, focuses on Paso Robles- and San Luis Obispo-grown grapes. Cabernet Sauvignon (★★★) is its best wine. The Chardonnay tends to be heavily oaked, while the Chenin Blanc, Sangiovese and Zinfandel, made in ripe, full-bodied styles, are sound wines.

TASTING NOTES

CABERNET SAUVIGNON PASO ROBLES (★★★): While early efforts with Cabernet were erratic, the most recent vintages are superior, showing better focus and more finesse. The 1991 (89 points), 1992 (88), 1993 (90), and 1994 (88) all were ripe, smooth and harmonious. Best to drink early on.

ADLER FELS ESTATE (★★)
Sonoma County
Founded: 1979. **Owner:** David Coleman & Ayn Ryan Coleman. **Winemaker:** David Coleman. **Second Label:** Leaping Lizard.

MAJOR WINES: PRICE, CASES, RATING
Chardonnay Sonoma County ($14, 2,131)	★★
Chardonnay Sonoma County Coleman Reserve ($15, 475)	★★
Fumé Blanc Sonoma County ($11, 2,150)	★★
Gewürztraminer Sonoma County ($11, 2,998)	★★
Sangiovese Mendocino County ($20, 1,291)	★★

ALSO PRODUCED
Fumé Blanc Sonoma County Organically Grown ($11, 542).

WINERY DATA
Case Production: 12,000. **Varietals Purchased:** Chardonnay (Sonoma County), Gewürztraminer (Sonoma County), Sangiovese (Mendocino County), Sauvignon Blanc (Sonoma County).

Owner-winemaker David Coleman is the free-thinking, free-spirited mind behind Adler Fels, a winery in the mountains overlooking Sonoma Valley. While this winery has been making wines for nearly two decades, it is still plagued by inconsistencies with every variety. Occasionally there's a brilliant breakthrough, such as the 1993 Sonoma County Chardonnay (91 points), but usually the wines are marked by off flavors and at best earn ★★.

TASTING NOTES

CHARDONNAY SONOMA COUNTY (★★): Very inconsistent; sometimes light and fruity, occasionally noteworthy.

FUMÉ BLANC SONOMA COUNTY (★★): Too often strays into weedy, grassy flavors that can be unappealing.

GEWÜRZTRAMINER SONOMA COUNTY (★★): Made in an off-dry, spicy style. Can be this winery's best.

SANGIOVESE MENDOCINO COUNTY (★★): Shares the inconsistency of the other wines, though the 1994 (87 points) featured chewy cherry and plum flavors.

ADOBE CANYON CELLARS see LANDMARK VINEYARDS

ALBAN VINEYARDS (★★★)
Edna Valley, San Luis Obispo County
Founded: 1986. **Owner:** Alban Family. **Winemaker:** John Alban.

MAJOR WINES: PRICE, CASES, RATING
Grenache Edna Valley Alban Vineyard ($28, 600)	★★★
Syrah Edna Valley Alban Estate Reva ($23, 1100)	★★★
Viognier Central Coast ($20, 2000)	★★
Viognier Edna Valley Alban Vineyard ($28, 750)	★★

ALSO PRODUCED
Roussanne Central Coast ($20, 500); Roussanne Edna Valley Alban Vineyard ($32, 500); Syrah Edna Valley Alban Estate Lorraine ($28, 100); Vin de Paille Red Edna Valley Alban Vineyard ($20, 300)

WINERY DATA
Case Production: 6,000. **Acres Owned:** 60 acres in Edna Valley. **Varietals by Acre:** Grenache (6 acres), Roussanne (10), Syrah (12), Viognier (32). **Vineyard Designations:** Alban Vineyard.

John Alban focuses exclusively on Rhône varietals grown in a family-owned 60-acre Edna Valley vineyard. Viognier captures spicy pear and floral flavors, while the reds, which have evolved from an earthy, herbal style to intensely flavored, deeply colored wines, are even better. The Grenache is rich and exotic, with wild berry flavors. The Syrah shows spicy, plummy, herbal and cherry-tinged notes. Worth watching.

TASTING NOTES

SYRAH EDNA VALLEY ALBAN ESTATE REVA (★★★): This wine is improving, showing riper fruit flavors and more complexity.
1995: Rich and smooth, with stewed plum, blackberry, tar and spice flavors, finishing with supple tannins. **89**
1994: Racy, with a beefy edge to the herb, cola and wild berry flavors, turning chewy. **88**

ALBINI FAMILY VINEYARDS (★★)
Russian River Valley, Sonoma County
Founded: 1991. **Owner:** Don & Lynne Albini. **Winemaker:** Don Albini.

MAJOR WINES: PRICE, CASES, RATING
Merlot Russian River Valley
($21, 392) ★★

WINERY DATA
Case Production: 500. **Acres Owned:** 1.5 in Russian River Valley. **Varietals by Acre:** Merlot (1.5 acres). **Varietals Purchased:** Merlot (Russian River Valley).

A family-run winery producing a sturdy mint- and currant-flavored Merlot from its small vineyard in Russian River Valley. Both the 1994 and 1995 (86 points each) are good, if short of exciting.

ALDERBROOK VINEYARDS & WINERY (★★★)
Dry Creek Valley, Sonoma County
Founded: 1981. **Owner:** George and Dorothy Gillemot. **Winemaker:** Kristi Koford.

MAJOR WINES: PRICE, CASES, RATING
Cabernet Sauvignon Sonoma County
($16, 3,000) ★★
Chardonnay Dry Creek Valley
($12, 20,000) ★★★
Chardonnay Dry Creek Valley Dorothy's Vineyard
($22, 1,000) ★★★
Gewürztraminer Russian River Valley Barrel Fermented
($12, 200) ★★
Gewürztraminer Russian River Valley Saralee's Vineyard
($11, 2,000) ★★
Merlot Sonoma County
($18, 2,000) ★★
Pinot Noir Russian River Valley
($16, 2,000) ★★
Sauvignon Blanc Dry Creek Valley
($11, 7,000) ★★
Viognier Russian River Valley
($18, 1,000) ★★
Zinfandel Russian River Valley Gamba Vineyard
($22, 200) ★★★★
Zinfandel Sonoma County OVOC
($16, 6,000) ★★★
Zinfandel Sonoma County George's Vineyards
($25, 600) ★★★★

ALSO PRODUCED
Syrah Russian River Valley ($16, 300).

WINERY DATA
Case Production: 50,000. **Acres Owned:** 63 acres in Dry Creek Valley. **Varietals by Acre:** Chardonnay (35 acres), Merlot (7), Sauvignon Blanc (14), Zinfandel (7). **Vineyard Designations:** Saralee's (Gewürztraminer), Dorothy's (Chardonnay), Gamba (Zinfandel). **Varietals Purchased:** Cabernet Sauvignon (Alexander Valley, Dry Creek Valley, Russian River Valley, Sonoma Valley), Merlot (Dry Creek Valley, Russian River Valley, Sonoma Valley), Pinot Noir (Russian River Valley), Syrah (Russian River Valley), Zinfandel (Alexander Valley, Dry Creek Valley, Russian River Valley, Sonoma Valley).

Chardonnay and Zinfandel have emerged as the quality leaders from this winery, which produces a wide array of mostly good ★★ wines from both estate and purchased grapes. As such, the appellations vary; usually either Dry Creek Valley or the broader Sonoma County name is used. The Zinfandel from Gamba Vineyard in Russian River is definitely worth watching (and drinking). It remains to be seen whether the other wines can rise to this level.

TASTING NOTES

CABERNET SAUVIGNON SONOMA COUNTY (★★): Variable quality, though the 1995 Sonoma County (89 points) featured attractive Cabernet flavors. Formerly called Cabernet Sauvignon Dry Creek Valley.

CHARDONNAY DRY CREEK VALLEY, DOROTHY'S VINEYARD AND SONOMA COUNTY (★★★): Represents a good value in complex, rich and flavorful Chardonnay that's close to outstanding.

GEWÜRZTRAMINER RUSSIAN RIVER VALLEY (★★): Fresh, elegant, slightly sweet and refreshing.

MERLOT SONOMA COUNTY (★★): Well-oaked style with firm tannins. It offers appealing Merlot flavors but lacks extra dimensions.

PINOT NOIR RUSSIAN RIVER VALLEY (★★): Medium weight, oaky, with pleasantly typical Pinot Noir flavors, but not a top-caliber Russian River wine.

SAUVIGNON BLANC DRY CREEK VALLEY (★★): Well made; tames the racy flavors of Sauvignon Blanc.

ZINFANDEL RUSSIAN RIVER VALLEY GAMBA VINEYARD (★★★★): Both the 1995 (92 points) and 1996 (89) Gamba Vineyard bottlings were rich and complex, loaded with dark fruit and concentrated wild berry flavors, making this an exciting addition to the winery's lineup.

ZINFANDEL SONOMA COUNTY OVOC (★★★): This bottling is intense and packed with fruit flavors.

ZINFANDEL SONOMA COUNTY GEORGE'S VINEYARDS (★★★★)
1997: A delicious orchestration of fruit and oak, with ripe, complex black cherry, plum and wild berry flavors and pretty, toasty, spicy oak adding texture and dimension. **92**

ALEXANDER VALLEY VINEYARDS (★★)
Alexander Valley, Sonoma County
Founded: 1975. **Owner:** Katie Wetzel Murphy.
Winemaker: Peter Burford.

MAJOR WINES: PRICE, CASES, RATING

Cabernet Franc Alexander Valley Wetzel Family Estate ($20, 500)	★★
Cabernet Sauvignon Alexander Valley Wetzel Family Estate ($18, 15,000)	★★
Chardonnay Alexander Valley Wetzel Family Estate ($12, 8,000)	★★
Chardonnay Alexander Valley Wetzel Family Estate Reserve ($20, 1,000)	★★
Chenin Blanc Alexander Valley Wetzel Family Estate Dry ($9, 1,200)	★★
Gewürztraminer North Coast New Gewürz ($9, 8,500)	★★
Merlot Alexander Valley Wetzel Family Estate ($17, 11,000)	★★
Syrah Alexander Valley Vyborny Vineyard ($22, 500)	★★
Zinfandel Alexander Valley Sin Zin ($16, 4,000)	★★

ALSO PRODUCED
Cabernet Sauvignon Alexander Valley Library Reserve ($24, 1,500).

WINERY DATA
Case Production: 51,200. **Acres Owned:** 115 acres. **Varietals by Acre:** Cabernet Sauvignon (47 acres), Chardonnay (27), Merlot (23), Pinot Noir (5), Syrah (6), Zinfandel (7). **Varietals Purchased:** Cabernet Sauvignon (Alexander Valley), Gewürztraminer (Mendocino), Syrah (Alexander Valley).

Alexander Valley Vineyards owes much of its reputation to its well-crafted, affordable wines. The Wetzel family came to the valley in 1962 and planted 115 acres of estate vineyards in the next decade. Cabernet remains the winery's strength, but quality has declined slightly, making this a ★★ winery across the board.

TASTING NOTES

CABERNET SAUVIGNON ALEXANDER VALLEY WETZEL FAMILY ESTATE (★★): The winery was a rising star in the mid-1980s on the basis of its rich, complex 1984, 1985 and 1986 Cabernet vintages, but the wines since have been more restrained, less flavorful and, to my taste, less exciting. These wines are best on release and for five to eight years, although the 1984 remains a big and potent wine. The 1994 (87 points) offered chewy berry and currant flavors, but it's been a long time since a Cabernet from this winery has earned an outstanding rating.

CHARDONNAY ALEXANDER VALLEY VARIOUS BOTTLINGS (★★): Smooth, delicate, sometimes merely simple and fruity.

MERLOT ALEXANDER VALLEY WETZEL FAMILY ESTATE (★★): Usually simple, clean and correct, lacking in extra facets.

ALLEN FAMILY see SEQUOIA GROVE VINEYARDS

ALTAMURA VINEYARDS & WINERY (★★★★)
Napa Valley
Founded: 1985. **Owner:** Frank & Karen Altamura.
Winemaker: Frank Altamura.

MAJOR WINES: PRICE, CASES, RATING
Cabernet Sauvignon Napa Valley
  ($40, 2,000)   ★★★★
Sangiovese Napa Valley
  ($28, 1,200)   ★★★★

WINERY DATA
Case Production: 3,500. **Acres Owned:** 59 acres in Napa Valley. **Varietals by Acre:** Cabernet Sauvignon (33 acres), Sangiovese (12), Sauvignon Blanc (12), Nebbiolo (2). **Varietals Purchased:** Cabernet Sauvignon (Napa Valley), Sangiovese (Napa Valley, Monterey County).

After starting as a Chardonnay specialist with a winery north of Napa, Altamura Vineyards shifted gears and now focuses on Cabernet and Sangiovese. In 1994, owners Frank and Karen Altamura ended a business relationship with Altamura's father, George, and began planting a new vineyard in the Wooden Valley area east of Napa near the Solano County line. Both of Altamura's red wines are composed of 65 to 70 percent estate-grown grapes, and eventually the Cabernet will be close to 80 percent estate-grown. A small portion of the Sangiovese comes from Mer Soleil Vineyard, Chuck Wagner's vineyard in Monterey. Quality of both the Cabernet and Sangiovese is very high.

TASTING NOTES

CABERNET SAUVIGNON NAPA VALLEY (★★★★): Has shown steady improvement and now merits special attention, as the wines are consistently rich, complex and beautifully balanced, with toasty oak shadings. No track record for aging yet, but has the right stuff.
1995: Ripe, smooth and smoky, with wild berry, black cherry, currant, plum and spice flavors deliciously woven together in a supple, complex, concentrated style. Tannins weigh in on the finish. **93**
1994: Big, ripe and well-oaked, with well defined currant, black cherry, herb and wild berry flavors, finishing with herb and coffee notes. **91**
1993: A wine of harmony and finesse; ripe, rich, complex, with lots of juicy cherry, currant, anise and light oak shadings. **92**
1992: Dark and complex, with spicy currant, plum and chocolate-cherry flavors that run deep, plus a mineral note. **92**
1991: Full-bodied, with a tight core of ripe cherry and plum flavors, turning more simple on the finish. **88**
1990: Showy and elegant, with ripe, smooth, supple black cherry, currant and vanilla-tinged oak shadings, finishing with mild, polished tannins. **88**

SANGIOVESE NAPA VALLEY (★★★★): Now one of the state's best, offering substance and depth.
1995: Tight and firm, with an earthy core of wild berry, black cherry, cedar and sage flavors, turning dry and tannic on the finish. **87**
1994: A wine of finesse and concentration, with spice, anise, cedar, currant and wild berry flavors turning rich and complex. **92**
1993: A complex, broad array of stewed plum, tar, coffee, mineral and blackberry flavors. **90**

AMADOR FOOTHILL WINERY (★★)
Shenandoah Valley, Amador County
Founded: 1980. **Owner:** Ben Zeitman, Katie Quinn.
Winemaker: Ben Zeitman, Katie Quinn.

MAJOR WINES: PRICE, CASES, RATING
Fumé Blanc Shenandoah Valley Amador Fumé ($8, 1,600)	★★
Sangiovese Shenandoah Valley Estate ($12, 600)	★★
Sémillon Shenandoah Valley Estate ($8, 350)	★★
Zinfandel Amador County Clockspring Vineyard ($11, 700)	★★
Zinfandel Shenandoah Valley Ferrero Vineyard ($12, 1,100)	★★

ALSO PRODUCED
Carignane Amador County Murrill Vineyard ($16, 200); Rosato of Sangiovese Shenandoah Valley ($8, 300); White Zinfandel Amador County ($6, 2,900); Zinfandel Amador County Murrill Vineyard ($11, 500).

WINERY DATA
Case Production: 9,000. **Acres Owned:** 10 acres in Shenandoah Valley. **Varietals by Acre:** Sangiovese (4 acres), Sauvignon Blanc (4), Sémillon (2). **Vineyard Designations:** Clockspring (Zinfandel), Ferrero Vineyard (Zinfandel), Murrill (Zinfandel, Carignane). **Varietals Purchased:** Carignane (Amador), Sauvignon Blanc (Shenandoah Valley), Zinfandel (Shenandoah Valley, Amador County).

Situated east of Plymouth in the Sierra foothills, Amador Foothill Winery produces Sangiovese, Sauvignon Blanc, Sémillon, and various Zinfandels, including vineyard-designated wines that reflect Zinfandel's austerity in the Sierra. None of the wines rises above a ★★ rating.

ANAPAMU see **GALLO OF SONOMA WINERY**

ANCIEN WINES (★★★)
Napa Valley
Founded: 1992. **Owner:** Ken Bernards. **Winemaker:** Ken Bernards.

MAJOR WINES: PRICE, CASES, RATING
Chardonnay Carneros ($28, 300)	★★★
Pinot Noir Carneros ($25, 350)	★★★

ALSO PRODUCED
Pinot Noir Sonoma Mountain Steiner Vineyard ($32, 60).

WINERY DATA
Case Production: 750. **Vineyard Designations:** Steiner Vineyard (Pinot Noir). **Varietals Purchased:** Chardonnay (Carneros), Pinot Noir (Carneros, Sonoma Mountain).

Former Truchard Vineyard winemaker Ken Bernards specializes in small lots of Pinot Noir and Chardonnay purchased from growers in Carneros and Sonoma Mountain. The Pinot Noir has been very good, occasionally rating outstanding. The 1996 (87 points) was dense with mineral, leather and plum flavors, while the 1994 (90) was more complex, with supple flavors of currant, mineral and earth. Worth watching.

S. ANDERSON VINEYARD (★★★★)
Stags Leap District, Napa Valley
Founded: 1971. **Owner:** Carol G. Anderson **Winemaker:** David DeSante. **Second Label:** Tivoli.

MAJOR WINES: PRICE, CASES, RATING
Blanc de Blancs Napa Valley ($36, 600)	★★★★
Blanc de Noirs Napa Valley ($22, 2,500)	★★★★
Brut Napa Valley ($24, 2,500)	★★★★
Brut Napa Valley Reserve ($32, 600)	★★★★
Cabernet Sauvignon Stag Leap District ($24, 1,500)	★★★
Cabernet Sauvignon Stags Leap District Richard Chambers Vineyard ($60, 700)	★★★★

Chardonnay Napa Valley Carneros
  ($22, 1,500)   ★★★
Chardonnay Napa Valley
  Proprietor's Reserve
  ($32, 600)   ★★★★
Chardonnay Stags Leap District
  ($22, 1,500)   ★★★
Diva Sparkling Napa Valley
  ($46, 600)   ★★★★
Merlot Stags Leap District Reserve
  ($32, 400)   ★★★
Rosé Sparkling Napa Valley
  ($28, 400)   ★★★

WINERY DATA
Case Production: 14,000. **Acres Owned:** 99 acres in Stags
Leap and Carneros (38 in Stags Leap District, 61 in Carneros).
Varietals by Acre: Chardonnay (28 Carneros, 30 Stags Leap),
Merlot (6 Stags Leap District), Pinot Noir (33 Carneros, 2 Stags
Leap District). **Vineyard Designations:** Richard Chambers
Vineyard (Cabernet Sauvignon). **Varietals Purchased:** Merlot,
Cabernet Franc, Cabernet Sauvignon (Stags Leap District).

S. Anderson Vineyard is best known for its delicious
sparkling wines, but it produces a variety of wines which
are very high in quality across the board. The winery's
best is the Cabernet Sauvignon from Richard Chambers
Vineyard, which merits special attention as one of the
best from the Stags Leap District. Both the Brut and
Blanc de Noirs are complex and feature ripe fruit flavors.
The Sparkling Rosé is less interesting.

The winery was founded by Stanley and Carol
Anderson in 1971. For years they commuted to Napa
Valley on weekends from their home in Pasadena to work
on their Yountville vineyard, and in 1979 they started making small lots of Chardonnay. Stanley died in 1994 just as
the winery began to raise quality levels to new highs.

TASTING NOTES

CABERNET SAUVIGNON STAGS LEAP DISTRICT (★★★)
1994: A bit nervy, with an odd, tangy, oaky edge which
somewhat overrides the currant and herb-tinged Cabernet
flavors. **89**
1993: Marked by strong menthol aromas and flavors,
with hints of currant and berry and a touch of spice. **87**

CABERNET SAUVIGNON STAGS LEAP DISTRICT RICHARD CHAMBERS VINEYARD (★★★★):
Supple and stylish,
with rich flavors, smooth tannins, lots of buttery oak and
a wonderful sense of harmony and finesse. The wines are
remarkably consistent in style and very appealing to
drink on release. Worth collecting.
1995: Delivers a complex array of earthy currant, black
cherry, wild berry and spice, but is quite elegant and
compact. **91**
1994: Tightly wound but quite complex, with a good
dose of oak. The smoky, meaty flavors compete with the
currant and plummy flavors. **91**
1993: An oaky style, but with enough ripe cherry and
berry flavors to give it balance and complexity. **90**
1992: Strikes a nice balance, with rich, earthy currant
and cherry flavors framed by nice toasty oak and leathery flavors. **89**
1991: Compact and vibrant, with an herbaceous edge to
the rich vanilla, currant and wild berry flavors, finishing
with firm tannins. **91**
1990: Tightly wound, but the currant, berry and spice flavors run deep, rich and supple, gaining complexity on
the finish. **91**
1989: A deep, densely flavored 1989 that delivers intense
black cherry, plum and currant flavors, shaded by vanilla,
nutmeg and chocolate notes. **90**

CHARDONNAY NAPA VALLEY CARNEROS (★★★)
1996: Clean and crisp, with a trim band of bright citrus,
pear and melon flavors. **87**
1995: Racy, with bracing acidity and strong citrus flavors—notably grapefruit—that are bright and distinctive. **91**
1994: Marked by strong citrus and spice flavors, with
mature pear and apple notes. **86**

CHARDONNAY NAPA VALLEY PROPRIETOR'S RESERVE (★★★)
1995: Serves up complex, concentrated flavors, with layers
of ripe pear, citrus, hazelnut and fig. **92**

CHARDONNAY STAGS LEAP DISTRICT (★★★★):
Despite
some variability in style, quality is usually very good and
occasionally outstanding.
1995: A racy, leesy style, with ripe pear and apple notes. **87**
1994: Trim and well balanced, with pleasant spice, vanilla and pear flavors that fan out on the finish. **90**

MERLOT STAGS LEAP DISTRICT RESERVE (★★★): Not in the same class as the Richard Chambers Cabernet, but it is ripe, fruity and marked by plum, cherry, wild berry and spicy flavors.

1995: Ripe and fruity, with plum, wild berry, cherry and menthol notes and supple tannins. **87**

1994: Young and vibrant, with a core of cherry, tea, herb and cedary oak flavors, turning crisp and tannic. **88**

ANDERSON'S CONN VALLEY VINEYARDS (★★★★)

Conn Valley, Napa Valley
Founded: 1983. **Owner:** The Anderson Family.
Winemaker: Gus & Todd Anderson.

MAJOR WINES: PRICE, CASES, RATING

Cabernet Sauvignon Napa Valley
  Estate Reserve
  ($40, 4,000-5,000)   ★★★★
Chardonnay Carneros Fournier Vineyard
  ($38, 1,000-1,500)   ★★★
Éloge Red Napa Valley
  ($45, 500-1,000)   ★★★
Pinot Noir Napa Valley Valhalla
  Vineyards
  ($40, 150-250)   ★★

ALSO PRODUCED

Pinot Noir Russian River Valley Dutton Ranch ($40, 200-300).

WINERY DATA

Case Production: 7,000. **Acres Owned:** 28 acres in Napa Valley. **Varietals by Acre:** Cabernet Sauvignon (23 acres), Cabernet Franc (1), Merlot (2), Pinot Noir (2). **Vineyard Designations:** Valhalla Vineyards, Dutton Ranch, Fournier Vineyard. **Varietals Purchased:** Chardonnay (Napa Valley), Pinot Noir (Russian River Valley).

Founded in 1983 by Gus Anderson in Conn Valley, a narrow valley east of Napa Valley, this family-owned and -operated winery specializes in complex and sumptuous Cabernets grown in a 28-acre vineyard. Legally, Conn Valley is part of the larger Napa Valley appellation, but

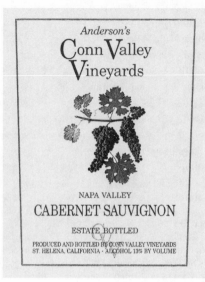

this is a distinctive vineyard yielding distinctive wines. Production is about 7,000 cases, including a Pinot Noir from purchased grapes. The debut 1993 vintage (86 points) of a Bordeaux-style blend called Éloge was marked by earthy, cedar flavors, not the rich fruit usually found in the winery's Cabernet Sauvignon; the 1995 debut of the elegant Chardonnay Napa Valley Fournier Vineyard (91) was more compelling.

TASTING NOTES

CABERNET SAUVIGNON NAPA VALLEY ESTATE RESERVE (★★★★): Dark, rich and well oaked, with supple herb, black currant and spice notes and firm but polished tannins. While most of the wines have earned outstanding marks, the 1995 was less compelling. Still, worth watching.

1995: Shows an elegant, understated style, with cedary tobacco and currant notes, but lacks richness and concentration. **87**

1994: A touch earthy, with a gamy edge. The core of cedar and currant is dense and intense, with big, chewy tannins. **91**

1993: A touch earthy and leathery, but with dense currant, coffee and cherry flavors and chewy tannins. **90**

1992: Beautifully crafted, with rich, complex cherry, plum, wild berry, anise, toast and vanilla notes that turn harmonious and supple. **93**

1991: Tannic and earthy, with a leathery edge to the currant and cherry flavors, but it softens on the finish. **88**

1990: Firm and intense, with rich, chewy cherry, chocolate and buttery oak flavors. Packs in lots of flavor, picking up mineral notes on the finish. **90**

1989: Smooth and ripe, with generous plum and currant aromas and flavors that finish with toast, spice and fruit notes. **88**

1988: Made in an earthy, minerally style, with dried currant, black cherry, anise, coffee, cedar and spicy notes. **87**

CHARDONNAY CARNEROS FOURNIER VINEYARD (★★★):
1995: Sleek and elegant, with a sharply focused core of ripe, rich peach, pear, ginger and spice flavors. **91**

ÉLOGE RED NAPA VALLEY (★★★)
1993: Struggles to find a focus amid earthy cedar and tannic notes; it finally straightens out at mid-palate, where plum and berry flavors emerge. **86**

PINOT NOIR NAPA VALLEY VALHALLA VINEYARDS (★★):
The first three vintages—1995 (87 points), 1993 (86) and 1991 (85)—earned good marks, with a style that featured earthy, beefy Pinot Noir flavors.

AQUA PUMPKIN CANYON see WILD HORSE WINERY & VINEYARDS

ARAUJO ESTATE WINES (★★★★★)
Calistoga, Napa Valley
Founded: 1990. **Owner:** Bart & Daphne Araujo.
Winemaker: Francoise Peschon.

MAJOR WINES: PRICE, CASES, RATING
Cabernet Sauvignon Napa Valley
  Eisele Vineyard
  ($100, 2,500)   ★★★★★
Sauvignon Blanc Napa Valley
  Eisele Vineyard
  ($22, 1,200)   ★★★
Syrah Napa Valley Eisele Vineyard
  ($50, 350)   ★★★★★

WINERY DATA
Case Production: 4,000. **Acres Owned:** 41 acres in Napa Valley. **Varietals by Acre:** Cabernet Franc (1 acre), Cabernet Sauvignon (28), Petit Verdot (1), Sauvignon Blanc (5), Syrah (5), Viognier (1).

Since the 1970s, Eisele Vineyard, situated at the foot of the Palisades mountains southeast of Calistoga, has proven to be one of California's greatest vineyards, with a distinguished track record for yielding consistently excellent, distinctive and ageworthy wines. In years such as 1974 (under the Conn Creek label), 1975, 1978, 1979, and 1985, the wines have shown uncommon richness, with thick, chewy, earthy tannins and a complex core of currant, berry and mineral flavors. They are also amazingly ageworthy, keeping their youthful, vibrant personalities for up to two decades.

The vineyard was originally planted by Milt and Barbara Eisele. In 1990, the Eiseles sold it to Bart and Daphne Araujo, who have continued to make genuinely sensational wines. The Araujos undertook a major overhaul, replanting many vines, adding new grape varieties (Petit Verdot, Syrah, Sangiovese, Sauvignon Blanc, and Viognier), building a handsome new winery and aging caves. Along with the superb Cabernet, the winery makes a small amount of equally stunning Syrah (500 cases) and a very fine Sauvignon Blanc.

TASTING NOTES

CABERNET SAUVIGNON NAPA VALLEY EISELE VINEYARD (★★★★★): Magnificent Cabernet, easily among the finest. Uniformly dark and rich with complex, concentrated fruit flavors and supple, polished tannins, marked by a characteristic mineral edge. Ages exceptionally well.
1995: Sleek, elegant, rich and concentrated, with sharply focused black cherry, currant, plum and wild berry flavors interspersed with cedary tobacco. **95**
1994: Massively proportioned; dense with cedar, cherry and currant flavors that are intense and well focused; finishes with a long, lively aftertaste. **96**
1993: Tight and complex, with tiers of spice, currant, plum and cherry flavors, picking up traces of herb, mineral and anise, and finishing with exotic, smoky fruit flavors. **93**

1992: Ultra rich and complex, with distinct vanilla bean, toasty oak and plush black cherry and berry flavors that are sharply focused. **96**

1991: A rich, concentrated, dark colored and deeply perfumed wine, packed with currant and mineral flavors and framed by light oak notes. Finishes with a long, full, broad aftertaste. **93**

SAUVIGNON BLANC NAPA VALLEY EISELE VINEYARD (★★★): Serves up supple, understated fig, melon and citrus notes, with vanilla and spice shadings. Has a small percentage of Viognier. The 1996 earned 87 points.

SYRAH NAPA VALLEY EISELE VINEYARD (★★★★★): This wine shares the Cabernet's power and finesse, with rich, thick, earthy currant and meaty flavors. No track record yet for aging, but it has all the right stuff. Limited production makes it hard to get.

1995: Smooth, rich and elegant, with polished currant, leather, anise, earth and mineral flavors that are complex, concentrated, long and sophisticated. **94**

ARBIOS (★★★)
Alexander Valley, Sonoma County
Founded: 1993. **Owner:** William Arbios. **Winemaker:** William Arbios.

MAJOR WINES: PRICE, CASES, RATING
Cabernet Sauvignon Alexander Valley
($32, 500-2,000) ★★★

WINERY DATA
Case Production: 2,000. **Varietals Purchased:** Cabernet Sauvignon (Alexander Valley).

Bill Arbios worked at Chateau Souverain, Lyeth, Wheeler and Jarvis before starting his own brand. He purchases Cabernet Sauvignon grapes from Smith-Reichel Vineyard in Alexander Valley and makes wine at the Associated Vintage Group custom crush facility in Graton. The 1995 Cabernet (88 points) was impressive, with tight spice, cedar, plum, and berry flavors.

ARCADIAN (★★★)
Santa Maria Valley, Santa Barbara County
Founded: 1996. **Owner:** Joseph Davis & Jill Goldworn. **Winemaker:** Joseph Davis.

MAJOR WINES: PRICE, CASES, RATING
Chardonnay Santa Maria Valley
  Bien Nacido Vineyard
  ($30, 2,000) ★★★

ALSO PRODUCED
Chardonnay Monterey Sleepy Hollow Vineyard ($30, 1,000); Pinot Noir Monterey Pisoni Vineyard ($45, 750); Pinot Noir Monterey Sleepy Hollow Vineyard ($25, 400); Pinot Noir Santa Maria Valley Bien Nacido Vineyard ($35, 500); Syrah Monterey Pisoni Vineyard (25, 250).

WINERY DATA
Case Production: 5,000. **Vineyard Designations:** Bien Nacido Vineyard (Chardonnay, Pinot Noir), Pisoni Vineyard (Pinot Noir, Syrah), Sleepy Hollow Vineyard (Chardonnay, Pinot Noir). **Varietals Purchased:** Chardonnay (Monterey, Santa Maria Valley), Pinot Noir (Monterey, Santa Maria Valley), Syrah (Monterey).

Joe Davis was winemaker for Morgan Winery (see entry) for 10 years before moving on to Bernardus in 1995 and then starting his own brand, Arcadian, in 1996. Operating out of the Central Coast Wine Warehouse, Davis focuses on vineyard-designated Pinot Noir, Chardonnay and Syrah from Central Coast vineyards. The 1996 Chardonnay Bien Nacido Vineyard (91 points) was fresh and crisp with a flinty edge to its peach, pear and nectarine flavors. Arcadian has locked on to excellent grape sources and if all goes well the wines should be excellent as well. A winery to watch.

ARCIERO WINERY (★★)
Paso Robles, San Luis Obispo County
Founded: 1985. **Owner:** Arciero Family, Kerry Vix, Vernon Underwood. **Winemaker:** Stephen Felten. **Second Label:** EOS, Canyon Ridge, Vineland.

MAJOR WINES: PRICE, CASES, RATING
Cabernet Sauvignon California
  ($10, 4,000) ★★
Chardonnay California
  ($10, 6,000) ★★

Muscat Canelli California
  ($7, 2,400)   ★★
Muscat Canelli Late Harvest Paso Robles
  ($14, 600)   ★★
Nebbiolo Paso Robles
  ($12, 1,200)   ★★
Sangiovese Paso Robles
  ($14, 1,200)   ★★
Zinfandel Paso Robles
  ($12, 2,250)   ★★
EOS Chardonnay Paso Robles
  Astreaus Vineyard
  ($16, 8,000)   ★★

ALSO PRODUCED
Chenin Blanc California ($6, 7,000); Petite Sirah Paso
Robles ($14, 1,000); White Zinfandel California ($6, 1,750);
EOS Cabernet Sauvignon Paso Robles Hyperion Vineyard
($16, 4,700); EOS Cabernet Sauvignon Paso Robles
Hyperion Vineyard ($16, 4,700); EOS Cabernet Sauvignon
Paso Robles Hyperion Vineyard ($16, 4,700).

WINERY DATA
Case Production: 220,000. **Acres Owned:** 702 acres in Paso
Robles. **Varietals by Acre:** Cabernet Franc (2 acres), Cabernet
Sauvignon (116), Chardonnay (206), Merlot (116), Muscat
Canelli (16), Nebbiolo (10), Petite Sirah (70), Pinot Grigio (2)
Sangiovese (16), Sauvignon Blanc (30), Zinfandel (118).
Varietals Purchased: Cabernet Sauvignon (Central Coast),
Chardonnay (Central Coast & California), Chenin Blanc
(California), Merlot (Central Coast), Syrah (Central Coast).

This large, ambitious winery produces a wide range of
primarily un-noteworthy wines. The Zinfandel is the
most consistent, although they've had some success with
their other reds, including Cabernet, Sangiovese and
Nebbiolo. A 1995 Zinfandel (87) was peppery and
herbal, but balanced with black cherry and vanilla notes.
In 1998, Arciero developed a new brand called EOS,
which may become the quality leader in the portfolio.

ARIES see **ROBERT SINSKEY VINEYARDS**

ARMIDA WINERY (★★)
Dry Creek Valley, Sonoma County
Founded: 1989. **Owner:** Bruce & Steve Cousins.
Winemaker: Michael Loykasek.

MAJOR WINES: PRICE, CASES, RATING
Merlot Russian River Valley
  ($18, 2,000)   ★★

ALSO PRODUCED
Chardonnay Russian River Valley ($16, 9,000); Chardonnay
Russian River Valley Reserve ($18, 400); Pinot Noir Russian
River Valley ($16, 1,000).

WINERY DATA
Case Production: 12,000. **Varietals Purchased:** Cabernet
Sauvignon (Dry Creek Valley), Chardonnay (Russian River
Valley), Merlot (Russian River Valley), Pinot Noir (Russian
River Valley), Zinfandel (Dry Creek Valley).

Brothers Bruce and Steve Cousins purchased Armida
from friend Robert Frugoli in 1994. The grapes used in
the wines still come from Frugoli's Russian River Valley
vineyards, but the long-term winemaking goal is to focus
on Dry Creek Valley Cabernet and Zinfandel. The 1994
Russian River Valley Merlot (88 points) was rich with
pure fruit flavors of blackberry and currant.

ARNS (★★★★)
Napa Valley
Founded: 1990. **Owner:** John Arns & Sandi Belcher.
Winemaker: Sandi Belcher.

MAJOR WINES: PRICE, CASES, RATING
Cabernet Sauvignon Napa Valley
  ($40, 400-1000)   ★★★★

WINERY DATA
Case Production: 400-1,000. **Acres Owned:** 7 in Napa Valley.
Varietals by Acre: Cabernet Sauvignon (7 acres).

Veteran vineyard consultant John Arns formed a
partnership with winemaker Sandi Belcher of Long
Vineyards to produce Cabernet from Arns' Napa
Valley vineyard. Consistently dark, concentrated and
firmly tannic, the Cabernet hit highs in 1993 (93
points) and 1995 (91), but leathery tannins kept it a
notch below the best in 1994 (89).

TASTING NOTES

CABERNET SAUVIGNON NAPA VALLEY (★★★★):
Impressive start, with dark, complex, tannic and seemingly ageworthy wines.
1995: Dark, ripe, rich and polished, with black cherry, chocolate, wild berry and spice. Gains complexity and nuance, but finishes with a touch of stemminess. **91**
1994: Tough and tannic, with a chewy, leathery flavor that overrides the core of spicy currant and mineral flavors. **89**
1993: Tightly wound, dark, ripe, rich and concentrated, with layers of currant, black cherry, anise and wild berry. **93**

ARROWOOD VINEYARDS & WINERY (★★★★★)
Sonoma Valley
Founded: 1986. **Owner:** Richard & Alis Arrowood.
Winemaker: Richard Arrowood & Michel Berthoud
Second Label: Domaine Grand Archer.

MAJOR WINES: PRICE, CASES, RATING
Cabernet Sauvignon Sonoma County
($17, 9,000) ★★★★
Cabernet Sauvignon Sonoma County
Réserve Spéciale
($50, 700) ★★★★★
Chardonnay Sonoma County
($24, 7,000) ★★★★
Chardonnay Sonoma County Cuvée
Michel Berthoud Réserve Spéciale
($33, 1,200) ★★★★★
Malbec Sonoma County
($37, 300) ★★★★
Merlot Sonoma County
($38, 4,500) ★★★★
Pinot Blanc Russian River Valley
Saralee's Vineyard
($33, 700) ★★★★
Syrah Russian River Valley
Saralee's Vineyard
($40, 300) ★★★★
Viognier Late Harvest Russian
River Valley Saralee's Vineyard Select
($30, 600) ★★★

White Riesling Late Harvest Russian
River Valley Oak Meadow Vineyard Select
($35, 240) ★★★★
White Riesling Late Harvest Russian
River Valley Preston Ranch Select
(Discontinued) ★★★★

Domaine Grand Archer Cabernet Sauvignon
Sonoma County
($17, 1,400) ★★★
Domaine Grand Archer Chardonnay
Sonoma County
($15, 1,800) ★★★
Domaine Grand Archer Merlot
Sonoma County
($20, 1,300) ★★

WINERY DATA
Case Production: 27,000. **Acres Owned:** 20 acres (10 in Sonoma Valley, 10 in Russian River Valley). **Varietals by Acre:** Cabernet Franc (2 acres), Malbec (2), Merlot (14), Petit Verdot (0.6), Syrah (1), Viognier (0.4). **Vineyard Designations:** Saralee's Vineyard (Pinot Blanc, Syrah, Viognier), Oak Meadow (White Riesling). **Varietals Purchased:** Cabernet Franc (Knights Valley), Cabernet Sauvignon (Alexander Valley, Dry Creek Valley, Sonoma Valley), Chardonnay (Russian River Valley, Sonoma Valley, Alexander Valley), Malbec (Alexander Valley), Merlot (Russian River Valley, Alexander Valley, Sonoma Valley), Petit Verdot (Knights Valley), Pinot Blanc (Russian River Valley), Syrah (Russian River Valley), Tannat (Russian River Valley), White Riesling (Russian River Valley, Alexander Valley), Viognier (Russian River Valley).

Richard and Alis Arrowood established this winery in Sonoma Valley in 1986, a few miles south of Chateau St. Jean, where Richard spent twelve distinguished years as winemaker. For a brief period, Arrowood oversaw winemaking at both wineries before severing his ties with St. Jean in 1990. Not surprisingly, Arrowood has built on his talents and strengths, which include his keen knowledge of Sonoma County vineyards (he's a native of Santa Rosa); a long association with St. Jean (where he made nearly a dozen vineyard-designated Chardonnays, Fumé Blancs, Rieslings and extraordinary dessert wines); connections with growers (such as the owners of Saralee's Vineyard), and a knack for producing complex and engaging wines regardless of the variety.

After a decade on his own, his wines continue to improve, and now rank among the finest in the state. The lineup of wines continues to expand as well, with specific varietals, reserve bottlings and vineyard-designated wines being added. The portfolio includes Cabernet Sauvignon, Chardonnay, Merlot, Pinot Blanc, and Syrah, along with dessert-style Viognier and White Riesling. Quality across the board is exceptionally high, with uniformly distinctive and beautifully crafted wines.

TASTING NOTES

CABERNET SAUVIGNON SONOMA COUNTY (★★★★): Supple and elegant, with polished currant, herb, coffee and cedary oak flavors followed by smooth tannins. A blend of Alexander Valley, Dry Creek, Knights Valley and Sonoma Valley grapes. Merlot and Malbec come from Rosewood Vineyard in the Russian River Valley, which gives the wine its tartness. It drinks well early on and ages well too.
1995: Supple and harmonious, with a complex array of cedar, plum and currant flavors, along with hints of coffee and anise; turns elegant. **88**
1994: Ripe and polished; a harmonious wine with pretty currant, plum and cherry notes and supple tannins. **91**
1993: Complex and well balanced; a fine interplay of ripe plum, currant, cherry, herb and olive flavors. **92**
1992: Big, ripe and well oaked, packed with ripe plum and black cherry flavors. Deep and nicely complex. **92**
1991: Supple and elegant, with layers of herb, currant, wild berry, coffee and cedary oak flavors; smooth tannins. **91**
1990: Smooth and elegant, a generous wine with supple currant and blackberry flavors, spicy herbal overtones and a lively berry finish. **91**
1989: Supple and generous, with a nice core of currant, black cherry and plum flavors. **88**
1988: Dry and tannic, like the vintage, with appealing ripe plum, black cherry, anise and cedary notes. **88**
1987: Supple and harmonious, with a velvety core of currant, cherry, chocolate and light toasty oak. **93**
1986: Fully mature and declining, with a modest band of cedar- and currant-accented Cabernet flavors. **83**
1985: Elegant and stylish, loaded with strawberry, cherry and spicy plum flavors and supple tannins. **90**

CABERNET SAUVIGNON SONOMA COUNTY RÉSERVE SPÉCIALE (★★★★★): With its broad, rich, complex flavors, pretty oak shadings and supple, polished tannins, this wine deserves to be ranked among the best in the California. No track record yet for aging, but has all the right ingredients.
1994: Beautifully crafted, complex and concentrated, with a tightly focused core of earthy, currant, black cherry, cedary oak and spicy nuances. **94**
1993: Firm and tight, with a rich, well-focused core of plum, currant, black cherry, cedary oak and spicy nuances. **92**
1992: Dark, rich, intense, with a seam of elegance to the bright, lively black cherry, plum and wild berry flavors. **92**
1989: Ripe and fleshy, with supple plum, cherry and currant flavors that are elegant and framed by pretty oak. **88**

CHARDONNAY SONOMA COUNTY (★★★★): Intense and spicy, with rich pear and apple flavors. Can age, but drinks well at two years.
1996: Toasty, smoky oak leads to a rich, complex, concentrated core of pear, spice, vanilla, honey and citrus notes. **91**
1995: Initially marked by strong citrus and grapefruit flavors, it works its way into more complex pear, apple and melon notes, finishing with buttery flavors. **92**
1994: Ripe, smooth and supple, with a pretty core of spicy pear, apple and melon notes, finishing with a fruity honey aftertaste. **88**

CHARDONNAY SONOMA COUNTY CUVÉE MICHEL BERTHOUD RÉSERVE SPÉCIALE (★★★★★): More sturdily built than the Sonoma County bottling, and appropriately different in style, with a little more of everything, including oak, creamy fruit flavors and intensity. Best early on, though it should age well for up to five years.
1996: Smooth, rich and harmonious, with pretty layers of ripe pear, fig, melon, toast, hazelnut and spice, finishing long and complex. **92**
1995: Intense and lively, with a complex, concentrated core of spice, fig, melon and pear. Shows remarkable finesse. **93**
1994: Wonderful balance between the crisp, well-focused honey, pear, spice and mineral flavors and the lightly toasty oak. **92**
1993: Rich and well focused, with complex and concentrated pear, fig, honey and toasty vanilla shadings; finishes long and smoky. **92**
1991: Supple, with generous spice, tangerine, pear and vanilla flavors that linger on a long and elegant finish. **90**
1990: Delicious and complex, with layers of honey, pear, apple and toast, shaded by smoky, buttery oak. **93**

MERLOT SONOMA COUNTY (★★★★): Shows complex yet supple coffee, herb, currant and spice notes. The texture is like a red Burgundy.

1995: Tight and firm, with a complex band of spicy currant, plum and tobacco flavors that are deep and complex. **92**

1994: Ripe, round, rich and smoky, with a supple core of ripe plum and black cherry, picking up a pleasant spice and vanilla edge. **92**

1993: Ripe, jammy flavors, with hints of currant and plum and a nice, toasty oak accent. **90**

1992: Ripe, supple and elegant, striking a nice balance between black cherry, plum and toasty oak flavors. **90**

1991: Complex and flavorful, with a rich, supple core of currant, cherry and spice flavors. **91**

1990: Complex, with beautifully integrated plum, currant and spice flavors framed by toasty, buttery oak. **91**

PINOT BLANC RUSSIAN RIVER VALLEY SARALEE'S VINEYARD (★★★★): True-to-form Pinot Blanc; lighter and more elegant than Chardonnay, with bright peach, fig and nectarine flavors.

1997: Smooth and creamy, with complex fig, pear, melon and spicy, citrus notes along with a touch of anise. **87**

1996: Sleek, elegant and brimming with ripe, juicy peach, pear and nectarine flavors and it's tightly focused from start to finish. **90**

SYRAH RUSSIAN RIVER VALLEY SARALEE'S VINEYARD (★★★★): Big, ripe, intense and concentrated, with a fleshy texture and lots of complex, detailed flavors.

1995: Dark, ripe, rich and concentrated, with exotic black cherry, plum and wild berry flavors; turns leathery and spicy, with supple tannins. **90**

VIOGNIER LATE HARVEST RUSSIAN RIVER VALLEY SARALEE'S VINEYARD SELECT (★★★): Captures the essence of this spicy varietal.

1994: Strong, spicy aroma and rich, complex honey, apricot, vanilla and nectarine flavors. **88**

WHITE RIESLING LATE HARVEST RUSSIAN RIVER VALLEY OAK MEADOW VINEYARD SELECT (★★★★): Sweet and delicate, with exotic guava, nectarine and apricot flavors.

1993: Gloriously sweet, rich, supple and complex; a many-layered swirl of honey, caramel, apricot, pear and exotic tropical fruit and spices, all balanced gorgeously on a fine thread of acidity. **100**

1991: Light, sweet and delicate, with exotic guava, nectarine and apricot aromas and flavors. The finish is sweet but balanced. **87**

WHITE RIESLING LATE HARVEST RUSSIAN RIVER VALLEY PRESTON RANCH SELECT (★★★★)
1995: Delicious apricot, cream and honey flavors in this elegant, richly flavored, sweet wine. **92**

ATLAS PEAK VINEYARDS (★★)
Atlas Peak, Napa Valley
Founded: 1986. **Owner:** Allied Domecq/Piero Antinori.
Winemaker: John Falcone.

MAJOR WINES: PRICE, CASES, RATING

Cabernet Sauvignon Atlas Peak ($16, 2,000)	★★
Cabernet Sauvignon Atlas Peak Consenso Vineyard ($24,1,000)	★★
Chardonnay Atlas Peak ($16, 6,000)	★★
Sangiovese Atlas Peak ($16, 20,000)	★★
Sangiovese Atlas Peak Reserve ($24, 1,000)	★★

WINERY DATA
Case Production: 30,000. **Acres Owned:** 475 acres in Atlas Peak. **Varietals by Acre:** Cabernet Franc (20 acres), Cabernet Sauvignon (125), Chardonnay (125), Merlot (70), Petit Verdot (10), Sangiovese (125).

One of the most ambitious, high profile, and capital-intensive undertakings of the 1980s, Atlas Peak Vineyards is also among the most disappointing. The wines, despite all the projections and expectations for excellence, have largely been ordinary and unexciting.

Atlas Peak Vineyards brought together the great Tuscan vintner Piero Antinori, Champagne master Christian Bizot and the drinks firm Whitbread with the goal of creating a Super Tuscan line of wines using Sangiovese, Cabernet and blends thereof, along with anything else that developed at the then-untested property. In 1985 the trio bought 800 acres—rising more than 1,000 feet above the Napa Valley floor—and a partially developed vineyard from William Hill. They now have some

475 acres under vines, planted primarily to Sangiovese, Cabernet, Chardonnay, and Merlot.

The winery has not developed as planned, however. In 1994, the partnership was reorganized, with Antinori acquiring the winery and vineyards from the other partners. Wine Alliance, Hiram Walker's California wine company (which also owns William Hill, Clos du Bois and Callaway), became the sales and marketing unit as well as the manager of the vineyards.

This winery does, however, still have considerable potential. Atlas Peak appears to be an ideal place to grow red wines, given the excellent quality of the many eastern hillside vineyards. And clearly it's too early to count Antinori out; his family has been in the wine business for more than 600 years. But considering how many grand Cabernets are being made in Napa Valley—and the uninspired nature of the winery's Sangiovese and Cabernet blends—disappointing seems the best adjective to describe Atlas Peak's efforts.

TASTING NOTES

CABERNET SAUVIGNON ATLAS PEAK (★★): As variable as the Consenso; dark and detailed one year, austere and uninspired the next.

CABERNET SAUVIGNON ATLAS PEAK CONSENSO VINEYARD (★★): Highly inconsistent: simple and modestly fruity one year, smooth, supple and flavorful the next.

SANGIOVESE ATLAS PEAK AND RESERVE (★★): Consistently earthy and dry, with medium-weight cherry and berry flavors; lacking in extra dimensions.

AU BON CLIMAT (★★★★)
Santa Barbara County
Founded: 1982. **Owner:** James Clendenen. **Winemaker:** James Clendenen. **Second Label:** Il Podere Dell' Olivos.

MAJOR WINES: PRICE, CASES, RATING

Chardonnay Arroyo Grande Valley Talley
  Reserve
  ($25, 1,000)   ★★★★
Chardonnay Edna Valley Alban Vineyard
  ($35, 650)   ★★★★
Chardonnay Santa Barbara County
  ($18, 5,500)   ★★★★
Chardonnay Santa Barbara County
  Le Bouge D'à Côté
  ($25,1,600)   ★★★★
Chardonnay Santa Barbara County
  Nuits-Blanches
  ($40, 400)   ★★★★
Chardonnay Santa Ynez Valley
  Sanford & Benedict Reserve
  ($35, 600)   ★★★★
Pinot Blanc Santa Barbara County
  Bien Nacido Reserve
  ($20, 300)   ★★★
Pinot Noir Arroyo Grande Valley
  Rosemary's Talley Vineyard
  ($50, 100)   ★★★★★
Pinot Noir Arroyo Grande Valley
  Piccho and Rincon
  ($40, 250)   ★★★
Pinot Noir Arroyo Grande Valley
  Rincon and Rosemary's
  ($40, 250)   ★★★★
Pinot Noir California Isabelle
  ($50, 200)   ★★★★
Pinot Noir Santa Barbara County
  La Bauge Au-dessus
  ($25, 750)   ★★★★
Pinot Noir Santa Maria Valley
  ($18, 5,000)   ★★★
Pinot Noir Santa Ynez Valley
  Sanford & Benedict Reserve
  ($35, 400)   ★★★
Pinot Noir Santa Ynez Valley
  Sanford & Benedict Vineyard
  ($35, 400)   ★★★

ALSO PRODUCED
Aligoté Central Coast ($12, 200); Pinot Blanc Santa Barbara County ($12, 1,200); Pinot Gris Santa Barbara County Bien Nacido Reserve ($20, 200).

WINERY DATA
Case Production: 16,000. **Acres Owned:** 50 acres leased in Bien Nacido Vineyard, Santa Barbara County. **Varietals by Acre:** Chardonnay (15 acres), Pinot Blanc (10), Pinot Gris (5), Pinot Noir (20). **Vineyard Designations:** Alban Vineyard (Chardonnay), Bien Nacido (Pinot Blanc, Pinot Noir), Sanford & Benedict (Pinot Noir), Piccho (Pinot Noir), Rancho Vinedo (Pinot Noir), Rincon

(Pinot Noir), Rosemary's (Pinot Noir), Talley Vineyard (Pinot Noir, Chardonnay). **Varietals Purchased:** Pinot Noir and Chardonnay (Arroyo Grande, Santa Barbara County).

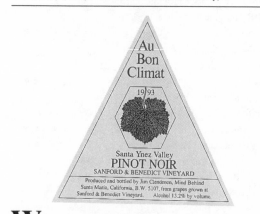

Without a doubt, Jim Clendenen continues to make some of the most highly individualistic, sometimes idiosyncratic and typically expressive wines in California, no matter which grapes he's working with. At times he's been on top of the Chardonnay and Pinot Noir worlds, riding the crest of a string of solid vintages. But he can also stumble and make some challenging wines that desperately need time, patience and understanding. My notes on Au Bon Climat's wines over the years show wild swings from highly manipulated, sometimes downright funky wines in difficult years to stylized, zesty, explosive barrel-fermented wines in others. At their best, these are brilliant, complex, truly intriguing and genuinely exciting Chardonnays, Pinot Blancs and Pinot Noirs.

As an unabashed lover of Burgundy wines, Clendenen's passion and dedication to the Burgundian style is unchallenged. Yet there are times when he seems to over-make (or under-make) his wines; they'll be missing the one or two ingredients that would allow them to achieve greatness. He seems less concerned with consistency of style or quality than with individually expressive wines.

Clendenen's winemaking career dates back to the 1970s, when he worked as a winemaker at Zaca Mesa. In 1982, he and Adam Tolmach (also a Zaca Mesa grad) started Au Bon Climat. After making wine at several rented locations, they settled in 1988 in a portion of Bien Nacido Vineyard's facilities in Santa Maria Valley. Clendenen also works with his wife, Morgan Toral, on her Cold Heaven label (see entry).

Clendenen is highly skilled at picking grape sources, and has a remarkable track record for excellence given that his sources are often pulled out from under him when vineyards are sold and contracts ended. Until recently, his wines have enjoyed cult status, winning the highest praise in some corners and eliciting raised eyebrows of doubt in others. ABC's best efforts, small 200- to 300-case lots of vineyard-designated wines, are often snapped up by devotees and thus are difficult to obtain, but they are usually vastly superior to his generic wines of the same type made in 1,000-case lots. It's not surprising that those who taste only the regular wines have no appreciation for what happens when it all comes together in one of ABC's bold and distinctive Reserve or vineyard-designated bottlings.

TASTING NOTES

CHARDONNAY ARROYO GRANDE VALLEY TALLEY RESERVE (★★★★): Inconsistent, but when it's right it offers a tremendously rich and concentrated mouthful of Chardonnay.
1996: Intense, with ripe, rich, creamy pear, fig, melon and apple flavors, turning complex. **92**
1993: Medium-bodied but well focused and flavorful, with toasty oak, ripe pear, honey and spicy citrus notes, turning complex and elegant on the finish. **90**

CHARDONNAY EDNA VALLEY ALBAN VINEYARD (★★★)
1996: A mild vegetal streak runs through the tart pear, spice and fig notes, but the finish is long and complex. **90**
1995: Tart green pear and pineapple flavors that lean toward the barely ripe side, with moderate depth. **87**

CHARDONNAY SANTA BARBARA COUNTY (★★★★): Bold, ripe and intense, rich and tightly wound, often earthy, leesy and marked by toasty oak, but also tremendously complex and full-bodied.
1995: Complex and full-bodied, with many juicy tiers of ripe pear, spice, hazelnut, honey and a touch of minerals. **90**

CHARDONNAY SANTA BARBARA COUNTY LE BOUGE D'À CÔTÉ (★★★★)
1996: Intense and a touch coarse, but the fruit flavors are ripe, complex and appealing, with earthy pear, spice and citrus notes. **88**
1995: Intense, complex and concentrated, with a tart edge to the ripe pear, citrus, honey and hazelnut flavors. **92**

1994: Flavorful, with ripe pear, peach, citrus and hazelnut notes that turn smooth and elegant on the long, complex finish. **87**

CHARDONNAY SANTA BARBARA COUNTY NUITS-BLANCHES (★★★)
1996: Tight and flinty, with complex, concentrated, pear, spice, cream and earthy citrus flavors that are deep and long. **90**

CHARDONNAY SANTA YNEZ VALLEY SANFORD & BENEDICT RESERVE (★★★★)
1996: Delicious, smooth, ripe and creamy, with pretty spice, nectarine, pear and fig flavors that are rich and concentrated. **92**
1995: Serves up fresh, ripe apple, pear and melon flavors; intense and concentrated, with a long, full finish. **91**
1994: Lithe, smooth and supple, with a pleasantly earthy accent to the hazelnut and green pineapple notes. **89**
1993: A deceptively subtle wine that builds richness and intensity, with complex spice, pear and pineapple flavors and toasty oak. **93**

PINOT BLANC SANTA BARBARA COUNTY BIEN NACIDO RESERVE (★★★)
1997: Smooth and rich, with a core of fig, grapefruit, and melon, turning tight and flinty on the finish, where the flavors linger. **89**
1996: A big, ripe, full-bodied wine, built around a core of fig and melon flavors. **87**
1995: A touch coarse, with earthy honey and leesy flavors. **86**

PINOT NOIR ARROYO GRANDE VALLEY PICCHO AND RINCON (★★★)
1996: Struggles to move into the fully ripened category, with cedary oak, blackberry, black cherry and spice flavors. **87**

PINOT NOIR ARROYO GRANDE VALLEY RINCON AND ROSEMARY'S (★★★★)
1994: A touch earthy and leathery, yet manages to deliver enough ripe cherry and plum flavors to give depth and complexity. **90**

PINOT NOIR ARROYO GRANDE VALLEY ROSEMARY'S TALLEY VINEYARD (★★★★★)

1996: Lean and leathery, with hard-edged tannins. It's best to wait on this one in the hopes that the plum and berry flavors will eventually emerge. **87**
1993: Ripe and smoky, with pretty black cherry, plum, anise and toasty oak flavors; shows uncommon richness and depth. **91**

PINOT NOIR SANTA BARBARA COUNTY BIEN NACIDO VINEYARD LA BAUGE
1995: Lean and spicy up front, with herb, tea and leathery notes, but the ripe cherry, cola and berry flavors fill out a complex finish. **92**

PINOT NOIR SANTA BARBARA COUNTY LA BAUGE AU-DESSUS (★★★★)
1996: Initially tight and earthy, but ripe cherry, loganberry and wild berry flavors emerge, giving this wine added depth and dimension. **87**
1994: Austere, with firm tannins, this is a tightly wound wine with a crisp band of cherry, cola and spice flavors, and a slight leathery edge. **86**

PINOT NOIR SANTA MARIA VALLEY (★★★): The least exciting Pinot Noir. Usually light and somewhat tart, although the style varies.
1997: Distinct for its tart sour cherry and wild berry flavors; made in a lighter, earthier style that is best suited for near-term consumption. **84**
1996: Light and spicy, with herb, rhubarb and cola edges to the tea and cherry-like flavors. **84**
1994: Combines ripe, bright and lively cherry, berry and cola notes, with good richness and intensity. **88**

PINOT NOIR SANTA YNEZ VALLEY SANFORD & BENEDICT RESERVE (★★★)
1995: A racy wine, with an earthy core of cherry and berry flavors and dry, earthy, tea-like tannins. **87**

PINOT NOIR SANTA YNEZ VALLEY SANFORD & BENEDICT VINEYARD (★★★): Variable. Sometimes tannic and stemmy; other times racy, with attractive herb and cherry flavors.
1996: Tough, with firm, stemmy tannins. It takes time to work into the earthy cherry and wild berry flavors, yet on the finish the flavors are appealing. **87**
1993: Well-oaked, but ripe wild berry and cherry flavors fill it in, making this wine both complex and elegant. **89**
1991: Rich, smooth and elegant, with intense spice, cherry, raspberry and earth notes that glide across the palate. **91**

AZALEA SPRINGS CELLARS (★★★)
Napa Valley
Founded: 1991. **Owner:** Norman & Norah Stone.
Winemaker: Kent Rasmussen.

MAJOR WINES: PRICE, CASES, RATING
Merlot Napa Valley
  ($30, 1,329)   ★★★

WINERY DATA
Case Production: 1,329. **Acres Owned:** 6 acres on Diamond Mountain, Napa Valley. **Varietals by Acre:** Merlot (6 acres).

This small Diamond Mountain producer has found a niche with Merlot, regularly producing very good, complex, cedar and currant-flavored wines like its 1995 vintage (88 points). The 1994 vintage (91) justifies a ★★★ rating for the winery overall, and indicates that there is potential for wines with greater depth and richness.

TASTING NOTES

MERLOT NAPA VALLEY (★★★): Charming Merlot from an area where it often doesn't excel. Makes it evident that Napa Valley is a fine place to grow this tricky grape.
1995: Intense, with complex cedar, spice, currant and berry flavors that are woven together nicely, turning supple on the finish. **88**
1994: Rich, smooth and full-bodied, with lots of plum, currant and cherry notes and a plush, complex texture. **91**
1992: The currant, coffee, cherry and anise notes are ripe, supple and well proportioned, turning crisp and tannic on the finish. **88**
1991: Smooth, plush and elegant, with a core of ripe, spicy currant, black cherry and plum flavors. **88**

BABCOCK VINEYARDS (★★★)
Santa Ynez Valley, Santa Barbara County
Founded: 1984. **Owner:** Walter, Mona & Bryan Babcock. **Winemaker:** Bryan Babcock.

MAJOR WINES: PRICE, CASES, RATING
Chardonnay Santa Barbara County
  ($18, 6,000)   ★★
Chardonnay Santa Ynez Valley Grand Cuvée
  ($30, 2,000)   ★★★★

Chardonnay Santa Ynez Valley
  Mt. Carmel Vineyard
  ($30, 800)   ★★★
Gewürztraminer Santa Ynez Valley
  Estate Grown
  ($16, 500)   ★★★
Pinot Gris Santa Barbara County
  ($14, 1,500)   ★★
Pinot Noir Santa Barbara County
  ($20, 2,000)   ★★★
Pinot Noir Santa Ynez Valley Grand Cuvée
  ($40, 500)   ★★★
Sangiovese Santa Barbara Valley Eleven Oaks
  ($30, 1,000)   ★★
Sauvignon Blanc Santa Barbara County
  Eleven Oaks
  ($20, 2,000)   ★★★★

ALSO PRODUCED
Chardonnay Santa Barbara County One Ton Per Acre ($20, 1,000); Chardonnay Santa Maria Valley Bien Nacido Vineyard Block W Gravelly Vein ($30, 900); Fathom Santa Barbara County ($30, 1,000); Pinot Noir Santa Ynez Valley Casa Cassara ($30, 500); Syrah Santa Barbara County Black Label Cuvée ($30, 1,000).

WINERY DATA
Case Production: 20,000. **Acres Owned:** 71 acres in Santa Ynez Valley. **Varietals by Acre:** Albariño (0.5 acres), Chardonnay (25), Gewürztraminer (5), Pinot Gris (5), Pinot Noir (25), Sauvignon Blanc (5), Syrah (5), Tempranillo (0.5). **Vineyard Designations:** Mt. Carmel Vineyard (Chardonnay, Pinot Noir). **Varietals Purchased:** Cabernet Franc (Santa Barbara County), Chardonnay (Santa Ynez Valley, Santa Barbara County), Pinot Gris (Santa Barbara County), Pinot Noir (Santa Ynez Valley, Santa Barbara County), Sangiovese (Santa Barbara County), Sauvignon Blanc (Santa Barbara County), Syrah (Santa Barbara County).

This family-owned winery now holds 71 acres in Santa Ynez Valley. While stylistic inconsistencies have hurt earlier vintages, things have begun settling down and better wines are emerging, led by the Chardonnay Grand Cuvee, Pinot Noir and Sauvignon Blanc from Eleven Oaks Ranch; the Gewürztraminer can also be very good. New bottlings of Pinot Noir, Syrah and a Cabernet Franc-Merlot-Cabernet Sauvignon called Fathom have joined the lineup. Experimental lots of two Spanish varieties, Albariño and Tempranillo, are on the way.

In 1995 Babcock formed a partnership with Anne Rice, author of *Interview With a Vampire*, and began producing Chardonnay, Syrah and a claret under the Cuvée Lestat designation. The labels for each of the wines displayed a different work of art by Stan Rice, the author's husband. The partnership, while amicable, was short-lived, and the wines have rejoined Babcock's other blends.

Tasting Notes

Chardonnay Santa Barbara County (★★)
1997: Crisp and earthy, it works its way into more complex, tangy nectarine, lemon-lime and citrus flavors, holding its focus through the finish. **88**

Chardonnay Santa Barbara County Cuvée Lestat (★★★★)
1996: Smooth, rich and creamy, with pear, fig, honey, vanilla and spicy oak flavors that gain momentum and linger on the finish. **90**

Chardonnay Santa Barbara County One Ton Per Acre (★★★)
1995: Lean, tight and focused, with a crisp core of tart, lemon-tinged pear and apple flavors. **89**

Chardonnay Santa Maria Valley Bien Nacido Vineyard Block W Gravelly Vein (★★★★)
1996: Rich and tightly focused, with elegant tropical fruit, apple and pear notes among the subtle oak shadings. **91**

Chardonnay Santa Ynez Valley Grand Cuvée (★★★★)
1996: A bright, rich, intensely concentrated wine packed with ripe, spicy pear, pineapple, guava and citrus flavors; turns complex on the finish. **92**
1995: Tight, rich, intense and lively, with a sharply focused core of pear, citrus and melon flavors. **90**

Chardonnay Santa Ynez Valley Mt. Carmel Vineyard (★★★)
1996: Lots of ripe, rich, complex fruit flavors and pretty oak nuances, with tiers of spicy pear, apple, melon and hazelnut notes. **92**
1994: Elegant and polished, with ripe pear and peach flavors and light oak and earthy shadings. **88**

Pinot Noir Santa Barbara County (★★★)

1997: Marked by a broad array of flavors, including spicy, earthy cola, wild berry, cherry, sage and spice; made in a medium-bodied, crisp, trim style. **87**
1996: Smooth and polished, with earthy, spicy, vegetal and peppery Pinot Noir flavors, turning murky on the finish. **86**
1995: Young, tight and focused, with intense black cherry, plum, anise and a hint of wild berry flavors that turn smooth on the finish. **91**

Pinot Noir Santa Ynez Valley Estate Grown (★★★): Will be labeled Grand Cuvée starting with the 1997.
1996: Rich and polished, with a well-focused center of black cherry, spice and wild berry flavors that pick up toasty oak, coffee and vanilla notes. **90**
1993: While dry and tannic, it offers glimpses of ripe black cherry, herb and cola notes. **84**

Sangiovese Santa Barbara County Eleven Oaks (★★)
1996: Complex, with pleasant cranberry, cherry and spicy notes, picking up cedary oak and firm tannins on the finish. **86**
1993: Soft and ripe, a prune flavor running through the velvety berry and floral notes. Modest tannins make it ready now. **85**

Sauvignon Blanc Santa Barbara County Eleven Oaks (★★★★)
1997: Tight, with a lemony core, fans out on the palate, showing hints of grapefruit, almonds, herbs and mineral notes. The finish is long and refreshing. **88**
1996: Slightly earthy and brightly textured with an herbal, grassy edge backed by grapefruit, lime and fig flavors. A forceful wine. **89**
1995: A zingy blend of ripe melon, passionfruit, lemon, orange and a delicate grassy tone, lightly framed by sweet oak. Complex and delicious. **91**
1994: Crisp and lively, with sharply focused onion-skin-scented pear, apple and citrus flavors. Long finish has herbal notes. **89**

Syrah Santa Barbara County Cuvée Lestat (★★★)
1996: Dark, ripe and firmly tannic; the core of fruit flavors is surrounded by spicy berry, mineral, leather and cedar notes. **88**

1995: Dark, intense and peppery, with a meaty, vegetal edge to the plum and wild berry flavors. **85**

BACIO DIVINO (★★★)
Napa Valley
Founded: 1993. **Owner:** Claus Janzen. **Winemaker:** Claus Janzen.

MAJOR WINES: PRICE, CASES, RATING
Cabernet Sauvignon-Sangiovese-Petite
  Sirah Napa
  ($50, 1,000)   ★★★

WINERY DATA
Case Production: 1,000. **Varietals Purchased**: Cabernet Sauvignon (Mount Veeder, Pope Valley), Petite Sirah (St. Helena), Sangiovese (Atlas Peak, Pope Valley).

A plush, complex and richly flavored 1995 Cabernet-Sangiovese-Petite Sirah (91 points) indicates that Claus Janzen, a marketing manager for Caymus Vineyards, is on the right track. Janzen purchases Napa Valley grapes for this atypical blend. Worth watching.

BAILEYANA VINEYARDS (★★)
San Luis Obispo County
Founded: 1971. **Owner:** Paragon Vineyard Co. Inc. **Winemaker:** Christian Roguenant.

MAJOR WINES: PRICE, CASES, RATING
Chardonnay Edna Valley
  ($17, 3000)   ★★

ALSO PRODUCED
Pinot Noir Edna Valley ($18, 400); Pinot Noir Edna Valley Reserve ($18, 400).

WINERY DATA
Case Production: 6,000. **Acres Owned:** 990 acres (889 in Edna Valley, 101 in Paso Robles). **Varietals by Acre:** Cabernet Sauvignon (138), Chardonnay (561), Pinot Gris (18), Pinot Noir (138), Sauvignon Blanc (50), Sémillon (5), Syrah (68), Zinfandel (13) **Varietals Purchased:** Chardonnay (Edna Valley, Monterey County), Pinot Noir (Edna Valley).

O wned by the Niven family's Paragon Vineyard Co., Baileyana has failed to produce exciting wines in recent years despite the family's nearly 1,000 vineyard acres in the Central Coast. The 1996 Chardonnay (82), while rich and intense, lacked finesse. In 1999, in a effort to increase quality, winemaker Christian Roguenant, formerly of Laetitia Winery, was hired and construction of a winery was begun. There are plans to produce 20,000 cases.

BANNISTER VINEYARDS (★★★)
Sonoma County
Founded: 1989. **Owner:** Marty Bannister. **Winemaker:** Marty Bannister.

MAJOR WINES: PRICE, CASES, RATING
Chardonnay Russian River Valley
  Allen Vineyard
  ($25, 300)   ★★★
Chardonnay Russian River Valley
  Porter-Bass Vineyard
  ($24, 300)   ★★★
Pinot Noir Anderson Valley
  Floodgate Vineyard
  ($24, 300)   ★★★
Zinfandel Dry Creek Valley
  Bradford Mountain Vineyard
  ($18, 400)   ★★
Zinfandel Russian River Valley
  Rochioli Vineyard
  ($18, 170)   ★★★

WINERY DATA
Case Production: 1,500. **Vineyard Designations**: Allen Vineyard (Chardonnay), Floodgate Vineyard (Pinot Noir), Porter-Bass Vineyard (Chardonnay), Seghesio Vineyards Keyhole Ranch (Pinot Noir). **Varietals Purchased:** Chardonnay (Russian River Valley), Pinot Noir (Anderson Valley and Russian River Valley), Zinfandel (Dry Creek Valley).

A fter years of operating VinQuiry, an independent wine laboratory in Healdsburg, Marty Bannister launched her own brand in 1989, focusing on Chardonnay, Pinot Noir and Zinfandel. So far the Chardonnay and Pinot Noir have performed on equally appealing levels, although the 1994 Zinfandel from Rochioli Vineyard may be the best wine she's made.

TASTING NOTES

CHARDONNAY RUSSIAN RIVER VALLEY ALLEN VINEYARD
(★★★): A fine wine from a great vineyard.
1995: Complex and lively, with a pretty band of ripe
pear, apple, light oak, spice and vanilla. **90**
1994: Delivers a range of citrus, orange blossom, ripe
pear and tart apple notes; a subtle, understated style with
light oak. **88**

PINOT NOIR ANDERSON VALLEY FLOODGATE VINEYARD
(★★★)
1996: Strives for delicacy and complexity with a range
of with earthy, spice, tea, cola and currant flavors. A
touch of heat throws off the balance. **82**
1995: Offers a broad range of flavors, with bright, spicy
blueberry fruit and traces of herb, mushroom, tea and
earth. **87**

ZINFANDEL DRY CREEK VALLEY BRADFORD MOUNTAIN
VINEYARD (★★)
1995: An elegant style that features ripe cherry and
plummy flavors and light oak. **85**
1993: Elegant, with a modest core of spicy, peppery
raspberry and cherry flavors. **86**

ZINFANDEL RUSSIAN RIVER VALLEY ROCHIOLI
VINEYARD (★★★)
1994: Starts earthy, but then delivers tart raspberry, wild
berry and blackberry flavors, turning rich and complex. **92**
1993: Marked by a tarry, earthy accent to the spicy wild
berry flavors; turns tannic on the finish. **85**

BARBOUR VINEYARDS (★★★★)
St. Helena, Napa Valley
Founded: 1995. **Owner:** Jim Barbour. **Winemaker:**
Heidi Peterson Barrett.

MAJOR WINES: PRICE, CASES, RATING
Cabernet Sauvignon Napa Valley
  Barbour Vineyards
  ($75, 200)   ★★★★

WINERY DATA
Case Production: 200. **Acres Owned:** 2 acres in St. Helena.
Varietals by Acre: Cabernet Sauvignon (2 acres).

Vineyard manager Jim Barbour, a Napa Valley native,
planted his 2-acre Cabernet vineyard with budwood from
Grace Family Vineyards. The wine, made by Heidi
Peterson Barrett at Grace, is dense, rich and concentrated, but is produced in tiny lots and sold only through
Barbour's and the Grace Family's mailing lists. The 1995
(92 points) and 1996 (91) are delicious, smooth and complex wines.

LAWRENCE J. BARGETTO WINERY (★★)
Santa Cruz Mountains
Founded: 1933. **Owner:** Bargetto Family. **Winemaker:**
Paul Wofford. **Second Label:** Chaucer, Coastal Cellars.

MAJOR WINES: PRICE, CASES, RATING
Cabernet Sauvignon Santa Cruz Mountains
  ($18, 1,200)   ★★
Chardonnay Central Coast
  ($10, 6,000)   ★★
Chardonnay Santa Cruz Mountains
  Regan Vineyards
  ($18, 2,000)   ★★
Dolcetto California
  ($15, 1,000)   ★★
Gewürztraminer Monterey
  ($10, 2,000)   ★★
Gewürztraminer Santa Cruz Mountains Dry
  ($12, 1,000)   ★★
Merlot California
  ($18, 3,000)   ★★

ALSO PRODUCED
Cabernet Sauvignon California ($10, 3,000); Merlot Santa
Cruz Mountains Regan Vineyards ($24, 800); Pinot Noir
Santa Cruz Mountains Regan Vineyards ($18, 1,000).

WINERY DATA
Case Production: 50,000. **Acres Owned:** 36 acres in Santa
Cruz Mountains. **Varietals by Acre:** Chardonnay (11 acres),
Merlot (13), Pinot Noir (6), Italian Varietals (6). **Vineyard
Designations:** Regan Vineyards (Chardonnay, Pinot Noir,
Merlot). **Varietals Purchased:** Cabernet Sauvignon (Santa Cruz
Mountains), Chardonnay (Central Coast), Dolcetto (Central
Coast), Gewürztraminer (Monterey, Santa Cruz Mountains).

One of the oldest wineries in the Santa Cruz Mountains, Bargetto is known locally for its berry and fruit wines under the Chaucer label. The winery has upgraded the quality of its varietal wines, moving from rustic to more supple and inviting, although inconsistencies still plague the lineup. Cabernet and Chardonnay under the Cypress label were good values, although that brand is being phased out. A new lineup under the Legacy Series brand was slated for 1999, including an Italian-inspired red blend of Nebbiolo, Dolcetto and Refosco.

BARNETT VINEYARDS (★★★)
Spring Mountain, Napa Valley
Founded: 1984. **Owner:** Fiona and Hal Barnett.
Winemaker: Charles Hendricks.

MAJOR WINES: PRICE, CASES, RATING
Cabernet Sauvignon Spring Mountain
  District
  ($35, 900)   ★★★
Cabernet Sauvignon Spring Mountain
  District Rattlesnake Hill
  ($50, 100)   ★★★★
Chardonnay Napa Valley
  ($18, 500)   ★★
Pinot Noir Santa Lucia Highlands
  ($20, 200)   ★★

ALSO PRODUCED
Merlot Spring Mountain District ($25, 300).

WINERY DATA
Case Production: 2,000. **Acres Owned:** 14 acres in the Spring Mountain District of Napa Valley. **Varietals by Acre:** Cabernet Franc (3 acres), Cabernet Sauvignon (9), Merlot (2). **Varietals Purchased:** Cabernet Sauvignon (Spring Mountain), Chardonnay (Napa Valley), Merlot (Spring Mountain), Pinot Noir (Santa Lucia Highlands).

Barnett Vineyards has experienced some ups and downs in wine quality. Of late, the Cabernets from their 14-acre vineyard on Spring Mountain have been impressive, while the Napa Valley Chardonnay and the Santa Lucia Highlands Pinot Noir have rated in the good-to-very good range. Both the 1996 Cabernet Spring Mountain (88 points) and the 1996 Cabernet Rattlesnake Hill (93) are dense and rich with earthy currant, anise and mineral flavors and firm tannins; the Rattlesnake Hill is a more complex, concentrated wine.

BARNWOOD (★★)
Santa Barbara County
Founded: 1994. **Owner:** Nebil Zarif & Selim Zilkha.
Winemaker: John Clark.

MAJOR WINES: PRICE, CASES, RATING
Sauvignon Blanc Santa Barbara County
  ($10, 2,500)   ★★

ALSO PRODUCED
Cabernet Sauvignon Santa Barbara County ($15, 1,200); Chardonnay Santa Barbara County ($16, 2,500); Merlot Santa Barbara County ($18, 1,800).

WINERY DATA
Case Production: 8,000. **Acres Owned:** 380 in Santa Barbara County. **Varietals by Acre:** Cabernet Franc, Cabernet Sauvignon, Chardonnay, Cinsault, Grenache, Merlot, Mourvèdre, Petite Syrah, Sauvignon Blanc, Syrah, Tempranillo, Viognier, Zinfandel. **Varietals Purchased:** Bien Nacido Vineyard (Chardonnay), Pisoni Ranch (Chardonnay, Pinot Noir).

Owners Nebil Zarif and Selim Zilkha made fortunes in the oil and gas industry before turning to wine. In 1994 Zarif purchased 30 acres in Cuyama Valley in Santa Barbara County and has since expanded the estate to 2,000 acres with 380 acres planted. John Clark, previously winemaker for Corbett Canyon and Central Coast Wine Warehouse and a co-owner of Brophy-Clark winery (see entry), is making Cabernet, Chardonnay, Merlot and Sauvignon Blanc from estate-grown grapes. The 1997 Sauvignon Blanc (85 points) was tight, refreshing and citrus-flavored. There are plans to plant an additional 700 acres by the year 2000. Zarif and Zilkha also own Laetitia winery (see entry).

BARON HERZOG (★–★★★★)
Saratoga, New York
Founded: 1985. **Owner:** David Herzog. **Winemaker:** Peter Stern. **Second Label:** Herzog, Weinstock, Joseph Zakon.

MAJOR WINES: PRICE, CASES, RATING

Cabernet Sauvignon Alexander Valley
Special Reserve
($26, 1,000) ★★★★

Cabernet Sauvignon Alexander Valley
Special Edition
($46, 230) ★★★★

Cabernet Sauvignon California
($14, 23,000) ★

Cabernet Sauvignon Napa Valley
Special Reserve
($30, 480) ★★★★

Chardonnay Alexander Valley
Special Reserve
($18, 450) ★★★

Chardonnay California
($13, 15,000) ★

Chardonnay Russian River Valley
Special Reserve
($21, 480) ★★★

Chenin Blanc Clarksburg
($8, 20,000) ★

Sauvignon Blanc California
($8, 4,900) ★

Zinfandel California
($13, 3,200) ★

ALSO PRODUCED

Gamay Paso Robles ($8, 5,201); White Zinfandel
California ($8, 38,000).

WINERY DATA

Case Production: 120,000. **Varietals Purchased**: Cabernet
Sauvignon (Alexander Valley, Napa Valley, Paso Robles),
Chardonnay (Alexander Valley, Russian River Valley), Chenin
Blanc (Clarksburg, Dunningan Hills), Gamay (Paso Robles),
Sauvignon Blanc (Clarksburg, El Dorado, Paso Robles), Zinfandel
(Clarksburg, El Dorado, Lodi, Tulare).

Baron Herzog is a New York-based kosher wine producer making inexpensive, simple wines from grapes purchased throughout California. Like other kosher wines, these are heat-pasteurized, but Herzog's wines receive a flash pasteurization treatment which is less detrimental to wine quality than other methods.

A line of surprisingly complex and flavorful reserve wines, made with top-quality Sonoma County and Napa Valley grapes, was released in 1998, suggesting interesting possibilities for Herzog's future. The first efforts include a rich, complex 1996 Russian River Valley Special Reserve Chardonnay (88 points); a concentrated though herbal 1995 Alexander Valley Special Reserve Cabernet (86); and a dazzling, ripe, creamy 1995 Alexander Valley Special Edition Cabernet (93) that shows off lots of toasted oak, currant, plum and spice flavors.

BARTHOLOMEW PARK WINERY (★★)
Sonoma Valley
Founded: 1993. **Owner:** James Bundschu. **Winemaker:**
Antoine Favero.

MAJOR WINES: PRICE, CASES, RATING

Cabernet Sauvignon Sonoma Valley
Alta Vista Vineyards
($30, 500) ★★

Cabernet Sauvignon Sonoma Valley
Desnudos Vineyard
($35, 500) ★★

Chardonnay Sonoma Valley Estate
Vineyards
($22, 300) ★★

Chardonnay Sonoma Valley Weiler
Vineyard
($21, 300) ★★

Merlot Sonoma Valley Alta Vista Vineyards
($25, 400) ★★

Merlot Sonoma Valley Desnudos Vineyard
($30, 400) ★★

Merlot Sonoma Valley Estate Vineyards
($32, 250) ★★

Merlot Sonoma Valley Weiler Vineyard
($25, 500) ★★

Pinot Noir Sonoma Valley Estate Vineyards
($23, 500) ★★

ALSO PRODUCED

Cabernet Sauvignon Napa Valley Parks Vineyard ($29,
300); Merlot Napa Valley Parks Vineyard ($25, 300).

WINERY DATA

Case Production: 3,500. **Acres Owned:** 47 acres in Sonoma
Valley. **Varietals by Acre:** Cabernet Sauvignon (8 acres),
Chardonnay (8), Merlot (18), Pinot Noir (7), Zinfandel (6).
Vineyard Designations: Alta Vista Vineyards (Cabernet
Sauvignon, Merlot), Desnudos Vineyard (Cabernet Sauvignon,
Merlot), Parks Vineyard (Cabernet Sauvignon, Merlot), Weiler

Vineyard (Chardonnay, Merlot). **Varietals Purchased:** Cabernet Sauvignon (Napa Valley, Sonoma Valley), Chardonnay (Sonoma Valley), Merlot (Napa Valley, Sonoma Valley).

Jim Bundschu, owner of Gundlach Bundschu Winery, also owns this smaller winery. Originally Hacienda Winery, this property became Bartholomew Park when then-owner Frank Bartholomew, an enterprising journalist who had earlier helped to revive Buena Vista, sold the Hacienda name to Bronco Wine Co.

Bundschu owns 47 acres; each of the wines made under the Bartholomew Park Winery label is either estate-bottled or vineyard-designated. So far, quality has ranged from average to very good, with no single varietal dominating.

TASTING NOTES

CABERNET SAUVIGNON VARIOUS BOTTLINGS (★★): The Sonoma Valley Alta Vista Vineyard 1994 (86 points) showed tar, cedar and beefy Cabernet flavors; the 1995 (80) was dry and simple, with herbal flavors and dry tannins. The Sonoma Valley Desnudos Vineyard showed a similar pattern; the 1994 (88) was better than the 1995 (82), with the former showing seductive blackberry and cherry flavors.

CHARDONNAY SONOMA VALLEY VARIOUS BOTTLINGS (★★): Neither the Estate Vineyard 1995 (81 points) nor the 1996 Weiler Vineyard (82) inspired much interest.

MERLOT VARIOUS BOTTLINGS (★★): None of the four different bottlings from 1995—a fine Merlot year—was terribly exciting.

PINOT NOIR SONOMA VALLEY ESTATE VINEYARDS (★★): There is plenty of room for improvement here.

BAYLISS & FORTUNE (★★)
Monterey County
Founded: 1997. **Owner:** Mildara Blass Inc. **Winemaker:** David O'Leary & Adam Marks.

MAJOR WINES: PRICE, CASES, RATING

Chardonnay Monterey County		
($12, 27,000)		★★
Merlot Monterey County		
($13, 16,000)		★★
Zinfandel Mendocino County		
($13, 9,000)		★★

WINERY DATA
Case Production: 80,000. **Acres Owned:** 420 acres in Pope Valley, Napa Valley. **Varietals by Acre:** Not yet planted. **Varietals Purchased:** Cabernet Sauvignon (Monterey County), Chardonnay (Monterey County), Merlot (Monterey County), Zinfandel (Mendocino County).

Mildara Blass Inc. was the first major Australian company to enter the California wine market with their own brand. Cabernet Sauvignon, Chardonnay and Merlot are made from grapes purchased in Monterey County; Zinfandel is made from Mendocino-purchased grapes. The wines are made at a custom crush facility owned by Golden State Vintners (Edgewood, Summerfield, etc.) in Monterey. Mildara Blass has also purchased a 420-acre property in Pope Valley, which will be planted with Cabernet Sauvignon, Merlot and Shiraz.

The winery's first releases were both pleasant and affordable. The 1997 Zinfandel (84 points) was smooth, with hints of cherry, herb and spice, while the 1997 Merlot (80) showed only a modest range of cherry flavors before drying out. The 1997 Chardonnay (83) was slightly sweet-tasting, with spicy pear and oak notes.

BAYVIEW CELLARS (★★)
Napa Valley
Founded: 1992. **Owner:** Ken Laird & John Richburg. **Winemaker:** John Richburg.

MAJOR WINES: PRICE, CASES, RATING

Cabernet Sauvignon Napa Valley		
($16, 700)		★★
Charbono Napa Valley		
($16, 500)		★★
Chardonnay Carneros		
($16, 1,200)		★★
Merlot Napa Valley		
($16, 200)		★★

ALSO PRODUCED
Gewürztraminer California ($9, 300); Sauvignon Blanc Napa Valley ($14, 600).

WINERY DATA

Case Production: 10,000. **Varietals Purchased:** Cabernet Sauvignon (Napa Valley), Charbono (Napa Valley), Chardonnay (Carneros), Gewürztraminer (California), Merlot (Napa Valley), Sauvignon Blanc (Napa Valley).

This partnership brings together long-time Inglenook-Napa Valley winemaker John Richburg with vineyard owner and manager Ken Laird, who oversees some 1,400 acres in vines from Carneros to St. Helena. So far the wines, including Napa Valley Cabernet Sauvignon, Charbono, Merlot, and Carneros Chardonnay, have been on the lean side and not very expressive. I've tasted many of Richburg's finer efforts at Inglenook, so I know he can make great wines, but as of yet, Bayview's wines have not lived up to his previous standards.

BEAUCANON WINERY (★)

Rutherford, Napa Valley
Founded: 1986. **Owner:** Jacques de Coninck. **Winemaker:** Louis de Coninck. **Second Label:** La Crosse.

MAJOR WINES: PRICE, CASES, RATING

Cabernet Sauvignon Napa Valley Reserve
($14, 2,200) ★

Chardonnay Napa Valley Jacques de Coninck
($28, 600) ★★

Chardonnay Napa Valley Reserve
($12, 2,500) ★★

Merlot Napa Valley Reserve
($15, 2,000) ★

WINERY DATA

Case Production: 30,000. **Acres Owned:** 244 acres in Napa Valley. **Varietals by Acre:** Cabernet Franc (5 acres), Cabernet Sauvignon (82), Chardonnay (85), Chenin Blanc (5), Merlot (67).

Owner Jacques de Coninck, who heads a large Bordeaux negociant house, J. Lebegue, owns some 244 acres spread throughout Napa Valley. But for whatever reason—grapes in poor areas or mediocre winemaking—Beaucanon's wines are well below average, ranging from weak and unbalanced to modestly pleasing. The winery is located on the west side of Highway 29 in Rutherford.

BEAULIEU VINEYARD (★★★★)

Rutherford, Napa Valley
Founded: 1900. **Owner:** International Distillers & Vintners. **Winemaker:** Joel Aiken.

MAJOR WINES: PRICE, CASES, RATING

Cabernet Sauvignon California Coastal
($9, 155,627) ★★

Cabernet Sauvignon Napa Valley
($15, 48,548) ★★

Cabernet Sauvignon Napa Valley George de Latour Private Reserve
($50, 14,764) ★★★★★

Cabernet Sauvignon Napa Valley Rutherford
($15, 108,885) ★★★

Cabernet Sauvignon Rutherford Clone 4/Clone 6 Signet Selection
($100, 289) ★★★★★

Chardonnay Carneros
($12, 45,074) ★★★

Chardonnay Carneros Reserve
($25, 9,985) ★★★★

Chardonnay California Coastal
($9, 141,163) ★★

Merlot California Coastal
($10, 75,576) ★★

Merlot Napa Valley
($15, 35,907) ★★

Petite Sirah Napa Valley Signet Collection
($14, 580) ★★★

Pinot Gris Napa Valley Signet Collection
($16, 225) ★★

Pinot Noir California Coastal
($10, 28,648) ★★

Pinot Noir Carneros
($13, 13,572) ★★★

Pinot Noir Carneros Reserve
($30, 3,901) ★★★

Sangiovese Napa Valley
($16, 2,472) ★★★

Sauvignon Blanc California Coastal
($7, 12,425) ★★

Syrah Dry Creek Valley Signet Collection
($25, 1,010) ★★★

Tapestry Red Napa Valley Reserve
($20, 11,686) ★★★★

Viognier Napa Valley Signet Collection
($16, 1,188) ★★★
Zinfandel California Coastal
($9, 31,194) ★★
Zinfandel Napa Valley
($12, 19,583) ★★★
Zinfandel Napa Valley Signet Collection
($20, 568) ★★★★

WINERY DATA
Case Production: 750,000. **Acres Owned:** 1,029 acres (338 in Calistoga, 275 in Carneros, 303 in Rutherford, 113 in St. Helena). **Varietals by Acre:** Cabernet Franc (16 acres), Cabernet Sauvignon (319), Chardonnay (124), Carignane (1), Marsanne (1), Merlot (85), Mourvèdre (1), Petite Sirah (1), Petit Verdot (8), Pinot Noir (136), Primitivo (1), Sauvignon Blanc (60), Valdiguié (11), Viognier (2), Sangiovese (1), Syrah (4), Roussanne (1), Touriga (1), Pinot Gris and Viognier (15), Zinfandel (241).

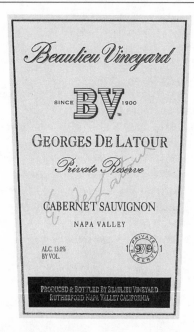

The amazing thing about Beaulieu Vineyard is that even with constant turmoil in its management ranks it is currently making the greatest wines in its fabled history. Not only is the flagship wine—the much-heralded BV Georges de Latour Private Reserve Cabernet Sauvignon—firmly among the finest in Napa Valley, but the entire lineup is better and more diverse than ever. New additions such as Tapestry Reserve (a Bordeaux-style blend), Zinfandel, Sangiovese and Syrah are all

welcome. Much of the credit for the step up in quality belong to its talented winemaker, Joel Aiken, who has become one of California's best.

One could easily write a book chronicling the history of Beaulieu and its vineyards, wines and cast of characters. Beaulieu (French for "beautiful place") was founded in 1900 by Frenchman Georges de Latour and modeled after the great French châteaux he admired. His splendid estate, across the highway from the winery, is still beautifully kept, with its towering trees, scenic gardens and panoramic views of the western foothills.

Georges de Latour had grand wines in mind when he selected property in Rutherford, the heart of Napa Valley. He began planting his first vineyard, BV No. 1, at the turn of the century, and followed seven years later with BV No. 2. Each of the vineyards, on the west side of Highway 29, measured nearly 100 acres.

For most of this century, BV's Private Reserve Cabernet was the most famous, and among the most prestigious, wines produced in California. Its long and distinguished reputation dates back to its first vintage in 1936. Through nearly 60 vintages, there have been many peaks and only a few low points for this wine. The great vintages from the 1930s and 1940s were made by the legendary Russian-born, French-trained winemaster André Tchelistcheff, who shaped the style of most of BV's early wines, and in the process helped establish Napa Valley's reputation for world-class Cabernet. Through the 1950s and 1960s, Tchelistcheff built on BV's greatness, continuing to refine its style and inspiring others to pursue fine wine in Napa Valley and elsewhere in California. Today, with literally scores of great California Cabernets being made, BV no longer dominates as it once did, yet this richly flavored, elegantly crafted wine has proven time and again to be consistently excellent and amazingly ageworthy.

Tchelistcheff also had successes with Chardonnay, and later, with Pinot Noir. BV's 1946 and 1947 vintages are reminders of how grand Carneros Pinot Noir can be. Under Tchelistcheff's direction, BV's wines steadily improved, production increased, and new wines were added, but the winery's strength remained its Cabernet. By the late 1960s, BV needed a cash infusion to revamp the winery, but the de Latour family could not afford to provide one. In 1969, the de Latours sold the winery to Heublein in Farmington, Conn.

By the time Tchelistcheff left BV in 1973, the winery had taken on a more corporate style, in which earnings and profits for shareholders shaped winemaking decisions. The winery's volume grew in subsequent years, reaching 450,000 cases by the early 1990s. BV remained a red wine house despite increased production of Chardonnay and Sauvignon Blanc, both of which were erratic in quality and style.

In 1994, with Aiken in charge, BV introduced Tapestry, its first Meritage, and a Merlot. The winery even tampered with its long-standing formula for BV Private Reserve: for the first time, the 1990 vintage was aged in both new French and American oak, and included 3 percent Merlot instead of the traditional 100 percent Cabernet. By the vintages of the mid-1990s, after a series of excellent years, BV's wines were still consistently improving, earning mostly high marks. The BV Coastal wines (previously known as Beautour) are usually good values.

TASTING NOTES

CABERNET SAUVIGNON CALIFORNIA COASTAL (★★): Conveys the impression that it's a Beaulieu Cabernet in name only, as it is light and herbal.

CABERNET SAUVIGNON NAPA VALLEY GEORGES DE LATOUR PRIVATE RESERVE (★★★★): Anchored by its superb Rutherford vineyards, this exemplifies a signature style of Napa Valley Cabernet. Ripe, rich and complex even in its earliest vintages; the latest vintages show a touch more oak. The wine ages gracefully, turning elegant and supple, and is never too tannic.

1995: Elegant, with ripe, plush currant, cherry, berry and spice flavors and complex cedar, anise, tobacco and mineral notes. **93**

1994: Firmly tannic, with a core of spicy currant and mineral-laced Cabernet flavors, plus cedary oak, coffee and sage notes. **93**

1993: Complex and harmonious, with a pretty core of ripe plum, cherry and currant flavors and shades of herb and cedary oak. **91**

1992: Austere, with a firm edge to the plum and cherry flavors; turns smooth and supple on the finish, with integrated tannins. **89**

1991: Smooth and elegant, with a cedar and spice edge to the cherry and currant flavors; turns tannic. **90**

1990: Ripe and spicy, with rich plum and cherry flavors that hold together nicely, finishing with fleshy tannins and good length. Impressive for its subtlety and finesse. **89**

1989: Crisp and austere, with a green edge to the tobacco and currant notes. **83**

1988: Simple, with a trim band of cedary currant, herb, anise and dried cherry flavors, turning dry on the finish. **84**

1987: Elegant and stylish, combining mature flavors with youthful ones. Shows cedar, currant and anise notes, finishing with soft, fleshy tannins. **91**

1986: Mature; a claret-style wine with dried cherry and anise notes. **87**

1985: Elegant and stylish, with layers of silky black cherry and currant aromas and flavors, a long, supple, lingering finish and fine, smooth tannins. Wonderful balance, with the depth and richness to age. **92**

1984: Ripe, smooth and elegant, with warm, rich and seductive currant and black cherry flavors, finishing with soft, fleshy tannins and fine depth. **90**

1983: Crisp, lean and tannic, but better balanced than most 1983s. **82**

1982: Mouthfilling and rich, with gorgeous fruit flavors. A well-knit wine on a firm framework. **88**

1981: A good but unexceptional wine, showing more gritty tannins than supple fruit. Well structured and balanced, but isn't a stand-out as a BV Private Reserve. **84**

1980: Bold and concentrated, a star of the 1980 vintage. Delicious, with ripe, massively rich, thickly concentrated layers of plum, cherry, currant and spicy oak flavors. **94**

1979: Smooth, complex and concentrated, a wine of enormous depth and finesse, with tiers of currant, black cherry and cedary oak flavors. **92**

1978: Mature, smooth, ripe and spicy, with a complex array of plum, currant, olive, cedar, tea and cherry flavors and elegant tannins. **90**

1977: A light and elegant wine in its youth, it has peaked and is now in decline, with diluted Cabernet flavors. **77**

1976: Very ripe and oaky, an unusually concentrated bottling with plum, cherry and raisin flavors, finishing with a chewy aftertaste. Despite its very ripe flavors and powerful personality, it hangs together quite well. **89**

1975: Smooth, elegant and harmonious, with smoky coffee and currant flavors and gentle tannins. **84**

1974: Despite bottle variation, at its best it reveals ripe, spicy currant and cherry flavors with a slightly nutty edge. **86**

1973: Once elegant and supple, this is a very good 1973 that has peaked. **85**

1972: A decent wine from a poor vintage, this one's past its prime. **72**

1971: Past its prime but holding, with light herb and currant notes. **78**

1970: A grand wine that's fully mature and still wonderfully complex, deep and intriguing, with layers of spice, currant, plum, cedar and herb flavors that turn rich, smooth and supple on the finish. **90**

1969: A graceful, elegant wine that continues to drink and age exceptionally well, with sweet, ripe, intense black cherry, plum and currant flavors framed by toasty oak. Great finesse and balance, with a long finish. This wine never underwent malolactic fermentation, which may account for its vibrant, youthful fruit profile. **90**

1968: The best wine of the decade at BV, with the 1969 its lone challenger, it's ripe, complex and enormously concentrated, with rich, focused plum, currant and black cherry flavors and a long, fruity aftertaste. **92**

1967: Tastes its age, but still has finesse and spicy black cherry flavors. **83**

1966: It's still a great drinking experience, with ripe black cherry, plum, anise and spice notes and a pretty touch of floral oak on the finish. Very persistent from start to finish. **87**

1965: Past its prime, this once very good wine is drying out. **78**

1964: My last note indicates this wine has dried out, with earthy, stemmy tea flavors. **70**

1963: The last time I tried this wine it offered a brief hint of dried cherry flavors, but quickly faded. It was good in its prime. **70**

1962: Fading, with anise and brown sugar flavors, but persistent on the finish. A good wine from a mediocre year. **73**

1961: Still elegant, with spicy tea and plum notes that fade and dry out. **76**

1960: In surprisingly good shape when I last tasted it. Fully evolved, with spicy herb, tea and plum flavors that dry out, but the flavors linger. Impressive color for a wine this age. **84**

1959: Long impressive for its elegance, grace and finesse. Fully mature, with ripe, rich, focused flavors, echoing spice, black cherry, currant and cedar notes on a long, lingering finish. Tastes as if it will age forever. **93**

1958: For me, this is the greatest Private Reserve produced in BV's first 30 years. It remains an incredibly delicious, wonderfully complex, delicate, deep and flavorful wine that is graced with layers of black cherry and spice flavors. Wine doesn't get much better. **98**

1957: Dried out and faded. Perhaps there is life in some bottles, but not in the ones I've tried, including several from the winery's cellars. **70**

1956: In its heyday a very fine wine, it's now fading, with tea, olive, plum and spice flavors. Worth the experience if you can find it. **87**

1955: Past its prime but still wonderful, with elegant, mature black cherry and olive flavors. **84**

1954: Aging well and still displaying a distinctive peppery edge to the dried cherry and plum flavors. **86**

1953: One of several great BV Private Reserves of the 1950s. This wine is aging amazingly well, with fresh, perfumed fruit aromas and elegant, supple black cherry, plum, herb and spice flavors. Long and complex on the finish. **92**

1952: A wine of great harmony, depth and complexity, delivering tiers of warm, rich, silky currant, black cherry, plum and spice flavors. An absolutely delicious wine with a long, full finish. **93**

1951: Considered by many the finest California Cabernet of this era. I've tried it more than a dozen times and it always shows very well. It's packed with rich, full-bodied plum, anise and black cherry flavors that are intense, concentrated and persistent. Recently I've tasted a dryness on the finish, so drink up. Worth going out of your way to try. **95**

1950: This wine has always reminded me of a Pinot Noir, with its lighter color, smooth, supple texture and rose petal aroma. It's a delicious wine, full of ripe plum, spice and cherry flavors and hints of rose on the finish. **89**

1949: This wine still displays a rich, intense personality with surprisingly firm tannins. The earthy black cherry and plum aromas and flavors are complex and lively for a wine this is age. **88**

1948: Every time I've tried this wine it has shown its age, with earthy, green, mature flavors. **73**

1947: From an excellent vintage, it shows incredible richness, complexity and harmony for a wine past its

50th birthday. There is still much to admire in this amazing wine that seems suspended in time. **93**

1946: Ripe, supple and generous even at this age, with plenty of black cherry, plum and spice nuances. **87**

1945: Oxidized. Enjoy as a taste of history. **70**

1944: It's not the Private Reserve bottling, but the regular '44 still possesses plenty of character for a wine this old. Tarry, earthy flavors show its maturity, but it's still enjoyable. **75**

1943: Very deep color, with spice, brown sugar and stewed plum flavors that offer fine depth, complexity and persistence. The texture is thick; the finish is the best part. **87**

1942: Dark color, with mature floral and fruit aromas and tight black cherry and earthy plum flavors. There's a metallic note on the finish, but otherwise it's quite complete and balanced. **85**

1941: Considered a fine year in Napa Valley, this '41 is an elegant, deep, rich wine with earthy black cherry and cedar flavors, gentle tannins and excellent length. **89**

1940: Dark in color, with deep cherry, currant and cedar flavors that are warm and spicy. The tannins are supple and there's plenty of fruit on the finish. **89**

1939: Dark in color, deep, rich and complex, with intriguing plum and black cherry flavors and subtle oak seasoning. Balanced and complex, better now than in previous tastings. Can still endure. **91**

1936: Smooth and elegant, with smoke, dry black cherry and spice notes. A timeless wine that's past its prime but not fatigued. **86**

CABERNET SAUVIGNON NAPA VALLEY RUTHERFORD (★★★): No longer a close second to the Private Reserve, this is still a solid Napa Valley Cabernet. It's not as rich or concentrated, but often shares the Reserve's ripe cherry and currant flavors. The 1994 (90 points) is a reminder of how delicious it can be.

CABERNET SAUVIGNON RUTHERFORD CLONE 4 AND CLONE 6 SIGNET COLLECTION (★★★★★): New additions such as Clones 4 and 6 are even more concentrated than the BV Private Reserve.

Clone 4 1995: Starts out with smoky, toasty oak, and then fills in the gaps with spicy cherry, currant and plum flavors and firm tannins. **92**

Clone 6 1994: Deeply concentrated, with rich currant, black cherry, herb, spice and vanilla tones. A wonderful aftertaste keeps pumping out the flavors. **93**

CHARDONNAY CARNEROS RESERVE (★★★★): The Reserve is increasingly more complex and concentrated, well-oaked and deftly balanced.

1995: Smooth, rich and creamy, with elegant, complex fig, melon, pear and citrus flavors that turn smoky. **93**

1994: Ripe, rich, smooth and harmonious, offering tiers of pear, honey, vanilla and spice as the flavors fan out. **91**

1993: Serves up fig, pear, apple and spice flavors in a round and forward style with toasty oak notes. **88**

MERLOT CALIFORNIA COASTAL (★★): Light and herbal, sometimes weedy.

MERLOT NAPA VALLEY (★★): Needs work; lacks depth and definition.

PETITE SIRAH NAPA VALLEY SIGNET COLLECTION (★★★)

1995: A dark, rich wine with black cherry, cassis and bell pepper notes and chewy tannins. **88**

PINOT GRIS NAPA VALLEY SIGNET COLLECTION (★★): Clean and refreshing, a nice alternative to Chardonnay and Sauvignon Blanc.

PINOT NOIR CALIFORNIA COASTAL (★★): Light, appealing, occasionally with berryish fruit.

PINOT NOIR CARNEROS RESERVE (★★★): More depth, purity of flavor and polish than the regular bottling.

1995: Wonderful ripe Pinot Noir flavors, with wild berry, black cherry, plum and spice notes, framed by light toasty oak that plays well with the fruitiness. **91**

1994: An elegant, exotic style, captures a wide range of flavors—black cherry, herb, spice and toasty, buttery oak. **90**

1993: Marked by strong, minty flavors that dominate the Pinot Noir flavors underneath. **83**

1990: Mature, drying, with a stemmy edge to the dried berry notes. **84**

PINOT NOIR NAPA VALLEY

1947: Not quite the richness and vibrancy of the 1946, but another masterpiece, warm, ripe, supple and complex, with tiers of anise and cherry, turning silky and smooth. Carneros-grown. **95**

1946: A fabulous wine with deep garnet color and smoky, meaty cherry, orange and stewed plum flavors that are smooth, crisp and lively. A delicious wine that shows no sign of tiring. Give it high marks for aging this long and this gracefully. **97**

Sangiovese Napa Valley (★★★): Rich and complex in 1994 (87 points) and 1995 (90), with dense, meaty flavors.

Sauvignon Blanc California Coastal (★★): Switched from Beautour to Coastal in 1998.

Syrah Dry Creek Valley Signet Collection (★★★): New to the line-up.
1995: Ripe, smooth and polished, with a sage and herbal edge to the meaty Syrah flavors. **91**

Tapestry Red Napa Valley Reserve (★★★★): A great addition to the portfolio. Typically tightly wound, dense and concentrated; this Cabernet blend is good early on but benefits from bottle age.
1995: Weaves together a supple, elegant band of cherry, currant, anise, sage and tarry notes, with a polished texture. **91**
1994: Dense and concentrated, with a tightly wound core of earthy currant, spice, plum and cherry flavors and firm tannins. **91**
1993: The ripe, supple cherry and spicy berry flavors are elegant but rather simple. **85**
1992: Features pretty mineral, currant, cherry and toasty oak flavors folded together in a neat, supple package. **88**
1991 Austere, with spice, currant, cherry and cedary oak flavors, all tightly wound and finishing with a tannic, herbal edge. **87**

Viognier Napa Valley Signet Collection (★★★): The initial release was very good, firm and focused with an unusually creamy finish.

Zinfandel California Coastal (★★): This wine is weedy and light, not as structured or complex as the Napa Valley bottlings.

Zinfandel Napa Valley (★★★)
1996: A lighter style Zinfandel, with lively berry, cherry and spice and firm tannins. **85**
1995: Ripe, rich and complex, with a jammy, pruny edge to the complex plum, cherry and raspberry flavors. **91**

Zinfandel Napa Valley Signet Collection (★★★★)
1997: A delicious Zinfandel; ripe, with plush blackberry, cherry, currant and spice flavors, zooming along on a long, rich, concentrated aftertaste and pretty, toasty oak notes. **93**

1995: Delicious, with complex spicy oak, ripe cherry, wild berry and currant flavors that are elegant and focused. **91**
1994: Shows a smooth and complex medley of spicy berry, cherry and plum flavors. **88**

Beckmen Vineyards (★★★)
Santa Barbara County
Founded: 1994. **Owner:** Thomas Beckmen. **Winemaker:** Steve Beckmen.

Major Wines: Price, Cases, Rating

Cabernet Sauvignon Santa Barbara County ($20, 1,000)	★★★
Chardonnay Santa Barbara County ($16, 3,300)	★★★
Sauvignon Blanc Santa Barbara County ($12, 1,100)	★★★
Syrah Santa Barbara County ($20, 1,000)	★★★

Winery Data
Case Production: 7,000. **Acres Owned:** 100 acres planted in Santa Barbara County. **Varietals by Acre:** Cabernet Franc (4 acres), Cabernet Sauvignon (20), Chardonnay (10), Grenache (19), Marsanne (4), Mourvèdre (4), Sauvignon Blanc (13), Syrah (26). **Varietals Purchased:** Cabernet Franc (Santa Ynez Valley), Cabernet Sauvignon (Santa Barbara County), Chardonnay (Santa Maria Valley), Grenache (Santa Ynez Valley), Merlot (Santa Ynez Valley), Mourvèdre (Santa Ynez Valley), Sauvignon Blanc (Santa Maria Valley), Syrah (Santa Barbara County).

Tom Beckmen, founder and C.E.O. of the music keyboard company Roland Corp., started Beckmen Vineyards with his son Steve. After a series of well-made, often distinctive Chardonnays, Cabernets and Sauvignon Blancs, their focus has moved toward Rhône varietals. The 1996 Syrah (89 points) was impressive for its firm structure and rich, jammy black currant, anise and plum flavors. Worth watching.

BEDFORD THOMPSON WINERY & VINEYARD (★★–★★★)
Santa Barbara County
Founded: 1994. **Owner:** David Thompson, Stephan Bedford. **Winemaker:** Stephan Bedford.

MAJOR WINES: PRICE, CASES, RATING
Chardonnay Santa Barbara County
($16, 800) ★★
Pinot Gris Santa Barbara County
($14, 150) ★
Syrah Santa Barbara County
($20, 1,500) ★★★

ALSO PRODUCED
Cabernet Franc Santa Barbara County ($20, 1,300); Gewürztraminer Santa Barbara County ($12, 300); Viognier Santa Barbara County ($18, 150).

WINERY DATA
Case Production: 4,200. **Acres Owned:** 42 acres in Santa Barbara County. **Varietals by Acre:** Cabernet Franc (9 acres), Chardonnay (3), Grenache (3), Mourvèdre (3), Petite Sirah (2), Pinot Gris (3), Syrah (19). **Varietals Purchased:** Gewürztraminer (Santa Barbara County), Pinot Gris (Santa Barbara County), Viognier (Santa Barbara County).

Following the lead of local vintners, Stephan Bedford and David Thompson are focusing on Cabernet Franc and Rhône varietals. The Syrah has been impressive; the 1995 (88 points) featured dense cherry, floral, plum and meaty, smoky flavors. So far, the white wines have been less distinctive. Should be worth watching.

BEHRENS & HITCHCOCK (★★★–★★★★)
Napa Valley
Founded: 1993. **Owner:** Les Behrens & Bob Hitchcock. **Winemaker:** Les Behrens.

MAJOR WINES: PRICE, CASES, RATING
Cabernet Sauvignon Napa Valley
  Inkgrade Vineyard
  ($30, 150) ★★★
Cabernet Sauvignon Napa Valley
  Kenefick Ranch Vineyard
  ($30, 300) ★★★★
Merlot Oakville
  ($28, 100) ★★★
Zinfandel Napa Valley
  ($24, 250) ★★★

ALSO PRODUCED
Cabernet Franc Napa Valley ($30, 400); Cuvée Lola Red Napa Valley ($45, 100); Merlot Napa Valley ($28, 700); Ode to Picasso Napa Valley ($45, 100); Petite Sirah Napa Valley ($26, 500); Syrah Napa Valley ($30, 300); Zinfandel Dry Creek Valley ($24, 100).

WINERY DATA
Case Production: 3,000. **Vineyard Designations**: Inkgrade Vineyard (Cabernet Sauvignon), Kenefick Ranch Vineyard (Cabernet Sauvignon). **Varietals Purchased:** Cabernet Franc (Napa Valley), Cabernet Sauvignon (Napa Valley), Merlot (Oakville, Napa Valley), Petite Sirah (Napa Valley), Syrah (Napa Valley), Zinfandel (Napa Valley, Dry Creek Valley).

Les Behrens and Bob Hitchcock make lots of good wines, often in very small quantities, and they're off to an encouraging start with their creative, well-crafted, stylistic wines made entirely from purchased grapes. A 1995 Napa Valley Cabernet TLK Ranch (91 points) showed complex, concentrated cherry and plum flavors while remaining smooth and elegant. (The TLK Ranch has since changed its name; it is now known as Kenefick Ranch Vineyard.) A 1994 Cabernet from Staglin Vineyard in Rutherford (92), a one-time production, features the smooth, rich, polished qualities that this winery is capable of. The 1995 Inkgrade offered a distinctive lead pencil and currant core, but was a bit on the stemmy side. Worth watching.

BEL ARBORS see FETZER VINEYARDS

BELL WINE CELLARS (★★)
Yountville, Napa Valley
Founded: 1991. **Owner:** Anthony Bell & John Baritelle. **Winemaker:** Anthony Bell. **Second Label:** Washington Street Cellars.

MAJOR WINES: PRICE, CASES, RATING
Cabernet Sauvignon Rutherford Baritelle Vineyards
  ($50, 2400) ★★

ALSO PRODUCED

Cabernet Sauvignon Sierra Foothills Brice Station Vineyard ($30, 960); Syrah Sierra Foothills Canterbury Vineyard ($30, 2,400); Viognier Santa Cruz Mountains ($26, 300).

WINERY DATA

Case Production: 6,000. **Vineyard Designations**: Baritelle Vineyards (Cabernet Sauvignon), Brice Station Vineyard (Cabernet Sauvignon), Hurley Vineyard (Merlot), Canterbury Vineyard (Syrah), Ziemann Vineyard (Viognier). **Varietals Purchased:** Cabernet Sauvignon (Rutherford, Sierra Foothills), Merlot (Rutherford), Syrah (Sierra Foothills), Viognier (Santa Cruz Mountains).

Former Beaulieu Vineyards winemaker Anthony Bell is part owner of this 6,000-case operation. The grapes used here are from John Baritelle Vineyards in Rutherford.

In recent vintages, this vineyard has failed to distinguish itself. The 1991 Cabernet Sauvignon Rutherford Baritelle Vineyards (83 points) was crisp, with sharp tannins. The 1992 (89) was better, with a rustic side to the currant and cherry flavors and more depth. But the 1994 (82), a great vintage for Napa Cabernet, turned out to be of medium weight and lacking in focus.

BELLA LONA see BRUTOCAO CELLARS

BELVEDERE WINERY (★★–★★★)
Russian River Valley, Sonoma County
Founded: 1982. **Owner:** William & Sally Hambrecht.
Winemaker: Kevin Warren.

MAJOR WINES: PRICE, CASES, RATING

Cabernet Sauvignon Dry Creek Valley	
($16, 4,900)	★★
Cabernet Sauvignon Dry Creek Valley Preferred Stock	
($25, 122)	★★
Chardonnay Alexander Valley	
($14, 10,000)	★★
Chardonnay Russian River Valley	
($18, 7,550)	★★★
Chardonnay Sonoma County	
($11, 34,000)	★★
Chardonnay Sonoma County Preferred Stock	
($22, 700)	★★★
Merlot Dry Creek Valley	
($16, 6,050)	★★
Merlot Dry Creek Valley Preferred Stock	
($22, 220)	★★★
Zinfandel Dry Creek Valley	
($18, 1,800)	★★

WINERY DATA

Case Production: 60,000. **Acres Owned:** 463 acres (301 in Alexander Valley, 60 in Anderson Valley, 98 in Dry Creek Valley, 4 in Russian River Valley). **Varietals by Acre:** Cabernet Franc (9 acres), Cabernet Sauvignon (74), Chardonnay (186), Gewürztraminer (13), Malbec (1), Merlot (81), Petit Verdot (7), Petite Sirah (2), Pinot Gris (5), Pinot Meunier (3), Pinot Noir (26), Sangiovese (5), Syrah (8), Zinfandel (43). **Varietals Purchased:** Chardonnay (Alexander Valley, Carneros, Russian River Valley), Zinfandel (Dry Creek Valley).

Bill Hambrecht, a San Francisco-based venture capitalist who is involved with a number of winery properties, assumed control of Belvedere in 1989. Chardonnay was traditionally the best wine made here, but quality took a dip in 1996. While the 1995 Chardonnays were impressive, including the Russian River Valley (91 points)—which featured complex and concentrated flavors of fig, melon and apricot—subsequent wines have shown only modest complexity and depth. The red wines have also been inconsistent, particularly the Merlot, which ranges from the mundane and tannic 1996 Dry Creek Valley (80) to the smooth, ripe and richly flavored 1994 Dry Creek Valley Preferred Stock (89).

BENESSERE (★★★)
St. Helena, Napa Valley
Founded: 1995. **Owner:** John & Ellen Benish.
Winemaker: Chris Dearden.

MAJOR WINES: PRICE, CASES, RATING

Sangiovese Napa Valley	
($25, 375)	★★★

WINERY DATA

Case Production: 1,500. **Acres Owned:** 33 acres in St. Helena. **Varietals by Acre:** Merlot (14.5 acres), Sangiovese (12), Sauvignon Blanc/Trebbiano (0.5), Syrah (1), Zinfandel (5). **Varietals Purchased:** Sangiovese (St. Helena, Sage Canyon, Sonoma County Green Valley), Zinfandel (Calistoga).

Tackling Sangiovese has proven difficult for most California wineries, but this new producer has chosen the fickle grape as its primary focus. The first vintage, an austere but flavorful 1995 Sangiovese (89 points) with licorice and black currant flavors, showed promise, while the 1996 (83) was simpler. Most of the large planting of Merlot on the property is being sold to Napa Valley wineries. Estate Zinfandel will be added in the future.

BENZIGER FAMILY WINERY (★★★)
Sonoma Mountain
Founded: 1981. **Owner:** Benziger Family. **Winemaker:** Joe Benziger & Terry Nolan.

MAJOR WINES: PRICE, CASES, RATING
Cabernet Franc Alexander Valley Imagery
($20, 600) ★★
Cabernet Sauvignon Sonoma County
($16, 29,820) ★★★
Cabernet Sauvignon Sonoma Mountain Reserve
($35, 1,018) ★★★
Chardonnay Carneros
($13, 44,040) ★★
Chardonnay Carneros Reserve
($25, 1,020) ★★★
Chardonnay Carneros Yamakawa Vineyards Reserve
($25, 300) ★★★★
Chardonnay Sonoma County
($13, 19,500) ★★★
Estate Tribute Sonoma Mountain Red
($25, 353) ★★★
Estate Tribute Sonoma Mountain White
($18, 307) ★★★
Fumé Blanc Sonoma County
($10, 15,205) ★★
Merlot Sonoma County
($16, 21,883) ★★
Merlot Sonoma County Reserve
($32, 720) ★★
Petite Sirah Paso Robles Imagery
($20, 472) ★★
Pinot Blanc North Coast Imagery
($18, 350) ★★★

Syrah Central Coast
($16, 1,400) ★★
Viognier Sonoma County Imagery
($18, 400) ★★
White Burgundy Napa Valley Imagery
($20, 1,300) ★★
Zinfandel Sonoma County
($18, 3,540) ★★

ALSO PRODUCED
Barbera Sonoma Valley Imagery ($20, 300); Malbec Alexander Valley Imagery ($20, 165); Pinot Noir California ($18, 730); Sangiovese Dry Creek Valley Imagery ($18, 480).

WINERY DATA
Case Production: 180,000. **Acres Owned:** 65 acres in Sonoma Mountain. **Varietals by Acre:** Cabernet Franc (7 acres), Cabernet Sauvignon (28), Malbec (2), Merlot (18), Petit Verdot (3), Sauvignon Blanc (3), Sémillon (3), Zinfandel (0.5). **Varietals Purchased:** Cabernet Sauvignon (Lake County, Mendocino County, Alexander Valley, Dry Creek Valley, Sonoma Valley), Malbec (Lake County, Alexander Valley), Merlot (Mendocino County, Sonoma Coast), Muscat Canelli (Lake County), Sauvignon Blanc (Lake County, Alexander Valley), Zinfandel (Lake County, Alexander Valley, Dry Creek Valley).

Benziger Family Winery, founded by Bruno Benziger and his family, started out as a small-scale operation in the sleepy hollow of Glen Ellen in Sonoma Valley. By the early 1980s, sales of its low-priced lines of Glen Ellen Proprietor's Reserve and M.G. Vallejo wines had rocketed past 3 million cases, making them two of the hottest brands of the decade. There was no doubt that these wines—Cabernet, Merlot, Chardonnay, Sauvignon Blanc and white Zinfandel—were sound values. The Benzigers showed a knack for finding high-quality bulk wines and good grape sources, and an ability to market their wares. In 1993, the Glen Ellen and M.G. Vallejo brands were sold to Heublein Inc.

In the mid-eighties, however—long before the sale to Heublein—the Benzigers began their return to the production of fine wines. The winery is still adjusting its new lineup, and makes about 180,000 cases, including several wines from its 85-acre estate vineyard on Sonoma Mountain. Most of these bottlings are solid and well made; occasionally, some are outstanding. The top-of-the-line wines, called Estate Tribute, are a red and a white

Meritage that both carry a Sonoma Mountain appellation. The Carneros Chardonnays show depth and complexity, while the Sonoma County Merlot, Pinot Blanc, Pinot Noir and Zinfandel display modest varietal character and are marked by creamy oak shadings. The Imagery Series features small lots of vineyard-designated wines that the winery dubs the winemaker's "Field of Dreams."

TASTING NOTES

CABERNET SAUVIGNON SONOMA COUNTY (★★★): Usually more rounded and supple than the Estate Tribute, with fleshier fruit flavors.

CHARDONNAY CARNEROS RESERVE (★★★)
1996: Ripe and creamy, with spicy peach, pear, fig and melon notes picking up pretty oak flavors. **91**
1995: Displays a complex interplay of rich fruit and spicy, vanilla-tinged oak, with hints of pear, apple, melon and apricot flavors. **91**

CHARDONNAY CARNEROS YAMAKAWA VINEYARDS RESERVE (★★★★)
1996: Well oaked, with rich, complex fig, pear, apricot and ginger notes. Holds its focus. **91**

ESTATE TRIBUTE SONOMA MOUNTAIN RED (★★★): This Cabernet blend consistently scores in the very good range, and is typically tightly wound, firmly tannic and built for aging.
1995: Tightly focused, with pretty, complex, black cherry, plum and currant flavors, hints of spice, herb and cedary oak accents. Finishes with a lingering aftertaste and hints of tea and spice. **89**
1994: Young, tight and tannic, but once you wade past the tannins the core of earthy currant, mint and spicy flavors are quite appealing. Firm tannins. **87**
1993: Tart and spicy, with a trim band of cherry and currant flavors that slowly unfold. Finishes with a dash of oak and herb and supple tannins. **87**
1992: Dark and intense, but with a measure of restraint. A Bordeaux-style blend featuring a range of herb, tea, cherry and currant flavors and finishing with a spicy accent and supple tannins. **87**
1991: Dominated by spicy, minty flavors, but with a pleasant core of currant and cherry flavors sitting underneath. Finishes with crisp tannins. **84**

BERINGER VINEYARDS (★★★–★★★★★)
Napa Valley
Founded: 1876. **Owner:** Beringer Wine Estates
Winemaker: Edward G. Sbragia.

MAJOR WINES: PRICE, CASES, RATING

Alluvium Blanc Knights Valley ($16, 15,000)	★★★
Alluvium Red Knights Valley ($25, 9,500)	★★★
Cabernet Sauvignon Howell Mountain Bancroft Vineyard ($80, 200)	★★★★★
Cabernet Sauvignon Knights Valley ($20, 59,000)	★★★
Cabernet Sauvignon Napa Valley Chabot Vineyard ($100, 200)	★★★★★
Cabernet Sauvignon Napa Valley Home Vineyard ($80, 200)	★★★★★
Cabernet Sauvignon Napa Valley Marston Vineyard ($80, 200)	★★★★★
Cabernet Sauvignon Napa Valley Private Reserve ($75, 11,500)	★★★★★
Cabernet Sauvignon Napa Valley State Lane Vineyard ($80, 200)	★★★★★
Chardonnay Napa Valley ($16, 90,000)	★★★
Chardonnay Napa Valley Private Reserve ($30, 19,900)	★★★★★
Chardonnay Napa Valley Sbragia Limited Release ($35, 1,900)	★★★★★
Merlot Howell Mountain Bancroft Ranch ($45, 7,000)	★★★★★
Nightingale Dessert Napa Valley ($22, 200)	★★★★★
Nouveau Red California ($7, 70,000)	★★
Pinot Noir Los Carneros Stanly Ranch ($30, 1,700)	★★★
Sauvignon Blanc Napa Valley ($9, 30,000)	★★★

Viognier Napa Valley
($32, 800) ★★★
Zinfandel North Coast
($12, 25,000) ★★

WINERY DATA

Case Production: 450,000 **Acres Owned:** 2,808 acres (1,807 in Napa Valley, 539 in Knights Valley, 125 in Howell Mountain, 184 in Carneros, 151 in Lake County). **Varietals by Acre:** Cabernet Franc (31 acres), Cabernet Sauvignon (774), Chardonnay (951), Malbec (15), Merlot (523), Pinot Noir (82), Riesling (35), Sauvignon Blanc (153), Sémillon (41), Viognier (27), Zinfandel (174). **Vineyard Designations:** Chabot Vineyard (Cabernet Sauvignon), Bancroft Vineyard (Cabernet Sauvignon), Marston Vineyard (Cabernet Sauvignon), Tre Colline Vineyard (Cabernet Sauvignon), Bancroft Ranch (Merlot), Stanly Ranch (Pinot Noir). **Varietals Purchased:** North Coast (Pinot Noir, Zinfandel, Gamay), California (Chenin Blanc, White Zinfandel).

In 1995, when the first edition of this book was published, my opening comment about Beringer was: "All things considered, Beringer Vineyards is a candidate for California's best all-around winery. It is doing many things exceptionally well—from its classy Reserve Chardonnays and Cabernets to its Howell Mountain Merlot and delicious Nightingale dessert wines—and nothing poorly." In 1997, the winery, long owned by Nestlé, was acquired by an investment group headed by Texas Pacific Group (TPG), and shortly thereafter, TPG made Beringer Wine Estates a publicly traded company. So far, all indicators show that TPG has every intention of maintaining Beringer's high standards. The winery owns or controls 2,800 acres mostly in Napa Valley and Knights Valley, including most of its best vineyards. Given the land's high caliber, this is a tremendous asset, and the best assurance of stability, consistency and quality grapes year after year.

Beringer has a proud history in Napa Valley. It was founded in 1876, by brothers Frederick and Jacob Beringer. Today, a re-tooled and modernized Beringer is one of Napa Valley's leading tourist attractions, as well as a first-rate winery. The historic Rhine House, an ornate Victorian structure, remains the centerpiece of this immaculately kept property. Visitors can tour the old stone caves where wines and barrels were once stored, and taste most of the wines, including some of the library reserves that are only sold at the winery. The winemaking takes place in a facility across the street which features a huge barrel-aging *chai*.

In 1972, Beringer became a whole new institution under the ownership of Nestlé, the Swiss food conglomerate, and the Labruyere family of Mâcon, France. By then the winery had fallen on hard times and the quality of its wines had steadily declined. The turnaround started with the hiring of Myron Nightingale, a savvy and talented winemaker who began to monitor quality more carefully, discarding offbeat, non-vintage wines and dramatically upgrading others. Moreover, Wine World Estates (the Nestlé division that is Beringer's corporate owner) lent considerable financial support, providing the winery with just about anything it needed to succeed, including the freedom to hire top professionals and let them manage the business.

The breakthrough vintage for the modern Beringer Vineyards came in 1977, when it introduced its first Private Reserve Cabernet, produced entirely from the Lemmon Ranch (now called Chabot) Vineyard in the hills east of St. Helena. That wine signaled the dawn of a new era. Since then, Beringer has built an impressive line of Reserve and vineyard-designated wines, including a classy Howell Mountain Merlot from Bancroft Ranch, a Meritage-style red and white from Knights Valley, and its dessert-style white, Nightingale. The winery's best-selling White Zinfandel is also very well made; it is best to drink it as you would a Riesling.

Even when the wines miss—which they rarely do—it only seems to inspire winemaker Sbragia to greater heights. A solid ★★★ Carneros Pinot Noir is among the latest additions to his long and remarkably successful product list.

TASTING NOTES

ALLUVIUM RED KNIGHTS VALLEY (★★★): Closing in on a ★★★★ rating. It's complex and concentrated, yet not on the scale of the Private Reserve. Drinks well early on for six to eight years after vintage. A blend of Merlot, Cabernet Sauvignon, Cabernet Franc, Petit Verdot and Malbec.

1995: Tightly focused, with a firm tannic backbone; a core of black cherry, plum and currant flavors picks up tea, herb and cedary notes. **90**

1994: Shows off appealing currant, coffee, berry and spicy flavors; the texture is supple and polished, and the finish is deceptively complex. **90**

1993: Ripe, smooth and spicy, with a pretty core of plum, currant and wild berry that turns elegant and complex, with anise and cedar notes. **90**

1992: Dark, ripe and well oaked, with strong toasty oak and roasted wood flavors that dominate the currant and black cherry underneath. **87**

1991: Ripe and firmly tannic, with spicy currant and plum flavors. Tight and compact, it will benefit from short-term cellaring. **88**

CABERNET SAUVIGNON HOWELL MOUNTAIN BANCROFT VINEYARD (★★★★★):

1994: Dark, ripe, rich and plush, with a wonderful core of dense currant, plum, black cherry and wild berry; gushes with concentrated fruit. **97**

CABERNET SAUVIGNON KNIGHTS VALLEY (★★★)

1995: A rich, potent, elegant wine, with ripe, polished currant, blackberry, cherry and spice flavors. **91**

1994: Tight and firmly tannic, it slowly unfolds to a core of ripe plum, black cherry, currant and spice. **91**

1993: Well crafted and elegant, with a range of ripe cherry, currant, herb and cedary oak flavors. **87**

CABERNET SAUVIGNON NAPA VALLEY CHABOT VINEYARD (★★★★★): Tighter, more compact and tannic than the Private Reserve; the focus is on vineyard expression, yielding a flavorful yet structured wine.

1994: A fruity style, with rich plum, black cherry and a dash of raspberry; ripe and jammy, turning tannic. **92**

1993: Austere and tightly wound, with firm tannins and attractive currant- and black cherry-laced fruit. **90**

1992: Dark, ripe, rich and concentrated, brimming with juicy plum, cherry, currant, anise and black cherry flavors. Shows lots of finesse. **93**

1991: Dark and intense, with floral and fruity aromas that turn elegant and supple, with a pretty core of black cherry, currant and plum, gaining a firm tannic edge. **93**

1990: Tight and deeply complex, with a core of rich, chewy currant, black cherry and cedary oak flavors, turning tannic on the finish. **92**

1989: Well crafted, bright and lively, with a wonderful integration of lush, elegant cherry, currant and spice notes. Tannins are firm but in check. **90**

1988: A lighter Chabot with a shallow nose and a narrow band of fruit flavor that has a raisiny edge, turning earthy and tarry on the finish. **84**

1987: Rich and intense, with mint-laced currant, berry, cherry and spice flavors, turning chewy with tannins. **93**

1986: Smooth and rich, with thick black cherry and currant flavors. Impeccably balanced, with a long, full finish. Amazingly complex; the best Chabot to date. **95**

1985: Mature, with herb, tar and earthy currant flavors that firm up on the finish. **86**

1984: A fine example of the rich, supple charm of the 1984 vintage, not as intense and backward as most bottlings from this vineyard. The bright plum, cherry and smoky anise flavors are attractive. **87**

1983: Austere, with drying tannins and a core of ample herb, currant, cherry and cedar flavors. Needs time to unfold. **85**

1982: Intense yet elegant, packed with fresh, ripe, juicy currant and cherry flavors, accented with a touch of mint, it's firm, lean and tannic. **89**

1981: Fully mature, with pure currant and berry flavors, ripe and full, with fine balance and plenty of mint and spice nuances. The tannins are deceptively soft; this wine has a fine backbone. **87**

CABERNET SAUVIGNON NAPA VALLEY MARSTON VINEYARD (★★★★★)

1994: Brimming with ripe, rich, concentrated cherry, currant, plum and anise flavors; a real mouthful of juicy Cabernet. **92**

CABERNET SAUVIGNON NAPA VALLEY PRIVATE RESERVE (★★★★★): Great grapes and equally great winemaking combine to give this wine a bold, rich, high-extract style, packed with complex flavors, potent but polished tannins, and excellent aging ability. Try it young, too, for its gobs of flavors.

1994: Beautifully integrated, muscular, dark, dense and enormously complex and concentrated, with shades of currant, black cherry, mineral, coffee, tar and anise. **95**

1993: Impressive intensity, richness, depth and concentration, this is a big yet elegant wine loaded with complex currant, leather, spice, sage and cedar flavors. **93**

1992: Complex, packing a load of ripe, juicy plum, black cherry, currant and spice flavors, all framed nicely by toasty, buttery oak. **95**

1991: Bright and lively, with a core of ripe, rich, juicy black cherry, currant, plum and anise flavors. Deep and complex, it finishes with strong fruit flavors and plush tannins. **95**

1990: Bold, rich and concentrated, with layers of ripe, spicy currant, black cherry and anise notes framed by toasty, buttery oak. Beautifully balanced, a wonderfully harmonious wine. **95**

1989: Rich and supple, with solid cherry, currant, plum and spice flavors that turn smooth and silky before the fine tannins kick in. **90**

1988: Mature, with earthy currant, anise, plum and cherry notes; turns dry and leathery on the finish. **88**

1987: Dark, ripe, intense and opulent; remarkably complex and youthful, with layers of currant, berry, herb, chocolate, mint, herb and spice, and supple tannins. **97**

1986: Mature; shows ripe, complex plum and currant flavors, with hints of anise and spice, turning dry and tannic. **89**

1985: Massive, ripe, rich and concentrated, with tiers of juicy cherry, currant, plum and spice flavors of uncommon depth and complexity. **97**

1984: A blockbuster, massively proportioned, extremely rich and powerful, packed with ripe fruit and layers of cherry, cedar, chocolate and toasty vanilla. It's a mouthful of Cabernet that has a silky texture to stand up to the tannins. **94**

1983: A tribute to concentrated fruit, it is now mature but still intense, with plenty of ripe, concentrated currant, herb and spice flavors. **89**

1982: Richly flavored and deftly balanced, with lush cedar, chocolate, plum and currant flavors that are long and full on the finish. **91**

1981: Thoroughly delicious, with its broad, rich, supple currant and anise notes and delicate tannins, it continues to improve with age and shows no sign of losing its charm. **91**

1980: Ripe, rich, lush and supple, fully mature, with cedar, currant, herb and mint flavors that are well integrated and complex. **89**

1978: Dark, ripe, rich and spicy, with a core of chocolate, currant, plum and cherry; aging beautifully. **92**

1977: Fully mature, with complex chocolate, herb, cedar and currant flavors that are rich and smooth, picking up a trace of tannin on the finish. **88**

CHARDONNAY NAPA VALLEY (★★★): Often merits outstanding marks, with ripe, rich, complex fruit and not as much new oak as the Private Reserve.

1997: Elegant, with apple, toast and citrus notes, finishing with complex toasted oak flavors. **87**

CHARDONNAY NAPA VALLEY PRIVATE RESERVE AND SBRAGIA LIMITED RELEASE (★★★★★): Nearly identical twins, featuring ripe, juicy, opulent fruit, lots of spicy toasty oak and amazing complexity. Sbragia tends to be a shade leaner. Best within the first one to three years; not one to cellar.

CHARDONNAY NAPA VALLEY PRIVATE RESERVE

1997: A tremendous effort. Ripe, complex, concentrated and spicy, with lots of pretty pear, nectarine, citrus and melon flavors, turning spicy with toasty oak. **93**

1996: Shows ripe pear, smoky oak, fig and vanilla flavors, turning rich and elegant and revealing a fine balance and integration of flavors. **95**

1995: Remarkable for its elegance, richness, finesse and complex integration of flavors, with tiers of ripe pear and spicy oak, and hints of citrus and pineapple. **94**

1994: Mature and declining, yet still rich, intense and deeply concentrated, with ripe pear, honey, hazelnut and butterscotch flavors. **90**

CHARDONNAY NAPA VALLEY SBRAGIA LIMITED RELEASE

1996: Big, ripe, rich and intense, with exotic, concentrated pear, fig, melon and toasty oak flavors. **94**

1995: A well-oaked style, with toasty, buttery flavors, but also a core of nectarine, pear, hazelnut and fig flavors that are ripe and concentrated. **93**

1994: A big, toasty wine that serves up layers of pear, fig, honey, melon and spice; rich and concentrated. **94**

MERLOT HOWELL MOUNTAIN BANCROFT RANCH (★★★★★): Arguably the best Merlot in California, it is dense, concentrated and enormously complex, if occasionally quite tannic as well. Despite its size and dimensions, it's best drunk two to five years after vintage.

1995: Complex, with a tight, tannic core of currant, anise, sage and spice and pretty vanilla-tinged oak shadings. **92**

1994: Ruggedly tannic, with a strong, earthy core of currant, sage and wild berry flavors. **89**

1993: Serves up a complex core of earthy cherry, currant and chocolate, and frames it with mineral flavors and a toasty oak overlay. **89**

1992: Smooth and harmonious, with a supple core of black cherry, currant, earth and toasty oak flavors that fold together nicely. **92**

1991: Complex and intriguing, with layers of cherry, currant, chocolate and buttery oak flavors that all fold together neatly. The flavors fan out on the finish, where it picks up a pretty vanilla edge. **90**

1990: Big, ripe, rich and tannic, packing in lots of currant, herb, cedar and spice notes and adding a toasty, smoky, woody overlay. **90**

1989: Enormously concentrated, smelling of smoke and coffee and tasting of chocolate and black cherry, with a long, toasty finish. **91**

1988: Rich and complex, lavishly spread with buttery oak and bursting with berry and currant flavors underneath. The tannins are well integrated. **90**

1987: Warm, ripe and generous, with plush, concentrated herb, plum, chocolate and toasty oak flavors and a finish that echoes the plum and herb notes. **91**

NIGHTINGALE DESSERT NAPA VALLEY (★★★★★): A delicious dessert wine, and one of the very best. Uncommon richness, complexity and depth of flavor. A blend of Sauvignon Blanc and Sémillon. Some years a second—and even a third—varietally labeled bottling is released.

1994: Smooth, ultrarich and distinctive, with its smoky fig, carmel, melon toasted marshmellow and oaky flavors, it's a broad, complex, potent wine. **94**

1990: Bold, ripe, smooth and creamy, with layers of lush fig, honey, pear, toast and tobacco flavors folding together on a rich, complex aftertaste. Delicious. **95**

Sauvignon Blanc 1990: Grassy, with sweet pear and candied fruit flavors that turn to dried apricot and nectarine on the finish. Impressive. **90**

Sémillon 1990: Ripe, smooth and supple, with rich, intense pear, fig and spice flavors that are deep and complex. **91**

1989: Racy and concentrated, with ripe, lush grass, fig, herb, butter and honey notes that turn complex and linger on the finish. **93**

1988: Complex, with an herbaceous edge to the ripe fig, honey, pear and toasty oak flavors. Turns elegant and refined on the finish. **91**

1987: Elegant and spicy, with sweet, ripe honey, pear, fig and toast notes. Finishes with a long, rich aftertaste, turning smoky and buttery. **92**

Sémillon 1987: Lush and creamy, with layers of honey, pear, fig and vanilla flavors that are complex and concentrated and a long, full finish. **93**

1986: Ripe and lush, with mint, butter, pear and fig flavors. Comes up short on the finish, but it's still impressive. **88**

1985: Has a minty edge, with ripe fig and apricot notes that turn spicy. **88**

Sauvignon Blanc 1985: Grassy, with ripe, lush fig and spice flavors that turn candied on the finish. Holds together, gaining complexity on the finish. **89**

Sémillon 1985: Decadent and smoky, a rich, lush, creamy wine with ripe fig, apricot and spice flavors. **89**

Sauvignon Blanc 1983: A racy, grassy wine that exaggerates the Sauvignon Blanc character, making for an intriguing range of flavors. Turns bitter on the finish, but still serves up lots of flavor. **87**

Sémillon 1983: It's a mature gold, with a smoky, charred edge to the ripe fig and apricot flavors. The finish is short. **84**

1982: Mature, with sweet, earthy fig, dried apricot and honey flavors. **87**

Sauvignon Blanc 1981: Complex, with roasted coffee, caramel and fig flavors. Very rich and opulent, showing a true Sauvignon Blanc character. **91**

Sémillon 1981: Ripe, plush and oily, with buttery fig and spice flavors that turn complex and earthy on the finish. **92**

1980: Deep gold, amazingly complex and supple, with smooth, rich apricot, butter, pear and toast flavors that turn to butterscotch and honey on the finish. Sensational. **99**

PINOT NOIR LOS CARNEROS STANLY RANCH (★★★): Improving, with more depth purer fruit and attractive oak shadings.

SAUVIGNON BLANC NAPA VALLEY (★★★): Getting better, with attractive fig, pea, herb and grassy flavors.

ZINFANDEL NORTH COAST (★★): Not as big and robust as most Beringer reds but improving. Made in a fruit-driven style, with supple pepper and wild berry flavors.

BERNARDUS WINERY (★★★★)
Carmel Valley, Monterey County
Founded: 1989. **Owner:** Ben Pon. **Winemaker:** Mark Chesebro

MAJOR WINES: PRICE, CASES, RATING

Chardonnay Monterey County
($19, 30,000) ★★★★
Marinus Red Carmel Valley
($36, 7,500) ★★★
Pinot Noir Santa Maria Valley
Bien Nacido Vineyard
($35, 1,500) ★★★
Sauvignon Blanc Monterey County
($14, 7,000) ★★★★

WINERY DATA
Case Production: 50,000. **Acres Owned:** 37 acres in Carmel Valley. **Varietals by Acre:** Cabernet Franc (2 acres), Cabernet Sauvignon (25), Merlot (9), Petit Verdot (1). **Vineyard Designations:** Bien Nacido Vineyard (Pinot Noir). **Varietals Purchased:** Chardonnay (Arroyo Seco, Carneros, Santa Maria, Edna Valley), Pinot Noir (Santa Barbara County), Sauvignon Blanc (Arroyo Seco), Sémillon (Napa Valley).

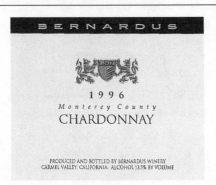

The wines from this Carmel Valley winery are well crafted, deliberate in style and getting better. Through his Berk Holdings, proprietor Bernardus (Ben) Pon owns 37 acres in Carmel Valley, planted primarily to Cabernet (23 acres) and Merlot (12). He buys Chardonnay, Sauvignon Blanc and Pinot Noir, the latter from Bien Nacido Vineyard. Don Blackburn departed as winemaker in 1998, and was replaced by Mark Chesebro. Two new Chardonnays are now in the works, one from Sangiacomo Vineyard in Carneros, and the other from Bien Nacido Vineyard in Santa Maria Valley.

TASTING NOTES

CHARDONNAY MONTEREY COUNTY (★★★★): Consistently bold, ripe and juicy, with a range of pear, citrus and pretty oak flavors.
1996: Distinctive for its bright citrus and lemony flavors, with touches of pear, spice, earth, oak and hazelnut added in. **91**
1995: Lots of rich, ripe pear, citrus, oak and spice notes, turning smooth and polished. **90**
1994: Bold and ripe, with rich pear, spice and honey flavors, and an elegant touch of hazelnut. **90**

MARINUS RED CARMEL VALLEY (★★★): A Bordeaux-style blend that's tightly wound and built for aging, but hasn't established a track record yet. So far, the 1994 has shown the most promise.
1995: Lean and a touch vegetal, with cedary oak and hints of tobacco and currant; it strives for complexity, and may well deliver some day. **86**
1994: Tight, rich and focused. Has a complex core of spicy currant, cedar, leather, anise and berry flavors, with notes of spice and mineral. **90**
1993: Intense and tannic, with chewy currant, cherry and anise flavors that are well focused and dry. **85**

PINOT NOIR SANTA MARIA VALLEY BIEN NACIDO (★★★): Excellent in 1994 and 1995, when it captured the decadent, earthy black cherry flavors of this vineyard and added a sense of elegance and finesse.
1996: Light, with tarry orange blossom, dried cherry and spicy notes; elegant, but a bit on the simple side. **85**
1995: A distinctly Santa Barbara Pinot Noir: complex, elegant and earthy, with spicy cherry, wild berry, tea, herb and sage notes. **91**
1994: Ripe, complex, with layers of pretty cherry, herb, berry and spice flavors, turning smooth and fleshy. **90**
1993: Of medium-weight; elegant, with spicy and peppery nuances and cherry and berry notes. **86**

SAUVIGNON BLANC MONTEREY COUNTY (★★★★): Well made, sleek and tangy, with depth and complexity.

ROBERT BIALE VINEYARDS (★★★★)
Napa Valley
Founded: 1991. **Owner:** Aldo Biale, Robert Biale, Al Perry & Dave Pramuk. **Winemaker:** Al Perry.

MAJOR WINES: PRICE, CASES, RATING

Petite Sirah Napa Valley Old Vineyards
($35, 225) ★★

Zinfandel Napa Valley Aldo's Vineyard
($25, 800) ★★★★

Zinfandel Napa Valley Falleri Vineyard
($25, 50) ★★★

Zinfandel Napa Valley Old Crane Ranch
($25, 700) ★★★

Zinfandel Sonoma Valley Monte Rosso
Vineyard
($25, 700) ★★★★

Zinfandel Sonoma Valley Valsecchi
Vineyard
($25, 175) ★★★

WINERY DATA

Case Production: 2,000. **Acres Owned:** 25 acres in Napa Valley. **Varietals by Acre:** Sangiovese (1), Sauvignon Blanc (4), Zinfandel (20 acres). **Vineyard Designations:** Aldo's Vineyard (Zinfandel), Old Crane Ranch (Zinfandel), Monte Rosso Vineyard (Zinfandel), Valsecchi Vineyard (Zinfandel), Falleri Vineyard (Zinfandel), Gaudi Carlt Vineyard (Barbera). **Varietals Purchased:** Barbera (Napa Valley), Petite Sirah (Napa Valley), Zinfandel (Napa Valley, Sonoma Valley).

Long-time Napa Valley grape-grower Aldo Biale's Zinfandel vineyard north of the city of Napa was planted in 1937 by his parents, Pietro and Christina Biale. In 1991, Biale formed a partnership with his son Robert and some associates to produce small lots of vineyard-designated red wines, with an emphasis on old-vine Zinfandel.

Over the last five years, the Biale's have considerably expanded their sources for Zinfandel and now make several separate bottlings, all from old-vine vineyards. Each wine is very distinctive, well made and emphasizes fruit and balance. Occasionally a late-picked style is made, featuring heightened ripeness and alcohol levels. An old-vine Petite Sirah is offered as well. Although the 2,000-case winery intends to stay small, the owners will continue to offer new vineyard-designated bottlings of Zinfandel and Petite Sirah as more sources of old-vine grapes become available.

TASTING NOTES

PETITE SIRAH NAPA VALLEY OLD VINEYARDS (★★)
1995: Delivers some tasty plum, cherry, floral and wild berry flavors, with firm, integrated tannins. **85**

ZINFANDEL NAPA VALLEY ALDO'S VINEYARD (★★★★):
The best of the Zinfandels, it's supple, balanced, with ripe, complex flavors.
1996: Ripe, with a jammy wild berry edge and hints of cherry, sage, cedar and spice flavors; turning spicy and elegant. **88**
1994: Rich, yet elegant, with tiers of ripe cherry, raspberry, mint and spice, finishing with a nuance of pretty oak. **93**
1993: Well focused, ripe and complex, with a seam of elegant cherry, plum and wild berry flavors that pick up a nice, toasty nuance. **91**
1992: Supple and fruity, with spicy strawberry and cherry notes that turn smooth and elegant on the finish. **84**
1991: Effusively fruity, with ripe, supple cherry and raspberry flavors that are spicy and elegant, finishing with soft tannins. **91**

ZINFANDEL NAPA VALLEY FALLERI VINEYARDS (★★★)
1995: Rough at this early stage, with a core of herb, sage, cherry and anise flavors, picking up a hint of cedar and smoky oak on the finish. **88**

ZINFANDEL NAPA VALLEY OLD CRANE RANCH (★★★)
1996: Serves up ripe, jammy, black cherry, blackberry, anise, sage and spice flavors; turns fleshy and supple on the finish. **89**
1995: Delicate, with an appealing core of plum and cherry flavors, turning simple on the finish. **85**

ZINFANDEL NAPA VALLEY OLD VINEYARDS LATE PICKED
1995: Sweet, with ripe, juicy cherry and berry flavors. **88**

ZINFANDEL NAPA VALLEY TWO VINEYARDS
1995: Smooth and elegant, with a core of plum, wild berry and cherry flavors, turning soft and fleshy on the finish. **88**

ZINFANDEL SONOMA VALLEY MONTE ROSSO VINEYARD (★★★★)
1996: Supple and focused, with coffee-laced wild berry and blackberry flavors, picking up complex mint, sage and cedary accents. **90**
1995: Intense and woody, with a slight vinegary edge to the earthy wild berry and cherry notes. **85**

ZINFANDEL SONOMA VALLEY VALSECCHI VINEYARD (★★★)
1996: Dark, ripe, rich and complex; brimming with juicy blackberry, black cherry and wild berry flavors that have a slightly jammy edge. **90**

BIG HORN see **PARDUCCI WINE CELLARS**

BLACK SEARS WINERY
Howell Mountain, Napa Valley
Founded: 1997. **Owner:** Joyce & Jerre Sears.
Winemaker: Ted Lemon.

MAJOR WINES: PRICE, CASES, RATING
Cabernet Sauvignon Howell Mountain Estate
 (TBA, 200)   NR

WINERY DATA
Acres Owned: 25 acres on Howell Mountain. **Varietals by Acre:** Cabernet Sauvignon (5 acres), Zinfandel (20).

Zinfandel lovers have grown accustomed to the fabulously complex Zinfandels that Turley Wine Cellars (see entry) makes from this Howell Mountain vineyard, so there's reason to expect this new winery is going to be a hit right off the bat. Ted Lemon will oversee the winemaking.

BOEGER WINERY (★★)
Placerville, El Dorado County
Founded: 1972. **Owner:** Greg & Susan Boeger.
Winemaker: Greg Boeger.

MAJOR WINES: PRICE, CASES, RATING
Barbera El Dorado
 ($14, 1,750)   ★★
Barbera El Dorado Vineyard Select
 ($20, 400)   ★★
Cabernet Sauvignon El Dorado
 ($12, 1,855)   ★★
Chardonnay El Dorado
 ($12, 1,120)   ★★
Majeure Red El Dorado
 ($15, 925)   ★★
Meritage Red El Dorado
 ($15, 975)   ★★
Merlot El Dorado
 ($15, 1,300)   ★
Miglióre Red El Dorado
 ($15, 185)   ★★
Milagro Red El Dorado
 ($15, 200)   ★★

Sauvignon Blanc El Dorado
 ($10, 1,550)   ★★★
Zinfandel El Dorado
 ($12, 900)   ★★
Zinfandel El Dorado Walker Vineyard
 ($15, 2,040)   ★★★

ALSO PRODUCED
Charbono El Dorado Arastra Vineyards ($15, 75); Muscat Canelli El Dorado ($8, 440); Pinot Noir El Dorado Irving Ranch ($15, 145); Viognier El Dorado ($16, 54); White Riesling El Dorado (10, 350); Zinfandel El Dorado Old Clone ($20, 278).

WINERY DATA
Case Production: 20,000. **Acres Owned:** 30 acres in El Dorado County. Lease 37 acres. **Varietals by Acre:** Barbera (20 acres), Cabernet Franc (3), Cabernet Sauvignon (10), Carignane (0.09), Chardonnay (9), Flora (0.4), Graciano (0.25), Grenache (1), Johannisberg Riesling (3), Malvasia Bianca (0.13), Mataro (0.63), Merlot (5), Muscat Canelli (1), Nebbiolo (0.63), Petit Verdot (0.82), Petite Sirah (1), Refosco (0.9), Sangiovese (0.7), Sauvignon Blanc (4), Sémillon (0.3), Syrah (0.94), Tempranillo (1), Viognier (0.1), Zinfandel (5). **Vineyard Designations:** Walker Vineyard (Zinfandel), Arastra Vineyards (Charbono). **Varietals Purchased:** Charbono (El Dorado), Petite Sirah (El Dorado), Pinot Noir (El Dorado), Sangiovese (El Dorado), Viognier (El Dorado), Zinfandel (El Dorado).

Boeger produces a variety of well-made, well-priced wines, the best values being the El Dorado and Walker Vineyard Zinfandels and the Sauvignon Blanc. The 1996 Walker Vineyard Zinfandel (85 points)—usually the best of the Zinfandels, with its ripe, earthy, cherry, plum and pepper notes—was slightly less complex than recent vintages. The Sauvignon Blanc is consistently very good; the 1997 vintage (88 points) featured some lovely crisp citrus and mineral flavors.

BOGLE VINEYARDS (★★)
Clarksburg, Sacramento County
Founded: 1979. **Owner:** Patty J. Bogle. **Winemaker:** Christopher Smith.

MAJOR WINES: PRICE, CASES, RATING
Cabernet Sauvignon California
 ($9, 10,000)   ★★

Chardonnay California
   ($7, 28,000) ★★
Chenin Blanc Clarksburg
   ($7, 300) ★★
Merlot California
   ($9, 50,000) ★★
Merlot Clarksburg Reserve
   ($18, 300) ★★
Petite Sirah California
   ($9, 26,000) ★★★
Sauvignon Blanc California
   ($7, 11,000) ★★★
Zinfandel California
   ($11, 6,000) ★★
Zinfandel California Old Vine Reserve
   ($18, 300) ★★

WINERY DATA
Case Production: 100,000. **Acres Owned:** 1,124 acres in Clarksburg. **Varietals by Acre:** Chardonnay (654 acres), Chenin Blanc (142), Merlot (119), Petite Sirah (38), Pinot Gris (5), Pinot Noir (25), Sauvignon Blanc (33), Viognier (5), Zinfandel (103).

Based in the Delta region of California's Central Valley, Bogle is a family-owned, value-oriented producer, making rustic reds and crisp, minerally white wines. The Petite Sirah is often the most flavorful and interesting in the winery's portfolio; the 1996 (88 points) was rich and generous, with effusive berry flavors and soft tannins. Of the whites, Sauvignon Blanc is the most reliable and well made, with flavors ranging from minerally and grassy in some years to lime and grapefruit, as in the 1997 (83).

BONNY DOON VINEYARD (★★★)
Santa Cruz Mountains
Founded: 1983. **Owner:** Grahm Family. **Winemaker:** Randall Grahm. **Second Label:** Ca' del Solo.

MAJOR WINES: PRICE, CASES, RATING
Chenin Blanc California Pacific Rim
   ($8, 2,600) ★★
Grenache California Clos de Gilroy
   ($8, 4,500) ★★
Le Cigare Volant Red California
   ($25, 3,000) ★★★

Mourvèdre California Old Telegram
   ($30, 1,000) ★★★
Muscat Canelli Monterey County
  Vin de Glaciere
   ($15, 13,500) ★★★★★
White Riesling California Pacific Rim
   ($8, 7,000) ★★

WINERY DATA
Case Production: 60,000. **Acres Owned:** 72 acres in Monterey. **Varietals by Acre:** Barbera (10 acres), Cinsault (5), Clinton (0.25), Delaware (0.25), Dolcetto (7), Friesa (7), Ives (0.25), Marsanne (1), Nebbiolo (3), Orange Muscat (15), Pinot Gris (5), Riesling (1), Syrah (15), Viognier (2). **Varietals Purchased:** Barbera (Monterey), Carignane (Contra Costa), Charbono (Napa), Grenache (Monterey), Mourvèdre (Contra Costa), Muscat Canelli (Monterey), Riesling (San Benito), Roussanne (Paso Robles), Sangiovese (Monterey), Syrah (Monterey), Syrah (Paso Robles), Zinfandel (Contra Costa).

At the time of this writing, Randall Grahm's career appears to be in limbo. He has indicated that he is weary of winemaking and perhaps ready for a change. In the past, his center of interest as a winemaker has zigzagged in several directions. He began as an advocate of Burgundian varieties (including an Oregon Pinot Noir), tinkered with Bordeaux-style wines (briefly making a Cabernet Sauvignon), gained fame as the head Rhône Ranger, and is now quite interested in Italian varieties (Nebbiolo, Barbera and Sangiovese).

Production from his winery is now approaching 60,000 cases of nearly 30 different wines, from table wines to blush wines to fine grappas and eaux-de-vie, which he makes for himself and other producers such as Sebastiani. Most of the wines are sound and well made, and a few, such as Le Cigare Volant, Muscat Canelli Vin de Glaciere, Grenache and Mourvèdre, demonstrate why his wines have such a devoted cult following.

Bonny Doon owns just over 70 acres in Monterey, mostly planted to small plots of Syrah, Barbera, Muscat, Nebbiolo and other obscure Italian clones. Many of the vineyards that he discovered in his early days of exploring Rhône varieties have since been purchased by others, drying up his sources. Still, he persists in his maverick ways. His best wine is the Vin de Glaciere (★★★★★), made from frozen, concentrated Muscat juice, which is deliciously fruity, with lively pineapple, apricot and citrus flavors.

TASTING NOTES

LE CIGARE VOLANT RED CALIFORNIA (★★★): Very good, but shy of outstanding. Smooth and spicy, with complex plum and wild berry flavors, it's a blend of Syrah, Grenache, Cinsault and Mourvèdre.

1996: Smells fruity, with hints of plum and wild berry flavor, yet turns dry and tannic on the palate, with less fruit evident. A blend of Syrah, Grenache, Cinsault and Mourvèdre. **85**

1995: Smooth and spicy, showing cherry and wild berry flavors before working into dry, leathery tannins that emerge on the finish. **88**

1994: Delivers lots of ripe, juicy plum and cherry flavors with zesty spice and leather accents. Turns elegant and complex on the finish. **87**

1993: Smooth-textured and lively wild berry and red cherry flavors tighten up on the finish. **85**

1991: Tight and firm but focused, with ripe, intense wild berry, cherry, spice and leather notes that are deep and complex. **88**

1990: Firm in texture, with focused blackberry and cherry flavors and an exotic edge of spice and black pepper notes. **87**

MOURVÈDRE CALIFORNIA OLD TELEGRAM (★★★)

1995: Appealing for its core of blackberry, mineral, tar, and spice flavors. Finishes with dry, fairly rugged tannins, but is tightly focused and flavorful. **89**

1993: Firm and spicy, a little chewy, but showing plenty of focused blackberry and tar flavors. **83**

1991: Shows a deft balance between ripe, supple, spicy fruit flavors and gentle, polished tannins. **87**

1990: Crisp and snappy, with tart, tight plum, currant and cherry flavors that are firmly tannic. **84**

1988: Vibrant cherry, blackberry and rose petal aromas and flavors that turn slightly tannic. **85**

1986: Ripe and rich, packed with blackberry flavors mixed with lots of black pepper and a touch of smoke. **90**

BONTERRA see FETZER VINEYARDS

BONVERRE see ST. SUPÉRY VINEYARD & WINERY

BOUCHAINE VINEYARDS (★★)
Carneros
Founded: 1981. **Owner:** Gerret & Tatiana Copeland. **Winemaker:** David Stevens.

MAJOR WINES: PRICE, CASES, RATING

Cabernet Franc Sonoma Valley Limited Release ($19, 300)	★★
Chardonnay Carneros ($18, 3,800)	★★
Chardonnay Carneros Estate Reserve ($24, 400)	★★
Gewürztraminer Russian River Valley ($12, 1,300)	★★
Pinot Noir Carneros ($19, 7,100)	★★
Pinot Noir Carneros Reserve ($27, 600)	★★

WINERY DATA
Case Production: 20,000. **Acres Owned:** 31 acres in Carneros. **Varietals by Acre:** Chardonnay (12 acres), Pinot Noir (19). **Varietals Purchased:** Cabernet Franc (Sonoma Valley, Napa Valley), Chardonnay (Carneros), Gerwürztraminer (Russian River Valley), Pinot Noir (Carneros).

This Carneros winery has never lived up to expectations, and seems content to churn out good, if rather ordinary, wines. Its wines have been well made throughout the years, but they are rarely exciting, providing modest varietal fruit but rarely showing the extra depth and complexity evident in the wines of the best Carneros producers of Chardonnay and Pinot Noir.

Founded in 1981 by a trio of investors—Gerret Copeland, an heir to the Du Pont estate; Richard Sutton; and Austin Kiplinger, publisher of the Kiplinger Washington newsletters and *Changing Times* magazine—it is now owned solely by Copeland. Jerry Luper, Bouchaine's original winemaker, made some good first wines; but they were somewhat inconsistent, which was not surprising as they came from disparate vineyard sources and bore appellations ranging from Alexander Valley to Winery Lake. A reorganization and Luper's departure to Rutherford Hill in 1986 led to a decision to concentrate more on Chardonnay and less on Pinot Noir.

The focus is now on Carneros Chardonnay, including Bouchaine's own 31-acre vineyard near the winery.

The Chardonnays, like the Pinot Noirs, are crisp and lean—although the Carneros Reserve has at times been fuller and richer than the regular Chardonnay bottling. The 1996 Chardonnay (87) had some rough spots, but its tart pear and citrus flavors were pleasant. It was tough to find the reserve quality among the stalky, bitter flavors in the 1995 Reserve Chardonnay (84)—a good example of this winery's inconsistency.

The Cabernet Franc from Sonoma Valley carries the varietal's signature herbal flavors and blueberry notes, but it is often a bit simple, though the 1994 (86 points) showed some complexity with its herb-tinged cherry and berry flavors. The Russian River Gewürztraminer is also usually simple, but it is refreshing and can be impressive, as was the 1995 Gewürztraminer (89 points), notable for its apricot and spicy grapefruit flavors.

Both the Pinot Noir and Pinot Noir Reserve are light in color, showing modest flavors; there is little to distinguish the two, although on occasion the Reserve offers more richness and complexity. The 1995 Pinot Noir Reserve (86) was smooth with earthy cherry and tea notes, showing only slightly more depth than the lightly fruity 1995 Pinot Noir (84).

THE BRANDER VINEYARD (★★–★★★)
Santa Ynez Valley, Santa Barbara County
Founded: 1975. **Owner:** Fred Brander. **Winemaker:** Fred Brander.

MAJOR WINES: PRICE, CASES, RATING
Bouchet Tête de Cuvée Red Santa Ynez Valley ($28, 150)	★★
Cabernet Franc Santa Ynez Valley High Density Vineyard ($32, 100)	★★
Cabernet Sauvignon Santa Ynez Valley ($19, 600)	★★
Cuvée Natalie White Santa Ynez Valley ($14, 400)	★★★
Cuvée Nicolas White Santa Ynez Valley ($22, 600)	★★★
Merlot Santa Ynez Valley ($19, 2000)	★
Sauvignon Blanc Santa Ynez Valley ($11, 4,800)	★★★
Sauvignon Blanc Santa Ynez Valley Au Naturel ($30, 600)	★★★

ALSO PRODUCED
Muscat Canelli Santa Barbara County ($10, 120).

WINERY DATA
Case Production: 12,000. **Acres Owned:** 40 acres in Santa Ynez Valley. **Varietals by Acre:** Cabernet Franc (3 acres), Cabernet Sauvignon (9), Chardonnay (6), Merlot (6), Pinot Gris (1), Pinot Noir (2), Sauvignon Blanc (13).

Owner-winemaker Fred Brander has chosen to focus on Sauvignon Blanc, one of the state's best and most distinctive wines. Tapping grapes from his 40 acres of vines in the Santa Ynez Valley, Brander's Sauvignon Blanc and two Sauvignon Blanc blends, Cuvée Nicholas (mostly Sauvignon) and Cuvée Natalie (Sauvignon with Riesling and Gewürztraminer), have all earned ★★★ for their style and complexity. The Bouchet Tête de Cuvée, a blend of Cabernet Sauvignon, Cabernet Franc and Merlot, and the Cabernet Franc both merit ★★. Each shows an herbal-vegetal character typical of this area. A similar character is also prominent in the Merlot (★).

AUGUST BRIGGS (★★★)
Napa Valley
Founded: 1995. **Owner:** August Briggs. **Winemaker:** August Briggs.

MAJOR WINES: PRICE, CASES, RATING
Cabernet Sauvignon Napa Valley ($30, 300)	★★★
Chardonnay Carneros Leveroni Vineyards ($25, 200)	★★★
Chardonnay Russian River Valley ($25, 200)	★★★
Pinot Noir Carneros ($25, 200)	★★
Pinot Noir Russian River Valley ($25, 200)	★★
Zinfandel Napa Valley ($20, 400)	★★★

ALSO PRODUCED
Cabernet Sauvignon Sonoma Mountain ($30, 300).

WINERY DATA
Case Production: 2,000. **Vineyard Designations:** Leveroni Vineyards (Chardonnay). **Varietals Purchased:** Cabernet Sauvignon (Napa Valley, Sonoma Mountain), Chardonnay (Carneros, Russian River Valley), Pinot Noir (Carneros, Russian River Valley), Zinfandel (Napa Valley).

After a decade of working for bulk brands and consulting for small labels, August "Joe" Briggs decided to get into the action himself. The quality of his first releases indicates that he is a producer to keep an eye on. Briggs makes Napa Valley Cabernet, Napa Valley Zinfandel and Pinot Noirs from Russian River and Carneros. But, thus far, his Chardonnays are the most impressive. The 1997 Russian River Chardonnay (91 points) and the 1997 Carneros Leveroni Vineyards Chardonnay (91), like Briggs's 1996 Chardonnays, are rich and show great finesse, offering supple flavors of pear, fig and apricot. Briggs's first Cabernet Sauvignon, a 1996 Napa Valley (91), is also outstanding, with a range of rich, complex, concentrated flavors and a long, lingering aftertaste.

BROPHY CLARK CELLARS (★★★)
Santa Maria Valley, Santa Barbara County
Founded: 1996. **Owner:** John & Kelly Brophy Clark.
Winemaker: John Clark.

MAJOR WINES: PRICE, CASES, RATING
Pinot Noir Arroyo Grande Valley ($18, 180)	★★★
Sauvignon Blanc Santa Barbara & San Luis Obispo Counties ($12, 350)	★★★

ALSO PRODUCED
Pinot Noir Santa Maria Valley ($24, 350); Syrah Santa Ynez Valley ($18, 225).

WINERY DATA
Case Production: 1,000. **Varietals Purchased:** Pinot Noir (Arroyo Grande Valley, Santa Maria Valley), Sauvignon Blanc (Santa Barbara County, San Luis Obispo County), Syrah (Santa Ynez Valley).

John Clark spent 13 years at Corbett Canyon Vineyards and now is winemaker for Laetitia and Barnwood wineries (see entries). Along with his wife Kelly Brophy Clark, a vineyard consultant, the two are now making Central Coast Pinot Noir, Syrah and Sauvignon Blanc. Their 1996 Arroyo Grande Pinot Noir (87 points) is made in an earthy style, with a lean core of black cherry and herb flavors.

DAVID BRUCE WINERY (★★★–★★★★)
Santa Cruz Mountains
Founded: 1964. **Owner:** David Bruce Winery Inc.
Winemaker: David Bruce.

MAJOR WINES: PRICE, CASES, RATING
Petite Sirah Central Coast ($18, 8,000)	★★★
Petite Sirah Paso Robles Ranchita Canyon Vineyard ($18, 600)	★★★★
Petite Sirah Paso Robles Shell Creek Vineyard ($18, 600)	★★★★
Pinot Noir Central Coast ($16, 12,000)	★★★
Pinot Noir Chalone ($32, 1,500)	★★★
Pinot Noir Russian River Valley ($30, 3,000)	★★★
Pinot Noir Russian River Valley Reserve (Discontinued)	★★★
Pinot Noir Santa Cruz Mountains ($25, 1060)	★★★★
Pinot Noir Santa Cruz Mountains Estate Reserve ($35, 500)	★★★★
Pinot Noir Sonoma County ($20, 8,000)	★★
Zinfandel Paso Robles Ranchita Canyon Vineyard ($15, 1741)	★★★

ALSO PRODUCED
Cabernet Sauvignon Santa Clara Valley ($20, 2,000); Chardonnay Santa Cruz Mountains ($18, 2,000); Syrah Paso Robles ($20, 1,500).

WINERY DATA

Case Production: 40,000. **Acres Owned:** 25 acres in Santa Cruz Mountains. **Varietals by Acre:** Chardonnay (5 acres), Pinot Noir (17), Syrah (3). **Vineyard Designations:** Ranchita Canyon Vineyard (Petite Sirah, Zinfandel). **Varietals Purchased:** Cabernet Sauvignon (Santa Clara Valley), Petite Sirah (Central Coast), Pinot Noir (Chalone, Central Coast, Santa Cruz Mountains, Sonoma County), Syrah (Paso Robles), Zinfandel (Paso Robles).

In the course of his nearly 40-year winemaking career, David Bruce's wines have undergone wild stylistic swings, from bizarre and flawed to brilliant and well crafted. Today, after a long period during the 1980s when his wines were erratic in quality, Bruce is back on target. He is now making the best wines of his career, focusing on Santa Cruz Mountain-grown Chardonnay and Pinot Noir, the latter from his estate vineyard.

A dermatologist by profession, Bruce began as a home winemaker in the late 1950s, and deserves credit for many pioneering efforts with grapes grown in different appellations. Bruce's experiments were hands-on. He worked at Martin Ray's winery and then crushed grapes at Ridge Vineyards, helping with the 1961 vintage of the Monte Bello Vineyard.

Bruce is known for his innovative wines, including a white Zinfandel made in the early 1960s; ultraripe, late-harvest Zinfandels; and some downright funky Pinot Noirs. His 25-acre vineyard, which he began planting in 1961, is divided between Chardonnay, Syrah and Pinot Noir, the latter now his best wine. Bruce makes no apologies for his wild stylistic swings. I used to keep the word "unpredictable" in mind when drinking his wines, but don't be surprised at the soulfulness and complexity of his latest offerings. His Petite Sirahs in particular have been enormously enjoyable, and he is making a better Chalone Vineyard Pinot Noir than Chalone.

TASTING NOTES

PETITE SIRAH CENTRAL COAST (★★★)
1996: Complex and well balanced, with dark, ripe fruit flavors, lots of plum and wild berry flavors and a dash of sage and spice. **90**

PETITE SIRAH PASO ROBLES RANCHITA CANYON VINEYARD (★★★★)
1997: Dark and intense, packed with rich wild berry, pepper, plum and anise flavors that saturate the palate. **91**

PETITE SIRAH PASO ROBLES SHELL CREEK VINEYARD (★★★★)
1996: Inky black in color, with rich, intense flavors and a range of meaty plum, black cherry, wild berry, sage, and plum flavors. **93**

PINOT NOIR CENTRAL COAST (★★★)
1997: Smooth, rich and polished, with a complex core of herb-laced black cherry, currant, plum and raspberry flavors; soars on the finish. **90**

PINOT NOIR CHALONE (★★★)
1996: Dry and tannic, with enough dried cherry, tea, mushroom, earth and sage flavors to fill in the gaps. **87**
1995: Well focused on supple fruit flavors, with the core of cherry, wild berry, tea, sage, mushroom, and spice. **92**
1994: Complex, with a smoky, meaty edge to the ripe plum and berry flavors, with vibrant tannins. **89**

PINOT NOIR RUSSIAN RIVER VALLEY (★★★)
1996: Simple, with modest dried cherry, plum, sage and herbal notes, finishing with firm tannins and ample oak. **82**
1991: Intense, with a core of raspberry, cherry, earth, sage and tar. **88**

PINOT NOIR RUSSIAN RIVER VALLEY RESERVE (★★★)
1995: Lots of ripe, juicy cherry, wild berry and raspberry flavors that are a bit on the tart side. **89**
1994: A delicate style, with a core of spice, black cherry, raspberry and hints of cola. **89**
1993: Mature, with hints of sage and wild berry, dried cherry and spice, showing some smoky nuances. **88**

PINOT NOIR SANTA CRUZ MOUNTAINS (★★★★)
1996: Tight, with a core of leather and anise-scented wild berry and cherry flavors; turns complex and spicy on the finish. **89**

1991: Elegant and supple, with bright cherry and berry flavors and a touch of smoke and anise. **88**

1990: Exotic, with its smoky anise, meat and wild berry flavors; intense and concentrated. **91**

PINOT NOIR SANTA CRUZ MOUNTAINS ESTATE RESERVE (★★★★): Dark in color, rich in flavor and firmly tannic; built to age.

1993: A touch earthy and leathery, with a drying edge and a modest core of cherry and berry fruit. **82**

1992: Dense and chewy, with compact spice and pepper flavors that echo black cherry, herb, mineral and anise. Turns earthy and tannic on the finish. **91**

1991: Lots of ripe, juicy cherry, plum, earth and berry notes and a touch of mineral and spice; firm on the finish. **92**

1990: Rich and silky-smooth; a wonderfully complex and inviting style, with tiers of ripe cherry, earth, tar, spice and a dash of mushroom. **93**

BRUTOCAO CELLARS (★–★★)
Mendocino County
Founded: 1986. **Owner:** Leonard J. Brutocao.
Winemaker: Fred Nickel. **Second Label:** Bella Lona.

MAJOR WINES: PRICE, CASES, RATING
Cabernet Sauvignon Mendocino County
   Bliss Vineyard
   ($15, 1,900)   ★★
Chardonnay Mendocino County
   Bliss Vineyard
   ($13, 2,000)   ★★★
Merlot Mendocino County
   ($18, 2,600)   ★
Sauvignon Blanc Mendocino County
   Bliss Vineyard
   ($11, 750)   ★
Zinfandel Mendocino County
   Bliss Vineyard
   ($14, 1,000)   ★★

Bella Lona White Mendocino County
   ($8, 1,450)   ★★

ALSO PRODUCED
Pinot Noir Mendocino County Feliz Vineyard ($18, 500).

WINERY DATA
Case Production: 10,000. **Acres Owned:** 466 acres in Mendocino County. **Varietals by Acre:** Cabernet Sauvignon (135 acres), Chardonnay (50), Chenin Blanc (11), French Colombard (3), Gewürztraminer (5), Merlot (51 acres), Pinot Noir (84), Sémillon (5), Zinfandel (22). **Vineyard Designations:** Bliss Vineyard (Merlot, Cabernet Sauvignon, Zinfandel, Chardonnay, Sauvignon Blanc), Feliz Vineyard (Pinot Noir).

Long-time grapegrower Leonard Brutocao launched his Hopland winery in 1986. Today, he farms 466 acres, more than half of which are devoted to Cabernet and Chardonnay. The 1995 Bliss Vineyard Chardonnay (88 points) is particularly impressive, with its zesty apple, pear and grapefruit flavors. The Cabernet (★★), Merlot (★), Sauvignon Blanc (★) and Zinfandel (★★) are, however, average or below average.

BRYANT FAMILY VINEYARD (★★★★★)
Napa Valley
Founded: 1987. **Owner:** Don & Barbara Bryant.
Winemaker: Helen Turley.

MAJOR WINES: PRICE, CASES, RATING
Cabernet Sauvignon Napa Valley
($100, 600)   ★★★★★

WINERY DATA
Case Production: 1,800. **Acres Owned:** 10 acres in Napa Valley. **Varietals by Acre:** Cabernet Sauvignon (10 acres). **Vineyard Designations:** Bryant Family Vineyard.

Bryant Family Vineyard, a 10-acre vineyard devoted exclusively to Cabernet, sits at the 1,500-foot elevation point on Pritchard Hill, amongst the hills east of St. Helena, near Chappellet. With Helen Turley in charge of winemaking, the focus is on low-yield (2 tons per acre), dense and concentrated wines, which are characterized by their pronounced fruitiness and polished tannins. Virtually all of the wine is sold by mailing list, so it is necessary to write to the winery in order to purchase the wines. With replantings, production should increase to 1,800 cases, which should make it easier to get your hands on some of these very collectable wines.

TASTING NOTES

CABERNET SAUVIGNON NAPA VALLEY (★★★★★): A bright new star. These are dense, massive, enormously complex and concentrated mountain-grown wines. Should age well.
1995: Dark, rich, plush and enormously extracted, it packs in lots of flavors: currant, black cherry, coffee, vanilla, herb, tea and spice. **97**
1994: An immense wine; rich, deep and concentrated, loaded with ripe, sweet currant and black cherry flavors and framed by pretty toasty, smoky oak. **94**
1992: Marked by a ripe, spicy quality; tightly wound and firmly tannic, but with a nice core of currant and berry flavors peeking through. **90**

BUEHLER VINEYARDS (★★★)
Napa Valley
Founded: 1978. **Owner:** John Buehler Sr. **Winemaker:** David Cronin.

MAJOR WINES: PRICE, CASES, RATING

Cabernet Sauvignon Napa Valley ($20, 5,000)	★★★
Cabernet Sauvignon Napa Valley Estate ($35, 1,300)	★★★
Chardonnay Russian River Valley ($15, 8,500)	★★
Chardonnay Russian River Valley Reserve ($30, 1,300)	★★★
White Zinfandel Napa Valley ($8, 25,000)	★
Zinfandel Napa Valley ($14, 5,000)	★★
Zinfandel Napa Valley Estate ($25, 1,300)	★★★

WINERY DATA
Case Production: 47,000. **Acres Owned:** 65 acres in Napa Valley. **Varietals by Acre:** Cabernet Sauvignon (45 acres), Zinfandel (20). **Varietals Purchased:** Cabernet Sauvignon (Napa Valley), Chardonnay (Russian River Valley), Zinfandel (Napa Valley).

Bechtel Corp. executive John Buehler Sr. purchased property for Buehler Vineyards in a narrow fold of hills east of St. Helena. After planting their vineyards, he and his son, John Jr., built a winery on the property and began making wine in 1978.

The early Buehler Cabernets were bold, ripe and distinctive, but then the winery went through a phase where its wines were leaner, trimmer and less complex. With the past few vintages, however, the winery has regained its form, its Cabernet and Cabernet Estate showing improved polish and richness. The estate-grown Zinfandel is also zesty, with pepper and wild berry flavors. The winery has been using Russian River grapes for its Chardonnay with increasing success. The Reserve featured generous fruit flavors in both 1995 (91 points) and 1996 (90).The regular Chardonnay scored in the mid-80s from 1994 through 1996.

TASTING NOTES

CABERNET SAUVIGNON NAPA VALLEY ESTATE (★★★): Regaining its earlier form. Shows more depth and complexity, with a sense of elegance and polish.
1995: A supple, fruity style, with bright, ripe, juicy Cabernet flavors, lots of cherry and berry notes and polished tannins. **88**
1994: Elegant and focused, with a core of tarry currant, mineral and spice flavors. **90**
1991: The best Buehler in years. Bold, ripe and complex, with attractive plum, currant and black cherry flavors that are rich and lively, with hints of mineral and earth. **91**

CHARDONNAY RUSSIAN RIVER VALLEY RESERVE (★★★)
1996: A gentle, elegant, subtle style, with pretty hints of pear, spice and melon, turning silky and earthy on the finish. **90**
1995: Rich and generous with its spicy pear and vanilla flavors; has a smoky oak aftertaste. **91**

BUENA VISTA WINERY (★★)
Carneros
Founded: 1857. **Owner:** Racke International. **Winemaker:** Judy Matulich-Weitz.

MAJOR WINES: PRICE, CASES, RATING

Cabernet Sauvignon Carneros ($16, 23,000)	★★
Cabernet Sauvignon Carneros Grand Reserve ($29, 900)	★★★

Chardonnay Carneros
($14,44,000) ★★

Chardonnay Carneros Grand Reserve
($24, 1,176) ★★★

Merlot Carneros
($19, 12,000) ★★

Merlot Carneros Grand Reserve
($28, 898) ★★

Pinot Noir Carneros
($16, 18,000) ★★

Pinot Noir Carneros Grand Reserve
($24, 1095) ★★

Riesling Carneros
($20, 403) ★★

Sauvignon Blanc Lake County
($9, 100,000) ★★

Zinfandel California
($20, 470) ★★

ALSO PRODUCED
Gewürztraminer Carneros ($10, 1,238).

WINERY DATA
Case Production: 200,000. **Acres Owned:** 895 acres in Carneros. **Varietals by Acre:** Cabernet Sauvignon (270 acres), Chardonnay (290), Gewürztraminer (1), Merlot (80), Pinot Noir (252), Riesling (1), Zinfandel (1). **Varietals Purchased:** Sauvignon Blanc (Lake County).

Buena Vista Winery is California's oldest premium winery. Founded in 1857 by Agoston Haraszthy of Hungary, it has undergone numerous changes, closing after the 1906 earthquake and re-opening in the late 1950s. But it wasn't until the late 1970s, when the winery was acquired by Racke International of Germany, that Buena Vista began to produce some impressive wines.

Buena Vista built a large winery in the Carneros district, and now owns 895 acres in the region. From 1978 to 1986, the winery made some very successful Cabernets under its Special Selection and Private Reserve designations (now called Grand Reserve), and also produced some fine Chardonnays and Merlots. In the late 1980s, however, the winery's vineyards came into full production, its case volume grew, and quality took a turn for the worse.

Today, Buena Vista's wines are still marred by inconsistencies. Its wines are too often lean, shallow and largely uninteresting. It's difficult to pinpoint a single cause,

but it appears that the winery has outgrown its ability to maintain quality. Buena Vista's two main lines of wines are the Carneros and the Grand Reserve bottlings, but there is little to distinguish the two, although the Grand Reserve wines have been improving slightly. The basic Chardonnay is light, fruity and appealing, but lacks depth; the Grand Reserve shows more complexity of late. The Merlots are lean and marked by herb and vegetal notes, with the Grand Reserve a shade richer. The Pinot Noirs are tart and simple. The best wines for years were the Lake County Sauvignon Blanc and Zinfandel, but they now carry a California appellation instead, and their quality has clearly declined.

In 1994, long-time winemaker Jill Davis departed for William Hill Winery in Napa, and was replaced by former Inglenook winemaker Judy Matulich-Weitz, who appears intent on re-establishing the brand. But the big question is whether the vineyards situated in cool areas can give her the fruit she needs. This winery is worth watching, if only to see whether it will turn itself around.

BURGESS CELLARS (★★★)
Napa Valley
Founded: 1972. **Owner:** Tom Burgess. **Winemaker:** Bill Sorenson.

MAJOR WINES: PRICE, CASES, RATING

Cabernet Sauvignon Napa Valley
Vintage Selection
($24, 8,000) ★★★

Chardonnay Napa Valley
($15, 10,000) ★★★

Chardonnay Napa Valley Triere
Vineyard Reserve
($30, 1,350) ★★★

Merlot Napa Valley
($22, 7,000) ★★

Zinfandel Napa Valley
($14, 5,000) ★★★

WINERY DATA
Case Production: 30,000. **Acres Owned:** 110 acres in Napa Valley. **Varietals by Acre:** Cabernet Sauvignon (30 acres), Chardonnay (25), Merlot (25), Zinfandel (30). **Vineyard Designations:** Triere Vineyard (Chardonnay).

Burgess Cellars operates out of a winery built in 1880 which lies at the foot of Howell Mountain. It was home to Lee Stewart's Souverain winery in the 1940's, but Tom Burgess, a former pilot, bought the property in 1972. Situated a few hundred feet above the Napa Valley floor, the winery is below the 1,400-foot elevation necessary to be considered part of the Howell Mountain appellation.

The 30,000-case winery specializes in Cabernet, Chardonnay, Merlot and Zinfandel. The wines are made under the direction of Bill Sorenson, who has been with Burgess since 1973. The winery owns 110 acres of grapes, including the Triere Vineyard in Yountville, which Sorenson uses for a vineyard-designated Chardonnay. Quality of the Chardonnay and Zinfandel has dipped a bit in the 1990s; recent Cabernets are also leaner than wines from the 1970s and 1980s. Burgess is, unfortunately, yet another winery where inconsistency is a problem.

TASTING NOTES

CABERNET SAUVIGNON NAPA VALLEY VINTAGE SELECTION (★★★): Leaner of late, but it can be elegant; older vintages have aged better than most.
1995: Firm and chewy, with a green olive edge to the black cherry and anise flavors. **85**
1994: Austere, with tight plum, anise, smoke and spice notes and earthy tannins. **87**
1993: Tight and well focused, with a core of cedar, currant, tobacco and spice, finishing with firm tannins. **88**
1992: Elegant and well crafted, with a nice balance between toasty, buttery oak notes and ripe cherry, plum and currant flavors. **90**
1991: Austere and tannic, with a narrow band of spicy currant and berry; lacking extra dimensions. **83**
1990: Balanced between ripe, spicy, supple fruit flavors and light oak shadings. **88**
1988: Austere, but with enough spicy currant and wild berry flavors to sustain it. **87**
1986: Hard and tannic, with intense currant, coffee and cherry flavors that are tightly wound. **88**
1985: Mature, but still showing plenty of flavor, with a minty currant edge. **89**
1978: Aging well, with attractive, ripe plum, spice, currant and cedary notes; a tightly framed wine. **89**

CHARDONNAY NAPA VALLEY TRIERE VINEYARD RESERVE (★★★): Variable quality is a concern. It can be brilliant, but often times it isn't.
1995: A bit coarse in texture, with the creamy, toasty oak nuances leading to a trim band of hazelnut and pear flavors; turns spicy and oaky, with the oak playing a dominate role. **90**

BYINGTON WINERY (★★★★)
Santa Cruz Mountains
Founded: 1987. **Owner:** Clyde D. Byington. **Winemaker:** Don Blackburn.

MAJOR WINES: PRICE, CASES, RATING

Cabernet Sauvignon Santa Cruz Mountains Twin Mountains ($14, 500)	★★
Chardonnay Napa Valley Twin Mountains ($15, 1,500)	★★★
Chardonnay Santa Cruz Dirk Vineyard ($25, 362)	★★★★
Chardonnay Santa Cruz Mountains ($20, 1,218)	★★★★
Chardonnay Santa Cruz Mountains Bald Mountain Vineyard ($25, 203)	★★★★
Pinot Noir Central Coast ($18, 800)	★★

ALSO PRODUCED
Cabernet Sauvignon Santa Cruz Mountains Bates Ranch ($23, 1,054)

WINERY DATA
Case Production: 20,000. **Acres Owned:** 9 acres in Santa Cruz Mountains. **Varietals by Acre:** Pinot Noir (9 acres). **Vineyard Designations:** Bald Mountain Vineyard (Chardonnay), Dirk Vineyard (Chardonnay). **Varietals Purchased:** Cabernet Sauvignon (Santa Cruz Mountains, Sonoma County), Chardonnay (Napa Valley, Santa Cruz Mountains), Pinot Noir (Central Coast).

Bill Byington, owner of Byington Steel, built a château-style winery on a hillside above Los Gatos in 1990, three years after starting his winery in rented space. There is a 9-acre Pinot Noir vineyard on the property, but most of the grapes are purchased from vineyards spread throughout California. A recent focus on Santa Cruz Mountain vineyards has coincided with an increase in the overall quality of the wines.

Chardonnay has proven to be the star of the portfolio, particularly the Santa Cruz Mountain appellation wines. The 1996 Bald Mountain Vineyard (90 points), 1996 Dirk Vineyard (91) and the regular 1996 Chardonnay (90) have similar qualities, remaining elegant despite their creamy textures and rich, complex flavors of pear, hazelnut and citrus. Pinot Noir and Cabernet have had limited success, but under new winemaker Don Blackburn, formerly of Bernardus, the red wines may well improve.

DAVIS BYNUM WINERY (★★)
Russian River Valley, Sonoma County
Founded: 1965. **Owner:** Davis Bynum. **Winemaker:** Gary Farrell. **Second Label:** River Bend.

MAJOR WINES: PRICE, CASES, RATING
Cabernet Sauvignon Russian River Valley
($15, 2,025) ★★
Cabernet Sauvignon Russian River Valley
Hedin Vineyard
($24, 625) ★★
Cabernet Sauvignon Russian River Valley
Laureles Vineyard
($20, 275) ★★
Chardonnay Russian River Valley Allen &
McIlroy Vineyards Limited Edition
($20, 700) ★★★
Chardonnay Russian River Valley Bohn
Vineyard
($22, 285) ★★
Eclipse Red Sonoma County
($28, 650) ★★
Fumé Blanc Russian River Valley
Shone Farm
($12, 4,500) ★★
Gewürztraminer Sonoma County
($10, 310) ★★
Merlot Russian River Valley Laureles
Vineyard
($22, 921) ★★
Pinot Noir Russian River Valley
($18, 2,900) ★★

Pinot Noir Russian River Valley Rochioli
Vineyard Le Pinot
($40, 160) ★★
Zinfandel Russian River Valley
Bohn Vineyard
($15, 2,025) ★★
Zinfandel Sonoma County Old Vine
($18, 2,999) ★★

WINERY DATA
Case Production: 15,000. **Acres Owned:** 25 acres in Russian River Valley. **Varietals by Acre:** Cabernet Franc (0.5 acres), Cabernet Sauvignon (0.15), Chardonnay (3), Malbec (0.5), Merlot (11), Petit Verdot (0.5), Pinot Noir (10). **Vineyard Designations:** Allen Vineyard (Chardonnay), Bohn Vineyard (Chardonnay), McIlroy Vineyard (Chardonnay), Rochioli Vineyard (Pinot Noir). **Varietals Purchased:** Cabernet Franc (Dry Creek), Cabernet Sauvignon (Russian River Valley), Chardonnay (Russian River Valley), Gewürztraminer (Dry Creek Valley, Russian River Valley), Pinot Noir (Russian River Valley), Sauvignon Blanc (Russian River Valley), Zinfandel (Alexander Valley, Russian River Valley).

Davis Bynum joined the California wine industry in 1965, after more than a decade of making wines at home. Through the years, his winery has produced many good wines, although they are rarely exceptional. Bynum has turned over many of the winemaking decisions to his sons and to his winemaker Gary Farrell, who remains a loyal employee despite having a highly successful brand of his own (see Gary Farrell listing).

Having been in the business for three decades, the Davis Bynum Winery has made just about every kind of wine imaginable, but its focus the past few years has been on Sonoma County and Russian River Valley Pinot Noir, Chardonnay, Merlot and Zinfandel. Bynum's best wines are his delicate Pinot Noirs, but they pale in comparison with the best from this area, despite the fact that his vineyard sources, the Rochioli and Allen vineyards, are first-rate.

BYRD-COOPER see NEYERS VINEYARDS

BYRON VINEYARDS & WINERY (★★★★)
Santa Maria Valley, Santa Barbara County
Founded: 1984. **Owner:** Robert Mondavi Corp. **Winemaker:** Byron "Ken" Brown.

MAJOR WINES: PRICE, CASES, RATING

Chardonnay Santa Maria Valley
($17, 25,000)   ★★★

Chardonnay Santa Maria Valley Estate
($32, 2,900)   ★★★★★

Chardonnay Santa Maria Valley Reserve
($24, 3,200)   ★★★★★

Pinot Blanc Santa Maria Valley Estate
($16, 845)   ★★★

Pinot Gris Santa Maria Valley Estate
($16, 650)   ★★★

Pinot Noir Santa Maria Valley
($18, 7,000)   ★★★

Pinot Noir Santa Maria Valley Reserve
($24, 1,600)   ★★★

WINERY DATA

Case Production: 55,000. **Acres Owned:** 582 in the Santa Maria Valley. **Varietals by Acre:** Chardonnay (387 acres), Grenache (5), Pinot Blanc (10), Pinot Gris (19), Pinot Noir (142), Syrah (12), Viognier (7). **Varietals Purchased:** Chardonnay (Santa Maria Valley), Pinot Gris (Santa Maria Valley), Pinot Blanc (Santa Maria Valley), Pinot Noir (Santa Maria).

After working for Zaca Mesa from 1978 to 1983, Byron "Ken" Brown founded his own winery in 1984. Despite a slow start, the winery has improved across the board, with some dazzling Chardonnays from old vines, polished Pinot Noirs, Sauvignon Blanc, Pinot Blanc and Pinot Gris. Since 1990, Byron has been owned by Robert Mondavi Corp., which built a new gravity-flow winery and has added considerable vineyard acreage, including a large portion of the former Tepusquet Vineyard and the Sierra Madre Vineyard. Byron's star is the Reserve

Chardonnay, which is planted on some of the oldest Chardonnay vines in the state. The Estate Chardonnay is new to the lineup and seems poised to surpass the Reserve as Byron's best wine. The Pinot Noir and Pinot Noir Reserve are worth watching, as they feature complex, earthy cherry, berry and leather flavors. A Rhône-style red is in the works.

TASTING NOTES

CHARDONNAY SANTA MARIA VALLEY ESTATE (★★★★★)

1995: Rich and expressive, with exotic tropical fruit flavors and lots of juicy pear, pineapple, citrus, mineral and spice notes. **92**

1994: Opulent, with racy pear and pineapple flavors; on the finish it turns smooth and silky, revealing more complexity and finesse. **92**

1993: A bold, complex wine that packs in lots of ripe pear, fig, honey and butterscotch flavors and frames them with toasty, smoky oak. **93**

CHARDONNAY SANTA MARIA VALLEY RESERVE (★★★★★): Beautifully crafted, ripe, opulent and detailed; rich in complex flavors. The Santa Barbara County Reserve was renamed to the more specific Santa Maria Valley appellation in 1995.

1996: Shows off ripe tangerine, citrus, pear and melon flavors that are a bit awkward now but are rich and concentrated, so short-term cellaring is advised. **89**

1994: An elegant, understated style with ripe pear, pineapple and citrus flavors framed in spicy, vanilla-scented oak. **90**

1992: Builds richness and complexity, with tight green apple and spice flavors that soften and swirl into honey and cream notes on the long finish. **92**

1991: Serves up ripe pear, apricot and honey notes, finishing with a rich, complex earthiness. **88**

1990: Ripe, intense, rich and creamy, with wonderful spice, pear, hazelnut, vanilla and honey notes that are complex and concentrated. **92**

PINOT NOIR SANTA MARIA VALLEY (★★★): Previously called Pinot Noir Santa Barbara County.

1996: Smooth and spicy, with a range of earthy cherry, cola, anise and sage flavors. **88**

1995: Intensely flavored, with rich, earthy cherry, wild berry and spicy features and a sense of finesse and elegance. **90**

1994: Intense and lively, with ample tannins; the supple cherry and berry flavors pick up herb and anise notes. **87**

PINOT NOIR SANTA MARIA VALLEY RESERVE (★★★): Dense and earthy, built for short-term aging of two to five years. Previously called Pinot Noir Santa Barbara County Reserve.

1995: Dense and earthy, unfolding to reveal a core of cherry, berry and beef flavors and dry tannins. **87**

1994: Rich, dense and smoky, with dry, leathery tannins and dashes of black cherry, olive and spice. **87**

1993: Ripe and intense, with exotic herb, spice and black cherry aromas and flavors. **88**

1991: Aging well, with complex spice, wild berry, earth and sage flavors that are young and firm. **87**

1990: Mature and elegant, with earthy, spicy flavors that slowly give way to a core of rhubarb, cherry, tar and citrus. **88**

CA' DEL SOLO see BONNY DOON VINEYARD

CACHAGUA see DURNEY VINEYARDS

CAFARO CELLARS (★★★)
St. Helena, Napa Valley
Founded: 1986. **Owner:** Joe Cafaro. **Winemaker:** Joe Cafaro.

MAJOR WINES: PRICE, CASES, RATING

Cabernet Sauvignon Napa Valley	
($35, 1,000)	★★★
Cabernet Sauvignon Napa Valley Reserva	
($60, 250)	★★★
Merlot Napa Valley	
($30, NA)	★★★

WINERY DATA
Case Production: 1,800. **Acres Owned:** 15 acres in Napa Valley. **Varietals by Acre:** Cabernet Franc, Cabernet Sauvignon, Merlot, Petit Verdot, Syrah. **Vineyard Designations:** Madrona Ranch **Varietals Purchased:** Cabernet Sauvignon (Carneros, Stags Leap District, Spring Mountain), Merlot (Carneros, Stags Leap District, Spring Mountain).

Joe Cafaro is a well known Napa Valley winemaker, having worked for Chappellet, Keenan, Acacia and Robert Sinskey as well as consulting for several other brands. In 1986, he began making small lots of Cabernet and Merlot from grapes purchased from different sub-appellations of Napa. Both wines are well crafted, and display a deliberate, tightly structured style. Both are blends of grapes grown in Carneros, Spring Mountain and the Stags Leap District. Given his dedication to these two wines, Cafaro remains worth watching.

TASTING NOTES

CABERNET SAUVIGNON NAPA VALLEY (★★★): The early vintages are more impressive than current efforts, which are tightly reined-in, well focused and in need of cellaring.

1995: Ripe and generous with its currant and spice flavors; picks up some nice hints of clove and anise. **87**

1994: Lean and trim, with smoky cedar, tobacco and anise notes, and tart currant and black cherry flavors. **89**

1993: Solid and intense, with ripe cherry, spice, herb and tar nuances and mild, integrated tannins. **87**

1992: Intense, broad-shouldered, with chunky currant, chocolate and wild berry flavors and rustic tannins. **88**

1991: Smooth and supple, with an attractive spicy currant and plum edge before the cedary oak and tannins kick in. Typical of the 1991 vintage with its understated flavors. Tasted out of magnum. **88**

1990: Lean and elegant, modestly concentrated and mildly tannic, with a spicy, peppery edge to the cherry and currant notes. **84**

1989: Crisp and firm, with ripe currant and cherry flavors that are bright and lively, but also quite tannic. **85**

1988: Tightly wound; focused, sporting a rich core of currant, black cherry, olive, herb, spice and cedary oak flavors. **88**

1987: Deep, dark, rich and plush, packed with currant, herb, black cherry and plum flavors. Wonderful harmony and finesse. **90**

1986: Elegant, with well defined, supple currant, plum and violet flavors that are quite harmonious. The delicious flavors sneak up on you. **93**

CABERNET SAUVIGNON NAPA VALLEY RESERVA (★★★): The Reserva line was added with the 1994 vintage. Like the recent regular bottlings, it has proved austere.

1994: A touch green and austere, with tightly wound currant, black cherry, green olive and bell pepper flavors. **89**

MERLOT NAPA VALLEY (★★★): Supple, elegant and well-crafted, with classic herb, currant and tobacco notes. Best to drink early, but can still age.
1995: Lean, a slightly green edge to the adequately ripe cherry and currant flavors; turns dry on the finish. **87**
1994: Herbal, with bell pepper, tart currant and cedary oak flavors and fleshy tannins. **88**
1990: Supple and elegant, with focused currant, plum and cherry flavors that turn smooth and fleshy. **87**
1988: Rich, lively and concentrated, packed with herb, cherry, plum and currant flavors that are a bit tight and tannic now, but show a sense of harmony and finesse. **89**

CAFE RED and **CAFE WHITE** see **FRICK WINERY**

CAIN VINEYARD & WINERY (★★★)
Spring Mountain District, Napa Valley
Founded: 1980. **Owner:** Jim & Nancy Meadlock.
Winemaker: Christopher Howell.

MAJOR WINES: PRICE, CASES, RATING
Cain Cuvée Red Napa Valley
  ($22, 10,000)   ★★
Cain Five Red Napa Valley
  ($50, 7,000)   ★★★
Sauvignon Blanc Monterey Ventana
  Vineyards Musqué
  ($20, 3,000)   ★★★

WINERY DATA
Case Production: 20,000. **Acres Owned:** 85 acres in Spring Mountain District. **Varietals by Acre:** Cabernet Franc (9 acres), Cabernet Sauvignon (52), Malbec (3), Merlot (19), Petit Verdot (2), Syrah (0.5). **Vineyard Designations:** Ventana Vineyards. **Varietals Purchased:** Cabernet Franc (Spring Mountain), Cabernet Sauvignon (Spring Mountain, Napa Valley), Merlot (Spring Mountain), Sauvignon Blanc (Monterey).

Jerry and Joyce Cain spared no expense when they bought and developed their steep, terraced vineyard at the top of Spring Mountain in Napa Valley and built a large stone-clad winery. In the late 1980s, the winery ran into financial difficulties, and in 1991 investor-partner Jim Meadlock bought out the Cains' interest and became the owner.

Cain Five, a blend of the five Bordeaux varieties grown in Cain's 85 acres of vineyard, has been the star offering, but now it is rivaled by a stylish Sauvignon Blanc called Musqué, produced from Ventana Vineyards in Monterey County. A third wine, Cain Cuvée—made from the Bordeaux varieties left over from Cain Five—can be solid, if leaner and more herbal, and is worthy of a ★★ rating.

TASTING NOTES

CAIN FIVE RED NAPA VALLEY (★★★): Intense and complex, this Cabernet blend has been quite herbal, earthy and leathery of late. While concentrated, the range of flavors often strays from the core of currant and black cherry, and the wine can be hard-edged. Aging well, but not wonderfully. At $50, this is expensive for what you get.
1995: Earthy and leathery, with herbaceous bell pepper and green bean notes that override the modest currant and cherry flavors. **89**
1994: Dark, dense and detailed, with a pleasant core of earthy currant, plum, cedar and spice, and intense tannins. **88**
1992: An herbal style with hints of black olive, cedar and currant, turning quite tannic. **86**
1991: Supple and complex, with a cedar and tobacco edge to the currant and spicy flavors, finishing with toasty oak and good length. **89**

1990: Big, ripe and fleshy, packed with juicy currant, tobacco, anise and spice flavors that are framed by toasty, buttery oak and firm but fleshy tannins. **91**

1989: Impressive for a 1989, with a focused, lively band of ripe, complex currant, cedar, tobacco and spice flavors. **87**

1987: Complex, with a range of flavors stretching from earthy currant to leather, cedar, anise and cherry; supple tannins. **89**

1986: Cedary currant, spice and earth notes are pleasant enough, but this wine is drying out. **85**

1985: An austere wine that leans toward the cedar-cigar box end of the Cabernet spectrum, with plum and currant flavors. **87**

CAKEBREAD CELLARS (★★★)
Rutherford, Napa Valley
Founded: 1973. **Owner:** The Cakebread Family.
Winemaker: Bruce Cakebread.

MAJOR WINES: PRICE, CASES, RATING

Cabernet Sauvignon Napa Valley ($30, 20,000)	★★★
Cabernet Sauvignon Napa Valley Benchland Select ($65, 900)	★★★
Cabernet Sauvignon Napa Valley Rutherford Reserve (Discontinued)	★★★
Cabernet Sauvignon Napa Valley Three Sisters ($65, 500)	★★★
Chardonnay Napa Valley ($25, 40,000)	★★★
Chardonnay Napa Valley Reserve ($37, 4,500)	★★★
Merlot Napa Valley ($29, 900)	★★★
Pinot Noir Napa Valley Carneros ($30, 500)	★★★
Sauvignon Blanc Napa Valley ($14, 20,000)	★★★
Zinfandel Howell Mountain ($21, 500)	★★★

WINERY DATA
Case Production: 75,000. **Acres Owned:** 77 acres in Napa Valley. **Varietals by Acre:** Cabernet Franc (2 acres), Cabernet Sauvignon (50), Sauvignon Blanc (25). **Varietals Purchased:** Cabernet Sauvignon (Napa Valley), Chardonnay (Carneros, Napa Valley), Merlot (Napa Valley), Pinot Noir (Carneros).

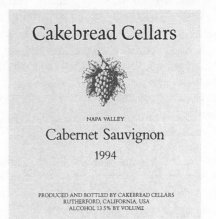

In the 1960s, freelance photographer Jack Cakebread discovered Napa Valley while on a photo assignment for a book on Napa wines. In 1971, he and his wife, Dolores, purchased a 22-acre vineyard in Rutherford, where the winery sits now, and began commuting from Oakland to Napa on weekends; they started their winery in 1973. Cakebread Cellars now owns 77 acres—mostly Cabernet Sauvignon and Sauvignon Blanc—and purchases Cabernet from the Stags Leap District, Chardonnay from Carneros and Merlot from Rutherford.

Cakebread has been a steady ★★★ performer through two decades, at times excelling at all four of the major wines it makes, including 400-case Reserve bottlings of a tightly structured Chardonnay and firmly tannic Cabernet. Carneros Pinot Noir 1994 (89 points) was a welcome addition. Syrah is also new to the mix, as are two new Cabernets—1995 Three Sisters Cabernet Sauvignon Napa Valley and 1995 Benchland Select Cabernet Sauvignon Napa Valley—both from the Rutherford area. It seems to me that winemaker Bruce Cakebread is producing the best wines of his career, making this winery a player once again on the Napa Valley scene.

Tasting Notes

Cabernet Sauvignon Napa Valley (★★★): Usually intense and firmly tannic, but it can be lean and hard as well as a touch bitter. At other times, it's lush and concentrated. It can also age well, as did the 1974.

1995: Earthy, with a tight core of plum and currant and a twinge of stemminess. **89**

1994: Dense, ripe, rich and chewy, with a complex, concentrated core of currant, plum and black cherry. **92**

1993: Simple, with modest ripe plum and cherry flavors and dashes of spice and herb. **82**

1991: Serves up crisp, ripe black cherry and plum flavors before the tannins kick in. **88**

1990: Spicy and herbal, with an elegant core of currant and cherry flavors. **83**

1989: Firm and generous, with a tight core of plum and spice notes. **87**

1988: Tight, with firm tannins, and chunky currant, black cherry, and plum flavors; turns simple. **87**

1987: Big, rich and lush, with intense, concentrated black cherry, currant and plum flavors that are broad and complex. **89**

1986: Fresh, clean and lively, with plenty of black cherry, mint, currant and plum flavors. **88**

1985: Lean and crisp, with medium-weight plum, currant, spice, cedar and tobacco notes. **84**

1984: Well focused vanilla, chocolate and black cherry flavors are framed by supple tannins and a pretty aftertaste. **87**

1983: A good 1983, but Cakebread's weakest vintage. Lean, thin and tannic; with ripe currant flavors that cannot match the tannins. **77**

Lot 2/1974: Deep, rich and plush, with mature but pleasing cedar, coffee, chocolate and currant flavors. One of the better 1974s, it is fully mature, complex and flavorful. The tannins turn smooth on the finish, with just a trace of dryness. Drink up. **91**

Cabernet Sauvignon Napa Valley Benchland Select (★★★)

1995: Well integrated and harmonious, if a bit rigid now. The fruit flavors are pure and well focused, with layers of coffee, currant, black cherry and cedar. Turns complex on the finish, where the flavors mesh together nicely. **90**

Cabernet Sauvignon Napa Valley Rutherford Reserve (★★★): Discontinued; grapes for this bottling are now split between the Benchland Select and the Three Sisters Cabernets.

1993: Crisp and clean, with ripe berry, cherry, currant, cedary oak and spicy nuances emerging from a lean frame. **87**

1992: Tight, lean, tannic and compact, with a narrow band of spicy currant, plum and berry flavors. **87**

1991: Intense, full-bodied, with a core of tarry, ripe plum and currant flavors and some herb and dill notes. **89**

1990: Dense and compact, with a chewy, weedy, earthy edge to the currant and berry notes. **87**

1988: An odd range of flavors taste alternately of plum brandy and ash. **81**

1987: Ripe, rich, plush currant, black cherry and spice notes turn intense and concentrated, finishing with fine depth and finesse. **88**

1986: Lean and tannic, with crisp plum and currant notes, a hard-edged wine. **80**

1985: Lean yet rich, with crisp acidity and fresh, ripe plum flavors of medium depth. **85**

1984: Generous and supple, with broad cherry and chocolate aromas and flavors. **85**

1983: Lean and firm, with a pretty core of black cherry and currant flavors and fine tannins. **88**

Cabernet Sauvignon Napa Valley Three Sisters (★★★)

1995: Austere and tightly wound, with black cherry, blackberry, strawberry and spice flavors. It turns quite tannic on the finish, however, so cellaring is advised. **89**

Chardonnay Napa Valley (★★★), Reserve (★★★): The Napa Valley bottling is made in a tight, non-malolactic style with green apple, melon, and fig flavors. The Reserve is richer and creamier but also clean and focused, with citrus and melon notes.

Chardonnay Napa Valley Reserve

1995: Ripe, clean and complex, with pretty spice, pear, vanilla and honey notes, finishing with toasty oak. **90**

1994: Well oaked, but enough ripe pear, citrus and spicy notes unfold to give it breadth and depth. **89**

Merlot Napa Valley (★★★): An impressive new addition which captures lots of Merlot flavor and sports a supple texture. The 1994 (89 points) was firm, tight and concentrated, and the 1995 (88) was ripe, rich and flavorful.

PINOT NOIR NAPA VALLEY CARNEROS (★★★): A ripe, full-bodied 1994 (89 points) with lots of plum, wild berry and leathery notes was followed by a lighter, earthier 1995 (84).

OLIVER CALDWELL CELLARS (★★★)
St. Helena, Napa Valley
Founded: 1996. **Owner:** Oliver & Karen Caldwell. **Winemaker:** Tom Eddy.

MAJOR WINES: PRICE, CASES, RATING

Cabernet Sauvignon Napa Valley Aïda Vineyard ($35, 400)	★★★
Petite Sirah Napa Valley Aïda Vineyard ($40, 150)	★★★
Zinfandel Napa Valley Aïda Vineyard ($30, 400)	★★★

WINERY DATA
Case Production: 1,500. **Acres Owned:** 17 acres in St. Helena. **Varietals by Acre:** Cabernet Sauvignon (6 acres), Merlot (2), Petite Sirah (4), Zinfandel (5). **Vineyard Designations:** Aïda Vineyard.

Art dealer Oliver Caldwell purchased the 17-acre Aïda Vineyard in Napa Valley in 1996. The old-vine Petite Sirah, Zinfandel and Cabernet Sauvignon grapes from the property were sold to local wineries (most notably Turley Wine Cellars) until Caldwell and his wife Karen decided to start their own label. Tom Eddy makes the wines at the Oakville Ranch Winery.

All of Caldwell's first releases were ripe, richly flavored, complex and intriguing. Based on the track record of the vineyard and winemaker, this winery is definitely worth watching.

TASTING NOTES

CABERNET SAUVIGNON NAPA VALLEY AÏDA VINEYARD (★★★)
1996: Zeros in on the ripe, tight core of black cherry and blackberry flavors, and keeps a vivid fruit profile. **88**

PETITE SIRAH NAPA VALLEY AÏDA VINEYARD (★★★)
1996: Dark, inky and complex, with tiers of earthy plum, leather, spice and cedar, fanning out and turning oaky but quite tannic on the finish. **87**

ZINFANDEL NAPA VALLEY AÏDA VINEYARD (★★★)
1996: A delicious wine; complex and concentrated, with ripe black cherry, wild berry, peppery and spicy nuances; turns smooth and supple. **92**

CALE FAMILY WINES (★★)
Sonoma Valley
Founded: 1990. **Owner:** Michael & Jeannie Cale. **Winemaker:** Kerry Damskey, Michael Cale.

MAJOR WINES: PRICE, CASES, RATING

Chardonnay Carneros Sangiacomo Vineyard ($22, 1,600)	★★★
Merlot Sonoma Valley Serres Ranch ($25, 1,000)	★★
Pinot Noir Carneros Sangiacomo Vineyard ($20, 400)	★★

WINERY DATA
Case Production: 3,000. **Vineyard Designations:** Sangiacomo Vineyard (Chardonnay, Pinot Noir), Serres Ranch (Merlot). **Varietals Purchased:** Chardonnay (Carneros), Merlot (Sonoma Valley), Pinot Noir (Carneros).

Cale has done well with Sangiacomo Chardonnay, regularly producing elegant, flavorful wines like the tightly wound 1996. New additions Pinot Noir and Merlot have been less exciting.

TASTING NOTES

CHARDONNAY CARNEROS SANGIACOMO VINEYARD (★★★)
1996: Ripe apple, citrus and pear flavors, with a dash of pineapple and a tart streak. **88**
1995: Clean, ripe and refreshing, with pretty pear, apple, melon and spice notes that fold together nicely. **90**

CALERA WINE CO. (★★★★)
Mount Harlan, San Benito County
Founded: 1975. **Owner:** Josh Jensen. **Winemaker:** Belinda Gould.

MAJOR WINES: PRICE, CASES, RATING

Chardonnay Central Coast ($16, 12,000)	★★★★

Chardonnay Mount Harlan ($30, 1,000)	★★★★
Pinot Noir Central Coast ($16, 12,000)	★★★
Pinot Noir Mount Harlan Jensen ($38, 1,200)	★★★★
Pinot Noir Mount Harlan Mills ($35, 1,100)	★★★★
Pinot Noir Mount Harlan Reed ($35, 400)	★★★
Pinot Noir Mount Harlan Selleck ($38, 500)	★★★
Viognier Mount Harlan ($30, 1,200)	★★★

WINERY DATA
Case Production: 30,000. **Acres Owned:** 47 acres in Mount Harlan. **Varietals by Acre:** Chardonnay (6 acres), Pinot Noir (36), Viognier (5). **Vineyard Designations:** Jensen (Pinot Noir), Mills (Pinot Noir), Reed (Pinot Noir), Seleck (Pinot Noir). **Varietals Purchased:** Chardonnay (Central Coast), Pinot Noir (Central Coast).

While touring France as a student at Oxford, Josh Jensen became fascinated by Burgundy. After working several harvests, he decided to grow Chardonnay and Pinot Noir in California. To that end, he began a statewide search for thin soils laced with limestone, and in 1974, he finally settled in the rugged Mount Harlan area of San Benito County, where he found a property with an old lime kiln. Today, Calera (lime kiln in Spanish) farms 47 acres, mostly planted to Pinot Noir. Calera makes vineyard-designated Pinots from four vineyard sites: Jensen (14 acres), Selleck (5 acres), Reed (5 acres) and Mills (11 acres).

Jensen strives for complexity in his Pinot Noir, with a dark, ultra-ripe, often jammy style full of intense flavors. Past efforts were occasionally funky and decadent, but lately the wines have been dramatic and well crafted, capable of aging for five to seven years. Wine from the Jensen Vineyard is usually the darkest and most complex. The Chardonnay is often quite toasty with new oak, and the Viognier is very intense and well made. Calera also produces a Chardonnay and a Pinot Noir from Central Coast grapes.

TASTING NOTES

CHARDONNAY CENTRAL COAST (★★★)
1997: Tight, tart and flinty, with a core of citrus, pear and earthy notes that are clean and lively. **87**
1996: Woody, with smoky, toasty notes, but also a rich core of ripe pear, fig, melon and citrus flavors. **90**
1995: Classy, smooth and ripe, with deep, creamy peach, pear, apple and vanilla flavors. **91**
1994: Smooth and rich, with toasty oak, pear, spice and honey notes, turning elegant. **90**

CHARDONNAY MOUNT HARLAN (★★★★): Intense, concentrated, and loaded with rich, compelling flavors.
1995: Smooth, ripe, rich and concentrated, with a focused core of spicy pear, hazelnut, fig, melon and light toasty oak. **90**
1994: Intense, lively, well focused and flavorful; rich, with pear, hazelnut, mineral and vanilla flavors. **91**
1992: Compact and concentrated, with ripe pear, pineapple, butterscotch and toasty oak flavors. **89**
1990: Ripe, fat and buttery, with creamy pear, earth and spice flavors that are smooth and fleshy, finishing with a rich, thick aftertaste. **89**

PINOT NOIR CENTRAL COAST (★★★)
1997: Spicy, with a vegetal, herbal streak running through the spicy cherry notes, it turns complex and a bit tannic. **86**

PINOT NOIR MOUNT HARLAN JENSEN (★★★★):
The best and most consistent of Calera's Pinots, this is usually very ripe, often exotic and typically complex and age-worthy.
1994: Lean and trim, with a complex, earthy currant and black cherry edge. **88**
1993: Distinct, exotic, ripe, racy fruit flavors, with layers of juicy cherry, wild berry and plum and a wonderful aftertaste. **91**
1992: Mature flavors and aromas, with a dry edge to the earthy cherry and mushroom flavors. **86**
1991: Aromatic with ripe, exotic wild berry and raspberry flavors that turn elegant and silky. **88**
1990: Bold and ripe, with a decadent edge of cherry and plum aromas and flavors. **87**
1989: Very dark and rich, packing a wallop of decadent and concentrated plum and cherry aromas and flavors. **89**

1988: Packed with rich, ultraripe black cherry, currant, herb and spicy earth flavors. Deeply flavored and very concentrated, with smooth, supple tannins. **92**

1987: Deep, rich, enormously complex and concentrated, with intense, sharply focused plum, currant, black cherry, raspberry, mineral and spice flavors. **93**

1986: A deliciously complex wine, with a magnificent interplay of plum, currant, nutmeg and vanilla flavors, a supple texture and vibrant acidity. **91**

1985: Effusively fruity, almost jammy, loaded with ripe, complex plum, cherry and raspberry flavors in a full-bodied, firmly-structured wine. **92**

PINOT NOIR MOUNT HARLAN MILLS (★★★): Excellent fruit intensity, though not as deep as the Jensen.

1994: Ripe and polished, with a focused core of cherry, sage, earth and spice, turning elegant. **88**

1993: Earthy, tannic and leathery, with cola, cherry, sage and spice flavors and a touch of cranberry. **86**

1992: Starts with ripe cherry and jammy raspberry notes, turning complex and racy on the finish. **91**

1990: Mature, with exotic, racy wild berry, cherry, anise and spicy nuances; turns complex. **90**

1989: A dramatic, complex Pinot Noir, rich, concentrated and effusively fruity, with tiers of black cherry, currant, anise and plum flavors that are broad and deep. **93**

1988: Dense and austere but has plenty of stuffing, with black cherry and currant flavors tightly wrapped in tannins. **89**

PINOT NOIR MOUNT HARLAN REED (★★★): Serves up a broad range of complex flavors.

1994: Earthy, with dried cherry and wild berry fruit, along with notes of tea and sage. **88**

1992: Elegant and fragrant, with a ripe, supple core of spicy cherry, raspberry and subtle earth notes. **91**

1989: A lean yet very ripe wine with jammy cherry flavors and a strong volatile edge. It's concentrated and earthy, finishing with potent berry flavors. **88**

1988: Ripe and intense, with pepper, stewed plum, herb and black cherry flavors that come with some alcoholic heat. **85**

1987: Spicy and slightly cooked, with cherry and beet flavors that are concentrated and rich, but also a bit earthy. **80**

PINOT NOIR MOUNT HARLAN SELLECK (★★★): Complex, often showing rich, almost tarry fruit flavors.

1993: A light Harlan, with herb, rhubarb and cola notes and a pretty dash of cherry and spice. **85**

1988: Ripe, with a complex raisiny edge, but also lots of spicy cherry and raspberry jam flavors that pick up a tarry edge. **89**

1987: Hard and tight now, but with a solid core of rich, concentrated, deeply perfumed black cherry, currant, plum and spice flavors. **92**

1986: Drinking well, with complex black cherry, spice and cedar flavors and a hint of earth, mushroom and smoked meat. **89**

VIOGNIER MOUNT HARLAN (★★★): Consistently rich, with exotic fruit and hazelnut flavors.

1997: A delicious wine; rich and unctuous, with layers of fig, apple, melon and citrus flavors. **89**

1995: Captures the ripe, rich and exotic flavors of this grape, with lots of ripe pear, citrus, spice and hazelnut flavors. **88**

1994: Elegant and refined, with attractive pear, spice and nectarine flavors. Becomes complex. **89**

CALISTOGA VINEYARDS see CUVAISON

CALLAWAY VINEYARD & WINERY (★★)
Temecula, Riverside County
Founded: 1969. **Owner:** Wine Alliance, Allied Domecq.
Winemaker: Dwayne Helmuth.

MAJOR WINES: PRICE, CASES, RATING

Cabernet Sauvignon California	
($11, NA)	★★
Chardonnay Temecula Calla-lees	
($10, NA)	★★
Chenin Blanc Temecula	
($6, NA)	★★
Dolcetto Temecula	
($16, NA)	★
Pinot Gris Temecula	
($14, NA)	★
Sauvignon Blanc Temecula	
($8, NA)	★★
Sweet Nancy Late Harvest Temecula	
($25, NA)	★★
Viognier Temecula	
($16, NA)	★★

WINERY DATA

Case Production: 250,000. **Acres Owned:** 750 acres in Temecula (20 year lease). **Varietals by Acre:** Cabernet Sauvignon (10 acres), Chardonnay (575), Chenin Blanc (10), Dolcetto (5), Merlot (20), Mourvèdre (5), Muscat Canelli (20), Nebbiolo (5), Pinot Blanc (20), Pinot Gris (10), Sauvignon Blanc (45), Syrah (5), Viognier (20). **Varietals Purchased:** Cabernet Sauvignon (California), Merlot (California).

Industrialist Ely Callaway, one-time president of Burlington Industries and now a golf club manufacturer, founded this winery in Temecula in 1974. He knew nothing about wine at the time, but claims he considered that an asset. The early years were rough going for this winery, as its trial-and-error experiments with different varietals led to some downright funky red wines characterized by earthy, rubbery flavors, and whites that were often oxidized. Callaway eventually grew tired of the wine business, realizing that Southern California's affection for his wines had its limits. He sold the winery to Hiram Walker in 1981, marking that company's entry into the California wine business (it also owns Clos du Bois and William Hill, and markets Atlas Peak Vineyards under its Wine Alliance umbrella). Wine Alliance set Callaway on a fast-paced growth cycle, expanding the vineyards to 750 acres, dropping reds, lees-aging its Chardonnay in stainless steel and adopting the motto "White Wine. It's All We Make".

Production is, at present, nearly 250,000 cases. The top-selling wine is the Calla-Lees Chardonnay, which, at its best, is fresh, fruity and without any oak flavors, but it can also be overly leesy, bordering on sour. The best overall wine is the Sauvignon Blanc, which is often delicious and flavorful, as the 1997 (88 points) proved to be. Sweet Nancy, a botrytis-style Chenin Blanc, can also be very good. Other wines produced are Viognier and White Riesling. In 1996 Callaway returned to reds with a California appellation Cabernet. Trials with Pinot Gris, Mourvèdre, Dolcetto and Nebbiolo are ongoing. In 1994, Callaway sold its vineyards, but signed a long-term agreement to buy grapes from the new owners. Expansion plans should bring production to 400,000 cases.

CAMBIASO see **DOMAINE ST. GEORGE**

CAMBRIA WINERY & VINEYARD (★★★)

Santa Maria Valley, Santa Barbara County
Founded: 1986. **Owner:** Barbara Banke & Jess Jackson. **Winemaker:** Fred Holloway.

MAJOR WINES: PRICE, CASES, RATING

Chardonnay Santa Maria Valley Katherine's Vineyard ($18, NA)	★★★★
Chardonnay Santa Maria Valley Reserve ($36, NA)	★★★
Pinot Noir Santa Maria Valley Julia's Vineyard ($24, NA)	★★★
Pinot Noir Santa Maria Valley Reserve ($40, NA)	★★★
Sangiovese Santa Maria Valley Tepusquet Vineyard ($18, NA)	★★★
Syrah Santa Maria Valley Tepusquet Vineyard ($18, NA)	★★★
Viognier Santa Maria Valley Tepusquet Vineyard ($18, NA)	★★★

WINERY DATA

Acres Owned: 1,232 acres in Santa Maria Valley. **Varietals by Acre:** Barbera (0.5 acres), Chardonnay (1,000), Pinot Blanc (0.5), Pinot Gris (3), Pinot Noir (201), Sangiovese (7), Syrah (10), Viognier (10). **Vineyard Designations:** Katherine's Vineyard (Chardonnay), Julia's Vineyard (Pinot Noir), Tepusquet Vineyard (Sangiovese, Syrah, Viognier).

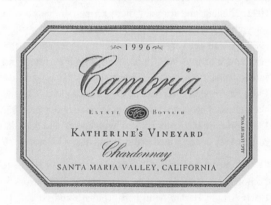

As Kendall-Jackson's Winery's demand for Chardonnay soared in the 1980s, it sought grapes throughout California. One of the best sources proved to be the Santa Maria Valley and the highly regarded, 2,000-acre Tepusquet Vineyard. In 1986, Jess Jackson began producing Cambria Chardonnay from Tepusquet. In 1987, Kendall-Jackson and Robert Mondavi Winery each bought part of the vineyard, with Kendall-Jackson acquiring nearly 1,000 acres, most of it in Chardonnay.

Today Cambria—which is considered a separate brand, even though wholly owned by Kendall-Jackson— holds 1,232 acres, including 1,000 acres of Chardonnay. While Chardonnay is its primary wine, Cambria has also enjoyed success with Pinot Noir, Sangiovese, Syrah and Viognier.

All of the wines are well made, complex and reasonably priced. The Katherine's Vineyard Chardonnay, however, has held a slight quality edge over the other wines of late. Given Cambria's considerable vineyard holdings in such a prime winegrowing area, it remains a winery worth considering.

TASTING NOTES

CHARDONNAY SANTA MARIA VALLEY KATHERINE'S VINEYARD (★★★★): Bold, ripe and intense, with bright, complex flavors and bracing acidity.

1996: Ripe and spicy, with a lively core of tangerine, pear, fig and melon flavors, and spicy vanilla notes. **90**

1995: Complex, with spicy citrus, tangerine, pear and pineapple notes that fan out nicely. **91**

1993: Bright and lively, with vivid, medium-weight pear, spice, honey and hazelnut notes that turn elegant. **87**

CHARDONNAY SANTA MARIA VALLEY RESERVE (★★★): A shade less complex than the Katherine's Vineyard bottling. Offers crisp acidity and pretty Chardonnay flavors. Best upon release.

1995: Crisp and flinty, with complex pear, peach and spicy oak flavors. **88**

1994: Well balanced, with a nice range of spicy, toasty pear and pineapple flavors. Complex and elegant. **88**

1993: Bold, ripe and harmonious, with rich pear, honey, butterscotch and spicy nuances, picking up a smoky leesy edge on the finish. Wonderful aftertaste. **91**

1992: Bold, ripe and complex, with tiers of fig, spice, oak, pineapple and citrus flavors that are rich and focused, picking up hints of honey and butterscotch on the finish. **91**

PINOT NOIR SANTA MARIA VALLEY JULIA'S VINEYARD (★★★): Remarkably consistent and smooth-textured, with supple flavors that range from herb to dark cherry. Well crafted.

1996: Intense and concentrated, with flavors of earth, spice, cranberry and cherry. **87**

1995: An earthy, beefy style with lots of herb, mushroom, tea and meaty notes. **87**

1994: Serves up a ripe, complex core of plum, cherry and wild berry flavors in an openly fruity style. **89**

1993: Exotic in its spiciness, with plush cherry, herb, tea and cedary oak flavors. **87**

1992: Tight, firm, with sharply-focused spice, black cherry, herb and cola flavors that are rich and concentrated. **87**

1991: Supple and elegant, with a smooth, fleshy texture and a core of rich, spicy herb and black cherry aromas and flavors. **87**

1989: Earthy, tarry and gamy, but has a nice core of cola and berry flavors, too. **80**

1988: Ripe, generous, silky and complex, with raspberry and plum flavors and hints of coffee, toast and chocolate on the long, complex finish. **88**

PINOT NOIR SANTA MARIA VALLEY RESERVE (★★★): Less consistent and complex than the Julia's Vineyard bottling, but well made.

1994: Distinctive, tight and complex, with an array of herb, spice, leather, mineral and cherry flavors. **88**

1993: A lighter style, with pretty herb, cola and black cherry flavors of modest proportion. **85**

1992: Pleasantly fruity, with herb and black cherry flavors. Finishes with firm tannins and a cola edge. **86**

SANGIOVESE SANTA MARIA VALLEY TEPUSQUET VINEYARD (★★★): Good color; impressive for its ripe zesty flavors.

SYRAH SANTA MARIA VALLEY TEPUSQUET VINEYARD (★★★): Deep in color; impressive for its intensity and purity of flavor. Worth watching.

1996: Smooth and racy, with herb-tinged cherry and berry flavors that turn elegant and supple. **87**

CANEPA CELLARS (★★★)

Alexander Valley, Sonoma County
Founded: 1991. **Owner:** James Canepa. **Winemaker:** Helen Turley.

MAJOR WINES: PRICE, CASES, RATING

Chardonnay Alexander Valley Gauer
  Vineyard Adobe III
  ($26, 614)   ★★★

WINERY DATA

Case Production: 700. **Vineyard Designations:** Gauer Vineyard. **Varietals Purchased:** Chardonnay (Alexander Valley).

Canepa produces only one wine—a Gauer Vineyard Chardonnay, which is often very good and occasionally outstanding. Gauer Vineyard, well known for its excellent Chardonnay grapes, was purchased by Jess Jackson in 1995, but Canepa has been able to continue buying grapes. Helen Turley makes the wine at the Napa Wine Co.

TASTING NOTES

CHARDONNAY ALEXANDER VALLEY GAUER VINEYARD ADOBE III (★★★)

1996: Pleasantly fruity and elegant, with ripe pear, fig and spicy notes and spicy, toasty flavors. **88**
1995: Very complex, with an intriguing interplay of ripe pear, apple, toast, fig and smoky, buttery flavors. **91**

CANYON RIDGE see ARCIERO WINERY

CANYON ROAD see GEYSER PEAK WINERY

CARDINALE (★★★★)

Oakville, Napa Valley
Founded: 1983. **Owner:** Jess Jackson. **Winemaker:** Charles Thomas.

MAJOR WINES: PRICE, CASES, RATING

Red Napa & Alexander Valleys
  ($70, 2,700)   ★★★★

WINERY DATA

Case Production: 3,000. **Acres Owned:** 162 acres (69 in Mount Veeder, 68 in Howell Mountain, 25 in Oakville). **Varietals by Acre:** Cabernet Sauvignon (94 acres), Chardonnay (8), Merlot (60).

Cardinale began as a high-end California-appellation Cabernet blend under the Kendall-Jackson umbrella of wines. In 1994, Kendall-Jackson owner Jess Jackson purchased the Robert Pepi Winery in Oakville, and in 1998 began construction of a new winery there which will become Cardinale's home, along with Kendall-Jackson's new Lokoya brand.

Cardinale's only wine is primarily a blend of Napa Valley and Sonoma County hillside grapes, and is made under the direction of Charles Thomas, a former winemaker for Robert Mondavi Winery. The most recent vintages have used grapes from Mount Veeder and Howell Mountain in Napa Valley and Gauer Ranch in Alexander Valley. The concept is to give the winemaker as much flexibility as possible in producing a highly complex wine. Don't be surprised, however, if Cardinale eventually becomes a Napa Valley-only wine as Kendall Jackson moves toward more vineyard-specific wines.

TASTING NOTES

RED NAPA & ALEXANDER VALLEYS (★★★★): Early vintages of this Cabernet blend were tight and tart and aged very poorly. More recent efforts are firm, with rich, complex fruit flavors and seemingly better aging potential.
1995: Manages to massage the tannins with supple currant and plum flavors, showing off cedar, spice and mineral accents. **92**
1993: Currant, cedar, plum and anise aromas and flavors strive for complexity, but the tannins swarm in, and it's dry and not terribly concentrated. **86**
1992: Dense and chewy, with an earthy, leathery accent to the currant, dried cherry and mineral flavors. More complex on the finish where the flavors fold together nicely. **89**
1991: Shows off its ripe black cherry, currant and wild berry flavors that stretch to a jammy edge, adding pretty spice and anise and firm tannins. **91**
1990: Bold, ripe, smooth and polished, with layers of plum, currant, cherry and blueberry flavors that are focused and lively. **90**
1989: An earthy, rough-hewn wine with chunky currant, herb and oak flavors. **86**
1988: Light and spicy, with ripe cherry and prune notes that pick up a touch of anise on a smooth finish. **85**

1987: Rich, ripe and concentrated, with plum, blueberry and currant flavors laced with spicy oak. Vanilla and cinnamon notes emerge on the long finish. **90**
1986: Lean and tannic, with intense, ripe aromas and flavors of currant and cherry and firm, crisp tannins. **86**
1985: Delivers a lot of richness and complexity, with pretty currant, cherry and plum flavors, finishing with toasty, buttery oak. **85**
1984: Ripe, with supple cassis and plum flavors framed by smoky, spicy oak notes. **84**

CARMENET WINERY (★★★)
Sonoma Valley
Founded: 1982. **Owner:** Chalone Wine Group Ltd.
Winemaker: Karl Wright.

MAJOR WINES: PRICE, CASES, RATING
Cabernet Sauvignon North Coast Dynamite
  ($17, 28,000)   ★★
Chardonnay Sonoma Valley Carneros
  Sangiacomo Vineyard
  ($18, 6,000)   ★★★
Meritage Sonoma Valley Moon Mountain
  Estate Reserve
  ($40, 5,000)   ★★★
Sauvignon Blanc-Sémillon Edna Valley
  Paragon Vineyard Reserve
  ($16, 4,400)   ★★
Zinfandel Contra Costa County Evanghelo
  Vineyard Delta Zin
  ($17, 2,000)   ★★

ALSO PRODUCED
Cabernet Franc Sonoma Valley Moon Mountain Vineyard ($25, 600); Cabernet Sauvignon North Coast Dynamite ($17, 2,200); Gewürztraminer Sonoma Valley ($14, 500); Merlot North Coast Dynamite ($17, 2,200); Zinfandel Port Contra Costa County ($17, 500).

WINERY DATA
Case Production: 50,000. **Acres Owned:** 97 acres in Sonoma Valley. **Varietals by Acre:** Cabernet Franc (22 acres), Cabernet Sauvignon (50), Malbec (3), Merlot (18), Petit Verdot (4). **Vineyard Designations:** Evanghelo Vineyard (Zinfandel), Sangiacomo Vineyard (Chardonnay). **Varietals Purchased:** Cabernet Franc (Napa Valley, Sonoma County, Mendocino County), Cabernet Sauvignon (Napa Valley, Sonoma County, Mendocino County), Chardonnay (Sonoma Valley, Carneros), Merlot (Napa Valley, Sonoma County, Sonoma Valley, Mendocino County, Carneros), Sauvignon Blanc (Edna Valley), Sémillon (Edna Valley), Zinfandel (Contra Costa County).

Situated in the sloping mountains that form the eastern border of Sonoma Valley, Carmenet Winery is part of Chalone Wine Estates, owners of Chalone Vineyards, Acacia Winery and Edna Valley Vineyards. Carmenet initially focused on Bordeaux-style reds (Cabernet and Merlot blends) and whites. Its estate vineyard—which sits 1,600 feet above the valley floor and is next to Louis Martini Winery's Monte Rosso vineyard—was formerly known as Glen Ellen Vineyard, and provided Cabernet grapes to Ridge, Kistler and Chateau St. Jean.

Carmenet's red Meritage, now called Moon Mountain Estate Reserve, is sturdy, roughly-hewn, chunky, oaky and occasionally rustic; it can also be complex. The very complex and concentrated Chardonnay, made from Sangiacomo Vineyard, has been a solid success. Karl Wright, an assistant winemaker at Ferrari-Carano Winery for eight years, took over as winemaker in 1998.

TASTING NOTES

CHARDONNAY SONOMA VALLEY CARNEROS SANGIACOMO VINEYARD (★★★)
1996: Tight and well focused, with spice, toasty oak, ripe pear and fig flavors that unfold nicely. **89**
1995: Rich and complex, with layers of ripe fig, apple, pear and spice flavors. Shows a wonderful sense of harmony and finesse. **92**

MERITAGE SONOMA VALLEY MOON MOUNTAIN ESTATE RESERVE (★★★): Tightly reined in and firmly tannic, sometimes to a fault, with crisp currant, cedar, tobacco and fruit flavors. Well-oaked and capable of aging, although the early vintages are still tough, unevolved and in danger of drying out.
1995: Complex and concentrated, with blackberry, currant, cedar, mineral and spice flavors. Finishes with firm, chewy tannins. **90**
1994: Smooth and ripe, with an array of currant, toasty oak and vanilla scents and hints of sage and tobacco. **90**
1993: Well focused, a pretty band of cedar, currant, coffee and light oak flavors, finishing with firm tannins. **87**

1992: Elegant and complex, with a pretty band of ripe cherry, currant, plum, anise and spice flavors and light toasty oak. **89**

1991: Smooth and mature, with hints of herb, currant and black cherry. **88**

1989: Offers cedar, cigar box and spicy black currant flavors that are intense, focused and concentrated. **88**

1988: Lavish, buttery oak notes dominating the currant and black cherry flavors. **87**

1987: Firm and intense, with well knit cherry, coffee, cedar, herb and currant flavors. **89**

1986: Dry, austere and tannic; very disappointing. **74**

1985: Elegant and stylish, with ripe plum and cherry flavors, accented by vanilla and tobacco nuances. **88**

1984: Mature, but the black cherry, currant and spice flavors are complex. **88**

1983: Tight and lean, mature and drying, leaving a hint of mint and plum. **83**

1982: Mature and turning earthy, with tannic currant and cedar flavors. **84**

CARNEROS CREEK WINERY (★★–★★★)
Carneros
Founded: 1972. **Owner:** Francis & Kathleen Mahoney, William Hambrecht. **Winemaker:** Melissa Moravec.

MAJOR WINES: PRICE, CASES, RATING
Chardonnay Carneros
  ($17, 2,500)   ★★
Pinot Noir Carneros
  ($18, 10,000)   ★★★
Pinot Noir Carneros Côte de Carneros
  ($15, 8,000)   ★★
Pinot Noir Carneros Fleur de Carneros
  ($12, 14,000)   ★★
Pinot Noir Carneros Signature Reserve
  ($40, 1,000)   ★★★

ALSO PRODUCED
Chardonnay Carneros Palombo Vineyard ($15, 4,000).

WINERY DATA
Case Production: 38,000. **Acres Owned:** 175 acres in Carneros. **Varietals by Acre:** Chardonnay (11 acres), Merlot (4), Pinot Noir (160). **Vineyard Designations:** Palombo Vineyard. **Varietals Purchased:** Pinot Noir (Carneros).

Owner-winemaker Francis Mahoney has been at the forefront of Pinot Noir clonal research and was an early advocate of the cool Carneros appellation for Pinot Noir. Dissatisfied with the Pinot Noir clones available when he started making wine, Mahoney embarked on an ambitious program to identify and test some 20 different clones. Mahoney's interest in winemaking grew out of an appreciation for wine that began when he worked as a wine retailer in San Francisco. In 1972, he and financial backer Balfour Gibson bought 30 acres in Carneros and planted 10 acres to vines, producing their first Pinot Noir in 1976.

Early on, Carneros Creek made a wide assortment of wines, such as Zinfandel from Napa and Amador Counties and Cabernet from the Stags Leap District, including a vineyard-designated Fay Vineyard bottling. But Pinot Noir has always been Mahoney's passion and his best wine. The winery now owns 175 acres, 160 of them planted to Pinot Noir. In 1998, venture capitalist and vintner William Hambrecht joined Carneros Creek as a minority partner. Hambrecht owns the Hambrecht Wine Group portfolio, which includes Belvedere Winery and Grove Street Winery.

None of Mahoney's wines are especially polished, and they often have a few rough edges that require short-term cellaring. The Carneros Chardonnay is ripe and fruity, with a subtle oak flavor. The Carneros Pinot Noir is of medium weight, with cherry and berryish flavors and mild tannins. The Fleur de Carneros is even lighter and often rather simple, designed for early consumption. The Signature Reserve Pinot Noir merits ★★★ overall, but in some years it has been outstanding.

TASTING NOTES

PINOT NOIR CARNEROS (★★★): Complex, occasionally outstanding, with earth, mineral and dark fruit notes.

PINOT NOIR CARNEROS SIGNATURE RESERVE (★★★): When it's good, it's very, very good and when it misses it isn't by much. The oldest vintages—from the mid-1970s—have aged well.

1995: An elegant, understated style, with tea, black cherry, spice and herbal notes, finishing with a beefy, meaty edge. **87**

1994: Smooth, ripe, supple and harmonious, with a complex band of cherry, cedar, earth and spice and lots of plum and cherry flavors coming through on the finish. **91**

1993: Firmly tannic and a bit dry, but the cherry and plum flavors are ripe and show more depth and richness than most from this vintage. **88**

1991: Drying out, but at an excellent drinking stage, as the Pinot Noir flavors are mature, with pleasant earth, mushroom and dried cherry and berry notes and a smooth texture. Shows a hint of raisin—hence the dryness. **88**

1989: Soft and fleshy, with an herbal edge to the currant, cola and berry flavors. **80**

1988: Intense and elegant, with chocolate and toasty oak aromas and rich, concentrated, complex black cherry and plum flavors. **89**

1987: A rich, supple wine with intense, concentrated spice, cola and cherry flavors rounded out by a touch of toasty oak. **87**

CARTLIDGE & BROWNE see EHLERS GROVE

CASE see ROBERT TALBOTT VINEYARDS

CASTALIA (★★★)
Russian River Valley, Sonoma County
Founded: 1992. **Owner:** Terry Bering. **Winemaker:** Terry Bering.

MAJOR WINES: PRICE, CASES, RATING
Pinot Noir Russian River Valley
  Rochioli Vineyard
  ($23, 300) ★★★

WINERY DATA
Case Production: 300. **Vineyard Designations:** Rochioli Vineyard. **Varietals Purchased:** Pinot Noir (Russian River).

As assistant winemaker at Rochioli Vineyard & Winery, Terry Bering has access to some great Pinot Noir grapes from the Rochiolis. Only a tiny amount of wine is produced each year under his own label, Castalia. When it's good, as was the 1994 (92 points), it can be rich and dazzling, but it can also suffer from a lack of balance and concentration, as did the 1996 (82).

CATACULA see GREEN & RED VINEYARD

CAYMUS VINEYARDS (★★★★★)
Rutherford, Napa Valley
Founded: 1972. **Owner:** Chuck Wagner. **Winemaker:** Chuck Wagner, Jon Bolta.

MAJOR WINES: PRICE, CASES, RATING
Cabernet Sauvignon Napa Valley
  ($65, 20,000) ★★★★★
Cabernet Sauvignon Napa Valley
  Special Selection
  ($135, 2,000) ★★★★★
Conundrum White California
  ($21, 18,000) ★★★★★
Sauvignon Blanc Napa Valley
  ($16, 18,000) ★★★★

WINERY DATA
Case Production: 70,000. **Acres Owned:** 73 acres in Napa Valley. **Varietals by Acre:** Cabernet Sauvignon (60 acres), Sauvignon Blanc (13). **Varietals Purchased:** Cabernet Franc (Napa Valley), Cabernet Sauvignon (Napa Valley), Chardonnay (Monterey County), Muscat (Monterey County), Sauvignon Blanc (Napa Valley), Sémillon (Monterey County), Viognier (Monterey County).

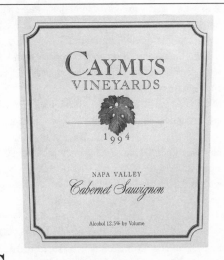

Caymus Vineyards is synonymous with classically proportioned, richly flavored Napa Valley Cabernet. Owner-founder Charlie Wagner, who was born and raised on this Rutherford estate, considers Caymus to be California's most consistent producer of great Cabernet. Given this winery's superb track record, it's difficult to disagree.

The Wagners are first and foremost great farmers—they know their land and vineyards well. Wagner's son Chuck is now in charge, refining and polishing what his father began. Chuck has also become a superb winemaker, branching out beyond Cabernet to make finely-crafted Sauvignon Blanc; unique blends such as Conundrum, a white wine made from a variety of grapes grown throughout the state; and even Chardonnay, with his Monterey-based Mer Soleil vineyard and brand.

The Wagner family began farming in Rutherford in 1906, planting vineyards in the late 1940s. After years of selling grapes to area wineries, the Wagners decided to try their hand at winemaking, naming their winery after the Caymus Indians, a tribe that once lived in Napa Valley. Charlie and Chuck Wagner made their first wines in 1972, among them a Cabernet. Beginning in 1975, Caymus chose its best barrels of Cabernet for its limited-production Special Selection, a 100 percent Cabernet bottling that's been made every year since 1975 except 1977, 1993 and 1996. Caymus Special Selection is an amazing line of distinctive, richly concentrated, wonderfully flavorful Cabernets. While Randy Dunn (Dunn Vineyards) worked as winemaker through 1984 and is often credited with crafting the great Caymus Cabernets, he is the first to point out that the strength of Caymus's wines lies in its vineyard and the quality of its grapes. Since Dunn left in 1984, Chuck Wagner has deftly demonstrated his ability to fine-tune these wines to near perfection.

While the Caymus lineup has, throughout the years, featured Zinfandel, Pinot Noir and Sauvignon Blanc, all from purchased grapes, today all that remains from that group is Sauvignon Blanc. Wagner has planted a Pinot Noir vineyard on the Sonoma Coast, but has yet to release a wine from that property.

In the late 1970s, the Wagners started a highly successful second label called Liberty School, which for years was a négociant brand that blended bulk wines. Recently, Caymus sold their majority stake in Liberty School to the Hope Family of Paso Robles, owners of Triana Winery. In 1989, Caymus added Conundrum, a white table wine that is a blend of Chardonnay, Sauvignon Blanc and Muscat from a broadly based California appellation; the result is best described as *sur lie* barrel-fermented Chardonnay meets lavishly oaked Sauvignon Blanc, along with a dash of spice.

While the Special Selection Cabernet reigns supreme, selling for $135 a bottle, the standard Caymus Cabernet Sauvignon Napa Valley is a lush and textured wine. It benefits from the Wagners' great vineyard connections, with grapes coming from both the hillsides and valley floor. Perhaps as a sign of the times and the growing recognition of the greatness of Napa Valley Cabernet, the 1995 vintage sold for $65 a bottle.

TASTING NOTES

CABERNET SAUVIGNON NAPA VALLEY (★★★★★): Once estate-bottled (through 1986), it is now a blend of valley floor and hillside grapes. While not as rich and opulent as the Special Selection, it nonetheless reflects the Caymus house style. Well-oaked, elegant and flavorful, it can age well, but it peaks at about five years.

1995: Seductive, with spicy, vanilla-scented oak leading to a rich, complex core of currant, black cherry, olive and plum flavors. **92**

1994: Bold, ripe, rich and flavorful, with layers of currant, black cherry, cedar and plum. A real mouthful. **95**

1993: Pleasant for its range of cherry, spice, cedar and currant flavors; complex, elegant and refined. **91**

1992: Possesses supple and harmonious black cherry, currant, plum and herb flavors that pick up an olive and spice edge. **89**

1991: Deep, rich and plush, with a core of ripe, seductive currant and black cherry flavors framed by pretty, toasty, buttery oak. One delicious mouthful of Cabernet. **91**

1990: Firm and focused, with spicy tobacco and chocolate overtones to the ripe prune and currant aromas and flavors. **90**

1989: Elegant and forward, well balanced and easy to drink, serving up a pretty array of currant, tea and oak flavors. **88**

1988: Smooth and velvety; a medium-weight wine with complex, subtle tobacco, chocolate, plum and currant aromas and flavors. **87**

1987: Cedar, vanilla, spice and currant aromas give way to similar flavors that are full-bodied and rich; a wonderful dose of oak and tannin balances the solid core of supple fruit. **92**

1986: Complex and elegant, with smoky chocolate, plum and cherry aromas and flavors; supple, smooth and amazingly long on the finish. **94**

1985: A beautifully defined Rutherford Cabernet; rich, lean and elegant, with layers of spice, cedar, plum and black cherry flavors that echo on the palate. **92**

1984: Richly flavored and supple, with ripe plum, herb and currant flavors. The tannins, while thick, are smooth and fleshy. **91**

1983: Showing its age, with mature cedar, tar and plum flavors. **84**

1982: This wine peaked in 1991, but in its youth it was one of the best 1982s. Now the currant, plum and herb flavors show their maturity, with dried fruit, anise and spice flavors coming through on the finish. Can age longer, but won't improve. **87**

1981: Ripe, forward and supple, with generous, fleshy plum, black cherry and cedar flavors, crisp acidity and smooth, polished tannins. **88**

1980: A deep, rich, concentrated wine with plenty of black cherry, currant and plum flavors, crisp acidity and tannins that are softening. Mature and at its peak. **90**

1979: Still youthful, dark and complex, with pretty spice, currant, herb, cherry and earth notes that are intense and elegant. Has a polished, supple texture. Aging exceptionally well. **91**

1978: Fading, though the dried plum, cherry and anise flavors have a pleasantly supple, earthy edge. **88**

1977: Light in body, with modest mint and cedar flavors that are simple and fading. **77**

1976: Mature, but holding its ripe, supple plum and black cherry flavors. **85**

1975: An elegant, generous wine with black cherry, plum and spice flavors that offer depth and complexity. **89**

1974: Very ripe and fruity on the nose, but with less flavor coming through. The fruit tastes hollow and less concentrated than in the past. **84**

1973: Mature, but still very complex, with a full bouquet of fruit and deep, rich flavors of black cherry, currant and anise. All silk and polish on the palate. **93**

1972: Fully mature now but holding its own, this is a ripe, supple, elegantly balanced wine. **83**

CABERNET SAUVIGNON NAPA VALLEY SPECIAL SELECTION (★★★★★): Uncommonly rich and complex; darkly colored, offering ripe cherry, plum, herb, spice and tea flavors supported by firm, thick and polished tannins. It spends three years in oak. Drinkable early on, reaching its peak at about age 6 to 10, it holds its fruit amazingly well and often outperforms the com-

petition in lesser years: witness the very fine 1988 and 1989 vintages. My most recent notes, however, show it's better earlier than later, with the 1987, 1988 and 1990 vintages already mature and ready to drink.

1995: Amazingly complex, with a wide range of currant, wild berry, herb, sage, coffee and tobacco. Gains nuance, delicacy, elegance and finesse, finishing with pretty oak shadings. **97**

1994: Big, ripe, rich and concentrated, with layers of currant, plum, black cherry, spice, cedary oak, and dashes of vanilla, tobacco and coffee notes. **95**

1992: Serves up elegant, ripe cherry, currant, cola and spice flavors, and frames them in toasty oak to round everything out nicely. **92**

1991: Another tremendous wine, with enormous richness, depth and complexities and classic layers of currant, plum, cherry and spice. Young and compact at this stage, tasted nearly a year before release and just after bottling. **95**

1990: Beautifully proportioned, rich and concentrated, with tiers of complex cherry, plum, currant and spice flavors and sweet tannins. There are pretty, toasty, buttery oak and vanilla flavors on the long, full finish. **98**

1989: Tight, tough, chewy, intense and tannic, but graced with a wealth of fruit flavors. The rich cherry, berry, prune and plum notes turn smoky and complex on the long, full finish. **90**

1988: Pure Caymus, with slightly muted currant, plum, dried cherry, anise and spicy flavors that are neatly layered. **88**

1987: Peaked early. Shows its age with a dry, earthy edge to the cherry, plum and currant flavors, and drying tannins. **88**

1986: Remarkably concentrated, elegant and refined. The range of herb, tea, ripe plum and cherry flavors stretches out, turning long and complex. **90**

1985: An extraordinary wine; enormously rich, complex and lively, with layers of cedar, plum, cassis and black cherry that gracefully unfold on the palate. The tannins are lean, fine and mouthwatering, giving the wine a steely backbone and great length. **95**

1984: A magnificent wine, tight, lean and concentrated, with deeply perfumed ripe plum, black cherry, anise and currant flavors. Turning supple and generous on the finish, this is one terrific wine that defines complexity. **90**

1983: Rich, intense, complex and concentrated, loaded with plum, currant, spice and toasty oak flavors. **91**

1982: Massively structured, intense, firm and compact, with ripe plum, currant, anise and oak flavors and a pretty chocolate and caramel aftertaste. **83**

1981: Tight, firm and concentrated, with ripe plum, currant and black cherry flavors that are rich and compact, elegant and focused. **88**

1980: Loaded with ripe plum, cherry, currant and anise flavors that are elegant and stylish, finishing with a pretty aftertaste and great length. **88**

1979: A gorgeous wine, rich, supple and complex, packed with ripe, vibrant currant, spice, cedar and anise flavors that are crisp, lively and long. **91**

1978: Very mature; nutty, with aldehydic notes and glimpses of plum, prune and cherry flavors that fade on the finish. **82**

1976: Rich and tannic, with a fair amount of oak and plenty of plum, currant and anise flavors. It's rather coarse. **87**

1975: A magnificent wine, loaded with fresh, ripe plum, cedar, currant and chocolate flavors that are supple and elegant. **92**

CONUNDRUM WHITE CALIFORNIA (★★★★★): Ripe and exotic, a distinctive, spicy wine that's rich and oaky; a blend of Chardonnay, Sémillon, Viognier, Sauvignon Blanc and Muscat.

SAUVIGNON BLANC NAPA VALLEY (★★★★): Barrel fermented and lavishly oaked, but with lots of intense varietal fruit flavors.

1997: A ripe, oaky style, this one leans toward butterscotch, fig and pear, with hints of lime on the finish. It is richly textured, though it lacks the focus and finesse of previous recent vintages. Still, quite good. **88**

CECCHETTI SEBASTIANI CELLAR (★★)
Sonoma County
Founded: 1985 **Owner:** Roy Cecchetti, Don Sebastiani.
Winemaker: Bob Broman. **Affliated Brands:** Pepperwood Grove, Quatro.

MAJOR WINES: PRICE, CASES, RATING

Cabernet Franc Napa Valley	
($30, 200)	★★
Cabernet Sauvignon Napa Valley	
($30, 400)	★★
Merlot Napa Valley	
($30, 400)	★★

WINERY DATA
Case Production: 30,000. **Varietals Purchased:** Cabernet Franc (Napa Valley), Cabernet Sauvignon (Napa Valley), Merlot (Napa Valley).

Don Sebastiani started this negociant brand with his brother-in-law, Roy Cecchetti, before he became involved with his family's winery. Sebastiani is now president of Sebastiani Vineyards, but he remains, along with Cecchetti, involved in the winemaking here. The 1993 Cabernet (89 points) and the 1992 Merlot (87) made from Napa Valley grapes were quite good. All of the winery's 30,000 cases are made from purchased bulk wine.

CELLAR MASTER'S SELECTION see EDNA VALLEY VINEYARD

CÉPAGE see JOULLIAN VINEYARDS LTD.

CHALK HILL WINERY (★★★★)
Chalk Hill, Sonoma County
Founded: 1982. **Owner:** Frederick & Peggy Furth.
Winemaker: William Knuttel.

MAJOR WINES: PRICE, CASES, RATING

Cabernet Sauvignon Chalk Hill	
($26, 11,000)	★★★
Chardonnay Chalk Hill	
($28, 38,000)	★★★★★
Chardonnay Chalk Hill Estate Vineyard	
Selection	
($40, 900)	★★★★★
Merlot Chalk Hill	
($30, 14,000)	★★★
Pinot Gris Chalk Hill Estate Vineyard	
Selection	
($22, 1,000)	★★★
Sauvignon Blanc Chalk Hill	
($20, 9,000)	★★★★
Sémillon Chalk Hill Botrytised Estate	
Vineyard Selection	
($48, 1,000)	★★★★★

WINERY DATA
Case Production: 75,000. **Acres Owned:** 286 acres in Chalk Hill. **Varietals by Acre:** Cabernet Franc (1 acre), Cabernet Sauvignon (33), Chardonnay (143), Malbec (6), Merlot (60), Petit Verdot (1), Pinot Gris (4), Sauvignon Blanc (28), Sauvignon Gris (1), Sémillon (9). **Vineyard Designations:** Chalk Hill Estate.

Chalk Hill Winery owners Fred and Peggy Furth own a vast estate in the Chalk Hill appellation, with 286 acres in vines comprising Chardonnay, Cabernet and Merlot. A San Francisco-based antitrust and class-action lawyer, Fred Furth began planting his vineyards in the 1970s. Chalk Hill's earlier wines were often flawed; the 1987 Cabernet was so tart and bizarre that it was eventually declassified and never sold under the Chalk Hill label.

Winemaker David Ramey arrived in 1990 and proceeded to craft a series of Chardonnays and Sauvignon Blancs that won wide acclaim and landed in *Wine Spectator*'s annual Top 100 on several occasions. The winery hasn't enjoyed the same level of success with its two reds—Cabernet Sauvignon and the newcomer Merlot—largely because the vineyard lies in a cool climate zone, where the grapes struggle to ripen and color. Ramey departed after the 1994 vintage, and former Saintsbury winemaker William Knuttel replaced him. With the Chardonnay and Sauvignon Blanc such steady and dramatic performers, Knuttel's challenge is to raise the level of the reds.

Chalk Hill Winery's strongest wine today is its Chardonnay, which has been amazingly good. The 1994 Cabernet just missed outstanding, with an earthy, leath-

ery edge to its ripe currant and sage flavors. The 1995 Merlot (87) showed a similar flavor profile. When the winery chooses to produce it, the late-harvest Sémillon can be stunning, as it was in 1994.

TASTING NOTES

CABERNET SAUVIGNON CHALK HILL (★★★): Highly variable, although recent vintages show added richness, with earthy currant and leather flavors and high-extract tannins. These wines have no track record for improving with age.

1995: Pleasantly fruity if a bit dry, with moderate intensity and hints of plum and currant. Becomes quite tannic. **85**

1994: Dense and a touch leathery, with herb, currant, plum and berry notes, finishing with dry, tealike tannins. **89**

1993: Marked by touches of herb and dill, but enough currant and berry flavors weave into the blend to give it dimension and complexity. **88**

1991: Tight and compact, with rich, complex currant, earth, tar and mineral flavors. Firmly tannic. **89**

1990: Dense, ripe, rich and concentrated, with focused currant, earth and black cherry flavors, picking up a touch of anise and spice on the finish. **89**

1989: Hard, tannic and barnyardy, and so earthy it's hard to like. **75**

1988: Smooth and silky, with well-modulated cherry and plum flavors. **87**

1987: A bizarre wine that is stripped of character. **70**

CHARDONNAY CHALK HILL (★★★★★): The 1990 set the standard, with its finesse and tiers of complex flavors. The next two bottlings failed to meet this standard, but from 1994 on this has been a deliciously rich, unctuous wine.

1996: A bold, ripe, complex and concentrated style that packs in lots of rich fig, pear, pineapple and smoky, toasty oak flavors. **93**

1995: Starts with a flinty, spicy edge to the ripe pear, grapefruit, guava and nectarine flavors, but then the flavors fan out and gain complexity. **93**

1994: Rich, intense and full-bodied. The ripe pear, spice, fig and honey flavors are framed nicely by toasty oak. **93**

CHARDONNAY CHALK HILL ESTATE VINEYARD
SELECTION (★★★★★)
1995: Lots of complexity and finesse, with smoky pear, apricot, fig, melon and citrus flavors that are rich and concentrated. **93**
1994: Complex, with an interplay of ripe pear, citrus, peach, fig, vanilla and spicy, toasty oak flavors. Turns elegant on the finish. **92**

SÉMILLON CHALK HILL BOTRYTISED ESTATE VINEYARD
SELECTION (★★★★★)
1994: Enormously complex and concentrated, with earthy fig, honey, pear and vanilla flavors swirling generously through the rich, sweet texture. **97**

CHALONE VINEYARD (★★★–★★★★★)
Chalone, Monterey County
Founded: 1969. **Owner:** Chalone Wine Group Ltd.
Winemaker: Dan Karlsen.

MAJOR WINES: PRICE, CASES, RATING
Chardonnay Chalone ($28, 27,000)	★★★★★
Chardonnay Chalone Reserve ($45, 750)	★★★★★
Chenin Blanc Chalone ($18, 100)	★★★★
Pinot Blanc Chalone ($18, 1,800)	★★★★
Pinot Blanc Chalone Reserve ($26, 300)	★★★★★
Pinot Noir Chalone ($27, 4,300)	★★★
Pinot Noir Chalone Reserve ($35, 300)	★★★

WINERY DATA
Case Production: 50,000. **Acres Owned:** 195 acres in Chalone.
Varietals by Acre: Chardonnay (110 acres), Chenin Blanc (8), Pinot Blanc (33), Pinot Noir (43), Viognier (0.5). **Varietals Purchased:** Chardonnay (Chalone), Pinot Noir (Chalone).

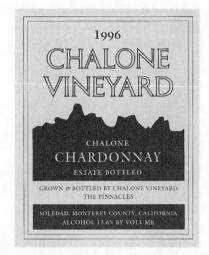

Chalone Vineyard is a highly regarded single-winery appellation in the Gavilan Mountains, located near the Pinnacles National Monument. Its history can be traced back to 1919, when a Frenchman named Tam began planting grapes in soils laced with limestone. Situated on a barren, windswept plateau 1,800 feet above sea level, the vineyard changed hands several times before Richard Graff purchased the property in 1965. Although the vineyard had suffered from neglect, the grapevines were still vital, and Graff began nourishing them back to health, battling an arid climate that often required him to haul water by truck to irrigate the vines.

Graff first produced wine from Chalone Vineyard in 1960, five years before purchasing the property. Working from a converted chicken coop that held 40 barrels, he produced 300 cases of Chardonnay. A year later, he made a sparkling wine, but it wasn't until 1966 that he started making small commercial lots of wine. The breakthrough came with the 1969 vintage of Chardonnay and Pinot Noir, both of which won critical acclaim, allowing Graff and his partner Philip Woodward to attract new investors. From there, Chalone began making small lots of Chardonnay, Pinot Noir and Chenin Blanc, the latter from vines planted by Tam around 1920; later, he added Pinot Blanc. In the 1970s, the vineyards were gradually expanded and production grew, although the winery didn't have electricity or a modern facility until the 1980s. Sadly, Richard Graff passed away in 1998.

The vineyard is now planted to Chardonnay, Pinot Noir, Pinot Blanc, Chenin Blanc and Viognier. The winery went public in 1984—the Rothschild family that owns Château Lafite-Rothschild is among the owners—and acquired Acacia Vineyards, Edna Valley Vineyards and Carmenet. Today, production is 50,000 cases, with two bottlings each—an Estate and a Reserve—of Chardonnay, Pinot Blanc and Pinot Noir. The Reserves come from the oldest vines. A second label, Gavilan, is being phased out, to be replaced by the Echelon brand.

Chalone's wines owe their distinctive style not only to unique soils and climate, but also to Graff's fascination with Burgundian vinification techniques. All of the white wines are barrel-fermented, aged *sur lie* and deftly balanced with oak. The Pinot Noir is fermented with a mixture of whole berries, wild yeast and some stem retention, although here the winery has been rethinking methods and is trying to make richer, fruitier wines with fleshier tannins.

Chalone's whites—Chardonnay and Pinot Blanc—are among the best in California, and have easily outpaced the winery's Pinot Noir for many years. New Pinot Noir and Syrah plantings are in the works, with Syrah expected to join Chalone's lineup soon. Dan Karlsen, a 17-year veteran who has worked at Domaine Carneros and briefly with Estancia in Napa Valley, replaced Michael Michaud as winemaker for the production of the 1998 vintage; whether Karlsen can improve on the Pinot Noir is a question of considerable interest to California winery-watchers.

TASTING NOTES

CHARDONNAY CHALONE (★★★★): Uncommonly rich and flavorful; deep in color, with tiers of complex flavors, bracing acidity, a broad, smooth texture and a flinty mineral aftertaste. Ages well.
1996: Elegant and complex; smooth, rich and flavorful, with a creamy texture and lots of ripe pear, apple, fig and melon notes. **91**
1995: Earthy, with a spicy mineral edge to the tightly wound pear and nectarine flavors and a classic wild mushroom edge. **91**
1994: Strikes a nice balance amongst ripe fig, honey, pear, mineral and melon flavors, which expand on the finish. **91**
1993: Smooth and polished, with spicy pear, fig and light toasty oak shadings; more complete than most 1993s. **87**

1992: Tight, firm and focused, with pretty pear, spice, honey and butter notes that pick up an oaky edge on a long full finish. **91**
1991: Soft, spicy and generous, with pear and lemon flavors at the core and all sorts of vanilla, hazelnut and nutmeg notes to make it complex. **91**
1990: Crisp and concentrated, with well defined apple, honey and spice aromas and flavors that fan out. **89**
1989: Earthy, smoky aromas lead to fig and grapefruit flavors, making for a very distinctive wine. **88**
1988: More forward and fruity than the Reserve, rich and complex, with firm fig, lemon, pear and spice flavors. **90**
1987: Earthy, rich and satiny, very smooth and distinctive, showing hints of toast, butterscotch, pear and lemon. **90**
1986: Amazingly delicious, rich, firm and complex, oozing with fresh, concentrated lemon, butterscotch, honey and toasty oak flavors. **94**

CHARDONNAY CHALONE RESERVE (★★★★★): These wines are selected from the oldest vines, and age exceptionally well. They often need three to five years to develop, which is very unusual for a California Chardonnay.
1994: Combines ripe, intense pear, honey and butterscotch flavors with a sense of elegance and finesse. **90**
1992: Ripe, smooth and creamy, with a pretty array of earthy pear, spice, honey and butterscotch flavors, picking up vanilla and toasty notes on a long, full finish. **93**
1991: The bright and lively pear, spice, citrus and pineapple flavors are ripe, rich and focused, with light, buttery oak shadings and a silky finish. **91**
1990: Firm, tight, complex, with spicy, earthy pear, pineapple and butter notes that are focused and elegant. **89**
1989: Pungent and earthy, with mature Chardonnay flavors that reflect ripe pear and honey notes. **82**
1988: Hints of smoke, flint, lime, pear and fig slowly come together on the finish. **89**
1985: Enormously rich and complex, deep and concentrated, with intense cream, fig, honey, pear and vanilla flavors that spread out and saturate the palate. **94**

PINOT BLANC CHALONE (★★★★): One of the best Pinot Blancs in California. Shares the richness, depth and intensity of the Chardonnay, often with similar flavors and weight. Ages amazingly well.

1993: Ripe, round and generous, with a spicy tang to the pear and apple flavors that linger on the finish. **88**

1992: Intense and spicy, with ripe pear and apple flavors and a coarse texture. Short-term cellaring won't hurt. **86**

1991: Deep, rich and concentrated, packed with ripe pear, peach, mineral and spicy oak shadings and graced with crisp, lively acidity. **92**

1990: Intense and lively, with rich pear and citrus notes that turn earthy and bitter. **80**

1989: Ripe and buttery, with pear and butterscotch flavors and enough elegance and suppleness to keep it from being ponderous. **88**

PINOT NOIR CHALONE (★★★): There's no disputing that these can be great wines, capable of long aging and, more importantly, of gaining complexity with age. They are, however, also austere and often tannic to a fault, marked by earthy plum and cherry notes that take on dried-fruit qualities with age. In the 1980s, the wines were thinner and more restrained than in the 1970s, and while the vintages of the 1990s show more polish and finesse, the group as a whole remains tannic and austere.

1996: Smooth and supple, with a range of tea, spicy cherry, mushroom and berry notes. Turning elegant and polished. **88**

1994: Serves up herb, cherry and sage notes, with supple tannins and smoke, plum and berry nuances. **88**

1992: Young, firm and tight, with crisp tannins. It unfolds slowly, revealing earthy, spicy, cherry and mushroom nuances. **87**

1991: Smooth and supple, well focused, with a pleasant core of cherry, earth and spice flavors that gains nuance and depth on the finish. **88**

1990: Marked by tart cherry and berry flavors, it's still vibrant, finishing with a dash of tar and anise. **87**

1989: A funky, earthy wine that has hints of lean raspberry and cherry flavors, turning bitter. **77**

1988: Pleasant enough, with floral and plum notes of modest depth. **83**

1987: Provides a core of decent spice, cherry and plum aromas and flavors, turning firm and tannic. **85**

1986: Dry, earthy and metallic, having lost its fruit. **78**

1985: Crisp and elegant, with spicy plum and anise notes of modest proportions. **84**

1984: Shows rich, spicy plum and mint flavors that are lean and focused, finishing with firm tannins, but also some fruit. **85**

1983: Elegant and well proportioned, it picks up a pleasant anise and earth aftertaste. **86**

1982: Intense and earthy, with ripe prune notes that are firm and tannic. **84**

1981: Aging well; a crisp, lean wine with hints of plum and anise, turning tannic and stemmy. **83**

1980: Rich, smooth, with spicy dried cherry and plum flavors and fine tannins, picking up a trace of oak. **85**

1979: Lean, trim, with tightly-focused spice, black cherry, anise and earth notes that are intense and lively. **88**

1977: Fully mature but aging well, with none of the tannic edge that often plagues Chalone Pinot Noirs. Complex and smooth, with earthy, gamy, sweet plum and cherry flavors, finishing with a spicy anise aftertaste. **92**

PINOT NOIR CHALONE RESERVE (★★★): The Reserve wines, made from vines planted in 1946, are sold primarily to Chalone Wine Group shareholders and have been uniformly hard and unyielding, although the 1990 has improved with bottle age.

1990: Distinct earth, pepper and spice notes and ripe cherry and berry flavors, turning crisp and elegant. **88**

1989: Tight and unyielding, with firm, hard-edged plum and spice flavors that turn tannic and drying. **83**

1988: Mature, with an earthy, smoky, leathery edge to the cherry and berry notes, but it's rough and tannic. **84**

1987: Broad and complex, with mineral and earth overtones to the ripe cherry and berry flavors. **86**

1986: Still austere, with earthy mushroom and berry notes; finishes with very dry tannins. **85**

1985: Hard, flat and oaky, a simple and disappointing wine that fails to excite. **75**

1984: A disjointed wine that has ripe, floral plum flavors but tastes lean and simple. **82**

1983: Age has been kind to this one, taking away some of the rough edges, but it remains curious, with funky, pungent, earthy flavors. **80**

1982: A funky, earthy, bitter wine that has seen better days. **70**

1981: Warm, ripe and supple, with a silky texture and complex flavors that echo ripe plum, earth, tar and anise, finishing with delicacy and finesse. **88**

1980: Holding but not gaining, with astringent, tannic, smoky anise, tar, dried plum and cherry flavors. **82**

CHAPPELLET VINEYARD (★★–★★★)
Napa Valley
Founded: 1967. **Owner:** Donn & Molly Chappellet.
Winemaker: Phillip Corallo-Titus.

MAJOR WINES: PRICE, CASES, RATING
Cabernet Sauvignon Napa Valley
  Signature
  ($24, 5,500)   ★★★
Chardonnay Napa Valley
  ($17, 3,100)   ★★
Chardonnay Napa Valley Signature
  ($24, 1,500)   ★★★
Chenin Blanc Napa Valley Dry
  ($11, 9,000)   ★★★
Chenin Blanc Napa Valley Moelleux
  ($34, 350)   ★★★
Chenin Blanc Napa Valley Old Vine Cuvée
  ($15, 4,000)   ★★★
Merlot Napa Valley
  ($22, 2,000)   ★★
Sangiovese Napa Valley
  ($22, 1,400)   ★★

ALSO PRODUCED
Cabernet Franc Napa Valley ($22, 300).

WINERY DATA
Case Production: 27,000. **Acres Owned:** 110 acres in Napa Valley. **Varietals by Acre:** Cabernet Franc (5 acres), Cabernet Sauvignon (27), Chardonnay (36), Chenin Blanc (23), Merlot (8), Petit Verdot (3), Sangiovese (8). **Varietals Purchased:** Chenin Blanc (Napa Valley), Merlot (Napa Valley).

Chappellet Vineyard sits on a rugged, forested slope of Pritchard Hill, east of St. Helena. In 1967, Donn and Molly Chappellet moved here from Los Angeles, where Donn had been running a successful industrial food vending business.

The Chappellets' mountain-grown wines have had their moments of glory, rising to prominence in the late 1960s on the merit of the 1968, 1969 and 1970 Cabernets, wines that were remarkable for their depth and complexity. Since then, the wines, including a Chardonnay, a Merlot and a generally well-crafted Chenin Blanc, have been marked by inconsistencies and stylistic swings. A succession of winemakers have overseen winegrowing at Chappellet: Philip Togni (of Philip Togni Vineyard), Joe Cafaro (of Cafaro Cellars), Tony

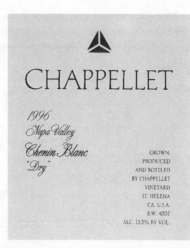

Soter (of Spottswoode Vineyard and Etude), Cathy Corison (of Corison Wines and Staglin Family Vineyards) and now, Phillip Corallo-Titus.

It seems apparent that the 110-acre vineyard, for all its terraced beauty, dictates the austere style and character shared by most of the estate-grown wines. The Chardonnay Napa Valley Signature 1996 (90 points), however, featured smooth, rich, creamy fig and pear flavors, a dramatic departure from the leaner, flinter efforts of the past. The Chenin Blanc Old Vine Cuvée is one of this winery's finest wines. The Merlot is made in a lean, trim, earthy style, while newcomer Sangiovese 1995 (87) offers elegant spice, currant and wild berry flavors.

TASTING NOTES

CABERNET SAUVIGNON NAPA VALLEY SIGNATURE (★★★): Always on the lean and tannic side, highly variable in quality. In some years it can be rich, with earthy currant, herb and spice notes, while retaining its austerity. Time does little to soften it.
1994: Decidedly herbal and cedary, with lots of tobacco, tar, spice, plum and berry notes, but it's quite tannic. **88**
1993: Tight, with a compact band of cedar, leather, green olive, herb and currant flavors. Finishes with strong, leathery tannins. **87**
1992: Intense, with spicy, leathery currant and anise flavors, but also some gritty tannins. **83**
1991: Firm and compact, with tight, earthy currant and herb flavors that fan out on the finish. Picks up hints of oak and spice along the way, making the flavors more interesting. **89**

1990: A bizarre wine with earthy, minty overtones that dominate the cedary currant flavors underneath. **80**

1989: Firm and focused but not very flavorful, with more mineral and earth flavors than fruit. **82**

1988: Toasty, spicy aromas and light fruit flavors indicate this is best for drinking in the near term. It's tasty and charming. **85**

Reserve 1987: Impressive for its rich core of earthy currant, mineral, cedar and spice, and its softening tannins. **90**

Reserve 1986: Sharply focused, with tart black cherry, anise and cedar flavors that are lean and elegant. Firmly tannic. **89**

Reserve 1985: Youthful and vibrant, tight and compact, with currant and black cherry flavors that are complex and concentrated. **88**

CABERNET SAUVIGNON NAPA VALLEY PRITCHARD HILL ESTATES
1992: Firm and substantially tannic, with a cedary rim around the tightly wound currant, tobacco and earth notes. **86**

CHARDONNAY NAPA VALLEY SIGNATURE (★★★): Shares the austerity of the Cabernet with its crisp, flinty, understated style. Avoids the heavy oak and malolactic character evident in so many Napa Chardonnays, but often comes across as simple. Holds its fruit well but rarely evolves into anything special.

CHENIN BLANC NAPA VALLEY DRY (★★★): One of California's best; tart, lean, dry and flinty, with crisp melon and citrus notes. Ages amazingly well.

1996: Tart and flinty, with lime, citrus, and hints of green apple and pear flavors that lack focus. **83**

1992: Bright and fruity, dry and spicy enough to weave some nice nuances around the delicate apple flavors. **85**

1991: Crisp, appley, a brightly focused wine with piney, leafy overtones. Graceful and lively on the finish. **85**

CHENIN BLANC NAPA VALLEY MOELLEUX (★★★)
1995: Sweet, with a sugary edge to the ripe peach, apricot and nectarine flavors, it finishes with a touch of orange peel and cream. **91**

MERLOT NAPA VALLEY (★★): Struggles to move beyond earthy, herbal flavors, while sharing the Cabernet's austerity and tannic edge.

CHATEAU JULIEN (★★)
Monterey County
Founded: 1982. **Owner:** Robert & Patty Brower. **Winemaker:** Bill Anderson, Marta Kraftzeck. **Second Label:** Emerald Bay, Garland Ranch, Mirage Vineyards.

MAJOR WINES: PRICE, CASES, RATING

Cabernet Sauvignon Monterey County Grand Reserve ($8, 3,600)	★★
Cabernet Sauvignon Monterey County Private Reserve ($20, 600)	★★
Chardonnay Monterey County Grand Reserve ($8, 3,600)	★★★
Chardonnay Monterey County Private Reserve Sur Lie ($15, 600)	★★
Merlot Monterey County Grand Reserve ($10, 4,500)	★★
Merlot Monterey County Private Reserve ($15, 600)	★★

ALSO PRODUCED
Gewurztraminer Monterey County ($8, 600); Riesling Monterey County ($8, 600); Sangiovese California ($15, 600); Sauvignon Blanc Monterey County Grand Reserve ($7, 2,000); Trebbiano California ($15, 600).

WINERY DATA
Case Production: 80,000. **Acres Owned:** 166 acres in Monterey County. **Varietals by Acre:** Cabernet Sauvignon (20 acres), Chardonnay (45), Merlot (45), Pinot Grigio (10), Sangiovese (16), Sauvignon Blanc (20), Syrah (10). **Varietals Purchased:** Cabernet Sauvignon/Chardonnay/Gewürztraminer/ Merlot/Riesling/Sangiovese/Sauvignon Blanc/Zinfandel (Monterey County), Trebbiano (California).

Wine quality has been extremely variable from this Carmel Valley producer. In previous years, Merlot seemed to be the mainstay, but recently Chardonnay has been the quality leader while the Merlot has slid to the level of the Cabernet. The 1995 Private Reserve Chardonnay (88 points) displayed a supple and understated style, with creamy pear, citrus and spice flavors. Both the 1995 and 1996 Grand Reserve Merlots (79) were simple, with herbal flavors and modest fruit. The same could be said for the tutti-frutti 1996 Grand Reserve Cabernet (75).

CHATEAU LA GRAND ROCHE see **FORMAN VINEYARD**

CHATEAU MONTELENA WINERY
(★★–★★★★★)
Calistoga, Napa Valley
Founded: 1882. **Owner:** James & Laura Barrett.
Winemaker: Bo Barrett. **Second Label:** Silverado Cellars.

MAJOR WINES: PRICE, CASES, RATING
Cabernet Sauvignon Napa Valley
  The Montelena Estate
  ($85, 12,000)   ★★★★★
Calistoga Cuvée Red Napa Valley
  ($22, 12,000)   ★★★
Chardonnay Napa Valley
  ($29, 12,000)   ★★★★
Johannisberg Riesling Potter Valley
  ($15, 1,000)   ★★

ALSO PRODUCED
Zinfandel-Sangiovese Napa Valley Saint Vincent ($25, 850).

WINERY DATA
Case Production: 40,000. **Acres Owned:** 125 acres in Napa Valley. **Varietals by Acre:** Cabernet Franc (8 acres), Cabernet Sauvignon (90), Merlot (5), Primitivo (5), Sangiovese (7), Zinfandel (10). **Vineyard Designations:** The Montelena Estate. **Varietals Purchased:** Chardonnay (Napa Valley), Johannisberg Riesling (Potter Valley).

Chateau Montelena is a medieval-looking stone winery north of Calistoga that dates back to 1882, but there's a gap of several decades between its first era and the modern one. In 1969, attorney Jim Barrett led a group of investors in purchasing the abandoned château, which began to produce wine again in 1972.

Mike Grgich (Grgich Hills Cellar), previously of Beaulieu Vineyard, made the first wines, and they were excellent. Montelena made headlines when its 1973 Chardonnay took first place in a famous blind tasting in Paris in 1976; the French wine critics judged it superior to a group of prestigious white Burgundies and other California Chardonnays.

Upon buying the winery, the owners began planting Cabernet, producing their first estate-bottled Cabernet in 1978. The vineyards now cover 125 acres and are planted primarily to Cabernet, with smaller amounts of Zinfandel, Cabernet Franc, Sangiovese, Merlot and Primitivo. Estate-grown Cabernet dominates the 40,000-case lineup, with 12,000 cases each of The Montelena Estate and Calistoga Cuvée. The winery's Chardonnay and Johannisberg Riesling are made from purchased grapes.

The Montelena Estate Cabernet is one of the most ageworthy wines made in California. The Chardonnay is made in a flinty style and is best with a few years of aging, though recent vintages have offered more up-front fruitiness. Winemaker Bo Barrett, owner Jim Barrett's son, has shown a deft hand at crafting complex, dense wines that reflect their *terroir*.

TASTING NOTES

CABERNET SAUVIGNON NAPA VALLEY THE MONTELENA ESTATE (★★★★★): Unusually dark, complex and tannic, this is a bold and assertive wine that packs in lots of rich currant, mineral, earth and cedary oak flavors while maintaining a sense of elegance and balance. Tannin management is the big challenge in some years, but in others these dense and chewy wines age magnificently, reaching their peak at about 10 years and lasting as much as 20. Until 1989, the label read "Napa Valley"; since 1990, the label has carried the designation "The Montelena Estate."
1995: A supple, forward wine that's ripe and fleshy, with complex currant, herb, tobacco, cedar and mineral flavors; not overly tannic. **92**
1994: Bold, tight and compact, with concentrated currant, black cherry, cedar and spice flavors, firming up on the finish. **91**
1993: Firm, intense and lively, with a complex core of currant, plum and berry, turning smoky and elegant on the finish. **92**
1992: Serves up a complex, supple band of cherry, plum, coffee and menthol flavors of good depth and concentration, before turning tannic. **91**
1991: Uncommonly dark and intense, even for this vintage, with a rich core of leathery currant, spice, cedar and anise flavors that are young and rambunctious. **92**

1990: A less tannic and more elegant Montelena with focused currant and black cherry flavors that turn supple on the finish. **90**

1989: Complex, ripe currant, anise and black cherry flavors, with a striking sense of balance and proportion. **90**

1988: Solid, firmly tannic and tightly focused, with earthy, leathery currant, anise, cedar, sage and spice notes. Finishes with chewy tannins. **88**

1987: Dark and very tightly wound, but the core of earthy currant, mineral, spice and cedar is focused, with soft tannins. **93**

1986: May well be the wine of the vintage. It's ripe, rich, complex and deeply concentrated, with a juicy core of black cherry and plum flavors. **96**

1985: Amazingly rich and concentrated, packed with black cherry, currant, cedar and spice flavors and wrapped in thick tannins that promise a long life. It's massive but elegant. **95**

1984: An enormous wine, that combining power and finesse with deep, rich, concentrated currant, black cherry and spicy plum flavors that are tight and closed now. **94**

1983: Still big and tannic but drying out, leaving more tannin and less currant and berry flavor to admire. **86**

1982: Elegant, with mature black cherry, plum and currant aromas and flavors, backed with toasty oak. **89**

1981: Simple by Montelena standards, with a narrow band of currant and spice flavors. **80**

1980: Mature, with generous ripe currant and berry notes that are beginning to fade and dry out. **86**

1979: Lean and elegant, fully mature, with black currant, mineral and cedar nuances that are rich and mature. **91**

1978: Luxurious, bright, rich, complex and concentrated, with black cherry, currant, vanilla, sage and mint notes. The tannins have softened. **92**

1977: Bold, ripe and still quite appealing, but it's showing its age and the fruit is beginning to dry out. Still, you get nice currant and berry flavors with earthy mineral nuances. **90**

1974: A bold, rich and fruity 1974 with gutsy tannins, still tightly closed and evolving. The ripe black cherry, currant and spice flavors are youthful and fresh but overshadowed now by the tannins. **90**

CALISTOGA CUVÉE RED NAPA VALLEY (★★★): The Calistoga Cuvée was new in 1990 and has varied in quality from simple and lean to smooth, rich and flavorful.

1996: Smooth, rich and complex, with a range of currant, bell pepper, herb, sage and tea flavors. **89**

1995: Openly fruity, with simple but pleasant cherry and berry flavors and just enough tannin to keep your interest. **82**

1994: Young, vibrant, a bit on the earthy, leathery side, but opens to reveal a rich core of currant, cherry and anise flavors that stay with you even as the tannins weigh in on the finish. **88**

1993: Well balanced, with pleasant cherry, plum and spice notes, with firm tannins on the finish. **86**

1992: Bold, ripe and supple, with rich, focused currant, black cherry, plum and exotic spice flavors. Builds richness, intensity and depth on a long, complex finish. **90**

CHARDONNAY NAPA VALLEY (★★★★): Although it hit some rough spots in the early 1990's, this wine is back on track, showing its characteristic crisp flintness and core of citrus and pears flavors. Ages well. The grapes are from the Dry Creek area of Napa Valley, which has a cool, mild, breezy climate that is ideally suited for Chardonnay.

1996: Crisp and elegant, with tart tangerine, citrus and lemony flavors, finishing with a leafy, peachy, hazelnut edge. Worth short-term cellaring. **90**

1995: Rich, intense and concentrated. The core of pear, citrus, nectarine, anise and fig picks up a leafy, earthy flavor. **90**

1994: Crisp and flinty, with a core of citrus and lemon that slowly fans out to feature pear, apple, spice and cinnamon notes. **91**

1992: Ripe and fruity, with rich pear, apple, melon and spice notes, turning smooth and polished on the finish, where the oak folds in. **88**

1986: Well defined and elegant, with spicy pear, apple and melon flavors. **90**

1985: Captures rich, ripe flavors of apple, pear and spice that play off each other. **90**

CHATEAU POTELLE (★★★–★★★★)
Mount Veeder, Napa Valley
Founded: 1988. **Owner:** Jean Noel & Marketta Fourmeaux. **Winemaker:** Marketta Fourmeaux.

MAJOR WINES: PRICE, CASES, RATING

Cabernet Sauvignon Mount Veeder V.G.S. ($39, 1,200)	★★★★
Chardonnay Central Coast ($14, 3,700)	★★

Chardonnay Mount Veeder V.G.S.
  ($35, 2,000)   ★★★★
Sauvignon Blanc Napa Valley
  ($11, 9,000)   ★★★
Zinfandel Amador County
  ($16, 3,000)   ★★
Zinfandel Mount Veeder V.G.S.
  ($32, 1,400)   ★★★★

WINERY DATA
Case Production: 22,000. **Acres Owned:** 83 acres (43 in Mount Veeder, 40 in Paso Robles). **Varietals by Acre:** Cabernet Sauvignon (14 acres), Chardonnay (16), Zinfandel (39) Syrah (14). **Varietals Purchased:** Chardonnay (Central Coast), Sauvignon Blanc (Napa Valley), Zinfandel (Amador County).

Bordeaux residents Jean-Noel and Marketta Fourmeaux came to Napa Valley in 1983 after studying the California wine business as emissaries of the French government.

Chateau Potelle's early wines were made from purchased grapes and often carried both the Napa and Alexander Valley appellations. Since the late 1980s, however, the 22,000-case operation, once home to the Vose Vineyard winery, has narrowed its focus to three excellent Mount Veeder-grown wines bottled under the V.G.S. designation (for Very Good Shit—really!): a superb Zinfandel, a classy Chardonnay, and an impressive Cabernet, augmented by Cabernet, Chardonnay and Sauvignon Blanc made from purchased grapes. The Fourmeaux family owns 43 acres on Mount Veeder and another 40 acres in Paso Robles, where the winery plans on planting Syrah and Zinfandel.

TASTING NOTES

CABERNET SAUVIGNON MOUNT VEEDER V.G.S. (★★★★): Steadily improving, revealing rich, complex, earthy currant flavors and tannins that are relatively tame for Mount Veeder. Worth collecting.
1994: This wine has substantial tannins, but it also has a smooth texture given its size, with spice, cedar, wild berry and currant flavors that are elegant and focused. **90**
1993: Dense and tight, with chewy tannins. It's backward in style, with a core of plum, earth, tar, pepper and cedar flavors. **88**
1992: Tight and green, with tart plum and berry notes. It's deeply concentrated, but backward and dense. **88**

1990: Dark and rich, with an earthy currant, oak and mineral edge that's deep and intense, finishing with firm tannins. **91**

CHARDONNAY MOUNT VEEDER V.G.S. (★★★★): The success of recent vintages is most impressive. These rich, intense, complex and well-oaked wines serve up lots of flavor.
1995: Smooth, ripe, rich and buttery, with a creamy texture and lots of complex pear, fig, melon and butterscotch flavors. **92**
1994: Young, intense and vibrant, with a complex, spicy edge to the ripe pear and apple flavors. Finishes with light oak shadings. **92**
1992: Rich and concentrated, offering an earthy, mature edge to the tiers of smoky pear, honey and toasty hazelnut notes. **91**

CHARDONNAY CENTRAL COAST (★★): Lighter than the V.G.S. but attractive enough, with subtle fruit flavors. Carried a Napa Valley appellation until 1995.

SAUVIGNON BLANC NAPA VALLEY (★★★): Bright and lively, with citrus and pear flavors.

ZINFANDEL MOUNT VEEDER V.G.S. (★★★★): Amazingly supple and complex given the tannin level in most Mount Veeder reds. This is a first-class effort featuring pretty raspberry, anise and buttery oak shadings. High-priced, but beautifully crafted. There was no 1991 vintage made.
1996: Ripe, with zesty wild berry, raspberry and cherry notes, it's crisp and elegant, with firm but well integrated tannins, finishing with earthy, tarry notes. **90**
1995: Deftly balanced, ripe and zesty, showing spice, earth, raspberry and dried cherry flavors. Rich, concentrated and focused. **91**
1994: Classy, loaded with rich, complex tiers of cherry, anise, wild berry and plum flavors, finishing with supple tannins and pretty oak nuances. **92**
1993: Intense and firmly tannic, but the spice, pepper and wild berry flavors ring true for Zinfandel. **88**
1992: Beautifully crafted, with layers of ripe, rich, supple raspberry, cherry and plum flavors. Turns smooth and polished on the finish, where the toasty, buttery oak adds depth. **92**
1990: Wonderful fruit intensity, concentration and complexity, with ripe black cherry, wild berry, currant, plum and spice flavors. **90**

CHATEAU SOUVERAIN (★★★–★★★★)
Alexander Valley, Sonoma County
Founded: 1944. **Owner:** Beringer Wine Estates.
Winemaker: Ed Killian.

MAJOR WINES: PRICE, CASES, RATING

Cabernet Sauvignon Alexander Valley ($17, 40,000)	★★★
Cabernet Sauvignon Alexander Valley Library Reserve ($45, 200)	★★★★
Cabernet Sauvignon Alexander Valley Winemaker's Reserve ($35, 2,000)	★★★★
Chardonnay Russian River Valley Winemaker's Reserve ($20, 1,000)	★★★★
Chardonnay Sonoma County ($13, 50,000)	★★★
Merlot Alexander Valley ($17, 24,000)	★★★
Sauvignon Blanc Alexander Valley ($9, 10,000)	★★★
Zinfandel Dry Creek Valley ($12, 10,000)	★★★

ALSO PRODUCED
Composée Red Alexander Valley ($NA, 400); Viognier Alexander Valley ($22, 200).

WINERY DATA
Case Production: 138,800. **Acres Owned:** 300 acres in Alexander Valley. **Varietals by Acre:** Cabernet Franc (10 acres), Cabernet Sauvignon (113), Malbec (5), Merlot (130), Mourvèdre (4), Sauvignon Blanc (23), Sémillon (8), Syrah (6), Viognier (1). **Varietals Purchased:** Cabernet Franc (Alexander Valley), Cabernet Sauvignon (Alexander Valley), Chardonnay (Alexander Valley, Carneros, Russian River Valley), Merlot (Alexander Valley), Sauvignon Blanc (Alexander Valley), Zinfandel (Dry Creek Valley).

Chateau Souverain's wines have improved considerably since it was acquired by Beringer Wine Estates in 1986, and it now ranks as one of Sonoma's best wineries, offering high quality and exceptional values.

For most of its history, the winery was undercapitalized and its wines were of variable quality. The original

Souverain Winery was founded by J. Leeland 'Lee' Stewart in 1944 in the old Rossini winery (now Burgess Cellars) in Napa Valley. After years of making highly-regarded Cabernets known for their elegance and finesse, Stewart sold the brand to Pillsbury, which built both the winery now known as Rutherford Hill, and, in 1973, a second winery at Chateau Souverain's current location in Alexander Valley. Unfortunately, the brand was to languish there for more than a decade.

In 1986, Wine World Inc., then owned by Nestlé, bought the winery and renamed it Chateau Souverain. Millions were spent to upgrade the facility, with the new owners buying new oak, securing top-quality grape sources and planting new vineyards, now totaling 300 acres in Alexander Valley.

Today, Chateau Souverain produces 138,000 cases, with a concentration on popular varietals such as Cabernet, Chardonnay, Merlot, Sauvignon Blanc and Zinfandel. Viogner and a Rhône-style red called Composée are new, limited-production additions. The Winemaker's Reserve bottlings of Cabernet and Chardonnay are Souverain's top wines, and nicely showcase the talents of winemaker Ed Killian.

TASTING NOTES

CABERNET SAUVIGNON ALEXANDER VALLEY (★★★): Supple, appealing, and well balanced, with herb, currant and spice notes and smooth, polished tannins. Made for early consumption.
1995: Complex, with smoky, earthy, meaty currant, anise and sage flavors that are tightly focused. Finishes with raw tannins. **89**

1994: Firm, intense and concentrated, with layers of currant, plum and black cherry fanning out, and herb and tar notes. **89**

1993: Smooth and elegant, with pretty herb, cherry and currant flavors and a nice touch of cedary oak. **86**

1992: Oak dominates, but underneath the currant, cherry and spice flavors are elegant and polished, finishing with a coffee and toasty oak aftertaste. **85**

1991: Dense and chocolaty, with spicy currant, vanilla and toasty oak flavors. **85**

1990: Solidly built and packed with complex, concentrated currant, plum, toast and tobacco flavors. **90**

CABERNET SAUVIGNON ALEXANDER VALLEY LIBRARY RESERVE (★★★★): Polished and well focused with layers of flavor. Rich, complex and concentrated.

1994: Ripe and polished, with layers of currant, black cherry, plum, anise and toasty-cedary oak, plus a dash of chocolate. **91**

1993: Dense, complex and richly flavored, with tiers of currant, chocolate and toasty oak and hints of herb and spice. **91**

CABERNET SAUVIGNON ALEXANDER VALLEY PRIVATE RESERVE

1987: Drying, with hints of earth, cedar, plum and currant, turning smoky on the finish. **87**

CABERNET SAUVIGNON ALEXANDER VALLEY WINEMAKER'S RESERVE (★★★★): Displays wonderful richness, depth and concentration, with pretty oak and plush tannins. Best early on, but drinkable up to 10 years from the vintage date.

1995: Smooth and supple, with polished notes of cedar, black cherry, currant, sage and spice, picking up a trace of coffee on the finish. **88**

1994: Beautifully orchestrated fruit and oak flavors, with tiers of currant, black cherry, herb, sage and spice and supple tannins. **93**

1993: Smooth, rich and harmonious, with a core of anise, currant, herb and spice flavors and well-polished tannins. **90**

1992: Rich and supple, with a pretty core of currant, plum and cherry and a nice overlay of oak. **89**

1991: A big, ripe, chewy wine with black cherry, plum and currant flavors framed by toasty, buttery oak. **91**

1988: A touch earthy and gamy, slowly works its way into hints of cherry, berry and cedar before turning dry. **84**

CHARDONNAY RUSSIAN RIVER VALLEY WINEMAKER'S RESERVE (★★★★): Impressive for its texture and complex flavors. The 1994 carried a Carneros appellation.

1996: Smooth, ripe and creamy, with hints of tropical fruit, ripe pear, fig and melon, plus a pretty touch of smoky, toasty oak. **92**

1995: Tightly wound, crisp and flinty; opens up to reveal more depth and intensity, with tiers of spicy apple, pear and citrus. **91**

1994: Ripe, smooth, elegant, with an alluring spectrum of spicy pear, honey, vanilla and toasty oak flavors. **91**

CHARDONNAY SONOMA COUNTY (★★★★): Rivals the Reserve for complexity, sharing its ripe, rich flavors, creamy texture and pretty oak shadings.

MERLOT ALEXANDER VALLEY (★★★): Smooth and elegant, not just an attempt to make a lighter Cabernet. Marked by herb, plum and cedary oak flavors; impressive for its delicacy and soft tannins. The 1996 (87 points) and 1995 (87) both offer spicy bell pepper and earthy flavors.

ZINFANDEL DRY CREEK VALLEY (★★★)

1995: Lively; brimming with blackberry, black cherry and vanilla notes that linger on the finish. **89**

1994: Light and simple, with a grapey cherry and berry accent to the not-quite-ripe flavors. **82**

1993: Smooth and well-integrated, modest cherry, spice and wild berry flavors finish off with soft tannins. **87**

CHATEAU ST. JEAN (★★★–★★★★★)
Sonoma Valley
Founded: 1973. **Owner:** Beringer Wine Estates. **Winemaker:** Steve Reeder.

MAJOR WINES: PRICE, CASES, RATING
Cabernet Sauvignon Sonoma County
Cinq Cépages
($24, 12,800)   ★★★★
Cabernet Sauvignon Sonoma
County Reserve
($45, 400)   ★★★★★

Chardonnay Alexander Valley
Belle Terre Vineyard
($24, 8,500)   ★★★★
Chardonnay Alexander Valley
Robert Young Vineyard
($24, 10,000)   ★★★★★
Chardonnay Alexander Valley
Robert Young Vineyard Reserve
($33, 1,500)   ★★★★★
Chardonnay Carneros Durell Vineyard
($24, 350)   ★★★★
Chardonnay Sonoma County
($13, 117,000)   ★★★
Fumé Blanc Russian River Valley
La Petite Etoile Vineyard
($13, 4,900)   ★★★
Fumé Blanc Sonoma County
($9, 16,000)   ★★
Johannisberg Sonoma County Riesling
($10, 4,200)   ★★★
Merlot Sonoma County
($18, 14,500)   ★★★
Merlot Sonoma County Reserve
($35, 500)   ★★★★
Pinot Noir Carneros Durell Vineyard
($30, 400)   ★★★

ALSO PRODUCED
Gewürztraminer Sonoma County ($10, 4,200);
Johannisberg Riesling Late Harvest Sonoma County
Belle Terre Vineyard Special Select ($25, 400).

WINERY DATA
Case Production: 235,000. **Acres Owned:** 117 acres (76 in
Sonoma Valley, 41 in Russian River Valley). **Varietals by Acre:**
Cabernet Franc (7 acres), Cabernet Sauvignon (10), Chardonnay
(24), Malbec (2), Merlot (24), Petit Verdot (0.7), Pinot Blanc
(3), Sauvignon Blanc (45), Viognier (2). **Vineyard
Designations:** Belle Terre Vineyard (Chardonnay, Johannisberg
Riesling), Durell Vineyard (Pinot Noir), La Petite Étoile
Vineyard (Sauvignon Blanc), Robert Young Vineyard
(Chardonnay). **Varietals Purchased:** Cabernet Sauvignon
(Alexander Valley), Chardonnay (Alexander Valley, Carneros),
Gewürztraminer (Sonoma County), Merlot (Alexander Valley),
Pinot Noir (Carneros), Riesling (Sonoma County).

Chateau St. Jean has always set impeccably high standards for its wines, and its current offerings—both reds
and whites—are the best ever. This beautiful château-
style winery moved to the forefront of California wine in
the 1970s with a series of vineyard-designated
Chardonnays, Fumé Blancs, Rieslings and dessert wines,
all of which ranked among the California elite.

St. Jean's talented winemaker, Richard Arrowood (see
Arrowood Vineyards & Winery) often went to extremes in
his winemaking; at one point, St. Jean had nine different
Chardonnays from one vintage on the market. The winery
was like an experimental lab for Arrowood's research with
Sonoma County's finest Chardonnay vineyards. Wines
from Robert Young, Belle Terre, Les Pierres (owned by
Sonoma-Cutrer), McCrea Vineyard, Beltane Ranch
(Kenwood), Frank Johnson Vineyard, Jimtown Ranch and
Wildwood Ranch were regulars in the St. Jean lineup,
along with lesser-known names like Gauer Ranch (now
owned by Kendall-Jackson Winery), Hunter Farms,
Bacigalupi and Riverview Vineyards. The research paid
off handsomely, and St. Jean (pronounced the American
way, 'jeen') emerged as California's foremost Chardonnay
specialist. Two bottlings in particular—from Robert
Young Vineyard and Belle Terre Vineyard—served as reference points for Alexander Valley Chardonnay.

In 1984, St. Jean founders (and Central Valley grape
growers) Robert and Edward Merzoian and Ken
Sheffield sold the winery to Suntory International for
$40 million. After the 1990 vintage, Arrowood left to
work full-time at his own winery. He was succeeded by
the equally capable Don Van Staaveren, who in turn
departed in 1997 to Codorniu (now Artesa) and was
replaced by Steve Reeder. The year 1997 also saw the
acquisition of St. Jean by Beringer Wine Estates.

There is much debate about whether the winery, which has grown to 235,000 cases, has maintained its standards. I would say that the answer is yes, although there have been significant changes, and there's no disputing that the competition has caught up with St. Jean.

Still, the Robert Young and Belle Terre Chardonnays are classy wines, as are the late-harvest Rieslings. The Fumé Blanc La Petite Étoile remains distinctive, and the Cabernet and Merlot Reserves are complex and beautifully balanced.

TASTING NOTES

CABERNET SAUVIGNON SONOMA COUNTY CINQ CÉPAGES (★★★★): Possessing a complex array of flavors and a sense of elegance, this blend of the five Bordeaux varieties has shown steady improvement,
1995: Ripe, smooth and elegant, with bright, complex black cherry, currant, plum and spicy notes. Finishes with well-integrated tannins. **91**
1994: Smooth and ripe, with a concentrated core of plum, cherry, currant and wild berry. The rich aftertaste keeps echoing fruit and light oak. **91**
1993: Elegant, with ripe, intense currant, coffee, cedar and cherry flavors. Maintains its balance and finesse. **91**
1992: Young and tight, with currant, herb, coffee and cedar flavors surrounded by chewy tannins. **89**
1991: Rich and complex, with full-bodied currant, anise, cherry and berry flavors framed by pretty, toasty oak. **91**
1990: Big, rich and dense, with rustic, chunky currant and oak flavors. **87**

CABERNET SAUVIGNON SONOMA COUNTY RESERVE (★★★★★): Bold and dramatic in the best years. Lavishly oaked and packed with flavor, with vintages such as 1987 aging very well. Ready to join the state's elite.
1993: Packs in gobs of ripe currant, plum, black cherry, cedar, anise, spice and toasty oak, and molds it into one delicious, complex wine. **93**
1992: Ripe and intense, with firm, chewy tannins. The ripe plum, currant and wild berry flavors pour through, revealing layers of complexity and depth. **92**
1991: Intense and tannic, but the currant, cedar and spice flavors manage to outshine the tannins, yielding complexity. **92**
1990: A bold, smooth, rich and exotic style of Cabernet that packs in lots of currant, cherry, mineral and toasty oak flavors. **95**

1989: Pleasant, with a trim, crisp band of cherry and plum flavors, finishing with a dry, tannic edge. **87**
1988: Complex, with creamy, toasty oak flavors and appealing cherry, herb and berry notes. The texture is supple. **88**
1987: At a nice drinking stage, with an impressive array of rich currant, smoke, spice and cedary aromas, turning soft on the finish. **90**

CABERNET SAUVIGNON SONOMA VALLEY GLEN ELLEN VINEYARD
1978: A touch nutty and tannic, it's holding up well. The earthy, spicy, peppery currant and cedar flavors turn chewy. **87**

CHARDONNAY ALEXANDER VALLEY BELLE TERRE VINEYARD (★★★★), RESERVE (★★★★): Rivals the Robert Young most years and surpasses it occasionally. Shares its elegance and finesse, often featuring tart apple and pineapple flavors.
1997: Intense, with ripe, spicy pear, fig and apricot flavors; picks up a touch of oak and nutmeg on the finish. **89**
1996: Elegant and understated, with ripe, spicy pear, fig and melon flavors that picks up a smoky, butterscotch edge. **91**
1995: Distinct for its spicy anise and oaky flavors. Enough ripe pear and apple fruit folds in to give it depth and complexity. **92**
1994: Rich, full-bodied, showing a complex core of ripe pear, nectarine, honey, spice and toasty oak flavors. **92**
1993: Ripe and spicy, with medium-weight pear, apple and light oak shadings. **86**
1992: Strikes a lovely balance between the ripe pear and peach flavors and pretty, toasty, buttery oak notes. **90**
1991: Focused and well proportioned, with toasty, buttery, ripe pear and honey notes. First Belle Terre to undergo malolactic fermentation. **88**
RESERVE 1991: Disjointed now, but remarkably youthful, with pine, spice and apple flavors that give way to smoky, toasty oak. Strives for complexity, turning a bit coarse and woody on the finish. **88**
1990: Ripe and crisp, with tasty green apple and pineapple flavors. **87**

CHARDONNAY ALEXANDER VALLEY ROBERT YOUNG VINEYARD (★★★★★): Exemplifies the pure spicy and elegant character of Alexander Valley Chardonnay with its tiers of honey, pear and apple flavors. Ages exceptionally well and often needs a year or two after release to blossom. Look for delicacy and finesse rather than sheer power.

1996: Generous with its ripe, up-front fruity flavors, showing apple, peach, pear and nectarine notes and a touch of nutmeg; it turns smooth and silky on the finish, unobstructed by oak. **91**

1995: Smooth, ripe and complex, with nectarine, pear and grapefruit notes that turn elegant and spicy. **91**

1994: Complex, with an interplay of ripe pear, apple, spice and cedary oak, plus a touch of dill. **92**

1993: Generous in its fruitiness, sporting layers of ripe pear, apple, vanilla and spice flavors. **90**

1992: A showy wine with toasty, buttery oak, pear, spice and nutmeg flavors. Combines harmony, intensity and finesse. **91**

1991: Elegant and intense, with spice, pear and fig flavors that stay focused through the finish. Balanced and lively. **89**

1990: Starts out slow, but the flavors build to a rich, complex finish. Serves up spicy pear, smoke, butter and fig flavors, with a long, full finish. **90**

Chardonnay Alexander Valley Robert Young Vineyard Reserve (★★★★★): The Reserve is similar to the regular bottling, but is aged longer and is marked by toasty oak flavors; it is produced only in magnums.

1995: Floral, with a spicy pear and nectarine core. An elegant, subtle wine that finishes with a cedary oak aftertaste. **88**

1994: Mature, with subtle, complex pear, citrus, earth and cedary notes that turn elegant and supple. **90**

1993: Mature, with a spicy edge to the pear, vanilla, nutmeg and light citrus notes, turning smooth and polished on the finish. **91**

1992: Complex, boasting a pretty array of honey, floral, pear and spice notes and following up with rich, deeply concentrated flavors. **94**

1991: Ripe and fruity, with a core of complex, supple pear, peach and toasty oak flavors that fold together nicely. **91**

1990: Youthful, rich and complex, with deeply concentrated pear, toast and spice flavors that are intense and lively. Packs in lots of flavor, with a long, full finish. **92**

Chardonnay Carneros Durell Vineyard (★★★★):
1997: Smooth, ripe and creamy, with anise, pear and fig flavors and notes of nutmeg and hazelnut on the finish. **92**

1996: Clean and fruity, with ripe, mature-tasting pear and apple flavors and touches of custard, anise and spice. **89**

Chardonnay Sonoma County (★★★): A medium-weight, middle-of-the-road style that's well done, striking a balance between ripe fruit flavors and light oak shadings. A good value.

Fumé Blanc Russian River Valley La Petite Étoile Vineyard (★★★): This bottling exaggerates the intensity and personality of the varietal, often straying into grassy onion flavors.

Merlot Sonoma County (★★★)
1996: Firm, yet supple, with focused, pretty black currant, cherry, tar, smoke and vanilla flavors. **88**

1995: Offers ripe cherry, berry, plum and spice flavors; picks up a complex notes of cedar and tobacco. **87**

1994: Serves up lots of sage, cedar and spice, and the supple plum and black cherry flavors show polish and finesse. **90**

1993: Ripe, smooth and harmonious, with well-focused core flavors of cherry, plum, spice and cedary oak. **90**

Merlot Sonoma County Reserve (★★★★)
1993: Elegant, deep and complex, with a pretty array of spicy cedar, currant, black cherry and berry flavors. **90**

1992: Marked by a touch of cedar and ash, it unfolds to show currant and berry flavors; quite intense, with concentrated tannins. **91**

1991: Ripe and intense. The pretty core of rich, spicy black cherry, tar, earth and anise flavors gains a pleasant, earthy character, has firm tannins. **92**

Pinot Noir Carneros Durell Vineyard (★★★)
1996: Smooth, ripe and harmonious, with supple plum and blackberry flavors and toasty oak shadings. **86**

1995: A beefy, meaty style, lots of smoky notes just enough leathery cherry and berry flavors to sustain it. **85**

Chateau St. Nicholas see The R.H. Phillips Vineyard

CHATEAU WOLTNER (★★–★★★)

Howell Mountain, Napa Valley
Founded: 1980. **Owner:** Francis & Francoise
DeWavrin-Woltner. **Winemaker:** Ted Lemon.

MAJOR WINES: PRICE, CASES, RATING

Chardonnay Howell Mountain	
($14, 7,500)	★★
Chardonnay Howell Mountain	
Frederique Vineyard	
($40, 250)	★★★
Chardonnay Howell Mountain	
St. Thomas Vineyard	
($23, 1,500)	★★★
Chardonnay Howell Mountain Titus Vineyard	
($40, 250)	★★★
Private Reserve Red Howell Mountain	
($50, 300)	★★

WINERY DATA

Case Production: 10,000. **Acres Owned:** 68 acres in Howell
Mountain. **Varietals by Acre:** Cabernet Franc (1.5 acres),
Cabernet Sauvignon (8.5), Chardonnay (53), Merlot (5).
Vineyard Designations: Frederique Vineyard (Chardonnay), St.
Thomas Vineyard (Chardonnay), Titus Vineyard (Chardonnay).

Howell Mountain is hearty-red-wine country to most,
but for a long time Francis and Françoise DeWavrin-
Woltner were devoted exclusively to a series of crisp,
flinty vineyard-designated Chardonnays. Despite hefty
red-wine credentials, these former owners of Bordeaux's
great Château La Mission-Haut Brion waited until the
1995 vintage before releasing their first Cabernet-based
red (85 points), an austerely-styled wine with earthy tannins and in need of cellaring.

Woltner's Chardonnays are characterized by a tight,
non-malolactic style, tart fruit and minimal, if any, oak
influence. Vintages from the 1980s have aged well, but
those from the early 1990s seem to have merely held up,
rather than improved from cellaring.

A generic Howell Mountain bottling is made from
wine not used in the vineyard-designated Chardonnays;
the 1997 (85) was tight and flinty. The Frederique
Vineyard, St. Thomas Vineyard, and Titus Vineyard bottlings are more alike than not.

At this point, Chateau Woltner appears to be at a crossroad. The Chardonnays, while good and distinctive, are not
among the leaders in California, and the Cabernet could
definitely use a little fine-tuning, polish and finesse.

TASTING NOTES

**CHARDONNAY HOWELL MOUNTAIN FREDERIQUE
VINEYARD (★★★):** Tightly wound and focused, with citrus and mineral flavors.
1996: Tight, green around the edges, with modestly ripe
peach, pear and nectarine flavors and a short finish. **86**
1995: Starts with green pear and apple flavors, then
slowly fans out, revealing hints of oak and fig. **88**
1993: Lean and tart, with a strong citrus edge to the crisp
apple and pear notes. Comes across as disjointed. **82**
1992: Tart and tightly wound, with spicy pear and mineral shadings, picking up light, toasty oak and nutmeg flavors that are crisp and persistent. **90**
1991: Crisp and lean, showing a coarse edge to the citrus
and pear flavors. **85**

**CHARDONNAY HOWELL MOUNTAIN ST. THOMAS
VINEYARD (★★★):** Austere, citrusy and flinty, but slightly less complex and compelling than the other bottlings.
1996: A touch earthy, it works its way into mineral, citrus, pear and spicy notes. **86**
1995: Tight and crisp; the core of fruit has flinty lemon
and tart pear edges. **87**
1994: Marked by a strong grapefruit and citrus edge. **89**
1993: Marked by tart, flinty pear and citrus flavors.
Simple at best. **83**
1992: Tart and intense, with a tightly wound core of
grapefruit, pineapple and light oak flavors. **88**
1990: Tight and taut, with crisp lemon, apple, nectarine
and pear flavors and subtle oak shadings. **90**

**CHARDONNAY HOWELL MOUNTAIN TITUS VINEYARD
(★★★):** Tends to be the most intense and concentrated,
but shares the tight, flinty, citrus and melon flavors of the
other vineyards.
1996: Tight, with complex peach, pear and citrus flavors
that are concentrated and long on the finish. **88**
1995: Lean and flinty, with lemony citrus, green pear
and apple notes. **88**
1994: Crisp and tightly wound, this young, concentrated
wine shows off a core of tart grapefruit, citrus and green
pear flavors. **89**
1993: Tart and flinty, with an earthy citrus edge, but not
much more in the way of fruit. **82**

1992: A lean, crisp wine with tart citrus and pear flavors, finishing with a hint of nutmeg and clove. **88**
1991: Lean and tight, with hints of pear and spice and light oak shadings that blend together nicely, finishing with delicate fruit nuances and buttery honey notes. **90**

PRIVATE RESERVE RED HOWELL MOUNTAIN (★★): 1995, the first vintage, was tight and overly tannic.

CHAUCER see **LAWRENCE J. BARGETTO WINERY**

CHAUFFE-EAU CELLARS (★★★)
Alexander Valley, Sonoma County
Founded: 1990. **Owner:** Keith Nelson & William R. Hunter. **Winemaker:** William R. Hunter. **Second Label:** Cirri.

MAJOR WINES: PRICE, CASES, RATING

Cabernet Sauvignon Alexander Valley Smith-Reichel Vineyard ($20, 250)	★★★
Chardonnay Carneros Sangiacomo Vineyard ($20, 900)	★★★
Pinot Noir Carneros ($22, 250)	★★

WINERY DATA
Case Production: 1,500. **Acres Owned:** 4 acres in Alexander Valley. **Varietals by Acre:** Syrah (4 acres). **Vineyard Designations:** Sangiacomo Vineyard (Chardonnay), Smith-Reichel Vineyard (Cabernet Sauvignon). **Varietals Purchased:** Cabernet Sauvignon (Alexander Valley), Chardonnay (Carneros), Pinot Noir (Carneros).

Keith Nelson and William Hunter oversee Chauffe-Eau, formerly the Vina Vista Winery, in Geyserville, where they produce 1,500 cases of Cabernet, Chardonnay (from Sangiacomo Vineyard) and Pinot Noir. When the first vintages came out, it was unclear where the winery was heading, but recently the wines have been very good. The 1996 Chardonnay Sangiacomo Vineyard (88 points) was well-oaked, elegant and complex, while the 1995 Cabernet Smith-Reichel Vineyard (88) was intense and tightly focused with layers of fruit flavors.

CHIMNEY ROCK WINERY (★★★)
Stags Leap District, Napa Valley
Founded: 1984. **Owner:** Sheldon & Stella Wilson. **Winemaker:** Douglas Fletcher.

MAJOR WINES: PRICE, CASES, RATING

Cabernet Sauvignon Stags Leap District ($28, 10,000)	★★★★
Cabernet Sauvignon Stags Leap District Reserve ($50, 250)	★★★★
Chardonnay Carneros ($17, 5,000)	★★
Élevage Red Stags Leap District ($44, 1,000)	★★★
Fumé Blanc Napa Valley ($13, 5,000)	★★

WINERY DATA
Case Production: 20,000. **Acres Owned:** 75 acres in Stags Leap District. **Varietals by Acre:** Cabernet Franc (5 acres), Cabernet Sauvignon (53), Merlot (14), Petit Verdot (3). **Varietals Purchased:** Chardonnay (Carneros), Sauvignon Blanc (Napa Valley).

Former Pepsi International executive Sheldon 'Hack' Wilson and his wife, Stella, bulldozed half the Chimney Rock Golf Course in the Stags Leap District to make way for their vineyard and their handsome Cape Dutch-style winery. The winery focuses on Stags Leap Cabernet, a Reserve Cabernet, Chardonnay from Carneros and Fumé Blanc. Both of the white wines have been erratic and on the lean, simple side. The early Cabernets were delicate, light and understated, often to a fault; they lacked the richness and depth found in so many other Stags Leap Cabernets. Recognizing this problem, Wilson and winemaker Douglas Fletcher added a Reserve wine and a Bordeaux-inspired red blend called Élevage (good breeding)—both of which offered more richness—and markedly improved the basic bottling. The Reserve in particular is now a plush, concentrated wine, and signals a remarkable rise in quality.

TASTING NOTES

CABERNET SAUVIGNON STAGS LEAP DISTRICT (★★★★): Has shown steady improvement and now merits outstanding ratings whether it carries the Napa Valley or more specific Stags Leap District appellation.

1996: Sleek and elegant, with ripe, spicy cherry, wild berry and strawberry flavors, it turns supple and polished on the finish. **90**

1995: Supple and harmonious; an elegant, rich and flavorful wine, with ripe currant, cherry, berry and spice notes. **90**

1994: Sharply focused, with a tightly wound core of ripe plum, black cherry and currant flavors that become elegant on the finish. **90**

1992: Spicy currant, earth and anise mark this medium-weight red, which lacks richness and depth. **83**

CABERNET SAUVIGNON STAGS LEAP DISTRICT RESERVE (★★★★): This wine has emerged as the star, increasingly showing more richness, depth and complexity.

1995: Has distinct smoky, toasty notes that ease into supple plum and berry flavors, but it lacks the extra dimensions that would justify this price. **87**

1994: Ripe, rich and deeply concentrated, with layers of black cherry, wild berry and currant flavors, and firm tannins. **91**

1993: Tight and firm, with crisp tannins and a complex, leathery core of currant, spice and cedar flavors. **90**

1992: Smooth and harmonious, with a lovely core of currant, coffee, cedar and spice, turning rich with plush, complex tannins. **92**

ÉLEVAGE RED STAGS LEAP DISTRICT (★★★): This blend has little more of everything than the earliest Cabernet vintages, from greater fruit extract to toastier oak.

1995: Elegant and understated; shows ripe, spicy cherry, wild berry and plum flavors, pretty oak, and soft, fleshy tannins. **89**

1994: Firm and structured, with a chewy, tannic edge to the earthy currant and leathery notes. **88**

1993: Firm, focused, with a band of ripe cherry, currant, spice and anise flavors, finishing with firm tannins. **88**

1992: Bright, with ripe, supple plum, berry and cherry flavors, finishing with mild, integrated tannins. **88**

1991: Strives for complexity with its smoky oak aromas and rich black cherry, currant and butter flavors. **88**

1990: Ripe and flavorful, with generous currant and blueberry aromas and flavors, finishing spicy and fresh. **88**

CHRISTOPHE VINEYARDS (★)
Napa Valley
Founded: 1984. **Owner:** Boisset U.S.A. **Winemaker:** William Arbios. **Second Label:** Joliesse.

MAJOR WINES: PRICE, CASES, RATING

Cabernet Sauvignon California ($10, 20,000)	★
Chardonnay California ($10, 20,000)	★
Pinot Noir California ($10, 10,000)	★
Sauvignon Blanc California ($9, 20,000)	★

WINERY DATA
Case Production: 70,000. **Varietals Purchased:** Cabernet Sauvignon (California), Chardonnay (California), Pinot Noir (California), Sauvignon Blanc (California).

This is a négociant brand, founded by French négociant Jean-Claude Boisset after he sold his winegrowing venture in Napa Valley (see St. Supéry). For years, Ginny Mills did a respectable job with wines such as Cabernet Sauvignon and Chardonnay, and in fact most of the wines under this label were good, and certainly good values. But Boisset has a history of letting quality slide with many of his wines, and this brand seems to be suffering, too. William Arbios, who has his own small Arbios brand (see entry) is now winemaker for Boisset U.S.A. The 1995 Cabernet (74 points) was simple with light cherry and oak flavors.

CHRISTOPHER CREEK WINERY (★★)
Russian River Valley, Sonoma County
Founded: 1972. **Owner:** Fred & Pamela Wasserman. **Winemaker:** Sebastian Pochan.

WINES PRODUCED: PRICE, CASES
Cabernet Sauvignon Dry Creek Valley Bradford Mountain Vineyard ($24, 350); Chardonnay Russian River Valley ($16, 300); Petite Sirah Russian River Valley ($18, 850); Syrah Russian River Valley ($18, 1,500); Syrah Russian River Valley Reserve ($22, 400).

WINERY DATA

Case Production: 5,000. **Acres Owned:** 11 acres in Russian River Valley. **Varietals by Acre:** Chardonnay (2 acres), Petite Sirah (4.5), Syrah (4.5). **Vineyard Designations:** Bradford Mountain Vineyard (Cabernet Sauvignon). **Varietals Purchased:** Cabernet (Dry Creek), Zinfandel (Dry Creek).

This small Russian River Valley winery has produced rustic Syrah and Petite Sirah for many years. In 1997 the vineyard and winery were purchased by the Wassermans, Central Valley orange growers. The Wassermans also own a 33-acre Dry Creek Valley Cabernet vineyard, although most of the grapes are sold to other wineries. The focus will continue to be Syrah and Petite Sirah, but Dry Creek Valley Cabernet from Bradford Mountain Vineyard and a Dry Creek Valley Zinfandel will be added in the future.

CINNABAR VINEYARDS (★★★)

Santa Cruz Mountains
Founded: 1986. **Owner:** Tom Mudd & Melissa Frank. **Winemaker:** George Troquato.

MAJOR WINES: PRICE, CASES, RATING

Cabernet Sauvignon Santa Cruz Mountains Saratoga Vineyard ($25, 2,000)	★★★
Chardonnay Santa Cruz Mountains ($23, 2,000)	★★★

ALSO PRODUCED

Chardonnay Central Coast ($17, 3,000); Merlot Central Coast ($18, 4,000); Pinot Noir Santa Cruz Mountains ($30, 1,500).

WINERY DATA

Case Production: 13,500. **Acres Owned:** 30 acres in the Santa Cruz Mountains. **Varietals by Acre:** Cabernet Franc (1 acre), Cabernet Sauvignon (8.5), Chardonnay (12), Merlot (1), Petit Verdot (.5), Pinot Noir (7). **Vineyard Designations:** Saratoga Vineyard (Cabernet Sauvignon). **Varietals Purchased:** Chardonnay (Santa Barbara County), Merlot (Santa Barbara County), Chardonnay (Santa Clara County), Merlot (Santa Clara County).

Cinnabar sits on a hilltop overlooking Saratoga and is owned by former Stanford research engineer Tom Mudd and his wife, Melissa Frank, who purchased the property in 1983. They use a mixture of estate-grown and purchased grapes to make their wine. The Cabernet from Saratoga Vineyard is the best wine; it is consistent in its high quality, and occasionally borders on outstanding. The Chardonnay has carried both Central Coast and Santa Cruz Mountains appellations, and there is a new Merlot from the Central Coast.

TASTING NOTES

CABERNET SAUVIGNON SANTA CRUZ MOUNTAINS SARATOGA VINEYARD (★★★)

1994: Ripe and jammy, with racy wild berry, black cherry and spicy nuances, finishing with chewy tannins. **88**
1993: Complex, with tiers of spicy currant, anise, tar and cedary oak nuances that fan out nicely. **89**
1992: Ripe and flavorful, with a distinct tobacco-leaf edge to the ripe plum and berry flavors and earthy tannins. **88**

CIRRI see CHAUFFE-EAU CELLARS

CK MONDAVI see CHARLES KRUG WINERY

CLAIBORNE & CHURCHILL VINTNERS (★★)

Edna Valley, San Luis Obispo County
Founded: 1983. **Owner:** Claiborne Thompson & Fredericka Churchill Thompson. **Winemaker:** Claiborne Thompson.

MAJOR WINES: PRICE, CASES, RATING

Chardonnay Edna Valley MacGregor Vineyard ($18, 350)	★★★
Gewürztraminer Cental Coast Alsatian Style Dry ($12, 2,500)	★★
Pinot Noir Edna Valley ($16, 200)	★
Riesling Central Coast Alsatian Style Dry ($12, 1,500)	★★

WINERY DATA

Case Production: 5,000. **Vineyard Designations:** MacGregor Vineyard (Chardonnay). **Varietals Purchased:** Chardonnay (Edna Valley), Gewürztraminer (Monterey, Santa Barbara County), Orange Muscat (Monterey), Pinot Noir (Edna Valley), Riesling (Monterey).

Claiborne Thompson was a college lecturer in old Norse and Scandinavian languages in Michigan before he moved to California and took a job working in the cellar at Edna Valley Vineyards. In 1983, Thompson and his wife, Fredericka Churchill, started their own winery, focusing on the production of white wines made from Edna Valley and Central Coast grapes. Their dry, crisp Gewürztraminer and Riesling are refreshing, if not exciting. The 1996 Chardonnay MacGregor Vineyard (87 points) was silky, with earthy citrus and pear flavors. The winery also makes the occasional Pinot Noir.

CLARK-CLAUDON VINEYARDS (★★★)
Oakville, Napa Valley
Founded: 1993. **Owner:** Thomas Clark & Laurie Claudon Clark. **Winemaker:** Gary Brookman.

MAJOR WINES: PRICE, CASES, RATING

Cabernet Sauvignon Napa Valley	
($45, 500)	★★★

WINERY DATA
Case Production: 500. **Acres Owned:** 20 acres in Napa Valley. **Varietals by Acre:** Cabernet Sauvignon (20 acres).

Tom and Laurie Clark of Clark-Claudon sell the majority of the Cabernet Sauvignon grapes from their Napa Valley vineyard to local wineries, but they are now retaining some and making small amounts of concentrated Cabernet under their own label. Their first wine, a 1993 Cabernet (90 points), was harmonious, with lots of complex spice, herb and fruit flavors. The 1994 (92 points) was even more intense, firm and concentrated, but while the very good 1995 (88 points), had rich, ripe flavors, it didn't have the finesse of the earlier vintages. Likely to have a promising future, this is a winery to watch.

CLAUDIA SPRINGS WINERY (★★)
Anderson Valley, Mendocino County
Founded: 1989. **Owner:** Claudia & Robert Klindt, Claudia & Warren Hein. **Winemaker:** Robert Klindt.

MAJOR WINES: PRICE, CASES, RATING

Chardonnay Anderson Valley	
($14, 250)	★★
Chardonnay Anderson Valley Reserve	
($20, 70)	★★
Pinot Noir Anderson Valley	
($18, 550)	★★
Zinfandel Redwood Valley	
($18, 375)	★★

WINERY DATA
Case Production: 1,200. **Varietals Purchased:** Chardonnay (Anderson Valley), Pinot Noir (Anderson Valley), Zinfandel (Redwood Valley).

This 1,200-case winery in Anderson Valley produces Pinot Noir, Chardonnay and Zinfandel from purchased grapes. None of the wines merit anything but passing interest at best. The 1996 Chardonnay Anderson Valley (84 points) was soft and creamy, while the Reserve Chardonnay Anderson Valley 1996 (83) tasted minerally with simple fruit flavors. The 1996 Pinot Noir Anderson Valley (81) was marked by light cherry and herb flavors, while Zinfandel Redwood Valley 1996 (81) was lean and awkward, with modest cherry notes.

CLINE CELLARS (★★–★★★)
Carneros
Founded: 1982. **Owner:** Fred & Nancy Cline. **Winemaker:** Matt Cline. **Second Label:** Jacuzzi Family Vineyards.

MAJOR WINES: PRICE, CASES, RATING

Carignane Contra Costa County	
($18, 2,983)	★★
Cotes D' Oakley Vin Rouge California	
($9, 20,240)	★★
Cotes D' Oakley Vin Blanc California	
($9, 6,328)	★★
Cotes D' Oakley Vin Gris California	
($9, 1,777)	★★
Marsanne Carneros	
($18, 843)	★★
Mourvèdre Contra Costa County	
($18, 2,850)	★★★

Muscat Canelli Sonoma Valley
($25, 220) ★★★

Roussanne Carneros
($24, 843) ★★

Syrah Contra Costa County
($24, 3,400) ★★

Viognier Carneros
($24, 978) ★★

Zinfandel California
($10, 46,000) ★★

Zinfandel Contra Costa County Ancient
Vines
($18, 7,900) ★★★

Zinfandel Contra Costa County Big Break
($24, 1,350) ★★★

Zinfandel Contra Costa County Bridgehead
($24, 1,380) ★★★

Zinfandel Contra Costa County Live Oak
($24, 675) ★★★

Zinfandel Contra Costa County Reserve
(Discontinued) ★★★

Winery Data

Case Production: 90,000. **Acres Owned:** 761 acres (251 in
Contra Costa County, 510 in Sonoma County). **Varietals by
Acre:** Alicante Bouchet (5 acres), Carignane (45), Chardonnay
(120), Grenache (5), Marsanne (100), Merlot (120), Palomino
(6), Pinot Gris (30), Pinot Noir (80), Roussanne (10), Syrah
(110), Viognier (30), Zinfandel (100). **Varietals Purchased:**
Muscat, Sauvignon Blanc, Syrah, Viognier, Zinfandel (all
Contra Costa County)

Brothers Fred and Matt Cline are grandsons of
Valeriano Jacuzzi, founder of the device and company
that bears his name. In 1982 Fred Cline decided to enter
the wine business using family-owned vineyards in
Oakley, a rural area in Contra Costa County. Not many
people think of Oakley as wine country, but Rhône varietals grow exceptionally well there. The family's 251
acres are planted to a wide range of varieties, including
Mourvèdre, Syrah, Zinfandel and Carignane.

In 1982 the Clines purchased the old Fripo Winery in
Oakley, but moved to Carneros in 1991, where the family
bought a horse ranch and some 40 acres of vineyard across
the highway from Viansa. Production has risen to 90,000
cases, including many small lots of designer wines.

Tasting Notes

Mourvèdre Contra Costa County (★★★): Marked
by distinctive, medium-weight tar, earth and raspberry
flavors and firm but supple tannins. A Reserve appears
occasionally.

**Zinfandel Contra Costa County Ancient Vines
(★★★):** Rustic, with wild berry and raspberry flavors; it
can be leathery.
1996: A ripe, full-bodied style, marked by an earthy,
tarry edge to the rich berry and plummy Zinfandel flavors. Turns dry and tannic on the finish, so a short time
in the cellar should help. **88**
1995: Lots of spice, ripe plum and berry flavors. This
robust, lively, complex wine is quite pleasing. Shows off
earthy bay leaf and minty notes on the finish. **87**

**Zinfandel Contra Costa County Big Break
(★★★):** Improving; some recent efforts were packed
with ripe, rich flavors.
1996: Very ripe, with a slightly jammy edge to the plum,
wild berry, anise, sage and cedary oak flavors. Fills out
on the palate, holding its flavors and keeping its focus,
even with its firm, dry tannins. **89**
1995: Starts out tough and chewy, then works its way
into more interesting blackberry and raspberry flavors.
Finishes with dry tannins. **84**
1994: A gutsy style, with ripe cherry and wild berry flavors and spicy, peppery nuances. The texture is smooth
and supple into the finish, where the tannins weigh in. **90**
1993: Distinct for its ripe chunky plum, berry and tarry
flavors and chewy tannins. **87**

**Zinfandel Contra Costa County Bridgehead
(★★★):** Big, ripe and concentrated, with a pretty array
of flavors.
1996: A tarry style of Zin that's quite ripe, with just a
glimmer of wild berry, stewed plum and cedary, spicy
notes appearing on the finish, where it turns a bit bitter
and stemmy. **86**
1995: Ripe and racy, with a spicy edge to the black cherry and wild berry flavors, finishing with firm tannins and
a hint of tar. **84**
1994: Tight and firm, with a compact core of wild berry,
cherry and plum flavors. Needs more time to open and
soften, but its solidly packed flavors show promise. **87**

1993: Appealing for its ripe, bright cherry and raspberry flavors that turn vibrant and complex, finishing with firm tannins. **87**

ZINFANDEL CONTRA COSTA COUNTY LIVE OAK VINEYARD (★★★)

1996: A dark, intense, meaty style, with lots of tar, stewed plum, wild berry and mineral flavors; turns thick and chewy on the finish, where the tannins are coarse and dry. **87**

ZINFANDEL CONTRA COSTA COUNTY RESERVE (★★★):

Vibrant, mouthfilling and well balanced, with plenty of dusty berry flavor.

1994: Despite a few tart notes, this is a rich, complex young wine, brimming with wild berry, cherry and raspberry flavors. It finishes with major-league tannins, but they're not biting. **89**

1993: Dense and chewy, with an intense core of tar, plum, spice and nutmeg, turning complex and tannic on the finish. Needs short-term cellaring. **88**

1992: Bright and vibrant, a firm and compact Zin that's weighted toward tarry berry and jam notes. **89**

1991: Tight, firm and focused, offering rich currant and raspberry aromas and flavors that are lively. **86**

CLOS DU BOIS WINERY (★★–★★★★)

Alexander Valley, Sonoma County
Founded: 1974. **Owner:** Wine Alliance, Allied Domecq.
Winemaker: Margaret Davenport.

MAJOR WINES: PRICE, CASES, RATING

Cabernet Sauvignon Alexander Valley Selection ($18, 10,000)	★★
Cabernet Sauvignon Alexander Valley Winemaker's Reserve ($50, 5,000)	★★★★
Cabernet Sauvignon Sonoma County ($15, 84,000)	★★
Cabernet Sauvignon Alexander Valley Briarcrest Vineyard ($21, 5,300)	★★★
Chardonnay Alexander Valley Alexander Valley Selection ($15, 150,000)	★★
Chardonnay Alexander Valley Calcaire Vineyard ($18, 11,500)	★★★
Chardonnay Dry Creek Valley Flintwood Vineyard ($17, 5,650)	★★★
Marlstone Vineyard Red Alexander Valley ($25, 12,000)	★★★
Merlot Alexander Valley Alexander Valley Selection ($20, 20,000)	★★★
Pinot Noir Sonoma County ($15, 3,000)	★★
Sauvignon Blanc Sonoma County ($9, 67,000)	★★
Zinfandel Sonoma County ($14, 20,000)	★★

WINERY DATA

Case Production: 890,000. **Acres Owned:** 650 acres in Alexander Valley. **Varietals by Acre:** Cabernet Sauvignon (100 acres), Chardonnay (350), Merlot (100), other (100). **Vineyard Designations:** Marlstone Vineyard (Cabernet Franc, Cabernet Sauvignon, Merlot, Petit Verdot, Malbec), Briarcrest Vineyard (Cabernet Sauvignon), Calcaire Vineyard. (Chardonnay), Flintwood Vineyard (Chardonnay). **Varietals Purchased:** Cabernet Sauvignon (Sonoma County), Chardonnay (Sonoma County), Merlot (Sonoma County), Pinot Noir (Sonoma County), Sauvignon Blanc (Sonoma County), Zinfandel (Sonoma County).

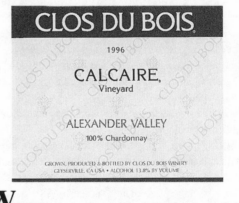

With 650 acres in vineyards and a modern new winery, Clos du Bois is a dominant force in Sonoma County wine. As it has grown in volume, Winemaker's Cabernet Reserve has become its best wine; its two vineyard-designated reds, the Marlstone blend and the Briarcrest Cabernet, are close runners-up. The rest of the main lineup of wines is good to very good, and can usually be had at very fair prices. Clos du Bois's wines are also widely distributed, another plus for consumers in many parts of the country.

The winery dates back to 1974, when businessman Frank Woods and a group of investors placed the acquisition of vineyards ahead of building a winery; winemaking was done out of a large warehouse in Healdsburg. In 1988, Clos du Bois was sold to Hiram Walker's Wine Alliance, which also owns Callaway and William Hill and markets Atlas Peak's wines.

Clos du Bois's 890,000-case output is focused on high-volume wines. Its biggest sellers are Sonoma County Cabernet, Alexander Valley Selection Chardonnay, Sonoma County Merlot and Sonoma County Sauvignon Blanc. This lineup is augmented by smaller lots of vineyard-designated Chardonnays: Calcaire in Alexander Valley and Flintwood in Dry Creek Valley. All in all, Clos du Bois offers a very good range of wines. The Briarcrest and Marlstone are worthy of collecting.

TASTING NOTES

CABERNET SAUVIGNON ALEXANDER VALLEY SELECTION (★★): Supple and elegant, with fine balance, cherry flavors, light oak shadings and mild tannins. Ages well over the short term. Can include up to 25 percent Cabernet Franc. The 1996 (83) offered simple cherry and berry flavors.

CABERNET SAUVIGNON ALEXANDER VALLEY BRIARCREST VINEYARD (★★★): The darkest and most concentrated of the wines, this 100 percent Cabernet is marked by intense berry, cherry and mineral flavors, and often by chewy tannins. Very consistent, with good but not great aging capability. Worth watching.
1995: Tightly wound, with a firm focus on the black cherry and blackberry flavors; complex, concentrated and firmly tannic. **91**
1994: Ripe, rich, focused, with a tight, complex core of currrant, black cherry, berry, coffee and spice flavors. **89**
1993: Tight and firm, with a chewy tannic edge to the spicy currant, herb and cedary oak flavors. **88**
1992: Attractive for its intense, complex plum, floral, wild berry flavors; turns supple and elegant on the finish. **89**
1991: A pleasant, well balanced wine with pretty plum and currant flavors that stay with you. **87**

1990: Broad, ripe and supple, with complex currant, anise, cherry and mineral flavors and soft tannins. **88**
1987: Shows wonderful harmony and finesse; rich and focused, with tiers of chocolate, cherry, currant and wild berry flavors, turning smooth and supple. **91**
1978: Aging well; complex and mature, with black cherry, wild berry, plum, herb and spice flavors. **88**

CABERNET SAUVIGNON ALEXANDER VALLEY WINEMAKER'S RESERVE (★★★★): Supple and elegant, with fine balance, cherry flavors, light oak shadings and mild tannins. Ages well over the short term. Can include up to 25 percent Cabernet Franc. The Reserve is worth watching.
1995: Smooth, ripe, supple and harmonious, with layers of plush currant, blackberry, sage, coffee, mineral, tea and spice. Keeps pumping out the flavors on the long, rich and polished finish. **92**
1991: Intense and concentrated, with layers of complex currant, black cherry and herb flavors. Finishes with a nice touch of oak. **92**

CHARDONNAY ALEXANDER VALLEY ALEXANDER VALLEY SELECTION (★★): Given its 150,000-case volume, this is a well-made wine, although recent vintages have been leaner, crisper and less satisfying than previous ones.

CHARDONNAY ALEXANDER VALLEY CALCAIRE VINEYARD (★★★): Consistent, but rarely outstanding. Made in a tight, firm style that accents pear, peach and spice notes.
1997: Openly fruity, with complex pear, apple, licorice and vanilla flavors, it's elegant and polished, finishing with a hint of grapefruit. **89**
1996: Clean, crisp and flinty, with an elegant, understated core of citrus, pear and lime. **87**
1995: Clean and lively, with a flinty edge to the pear, spice, apple and light oak shadings. **89**
1994: Bright and lively, with a core of ripe pear, grapefruit, honey and light toasty oak notes that fold together nicely. **91**

CHARDONNAY DRY CREEK VALLEY FLINTWOOD VINEYARD (★★★): Bolder and riper than Calcaire. Usually very well made, but can vary at times.
1996: Elegant, with floral, pear, citrus and spice notes, turning flinty with a mineral edge. **87**
1995: Smooth and polished, with an elegant core of creamy pear, citrus, vanilla, herb and sage flavors. **88**

1994: Fragrant, with spicy apple, fig and pear notes of moderate richness and depth, turning elegant and complex on the finish. **89**

MARLSTONE VINEYARD RED ALEXANDER VALLEY (★★★): A blend of Cabernet Sauvignon, Merlot and Cabernet Franc, it is supple and elegant, well oaked and marked by herb and cherry flavors and fleshy tannins. Appealing early on, and for up to six to eight years.

1995: Smells exotic and complex, with a broad range of dried cherry, currant, plum, anise, cedar and earth flavors. Holds its focus. **91**

1994: Elegant, understated, with ripe plum, currant, spice and herbal notes and fine balance. **90**

1992: Well oaked, with toasty, buttery flavors and ripe cherry, plum, herb and coffee notes on a supple finish. **89**

1991: Shows ripe plum, cranberry, cherry and cedary oak flavors that are well focused. **88**

1990: Forward and fleshy, with lots of appealing berry and plum flavors dressed up with spicy oak. **88**

1989: Crisp, firm and elegant, with lively black cherry, anise, herb and currant flavors. **84**

1987: A tightly knit, harmonious wine with rich, intense currant, herb, spice, chocolate and berry flavors that are neatly woven together. **90**

1986: Soft and supple, with modest herb, vanilla and cherry flavors and hints of beets and dill on the finish. **85**

1985: Lavishly oaked, rich and supple, with pronounced herb and cedar notes and concentrated olive, black cherry, anise and spice flavors. **88**

1978: Mature and fading, with dry, earthy, tarry mushroom flavors and slightly sour, dirty notes. **74**

MERLOT ALEXANDER VALLEY ALEXANDER VALLEY SELECTION (★★★): Once the most consistent and well balanced of the Clos du Bois reds, before the rise in quality of the Cabernets. Now it is typically smooth and supple, but not especially concentrated. The 1995 (86 points) was bright with smooth currant flavors. Carried a Sonoma County appellation until 1994.

PINOT NOIR SONOMA COUNTY (★★): Simple and light, with cherry and berry notes of modest proportion.

SAUVIGNON BLANC SONOMA COUNTY (★★): Typically bright and lively, with grassy citrus, pear and fig flavors. The 1997 (84 points) was bright and lemony early on.

ZINFANDEL SONOMA COUNTY (★★): Made in a smooth, balanced style, it's an easy-drinking wine with cherry and berry flavors.

CLOS DU VAL WINE CO. (★★–★★★★)
Stags Leap District, Napa Valley
Founded: 1972. **Owner:** John Goelet. **Winemaker:** Bernard Portet. **Second Label:** Le Clos.

MAJOR WINES: PRICE, CASES, RATING

Cabernet Sauvignon Napa Valley ($24, 32,000)	★★
Cabernet Sauvignon Napa Valley Reserve ($50, 1,800)	★★★★
Cabernet Sauvignon Stags Leap District (Discontinued)	★★
Chardonnay Napa Valley Carneros Estate ($16, 24,000)	★★
Chardonnay Napa Valley Carneros Estate Reserve ($25, 500)	★★★
Merlot Napa Valley ($28, 5,000)	★★
Pinot Noir Napa Valley Carneros ($20, 3,000)	★★
Sémillon Stags Leap District ($15, 1,000)	★★★
Zinfandel California ($15, 4,000)	★★

ALSO PRODUCED
Ariadne Napa Valley ($25, NA).

WINERY DATA
Case Production: 80,000. **Acres Owned:** 252 acres in Carneros, Stags Leap District and Yountville (118 in Carneros, 126 in Stags Leap District, 8 in Yountville). **Varietals by Acre:** Cabernet Franc (6 acres), Cabernet Sauvignon (80), Chardonnay (96), Merlot (31), Pinot Noir (22), Sangiovese (5), Sémillon (1), Zinfandel (11). **Varietals Purchased:** Cabernet Franc (Napa Valley), Cabernet Sauvignon (Napa Valley), Merlot (Napa Valley), Sauvignon Blanc (Napa Valley), Sémillon (Napa Valley), Zinfandel (El Dorado).

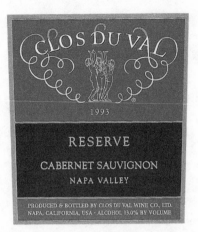

Clos Du Val is owned by John Goelet, a wealthy New York businessman who hired Bernard Portet in 1970 to develop a California-based winery. Portet settled on a site in the Stags Leap District because it was cooler than areas farther up the valley, and because local growers such as Nathan Fay (of Fay Vineyard) made excellent homemade Cabernets with more polish and finesse than many others in Napa.

Clos Du Val rose to prominence under Portet's direction in the 1970s and early 1980s on the strength of its red wines–Cabernet Sauvignon, a Cabernet Reserve, Merlot and Zinfandel, each from estate-grown grapes in the Stags Leap District. Portet displayed a deft hand with each of these four, creating wines of elegance and finesse uncommon in Napa Valley. With the Reserve, for instance, Portet was among the first to use Merlot to soften and tame Cabernet's aggressive tendencies. Clos Du Val's Merlots, supported by a small dose of Cabernet Sauvignon, were among the most complex and complete wines of the 1970s and 1980s, as vintners were beginning to focus on Merlot and quality was beginning to improve. With Zinfandel, too, Portet created a supple, polished style of wine that toned down Zinfandel's sometimes racier flavors.

By the 1990s, however, only the Reserve had held its own in terms of quality and style; both the Merlot and the Zinfandel have since become increasingly simpler and less compelling. One key reason for this inconsistency is that the winery's vineyards have gone into decline, forcing Clos Du Val to buy grapes from elsewhere in the valley. (The vineyards have recently been replanted). Thus, the Cabernet no longer says Stags Leap District, but car-

ries the broader Napa Valley name. Similarly, the Zinfandel has gone from Stags Leap to Napa-El Dorado to an even larger California appellation.

With white wines, particularly Chardonnay, Clos du Val has leaned toward crisp flavors. Pinot Noir, too, is very light and ordinary, especially when compared with other, more exciting wines being made from Carneros-grown grapes. Portet is intent on making better wines now, as the Reserve Chardonnay 1995 (91 points) indicates. Quality should improve when the replanted vineyards begin to bear fruit.

TASTING NOTES

CABERNET SAUVIGNON NAPA VALLEY (★★): Less interesting of late. The 1994 (86 points) and 1993 (83) were good, but well off the pace.

CABERNET SAUVIGNON NAPA VALLEY RESERVE (★★★★): Clos du Val's best wine, period. Deftly balanced, with a tight, narrow beam of supple currant and herb flavors, a nice touch of oak and firm but polished tannins. Can age well; is best at six to ten years.
1994: Rich, with pretty currant, coffee, anise, sage and cedar flavors that are elegant and understated, finishing with supple tannins. **91**
1993: Smooth and ripe, with rich, complex flavors of juicy currant, cherry, plum and wild berry. **91**
1992: Tight and tannic, but with a well-focused core of earthy currant and cedar flavors. **89**
1990: Light for a 1990 Reserve; has elegant cherry, currant and earthy notes and a sense of finesse, but it lacks richess. **88**
1988: Ripe and full-bodied; earthy, with clay, cedar, spice, currant and black cherry flavors. **88**
1987: Rich and polished; very complex and compelling, with layers of currant, anise, cedar, tea, sage and spice that turn silky. **93**
1985: Rich, elegant, tightly wound, with bright cherry, cedar, anise and plum flavors that are long and satisfying. Has excellent structure and depth. **94**
1982: Showing attractive bottle bouquet and some maturity and development, with cedar, chocolate, plum and tobacco flavors. It's a rich, tannic, full-bodied wine. **88**
1979: Mature now, it is supple and generous, with cedar, tobacco, cherry and currant flavors that pick up an anise edge. Past its prime but very appealing. **90**

1978: Mature, complex and a bit drying, with ripe cherry and currant flavors that are elegant but fading. **88**

CABERNET SAUVIGNON STAGS LEAP DISTRICT (★★): No recent bottlings, as the vineyards are being replanted.
1990: Austere and tannic, with just a glimpse of fruit peeking through. **84**
1989: Lean and firm, with a narrow band of currant and cedar notes. **83**
1988: Tight, with currant, cherry and plum flavors and mild tannins. **86**
1987: Ripe and supple, with rich, generous plum, currant, black cherry, chocolate and spicy vanilla notes that are elegant and concentrated. **90**
1986: Impressive, rich and supple, with bright black cherry and subtle earth notes, plus hints of anise, cedar and coffee. **89**
1985: Elegant and refined, with sharply focused black cherry, currant and cedar flavors, finishing with fine tannins. **91**
1984: Ripe, open, generous, with firm currant and black cherry flavors and hints of tobacco on the finish. **92**

CHARDONNAY NAPA VALLEY CARNEROS ESTATE (★★); RESERVE (★★★): Very inconsistent, though both 1995 bottlings—the Estate (90 points) and the Reserve (91)—earned outstanding marks for their richness, depth and creamy, polished, lovely flavors. There is no reason why this wine can't be better considering the winery's extensive Carneros vineyards.

MERLOT NAPA VALLEY (★★): It's been a long time since this wine wowed anyone. Recent vintages, such as 1995 (86 points) and 1994 (88), were improvements; new vines should help. Until 1994, carried a Stags Leap District appellation.

ZINFANDEL CALIFORNIA (★★): In the past, has carried Napa and El Dorado County appellations. Like the Merlot, it's been less interesting of late, and now with a California appellation it's far less distinctive.

CLOS LACHANCE WINES (★★★)
Santa Cruz Mountains
Founded: 1992. **Owner:** Bill & Brenda Murphy.
Winemaker: Jeff Ritchey. **Second Label:** Colibri.

MAJOR WINES: PRICE, CASES, RATING
Cabernet Sauvignon Santa Cruz Mountains
($22, 1,025) ★★
Chardonnay Santa Cruz Mountains
($22, 3,000) ★★★
Chardonnay Santa Cruz Mountains
Vintner's Reserve
($29, 300) ★★★
Pinot Noir Santa Cruz Mountains
($19, 300) ★★

ALSO PRODUCED
Chardonnay Napa Valley ($18, 180); Merlot Central Coast ($18, 1,000).

WINERY DATA
Case Production: 15,000. **Acres Owned:** 0.75 acres in Santa Cruz Mountains. **Varietals by Acre:** Chardonnay (0.75 acres). **Varietals Purchased:** Cabernet Franc (Santa Cruz Mountains), Cabernet Sauvignon (Santa Cruz Mountains), Chardonnay (Santa Cruz Mountains, Napa Valley), Merlot (Santa Cruz Mountains), Nebbiolo (Santa Cruz Mountains), Zinfandel (Santa Cruz Mountains, El Dorado).

Clos LaChance has grown considerably since it was founded in 1992. It now produces 15,000 cases, though most of that is bottled under the second label, Colibri. Santa Cruz appellation Chardonnay, Cabernet and Pinot Noir are presently this winery's focus; however, wines ranging from Santa Cruz Mountain Nebbiolo to El Dorado Zinfandel, all made from purchased grapes, will be added in the future. Rich, concentrated Santa Cruz Chardonnays, like the 1996 Vintner's Reserve, are Clos LaChance's best wines.

TASTING NOTES

CHARDONNAY SANTA CRUZ MOUNTAINS VINTNER'S RESERVE (★★★)
1996: Ripe, rich and concentrated. Sharply focused, with pretty mineral, pear, spice and earth notes that echo on the complex aftertaste. **90**

CHARDONNAY SANTA CRUZ MOUNTAINS (★★★)
1996: Ripe, with concentrated, pear, spice, fig and earthy Chardonnay flavors. **88**
1995: Smooth, ripe and buttery, with a rich core of pear, apple, oak and spice flavors that turn rich and creamy. **92**
1994: Bold, ripe and generous, with buttery pear, fig and melon notes; finishes with a smoky, toasty oak edge. **89**

CLOS PEGASE (★★–★★★)

Calistoga, Napa Valley
Founded: 1984. **Owner:** Jan and Mitsuko Shrem.
Winemaker: Steven Rogstad.

MAJOR WINES: PRICE, CASES, RATING

Cabernet Sauvignon Napa Valley
   ($25, 7,500)   ★★★
Cabernet Sauvignon Napa Valley
   Hommage Artist Series Reserve
   ($50, 900)   ★★★
Chardonnay Carneros Mitsuko's Vineyard
   ($20, 11,000)   ★★★
Merlot Napa Valley Carneros
   ($23, 14,000)   ★★

ALSO PRODUCED

Cabernet Franc Napa Valley ($20, NA); Chardonnay
Carneros Mitsuko's Vineyard Reserve ($30, 700); Pinot
Noir Carneros Mitsuko's Vineyard ($19, NA); Vin Gris of
Merlot Carneros ($13, NA).

WINERY DATA

Case Production: 40,000. **Acres Owned:** 278 acres (229 in
Carneros, 49 in Napa Valley). **Varietals by Acre:** Cabernet Franc
(6 acres), Cabernet Sauvignon (46), Chardonnay (131), Malbec
(3), Merlot (72), Petit Verdot (3), Pinot Noir (11), Sauvignon
Blanc (6). **Vineyard Designations:** Mitsuko's Vineyard.

In Clos Pegase, Jan and Mitsuko Shrem have built one of
Napa Valley's showcase wineries. Post-modernist architect
Michael Graves designed this elaborate estate south of
Calistoga near Sterling Vineyards. After buying grapes for
several years and making mainstream wines, the Shrems
began acquiring vineyards of their own in an effort to raise

quality. They now own 433 acres (278 planted), including
200-plus in Carneros planted primarily to Chardonnay.
Shrem also grows Cabernet (46 acres) and Merlot (72 acres).

Recent efforts with the Cabernet Hommage Artist
Series Reserve have shown more depth and complexity,
but at $50 a bottle it's overpriced for what you get. The
Napa Valley Cabernet has been very good, and the
Chardonnay Carneros Mitsuko's Vineyard has moments
of excellence, such as the 1995 (90 points). The Merlot,
now sporting a Napa Valley Carneros appellation, has
also had its bright spots, with the 1992 (90) the best off
the most recent efforts. The 1995 (84) and 1996 (86) vintages were less impressive. Considering all the effort and
money the Shrems have put into Clos Pegase, this should
be a winery to watch—if only to see whether it can reach
the upper echelon of Napa Valley wineries.

TASTING NOTES

CABERNET SAUVIGNON NAPA VALLEY (★★★): Highly
variable. The superb, Bordeaux-style 1990 was a big
breakthrough and the 1996 equally outstanding, but the
quality of intervening vintages was more modest.
1996: Smooth and elegant on the palate, yet with plenty
of structure and staying power. Flavors are well integrated, with black currant, blackberry, herb, tobacco and
chocolate in evidence. Finishes long; should improve
nicely in the cellar. **91**
1994: Marked by a slight gamelike edge, but offers
enough currant, cherry, sage and spice flavors to hold
your interest. **86**
1993: Smooth and harmonious, with an earthy edge to
the plum and currant flavors. Finishes with firm, plush
tannins. **87**
1992: Tightly wound, rich, firm core of cherry, currant and
anise flavors, picking up an earthy, toasted oak edge. **88**
1991: While this is a firmly austere and tannic wine, it's
also quite flavorful, with layers of currant, cedar, spice
and tobacco. **87**
1990: Firm and intense with solid cherry, currant and plum
flavors that gently unfold into a spicy, concentrated wine. **91**

**CABERNET SAUVIGNON NAPA VALLEY HOMMAGE ARTIST
SERIES RESERVE (★★★):** A blend of Cabernet and
smaller amounts of Merlot and Cabernet Franc. It's been
a rustic, tannic wine in the past, but recent vintages have
been richer and more polished.

1995: Elegant and supple, with pretty plum, currant and black cherry notes; dashes of mint and sage add complexity. **89**
1994: Distinctive, with cedary oak, ripe plum and cherry flavors, and hints of strawberry and blueberry. **90**
1993: Impressive for its elegance and finesse, this wine delivers a pleasant core of cherry, currant and wild berry flavors. **88**
1991: A good wine with ripe currant and plum flavors, but it comes across as awkward and hollow in the middle, finishing with crisp tannins. **85**
1990: Crisp, harmonious, gaining some flesh and silkiness as it unfolds its cherry, prune and spice flavors. **86**

CHARDONNAY CARNEROS MITSUKO'S VINEYARD (★★★): Occasionally outstanding, but usually comes up just short. Elegant and polished, but can be tart.
1996: Elegant and intense, with cedary oak and ripe pear flavors that finish with a togh of spice and citrus. **87**
1995: Appealing for its ripe, smooth core of spice, pear, apple and melon; becomes elegant and sophisticated. **90**
1994: Young, tart, adding a distinct lemony flair to the ripe pear and spice flavors. Toasty oak shows on the elegant finish. **90**

MERLOT NAPA VALLEY CARNEROS (★★): Fails to excite. It's variable in quality, and is often tannic and lean.

COASTAL CELLARS see LAWRENCE J.
BARGETTO WINERY

COBBLESTONE see PARAISO SPRINGS VINEYARDS

CODORNIU NAPA (★★★)
Carneros
Founded: 1991. **Owner:** Codorniu S.A. (Spain). **Winemaker:** Don Van Staaveren (table); Todd Graff (sparkling).

MAJOR WINES: PRICE, CASES, RATING
Blanc de Blancs Napa Valley
  ($22, 300) ★★★
Brut Napa Valley
  ($15, 25,000) ★★★

Reserve Napa Valley
  ($25, 300) ★★★
Rosé Napa Valley
  ($18, 1,000) ★★★

WINERY DATA
Case Production: 35,000. **Acres Owned:** 172 acres in Carneros. **Varietals by Acre:** Chardonnay (101 acres), Pinot Noir (65), new rootstock (6). **Varietals Purchased:** Cabernet Franc (Napa Valley), Cabernet Sauvignon (Alexander, Napa, Sonoma Valleys, Carneros, Rutherford Bench), Chardonnay (Napa Valley), Malbec (Napa Valley), Merlot (Napa, Sonoma Valleys), Muscadelle de Bordelais (Sonoma Valley), Pinot Noir (Santa Barbara County, Santa Maria Valleys, Russian River, Willamette in Oregon), Sauvignon Blanc (Napa Valley), Zinfandel (Sonoma Valley).

Spanish sparkling-wine giant Codorniu, which has been making wine in Spain since 1872, followed the foreign investment trail to California in the late 1980s, settling in Carneros. The company built a handsome, modern winery into a hillside so as to blend in with the rural area. Codorniu owns 172 acres in Carneros, largely Chardonnay (101 acres) and Pinot Noir. They also buy some of their grapes from growers in Carneros and Napa Valley.

All four of the non-vintage sparkling wines are very clean and well made. The Blanc de Blancs and Reserve are sold only at the winery.

In 1997, the winery decided to venture into table wines, and hired the talented Don Van Staaveren from Chateau St. Jean. The plan is to produce a broad lineup that should include Cabernet, Chardonnay, Merlot, Pinot Noir and Sauvignon Blanc. In 1999, Codorniu Napa announced that it would change its name to Artesa. Worth watching.

DAVID COFFARO VINEYARD & WINERY (★★★★)
Dry Creek Valley, Sonoma County
Founded: 1994. **Owner:** David Coffaro. **Winemaker:** David Coffaro.

MAJOR WINES: PRICE, CASES, RATING
Cabernet Sauvignon Dry Creek Valley
  Coffaro Estate Vineyard
  ($19, 300) ★★★
Carignane Dry Creek Valley
  ($23, 250) ★★★

Estate Cuvée Dry Creek Valley
  Coffaro Estate Vineyard
  ($23, 700)   ★★★★
Petite Sirah Dry Creek Valley
  ($23, 250)   ★★★★
Sauvignon Blanc Late Harvest
  Dry Creek Valley
  ($23, 75)   ★★★★
Zinfandel Dry Creek Valley
  Coffaro Estate Vineyard
  ($23, 800)   ★★★★

ALSO PRODUCED
Aca Modot Red Dry Creek Valley ($30, 700); Sauvignon
Blanc Dry Creek Valley ($12, 200). Neighbors' Cuvée
Red Dry Creek Valley ($23, 600).

WINERY DATA
Case Production: 2,900. **Acres Owned:** 19 acres in Dry Creek.
Varietals by Acre: Cabernet Sauvignon (2 acres), Carignane (3),
Mourvèdre (0.5), Petite Sirah (3), Sauvignon Blanc (2), Syrah
(0.5), Zinfandel (8). **Varietals Purchased:** Cabernet Sauvignon
(Dry Creek Valley), Syrah (Dry Creek Valley), Zinfandel (Dry
Creek Valley).

David Coffaro is proof that if your vineyard is planted
with the right grapes and you pay attention to the details in
the vineyard and winery, you can make delicious wines. A
home winemaker turned pro, Coffaro farms nearly 20 acres
in Dry Creek Valley planted mostly to reds, from which he
makes ripe, juicy, complex wines at reasonable prices.
Moreover, he is boosting production to nearly 3,000 cases
and expanding his offerings. New to the lineup are a
Cabernet blend called Aca Modot and a Cabernet, Zinfandel,
Syrah and Petite Sirah blend called Neighbors' Cuvée.

His vineyard is a prototype for classic Dry Creek
Valley reds and a good example of why Zinfandel often
overshadows Cabernet. I typically give higher marks to
the Zinfandel and to the Estate Cuvée than to his
Cabernet, which is a shade lighter. Still, this is an
unabashedly consumer-friendly winery, setting and
achieving high winegrowing standards at excellent
prices.

TASTING NOTES

**CABERNET SAUVIGNON DRY CREEK VALLEY COFFARO
ESTATE VINEYARD (★★★):** Elegant and deftly balanced,
with the emphasis on ripe, fleshy, berry flavors and soft
tannins. Best to drink early on.
1995: Ripe, juicy, up-front fruit, with flashes of black
cherry, plum and berry flavors and mild tannins. **87**
1994: Ripe, smooth and harmonious, with attractive layers of plum, cherry, currant and cedary oak flavors. **88**

**ESTATE CUVÉE DRY CREEK VALLEY COFFARO ESTATE
VINEYARD (★★★★):** A blend of Cabernet, Zinfandel,
Carignane, Petite Sirah, Merlot, and Cabernet Franc; it
gets its fruity complexity straight from the grapes.
1995: Smooth, ripe and fruity, with lots of cherry, wild
berry, plum and currant notes and fleshy tannins. **88**
1994: Combines ripe, complex cherry, plum and
raspberry flavors in a supple texture, with an intriguing
aftertaste. **90**

**ZINFANDEL DRY CREEK VALLEY COFFARO ESTATE
VINEYARD (★★★★):** Classy and ripe, with lots of raspberry and cherry flavors and silky tannins.
1996: Ripe and lively, with plum, blueberry, raspberry
and spice flavors and lingering tannins. **90**
1995: Complex, with elegant cherry, raspberry and spice
notes that turn supple and peppery. **90**
1994: Ripe and yummy, with zesty cherry, plum and wild
berry flavors that turn elegant and spicy. **91**

B. R. COHN (★★–★★★★)
Sonoma Valley
Founded: 1984. **Owner:** Bruce R. Cohn. **Winemaker:**
Mikael Gulyash.

MAJOR WINES: PRICE, CASES, RATING
Cabernet Sauvignon Sonoma Valley
  Olive Hill Estate Vineyard
  ($35, 4,000)   ★★★★
Cabernet Sauvignon Sonoma Valley
  Olive Hill Estate Vineyard Special Selection
  ($80, 700)   ★★★★
Cabernet Sauvignon Sonoma Valley
  San Luis Obispo County Silver Label
  ($14, 10,000)   ★★
Chardonnay Carneros Joseph Herman
  Vineyard Reserve
  ($28, 1,500)   ★★★
Chardonnay Sonoma Valley
  ($14, 3,500)   ★★★

Merlot Sonoma Valley Olive Hill
Estate Vineyard
($28, 950)   ★★★
Pinot Noir Sonoma Valley Olive Hill
Estate Vineyard
($28, 190)   ★★

WINERY DATA
Case Production: 21,000. **Acres Owned:** 61 acres in Sonoma Valley. **Varietals by Acre:** Cabernet Sauvignon (46 acres), Chardonnay (12), Merlot (2), Pinot Noir (1). **Vineyard Designations:** Olive Hill Vineyard (Cabernet Sauvignon, Merlot), Joseph Herman Vineyard (Chardonnay). **Varietals Purchased:** Chardonnay (Carneros).

Owner Bruce Cohn managed rock and roll bands in the 1970s and 1980s before buying the Olive Hill Vineyard in Sonoma Valley. For years, Cohn, manager of the Doobie Brothers and Night Ranger, sold grapes to Kenwood, Ravenswood and Gundlach Bundschu. In 1984 Cohn decided to produce his own estate-grown Cabernet, hiring Helen Turley to oversee winemaking. Cohn's best wines remain his two estate-grown Cabernets, Olive Hill and Olive Hill Special Selection, both of which are ripe, rich and full bodied, well-oaked and worthy of cellaring. Cohn also produces an Olive Hill Merlot and Pinot Noir.

A Silver Label Cabernet has carried appellations ranging from Napa Valley to North Coast to San Luis Obispo. Two bottlings are made with Chardonnay, with the Joseph Herman Vineyard Carneros Reserve holding an edge over a Sonoma Valley bottling.

TASTING NOTES

CABERNET SAUVIGNON SONOMA VALLEY OLIVE HILL ESTATE VINEYARD (★★★★): Ripe, complex, concentrated. Ages well, though it is best between five and seven years from the vintage.
1995: Austere, dense and complex, with a trim band of currant, tar, sage and berry and firm tannins. **91**
1994: Dark, immense and firmly tannic, with lots of oak, currant and berry flavors and firm tannins. **89**
1993: Dark, dense and tannic, with a rich, well-focused core of currant and cherry flavors. **90**
1991: Ripe and juicy, with rich, supple black cherry, anise and cedary notes, finishing with fine tannins. **90**

1990: Ripe, smooth, rich and complex, with pretty, toasty, buttery oak and layers of cherry, currant, anise and plum flavors. **90**
1989: Smooth and generous, with ample plum, currant, vanilla and toast flavors. **84**
1988: Features ripe currant, herb, olive and toasty oak flavors, with spicy notes. **87**
1987: Features drying fruit and tannins; mature, with spicy, cedary oak nuances and a modest core of currant and berry. **87**
1986: Has reached a fine drinking plateau, with soft tannins and rich, sweet plum, black cherry, black olive and herbal notes. **91**
1985: Complex and enticing, with bold, ripe, juicy currant, black cherry and anise flavors that fan out, finishing with firm tannins and subtle nuances. **94**
1984: Fully mature, with a decadent, earthy, dry tannic edge to the ripe currant and spicy berry flavors. Finishes with a dry, oaky aftertaste. **85**

CABERNET SAUVIGNON SONOMA VALLEY OLIVE HILL ESTATE VINEYARD SPECIAL SELECTION (★★★★): A new addition, the Special Selection is a bigger version of the regular Olive Hill Cabernet. It's well-oaked, supple and seductive, with ripe, juicy currant flavors, spicy notes and big, polished tannins.
1995: Ripe and harmonious, with pretty black cherry, wild berry, currant and plum flavors and firm tannins. **90**

CHARDONNAY CARNEROS JOSEPH HERMAN VINEYARD RESERVE (★★★): Intense and concentrated, but needs short-term cellaring to soften.
1996: Shows spicy, toasty, vanilla-scented oak flavors, backed up by notes of ripe pear and apple. **87**
1995: Complex, elegant, with a pretty band of ripe pear, apple and citrus flavors; turning creamy on the finish. **91**

CHARDONNAY SONOMA VALLEY (★★★): Variable, but can be complex, with spicy apple and pear flavors.
1996: A touch leafy, it works its way into spicy pear and apple flavors, with light oak shadings. Good, but lacks focus, and finishes with an earthy aftertaste. **87**
1995: Complex, with a rich core of ripe pear, apple and spice flavors, and an attractive oak seasoning which keeps the flavors lively through the finish. **89**

MERLOT SONOMA VALLEY OLIVE HILL ESTATE VINEYARD (★★★): Estate-grown since the 1994 vintage, the Merlot, though not as exciting as the Cabernet, is showing improvement. Earlier bottlings carried a Napa-Sonoma appellation.

1995: Shows depth, richness and complexity, with firm, tight currant, anise, cedar, sage and herb notes that fan out nicely on the finish. **88**

1994: Marked by a strong oaky character, the dill and berry flavors are pleasant, but it turns astringent on the finish. **83**

PINOT NOIR SONOMA VALLEY OLIVE HILL ESTATE VINEYARD (★★): The 1995 (84) was tart, with a sharp edge to the earthy mushroom flavors.

COLD HEAVEN (★★)
Santa Barbara County
Founded: 1996. **Owner:** Morgan Toral & Jim Clendenen. **Winemaker:** Morgan Toral.

MAJOR WINES: PRICE, CASES, RATING
Pinot Noir Santa Barbara County
  Bien Nacido Vineyard
  ($25, 600) ★★
Viognier Santa Barbara County
  ($18, 1,000) ★★
Viognier Santa Barbara County
  Sanford and Benedict Vineyard
  ($25, 500) ★★

ALSO PRODUCED
Viognier San Luis Obispo County Alban Vineyard ($30, 300).

WINERY DATA
Case Production: 3,000. **Acres Owned:** 3 acres in Santa Maria Valley. **Varietals by Acre:** Viognier (3 acres). **Vineyard Designations:** Alban Vineyard (Viognier), Bien Nacido Vineyard (Pinot Noir), Sanford and Benedict Vineyard (Viognier). **Varietals Purchased:** Pinot Noir (Santa Maria Valley), Viognier (Santa Inez Valley, Edna Valley).

Morgan Toral and husband Jim Clendenen of Au Bon Climat are partners in Cold Heaven, with Toral directing the winemaking. The couple have chosen an unlikely focus: Viognier, along with a Bien Nacido Vineyard Pinot Noir. The intial releases have been good, if not necessarily representative of Clendenen's full potential. This is a winery to keep an eye on.

COLGIN (★★★★★)
St. Helena, Napa Valley
Founded: 1992. **Owner:** Ann Colgin **Winemaker:** Mark Aubert.

MAJOR WINES: PRICE, CASES, RATING
Cabernet Sauvignon Napa Valley
  Herb Lamb Vineyard
  ($90, 400) ★★★★★

WINERY DATA
Case Production: 400. **Acres Owned:** 2.5 acres in Napa Valley. **Varietals by Acre:** Cabernet (2.5 acres). **Vineyard Designations:** Herb Lamb Vineyard. **Varietals Purchased:** Cabernet Sauvignon (Napa Valley).

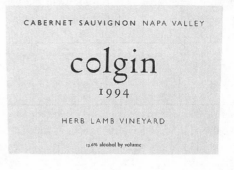

Ann Colgin bought and sold art before catching the wine bug, and is now employed by Sotheby's auction house as a wine auctioneer and wine specialist, seemingly a good fit. She and her former husband Fred Schrader began by buying Cabernet from the 7-acre Herb Lamb Vineyard at the base of Howell Mountain, with Helen Turley overseeing winemaking and sharing in profits. Colgin has since acquired a small vineyard north of St. Helena on the west side of Highway 29 near Freemark Abbey. It's a property of historical significance, the one-time residence of Josephine Tychson, one of California's first women winemakers and founder of Freemark Abbey. Colgin's Cabernets, dating to 1992, have been nothing short of sensational—definitely worth collecting and drinking.

In 1999, Mark Aubert, previously at Peter Michael Winery (see entry), replaced Turley as winemaker. Given Aubert's talent, the wine's quality should be in safe hands.

TASTING NOTES

CABERNET SAUVIGNON NAPA VALLEY HERB LAMB VINEYARD (★★★★★): Uniformly dark, rich and deeply concentrated. Packed with flavor and built to age; early indications indicate future success.

1995: Dense and powerful. A majestic wine, packed with rich, earthy currant, black cherry, mineral, sage, coffee and spice flavors. **94**

1994: Brilliant and complex, with a rich array of currant, cherry, plum and spice flavors, and a pretty, toasty oak overlay. **95**

1993: Amazingly rich, plush and seductive; jam-packed with layers of concentrated plum, currant, cherry and berry flavors. **96**

1992: Dark, intense, concentrated, with rich black cherry and currant flavors and lots of spice and finesse. **92**

COLIBRI see CLOS LaCHANCE WINES

COLLIER FALLS (★★★)
Dry Creek Valley, Sonoma County
Founded: 1997. **Owner:** Barry & Susan Collier.
Winemaker: Alex MacGregor.

MAJOR WINES: PRICE, CASES, RATING

Zinfandel Dry Creek Valley ($22, 500)	★★★

WINERY DATA
Case Production: 500. **Acres Owned:** 26 acres in Dry Creek Valley. **Varietals by Acre:** Cabernet Franc (0.5 acres), Cabernet Sauvignon (6), Petite Sirah (1), Petit Verdot (0.5), Primitivo (9), Zinfandel (9).

Los Angeles television and film producer Barry Collier and his wife, Susan, purchased a portion of Meeker Vineyard's old Dry Creek property in 1997 and set out to make wine. The two studied viticulture and expanded the original 8-acre hillside Zinfandel vineyard to 26 acres, doing much of the work themselves. Their first wine, a 1997 Zinfandel (89 points), was deliciously complex, with smooth, ripe wild berry and spice flavors. Cabernet, Petite Sirah and Primitivo will be added with the 1999 vintage.

COMPASS see DREYER SONOMA WINERY

CONCANNON VINEYARD (★★)
Livermore Valley, Alameda County
Founded: 1883. **Owner:** Tesla Vineyards L.P.
Winemaker: Tom Lane.

MAJOR WINES: PRICE, CASES, RATING

Assemblage Red Livermore Valley Reserve ($17, 1,839)	★★
Assemblage White Livermore Reserve ($13, 394)	★★
Cabernet Sauvignon Central Coast ($10, 15,600)	★★
Chardonnay Central Coast ($10, 14,970)	★★
Chardonnay Livermore Valley Reserve ($16, 792)	★★
Gewürztraminer Arroyo Seco Monterey ($9, 223)	★★
Petite Sirah California ($10, 19,550)	★★
Petite Sirah Central Coast Reserve ($20, 1,472)	★★
Sauvignon Blanc Livermore Valley ($8, 2,400)	★★

ALSO PRODUCED
Righteously Rosé Central Coast ($9, 505).

WINERY DATA
Case Production: 90,000. **Acres Owned:** 191 acres in Livermore Valley. **Varietals by Acre:** Cabernet Sauvignon (38 acres), Cinsault (3), Marsanne (2), Merlot (6), Mourvèdre (4), Petite Sirah (49), Petit Verdot (6), Roussanne (2), Sauvignon Blanc (58), Sémillon (11), Syrah (10), Viognier (2). **Varietals Purchased:** Cabernet Sauvignon (Livermore Valley, Monterey, Paso Robles, San Benito), Chardonnay (Arroyo Seco, Livermore Valley, Paso Robles, San Benito), Cinsault (Monterey), Gewürztraminer (Monterey), Marsanne (Central Coast), Merlot (Contra Costa County, Monterey), Mourvèdre (Conta Costa County), Muscat (Yolo County), Orange Canelli (Yolo County), Petite Sirah (Lodi, Monterey, Paso Robles), Pinot Blanc (Monterey), Roussanne (Central Coast), Sauvignon Blanc (Monterey), Sémillon (Monterey), Syrah (Contra Costa County), Viognier (Central Coast), White Riesling (Monterey), Zinfandel (Contra Costa County).

Irish entrepreneur James Concannon founded this winery in Livermore Valley in 1883, some 18 years after arriving in the U.S. at the age of 18. Concannon remained family-owned, producing a wide range of wines, until the 1980s, when ownership changed hands several times. The property passed from Distillers Co. to a partnership headed by Sergio Traverso and Deinhard, to Deinhard by itself, and then to Wente, which took over in 1992.

Through the years Concannon's wines have been consistently good but never great. The winery owns 191 acres in Livermore Valley and produces 90,000 cases, including Cabernet, Chardonnay, Merlot, Petite Sirah, and Sauvignon Blanc. They come from a variety of appellations stretching from Livermore Valley to the Central Coast; all earn ★★ ratings.

CONN CREEK WINERY (★★–★★★★)
St. Helena, Napa Valley
Founded: 1974. **Owner:** Stimson Lane Vineyards.
Winemaker: David Moore.

MAJOR WINES: PRICE, CASES, RATING
Anthology Red Napa Valley
  ($37, 2,000) ★★★★
Cabernet Sauvignon Napa Valley
  Limited Release
  ($20, 2,000) ★★

WINERY DATA
Case Production: 4,000. **Acres Owned:** 3 acres. **Varietals by Acre:** Cabernet Sauvignon (3 acres). **Varietals Purchased:** Cabernet Franc (Napa, St. Helena), Cabernet Sauvignon (Napa, Rutherford, Calistoga, St. Helena), Merlot (Napa, St. Helena).

Conn Creek Winery is in the midst of re-establishing itself. Bill Collins founded the winery in 1973 and produced a number of memorable Cabernets, particularly the magnificent 1973 from Steltzner Vineyard and a monumental 1974 from Eisele Vineyard. Both wines were produced by Lyncrest Winery before it went out of business. Collins expanded into Chardonnay and built a modern winery on the Silverado Trail in 1980, but by 1986 production outpaced sales and the winery was sold to Stimson Lane, a unit of U.S. Tobacco Co. Today, Conn Creek's production is 4,000 cases, and the current owners are working to upgrade quality and rebuild the winery's reputation. The Meritage-style red, Anthology, has been excellent, with rich, complex flavors and supple texture.

TASTING NOTES

ANTHOLOGY RED NAPA VALLEY (★★★★): Amazingly complex and well crafted, with dense flavors and full-blown tannins.
1994: Complex, concentrated and well structured, with an intriguing array of ripe currant, plum and cedary oak. A tightly wound and well focused style with supple tannins and a fine length. **90**
1993: Appealing for its supple texture and bright, forward flavors—layers of juicy cherry, currant, plum and berry. Finishes with a spicy anise aftertaste and notes of tar, herb and cedary oak. **93**
1992: Firm and tannic, but the ripe fruit flavors are pretty, with plum, wild berry and cherry notes filling out the sage and spice notes. **90**
1991: Complex and elegant, with supple, polished currant, black cherry, plum and vanilla flavors that fold together nicely, finishing with a long, full aftertaste and pretty fruit flavors that linger. A wine of harmony and grace. **93**

CABERNET SAUVIGNON NAPA VALLEY LIMITED RELEASE (★★)
1994: On the lighter side, with a modest band of cedar, celery and currant flavors; a glint of leather and oak fold in on the finish. Lacks focus and harmony, turning dry on the finish. **84**
1993: A middle-of-the-road style. Shows ripe plum, berry and cherry flavors. Turns simple on the finish, where tannins and herbal notes dominate. **84**
1992: Ripe and fruity, with spicy plum, cherry and currant flavors. An elegant, well-crafted wine that's tempting to drink now, but has intensity and depth. **88**

CONSTANT (★★★★)
Diamond Mountain, Napa Valley
Founded: 1995. **Owner:** Fred & Mary Constant.
Winemaker: Philippe Melka.

MAJOR WINES: PRICE, CASES, RATING
Diamond Mountain Vineyard Napa Valley
  ($95, 250) ★★★★

WINERY DATA

Case Production: 4,000. **Acres Owned:** 24 acres in Diamond Mountain. **Varietals by Acre:** Cabernet Franc (2 acres), Cabernet Sauvignon (15), Merlot (1), Syrah (5), Viognier (1). **Vineyard Designation:** Diamond Mountain Vineyard (Cabernet Blend).

Fred and Mary Constant, who own the wine country radio stations KRSH "the crush" and KGRP "the grape," sold grapes from their Diamond Mountain vineyard for 18 years before making their first wine. The vineyard, originally planted in the late 1890s, lies at 2,000 feet of elevation near the crest of Diamond Mountain. In 1984 much of the vineyard was replanted, primarily to Bordeaux varietals and recently small amounts of Syrah and Viognier.

The 1995 Diamond Mountain Vineyard, a blend of Cabernet Sauvignon, Cabernet Franc and Merlot, was rich, plush and deeply concentrated. While the first vintages are limited, the Constants plan to produce as many as 4,000 cases in the future.

COOPER-GARROD VINEYARDS (★★)

Santa Cruz Mountains
Founded: 1994. **Owner:** Garrod Farms. **Winemaker:** George Cooper.

MAJOR WINES: PRICE, CASES, RATING

Cabernet Franc Santa Cruz Mountains
($20, 850)   ★
Cabernet Sauvignon Santa Cruz Mountains
($35, 1,300)   ★★
Chardonnay Santa Cruz Mountains
($20, 850)   ★★

WINERY DATA

Case Production: 4,000. **Acres Owned:** 21 acres in the Santa Cruz Mountains. **Varietals by Acre:** Cabernet Franc (5 acres), Cabernet Sauvignon (11), Chardonnay (5).

Formerly a research pilot for NASA, George Cooper started this family-owned winery in 1994. The estate-bottled Cabernet and Chardonnay have been very good, if a bit inconsistent, while the Cabernet Franc has been just average.

FRANCIS COPPOLA DIAMOND SERIES & FRANCIS COPPOLA PRESENTS see NIEBAUM-COPPOLA ESTATE WINERY

CORBETT CANYON VINEYARDS (★)

Edna Valley, San Luis Obispo County
Founded: 1979. **Owner:** The Wine Group Inc.
Winemaker: Denise Shurtleff.

MAJOR WINES: PRICE, CASES, RATING

Cabernet Sauvignon California
 Coastal Classic
 ($6, NA)   ★
Chardonnay Santa Barbara County Reserve
 Los Alamos Vineyards
 ($10, NA)   ★
Chardonnay California
 Coastal Classic
 ($6, NA)   ★
Merlot California Coastal Classic
 ($6, NA)   ★
Merlot California Reserve
 ($10, NA)   ★
Sauvignon Blanc California Coastal Classic
 ($5, NA)   ★
Sauvignon Blanc Temecula Reserve
 ($10, NA)   ★

ALSO PRODUCED

White Zinfandel California Coastal Classic ($6, NA), Zinfandel California Coastal Classic ($6, NA).

WINERY DATA

Case Production: 2.4 million. **Acres Owned:** 70 acres. **Varietals by Acre:** Chardonnay (70 acres). **Vineyard Designations:** Los Alamos Vineyards (Chardonnay). **Varietals Purchased:** Cabernet Sauvignon (California), Chardonnay (California), Merlot (California), Sangiovese (California), Shiraz (California), Zinfandel (California).

This is the largest winery in the Central Coast and one of California's most successful bulk producers, but Corbett Canyon's wines are at best ordinary. Most of the wines sell for less than $10, but even so, they're hardly a bargain.

CORISON WINES (★★★)
Napa Valley
Founded: 1987. **Owner:** Cathy Corison. **Winemaker:** Cathy Corison.

MAJOR WINES: PRICE, CASES, RATING
Cabernet Sauvignon Napa Valley
($40, 2,700) ★★★

WINERY DATA
Case Production: 2,700. **Acres Owned:** 9 acres in Napa Valley. **Varietals by Acre:** Cabernet Sauvignon (9 acres). **Varietals Purchased:** Cabernet Sauvignon (Napa Valley).

Long-time Napa Valley winemaker Cathy Corison worked at Freemark Abbey, Chappellet (for 10 years) and Yverdon before starting her Cabernet-only label with the 1987 vintage. Initially Corison bought all her grapes from growers throughout Napa Valley (Vine Hill Ranch, Morisoli Vineyard, Garvey Vineyard), believing her blended wine was more complex than that of any of the vineyards on their own. She has since purchased a small 9-acre Cabernet vineyard which will eventually be bottled as a vineyard-designated wine. Plans are also in the works for a winery south of St. Helena.

TASTING NOTES

CABERNET SAUVIGNON NAPA VALLEY (★★★): Deftly balanced between ripe, supple currant flavors and toasty oak; a graceful and polished style. Drinks well early and has a good track record for aging.
1995: Starts with lots of anise, plum and wild berry, but then tightens up, turning crisp, lean and concentrated. **89**
1994: Tight early on, with glimpses of plum and blackberry flavors peeking through the tannins. **87**
1993: Elegant, with smoky, toasty oak shadings and a ripe core of cherry and berry flavors. **87**
1992: Bold, ripe, rich and concentrated, with layers of plum and currant flavors, accented by anise and toasty oak. **92**
1991: Leather, coffee and currant flavors strive for complexity but it turns dry and tannic on the finish. **89**
1990: Smooth and generous, with ripe currant, cherry and chocolate aromas and flavors, all of it holding together in elegance and harmony. **90**
1989: Firm and focused, with strong herbal aromas and flavors and a nice core of ripe currant and black cherry flavors. **88**

1988: Solid, with ripe, plummy currant, anise, mineral and sage flavors that are intense and firmly tannic before turning dry on the finish. **84**
1987: Smells ripe, intense and fruity, but tastes dry and tannic, with complex cherry and currant flavors. **89**

CORNERSTONE CELLARS (★★★★)
Napa Valley
Founded: 1991. **Owner:** Bruce Scotland, David Sloas & Michael Dragutsky. **Winemaker:** Bruce Scotland. **Affiliated Brands:** L'Ecosse, Tay.

MAJOR WINES: PRICE, CASES, RATING
Cabernet Sauvignon Howell Mountain
 Beatty Ranch
 ($40,100) ★★★★
Zinfandel Howell Mountain Beatty Ranch
 ($25, 700) ★★★

L'Ecosse Cabernet Franc Napa Valley Cuvée
 Homage de Jeanne dArc
 ($24, 1,200) ★★★
L'Ecosse Pinot Noir Atlas Peak
 ($22, 600) ★★
L'Ecosse Pinot Noir Russian River Valley
 ($30, 250) ★★
Tay Cabernet Sauvignon Napa Valley
 ($40, 550) ★★★★

ALSO PRODUCED
Cabernet Sauvignon Howell Mountain Black-Sears Vineyard ($40, 680); L'Ecosse Dolcetto Napa Valley ($18, 576); L'Ecosse Malbec Napa Valley ($24, 400).

WINERY DATA
Case Production: 1,400. **Acres Owned:** 13 acres on Howell Mountain. **Varietals by Acre:** Cabernet Sauvignon (13 acres). **Vineyard Designations:** Beatty Ranch (Cabernet Sauvignon, Zinfandel), Black-Sears Vineyard (Cabernet Sauvignon). **Varietals Purchased:** Cabernet Franc (Napa Valley), Cabernet Sauvignon (Howell Mountain, Napa Valley), Dolcetto (Napa Valley), Malbec (Napa Valley), Pinot Noir (Atlas Peak, Russian River Valley), Zinfandel (Howell Mountain).

Bruce Scotland worked as a wine retailer and for several wineries before launching Cornerstone with the 1991 vintage. Through a friendship with Randy Dunn,

Scotland buys Howell Mountain Cabernet and Zinfandel from Beatty Ranch, one of Dunn's Cabernet sources. The Black-Sears Vineyard on Howell Mountain is another source of Zinfandel. Scotland also recently purchased 13 acres of Cabernet Sauvignon on Howell Mountain which will go into the Cornerstone Cabernet.

Scotland owns two other labels, L'Ecosse and Tay. Tay has been a one-wine brand with a focus on Napa Valley Cabernet Sauvignon. L'Ecosse gives Scotland an opportunity to work with a variety of wines: Malbec, Dolcetto, Cabernet Franc and Pinot Noir, all of which are well made.

TASTING NOTES

CABERNET SAUVIGNON HOWELL MOUNTAIN BEATTY RANCH (★★★★): A solid and steady performer in the 1990s, made in a big, rich, earthy style. No track record yet for aging, but appears to have the proper ingredients to do so. The 1995 carried a Napa Valley designation.
1995: Earthy up front, but complex as well, with ripe berry and cherry flavors among the fleshy, elegant tannins. **90**
1994: Dense and chewy, with firm, earthy tannins. The currant and cherry notes have cedary oak and tarry edges. **93**
1993: Smooth, rich and complex, with tiers of spicy currant, cherry, toasty oak and cedar notes; the tannins emerge on the finish. **93**
1992: Elegant, with a well-focused band of currant, spice and black cherry flavors; finishes with firm, complex tannins. **90**
1991: Ripe, generous, with tight, focused currant, plum and black cherry flavors that are plush and concentrated, finishing with a long, complex, tannic aftertaste. **93**

ZINFANDEL HOWELL MOUNTAIN BEATTY RANCH (★★★★): An intense and beautifully focused, classy Howell Mountain Zinfandel.
1994: Tight, firm and intense, with a complex core of earth, herb, and raspberry flavors and dashes of herb and spice. **91**

ZINFANDEL HOWELL MOUNTAIN CUVÉE MYSTERIEUSES
1994: Beautifully focused, with tiers of black cherry, herb, spice and light toasty oak flavors. **91**

COSENTINO WINERY (★★★)
Oakville, Napa Valley
Founded: 1980. **Owner:** Vintage Grapevine Inc.
Winemaker: Mitch Cosentino. **Second Label:** Crystal Valley Cellars, The Yountville Winery.

MAJOR WINES: PRICE, CASES, RATING
Cabernet Sauvignon Napa Valley ($18, 2,500) ★★★
Cabernet Sauvignon Napa Valley Reserve ($40, 400) ★★★★
Chardonnay Napa County ($18, 3,000) ★★★
Chardonnay Napa Valley The Sculptor Reserve ($30, 700) ★★★
Il Chiaretto Red California ($15, 1,300) ★★★
Gewürztraminer Napa Valley ($18, 430) ★★
M. Coz Red Napa Valley Meritage ($75, 450) ★★★
Merlot Napa Valley Oakville Estate ($60, 400) ★★★
Merlot Napa Valley Reserve ($34, 700-1,000) ★★★
Merlot North Coast ($25, 600) ★★★
The Novelist White California Meritage ($16, 3,000) ★★★
Pinot Noir Carneros ($30, 1,000) ★★
Pinot Noir Napa Valley ($25, 800) ★★★
Pinot Noir Russian River Valley ($60, 250) ★★★
The Poet Red Napa Valley Meritage ($40, 1,400) ★★★
Tenero Rosso California ($13, 400) ★★
Zinfandel California CigarZin ($16, 3,000) ★★★
Zinfandel California The Zin ($22, 2,100) ★★★

ALSO PRODUCED
Cabernet Franc Napa Valley ($22, 400-600); Nebbiolo Sonoma County ($18, 200); Pinot Noir Sonoma County

($20, 300); Port California ($23, 500); Sangiovese Napa County Il Tesoro ($18, 300-500); Vin Sante California Francesca d'Amore ($23, 200); Viognier California Vin Doux Viognier Kay ($23, 300); Zinfandel Late Harvest Napa Valley ($23, 200); Zinfandel California Zinport ($23, 300-500).

WINERY DATA
Case Production: 27,000. **Acres Owned:** 4 acres in Oakville, 25 acres leased in Napa Valley. **Varietals by Acre:** Merlot (4 acres), Cabernet Sauvignon (11), Chardonnay (5), Gewürztraminer (2), Merlot (5), Pinot Noir (2). **Varietals Purchased:** Cabernet Franc (St. Helena, Napa Valley, Oakville, Russian River Valley), Cabernet Sauvignon (St. Helena, Napa Valley, Oakville, Sonoma Valley), Chardonnay (Napa Valley), Merlot (Napa Valley, Lodi), Nebbiolo (Sonoma Valley), Pinot Noir (Carneros, Russian River Valley), Sangiovese (Napa Valley), Sauvignon Blanc (Napa Valley, Lodi), Sémillon (Napa Valley), Zinfandel (Russian River Valley, Napa Valley, Lodi).

Mitch Cosentino's assortment of wines are occasionally brilliant, complex and well-crafted, but can also miss the elements that make his best wines so appealing. Formerly a wine wholesaler, Cosentino started a winery in Modesto, which he once proclaimed the second-largest winery in that Central Valley city (Gallo, the world's largest winery, is headquartered there too); he bottled wines there under the Crystal Valley Cellars brand.

Beginning in the early 1980s, Cosentino began focusing on North Coast wines, and in 1990 he built a winery in Oakville next door to Mustard's Grill. Except for the 4 acres of Merlot planted near his winery, he still buys most of his grapes. In 1992, Cosentino took on partners, and Vintage Grapevine Inc. is now the owner. The 27,000-case product line is mostly small case lots with eclectic brand names: The Novelist (a white Meritage), The Poet (a red Meritage), The Sculptor (a *sur lie* Chardonnay), "CigarZin" (a late-harvest-style Zinfandel) and The Zin (a Zinfandel from Alexander Valley). Having learned a lesson about names—the wine now called 'M. Coz' originally debuted as just 'Coz' and caused the owner of Château Cos-d'Estournel to threaten legal action—Cosentino registered "CigarZin" as a trademark.

TASTING NOTES

CABERNET SAUVIGNON NAPA VALLEY RESERVE (★★★★): Usually Cosentino's best; made in a complex, elegant style.
1995: Smooth, rich and polished, with plush plum, currant, black cherry and wild berry flavors that expand on the palate. **91**
1994: Supple and harmonious, with spicy currant and wild berry flavors that build in intensity. **89**
1993: Packs in ripe, rich black cherry, plum and currant flavors, with hints of anise, cedar and spice adding dimension. **91**
1991: Lithe, juicy and refreshing flavors focusing on plum, berry and vanilla; matches grace with strength. **90**

CHARDONNAY NAPA VALLEY THE SCULPTOR RESERVE (★★★): The Sculptor Reserve is the best of the Chardonnays. Ripe and fruity, the 1995 (91 points) and 1996 (90) were both superlative efforts.

M. COZ RED NAPA VALLEY MERITAGE (★★★): Very well made, and can be outstanding. Well-oaked and richly flavored.
1995: Racy, with earthy blackberry, cherry, currant and spice flavors; turns simpler on the finish, with mild tannins. **88**
1994: Tight and tannic, with rich, dense mineral, tar, currant, plum and spice flavors. **91**
1993: A big, ripe and intense style, with firm, crisp tannins and ripe currant, coffee and cedar flavors. **88**
1992: Well-oaked; vanilla bean and toasty notes are packed in with lots of plush currant, black cherry, anise and spice flavors. **92**
1991: Strikes a nice balance between ripe, spicy fruit flavors and buttery oak, but it needs time. **89**
1990: Elegant and richly fruity, with wonderful currant, black cherry, vanilla and cedar flavors gently unfolding, finishing with excellent length and fine tannins. **92**

MERLOT NAPA VALLEY OAKVILLE ESTATE (★★★): Impressive for its grace and finesse. Offers polished tannins and rich flavors of fruit and oak.
1996: Packs in lots of flavor; well-oaked, with a core of plum and cherry plus some funky, earthy flavors. **88**
1995: Rich and polished, with layers of ripe cherry and currant, framed by vanilla and light toasty oak. **92**
1994: Smooth, polished, with a rich core of currant, chocolate and berry notes that finish with soft tannins. **87**

1993: Ripe and complex, with appealing plum, black cherry, herb, cedar and toasty oak notes. **89**

MERLOT NAPA VALLEY RESERVE (★★★): Concentrated, with rich, complex flavors.
1996: Supple and complex. The well-focused currant, plum, earth and cherry flavors pick up some toasty oak notes. **88**
1994: Smooth and seductive, with lavish oak; the silky texture lets the currant, herb and anise flavors flow. **91**

MERLOT NORTH COAST (★★★): Not as complex as the Reserve and Estate, the North Coast is nonetheless smooth, polished and drinks well young.

THE NOVELIST WHITE CALIFORNIA MERITAGE (★★★): A Sauvignon Blanc-Sémillon blend; carried a Napa Valley appellation until 1996.
1997: Herbal, with a solid grapefruit and grass core. Bright acidity in this old-style yet fairly complex wine. Finishes with a hint of ripe fig. **87**
1996: A nice blend of grapefruit, lemon, melon, celery and grass notes, finishing bright and clean. Refreshing. **87**

PINOT NOIR CARNEROS (★★): The Carneros bottling varies in quality. The 1996 (84 points) was light in color and body and the 1994 (84) similarly lacked richness in what was elsewhere a great year. Needs work.

PINOT NOIR NAPA VALLEY (★★★): Variable, but often very good, especially in the better years. The 1995 (89 points) was smooth and complex.

PINOT NOIR RUSSIAN RIVER (★★★): The Russian River efforts in 1996 (89 points) and 1994 (88) offered more depth and range of flavors than did the Carneros or Napa Valley.

THE POET RED NAPA VALLEY MERITAGE (★★★): A red Meritage that is very good and can be outstanding.
1995: A clean, well-proportioned, claret-style wine, with spicy currant, berry, plum and cedary oak flavors and integrated tannins. **88**
1994: Dark, ripe and concentrated, with a core of earthy currant, cedar, spice and tar flavors, plus hints of vanilla and chocolate. **89**
1993: Ripe and complex, with tiers of ripe cherry, currant, plum and anise flavors, and just-right doses of oak and tannin. **91**
1992: Clean and correct, with a ripe plum and currant edge, turning firm and chunky on the finish. **87**

ZINFANDEL CALIFORNIA CIGARZIN (★★★): CigarZin is made in a late-harvest style, with a touch of raisiny Port-like flavor.

ZINFANDEL CALIFORNIA THE ZIN (★★★): A solid wine; very ripe and jammy, with the tannins in check.

H. COTURRI & SONS LTD. (★★–★★★)
Sonoma Mountain
Founded: 1979. **Owner:** The Coturri Family. **Winemaker:** Tony Coturri. **Second Label:** Jessandra Vittoria.

WINES PRODUCED: PRICE, CASES
Assemblage Red Sonoma Valley ($25, 200); Cabernet Sauvignon Sonoma Valley ($25, 600); Cabernet Sauvignon Sonoma Valley Jessandra Vittoria Vineyard ($25, 600); Merlot Sonoma Valley Maclise Vineyards ($23, 500); Santa Vittoria Red Sonoma Valley Jessandra Vittoria Vineyard ($28, 1,200); Zinfandel Sonoma Mountain ($22, 350); Zinfandel Sonoma Valley Chauvet Vineyards ($16, 1,700); Zinfandel Sonoma Valley Freiberg Vineyards ($23, 500); Zinfandel Sonoma Valley P. Coturri Family Vineyards ($23, 250)

WINERY DATA
Case Production: 6,000. **Acres Owned:** 7 acres in Sonoma Mountain. **Varietals by Acre:** Zinfandel (7 acres). **Vineyard Designations:** Chauvet Vineyards (Zinfandel), Freiberg Vineyards (Zinfandel), Jessandra Vittoria Vineyard (Cabernet Sauvignon, Sangiovese), Maclise Vineyards (Merlot). **Varietals Purchased:** Cabernet Sauvignon (Sonoma Valley), Merlot (Sonoma Valley), Sangiovese (Sonoma Valley), Zinfandel (Sonoma Valley).

Few wineries have divided critics as Coturri has. This 6,000-case winery in Glen Ellen was among the first—if not the first—to take organic farming and winemaking to the limit, using everything from organic fertilizers to wild yeast fermentations. Over the years a number of bizarre wines have emerged, marked by earthy, funky, sometimes dirty and volatile flavors; but there have also been very good wines like the 1990 Zinfandel Chauvet Vineyards, a ripe, hot, sweet and raisiny sort of junior Port which, while extreme in style, has no defects. The 1994 Zinfandel Sonoma Mountain (88 points) was more mainstream, with ripe, juicy flavors of brambly berry, cherry, anise and oak notes. The product mix also includes Cabernet, Merlot, a Cabernet-Merlot blend called Assemblage and a Cabernet-Sangiovese blend called Santa Vittoria.

COUNTERPOINT see LAUREL GLEN VINEYARD

ROBERT CRAIG (★★★★★)
Napa Valley
Founded: 1992. **Owner:** Robert & Lynn Craig, Derek Ruston, Michael Nugent, Michael Adams. **Winemaker:** Rudy Zuidema & Robert Craig.

MAJOR WINES: PRICE, CASES, RATING

Affinity Red Napa Valley
($34, 2,600) ★★★★★
Cabernet Sauvignon Howell Mountain
($34, 600) ★★★★★
Cabernet Sauvignon Mount Veeder
($34, 1,800) ★★★★★

ALSO PRODUCED
Chardonnay Napa Valley Carneros ($22, 200); Syrah Paso Robles ($24, 200).

WINERY DATA
Case Production: 6,000. **Acres Owned:** 7 acres in Napa Valley. **Varietals by Acre:** Cabernet Sauvignon (7 acres). **Varietals Purchased:** Cabernet Franc (Mount Veeder, Howell Mountain), Cabernet Sauvignon (Napa Valley, Howell Mountain, Mount Veeder), Chardonnay (Napa Valley, Carneros), Merlot (Napa Valley, Mount Veeder, Howell Mountain), Syrah (Paso Robles).

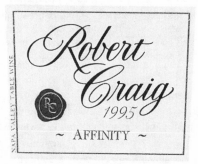

The emergence of Robert Craig as a first-class winemaker is one of the highlights of the 1990s. While a relative newcomer as a solo act, Craig has definitely been around. In the 1970s, he worked with William Hill's partners when Hill began developing mountain vineyard products. From 1981 through 1990, he was the general manager for The Hess Collection. Craig started his own wine brand in 1992, focusing on Cabernet and Cabernet blends, using grapes from Howell Mountain (Dennis John's White Cottage Ranch vine-

yard) and Mount Veeder (PymRay Vineyards, owned by comedian/actor Robin Williams). In 1995, he bought a 7-acre vineyard north of Napa, which is also planted to Cabernet. He now has plans to build a winery on Howell Mountain.

The first wines from the 1992 vintage were made in a lean, austere style. The 1993 wines were similar, but showed a shade more depth and richness; the 1994s were riper and fleshier. Affinity is a Bordeaux-style blend, made from Rutherford- and Carneros-grown grapes. A Napa Valley Carneros Chardonnay and a Paso Robles Syrah are new additions to Craig's product mix.

TASTING NOTES

AFFINITY RED NAPA VALLEY (★★★★★): This Bordeaux-inspired blend continues to improve and impress, and it should only get better given Craig's high standards. No track record yet for aging, but it has the right ingredients.
1996: Smooth and supple, with a tasty core of black cherry, currant, anise, sage, cedar and spice flavors that are rich, concentrated, long and lingering. **92**
1995: A dense and backward style; filled with complex currant and black cherry flavors and nuances of cedar, leather and spice. **91**
1994: Rich and plush, with a pretty core of ripe black cherry, currant, anise and plum flavors, turning silky and polished on the finish. **94**
1993: Starts off complex, with currant and cherry flavors, but turns austere, adding crisp acidity and firm tannins. **87**

CABERNET SAUVIGNON HOWELL MOUNTAIN (★★★★★): Reflects the austerity and earthiness of the appellation, yet manges to polish and tame the tannins with its supple texture.
1995: Ripe, rich and polished, with earth, mineral, plum, blackberry and currant flavors that are deep and concentrated. **91**
1994: Remarkably elegant, with layers of currant, anise, cedar, sage and spice, a mineral edge and dry tannins. **90**
1993: Smooth and harmonious, with dark cherry, plum, currant and cedary oak flavors, turning smoky on the finish. **89**

CABERNET SAUVIGNON MOUNT VEEDER (★★★★★): This appellation is also noted for its rugged tannins, yet Craig brings a measure of elegance and finesse to these grapes.
1995: Tightly wound, with firm tannins built around a core of earthy currant, mineral, coffee, sage and cedar flavors. **91**

1994: Strikingly elegant for a Mount Veeder Cabernet, with lots of delicious black cherry, herb, mineral, spice and anise flavors. **94**

1993: Plush, harmonious, complex and well crafted, featuring currant, earth, anise and cedary oak flavors. **90**

CABERNET SAUVIGNON NAPA VALLEY
1992: Intense, concentrated, crisp and tannic, showing currant, plum and anise flavors. **87**

CREEKSIDE see IRONSTONE VINEYARDS

CRESTON MANOR VINEYARDS & WINERY (★★)
Paso Robles, San Luis Obispo County
Founded: 1981. **Owner:** Creston Manor Associates Ltd.
Winemaker: Tim Spears.

MAJOR WINES: PRICE, CASES, RATING

Cabernet Sauvignon Paso Robles
($15, 2,000) ★★
Cabernet Sauvignon Paso Robles
Winemaker's Selection
($20, 500) ★★
Chardonnay Paso Robles
($13, 3,000) ★★
Merlot Paso Robles
($16, 1,500) ★★
Pinot Noir Paso Robles
($10, 2,000) ★
Sauvignon Blanc Paso Robles
($10, 1,000) ★★
Zinfandel Paso Robles
($10, 1,000) ★

WINERY DATA
Case Production: 12,000. **Acres Owned:** 121 acres in Paso Robles. **Varietals by Acre:** Cabernet Franc (1 acre), Cabernet Sauvignon (33), Chardonnay (28), Chenin Blanc (3), Merlot (2), Pinot Noir (14), Sauvignon Blanc (18), Sémillon (5), Zinfandel (17).

Creston was founded by a group of Los Angeles investors headed by Christina Crawford, daughter of actress Joan Crawford. The 121-acre vineyard sits high atop a remote hill at an elevation of 1,700 feet.

Ownership changed hands in 1987; Alex Trebek (of *Jeopardy* fame) is now majority partner.

Creston wines have been disappointing, rating ★ to ★★ at best, but recent efforts to increase quality could have a positive effect. A new winemaker, Tim Spears (previously at Justin and Meridian) has been hired, and the winery is now focusing on Cabernet, Merlot, Syrah and Zinfandel. Chardonnay, Pinot Noir and Sauvignon Blanc have been dropped from the lineup, and plans are underway to replant the vineyard. For the time being, case production is down considerably, dropping from 40,000 in 1995 to 12,000.

CRICHTON HALL (★–★★)
Napa Valley
Founded: 1983. **Owner:** Richard & Judith Crichton.
Winemaker: Richard Crichton.

MAJOR WINES: PRICE, CASES, RATING
Chardonnay Napa Valley Crichton Hall
Vineyard
($21, 3,000) ★★
Merlot Napa Valley
($26, 1,200) ★★
Pinot Noir Napa Valley Carneros
($25, 700) ★

WINERY DATA
Case Production: 5,000. **Acres Owned:** 17 acres in Napa Valley. **Varietals by Acre:** Chardonnay (17 acres). **Vineyard Designations:** Crichton Hall Vineyard (Chardonnay). **Varietals Purchased:** Merlot (Napa Valley), Pinot Noir (Napa Valley Carneros).

Owners Judith and Richard Crichton produce 5000 cases of Chardonnay, Merlot and Pinot Noir from their 17-acre vineyard. Their best wine is the Chardonnay; the 1996 (88 points) is tight and flinty, with pear, anise and hazelnut notes. The Merlot and Pinot Noir are average to below average in quality.

CRONIN VINEYARDS (★★★)
Santa Cruz Mountains
Founded: 1980. **Owner:** Duane & Nancy Cronin.
Winemaker: Duane Cronin. **Second Label:** Portola
Hills.

MAJOR WINES: PRICE, CASES, RATING

Cabernet Sauvignon Santa Cruz Mountains
($23, 229) ★★★
Chardonnay Alexander Valley
Stuhlmuller Vineyard
($18, 450) ★★★
Chardonnay Santa Cruz Mountains
($20, 650) ★★★
Chardonnay Santa Cruz Mountains
Nancy's Cuvée
($28, 120) ★★★★
Concerto Red Stags Leap District
Robinson Vineyard
($23, 346) ★★★
Pinot Noir Santa Cruz Mountains
($23, 216) ★★

WINERY DATA

Case Production: 2,000. **Acres Owned:** 1 acre in Santa Cruz
Mountains. **Varietals by Acre:** Cabernet Sauvignon (0.5 acres),
Chardonnay (0.5). **Vineyard Designations:** Stuhlmuller
Vineyard (Chardonnay), Robinson Vineyard (Cabernet Franc,
Cabernet Sauvignon, Merlot). **Varietals Purchased:** Cabernet
Franc (Stags Leap District), Cabernet Sauvignon (Santa Cruz
Mountains, Stags Leap District), Chardonnay (Alexander Valley,
Santa Cruz Mountains), Merlot (Stags Leap District), Pinot Noir
(Santa Cruz Mountains).

Former Silicon Valley computer programmer Duane
Cronin began making wine in the basement of his home
in Woodside (south of San Francisco) as a sideline, initially focusing on small lots of Chardonnay. Cronin

Vineyards is still small-scale, making a total of 2,000
cases and Chardonnay is still its strongest wine, although
the Cabernet can be exceptional. The Pinot Noir from
Peter Martin Ray Vineyard in the Santa Cruz Mountains
has also improved.

Cronin purchases grapes from key appellations
throughout California, utilizing Burgundian vinification
techniques for his Chardonnay and Pinot Noir. He produces several Chardonnays in most years, the best of
which come from the Santa Cruz Mountains. Often,
however, these are rivalled in quality by bottlings from
Monterey County and Stuhlmuller Vineyard in Alexander
Valley. Concerto is a new Meritage blend that's mostly
Cabernet, and is made entirely of grapes from Robinson
Vineyard in Stags Leap District. Cronin occasionally
makes a Zinfandel.

TASTING NOTES

**CABERNET SAUVIGNON SANTA CRUZ MOUNTAINS
(★★★):** Quality varies in this cooler climate. The wine
is often ripe and exotic, with cherry and chocolate flavors, but it can be tannic and leathery.
1994: A medium-weight, moderately rich wine with pretty
oak, marked by cedar, black olive, spice and berry notes. **88**
1992: Rustic at first, with an earthy, leathery, and cedary
edge, but enough plum and cherry flavors emerge to provide a hint of elegance. **88**
1991: Rustic, firm tannins and a slightly metallic edge
overlay a tight core of mineral and currant flavors. **89**

**CHARDONNAY ALEXANDER VALLEY STUHLMULLER
VINEYARD (★★★):** Usually vibrant, with ripe peachy
flavors. The 1995 (91 points) was elegant, with creamy
oak, while the 1994 (87) was more restrained.

CHARDONNAY SANTA CRUZ MOUNTAINS (★★★):
Intense, earthy and well oaked; marked by rich, complex
flavors, finishing with elegance and grace. The 1994,
though, missed the mark.

**CHARDONNAY SANTA CRUZ MOUNTAINS NANCY'S CUVÉE
(★★★★):** Cronin's version of a reserve wine, this is blended from various Santa Cruz Mountain vineyards. Marked
by intense fruit and mineral flavors and a supple texture.

**CONCERTO RED STAGS LEAP DISTRICT ROBINSON
VINEYARD (★★★):** Recent vintages show more depth
and richness, displaying flavors of ripe plum.

1994: Plump, with rich, supple plum, cherry, wild berry and currant flavors and a nice dash of spicy, cedary oak. **90**

1993: Elegant, with supple cherry and berry flavors that are deep and concentrated. **88**

1992: Vibrant, ripe and rich cherry, currant and plum flavors pick up dashes of spice and oak on the finish. The supple texture is pure Stags Leap. **93**

1991: Firm and tannic, with ripe cherry and currant flavors flanked by anise and cedary oak. **87**

1990: Lean and a bit green, with firm tannins and a tight oak overlay, but enough currant and cherry flavors emerge; patience required. **82**

1989: Shows off ripe, tart, bright black cherry and currant flavors up front, but turns austere and thins out on the finish. **85**

1988: Plenty of supple cherry and currant flavors in this appealing wine. **86**

1987: Offers bright, pure currant and cherry flavors accented with nutmeg, cedar and vanilla. **89**

1986: Alluring wild berry and currant flavors turn supple, with fine tannins and fruit echoing on the finish. **88**

PINOT NOIR SANTA CRUZ MOUNTAINS (★★): Excellent in 1992 (89 points), with complex dried cherry, earth and mushroom flavors, but it was less exciting in 1993 (86) and 1994 (85).

CRYSTAL VALLEY CELLARS see COSENTINO WINERY

CULBERTSON see THORNTON

CUVAISON (★★★–★★★★)
Calistoga, Napa Valley
Founded: 1969. **Owner:** Thomas Schmidheiny. **Winemaker:** John Thacher. **Second Label:** Calistoga Vineyards.

MAJOR WINES: PRICE, CASES, RATING

Cabernet Sauvignon Napa Valley ($28, 4,500)	★★★
Cabernet Sauvignon Napa Valley ATS ($50, 250)	★★★★
Chardonnay Napa Valley Carneros ($19, 42,000)	★★★
Chardonnay Napa Valley Carneros ATS ($45, 350)	★★★★
Chardonnay Napa Valley Carneros Reserve ($28, 2,500)	★★★★
Merlot Napa Valley ATS ($50, 350)	★★★★
Merlot Napa Valley Carneros ($31, 9,000)	★★★
Pinot Noir Napa Valley Carneros ($23, 2,500)	★★★
Pinot Noir Napa Valley Carneros Eris ($21, 2,500)	★★★

ALSO PRODUCED
Zinfandel Napa Valley ($21, 600).

WINERY DATA
Case Production: 65,000. **Acres Owned:** 274 acres in Carneros. **Varietals by Acre:** Chardonnay (196 acres), Merlot (44), Pinot Noir (34). **Varietals Purchased:** Cabernet Sauvignon (Napa Valley), Zinfandel (Napa Valley).

Founded in 1969, Cuvaison has gone through a succession of owners and styles. Its early wines, made by Philip Togni, were eccentric to a fault, with Cabernets and Zinfandels marked by high alcohol levels, heavy oak and gritty tannins, and Chardonnays that were bold and assertive, reflecting the style of the era. Since John Thacher took over in 1983, quality has been steady as production has leveled off at 65,000 cases.

The Schmidheiny family of Switzerland bought Cuvaison in 1986 and invested heavily in vineyards, the most ambitious being a 274-acre estate in Carneros where the winery grows all of its Chardonnay (more than 40,000 cases, including a Reserve), Merlot and Pinot Noir. Cabernet and Zinfandel are purchased. All of Cuvaison's wines are well-made; of late, a few select bottlings have been exceptional, and occasionally tremendous. All of the wines share a distinctive house style, with ripe, focused, supple fruit flavors, good intensity, fine balance and a sense of harmony and finesse.

TASTING NOTES

CABERNET SAUVIGNON NAPA VALLEY (★★★): Typically firm and intense, with a solid core of currant, herb and oak flavors. The wines have been fruitier and fleshier of late.
1995: A ripe, smooth and polished style, with supple currant, earth, anise and cedar notes. **88**
1994: Harmonious; the earthy currant, cedar and spice flavors finish with firm but supple tannins. **89**
1993: Tight, firm and tannic, yet enough earthy currant and cherry flavors emerge to provide balance. **87**
1992: Austere, with a trim band of currant, earth, cedar and spice, finishing with firm tannins. **88**
1991: Firm and intense, with a core of ripe, rich currant, cherry and spicy oak flavors. **88**
1990: Tight and a little on the tough side, with a beam of cherry, currant and berry flavors pushing through on the finish, picking up a trace of tobacco. **88**
1987: Lively, with lots of ripe cherry and berry notes, hints of cedar and spice and a nibble of chocolate. **90**
1986: Mature, with herb and black cherry flavors that are losing intensity; the tannins hold the upper hand. **89**

CABERNET SAUVIGNON NAPA VALLEY ATS (★★★★)
1994: Cuvaison's best Cabernet ever, showing extra richness and dimension; plush tannins surround the rich currant, spice, herb and mineral flavors. **92**

CHARDONNAY NAPA VALLEY CARNEROS (★★★): Deftly balanced, complex and intense, with rich fruit and pretty oak shadings.

CHARDONNAY NAPA VALLEY CARNEROS ATS (★★★★): Shows tremendous complexity and intensity. The ATS is superior to the Reserve.
1995: Aromatic with lots of complex spice, pear, hazelnut, melon and fig flavors that are concentrated and smooth. **93**
1994: Delicious, rich and sharply focused; the core of pear, fig, hazelnut, melon and apricot flavors turns smooth in texture on the finish. **93**

CHARDONNAY NAPA VALLEY CARNEROS RESERVE (★★★★): Impressive for its finesse and concentration.
1996: Starts with dusty, earthy oak flavors and then focuses on an intensely wound core of anise, mineral, pear and fig-laced flavors that are rich and concentrated. **92**
1995: Great finesse, texture and balance, with delicately spicy pear, peach and apple flavors. **90**

1994: Well-focused, ripe pear, honey, apple and citrus flavors turn smoky, complex and creamy. **92**

MERITAGE RESERVE NAPA VALLEY
1991: Elegant and well balanced, if on the crisp side, with ample cherry and berry fruit. **86**

MERLOT NAPA VALLEY ATS (★★★★)
1994: Smooth, with herb, leather and spicy stewed plum flavors, turning supple and polished, gaining nuance and complexity on the long, rich finish. **91**

MERLOT NAPA VALLEY CARNEROS (★★★): Usually quite good, if just shy of great. Ready to drink now, or can be cellared short-term. The 1984 remains stunning.
1995: Smooth and plush, with an elegant array of coffee, currant, berry and plum flavors. **88**
1994: Shows off earthy, herbal flavors, with a range of currant and anise notes that provide complexity. **89**

PINOT NOIR NAPA VALLEY CARNEROS (★★★): Shows delicacy and finesse in a medium-weight style; could use a little more richness.
1995: The best ever. Bold and ripe, with layers of black cherry, plum, wild berry and smoky, toasty oak flavors; shows depth and complexity. **91**

PINOT NOIR NAPA VALLEY CARNEROS ERIS (★★★): The Eris bottling aims for more finesse, and usually succeeds.
1996: Delivers ripe cherry, berry and cola flavors and a touch of oak that adds dimension. **86**
1995: Plush and complex. The dark, concentrated plum, wild berry and black cherry flavors have earthy mushroom nuances. **89**

CYPRESS see J. LOHR WINERY

DA VINCI see RENAISSANCE VINEYARD & WINERY INC.

DALLA VALLE VINEYARDS (★★★★★)
Oakville, Napa Valley
Founded: 1986. **Owner:** Naoko Dalla Valle.
Winemaker: Mia Klein.

MAJOR WINES: PRICE, CASES, RATING

Cabernet Sauvignon Napa Valley
  ($50, 2,200)   ★★★★★
Maya Red Napa Valley
  ($80, 500)   ★★★★★
Sangiovese Napa Valley Pietre Rosse
  ($25, 500)   ★★

WINERY DATA

Case Production: 3,500. **Acres Owned:** 25 acres in Oakville, Napa Valley. **Varietals by Acre:** Cabernet Franc (2 acres), Cabernet Sauvignon (21), Sangiovese (2). **Varietals Purchased:** Sangiovese (Napa Valley).

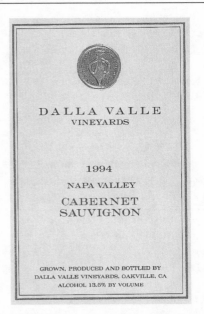

Dalla Valle was one of the most exciting new wineries to emerge in California in the 1980s. In 1982, Gustave and Naoko Dalla Valle moved to Napa and built their spectacular Mediterranean-style estate in the hills above the Silverado Trail in the Rutherford district. Now, in the 1990s, the winery has hit full stride with two mountain-grown reds: a rich, dense Cabernet Sauvignon, and a vineyard-designated blend of Cabernet and Cabernet Franc called Maya (the name of the owners' daughter).

These are very distinctive wines indeed, grown on a sloping hillside of reddish-brown soil. While it remains to be seen how well the wines will age, right now they are impressive for their flavor and style. Cabernet is the main wine from this 25-acre estate vineyard, with 2,200 cases made; Maya is a 400-500-case brand made from a 4-acre plot. Pietre Rosse is a Tuscan-inspired Sangiovese, but so far it is not in the same class as the other reds. Credit goes to winemaker Heidi Peterson Barrett for the early successes, but she was replaced by Tony Soter and Mia Klein with the 1996 vintage; Soter has since left to focus on his brand, Etude.

TASTING NOTES

CABERNET SAUVIGNON NAPA VALLEY (★★★★★): Early vintages were hard and austere and didn't undergo malolactic fermentation, but the wine's full potential was realized beginning with the 1990 vintage.

1995: A dark, sharply focused and richly flavored wine, brimming with pure cherry, currant, mineral, sage and spice. Has the tannic strength to age well into the 21st century. **94**

1994: Dense, rich and concentrated, with tiers of currant, black cherry, anise and cedar and tight, firm tannins. **93**

1993: Tight and focused, showing a firm band of currant and plum flavors, with a spicy, cedary accent and gritty tannins. **88**

1992: Ripe, dark, complex and concentrated, with a solid core of black cherry and currant flavors and toasty oak notes. **92**

1991: An exotic wine with ripe, spicy black cherry and wild berry flavors that add an intriguing flavor profile. Well balanced, with richness, depth and concentration, finishing with firm tannins. **91**

1990: Deep, dense and delicious, bursting with plum, currant, chocolate and spice aromas and flavors; generous and concentrated, an elegant wine with power. **93**

1989: Crisp and intense, this is a lean, austere 1989 that offers a tight, compact core of cherry and currant flavors. **84**

1988: Tight and closed, with a nice core of plum and currant flavors. **88**

1987: Shows polish and finesse, with complex, concentrated currant, mint and mineral flavors. **89**

1986: Hard, tannic, austere, even stemmy in texture; a tough wine to warm up to, with firm currant, herb and beefy flavors. **84**

MAYA RED NAPA VALLEY (★★★★★): Uncommonly dark and potent, with tiers of flavor and firm tannins. This Cabernet blend seems well built to age, but it's enjoyable early on.

1995: Dark, intense and deeply concentrated, with a tight beam of currant, blackberry and cherry-laced fruit and tannins woven in. **95**

1994: Beautifully crafted, tight and intense, with a big, ripe, rich core of spicy currant, plum and berry flavors, finishing with a complex earthy mineral edge. **95**

1993: Magnificent; loaded with complex flavors, with plush tannins and tiers of currant, anise, mineral and cedar that flow on and on. **96**

1992: Beautifully balanced, dark, rich and supple, with brilliant, complex currant, plum, herb and mineral flavors that run deep and concentrated, turning elegant. **94**

1991: Bold and ripe, showing delicious currant, black cherry and plum flavors before the firm tannins kick in. **90**

1990: Dark and inky, with ripe, rich, complex currant, plum, cherry and spice flavors that turn smoky and buttery on the finish, with mineral, herb and coffee notes. **90**

1989: Smooth and polished, with generous, spicy vanilla aromas and black cherry, plum and currant flavors that linger on the solid finish. Has lots of personality. **91**

1988: Rich and elegant, with tight currant, plum and cherry flavors that hang in there on the finish, where the tannins firm up. **86**

SANGIOVESE NAPA VALLEY PIETRE ROSSE (★★): Showed improvement with the 1996 (85 points) and 1995 (86), offering fruitier wines on a small scale.

DANIEL LAWRENCE (★–★★)
Sonoma County
Founded: 1994. **Owner:** Daniel Horsch. **Winemaker:** Michael Draxton. **Second Label:** Sequoia Ridge.

MAJOR WINES: PRICE, CASES, RATING

Chardonnay Carneros	
($12, 1,200)	★
Chardonnay Santa Cruz Reserve	
($15, 700)	★
Syrah Alexander Valley Reserve	
($13, 2,100)	★★

ALSO PRODUCED
Cabernet Sauvignon Alexander Valley ($15, 500); Gewürztraminer Monterey ($8, 600); Sangiovese Alexander Valley ($12, 200).

WINERY DATA
Case Production: 5,000. **Varietals Purchased:** Cabernet Sauvignon (Alexander Valley), Chardonnay (Carneros, Santa Cruz Mountains), Gewürztraminer (Monterey), Merlot (Alexander Valley), Sangiovese (Alexander Valley), Syrah (Alexander Valley).

Founded by Dan Horsch and his father, Lawrence, Daniel Lawrence began as a value-oriented brand. Today, it is moving toward small-production, moderately priced wines. But while Daniel Lawrence is being downsized, its second label, Sequoia Ridge, is expanding, with a goal of 250,000 cases by 2003. All of the wines are custom crushed by Associated Vintage Group, which is also a partner in the Sequoia Ridge brand.

The quality of the Daniel Lawrence wines has been variable: mostly average to below average. The best wine so far has been the earthy, minerally 1996 Alexander Valley Syrah Reserve (86 points).

DARK STAR CELLARS (★★)
Paso Robles, San Luis Obispo County
Founded: 1994. **Owner:** Dark Star Cellars Ltd. **Winemaker:** Norm Benson.

MAJOR WINES: PRICE, CASES, RATING

Cabernet Sauvignon Paso Robles	
($19)	★★
Merlot Paso Robles	
($18)	★★
Ricordati Red Paso Robles	
($20)	★★
Zinfandel Paso Robles	
($18)	★★

ALSO PRODUCED
Chardonnay Paso Robles ($14); Syrah Paso Robles ($19).

WINERY DATA
Case Production: 2,500. **Varietals Purchased:** Cabernet Sauvignon (Paso Robles), Chardonnay (Paso Robles), Merlot (Paso Robles), Syrah (Paso Robles), Zinfandel (Paso Robles).

Norm Benson uses purchased grapes from the Paso Robles area for his small, red wine-focused winery. The mix includes Cabernet, Ricordati (a Cabernet blend), Cabernet Franc, Merlot and Zinfandel, with the last the best so far—the 1996 scored 88 points. Chardonnay and Syrah have recently joined the product list.

DASHE CELLARS (★★★)
Sonoma County
Founded: 1996. **Owner:** Michael & Anne Dashe.
Winemaker: Michael Dashe.

MAJOR WINES: PRICE, CASES, RATING
Zinfandel Dry Creek Valley
  ($18, 1,300)   ★★★

ALSO PRODUCED
Merlot Mendocino ($NA, 1,000); Sangiovese Dry Creek ($18, 700); Zinfandel Late Harvest ($20, 150); Zinfandel Russian River Valley ($25, 1,500).

WINERY DATA
Case Production: 5,000. **Varietals Purchased:** Cabernet Sauvignon (Alexander Valley), Carignane (Dry Creek Valley), Merlot (Mendocino County), Sangiovese (Dry Creek Valley), Zinfandel (Russian River Valley, Alexander Valley, Dry Creek Valley).

Mike Dashe left his winemaking position at Ridge's Sonoma facility (the old Lytton Springs Winery) to start his own label. The wines are all made from purchased grapes, and are being made in an Alameda warehouse next door to Rosenblum Cellars. Dashe's first wine, a 1996 Dry Creek Valley Zinfandel (87 points), showed ripe wild berry, raspberry and spice flavors and a complex, fruity finish. In addition to various Zinfandels, Dashe makes an Alexander Valley Cabernet, a Dry Creek Valley Sangiovese, and a Merlot from Mendocino County.

DAVID ARTHUR VINEYARDS (★★★★)
Napa Valley
Founded: 1985. **Owner:** David and Robert Long.
Winemaker: Bob Egelhoff.

MAJOR WINES: PRICE, CASES, RATING
Cabernet Sauvignon Napa Valley
  ($45, 1,000)   ★★★★
Cabernet Sauvignon Napa Valley
  Elevation 1147
  ($75, 1,000)   ★★★★
Chardonnay Napa Valley Reserve
  ($28, 500-1,500)   ★★
Meritaggio Red Napa Valley
  ($32, 800)   ★★★

WINERY DATA
Case Production: 3,000. **Acres Owned:** 47 in Napa Valley.
Varietals by Acre: Cabernet Franc (1.5), Cabernet Sauvignon (15), Chardonnay (25 acres), Merlot (1.5), Petit Verdot (1.5), Sangiovese (2.5).

Located in the hills east of St. Helena near Chappellet, this small, family-owned winery produces Chardonnay, two Cabernets and a Cabernet blend from grapes grown on their 47-acre vineyard. The Chardonnays are good, tending toward crisp apple and pear flavors. The Chardonnay Reserve 1997 (88 points) is complex and concentrated, with crisp flavors of melon and pear.

The winery's strength lies in its Cabernets, the best being the expensive, limited production Elevation 1147, though the Napa Valley and Meritaggio are also excellent. The 1996 Elevation 1147 (95) is smooth and rich with a plush, complex range of chocolate, berry, spice and cedar flavors and a long, complex finish. The 1996 Cabernet Sauvignon Napa Valley (94) is also rich and plush and shows concentrated layers of currant, blackberry, black cherry, spice and nutmeg flavors. The 1996 Meritaggio (91), though less opulent and featuring more earthy, leathery flavors than the other Cabernets, is impressive for its complexity. This is a winery to watch.

DAYDREAM CELLARS see REVERIE WINERY

D-CUBED CELLARS (★★)
Napa Valley
Founded: 1994. **Owner:** Duane & Sherri Dappen.
Winemaker: Duane Dappen.

MAJOR WINES: PRICE, CASES, RATING

Zinfandel Howell Mountain ($20, 330)	★★★
Zinfandel Napa Valley ($17, 500)	★★

WINERY DATA

Case Production: 830. **Acres Owned:** 2 acres in Howell Mountain. **Varietals by Acre:** Zinfandel (2 acres). **Varietals Purchased:** Zinfandel (Howell Mountain, Napa Valley).

Winemaker Duane David Dappen had worked for Storybook Mountain, Grgich Hills and Rombauer before starting his own label in 1994. (The name D-Cubed comes from his initials). Dappen produces two Zinfandels—one from Howell Mountain and the other from Napa Valley—which have been excellent-to-good since the first vintage. Complex, earthy, spicy and marked by wild berry flavors, the Howell Mountain Zinfandel has been more interesting, while the Napa Valley Zinfandel shows good balance but more modest flavors.

TASTING NOTES

ZINFANDEL HOWELL MOUNTAIN (★★★)
1996: A racy style that's tart and firm, with spicy wild berry, black pepper and bell pepper flavors. **87**
1995: Smooth and supple, with an earthy, spicy edge to the cherry and wild berry flavors. **89**
1994: Brimming with ripe, juicy, spicy wild berry, raspberry and cherry notes, turning tarry with ripe tannins. **90**

ZINFANDEL NAPA VALLEY (★★)
1996: Appealing, if modest, with ripe, supple plum and berry flavors and firm tannins. **84**

DE LOACH VINEYARDS (★★–★★★★)

Russian River Valley, Sonoma County
Founded: 1975. **Owner:** Cecil De Loach. **Winemaker:** Dan Cederquist.

MAJOR WINES: PRICE, CASES, RATING

Cabernet Sauvignon Russian River Valley ($18, 6,600)	★★
Cabernet Sauvignon Russian River Valley O.F.S. ($28, 2,000)	★★★
Chardonnay Russian River Valley ($18, 39,000)	★★★
Chardonnay Russian River Valley O.F.S. ($28, 8,000)	★★★★★
Chardonnay Sonoma Cuvée ($14, 42,000)	★★★
Fumé Blanc Russian River Valley ($14, 5,000)	★★★
Gewürztraminer Russian River Valley ($12, 3,500)	★★
Merlot Russian River Valley ($18, 1,000)	★★
Petite Sirah Russian River Valley Flagstaff Ranch ($20, 1,000)	★★
Pinot Noir Russian River Valley ($16, 3,500)	★★★
Pinot Noir Russian River Valley O.F.S. ($28, 750)	★★★
White Zinfandel Sonoma County ($8, 24,000)	★
Zinfandel Russian River Valley Barbieri Ranch ($28, 500)	★★★
Zinfandel Russian River Valley Estate ($28, 500)	★★★
Zinfandel Russian River Valley Gambogi Ranch ($28, 500)	★★★
Zinfandel Russian River Valley O.F.S. ($28, 500)	★★★★
Zinfandel Russian River Valley Papera Ranch ($28, 500)	★★★
Zinfandel Russian River Valley Pelletti Ranch ($28, 500)	★★★
Zinfandel Russian River Valley Saitone Ranch ($28, 500)	★★★

ALSO PRODUCED

Chardonnay Russian River Valley Olivet Ranch ($20, 3,500).

WINERY DATA

Case Production: 145,000. **Acres Owned:** 674 acres (602 in Russian River Valley, 72 in Butte County). **Varietals by Acre:**

Cabernet Franc (6 acres), Cabernet Sauvignon (80), Chardonnay (188), Gewürztraminer (16), Merlot (36), Pinot Noir (35), Petite Sirah (15), Sangiovese (6), Sauvignon Blanc (25), Zinfandel (267). **Vineyard Designations:** Barbieri Ranch (Zinfandel), Flagstaff Ranch (Petite Sirah), Gambogi Ranch (Zinfandel), Olivet Ranch (Chardonnay), Papera Ranch (Zinfandel), Pelletti Ranch (Zinfandel), Saitone Ranch (Zinfandel). **Varietals Purchased:** Chardonnay (Russian River Valley), Sauvignon Blanc (Russian River Valley).

In 1975, Cecil de Loach took an early retirement from the San Francisco Fire Department, and winemaking became his and his wife Christine's full-time profession. Their winery was founded in 1975, six years after the couple bought their property on Olivet Lane in the Russian River Valley. The original property had 24 acres planted to Zinfandel, dating back to 1905. Two years later, they added another 27-acre vineyard nearby, where the winery now sits.

In many respects, De Loach Vineyards is a prototype of how California wineries have evolved through the 1990s. Long one of California's steadiest performers, the De Loachs are now not only making better wines; they're also making more of them, by tapping into specific vineyard sites. Case in point: For years De Loach made a Zinfandel (and lots of White Zinfandel), but now they've separated their Zinfandels by vineyard, coming up with seven different bottlings.

Their main wines—Cabernet and Chardonnay—now have a reserve-style bottling under the O.F.S. (Our Finest Selection) label. They've also added Merlot, Pinot Noir and Petite Sirah to the mix, to go along with their

Gewürztraminer. On top of all this, the winery now owns 602 acres in Russian River and another 72 acres in Butte County, allowing them to control their grape sources, and thus the winery's destiny. In effect, DeLoach has expanded to cover as many bases as possible, yet they still manage to make very high-quality wines.

All of the wines are well-made, but the Chardonnay Russian River Valley O.F.S., an uncommonly rich, elegant and flavorful wine that ranks among California's best, has been the star. White Zinfandel has also been a big hit, with case volume sales that generate cash and help pay the bills. Furthermore, the vineyard-designated Zinfandels make a great study in microclimates of the Russian River Valley. All in all, this winery just keeps making more and better wines.

TASTING NOTES

CABERNET SAUVIGNON RUSSIAN RIVER VALLEY O.F.S. (★★★): Ripe, dark and concentrated; improving of late, offering lots of complex flavors.
1994: Dark, ripe and richly flavored, with layers of black cherry, currant, anise and spice, turning supple and harmonious. **90**
1993: A nice core of earthy currant, mineral, tar and cedary notes and a dash of oak and firm tannins. **87**
1992: Tight and focused, with currant and cherry flavors that fan out, picking up herb and cedary notes. **89**
1991: Compact and well focused, offering pleasant earth, berry and cherry notes and a long finish. **89**

CHARDONNAY RUSSIAN RIVER VALLEY O.F.S. (★★★★★): Typically opulent and well oaked, but also elegant and refined, rendering a wine of complexity and finesse.
1996: A rich concentration of flavors, it's tight, ripe and focused, with complex notes of pear, fig, apricot, anise and spice. **92**
1995: Brilliant, ripe and complex, with juicy, lively pear, spice, apple and hazelnut notes. **92**
1994: Pleasantly fruity, with a nice array of pear, citrus, honey and butterscotch flavors. **89**

PINOT NOIR RUSSIAN RIVER VALLEY O.F.S. (★★★): Appears ready to join the elite of Russian River Pinot Noirs; rich in fruit and elegant in style.
1996: Elegant and understated, with herb, tea, strawberry, cherry, leather and spice flavors, turning firm and tannic. **89**

1995: Ripe, rich and focused, with a sense of elegance and delicacy and earthy cherry and wild berry flavors. **89**
1994: Complex, with ripe cherry, currant, herb and spice notes and pretty oak flavors. **89**
1992: Moves past its initial earthiness to reveal a supple core of plum- and cherry-laced Pinot Noir fruit. **88**

ZINFANDEL RUSSIAN RIVER VALLEY BARBIERI RANCH (★★★): Leans toward the tart side, with intense, sometimes gritty tannins and peppery notes.
1997: Smooth, rich and polished, with layers of plush cherry, raspberry, and blackberry flavors; tightly focused and long on the finish. **90**
1996: Ripe and intense, with firm, gritty tannins, it serves up a modest range of tart wild berry and cherry-laced fruit. **86**
1995: On the tart side, with a sharply focused band of cherry, wild berry and raspberry fruit and a peppery edge. **88**
1994: Tightly wound, with tart plum, cherry and berry flavors building on the finish. **85**
1993: Elegant and well focused; pours out its bright, lively cherry, raspberry and peppery notes. **88**

ZINFANDEL RUSSIAN RIVER VALLEY ESTATE (★★★): Consistently good. Medium-bodied, with flavors varying from ripe raspberry to earthy cherry and herb-tinged fruit notes.
1997: Crisp and a touch flinty, with a slight smoky edge to the tannic cherry and raspberry notes, but the flavors linger and fan out nicely. **88**

ZINFANDEL RUSSIAN RIVER VALLEY GAMBOGI RANCH (★★★): Can be tart, with cherry, berry and jammy notes appearing in the riper years.
1997: Tart and spicy, with wild berry, blackberry, anise and sage flavors; tightly focused through the finish. **87**
1996: A lighter style, with earthy, bell pepper flavors and barely ripe berry and cherry flavors. **84**
1995: Fresh and lively; a shade tart, with bright berry and cherry flavors that pick up a hint of jamminess. **88**
1994: Tightly wound; marked by tart cherry and berry notes, but the flavors fan out nicely on the finish. **87**
1993: A touch earthy and austere, but it opens up to show off a range of cherry and berry flavors. **86**

ZINFANDEL RUSSIAN RIVER VALLEY O.F.S. (★★★★): A high-extract, high-alcohol, jam-packed style that borders on late harvest, and is simply delicious.

1997: Starts with creamy, toasty oak and then works in ripe cherry, wild berry raspberry and spice flavors that weave together nicely. **89**
1996: Smooth, polished, elegant and focused, with complex wild berry, black cherry, earth and spice flavors. **90**
1995: Gushing with ripe, juicy raspberry, wild berry, spice and cherry flavors, turning plush and rich. **92**
1994: A complex, broad, ripe range of cherry, herb and wild berry flavors. **88**

ZINFANDEL RUSSIAN RIVER VALLEY PAPERA RANCH (★★★): Serves up lots of complex flavors, with jammy cherry and berry nuances.
1997: Clean, ripe and fruity, with a pretty, complex array of plum, blackberry, cedar and spice flavors, and firm tannins. **88**
1996: Pleasant for its wild berry, anise, sage and raspberry notes, finishing with firm tannins. **87**
1995: Ripe and full-bodied, with jammy wild berry, cherry and plum-laced fruit and hints of pepper and spice. **90**
1994: Slightly earthy and tannic, with tart wild berry and cherry flavors showing through on the finish. **87**
1993: Of medium-weight, with zesty, elegant earthy berry and cherry flavors. **86**

ZINFANDEL RUSSIAN RIVER VALLEY PELLETTI RANCH (★★★): Shows lots of rich cherry and wild berry flavors in the best years, but can also be tart and lean.
1997: Supple and balanced, with a pretty array of blackberry, wild berry, sage, cedar and spice and a burst of fruit. **90**
1996: Marked by earthy nuances and tart, moderately ripe cherry and wild berry flavors. **86**
1995: Ripe and complex, with lots of cherry, wild berry and raspberry fruit that's pure and plush. **90**
1994: Impressive for its pretty cherry, berry and cranberry flavors, finishing with earthy tannins. **86**
1993: Full, rich and ripe, with cherry jam and raspberry flavors, turning smooth and polished. **88**
1991: Tart, crisp and lively, with a narrow, focused band of rich raspberry and wild berry flavors. **86**
1990: Tight and tannic, with a solid core of blackberry and black cherry aromas and flavors. **87**

ZINFANDEL RUSSIAN RIVER VALLEY SAITONE RANCH (★★★): Sometimes smoothly textured, and other times crisp and tannic, but it maintains a complex core of pepper, strawberry and plum flavors.

1997: Smooth, ripe and creamy, with rich blackberry, raspberry, plum and strawberry flavors, gaining richness and depth. **89**

1996: Fresh, crisp and snappy, with crushed pepper, wild berry, raspberry and cherry notes. **88**

1995: Complex and flavorful, with a fine interplay of cherry, wild berry, currant and plum flavors and firm tannins. **89**

DE LORIMIER WINERY (★★–★★★)

Alexander Valley, Sonoma County
Founded: 1986. **Owner:** Alfred & Sandra de Lorimier.
Winemaker: Donald H. Frazer.

MAJOR WINES: PRICE, CASES, RATING

Chardonnay Alexander Valley ($16, 1,500)	★★
Merlot Alexander Valley ($18, 1,800)	★★
Mosaic Meritage Red Alexander Valley ($24, 1,500)	★★
Sauvignon Blanc Alexander Valley ($18, 2,500)	★★★
Spectrum Meritage White Alexander Valley ($14, 1,500)	★★★

ALSO PRODUCED

Chardonnay Alexander Valley Clonal Select ($24, 500); Malbec Alexander Valley ($20, 500); Sémillon Alexander Valley ($16, 500).

WINERY DATA

Case Production: 11,000. **Acres Owned:** 83 acres in Alexander Valley. **Varietals by Acre:** Cabernet Franc (3 acres), Cabernet Sauvignon (14), Chardonnay (22), Malbec (2), Merlot (22), Petit Verdot (1), Sangiovese (1), Sauvignon Blanc (11), Sémillon (4), Viognier (1), Zinfandel (2).

Owned by surgeon Alfred de Lorimier, this winery is situated near Geyserville at the northern end of Alexander Valley. The winery draws from its 83 acres of vineyard, which provides all the grapes for its wines.

Quality across the board is in the good-to-very-good range, with only the 1995 Sauvignon Blanc (90 points) earning an outstanding mark of late.

TASTING NOTES

CABERNET BLEND ALEXANDER VALLEY MOSAIC MERITAGE (★★): This wine usually scores in the mid-80s range; the 1995 (85 points) was lean and spicy.

CHARDONNAY ALEXANDER VALLEY (★★): Typically spicy with good intensity and focus, but not exceptional. The 1996 (87 points) had attractive flavors.

SAUVIGNON BLANC ALEXANDER VALLEY (★★★): The 1997 (86 points) was refreshing, with flinty citrus notes.

SPECTRUM MERITAGE WHITE ALEXANDER VALLEY (★★★): The 1995 (87 points) was marked by pineapple and herb flavors.

DECOY see DUCKHORN VINEYARDS

DEHLINGER WINERY (★★★★–★★★★★)

Russian River Valley, Sonoma County
Founded: 1975. **Owner:** Tom Dehlinger. **Winemaker:** Tom Dehlinger.

MAJOR WINES: PRICE, CASES, RATING

Cabernet Sauvignon Russian River Valley ($26, 700)	★★★★
Chardonnay Russian River Valley ($20, 3,000)	★★★★
Pinot Noir Russian River Valley ($30, 1,600)	★★★★★
Pinot Noir Russian River Valley Goldridge Vineyard ($25, 1,200)	★★★★★
Pinot Noir Russian River Valley Octagon Vineyard ($35, 350)	★★★★★
Pinot Noir Russian River Valley Reserve ($35, 500)	★★★★★
Syrah Russian River Valley ($28, 700)	★★★★★
Syrah Russian River Valley Goldridge Vineyard ($24, 400)	★★★★

WINERY DATA
Case Production: 9,000. **Acres Owned:** 45 acres in Russian River Valley. **Varietals by Acre:** Cabernet Sauvignon (7 acres), Chardonnay (16), Merlot (3), Pinot Noir (16), Syrah (3). **Vineyard Designations:** Goldridge Vineyard (Pinot Noir, Syrah), Octagon Vineyard (Pinot Noir).

1995

DEHLINGER

Pinot Noir

RUSSIAN RIVER VALLEY
ESTATE BOTTLED

PRODUCED AND BOTTLED BY THE DEHLINGER WINERY, SEBASTOPOL, CA. CONTAINS SULFITES. ALC. 14.5% BY VOL.

If one were to take a vote on California's best winemakers, Tom Dehlinger would surely end up among the top dozen or so, and he would just as assuredly rank number one on many ballots. Using grapes grown on a 45-acre family-owned vineyard in Russian River Valley near Sebastopol, where he's shown a master's hand in crafting intensely flavored, richly concentrated, succulent wines. His best wines are the Burgundian varietals Chardonnay and Pinot Noir, along with Syrah.

His vineyard is best suited to Chardonnay (16 acres) and Pinot Noir (16 acres), which ripen fully; his Cabernet Sauvignon and Cabernet Franc often seem to struggle because of the cool climate, resulting in wines marked by green herb and bell pepper notes coupled with gritty tannins. Once part of the lineup, Merlot and Zinfandel have now been dropped because they failed to ripen interestingly. When it comes to Dehlinger's wines, the advice is simple: if you see his name on a wine bottle, buy it.

TASTING NOTES

CABERNET SAUVIGNON RUSSIAN RIVER VALLEY (★★★★): The style is consistent and improving, with riper flavors, darker colors and smoother tannins. Ages well, as is evidenced by the very fine 1986 vintage.
1994: Intense and lively, with ripe, juicy, sharply focused cherry, raspberry and wild berry flavors. **91**

1992: Ripe, spicy layers of plum, cherry and currant flavors, with firm, balanced tannins. **86**
1986: Big and ripe, with power and finesse; shows hints of bell pepper and herb and lots of currant, plum and berry flavors. **91**

CHARDONNAY RUSSIAN RIVER VALLEY (★★★): Can be exceptional; rich in fruit, smooth in texture and delicious to drink.
1996: Tight, with a crisp, focused band of ripe pear, apple, citrus and mineral flavors which fan out on the finish. **90**
1995: Openly fruity, with a pleasing earthy edge to the ripe pear, fig and melon flavors; picks up a trace of citrus and grapefruit. **93**
1994: Smooth and subtle, with a polished texture and ripe pear, spice and hazelnut notes. **88**

PINOT NOIR RUSSIAN RIVER VALLEY (★★★★★): Getting riper, fuller, more flavorful and more supple in texture with every vintage.
1996: Pleasantly balanced and flavorful, with pretty plum, black cherry and wild berry notes. **88**
1995: Wonderful depth, richness, concentration and purity of flavor, with layers of ripe, supple plum, black cherry, currant and berry flavors. **94**
1994: Lots of broad, ripe, complex tiers of black cherry, spice, mineral and wild berry flavors that linger. **90**
1993: Medium-bodied, with a modest core of black cherry jam, it turns elegant and supple. **88**
1992: Tight and chewy, but the black cherry and cedary oak flavors that do emerge are pleasing, if tannic. **88**
1991: Less rich and concentrated than the Reserve, but very fine nonetheless, with supple herb, cherry and spice notes. **87**
1990: Dark, rich and effusively fruity, with layers of delicious ripe cherry, berry and currant-tinged fruit. **93**

PINOT NOIR RUSSIAN RIVER VALLEY GOLDRIDGE VINEYARD (★★★★): Delicious fruit; dark, ripe and opulent, seductive in style.
1996: The fleshy texture leads to a supple core of black cherry, wild berry, plum and spice, accented by pretty vanilla-tinged oak. **89**
1995: Smooth, ripe, rich and complex, with a pretty array of ripe cherry, spice, cedar, anise and rhubarb flavors. **91**

1994: Tight, firm and concentrated, showing an array of currant and wild berry fruit and hints of anise, with mineral and oak shadings. **92**

PINOT NOIR RUSSIAN RIVER VALLEY GOLDRIDGE VINEYARD 20-YEAR-OLD VINES
1994: Delicious, broad, ripe and juicy, with tiers of black cherry, currant, plum and wild berry, turning smooth and supple. **93**

PINOT NOIR RUSSIAN RIVER VALLEY OCTAGON VINEYARD (★★★★★): May be the best of the multiple bottlings. Very rich, concentrated, broad and plush.
1995: Rich and concentrated, with spicy cherry, wild berry, raspberry and plummy notes; impeccably balanced. **92**
1994: A ripe, fleshy, juicy Pinot Noir, with layers of plum, cherry, spice and anise notes that turn smooth and supple. **92**

PINOT NOIR RUSSIAN RIVER VALLEY RESERVE (★★★★★): The Reserve is quickly joining the elite of California, with uncommonly dark color and depth of flavor. Ages well.
1994: Smooth, ripe, supple and polished, with tiers of black cherry, plum, currant and wild berry flavors, turning smoky and silky. **93**
1992: Intense and tightly wound; remarkable for its depth and flavor, with mineral, black cherry and cedary oak aromas and firm tannins. **91**
1991: Big, dark, ripe and intense, loaded with supple currant, black cherry, spice, mineral and mushroom flavors, and framed by toasty oak. **94**

SYRAH RUSSIAN RIVER VALLEY (★★★★★): This wine has enormous depth and richness, with meaty mineral flavors that run deep.
1995: Smooth, rich, plush and concentrated, with layers of juicy blackberry, cherry, plum, anise, currant and mineral flavors, finishing with a touch of oak and earthiness. **94**
1994: Dark, ripe, rich and meaty, with lots of chewy currant-, plum- and black cherry-laced fruit that is bold and sharply focused. **92**
1993: Dark, chewy and rich, with plum, black cherry, mineral and spice notes, finishing with a hint of leather and tobacco. **90**

1992: Uncommonly dark, with deep purple hues and a rich, plush core of plum, cherry, currant and mineral flavors. Serves up a big, bold mouthful of Syrah. Ready now but worthy of cellaring short-term. **93**

DEL DOTTO (★★★★)
Rutherford, Napa Valley
Founded: 1995. **Owner:** John Del Dotto. **Winemaker:** Nils Venge.

MAJOR WINES: PRICE, CASES, RATING

Cabernet Sauvignon Napa Valley ($43, 500)	★★★★
Giovanni's Tuscan Red Napa Valley Reserve ($30, 190)	★★★★

WINERY DATA
Case Production: 780. **Acres Owned:** 11 acres in Rutherford. **Varietals by Acre:** Cabernet Franc (1.5 acres), Cabernet Sauvignon (7), Merlot (1.5), Sangiovese (1).

Real estate entrepreneur David Del Dotto has had a string of successes with his Napa Valley Cabernet Sauvignon. The 1993, 1994 and 1995 vintages (all 92 points) are remarkably stylish, balancing intensely concentrated fruit, mineral and spice flavors with plush tannins and lavish oak. A 1995 Cabernet-Sangiovese blend called Giovanni's Tuscan Red Napa Valley Reserve (91) was also outstanding, with creamy black cherry, strawberry, black olive and spice flavors and a long, polished finish. The case production is slowly increasing. Worth watching.

TASTING NOTES

CABERNET SAUVIGNON NAPA VALLEY (★★★★): Beautifully crafted and remarkably stylish, balancing intensely concentrated fruit, mineral and spicy flavors with plush tannins and lavish oak.

GIOVANNI'S TUSCAN RED NAPA VALLEY RESERVE (★★★★): A blend of 70 percent Cabernet and 30 percent Sangiovese.

DELECTUS (★★★)
Napa Valley
Founded: 1995. **Owner:** Gerhard & Linda Reisacher.
Winemaker: Gerhard Reisacher.

MAJOR WINES: PRICE, CASES, RATING
Cabernet Sauvignon Napa Valley
($42, 1,000)   ★★★
Merlot Oakville Stanton Vineyard
($38, 500)   ★★★

WINERY DATA
Case Production: 1,500. **Vineyard Designations:** Stanton Vineyard (Merlot). **Varietals Purchased:** Cabernet Sauvignon (Napa Valley), Merlot (Oakville).

Gerhard Reisacher was an enologist and viticulturalist for Clos Du Val before starting Delectus. While the 1994 Napa Valley Cabernet Sauvignon was very good, the 1995 was outstanding. The 1996 Merlot Stanton Vineyard (87 points) was ripe and juicy, with intriguing spice and herb flavors.

TASTING NOTES

CABERNET SAUVIGNON NAPA VALLEY (★★★)
1995: Ripe and supple, with an elegant range of currant, chocolate, cherry, cedar, anise and spicy wood flavors. **91**
1994: Tightly wound, with firm tannins and a narrow band of currant and black cherry fruit. **88**

DEUX AMIS (★★)
Dry Creek Valley, Sonoma County
Founded: 1987. **Owner:** James Penpraze & Phyllis Zouzounis. **Winemaker:** Phyllis Zouzounis.

MAJOR WINES: PRICE, CASES, RATING
Zinfandel Dry Creek Valley
Rued Vineyard
($20, 200)   ★★★
Zinfandel Sonoma County
($15, 1,500)   ★★

ALSO PRODUCED
Petite Sirah Sonoma County ($20, 100).

WINERY DATA
Case Production: 2,000. **Vineyard Designations:** Rued Vineyard (Zinfandel). **Varietals Purchased:** Petite Sirah (Alexander Valley), Zinfandel (Dry Creek, Alexander Valley).

Phyllis Zouzounis, the winemaker at Mazzocco, and James Penpraze started this small winery in 1987. The wine is made from purchased Zinfandel and Petite Sirah grapes in a rented space. Two Zinfandels were made from the 1995 vintage: a Rued Vineyard Dry Creek Valley (87 points), which is marked by spicy, peppery raspberry flavors; and a Sonoma County bottling (83), which had more subtle flavors and less pizzazz.

DI BRUNO (★★★)
Santa Ynez Valley, Santa Barbara County
Founded: 1996. **Owner:** Bruno D'Alfonso.
Winemaker: Bruno D'Alfonso.

MAJOR WINES: PRICE, CASES, RATING
Pinot Grigio Santa Ynez Valley
Sanford & Benedict Vineyard
($14, 350)   ★★★

ALSO PRODUCED
Sangiovese Santa Ynez Valley Stolpman Vineyard ($NA, 750).

WINERY DATA
Case Production: 2,000. **Vineyard Designations:** Sanford & Benedict Vineyard (Pinot Grigio), Stolpman Vineyard (Sangiovese). **Varietals Purchased:** Pinot Grigio (Santa Ynez Valley), Sangiovese (Santa Ynez).

Talented Sanford Winery winemaker Bruno D'Alfonso has made his solo debut with a 1996 Pinot Grigio (87 points) from the Sanford & Benedict Vineyard. His Sangiovese is too new to be rated here.

DIAMOND CREEK VINEYARDS (★★★★★)
Diamond Mountain, Napa Valley
Founded: 1968. **Owner:** Al & Adelle Brounstein.
Winemaker: Phil Steinschriber

MAJOR WINES: PRICE, CASES, RATING

Cabernet Sauvignon Napa Valley
  Gravelly Meadow
  ($100, NA)   ★★★★★

Cabernet Sauvignon Napa Valley
  Gravelly Meadow
  Microclimate 1, Microclimate 2
  ($150, NA)   ★★★★★

Cabernet Sauvignon Napa Valley
  Lake Vineyard
  ($300, NA)   ★★★★★

Cabernet Sauvignon Napa Valley
  Red Rock Terrace
  ($100, NA)   ★★★★★

Cabernet Sauvignon Napa Valley
  Red Rock Terrace Microclimate 1,
  Microclimate 2, Microclimate 3
  ($150, NA)   ★★★★★

Cabernet Sauvignon Napa Valley
  Volcanic Hill
  ($100, NA)   ★★★★★

Cabernet Sauvignon Napa Valley
  Volcanic Hill Microclimate 1, Microclimate 2,
  Microclimate 3, Microclimate 4
  ($150, NA)   ★★★★★

WINERY DATA

Case Production: 3,500. **Acres Owned:** 22 acres in Calistoga. **Varietals by Acre:** Cabernet Franc, Cabernet Sauvignon, Merlot, Petit Verdot. **Vineyard Designations:** Volcanic Hill, Red Rock Terrace, Gravelly Meadow, Lake Vineyard.

In 1968, a year after buying a 79-acre parcel in the narrow canyon that lines Diamond Creek, Al Brounstein began clearing the hillsides, and discovered that he had three distinctly different soil types and exposures. He planted the three sites to a mixture of Bordeaux varieties, using budwood from Bordeaux's first growths, which he smuggled into the U.S. Upon making his first Cabernets in 1972, he wondered whether the vineyards would yield distinctively different wines.

Brounstein found that each of the vineyards had a unique personality, and named them after their respective soil compositions. Volcanic Hill is 8 acres of volcanic ash on a south-facing slope. Red Rock Terrace is 7 acres of iron-rich, reddish clay on a steeper grade with a northerly exposure. Gravelly Meadow is a flatter 5 acres of rocky, gravelly soil.

Brounstein eventually planted a fourth vineyard, a three-quarter-acre parcel called Lake Vineyard. Since 1978, Lake Vineyard's grapes have been bottled separately in years when they're distinctive; otherwise, they become part of the Gravelly Meadow blend. In 1991, Brounstein began separating lots from within the vineyards, calling these special bottlings "Microclimates." Thus, it's possible that six to eight different bottlings could appear in any given vintage, depending upon how many Microclimate bottlings are produced.

The Brounsteins planned from the beginning to be California's first Cabernet-only estate, and they have remained true to this intention. The three main wines, grown at a 600-foot elevation, share a rustic, mountain-grown austerity, the result of small berries and low crop yields. Intense and tannic when young, Diamond Creek's Cabernets are also deeply colored and enormously concentrated, capable of aging and gaining complexity for up to two decades.

After a mild quality decline in the 1980s, Brounstein fine-tuned his vineyards, and the Cabernets of the 1990s have been tremendous. Production peaks at 3,500 cases in good years, but is often much less. Because of the wines' distinctive qualities and limited production (often just a few hundred cases of each wine are produced), prices have soared. The three main bottlings sell for $100 to $150, and the Lake Vineyard sells briskly at $300 a bottle, making it California's most expensive wine. Brounstein periodically bottles a three-vineyard blend, which he uses for charity wine auction donations.

Jerry Luper made the wines through the 1990 vintage; Phil Steinschriber deserves the credit for the succeeding vintages. Having tasted Diamond Creek Cabernets on many occasions, I have not only found them to be distinctive, but I've found that they age exceptionally well. Interestingly enough, in vertical tastings, no single vineyard excels in any predictable fashion.

TASTING NOTES

CABERNET SAUVIGNON NAPA VALLEY GRAVELLY MEADOW (★★★★★): Gravelly Meadow tends toward more herb and mineral flavors. Ages exceptionally well; can be aged for up to 20 years.

1996: Austere and on the earthy side, but it serves up a nice band of clay-tinged currant, plum and wild berry flavors before the tannins take over. **91**

1995: Simply delicious, with an amazing amount of complex fruit and tiers of currant, black cherry, plum and spice flavors. **94**

1994: Elegant, sophisticated, and complex, with notes of ripe cherry, sweet plum, spicy anise and cedar. **93**

1993: Marked by mint and herbal flavors and notes of coffee and currant. **86**

1992: Supple and showy, with ripe, polished plum, cherry and wild berry fruit, turning elegant on the finish. **92**

1991: Solid, dense and chewy, with a wonderful core of currant, blackberry and spice. Intense and concentrated, it is approachable now, but is sure to improve. **92**

Microclimate 1991: Tight, firm and concentrated, with a complex core of spicy currant and wild berry flavors. **90**

1990: Austere, with a stony, flinty edge to the currant and berry flavors and muscular tannins. **88**

1989: Typically earthy and complex, with lingering layers of clay, spice, berry and cherry flavors. **89**

1988: Lean and tannic but well focused, with spicy cedar aromas and flavors and cranberry and black cherry notes. **87**

1987: An earthy wine. Crisp and intense, with hints of currant; it still needs some time. **89**

1986: Tremendous depth, richness and complexity, with youthful, vibrant currant, berry, cherry and spice flavors. **92**

1985: Hard, tart and tannic, this is a very austere Gravelly Meadow that serves up a firm core of cedar and black cherry flavors. A long-ager. **92**

1984: Tight and well focused, with complex currant- and berry-laced fruit that picks up intensity on the finish. **90**

1983: Shows off an impressive amount of vibrant plum and berry fruit for such a difficult and tannic vintage. **88**

1982: Elegant and complex, with an understated style and mature currant, anise, sage, tea and tar flavors. **88**

1981: Racy, with an herbaceous streak running through the earthy currant notes. **84**

1980: A rich, complex wine that displays layers of black cherry, currant and cedar flavors that are well integrated, finishing with a touch of coffee and anise. **92**

1979: Elegant, with a spicy, earthy, cedary edge that blends in nicely with the herb and black cherry flavors. **92**

1978: Rich and complex, with earthy currant, sage, tar and spice flavors; mineral notes appear on the finish. **91**

1977: A durable 1977, it is rich, thick and earthy, with mineral, currant and black cherry flavors that are austere. **89**

1976: Drying, with mature, complex Cabernet flavors; finishes with notes of sage and tea. **84**

1975: Dense, with an earthy, slightly medicinal edge. Also a touch raisiny, with some currant and cranberry notes. **90**

1974: Fully mature. Still austere, with earthy currant, mineral and spice notes; turns complex on the finish. **88**

CABERNET SAUVIGNON NAPA VALLEY GRAVELLY MEADOW–LAKE VINEYARD BLEND

1992: Subtle, with complex, earthy currant- and berry-laced fruit; exhibits delicacy and finesse. **90**

1991: Bright and chewy, with a solid core of currant and berry flavors. Almost floral at the edges, this is an elegant wine behind the layer of tannins. **92**

CABERNET SAUVIGNON NAPA VALLEY LAKE VINEYARD

(★★★★★): Usually the most supple and richly flavored wine, it is dense, complex and ageworthy.

1996: Ripe, smooth and elegant, with pretty black cherry, tart plum, herb and cedary oak notes, turning supple and polished. A wonderful integration of fruit and tannins. **92**

1994: Dramatic, dark and complex, with a firm tannic backbone for the rich mineral, currant, earth, spice and cedar notes. **94**

1992: Showy early, with more buttery oak than usual, and also very supple, with tiers of currant, herb, spice and chocolate notes. **94**

1990: Graceful and harmonious, with rich, complex spicy, currant, cedar and anise flavors. **92**

1987: Wonderful aromatics and flavors, with ripe plum, black cherry and spicy nuances and a strong anise aftertaste. **93**

1984: Intense and lively, with enormously deep, concentrated flavors; shows rich, chocolaty currant, berry and black cherry fruit. **94**

1978: An extraordinary wine; atypical for Diamond Creek, with its lush, rich, fleshy texture and opulent plum, currant, and black cherry- and berry-scented fruit. **97**

CABERNET SAUVIGNON NAPA VALLEY RED ROCK TERRACE

(★★★★★): Red Rock Terrace is usually more elegant and refined, but it ages very well, with bright cherry and currant flavors.

1996: Sleek and elegant, with ripe, spicy Cabernet flavors that echo berry, plum and currant fruit, with hints of tea, sage, cedar and earth; finishes with supple tannins. **92**

Microclimate 3 1996: Dense and concentrated, with a rich, classy array of currant, black cherry, exotic spice, mineral and cedar flavors. It's tightly focused and quite complex, with a long, rich aftertaste. **94**

1995: A lovely orchestration of complex cherry, currant, and floral flavors and a long, graceful finish. **95**

1994: Ripe, bold and generous; deeply concentrated, with rich black cherry, currant, plum and wild berry notes and firm tannins. **92**

Microclimate 1994: Intense, with brilliant fruit concentration and deep, perfumed currant, cedar, anise, berry flavors that linger on the finish. **93**

Microclimate 2 1994: Deeply concentrated, with complex, ripe, supple flavors of currant, cherry, spice and mineral and light, cedary oak nuances. **93**

1993: Medium-bodied, intense and tannic, with a modest core of currant, cedar and berry notes. **85**

1992: Ripe and spicy, with rich black cherry, currant, anise and cedary oak flavors that are focused and lively. **91**

1991: Wonderfully perfumed currant, plum and wild berry fruit; turning rich, intense, focused, and concentrated on the finish. **94**

1990: Herbaceous and racy, with a fleshy edge to the earthy currant notes; turning supple on the finish. **89**

1989: Tough and tannic, with concentrated red cherry, currant and black pepper aromas and flavors that persist onto a long finish. **88**

1988: Deep, earthy black cherry, leather, cedar and spice flavors; complex and concentrated. **89**

1987: Earthy, with a brickish edge to the currant, anise and spice flavors. Fully mature now with soft, fleshy tannins. **88**

1986: Dark, ripe, rich and concentrated, with vibrant, complex notes of currant, black cherry, tar, sage and spice. **92**

1985: Elegant and refined, with tiers of ripe, spicy black cherry, currant and berry. **90**

1984: Ripe and flavorful, with pretty floral, plum, cherry and spicy nuances, turning complex on the finish. **92**

1983: Lean and austere, which is typical of the vintage; with crisp cherry and currant fruit. **84**

1982: A rich, dark-colored wine that's remarkably complex, with earthy currant, herb and tea flavors. **90**

1981: An elegant style that's complex and flavorful, with ripe, spicy cherry and berry fruit. **88**

1980: Has the subtle nuances you hope for in a mature wine, with complex cherry, currant, herb and berry notes. **88**

1979: Austere but classy; tightly wound, with pretty, mature black cherry- and currant-laced fruit. **90**

1978: A grand wine that's still youthful, with ripe, juicy cherry and plummy Cabernet fruit, turning elegant on the finish. **96**

First Pick 1977: Still dark and firmly tannic, but the rich, earthy currant, anise and mineral flavors are complex and concentrated, pumping out lots of flavor on a long, full finish. **88**

Second Pick 1977: A lean wine with a modest proportion of red cherry fruit. **84**

1976: Drying, with a metallic edge, but the core of flavor is built around earthy, meaty currant, cherry, anise and mineral flavors. **88**

1975: Dark, dense, and enormously complex and concentrated, with rich currant, mineral, anise, sage and cedar notes. **94**

1974: Deeply colored, with wonderfully complex and youthful aromas. The spicy, grapey currant flavors pick up an anise note on a long, full finish. **92**

1972: Very complex, with a broad range of earthy currant, plum, berry, sage and spice flavors. **90**

CABERNET SAUVIGNON NAPA VALLEY THREE VINEYARD BLEND (★★★): Unique because it's a blend, but it's not in the same class as the other wines.

1990: Ruggedly tannic; even backward, with a decidedly earthy quality. **88**

1989: Solid, crisp and austere, with light, pleasant currant, berry and cherry fruit. **87**

1985: Complex and flavorful, with firm currant, black cherry, anise, herb and spicy nuances. **90**

1981: Elegant, with simple spice and herbal notes. **84**

CABERNET SAUVIGNON NAPA VALLEY VOLCANIC HILL (★★★★★): Volcanic Hill is usually the earthiest and most tannic of these wines. It is uncommonly dark, and has a long life.

1996: Ripe and intense, with a chalky edge to the concentrated wild berry, currant, sage, anise and spicy flavors; the tannins are tight and chewy. **92**

1995: Intense and deeply concentrated, with an abundance of ripe, rich and lively currant, black cherry and chocolate nuances. **94**

1994: Firm, dense and rich, with earthy currant, anise, mineral and berry flavors showing through before the tannins weigh in. **93**

1993: Ripe and intense, with a tightly wound core of earthy currant, herb, tobacco and spice flavors. **88**

1992: Openly fruity, dense, ripe, rich and concentrated, with tiers of currant, plum and cherry. **92**

1991: Wonderfully rich and concentrated, with a complex array of currant, berry, spice, anise and cedar flavors. **93**

Microclimate 1991: Tightly wound, with a trim band of spicy currant, plum and cedar notes, turning tannic on the finish. **92**

1990: Intense, lively, complex and concentrated; rich with vibrant currant, plum, cherry and spice nuances; long and lingering on the finish. **93**

1989: Surprisingly ripe and complex, it shows off attractive earthy, clay-laced currant flavors, and finishes with a long, full aftertaste. **89**

1988: Austere, even grapey, with a narrow range of cherry and currant flavors, turning dry on the finish. **87**

1987: Marked by earthy clay-, tea- and sage-like aromas supported by rich currant, cedar, tar and spicy nuances. **88**

1986: Dark, dense, ripe, and flavorful, with complex mint, currant, blackberry and earthy nuances. **92**

1985: Austere and restrained, yet complex, with firm currant, spice, cedar and sage notes. **90**

1984: Tremendous concentration and complexity; ripe and vibrant, with cherry, currant, anise, sage and cedar flavors that linger. **93**

1983: Lean and tight, it slowly fans out to show complex currant, sage and spice nuances. **88**

1982: Austere, with a twinge of herbaceousness; tightly wound spice, mineral, sage and currant flavors. **87**

Special Select 1982: Complex, with a pleasant earthiness to the currant and spicy clay-like aftertaste. **88**

1981: Displays a healthy, dark color, earthy, leathery Cabernet flavors and a good length. **88**

1980: Dark, dense and chewy, with complex notes of earth, meaty currant, spice and tar. **91**

1979: Youthful, as is evidenced by its currant and grape core, picking up complex mineral, sage and cedary notes on the finish. **91**

First Pick 1979: Tremendous complexity and concentration, with appealing, earthy currant, mineral and spice flavors. **93**

1978: Still dense, chewy, and richly flavored; packed with earthy, leathery currant, spice and mineral notes that linger. **93**

1977: Austere, with some bottle variation, it is fully mature but still deeply colored, with an earthy mineral and currant edge and drying tannins on the finish. **85**

1976: Mature, with a dry mineral edge to the flinty currant and cedary flavors. **88**

1975: A powerful wine with enormous depth, richness and flavor and dense, earthy mineral, currant, herb, sage and tea notes. **94**

1974: Fading now after a long successful run; turning dry and earthy, with sage and mineral flavors. **86**

1973: Austere, with a thin band of mature Cabernet flavors. **82**

1972: Youthful and complex, with plum, earth and mushroom flavors and a fine balance and length. **90**

DICKERSON VINEYARD (★★-★★★)
Napa Valley
Founded: 1971. **Owner:** William Dickerson.
Winemaker: Joel Peterson.

MAJOR WINES: PRICE, CASES, RATING

Merlot Napa Valley Limited Reserve ($16, 250)	★★
Ruby Cabernet Limited Reserve ($10, 250)	★★
Zinfandel Napa Valley Limited Reserve ($22, 200)	★★★

ALSO PRODUCED
Red Napa Valley ($11, 350).

WINERY DATA
Case Production: 800. **Acres Owned:** 17.5 acres in Napa Valley. **Varietals by Acre:** Cabernet Franc (0.5 acres), Cabernet Sauvignon (0.5), Merlot (3.5), Ruby Cabernet (3), Zinfandel (10).

Dickerson Vineyard in Napa Valley has long been a source of superb Zinfandel for Ravenswood. In the mid-1990s, it also became a brand in its own right, with Ravenswood's Joel Peterson making small lots of Zinfandel, Merlot and Ruby Cabernet from the vineyard in Rutherford. The Zinfandel grown here is marked by minty overtones and black cherry flavors in both the Dickerson and the Ravenswood bottlings. Dickerson's total production is 800 cases, with the wines made at Ravenswood. Once worthy of a solid ★★★ rating, the quality has unfortunately dipped a bit.

DOLCE see FAR NIENTE WINERY

DOMAINE CARNEROS (★★★)

Carneros
Founded: 1987. **Owner:** Domaine Carneros Ltd.
Winemaker: Eileen Crane.

MAJOR WINES: PRICE, CASES, RATING

Brut Carneros
    ($18, 30,000) ★★★
Le Reve Blanc de Blancs Carneros
    ($35, 3,000) ★★★★
Pinot Noir Carneros
    ($22, 6,300) ★★★
Pinot Noir Carneros The Famous Gate
    ($35, 1,000) ★★★

WINERY DATA

Case Production: 40,000. **Acres Owned:** 200 acres in Carneros (60 of the 200 acres are leased). **Varietals by Acre:** Chardonnay (109 acres), Pinot Blanc (5), Pinot Meunier (6), Pinot Noir (80). **Varietals Purchased:** Pinot Noir (Carneros).

This beautiful château's primary owner is Taittinger, the prestigious French Champagne producer, and its sparkling wines are uniformly ★★★-★★★★ performers. From its stately locale on Highway 121, Domaine Carneros is home to some of California's most delicate and elegant sparkling wines. The wines are made under the direction of Eileen Crane, who, after a stint at Domaine Chandon, helped build Gloria Ferrer, where she made its first wines. Domaine Carneros owns 140 acres, and leases another 60; Chardonnay and Pinot Noir (the latter being a new addition) are the principal grapes, with smaller amounts of Pinot Blanc and Pinot Meunier also grown. The Pinot Noir bottlings are off to a good start.

TASTING NOTES

PINOT NOIR CARNEROS (★★★)
1996: Smooth, ripe and moderately rich, with a pretty core of black cherry, plum and anise flavors and notes of mineral and leather. **88**
1995: Supple and complex, with a range of ripe, spicy cherry, plum and earthy notes that are focused. **88**
1994: Tight and appealing, with a band of plum and cherry flavors and a hint of spice. **87**

1993: Smooth, with a supple, polished texture; the elegant black cherry, vanilla and plum flavors turn silky. **90**

PINOT NOIR CARNEROS THE FAMOUS GATE (★★★)
1995: Silky and elegant, with pretty plum, wild berry and cherry flavors, framed by light, toasty oak. **88**
1994: Marked by herb, cherry, earth and mushroom flavors, it's gentle, supple and complex. **88**
1993: Medium-bodied and earthy, with a spicy edge to the ripe plum and black cherry fruit, turning tannic. **87**

DOMAINE CHANDON (★★★)

Yountville, Napa Valley
Founded: 1973. **Owner:** Louis Vuitton-Moët-Hennessey.
Winemaker: Dawnine Dyer.

MAJOR WINES: PRICE, CASES, RATING

Blanc de Noirs Carneros
    ($15, 125,000) ★★★
Brut Sonoma-Napa Counties
    ($15, 275,000) ★★★
Étoile Napa Valley
    ($31, 10,000) ★★★
Étoile Rosé Napa Valley
    ($34, 2,000) ★★★
Fleur de Vigne Napa-Sonoma Counties
    ($15, 3,000) ★★
Reserve Cuvée Napa County
    ($24, 20,000) ★★★

WINERY DATA
Case Production: 450,000. **Acres Owned:** 1,102 acres in Napa Valley and Sonoma County (427 in Napa Valley, 675 in Sonoma County). **Varietals by Acre:** Cabernet Sauvignon (48 acres), Chardonnay (222), Pinot Blanc (41), Pinot Meunier (103), Pinot Noir (670), other (18). **Varietals Purchased:** Chardonnay (Carneros, Russian River Valley), Pinot Blanc (Napa Valley, Carneros, Monterey), Pinot Meunier (Napa Valley), Pinot Noir (Carneros, Russian River Valley, Monterey).

In 1973, Moët & Chandon became the first French Champagne-maker to set its sights on a large-scale sparkling wine operation in California, settling in Napa Valley near the Veteran's Home in Yountville. The first vintages were made at Trefethen, but the operation moved in 1977, when a beautiful winery and surrounding grounds were completed. By the 1980s, Chandon was making 100,000 cases a year. About a half-dozen Champagne houses have since followed Moët's lead and built sparkling wine facilities in California, as have the two major Spanish cava makers, the Ferrer family (Freixenet in Spain, Gloria Ferrer in Carneros) and Codorniu (Codorniu Napa).

For more than two decades, Domaine Chandon has come to symbolize Moët's long-term commitment to international investment and uniformly high standards. Consistency of style is Chandon's strength, even as case production hovers around 450,000 cases. It is a steady, dependable brand whose only fault may be that it rarely takes chances with its cuvées. Much of this consistency is due to the winemaking skills of Dawnine Dyer, who joined the winery in 1976 and has been well trained by her French counterparts. The product mix features non-vintage Brut, Brut Cuvée, Blanc de Noirs, Étoile and Reserve. There's also a rosé which is marked by complex strawberry, cherry and vanilla notes.

DOMAINE DE LA TERRE ROUGE (★★★)
California Shenandoah Valley, Amador County
Founded: 1984. **Owner:** William and Jane O'Riordan Easton. **Winemaker:** William Easton. **Second Label:** Easton.

MAJOR WINES: PRICE, CASES, RATING
Enigma White Sierra Foothills
  ($16, 750)   ★★★
Noir Sierra Foothills
  ($16, 1,000)   ★★★
Noir Sierra Foothills Grande Année
  ($20, 1,000)   ★★★
Syrah Shenandoah Valley Sentinel Oak
  Vineyard
  ($25, 1,200)   ★★★
Syrah Sierra Foothills
  ($18, 400)   ★★★
Tête-a-Tête Red Sierra Foothills
  ($12, 1,000)   ★★
Viognier Shenandoah Valley
  ($25, 300)   ★★★

Easton Natoma Sauvignon Blanc Blend
  Sierra Foothills
  ($20, 800)   ★★

Easton Zinfandel Fiddletown
  ($20, 800)   ★★★
Easton Zinfandel Shenandoah Valley
  ($18, 1,500)   ★★★

ALSO PRODUCED
Mourvèdre Amador County ($16, 400); Muscat à Petits Grains ($15, 500); Vin Gris d'Amador Sierra Foothills ($9, 500); Easton Barbera Shenandoah Valley ($18, 500); Easton Zinfandel Amador County ($12, 1,500).

WINERY DATA
Case Production: 12,000. **Acres Owned:** 10 acres in Fiddletown. **Varietals by Acre:** Syrah (8 acres), Viognier (2). **Varietals Purchased:** Barbara (Shenandoah Valley), Cabernet Sauvignon (Sierra Foothills), Cinsault (Sierra Foothills), Marsanne (Sierra Foothills), Mourvèdre (Amador County), Roussanne (Sierra Foothills), Sauvignon Blanc (Sierra Foothills), Syrah (Sierra Foothills), Viognier (Sierra Foothills), Zinfandel (Shenandoah Valley).

The emergence of this Amador Foothills winery has been a welcome surprise; some delicious Rhône-style reds and whites are being produced here, proving that this area still has untapped potential. One-time San Francisco Bay Area wine merchant Bill Easton has developed a 10-acre vineyard in Fiddletown, and also uses purchased grapes for this 12,000-case winery. The reds, led by Syrah, dominate, but the Viognier is also very tasty, as is the Marsanne-Viognier-Roussanne blend called Enigma. The Noir Rhône blends are a mix of Grenache, Mourvèdre and Syrah; the 1994 Noir Grand Année (87 points) offered ripe plum, wild berry and complex sage notes. (The other red Rhône blend, Tête-a-Tête, comprises the same grapes, but is more for early drinking.)

Easton also produces Barbera, Sauvignon Blanc and Zinfandel, and keeps them separate from the Rhône-style Terre Rouge wines by bottling them under his Easton label. The Zinfandels—a Fiddletown and a Shenandoah Valley—are both complex, supple wines that show off the earthy, rustic prune and plum flavors of Amador County.

TASTING NOTES

SYRAH SIERRA FOOTHILLS (★★★): Shows the potential for this grape when it is properly grown and vinified.

DOMAINE MICHEL see MICHEL-SCHLUMBERGER

DOMAINE SAINT GEORGE (★-★★)
Sonoma County
Founded: 1985. **Owner:** Pan Magna Group. **Winemaker:** Bob Fredson. **Second Label:** Oak Vineyards, Cambiaso.

MAJOR WINES: PRICE, CASES, RATING
Cabernet Sauvignon Alexander Valley Premier Cuvée ($12, 4,000)	★★
Cabernet Sauvignon California Select Reserve ($8, 75,000)	★
Chardonnay California Select Reserve ($8, 90,000)	★
Chardonnay Chalk Hill Premiere Cuvée ($12, 7,000)	★★
Merlot Alexander Valley Premiere Cuvée ($12, 4,000)	★★
Merlot California Select Reserve ($8, 50,000)	★
Pinot Noir Santa Barbara County Premiere Cuvée ($13, 2,000)	★
Sauvignon Blanc California Select Reserve ($7, 40,000)	★

WINERY DATA
Case Production: 350,000. **Acres Owned:** 22 acres in Russian River Valley. **Varietals by Acre:** Cabernet Sauvignon (12 acres), Merlot (10). **Varietals Purchased:** Cabernet Sauvignon (Dry Creek Valley, Alexander Valley), Chardonnay (Alexander Valley, Dry Creek Valley, Chalk Hill, Monterey), Merlot (Alexander Valley).

Domaine Saint George produces Cabernet, Chardonnay, Merlot and Pinot Noir in the old Cambiaso winery in Russian River Valley. Two tiers of wines are produced—a California appellation Select Reserve, and an appellation-specific Premiere Cuvée—both of which are value-oriented. The Premiere Cuvée wines have a slight quality edge over the Select Reserve wines, though neither are terribly exciting. The 1996 Alexander Valley Merlot Premiere Cuvée (85 points) was the best in recent years, with pleasant, lightly herbal, lively fruit flavors and soft tannins.

DOMAINE SAINT GREGORY (★★)
Mendocino County
Founded: 1988. **Owner:** Gregory & Trudi Graziano. **Winemaker:** Gregory Graziano. **Second Label:** Monte Volpe.

MAJOR WINES: PRICE, CASES, RATING
Domaine Saint Gregory Pinot Blanc Mendocino ($15, 1,000)	★★
Domaine Saint Gregory Pinot Noir Mendocino ($18, 1,000)	★★
Monte Volpe Vineyards Barbera California ($12, 1,500)	★★
Monte Volpe Vineyards Dolcetto Mendocino ($16, 1,500)	★★
Monte Volpe Vineyards Moscato Mendocino ($10, 1,000)	★★
Monte Volpe Vineyards Nebbiolo Mendocino ($18, 600)	★★
Monte Volpe Vineyards Peppolino Mendocino ($30, 300)	★★
Monte Volpe Vineyards Pinot Bianco Mendocino ($12, 1,800)	★★
Monte Volpe Vineyards Pinot Grigio Mendocino ($14, 1,000)	★★
Monte Volpe Vineyards Sangiovese Mendocino ($18, 2,000)	★★
Monte Volpe Vineyards Tocai Friulano Mendocino ($14, 1,000)	★★

ALSO PRODUCED
Domaine Saint Gregory Pinot Noir Rosé Mendocino ($10, 100); Domaine Saint Gregory Valdiguié Mendocino ($10, 200); Monte Volpe Vineyards Arneis ($12, 300); Monte Volpe Vineyards Barbera Riserva ($18, 200); Monte Volpe Vineyards Sangiovese Riserva ($25, 300); Monte Volpe Vineyards Tanaro ($18, 200).

WINERY DATA
Case Production: 15,000. **Varietals Purchased:** Arneis (Mendocino County), Barbera (Mendocino County), Dolcetto

(Mendocino County), Montepulciano (Mendocino County), Moscato (Mendocino County), Nebbiolo (Mendocino County), Pinot Blanc (Mendocino County), Pinot Gris (Mendocino County), Pinot Noir (Mendocino County), Sangiovese (Mendocino County), Tocai Friulano (Mendocino County).

Gregory Graziano founded this winery in Ukiah in 1988, producing an eclectic lineup of wines that includes Pinot Blanc, Pinot Noir and Valdiguie from Mendocino and an assortment of Italian-style wines such as Moscato, Nebbiolo, Pinot Bianco and Sangiovese. The Italian-styled wines are bottled under the Monte Volpe brand.

DOMINUS ESTATE (★★★★★)
Yountville, Napa Valley
Founded: 1982. **Owner:** Christian Moueix. **Winemaker:** Jean-Claude Berrouet. **Second Label:** Napanook.

MAJOR WINES: PRICE, CASES, RATING
Dominus Estate Yountville
($90, 10,000)   ★★★★★

ALSO PRODUCED
Napanook Yountville ($30, 5,000).

WINERY DATA
Case Production: 15,000. **Acres Owned:** 122 acres in Napa Valley. **Varietals by Acre:** Cabernet Franc (15 acres), Cabernet Sauvignon (82), Merlot (20), Petit Verdot (5).

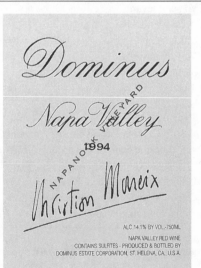

Dominus Estate began in 1982 as a highly publicized joint venture between Christian Moueix of Château Petrus and the daughters of John Daniel—Robin Lail and Marcia Smith—the owners of Napanook Vineyard, an enterprise which they inherited from their father (John Daniel also owned Inglenook through 1964). The partnership came in the wake of the even higher-profile Mondavi-Rothschild Opus One venture three years earlier, and underscored the Bordelais' admiration for Napa Valley's rich Cabernet heritage.

Dominus brought together Moueix's winemaking talents—honed and refined in Pomerol, where his family owns several esteemed châteaux—with that of Lail and Smith. A source of the fine Cabernet grapes used by Daniel during his glory days at Inglenook, the vineyard is known for producing dense and tannic wines which for years provided the backbone for many grand Inglenook Cask Cabernets.

Few California wines have divided the critics like the early Dominus bottlings, with their rich, earthy flavors and fairly massive tannins. Without a doubt, Dominus had a rugged first decade, as Moueix and his staff wrestled with a vineyard that yields rustic, often chewy wines. Their debut 1983 vintage—an unusually tannic year in Napa anyway—showed the signature of this vineyard in spades. In the years 1984 through 1986, efforts were made to refine the style and tame the tannins, with varying degrees of success. By 1987, Dominus was showing even more precision in its balance and flavor, and in years such as 1989, a difficult year for most Napa Cabernets, Dominus proved amazingly complex and well crafted. Vintages from the 1990s—particularly 1991 and 1994—show that Moueix and his winemaking team now have a much better handle on the vineyard and the wine.

In 1994, Lail and Smith bowed out of the Dominus venture, selling their interest to Moueix and leaving him as sole proprietor of the 122-acre Napanook property and the Dominus brand. Lail went on to form her own winery, Lail Vineyards. Dominus, meanwhile, remains worth collecting.

TASTING NOTES

DOMINUS ESTATE YOUNTVILLE (★★★★★): As distinctive and divisive a wine as is produced in Napa, but a true reflection of the *terroir*, and of what a vineyard has to offer. This wine is dense, dark, chewy and tannic, often with earthy, leathery notes, but it also has a core of rich currant and berry flavors. The best wines are the 1991 and 1994; the 1993 vintage was skipped, while the 1995 was clearly light for the vintage and the property.

1996: Bordeaux-like in style; ripe, polished, and rich, with complex currant, earth, cherry and berry flavors, and plenty of spicy, peppery notes. Finishes with polished tannins. **92**

1995: A lighter style, with a supple, polished texture and some vegetal notes that work their way into cherry and plum flavors. **88**

1994: Complex and concentrated, with a pretty, earthy core of anise and currant flavors, finishing with coffee and spice notes and fleshy tannins. **96**

1992: Smooth and supple, with silky tannins and a complex array of ripe plum, currant, mineral, sage and spice flavors. **92**

1991: Opens with earthy, cedary notes, but turns supple, with a core of currant, tobacco, mineral and anise flavors. **93**

1990: Big, rich and chewy, this is a high-extract wine packed with currant, mineral, earth and spice flavors of remarkable depth and breadth. It finishes with firm tannins, but is impeccably balanced. **93**

1989: Rich, dense and leathery, with a core of tight currant, earth, coffee, cedar and anise flavors, it's deeply concentrated and firmly tannic. The texture is smooth and silky. This wine has more balance and finesse than most 1989s. **92**

1988: Complex, with elegant flavors, including gamy notes, currant, anise and spice flavors, and leathery tannins. **87**

1987: Complex, with earthy currant, cherry, anise and mineral flavors that work well with the supple texture and fine length. **92**

1986: Rugged, with earthy, leathery notes, picking up complex mineral, currant and cedar flavors, turning dry. **88**

1985: A complex and harmonious wine that shows subtlety and finesse, with earthy currant, tar, cedar and tobacco flavors that are focused, finishing with smooth tannins. **88**

1984: Mature, with appealing currant, spice and cedar flavors, but also a firm dose of tannin. **85**

1983: Has developed nicely, with rich, earthy, tannic currant and tar flavors. Lively acidity keeps the flavors alive, and the texture is softening. **85**

DOVER CANYON WINERY (★★)
Paso Robles, San Luis Obispo County
Founded: 1992. **Owner:** Dan Panico. **Winemaker:** Dan Panico.

MAJOR WINES: PRICE, CASES, RATING
Cabernet Sauvignon Paso Robles
 ($18, 300)   ★★
Rhône Reserve
 ($17, 200)   ★★
Zinfandel Templeton Gap
 ($18, 600)   ★★

ALSO PRODUCED
Chardonnay Paso Robles Cougar Ridge Vineyard ($16,400); Menage Meritage Blend ($28, 300); Merlot Reserve Paso Robles ($17, 200); Roussanne Paso Robles ($20, 200); Viognier Paso Robles ($18, 200).

WINERY DATA
Case Production: 4,000. **Vineyard Designations:** Cougar Ridge Vineyard. **Varietals Purchased:** Cabernet Sauvignon (Paso Robles), Chardonnay (Paso Robles), Merlot (Paso Robles), Roussanne (Paso Robles), Syrah (Paso Robles), Viognier (Paso Robles), Zinfandel (Paso Robles).

This small new Paso Robles-based winery makes a variety of wines—from extracted, alcoholic Zinfandels, to well-structured, flavorful Cabernets and bright, effusively fruity Rhône-style white wines. While early releases have been good, it is too early to tell at this point where this winery is headed.

DRAXTON (★★)
Alexander Valley, Sonoma County
Founded: 1995. **Owner:** Carol & Mike Draxton. **Winemaker:** Mike Draxton. **Second Label:** El Roy.

MAJOR WINES: PRICE, CASES, RATING
Sauvignon Blanc Alexander Valley
 Big River Ranch
 ($13, 500)   ★★

ALSO PRODUCED
El Roy Red Alexander Valley ($20, 400); Merlot Alexander Valley Farrow Ranch ($25, 500).

WINERY DATA
Case Production: 1,500. **Acres Owned:** 85 acres in Alexander Valley. **Varietals by Acre:** Cabernet Franc (5 acres), Cabernet Sauvignon (12), Chardonnay (25), Malbec (3.5), Merlot (34), Petit Verdot (1.5), Syrah (4). **Vineyard Designations:** Big River Ranch (Sauvignon Blanc), Farrow Ranch (Merlot). **Varietals Purchased:** Sauvignon Blanc (Alexander Valley).

Mike Draxton worked as assistant winemaker with Daryl Groom at Geyser Peak for five years, and was winemaker for Geyser Peak's Canyon Road brand before he and his wife launched their own brand using grapes grown on their Alexander Valley vineyard. Grape growing is their primary business, and the winery is expected to expand slowly, as the brand becomes established. The 1995 Sauvignon Blanc (88 points) was clean and crisp, with minerally citrus flavors.

DREYER SONOMA WINERY (★★)
Sonoma County
Founded: 1980. **Owner:** Dreyer Family. **Winemaker:** Kerry Damskey. **Second Label:** Compass.

MAJOR WINES: PRICE, CASES, RATING
Cabernet Sauvignon Sonoma County
($11, 1,200) ★★
Chardonnay Sonoma County
($10, 5,000) ★★

ALSO PRODUCED
Compass Merlot ($9, 2,500).

WINERY DATA
Case Production: 10,000. **Acres Owned:** 120 acres in Sonoma County. **Varietals by Acre:** Cabernet Sauvignon (40 acres), Merlot (80). **Varietals Purchased:** Cabernet Sauvignon (Sonoma County), Chardonnay (Sonoma County).

Well-made, inexpensive wines of modest depth and flavor are the norm for this family-owned brand. The wines are made to the Dreyers' specifications by the Associated Vintage Group. The 1996 Sonoma County Cabernet (84 points) was a good value, with blackberry, herb and currant flavors and powdery tannins.

DRY CREEK VINEYARD (★★★)
Dry Creek Valley, Sonoma County
Founded: 1972. **Owner:** David S. Stare. **Winemaker:** Jeff McBride.

MAJOR WINES: PRICE, CASES, RATING
Cabernet Sauvignon Dry Creek Valley
($19, 11,000) ★★★
Cabernet Sauvignon Dry Creek Valley
Reserve
($27, 2,000) ★★★
Cabernet Sauvignon Sonoma County
($19, 11,000) ★★★
Chardonnay Sonoma County
($15, 24,000) ★★★
Chardonnay Sonoma County Reserve
($20, 8,500) ★★★
Chenin Blanc Clarksburg Dry
($8, 8,500) ★★
Fumé Blanc Dry Creek Valley Reserve
($16, 8,100) ★★★
Fumé Blanc Sonoma County
($12, 33,500) ★★★
Meritage Red Dry Creek Valley
($25, 5,000) ★★★
Merlot Dry Creek Valley Reserve
($30, 4,500) ★★★
Merlot Sonoma County
($19, 7,500) ★★
Zinfandel Sonoma County Old Vines
($16, 10,500) ★★★
Zinfandel Sonoma County Reserve
($25, 1,400) ★★★

WINERY DATA
Case Production: 120,000. **Acres Owned:** 138 acres (73 in Alexander Valley, 30 in Dry Creek Valley, 35 in Russian River Valley). **Varietals by Acre:** Cabernet Sauvignon (19 acres), Chardonnay (33), Merlot (18), Sauvignon Blanc (44), Zinfandel (24). **Varietals Purchased:** Cabernet Franc (Dry Creek Valley, Sonoma Valley), Cabernet Sauvignon (Dry Creek Valley, Alexander Valley, Knight's Valley), Chardonnay (Dry Creek Valley, Alexander Valley, Russian River Valley), Chenin Blanc (Clarksburg), Merlot (Dry Creek Valley, Alexander Valley), Petite Sirah (Dry Creek Valley, Sonoma Valley, Russian River Valley), Petit Verdot (Knights Valley, Sonoma Valley, Dry Creek Valley), Sauvignon Blanc (Dry Creek Valley, Alexander Valley), Zinfandel (Dry Creek Valley, Russian River Valley, Alexander Valley, Sonoma Valley).

When David Stare built Dry Creek Vineyards in 1972—the first winery to be constructed in Dry Creek Valley since the end of Prohibition—he initially focused on Chenin Blanc from the Delta and Sauvignon Blanc from Sonoma County. Stare, along with Robert Mondavi, deserves credit for championing Sauvignon Blanc through the 1970s and 1980s, raising its quality and bringing it the recognition it deserves. Dry Creek Vineyard still relies heavily on its Sonoma County Fumé Blanc and standard Sonoma County Chardonnay for nearly half of its 120,000-case output, but recently the reds have been more interesting. In tastings of older vintages, I've been impressed by how well the wines age and retain their elegance.

TASTING NOTES

CABERNET SAUVIGNON DRY CREEK VALLEY (★★★): Medium-bodied and well made for drinking young.
1996: Attractive for its assertive, up-front fruitiness, with plum, wild berry, black cherry and anise notes. **88**
1994: Solid, with a band of cherry, currant, herb and cedary oak flavors that finish with mild tannins. **86**
1993: Very ripe and cedary, with plum and cherry notes that are bright and jammy, finishing with dry tannins. **88**
1992: Elegant, smooth and polished, sporting refined cherry, currant, berry and spice notes. **89**

CABERNET SAUVIGNON DRY CREEK VALLEY RESERVE (★★★): Pleasantly fruity, with bright berry and raspberry flavors, a supple texture and mild tannins.
1995: Shows off ripe, spicy flavors and a center of wild berry, cherry and plum fruit, turning minty and tannic. **86**
1994: Of medium-weight, with ripe cherry, currant, anise and cedary flavors and soft, fleshy tannins. **87**
1993: Offers a decent core of wild berry, blackberry and cherry flavors, with crisp tannins a hint of dill from the oak. **83**

FUMÉ BLANC DRY CREEK VALLEY RESERVE (★★★): Bright, sometimes racy, with complex flavors.

FUMÉ BLANC SONOMA COUNTY (★★★): A touch grassier than the Reserve, but it is likewise well made.

MERITAGE RED DRY CREEK VALLEY (★★★): The finest of the red wines. Complex and refined, this wine is always very good, and often borders on outstanding.
1995: Showy, with its up-front cherry, spice, cedar and wild berry fruit, turning supple and harmonious. **89**
1994: Supple and elegant, with a cedary oak edge to the ripe plum and cherry flavors and fleshy tannins. **88**
1993: Effusive cherry, berry and currant flavors; a fruity, elegant style with supple tannins. **89**
1990: An herbal, oaky wine with ripe, chunky currant, plum and wild berry flavors. **89**
1988: Smooth and tasty, with a smoky, gamy edge to the well defined cherry and spice flavors. **86**
1987: Attractive for its balance of ripe currant, plum, anise and cherry flavors and toasty oak shadings. Still tannic, but shows a suppleness on the finish. **87**
1986: A ripe, jammy, moderately distinctive wine that has well-integrated, pleasant soy, cherry, cedar and coffee flavors. **80**
1985: Herb-scented red cherry and strawberry flavors compete with spicy oak for attention in this silky, concentrated wine. **88**

MERLOT DRY CREEK VALLEY RESERVE (★★★): The Reserve is riper and more full-bodied than the regular bottling.
1995: Tight and tannic, with a pleasant band of cedary currant, cherry, berry and spice flavors. **85**
1994: Smooth and herbal, with a cherry, currant and cedary oak edge and supple tannins. **88**
1993: Ripe and full, with firm tannins and ripe cherry and plum flavors, along with jammy anise and cedary oak notes. **87**

MERLOT SONOMA COUNTY (★★): Struggles for consistency, as is the case with most Merlots.

ZINFANDEL SONOMA COUNTY OLD VINES (★★★)
1995: A racy, spicy style with wild berry, jam, bay leaf and minty flavors that are a bit off-beat. **85**
1994: Ripe, smooth and juicy, with pretty black cherry, currant and plummy notes that turn smooth. **89**
1993: Well balanced, with a nice array of wild berry and cherry flavors and a sense of finesse. **88**
1991: Elegant, with a fine balance between its ripe plum and cherry fruit and smooth, supple tannins. **88**

ZINFANDEL SONOMA COUNTY RESERVE (★★★): Very ripe and jammy, with tarry cherry and raspberry flavors and fine tannins.
1995: Elegant, with ripe, almost jammy cherry, plum and blueberry fruit, pretty floral aromas and supple tannins. **88**
1994: Racy and well oaked, with a waxy, dill edge to the wild berry and black cherry core of fruit. **89**
1993: Of medium weight; smooth and spicy, with a touch of strawberry jam. **83**
1991: Deep and impressive, with a rich core of plum, cherry and raspberry flavors. **88**

DUCKHORN VINEYARDS (★★★–★★★★)
St. Helena, Napa Valley
Founded: 1976. **Owner:** Dan & Margaret Duckhorn and partners. **Winemaker:** Tom Rinaldi. **Second Label:** Decoy, Paraduxx, Goldeneye, King Eider.

MAJOR WINES: PRICE, CASES, RATING
Cabernet Sauvignon Napa Valley
($40, 5,000)   ★★★★
Merlot Napa Valley
($28, 12,000)   ★★★★
Merlot Napa Valley Estate Grown
($50, 300)   ★★★★
Merlot Napa Valley Howell Mountain
($40, 2,000)   ★★★★
Merlot Napa Valley Three Palms Vineyard
($45, 700)   ★★★
Sauvignon Blanc Napa Valley
($15, 15,000)   ★★★

WINERY DATA
Case Production: 50,000. **Acres Owned:** 229 acres (63 in Anderson Valley, 63 in Howell Mountain, 85 in Napa Valley, 21 in St. Helena). **Varietals by Acre:** Cabernet Franc (11 acres), Cabernet Sauvignon (52), Chardonnay (9), Gewürztraminer (2), Merlot (62), Petit Verdot (6), Pinot Noir (52), Sauvignon Blanc (10), Sémillon (7), Syrah (1), Viognier (2), Zinfandel (15). **Vineyard Designations:** Three Palms Vineyard (Merlot). **Varietals Purchased:** Cabernet Franc (Napa Valley, St. Helena, Carneros, Rutherford, Howell Mountain), Cabernet Sauvignon (Napa Valley, St. Helena, Carneros, Oakville, Howell Mountain), Chardonnay (Anderson Valley), Merlot (Napa Valley, St. Helena, Carneros, Rutherford, Oakville, Howell Mountain), Pinot Noir (Anderson Valley, Russian River Valley), Zinfandel (Anderson Valley, Napa Valley), Sauvignon Blanc (Napa Valley, Oakville), Sémillon (Napa Valley).

Duckhorn Vineyards specializes in hearty, rich and tannic red wines, notably Cabernet and Merlot. Each is well crafted and among Napa's finest, but the winery is best known as a champion of Merlot, the wine that first captured its imagination in the early 1970s. The winery produced its first wines in 1978.

Until recently, Duckhorn's three main red wines—Napa Valley Cabernet Sauvignon and Merlot, and a Three Palms Vineyard Merlot—were made entirely from purchased grapes grown from Carneros to Howell Mountain, and included such prizes as Spottswoode-grown Cabernet. It is Duckhorn's belief that given the right mixture of vineyards, grapes and final wine selection, one can craft a complex and consistent wine each year. Tom Rinaldi, the winemaker since 1978, has been exceedingly successful in achieving that aim. But Duckhorn also realized that control of grape sources is essential to quality, and the winery has since purchased its own property, which now totals 229 acres in vines, most of it Cabernet Sauvignon and Merlot.

TASTING NOTES

RED HOWELL MOUNTAIN
1992: Firm, ripe and intense, with tiers of currant, anise and mineral flavors and chewy tannins. **88**

CABERNET SAUVIGNON NAPA VALLEY (★★★★): Hits all the right notes, with consistently fine, complex and concentrated wines that are deftly balanced and improve with age.
1995: Complex but distinctive, with an elegant core of earthy clay, currant and black cherry flavors. **89**
1994: Immense, deeply concentrated and quite tannic, with currant, plum and berry flavors that linger. **90**

1993: Young and tight, with ripe cherry and cedary oak flavors that are pleasant, if austere. **87**

1992: Smooth and harmonious, with pretty plum, black cherry and currant notes, turning tannic and complex. **90**

1990: Young, firm and intense, with a core of rich, complex, concentrated currant, cherry, anise and toasty, buttery oak flavors. A wine of great harmony and finesse. **93**

1989: Firm and spicy, with lots of minty, earthy tobacco overtones to the ripe currant, cherry and raisin flavors. **83**

1988: Ripe, supple and balanced, with juicy black cherry, currant, spice and cedary notes. **88**

1987: Supple, complex, and smooth in texture, with an appealing core of currant, black cherry, anise, spice and cedar flavors. **92**

1986: Ripe, intense and concentrated, with rich, complex layers of earthy currant, mineral, plum, anise and cedar flavors. **94**

1985: Serves up a massive concentration of rich, deep fruits and tannins. The compact black currant, cedar and plum flavors are dense and structured. **92**

1984: Deep, powerful and tightly structured, with plum, black currant, cedar and earth flavors tightly woven together. **91**

1983: Mature, with cedar, plum, cherry and anise flavors that are ripe, supple and elegant. **86**

1982: Very impressive considering the vintage, displaying generous, ripe, supple, elegant plum, black cherry and currant flavors and a touch of chocolate. Not quite possessed of the depth of 1978 and 1980, but still well balanced. **88**

1981: Lean and mature, drinking well, with ample currant and spice flavors that are very attractive. **86**

1980: Impressive for its deep currant, mint and earth notes. **91**

1978: Tight, firm and tannic, but aging nicely, with a solid core of spicy currant and cedar flavors and a long, full, focused finish. **92**

Merlot Napa Valley (★★★★): While a less consistent wine than the Cabernet, this is still among California's finest. Very well crafted, if at times a bit heavy-handed; highly reliant on Cabernet for its tannic backbone. Ages well for up to 10 years.

1996: Earthy, gamy and leathery, with a twinge of currant and a slight bitterness; the core of Merlot fruit struggles to find a focus. **87**

1995: Complex in flavor, with currant, cedar, spice and anise notes; deftly balanced. **88**

1994: Starts out earthy, but works in complex cherry, currant, anise and cedar flavors, turning tannic. **90**

1993: Intense and well-focused, with a rich, supple core of earthy currant, herb and cherry flavors that are tannic. **90**

1992: Tart and grapey, with herb, spice, currant and cherry flavors that finish with a cedary oak edge. **88**

1990: Alluring, rich and complex, with currant, plum and herb characteristics. Tight and tannic, with strong oak and leather flavors. **89**

1989: Brimming with ripe, rich currant and black cherry flavors, this wine exhibits the vitality of youth and sustains it through the finish. **86**

1988: Bright and lively; medium-bodied, with pretty currant, cherry, herb and spice flavors that turn tannic. **86**

1987: Enormously deep, gutsy and complex, with rich, earthy currant, herb, toast and cedar flavors that are sharply focused and long on the finish. **93**

1986: Tight and lean, with austere cherry and currant flavors and gripping tannins. **85**

1985: Duckhorn's finest to date, it possesses deep, rich, intense, powerful, complex currant, black cherry, anise and herb flavors that are tight, focused and long on the finish. **95**

1984: Tight, firm and tannic, with earthy currant, cedar, herb and spice notes. Youthful, powerful and just reaching maturity. **92**

1983: Deep, rich, complex and earthy, but the tightly focused currant, berry, anise and herb flavors pour through. Still a bit tannic. **90**

1982: Rich, complex and focused, with ripe currant, earth, cedar and cherry flavors that are neatly woven together and a long, complex finish. **92**

1981: Intense and focused, with earthy, meaty currant and anise flavors backed by firm, tight tannins. **87**

1980: Ripe and fruity, with supple currant, cranberry, cedar and anise flavors that are bright and focused. The tannins are softening. **91**

1979: Elegant and supple; fully mature, with herb, olive, currant and black cherry flavors that are focused and lively. Impressive for its length and finesse. **91**

Merlot Napa Valley Estate Grown (★★★★)

1995: Dense, chewy, and rich, with a full array of earthy currant, mineral, anise, sage, tea and spice flavors. **92**

MERLOT NAPA VALLEY HOWELL MOUNTAIN (★★★)

1994: Firm in oak and tannin, the core of flavors is built around earthy currant, wild berry and cherry-laced fruit. **89**

1993: Lean and crisp, with a spicy, mineral edge to the earthy cherry and berry flavors. **88**

MERLOT NAPA VALLEY THREE PALMS VINEYARD

(★★★): Three Palms Vineyard renders an austere wine that often shows more tannin than fruit, but the style is distinctive and consistent.

1995: Trim, with crisp mineral and currant flavors that are tight and firmly tannic. **87**

1988: Tight and firm, with pretty currant, cranberry, tea and spice flavors that are well integrated and supported by firm tannins. Finishes with an earthy note. **87**

1987: Rich, concentrated and sharply focused, the currant, plum, chocolate, anise and vanilla flavors are bright and lively, with firm but smooth tannins. **90**

1986: Tough, dry and earthy, with barnyard flavors competing with the currant and berry notes. Backward and unevolved. **84**

1985: Sharply focused, deftly balanced, youthful and tight, with firm currant and black cherry flavors. A seam of elegance runs through this tight, tannic wine. **91**

1984: Ripe and supple, with pretty currant, berry and cherry notes, finishing with firm, dry tannins and oaky vanilla shadings. **87**

1983: Rich, complex and smoky, with tight, sharply focused currant, tar, anise and black cherry flavors. Enormously complex, earthy and concentrated. **92**

1981: An earthy wine; lean and focused, with oaky currant, spice, cedar and tobacco notes and firm tannins. **87**

1978: Ripe and fruity, with concentrated currant, plum and cherry flavors, finishing with firm tannins and good length. **88**

DUNCAN PEAK VINEYARDS (★★)

Mendocino County
Founded: 1986. **Owner:** Hubert & Resa Lenczowski.
Winemaker: Hubert & Resa Lenczowski.

MAJOR WINES: PRICE, CASES, RATING

Cabernet Sauvignon Mendocino County
($25, 500) ★★

WINERY DATA

Case Production: 500. **Acres Owned:** 8 acres in Mendocino County. **Varietals by Acre:** Cabernet Sauvignon (8 acres).

Attorney Hubert Lenczowski and his wife Resa produce 500 cases of Cabernet from a family-owned ranch near Hopland. While the wines are usually very good—like the 1995 Cabernet (87 points), which featured lovely notes of blueberry, herb and anise—they have never been outstanding.

DUNN VINEYARDS (★★★★★)

Howell Mountain, Napa Valley
Founded: 1979. **Owner:** Randy & Lori Dunn.
Winemaker: Randy Dunn.

MAJOR WINES: PRICE, CASES, RATING

Cabernet Sauvignon Howell Mountain
($45, 2,700) ★★★★★
Cabernet Sauvignon Napa Valley
($39, 1,700) ★★★★

WINERY DATA

Case Production: 5,000. **Acres Owned:** 14 acres in Howell Mountain. **Varietals by Acre:** Cabernet Sauvignon (11 acres), Petite Sirah (3). **Varietals Purchased:** Cabernet Sauvignon (Howell Mountain).

Randy Dunn worked at Caymus Vineyards from 1975 to 1984, helping to refine the style of its Special Selection Cabernet. In 1978, with the help of Caymus's owners, Charlie and Lorna Wagner, Dunn and his wife, Lori, bought and revived an old 5-acre Cabernet vineyard on Howell Mountain. The Dunns made their first Cabernet in 1979, with Randy Dunn working at Caymus on weekdays and at Dunn Vineyards on weekends. The Dunns gradually built their production up to 5,000 cases, roughly divided between an inky Howell Mountain Cabernet and an almost-as-inky Napa Valley bottling made from purchased grapes.

After the 1984 vintage, Dunn left Caymus and signed on as a consultant with several other wineries. By 1993, however, he had severed his ties with all clients in order to focus on his own winery. In 1991, the Dunns bought the old Park-Muscadine Vineyard, a 47-acre parcel with 15 acres in vines—mostly Zinfandel and Petite Sirah—and replanted the vineyard to Cabernet.

Dunn's Cabernets are massive, complex and enormously concentrated. Both the Napa Valley and Howell Mountain bottlings have been amazingly consistent over the years. (This was a hallmark of Dunn's work at Caymus, too.) The Napa Valley bottling owes part of its intensity to the healthy portion of Howell Mountain grapes that Dunn blends in for color and backbone. Even in off years, the strength of the Howell Mountain vineyard's personality has come through. Older vintages dating back to 1979 and 1980 are still deeply colored, youthful and vibrant and appear to have the stuffing to age 25 to 30 years—maybe even longer.

TASTING NOTES

CABERNET SAUVIGNON HOWELL MOUNTAIN (★★★★★): Uncommonly dark and immense, with tiers of earthy currant, mineral, spice and cedar flavors. While tannic, it's also richly fruity; built for the long haul, it ages well.

1995: Austere, with firm tannins, this tightly wound wine needs time to unfold, but when it does, it reveals layers of dense currant, anise, mineral, sage and spice, tightening up on the finish. **93**

1994: A big, ripe, earthy style that manages to stuff plenty of currant, mineral, black cherry and spicy fruit into the bottle. **91**

1993: Tight; marked by cedary flavors, it works its way into a core of currant, sage, mineral and spice, turning tannic. **90**

1990: Dark in color, with very ripe, opulent and fleshy fruit flavors and an oaky edge, but it's tightly wound and compact now, finishing with chewy tannins and a burst of cherry and mineral. **92**

1989: Youthful, dark, tart and potent, showing layers of intense currant, anise, black cherry and cedar flavors. Has an earthy, oaky edge and is uncommonly tight and focused for an '89. **91**

1988: Shows a fine depth, richness and concentration, with a core of earthy currant, mineral, and raspberry notes. **89**

1987: Dark, ripe, intense and hard-edged; packed with a rich, earthy core of currant, mineral, anise, sage and cedar flavors. **92**

1986: Big, ripe, intense and expressive, with tiers of concentrated, earthy currant, mineral, cedar and spice flavors that turn elegant. **94**

1985: Tight, firm and structured, with compact, deeply concentrated currant, anise and floral flavors. **91**

1984: A bold, rich, dramatic wine, packed with dense, chewy, deeply concentrated plum, currant and anise flavors. Fruit pours through on the finish. **96**

1983: Tart and earthy, also quite tannic, but loaded with currant, spice and cherry flavors. The finish is tannic too, but the fruit hangs in there. **91**

1982: Remains the star of the vintage, with its core of rich fruit and earthiness. Packed with complex currant and black cherry flavors. **94**

1981: Tight and compact, with deep, powerful, chewy currant and black cherry flavors. The tannins are thick but elegant and the finish picks up a touch of earthiness. Youthful and impressive. **93**

1980: Massive and inky, this wine is packed with ripe plum, currant and black cherry flavors and pretty spice and cinnamon scents. Won't shortchange you on tannin either. **95**

1979: Sharply focused, with deep, rich, thick layers of fruit that echo plum, cassis and black currant flavors. Firm but polished, it's mature and drinkable now but should hold up through the next decade with ease. **92**

CABERNET SAUVIGNON NAPA VALLEY (★★★★): Shares many of the Howell Mountain's characteristics and can rival it in some years, but it's a shade lighter and matures more quickly.

1995: Tight, with an austere band of cedar, currant, mineral and sage flavors, finishing with firm, earthy tannins. Needs some time. **89**

1994: Inky dark, intense and tannic, packing in a tightly wound core of currant, mineral, plum and earthy flavors. **88**

1993: A lean, muscular style, with the cedary oak, currant, anise and spice flavors struggling with the tannins. **89**

1992: Grapey; a high-extract style, with rich currant, mineral, leather and herb flavors and chewy tannins. **88**

1991: Despite its deep color, firm tannins and fruit concentration, this wine is still rough and tumble, with earthy, oaky flavors that override the backward berry and currant notes. In two tastings, this wine showed more like a barrel sample than a finished wine. **90**

1990: Dense, ripe and concentrated, with a tough edge of tannin but plenty of berry, currant and plum flavors showing through. A massive wine that holds together nicely. **92**

1989: Deep, dark and tannic, this is an enormously concentrated and intense wine that packs in more power and flavor than most 1989s. It has rich currant, herb, mineral and spicy berry flavors and firm tannins. **89**

1988: Youthful and unevolved but showing the same strength of character found in other Dunn Napa Valley bottlings. Packs in plenty of black cherry, currant and raspberry flavors, finishing with firm tannins. **90**

1987: A bold, rich, dramatic wine with loads of raspberry, plum and black cherry flavors. Elegant, refined, and beautifully balanced. **90**

1986: Remarkably elegant and concentrated, with pure, ripe plum and currant flavors. Picks up a touch of mint and bay leaf on the finish, and it's tannic, but the fruit comes through on the finish. **93**

1985: Tough and tannic in this tasting, but with a core of rich, firm plum and currant flavors. The finish is long and tannic. **93**

1984: Broad, rich and complex, with tiers of plum, black cherry, currant and spice flavors. Wonderful balance and depth of flavor. The fruit intensity builds on the finish. **93**

1983: A very complete '83, with tart, ripe black cherry and currant flavors. Has the vintage's tannic edge and may always be a bit tannic, but overall it's complex and intriguing. **91**

1982: The earthy tar and rose petal aromas are mature, with soft tannins, but there are plenty of deep, rich plum and black cherry aromas and flavors to back it up. Has peaked. **91**

DUNNEWOOD VINEYARDS & WINERY (★-★★)
Mendocino County
Founded: 1988. **Owner:** Canandaigua Wine Co. **Winemaker:** George Phelan.

MAJOR WINES: PRICE, CASES, RATING
Cabernet Sauvignon North Coast
  ($8, 34,000) ★
Chardonnay North Coast
  ($8, 100,000) ★
Merlot North Coast
  ($8, 55,000) ★
Pinot Noir North Coast
  ($7, 7,500) ★
Zinfandel Mendocino
  ($7, 8,000) ★

ALSO PRODUCED
Cabernet Sauvignon Alexander Valley Dry Silk ($11, 3,500); Cabernet Sauvignon Napa Valley Dry Silk ($11, 3,500); Chardonnay Carneros Dry Silk ($11, 8,000); Sauvignon Blanc Mendocino ($7, 5,900); White Zinfandel California ($6, 6,500).

WINERY DATA
Case Production: 250,000. **Acres Owned:** 11 acres in Mendocino. **Varietals by Acre:** Chardonnay (11 acres). **Varietals Purchased:** Cabernet Sauvignon (Mendocino), Chardonnay (Mendocino), Merlot (Mendocino), Pinot Noir (Mendocino), Sauvignon Blanc (Mendocino), Zinfandel (Mendocino).

This is not a joint venture between Dunn and Spottswoode, but a brand introduced in 1988 by Guild Wineries. It is now part of the Canandaigua Wine Co. The quality of its wines—Cabernet, Chardonnay, Merlot and Zinfandel—has, unfortunately, slowly eroded over the years. The Cabernet, for instance, has gone from a Napa Valley appellation to a North Coast appellation. All of the wines are made in Mendocino. Sauvignon Blanc and Pinot Noir are also part of the 250,000-case production, which could easily get larger or smaller in coming years.

DUNNING VINEYARDS (★★)
Paso Robles, San Luis Obispo County
Founded: 1994. **Owner:** Dunning Family. **Winemaker:** Robert Dunning.

MAJOR WINES: PRICE, CASES, RATING
Cabernet Sauvignon Paso Robles
  Westside
  ($15, 350) ★★
Chardonnay Paso Robles Westside
  ($15, 350) ★★
Merlot Paso Robles Westside
  ($18, 300) ★★

WINERY DATA
Case Production: 1,000. **Acres Owned:** 16 acres in Paso Robles. **Varietals by Acre:** Cabernet Franc (1), Cabernet Sauvignon (3), Chardonnay (10), Merlot (2).

Robert Dunning produces small lots of estate-grown Cabernet, Chardonnay and Merlot, all of which have been rustic but flavorful. The reds have been the best; the 1995 Cabernet (87 points) was supple, with black cherry flavors, and the 1996 Merlot (86) displayed smoky licorice, black cherry and herb notes.

DURNEY VINEYARDS (★-★★)
Carmel Valley, Monterey County
Founded: 1968. **Owner:** Durney Winery Inc. **Winemaker:** Rex Smith. **Second Label:** Cachagua.

MAJOR WINES: PRICE, CASES, RATING

Cabernet Sauvignon Carmel Valley ($25, 6,000)	★★
Chardonnay Carmel Valley ($18, 3,000)	★★
Pinot Noir Carmel Valley ($18, 350)	★
Cachagua Cabernet Sauvignon Cuvée Carmel Valley ($15, 6,000)	★
Cachagua Chardonnay Carmel Valley ($12, 1,000)	★

ALSO PRODUCED
Chenin Blanc Carmel Valley ($10, 3,000); Late Harvest Riesling ($12, 700).

WINERY DATA
Case Production: 20,000. **Acres Owned:** 92 acres in Carmel Valley. **Varietals by Acre:** Cabernet Sauvignon (28 acres), Chardonnay (28), Chenin Blanc (27), Merlot (9).

Durney Vineyard was the long-time dream of Dorothy and the late William Durney (William died in 1989). In 1968, the Durneys were among the first to plant grapes in Carmel Valley, on property they bought in 1954. Today, the vineyard rises to 1,200 feet, and is planted mostly to Cabernet, Chardonnay, Chenin Blanc and Merlot.

While the style of the Cabernet was once deliberate and consistent, the wines now seem to be overly tannic and hollow. I've tasted these Cabernets on many occasions, and tannins do not frighten me, but these wines are simply too chewy and rustic to ever come into balance. Closer attention must be paid to the winemaking if this winery wants to be given serious consideration.

EASTON see DOMAINE DE LA TERRE ROUGE

EBERLE WINERY (★★★)
Paso Robles, San Luis Obispo County
Founded: 1984. **Owner:** Ltd. Partnership - Gary Eberle, General Partner. **Winemaker:** Bill Sheffer.

MAJOR WINES: PRICE, CASES, RATING

Barbera Paso Robles Steinbeck ($22, 300)	★★
Cabernet Sauvignon Paso Robles Estate ($20, 6,500)	★★
Chardonnay Paso Robles Estate ($14, 2,500)	★★
Muscat Canelli Paso Robles Estate ($10, 1,500)	★★
Syrah Paso Robles Fralich ($18, 1,000)	★★★
Syrah Paso Robles Steinbeck ($18, 1,800)	★★★
Zinfandel Paso Robles Sauret ($18, 1,500)	★★★
Zinfandel Paso Robles Steinbeck ($16, 500)	★★

ALSO PRODUCED
Côtes-du-Robles Red Paso Robles ($13, 2,000); Glenrose Viognier Paso Robles ($22, 350); Laudidsen Counoise Paso Robles ($11, 750).

WINERY DATA
Case Production: 19,000. **Acres Owned:** 40 acres in Paso Robles. **Varietals by Acre:** Cabernet Sauvignon (20 acres), Chardonnay (16), Muscat Canelli (4). **Vineyard Designations:** Fralich (Syrah), Sauret (Zinfandel), Steinbeck (Syrah, Zinfandel). **Varietals Purchased:** Barbera (Paso Robles), Counoise (Paso Robles), Grenache (Paso Robles), Mourvèdre (Paso Robles), Syrah (Paso Robles), Viognier (Paso Robles), Zinfandel (Paso Robles).

Former Penn State defensive tackle Gary Eberle became involved in Paso Robles winemaking in 1977 with the founding of Estrella River Winery, which has since been re-made into the home of Meridian Vineyards. After some success with several wine varieties, Eberle departed following a family dispute and started his own winery in 1981, producing Paso Robles-grown Cabernet, Chardonnay, Muscat, Syrah and Zinfandel.

To my taste, the two best wines are the dark, rich Zinfandel from Sauret Vineyard and the supple Syrahs from Fralich and Steinbeck vineyards. His Cabernet has shown promise at times, particularly the 1991 Paso Robles Reserve (91 points), but is variable in quality. The Chardonnay is the least interesting, while the off-dry Muscat and Viognier appear to be tasting room wines aimed at visitors rather than serious wines. Look for the Syrah and the Zinfandel.

TASTING NOTES

SYRAH PASO ROBLES FRALICH (★★★)
1993: Dark, ripe and intense, with a rich, earthy edge to the supple black cherry and currant flavors. Turns complex on the finish, where the toasty oak folds in. **89**

SYRAH PASO ROBLES STEINBECK (★★★)
1995: Ripe, rich and concentrated, with supple layers of plum, wild berry, cherry and spice. **88**

ZINFANDEL PASO ROBLES SAURET (★★★)
1996: Firmly tannic; ripe, with black cherry and wild berry fruit, turning even earthier and more tannic on the finish. **85**
1995: Serves up lots of ripe, juicy cherry and wild berry flavors and a nice pepper and anise edge. **90**
1994: Dusty and earthy, with complex anise, cherry and berry flavors that are polished. **87**

ECHELON VINEYARDS (★★)
Central Coast
Founded: 1998. **Owner:** Chalone Wine Group Ltd.
Winemaker: Larry Brooks.

MAJOR WINES: PRICE, CASES, RATING
Chardonnay Central Coast
($12, 68,000) ★★

Pinot Noir Central Coast
($13, 23,000) ★★

ALSO PRODUCED
Merlot Central Coast ($12, 45,000).

WINERY DATA
Case Production: 127,000. **Varietals Purchased:** Chardonnay (Central Coast), Merlot (Central Coast), Pinot Noir (Central Coast).

This new value-oriented brand of wines from the Chalone Wine Group focuses on Chardonnay, Merlot and Pinot Noir made from Central Coast grapes. The debut wines are good values.

TOM EDDY (★★★★)
Napa Valley
Founded: 1990. **Owner:** Tom & Kerry Eddy.
Winemaker: Tom Eddy.

MAJOR WINES: PRICE, CASES, RATING
Cabernet Sauvignon Napa Valley
($60, 1,000) ★★★★

WINERY DATA
Case Production: 1,000. **Varietals Purchased:** Cabernet Sauvignon (Diamond Mountain, Dry Creek Valley, Howell Mountain, Napa Valley).

Tom Eddy, one-time winemaker for The Christian Brothers and Souverain, started his own wine brand with the 1991 vintage, and now produces 1000 cases of Cabernet Sauvignon. The grapes come from three vineyards—Bella Vista on Diamond Mountain, Vyborny Ranch in Oakville and Beatty Ranch on Howell Mountain; the blend includes about 10 percent Vyborny Ranch Merlot. A Napa Chardonnay is set to follow. Production is expected to grow to 2,500 cases by 2000.

TASTING NOTES

CABERNET SAUVIGNON NAPA VALLEY (★★★★): Strives for elegance and finesse and succeeds, with ripe, complex flavors and supple tannins. The 1991 is aging very well.
1995: Seductive, smooth and polished, with currant, anise, cherry, sage and leathery notes, finishing with a

complex array of flavors, including a touch of coffee. **92**
1994: Restrained, with understated but complex black cherry, tart plum, spice and wildberry flavors that linger on the finish. **90**
1993: Lean and trim, with a pretty, earthy edge to the ripe currant and berry flavors, picking up leather and cedar notes on the finish. **90**
1992: Attractive plum, herb, cherry and cedary oak flavors finish with firm tannins. **88**
1991: Rich, supple and complex, with an array of pretty plum, currant, black cherry, anise and mineral flavors, finishing with smooth, polished tannins. **91**

EDGEWOOD (★★)
Napa Valley
Founded: 1994. **Owner:** Golden State Vintners.
Winemaker: Eric Laumann. **Second Label:** Monthaven.

MAJOR WINES: PRICE, CASES, RATING
Edgewood Cabernet Franc Napa Valley
($20, 2,000) ★★
Edgewood Cabernet Sauvignon
Napa Valley
($20, 4,000) ★★
Edgewood Malbec Napa Valley
($20, 1,000) ★★
Edgewood Merlot Napa Valley
($20, 4,000) ★★
Edgewood Petite Sirah Napa Valley
($15, 1,000) ★★
Edgewood Zinfandel Napa Valley
($15, 2,000) ★★

Monthaven Cabernet Franc Napa Valley
($10, 5,000) ★★
Monthaven Cabernet Sauvignon
Napa Valley
($10, 10,000) ★★
Monthaven Chardonnay Napa Valley
($10, 10,000) ★★
Monthaven Sauvignon Blanc
Napa Valley
($7, 1,000) ★★
Monthaven Syrah California
($10, 3,000) ★★

Monthaven Viognier California
($10, 3,000) ★★

ALSO PRODUCED
Edgewood Napa Valley Captains Cuvée ($30, 500); Edgewood Petit Verdot Napa Valley ($20, 500).

WINERY DATA
Case Production: 50,000. **Acres Owned:** 30 acres in Napa Valley. **Varietals by Acre:** Cabernet Sauvignon (30 acres). **Varietals Purchased:** Cabernet Franc (Napa Valley), Cabernet Sauvignon (Napa Valley), Malbec (Napa Valley), Merlot (Napa Valley), Petite Sirah (Napa Valley), Petit Verdot (Napa Valley), Zinfandel (Napa Valley).

Edgewood is owned by Golden State Vintners, a wine corporation which produces a number of bulk-style wines and controls 10,030 vineyard acres, most of which are located in the Central Valley. Concentrating on rustic, tannic Napa Valley red wines, Edgewood has had some success, particularly with Cabernet and Merlot, but the direction of its style and quality is still unclear. The 1994 vintage was a high point, with most wines scoring in the high 80s. The 1994 Cabernet (88 points) was austere but well-focused, with complex currant, plum and spice notes.

The second label, Monthaven, tends to be a better value, but the wines, like Edgewood's, are rustic, with tannic, earthy reds and minerally, earthy and occasionally coarse white wines. The 1995 Syrah California (87 points) was rich and smoky with a slight bitterness, while the 1996 Viognier California (85) showed bright, crisp grapefruit and pineapple flavors.

EDMEADES VINEYARDS (★★★)
Anderson Valley, Mendocino County
Founded: 1962. **Owner:** Jess Jackson. **Winemaker:** Van Williamson.

MAJOR WINES: PRICE, CASES, RATING
Chardonnay Anderson Valley
($18, 7,400) ★★★
Gewürztraminer Anderson Valley
($16, 446) ★★★
Pinot Noir Anderson Valley
($20, 5,700) ★★★

Zinfandel Mendocino
(\$18, 9,000) ★★★
Zinfandel Mendocino Ciapusci
(\$25, 400) ★★★
Zinfandel Mendocino Zeni
(\$25, 650) ★★★
Zinfandel Russian River Valley
Hartford Court
(Discontinued) ★★★

ALSO PRODUCED
Petite Sirah Anderson Valley Eaglepoint (\$NA, NA);
Zinfandel Mendocino Ridge (\$NA, NA).

WINERY DATA
Case Production: 25,200. **Acres Owned:** 62 acres in Anderson Valley. **Varietals by Acre:** Chardonnay (34 acres), Pinot Noir (28). **Vineyard Designations:** Ciapusci Vineyard (Zinfandel), Eaglepoint Ranch (Petite Sirah), Zeni Vineyard (Zinfandel). **Varietals Purchased:** Chardonnay (Anderson Valley), Gewürztraminer (Anderson Valley), Petite Sirah (Anderson Valley), Pinot Noir (Anderson Valley), Zinfandel (Mendocino).

Edmeades is now part of Kendall-Jackson's portfolio of wineries. Donald Edmeades planted several varieties of grapes in Anderson Valley in the late 1960s, but it wasn't until 1972, after his death, that his son Deron started a winery. Jed Steele, who went on to greater fame with Kendall-Jackson and now his own Steele Wines, was one of the first winemakers at Edmeades.

This small winery initially focused on vineyard-designated Zinfandels, among other wines, creating reputations for Zeni, DuPratt and Pacini vineyards as fine Zinfandel sources. In 1988, Jackson bought the winery and has since replanted its 62 acres of vines to Chardonnay and Pinot Noir. Today's wine lineup also includes Mendocino Zinfandel (carrying the Zeni, Ciapusci and Hartford vineyards designations), and Gewürztraminer made in a vivid style, with litchi, rose petal and spice flavors. Quality across the board remains high, with distinctive, *terroir*-driven wines. On the whole, these wines are worth buying, especially the Zinfandels.

TASTING NOTES

CHARDONNAY ANDERSON VALLEY (★★★): Clean and complex, with both 1994 and 1995 scoring 88 points.

PINOT NOIR ANDERSON VALLEY (★★★): Very appealing, with juicy fruit and earthy mineral flavors.
1996: Ripe, with juicy plum and strawberry flavors; turns rich and complex on the finish, with lots of fruity notes. **88**

ZINFANDEL MENDOCINO CIAPUSCI (★★★): Some vintage variations in terms of density and tannins, but usually the cherry- and berry-laced flavors shine through.
1996: Lots of supple cherry and wild berry flavors that are plush with spice, anise and cedary notes and mild tannins. **88**

ZINFANDEL MENDOCINO ZENI (★★★): Marked by classic peppery Zinfandel notes, it can also run to the tannic side.
1996: Peppery, with earthy, tar, raspberry and wild berry flavors; made in a distinctive style, with firm, dry tannins. **88**
1993: Tight and firm, with a hard tannic edge. The chewy core of earthy raspberry and spice takes a while to work through, but it turns more palatable on the finish, where it picks up oak and peppery notes. **88**

ZINFANDEL RUSSIAN RIVER VALLEY HARTFORD COURT (★★★): The 1994 (92 points) was a real stunner, with buttery oak buttressing the core of cherry, currant and herb-laced flavors.

EDMUNDS ST. JOHN (★★★)
Alameda County
Founded: 1985. **Owner:** Steve Edmunds & Cornelia St. John. **Winemaker:** Steve Edmunds.

MAJOR WINES: PRICE, CASES, RATING
Les Côtes Sauvages Red Sonoma/Mendocino
(\$20, 500) ★★★
Syrah Sonoma County Fenaughty Vineyard
(\$30, 300) ★★★
Syrah Sonoma Valley Durell Vineyard
(\$30, 700) ★★★
Zinfandel Amador County
(Discontinued) ★★★

ALSO PRODUCED
Sangiovese El Dorado Matagrano Vineyard (\$NA, 300); Syrah El Dorado County (\$20, 3500); Syrah Sonoma Valley Parmelee Hill (\$30, 500); Viognier Sonoma Valley Durell Vineyard (\$NA, 300).

WINERY DATA**Case Production:** 4,000. **Acres Owned:** 5 acres in El Dorado. **Varietals by Acre:** Syrah (5 acres). **Vineyard Designations:** Durell Vineyard (Syrah, Viognier), Fenaughty Vineyard (Syrah), Parmelee Hill (Syrah), Matagrano Vineyard (Sangiovese). **Varietals Purchased:** Grenache (Mendocino County), Sangiovese (El Dorado County), Syrah (Sonoma Valley, El Dorado County), Viognier (Sonoma Valley).

Steve Edmunds was one of the original Rhône Rangers, and he has doggedly pursued old-vine vineyards throughout California. His search has led him to Placerville in the Sierra Nevada foothills, and to Knights Valley, Sonoma Valley, Mount Veeder and Oakley in Contra Costa County. He has crafted many exciting wines in the process, using Syrah from Durell Vineyard, Grenache, Zinfandel, Carignane, Mourvèdre, Viognier and others. The down side to his vineyard discoveries, however, is that other wineries often move in on his grape sources once they taste how good his wines are.

Edmunds's best wines have been the Durell Syrah, a Zinfandel, and a Rhône blend he calls Les Côtes Sauvages. His eclectic product mix varies each year. He'll often introduce surprises into the lineup, finding small batches of grapes and vinifying them into exciting wines, as he has done with rich and complex bottlings of Pinot Grigio and Viognier. The winery is housed in a warehouse between Berkeley and Oakland; production hovers around 4,000 cases. Don't be surprised by anything that shows up under his label.

TASTING NOTES

SYRAH SONOMA VALLEY DURELL VINEYARD (★★★): Typically well crafted, rich, meaty and peppery.
1996: A rustic style that's earthy and gamy, with leather, pepper and mineral flavors preceding a core of meaty plum and berryish flavors that stumble toward the finish line, turning tannic. **87**
1995: Dark color, with rich, complex, meaty currant, plum and wild berry flavors that are tightly wound, finishing with firm but polished tannins. **88**
1994: Dark, ripe and peppery, with a leathery edge to the plum wild berry flavors. Finishes with firm tannins. **87**
1991: Another superb Syrah that combines tight, firm, rich and opulent currant and raspberry flavors with pretty oak and toast shadings. **91**

1990: Bold, rich and compelling, with ripe, opulent currant and raspberry flavors, finishing with a spicy, complex aftertaste. Very impressive. **90**

ZINFANDEL AMADOR COUNTY (★★★): Manages to deliver flavor without heavyweight tannins.
1995: Serves up a medley of cherry, berry and spice flavors. **86**

EDNA VALLEY VINEYARD (★★★)
Edna Valley, San Luis Obispo County
Founded: 1980. **Owner:** Chalone Wine Group Ltd., in partnership with Paragon Vineyard Company. **Winemaker:** Clayton R. Brock. **Second Label:** Cellar Master's Selection.

MAJOR WINES: PRICE, CASES, RATING
Chardonnay Edna Valley Paragon Vineyard
($17, 110,000) ★★★
Pinot Noir Edna Valley Paragon Vineyard
($19, 7,000) ★★

ALSO PRODUCED
Brut Edna Valley ($25, 400); Chardonnay Edna Valley Paragon Vineyard Reserve ($23, 2,500); Muscat Canelli Santa Barbara County Carrari Vineyard Winemaker's Selection Label ($9, 800); Rosé Edna Valley Paragon Vineyard Vin Rouge ($12, 635); Syrah Santa Ynez Valley Fess Parker Vineyard Winemaker's Selection Label ($20, 1,000); Viognier Paso Robles Fralich Vineyard Winemaker's Selection Label ($18, 1,000).

WINERY DATA
Case Production: 120,000. **Acres Owned:** 560 acres in Edna Valley (owned by Paragon Vineyards Company). **Varietals by Acre:** Chardonnay (500 acres), Pinot Noir (60). **Vineyard Designations:** Paragon Vineyard (Chardonnay, Pinot Noir), Fess Parker Vineyard (Syrah), Fralich Vineyard (Viognier). **Varietals Purchased:** Muscat Cannelli (Santa Barbara County), Viognier (Paso Robles), Syrah (Santa Ynez Valley).

Edna Valley Vineyards grew out of the Niven family's Paragon Vineyards. They began planting in the early 1970s, developing several hundred acres, most of them Chardonnay. In 1980, Chalone Vineyards began buying this Chardonnay and bottling it under the Edna Valley label. The two interests eventually formed a joint venture, and by 1990 Paragon was closely tied to the

Chalone Wine Group, owning 560 acres of vineyards, 500 of which are planted to Chardonnay. The Chardonnay has been variable, but the 1995 and 1996 vintages were better and more consistent.

TASTING NOTES

CHARDONNAY EDNA VALLEY PARAGON VINEYARD (★★★): Recent vintages are more elegant and refined than those from the 1980s and early 1990s, which tended to be heavier.
1996: Clean and refreshing, with lively, well focused pear, apple and peach fruit flavors and spicy nuances. **89**
1995: Distinct and focused, with ripe peach, fig and apricot flavors and light oak shadings. **89**

MERRY EDWARDS (★★★)
Russian River Valley, Sonoma County
Founded: 1997. **Owner:** Meredith Vineyard and Estate. **Winemaker:** Merry Edwards.

WINES PRODUCED: PRICE, CASES
Pinot Noir Russian River Valley ($28, 1,750); Pinot Noir Russian River Valley Olivet Lane ($42, 450); Pinot Noir Russian River Valley Windsor Gardens ($NA, 250).

WINERY DATA
Case Production: 2,400. **Acres Owned:** 24 acres in Russian River Valley. **Varietals by Acre:** Pinot Noir (24 acres). **Vineyard Designations:** Olivet Lane (Pinot Noir). **Varietals Purchased:** Pinot Noir (Russian River Valley).

Merry Edwards, who has been a winemaker for 25 years, started anew in 1997, using grapes from a 24-acre vineyard in Russian River, and from Olivet Lane. Her first releases were very good. She has worked for Mount Eden, Matanzas Creek and B.R. Cohn, and for a brief time owned The Merry Vintners. Edwards knows how to make good wines; it is worth watching to see if she can do it, consistently, again.

EHLERS GROVE (★-★★★)
Napa Valley
Founded: 1993. **Owner:** Tony Cartlidge, Glenn Browne, Greenfield Wine Co. **Winemaker:** Paul Moser. **Second Label:** Cartlidge & Browne.

MAJOR WINES: PRICE, CASES, RATING
Ehlers Grove Cabernet Sauvignon
Napa Valley Winery Reserve
($23, 300)   ★★★
Ehlers Grove Chardonnay Napa Valley
Winery Reserve
($25, 250)   ★★★
Ehlers Grove Sauvignon Blanc Napa Valley
Winery Reserve
($15, 500)   ★★★

Cartlidge & Browne Chardonnay California
($10, 25,000)   ★
Cartlidge & Browne Pinot Noir California
($12, 2,500)   ★
Cartlidge & Browne Zinfandel California
($10, 7,500)   ★

ALSO PRODUCED
Ehlers Grove Dolcetto Napa Valley ($15, 500).

WINERY DATA
Case Production: 36,500. **Varietals Purchased:** Cabernet Sauvignon (Napa Valley), Chardonnay (Carneros, Napa Valley), Dolcetto (Napa Valley), Merlot (Lodi), Pinot Noir (Carneros, Sonoma County), Sauvignon Blanc (Napa Valley), Zinfandel (Lodi).

Most of this winery's production is directed to their Cartlidge & Browne label, which focuses on simple, value-oriented wines made from grapes purchased throughout California. Showing more flavor and complexity are the Ehlers Grove wines, which are made in small lots (500 cases or less) and are more expensive. The Ehlers Grove wines can be very good; especially fine was the ripe, rich 1996 Chardonnay (88 points) and the bright, citrus-flavored 1996 Sauvignon Blanc (88).

VOLKER EISELE (★★★)
Chiles Valley District, Napa Valley
Founded: 1991. **Owner:** Volker & Liesel Eisele. **Winemaker:** Volker Eisele.

MAJOR WINES: PRICE, CASES, RATING
Cabernet Sauvignon Napa Valley
Chiles Valley District
($30, 1,200)   ★★★

Case Production: 1,200. **Acres Owned:** 60 acres in Chiles Valley District, Napa Valley. **Varietals by Acre:** Cabernet Franc (6 acres), Cabernet Sauvignon (43), Merlot (8), Sémillion/ Sauvignon Blanc (3).

Located in Chiles Valley, Volker Eisele bears no relationship to the Eisele Vineyard in Calistoga owned by the Araujo family. In the 1980s, Vichon bought Cabernet from this property.

I have tasted many wines from this vineyard and none have been spectacular. A consistent style does exist, however: the wines are typically of medium weight, with good intensity, but lack the plusher flavors found in the best Napa Cabernets. The owners are intent on raising quality, though, and the most recent vintages have been more appealing.

TASTING NOTES

CABERNET SAUVIGNON NAPA VALLEY CHILES VALLEY DISTRICT (★★★)

1995: Smooth and spicy, with currant, tobacco, anise and cedary flavors, turning elegant. **88**
1994: Features cherry and currant fruit, along with flavors of anise and sage. **87**
1993: Well-made, showing a green olive edge. **88**

EL MOLINO WINERY (★★★★)

St. Helena, Napa Valley
Founded: 1871. **Owner:** Reginald B. Oliver & Marie Mason Oliver. **Winemaker:** Scott McLeod.

MAJOR WINES: PRICE, CASES, RATING

Chardonnay Napa Valley	
($38, 1,000)	★★★★
Pinot Noir Napa Valley	
($42, 1,000)	★★★

Case Production: 2,000. **Acres Owned:** 58.5 acres. (58 in Rutherford, 0.5 in St Helena). **Varietals by Acre:** Cabernet Sauvignon (21.5 acres), Chardonnay (32), Merlot (2), Pinot Noir (2). **Varietals Purchased:** Pinot Noir (Carneros).

El Molino is a restored winery situated north of St. Helena. Originally built in 1871, it was refurbished and re-introduced as a brand by Reg Oliver in 1981. El Molino's Chardonnays and Pinot Noirs have moved to the forefront of the California scene, despite the fact that the winery keeps a low profile and that its wines are difficult to obtain (most are sold only to restaurants and mailing-list customers). Nevertheless, these wines are worth the search.

Production runs about 2,000 cases, 1,000 of which are Pinot Noir. At first, the Pinot came from Abbott's Vineyard in Carneros, but in 1990 the source changed to two other vineyards: Hyde Vineyards, and a vineyard owned by Carneros Valley Investors (CVI), with a small amount of Oliver's Rutherford-grown Pinot Noir mixed into the blend. The Chardonnay is 100 percent Rutherford-grown from Oliver's Star Vineyard. Until recently, the appellation on the label read St. Helena, Napa County; the current label simply reads Napa Valley.

Oliver owns 58 acres in Rutherford, which are dominated by Chardonnay and Cabernet; some of the Chardonnay is sold to Ric Forman of Forman Vineyard. Scott McLeod of Niebaum-Coppola Estate oversees winemaking. The wines are given minimal handling and display rich, complex flavors, though of late the Chardonnay has shown an edge in quality over the Pinot Noir.

TASTING NOTES

CHARDONNAY NAPA VALLEY (★★★★): Uncommonly rich, deep and complex, with tiers of flavor and a wonderful sense of harmony and finesse. It does not undergo malolactic fermentation, and it ages very well.
1996: Crisp, flinty and subtle, with a complex array of ripe pear, fig, melon, toast and spice flavors. **90**
1995: Sharply focused, with flavors built around ripe pear, nectarine, fig and melon, turning complex and spicy. **91**

1994: Offers complex, ripe pear, spice and honey notes, with light oak shadings folding in. **91**

1993: Complex, with an appealing core of ripe pear and apple notes and just the right amount of oak shading. **88**

1992: Elegant and refined, with layers of complex pear, fig and spice flavors. Youthful and tight now, but the flavors run deep and long. **91**

1991: Silky, elegant, youthful and tight, with pretty, fresh, ripe pear and spice flavors that linger. **92**

1990: Big, ripe and concentrated, with layers of complex fig, pear, spice and honey flavors that turn to smoky butterscotch and vanilla on the finish. Delicious. **95**

PINOT NOIR NAPA VALLEY (★★★): Marked by ripe cherry and spice flavors, along with deft oak shadings. Ages well. The appellation has changed with the vineyard sources over the years.

1995: Lean and trim, with a well focused band of spice, cola, mushroom and berry flavors. **88**

1994: Rich, with complex layers of black cherry, plum and berry notes and a nice dash of toasty, smoky oak and herb flavors. **89**

1993: Solid, with a pleasant core of ripe plum and cherry flavors, turning hard and tannic. **87**

1992: Bold, ripe, rich and complex, with cherry, plum and spice flavors that linger. Supple, yet tannic. **91**

1991: Elegant and refined, with complex smoke, black cherry, wild berry and plum flavors that turn silky. **88**

1990: Fully mature, with earthy mushroom, dried cherry and rhubarb flavors that turn decadent. **89**

EL ROY see DRAXTON

ELAN (★★★)
Atlas Peak, Napa Valley
Founded: 1992. **Owner:** Elliott-Smith Family.
Winemaker: Patrick Elliott-Smith.

MAJOR WINES: PRICE, CASES, RATING
Cabernet Sauvignon Atlas Peak
  ($34, 400)   ★★★

WINERY DATA
Case Production: 700 cases. **Acres Owned:** 23 acres in Atlas Peak, Napa Valley. **Varietals by Acre:** Cabernet Franc (1 acre), Cabernet Sauvignon (19), Merlot (3).

In the mid-1970s, Patrick Elliot-Smith settled on Atlas Peak to grow grapes. He and his wife, Linda, now control 23 acres, and sell most of the grapes to other wineries. They do, however, produce a small amount of smooth, rich, intensely flavored Cabernet. The 1992 (91 points) was very complex, while the 1994 (88) was elegant, showing earthy, herbaceous flavors.

ELEVEN OAKS see BABCOCK VINEYARDS

ELYSE WINES (★★★)
Napa Valley
Founded: 1987. **Owner:** Nancy & Ray Courson.
Winemaker: Ray Courson.

MAJOR WINES: PRICE, CASES, RATING
Cabernet Sauvignon Napa Valley
  Morisoli Vineyard
  ($40, 450)   ★★★
Cabernet Sauvignon Napa Valley
  Tietjen Vineyard
  ($30, 142)   ★★
Zinfandel Howell Mountain
  ($25, 500)   ★★★
Zinfandel Napa Valley Coeur du Val
  ($20, 650)   ★★★
Zinfandel Napa Valley Morisoli Vineyard
  ($22, 1,400)   ★★★

ALSO PRODUCED
Napa Valley Malvasia Bianca & Chenin Blanc ($25, 110); Nero Misto Napa Valley Field Blend ($20, 450); Rosé Napa Valley ($15, 110); Syrah Napa Valley ($28, 650).

WINERY DATA
Case Production: 6,000. **Acres Owned:** 1.5 acres in Napa Valley. **Varietals by Acre:** Cabernet Sauvignon (1.5 acres). **Vineyard Designations:** Morisoli Vineyard (Cabernet Sauvignon, Zinfandel), Tietjen Vineyard (Cabernet Sauvignon). **Varietals Purchased:** Cabernet Sauvignon (Napa Valley), Chenin Blanc (Napa Valley), Cinsault (Napa Valley), Grenache (Napa Valley), Malvasia Bianca (Napa Valley), Mourvèdre (Napa Valley), Napa Gamay (Napa Valley), Petite Sirah (Napa Valley), Syrah (Napa Valley), Zinfandel (Napa Valley).

Nancy and Ray Courson started Elyse in 1987, intially focusing on Zinfandel from Morisoli Vineyard in Rutherford, which was planted in 1915. They then added a red table wine called Nero Misto ("Mixed Black," a blend of Petite Sirah, Zinfandel, Alicante, Grenache, Grand Noir, Carignane and Mondeuse), a Howell Mountain Zinfandel, a Zinfandel blend called Coeur du Val, a Morisoli Cabernet, and a Syrah. All grapes are purchased. All of the wines are made in a deliberately austere style which is very consistent.

TASTING NOTES

CABERNET SAUVIGNON NAPA VALLEY MORISOLI VINEYARD (★★★)
1993: Ripe and flavorful, with black cherry, cedar, currant, anise and tar flavors and firm tannins. **87**
1992: Tightly wound, with strong anise and black cherry flavors, it's intense, tannic and compact. **89**

ZINFANDEL HOWELL MOUNTAIN (★★★): Austere, tannic and more peppery than the Morisoli bottling.
1994: Ripe and perfumed, sporting pretty aromatics, firm tannins and bright, elegant cherry and berry flavors. **87**
1993: Tight and firm, with an austere band of earthy, spicy wild berry flavors. Hard tannins on the finish. **85**
1992: Pure Zinfandel from start to finish, with spicy pepper, wild berry and raspberry notes that pick up a pleasant earthy nuance on the finish, where the crisp, dry tannins come through. **87**
1991: Firm, ripe and focused, offering generous blackberry and spice aromas and flavors. The finish is firm and tannic, with plenty of flavor. **85**

ZINFANDEL NAPA VALLEY MORISOLI VINEYARD (★★★): Fruitier than the Howell Mountain bottling, this Rutherford-area Zinfandel offers black cherry and raspberry flavors that are rich and focused.
1996: Juicy, with complex, spicy wild berry, cherry and raspberry flavors, tasting a touch sweet with ripe, plush tannins. **88**
1994: Well balanced and pleasant to drink, in a claret style that avoids excess. Flavorful, with bright ripe cherry, strawberry and spice. **88**
1993: Floral and aromatic, followed by tight raspberry and cherry flavors of modest depth and richness. **84**

1992: The black cherry and raspberry flavors are bright and lively, well focused and spicy, turning firm and tannic on the finish. **88**
1991: Tart, tight and focused, with bright cherry, plum and raspberry flavors that turn vivid and lively, with mild tannins. **87**
1990: Ripe, generous and flavorful, with plum, blackberry and vanilla aromas and flavors that remain rich and fruity through the finish. **88**
1989: Lean and sharply focused, with bright raspberry and spice aromas and flavors that are tart and lively on the finish. **85**

EMERALD BAY see CHATEAU JULIEN

EMMOLO (★★-★★★)
Rutherford, Napa Valley
Founded: 1994. **Owner:** Cheryl Emmolo. **Winemaker:** Bob Pepi Jr.

MAJOR WINES: PRICE, CASES, RATING
Merlot Rutherford ($25, 300)	★★★
Sauvignon Blanc Rutherford ($12, 800)	★★

WINERY DATA
Case Production: 1,000. **Acres Owned:** 80 acres owned by Emmolo Family (47 in Rutherford, 33 in Stags Leap). **Varietals by Acre:** Cabernet Franc (11 acres), Chardonnay (14), Malbec (8), Merlot (24), Sauvignon Blanc (23).

Many vintners make the passage from vine to wine, but few do it as literally or as naturally as Cheryl Emmolo. This Napa Valley native's grandfather started a rootstock nursery in St. Helena in 1923, and her family owns a 43-acre vineyard on Mee Lane in Rutherford. She was married to Chuck Wagner, the winemaker at Caymus Vineyards for 15 years. In short, she's been immersed in the wine business her whole life.

In 1994, after years of contemplation, Emmolo started her wine company, focusing on two wines: barrel-fermented Sauvignon Blanc and Merlot. Her family still sells most of their grapes to Robert Mondavi Winery, The Hess Collection and Villa Mt. Eden, but now Emmolo has her own seven rows of Sauvignon Blanc, which she makes in a modestly varietal style.

Emmolo's present plans are to expand Merlot production. The 1996 vintage (87 points) served up ripe plum, black cherry and wild berry fruit flavors.

EOS see ARCIERO WINERY

ERIC ROSS (★★)
Russian River Valley, Sonoma County
Founded: 1994. **Owner:** Eric Luse, John Ross Storey.
Winemaker: Eric Luse, John Ross Storey.

MAJOR WINES: PRICE, CASES, RATING

Chardonnay Russian River Valley	
($15, 320)	★★
Merlot Russian River Valley Occidental	
Vineyard	
($25, 246)	★★
Zinfandel Russian River Valley	
($19, 148)	★★
Zinfandel Russian River Valley	
Occidental Vineyard Old Vine	
($28, 485)	★★

ALSO PRODUCED
Zinfandel Port Russian River Valley ($25, 43).

WINERY DATA
Case Production: 2,200. **Vineyard Designations:** Occidental Vineyard (Merlot, Zinfandel). **Varietals Purchased:** Chardonnay (Russian River Valley), Merlot (Russian River Valley), Zinfandel (Russian River Valley).

Photographers for competing San Francisco newspapers, Eric Luse of the *Chronicle* and John Storey of the *Examiner,* started Eric Ross Winery (Ross is Storey's middle name) in 1994. The wines have been good, if uneven. Merlot has varied from the 1995 Sonoma County (88 points), which was ripe with intense wild berry flavors, to the 1996 Russian River Valley (84), a pleasant blend of licorice and black cherry flavors that lacked finesse. The 1995 Zinfandel Old Vine (88) showed rich, lively tart cherry, pepper and tea flavors and was more interesting than the 1996 offerings, including the Zinfandel Russian River Valley (84) and the Merlot

Russian River Valley Occidental Vineyard (85), both of which had focused, tart raspberry and plum flavors, but modest depth.

ESHCOL see TREFETHEN VINEYARDS

ESTANCIA ESTATES (★★-★★★★)
Alexander Valley, Sonoma & Monterey Counties
Founded: 1986. **Owner:** Canandaigua Wines.
Winemaker: Larry Levin, Phil Fransioni.

MAJOR WINES: PRICE, CASES, RATING

Cabernet Sauvignon California	
($12, 45,000)	★★
Cabernet Sauvignon Sonoma County	
($12, 45,000)	★★
Chardonnay Monterey County Reserve	
($19, 4,000)	★★★★
Chardonnay Monterey Pinnacles	
($11, 100,000)	★★
Duo Red Alexander Valley	
($22, 3,000)	★★★
Fumé Blanc Monterey Pinnacles	
($10, 5,000)	★★★
Meritage Red Alexander Valley	
($22, 10,000)	★★★★
Merlot Alexander Valley	
($14, 9,000)	★★
Pinot Noir Monterey Pinnacles	
($12, 25,000)	★★
Pinot Noir Monterey Reserve	
($18, 750)	★★★

WINERY DATA
Case Production: 250,000. **Acres Owned:** 1,054 acres (847 in Monterey, 280 in Alexander Valley). **Varietals by Acre:** Cabernet Franc (21), Cabernet Sauvignon (170), Chardonnay (529), Gewürztraminer (25), Malbec (2), Merlot (2), Petit Verdot (2), Pinot Gris (26), Pinot Noir (267), Sangiovese (10).

Estancia offers some of the best values in California. The winery is now owned by Canandaigua Wines, which purchased Estancia, along with Franciscan and Mount Veeder Winery in 1999. The grapes are sourced from Estancia's considerable vineyard holdings, which grow all the major varieties except Zinfandel. Most of its whites come from Monterey County and most of the reds are grown in Alexander Valley.

Across the board, the wines are well crafted, with bright flavors, elegant structures and supple textures. They are ideal for everyday drinking, and on occasion they're worthy of tucking away in your cellar for a short period of time. The best wines are the Chardonnay Reserve from Monterey County, and the Meritage Red from Alexander Valley. Worth buying.

TASTING NOTES

CABERNET SAUVIGNON CALIFORNIA (★★)
1996: Richly textured, with smoky oak, black currant and herbal, licorice notes. Finishes moderately with mild tannins. **86**

CHARDONNAY MONTEREY COUNTY RESERVE (★★★):
Elegant, rich and creamy, with a complex range of fig, pineapple, melon, spice and nut flavors.

DUO RED ALEXANDER VALLEY (★★★):
This is a successful blend of Cabernet (70 percent) with Sangiovese; worth watching.
1996: Rich and complex, with pretty plum, wild berry, cherry and spice flavors, turning supple and polished on the finish. **89**

FUMÉ BLANC MONTEREY PINNACLES (★★★):
Intense, with rich, layered flavors and pretty oak notes. The 1996 (87 points) served up lots of pear, fig and sweet pea flavors.

MERITAGE RED ALEXANDER VALLEY (★★★★):
Defines Alexander Valley fruit and elegance, with supple tannins and a pretty mix of cherry, currant and herbal flavors.

PINOT NOIR MONTEREY RESERVE (★★★)
1995: Features ripe cherry, plum and prominent oak flavors, finishing with firm but polished tannins and a good length. **88**

ETUDE WINES (★★★★★)
Napa Valley
Founded: 1982. **Owner:** Tony & Michelle Soter.
Winemaker: Scott Rich.

MAJOR WINES: PRICE, CASES, RATING
Cabernet Sauvignon
  Napa Valley
  ($40, 1,400)   ★★★★★
Pinot Blanc Carneros
  ($20, 1,100)   ★★★
Pinot Noir Carneros
  ($30, 5,000)   ★★★
Pinot Noir Rosé American
  ($14, 700)   ★★★

ALSO PRODUCED
Pinot Gris Carneros ($20, 50).

WINERY DATA
Case Production: 8,000. **Varietals Purchased:** Cabernet Sauvignon (Napa Valley), Pinot Blanc (Carneros), Pinot Gris (Carneros), Pinot Noir (Carneros).

Tony Soter has had a great influence on California winemaking. His first significant impact was as winemaker at Spottswoode in the 1980s, where he fine-tuned the vineyard and created a specific style of Cabernet. He also worked for Araujo, Niebaum-Coppola, Dalla Valle and Moraga before ending his consulting career in 1999 to concentrate on Etude.

Soter started Etude Wines in 1982, focusing initially on Napa Valley Cabernet before branching out into Carneros Pinot Noir, Napa Pinot Blanc and a rosé of Pinot Noir, all of which are exceptionally well made. Soter's Carneros Pinot Noir is refined, elegant and very consistent. His Pinot Blanc captures the peachy-citrus-mineral essence of the wine, giving it a sense of finesse and complexity. Still, the star in his lineup is Cabernet.

While it's true that the most consistently excellent, expressive wines come from specific vineyard sites, this is not the only way to assure high quality, as is evidenced by Etude's wines. Soter owns no vineyards, yet he is able to work with growers to achieve his goals of low crop loads and ripe grapes, and has succeeded in making a string of excellent wines.

TASTING NOTES

CABERNET SAUVIGNON NAPA VALLEY (★★★★★):
Typically dark, rich, complex and supple; high in extract, with firm tannins and minty, herbal currant flavors. Steadily improving; older vintages have aged well. Worth collecting.
1995: Sleek and elegant, with complex, detailed flavors of anise, cedar, currant and black cherry; turns elegant and supple on the finish, where hints of olive and spice emerge. **92**
1994: Remarkably complex, with tiers of ripe, juicy currant, plum, cherry and berry flavors framed by spicy, toasty oak. **93**
1993: Smooth and harmonious, with layers of spice, currant and plum flavors that fold together nicely. **90**
1992: Dark, rich and harmonious, with complex plum, currant, cherry, vanilla and toasty oak flavors that are tightly wound. **93**
1991: Smooth and elegant, with a focused band of spice, currant and cedary oak that gently unfolds, turning supple and polished. **90**
1990: Bold and ultra-ripe, bordering on jammy, with supple black cherry and plum flavors, framed by spicy oak, but the fruit pours through and the texture is polished. **91**
1989: Tight, firm and focused, deftly balancing the ripe, spicy currant flavors and cedary oak shadings. **87**
1987: Rich, complex and concentrated, with a dense core of mint, chocolate, currant and berry flavors. **92**
1986: Deep, rich, intense and fruity, with cedar, currant, plum and spice flavors that are tightly wound and compact. Needs to shed some tannin. **92**
1985: Packed with plum, cherry, anise and spice flavors and firm with tannins and oak, it offers deeply concentrated flavors that are just beginning to reveal their potential. **90**

PINOT NOIR CARNEROS (★★★): These wines have steadily improved since the first vintage in 1984, with recent efforts showing a measure of delicacy and finesse, plus complex cherry and plum flavors and a silky texture. Best upon release.
1996: Dense, concentrated and tannic, with an earthy, leathery, beefy edge to the ripe cherry, berry and plummy notes. **88**
1995: Smooth and polished, with a dash of cherry, herb, sage and cedary oak. **88**
1994: Silky in texture, with a subtle, elegant core of spice, cherry and wild berry flavors. **88**

1993: Light in body and flavor, with an earthy, slightly bitter edge to the cherry and berry fruit. **84**
1992: Smooth and elegant, with a pretty beam of ripe black cherry, currant and light oak shadings. Finishes with a delicate edge. **89**
1991: Spicy and floral, with a touch of mint, this is a firm, closed wine that slowly reveals a core of earthy black cherry and plum flavors. **89**

FANTAISIE see **FOLIE À DEUX WINERY**

FANUCCHI VINEYARDS (★-★★★)
Russian River Valley, Sonoma County
Founded: 1992. **Owner:** Peter Fanucchi. **Winemaker:** Peter Fanucchi.

MAJOR WINES: PRICE, CASES, RATING

Trousseau Gris Russian River Valley	
Fanucchi Wood Road Vineyard	
($13, 335)	★
Zinfandel Russian River Valley	
Fanucchi Wood Road Vineyard Old Vine	
($34, 498)	★★★

WINERY DATA
Case Production: 1,100. **Vineyard Designations:** Fanucchi Wood Road Vineyard. **Varietals Purchased:** Trousseau Gris (Russian River Valley), Zinfandel (Russian River Valley).

Peter Fanucchi manages his mother's 92-year-old, seven-acre block of Zinfandel and a 10-acre Trousseau Gris vineyard in Russian River Valley. Most of the Zinfandel is sold to Hartford Court, but Fanucchi also makes a small amount of rich, distinctive Zinfandel under his own label. While the Trousseau Gris can be refreshing, it is more of a curiosity. Worth watching.

TASTING NOTES

ZINFANDEL RUSSIAN RIVER VALLEY OLD VINE (★★★)
1996: Ripe and full-bodied, with a jammy edge to the earthy plum and wild berry flavors. **89**
1995: Dark, ripe, rich and polished, with complex black cherry, wild berry, raspberry, tar and spice flavors. **91**

FAR NIENTE WINERY (★★★★–★★★★★)
Oakville, Napa Valley
Founded: 1979. **Owner:** Gil Nickel. **Winemaker:** Ashley Heisey. **Second Label:** Dolce.

MAJOR WINES: PRICE, CASES, RATING
Cabernet Sauvignon Napa Valley
($70, 14,000)   ★★★★
Chardonnay Napa Valley
($40, 24,000)   ★★★★

Dolce Sémillon-Sauvignon Blanc Blend
Late Harvest Napa Valley
($60, 2,500)   ★★★★★

WINERY DATA
Case Production: 36,000. **Acres Owned:** 183 acres in Napa Valley. **Varietals by Acre:** Cabernet Franc (8 acres), Cabernet Sauvignon (63), Chardonnay (72), Merlot (18), Sauvignon Blanc (8), Sémillon (14). **Varietals Purchased:** Cabernet Sauvignon (Napa Valley), Chardonnay (Napa Valley), Merlot (Napa Valley).

Oklahoma nurseryman Gil Nickel outbid Robert Mondavi, among others, to buy this prized property in Oakville, situated west of Highway 29. The vineyard is next door to Martha's Vineyard, famous for Cabernet under the Heitz Cellars label, and Mondavi's To-Kalon Vineyard—two great Cabernet sites. Nickel spent a small fortune restoring the ruggedly handsome stone winery which dates back to 1885, tunneling extensive barrel-aging caves and replanting the vineyards.

Each of Far Niente's wines are excellent, though the best might be a Sémillon-based dessert wine called Dolce. The winery draws from 183 acres of vineyard (mostly in the Coombsville area east of Napa), primarily planted to Chardonnay and Cabernet, as well as from some other Bordeaux varieties planted around the winery.

TASTING NOTES

CABERNET SAUVIGNON NAPA VALLEY (★★★★): Initially plagued by uneven quality, recent vintages of the 1990s offer better depth and balance and are true to their years. Ages well.
1995: Tight, complex and concentrated, with a pretty core of spicy currant, anise, tar, sage and cedar, turning supple. **92**
1994: Rich, complex and harmonious, with spicy currant, cherry, anise and light oak flavors. **91**

1993: Intense and flavorful, with the plum and currant notes gaining a leathery, slightly bitter edge. **86**
1992: Big, ripe and complex, with tiers of rich plum, currant and black cherry fruit, turning supple and elegant. **93**
1991: Supple and elegant, with a band of spicy currant, black cherry, cedar, anise and light oak flavors. Impressive for its balance, delicacy and fine tannins. **88**
1990: Youthful, firm, tannic and leathery, showing toasty new oak notes, but also nice currant and spice flavors that stay with you on the finish. **89**
1989: Smoky, with smooth, supple cedar, tobacco and currant flavors that are well balanced and well mannered for an '89. Hints of herb and chocolate emerge on the aftertaste. **86**
1988: Balanced, with ripe, spicy currant, plum and cedary notes, turning supple. **88**
1987: Smooth and elegant, with ripe cherry, currant and spicy flavors, turning smoky. **91**
1986: Mature and fading; a touch earthy, with pleasant currant, cherry and toasty oak flavors. **87**
1985: Rich and concentrated, with coffee, cedar, black cherry and spicy oak flavors, finishing with a hint of earthiness. **90**
1984: Bold, ripe, rich and supple, with opulent, sharply focused black cherry, plum and currant flavors and soft tannins. Plenty of depth and intensity behind the fruit. **92**
1983: Austere and dry as 1983s go, but with some attractive Cabernet flavors as well, with hints of berry, cherry and plum flavors framed by cedary oak. **84**
1982: Mature and past its prime, with dry cedar, currant and earth notes. **81**

CHARDONNAY NAPA VALLEY (★★★★): Quality has been more variable of late, with some excellent wines, like the 1995, and others that seem less inspired.
1997: Tight, with a flinty, mineral edge to the center of pear, nutmeg and hazelnut flavors; needs some time to unfold, so short-term cellaring is advised. **88**
1996: Tight, with a crisp edge to the core of citrus and grapefruit flavors, finishing with a concentrated lemony aftertaste. **90**
1995: Bright and ripe, with brilliant, juicy pear, apple, spice and citrus notes and subtle oak shadings. **92**

DOLCE SÉMILLON-SAUVIGNON BLANC BLEND LATE HARVEST NAPA VALLEY (★★★★★): Uncommonly complex and flavorful, with brilliant fruit flavors and amazing length.

1996: A touch earthy; rich with fig, pear and mushroom notes. **90**

1995: Sweet and elegant, with layers of honey and pear flavors. **90**

1994: Smooth, silky, supple and sweet, with lovely honey-scented pear and peach flavors that linger enticingly on the finish. **92**

1993: Wonderfully rich and complex, with tiers of honey, pear, apricot, butterscotch, vanilla and spice, all unfolding gracefully on the palate, where they're smooth and elegant. Finishes with a long, smooth, refined aftertaste. **92**

1992: Sweet, with a ripe sugary edge, turning to apricot, pear, honey and spice, and a note of green tobacco. **89**

1991: Brilliant yellow; rich with fig, apricot, honey, pear and spice, with toasty buttery oak on the finish. **91**

1990: Wonderfully complex, with honey, spice and fig aromas and flavors; nectarine and anise notes turn smooth and fleshy on a long, full finish. **95**

1989: Bold, ripe and complex, with intense, rich pear, spice, butter, nutmeg and honey flavors that fan out on the palate. Harmonious and elegant, with layers of apricot and butterscotch nuances emerging on the finish. **93**

GARY FARRELL WINES
(★★★–★★★★★)
Russian River Valley, Sonoma County
Founded: 1982. **Owner:** Gary Farrell. **Winemaker:** Gary Farrell.

MAJOR WINES: PRICE, CASES, RATING

Cabernet Sauvignon Sonoma County Hillside
Selection
($28, 500) ★★★

Cabernet Sauvignon Sonoma County
Ladi's Vineyard
($28, 500) ★★★

Chardonnay Russian River Valley Allen
Vineyard
($28, 500) ★★★★★

Chardonnay Russian River Valley
Rochioli Vineyard
($28, 500) ★★★★

Chardonnay Santa Barbara County
Bien Nacido Vineyard
($22, 550) ★★★★

Merlot Russian River Valley
($22, 500) ★★★

Merlot Sonoma County Ladi's Vineyard
($28, 500) ★★★

Pinot Noir Russian River Valley
($22, 1,800) ★★★

Pinot Noir Russian River Valley Allen
Vineyard
($40, 500) ★★★★★

Pinot Noir Russian River Valley
Rochioli Vineyard
($50, 150) ★★★★★

Pinot Noir Santa Barbara County
Bien Nacido Vineyard
($28, 500) ★★★

Zinfandel Russian River Valley
($20, 800) ★★★

Zinfandel Russian River Valley
Collins Vineyard
(Discontinued) ★★★

Zinfandel Sonoma County Old Vine Selection
($25, 1,000) ★★★

ALSO PRODUCED
Chardonnay Sonoma County Ash Creek Vineyard ($28, 700); Zinfandel Dry Creek Valley Bradford Mountain ($25, 300); Zinfandel Dry Creek Valley Maple Vineyard ($25, 300).

WINERY DATA
Case Production: 10,000. **Acres Owned:** 24 acres in Russian River Valley. **Varietals by Acre:** Pinot Noir (12), Chardonnay (4), Merlot (4), Zinfandel (4). **Vineyard Designations:** Allen Vineyard (Chardonnay, Pinot Noir), Ash Creek Vineyard (Chardonnay), Bien Nacido Vineyard (Pinot Noir), Ladi's Vineyard (Cabernet Sauvignon, Merlot), Maple Vineyard (Zinfandel), Rochioli Vineyard (Chardonnay, Pinot Noir). **Varietals Purchased:** Cabernet Sauvignon (Sonoma County), Chardonnay (Russian River Valley, Sonoma), Merlot (Sonoma County, Russian River Valley), Pinot Noir (Russian River Valley, Santa Barbara County), Zinfandel (Dry Creek Valley).

Since the late 1980s, Gary Farrell's wines have quickly risen to the top of the class in California. Farrell began his career as the winemaker for Davis Bynum Winery, where he still is a consultant, but in 1982 he began making small lots of wine under his own label. The quality, particularly of the Chardonnay and Pinot Noir from Allen and Rochioli Vineyards, places his wines among the best; the quality of the Zinfandel is close behind, slightly ahead of the Cabernet and Merlot. Regardless of how one judges these finely crafted wines, there's a definite sense of style that runs through them.

While Farrell didn't own any vineyards until recently, his contacts are first-rate: he buys Chardonnay and Pinot Noir from both Allen Vineyard and Rochioli Vineyards, Bien Nacido Chardonnay and Pinot Noir, and Ladi's Vineyard Cabernet and Merlot. Production is about 10,000 cases. Farrell recently planted 24 acres in Russian River Valley at a site upon which he has plans to build a winery.

Tasting Notes

Cabernet Sauvignon Sonoma County Ladi's Vineyard (★★★): Not quite in the same league as Farrell's best, but still very classy, consistent and distinctive.
1994: Of medium weight, with a modest array of light cherry- and berry-laced fruit and crisp tannins. **83**
1993: Young, firm and tight, with a ripe core of plum, black cherry, anise and cedar flavors. **88**
1992: Full-bodied, with flavors of ripe cherry and currant slowly unfolding to reveal depth and richness. **89**

Chardonnay Russian River Valley
1994: Ripe and exotic; distinctive for its range of tangerine, orange, nectarine, pear and fig-laced flavors. **92**

Chardonnay Russian River Valley Allen Vineyard (★★★★): Intense, lively, rich and complex, with bright, focused flavors and supreme balance. Ages well.
1996: Ripe, rich and concentrated; brimming with tiers of tightly focused pear, fig, apple and apricot fruit. **93**
1995: Has a distinctly flinty, minerally edge; the core of pear, citrus, grapefruit and light oak is rich and complex. **92**
1994: Bold, intense and rich with pear, honey, toast and spice flavors. **92**

Chardonnay Russian River Valley Rochioli Vineyard (★★★★)
1997: Complex—from its initial toasty oak flavors and ripe pear, apple and spicy nuances to its rich butterscotch aftertaste. **91**

Chardonnay Santa Barbara County Bien Nacido Vineyard (★★★★)
1996: Clean and crisp, with a flinty pear and citrus edge; shows a subdued style that's been tightly reined in. **86**
1995: Serves up ripe, bright, juicy tropical fruit, with fig,

apricot and apple flavors and just a hint of oak. **91**

Merlot Sonoma County Ladi's Vineyard (★★★): Much the same as the Cabernet: a tightly focused, well-crafted wine that needs cellar time.
1995: Firm and compact, with a narrow range of cedar, currant, herb and tar flavors, turning tannic and leathery. **86**
1994: Tough and chewy, with firm tannins and appealing herb, sage and tart black cherry flavors. **87**
1993: Attractive cherry and currant flavors are lean and balanced, with modest richness. **87**

Pinot Noir Russian River Valley (★★★): Bright and lively, with rich, concentrated fruit flavors; supple and complex.
1996: Bright, with ripe cherry, blackberry and plummy notes, it's tight and trim, turning supple, creamy and complex. **89**
1995: Lean and trim, with a modest band of black cherry, spice, currant and berry flavors. **87**
1994: Tight, with a tannic edge to the ripe plum and cherry flavors, adding hints of coffee and oak and smoothing out. **90**

Pinot Noir Russian River Valley Allen Vineyard (★★★★★): Deep, with broad, amazingly complex flavors.
1995: Well focused on the core of plum and wild berry fruit, it's tightly wound, with firm tannins and a tea-like edge. **90**
1994: Tight, with a firm, tannic core of ripe currant, plum and wild berry flavors and hints of anise, cedar, nutmeg and spice. **92**
1992: Serves up ripe plum and raspberry flavors of moderate richness and intensity, but it turns tight, tannic and compact on the finish. **88**
1991: Bright, ripe, intense and focused, the rich fruit flavors turn elegant and graceful, finishing with moderate tannins. **87**
1990: Rich, dense and earthy, with complex cherry, mushroom, anise and spicy flavors that are deep and concentrated. **93**
1986: Mature, with plum, cherry and wild berry notes that are soft and fleshy, with hints of earth and mushroom. **91**

Pinot Noir Russian River Valley Olivet Lane Vineyard
1994: Young and tight, with a crisp edge to the plum and berry flavors, along with herb and oak notes. **88**

PINOT NOIR RUSSIAN RIVER VALLEY ROCHIOLI VINEYARD (★★★★★): As you might expect from this great vineyard: tremendous flavor, complexity and finesse.

1995: Tight and complex, with a band of tart berry, wild berry, strawberry, herb and spice, with firm tannins. **92**

1994: Shows tremendous complexity and finesse, with a wealth of ripe cherry, currant and plum flavors that are amazingly well focused. **94**

PINOT NOIR SANTA BARBARA COUNTY BIEN NACIDO VINEYARD (★★★)

1996: Of medium weight, with fresh berry and strawberry flavors, finishing with a dash of pepper and oak. **87**

ZINFANDEL RUSSIAN RIVER VALLEY (★★★)

1995: Ripe, with juicy, polished spice, anise, tar, raspberry, cherry and plum flavors. **90**

ZINFANDEL RUSSIAN RIVER VALLEY COLLINS VINEYARD (★★★)

1994: Shows solid, complex black cherry, cedar, spice and tar notes; this is definitely a cellar-worthy wine. **88**

1993: Dark, tight and intensely wound, with chunky, focused currant and raspberry flavors. **89**

FATHOM see BABCOCK VINEYARDS

FERRARI-CARANO WINERY (★★★-★★★★★)
Dry Creek Valley, Sonoma County
Founded: 1981. **Owner:** Don & Rhonda Carano.
Winemaker: George Bursick.

MAJOR WINES: PRICE, CASES, RATING

Cabernet Sauvignon Sonoma County ($28, 14,500)	★★★
Chardonnay Alexander Valley ($21, 35,000)	★★★★★
Chardonnay Alexander Valley TreMonte ($38, 950)	★★★★★
Chardonnay Napa-Sonoma Counties Reserve ($34, 4,000)	★★★★★
Eldorado Gold Late Harvest Dry Creek Valley ($23, 300)	★★★★
Fumé Blanc Sonoma County ($12, 50,000)	★★★
Fumé Blanc Sonoma County Reserve ($18, 5,000)	★★★
Merlot Sonoma County ($23, 21,000)	★★★
Siena Red Sonoma County ($28, 7,500)	★★★★
Trésor Red Sonoma County Reserve ($55, 1,200)	★★★★
Zinfandel Sonoma County ($18, 7,500)	★★★

WINERY DATA
Case Production: 150,000. **Acres Owned:** 647 acres (Alexander Valley, Carneros, Dry Creek Valley, Russian River Valley). **Varietals by Acre:** Alicante Bouschet (4 acres), Cabernet Franc (4), Cabernet Sauvignon (61), Chardonnay (255), Carignane (1), Grenache (6), Malbec (28), Merlot (93), Petite Sirah (1), Petit Verdot (18), Pinot Noir (9), Sangiovese (47), Sauvignon Blanc (75), Syrah (29), Sémillon (1), Zinfandel (15) **Vineyard Designations:** TreMonte (Chardonnay).

Ferrari-Carano is the ambitious, fast-paced and highly successful undertaking of hoteliers Don and Rhonda Carano, owners of the Eldorado Hotel and Casino and partners in the relatively new Silver Legacy casino, both in Reno, Nevada. Beginning in 1979, the Caranos began buying vineyard property in northern Sonoma County. They have since expanded their holdings, investing millions in acquiring and planting vineyards. Today, they own 647 acres in more than a dozen locations, from Alexander Valley to Dry Creek Valley to Carneros. Their beautiful, state-of-the-art winery, barrel-aging *chai* and showcase Villa Fiore estate are situated in Dry Creek Valley.

Ferrari-Carano first made its mark with Chardonnay and Fumé Blanc. After having mastered those wines as well as any producer in California, the winery has moved on to an impressive array of reds, making classy

Cabernet, Merlot and Zinfandel, exciting Reserve Cabernet (called Trésor), and the absolutely delicious Sangiovese-Cabernet-Merlot blend called Siena. Recently, all the reds have shown even more depth, richness and complexity, a factor Carano and winemaker George Bursick attribute to their mountain-grown grapes. The most important mountain vineyard has nearly 100 acres in vines in an area where Chalk Hill, Alexander Valley and Knights Valley meet. By the year 2000, the winery may well be producing 100 percent mountain-grown reds (except for Pinot Noir). To top things off, the winery also produces a plush dessert wine called Eldorado Gold. About the only wine Bursick has tried and not yet mastered is Pinot Noir, but he is enthusiastic about the winery's new vineyard in Russian River Valley. This entire lineup is still on solid ground.

TASTING NOTES

CABERNET SAUVIGNON SONOMA COUNTY (★★★): Deftly balanced, with both the 1993 and 1994 (87 points) showing ripe fruit flavors with mostly supple tannins. It is best to drink this wine early.

CHARDONNAY ALEXANDER VALLEY (★★★★★)
1996: Elegant, even delicate, with complex, spicy pear, apple, melon and light oak shadings. **90**
1995: Deliciously complex, with rich tropical fruit, pear, melon, fig and butterscotch flavors. **92**

CHARDONNAY ALEXANDER VALLEY TREMONTE (★★★★★): Intense, vibrant and concentrated; typically delicious.
1996: Smooth, ripe, rich and creamy, with pretty apple, pear and spicy fig and vanilla-oak shadings. **92**
1995: Complex, with smoky, toasty oak and a core of pear, melon, fig and spice flavors that are concentrated. **92**
1994: Openly fruity, remarkably complex and subtle, with ripe pear, peach, nectarine and pretty, toasty, smoky oak. **91**

CHARDONNAY NAPA-SONOMA COUNTIES RESERVE (★★★★★): A shade leaner and less opulent than the regular bottling, it's still finely tuned and very complex.
1995: Loads of ripe, rich, complex and concentrated fruit flavors, with tiers of pear, tropical fruit, fig, melon and citrus shadings. **93**
1994: Remarkably complex, with brilliant pear, honey, spice and buttery flavors, turning smooth and creamy. **93**

ELDORADO GOLD LATE HARVEST DRY CREEK VALLEY (★★★★): Fat, ripe and packed with peach, pear, fig and nectarine flavors. Best to drink early.
1996: Cedar, tobacco, pear and caramel flavors fold together, picking up a vanilla edge. **89**
1994: Silky, elegant, round and sweet, the floral pear, pineapple, apricot and vanilla flavors are nicely layered. **91**

FUMÉ BLANC SONOMA COUNTY (★★★), RESERVE (★★★★): Lots of complex varietal flavors. The Reserve turns up the intensity and folds in pretty oak shadings.

MERLOT SONOMA COUNTY (★★★): Tends to be crisper and offers less depth than the other Ferrari-Carano wines. The most recent vintages have scored in the mid-80s.

SIENA RED SONOMA COUNTY (★★★★): A blend of roughly 40 percent Sangiovese, 50 percent Cabernet and 10 percent Merlot, this is a complex and intriguing wine that combines rich raspberry and spice flavors with a supple elegance.
1995: Smooth, ripe, rich and concentrated, with complex black cherry, raspberry, anise, sage and spice flavors. **91**
1994: Smooth, ripe and harmonious, with a core of black cherry, plum, anise and berry notes and supple tannins. **89**
1993: Smooth and harmonious, with a supple core of black cherry, wild berry, coffee and spicy flavors. **90**
1992: Stretches the flavor range from blackberry and currant to tar and anise, then turns elegant, finishing with a cedary oak edge. Needs short-term cellaring. **89**
1992: Bright, crisp and complex, with compelling, spicy black cherry and raspberry flavors that are well balanced, focused and lively. **90**

TRÉSOR RED SONOMA COUNTY RESERVE (★★★★): This wine is Ferrari-Carano's reserve Cabernet blend.
1993: Tightly packed with ripe, rich plum, black cherry, currant and spice, this is a muscular, tannic wine. **92**
1992: Complex, with tiers of currant, spice, cedar and dill, turning elegant and supple on the finish. **91**
1991: Big, ripe and ruggedly tannic, this blockbuster is rich with spicy cherry, wild berry and currant flavors and firm tannins. **90**
1990: Dark, ripe, bold and opulent, with plush black cherry, plum, anise and mineral flavors and a dash of herb and tobacco. **91**

ZINFANDEL SONOMA COUNTY (★★★): Usually shows off ripe cherry and raspberry flavors in a medium-weighted, balanced style.

GLORIA FERRER CHAMPAGNE CAVES (★★★–★★★★)

Carneros
Founded: 1982. **Owner:** Freixenet S.A. **Winemaker:** Bob Iantosca.

MAJOR WINES: PRICE, CASES, RATING

Blanc de Noirs Carneros	
($15, 21,000)	★★★
Brut Carneros Cuvée Late Disgorged	
($27, 1,500)	★★★★
Brut Rosé Carneros	
($26, 1,000)	★★★
Brut Sonoma	
($15, 40,000)	★★★
Chardonnay Carneros	
($19, 9,500)	★★★★
Pinot Noir Carneros	
($19, 3,500)	★★

WINERY DATA
Case Production: 80,000. **Acres Owned:** 200 acres in Carneros. **Varietals by Acre:** Chardonnay (65 acres), Pinot Noir (135). **Varietals Purchased:** Chardonnay (Carneros), Pinot Noir (Carneros).

After watching the success of Domaine Chandon and a handful of other French Champagne houses, Freixenet, the giant Spanish sparkling wine firm, moved into California in 1986, planting 200 acres of vineyards and constructing a large winery along the western edge of Carneros. Their sparkling wines have been on solid footing from the start; well made and very consistent, they are highly reliant on Pinot Noir, which accounts for 135 acres of the vineyard.

In the early 1990s, the winery began making excellent Chardonnay and very good Pinot Noir table wines. The winery's 80,000-case output is dominated by 40,000 cases of the Sonoma Brut (mostly Pinot Noir), with smaller lots of Brut Rosé, Carneros Cuvée and a Blanc de Noirs. The big surprise is the Chardonnay, which is rich, toasty and elegant, with lots of flavor. The Pinot Noir is lighter, and is attractive for its berryish flavors.

CHARDONNAY CARNEROS (★★★★)
1997: Bright and focused, with a tight core of pear, pineapple and citrus, adding a touch of mineral and earthiness on the finish. **91**

1996: Ripe, rich and full-bodied, loaded with complex, concentrated fig, pear, melon and honey flavors that persist on the finish. **90**

FETZER VINEYARDS (★★)

Mendocino County
Founded: 1968. **Owner:** Brown-Forman Corporation. **Winemaker:** Dennis Martin. **Second Label:** Bonterra, Bel Arbors.

MAJOR WINES: PRICE, CASES, RATING

Cabernet Sauvignon California Valley Oaks	
($9, 375,000)	★★
Cabernet Sauvignon Napa Valley Reserve	
($24, 2,000)	★★★
Cabernet Sauvignon North Coast Barrel Select	
($14, 32,000)	★★
Chardonnay California Sundial	
($9, 1,000,000)	★★
Chardonnay Mendocino County Barrel Select	
($12, NA)	★★★
Chardonnay Mendocino County Reserve	
($18, 2,000)	★★★
Gewürztraminer California	
($7, 300,000)	★★
Gewürztraminer Mendocino County Dry Reserve	
($18, 1,500)	★★
Johannisberg Riesling California	
($7, 100,000)	★★
Merlot California Eagle Peak	
($9, 650,000)	★★
Merlot North Coast Barrel Select	
($14, NA)	★★
Merlot North Coast Reserve	
($24, 1,000)	★★
Pinot Noir Santa Barbara County Bien Nacido Vineyards Reserve	
($24, 2,000)	★★
Pinot Noir North Coast Barrel Select	
($13, NA)	★★

Sauvignon Blanc Echo Ridge California
  ($8, 50,000)   ★★
Sauvignon Blanc Mendocino County
  Barrel Select
  ($10, NA)   ★★
Zinfandel California Home Ranch
  ($9, 50,000)   ★
Zinfandel Mendocino County Barrel Select
  ($9, 24,000)   ★★

Bonterra Cabernet Sauvignon
  North Coast
  ($13, 25,000)   ★★
Bonterra Chardonnay Mendocino County
  ($13, 70,000)   ★★★
Bonterra Sangiovese Mendocino County
  ($22, 1,000)   ★
Bonterra Syrah Mendocino County
  ($22, 2,000)   ★★★
Bonterra Viognier Mendocino County
  ($22, 2,000)   ★★★

WINERY DATA

Case Production: 2.5 million. **Acres Owned:** 367 acres in Mendocino County. **Varietals by Acre:** Cabernet Sauvignon (100 acres), Chardonnay (150), Merlot (20), Sangiovese (7), Sauvignon Blanc (40), Viognier (40), Zinfandel (10). **Vineyard Designations:** Bien Nacido Vineyards (Pinot Noir). **Varietals Purchased:** Cabernet Sauvignon/Chardonnay/Merlot/Zinfandel (Mendocino County, Monterey County, San Joaquin County, San Luis Obispo County, Sonoma County).

Lumberman Barney Fetzer and his family settled into grape growing in Mendocino in the 1960s, making their first wines in 1968. By 1980, Fetzer was growing rapidly and had surpassed even Parducci in case volume, offering a wide range of well-crafted, value-oriented wines, including large volumes of White Zinfandel, Gewürztraminer, Fumé Blanc, Chardonnay, Zinfandel, Petite Sirah, Cabernet and Pinot Noir. Bel Arbors was later added as a lower-priced second label.

Fetzer Vineyards has enjoyed many successes; brands such as Sundial Chardonnay have soared to 1 million cases with ease. By the end of the 1980s, Fetzer was one of the fastest growing and most profitable wineries in California, selling 2.5 million cases.

In 1992, the Fetzer family decided to sell the winery to Brown-Forman Corp., an international beverage alcohol company. The Fetzers retained most of their vineyards, agreeing to sell the grapes back to their former winery.

Under the direction of president and former winemaker Paul Dolan, the Reserve Cabernets and Chardonnays have improved significantly over time, though they've tapered off a bit in quality lately. A second tier of Barrel Select wines has also maintained high standards of quality at affordable prices. In fact, quality is good overall, but none of the wines in this vast lineup are among the best of their kind.

TASTING NOTES

CABERNET SAUVIGNON NAPA VALLEY RESERVE (★★★): The move to Napa Valley grapes indicates an intention to make superior quality wines. The 1994 (88 points) was a complex wine with cherry and blackberry fruit flavors.

FICKLIN VINEYARDS (★★★)
Madera, Fresno County
Founded: 1946. **Owner:** Ficklin Family. **Winemaker:** Peter Ficklin.

MAJOR WINES: PRICE, CASES, RATING

Port California Special Bottling
  ($25, 1,000)   ★★★
Port California Ten-Year-Old Tawny
  ($22, 1,200)   ★★★
Port California Tinta
  ($13, 10,000)   ★★

WINERY DATA

Case Production: 9,000. **Acres Owned:** 30 acres in Madera. **Varietals by Acre:** Tinta Cão/Tinta Madeira/Touriga/Souzão (30 acres).

Ficklin has been making Port-style dessert wines in the Central Valley since 1948, when Walter Ficklin determined that traditional Port varieties—Tinta Madeira, Touriga, Tinta Cão and Souzão—were the best bets for this hot climate. The family-owned winery has 30 acres in Madera, and makes about 9,000 cases a year, the main wine being the non-vintage Tinta Port, with a vintage-dated bottling appearing in select years. Mature upon release, the Tinta Port can be very good, with sweet plum and spice nuances, but it is not in the same class as true vintage Port from Portugal.

FIDDLEHEAD CELLARS (★★–★★★)
Santa Ynez Valley, Santa Barbara County
Founded: 1989. **Owner:** Kathy Joseph. **Winemaker:** Kathy Joseph.

MAJOR WINES: PRICE, CASES, RATING
Pinot Noir Santa Maria Valley
  ($35, 1,000)   ★★★

ALSO PRODUCED
Pinot Noir Willamette Valley ($36, 1,000); Sauvignon Blanc Santa Ynez Valley ($20, 1,000).

WINERY DATA
Case Production: 3,000. **Acres Owned:** 100 acres in Santa Ynez Valley. **Varietals by Acre:** Pinot Noir (100 acres). **Varietals Purchased:** Pinot Noir (Santa Maria Valley, Willamette Valley-Oregon), Sauvignon Blanc (Santa Ynez Valley).

Kathy Joseph made wine at Robert Pecota Winery in Napa Valley before branching out on her own in 1989. Her focus is on Pinot Noir from Santa Maria Valley and from Oregon, and on Sauvignon Blanc from the Santa Ynez Valley.

Using purchased grapes, Joseph produces up to 3,000 cases a year from her winery in Davis. Her initial efforts with Pinot Noir were impressive for their finesse and delicacy. In 1998, she completed a deal to acquire property in Santa Ynez, where she's planted nearly 100 acres of Pinot Noir, a portion of which she will share with Meridian Vineyards.

TASTING NOTES

PINOT NOIR SANTA MARIA VALLEY (★★★): Captures the essence of Santa Maria Valley, yet tames the herbal, earthy flavors that often appear in these wines.
1992: Attractive for its supple, delicate texture and alluring black cherry, cola, herb and spice flavors. Unfolds gently, turning supple and complex. **88**

FIELD STONE WINERY (★★–★★★)
Alexander Valley, Sonoma County
Founded: 1977. **Owner:** John & Katrina Staten. **Winemaker:** Tom Milligan.

MAJOR WINES: PRICE, CASES, RATING
Cabernet Sauvignon Alexander Valley
  ($20, 2,000)   ★★
Cabernet Sauvignon Alexander Valley
  Staten Family Reserve
  ($28, 600)   ★★★
Chardonnay Sonoma County
  ($16, 1,500)   ★★★
Gewürztraminer Sonoma County
  ($10, 1,500)   ★★
Sauvignon Blanc Sonoma County
  ($12, 1,200)   ★★

ALSO PRODUCED
Chardonnay Carneros Staten Family Reserve ($20, 400); Petite Sirah Alexander Valley Staten Family Reserve ($20, 550).

WINERY DATA
Case Production: 10,000. **Acres Owned:** 15 acres in Alexander Valley. **Varietals by Acre:** Cabernet Sauvignon (5 acres), Merlot (3), Petite Sirah (6), Viognier (1). **Varietals Purchased:** Cabernet Sauvignon (Alexander Valley), Chardonnay (Carneros, Russian River Valley), Gewürztraminer (Sonoma County), Sauvignon Blanc (Dry Creek Valley).

Owners John and Katrina Staten planted Field Stone's vineyards in the 1960s, a full decade before they built an underground winery. The Statens made their first wines in 1977. The focus is on small case lots of Cabernet, Chardonnay, Sauvignon Blanc, Gewürztraminer and Petite Sirah, all of which share a rustic style.

The wines are good—occasionally very good—as was the 1994 Cabernet Sauvignon Staten Family Reserve (88 points), which featured complex flavors of cassis, blackberry, licorice and herb on a lean frame. The regular 1994 Cabernet Sauvignon (84) was supple, with a core of tar, mineral and black currant flavors. A rich, tropical fruit-flavored 1996 Chardonnay (87) was full-bodied, with lots of toasted oak.

FIFE VINEYARDS (★★★★)
Spring Mountain District, Napa Valley
Founded: 1991. **Owner:** Dennis Fife & Family.
Winemaker: John Buechsenstein.

MAJOR WINES: PRICE, CASES, RATING

Cabernet Sauvignon Spring Mountain
District Reserve
($35, 2,000) ★★★

Merlot Napa Valley
($20, 1,000) ★★★

Petite Sirah Redwood Valley Redhead
Vineyard
($20, 1,000) ★★★

Red Napa Valley Max Cuvée
($30, 1,000) ★★★★

Zinfandel Mendocino
($17, 2,500) ★★★

Zinfandel Napa Valley Old Vines
($20, 1,500) ★★★

Zinfandel Redwood Valley Redhead Vineyard
($20, 1,500) ★★★

ALSO PRODUCED

Barbera Lodi Borra Vineyard ($16, 1, 000); Cabernet
Sauvignon Napa Valley Estate Vineyard ($24, 230).

WINERY DATA

Case Production: 10,000. **Acres Owned:** 60 acres (40 in Napa
Valley, 20 in Mendocino). **Varietals by Acre:** Cabernet
Sauvignon (20 acres), Merlot (3), Petite Sirah (13), Syrah (10),
Zinfandel (14). **Vineyard Designations:** Borra Vineyard
(Barbera), Redhead Vineyard (Zinfandel). **Varietals Purchased:**
Cabernet Franc (Napa Valley), Cabernet Sauvignon (Napa
Valley), Carignane (Mendocino), Cinsault (Mendocino),
Grenache (Mendocino), Merlot (Napa Valley), Mourvèdre
(Mendocino), Petite Sirah (Mendocino, Napa Valley), Syrah
(Mendocino, Napa Valley), Zinfandel (Mendocino, Napa
Valley).

After leaving Ingle-nook-Napa Valley, where he served as president and general manager in the 1980s, Dennis Fife launched his own small winery. Fife's focus is on hearty, tannic reds, including Cabernet and Merlot; also impressive are some of the Zinfandel and Petite Sirah bottlings, many of which are vine-yard-designated. All of the wines are varietally expressive, distinctive, well-made and fun to drink. In 1998, Fife acquired the former Yverdon property on Spring Mountain, and now owns 60 acres: 40 in Napa Valley, and 20 in Mendocino. Worth watching and collecting.

TASTING NOTES

**CABERNET SAUVIGNON NAPA VALLEY ESTATE VINEYARD
1995:** Tightly focused, with a core of currant, cedar, plum and vanilla, turning complex and tannic. **90**

**CABERNET SAUVIGNON SPRING MOUNTAIN DISTRICT
RESERVE (★★★):** Shows promise in a dense, high-extract, firmly tannic style. A 1995 Reserve Estate Vineyard (90 points) was tightly focused on a core of currant, cedar, plum and vanilla flavors.
1995: Dense, tight, massive and chewy, with a solid dose of oak and a core of currant, sage, anise, tar and mineral flavors. **88**
1993: Big, ripe and intense, with smoky currant, black cherry, mineral, anise and earthy tannins. **90**

MERLOT NAPA VALLEY (★★★): Not quite in the same class as the other reds, but the 1996 (88 points) did show richness and concentration, with cherry, berry and vanilla scents.

PETITE SIRAH NAPA VALLEY
1994: Spicy, with a core of earthy currant and cherry; turns simpler on the finish. **87**

PETITE SIRAH NAPA VALLEY OLD VINES
1993: Captures the essence of Petite Sirah, with its grapey, spicy, peppery flavors and tame tannins. **88**

PETITE SIRAH REDWOOD VALLEY REDHEAD VINEYARD (★★★): Named after his wife, food and wine writer Karen MacNeil, this is a dense, high-extract wine with lots of flavor and personality.
1996: The enormous tannins override the peppery wild berry, cherry, leather and sage notes. **85**
1995: Distinct for its spicy, peppery aromas and chewy, gritty tannins, with wild berry and black cherry fruit. **89**

RED NAPA VALLEY MAX CUVÉE (★★★★): The most exciting wine right now, with lots of exotic, complex flavors.
1995: Serves up complex smoky, meaty Petite Sirah-like flavors along with ripe cherry and berry fruit. **89**
1994: Delicious, with ripe, juicy plum and cherry flavors, a dash of spice and pretty oak, but most importantly, lots of exotic fruit. **93**

ZINFANDEL NAPA VALLEY OLD VINES (★★★): Has varied in quality and style, but still a complex and interesting wine. Has gone by the name Vielles Vignes (Old Vines) as well.
1996: A touch green, it's quite light, showing moderately ripe plum and berry fruit and dry tannins. **84**
1995: Ripe and toasty, with a smoky, meaty edge to the raspberry and wild berry flavors and firm tannins. **89**
1994: Well oaked and a touch earthy, with ripe plum, anise and wild berry flavors and firm tannins. **88**
1992: Ripe, with intense black cherry and plum flavors, with hints of anise, cedar, blueberry and spice showing through. **89**

ZINFANDEL REDWOOD VALLEY REDHEAD VINEYARD (★★★): This wine dipped in quality with the 1996 vintage, but prior to that, it delivered lots of ripe, juicy flavors.
1996: Firm and tight, with intense cherry- and berry-laced fruit that finishes with crisp, lean tannins. **86**
1995: Marked by grapey plum and wild berry flavors, turning dry and tannic. **88**
1994: Ripe and juicy, with a racy edge to the cherry, raspberry and spicy, peppery nuances and firm tannins. **91**

FIRESTONE VINEYARD (★★★)
Santa Ynez Valley, Santa Barbara County
Founded: 1972. **Owner:** Adam B. Firestone.
Winemaker: Alison Green-Doran. **Second Label:** Prosperity.

MAJOR WINES: PRICE, CASES, RATING

Cabernet Sauvignon Santa Ynez Valley ($14, 29,000)	★★
Chardonnay Santa Ynez Valley ($13, 26,000)	★★★
Johannisberg Riesling Santa Barbara County Selected Harvest ($15, 800)	★★★
Merlot Santa Ynez Valley ($13, 25,000)	★★
Sauvignon Blanc Santa Ynez Valley ($9, 10,000)	★★★

WINERY DATA
Case Production: 200,000. **Acres Owned:** 228 acres in Santa Ynez Valley. **Varietals by Acre:** Cabernet Franc (10 acres), Cabernet Sauvignon (31), Chardonnay (60), Gewürztraminer (14), Merlot (36), Pinot Noir (6), Riesling (40), Sauvignon Blanc (12), Syrah (19). **Varietals Purchased:** Chardonnay (Santa Ynez Valley), Gewürztraminer (Santa Barbara County), Merlot (Santa Ynez Valley), Sauvignon Blanc (Santa Ynez Valley).

Firestone tire heir Brooks Firestone and his wife Kate pioneered winegrowing in Santa Ynez Valley in 1972, when they planted a vineyard that now covers 228 acres and is home to a picturesque winery. Across the board, the wines are well made, sharing a house style of light- to-medium fruit intensity; while they do not overpower, they offer enough delicacy and finesse to succeed. Lately each of the main wines has shown a shade more depth of flavor, with whites holding a quality edge over the reds, which tend to stray into herbaceous flavors. The Cabernet and Merlot are often strongly marked by herb, tobacco and vegetal notes, but they also have smooth, supple textures.

FISHER VINEYARDS (★★★)

Sonoma County
Founded: 1973. **Owner:** Fred Fisher. **Winemaker:**
Mitch Firestone-Gillis.

MAJOR WINES: PRICE, CASES, RATING

Cabernet Sauvignon Napa Valley
Lamb Vineyard
($50, 400)   ★★★★
Cabernet Sauvignon Sonoma County
Wedding Vineyard
($64, 350)   ★★★
Chardonnay Sonoma County
Coach Insignia
($26, 3,500)   ★★★
Chardonnay Sonoma County Whitney's
Vineyard
($30, 400)   ★★★
Coach Insignia Red Napa Valley
($30, 2,650)   ★★★
Merlot Napa Valley RCF Vineyard
($26, 700)   ★★★

WINERY DATA

Case Production: 8,000. **Acres Owned:** 88 acres (31 in
Sonoma County, 57 in Napa Valley). **Varietals by Acre:**
Cabernet Sauvignon (34 acres), Chardonnay (18), Merlot (6),
Rootstock (30). **Vineyard Designations:** Lamb Vineyard
(Cabernet Sauvignon), RCF Vineyard (Merlot), Wedding
Vineyard (Cabernet Sauvignon), Whitney's Vineyard
(Chardonnay). **Varietals Purchased:** Cabernet Sauvignon
(Napa Valley), Chardonnay (Sonoma County), Merlot (Sonoma
County).

Fred and Juelle Fisher planted their initial 20-acre vineyard on the mountain-top ridge that separates Napa and
Sonoma counties, and then built a beautiful winery from
trees cut on their property. The Fishers first succeeded
with Chardonnay from their estate vineyard—particularly
an ageworthy bottling called Whitney's Vineyard—and
then moved into Cabernet from purchased grapes. Their
best Cabernet comes from the Lamb Vineyard (no relation to Herb Lamb Vineyard, used by Colgin), situated in
Napa off the Silverado Trail; it has shown signs lately of
becoming an important producer of dense, complex
Cabernets. So, while Chardonnay once ruled at this winery, it's Cabernet that holds the upper hand these days—
for that reason, it remains especially worth watching.

TASTING NOTES

**CABERNET SAUVIGNON NAPA VALLEY LAMB VINEYARD
(★★★★):** This appears to be the upcoming star, with
two tremendous vintages in 1993 and 1994—both are
big, rich and structured.
1994: Big, ripe, intense and concentrated, with a firmly tannic core of earthy currant, spice, plum and cherry flavors. **92**
1993: Tight, tannic and firmly structured, with ripe cherry and currant flavors that turn supple and rich with
complexity. **90**

**CABERNET SAUVIGNON SONOMA COUNTY WEDDING
VINEYARD (★★★):** Steadily improving, though it still
has to work off some chewy, gritty tannins. Best to cellar
for a while.
1995: Earthy, oaky and intense, with powerful wild berry,
currant, mineral and spice flavors and chewy tannins. **89**
1994: Tough and leathery, with chewy, gritty tannins and
tightly wound fruit flavors that need cellaring. **88**
1993: Firm, ripe and intense; gritty in texture, with tiers
of currant, mint, cherry and berry flavors that fold
together. **90**
1991: A gamy wine with dry, plush tannins and an earthy
streak, but also appealing currant and chocolate flavors. **88**

**CHARDONNAY SONOMA COUNTY COACH INSIGNIA
(★★★):** Very good. Often ripe and spicy, but not as
complex as vintages from the 1980s.

**CHARDONNAY SONOMA COUNTY WHITNEY'S VINEYARD
(★★★):** This wine has lost its edge, with the 1994 (87
points) mature upon release; the 1995 (89) was very
good, but a touch bitter.

COACH INSIGNIA RED NAPA VALLEY (★★★): Intense and
muscular, with tannin control the main issue. This wine
has carried several appellations over the years, but now
focuses on Napa Valley.
1996: Intense and concentrated, with a rich core of
earthy currant, leather, anise, mineral and sage. It takes a
bit of time to open, but offers lots of complex, concentrated fruit flavors. **91**
1995: Smooth, with pretty black cherry, plum and wild
berry fruit flavors and integrated tannins. **88**
1994: Solid, with a nice core of earthy currant, cedar and
tar flavors, it's nicely balanced, if a bit too tannic. **87**
1993: Ripe and chunky, with currant, plum and berry flavors, but it lacks focus and harmony. **85**

1991: The tight, rich, intense plum and currant flavors are framed by toasty, cedary oak. **84**

1990: Rich, dark, complex and concentrated; packed with dense currant, anise, cedar and spice flavors. **90**

1986: Mature, with drying tannins and a modest array of cherry, herb and cedar-tinged flavors. **86**

MERLOT NAPA VALLEY RCF VINEYARD (★★): The three earlier vintages—1993, 1994 and 1995—scored 84 points, just missing the richness that often betrays Merlot.

1996: Smooth, with herb- and oak-laced Merlot flavors and nuances of currant, spice and wild berry; finishing with leathery tannins. **87**

FLORA SPRINGS WINE CO.

(★★★–★★★★★)

St. Helena, Napa Valley
Founded: 1978. **Owner:** Komes & Garvey Families.
Winemaker: Ken Deis.

MAJOR WINES: PRICE, CASES, RATING

Cabernet Sauvignon Napa Valley
($20, 900) ★★★

Cabernet Sauvignon Pope Valley
Cypress Ranch
($38, 1,200) ★★★

Cabernet Sauvignon Rutherford
Hillside Reserve
($70, 750) ★★★★★

Chardonnay Carneros Napa Valley
Lavender Hill Vineyard
($24, 840) ★★★★

Chardonnay Napa Valley
($15, 3,000) ★★★★

Chardonnay Napa Valley Reserve
($20, 7,500) ★★★★★

Merlot Napa Valley
($20, 10,000) ★★★

Merlot Rutherford Windfall Vineyard
($40, 250) ★★★

Pinot Noir Carneros Lavender Hill
Vineyard
($30, 615) ★★★

Sangiovese Napa Valley
($16, 3,500) ★★★

Sauvignon Blanc Napa Valley Soliloquy
($17, 1,000) ★★★

Sauvignon Blanc Napa Valley
($15, 3,800) ★★★

Trilogy Red Napa Valley
($40, 3,500) ★★★★

ALSO PRODUCED

Pinot Grigio Oakville Napa Valley ($12, 700); Sangiovese Rosata Napa Valley ($12, 800).

WINERY DATA

Case Production: 40,000. **Acres Owned:** 476 acres (19 in Carneros, 110 in Oakville, 156 in Pope Valley, 110 in Rutherford, 81 in St. Helena). **Varietals by Acre:** Cabernet Franc (5 acres), Cabernet Sauvignon (186), Chardonnay (62), Malbec (4), Merlot (88), Sangiovese (14), Sauvignon Blanc (38), Pinot Grigio (12), Pinot Noir (3), Petit Verdot (2), Zinfandel (62). **Vineyard Designations:** Cypress Ranch (Cabernet Sauvignon), Lavender Hill Vineyard (Chardonnay, Pinot Noir), Windfall Vineyard (Merlot).

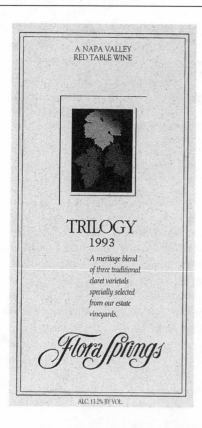

A NAPA VALLEY
RED TABLE WINE

TRILOGY
1993

*A meritage blend
of three traditional
claret varietals
specially selected
from our estate
vineyards.*

Flora Springs

ALC. 13.2% BY VOL.

Flora Springs' early successes with Chardonnay have now been matched—even surpassed—by its extraordinary Cabernet Rutherford Hillside Reserve. The winery dates back to 1977, when Jerry and Flora Komes purchased the old Louis M. Martini Winery (ca. 1888) on Zinfandel Lane south of St. Helena. Jerry Komes had worked for Bechtel Corp., and had retirement in mind when he and his wife moved to Napa. But their grown children soon joined them, and their plans were revised; the family bought vineyard land that now totals 476 acres, making them one of the largest vineyard owners in Napa Valley.

Flora Springs' wines debuted with the 1978 vintage. Two years later, Ken Deis, a former Heitz Cellars winemaker, joined the team, guiding the winery in its focus on using the best grapes from its best vineyards.

Cabernet Sauvignon plantings dominate (186 acres), including property in Pope Valley, which is bottled under the Cypress Ranch designation. Chardonnay (62 acres) and Merlot (88 acres) are also widely planted. Chardonnay has always been excellent, with its richness and complexity; it remains the winery's best white, now with three different bottlings. Flora Springs was among the first to explore Meritage-style reds with its Trilogy, an elegant, flavorful blend of roughly equal parts Merlot, Cabernet Sauvignon and Cabernet Franc. It also offers a Meritage white called Soliloquy. Sangiovese and Pinot Noir are new additions.

TASTING NOTES

CABERNET SAUVIGNON RUTHERFORD HILLSIDE RESERVE (★★★★★): Steadily improving, as the winery isolates the best grapes—those grown on a sloping hillside in Rutherford—for this wine. These are dynamite wines that should age well. Previously called the Napa Valley Rutherford Reserve.

1995: Smooth, plush and elegant, with pretty plum, currant and black cherry flavors that are complex and concentrated. **90**

1994: Dense and tightly built, with rich, smoky currant, blackberry, cherry and cedary notes and full, plush tannins. **96**

1993: Lots of ripe cherry, strawberry jam and berry flavors, with hints of blackberry, currant, and black cherry and supple tannins. **92**

1992: Sharply focused, with a bright, rich core of plum, currant and black cherry fruit that turns supple and elegant. Wonderful depth. **96**

1991: A stylish wine that packs in lots of ripe, rich flavors and then polishes them with toasty, buttery oak. The currant, plum and cherry flavors are bright and lively, picking up spicy herb and tobacco notes on a long, full finish. **97**

1990: Shows depth and substance, with compact currant and spice flavors. **88**

CHARDONNAY CARNEROS NAPA VALLEY LAVENDER HILL VINEYARD (★★★★): A vineyard-designated Chardonnay that is rich, creamy and complex.

1995: Ripe and complex, with a well focused core of apple, pear, spice and light oak shadings, turning silky. **92**

1994: Balanced, with ripe pear, apple and nectarine flavors and elegant toasty oak. **89**

CHARDONNAY NAPA VALLEY (★★★★): Ripe, rich and intense.

1997: An up-front, ripe, fruity style, with rich pear, fig, apple and melon flavors that turn smooth and creamy on the finish, where it picks up a hint of hazelnut and shows off its juicy, nectarine fruit flavors. **91**

1996: Starts out earthy and leafy, with smoky, toasty oak and rich, intense pear, hazelnut and spice coming through. **91**

1995: An exotic, spicy, complex wine with grapefruit, pear, citrus and melon flavors. **88**

CHARDONNAY NAPA VALLEY RESERVE (★★★★★): Silky and concentrated, with remarkable depth and finesse.

1995: Intense, lively and concentrated, with a slightly earthy, minerally edge to the creamy pear, citrus, melon and light, spicy oak. **93**

MERLOT NAPA VALLEY (★★★): Not as rich, complex or consistent as the Cabernet Reserve, but it can be supple and harmonious, as it was in 1993 (87 points) and 1994 (87). The 1996 (82) was earthy and lacking in fruit.

PINOT NOIR CARNEROS LAVENDER HILL VINEYARD (★★★): This wine is new. The 1996 (88 points) was graceful, with complex cherry, berry and spice flavors.

SANGIOVESE NAPA VALLEY (★★★): We've seen both a hit and a miss with this wine. The 1995 (92 points) was one of the best vintages—ripe and complex, with lots of flavors. Its successor, the 1996 (82), was earthier.

SAUVIGNON BLANC (★★★): Can carry either the Napa Valley or California appellation, though the former is superior. Soliloquy is richer and more complex; the 1995 (89 points) was creamy, with grapefruit and passion fruit flavors.

TRILOGY RED NAPA VALLEY (★★★★): This Cabernet blend can be brilliant, complex and elegant. The best capture ripe, rich, supple fruit flavors, with mild tannins and lots of finesse.

1995: Smooth, ripe and spicy; a complex, elegant style, with cherry, plum and berry flavors and attractive spicy nuances. **88**

1994: A hearty, rustic style, with chewy tannins and a spicy mineral edge to the currant and wild berry flavors. **90**

1993: Ripe and juicy, with an alluring core of black cherry, currant, plum and berry flavors and hints of spice. **89**

1992: Well oaked, dark and intense, with a rich core of black cherry, currant, olive and toasty oak. **92**

1991: A racy Trilogy with distinctive earthy, leathery flavors that override the currant, cherry and cedary oak notes. **89**

1990: Lean and austere, with a tight band of complex currant, berry and cedary oak flavors. **85**

1988: A simple core of tarry currant, sage and cedary flavors and dry tannins. **84**

1986: Simple and diluted, in sharp contrast to the richer, full-bodied efforts of other '90s vintages. **82**

FLOWERS (★★★★)

Sonoma Coast
Founded: 1990. **Owner:** Walt & Joan Flowers.
Winemaker: Greg La Follette.

MAJOR WINES: PRICE, CASES, RATING

Chardonnay Porter-Bass Vineyards Sonoma County ($38, 180)	★★★★
Chardonnay Sonoma Coast ($32, 1,280)	★★★★
Chardonnay Sonoma Coast Camp Meeting Ridge ($36, 2,000)	★★★★
Pinot Noir Carneros ($32, 850)	★★★
Pinot Noir Sonoma Coast Camp Meeting Ridge ($42, 1,000)	★★★★
Pinot Noir Sonoma Coast Camp Meeting Ridge Moon Select ($45, 135)	★★★★
Pinot Noir Sonoma Coast Hirsch ($42, 225)	★★★

ALSO PRODUCED

Pinot Noir Sonoma Coast ($NA, 1,000).

WINERY DATA

Case Production: 6,500. **Acres Owned:** 50 acres in the Sonoma Coast. **Varietals by Acre:** Chardonnay (21 acres), Pinot Noir (29). **Vineyard Designations:** Camp Meeting Ridge (Chardonnay, Pinot Noir), Hirsch (Pinot Noir), Porter-Bass Vineyards (Chardonnay). **Varietals Purchased:** Chardonnay (Sonoma Coast), Pinot Noir (Carneros, Sonoma Coast).

Flowers has quickly become one of the most promising new wineries in California. Owners Walt and Joan Flowers began planting their steep hillside vineyard in 1989, but allowed Kistler Vineyards to establish a name for their Camp Meeting Ridge Vineyard before they released any of their own wines.

The first vintages of Flowers' wines have been remarkably complex and concentrated, from a silky 1995 Chardonnay (91 points)—which had layers of rich, focused flavors—to their 1996 Pinot Noir (92) and 1996 Pinot Noir Moon Select (94), both of which featured intense, detailed dark cherry, berry and spice flavors.

With 23 acres already producing, and another 20 acres of Pinot Noir and 7 acres of Chardonnay recently planted, Flowers does not need to worry about grape sources. A large, thoughtfully designed winery ensures that they have complete control of the winemaking. Definitely a winery to watch.

TASTING NOTES

CHARDONNAY SONOMA COAST (★★★★)

1997: A rich, resiny flavor gives this wine an earthy introduction. With aeration the core of pear, peach and nectarine flavors emerge, finding focus on the long flavorful finish. **91**

CHARDONNAY SONOMA COAST CAMP MEETING RIDGE (★★★★)

1995: Wonderfully rich and complex, with layers of spicy pear, apple, citrus and melon flavors that are sharply focused and long and intense on the finish, where the texture turns silky. **91**

CHARDONNAY PORTER-BASS VINEYARDS SONOMA COUNTY (★★★★)
1997: Intensely flavored and sharply focused, with brilliant flavors, ranging from ripe tart pear, nectaine, peach, fig and spicy, buttery oak. Flavors evolve, gaining depth and nuance. **93**

PINOT NOIR CARNEROS (★★★)
1997: Bright and ripe, with tight, intense cherry, cola, anise, spice and cedary notes, finishing with complex earthy notes. **87**

PINOT NOIR SONOMA COAST CAMP MEETING RIDGE (★★★★)
1996: Dark, ripe, complex and concentrated, with detailed black cherry, wild berry, plum, coffee and spicy notes fanning out on the finish, where the tannins are fine but firm. **92**

PINOT NOIR SONOMA COAST CAMP MEETING RIDGE MOON SELECT (★★★★)
1996: Intense, with lively complex, dense and chewy black cherry, plum, wild berry and spicy notes that run deep and concentrated, finishing with a long aftertaste. **94**

PINOT NOIR SONOMA COAST HIRSCH (★★★)
1997: Appealing for its upfront fruitiness, with ripe plum, blackberry, cherry and cedary oak, finishing with complex tannins. **89**

THOMAS FOGARTY WINERY (★★★)
Santa Cruz Mountains
Founded: 1981. **Owner:** Thomas Fogarty. **Winemaker:** Michael Martella.

MAJOR WINES: PRICE, CASES, RATING
Cabernet Sauvignon Napa Valley
($22, 500) ★★★
Chardonnay Santa Cruz Mountains
($19, 4,000) ★★★★
Chardonnay Santa Cruz Mountains Estate
Reserve
($28, 500) ★★★★
Gewürztraminer Monterey County
($13, 4,000) ★★★

Pinot Noir Santa Cruz Mountains Estate
($25, 600) ★★★
Pinot Noir Santa Cruz Mountains Estate
Reserve
($30) ★★★
Sangiovese Santa Cruz Mountains Estate
Reserve
($28, 100) ★★★

ALSO PRODUCED
Cabernet Sauvignon Santa Cruz Mountains ($NA, 500); Merlot Santa Cruz Mountains ($24, 600).

WINERY DATA
Case Production: 16,000. **Acres Owned:** 22 acres in Santa Cruz Mountains. **Varietals by Acre:** Chardonnay (12 acres), Merlot (2), Pinot Noir (7), Sangiovese (1). **Varietals Purchased:** Cabernet Sauvignon (Napa Valley, Santa Cruz Mountains), Chardonnay (Santa Cruz Mountains), Gewürztraminer (Monterey), Merlot (Santa Cruz Mountains).

Cardiovascular surgeon Thomas Fogarty founded his winery in 1981 in the San Francisco Peninsula area known as Portola Valley. He planted Chardonnay and Pinot Noir between 1978 and 1980, and has since added small amounts of Merlot and Sangiovese. Cabernet and other varieties are purchased. Fogarty makes 16,000 cases a year, mostly very good to outstanding in quality. The focus is on estate-grown wines, but many of the wines throughout the years have been made from assorted grapes and appellations.

TASTING NOTES

CABERNET SAUVIGNON VARIOUS BOTTLINGS (★★★): Usually on sound footing regardless of where it's grown. The Napa Valley 1995 (88 points) was firm, with a blend of currant, anise and herb flavors. The Napa Valley Vallerga Vineyards 1992 (90) was well oaked and very concentrated.

CHARDONNAY VARIOUS BOTTLINGS (★★★★): Each of these wines is intense and concentrated, with the Santa Cruz Mountains Estate Reserve the most consistent and ageworthy.

PINOT NOIR SANTA CRUZ MOUNTAINS VARIOUS BOTTLINGS (★★★): Two, sometimes three, Santa Cruz Mountains bottlings are made, each typically austere, tannic and earthy, with mushroom and berry flavors.

Sangiovese Santa Cruz Mountains Estate Reserve (★★★): Only a tiny amount is made from a half-acre of vines, but the 1996 (88 points) was dark, ripe, rich and concentrated.

FOLEY ESTATE (★★★)
Santa Barbara County
Founded: 1997. **Owner:** Willian P. Foley. **Winemaker:** Alan Phillips.

MAJOR WINES: PRICE, CASES, RATING
Sauvignon Blanc Santa Barbara County
  ($14, 688)   ★★★

ALSO PRODUCED
Cabernet Sauvignon Santa Ynez Valley Santa Barbara La Cuesta Vineyard ($25, 900); Chardonnay Santa Barbara ($16, 2,643); Chardonnay Santa Maria Valley Bien Nacido Vineyard ($20, 386); Merlot Santa Ynez Valley Santa Barbara La Cuesta Vineyard ($20, 223); Pinot Noir Santa Maria Valley Santa Maria Hills ($25, 625).

WINERY DATA
Case Production: 9,000. **Acres Owned:** 24 acres in Santa Ynez Valley. **Varietals by Acre:** Cabernet Sauvignon (18 acres), Merlot (3), Sauvignon Blanc (3). **Vineyard Designations:** Bien Nacido Vineyard (Chardonnay), La Cuesta Vineyard (Cabernet Sauvignon, Merlot). **Varietals Purchased:** Chardonnay (Santa Maria Valley), Pinot Noir (Santa Maria Valley).

Businessman Bill Foley, chairman and CEO of CKE Enterprises (owner of restaurant chains) and chairman and CEO of Fidelity National Title Co., added wine to his array of businesses when he purchased the old J. Carey Winery in 1997. Alan Philips, formerly of Byington Winery (where he crafted a number of outstanding, rich and complex Chardonnays) has been put in charge of winemaking.

Foley is focusing on estate-grown Cabernet, Merlot and Sauvignon Blanc as well as Pinot Noir and Chardonnay from other Santa Barbara County vineyards. Production will remain close to 10,000 cases. The 1997 Sauvignon Blanc (90 points) was rich and elegant with fresh sweet pea, fig, melon, citrus and herb notes.

Foley is also developing another Santa Barbara winery called LinCourt Vineyards. Worth watching.

FOLIE À DEUX WINERY (★★)
St. Helena, Napa Valley
Founded: 1982. **Owner:** Richard Peterson. **Winemaker:** Scott Harvey. **Second Label:** Fantaisie.

MAJOR WINES: PRICE, CASES, RATING
Cabernet Sauvignon Napa Valley
  ($18, 1,360)   ★★
Cabernet Sauvignon Napa Valley Reserve
  ($25, 2,150)   ★★
Chardonnay Napa Valley Reserve
  ($25, 580)   ★★
Zinfandel Amador County Old Vine
  ($18, 1,540)   ★★
Zinfandel Fiddletown Eschen Vineyard
  Old Vine
  ($22, 470)   ★★

ALSO PRODUCED
Chardonnay California ($14, 3,875); Sangiovese Amador County ($16, 375); Syrah Amador County ($22, 570).

WINERY DATA
Case Production: 20,000. **Acres Owned:** 12 acres in Napa Valley. **Varietals by Acre:** Cabernet Sauvignon (12 acres). **Vineyard Designations:** Eschen Vineyard (Zinfandel). **Varietals Purchased:** Chardonnay (Monterey County, Nevada County), Sangiovese (Amador County), Syrah (Amador County), Zinfandel (Amador County).

Founded in 1981 by Larry and Evie Dizmang, two mental health professionals, this winery bears a name meaning "a shared fantasy" (the label is a parody of the Rorschach test). Under the ownership of the Dizmangs, Folie à Deux made a wide variety of wines, including Cabernet, Chardonnay, Chenin Blanc and Zinfandel. In 1995, the Dizmangs sold the winery to a group of investors headed by Richard Peterson, a wine industry veteran who had done stints at Beaulieu Vineyard, The Monterey Vineyard and Montpellier before taking over this Napa winery.

The winery owns but 12 acres of Cabernet Sauvignon. Scott Harvey has been hired as winemaker; given his talent and success at Renwood Winery in Amador County, where he made some delicious Barberas and Zinfandels, quality should improve significantly. If need be, Peterson could also call upon his daughter, the highly regarded Heidi Peterson Barrett, to help fine-tune things. Though the winery is in transition, with no standout wines that merit more than a ★★ rating, it should be worth watching in the future.

FOPPIANO VINEYARDS (★★)

Russian River Valley, Sonoma County
Founded: 1896. **Owner:** Louis J. Foppiano.
Winemaker: Bill Regan. **Second Label:** Fox Mountain,
Riverside Farms.

MAJOR WINES: PRICE, CASES, RATING

Cabernet Sauvignon Russian River Valley
($14, 4,000) ★★
Merlot Russian River Valley
($16, 4,000) ★★
Petite Sirah Russian River Valley
($14, 6,000) ★★★
Pinot Noir Russian River Valley
($16, 1,000) ★★
Zinfandel Dry Creek Valley
($14, 2,000) ★★

WINERY DATA
Case Production: 100,000. **Acres Owned:** 119 acres in
Russian River Valley. **Varietals by Acre:** Cabernet Franc (6
acres), Cabernet Sauvignon (16), Chardonnay (30), Merlot (11),
Petite Sirah (36), Pinot Noir (5), Sauvignon Blanc (15).
Varietals Purchased: Zinfandel (Dry Creek Valley).

Foppiano Vineyards passed the century mark in 1996.
Today it is a highly modernized winery, producing
100,000 cases of wine under three labels: Fox Mountain,
Foppiano and Riverside Farms white Zinfandel,
Cabernet, Chardonnay and Zinfandel. Many of the
grapes come from the winery's 119 acres of vines in
Russian River Valley. The Petite Sirah is the best
Foppiano wine; the Dry Creek Valley Zinfandel also
impressed me with its spice, earth and raspberry notes.

TASTING NOTES

PETITE SIRAH RUSSIAN RIVER VALLEY (★★★):
Typically ripe, expressive wines that are also tannic, but
they deserve good marks for their distinctive features.
1995: Intense, with a spicy, leathery, meaty edge to the
core of tannic plum and wild berry flavors. **87**
1994: Big, ripe and expressive, with a mouthful of chewy
tannins. **86**

FORMAN VINEYARD (★★★★★)

St. Helena, Napa Valley.
Founded: 1983. **Owner:** Ric Forman. **Winemaker:** Ric
Forman. **Second Label:** Chateau La Grand Roche.

MAJOR WINES: PRICE, CASES, RATING

Cabernet Sauvignon Napa Valley
($38, 1,900) ★★★★★
Chardonnay Napa Valley
($29, 1,900) ★★★★★
Merlot Napa Valley
($36, 500) ★★★

WINERY DATA
Case Production: 4,000. **Acres Owned:** 87 acres (9 in St.
Helena, 63 in Rutherford, 15 in Napa Valley). **Varietals by
Acre:** Cabernet Franc (1 acre), Cabernet Sauvignon (36),
Chardonnay (40), Merlot (9), Petit Verdot (1).

Ric Forman has filled his life with Napa Valley wine,
and has had a hand in developing many important wines.
While a student at U.C. Davis, he worked at Stony Hill,
the famous Napa Valley Chardonnay estate. After school
he worked briefly at Robert Mondavi Winery. In 1968, he
was hired at age 24 to be winemaker for the new Sterling
Vineyards winery, where he worked until 1978, in the
process developing new wines such as Sauvignon Blanc
and Merlot while defining the Sterling Reserve
Cabernets. Following Sterling, he did a brief stint at
Newton before starting his own winery in the hills east of
St. Helena near the Meadowood Resort.

Forman owns 87 acres of vineyard, mostly
Chardonnay and Cabernet, and his focus is on those two
wines. His Cabernet is a Bordeaux-inspired blend con-
taining Merlot and Cabernet Franc, while his Chardonnay
is made in a traditional California style, with no malolactic fermentation or emphasis on heavy oak or natural
yeasts. His Merlot is new, and the first few vintages have
been distinctive, if weighted to the tannic side of the
grape.

TASTING NOTES

CABERNET SAUVIGNON NAPA VALLEY (★★★★★): Aims
for finesse and understated flavors. Rarely overwhelms,
but charms with its subtlety and grace. Packs in lots of
complex flavors, but finesse and grace are its signature.
Ages very well.

1995: Ripe, rich, smooth and concentrated; sharply focused on the currant, black cherry, sage, cedar and spice flavors. **91**

1994: Elegant, smooth and smoky, with a leather and herb edge to the currant, mineral, and berry flavors. **92**

1993: Tight, with crisp cedar, cherry and currant flavors and a firmly tannic finish. **88**

1992: Weaves together a pretty array of ripe cherry, currant and spicy oak flavors, with an earthy edge. Very well focused, young and vibrant. **92**

1991: Inky and raw like a barrel sample, but it serves up lots of concentrated currant, spice and cherry flavors, finishing with a peppery, tannic edge. **89**

1990: Sleek and elegant, with tight, firm, focused herb, currant, cedar and spice flavors. This youthful and concentrated wine finishes with fine tannins, but needs short-term cellaring to soften and develop. **90**

1989: Ripe and supple, a fleshy wine with a soft texture and enough backbone to carry the currant and spice flavors. It hints at anise and herbs, but remains fruity. **88**

1988: The initial gaminess turns earthy, with complex currant, cedar and spice flavors. **86**

1987: Grows beyond the initial meaty, earthy flavors to present notes of currant, cherry, plum, cedar and tar, with a complex finish. **90**

1986: Ripe and rich; high in extract, with currant, plum and mineral flavors, cedary oak nuances and chewy tannins. **92**

1985: Very rich and cedary, with a touch of elegance and finesse and deep currant, spice and plum flavors. Finishes with fine, smooth tannins; it's focused, long and complex. **93**

1984: Rich, forward and delicious, a splendid Cabernet with supple, layered black cherry, currant and anise flavors framed by toasty oak and smooth tannins. **92**

1983: Mature and drinking well, holding its core of rich, complex currant, berry and spice flavors. **90**

CHARDONNAY NAPA VALLEY (★★★★★): Starts out crisp and tight, but blossoms in the bottle, showing flinty apple and citrus notes. Best with short-term cellaring.

1997: Ripe and intense, with a tight core of pear, fig, spice and nutmeg flavors, finishing with a citrus edge. **89**

1996: Lively, with zesty grapefruit, lemon, pear and fig flavors that are rich and concentrated. **90**

1995: Complex, with an array of ripe pear, smoky oak, toast, hazelnut and buttery flavors. **91**

1994: Intense, elegant and ripe, with pear, spice, melon and fig notes, finishing with toasty oak nuances. **91**

1992: Crisp and lean, with lots of spice notes, but also sharply focused apple, pear and nectarine flavors. **89**

1991: Tart, lean and crisp, with spicy lemon, honey, pear and toast notes. Youthful, concentrated and full of flavor, but will require time to open and become more generous. **89**

1990: Tight, firm and crisp, with intense, focused pear, pineapple, peach and citrus flavors and a pretty overlay of toasty, buttery oak notes. **90**

MERLOT NAPA VALLEY (★★★): Tannin control has been an issue with the first few vintages, but this is a tricky grape to master, even for those with experience.

1996: Starts out earthy and gamy, with chewy, leathery tannins; dense from beginning to end, with glimpses of currant and black cherry fruit, turning austere on the finish. **88**

1995: Dry, ruggedly earthy, and tannic, with leathery flavors that require patience. **85**

1994: Enormously tannic, with a smoky, leathery edge to the currant, cedar and plum notes. **89**

FOX MOUNTAIN see FOPPIANO VINEYARDS

FOXEN VINEYARD (★★★)
Santa Maria Valley, Santa Barbara County
Founded: 1987. **Owner:** Richard Dore, Bill Wathen.
Winemaker: Bill Wathen.

MAJOR WINES: PRICE, CASES, RATING

Cabernet Franc Santa Maria Valley Tinaquaic Vineyard ($24, 500)	★★★
Cabernet Sauvignon Santa Barbara County ($24, 2,000)	★★★
Cabernet Sauvignon Santa Valley Mamere Vineyard ($40, 50)	★★
Chardonnay Santa Maria Valley ($20, 2,500)	★
Chardonnay Santa Maria Valley Estate Tinaquaic Vineyard ($30, 500)	★
Merlot Santa Barbara County ($24, 300)	★★

Pinot Noir Santa Maria Valley
($24, 3,000) ★★★
Pinot Noir Santa Maria Valley
Bien Nacido Vineyard
($30, 500) ★★★
Pinot Noir Santa Maria Valley
Julia's Vineyard
($25, 300) ★★★
Pinot Noir Santa Ynez Valley
Sanford & Benedict
($30, 500) ★★★
Syrah Santa Ynez Valley Morehouse
Vineyard
($30, 500) ★★★
Viognier Santa Ynez Valley
Rothberg Vineyard
($25, 500) ★★★

ALSO PRODUCED
Chenin Blanc Santa Barbara County ($24, 300); Syrah
Santa Barbara County ($20, 1,000).

WINERY DATA
Case Production: 12,000. **Acres Owned:** 10 acres in the Santa
Maria Valley. **Varietals by Acre:** Cabernet Franc (1 acre),
Cabernet Sauvignon (1), Chardonnay (7), Merlot (2). **Vineyard
Designations:** Bien Nacido Vineyard (Pinot Noir), Julia's
Vineyard (Pinot Noir), Mamere Vineyard (Cabernet Sauvignon),
Morehouse Vineyard (Syrah), Rothberg Vineyard (Viognier),
Sanford & Benedict Vineyard (Pinot Noir), Tinaquaic Vineyard
(Cabernet Franc, Chardonnay). **Varietals Purchased:** Cabernet
Franc (Los Alamos Valley), Cabernet Sauvignon (Santa Maria
Valley, Santa Ynez Valley), Chardonnay (Santa Maria), Chenin
Blanc (Los Alamos Valley), Merlot (Santa Maria Valley, Los
Alamos Valley), Mourvèdre (Santa Ynez Valley), Pinot Noir
(Santa Maria, Santa Ynez Valley), Syrah (Los Alamos Valley,
Santa Ynez Valley), Viognier (Santa Ynez Valley).

Richard Dore, a member of the Foxen family, long-
time cattle ranchers in Santa Maria, and Bill Wathen, former vineyard manager of Rancho Sisquoc and Chalone,
started Foxen Vineyard in 1987. The wines have gone
from good to better, with each vintage showing more
promise. There have, however, been a few dips, including
vintages where the wines were not as satisfying and complete as they should have been.

The winery produces 12,000 cases, with a lineup that
includes Cabernet, Chardonnay, Merlot, Pinot Noir (several bottlings), Syrah and Viognier. All of the reds are

solid, but the most striking is perhaps the Santa Barbara
Cabernet, which of late has been right on the mark,
despite that it comes from an area where this varietal is
often marred by vegetal flavors. The Chardonnay has
been hit or miss—generally not a good sign.

TASTING NOTES

**CABERNET FRANC SANTA MARIA VALLEY TINAQUAIC
VINEYARD (★★★):** Elegant, complex and one of the best
in the state.

**CABERNET SAUVIGNON SANTA BARBARA COUNTY
(★★★):** Unusually good, especially for the area; the
1994 (88 points) was ripe, with a core of plum and wild
berry flavors.

CHARDONNAY VARIOUS BOTTLINGS (★★): Highly variable, from lows in 1995 (68 points), when it was pungently earthy, to much better examples, such as the Santa
Maria Valley 1996 (88), which was intense and lively,
with a range of attractive flavors.

MERLOT SANTA BARBARA COUNTY (★★): Can be brilliant, with high marks in 1995 (88 points). Smooth and
supple, if slightly vegetal in flavor.

PINOT NOIR VARIOUS BOTTLINGS (★★★): The Santa
Maria Valley 1995 (86 points) was rather rich and exotic,
if a shade earthy. The Santa Maria Valley Bien Nacido
Vineyard is usually superior, and was best in 1993 (90).
A Julia's Vineyard 1996 (88) was smooth, with racy cola
and black cherry fruit. A Sanford & Benedict Vineyard
bottling is also made; the 1995 (88) was elegant and flavorful.

**SYRAH SANTA YNEZ VALLEY MOREHOUSE VINEYARD
(★★★):** Impressive so far. The 1995 (92 points) was
smooth, rich and complex, with layers of black cherry,
spice and mint; the 1994 (88) was dark, ripe and peppery.
Worth watching.

**VIOGNIER SANTA YNEZ VALLEY ROTHBERG VINEYARD
(★★★):** The 1997 (89 points) was bright and lively, with
a wide range of complex flavors. Worth watching.

FOX RIDGE see **GEYSER PEAK WINERY**

FRANCISCAN OAKVILLE ESTATE
(★★★–★★★★)
Oakville, Napa Valley
Founded: 1973. **Owner:** Canandaigua Wines.
Winemaker: Larry Levin.

MAJOR WINES: PRICE, CASES, RATING
Cabernet Sauvignon Napa Valley
($17, 18,000)   ★★★
Chardonnay Napa Valley
($15, 15,000)   ★★★★
Chardonnay Napa Valley Cuvée Sauvage
($30, 3,500)   ★★★★
Magnificat Red Napa Valley Oakville Estate
($30, 5,000)   ★★★★
Merlot Napa Valley
($17, 15,000)   ★★
Zinfandel Napa Valley
($15, 2,000)   ★★★

WINERY DATA
Case Production: 65,000. **Acres Owned:** 216 acres in Oakville. **Varietals by Acre:** Cabernet Franc (18 acres), Cabernet Sauvignon (65), Chardonnay (22), Malbec (2.5), Merlot (80), Petit Verdot (2.5), Zinfandel (26).

Talk about turnarounds. In its first phase, from 1972 to 1985, Franciscan appeared to be headed for disaster. Its product mix included low-priced Burgundies, weedy Cabernets and oxidized Chardonnays. This mediocrity was all the more curious since one of its early owners was Justin Meyer (from 1975-1979), whose Silver Oak Cellars produced deliciously well-focused Cabernets. Further, the winery had vineyards in good, if not great, locations in both Napa and Alexander valleys.

In 1979, the Eckes family of Germany bought Franciscan, and in 1985, Agustin Huneeus (of Seagram, Concannon, Souverain and Quintessa) joined as president, re-directing the winery with a skilled staff, centralizing winemaking in Rutherford, and separating the vineyards by brands: Napa Valley grapes were used for Franciscan's wines, and Alexander Valley grapes were used for Estancia's.

Franciscan owns 216 acres in Oakville, with Cabernet, Chardonnay, Merlot and Zinfandel the major grapes. Production is 65,000 cases, with the Cabernet blend Magnificat and Chardonnay Cuvée Sauvage the top two wines. Quality across the lineup is solid and usu-

ally offers good value. Larry Levin is the new winemaker as of 1998, having moved to Napa from Dry Creek Vineyard in Sonoma.

In 1999, Canandaigua Wines, known for its low-priced mass-produced wines, purchased the Franciscan portfolio—including Franciscan Oakville Estate, Mount Veeder Winery and Estancia Winery, as well as nearly 1,600 vineyard acres—for $240 million. This occurred shortly after Canandaigua's purchase of Simi Winery in Sonoma County, and is an indication of the trend toward consolidation in the California wine industry.

TASTING NOTES

CABERNET SAUVIGNON NAPA VALLEY (★★★): Supple, fruity, complex, creamy and harmonious, with both the 1994 and 1995 vintages receiving 88 points.

CHARDONNAY NAPA VALLEY (★★★★): Complex, focused and rich in fruit.

CHARDONNAY NAPA VALLEY CUVÉE SAUVAGE (★★★★): Rich, concentrated and well oaked.

MAGNIFICAT RED NAPA VALLEY OAKVILLE ESTATE (★★★★): Poised for excellence, this Cabernet blend captures the rich fruit flavors of Oakville and is complex and elegant.
1995: Ripe with integrated flavors and a core of black cherry, plum and wild berry fruit flavors. Finishes with spice, cedar, sage and mineral notes. The tannins fold in nicely. **89**
1994: Complex, with ripe cherry, cedar and currant, with a dash of anise and spice, finishing with firm but polished tannins. Turns elegant and supple on the finish. **89**
1993: Elegant and sophisticated, a complex blend of flavor and texture—bright, lively cherry, plum and currant flavors and a smooth, supple texture. The tannins are there, for sure, but the fruit flavor works its way past them for a fine finish. **91**
1991: Well oaked, with a buttery edge and a medium-bodied core of plum, cherry, anise and spice. Merits attention for its suppleness and finesse. Picks up a pruney edge on the aftertaste. **89**

MERLOT NAPA VALLEY (★★): More variable of late, but the 1993 (89 points) was smooth and smoky, with rich fruit. The 1994 (84) was tougher and more tannic and in need of cellaring. The 1995 (86) stretched the range of flavors from cherry to bell pepper.

PETER FRANUS WINE CO. (★★★)
Napa Valley
Founded: 1987. **Owner:** Peter Franus. **Winemaker:** Peter Franus.

MAJOR WINES: PRICE, CASES, RATING
Cabernet Sauvignon Napa Valley
($28, 1,500)   ★★★
Zinfandel Contra Costa County Planchon Vineyard
($17, 1,000)   ★★★
Zinfandel Mount Veeder Brandlin Ranch
($20, 1,500)   ★★★
Zinfandel Napa Valley Hendry Vineyard
(Discontinued)   ★★★

ALSO PRODUCED
Sauvignon Blanc Napa Valley ($15, 200); Zinfandel Napa Valley ($16, 1,000).

WINERY DATA
Case Production: 5,000. **Acres Owned:** 12 acres in Mount Veeder (leased). **Varietals by Acre:** Zinfandel (12 acres). **Vineyard Designations:** Brandlin Ranch (Zinfandel), Planchon Vineyard (Zinfandel). **Varietals Purchased:** Cabernet Sauvignon (Napa Valley), Sauvignon Blanc (Napa Valley), Zinfandel (Contra Costa, Napa Valley).

Peter Franus left a career as a journalist to take up winemaking, working briefly at Chalone and William Hill Winery before settling in as winemaker at Mount Veeder Winery from 1981 to 1992. In 1987, Franus began making small lots of Zinfandel in a rented Napa warehouse that he shared with Mike Havens; the two now operate out of the former Lakespring Winery near Yountville. Part of Franus's fascination with Zinfandel stems from the excellent vineyards on Mount Veeder. He has settled on two key vineyards, George Hendry Vineyard and Brandlin Vineyard, which he bottles separately with vineyard designations. He has also made a Hendry Vineyard Cabernet, which is spicy and elegant. Future growth will come as Franus finds additional vineyards worthy of being bottled as vineyard-designated wines, for example his Contra Costa County Planchon Vineyard 1996 Zinfandel (89 points), made from purchased grapes, which displays a wide array of complex, concentrated flavors.

TASTING NOTES

CABERNET SAUVIGNON NAPA VALLEY (★★★): New to the lineup, but given the winemaker's experience with this grape, it should be a good match. The 1995 (88 points) was firm, with ripe cherry, coffee and grainy tannins; best to cellar.

ZINFANDEL MOUNT VEEDER BRANDLIN RANCH (★★★): Austere but well focused, with tight fruit flavors and ample tannins.
1995: Intense, with lots of wild berry, black cherry, spice, pepper and sage notes; turns tight and tannic. **88**
1992: Serves up classic Zinfandel flavors, with its well focused spice, pepper and wild berry notes. **88**
1991: Tight and austere, with firm, chewy tannins, but enough cherry and raspberry flavors underneath to merit attention. **86**

ZINFANDEL NAPA VALLEY HENDRY VINEYARD (★★★): Ripe and intense, with more depth and complexity than the Brandlin.
1993: Compact, with a green tea edge, leathery notes and rugged, tannic berry-ish flavors. **85**
1992: Ripe and spicy, with bright, rich, lively raspberry, anise and black cherry flavors that are firmly tannic and framed by light oak. **89**
1991: Ripe and intense, with tart, vivid, concentrated, sharply focused berry, pepper, cherry and floral aromas and flavors that turn rich and complex. **90**
1990: Bold, ripe and flavorful, with rich, intense cherry, plum and raspberry flavors that are long and peppery on the palate. **89**

FRAZIER (★★★)
Coombsville, Napa Valley
Founded: 1995. **Owner:** Bill Frazier. **Winemaker:** John Gibson.

MAJOR WINES: PRICE, CASES, RATING
Cabernet Sauvignon Napa Valley Lupine Hill Vineyard
($40, 2,400)   ★★★
Merlot Napa Valley Lupine Hill Vineyard
($35, 600)   ★★★

WINERY DATA
Case Production: 3,000. **Acres Owned:** 20 acres in Napa.
Varietals by Acre: Cabernet Franc (1 acre), Cabernet Sauvignon (14), Merlot (4), Petit Verdot (1). **Vineyard Designations:** Lupine Hill Vineyard (Cabernet Sauvignon, Merlot).

Retired airline pilot Bill Frazier has produced complex, flavorful Cabernet Sauvignon and Merlot from his Lupine Hill Vineyard in the Coombsville area east of the city of Napa. The wines are made by John Gibson (Snowden) at the Napa Wine Co. The 1995 Cabernet (88 points) was plush, with black currant, herb and cedar flavors and a long finish. The 1995 Merlot (85) was complex, featuring earthy, leathery flavors followed by nuances of currant, anise and sage. Worth watching.

FREEMARK ABBEY WINERY
(★★–★★★★)
St. Helena, Napa Valley
Founded: 1967. **Owner:** Carpy Family, Jaeger Family, John Bryan Family, Warren Family, Laurie Wood Family, Ted Edwards, Webb Family, Dick Heggin. **Winemaker:** Ted Edwards.

MAJOR WINES: PRICE, CASES, RATING

Cabernet Sauvignon Napa Valley ($24, 12,000)	★★★
Cabernet Sauvignon Napa Valley Bosché Vineyard ($44, 3,000)	★★★★★
Cabernet Sauvignon Napa Valley Sycamore Vineyards ($34, 2,200)	★★★★
Chardonnay Napa Valley ($18, 10,000)	★★★
Chardonnay Napa Valley Carpy Ranch ($24, 2,000)	★★★★
Johannisberg Riesling Late Harvest Napa Valley Edelwein Gold ($40, 1,300)	★★★★
Merlot Napa Valley ($20, 10,000)	★★★

WINERY DATA
Case Production: 45,000. **Acres Owned:** 295 acres in Napa Valley. **Varietals by Acre:** Cabernet Franc (12 acres), Cabernet Sauvignon (82), Chardonnay (70), Merlot (90), Petite Sirah (10), Petit Verdot (10), Sangiovese (6), Viognier (7), White Riesling (8). **Vineyard Designations:** Bosché (Cabernet Sauvignon), Carpy Ranch (Chardonnay), Sycamore Vineyard (Cabernet Sauvignon). **Varietals Purchased:** Cabernet Sauvignon (Napa Valley).

Freemark Abbey Winery remains a steady, under-appreciated producer of Cabernet Sauvignon from both Bosché Vineyard and Sycamore Vineyards in Rutherford. These are not blockbusters; rather, they are wines of finesse and polish. They are rarely mentioned as among Napa's finest, but in fact they're exceptionally well made, age well, and are very consistent from year to year. Chardonnay and Merlot are also in the good to very good category.

A group of seven partners, including long-time winegrower Chuck Carpy and legendary winemaker Brad Webb, founded the winery in 1967, before the start of the 1970s California wine boom. Many fine winemakers have passed through its cellars, including Jerry Luper (Chateau Montelena, Diamond Creek), Mike Richmond (Acacia, Carmenet) and Ted Edwards, the current steward. Early on, Freemark Abbey had a big advantage over its competition, because its partners knew the best areas in the valley for grapes; witness their recognition of the Bosché Vineyard in Rutherford. For years, the grapes from that property went into Beaulieu Vineyard Private Reserve, and BV set aside special lots bottled especially for proprietor John Bosché. But in 1968, Bosché asked Carpy to make wine from his vineyard, and by 1969 Bosché Cabernet had become a staple in Freemark Abbey's lineup, to be joined later by a Cabernet from Sycamore Vineyards.

TASTING NOTES

CABERNET SAUVIGNON NAPA VALLEY (★★★): Can be a very good value. The 1994 (89 points) and 1995 (89) offer a solid core of complex currant, herb, black cherry and spice flavors.

CABERNET SAUVIGNON NAPA VALLEY BOSCHÉ VINEYARD (★★★★★): Among the most elegant and refined of the great Rutherford Cabernets. This is a classy, supple, well integrated wine that is very consistent and ageworthy.

1994: Ripe, rich and complex, with a supple, elegant texture and a wonderful array of flavors. **91**

1993: Rich and complex, with a tight, well focused core of currant, black cherry, anise, sage and spice flavors. **92**

1992: Ripe, smooth and harmonious, with a delicious core of plum and wild berry flavors that unfold gracefully. **93**

1991: Firm, rich and focused, with complex cherry, currant and anise flavors that linger. Beautifully balanced. **90**

1990: Complex and concentrated, classic Bosché with its core of ripe, supple currant and black cherry flavors. **90**

1989: Lean and crisp, with a narrow range of earthy currant, black cherry and cedary oak flavors. **87**

1988: Austere, with dry tannins and a modest core of dried cherry and currant flavors framed by light sage and oak. **83**

1987: Lean and trim, with crisp tannins and an earthy edge to the herb, green olive and currant notes. **88**

1986: Tart, with a cedary accent to the anise and cherry flavors, turning dry on the finish. **78**

1985: Lean, tight and concentrated, with firm black cherry, plum, currant, earth and cedar flavors that are intense and lively. The finish is narrow and focused. **90**

1984: Chunky, showing mature currant, black cherry, cedar and spice notes before firm tannins kick in. **87**

1983: A little rough around the edges now, this is a serious, intense wine with high acid, lots of tannins and loads of complex plum, cherry and anise flavors that are very well focused. **86**

1982: Tough, lean and tannic, with herb, cherry, spice and currant flavors, but it's still elegant. **88**

1981: Has pretty black cherry flavors and is leaner and more compact on the palate than the nose suggests. **86**

1980: Rich and ripe, with sharply defined fruit flavors and a touch of herb, cherry and anise. **88**

1979: Mature but still dense and concentrated, with compact currant, anise and cedar notes, finishing with firm tannins. Still excellent. **88**

1978: Mature and fading, with drying cedar and currant flavors. After a long run in prime condition, it has passed its peak. **87**

1976: Ripe, jammy and chunky, turning dry and austere on the finish. **84**

1975: Deeply colored but fading, with pleasant dried cherry and currant flavors. **85**

1974: Showing its age but retaining its elegant personality, it's drying out and losing its fruit, but there are just enough complexity and finesse to hold your interest. Drink up if you still have a bottle. **85**

1973: Smooth and polished, with a core of pretty, mature currant, anise and smoky cedar notes. Still delicious. **89**

1971: From a difficult vintage, this 1971 is an extraordinary wine that has aged extremely well. It's fully mature and elegant, with complex, mature toast, cedar, plum and currant flavors. **86**

1970: Amazingly rich and elegant, with supple cedar, black cherry and currant flavors, smooth tannins and a long, delicious finish. Complex and enticing. **91**

CABERNET SAUVIGNON NAPA VALLEY SYCAMORE VINEYARDS (★★★★): Lacks the depth of Bosché, but can be very good. It's marked by herb, currant and cedar flavors.

1993: Tight, with pretty plum, black cherry, herb and mineral flavors and firm but polished tannins coming through on the finish. **89**

1992: Mature and supple, with complex currant, plum, cedar and coffee flavors and polished tannins. **89**

1991: Smooth, with a supple texture, ripe tannins and a pleasing core of cherry and wild berry flavors, with firm tannins. **88**

1990: Ripe and generous, with a mouthful of black cherry and spicy toast flavors and fine tannins. **88**

1988: Nicely balanced, with a modest range of herb, currant and spicy notes, turning simple. **86**

1987: Firm, with chewy tannins and a meaty, herbal edge to its Cabernet flavors. **84**

CHARDONNAY VARIOUS BOTTLINGS (★★): Carpy Ranch is made in a tight, flinty style, with the emphasis on rich pear and spicy oak. The Napa Valley bottling is good, with attractive fruit.

JOHANNISBERG RIESLING LATE HARVEST NAPA VALLEY EDELWEIN GOLD (★★★★): Among the best in California of this type, it ages well and gains depth, with rich, complex apricot and honey notes.

1991: Ripe, buttery, rich and sweet, with all kinds of spice, honey and butter notes gracing the sweet pineapple, fig and pear flavors. **92**

1989: With its golden color and honey, apricot and spice aromas and flavors, this is a knockout from the first whiff to the last echo of the long finish. A rich, sweet, seductive wine. **92**

MERLOT NAPA VALLEY (★★★): Improving; the 1995 (88 points) was rich and complex, with lots of currant, cherry, herb, cedar and spice flavors. Both the 1994 and 1993 scored 87 points.

FREESTONE see VON STRASSER

FRICK WINERY (★★)
Dry Creek Valley, Sonoma County
Founded: 1976. **Owner:** Bill Frick & Judith Gannon. **Winemaker:** Bill Frick. **Second Label:** Cafe Red, Cafe White.

MAJOR WINES: PRICE, CASES, RATING

Cabernet Sauvignon Dry Creek Valley	
($21, 350)	★★★
Cinsault Dry Creek Valley	
($15, 400)	★★
Merlot Dry Creek Valley	
($20, 1,000)	★★
Syrah Dry Creek Valley	
($21, 500)	★★
Viognier Dry Creek Valley	
($21, 150)	★★

ALSO PRODUCED
Cinsault Rosé Dry Creek Valley ($10, 150).

WINERY DATA
Case Production: 2,000. **Acres Owned:** 6 acres in Dry Creek Valley. **Varietals by Acre:** Syrah (4 acres), Viognier (2). **Varietals Purchased:** Merlot (Dry Creek Valley), Cinsault (Dry Creek Valley).

The Frick Winery has moved almost as often as its grape sources have changed. It began in an abandoned gas station in Bonny Doon in the Santa Cruz Mountains, moved to a warehouse in Santa Cruz and now operates six acres in Dry Creek Valley. The label looks as if it were penned by Ralph Steadman, and the wines are ripe, bold and full-blown but inconsistent. I liked the 1994 Cabernet Sauvignon Dry Creek Valley (89 points) for its complex flavors. Cinsault, Merlot, Syrah, Viognier and Zinfandel are all ★★ performers.

J. FRITZ (★★★)
Dry Creek Valley, Sonoma County
Founded: 1979. **Owner:** J. Fritz. **Winemaker:** Jim Coughlin.

MAJOR WINES: PRICE, CASES, RATING

Chardonnay Russian River Valley Dutton Ranch	
($20, 3,000)	★★★★
Chardonnay Russian River Valley Dutton Vineyard Ruxton Ranch	
($26, 450)	★★★
Chardonnay Russian River Valley Dutton Vineyard Shop Block	
($30, 300)	★★★★
Chardonnay Russian River Valley Poplar Vineyard	
($22, 500)	★★★
Melon Russian River Valley	
($14, 750)	★★
Sauvignon Blanc Dry Creek Valley Jenner Vineyard	
($12, 1,500)	★★★
Sauvignon Blanc Russian River Valley Poplar Vineyard	
($12, 500)	★★★
Zinfandel Dry Creek Valley Old Vine	
($20, 1,000)	★★★
Zinfandel Dry Creek Valley Rogers Reserve Eighty-Year-Old Vines	
($26, 150)	★★★

ALSO PRODUCED
Cabernet Sauvignon Dry Creek Valley ($20, 150); Merlot Dry Creek Valley Estate ($18, 700); Zinfandel Late Harvest Dry Creek Valley Redwood Hill ($18, 450).

WINERY DATA
Case Production: 15,000. **Acres Owned:** 130 acres (30 in Dry Creek, 100 in Russian River). **Varietals by Acre:** Chardonnay (100 acres), Sauvignon Blanc (20), Zinfandel (10). **Vineyard Designations:** Dutton Ranch (Chardonnay), Jenner Vineyard (Sauvignon Blanc), Poplar Vineyard (Chardonnay, Sauvignon Blanc), Redwood Hill (Zinfandel). **Varietals Purchased:** Chardonnay (Russian River), Sauvignon Blanc (Russian River), Zinfandel (Dry Creek).

Arthur and Barbara Fritz founded this 15,000-case winery in 1979. Through the years the wines have lacked consistency, but the most recent offerings have shown a marked improvement. For a brief period, Helen Turley worked with these wines, aiming for riper, richer flavors—a strategy that has paid off.

TASTING NOTES

CHARDONNAY RUSSIAN RIVER VALLEY VARIOUS BOTTLINGS (★★★): The Dutton Ranch bottling (★★★★) exhibits the rich, complex flavors that come from the Chardonnay grapes that are grown there. The 1996 (91 points) offers ripe pear, hazelnut and spicy nuances. The Poplar Vineyard 1996 (★★★) leaned more toward floral and citrus flavors.

SAUVIGNON BLANC VARIOUS BOTTLINGS (★★★): In 1996, two bottlings were made from grapes from Dry Creek Valley and Russian River Valley. The Dry Creek 1996 Jenner Vineyard (87 points) was rich and buttery, while the Russian River Poplar Vineyard 1996 (89) featured bright grapefruit and hazelnut flavors.

ZINFANDEL DRY CREEK VALLEY VARIOUS BOTTLINGS (★★★): The 1996 Old Vine (88 points) had well-focused wild berry, black cherry and strawberry flavors. The 1996 Rogers Reserve Eighty-Year-Old Vines (86) was crisper, without the depth of the Old Vine.

FROG'S LEAP (★★★)
Rutherford, Napa Valley
Founded: 1981. **Owner:** John & Julie Williams. **Winemaker:** John Williams.

MAJOR WINES: PRICE, CASES, RATING
Wine	Rating
Cabernet Sauvignon Napa Valley ($24, 6,500)	★★★
Chardonnay Carneros ($22, 6,900)	★★★
Merlot Napa Valley ($22, 8,600)	★★★
Sauvignon Blanc Napa Valley ($13, 16,000)	★★
White Leapfrögmilch Napa Valley ($16, 1,900)	★★
Zinfandel Napa Valley ($16, 7,100)	★★★

WINERY DATA
Case Production: 47,000. **Acres Owned:** 135 acres in Rutherford. **Varietals by Acre:** Cabernet Sauvignon (20 acres), Chenin Blanc (6), Merlot (35), Petite Sirah (3), Sauvignon Blanc (50), Sémillion (6), Zinfandel (15). **Varietals Purchased:** Cabernet Sauvignon (Carneros, Oakville, Rutherford), Chardonnay (Carneros), Merlot (Carneros, Rutherford), Sauvignon Blanc (Yountville), Zinfandel (St. Helena).

In 1981 Frog's Leap was founded by Larry Turley, his former wife, Jeannine, and John and Julie Williams. The wine was made on Turley's property, where frogs—whose legs were destined for fine restaurants—once were raised. Frog's Leap's initial focus was on Sauvignon Blanc; Cabernet, Chardonnay, Merlot, Zinfandel, and occasionally a late-harvest wine called Late Leap were added later. In 1993 Turley formed Turley Wine Cellars, focusing on Zinfandel and hearty reds, while the Williamses took on new partners, building the current winery in Rutherford near Caymus. Production is at 47,000 cases, with grapes coming from 135 acres in the Rutherford area.

TASTING NOTES

CABERNET SAUVIGNON NAPA VALLEY (★★★): Elegant and usually quite fruity, with mild tannins; made in a ready-to-drink style. Both the 1994 (88 points) and 1995 (88) offered lots of ripe, juicy Cabernet flavors. Best to drink early on, though it ages well.

CHARDONNAY CARNEROS (★★★): Inconsistent. At its best, it's marked by crisp acidity and attractive flavors.

MERLOT NAPA VALLEY (★★★): Consistent, with the 1993 (87 points), 1994 (87) and 1995 (86) vintages all well made. The latter vintage was marked by an earthy streak, but it also showed complex currant and berry flavors.

SAUVIGNON BLANC NAPA VALLEY (★★): Quality has declined, hitting a low with the 1995 (76 points), in which tart, unripe flavors abounded. The 1996 (83) was better, but it's still rather ordinary.

ZINFANDEL NAPA VALLEY (★★★): This is perhaps the winery's best wine of late. The 1994 (89 points) featured tart, earthy wild berry, cherry, raspberry and spice flavors. The 1995 (87) was more elegant, with pretty plum and cherry flavors.

THE GAINEY VINEYARD (★★★)
Santa Ynez Valley, Santa Barbara County
Founded: 1984. **Owner:** Daniel J. & Daniel H. Gainey.
Winemaker: Kirby Anderson.

MAJOR WINES: PRICE, CASES, RATING

Chardonnay Santa Barbara County	
Limited Selection	
($25, 1,000)	★★★★
Pinot Noir Santa Maria Valley	
Limited Selection	
($25, 1,000)	★★★
Riesling Santa Ynez Valley	
($10, 2,000)	★★

ALSO PRODUCED
Cabernet Franc Santa Ynez Valley Limited Selection ($20, 400); Chardonnay Santa Barbara County ($15, 3,000); Merlot Santa Ynez Valley ($18, 2,000); Sauvignon Blanc Santa Ynez Valley Limited Selection ($16, 2,000).

WINERY DATA
Case Production: 15,000. **Acres Owned:** 115 acres in Santa Ynez Valley. **Varietals by Acre:** Cabernet Franc (7 acres), Chardonnay (40), Merlot (25), Pinot Noir (4), Riesling (7), Sauvignon Blanc (18), Sémillon (4), Syrah (10). **Varietals Purchased:** Chardonnay (Santa Ynez, Santa Maria Valley), Pinot Noir (Santa Maria Valley).

The Gainey Vineyard is 115 acres of vineyard carved out of a much larger 1,800-acre ranch devoted to farm animals and a variety of crops. The winery was once headed by winemaker Richard Longoria, who departed to form his own winery (see Longoria listing). Of the 15,000 cases produced, the Chardonnay Limited Selection is clearly the quality leader.

TASTING NOTES

CHARDONNAY LIMITED SELECTION (★★★★): Carries both the Santa Barbara County and the narrower Santa Ynez appellations; under either designation, this is a very well made, complex, exotic wine.

CHARDONNAY SANTA BARBARA COUNTY LIMITED SELECTION (★★★★)
1996: An exotic yet elegant style, with an earthy streak to ripe pear, fig, apricot and melon flavors. **91**

CHARDONNAY SANTA YNEZ VALLEY LIMITED SELECTION
1995: Ripe and full-bodied, with complex, exotic, creamy pear, pineapple, citrus, honey and hazelnut flavors. **93**
1994: Pleasantly balanced, ripe and elegant, with layers of rich pear, honey, vanilla and spice flavors. **88**

PINOT NOIR SANTA MARIA VALLEY LIMITED SELECTION (★★★): The 1996 (87 points) served up a range of black cherry, spice herb and rhubarb flavors.

GALANTE VINEYARDS (★★★)
Carmel Valley, Monterey County
Founded: 1994. **Owner:** Jack Galante. **Winemaker:** Jack Galante.

MAJOR WINES: PRICE, CASES, RATING

Cabernet Sauvignon Carmel Valley Estate	
Blackjack Pasture	
($35, 1,000)	★★★
Cabernet Sauvignon Carmel Valley Estate	
Red Rosé Hill	
($25, 1,300)	★★★
Merlot Carmel Valley Estate	
($30, 125)	★★★

ALSO PRODUCED
Cabernet Sauvignon Carmel Valley Estate Rancho Galante ($18, 1,200); Sauvignon Blanc Carmel Valley Estate ($18, 100).

WINERY DATA
Case Production: 4,000. **Acres Owned:** 70 acres in Carmel Valley. **Varietals by Acre:** Cabernet Sauvignon (57 acres), Merlot (2), Pinot Noir (8), Sauvignon Blanc (2), Viognier (1).

Located in Carmel Valley, Galante Vineyards was better known for being one of the largest commercial rose growers in California until they began producing wines in 1994. The early releases of Cabernet and Merlot have been tightly wound, concentrated wines with ripe currant, anise and herb flavors. The 1995 Cabernet Sauvignon Blackjack Pasture (90 points) was slightly richer and more complex than the 1995 Red Rose Hill (88).

GALLO OF SONOMA WINERY
(★★★–★★★★★)
Dry Creek Valley, Sonoma County
Founded: 1977. **Owner:** The Gallo Family.
Winemaker: Marcello Monticelli and Gina Gallo.
Second Label: Anapamu, Indigo Hills, Marcelina, Turning Leaf, Rancho Zabaco.

MAJOR WINES: PRICE, CASES, RATING

Cabernet Sauvignon Dry Creek Valley Frei Ranch Vineyard ($18, 5,600)	★★★
Cabernet Sauvignon Dry Creek Valley Stefani Vineyard ($20, 7,000)	★★★
Cabernet Sauvignon Northern Sonoma Estate Bottled ($55, 2,400)	★★★★★
Cabernet Sauvignon Sonoma County ($10, 35,000)	★★
Chardonnay Dry Creek Valley Stefani Vineyard ($16, 17,000)	★★★★
Chardonnay Northern Sonoma Estate Bottled ($45, 1,000)	★★★★★
Chardonnay Russian River Valley ($11, 35,000)	★★
Chardonnay Russian River Valley Laguna Ranch ($18, 17,000)	★★★★
Merlot Northern Sonoma ($14, 5,000)	★★★
Merlot Sonoma County ($10, 63,000)	★★★
Pinot Noir Russian River Valley ($10)	★★
Valdiguié Alexander Valley Barrelli Creek Vineyard ($14, 4,000)	★★
Zinfandel Alexander Valley Barrelli Creek Vineyard ($18, 2,000)	★★★
Zinfandel Dry Creek Valley Chiotti Vineyard ($18, 2,000)	★★★
Zinfandel Dry Creek Valley Frei Ranch Vineyard ($18, 10,000)	★★★
Zinfandel Dry Creek Valley Stefani Vineyard ($18, 2,200)	★★★
Zinfandel Sonoma County ($10, 10,000)	★★★

ALSO PRODUCED
Sauvignon Blanc Carmel Valley Estate ($18, 100); Merlot Alexander Valley Barrelli Creek Vineyard ($18); Merlot Dry Creek Valley Frei Ranch Vineyard ($14); Sangiovese Alexander Valley; Barrelli Creek Vineyard ($16).

WINERY DATA
Acres Owned: 3,005 acres (610 in Alexander Valley, 965 in Dry Creek Valley, 1,170 in Russian River Valley, 260 in Sonoma Coast). **Varietals by Acre:** Barbera, Cabernet Sauvignon, Chardonnay, Merlot, Sangiovese, Valdiguié, Zinfandel. **Vineyard Designations:** Barrelli Creek Vineyard (Barbera, Cabernet Sauvignon, Merlot, Sangiovese, Valdiguié, Zinfandel), Frei Ranch Vineyard (Cabernet Sauvignon, Merlot, Zinfandel), Laguna Ranch Vineyard (Chardonnay), Stefani Vineyard (Cabernet Sauvignon, Chardonnay).

After decades of mass-producing value-oriented wines, from Hearty Burgundy to Bartles & Jaymes wine coolers, the world's largest winery (more than 70 million cases and more than $1 billion in sales annually) has focused on super-premium wines from its considerable Sonoma County vineyard holdings, and further emphasized its estate-grown Cabernet, Chardonnay, Merlot and Zinfandel. The shift to the high end of the wine market came late in the distinguished winemaking careers of Ernest and Julio Gallo. Both brothers were in their 80s when the first Gallo Northern Sonoma Cabernet appeared at $55 a bottle, accompanied by a $45 Chardonnay—nearly 60 years after they founded their winery in Modesto in 1933.

Plans to focus on fine wines grown in Sonoma and Napa were in the works for decades, but the Gallos kept their intentions a well-guarded secret. Once they started planting thousands of acres of grapes throughout Northern Sonoma, though, it became apparent that they were going to be making great wines, as wine drinkers increasingly clamored for vineyard-designated and appellation-oriented wines. The first serious attempt with Cabernet in 1978 aged very well for the first decade of its life; the wines thereafter were leaner and trimmer, until the 1990 and 1991 Northern Sonoma vintages, which were outstanding.

The Gallos were long-time buyers of top-quality Napa and Sonoma grapes, at times purchasing anywhere from 25 percent to 40 percent of the grapes and bulk wines from those areas. In the 1970s the Gallos decided to put money into Sonoma County vineyard land, buying the old Frei Ranch, which now totals 710 acres of grapes, including Cabernet, Merlot, Zinfandel and others in Dry Creek Valley (where a huge new winery has been built); the Laguna Ranch, which encompasses 360 acres of Chardonnay in a cool spot in Russian River Valley; 200 acres at Stefani Vineyard in Dry Creek; and another 610 acres of sweeping vineyards in Alexander Valley around the hamlet of Asti. The Asti area vineyards are planted to a wide assortment of mostly red-wine grapes—Syrah, Sangiovese, Zinfandel and the like—which Gallo now vinifies as well. And a number of new brands—Anapamu, Indigo Hills, Marcelina, Turning Leaf and Zabaco—have been launched recently.

Just about anything's possible, given the quality of Gallo's vineyards, winemaking know-how, research capabilities and determination to rise to the top of the quality charts. My notes focus on the Sonoma County (Gallo of Sonoma) estate-bottled (Northern Sonoma), and vineyard-designated wines. Most of Gallo's other bottlings are clean, well made and easy to drink, even if they do not excite as the new wines do. Sadly, Julio Gallo died in 1993, but his clear vision of quality lives on in these new wines.

TASTING NOTES

CABERNET SAUVIGNON DRY CREEK VALLEY FREI RANCH VINEYARD (★★★): Steadily improving, dark, ripe and fruity. Worth watching.
1994: Dark, ripe, plump and juicy; brimming with lively black cherry, plum and wild berry flavors and smooth, ripe tannins. **91**

1993: Dense and chewy, with a firm wall of tannins and a core of tarry plum and dried cherry. **87**
1992: Ripe, rich and intense, with a tightly wound core of currant, anise, plum and cherry flavors, turning tannic. **89**

CABERNET SAUVIGNON DRY CREEK VALLEY STEFANI VINEYARD (★★★)
1994: Bright and lively, with an earthy streak that runs through the bright wild berry, cherry and plumy flavors. **89**

CABERNET SAUVIGNON NORTHERN SONOMA ESTATE BOTTLED (★★★★★): This wine could carry the Dry Creek appellation, as it is entirely from the Gallos' Frei Ranch Vineyard. Introduced with the 1990 vintage, it combines rich, complex fruit flavors with a sense of elegance and finesse, showing off a nice array of toasty oak flavors.
1994: Elegant, with ripe, fleshy cherry, currant, anise, cedar and spice flavors, finishing with supple tannins. **92**
1993: Dry and earthy, yet focused, with a core of plum and cherry flavors that are ripe, dense and complex. **90**
1992: Ripe, rich and complex; tight and firm, with currant, mineral, anise and berry flavors that linger. **92**
1991: Youthful and vibrant, with ripe, rich, supple spice, cherry and berry flavors that run deep. A concentrated wine with a long and full finish. **91**
1990: Ripe and spicy, supple and complex, with concentrated currant, spice, cedar and black cherry flavors that are beautifully focused and rich. Combines a wealth of flavor with elegance and finesse. **93**

CHARDONNAY DRY CREEK VALLEY STEFANI VINEYARD (★★★★)
1996: A crisp, flinty style, with fresh pear, quince and tart apple flavors. Turns elegant on the finish. **88**
1995: Lively and complex, with spicy pear, apple and nutmeg notes, turning smooth and silky, with a smoky aftertaste. **91**

CHARDONNAY NORTHERN SONOMA ESTATE BOTTLED (★★★★★): Truly exceptional Chardonnay; rich, complex, detailed, elegant and long on the finish.
1996: Deliciously fruity, elegant, ripe, rich and concentrated, with tiers of spicy pear, fig, apricot and melon, finishing with a complex spicy oak aftertaste. **93**
1995: Toasty, smoky oak leads to a rich, complex range of fig, pear, spice and melon flavors that are long and lively. **94**
1994: Elegant and complex, with layers of ripe, rich pear, fig, melon and citrus flavors accented by a smoky, toasty note. **92**

CHARDONNAY RUSSIAN RIVER VALLEY LAGUNA RANCH
(★★★★): Pushing a ★★★★★ rating. It's seductive and very complex, having been grown in a prime area for Chardonnay.
1996: Delicious, rich, flavorful and loaded with spice, pear, apple, fig and melon flavors. **91**
1995: Bright and lively, with a juicy core of citrus, pear and spice flavors and firm acidity. Turns elegant on the finish. **90**
1994: Combines smoky oak and exotic layers of earthy pear, grapefruit and spice flavors, turning elegant and delicate. **92**

MERLOT SONOMA COUNTY (★★★): Steadily improving; the 1996 (86 points) is firmly tannic, with earthy currant, tea and sage flavors.

ZINFANDEL VARIOUS BOTTLINGS (★★★): Julio Gallo's favorite wine continues to impress. It is made from several different vineyards.
ZINFANDEL ALEXANDER VALLEY BARRELLI CREEK VINEYARD (★★★)
1995: Ripe, with lovely jam, wild berry, cherry and plum-laced flavors. Complex, concentrated, well proportioned and long and fruity on the aftertaste, where the tannins are smooth and rich. **90**
ZINFANDEL DRY CREEK VALLEY CHIOTTI VINEYARD (★★★)
1995: Starts out earthy, but slowly works its way into the fruit spectrum, with wild berry, raspberry, tar and sage notes. **90**
ZINFANDEL DRY CREEK VALLEY FREI RANCH VINEYARD (★★★)
1995: Firm, tightly wound and well focused, with ripe, complex raspberry, cherry, earth and cedary notes. Elegant and refined. **87**
1994: Austere, with a dry edge to the modest plum and wild berry flavors; the dryness on the finish is difficult to overlook. **84**
1993: Supple, with ripe cherry and berry flavors, finishing with fine tannins and a soft edge. **87**
1990: Smells fruity, with berry and jam flavors, then it turns dry, with sage, wild berry, smoke and tarry notes, finishing with firm tannins. **88**

ZINFANDEL DRY CREEK VALLEY STEFANI VINEYARD (★★★)
1996: Bright and lively, with nuances of creamy oak and zesty cherry and berry flavors that are fresh and snappy, finishing with a dash of tar and cedar. **89**

GARLAND RANCH see CHATEAU JULIEN

GARRETSON WINE CO. (★★★)
Paso Robles, San Luis Obispo County
Founded: 1997. **Owner:** Matt & Amie Garretson.
Winemaker: Matt Garretson.

MAJOR WINES: PRICE, CASES, RATING
Eau de Vie Edna Valley Cuvée
  Ella Alban Vineyards
  ($120, 100)   ★★★★

ALSO PRODUCED
Rosé Central Coast The Celeidh ($16, 300); Syrah Paso Robles The Aisling ($20, 500).

WINERY DATA
Case Production: 1,000. **Varietals Purchased:** Grenache (Central Coast), Roussanne (Edna Valley), Syrah (Central Coast, Paso Robles), Viognier (Edna Valley).

Matt Garretson, brand manager for Wild Horse Winery and organizer of the Hospice du Rhône, an annual Rhône varietal-focused event in Paso Robles, started his own brand in 1997. So far Garretson has two wines (a Rhône blend Rosé and Syrah) and an *eau-de-vie*, but the portfolio is likely to expand as the brand gets established. Grapes are purchased from a number of Central Coast vineyards. Garretson's impressive *eau-de-vie* was made by distilling a blend of Roussanne and Viognier wines, rather than just the grape skins, making a smooth, elegant spirit, with flavors of orange peel. A winery to watch.

DANIEL GEHRS WINES (★★★)
Santa Barbara County
Founded: 1990. **Owner:** Daniel & Robin Gehrs.
Winemaker: Daniel Gehrs.

MAJOR WINES: PRICE, CASES, RATING
Chenin Blanc Monterey Carmel Vineyard
Le Chenière
($10, 1,100) ★★★
Pinot Blanc Monterey Carmel Vineyard
($12, 1,500) ★★
Pinot Noir Santa Barbara County
($20, 500) ★★
Sauvignon Blanc Monterey Carmel
Vineyard
($11, 1,500) ★★★
Syrah Paso Robles
($18, 780) ★★★
Viognier Santa Barbara County
($18, 450) ★★★

ALSO PRODUCED
Cabernet Franc Santa Barbara County ($14, 750).

WINERY DATA
Case Production: 5,500. **Vineyard Designations:** Carmel Vineyard. **Varietals Purchased:** Cabernet Franc (Santa Barbara), Chardonnay (Santa Barbara County), Chenin Blanc (Monterey), Pinot Blanc (Monterey), Pinot Noir (Santa Barbara), Syrah (Paso Robles).

Daniel Gehrs founded his own brand in 1991 while he was still winemaker at Zaca Mesa; he left there in 1998 in order to focus on his label full time. Gehrs's portfolio has expanded from Loire-style whites like Chenin Blanc, Pinot Blanc and Muscadet to include the Rhône varietals Syrah and Viognier, with which he was very successful at Zaca Mesa. Gehrs's old-vine Chenin Blanc from Carmel Valley is one of California's more distinctive; the 1996 (88 points) showed complex, herb-tinged lemon and grapefruit flavors.

GEORIS WINERY (★★)
Carmel Valley, Monterey County
Founded: 1982. **Owner:** Walter Georis. **Winemaker:** Water Georis.

MAJOR WINES: PRICE, CASES, RATING
Merlot Carmel Valley
($24, 1,700) ★★

WINERY DATA
Case Production: 1,700. **Acres Owned:** 28 acres in Carmel Valley. **Varietals by Acre:** Cabernet Sauvignon (4 acres), Merlot (24).

Walter Georis has gone from surf rock (Endless Summer soundtrack) to Birkenstock salesman to restaurateur (Casanova in Carmel) to wine. He now makes a dense and chewy Merlot from estate-grown vines in Carmel Valley. Production has risen from a few hundred cases to 1,700 as the vineyard has grown to 28 acres, 24 of that Merlot. The goal is to produce a long-lived Merlot and possibly a Cabernet. The Merlot certainly has the tannin and concentration to endure, but the question is whether it will ever soften up and evolve into something more complex. The jury is still out.

TASTING NOTES

MERLOT CARMEL VALLEY (★★): The 1994 (80 points) was hard and green, with dry, leathery tannins. A more appealing effort in 1992 (89) was smoother and more polished, with berry and sage flavors.

GEYSER PEAK WINERY (★★★)
Alexander Valley, Sonoma County
Founded: 1880. **Owner:** Jim Beam Brands. **Winemaker:** Daryl Groom. **Second Label:** Canyon Road, Fox Ridge, Venezia.

MAJOR WINES: PRICE, CASES, RATING
Alexandre Cabernet Blend
Alexander Valley Reserve
($32, 4,800) ★★★★
Cabernet Sauvignon Alexander Valley
Reserve
($29, 8,100) ★★★

Cabernet Sauvignon Sonoma County
($16, 4,500) ★★★

Chardonnay Alexander Valley Reserve
($23, 1,250) ★★★

Chardonnay Sonoma County
($14, 80,000) ★★★

Johannisberg Riesling California
($8, 39,000) ★★

Merlot Alexander Valley Reserve
($32, 1,400) ★★★

Merlot Sonoma County
($17, 43,000) ★★★

Sauvignon Blanc Sonoma County
($9, 39,000) ★★★

Shiraz Sonoma County
($16, 5,000) ★★★

Shiraz Sonoma County Reserve
($32, 920) ★★★

Zinfandel Sonoma County
($17, 5,000) ★★

Canyon Road Cabernet Sauvignon
California
($8, 66,000) ★★

Canyon Road Chardonnay California
($8, 75,000) ★★

Canyon Road Merlot California
($9, 70,000) ★★

Canyon Road Sauvignon Blanc
California
($7, 15,000) ★★

Venezia Cabernet Sauvignon
Alexander Valley
($24, 2,350) ★★★

Venezia Chardonnay Alexander Valley
($20, 1,780) ★★★

Venezia Chardonnay Napa Valley
($20, 1,000) ★★★

Venezia Sangiovese Mendocino County
Eagle Point Ranch
($24, 350) ★★★

Venezia Sangiovese North Coast
Nuovo Mondo
($24, 2,450) ★★

Venezia Sangiovese Russian River Valley
Alegria Vineyard
($24, 620) ★★★

ALSO PRODUCED
Gamay California ($8, 15,000); Venezia Meritage Sonoma County ($20, 1,350).

WINERY DATA
Case Production: 500,000. **Acres Owned:** 122 acres in Alexander Valley. **Varietals by Acre:** Cabernet Sauvignon (10 acres), Chardonnay (37), Malbec (5), Merlot (22), Petite Sirah (2), Petit Verdot (5), Sangiovese (4), Sauvignon Blanc (25), Shiraz (12). **Varietals Purchased:** Cabernet Sauvignon (Sonoma County), Chardonnay (Sonoma County), Johannisberg Riesling (California), Merlot (Sonoma County), Sauvignon Blanc (Sonoma County), Zinfandel (Sonoma County).

Few wineries have had as dramatic and changeable a history as Geyser Peak. It was founded in 1880, and for most of its existence its wines were mired in mediocrity. Schlitz, the Milwaukee brewer, tried to revive the winery in 1972 by remodeling it and modernizing the equipment, retooling it for mass production. In 1982 Schlitz sold Geyser Peak to Santa Rosa businessman Henry Trione, who bought the winery with hopes of making fine wines. Trione had one big advantage: he owned a source of grapes for fine wine—nearly 1,000 acres of vineyard in the Alexander and Russian River valleys. But still the winery struggled, finally selling off its Summit line of jug wines and then slowly upgrading the quality of its estate-grown wines.

In 1989, Penfolds, the Australian wine company, bought a 50 percent interest (which it later sold back to the Triones) and sent its talented winemaker, Daryl Groom, to work with the vineyards and winery. After his arrival (and even a bit before), quality surged, with an across-the-board improvement; the reds have been rich and supple and the whites bright and fruity. In 1997, however, Trione sold the winery to Fortune Brands, makers of Jim Beam Brands, for $100 million. The deal included the sale of 140 acres of property, including 122 acres of vineyard in Alexander Valley. As of 1999, Daryl Groom was still in charge of winemaking, with the future direction of the winery yet to be determined.

TASTING NOTES

ALEXANDRE CABERNET BLEND ALEXANDER VALLEY RESERVE (★★★★): Ripe, intense and complex, like the Reserve Cabernet, and steadily improving. A Cabernet blend worth watching.

1995: Tight and well-oaked, with complex cedar, plum, currant, anise, cherry and spice flavors, turning tannic and showing a mineral edge. **90**

1994: Well focused, with a ripe, complex core of cherry, currant and berry flavors, turning smooth, with pretty oak. **91**

1993: Complex, with an array of spicy currant, plum and berry flavors and smooth, supple tannins. **88**

1990: Smooth, plush and elegant, with tiers of spicy currant, black cherry, anise and cedar flavors, this is an invitingly complex and vibrant wine. **90**

1987: Rich, intense and concentrated, with ripe plum, currant, black cherry and anise flavors, picking up a dash of spicy oak. **92**

1986: This austere wine has plenty of herb, dill and oak notes graced by pretty plum and currant flavors that are elegant. **89**

CABERNET SAUVIGNON ALEXANDER VALLEY RESERVE (★★★): Impressive. Recent vintages showed richness and finesse, complex flavors and supple tannins.

1995: Dark, ripe, rich and concentrated, with pretty black cherry, currant, anise and sage flavors and pretty toasty oak. **89**

1994: Well-oaked and marked by herb and cedary notes, it unfolds to offer currant and black cherry fruit. **89**

1993: Smooth and polished, with a marked herbal edge to the ripe berry and cherry flavors. **88**

1991: Ripe and generous, a smooth-textured wine with broad currant, black cherry and berry flavors shaded with spicy oak and a touch of herb. **90**

1990: Strives for complexity and elegance, offering bright, ripe currant and raspberry flavors that are intense, yet it's crisp and spicy, with pretty oak seasoning. **90**

1987: Offers ripe, juicy cherry, currant and plummy flavors with dill-laced oak, turning dry and tannic. **89**

CHARDONNAY ALEXANDER VALLEY RESERVE (★★★): Typically ripe and creamy, with elegant spicy pear, fig and melon flavors. The 1996 (89 points) was consistent with the style.

MERLOT VARIOUS BOTTLINGS (★★★): Both the Sonoma County and Alexander Valley Reserve fall into the good-to-very good range. The 1995 Reserve (88 points) was ripe, complex and chewy, with a range of plum, mineral, sage, tea and herbal notes.

SHIRAZ SONOMA COUNTY RESERVE (★★★)
1995: Rich, plum and earth tones with bright blackberry and mineral flavors. **87**

GIRARD see RUDD ESTATE

GLASS MOUNTAIN QUARRY see MARKHAM VINEYARDS

GLEN ELLEN WINERY (★)
California
Founded: 1983. **Owner:** Diageo PLC. **Winemaker:** Charlie Tsegeletos.

MAJOR WINES: PRICE, CASES, RATING

Cabernet Sauvignon California Proprietor's Reserve ($6, NA)	★
Chardonnay California Proprietor's Reserve ($6, NA)	★
Merlot California Proprietor's Reserve ($7, NA)	★
Sauvignon Blanc California Proprietor's Reserve ($6, NA)	★★
White Zinfandel California Proprietor's Reserve ($5, NA)	★
Zinfandel California Proprietor's Reserve ($6, NA)	★

ALSO PRODUCED
Gamay Beaujolais California Proprietor's Reserve ($5, NA); Red Table Wine California Proprietor's Reserve ($5, NA); White Table Wine California Proprietor's Reserve ($5, NA).

WINERY DATA
Case Production: 3.3 million. **Varietals Purchased:** Cabernet Sauvignon (California), Chardonnay (California), Merlot (California), Sauvignon Blanc (California), Zinfandel (California).

Glen Ellen Winery was founded in 1980 by the Benziger family (see Benziger Family Winery). Production had reached nearly 4 million cases by the time the Benzigers sold it to Heublein in 1993, and its success helped fuel the entire so-called "fighting varietal" class of wines, usually priced at $4 to $7. The winery discovered vineyard sources throughout California and developed a sophisticated network for buying, blending and bottling bulk wines. Quality across the board was good for quite a while, with a full range of popular varietals from Cabernet to white Zinfandel, all carrying the California appellation and labeled "Proprietor's Reserve." Lately, however, quality has declined, with many simple, diluted, marginally drinkable wines.

GODWIN see **MARK WEST**

GOLDENEYE see **DUCKHORN VINEYARDS**

GRACE FAMILY VINEYARDS (★★★★★)
St. Helena, Napa Valley
Founded: 1983. **Owner:** Richard & Ann Grace.
Winemaker: Heidi Peterson Barrett.

MAJOR WINES: PRICE, CASES, RATING
Cabernet Sauvignon Napa Valley
($75, 200)   ★★★★★

WINERY DATA
Case Production: 200. **Acres Owned:** 2 acres in Napa Valley.
Varietals by Acre: Cabernet Sauvignon (2 acres).

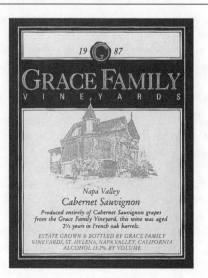

Stockbroker Richard Grace and his wife Ann planted a one-acre vineyard in front of their home in 1976, using budwood from Bosché Vineyard, and two years later they got their first real crop. The ripening grapes looked so appealing that Richard asked Charlie Wagner of Caymus Vineyard to examine them and determine whether it would be possible to make wine out of them. Wagner took a look, then crushed the grapes. Once it was apparent that the wine was pretty good, Wagner made a special vineyard-designated bottling of Grace Family Vineyard under the Caymus label. That arrangement continued through the 1982 vintage. In 1983, Grace began to sell his wine under his own label, added a second acre to his vineyard, and built a beautiful miniature winery.

The wines, which are 100 percent Cabernet, are ripe, supple and beautifully crafted, with bright, opulent flavors. The winemaking style has changed over the years, shifting from Caymus's lengthy barrel aging to less time in the barrel, but quality remains exceptionally high, and the wine is scarce even at $75 a bottle. The wines are all sold directly to individuals, restaurants and wine shops through Grace's mailing list, which also sells wine from two other vineyard estates: Vineyard 29 and Barbour (see entries), both of which produce delicious wines from small vineyards planted with the Grace clone.

The already small production of Grace Cabernet dropped dramatically from 1995 through 1997 when the vineyard began suffering from oak root fungus, and was replanted in stages. In 1995, Grace produced 435 magnums; in 1996 and 1997, 435 liter-sized bottles were produced. Production was back up in 1998, with the addition of a leased acre grown on a neighboring property. Grace expects to produce approximately 600 cases in the future.

TASTING NOTES

CABERNET SAUVIGNON NAPA VALLEY (★★★★): Rich and elegant in style. Loaded with fruit flavors, and marked by soft, fleshy tannins. Ages very well, but peaks at three to five years. This wine is definitely a top priority for collectors.
1995: Tight, with dense, rich, well focused cherry, plum and currant fruit that is bright and vivid. **92**
1994: Big, tight and concentrated, with a brilliant, complex core of currant, black cherry, cedary oak and spicy nuances. **94**

1993: Lean and a touch leathery, offering more oak and cedary flavors than fruit. **85**

1991: Lean and earthy, with firm tannins that dominate the spicy currant and cedar flavors. **88**

1990: Wonderfully complex, showing a toasty, smoky, buttery oak overlay to the ripe currant and cherry flavors underneath. The tannins are chewy and firm, but softening. **92**

1989: Plush and opulent, with supple currant, cherry and spice notes framed by light oak shadings. **88**

1988: Dense in color and flavor, rich and concentrated, with tiers of ripe black cherry, plum and currant flavors and spicy, toasty oak notes. **88**

1987: Remains showy, with a bounty of silky currant, plum, and spicy Cabernet flavors that are long and complex. **94**

1986: Impressive for its range of flavors, touching on cedar, spice, currant and cherry, turning smooth. **91**

1985: Amazingly complex, supple and elegant, offering rich, concentrated, beautifully defined cassis, currant and plum flavors with a touch of anise and toasty oak on the finish. **95**

1984: Enticingly generous and forward, mature now, with deep, rich, lush plum, cassis and cherry flavors that are framed by toasty French oak. The tannins are soft and fleshy. **92**

1983: Absolutely delicious, ripe, rich, round and deep, with complex plum, black cherry and currant flavors that are plush and elegant, finishing with fine tannins. Wonderful complexity, harmony and finesse. **93**

1982: Lean, tight and delicate, with plenty of sharply focused plum, cassis and currant flavors and a good dose of oak. **89**

1981: Effusively fruity and forward, with elegant, supple cherry and plum aromas and flavors. Mature now. **88**

1980: Mature but still showing rich, concentrated and focused black cherry and plum flavors, with layers of cedar and vanilla. **92**

1979: Defines the Grace Vineyard's richness, suppleness and elegance, with rich chocolate, plum and cherry flavors that are delicately balanced. Mature. **92**

1978: Mature, with drying flavors, but there's still much to admire in the elegant spice, cassis, currant and black cherry flavors. **86**

GRAND ARCHER see **ARROWOOD VINEYARDS & WINERY**

GREEN & RED VINEYARD (★★★)
Chiles Valley District, Napa Valley
Founded: 1977. **Owner:** Jay & Pam Hemingway.
Winemaker: Jay Hemingway. **Second Label:** Catacula.

MAJOR WINES: PRICE, CASES, RATING
Chardonnay Napa Valley Catacula Estate Vineyard ($18, 200)	★★
Gamay Napa Valley ($14, 350)	★★
Zinfandel Napa Valley Chiles Mill Vineyard ($18, 1,279)	★★★★
Zinfandel Napa Valley Chiles Valley Vineyard ($17, 1,493)	★★★

ALSO PRODUCED
Sauvignon Blanc Napa Valley Chiles Valley ($18, 150); Zinfandel California ($12, 380).

WINERY DATA
Case Production: 6,000. **Acres Owned:** 30 acres in Chiles Valley District, Napa Valley. **Varietals by Acre:** Chardonnay (3 acres), Zinfandel (27). **Vineyard Designations:** Catacula Vineyard (Chardonnay), Chiles Mill Vineyard (Zinfandel). **Varietals Purchased:** Sauvignon Blanc (Napa Valley), Zinfandel (Napa Valley, Lodi).

Jay Hemingway makes a very distinctive, spicy, peppery Zinfandel from his Chiles Valley property, which is planted mostly to Zinfandel (27 acres); there are also three acres of Chardonnay, which he bottles under the Catacula Vineyard designation. While the Chardonnay is worthy of a ★★ rating, it's the Zinfandel that's worth seeking out.

TASTING NOTES

ZINFANDEL NAPA VALLEY CHILES MILL VINEYARD (★★★★): Very consistent. Of medium weight, with tart berry, spice and pepper notes.

1997: Jammy, with ripe black cherry, raspberry, boysenberry and spicy flavors that are rich and elegant; finishing with a twist of pepper. **93**

1996: The berry- and cherry-laced fruit is ripe and pleasant, and has a light peppery note, but is lacking in depth and is somewhat one-dimensional. It should be given short-term cellaring; hopefully, it will fill out a bit. **85**

1995: Young, vibrant and fruity, with boysenberry, raspberry, anise and pepper flavors. **90**

1994: Elegant, refined, tart cherry and berry flavors that gain a spicy, anise edge on the aftertaste, where the texture is smooth and the tannins fine. **88**

1993: Intense yet elegant; focused on the spicy cherry, wild berry and light jammy notes. Has firm tannins to frame the flavors. **90**

ZINFANDEL NAPA VALLEY CHILES VALLEY VINEYARD (★★★)

1997: Ripe and effusively fruity, with layers of plum, black cherry, raspberry, anise, sage and cedar, finishing with a long, rich aftertaste that keeps pumping out the fruit. **92**

GREENWOOD RIDGE VINEYARDS
(★★★–★★★★)

Mendocino Ridge, Mendocino County
Founded: 1980. **Owner:** Allan Green. **Winemaker:** Allan Green.

MAJOR WINES: PRICE, CASES, RATING

Cabernet Sauvignon Mendocino Ridge ($32, 800)	★★★
Chardonnay Mendocino Ridge DuPratt Vineyard ($22, 800)	★★★★
Merlot Mendocino Ridge ($22, 1,000)	★★★
Pinot Noir Anderson Valley ($22, 1,000)	★★★
Sauvignon Blanc Mendocino Ridge ($11, 1,000)	★★★
White Riesling Mendocino Ridge ($11, 800)	★★★
White Riesling Late Harvest Mendocino Ridge ($18, 250)	★★★★
Zinfandel Mendocino Ridge ($16, 600)	★★★
Zinfandel Sonoma County Scherrer Vineyard ($18, 1,000)	★★★★

WINERY DATA

Case Production: 7,000. **Acres Owned:** 16 acres in Mendocino Ridge. **Varietals by Acre:** Cabernet Sauvignon (4 acres), Merlot (4), Pinot Noir (4), White Riesling (4). **Vineyard Designations:** Du Pratt Vineyard (Chardonnay), Scherrer Vineyard (Zinfandel). **Varietals Purchased:** Chardonnay (Mendocino Ridge), Pinot Noir (Anderson Valley), Sauvignon Blanc (Mendocino), Zinfandel (Mendocino, Sonoma).

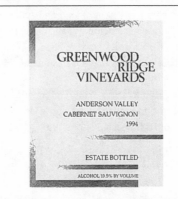

Greenwood Ridge Vineyards rests at the 1,200-foot elevation above Anderson Valley, surrounded by a towering forest of trees. The winery produces 7,000 cases of wine a year from a combination of its own 16-acre vineyard and purchased grapes, mostly from elsewhere in the newly formed Mendocino Ridge appellation. The wines have shown a steady improvement in recent vintages, especially the Pinot Noir and Zinfandel. A 1992 Cabernet Sauvignon from Villa Mt. Eden is ample evidence of the ripeness achievable at this location. Production is more or less evenly divided among Cabernet, Chardonnay (DuPratt Vineyard), Merlot, Pinot Noir, Sauvignon Blanc (Ferrington Vineyard), Riesling (including a late harvest) and Zinfandel from Scherrer Vineyard in Sonoma.

Greenwood Ridge has been changing many of their appellations to Mendocino Ridge since the creation of this AVA in 1997.

TASTING NOTES

CABERNET SAUVIGNON MENDOCINO RIDGE (★★★): Best in warmer, riper years, such as 1994.

1995: Firm but smoothly textured, this one offers subtle cola, coffee, black currant, licorice, herb and cedar notes. Falters a little, though, with a tart, slightly unripe finish, but still quite lovely. **86**

1994: Shows off sage and bell pepper notes before working its way into truer Cabernet flavors, including layers of currant, plum and light toasty oak. Finishes with firm tannins. **89**

CHARDONNAY MENDOCINO RIDGE DUPRATT VINEYARD (★★★★): Made in a fruity, sometimes grassy style that is well balanced.

1996: An openly fruity style. Floral and spicy, with well focused and ripe apple, melon, fig and citrus flavors. **88**

1995: Marked by a spicy, grassy edge, with ripe pear, apple and hazelnut notes that are fresh and lively, finishing with trace of grapefruit. **88**

1994: Ripe and refreshing, featuring complex pear, tangerine, honey and spice flavors and a delicate finish. Impressive for its finesse and grace. **90**

MERLOT MENDOCINO RIDGE (★★★): Quite tasty in 1993 and 1995 when the grapes were fully ripened; less impressive in 1996 (84 points) when it was more austere.

1995: Serves up lots of ripe, bright fruit, with ripe plum, cherry and berry notes. Finishes with soft, fleshy tannins. **89**

1994: A bit stalky, with cedar and currant flavors and a dash of bell pepper and oregano, it's a good red, but it won't remind you much of Merlot. **84**

1993: Rich and well focused, with chewy currant, black cherry, plum and berry notes. Picks up a spicy anise edge, with light toasty oak. Finishes with firm tannins. **89**

PINOT NOIR ANDERSON VALLEY (★★★): Keeps on getting better, with more and more depth and richness.

1996: Smooth, ripe and juicy, with pretty plum, black cherry and light oak shadings. Turns elegant and supple on the finish, with a delicate fruity aftertaste. **88**

1995: Captures lots of pretty fruit flavors, with plum, cherry, strawberry and watermelon notes. Keeps its flavors on a long, lingering finish, where it picks up a trace of earthy and smoky notes. **88**

1994: Dark in color, with ripe, rich and intense flavors. The cherry and berry notes show nicely through the supple tannins. Impressive for its purity of flavor. **90**

1990: Complex, with refreshing wild berry-, raspberry- and cherry-laced notes that linger on the finish. Appealing for its up-front pure fruitiness. **89**

PINOT NOIR MENDOCINO COUNTY

1991: Impressive for its smooth, supple texture and tannins, with attractive, ripe, sweet plum, black cherry and

wild berry flavors, turning complex and picking up a rich mushroom aftertaste. **88**

ZINFANDEL MENDOCINO RIDGE (★★★)

1996: Supple and generous, with plum and berry flavors, a nice edge of acidity and pretty oak. **88**

ZINFANDEL SONOMA COUNTY SCHERRER VINEYARD (★★★★): A medium-weight but flavorful style; made from purchased grapes.

1996: Has a pleasant core of earthy cherry, wild berry, light vanilla oak and spice. **86**

1995: A well-oaked style with toasty, buttery nuances and lots of wild berry, black cherry and spicy flavors. Has a nice sense of balance and proportion and a long, lingering finish. **89**

1994: Complex and graceful, featuring lots of cherry and raspberry notes; gaining a sense of elegance and finesse on the finish, where the flavors fold together nicely. **90**

1991: Still holding its fruit quite well, with plum, cherry and raspberry flavors that are ripe and lively. Finishes with a pretty floral aftertaste. **88**

GREGORY GRAHAM (★★★)
Napa Valley
Founded: 1992. **Owner:** Gregory Graham. **Winemaker:** Gregory Graham.

MAJOR WINES: PRICE, CASES, RATING

Pinot Noir Carneros	
($24, 800)	★★
Viognier Knights Valley	
($24, 600)	★★★★
Viognier Napa Valley	
($24, 650)	★★★

ALSO PRODUCED
Syrah Napa Valley ($20, 150).

WINERY DATA
Case Production: 2,000. **Varietals Purchased:** Pinot Noir (Carneros), Syrah (Napa Valley), Viognier (Knights Valley, Napa Valley).

Gregory Graham, the winemaker for Rombauer, has done a remarkable job of improving its wines—Chardonnay in particular—but other varieties have been enhanced as well. For his own label, he buys all of the grapes, fashioning some delicious wines. His Knights Valley Viognier is especially rich and flavorful; both the 1995 and 1996 scored 88 points. His 1994 Napa Valley Viognier (90 points) was among the best I've tasted from California. The Carneros Pinot Noir has yet to prove itself; the 1994 (83) was earthy and tannic. A Napa Valley Syrah is also in the works. Worth watching.

GRGICH HILLS CELLAR
(★★★–★★★★★)
Rutherford, Napa Valley
Founded: 1977. **Owner:** Mike Grgich, Austin Hills.
Winemaker: Mike Grgich.

MAJOR WINES: PRICE, CASES, RATING

Cabernet Sauvignon Napa Valley
  ($35, 15,000) ★★★★
Cabernet Sauvignon Napa Valley
  Yountville Selection
  ($65, 1,500) ★★★★
Chardonnay Napa Valley
  ($30, 30,000) ★★★★★
Fumé Blanc Napa Valley
  ($18, 13,000) ★★★★
Violetta Late Harvest Napa Valley
  ($50, 1,000) ★★★★★
Zinfandel Sonoma County
  ($18, 11,000) ★★★

ALSO PRODUCED

Chardonnay Napa Valley Carneros Selection ($40, 3,000).

WINERY DATA

Case Production: 75,000. **Acres Owned:** 171 acres in Napa Valley. **Varietals by Acre:** Cabernet Sauvignon (45 acres), Chardonnay (119), Sauvignon Blanc (1), Zinfandel (6). **Varietals Purchased:** Cabernet Sauvignon (Napa Valley), Chardonnay (Napa Valley), Sauvignon Blanc (Napa Valley), Zinfandel (Sonoma).

Croatian-born winemaker Miljenko "Mike" Grgich had impeccable credentials by the time he and Hills Bros. Coffee heir Austin Hills founded Grgich Hills Cellar in 1977. Grgich came to California in 1958, having earned a degree in wine science from Zagreb University in Croatia. He worked with Lee Stewart at Souverain, Robert Mondavi at Mondavi's winery and

André Tchelistcheff at Beaulieu Vineyard, before being hired by Chateau Montelena for the 1972 vintage. His second vintage of Chardonnay at Montelena, the 1973, wowed the wine world, placing first in the famous Paris Tasting of 1976, when French critics judged it superior to the finest white Burgundies in a blind tasting.

At Grgich Hills the Chardonnays have always been brilliantly crafted, and the rest of the wines—including Fumé Blanc, Cabernet, Zinfandel and a dessert wine—are also impressive. The winery has substantial vineyard holdings in Napa and Carneros, with Chardonnay the leader at 119 acres. Output has been at about 75,000 cases. While I'm still a big fan of the Chardonnay, the Cabernet can be excellent, the Fumé Blanc classy and, on occasion, the Zinfandel makes a statement.

TASTING NOTES

CABERNET SAUVIGNON NAPA VALLEY (★★★★): Better balanced of late, though it is sometimes austere and lean. The best vintages offer ripe, complex fruit flavors and more finesse.
1995: Shows elegance and finesse with its supple, fleshy, plummy fruit, hints of cedar and spice, and polished tannins. **91**
1994: Tart, with herb, spice, tea, currant and wild berry flavors and smooth, polished tannins. **88**
1993: Well made, with an array of ripe plum, cherry and toasty oak flavors and moderate tannins. **88**
1992: Lean, tart and tannic, with just a glimpse of cherry and cedar flavors peeking through. **79**
1991: Trim, with a green tea and herbal edge to the flavors; lacking in richness. **83**
1987: Harmonious, with ripe plum, cherry and berry notes, a dash of cedar and dill and soft tannins. **88**
1986: Complex, with mature ripe cherry and plum flavors, pretty oak and polished tannins. **89**

CABERNET SAUVIGNON NAPA VALLEY YOUNTVILLE SELECTION (★★★★): Well made, though its shares the Napa Valley Cabernet's austerity. Not made every year.
1994: Austere, with a focused band of earthy currant, cedar, tar and spice flavors. Firms up on the finish, where the tannins are dry. Give it some time in the cellar. **91**
1991: Sturdy, displays ripe currant and hints of plum and vanilla flavors as the intensity builds. **89**

CHARDONNAY NAPA VALLEY (★★★★★): Intense, focused, elegant and richly flavored, the style remains refined and flavorful.

1996: Crisp, with a lemon, citrus, grapefruit edge to the pear and toasty oak flavors, turning complex on the finish. **89**

1995: Ripe and elegant, with a spicy core of pear, apple, citrus and melon fruit; revealing increasingly more depth. **92**

1994: Crisp and flinty, with a well focused core of pear, citrus, lemon and spice flavors, graced by a pretty overlay of toasty oak. **90**

FUMÉ BLANC NAPA VALLEY (★★★★): Lively, with grassy, citrusy, passionfruit and nectarine flavors. The 1995 (89 points) was right on the mark.

VIOLETTA LATE HARVEST NAPA VALLEY (★★★★★): A blend of Riesling, Johannisburg Riesling and Chardonnay that's typically delicious, rich and succulent.

1994: Rich, honeyed and elegant, its concentrated orange and apricot flavors are wrapped in layers of vanilla, nutmeg and cream. **95**

ZINFANDEL SONOMA COUNTY (★★★): Improving, now showing an elegant, understated style. The 1995 (88 points) was ripe and alive, with cherry and raspberry flavors. The 1994 (87) was marked by earthy plum and tarry notes.

GROTH VINEYARDS & WINERY (★★★★)

Oakville, Napa Valley
Founded: 1982. **Owner:** Dennis & Judy Groth.
Winemaker: Michael Weis.

MAJOR WINES: PRICE, CASES, RATING

Cabernet Sauvignon Napa Valley ($31, 15,000)	★★★★
Cabernet Sauvignon Napa Valley Reserve ($125, 1,500)	★★★★★
Chardonnay Napa Valley ($18, 12,500)	★★★
Merlot Napa Valley ($31, 3,000)	★★★
Sauvignon Blanc Napa Valley ($14, 17,500)	★★★

WINERY DATA

Case Production: 50,000. **Acres Owned:** 140 acres in Napa Valley. **Varietals by Acre:** Cabernet Sauvignon (31 acres), Chardonnay (58), Merlot (27), Sauvignon Blanc (24). **Varietals Purchased:** Cabernet Sauvignon (Oakville), Merlot (Oakville), Sauvignon Blanc (Napa Valley).

Dennis Groth left the high-tech life at Atari Computer for Napa wine, buying a large property in Oakville in 1982 and promptly hiring Nils Venge, then winemaker at Villa Mt. Eden Winery, Groth's neighbor to the east. The winery now makes five wines, all estate-grown except for the Sauvignon Blanc, with the Cabernets being the standouts. Groth owns 140 acres in Napa, with 31 of them devoted to Cabernet. Chardonnay, Merlot and Sauvignon Blanc are also grown.

Cabernet Sauvignon Napa Valley Reserve is the star, but because it ripens late in this cool spot in the valley, it is often among the last picked in the Napa Valley. When it ripens fully, it makes a thick, dense, enormously complex wine that offers an uncommonly wide range of succulent flavors, from currant to mineral to herb and spice, with firm but fleshy tannins and ample oak shadings. In cooler years, when the grapes are less ripe at harvest, the wines are clearly marked by green vegetal flavors that echo coffee, tobacco and green beans. Groth has decided it's wiser to wait and hope the grapes reach 24 degrees Brix in sugar content rather than pick early (and in years such as 1998, harvest runs into November). The other wines are improving. Production has leveled off at 50,000 cases.

In 1994 Groth and Venge parted ways, with Venge focusing on his Venge and Saddleback Cellars brands; Michael Weis, late of Vichon, took over as winemaker in 1994.

TASTING NOTES

CABERNET SAUVIGNON NAPA VALLEY (★★★★): This standard estate bottling usually mirrors the Reserve, and can be rich and supple, although not quite as grand or as concentrated.

1995: Elegant and complex, it offers a pretty array of cherry, plum, currant and sage flavors built around ripe, firm tannins. **90**

1994: Of medium weight, with attractive cedar, herb, and currant notes, it's mildly tannic, and has a supple texture. **88**

1993: Ripe, with chunky cherry and currant flavors, a touch of earthiness and some coffee and weedy herbal notes. **88**

1992: Gains complexity as the flavors unfold, revealing layers of currant, cedar, coffee and spice, turning herbal. **91**
1991: The currant and coffee flavors are rich and intense, laced with cedary oak and herbal notes, finishing with a weedy black currant and chocolate edge. Firmly tannic. **90**
1990: Dense and concentrated, this is a dark, chunky wine that has plenty of flavor, running from plum and currant to herb and tobacco, echoing coffee and spice on the finish. **90**
1986: An earthy coffee accent leads to a center of currant and berry flavors, then turns supple and complex. **90**

CABERNET SAUVIGNON NAPA VALLEY RESERVE (★★★★★): In ripe years this wine can be stunning, amazingly complex and jam-packed with rich flavors. Improves with age.
1995: Smooth, ripe and polished, with rich, complex layers of currant, herb, cedar, tar, black cherry and spice, finishing with a long, supple aftertaste. **95**
1994: Enormously complex and tightly wound, with ripe, firm tannins and rich, complex, concentrated cherry, wild berry, plum, cedar, coffee and spice flavors. **96**
1992: Dark, thick, smooth and polished, this plush young Cabernet is brimming with ripe cherry, currant and berry flavors that turn exotic. **98**
1991: Distinctive for its richness and depth, but marked by herb, bell pepper and racy currant flavors that offer uncommon depth and complexity in a distinct style. **95**
1990: A supple and seductive wine that's silky and complex, with tiers of currant, cherry, cedar, herb and mineral flavors that stay with you on a long, full, rich finish. A beautiful harmony of flavors. **94**
1989: Distinctive for its coffee, olive and cedar nuances, it also serves up ripe, rich, concentrated currant, chocolate and black cherry flavors, picking up a prune note on the finish. **87**
1988: Offers a range of coffee, herb, currant, cedar and spice flavors, finishing with nuances of bay leaf, green bean, tobacco and mineral. **88**
1987: Smooth and supple; marked by herb, sage, tea, ash and bell pepper flavors, along with notes of ripe black cherry, stewed plum and currant. **90**
1986: Rich, complex, deep and concentrated, with a broad array of spicy currant, coffee, herb, tea and black cherry flavors. **92**
1985: Dark in color, with wonderful, perfumed aromas of currant, cherry, mineral and spice and a broad, rich, supple, silky texture that carries the flavors on a long,

full, delicious aftertaste. Picks up herb, tea, cocoa and vanilla nuances. A tremendous wine, pure and simple. **97**
1984: A wonderful rich and complex mouthful of Cabernet. Typical weedy currant, cedar, coffee and spice flavors turn smooth and silky, with soft, fleshy tannins on the finish, where it picks up a pretty vanilla taste. **92**
1983: Fuller and richer than the regular bottling but showing a similar stage of maturity, with the cedar, earth, green olive, tar and currant flavors turning leafy and tannic. **88**

CHARDONNAY NAPA VALLEY (★★★): Improving. The 1996 (88 points) is well oaked, with complex pear and citrus notes.

MERLOT NAPA VALLEY (★★★): Improving overall. The 1994 (87 points) marked by herbal, currant and berry flavors. The 1992 (89) was intense and concentrated.

SAUVIGNON BLANC NAPA VALLEY (★★★): Inconsistent, sometimes lacking intensity, but the 1999 (87 points) was silky, with citrus and passionfruit flavors.

GUENOC WINERY (★★–★★★★★)
Guenoc Valley
Founded: 1981. **Owner:** Orville Magoon. **Winemaker:** Malcolm Seibly.

MAJOR WINES: PRICE, CASES, RATING	
Cabernet Sauvignon California ($11, 30,000)	★★
Cabernet Sauvignon Napa Valley Beckstoffer Vineyard Reserve ($41, 1,900)	★★★★
Cabernet Sauvignon Napa Valley Bella Vista Vineyard Reserve ($26, 800)	★★★★
Cabernet Sauvignon North Coast ($16, 14,000)	★★
Chardonnay California ($11, 30,000)	★★
Chardonnay Guenoc Valley Genevieve Magoon Vineyard Estate Reserve ($25, 3,000)	★★★★★
Chardonnay Guenoc Valley Genevieve Magoon Vineyard Unfiltered Estate Reserve ($30, 400)	★★★★★

Chardonnay North Coast
($16, 18,000) ★★★

Meritage Red California
($19, 5,000) ★★★

Meritage Red California North Coast Langtry
($50, 3,500) ★★★★

Meritage White Blend
Guenoc Valley Langtry
($21, 2,600) ★★★

Petite Sirah California
($16, 11,000) ★★★

Port California
($25, 500) ★★★

Sauvignon Blanc California
($8, 13,000) ★★

Sauvignon Blanc North Coast
($14, 5,000) ★★

Zinfandel California
($11, 5,000) ★★

WINERY DATA
Case Production: 145,000. **Acres Owned:** 388 acres (43 in Napa Valley, 345 in Guenoc Valley). **Varietals by Acre:** Cabernet Franc (11 acres), Cabernet Sauvignon (42), Carmenère (1), Chardonnay (176), Gros Verdot (1), Malbec (3), Marsanne (1), Merlot (28), Petit Verdot (18), Petite Sirah (52), St.-Macaire (1), Sauvignon Blanc (43), Sémillon (8), Viognier (4). **Varietals Purchased:** Cabernet Franc (Lake), Cabernet Sauvignon (Lake, Lodi, Paso Robles, Napa), Chardonnay (Mendocino, Sonoma, Lodi, Paso Robles, Yolo), Chenin Blanc (Lodi), Petite Sirah (Mendocino, Lake), Sauvignon Blanc (Mendocino, Paso Robles, Lake).

In an unusual land swap, in 1963 the Magoon family traded 23 acres of prime Hawaiian real estate for 23,000 acres in rural Lake County. This land, which dips into Napa County, is the foundation for Guenoc, the winery, and Guenoc Valley, the nation's first single-proprietor American Viticultural Area, covering 1,200 acres. Grapes had been grown in the area beginning in 1854, and this scenic estate was once home to the famous Victorian actress Lillie Langtry, who settled there in 1888 with the intention of making the greatest claret in the country. Langtry took her winemaking seriously, producing wine until 1906, when she returned to France.

At Genevieve Magoon's urging, her sons Orville and Eaton decided to try something "more romantic" than running cattle and mowing hay, and they began studying wine-grape growing. In the late 1960s they began to plant an extensive vineyard, utilizing Orville's passion for precision and the wine know-how of Roy and Walt Raymond of Raymond Vineyards, who helped in the vineyard design and who oversaw production of the early wines, beginning in 1976. The Magoons restored the Langtry house and proceeded to build a modern winery. By the mid-1980s their efforts began to pay off with increasingly better wines.

Today, the winery farms nearly 400 acres, with Chardonnay (176 acres) the dominant grape, followed by Cabernet Sauvignon (42), Sauvignon Blanc (42) and Petite Sirah (52). Production is 145,000 cases, including a second label, Langtry. All the wines are well made, clean and balanced, but a few stand out: the Beckstoffer Napa Valley Reserve Cabernet, Genevieve Magoon Reserve Chardonnay and Langtry Estate Meritage Red and White.

In 1999, Magoon was considering selling all, or a portion, of his winery and property.

TASTING NOTES

CABERNET SAUVIGNON NAPA VALLEY BECKSTOFFER VINEYARD RESERVE (★★★★): From grapes grown in a 5-acre vineyard near Spottswoode in St. Helena. Each of the vintages has been superb, with ripe, rich, complex fruit flavors, polished tannins and a sense of harmony and finesse.
1995: Intense, juicy, and a touch tart, but with plenty of plum and wild berry flavors; clamps down on the finish, where the tannins are firm. **89**
1994: Sharply focused and deeply concentrated, with a pretty core of ripe cherry, currant, plum and berry flavors, showing polish and finesse. **93**
1993: Vibrant, with a tart narrow band of cherry and wild berry flavors, turning tannic. **88**

1992: Tight and intense, with a trim band of spice, currant, black cherry and tobacco flavors, turning tannic. **90**

1991: Young and tight but well focused and concentrated, serving up complex herb, currant and black cherry flavors that turn supple and elegant on the finish. Shows a measure of finesse and restraint. **94**

1990: Ripe and aromatic, rich and flavorful, with a tight, solid core of black cherry, cedar, currant and spice flavors that fan out. Supple and generous, yet with a firm backbone. **92**

1989: Ripe and rich, with generous loganberry and blackberry flavors that keep bubbling up on the finish. Shades of coffee, smoke and spice make it interesting. Has tannin to lose. **88**

1987: Youthful and vibrant, with rich currant, cedar, black cherry and anise flavors and a firm but supple wall of tannins. **91**

CABERNET SAUVIGNON NAPA VALLEY BELLA VISTA VINEYARD RESERVE (★★★★): Another impressive Cabernet; complex, elegant and understated.

1995: Spicy, with bright, tart acidity and a distinct jalapeño pepper edge to the chunky, intense unevolved fruit flavors. Time may work in its favor. **87**

1994: Smooth, ripe and juicy, with a pretty array of plum, cherry and berry flavors; finishing with firm, supple tannins. **90**

1993: Distinctive for its spicy cherry and wild berry flavors, gaining complexity and finesse on the finish. **88**

1992: Tight and compact, with a firm band of anise, currant, black cherry and cedary oak, turning tannic and austere. **90**

CHARDONNAY GUENOC VALLEY GENEVIEVE MAGOON VINEYARD ESTATE RESERVE (★★★★★): Remarkably complex, sophisticated and richly flavored.

1996: Intense and lively, with an elegant core of citrus, grassy pear and spice. Finishes with subtle oak shadings. **90**

1995: Smooth, ripe and harmonious, with a complex core of concentrated pear, spice, apple and hazelnut flavors. **92**

1994: The pear and tangerine flavors are marked by grassy nuances and hold together nicely. **88**

CHARDONNAY GUENOC VALLEY GENEVIEVE MAGOON VINEYARD UNFILTERED ESTATE RESERVE (★★★★★): The Unfiltered version often carries slightly more richness and complexity than the above reserve.

1996: Starts out lean and trim, but slowly builds in complex citrus, pear and apple flavors that turn flinty with a mineral edge. **92**

1995: Delicious, with layers of flavor ranging from ripe pear, fig and apple to spice, anise, vanilla and cedar. **93**

1994: Intense, elegant, attractive and lingering, with pear, spice, fig, and melon notes. **88**

MERITAGE RED CALIFORNIA NORTH COAST (★★★)

1994: Tightly wound, with a firm core of mint, herb, currant, and blackberry flavors and firm tannins. **86**

1992: Elegant, with a pretty core of plum, wild berry and spice flavors, finishing with smooth, plush tannins. **88**

MERITAGE RED CALIFORNIA NORTH COAST LANGTRY (★★★★)

1994: Fruity, with a supple texture and appealing plum and cherry flavors that build intensity and turn complex. **90**

1995: A rustic, earthy, firmly tannic style, it slowly opens to a core of black cherry, plum and berry fruit, and rugged tannins. **88**

1991: A stylish wine with layers of plum, cherry, raspberry and herb flavors that stay focused and linger on a long finish. Picks up cedary oak on the aftertaste and the tannins are firm and polished. **90**

1990: Firm and focused, with a tight core of currant, spice and cedar flavors that finish with fine tannins and good length. **89**

MERITAGE SAUVIGNON BLANC GUENOC VALLEY LANGTRY (★★★): This wine successfully unites Sauvignon Blanc and Sémillon. The 1997 (88 points) was fresh and lively, with grassy melon and citrus notes.

PETITE SIRAH CALIFORNIA (★★★): This wine can carry either the North Coast or the California appellation, and usually tames the grape's tannic tendencies. The 1996 (84 points) was dry and pruney, but the 1992 (89) was supple, aromatic and richly fruity.

HAHN ESTATES see SMITH & HOOK

HAMEL WINES (★★★)
Sonoma County
Founded: 1994. **Owner:** Kevin & Yvonne Hamel.
Winemaker: Kevin Hamel.

MAJOR WINES: PRICE, CASES, RATING
Syrah Russian River Valley
    ($24, 600)   ★★★

WINERY DATA
Case Production: 600. **Varietals Purchased:** Syrah (Dry Creek Valley, Russian River Valley).

Kevin Hamel, winemaker for Preston Vineyards and his wife Yvonne began their Syrah-focused brand in 1994 with purchased grapes. All of the wines have been very good to outstanding. While the production is limited at this time, it could reach 3,000 cases once new vineyard contracts begin to yield grapes.

TASTING NOTES

SYRAH RUSSIAN RIVER VALLEY (★★★): Dark, rich and concentrated, with dark fruit and meaty flavors. The 1996 was leaner and more austere than earlier wines. (Can carry either a Russian River or Sonoma County appellation).
1996: Firm, dry and tannic, with a tight core of wild berry, plum, sage and spice. **86**
1995: Inky dark color, dense and concentrated, with a potent core of rich currant, plum, mineral and spice, finishing with a classic smoky, meaty edge and thick but plush tannins. **92**
1994: Dark, ripe, rich and spicy, with a tannic leathery edge to the black cherry and wild berry flavors. **88**

HANDLEY CELLARS (★★–★★★)
Anderson Valley, Mendocino County
Founded: 1982. **Owner:** Milla Handley, Raymond Handley, Rex McClellan. **Winemaker:** Milla Handley.

MAJOR WINES: PRICE, CASES, RATING
Chardonnay Anderson Valley Estate
  ($17, 2,500) ★★
Chardonnay Dry Creek Valley
  Handley Vineyard
  ($17, 3,000) ★★★
Gewürztraminer Anderson Valley
  ($13, 500) ★★
Pinot Gris Anderson Valley
  ($18, 500) ★★
Pinot Meunier Anderson Valley
  ($19, 700) ★★
Pinot Noir Anderson Valley Estate Reserve
  ($30, 150) ★★
Pinot Noir Anderson Valley
  ($21, 1,800) ★★
Sauvignon Blanc Dry Creek Valley
  Handley Vineyard
  ($13, 2,500) ★★★
Sparkling Brut Anderson Valley
  ($20, 500) ★★★
Sparkling Brut Rosé Anderson Valley
  ($22, 250) ★★★

ALSO PRODUCED
Riesling Late Harvest Anderson Valley ($14, 500).

WINERY DATA
Case Production: 14,000. **Acres Owned:** 47 acres (27 in Anderson Valley, 20 in Dry Creek Valley). **Varietals by Acre:** Chardonnay (22 acres), Gewürztraminer (2), Pinot Noir (13), Sauvignon Blanc (10). **Varietals Purchased:** Gewürztraminer (Anderson Valley), Pinot Noir (Anderson Valley), Riesling (Anderson Valley).

Milla Handley worked at Chateau St. Jean and Edmeades before starting Handley Cellars in 1982. At Handley, the focus is on Chardonnay (Anderson and Dry Creek bottlings), Gewürztraminer, Pinot Noir and Sauvignon Blanc, largely from the winery's 47 acres of vines. All of these wines share a simple, fruity and easy-to-drink house style. Handley also produces a line of sparkling wines that are worth seeking out; the Brut's 1992 and 1993 vintages earned 89-point ratings for their bright, complex fruit flavors. Gewürztraminer and Sauvignon Blanc merit ★★ and ★★★ ratings.

HANNA WINERY (★★)
Russian River Valley, Sonoma County
Founded: 1985. **Owner:** Elias Hanna. **Winemaker:** Jeff Hinchliffe.

MAJOR WINES: PRICE, CASES, RATING
Cabernet Sauvignon Alexander Valley
  ($20, 4,900) ★★
Chardonnay Russian River Valley
  ($16, 9,000) ★★
Merlot Alexander Valley
  ($21, 2,900) ★★
Pinot Noir Russian River Valley
  ($21, 600) ★★

Sauvignon Blanc Reserve
  Russian River Valley
  ($21, 1,000)   ★★
Sauvignon Blanc Russian River Valley
  ($12, 13,000)   ★★
Zinfandel Alexander Valley Pourroy
  Vineyard Reserve
  ($35, 125)   ★★★

ALSO PRODUCED
Syrah Alexander Valley ($16, 400); Zinfandel Alexander Valley ($12, 1,300).

WINERY DATA
Case Production: 35,000. **Acres Owned:** 225 acres (90 in Alexander Valley, 60 in Sonoma Valley, 75 in Russian River Valley). **Varietals by Acre:** Cabernet Franc (7 acres), Cabernet Sauvignon (58), Chardonnay (70), Merlot (54), Nebbiolo (4), Pinot Noir (13), Sangiovese (3), Sauvignon Blanc (8), Syrah (5), Zinfandel (3). **Vineyard Designations:** Pourroy Vineyard (Zinfandel). **Varietals Purchased:** Sauvignon Blanc (Russian River Valley), Zinfandel (Alexander Valley).

Heart surgeon Elias Hanna has substantial vineyard holdings, with 225 acres in vines spread throughout Alexander Valley, Russian River and Sonoma Valley. The 35,000-case winery is located west of Santa Rosa. Hanna produces Cabernet, Chardonnay, Merlot, Sauvignon Blanc, and a Russian River Pinot Noir that joined the lineup in 1992. So far, the wines have been above average, with Zinfandel from Pourroy Vineyard in Alexander Valley the quality leader. Despite many vintages and the many vineyards under its management, however, Hanna has produced few wines worth getting truly excited about.

TASTING NOTES

ZINFANDEL ALEXANDER VALLEY POURROY VINEYARD RESERVE (★★★): The 1995 (90 points) displayed ripe, racy cherry, wild berry and raspberry flavors, and lots of zest. The 1996 Reserve (83) tilted more toward oak, with modest Zinfandel flavors.

HANZELL VINEYARDS (★★★–★★★★★)
Sonoma Valley
Founded: 1957. **Owner:** de Brye Family. **Winemaker:** Bob Sessions.

MAJOR WINES: PRICE, CASES, RATING
Cabernet Sauvignon Sonoma Valley
  (Discontinued)   ★★
Chardonnay Sonoma Valley
  ($35, 1,750)   ★★★★★
Pinot Noir Sonoma Valley
  ($35, 700)   ★★★

WINERY DATA
Case Production: 3,000. **Acres Owned:** 25 acres in Sonoma Valley. **Varietals by Acre:** Chardonnay (15 acres), Pinot Noir (10).

An appreciation of great Burgundies like Montrachet and Romanée-Conti inspired James D. Zellerbach to build Hanzell Vineyards on a hill overlooking the city of Sonoma. A member of the family that owned the paper products firm Crown Zellerbach Corp., Zellerbach honed his appreciation for fine wine while serving as U.S. ambassador to Italy. He decided to duplicate Burgundian winemaking techniques with hopes of making California-style red and white "Burgundies." In 1952, he began planting his vineyard, and four years later he built a winery, which he named after himself and his wife, Hanna, combining her first name with his last. He spared no expense to build this tiny jewel of a winery, a miniature replica of the famous Clos de Vougeot in Burgundy.

The first Chardonnay vintage in 1956 only produced enough wine to fill one large bottle. His luck steadily improved, however, and what followed was a 30-year-plus string of superb Chardonnays; these were among the first (if not the first) in California to age in new French oak barrels. Later came equally attractive and compelling Pinot Noirs. Brad Webb, a highly respected winemaker, oversaw production, utilizing advanced techniques such as temperature-controlled stainless steel tanks for fermentation. This grand experiment ended rather abruptly, however, when Zellerbach died in 1963 and his wife sold the winery. Their entire inventory of wines was sold at auction, including two vintages of Chardonnay and one of Pinot Noir that were purchased by Heitz Wine Cellars in Napa Valley.

No wines were made in 1963 or 1964, but new owners Douglas and Mary Day resumed winemaking in

1965. In 1973, Bob Sessions became winemaker and general manager of Hanzell, after having worked at Mayacamas. In 1976, Barbara de Brye of Great Britain purchased Hanzell. Being a claret drinker, she had some five acres of Bordeaux grape varieties rooted in a separate vineyard, and from 1979 to 1992 Hanzell produced a Cabernet. Following de Brye's death in 1991, a decision was made to discontinue Cabernet, and the vines were grafted over to Pinot Noir.

Hanzell's success with Chardonnay and Pinot Noir secured its reputation. The Chardonnay, though barrel-aged, is not made using strict Burgundian techniques, despite Zellerbach's original intentions; it is fermented in stainless steel and is not lees aged, nor does it undergo a full malolactic fermentation. Still, it has proved to be unusually long-lived and distinctly complex by both Californian and European standards. Pinot Noir has been more variable, as it almost always is, although the string of vintages from 1961 to 1981 revealed a number of truly remarkable wines with tremendous depth, complexity and aging capacity. Since 1982, however, the Pinot Noir has been in a slump, lacking focus and often marred by herbal flavors, and, while firmly structured, needing more fruit and richness. Winemaker Sessions is at a loss to explain why the style shifted so dramatically, since no winemaking or vineyard practices changed. By the end of the 1980s, Hanzell Pinot Noir had lost most of its luster; sales were slow and the winery decided to rethink its style, aiming for riper fruit, lighter tannins and a little more toasty oak.

Hanzell's Cabernet never really blossomed the way de Brye had hoped it would. While the vineyard seemed to be in a good location, the wines were unusually austere and tannic, with earthy herb and currant flavors. I have tasted the Cabernets on several occasions, and it appears that Hanzell made the right decision in dropping it and refocusing on what made it famous in the first place. Production is about 3,000 cases from 25 acres of vineyards. A new Pinot Noir vineyard was being planted in 1999 on a more northeasterly slope. For now, Chardonnay is the wine to buy; the Pinot Noir is more challenging, though it is fun to drink—think of it as a Syrah-style Pinot.

TASTING NOTES

CABERNET SAUVIGNON SONOMA VALLEY (★★): Austere and marked by earthy tannins, with herb and currant fla-vors. Very consistent over the years, although it never lived up to expectations. Discontinued in 1992.

CHARDONNAY SONOMA VALLEY (★★★★★): Tight and flinty early on, with citrus and pear notes, but remarkably concentrated and ageworthy, gaining depth and richness with time. Peaks after most Chardonnays have faded.

1996: Distinct for its spicy grapefruit and citrus flavors, it's an intensely flavored, racy, complex wine that slowly unfolds, gaining complexity and nuance on the finish. **92**

1995: Beautifully crafted, rich and harmonious, with tiers of ripe pear, fig, citrus, lemon and light oak shadings. Really zooms on the finish, where the flavors are complex and concentrated. **92**

1994: Spicy, perfumed aromas lead to an elegant, complex array of ripe pear, tart pineapple, citrus and light oak flavors. **90**

1993: Fresh and lively if a bit on the crisp, tart side, this shows a nice range of ripe apple, pear and melonlike flavors with hints of spice and light oak. Finishes with a zesty aftertaste. **90**

1992: Clean and compact, featuring a ripe core of pear, apple and light oak shadings. **87**

1991: Big, ripe and assertive, with nectarine, pear and spice notes that stay focused on the finish. **91**

1990: Broad, ripe, lively and intensely fruity, with rich, concentrated and sharply focused pear, pineapple and citrus notes. **89**

1988: Fresh and aromatic, with tight pear, lemon, fig and melon flavors that are rich, elegant and very well balanced. **90**

1987: Has plenty of fresh, clean, ripe pear and citrus aromas and flavors that turn elegant and subtle on the finish. **89**

1986: Very ripe and forward, quite woody, with pretty pineapple, pear, apple and spice flavors of great intensity and depth. **87**

1985: Excellent balance, intensity and depth; may become a classic. It combines ripe, rich pineapple, pear, spice and citrus notes that show remarkable finesse and elegance, and there's a smoky aftertaste. **90**

1982: Elegant and stylish, with pretty honey, lemon, pear and spice flavors and a wonderful balance of fruit and oak. More subtle than many Hanzells. **89**

1981: Forward and fruity, with fresh, lively lemon, pear and pineapple flavors and good intensity and depth. **86**

1980: Enormous depth and concentration, very ripe and rich, with fig, pear and honey flavors. Big and full-blown. **90**

1979: Elegant and spicy, with the pear and melon flavors beginning to dry out, becoming somewhat coarse. Still, there's plenty to like in this wine. **85**

1978: Incredibly rich, ripe, smooth and buttery, with intense fig, pear, spice and lemon flavors, finishing with lovely honey notes and a long, creamy aftertaste. **95**

PINOT NOIR SONOMA VALLEY (★★★): Until the 1982 vintage, this was the most ageworthy Pinot Noir in California; it was an amazingly complex, intricate and durable wine. Quality since has varied, though the 1990s vintages are better.

1995: Mature, with an earthy streak running through the dried cherry and berryish fruit, turning firm and structured on the finish, where it becomes more complex. **87**

1994: Earthy, with a meaty streak, and hints of plum and dried cherry fruit. This is a tight, backward wine that needs time. **87**

1993: Shows off some mature aromas and flavors, with earthy sage, tar, spice and plummy notes, turning complex on the finish where rose petal and cherry notes fold in. **87**

1992: Mature in color with attractive earth and mushroom flavors, hints of dried cherry, tar and spice, finishing with firm tannins and a slight bitter edge. True to style Hanzell Pinot Noir, showing its earthier side. **86**

1991: Earthy with spicy stewed plum and anise flavors and firm, intense tannins. **86**

1990: Rustic, with chunky, earthy plum and black cherry flavors that are in an awkward phase. However, the core of complex tar and rose petal notes should be more compelling with time. **85**

1989: Light and fruity, with toasty strawberry, plum and currant flavors that are intense and lively. **88**

1988: Ripe and flavorful, with intense cherry, currant, plum and spice flavors that are full, rich and supple, intense and concentrated. Tannins are firm. **88**

1987: Charming in its own way, with fresh, ripe, intense and sharply focused strawberry, cherry and tarry anise notes. **87**

1986: Earthy, Syrah-like flavors are firm and tight. **87**

1985: Austere, with a narrow band of anise, cherry and strawberry notes and good depth and intensity. **85**

1984: Austere and thin in flavor, but the tannins and dry oak flavors are substantial. **80**

1983: Light and simple, with spicy anise and cedar notes and coarse tannins. **83**

1982: Weedy and earthy, with chewy tannins. **77**

1981: Ripe and forward, with cherry and plum flavors that are bright and lively. **83**

1980: Earthy and herbal, with weedy currant and spice flavors that turn tarry. **84**

1979: Another stunning Hanzell, with bold, ripe, complex flavors that echo plum, raisin, currant and black cherry. Youthful and vibrant, with great length. **95**

1978: Ultra-ripe and raisiny, with roasted plum and currant flavors. A big, potent wine that's tight and lacking the extra complexity found in most Hanzells. **87**

1977: Elegant and intense, with currant and plum flavors. **87**

1976: Ripe and chewy, enormously concentrated, with chunky plum, prune and currant flavors. Tells the story of the vintage. **91**

1975: Supple and fruity, round and fleshy, with spicy plum, currant and tar notes. **92**

1974: Ultra-ripe and flavorful, not unlike the 1974 Cabernets. Tiers of black cherry, plum, currant, tar and anise flavors unfold into an elegant finish, where a touch of cedar and spice add extra complexity. **91**

1973: Smooth and elegant for Hanzell. This wine combines ripe, spicy cherry and plum aromas and flavors with a measure of elegance and finesse, finishing with firm, drying tannins that let the flavors pour through. **89**

1972: Ripe and vibrant, with deep, rich, intense plum, currant and cherry flavors that are lively and potent, finishing with a burst of spice. A powerful, amazing wine that's held its youthful personality. Could be the best wine of the entire '72 vintage. **93**

1971: Bold, ripe and intense, deeply concentrated and full of spicy plum, currant, anise and rose petal flavors, with firm, dry tannins and plenty of length. Showing a trace of oxidation on the finish, but this wine has the depth and richness to age on. **92**

1970: Fully mature and at a fine drinking stage. Less opulent and ripe than either 1968 or 1969, it is more refined, with delicate plum, anise and dried cherry notes. What's most striking is the long, smooth, elegant finish. **90**

1969: Firm and tight, with ripe plum and currant flavors that are reminiscent of the 1968 except on a smaller scale. Appealing in its austerity, with tar and rose petal notes that come through on the finish. **87**

1968: Ultra-ripe and raisiny, this comes from a famous vintage of ripe wines. While it's deep and concentrated and Port-like, the plum, currant and cherry flavors manage to retain their balance and appeal. A distinctive, long-lived, potent wine that's firmly tannic. **89**

1967: A hard, tight wine that shows more tannin and oak than most Hanzells this age. Despite its austerity there are nice cherry and currant aromas and flavors that stay with you. **86**

1966: Mature but holding, it has a soft texture and ripe, polished, earthy plum and cherry flavors framed by cedary oak. **87**

1965: In fantastic condition, much like the 1961 vintage. The fruit is ripe and sweet, with layers of plum, cherry, currant and vanilla flavors that are intense, focused and lively, finishing with a sweet plum, smoke and rose petal edge. **93**

Heitz Bottling 1962: Tart, crisp and gamy, with volatile fruit flavors that are fading, picking up cedary notes on the finish. A wine that still shows decent fruit, but doesn't have the stellar quality of the 1961. Worth the experience, though. **78**

Heitz Bottling 1961: In absolutely fantastic condition, ripe, rich, sweet and concentrated, with intense tar, plum, currant and cherry flavors that run deep and complex. Despite a good dose of alcohol, it's smooth and focused. The finish is long and wonderfully complex, with tiers of dried fruit flavors. **97**

HARLAN ESTATE (★★★★★)
Oakville, Napa Valley
Founded: 1988. **Owner:** William Harlan. **Winemaker:** Robert Levy.

MAJOR WINES: PRICE, CASES, RATING
Cabernet Blend Napa Valley
   ($120, 1,500)   ★★★★★

WINERY DATA
Case Production: 1,500. **Acres Owned:** 32 acres in Oakville.
Varietals by Acre: Cabernet Franc (0.5 acres), Cabernet Sauvignon (21), Merlot (6), Petit Verdot (4.5).

William Harlan built a lucrative real estate development firm in San Francisco before turning his sights to winemaking in Napa Valley, where he is now part owner of the Meadowood Resort in St. Helena. He zeroed in on the Oakville area as a location for his own winery, a 32-acre hillside vineyard situated high above the famed Martha's Vineyard. Harlan's vineyard is planted primarily to Bordeaux varieties, led by Cabernet Sauvignon.

Harlan's operation is without doubt one of the most exciting in Napa Valley today. I have tried these wines on numerous occasions and am truly amazed by how rich, detailed, complex and beautifully crafted they are. Bob Levy is the winemaker, and is often advised by noted Bordeaux enologist Michel Rolland (of Château Le Bon Pasteur and others). Quality is extremely high; worth collecting.

TASTING NOTES

NAPA VALLEY (★★★★★): These are stunning wines, with uncommon richness, depth and complexity, plush, concentrated flavors and thick, polished tannins.

1995: A tremendous effort; extra flavor dimensions that are complex and concentrated; loaded with layers of spicy mint, currant, black cherry, cedar and tobacco. **96**

1994: Muscular, beautifully focused, rich and complex, with layers of deep currant, spice and black cherry that are concentrated and lively. **95**

1993: Beautifully crafted, seamless, and deeply concentrated with lots of ripe, juicy currant, wild berry and plum fruit and a smoky, cedary edge. **93**

1992: Delicious, with ripe, rich, supple layers of toasty oak, cherry and currant. Well focused, with polished tannins that are long on the finish. **93**

1991: Intense and elegant, with a sharply focused core of currant, black cherry, cedar and spice, finishing with a long aftertaste. **92**

1990: Deep, rich, dark and harmonious, with bold, round, supple and complex tiers of black cherry, currant and plum flavors and with thick, plush tannins. **93**

HARMONY CELLARS (★★)
San Luis Obispo County
Founded: 1989. **Owner:** Charles & Kimberley Mulligan. **Winemaker:** Chuck Mulligan. **Second Label:** Noel Vineyards.

MAJOR WINES: PRICE, CASES, RATING

Cabernet Sauvignon Paso Robles	
($14, 400)	★★
Chardonnay San Luis Obispo County	
($14, 640)	★★
Pinot Noir San Luis Obispo County	
($14, 300)	★★

ALSO PRODUCED
Johannisberg Riesling Paso Robles ($9, 600); White Zinfandel Paso Robles ($7, 600); Zinfandel Paso Robles; ($14, 100); Zinfandel Paso Robles Zinjoli; ($9, 300).

WINERY DATA
Case Production: 4,000. **Acres Owned:** 1.5 acres in San Luis Obispo County. **Varietals by Acre:** Chardonnay (1.5 acres). **Varietals Purchased:** Cabernet Sauvignon (Paso Robles), Chardonnay (San Luis Obispo County), Pinot Noir (San Luis Obispo County), Riesling (Paso Robles), Zinfandel (Paso Robles).

This winery has released three wines—Cabernet, Chardonnay and Pinot Noir—all of which are Paso Robles-grown. The best wine I've tasted was the 1994 Pinot Noir (88 points), which offered appealing ripe cherry and raspberry fruit.

HARRISON WINERY & VINEYARDS (★★★–★★★★)
Napa Valley
Founded: 1989. **Owner:** Lyndsey Harrison. **Winemaker:** Lyndsey Harrison. **Second Label:** Zebra Zin.

MAJOR WINES: PRICE, CASES, RATING

Cabernet Sauvignon Napa Valley	
($40, 900)	★★★★
Cabernet Sauvignon Napa Valley Reserve	
($60, 45)	★★★
Chardonnay Napa Valley	
($35, 600)	★★★★
Merlot Napa Valley	
($33, 300)	★★★

ALSO PRODUCED
Zebra Zin Napa Valley ($18, 300).

WINERY DATA
Case Production: 2,500. **Acres Owned:** 17 acres in Napa Valley. **Varietals by Acre:** Cabernet Sauvignon (9 acres), Chardonnay (8). **Varietals Purchased:** Merlot (Napa Valley), Zinfandel (Napa Valley).

In 1987, Michael and Lyndsey Harrison bought an established 17-acre vineyard on Pritchard Hill along the eastern hills of Napa Valley. They made their first wine, a Cabernet, followed two years later by a Chardonnay, both of which were estate-grown. The early wines were solid, complex and rich in varietal fruit. Production hovers around 2,500 cases, divided more or less equally between the two wines. Zinfandel appears occasionally. Sadly, Michael Harrison died in 1999.

TASTING NOTES

CABERNET SAUVIGNON NAPA VALLEY (★★★★): Variable in quality. The 1989 and 1990 were rich and dark, but subsequent vintages have been tighter and more austere. The 1992, 1994 and 1996 were more complex.

1996: Delivers plenty of ripe, complex black cherry, currant, berry and mineral flavors and frames them with notes of sage and cedary oak. **91**

1994: A supple, elegant, understated style, with a complex array of currant, earth, cedar, spice and coffee notes. **93**

1993: Displays pleasant, moderately rich currant and cherry flavors, but loses some of its intensity on the finish. **87**

1992: Packs in lots of flavor; layered with currant, plum, cherry and mint nuances, shows excellent depth and richness. **90**

1991: A dark, tight, intense and tannic wine with sharply focused currant, plum and tart berry flavors. **86**

1990: Young, ripe and intense, with a tight, firm core of currant, cherry and spicy oak flavors. Raw and unevolved now, but shows intensity and depth. **87**

1989: Bold, dark, ripe and concentrated, with sharply focused currant, black cherry, plum and spice flavors that have just the right touch of tannin and oak. Intense and powerful. **88**

CABERNET SAUVIGNON NAPA VALLEY RESERVE (★★★)

1994: Earthy, with a dusty, oaky edge and dry, chewy tannins; it works its way into dense, rough-hewn currant, mineral and sage notes. **88**

1990: Ripe, rich, smooth and supple, with polished currant, oak and spice flavors. This full-bodied wine is compact and tightly wound, finishing with chewy tannins. **91**

CHARDONNAY NAPA VALLEY (★★★★): This is a pleasant surprise; consistently excellent, with lots of spicy Chardonnay fruit flavors.

1996: An ultra-rich style that's visibly unfined and unfiltered, with exotic, buttery pear, fig, apricot and spicy, toasty oak flavors. **92**

1995: A touch earthy, but some interesting flavors emerge; with tiers of pear, spice, melon, and a hint of spicy oak. **90**

1994: Smooth, ripe and creamy, the pretty honey, pear, spice and vanilla flavors pick up a trace of tangerine and nutmeg on the finish. **90**

MERLOT NAPA VALLEY (★★★)

1995: Supple and elegant, with ripe, spicy cherry, wild berry, strawberry and minty flavors, it exhibits finesse and is nicely polished. **89**

1994: Austere, with spice, cedar, herb and tobacco notes and just a hint of currant and cherry flavor emerging from the tannins. **87**

HARTFORD COURT WINERY (★★★)
Green Valley, Sonoma County
Founded: 1993. **Owner:** Jennifer Jackson-Hartford, Don Hartford & Laura Jackson-Giron. **Winemaker:** Mike Sullivan.

MAJOR WINES: PRICE, CASES, RATING

Chardonnay Russian River Valley Seascape Vineyard ($35, 450)	★★★
Pinot Noir Russian River Valley Arrendell Vineyard ($45, 400)	★★★
Pinot Noir Russian River Valley Dutton Ranch Sanchietti Vineyard ($40, 400)	★★★
Pinot Noir Sonoma Coast ($35, 250)	★★★
Zinfandel Russian River Valley Fanucchi Vineyard ($30, 450)	★★★
Zinfandel Russian River Valley Hartford Vineyard ($35, 450)	★★★

WINERY DATA

Case Production: 2,450. **Acres Owned:** 45 acres in Russian River. **Varietals by Acre:** Chardonnay (6 acres), Pinot Noir (30), Zinfandel (9). **Vineyard Designations:** Arrendell Vineyard (Pinot Noir), Dutton Ranch Sanchietti Vineyard (Pinot Noir), Fanucchi Vineyard (Zinfandel), Hartford Vineyard (Zinfandel), Seascape Vineyard (Chardonnay). **Varietals Purchased:** Pinot Noir (Russian River), Zinfandel (Russian River).

Part of the Kendall-Jackson group of wineries, Hartford Court continues to make impressive wines that come up just short of outstanding. Given the owners' drive for success, however, I expect that these wines will move up in quality soon. The focus is on Russian River appellation grapes, and the lineup now appears settled. Worth buying.

TASTING NOTES

PINOT NOIR RUSSIAN RIVER VALLEY ARRENDELL VINEYARD (★★★)

1996: Tight, with firm tannins and hints of cola, black cherry, sage and spice; finishing with a spicy blackberry flavor. **88**

1995: Tough, earthy and leathery, with just enough ripe plum and black cherry fruit to sustain it. **85**

1994: Smooth, ripe, rich and polished, it delivers a complex array of plum, cherry, wild berry and toasty oak flavors. **89**

PINOT NOIR RUSSIAN RIVER VALLEY DUTTON RANCH SANCHIETTI VINEYARD (★★★)

1996: Complex, with a pretty, focused array of black cherry, blackberry, vanilla, spice, cola and tea flavors. **88**

1995: Lightly flavored, elegant and delicate, with earthy cherry and raspberry flavors that are clean and simple. **87**

1994: Appealing for its ripe, sweet plum and black cherry flavors, it shows a shade more tannin on the finish. **86**

PINOT NOIR SONOMA COAST (★★★)

1996: Tight and compact, with complex flavors of black cherry, blackberry, herb, sage and spice. **88**

1995: Smooth and elegant, with subtle herb, cherry, tea, earth and spice notes, firming up on the finish. **87**

ZINFANDEL RUSSIAN RIVER VALLEY HARTFORD VINEYARD (★★★): The brilliant 1994 (90 points) served up lots of complex raspberry and cherry flavors and lots of finesse. Worth watching.

1996: Folds together lots of ripe cherry, plum, and blackberry flavors and finishes with a dash of cedar and spice. **87**

1995: Offers harmony and finesse; nicely balanced between its cherry- and raspberry-laced fruit and its light oak shadings. **90**

HARTWELL VINEYARDS (★★★★)

Stags Leap District, Napa Valley
Founded: 1986. **Owner:** Bob Hartwell. **Winemaker:** Celia Masyczek.

MAJOR WINES: PRICE, CASES, RATING

Cabernet Sauvignon Stags Leap District Grace ($65, 300)	★★★★
Cabernet Sauvignon Stags Leap District Sunshine Vineyard ($50, 700)	★★★★
Chardonnay Stags Leap District ($30, 300)	★★★★

WINERY DATA
Case Production: 1,500. **Acres Owned:** 20 acres in Stags Leap District. **Varietals by Acre:** Cabernet Sauvignon (13 acres), Merlot (5), Chardonnay (2). **Vineyard Designations:** Grace Vineyard (Cabernet Sauvignon), Sunshine Vineyard (Cabernet Sauvignon).

This 20-acre vineyard in the Stags Leap District is owned by Bob Hartwell. The wines used to be made at and marketed by Grace Family Vineyard in St. Helena, but in 1997, Hartwell decided to build a winery on his property.

The Hartwell Grace Cabernet is made from a one-acre plot of Cabernet in Hartwell's Stags Leap vineyard. The first Hartwell vintage was in 1990; the wine's production lapsed for one year, 1995, when the vineyard, a phylloxera victim, needed to be replanted. First made in 1993, Sunshine Vineyard Cabernet comes from another portion of Hartwell's vineyard, planted on the same terraced hillside as the original section. A small amount of Chardonnay is produced as well. Production has moved from the hard-to-find level to greater abundance, with 1,500 cases produced.

TASTING NOTES

CABERNET SAUVIGNON STAGS LEAP DISTRICT GRACE (★★★★)

1994: Tight and rich, with a concentrated core of ripe plum, currant and black cherry and a nice edge of toasty, cedary oak. **94**

1992: Supple and harmonious, with a pretty core of polished cherry and berry flavors, finishing with a dash of toasty oak. **90**

1991: Ripe, round, smooth and supple, this wine delivers a pretty core of currant, cedar and spice flavors, finishing with smooth tannins and toasty oak nuances. **92**

CABERNET SAUVIGNON STAGS LEAP DISTRICT SUNSHINE VINEYARD (★★★★): Very impressive; poised to join the ★★★★★ club.

1995: Well balanced, supple and harmonious, with spicy currant, black cherry and anise flavors; turning earthy and complex on the finish. **92**

1994: Elegant and richly flavored, with pretty plum, wild berry and cherry fruit and soft, supple tannins. **89**

CHARDONNAY STAGS LEAP DISTRICT (★★★★): New to the lineup, and headed in the right direction. Worth watching.

1997: Smooth, ripe and creamy, with tiers of pear, fig, melon and citrus flavors that turn complex and linger on the finish. **90**

HAVENS WINE CELLARS (★★★)
Napa Valley
Founded: 1984. **Owner:** Michael & Kathryn Havens, Jon Scott, Russell Lane. **Winemaker:** Michael Havens.

MAJOR WINES: PRICE, CASES, RATING
Merlot Carneros Reserve ($28, 3,000)	★★★
Merlot Napa Valley ($20, 9,000)	★★★
Red Bourriquot Napa Valley ($28, 1,000)	★★★
Sauvignon Blanc Napa Valley ($12, 1,1000)	★★
Syrah Carneros ($20, 1,000)	★★★

WINERY DATA
Case Production: 15,000. **Acres Owned:** 12 acres in Napa Valley. **Varietals by Acre:** Sauvignon Blanc (4 acres), Syrah (8). **Varietals Purchased:** Cabernet Franc (Carneros, Napa Valley), Merlot (Carneros, Napa Valley), Syrah (Carneros).

Michael Havens earned a doctorate in humanities and became a college professor before turning his hobby of home winemaking into a full-time vocation. In 1983, Havens purchased a 3-acre parcel of land in Carneros next to Truchard Vineyard, and bought grapes from Truchard for his Merlot. He later joined Truchard as winemaker when the Truchard family started its winery in 1989. In 1994, he left Truchard to focus on his own brand, which has grown to 15,000 cases. Napa Valley Merlot is the leader; the rest of the lineup is comprised of a Reserve Merlot from Carneros, a Napa Valley Sauvignon Blanc and a Carneros Syrah.

TASTING NOTES

MERLOT NAPA VALLEY (★★★): Good, occasionally earthy, but not among the best. The 1996 (84 points) offered more earth and leather than pure fruit.

SYRAH CARNEROS (★★★): Dense and earthy in 1995 (83 points), but concentrated. Later efforts have been more impressive.

HAWK CREST see STAG'S LEAP WINE CELLARS

HAWLEY WINES (★★)
Dry Creek Valley, Sonoma County
Founded: 1996 **Owner:** John & Dana Hawley. **Winemaker:** John Hawley.

MAJOR WINES: PRICE, CASES, RATING
Merlot Dry Creek Valley ($28, 750)	★★
Viognier Dry Creek Valley ($22, 400)	★★

WINERY DATA
Case Production: 1,500. **Acres Owned:** 10 acres in Dry Creek Valley. **Varietals by Acre:** Cabernet Sauvignon (2 acres), Merlot (7), Viognier (1). **Varietals Purchased:** Viognier (Dry Creek Valley).

John Hawley, former winemaker for Kendall-Jackson, formed his own label in 1996 though he still works for K-J on a consulting basis. Hawley makes Merlot, Cabernet and Viognier from his Dry Creek Valley vineyard and plans to add Pinot Noir and Chardonnay, made from purchased grapes, to his line in the future. The initial releases of Viognier and Merlot were lean, with modest depth of flavor. The wines seem to be improving, however, as the 1997 Viognier (87 points) showed more complex, ripe fruit flavors.

HAYWOOD VINTNER'S SELECT see HAYWOOD WINERY

HAYWOOD WINERY (★★–★★★)

Sonoma County
Founded: 1980. **Owner:** Racke USA **Winemaker:** Judy Matulich Weitz. **Second Label:** Haywood Vintner's Select.

MAJOR WINES: PRICE, CASES, RATING

Cabernet Sauvignon California	
($9, 60,000)	★★
Chardonnay California	
($9, 90,000)	★★
Merlot California	
($9, 30,000)	★★
Zinfandel Sonoma Valley Los Chamizal Vineyard	
($19, 4,000)	★★★
Zinfandel Sonoma Valley Los Chamizal Vineyard Rocky Terrace	
($29, 1,000)	★★★★

WINERY DATA

Case Production: 180,000. **Acres Owned:** 60 acres in Sonoma Valley. **Varietals by Acre:** Cabernet Franc (3 acres), Cabernet Sauvignon (17), Merlot (3), Zinfandel (37). **Vineyard Designations:** Los Chamizal (Zinfandel). **Varietals Purchased:** Cabernet Sauvignon (California), Chardonnay (California), Merlot (California).

Former building contractor Peter Haywood planted a 90-acre vineyard in the hills above Sonoma in the late 1970s before starting his winery in 1980. Haywood's greatest success was with his mountain-grown Los Chamizal Vineyard Zinfandel; with its intense, spicy, peppery fruit flavors, it was considered to be among the best in Sonoma during the 1980s. The Cabernet, however, was marked by unusually high acidity levels, and the Chardonnay struggled as well. By the late 1980s, the winery was experiencing financial difficulties, and Haywood sold the brand to Racke USA, owner of Buena Vista Winery, and production shifted there. The winery facility was sold to Ravenswood. Zinfandel from Los Chamizal remains the best wine; the average-quality Cabernet and Chardonnay now carry a California appellation and Vintner's Select designations, and are barely worthy of a ★★ rating.

TASTING NOTES

ZINFANDEL SONOMA VALLEY LOS CHAMIZAL VINEYARD (★★★): A very consistent vineyard, producing crisp wines with earthy raspberry and spice flavors.
1995: This elegant wine offers medium-weight cherry, wild berry and spice flavors and mild tannins. **87**
1994: Smooth, ripe and polished, with a supple range of cherry, anise, raisin, raspberry, sage, smoke and tea flavors. **88**
1993: A touch earthy, with herb, sage, cherry, currant and cedary notes, turning tannic on the finish. **88**

ZINFANDEL SONOMA VALLEY LOS CHAMIZAL VINEYARD ROCKY TERRACE (★★★★): The better portion of the vineyard gets riper and more supple; very complex and under-rated. Worth collecting.
1995: Beautifully crafted. Intense, ripe, rich and distinctive, with spice, mineral, sage, earth and wild berry flavors. **90**
1994: Combines ripe, mature cherry, raspberry and anise flavors with firm tannins and a sense of elegance. **89**

HEITZ WINE CELLARS (★★–★★★★★)

Napa Valley
Founded: 1961. **Owner:** Heitz Wine Cellars. **Winemaker:** David Heitz.

MAJOR WINES: PRICE, CASES, RATING

Cabernet Sauvignon Napa Valley	
($21, NA)	★★★
Cabernet Sauvignon Napa Valley Martha's Vineyard	
($65, NA)	★★★★★
Cabernet Sauvignon Napa Valley Bella Oaks Vineyard	
($28, NA)	★★★
Cabernet Sauvignon Rutherford Trailside Vineyard	
($48, NA)	★★★★

ALSO PRODUCED

Chardonnay Napa Valley ($11); Grignolino Port Napa Valley ($18); Grignolino Rosé Napa Valley ($7); Pinot Noir Napa Valley ($15); Port Napa Valley Vintage; ($35); Zinfandel Napa Valley; ($13).

WINERY DATA

Case Production: 38,000. **Acres Owned:** 350 acres (101 in Rutherford, 249 in Pope Valley & Napa Valley). **Varietals by Acre:** Cabernet Sauvignon (195 acres), other (155). **Vineyard Designations:** Bella Oaks (Cabernet Sauvignon), Martha's Vineyard (Cabernet Sauvignon), Trailside Vineyard (Cabernet Sauvignon). **Varietals Purchased:** Cabernet Sauvignon (Rutherford, Oakville), Chardonnay (Carneros).

VINTAGE 1991 — Bottle — BOTTLED SEPTEMBER 1995 of a total of 32,256 Bottles — **Heitz Cellar** — NAPA VALLEY — CABERNET SAUVIGNON — Trailside Vineyard — ALCOHOL 13.5% BY VOLUME — PRODUCED AND BOTTLED IN OUR CELLAR BY HEITZ WINE CELLARS — ST. HELENA, CALIFORNIA, U.S.A.

Joe Heitz will be best remembered for his minty, currant-laced Martha's Vineyard Cabernet Sauvignons, which helped catapult Napa Valley wines to international fame. Heitz moved to Napa Valley in the 1950s with his wife, Alice, and worked in the wine lab at Beaulieu Vineyard with André Tchelistcheff for several years. In 1961 he and Alice bought a small winery on Highway 29 (now the Heitz tasting room) and began buying bulk wines, blending them and selling them under the Heitz Wine Cellars label. Heitz had a hand in many of the wines being crafted in Napa in that era, including Stony Hill's; he had a close relationship with Fred and Eleanor McCrea, Stony Hill's owners.

Heitz was also friends with wine connoisseur Barney Rhodes, one of the investors who helped finance Heitz Cellars early on by buying two vintages of Hanzell Chardonnay and Pinot Noir at auction, which Heitz bottled and sold under his label to wide critical acclaim. More significantly, Rhodes and his wife, Belle, planted the first 12 acres of what became the 34-acre Martha's Vineyard after Tom and Martha May bought it in 1964. In 1965 Heitz made his first Cabernet, and a year later agreed to buy the Mays' Martha's Vineyard Cabernet. It proved so distinctive that Heitz decided to bottle it separately. The Mays too

became partners in the Heitz business, along with Harolyn and Bob Thompson (the latter being the wine writer and author of *The Wine Atlas of California*).

Heitz's specialty was always Cabernet. He made some good Zinfandels, a Grignolino Rosé, and occasionally a good Chardonnay, but wines such as Pinot Noir were never above average.

Heitz's son David has been the winemaker for almost a decade and he continues to make a very fine Martha's Vineyard Cabernet, along with an impressive Cabernet from the family's Trailside Vineyard near Conn Creek Winery on Silverado Trail. The other major vineyard-designated Cabernet comes from the Bella Oaks Vineyard in Rutherford, owned by the Rhodeses. The Heitz family understands the importance of controlling their grape sources, and has steadily been adding vineyard property. They now own 350 acres of vineyards, including 101 acres in Rutherford. They also have extensive holdings in Pope Valley, which contribute to their regular Napa Valley Cabernet. Note: there is no Martha's after 1992 because the vineyard was replanted.

TASTING NOTES

CABERNET SAUVIGNON NAPA VALLEY (★★★): More rustic these days, but usually solid, marked by cedary currant and spice notes. Often, it benefits from small doses of Martha's, Bella's and Trailside grapes. Bottlings from the 1960s and 1970s were frequently superb.
1994: Spicy and peppery, medium weight, with a modest range of dried cherry and berry fruit that turns dry and austere. Good but nothing more. **84**
1993: Starts out tight and compact, it slowly opens to more rich and supple flavors, with currant, berry and plummy notes. Finishes with dry tannins. **88**
1992: Solid Cabernet, with a core of rich, earthy currant and berry flavors and a hint of cedar and spice on the firm finish. **89**
1991: Marked by a dank, earthy, rustic aroma, it's more satisfying on the palate as the spicy Cabernet flavors unfold slowly, turning supple in texture. **85**
1990: Strikes a nice balance between spicy, cedary oak and ripe cherry and currant flavors, turning smooth and supple on the finish. Has good intensity and depth. **90**

CABERNET SAUVIGNON NAPA VALLEY BELLA OAKS VINEYARD (★★★)

1994: Medium ruby red, similar medium weight, with dried plum, red cherry and berryish notes that while elegant and spicy never really frame a tight focus. **87**

1993: Complex and somewhat austere; unfolds to a broad range of currant, spice, sage and cedary notes. **91**

1986: Still marked by a cedary, mossy edge, giving the cherry and currant flavors a tinge of sourness. **78**

CABERNET SAUVIGNON NAPA VALLEY MARTHA'S VINEYARD (★★★★★):
From 1966 to 1980, this was the star of Napa Valley Cabernets, with its signature deep color and rich, minty chocolate, currant and blackberry flavors. The wines of the 1980s have been good but variable, as the style has gotten more rustic. The entire vineyard has been replanted and there hasn't been a bottling since the 1992 vintage.

1992: Smooth, rich and harmonious, with a distinct minty edge to the currant and black cherry fruit, turning supple on the finish. **93**

1991: Shows off its minty currant overtone, with tightly wound, complex sage and cherry notes. **91**

1990: Marked by mint and currant with a cedary oak edge, turning smooth and supple with good depth and intensity before finishing with firm tannins. **90**

1989: Dark, rich and intensely flavored, this is a youthful and tightly wound Martha's that's opening up, with spicy mint, cherry and currant flavors that turn supple and generous on the finish. **90**

1988: A successful 1988 that combines the classic Martha's cedar and mint notes with supple currant and spice flavors. **87**

1987: There was some bottle variation, but the best ones were spicy, with minty currant and chocolate aromas and flavors and supple tannins. **92**

1986: Smooth and spicy, with rich currant, chocolate and mineral flavors adding dimension and depth. **91**

1985: Wonderfully rich, elegant and complex, with tiers of currant, black cherry, spice and mint flavors that are deep and concentrated. **94**

1984: Beautifully defined and richly concentrated, with deep, complex, vibrant black cherry, currant, cedar and creamy vanilla flavors that are impeccably balanced. **92**

1983: Supple for the vintage, with chocolate, currant and plum flavors that pick up firm, hard tannins on the finish. **88**

1982: Powerful and concentrated, yet with rounded edges that display depth and finesse. A beautifully crafted wine with lots of mint and currant flavors. **90**

1981: Deep and intense, with a rich concentration of ripe currant, plum and cherry flavors with cedar and mint notes. Has great harmony, balance and finesse. **89**

1980: Very forward and flavorful, with ripe, generous, bright cherry, plum, anise and cedar nuances that are beautifully focused and very long on the finish. **91**

1979: A rich, bold, dramatic Martha's, intense yet elegant and supple, with round, smooth tannins and a long, gorgeous aftertaste that echoes the mint, fruit and floral notes. **93**

1978: Classic Martha's Vineyard: minty, spicy, elegant and aging exceptionally well, with currant, black cherry, anise, cedar and plum flavors. **91**

1977: Mature, with generous ripe cherry, plum and currant flavors, a nice overlay of peppery, cedary oak and fine balance and length. **90**

1976: Mature, with ripe but drying plum and currant flavors and a good dose of tannin. **85**

1975: Mature but intense, with complex cedar, chocolate and cherry flavors that are softening. **92**

1974: Now at its best, this classic offers extraordinary richness, depth and complexity, with deep currant, mint, spice and cassis flavors. **97**

1973: Impressive for its rich core of cedar, chocolate and currant flavors and smooth, supple texture. Mature. **92**

1972: A weak vintage with modest, drying flavors. **75**

1970: Mature but aging magnificently, with tiers of complex currant, mint, anise and cedar flavors. Deep, rich and concentrated. **92**

1969: Elegant, with great intensity and depth and the characteristic Martha's mintiness that complements the rich currant and cherry flavors. Great length on the finish. **95**

1968: A big, deep, extremely rich and concentrated wine, packed with complex, ripe currant, cedar and spice flavors that are fully mature, with great persistence and depth of flavor on the finish. A stunning wine. **92**

1967: Holding up; it's a bit earthy, with bright cherry, cedar and spice flavors that are lively on the finish. **86**

1966: Still a marvelous wine, with complex currant, earth, mint and cherry flavors and a delicate touch of cedar and cinnamon on the finish. Perfectly balanced. **91**

CABERNET SAUVIGNON RUTHERFORD TRAILSIDE VINEYARD (★★★★):
This property, on rich soils near Caymus, serves Heitz well—it's great Cabernet country.

1993: Complex, with ripe, juicy currant, black cherry and spice and plenty of toasty vanilla-laced oak. **92**
1992: Smooth, ripe and harmonious, with a supple core of currant, herb, dill and sage notes and a hint of coffee. **90**
1991: Well oaked, with a leathery edge to the mature currant and plum flavors, turning cedary on the finish. **88**
1990: Mature cedar and coffee flavors appear alongside complex, yet harmonious nuances of anise, cherry, plum and currant. **91**
1989: Intense and lively, rich and supple, with tiers of spicy currant, black cherry, vanilla and toasty oak flavors. A wonderful sense of harmony and finesse. **89**

H.W. HELMS SEE LIVINGSTON VINEYARDS

HENDRY RANCH (★★★)
Napa Valley
Founded: 1992. **Owner:** George Hendry, Susan Ridley, Jeff Miller. **Winemaker:** Robert Mueller.

MAJOR WINES: PRICE, CASES, RATING
Cabernet Sauvignon Napa Valley Block 8
  ($25, 875)   ★★★
Chardonnay Napa Valley Block 9
  ($23, 900)   ★★★
Zinfandel Napa Valley Block 7
  ($18, 2,000)   ★★★

ALSO PRODUCED
Chardonnay Napa Valley Block 10 ($20, 300); Pinot Noir Napa Valley Hendry Vineyard ($24, 325); Zinfandel Napa Valley Hendry Block 23 ($18, 300).

WINERY DATA
Case Production: 4,700. **Acres Owned:** 118 acres in Napa. **Varietals by Acre:** Cabernet Franc (1 acre), Cabernet Sauvignon (21), Chardonnay (47), Malbec (3), Merlot (3), Petit Verdot (1), Pinot Gris (2), Pinot Noir (14), Primitivo (5), Sauvignon Blanc (3), Zinfandel (18). **Vineyard Designations:** Hendry Vineyard.

George Hendry, president of Cyclotron Inc., a company that designs and manufactures particle accelerators for medical purposes, grew up in Napa. In 1939 his parents began planting what is now a 118-acre vineyard at the base of Mount Veeder. Because the vineyard's elevation is below the Mount Veeder appellation line, it carries a Napa Valley designation. For several years, Rosenblum and Franus have produced very fine vineyard-designed Zinfandels from this vineyard, and in 1992 Hendry began bottling his own Zinfandels. In 1995 he added a Cabernet Sauvignon. Worth watching.

TASTING NOTES

CABERNET SAUVIGNON NAPA VALLEY BLOCK 8 (★★★): No track record yet, but the 1995 (90 points) was distinctively minty, with bay leaf, currant, berry, cedar and spice.

CHARDONNAY NAPA VALLEY BLOCK 9 (★★★): The first effort in 1996 (88 points) offered ripe pear, apple, melon and spicy fruit flavors.

ZINFANDEL MOUNT VEEDER BRANDLIN VINEYARD (★★★)
1994: Distinct for its mint, spice and cedar notes, the ripe berry and cherry fruit unfold gracefully. **88**
1992: Has the typical briar and black pepper flavors, but the finish clamps down and turns dry. **86**

ZINFANDEL NAPA VALLEY BLOCK 7 (★★★)
1994: Smooth, ripe and polished, with a jammy cherry and wild berry edge to the flavors and supple tannins. **90**
1992: Young and intense, with a tightly wound core of wild berry, cherry, anise and spice flowing through it. **88**

HERITAGE see SEBASTIANI SONOMA CASK CELLARS

HERZOG see BARON HERZOG

THE HESS COLLECTION WINERY (★★★–★★★★)
Mount Veeder, Napa Valley
Founded: 1985. **Owner:** Hess Holding A.G. **Winemaker:** Dave Guffy. **Second Label:** Hess Select.

MAJOR WINES: PRICE, CASES, RATING
Cabernet Sauvignon Mount Veeder
  Napa Valley
  ($25)   ★★★★
Cabernet Sauvignon Mount Veeder
  Napa Valley Reserve
  ($45)   ★★★★

Chardonnay Napa Valley
($18) ★★★★

Merlot Mount Veeder Napa Valley
($23) ★★★

Zinfandel Napa Valley
($18) ★★★

WINERY DATA

Acres Owned: 725 acres (100 in Napa Valley, 275 in Mount Veeder, 350 in Monterey). **Varietals by Acre:** Chardonnay (475 acres), Cabernet Sauvignon (235), Merlot (15). **Varietals Purchased:** Chardonnay (Napa Valley, Carneros, Monterey), Cabernet Sauvignon (California, Napa Valley).

Swiss entrepreneur Donald Hess came to California in 1978 searching for new springs to expand Valser, his mineral water company. He immediately took a liking to Napa Valley wines and decided to start a winery after carefully studying the success of Robert Mondavi. Being Swiss, he liked the mountains, and bought more than 500 acres of land on Mount Veeder, including several hundred already planted to vines by William Hill. Hess has since expanded his Mount Veeder plantings to cover some 275 acres. He has also added 100 acres of vines in American Canyon, south of the city of Napa near the Napa County Airport, along with 350 acres in Monterey County. Grapes from those two areas are used primarily for the Hess Select, California appellation wines. Additional plantings are slated for Pope Valley and American Canyon, which will make Hess one of the largest owners of super premium-quality grapes in California.

Instead of building a new winery, Hess wisely approached Christian Brothers about using its abandoned Mont La Salle Winery on Mount Veeder; Hess signed a 50-year lease and began an extensive remodeling that resulted in not only a modernized, high-tech, tourist-friendly winery, but also a museum to house Hess's magnificent modern art collection (hence the winery's double-entendre name). While the initial focus was on Mount Veeder estate-grown Cabernet and Chardonnay, Merlot has since been added. Winemaker Randle Johnson has fine-tuned the style to capture the depth and intensity of Mount Veeder-grown grapes, balancing it well with oak and a sense of elegance. The Hess Select Cabernet and Chardonnay are steady ★★ performers and good values.

TASTING NOTES

CABERNET SAUVIGNON MOUNT VEEDER NAPA VALLEY (★★★★): Dark, intense and concentrated; capable of uncommon depth and complexities while keeping the tannins under control. This remains one of the best values in estate-grown cellar worthy Napa Valley Cabernet.

1995: Smooth, lush and polished, with a pretty array of currrant, black cherry, anise, earth, sage and tarry-leathery flavors building to a sharp focus, and then holding it. Needs time, though. **92**

1994: Solid with ripe, intense, earthy currant, black cherry and berry flavors and a dash of mint and cedar. Turns complex on the finish, where the flavors fold together nicely. **88**

1993: Clean and crisp, with a trim band of ripe currant, chocolate, berry and cedar notes. **88**

1992: Very rich and intense, deeply complex and concentrated, offering tiers of plum, blackberry, currant and spice, and picking up nice, spicy oak notes on the finish. **90**

1991: There's a wonderful sense of harmony and finesse, with ripe, concentrated currant, plum and black cherry flavors and spicy oak notes that add complexity. **92**

1990: Firm and compact, with a tight band of chunky currant, plum, spice and oak flavors. **90**

1989: Lean, green and herbal, with tough, chewy tannins that override the plum and cherry flavors. **82**

1988: Fine balance for an 88, with ripe currant, olive, coffee, herb and tea notes, finishing with a nice balance between tannin and fruit. **87**

1987: Smooth and supple—especially compared with the Hess Reserve, which is quite tannic—this is a complex and harmonious wine with layers of currant, cedar, spice, sage, tar, chocolate and berry, finishing with intensity and a firm tannic edge marked by earthiness. **94**

1986: Shows the same ripe, vibrant cherry, wild berry and spice flavors that have made it likable ever since its release. What it may lack in tannin and extraction, compared to the reserve, it makes up in youthful vitality. **90**

1985: A terrific wine, lavishly oaked, rich, smooth, supple and concentrated, with great depth and intensity and delicious black cherry, cedar, vanilla and anise flavors. **92**

1983: Still lean and austere, offering ripe cherry, currant and cedar flavors of moderate depth and intensity. **84**

CABERNET SAUVIGNON MOUNT VEEDER NAPA VALLEY RESERVE (★★★★)

1994: Intense and tannic, this one's definitely for the cellar, with its tightly wound band of currant, blackberry and earthy mineral nuances. Finishes with tight, firm tannins. **90**

1993: Dark in color, but lean on the palate, with tart cherry and wild berry flavors that slowly unfold. A wine that will need time to open and show its best. Finishes with rich fruit and firm tannins. **90**

1992: Complex, with an elegant band of currant, anise, cedar and spice flavors, showing a hint of mineral on the aftertaste. For all its intensity and concentration, it's texture is smooth and polished. **90**

1991: Very intense and minty, a rich, concentrated, vibrant and tightly wound young red that slowly opens to reveal a complex core of plum and currant. The tannins are major-league. **91**

1990: Bold, rich and intensely concentrated, with compact, tannic fruit flavors. On the finish the spicy black cherry, currant and mineral notes are focused and complex. **90**

1989: An oaky wine, but the currant, wild berry and black cherry flavors are now coming to the front, giving it a greater sense of proportion and depth. Complex and concentrated. **89**

1988: Austere style, with lots of mint, herb, sage and tannin, without the supple tannins and rich fruit to support it. Appears headed toward drying out. **85**

1987: Firm, dark, ripe and intense, a young, vibrant wine with lots of earthy currant, spice, cedar and sage notes, finishing with a tight band of tannin but also good length. **94**

1986: Dense and concentrated, packed with ripe, rich flavors of earthy currant, mineral, anise, tar and spice. Finishes with firm, chewy tannins, but plenty of fruit flavor works its way through, providing depth and complexity. **91**

1984: Still bold, ripe and complex, with currant, spice, anise and cherry flavors, straddling the line between youth and maturity, picking up cedar and coffee notes from age. **91**

1983: Lean and austere, with tight tannins and sharply defined black cherry and currant flavors. **88**

CHARDONNAY NAPA VALLEY (★★★★): Usually tight and flinty, which is in sync with the appellation. Can age well.

1997: Bright, complex grapefruit, melon, pear and spice flavors framed by pretty toasty oak. **90**

MERLOT NAPA VALLEY (★★★): Shares the Cabernet's austerity and firm tannins, but is typically Merlot in its struggle to find a rich core of fruit at mid-palate.

HESS SELECT see **THE HESS COLLECTION WINERY**

HIDDEN CELLARS WINERY (★★★)
Mendocino County
Founded: 1991. **Owner:** Parducci Wine Cellars, Carl Thoma. **Winemaker:** Dennis Patton.

MAJOR WINES: PRICE, CASES, RATING

Carignane Mendocino Hillside ($13, 2,200)	★★★
Petite Sirah Mendocino ($18, 1,076)	★★★
Petite Sirah Mendocino Eaglepoint Ranch ($28, 242)	★★★★
Sauvignon Blanc Mendocino ($13, 2,100)	★★
Sorcery Zinfandel Blend Mendocino ($28, 920)	★★★
Syrah Mendocino ($16, 588)	★★★
Zinfandel Mendocino Eaglepoint Ranch ($28, 241)	★★★★
Zinfandel Mendocino Ford-Hitzman ($32, 218)	★★★
Zinfandel Mendocino Old Vine ($18, 4,470)	★★★

WINERY DATA
Case Production: 25,000. **Vineyard Designations:** Eaglepoint Ranch (Petite Sirah, Zinfandel), Ford-Hitzman (Zinfandel). **Varietals Purchased:** Carignane (Mendocino), Petite Sirah (Mendocino), Sauvignon Blanc (Mendocino), Syrah (Mendocino), Zinfandel (Mendocino).

Dennis Patton founded Hidden Cellars in Talmage, east of Ukiah, and built the brand up to 25,000 cases with a product mix that includes Chardonnay, a white Meritage called Alchemy, Johannisberg Riesling, Sauvignon Blanc and Zinfandel, all from purchased Mendocino County grapes. The lineup is solid, as Patton has zeroed in on many of the varieties that grow well in Mendocino County.

Parducci Wine Cellars purchased Hidden Cellars in 1999, keeping Dennis Patton on as winemaker, and expanding their holdings in Mendocino County.

TASTING NOTES

SYRAH MENDOCINO (★★★)
1996: Plush and elegant, with silky tannins and finely detailed, yet subtle herb, blackberry, pepper and sage notes. **89**

WILLIAM HILL WINERY (★★)
Napa Valley
Founded: 1976. **Owner:** Allied Domecq. **Winemaker:** Jill Davis.

MAJOR WINES: PRICE, CASES, RATING
Cabernet Sauvignon Napa Valley	
($16, 20,000)	★★
Cabernet Sauvignon Napa Valley Reserve	
($27, 5,000)	★★
Chardonnay Napa Valley	
($15, 44,000)	★★★
Chardonnay Napa Valley Reserve	
($20, 8,000)	★★★
Merlot Napa Valley	
($19, 20,000)	★★

WINERY DATA
Case Production: 97,000. **Acres Owned:** 125 acres in Napa Valley. **Varietals by Acre:** Cabernet Sauvignon (90 acres), Chardonnay (19), Merlot (11), Petit Verdot (5). **Varietals Purchased:** Cabernet Franc (Napa Valley), Cabernet Sauvignon (Napa Valley), Chardonnay (Napa Valley, Carneros), Merlot (Napa Valley), Petit Verdot (Napa Valley).

In the early 1970s, William Hill moved to Napa Valley and developed a vineyard on Diamond Mountain (now Sterling's Diamond Mountain Ranch) before moving south to Mount Veeder, where he planted his own vineyard, and then started William Hill Winery in 1976. A true believer in mountain-grown grapes, Hill favored intensity and concentration in his wines. The first commercial wines were the 1978 Cabernet and the 1980 Chardonnay, both excellent in their time; the former is perhaps to this day the finest wine ever bottled under this label. The Cabernets through 1983 were entirely Mount Veeder-grown. By the mid-1980s, however, Hill began blending grapes from his estate vineyard in Soda Canyon, and quality began to decline. He also continued investing in and developing vineyards, most notably the Atlas Peak Vineyards.

In 1985 Hill sold the Atlas Peak Vineyards, and three years later, needing cash to build a winery, he entered into an agreement that led to the sale of his name and winery to The Wine Alliance—a subsidiary of the British drinks firm Allied Domecq which also owns Clos du Bois and Callaway (see listings). In 1993, Hill severed his ties with The Wine Alliance and embarked on plans to develop Domain Hill & Mayes, a diversified wine company based on vineyard estates, with John Mayes, a longtime business associate. Although Hill sold his 70-acre Mount Veeder vineyard to Kendall-Jackson in 1994, he still has widespread vineyard holdings throughout Napa, Sonoma and Mendocino counties, and has branched out into Oregon with Van Duzer.

After an impressive start, by the late 1980s William Hill Winery had settled into producing a line of good but unexceptional wines. The winery has experienced tremendous growth, and production rose to 125,000 cases, with Cabernet and Chardonnay, both regular and Reserve bottlings, remaining the primary focus. Merlot and Sauvignon Blanc have now been added to the product mix. In 1994, The Wine Alliance hired Jill Davis from Buena Vista Winery to oversee winemaking.

It is still unclear whether the winery has the grape sources or desire to rise to the top. As of now, the whole line of William Hill wines is dead center middle-of-the-road.

TASTING NOTES

CABERNET SAUVIGNON NAPA VALLEY & RESERVE (★★): Once deep, ripe and complex, recent vintages have all been merely good, with the 1994, 1995 and 1996—all tremendous vintages—scoring only 86 points. These wines tend to be lean, earthy and lacking in rich, polished fruit. The Reserve is reserve in name only, bearing no resemblance to a wine of extra dimension.
1979: Smooth, supple and seductive, with attractive cedar and cigar box aromas and ripe black cherry, currant and spice notes. **90**
1978: Deeply colored and richly flavored, it gushes with fruit, with a tight core of currant, cherry and wild berry flavors that pick up pretty chocolate and buttery oak nuances on the finish. Still firmly tannic, but at its peak. **92**

CHARDONNAY NAPA VALLEY & RESERVE (★★): Simply lacks the extra flavor dimensions, aromas and complexities of the best being made. The Reserve has had moments of promise, with the 1995 (89 points) the best in memory.

MERLOT NAPA VALLEY (★★): A classic example of a winery following trends, with no real source or passion to make great Merlot.

HITCHING POST (★★★)
Santa Maria Valley, Santa Barbara County
Founded: 1984. **Owner:** Frank Ostini & Gray Hartley.
Winemaker: Frank Ostini & Gray Hartley.

MAJOR WINES: PRICE, CASES, RATING
Pinot Noir Central Coast
($18, 400)   ★★
Pinot Noir Santa Maria Valley
($20, 700)   ★★★
Pinot Noir Santa Maria Valley Bien Nacido
Vineyard
($25, 550)   ★★★
Pinot Noir Santa Ynez Valley
Sanford & Benedict Vineyard
($30, 150)   ★★★★
Syrah Santa Ynez Valley Fess Parker Vineyard
($20, 200)   ★★★

ALSO PRODUCED
Pinot Noir Santa Barbara County Highliner ($40, 200).

WINERY DATA
Case Production: 2,600. **Vineyard Designations:** Bien Nacido Vineyard (Pinot Noir), Fess Parker Vineyard (Syrah), Sanford & Benedict Vineyard (Pinot Noir). **Varietals Purchased:** Pinot Noir (Santa Maria Valley, Santa Ynez Valley), Syrah (Santa Ynez Valley).

Frank Ostini owns the Buellton-based Hitching Post restaurant and wine brand, which uses grapes purchased from Santa Maria Valley and the Sanford & Benedict Vineyard in Santa Ynez Valley. Through the years, several winemakers have assisted Ostini, including Lane Tanner (his former wife) and Jim Clendenen of Au Bon Climat. I have tasted most of the Hitching Post Pinot Noirs, and there's no mistaking their generally high quality —all the more impressive given Pinot's difficult personality. The wines reflect their appellations, with ripe black cherry, herb and cola notes, and clearly strive for elegance and finesse. Production has risen from a few hundred cases in 1994 to 2,600 cases today, and Syrah from Fess Parker Vineyard has also become part of the lineup. The Hitching Post restaurant is an excellent choice for older vintages and a fun place to eat and drink. Worth going out of your way for.

TASTING NOTES

PINOT NOIR SANTA MARIA VALLEY (★★★): Often rustic, but improving and showing more consistency.
1991: Earth, sage and herb aromas give way to earthy cherry flavors, finishing with a spicy edge. **86**
1990: Ripe and fruity for a young Hitching Post Pinot, with intense, complex, concentrated plum, cherry, anise and oak flavors. **91**
1989: Lots of flavor, with cola, currant, plum and spice notes in a tight, compact, complex package, finishing with subtle oak shadings. **88**
1988: Remarkably complex, with ripe, intense, grapey flavors that take on an earthy, leathery edge, especially on the finish, where the tannins kick in. This is a tough, gutsy wine. **90**
1987: Classic Hitching Post Pinot Noir, intense and potent, with wonderful cola, plum, cherry and spice flavors and a texture that's developing silk and polish, but at the same time is very firm and intense. **92**

PINOT NOIR SANTA MARIA VALLEY BIEN NACIDO VINEYARD (★★★): Consistently well made, with complex flavors and fine balance.
1995: Smooth and spicy; a racy style with cola, cherry, berries and cedary notes, turning complex on the finish. **88**
1994: Smooth and polished, with a supple array of spicy cherry, currant, herb and cedary oak flavors. Turns complex and elegant on the finish, where the flavors linger. **89**
1993: Supple and refined plum, cherry, cola and spice flavors that remain focused. Gains complexity and finesse on the finish. **88**

PINOT NOIR SANTA MARIA VALLEY SIERRA MADRE & RIVERBENCH VINEYARDS
1995: Distinct, with a smoky, gamy, meaty edge; the currant and cherry core adds depth and dimension. **87**

PINOT NOIR SANTA YNEZ VALLEY SANFORD & BENEDICT VINEYARD (★★★★): Usually the best. Serves up a wide array of flavors, and can age well for several years.
1995: Firmly tannic, but the core is complex, with intense spice, meaty-beefy notes and mushroom and dried cherry flavors. **90**

1993: Intense and lively cherry and currant flavors; somewhat astringent with a green tea-like edge. **88**
1991: Lean and earthy, with a leathery edge to the black cherry and spice flavors, finishing with firm, drying tannins. **86**
1989: From a great vintage in Santa Ynez Valley, this is a ripe, intense and fruity wine with a big spine and a distinctive Pinot Noir character. **88**

PAUL HOBBS (★★★–★★★★)

Russian River Valley, Sonoma County
Founded: 1991. **Owner:** Paul Hobbs. **Winemaker:** Paul Hobbs.

MAJOR WINES: PRICE, CASES, RATING

Cabernet Sauvignon Howell Mountain Liparita Vineyard ($45, 656)	★★★
Cabernet Sauvignon Napa Valley Carneros Hyde Vineyard ($40, 873)	★★★★
Chardonnay Russian River Valley Walker Station Vineyard ($45, 306)	★★★★
Chardonnay Sonoma Mountain Richard Dinner Vineyard ($39, 999)	★★★★
Chardonnay Sonoma Mountain Richard Dinner Vineyard Cuvée Augustina ($60, 100)	★★★★
Chardonnay Sonoma Valley Kunde Vineyard ($35, 434)	★★★★
Pinot Noir Carneros Hyde Vineyard ($30, 868)	★★

ALSO PRODUCED

Merlot Napa Valley Michael Black Vineyard ($38, 950).

WINERY DATA

Case Production: 7,000. **Acres Owned:** 15 acres in Russian River Valley. **Varietals by Acre:** Pinot Noir (15 acres). **Vineyard Designations:** Richard Dinner Vineyard (Chardonnay), Hyde Vineyard (Cabernet Sauvignon, Pinot Noir), Kunde Vineyard (Chardonnay), Liparita Vineyard (Cabernet Sauvignon), Michael Black Vineyard (Merlot). **Varietals Purchased:** Cabernet Sauvignon (Carneros, Howell Mountain), Chardonnay (Sonoma Valley, Sonoma Mountain), Merlot (Napa Valley), Pinot Noir (Carneros).

Paul Hobbs worked with Opus One in the early 1980s and was winemaker at Simi from 1985 to 1991 before launching his own brand, using space at Kunde Estate Winery in Kenwood and purchasing grapes from a number of excellent sources. Hobbs's 7,000-case lineup includes Cabernet and Pinot Noir from Hyde Vineyard in Carneros, Chardonnay from Richard Dinner Vineyard on Sonoma Mountain, a second Cabernet from Liparita Vineyard on Howell Mountain and Merlot from Michael Black Vineyard near Napa. All of the early wines have been impressive, with the exception of the Pinot Noir, which is lagging a bit. Hobbs is also a consultant to several wine ventures, including clients in Chile and Argentina. Land has been cleared for a planting of 15 acres in Russian River Valley. Worth buying.

TASTING NOTES

CABERNET SAUVIGNON HOWELL MOUNTAIN LIPARITA VINEYARD (★★★): Can be brilliant, but often it struggles to work out of its earthiness.

CABERNET SAUVIGNON NAPA VALLEY CARNEROS HYDE VINEYARD (★★★★): Repeatedly impressive, with a range of intense, complex flavors.
1994: Smooth and polished, with complex dill, sage, tea and currant flavors, turning complex and harmonious on the finish. **89**
1993: Marked by herb and black olive flavors with hints of currant and strawberry, turning elegant on the finish. **89**
1992: Intense and concentrated, with complex, earthy currant, mineral, berry and spice flavors and substantial tannins. **93**
1991: Firm, ripe and intense, with a rich, focused core of currant, black cherry, mineral and herb notes. Turns supple and complex on the finish, where the tannins and buttery oak kick in. **91**

CHARDONNAY SONOMA MOUNTAIN RICHARD DINNER VINEYARD (★★★★): Pushing for ★★★★★, this can be a tremendously complex and concentrated wine, with 1995 the benchmark so far.
1996: An appealing, fruit-driven style, with ripe apple, pear, nectarine, melon and spice, turning complex on the finish. **91**
1995: Amazingly elegant, ripe and flavorful, with a wonderful core of ripe pear, apple, spice and melon flavors. **94**
1994: Well-oaked, with mature, medium-bodied honey, citrus and earthy pear notes, turning elegant on the finish. **89**

CHARDONNAY SONOMA MOUNTAIN RICHARD DINNER VINEYARD CUVÉE AGUSTINA (★★★★)
1996: Elegant, with a pretty array of ripe pear, spice, fig and melon, picking up hints of hazelnut and toasty, buttery oak. Finishes with a long stream of complex flavors. **92**

CHARDONNAY SONOMA VALLEY KUNDE VINEYARD (★★★★)
1996: Ripe, fruity and complex, with polished, elegant pear, spice, fig and melon notes. **91**
1995: Bold and exotic, with layers of juicy pear, apple, fig, melon and light toasty oak shadings, turning complex on the finish. **93**

PINOT NOIR CARNEROS HYDE VINEYARD (★★): No miracles here yet, but the 1994 was impressive, so it's definitely worth watching.

HONIG CELLARS (★★–★★★)
Rutherford, Napa Valley
Founded: 1964. **Owner:** Bill & Nancy Honig, Dan & Sue Weinstein, Honig Family. **Winemaker:** Kristin Belair.

MAJOR WINES: PRICE, CASES, RATING
Cabernet Sauvignon Napa Valley	
($22, 3,000)	★★★
Sauvignon Blanc Napa Valley	
($12, 20,000)	★★
Sauvignon Blanc Napa Valley Reserve	
($16, 3,000)	★★

WINERY DATA
Case Production: 30,000. **Acres Owned:** 51 acres in Rutherford. **Varietals by Acre:** Cabernet Sauvignon (19 acres), Sauvignon Blanc (32). **Varietals Purchased:** Cabernet Sauvignon (Rutherford), Sauvignon Blanc (Rutherford).

In 1966, Louis Honig bought a partially planted 67-acre property in Rutherford from Charlie Wagner of Caymus, and began replanting the remaining acreage. In 1980, Honig's son Bill, better known then as California's former Superintendent of Schools, and Daniel Weinstein, his son-in-law, began making small lots of Sauvignon Blanc, which has steadily increased to about 28,000 cases. Cabernet Sauvignon has also become part of the product mix (3,000 cases). Kristin Belair, former winemaker at Turnbull, has now succeeded James Hall as winemaker, with Hall having moved on to his own successful venture, Patz & Hall. Sauvignon Blanc remains this winery's best, though the 1995 Cabernet Sauvignon (89 points) proved to be a pleasant surprise.

HOP KILN WINERY (★★–★★★)
Russian River Valley, Sonoma County
Founded: 1975. **Owner:** Marty Griffin Jr. **Winemaker:** Steve Strobl.

MAJOR WINES: PRICE, CASES, RATING
Marty Griffin's Big Red California	
($10, 4,800)	★★
Zinfandel Sonoma County	
($16, 2,170)	★★★
Zinfandel Sonoma County Primitivo	
($22, 460)	★★★

ALSO PRODUCED
A Thousand Flowers White Russian River Valley ($8, 2,778); Chardonnay Russian River Valley M. Griffin Vineyard ($18, 450); Riesling Russian River Valley M. Griffin Vineyard ($10, 628); Sauvignon Blanc Russian River Valley ($11, 420); Valdiguié Russian River Valley M. Griffin Vineyard ($20, 400); Zinfandel Late Harvest Russian River Valley M. Griffin Vineyard ($15, 958).

WINERY DATA
Case Production: 12,000. **Acres Owned:** 43 acres in Russian River Valley. **Varietals by Acre:** Cabernet Sauvignon (3 acres), Chardonnay (6), Gewürztraminer (4), Johannisberg Riesling (8), Valdiguié (4), Zinfandel (18). **Vineyard Designations:** M. Griffin Vineyard (Chardonnay, Riesling, Valdiguié, Zinfandel). **Varietals Purchased:** Gewürztraminer (Russian River Valley), Sauvignon Blanc (Russian River Valley).

After studying winemaking in Italy in 1964, Marty Griffin started making Zinfandel as a home winemaker. In 1975, he decided to go commercial and started a winery, focusing on Zinfandel, his favorite wine.

Griffin holds the trademark for the name Primitivo, the southern Italian grape that may have genetic links to Zinfandel. The vines for the Primitivo bottling, which must be at least 50 years old, yield a very intriguing Zinfandel, with bold ripe fruit flavors, a deep color and gutsy tannins. Roughly half of Griffin's acres are planted to red grapes, including Zinfandel and Cabernet, and he also buys grapes from area vineyards. Chardonnay, Gewürztraminer and Riesling are rooted in his vineyard as well. He makes a blend called Marty Griffin's Big Red, a mixture of Zinfandel, Petite Sirah, Napa Gamay and Cabernet that is often a rich, hearty wine and an excellent value. (One year, a California wine competition awarded Big Red a gold medal over Opus One, favoring power and intensity over harmony and finesse.) The winery is modeled after a hop kiln from 1905, and is well worth a visit.

TASTING NOTES

ZINFANDEL SONOMA COUNTY (★★★): The 1995 (90 points) was complex, with supple black cherry, wild berry and raspberry notes. The 1996 (85) was lighter, a touch green and tannic.

ZINFANDEL SONOMA COUNTY PRIMITIVO (★★★): Made from old vines, recent vintages have been leaner, greener and more tart. The 1996 (84 points), 1995 (87) and 1994 (81) were not very interesting wines, considering the high quality of the vintages.

HOWELL MOUNTAIN VINEYARDS (★★★★)
Howell Mountain, Napa Valley
Founded: 1988. **Owner:** Mike Beatty, Joyce Black Sears, Jerre Sears. **Winemaker:** Ted Lemon.

MAJOR WINES: PRICE, CASES, RATING

Zinfandel Howell Mountain (Discontinued)	★★★
Zinfandel Howell Mountain Beatty Ranch ($32, 250)	★★★★
Zinfandel Howell Mountain Black Sears Vineyard ($32, 250)	★★★★
Zinfandel Howell Mountain Old Vine ($24, 1,300)	★★★★

ALSO PRODUCED
Cabernet Sauvignon Howell Mountain Black Sears Vineyard Beatty Ranch ($40, 500).

WINERY DATA
Case Production: 2,300. **Acres Owned:** 80 acres on Howell Mountain. **Varietals by Acre:** Cabernet Sauvignon (40 acres), Zinfandel (40). **Vineyard Designations:** Beatty Ranch (Zinfandel), Black Sears (Zinfandel).

This is a promising new venture, joining two well-known Howell Mountain vineyards with skilled winemaker Ted Lemon. Both Beatty Ranch and Black Sears vineyards are known for excellent quality and distinctive wines. With Lemon in charge, the wines should be right on target.

TASTING NOTES

ZINFANDEL HOWELL MOUNTAIN (★★★)
1995: A ripe, high-octane style, with juicy plum and wild berry flavors, turning slightly hot on the finish, where a peppery note comes through. The fruit comes from the Black Sears Vineyard. **89**
1994: Classic spice and pepper aromas with hints of cherry, sage, and wild berry characterize this ripe, lean, elegant young wine. Finishes with firm tannins. **88**

ZINFANDEL HOWELL MOUNTAIN BEATTY RANCH (★★★★)
1997: Tight, firm and fleshy, with a complex array of sage, anise, mineral and spice, finishing with a tightly focused core of flavorful tannins. **91**

ZINFANDEL HOWELL MOUNTAIN BLACK SEARS VINEYARD (★★★★)
1997: A mouthful of ripe, plush, lush cherry, wild berry, cedar and spice, it's wall to wall Zinfandel, with amazing depth and complexity. **93**

ZINFANDEL HOWELL MOUNTAIN OLD VINE (★★★★)
1997: Tightly focused, rich and complex, with peppery, earthy cherry, wild berry, anise, sage and cedary flavors, finishing with firm, but flavorful tannins. **91**

HUNTER ASHBY see **RUTHERFORD HILL WINERY**

ROBERT HUNTER WINERY (★★★)
Sonoma Valley
Founded: 1975. **Owner:** Robert E. Hunter Jr.
Winemaker: Rob Hunter III.

MAJOR WINES: PRICE, CASES, RATING
Brut de Noirs Sonoma Valley
  Extended Tirage
  ($25, 1,000)   ★★★

WINERY DATA
Case Production: 1,000. **Acres Owned:** 42 acres in Sonoma Valley. **Varietals by Acre:** Cabernet Franc (1 acre), Cabernet Sauvignon (6), Chardonnay (20), Malbec (1) Merlot (4), Petit Verdot (1), Pinot Noir (9 acres).

Sonoma Valley grape grower Robert Hunter sold Chardonnay and Pinot Noir to Sonoma wineries before starting his *méthode champenoise* sparkling wine brand, which is now made in 1,000-case quantities by his son, Rob Hunter, who is also winemaker at Sterling Vineyards. Quality is usually very good in his vintage-dated Blanc de Noirs.

HUSCH (★★)
Anderson Valley, Mendocino County
Founded: 1971. **Owner:** H. A. Oswald Jr. Family.
Winemaker: Fritz Meier.

MAJOR WINES: PRICE, CASES, RATING
Cabernet Sauvignon Mendocino La Ribera
Vineyards
  ($17, 4,000)   ★★★
Chardonnay Mendocino
  ($13, 10,000)   ★★
Pinot Noir Anderson Valley
  ($18, 4,000)   ★
Pinot Noir Anderson Valley Reserve
  ($29, 500)   ★★
Sauvignon Blanc Mendocino La Ribera
  Vineyards
  ($11, 8,000)   ★★

ALSO PRODUCED
Cabernet Sauvignon Mendocino Reserve ($27, 400); Carignane Mendocino Old Vines ($12, 400); Chardonnay Anderson Valley Special Reserve ($22, 600); Chardonnay Mendocino La Ribera Vineyards ($16, 700); Chenin Blanc Mendocino ($9, 2,000); Gewürztraminer Anderson Valley ($11, 3,000); Gewürztraminer Late Harvest Anderson Valley ($14, 300); Muscat Canelli Mendocino ($14, 700); Sauvignon Blanc Blend Mendocino La Ribera Vineyards Blanc ($7, 1,000); Mendocino La Ribera Vineyards Red ($9, 800).

WINERY DATA
Case Production: 36,000. **Acres Owned:** 206 acres (81 in Anderson Valley, 125 in Mendocino). **Varietals by Acre:** Cabernet Sauvignon (21 acres), Chardonnay (89), Gewürztraminer (13), Pinot Noir (22), Sauvignon Blanc (40), other (21). **Vineyard Designations:** La Ribera Vineyards (Cabernet Sauvignon, Chardonnay, Sauvignon Blanc).

In 1971 Tony Husch established the first winery in Anderson Valley since Prohibition, but his business success was mixed and he sold it in 1979 to the Oswald family, longtime grape growers. The winery now has 206 acres in vines: Chardonnay (89 acres) dominates, followed by Sauvignon Blanc (40), and Pinot Noir and Cabernet (roughly 20 acres each). The winery's 36,000-case output includes those varietal wines, along with Chenin Blanc and Gewürztraminer, all estate-grown. Three wines, the Cabernet, Chardonnay and Sauvignon Blanc, carry a La Ribera Vineyards designation. Though the wines are good values, quality has leveled off and none of the wines merit more than a ★★★ rating.

ICI/LA-BAS see **AU BON CLIMAT**

IL PODERE DELL' OLIVOS see **AU BON CLIMAT**

INDIAN CREEK see **NAVARRO VINEYARDS**

INDIGO HILLS see **GALLO OF SONOMA WINERY**

IRON HORSE VINEYARDS (★★★)
Green Valley, Sonoma County
Founded: 1976. **Owner:** Audrey & Barry Sterling, Joy Sterling, Forrest Tancer, Laurence & Terry Sterling. **Winemaker:** Forrest Tancer.

MAJOR WINES: PRICE, CASES, RATING

Blanc de Blancs Sonoma Green Valley LD
($45, 1,000) ★★★★
Brut Rosé Sonoma Green Valley
($22, 1,000) ★★★
Brut Sonoma Green Valley Classic Vintage
($20, 10,000) ★★★
Brut Sonoma Green Valley LD
($45, 1,000) ★★★
Cabernet Sauvignon Alexander Valley T-T Vineyards
($18, 2,000) ★★
Chardonnay Sonoma Green Valley
($18, 10,000) ★★★
Fumé Blanc Alexander Valley T-T Vineyards
($16, 3,000) ★★★
Pinot Noir Sonoma Green Valley
($18, 3,000) ★★
Sangiovese Alexander Valley T-T Vineyards
($18, 1,000) ★★★
Sparkling Sonoma Green Valley Russian Cuvée
($20, 1,000) ★★★
Sparkling Sonoma Green Valley Vrais Amis
($22, 1,000) ★★★
Sparkling Sonoma Green Valley Wedding Cuvée
($20, 2,500) ★★★
Viognier Alexander Valley T-T
($16, 1,000) ★★★

WINERY DATA
Case Production: 40,000. **Acres Owned:** 242 acres (190 in Sonoma County-Green Valley, 52 in Alexander Valley). **Varietals by Acre:** Cabernet Franc (2 acres), Cabernet Sauvignon (13), Chardonnay (110), Merlot (3), Pinot Noir (80), Sangiovese (6), Sauvignon Blanc (14), Viognier (14). **Vineyard Designations:** T-T (Cabernet Sauvignon, Fumé Blanc, Sangiovese, Viognier).

Barry and Audrey Sterling founded this winery in 1976, naming it after a railroad stop called Iron Horse. There are 242 acres in vines, with Green Valley-grown Chardonnay and Pinot Noir dominating; a large portion of each goes into the winery's line of sparkling wines. Under the direction of winemaker and part-owner Forrest Tancer, the 40,000-case Iron Horse Vineyards' product mix ranges from Cabernet, Chardonnay and Pinot Noir to vintage-dated sparkling wines. Quality is solid across the board, with the sparkling wines among the most consistent and best in California.

TASTING NOTES

CABERNET SAUVIGNON ALEXANDER VALLEY T-T VINEYARDS (★★): Variable, the 1995 (78 points) was awkward, but the 1996 (88) was rich, focused and elegant.

CHARDONNAY SONOMA GREEN VALLEY (★★★): Lean, tart and simple, with the emphasis on flinty pear and citrus notes.

FUMÉ BLANC ALEXANDER VALLEY T-T VINEYARDS (★★★): Bright, with lots of crisp, clean melon, peach, citrus and mineral notes.

MERLOT ALEXANDER VALLEY T-T VINEYARDS (★★): An austere style, with a narrow range of flavors.

PINOT NOIR SONOMA GREEN VALLEY (★★)
1996: The best yet—smooth and ripe, with cherry, sage, toast and anise notes. Earlier vintages struggled to reach riper fruit levels. **88**

SANGIOVESE ALEXANDER VALLEY T-T VINEYARDS (★★★): Has shown promise, though the 1996 (86 points) and 1995 (82) were trimmer than 1994 (88).

IRONSTONE VINEYARDS (★★)
Calaveras County, Sierra Foothills
Founded: 1989. **Owner:** Kautz Family. **Winemaker:** Steve Miller. **Second Label:** Creekside.

MAJOR WINES: PRICE, CASES, RATING

Cabernet Franc California
($10, 13,000) ★★
Cabernet Sauvignon California
($10, 13,000) ★
Chardonnay California
($10, 13,000) ★
Meritage Red California
($40, 600) ★★
Merlot California
($10, 33,000) ★★

Shiraz California
($12, 3,000)   ★★

ALSO PRODUCED
Chardonnay California Library ($14, 600); Fumé Blanc California ($9, 1,000); Symphony California Obsession ($8, 6,000).

WINERY DATA
Case Production: 250,000. **Acres Owned:** 5,600 in Calaveras County, Sacramento County and San Joaquin County. **Varietals by Acre:** Cabernet Franc, Cabernet Sauvignon, Chardonnay, French Colombard, Malbec, Merlot, Napa Gamay, Petite Sirah, Petit Verdot, Sauvignon Blanc, Shiraz, Souzao, Symphony, Viognier, Zinfandel.

Long-time Central Valley farmers, the Kautz family started their winery in 1989 on property they acquired in Calaveras County. With vineyards in Calaveras County, Sacramento County and San Joaquin County, Kautz produces a range of value-oriented red and white wines. The reds are often simple and marked by herbal notes; the most interesting has been a 1995 Shiraz (87 points), which was well balanced, with plum and anise flavors. The whites are simple and straightforward.

J WINE CO. (★★–★★★★)
Russian River Valley, Sonoma County
Founded: 1987. **Owner:** Judy Jordan. **Winemaker:** Oded Shakked.

MAJOR WINES: PRICE, CASES, RATING
Sparkling Sonoma County
($28, 25,000)   ★★★★
Pinot Noir Russian River Valley
($20)   ★★
Pinot Noir Russian River Valley
Nicole's Vineyard
($33)   ★★

WINERY DATA
Case Production: 30,000. **Acres Owned:** 200+ in Russian River Valley. **Varietals by Acre:** Chardonnay, Pinot Noir, Pinot Meunier. **Vineyard Designations:** Nicole's Vineyard (Pinot Noir).

This winery is owned by Judy Jordan, daughter of Jordan Vineyards & Winery owner Tom Jordan, and run as a separate entity. The focus is on its sparkling wine, simply called

J, and on Pinot Noir. While the J is usually in the ★★★–★★★★ range, with bright, complex fruit flavors, the Pinot Noir is light and simple, barely worth a ★★ rating.

JACUZZI FAMILY VINEYARDS
see CLINE CELLARS

JADE MOUNTAIN (★★)
Napa Valley
Founded: 1988. **Owner:** James C. Paras. **Winemaker:** Douglas Danielak.

MAJOR WINES: PRICE, CASES, RATING
Côtes du Soleil Syrah Blend California
($13, 550)   ★★
La Provençale Syrah Blend California
($17, 750)   ★★
Merlot Mount Veeder
($36, 900)   ★★
Merlot Napa Valley Caldwell Vineyard
($30, 900)   ★★
Mourvèdre California Evangelho Vineyard
($22, 1,400)   ★★
Syrah Mount Veeder
($40, 550)   ★★
Syrah Napa Valley Hudson Vineyard
($23, 750)   ★★
Viognier Mount Veeder
($32, 600)   ★★

WINERY DATA
Case Production: 7,000. **Acres Owned:** 23 acres in Mount Veeder. **Varietals by Acre:** Cabernet Sauvignon (3 acres), Grenache (2), Merlot (8), Syrah (7), Viognier (3). **Vineyard Designations:** Caldwell Vineyard (Merlot), Evangelho Vineyard (Mourvèdre), Hudson Vineyard (Syrah). **Varietals Purchased:** Merlot (Napa), Mourvèdre (California), Syrah (Napa).

Douglas Danielak believes Syrah will be California's star grape in the future, and thus has committed himself to this variety and blends thereof. This 7,000-case winery leases space from White Rock Vineyards in the hills east of Napa, and uses grapes from a variety of sources, including Merlot from Caldwell and its own Jade Mountain Ranch (part of the old Veedercrest vineyard). Although I've liked the wines in the past, there has been little progress in quality with recent vintages, and none of the wines merit more than a ★★ rating. This winery should really be doing better, given all the effort its put into its vineyards and wines.

JAFFURS (★★★)
Santa Barbara County
Founded: 1994. **Owner:** Craig & Lee Jaffurs. **Winemaker:** Craig Jaffurs.

MAJOR WINES: PRICE, CASES, RATING

Wine	Rating
Grenache Santa Barbara County Stolpman Vineyard ($20, 500)	★★★
Syrah Blend Santa Barbara County Cuvée ($19, 400)	★★★
Syrah Santa Barbara County ($22, 1,000)	★★★
Syrah Santa Barbara County Bien Nacido Vineyard ($27, 50)	★★★
Syrah Santa Barbara County Thompson Vineyard ($27, 50)	★★★★
Viognier Santa Barbara County ($22, 450)	★★★

ALSO PRODUCED
Mourvèdre Santa Barbara Stolpman Vineyard ($20, 380); Roussanne Santa Barbara County Stolpman Vineyard ($18, 150).

WINERY DATA
Case Production: 2,800. **Vineyard Designations:** Bien Nacido Vineyard (Syrah), Stolpman Vineyard (Grenache, Roussanne), Thompson Vineyard (Syrah). **Varietals Purchased:** Grenache (Santa Barbara), Mourvèdre (Santa Barbara), Roussanne (Santa Barbara), Syrah (Santa Barbara, San Luis Obispo), Viognier (Santa Barbara).

Jaffurs specializes in Santa Barbara County Rhône varietals, purchasing grapes from a number of local growers. All of the wines are well made, with distinct varietal flavors. The Syrah has been consistently dark and complex, with rich fruit flavors. The 1996 Syrah Thompson Vineyard (89 points) was the best of recent efforts, showing more richness and depth than the impressive 1996 Bien Nacido Syrah (88) and the 1996

Santa Barbara County Syrah (86). The 1996 Viognier (88) was also very good, displaying a thick rich texture and bright citrus and tropical fruit flavors. Jaffurs plans to add other vineyard-designated Syrahs, including Stolpman Vineyard, with future vintages.

TOBIN JAMES CELLARS (★★)
Paso Robles, San Luis Obispo County
Founded: 1985. **Owner:** Tobin James Shumrick, Lance and Claire Silver. **Winemaker:** Tobin James Shumrick.

MAJOR WINES: PRICE, CASES, RATING

Wine	Rating
Cabernet Franc Paso Robles ($18, 300)	★
Cabernet Sauvignon Paso Robles ($14, 1,200)	★
Chardonnay Paso Robles ($13, 1,200)	★
Chateau le Cacheflo Red Paso Robles ($10, 500)	★★
Merlot Paso Robles ($16, 600)	★
Pinot Noir Monterey ($16, 500)	★★
Syrah Paso Robles ($15, 1,500)	★★★
Zinfandel Paso Robles ($15, 2,800)	★★
Zinfandel Paso Robles James Gang Reserve ($22, 450)	★★★

ALSO PRODUCED
Cabernet Sauvignon Paso Robles James Gang Reserve ($20, 400); Muscat Late Harvest ($30, 350); Sangiovese Paso Robles ($15, 200); Sauvignon Blanc Paso Robles ($11, 200); Viognier Paso Robles ($20, 200); Zinfandel Late Harvest Paso Robles ($16, 1,000); Zinfandel Late Harvest Paso Robles Charisma ($20, 1,400).

WINERY DATA
Case Production: 14,000. **Acres Owned:** 16 acres in Paso Robles. **Varietals by Acre:** Cabernet Franc (3 acres), Cabernet Sauvignon (3), Merlot (3), Syrah (2), Zinfandel (5). **Varietals Purchased:** Cabernet Franc (Paso Robles), Cabernet Sauvignon (Paso Robles), Chardonnay (Paso Robles, Santa Barbara), Merlot (Paso Robles), Mourvèdre (Paso Robles), Sangiovese (Paso Robles), Syrah (Paso Robles), Zinfandel (Paso Robles).

Tobin James "Toby" Shumrick worked for Eberle Winery in the early 1980s before moving on to Peachy Canyon Winery in 1984, where he started his own brand. He has focused on Paso Robles-grown Cabernet, Chardonnay and Zinfandel (including standard, Reserve and late-harvest bottlings), along with Pinot Noir purchased from Monterey. Paso Robles Syrah and Viognier are new additions and the Syrah has been impressive. Most of the wines carry exotic nicknames, such as Big Shot and Blue Moon Reserve Zinfandels, Made in the Shade Merlot, Private Stash Cabernet and Solar Flair, a dessert-style Zinfandel. Overall quality is good but the wines are often unusual if not simply funky. The best wines of late have been the Zinfandels and Syrah. The 1996 Merlot 7th Heaven (82 points) showed modest amounts of cherry and spice while the 1996 Zinfandel Ballistic (83) was light but had a wider range of pepper, dried strawberry, plum and earthy, herbal notes. The 1996 Syrah Bulls Eye (87) was a rich-textured, flavorful blend of blueberry, black cherry, spice and earth flavors.

JARVIS (★★★)
Napa Valley
Founded: 1995. **Owner:** William & Leticia Jarvis.
Winemaker: Dimitri Tchelistcheff.

MAJOR WINES: PRICE, CASES, RATING
Cabernet Franc Napa Valley
    ($44, 250)   ★★★
Cabernet Sauvignon Napa Valley
    ($58, 3,000)   ★★★
Cabernet Sauvignon Napa Valley Lot 4
    ($58, 3,000)   ★★★
Chardonnay Napa Valley
    ($48, 400)   ★★★
Lake William Red Napa Valley
    ($48, 750)   ★★★★
Merlot Napa Valley
    ($46, 500)   ★★★

ALSO PRODUCED
Cabernet Sauvignon Napa Valley Reserve ($75, 300); Chardonnay Napa Valley Reserve; ($48, 400).

WINERY DATA
Case Production: 7,000. **Acres Owned:** 37 acres in Napa Valley. **Varietals by Acre:** Cabernet Franc (3 acres), Cabernet Sauvignon (21), Chardonnay (9.5), Malbec (1), Merlot (2), Petit Verdot (0.5).

William and Leticia Jarvis own a rolling 1,400-acre country estate in the hills east of Napa, where they've planted 37 acres of vines, most of them Bordeaux varieties. They have also tunneled out a 45,000-square-foot subterranean winery at a cost of more than $20 million.

In 1992, the winery, under the direction of Dimitri Tchelistcheff, produced its first estate-grown wines: Cabernet Franc, Cabernet Sauvignon and Chardonnay; a Merlot followed in 1993. The vineyard is rooted in three different areas on the property, at an elevation of 1,000 feet above sea level. The debut wines were very impressive for their elegance and finesse. Worth watching.

TASTING NOTES

CABERNET SAUVIGNON NAPA VALLEY (★★★): Impressive, though its potential seems unfulfilled at this point. Worth watching.
1994: Sleek and supple, with a range of currant and cherry flavors that build, gaining nuance and finesse and a touch of earthiness towards the finish. **89**
1993: Smooth, ripe and fleshy, with a core of currant, black cherry, cedar and spice flavors. **88**
1992: Supple and polished, with ripe black cherry, currant, cedar and tobacco notes, finishing with mild tannins. **90**

CABERNET SAUVIGNON NAPA VALLEY LOT 4 (★★★)
1993: Smooth, elegant and polished, with supple currant, cedar, cherry and spice flavors. **88**

CHARDONNAY NAPA VALLEY (★★★): Sleek and subtle, with the 1994 (87 points) built around ripe pear and citrus flavors.

LAKE WILLIAM RED NAPA VALLEY (★★★★) The best of the wines, it's complex, elegant, and rich in flavor.
1993: A tight band of cherry, herb, tobacco and currant flavors with an olive edge turns smooth on the finish. **90**

JAYSON see PAHLMEYER

JC CELLARS (★★★)
Alameda County
Founded: 1996. **Owner:** Jeffrey & Alexandra Cohn.
Winemaker: Jeffrey Cohn.

MAJOR WINES: PRICE, CASES, RATING
Petite Syrah St. Helena Napa Valley
  St. George Vineyard
  ($35, 75)   ★★★
Syrah Santa Barbara Mesa Vineyard
  ($20, 125)   ★★★
Zinfandel Redwood Valley Mendocino
  Rhodes Vineyard
  ($26, 125)   ★★★★
Zinfandel Russian River Valley
  Sonoma Alegria Vineyard
  ($28, 125)   ★★★
Zinfandel St. Helena Napa Valley
  Balduc Vineyard
  ($30, 75)   ★★★

ALSO PRODUCED
Petite Sirah Calistoga Napa Valley Frediani Vineyard ($28, 100); Red Mount Veeder Napa Valley Yates Ranch ($35, 75); Syrah Monterey Ventana Vineyard ($20, 75); Syrah Monterey Ventana Vineyard Reserve ($25, 40).

WINERY DATA
Case Production: 750. **Vineyard Designations:** Alegria Vineyard (Zinfandel), Balduc Vineyard (Zinfandel), Frediani Vineyard (Petite Sirah), Mesa Vineyard (Syrah), Rhodes Vineyard (Zinfandel), St. George Vineyard (Petite Syrah), Ventana Vineyard (Syrah), Yates Ranch (Cabernet Blend). **Varietals Purchased:** Cabernet Franc (Napa Valley), Cabernet Sauvignon (Mount Veeder), Merlot (Napa Valley), Petite Syrah (Calistoga, Napa Valley, St. Helena), Syrah (Mendocino, Monterey, Santa Barbara), Zinfandel (Redwood Valley, Mendocino, Russian River Valley, Sonoma, St. Helena, Napa).

Jeff Cohn, the enologist for Rosenblum Cellars (see entry), makes his own wines from purchased grapes in Rosenblum's Alameda facility. The first wine, a 1996 Redwood Valley Rhodes Vineyard Zinfandel (91 points), was one of the better 1996 Zinfandels produced in California that year. Cohn plans to add a number of other small-production wines, including vineyard-designated Syrah, Petite Syrah and a Cabernet blend. A winery to watch.

JEKEL VINEYARDS (★★)
Monterey County
Founded: 1978. **Owner:** Brown-Forman Corp.
Winemaker: Rick Boyer.

MAJOR WINES: PRICE, CASES, RATING
Cabernet Sauvignon Monterey
  ($15, 26,000)   ★★
Chardonnay Monterey Gravelstone
  ($12, 60,000)   ★★
Johannisberg Riesling Late Harvest
  Monterey
  ($14, 1,500)   ★★★
Johannisberg Riesling Monterey
  ($10, 16,000)   ★★
Merlot Monterey
  ($16, 26,000)   ★★
Pinot Noir Monterey
  ($14, 3,000)   ★
Red Sanctuary Monterey Sanctuary Estate
  ($26, 300)   ★★

ALSO PRODUCED
Cabernet Franc Monterey Sanctuary Estate ($15, 300); Malbec Monterey Sanctuary Estate ($15, 300); Petit Verdot Monterey Sanctuary Estate ($15, 300); Syrah Monterey Sanctuary Estate ($15, NA).

WINERY DATA
Case Production: 150,000. **Acres Owned:** 316 acres in Monterey. **Varietals by Acre:** Cabernet Franc (9 acres), Cabernet Sauvignon (41), Chardonnay (145), Johannisburg Riesling (19), Malbec (4), Merlot (60), Muscat (4), Petit Verdot (10), Pinot Noir (22), Syrah (2).

Bill and Gus Jekel made a major commitment to Monterey County, planting vineyards in the 1970s and launching their winery in 1978. The focus was on Cabernet, Chardonnay and Riesling. At first, the whites held a distinct edge in quality, while the Cabernet struggled to ripen beyond the herb, bell pepper and tobacco flavors that so often characterize Cabernets grown in a climate that is too cool. But despite these challenges, Jekel enjoyed success with its Cabernet, winning a following even while critics often panned the wines.

By the late 1980s, however, Monterey Cabernets had such a poor reputation that sales were seriously damaged, and the Jekels decided to sell the winery and vineyards.

In 1990, Jekel became part of the ill-fated Vintech group, which failed financially. The Jekels resumed ownership of the winery, only to sell it to Brown-Forman, an international beverage alcohol company that also owns Jack Daniel's and Fetzer Vineyards.

JEPSON VINEYARDS (★★★)
Mendocino County
Founded: 1985. **Owner:** Robert & Alice Jepson. **Winemaker:** Kurt Lorenzi.

MAJOR WINES: PRICE, CASES, RATING
Blanc de Blanc Mendocino County
  Burnee Hill Vineyard
  ($19, 1,500) ★★★
Brandy Mendocino County
  ($34, 800) ★★★
Chardonnay Mendocino County
  ($15, 7,700) ★★★
Sauvignon Blanc Mendocino County
  ($11, 6,500) ★★★
Viognier Mendocino County
  ($15, 1,500) ★★

ALSO PRODUCED
Merlot Mendocino County ($18, 3,000).

WINERY DATA
Case Production: 20,000. **Acres Owned:** 106 acres in Mendocino County. **Varietals by Acre:** Chardonnay (68 acres), French Colombard (10), Sauvignon Blanc (18), Syrah (6), Viognier (4). **Vineyard Designations:** Burnee Hill Vineyard (Chardonnay). **Varietals Purchased:** Merlot (Mendocino), Viognier (Mendocino).

Banker Robert Jepson purchased the former Estate William Baccala facility in 1985, in the process acquiring a modern winery, 106 acres of vineyard and an alambic still. The winery's focus is on Sauvignon Blanc, Chardonnay and sparkling wine, along with Merlot, Viognier and a brandy. Quality varies, but the Sauvignon Blanc and sparkling wines are usually crisp and refreshing.

JESSANDRA VITTORIA see H. COTURRI & SONS LTD.

JOLIESSE see CHRISTOPHE VINEYARDS

JORDAN VINEYARD & WINERY (★★★)
Alexander Valley, Sonoma County
Founded: 1972. **Owner:** Tom Jordan. **Winemaker:** Rob Davis.

MAJOR WINES: PRICE, CASES, RATING
Cabernet Sauvignon Alexander Valley
  ($33, 60,000) ★★★
Chardonnay Sonoma County
  ($22, 30,000) ★★★

WINERY DATA
Case Production: 90,000. **Acres Owned:** 391 acres (324 in Alexander Valley, 67 in Russian River Valley). **Varietals by Acre:** Cabernet Sauvignon (220 acres), Merlot (52), Chardonnay (119). **Varietals Purchased:** Cabernet Sauvignon (Alexander Valley, Mendocino County), Chardonnay (Russian River Valley, Mendocino County), Merlot (Alexander Valley, Dry Creek, Mendocino County).

Denver oil and gas executive Tom Jordan and his wife, Sally, spent a small fortune on vineyards, and on building a lavish Bordeaux-style château in Alexander Valley. The château was completed in 1976, and in that year, Jordan made its first Cabernet from purchased grapes. By 1978, the estate vineyards were mature enough for the first estate-bottled Cabernet.

The 1976 Jordan Cabernet was a big success from the moment it was introduced in 1980, memorable for its bright fruit flavors, spicy cinnamon and cedary oak nuances and smooth, polished texture. The Jordan Cabernets are wonderful to drink on release and for the first few years thereafter, making them perfect for restaurant sales, but they are not cellar-worthy. Chardonnay was introduced in the mid-1980's, but has not enjoyed the same success as the Cabernets; over the years, the style has swung from ultra-ripe and oaky to earthy and unfocused. J, the sparkling wine, was introduced with the 1987 vintage as a business venture between Jordan and his daughter Judy, and now operates separately from Jordan (see J entry). The winery owns 391 acres of vineyard, with production at about 90,000 cases. Jordan has now settled into a comfortable house style with both wines, even if they're well away from the cutting edge.

TASTING NOTES

CABERNET SAUVIGNON ALEXANDER VALLEY (★★★):
Supple, elegant and refined, with a polished texture, herb, cherry and currant flavors and soft tannins. Best early on; ideal for restaurants. Replanting of key vineyards, due to phylloxera, made this wine no longer "Estate Bottled" as of the 1994 vintage, so a modest stylistic change may be forthcoming. The wines will be "Estate Bottled" again with the 2001 vintage.
1994: Tight, firmly tannic and well focused, with complex cherry, currant, menthol and cedary flavors. Firm and tannic on the finish. **88**
1993: More tannic than usual for Jordan, with just enough ripe cherry and plum flavors to hold your interest. Slowly opens to reveal more fruit flavors, with hints of currant and spice. **87**
1992: Dry and tannic, with a musty, earthy note to the wild berry and cherry flavors. Finishes with dry tannins. **83**
1991: Supple and elegant, with smooth, polished, medium-weight cherry, currant, herb and anise notes and with mild tannins. **87**
1990: Supple and elegant, with spicy black cherry and plum notes and mild tannins. **87**
1986: This wine has been mature for years. What's left is a modest range of cedary cherry and currant flavors with notes of herb, especially dill. **82**

CHARDONNAY SONOMA COUNTY (★★★): Improving after an awkward start, when the wines seemed overly heavy and woody. Now they're more elegant—both the 1994 (89 points) and 1995 (88) were impressive.

JOSEPH ZAKON see BARON HERZOG WINE CELLARS CO.

JOULLIAN VINEYARDS (★★)
Carmel Valley, Monterey County
Founded: 1989. **Owner:** E.C. Joullian, R.L. Sias.
Winemaker: Ridge Watson. **Second Label:** Cépage.

MAJOR WINES: PRICE, CASES, RATING
Cabernet Sauvignon Carmel Valley
($16, 2,744) ★★
Chardonnay Monterey
($16, 6,750) ★★
Chardonnay Monterey Family Reserve
($24, 656) ★★
Merlot Carmel Valley Family Reserve
($25, 223) ★★
Sauvignon Blanc Carmel Valley
($14, 2,941) ★★
Sauvignon Blanc Carmel Valley Family Reserve
($17, 567) ★★★

ALSO PRODUCED
Zinfandel Carmel Valley Sias Cuvée ($16, 456).

WINERY DATA
Case Production: 15,000. **Acres Owned:** 40 acres in Carmel Valley. **Varietals by Acre:** Cabernet Franc (1 acre), Cabernet Sauvignon (14), Chardonnay (11), Merlot (2), Sauvignon Blanc (8), Sémillion (2), Zinfandel (2). **Varietals Purchased:** Chardonnay (Monterey).

Joullian Vineyards has been producing wines of modest quality in Carmel Valley for more than a decade now. The reds often stray toward herbal or beefy flavors, while the marginally better whites (with Sauvignon Blanc the quality leader) are made in a pleasant, crisp, minerally style.

JUDD'S HILL (★★★)
Napa Valley
Founded: 1989. **Owner:** Bunnie & Art Finkelstein.
Winemaker: Art Finkelstein. **Second Label:** Zahariah.

MAJOR WINES: PRICE, CASES, RATING
Cabernet Sauvignon Napa Valley
($32, 2,000) ★★★
Merlot Napa Valley Juliana Vineyards
($30, 500) ★★★
Pinot Noir Napa Valley
($20, 300) ★★

ALSO PRODUCED
Merlot Knights Valley Summers Ranch ($30, 500);
Merlot Napa Valley Orchard Creek Vineyards ($NA).

WINERY DATA
Case Production: 3,000. **Acres Owned:** 14 acres in Napa Valley. **Varietals by Acre:** Cabernet Franc (1 acre), Cabernet Sauvignon (11), Merlot (2). **Vineyard Designations:** Juliana Vineyards (Merlot), Summers Ranch (Merlot), Orchard Creek Vineyards (Merlot). **Varietals Purchased:** Cabernet Franc (Napa Valley), Cabernet Sauvignon (Napa Valley), Merlot (Napa Valley, Knights Valley), Pinot Noir (Napa Valley).

Art and Bunnie Finkelstein were co-founders and former owners of Whitehall Lane Winery in St. Helena before they sold that winery and started Judd's Hill, which is named after their son. The initial focus was on estate-grown Cabernet from their property in Napa Valley east of St. Helena, with the winery situated beneath their home. They've since added Merlot from Juliana Vineyard in Pope Valley; the 1995 (88 points) is a bright, elegant, tasty wine. A less compelling Pinot Noir 1996 (84), was light and herbal, with a touch of stemminess to the modest cherry notes. The Cabernet has had some promising moments, and is worth watching.

TASTING NOTES

CABERNET SAUVIGNON NAPA VALLEY (★★★): Off to a good start. Impressive for its richness, depth and purity of flavor. No track record for aging, but the wines drink well on release. Worth watching.

1995: Complex and elegant, with ripe plum, blueberry, spice and earthy mineral notes, turning tannic on the finish. **90**

1994: Elegant and refined, with complex currant, iodine, mint, spice and cedary flavors. **87**

1993: Smooth in texture, with ripe cherry and currant flavors; turns complex and supple on the finish. **88**

1992: Rich and plush, with an exotic core of rich currant, black cherry and wild berry flavors, turning tannic on the finish. **91**

1991: Packs in lots of ripe, juicy plum and currant flavors, with an elegant, supple, polished texture, picking up subtle herb, tea, spice and tobacco notes. **93**

1990: Framed with buttery oak, it is lean, elegant and compact, with cherry and currant flavors that are tightly wrapped. **89**

1989: Offers a pretty dose of cherry and currant flavors, with coffee, vanilla and cola notes that turn intense and tannic. **89**

JUSTIN VINEYARDS & WINERY (★★★)

Paso Robles, San Luis Obispo County
Founded: 1982. **Owner:** Justin & Debby Baldwin.
Winemaker: Jeff Branco.

MAJOR WINES: PRICE, CASES, RATING

Cabernet Franc Paso Robles ($23, 500)	★★★
Cabernet Sauvignon Paso Robles ($20, 9,000)	★★★
Cabernet Sauvignon San Luis Obispo County Reserve (Discontinued)	★★★
Chardonnay Paso Robles ($19, 2,000)	★★★
Isosceles Red Paso Robles ($37, 4,000)	★★★
Merlot Paso Robles ($23, 500)	★★★

ALSO PRODUCED

Justification Red Paso Robles ($25, 3,000); Nebbiolo Paso Robles ($23, 200); Obtuse Port Paso Robles ($23, 800); Orange Muscat Paso Robles ($23, 200); Sangiovese Paso Robles ($23, 200); Sauvignon Blanc Paso Robles ($13, 3,000); Syrah Paso Robles ($20, 500).

WINERY DATA

Case Production: 25,000. **Acres Owned:** 75 acres in Paso Robles. **Varietals by Acre:** Cabernet Franc (10 acres), Cabernet Sauvignon (30), Chardonnay (20), Merlot (10), Nebbiolo (1), Orange Muscat (1), Sangiovese (1), Syrah (2). **Varietals Purchased:** Cabernet Sauvignon (Paso Robles), Sauvignon Blanc (Paso Robles), Syrah (Paso Robles).

Investment banker Justin Baldwin began planting his 75-acre vineyard 15 miles west of Paso Robles in the early 1980s, making his first wine with the 1987 vintage. Production has since risen to 25,000 cases, and quality is high. All of the wines in the lineup—Cabernet Sauvignon, Cabernet Franc, Isosceles Cabernet blend, Merlot and Chardonnay—strive for deep, ripe, rich flavors, and so far have been on target more often than not. Given these successes, it's a winery worth watching.

TASTING NOTES

CABERNET SAUVIGNON SAN LUIS OBISPO COUNTY, RESERVE (★★★): Rivals Isosceles for its richness and complexity. Shows the potential for this variety from this area.
1994: Smooth, supple and harmonious, with a complex core of currant, cherry, light toasty oak and spicy nuances. **89**
1993: Sophisticated, with a complex, intriguing interplay of ripe, spicy cherry, berry, currant and sage notes. **92**
1992: Complex, with pretty, toasty oak, wild berry and cherry flavors, finishing with mild tannins. **88**

CHARDONNAY PASO ROBLES (★★★): Typically very ripe, rich and deeply colored. The 1994 (89 points) served up fig, pear, honey and butterscotch flavors.

ISOSCELES RED PASO ROBLES (★★★): Somewhat variable in quality, though it's still among the richest, deepest and most complex Cabernet-based reds outside Napa or Sonoma.
1994: Smooth and flavorful, with a pretty array of cherry, berry and chocolate flavors, turning plush and complex on the finish. **92**
1993: Firm, ripe and intense, with tiers of currant, cedar, anise, spice and leather flavors. **87**
1992: Smooth and polished; packed with complex flavors, weaving together currant, coffee, cedar and cherry notes. **92**

MERLOT PASO ROBLES (★★★): Has shown promise. The 1992 (91 points) was dense and concentrated, and was followed by the successful 1993 (89), another sharply focused wine. The 1994 (86) was heavily oaked early on.

RED PASO ROBLES RESERVE
1987: Still firmly tannic, with an earthy, cedary edge to the ripe Cabernet flavors. **90**

KARL LAWRENCE (★★★)
Rutherford, Napa Valley
Founded: 1991. **Owner:** Michael Trujillo, Bryan Henry, Ric Henry. **Winemaker:** Michael Trujillo.

MAJOR WINES: PRICE, CASES, RATING
Cabernet Sauvignon Howell Mountain ($28, 600)	★★★

WINERY DATA
Case Production: 600. **Acres Owned:** 5 acres in Howell Mountain. **Varietals by Acre:** Cabernet Sauvignon (5 acres). **Varietals Purchased:** Cabernet Sauvignon (Howell Mountain, Rutherford).

Sequoia Grove winemaker and co-owner Michael Trujillo and fellow co-owner Bryan Henry have used a compilation of their own middle names to form this 600-case brand, which uses grapes from a 5-acre vineyard on Howell Mountain.

TASTING NOTES
CABERNET SAUVIGNON HOWELL MOUNTAIN (★★★)
1994: A bit rustic, with earthy currant and cherry flavors. **88**
1993: Attractive with currant, cherry and berry flavors and a spicy oak accent. **88**

KARLY WINES (★★–★★★)
Amador County
Founded: 1980. **Owner:** Buck Cobb. **Winemaker:** Buck Cobb.

MAJOR WINES: PRICE, CASES, RATING
Marsanne Amador County ($20, 800)	★★★
Orange Muscat Amador County ($15, 600)	★★
Sauvignon Blanc Amador County ($10, 2,000)	★★★
Syrah Amador County ($20, 900)	★★★
Zinfandel Amador County ($14, 2,500)	★★
Zinfandel Amador County Pokerville ($10, 4,000)	★★
Zinfandel Amador County Warrior Fires ($20, 1,200)	★★★

ALSO PRODUCED
El Alacron Red Amador County ($30, 500); Zinfandel Amador County Sadie Upton ($20, 500).

WINERY DATA

Case Production: 11,000. **Acres Owned:** 20 acres in Amador County. **Varietals by Acre:** Marsanne (3 acres), Mourvèdre (2), Orange Muscat (1), Petite Sirah (2), Sauvignon Blanc (6), Syrah (3), Zinfandel (3).

Larry "Buck" Cobb and his wife, Karly, founded this 11,000-case Amador-based winery in 1980, using their 20-acre vineyard as an anchor, and buying other grapes to augment their lineup. Zinfandel, particularly the Amador County Warrior Fires bottling, is their best and most reliable wine, although all the wines are well made, fairly priced and reflective of their appellations. The Sauvignon Blanc also merits special attention.

TASTING NOTES

ZINFANDEL AMADOR COUNTY WARRIOR FIRES (★★★): Pushes Zinfandel to the limit; very ripe, dark and complex. **1996:** Austere and leathery, but consistent with the vintage. **87**
1995: Very ripe, expressive and concentrated, with a rich core of earthy wild berry, cherry and plum notes. **89**
1994: Dark, rich and plush, with layers of complex currant, cherry, plum and berry notes and firm tannins. **90**

KEEGAN CELLARS (★★)

Napa Valley
Founded: 1994. **Owner:** Eugenia Keegan. **Winemaker:** Eugenia Keegan.

MAJOR WINES: PRICE, CASES, RATING

Chardonnay Knights Valley
($20, 150)   ★★
Pinot Noir Russian River Valley
($20, 750)   ★★

ALSO PRODUCED

Chardonnay Carneros ($20, 100); Zinfandel Alexander Valley ($18, 150); Zinfandel Dry Creek Valley; ($18, 100).

WINERY DATA

Case Production: 1,200. **Acres Owned:** 4 acres in Russian River Valley (leased). **Varietals by Acre:** Pinot Noir (4 acres). **Varietals Purchased:** Chardonnay (Carneros, Knights Valley), Pinot Noir (Russian River Valley), Zinfandel (Alexander Valley, Dry Creek Valley).

Eugenia Keegan began her winemaking career working with Joseph Swan. She then served as president of Bouchaine Vineyards from 1986 through 1995, making her first Pinot Noir in 1994. She hopes to eventually plant her own vineyard on the Sonoma coast, build a small gravity-flow winery and make an estate-bottled Pinot Noir.

The Chardonnay from Knights Valley appeared in 1995; also in the works is a small lot of Alexander Valley Zinfandel. So far, the Pinot Noir has been light and elegant, with the 1994 (87 points) offering more fruit than the 1996 (82).

ROBERT KEENAN WINERY (★★)

Spring Mountain District, Napa Valley
Founded: 1974. **Owner:** Robert Keenan. **Winemaker:** Nils Venge.

MAJOR WINES: PRICE, CASES, RATING

Cabernet Sauvignon Napa Valley
($23, 3,000)   ★★
Chardonnay Napa Valley
($17, 2,000)   ★★
Merlot Napa Valley
($30, 4,000)   ★★

WINERY DATA

Case Production: 9,000. **Acres Owned:** 48 acres in Spring Mountain, Napa Valley. **Varietals by Acre:** Cabernet Franc (4 acres), Cabernet Sauvignon (16), Chardonnay (6), Merlot (22). **Varietals Purchased:** Merlot (Carneros).

Robert Keenan purchased the old defunct Conradi Winery at the 1,700-foot level on Spring Mountain in 1974, replanting some 48 acres to Cabernet, Cabernet Franc, Chardonnay and Merlot and introducing his first wines with the 1977 vintage. After a string of high-extract, overly tannic and excessively oaky wines in the late 1970s, Keenan redefined the winery's style with an impressive series of opulent, polished Cabernets, but by the end of the 1970s the wines had turned leaner and more austere. Merlot, made partly from Carneros-grown grapes, also seemed to peak in quality in the mid-1980s, as recent vintages have been less interesting. The Chardonnays are made in a lean, crisp style. Nils Venge, owner/winemaker of Saddleback Cellars and formerly the winemaker at Groth, is now a consultant here, but the wines still need work. The Cabernet and Merlot are both very austere and hard-edged, while the Chardonnay has been unusually lean and tart, with bracing acidity.

KELTIE BROOK see MACROSTIE WINES

KENDALL-JACKSON WINERY
(★★–★★★★)
Santa Rosa, Sonoma County
Founded: 1982. **Owner:** Jess Jackson. **Winemaker:** Randy Ullom.

MAJOR WINES: PRICE, CASES, RATING

Cabernet Sauvignon Alexander Valley Buckeye Vineyard Single Vineyard Series ($33, 2,431)	★★★
Cabernet Sauvignon California Grand Reserve ($50, 4,318)	★★★★
Cabernet Sauvignon California Vintner's Reserve ($18, 250,000)	★★
Chardonnay Arroyo Seco Monterey Paradise Vineyard Single Vineyard Series ($20, 9,622)	★★★
Chardonnay California Grand Reserve ($26, 82,706)	★★★★
Chardonnay California Vintner's Reserve ($15, 2,750,000)	★★★
Chardonnay Santa Maria Valley Camelot Vineyard Single Vineyard Series ($18, 53,280)	★★★★
Gewürztraminer California Vintner's Reserve ($10, 455)	★★
Johannisberg Riesling California Vintner's Reserve ($11, 45,499)	★★
Merlot Alexander Buckeye Vineyard Single Vineyard Series ($29, 2,545)	★★
Merlot California Grand Reserve ($39, 6,118)	★★★
Merlot California Vintner's Reserve ($19, 272,000)	★★
Pinot Noir California Grand Reserve ($30, 364)	★★
Pinot Noir California Vintner's Reserve ($15, 65,000)	★★
Sauvignon Blanc California Grand Reserve ($20, 201)	★★
Sauvignon Blanc California Vintner's Reserve ($11, 222,000)	★★
Syrah California Grand Reserve ($25, 253)	★★
Syrah California Vintner's Reserve ($16, 900)	★★★
Viognier California Grand Reserve ($25, 1,000)	★★
Zinfandel California Grand Reserve ($25, 2,000)	★★★
Zinfandel California Vintner's Reserve ($18, 50,000)	★★

ALSO PRODUCED
Cabernet Franc Alexander Valley Buckeye Vineyard Single Vineyard Series ($24, 299); Syrah Sonoma Valley/Carneros Durell Vineyard Single Vineyard Series ($25, 478); Sémillon California Vintner's Reserve ($25, 250); Viognier California Vintner's Reserve ($25, 1,000); White Meritage California Grand Reserve ($25, 600).

WINERY DATA
Case Production: 4 million. **Acres Owned:** 6,672 acres owned throughout California. **Varietals by Acre:** Barbera (1 acre), Cabernet Franc (25), Cabernet Sauvignon (645), Chardonnay (4,703), Chenin Blanc (3), Johannisberg Riesling (35), Merlot (511), Muscat (4), Petit Verdot (1), Pinot Gris (3), Pinot Noir (471), Sangiovese (20), Sauvignon Blanc (120), Sémillion (31), Symphony (19), Syrah (21), Viognier (19), Zinfandel (40).

The emergence, growth and diversification of Kendall-Jackson's contingent of wineries is one of the most fascinating wine stories in California as the century ends. San Francisco attorney Jess Stonestreet Jackson started planting wine grapes at his Lake County retreat in 1974, before deciding to try his hand at winemaking in 1982. An arrested fermentation of his first wine led to a sweet Chardonnay with residual sugar, but Jackson sold the wine anyway and it proved enormously popular with consumers. Building on the straightforward fruitiness of its Vintner's Reserve Chardonnay, Kendall-Jackson grew quickly through the 1980s, reaching several hundred thousand cases by decade's end. It now produces an estimated 4 million cases, making it one of the most prolific wine companies in California.

From early on, Jed Steele (Steele Wines) made the Kendall-Jackson wines, building volume by securing grape sources throughout Napa and Sonoma and the Central Coast, where excellent Chardonnay vineyards in Santa Maria Valley and Santa Barbara lay. One major coup came with the purchase of the 1,000-acre Tepusquet Vineyard in Santa Maria. Those grapes helped fuel K-J's growth, and provided the foundation for Cambria Winery. Jackson then acquired Edmeades in 1988, and Stephen Zellerbach, which he renamed "Stonestreet," in 1989. In 1994, he acquired Vinwood, a large modernized winemaking facility north of Healdsburg, and Robert Pepi Winery in Napa Valley. K-J keeps adding vineyards —it now has some 6,672 acres in vines—including 4,703 planted to Chardonnay—as well as new brands, with Cardinale, Hartford Court, Kristone, La Crema and Lokoya joining the lineup.

While Chardonnay and Cabernet roll up big sales numbers, K-J also focuses on designer wines. Jackson gave Steele enough leeway to experiment with smaller lots of wines; when Steele found the right grapes, he kept the wine separate, leading to vineyard-designated Chardonnay, Zinfandel and Syrah, usually made in 200- to 500-case lots. K-J's finest wines are now bottled under the Grand Reserve designation. The Grand Reserve Cabernet, Chardonnay, and occasionally, the Zinfandel are the best wines. The remainder of the lineup, using the Vintner's Reserve designation, remain good values.

The wines are now made under the direction of winemaker Randy Ullom.

TASTING NOTES

CABERNET SAUVIGNON CALIFORNIA GRAND RESERVE (★★★★): Richer and more polished than the Vintner's Reserve, with currant and cherry flavors and more toasty oak. Showing steady improvement. Typically a blend of select grapes from Napa and Alexander Valleys.
1995: A complex, well structured, intensely flavored wine, with layers of currant, plum, black cherry and wild berry fruit. Finishes with ripe, well integrated tannins. **90**
1994: Crisp, with firm tannins and just enough spicy currant and berry flavors to give it the depth and complexity one hopes for at this price. **87**

1992: Dense and chewy, but it has all the right ingredients for greatness. Shows tiers of black cherry, currant, anise and plum, and finishes with chunky tannins that let the fruit glide through to the spicy finish. **91**
1991: Bright, ripe and rich, with layers of currant, black cherry and spice flavors that are focused and concentrated. **89**
1990: Ripe and generous, with a strong current of fruit flavors, firm tannins and an herbal edge. **90**

CHARDONNAY CALIFORNIA GRAND RESERVE (★★★★): Draws on K-J's considerable Chardonnay holdings. Consistently well made, rich in flavor and elegant in style. The 1996 (89 points) was a shade less complex than the excellent 1995 (91) and 1994 (90).

KATHRYN KENNEDY WINERY (★★–★★★★)
Santa Cruz Mountains
Founded: 1979. **Owner:** Kathryn Kennedy. **Winemaker:** Marty Mathis.

MAJOR WINES: PRICE, CASES, RATING
Cabernet Sauvignon Santa Cruz Mountains Estate ($100, 600)	★★★★
Lateral Red California ($30, 1,000)	★★
Syrah Santa Cruz Mountains Maridon Vineyard ($40, 300)	★★★★

ALSO PRODUCED
Chenin Blanc-Viognier Blend California ($18, 200).

WINERY DATA
Case Production: 3,000. **Acres Owned:** 9 acres in Santa Cruz Mountains. **Varietals by Acre:** Cabernet Sauvignon (8 acres), Tempranillo (1). **Varietals Purchased:** Cabernet Franc (California), Cabernet Sauvignon (California), Chenin Blanc (California), Merlot (California), Sangiovese (Santa Cruz Mountains), Syrah (Santa Cruz Mountains), Viognier (California).

Kathryn Kennedy initially established this 9-acre vineyard to protect her land from real estate developers who were coveting her property. But she also took winegrowing seriously from the start, attending viticultural and winemaking classes, and ultimately decided to focus on making Cabernet. She later added a second wine, a Merlot-Cabernet Franc-Cabernet Sauvignon blend called

Lateral, made from purchased grapes from vineyard sources as diverse as Napa, Nevada County, Monterey and Santa Cruz.

The bright new star is the stunning Syrah 1996 Santa Cruz Mountains Maridon Vineyard, (91 points), which offers rich, smooth plum, wild berry, spice and pretty oak shadings. Given the pressures to develop in this area, with prices running to several hundred thousand dollars an acre, Kathryn Kennedy's vineyard is clearly a labor of love.

TASTING NOTES

LATERAL RED CALIFORNIA (★★): Once a steady ★★★ performer that looked like it might rate higher, but recent vintages have been less impressive, with muddled flavors. The 1995 (83 points) and 1996 (86) had flavor, but no polish or finesse. Still, it's worth watching to see if there is a turnaround.

CABERNET SAUVIGNON SANTA CRUZ MOUNTAINS ESTATE (★★★★): Aptly reflects the appellation, with its earthy currant and herb flavors and firm tannins, but it can be ripe and opulent too. Ages well.
1995: Tight, lean and very concentrated, with a distinctive earthy, dusty blackberry flavor, finishing with complexity and length. **88**
1993: A tight, tart, richly flavored wine with a tightly packed core of currant and berry, with firm, rustic tannins, but on the finish, the flavors are long and true. **91**
1992: An attractive blend of ripe plum, cherry and currant flavors. Finishes with a slightly nutty edge to the tannins. **87**
1991: Walks a tightrope between its earthy juniper berry and peppery cherry notes. Firmly tannic. **87**
1990: Earthy and oaky, with a potent tannin level, but it does have rich, earthy currant and spice flavors. **89**
1989: Tight and firm, with intense black cherry, currant, herb and cedary oak flavors. **87**
1988: Smooth, lush and polished, with supple, complex anise, currant and plum aromas and flavors, mild tannins and herbal oak shadings. **88**
1987: Aging beautifully, with a healthy dark color, lots of rich currant, black cherry, chocolate and spice flavors, and a smooth, polished texture, right up until the finish, where it dries ever so slightly with tannin. **92**
1986: Rich and polished, with a complex bouquet of black cherry and currant aromas and flavors and spicy, buttery oak shadings. **89**

1985: Broad, ripe and complex, with concentrated currant, herb, spice and cherry flavors that are intense and framed by spicy, toasty oak and firm tannins. **91**
1984: Opulent, with rich, ripe currant, plum and black cherry flavors framed by toasty, spicy oak. **88**

KENWOOD VINEYARDS (★★–★★★★★)
Sonoma Valley
Founded: 1970. **Owner:** Gary Heck. **Winemaker:** Mike Lee.

MAJOR WINES: PRICE, CASES, RATING	
Cabernet Sauvignon Sonoma Valley ($18, 24,000)	★★
Cabernet Sauvignon Sonoma Valley Artist Series ($50, 3,250)	★★★★★
Cabernet Sauvignon Sonoma Valley Jack London Vineyard ($25, 10,000)	★★★
Chardonnay Sonoma County ($15, 42,000)	★★★
Chardonnay Sonoma-Santa Maria Reserve ($22, 3,200)	★★★★
Merlot Sonoma County ($20, 16,000)	★★
Merlot Sonoma Valley Estate ($22, 1,800)	★★
Merlot Sonoma Valley Jack London Vineyard ($25, 5,400)	★★
Merlot Sonoma Valley Massara ($25, 1,000)	★★
Pinot Noir Russian River ($17, 12,000)	★★
Pinot Noir Russian River Olivet Lane ($25, 450)	★★
Pinot Noir Sonoma Valley Jack London Vineyard ($20, 700)	★★
Sauvignon Blanc Sonoma County ($10, 80,000)	★★★
Sauvignon Blanc Sonoma Valley Reserve ($15, 3,000)	★★★

Zinfandel Geyserville Mazzoni
   ($20, 900)   ★★★
Zinfandel Sonoma Valley
   ($15, 12,000)   ★★★
Zinfandel Sonoma Valley
   Jack London Vineyard
   ($20, 6,000)   ★★
Zinfandel Sonoma Valley Nuns Canyon
   ($20, 700)   ★★★
Zinfandel Sonoma Valley Upper Weise
   ($20, 2,000)   ★★

ALSO PRODUCED
Gewürztraminer Sonoma Valley ($11, 1,400); Red
California Vintage ($8, 8,500); White California Vintage
($8, 13,000); White Zinfandel California ($8, 13,000);
Zinfandel Sonoma Valley Nora's ($20, 200).

WINERY DATA
Case Production: 319,000. **Acres Owned:** 263 acres in
Sonoma Valley. **Varietals by Acre:** Cabernet Sauvignon (30
acres), Chardonnay (83), Merlot (40), Sauvignon Blanc (30),
Petite Sirah (5), Petit Verdot (5), Pinot Blanc (15), Sangiovese
(15), Syrah (15), Zinfandel (25). **Vineyard Designations:** Jack
London Vineyard (Cabernet Sauvignon, Merlot, Pinot Noir,
Zinfandel), Massara (Merlot), Mazzoni (Zinfandel), Nora's
(Zinfandel), Nuns Canyon (Zinfandel), Olivet Lane (Pinot Noir),
Upper Weise (Zinfandel). **Varietals Purchased:** Cabernet
Sauvignon (Sonoma County), Chardonnay (Sonoma County),
Gewürztraminer (Sonoma Valley), Merlot (Sonoma County),
Pinot Noir (Russian River), Sauvignon Blanc (Sonoma Valley),
Zinfandel (Sonoma Valley).

Gary Heck, owner of Korbel Champagne Cellars, took
sole possession of this venerable Sonoma Valley winery
in 1998. While quality remains high, the future direction
of the winery may be determined by the extent of its
growth, and whether Mike Lee remains in charge of winemaking.

The winery was founded by Lee's two brothers in partnership with a close friend. John Sheela's family farmed
grapes in the Central Valley, leading him to believe that
fine wine might have a future in California. When the old
Pagani Winery in Kenwood came up for sale, Sheela put
together a consortium to buy it in 1970, which included
his college roommate and future brother-in-law, Marty
Lee, and eventually more of the Lee family, including
Marty's parents and his younger brother Mike.

Progress with all of Kenwood's wines remained
steady during its revival under the Sheela-Lee regime,
with reds getting a slight nod over whites overall. The
winery had a huge amount of success with Sauvignon
Blanc, however, and improved its Chardonnay, often
making a brilliant Reserve of the latter. Efforts with several vineyard-designated Pinot Noirs and Zinfandels
showed that the winery was determined to focus on
unique vineyards.

Today, the winery owns 263 acres of vines in Sonoma
Valley, 100 of those planted from 1997 to 1998. Kenwood
prefers hillside-grown grapes, and has contracts to buy from
several key vineyards for its vineyard-designated wines,
among them Milo Shepard's Jack London Vineyard at the
base of Sonoma Mountain for Cabernet, Merlot, Pinot Noir
and Zinfandel; Olivet Lane in Russian River Valley for
Pinot Noir and Nuns Canyon in Sonoma Valley for
Zinfandel. The flagship wine is the Artist Series Cabernet.
The winery commissions a leading artist to design or sell a
piece of art for use on the label, (à la Mouton-Rothschild)
then selects the best lots of Cabernet. Production climbed
from 210,000 cases in 1995 to 319,000 in 1998, with new
wines continously being added to the mix.

Any winery that grows too large too quickly will face
quality control issues. So far, Kenwood has kept quality levels high, and for this reason it remains a winery to watch.

TASTING NOTES

**CABERNET SAUVIGNON SONOMA VALLEY ARTIST SERIES
(★★★★★):** The Artist Series ranks among the state's
best, its only shortcoming being that it can be exceedingly tough and tannic. But it can also be unusually supple
and charming in so-called off vintages, and it ages quite
well.
1994: Beautifully crafted, sleek and elegant; sharply
focused on the core of ripe, rich, cherry, currant, plum
and berry flavors. **93**
1993: Tight and firm, with chewy tannins and a core of
spicy currant, earth, anise and cedary oak flavors. Turns
tannic on the finish. **90**
1992: Marked by herb and cedar flavors, its currant and
plum nuances are a bit muted and struggle against the
tannins. **91**
1991: Firm and compact, with a tight, narrow band of
spicy currant, cedar, oak and mineral notes. Picks up an
earthy edge on the finish, but hangs together. **90**

1990: Hard-edged and tannic, with mint, herb and tart berry flavors framed by cedar notes. **86**

1989: Firm, rich and deeply flavored, packed with spicy currant, plum and cherry flavors framed by spicy, buttery oak notes. **91**

1988: Firm, tight and tannic; an austere style, with a trim band of spicy, earthy currant and tobacco flavors. **86**

1987: Smooth, ripe and complex, with a pretty array of spicy currant, black cherry, anise, sage and cedary oak flavors. **91**

1986: Tight and tannic, with ripe, complex, earthy currant, mineral, cedar and spice flavors that linger on the finish. **90**

1985: Elegant and refined, typical of the vintage, offering plenty of currant, cassis, cedar and spice flavors, fine tannins and good length. **91**

1984: Big, ripe and deeply concentrated, with complex black cherry, spice and plum flavors to match firm tannins. **93**

1983: Mature, still lean and firm, with elegant fruit flavors, fine tannins and a pretty spice and cedar aftertaste. **87**

1982: Tight, lean and concentrated, with spice, cedar, earth and plum flavors now emerging from the tannins. **87**

1981: Aging well, with ripe plum, currant and cassis flavors and a fleshy texture. **89**

1980: A weedy, vegetal wine that lacks the appeal of most Artist Series bottlings. **80**

1979: Mature and drying, but holding its complex chocolate, plum, anise and spice flavors. **90**

1978: This wine has aged well, and is now fully mature, with smooth, supple, elegant notes of currant, cedar, anise and sage. **87**

1977: Mature and declining, with modest plum, anise and mint flavors. **82**

1976: Fading, with pungent earthy flavors. **75**

1975: Well past its prime but valuable as a collectible, so if you still have a bottle, don't open it. **73**

CABERNET SAUVIGNON SONOMA VALLEY JACK LONDON VINEYARD (★★★): This wine continues to get better. It ages very impressively, the ruggedly earthy tannins subsiding with age. Very distinctive.

1995: Tight and trim, with a focused, austere band of spicy currant, cedar and cherry flavors, turning supple on the finish. **89**

1994: Rugged, with earthy, claylike tannins and hints of currant, sage and leather. **88**

1993: An herbal style with hints of sage and anise, but the currant, cherry and berry flavors turn tannic on the finish. **88**

1992: Ripe and plush, showing herb- and currant-laced Cabernet fruit, toasty oak and supple tannins. **87**

1987: Smooth and supple, with a rich, smoky edge to the ripe currant- and plum-laced fruit. **89**

1986: Remarkably tame, with mature tannins and earthy currant, spicy oak, herb and mineral flavors. **89**

ZINFANDEL SONOMA VALLEY NUNS CANYON (★★★): This single-vineyard Zinfandel has emerged as the best so far, with impressive wines that are variable in style.

1996: A touch earthy, with herb and sage overtones, the core of flavors is built around ripe cherry, blackberry, tea and spice, with mild tannins. **88**

1995: There's a green, slightly unripe streak that runs through this wine, interrupting the core of sage and wild berry. **84**

1994: Tart and earthy, but hits plenty of the right notes with its core of black cherry, raspberry, spice and anise, finishing with a good dose of tannins. **89**

1993: Well oaked, with toasty vanilla flavors, the ripe cherry and wild berry flavors come through in fine fashion, giving this wine a smooth, silky texture and finishing with classic Zinfandel peppery notes. **90**

KEYHOLE RANCH see SEGHESIO WINERY

A.S. KIKEN WINERY see REVERIE WINERY

KISTLER VINEYARDS (★★★★★)
Russian River Valley, Sonoma County
Founded: 1978. **Owner:** Kistler Vineyards.
Winemaker: Steve Kistler.

MAJOR WINES: PRICE, CASES, RATING

Chardonnay Carneros Hudson Vineyard		
($48, 288)		★★★★★
Chardonnay Carneros Hyde Vineyard		
($45, 566)		★★★★★
Chardonnay Russian River Valley		
Dutton Ranch		
($45, 1,876)		★★★★★

Chardonnay Russian River Valley
Vine Hill Road Vineyard
($45, 2,782)   ★★★★★

Chardonnay Sonoma Coast
($31, 7,017)   ★★★★★

Chardonnay Sonoma Coast Camp
Meeting Ridge
($45, 282)   ★★★★★

Chardonnay Sonoma County
Cuvée Cathleen
($50, 540)   ★★★★★

Chardonnay Sonoma Mountain
McCrea Vineyard
($45, 2,782)   ★★★★★

Chardonnay Sonoma Valley
Durell Vineyard
($45, 2,735)   ★★★★★

Chardonnay Sonoma Valley
Kistler Estate Vineyard
($45, 522)   ★★★★★

Pinot Noir Russian River Valley
Kistler Vineyard
($55, 733)   ★★★★★

Pinot Noir Sonoma Coast
Camp Meeting Ridge
($38, 190)   ★★★★★

Pinot Noir Sonoma Coast Cuvée Catherine
($45, 192)   ★★★★★

Pinot Noir Sonoma Coast Hirsch Vineyard
($50, 164)   ★★★★★

WINERY DATA
Case Production: 23,000. **Acres Owned:** 120 acres (50 in Russian River Valley, 5 on Sonoma Coast, 35 on Sonoma Mountain, 30 in Sonoma Valley). **Varietals by Acre:** Chardonnnay (93 acres), Pinot Noir (27). **Vineyard Designations:** Camp Meeting Ridge (Chardonnay, Pinot Noir), Durell Vineyard (Chardonnay), Dutton Ranch (Chardonnay), Hirsch Vineyard (Chardonnay, Pinot Noir), Hudson Vineyard (Chardonnay), Hyde Vineyard (Chardonnay), Kistler Vineyard (Chardonnay, Pinot Noir), McCrea Vineyard (Chardonnay), Vine Hill Vineyard (Chardonnay). **Varietals Purchased:** Chardonnay (Sonoma Coast, Russian River Valley, Sonoma Valley, Carneros), Pinot Noir (Sonoma Coast).

Steve Kistler's name has become synonymous with brilliantly crafted wines. He studied English at Stanford, hoping for a career as a writer, but found winemaking more

to his liking. In the late 1970s, he teamed up with Mark Bixler, a chemistry wiz, and with the backing of the Kistler family, the duo founded Kistler Vineyards in 1978.

Considering how consistently excellent Kistler's ten different Chardonnays are, one could make a strong case for crowning him king of California Chardonnay. There are a few Chardonnays in the state that rival Kistler's, but no one is putting out as many of such extraordinarily high quality. It is mind-boggling how complex and intricate these wines are every year, and while each of the bottlings has distinctive features, they are more alike than not.

The winery's 23,000 cases are dominated by Chardonnay. It's vineyard holdings now measure 120 acres, including 93 in Chardonnay and 27 in Pinot Noir. The Chardonnays are all barrel-fermented, undergo full malolactic fermentation and are aged on their lees, with wild (or natural) yeast fermentations often part of the formula. Kistler is a big fan of different yeast strains, using them to achieve the broadest range of flavors possible. He prefers his wines to have a doughy, hazelnut flavor, a character sometimes found in great white Burgundies; this effect is partially achieved through his vinification techniques. The wines typically display a bold, rich, creamy texture, with tiers of fruit and spice flavors and remarkably long finishes.

Cabernet appears to been dropped from the lineup, but Pinot Noir is filling in the gap quite nicely, with up to five different bottlings from Russian River and Sonoma Coast vineyards. I hesitate to use the word incredible in describing wines or winemakers, but it's tempting with Kistler. Worth collecting.

TASTING NOTES

CHARDONNAY CARNEROS HUDSON VINEYARD (★★★★★): New to the lineup, but others have made great wines from this property.
1996: A wonderful range of ripe, exotic, complex flavors, with tiers of concentrated, earthy pear, lemon, citrus, fig and apricot, gaining a sense of elegance and finesse rarely found in California Chardonnay. **97**
1995: Complex, with a core of flinty grapefruit, citrus and pear fruit flavors; tightly wound and sharply focused. **92**

CHARDONNAY CARNEROS HYDE VINEYARD (★★★★★): Another new property, brilliant with his first wine.

1996: Intense, with complex, earthy pear, fig, melon, citrus and hazelnut flavors that are remarkably elegant and sophisticated; long and lingering on the finish. **96**

CHARDONNAY RUSSIAN RIVER VALLEY DUTTON RANCH (★★★★★): Kistler has been making Chardonnay from this vineyard for more than a decade; its silkiness never fails to amaze.

1996: Starts out smoky and toasty, turning focused on the ripe pear, fig, apricot and anise flavors, with a touch of hazelnut on the aftertaste. **93**

1995: Smoky and oaky, with a rich, complex, concentrated core of fig, pear, anise, hazelnut and cedary oak flavors. **91**

1994: Delicious. Brimming with ripe, juicy pear, apple, apricot and exotic spicy notes and toasty oak nuances. **94**

1993: Smooth textured, elegant and understated, with a nice core of citrus, pear, cream and hazelnut flavors. **92**

1992: Intense and lively, with layers of tightly wound pear, spice, vanilla and nutmeg flavors, held together by crisp acidity and finishing with a long, full aftertaste that lingers. **92**

1991: Ripe and refreshing, with rich, intense pear, spice, hazelnut and earth flavors that turn silky. **92**

CHARDONNAY RUSSIAN RIVER VALLEY VINE HILL ROAD VINEYARD (★★★★★): Consistently sensational.

1996: Tight and flinty, with rich pear, fig, anise, vanilla and hazelnut flavors that start out subtle, building up to a rich, complex aftertaste. **93**

1995: Crisp and lively, with a rich, concentrated, tightly wound band of nectarine, pear, citrus and spice flavors. **94**

1994: Showing amazing depth and finesse, this wine is smooth, rich and creamy, with layers of pear, vanilla, fig, anise, smoke, butter and spice. **95**

1993: Complex, with tiers of rich, polished honey, pear and hazelnut flavors that expand and linger on the finish. **92**

1992: Ripe, rich and exotic, with layers of pear, toast, hazelnut and smoky oak, all folding together into a complex and concentrated wine. **91**

1991: Rich and complex, combining a generous core of pear, pineapple, spice and earth notes with a smooth, supple texture, turning smoky and toasty. **92**

1990: Complex and deep, with rich, ripe pear, apple and spice flavors framed by toasty, buttery oak notes. **90**

CHARDONNAY SONOMA COAST (★★★★★): Bold, ripe and intense; cool climate Chardonnay at its finest.

1995: Bold, ripe, rich and complex, with exotic fig, pear, melon and spicy, toasty oak flavors. **92**

1993: Well oaked, with smoky, toasty oak flavors, but a pretty core of elegant pear and spice, picking up the hazelnut notes, finishing with a complex aftertaste. **89**

CHARDONNAY SONOMA COAST CAMP MEETING RIDGE (★★★★★): Ultra-rich and complex, showing fabulous fruit.

1996: Rich, smoky and exotic, with toasty oak, vanilla, fig, pear and hazelnut flavors that are deeply concentrated and long and complex on the finish. **97**

1995: Rich and unctuous; bold, flavorful and fleshy, with layers of ripe pear, fig, citrus, pretty oak and honeysuckle flavors. **95**

CHARDONNAY SONOMA COUNTY CUVÉE CATHLEEN (★★★★★): Carries the broader Sonoma County appellation, and is a blend of different vineyards, which only serves to highlight Kistler's talents. As delicious as the others.

1994: Ripe, rich and opulent, with tiers of spicy pear, apple, melon and citrus, finishing with complex flavors of oak. **93**

1993: Ultra-rich and flavorful, with layers of ripe pear, honey, butterscotch and spice unfolding into a long, complex aftertaste. **90**

1992: Remarkably complex with ripe, rich pear, fig and smoky oak flavors, turning complex and lingering on the finish. **92**

CHARDONNAY SONOMA MOUNTAIN MCCREA VINEYARD (★★★★★): Brilliant, rich and flavorful; enormously complex.

1996: Tightly reined in, intense and deeply concentrated, with an elegant, bright core of pear, anise, hazelnut, citrus and honeyed notes, lingering long and lively on the finish. **96**

1995: Shows wonderful depth; smooth, rich and polished, with a succulent core of ripe pear, spice, hazelnut, fig and honey flavors. **93**

1994: Delivers a rich core of flinty mineral and spice-laced pear and anise notes; flavors are complex and concentrated. **95**

1993: Rich and concentrated, with subtle flavors of honey, pear, pineapple, vanilla and hazelnut shadings. **91**

1992: Youthful and tight, with smoky, toasty pear and spice flavors slowly unfolding, revealing more depth and complexity. **92**

1991: Bold, ripe and complex, loaded with tiers of citrus, pear, fig and spicy wood nuances that turn smooth and creamy. **91**

1990: Exuberantly fruity and full-bodied, with tons of grapefruit, pear, cream, butter and vanilla flavors. **92**

CHARDONNAY SONOMA VALLEY DURELL VINEYARD (★★★★★): Another Kistler staple, it's been a great wine year after year. Seemingly a perfect area for this grape. Former designation was Sand Hill.

1996: Big, bold, rich and creamy, with tiers of vanilla, pear, anise, fig and melon, it's a delicious mouthful of Chardonnay, finishing with smoke and nectarine flavors. **95**

1995: Remarkably complex and concentrated, serving up lots of intense fruit flavors, with notes of ripe pear, citrus, fig, toasty oak and hazelnut. **93**

1993: Smooth, ripe and harmonious, with a rich complex core of pear, hazelnut, honey and spice notes, finishing with a smoky oak aftertaste. **91**

1992: Ripe and assertive, brimming with rich pear and apple flavors framed by toasty oak, spicy pear and honey notes. **91**

1991: Tight and concentrated, with a toasty oak edge, this is rich and flavorful, showing pear, apple and spice flavors. **90**

1990: Rich, dense and enormously concentrated, with toasty, buttery notes over tight peach and pear flavors that turn creamy. **93**

CHARDONNAY SONOMA VALLEY KISTLER ESTATE VINEYARD (★★★★★): Kistler's vineyard on the east side of Sonoma Valley. Wonderful Chardonnay.

1996: Tight, rich and concentrated, with a pretty array of creamy oak, custard, citrus, and pear flavors that fan out and gain nuance.

1994: Ripe, vibrant and concentrated, with a core of smoky pear, spice and citrus, turning buttery on the finish. **92**

1993: Smooth and creamy, with rich, subtle flavors that develop and expand to reveal a complex core of ripe pear, butter and hazelnut. **94**

1992: A rich, high-extract, enormously complex blend of ripe pear, apple and spice flavors and toasty, smoky, buttery oak nuances. **94**

1991: Bright and lively, with juicy pear, apple and

pineapple flavors that are framed by pretty, toasty, buttery oak flavors, turning elegant and smoky. **90**

1990: Enormously complex and deep, with rich, concentrated pear, pineapple, citrus and hazelnut flavors that glide across the palate. Finishes with a long, smoky, toasty aftertaste. **92**

PINOT NOIR RUSSIAN RIVER VALLEY KISTLER VINEYARD (★★★★★): Ripe, rich, complex and concentrated, with pretty oak and polished tannins.

1996: Deliciously rich and focused, with a bright core of ripe plum, black cherry, anise, cedar and spice, impressively gaining nuance and complexity on the finish, where the flavors sail on. **92**

PINOT NOIR SONOMA COAST CAMP MEETING RIDGE (★★★★★): New from the Flowers' (see entry) Camp Meeting Ridge property, it is amazingly complex and well crafted. Worth watching.

1994: Impressive, with a dense, concentrated core of black cherry, plum and berry fruit; picking up some pretty oak shadings and a meaty, tannic edge on the finish. **94**

PINOT NOIR SONOMA COAST CUVÉE CATHERINE (★★★★★): Dark, rich and flavorful; beautifully crafted.

1996: Wonderfully pure fruit; ripe, rich, and focused, with complex plum, raspberry, blueberry and spice, picking up light, toasty oak on the finish, and showing enough tannic strength to merit short term cellaring. **92**

1994: A dark, plummy color, with lots of ripe, rich black cherry, plum, spice and light toasty oak flavors; balanced, long and complex. **95**

1992: Offers complex flavors, with toasty, buttery oak and pretty plum and black cherry flavors. **90**

PINOT NOIR SONOMA COAST HIRSCH VINEYARD (★★★★★): This popular vineyard yields some exotic wild berry and spicy flavors, and can be tannic. Still, it's a delicious expression of a vineyard.

1995: Dense, dark and concentrated, with a tightly wound core of wild blackberry, cherry, anise, sage and spice flavors. **90**

KONGSGAARD WINES (★★★★★)

Napa Valley
Founded: 1996. **Owner:** John Kongsgaard.
Winemaker: John Kongsgaard.

MAJOR WINES: PRICE, CASES, RATING

Chardonnay Napa Valley
  ($55, 600) ★★★★★

ALSO PRODUCED

Syrah Carneros Hudson Vineyard (NA).

WINERY DATA

Case Production: 1,200. **Acres Owned:** 7 acres in Napa Valley.
Varietals by Acre: Chardonnay (7 acres). **Vineyard
Designations:** Hudson Vineyard (Syrah). **Varietals Purchased:**
Syrah (Carneros).

Using a family-owned, seven-acre Chardonnay property on a rocky knoll east of the city of Napa, John Kongsgaard, a Napa native, has started his own brand. The focus is on Chardonnay and Syrah, with grapes for the latter coming from Hudson Vineyard. Kongsgaard has had a distinguished career, most notably spending more than a decade at Newton. Today, he is also involved with Luna, Livingston and Arietta.

TASTING NOTES

CHARDONNAY NAPA VALLEY (★★★★★)

1996: A sensational debut. Wonderful complexity and richness of flavors, with ripe, smooth fig, anise, and pear woven together, finishing long and lively. **95**

F. KORBEL AND BROS. (★★)

Russian River Valley, Sonoma County
Founded: 1882. **Owner:** Gary Heck. **Winemaker:** Paul
Ahvenainen.

MAJOR WINES: PRICE, CASES, RATING

Blanc de Noirs California
  ($10, 20,000) ★★
Blanc de Noirs Russian River Valley
  Vintage ($14, 2,500) ★★
Brut California
  ($10, 650,000) ★★
Brut Rosé California Artist Series
  ($13, 30,000) ★★

Sparkling California Chardonnay
  Champagne ($13, 100,000) ★★
Sparkling California Extra Dry
  ($10, 250,000) ★★
Sparkling California Kosher
  ($12, 5,000) ★★
Sparkling California Sec
  ($10, 1,500) ★★
Sparkling Sonoma County Natural
  ($12, 37,000) ★★
Sparkling Sonoma County Rouge
  ($10, 1,500) ★★

WINERY DATA

Case Production: 1.2 million. **Acres Owned:** 1,064 acres (604 in Yolo County, 460 in Sonoma). **Varietals by Acre:** Chardonnay, Chenin Blanc, Sauvignon Blanc (604 acres), Pinot Noir, Chardonnay (460).

Korbel Champagne Cellars in Russian River is a beautiful old winery with scenic landscaped gardens and brilliant flower arrangements. It is one of the largest wineries in California, producing roughly 1.2 million cases of *méthode champenoise* sparkling wine. The Brut, Brut Natural, Blanc de Blancs, Blanc de Noirs and Rosé are all good values. The winery added Sonoma County Chardonnay and Alexander Valley Cabernet in the 1990s, both of which are quite good.

KRISTONE CHAMPAGNE CELLARS (★★★)

Santa Maria Valley, Santa Barbara County
Founded: 1987. **Owner:** Jess Jackson & Barbara Banke.
Winemaker: Harold Osborne.

MAJOR WINES: PRICE, CASES, RATING

Blanc de Blancs California
  ($30, 2,000) ★★★
Blanc de Noirs California
  ($30, 2,000) ★★★
Brut Rosé California
  ($30, 1,000) ★★★

WINERY DATA

Case Production: 5,000. **Varietals Purchased:** Chardonnay (Santa Maria Valley), Pinot Blanc (Monterey County), Pinot Noir (Santa Maria Valley), Syrah (Santa Maria Valley).

This enterprise began as an ambitious attempt to make bold, rich, ultra-ripe sparkling wine by using very ripe grapes, barrel-aging the cuvées and then extending the time *en tirage*. The results have been mixed: some wines are attractive, while others have tasted dull and oxidized. Initial releases were in the $60 range, but the price has been cut in half and no recent vintage-dated wines have been released.

CHARLES KRUG WINERY (★★)
St. Helena, Napa Valley
Founded: 1861. **Owner:** Peter Mondavi Family.
Winemaker: Jac Cole. **Second Label:** CK Mondavi.

MAJOR WINES: PRICE, CASES, RATING
Cabernet Sauvignon Napa Valley
($14, 21,200) ★★
Cabernet Sauvignon Napa Valley
Vintage Selection
($38, 3,100) ★★★
Chardonnay Napa Valley Carneros Reserve
($19, 1,840) ★★
Chardonnay Napa Valley
($13, 11,600) ★★
Merlot Napa Valley Carneros Reserve
($19, 2,150) ★★
Merlot Napa Valley
($14, 6,200) ★★
Pinot Noir Napa Valley
($14, 6,700) ★★
Red Napa Valley Generations
($25, 1,910) ★★★
Sangiovese Napa Valley Reserve
($14, 1,675) ★★
Sauvignon Blanc Napa Valley
($10, 2,000) ★★
Zinfandel Napa Valley
($10, 2,600) ★★

WINERY DATA
Case Production: 985,000. **Acres Owned:** 470 acres in Carneros and Napa Valley. **Varietals by Acre:** Cabernet Franc (5 acres), Cabernet Sauvignon (142), Chardonnay (71), Chenin Blanc (59), Riesling (58), Merlot (54), Pinot Noir (49), Sangiovese (10), Sauvignon Blanc (22). **Varietals Purchased:** Cabernet Franc (Napa Valley), Cabernet Sauvignon (Napa Valley), Chardonnay (Napa Valley), Zinfandel (Napa Valley).

Russian immigrant Charles Krug founded this winery in St. Helena in 1861, establishing a 540-acre estate and vineyard. At the end of the 19th century, however, phylloxera and Prohibition spelled doom for the winery, forcing its closure. Then, in 1943, another immigrant, Italian-born Cesare Mondavi, bought the winery at the urging of his son Robert, who had scouted Napa Valley with an eye to moving his family's wine business there from Lodi. The Mondavi era featured Cesare and sons Robert and Peter overseeing winemaking, production and marketing. Charles Krug's flagship wine was the Vintage Selection Cabernet, which the winery started producing in 1946. Krug's quality and volume grew through the 1960s, and Krug became one of Napa's "big four," along with Beaulieu, Inglenook and Louis Martini.

In the early 1960s, family tensions over wine styles and future directions led to a bitter falling out between Robert and Peter, with Robert departing to start his own winery in 1966, and Peter remaining in charge of Charles Krug. Robert prevailed in a lawsuit against his family, which resulted in the diversion of both money and key vineyards from the Krug winery. A period of decline followed in the early 1970s. The Vintage Selection Cabernet held its own for a while, but became less exciting when the vineyard source shifted to western Yountville.

By the mid-1980s, Krug was back on solid footing following a major renovation. Today, while its wines have undoubtedly improved, they are still more mainstream than cutting edge. Occasionally, though, wines such as the 1990 and the 1992 Carneros Reserve Chardonnay show the potential of the winery's considerable vineyard holdings throughout the valley, which measure some 470 acres spread out from Carneros to Napa Valley proper.

KUNDE ESTATE WINERY (★★★)
Sonoma Valley
Founded: 1989. **Owner:** Kunde Family. **Winemaker:** David Noyes.

MAJOR WINES: PRICE, CASES, RATING
Cabernet Sonoma Valley
($20, 6,000) ★★
Cabernet Sonoma Valley Reserve
($24, 900) ★★

Chardonnay Sonoma Valley
($15, 40,000) ★★★

Chardonnay Sonoma Valley Kinneybrook
($20, 1,000) ★★★

Chardonnay Sonoma Valley Reserve
($22, 2,000) ★★★

Chardonnay Sonoma Valley Wildwood
($20, 1,000) ★★★

Merlot Sonoma Valley
($17, 35,000) ★★

Sauvignon Blanc Sonoma Valley
Magnolia Lane
($11, 10,000) ★★

Syrah Sonoma Valley
($18, 1,000) ★★★

Viognier Sonoma Valley
($18, 2,000) ★★★

Zinfandel Sonoma Valley
($15, 7,000) ★★

Zinfandel Sonoma Valley Robusto
($24, 450) ★★★★

Zinfandel Sonoma Valley
Shaw Vineyard Century Vine
($15, 2,000) ★★

WINERY DATA
Case Production: 100,000. **Acres Owned:** 750 acres in Sonoma Valley. **Varietals by Acre:** Cabernet Sauvignon (120 acres), Chardonnay (190), Merlot (150), Sauvignon Blanc (55), Viognier (15), Zinfandel (90), 16 other varietals (130).
Vineyard Designations: Kinneybrook (Chardonnay), Wildwood (Chardonnay), Shaw (Zinfandel), Magnolia Lane (Sauvignon Blanc).

The Kundes started planting grapes in Sonoma Valley in 1904. Their hillside vineyards were long a source of grapes for Sebastiani Vineyards, which bought most of their produce until 1990. Sebastiani used parts of Kunde's vineyard for its vineyard-designated wines: Bell, Kinneybrook and Wildwood.

In 1989, Kunde Estate Winery got off to a good start with a series of wines, including Chardonnay, Meritage red and Zinfandel. Quality varied in subsequent vintages, however, possibly due to an overly rapid expansion: the winery has quickly grown from 32,000 cases to its current 100,000. Kunde Estate is spread out over 2,000 acres, with 750 planted to grapes in seven different

microclimates that rise 1,200 feet above the valley floor. An additional 50 acres of vines per year have been slated for planting.

TASTING NOTES

CHARDONNAY SONOMA VALLEY KINNEYBROOK (★★★): The most consistently excellent bottling from this winery, this is an elegant, flavorful wine.
1996: Ripe, rich and smoky, with a tight, complex band of fig, toast, pear and apricot flavors that fan out on the finish, gaining nuance and complexity. **90**
1995: Ripe and spicy, with a solid core of pear, vanilla, hazelnut and nutmeg, showing a trace of alcohol on the finish, where the flavors turn complex. **88**
1994: An elegant and detailed young wine with bright, vivid pear, spice and citrus flavors that keep their focus on a long, complex finish. **89**

ZINFANDEL SONOMA VALLEY VARIOUS BOTTLINGS (★★): The star is the Robusto, which with the 1995 (94 points) showed how rich and seductive Zinfandel can be; it displayed tiers of coffee, currant, spice and anise, turning polished.

KYNSI (★★★)
Edna Valley, San Luis Obispo County
Founded: 1995. **Owner:** Don & Gwen Othman.
Winemaker: Don & Gwen Othman.

MAJOR WINES: PRICE, CASES, RATING
Pinot Noir Edna Valley
($20, 400) ★★★

Syrah San Luis Obispo County
($20, 295) ★★★

ALSO PRODUCED
Chardonnay Edna Valley Edna Ranch ($20, 200); Chardonnay Santa Ynez Valley Edna Ranch ($20, 200); Pinot Noir Santa Maria Valley Sanford & Benedict Vineyard ($25, 400).

WINERY DATA
Case Production: 1,500. **Vineyard Designations:** Sanford & Benedict Vineyard (Pinot Noir), Edna Ranch (Chardonnay).
Varietals Purchased: Chardonnay (Edna Valley, Santa Ynez Valley), Pinot Noir (Edna Valley, Santa Maria Valley), Syrah (Paso Robles, Santa Maria Valley).

Housed in an old dairy building in San Luis Obispo, Kynsi produces small lots of Chardonnay, Pinot Noir and Syrah. Co-owner Don Othman invented "Bulldog Pup," a gas-pressure racking tool used in the winemaking process.

The 1995 Edna Valley Pinot Noir (88 points) was elegant and spicy, with wild berry and cherry flavors, while the 1995 Chardonnay Sanford & Benedict Vineyard (88) was appealing for its citrusy pear and spice flavors. The 1995 Syrah (86) was of medium weight, with plum, wild berry and sage flavors. While the initial wines were very good, it is worth watching to see if the wines improve.

L'ECOSSE see CORNERSTONE CELLARS

L'ETAGE see SCHUG CARNEROS ESTATE WINERY

LA CREMA (★★★)
Russian River Valley, Sonoma County
Founded: 1979. **Owner:** Jennifer Jackson-Hartford & Laura Jackson-Giron. **Winemaker:** Dan Goldfield.

MAJOR WINES: PRICE, CASES, RATING

Chardonnay Sonoma Coast	
($15, 40,000)	★★★
Chardonnay Sonoma Coast Reserve	
($26, 1,500)	★★★
Pinot Noir Sonoma Coast	
($15, 20,000)	★★★
Pinot Noir Sonoma Coast Reserve	
($26, 1,500)	★★★
Zinfandel Sonoma Coast Reserve	
($20, 2,000)	★★★

WINERY DATA
Case Production: 65,000. **Acres Owned:** 250 acres in Russian River. **Varietals by Acre:** Chardonnay (125 acres), Pinot Noir (120), Zinfandel (5). **Varietals Purchased:** Chardonnay (Sonoma Coast), Pinot Noir (Sonoma Coast), Zinfandel (Russian River, Sonoma Coast).

Burgundy-inspired La Crema changed hands twice before it was purchased by Jess Jackson of Kendall-Jackson in 1993. It was founded in 1979 as La Crema Vinera in a dreary warehouse in Petaluma, and remained there until 1983, when New Yorker Jason Korman and a group of investors bought the brand. The new owners expanded production and introduced a line of cash-flow wines, but financial problems and subsequent bankruptcy eventually forced them sell the winery to Jackson. The Chardonnays and Pinot Noirs have both been steady performers. With recent vintages, Sonoma County and a narrower Sonoma Coast appellation have been replacing the broader California appellation. Zinfandel has also been added.

The winery's philosophy remains that complex wines are best created through blending different vineyards. "In an average year, could a little Chambertin help a Richebourg?" reasoned winemaker Dan Goldfield, who set the style. "Yes, it can." Goldfield left La Crema in 1999 to pursue other winemaking possibilities, and hasn't been replaced as of this writing. Jackson's daughters are listed as the owners of this winery.

TASTING NOTES

CHARDONNAY SONOMA COAST VARIOUS BOTTLINGS (★★★): Improved, with the 1995 (90 points) marked by creamy pear and peach flavors, while the Reserve 1995 (88) tasted leaner and less complex. The 1996 Reserve (87) was intense, with a narrow range of flavors.

PINOT NOIR SONOMA COAST RESERVE (★★★): A touch austere; built for cellaring to let the tight cherry, cola, tea and spice flavors evolve. The Reserve 1995 (88 points) and Reserve 1996 (87) were well balanced.

ZINFANDEL SONOMA COAST RESERVE (★★★): New as of 1995 (87 points), with grapey cherry, snappy raspberry and wild berry flavors.

LA CROSSE see BEAUCANON WINERY

LA FAMIGLIA DI ROBERT MONDAVI (★★)

Oakville, Napa Valley
Founded: 1995. **Owner:** Robert Mondavi Corp.
Winemaker: Heather Pyle.

MAJOR WINES: PRICE, CASES, RATING

Barbera California
  ($18, NA)   ★★
Moscato Bianco California
  ($12, NA)   ★★
Nebbiolo California
  ($12, NA)   ★★
Pinot Grigio California
  ($16, NA)   ★★
Sangiovese California
  ($22, NA)   ★★

ALSO PRODUCED

Sangiovese California Riserva ($35, NA).

WINERY DATA

Case Production: 40,000. **Acres Owned:** 39 acres (2 in Carneros, 30 in Napa Valley, 7 in Stags Leap). **Varietals by Acre:** Barbera (7 acres), Pinot Grigio (12), Sangiovese (18), Tocai Friulano (2). **Varietals Purchased:** Barbera (North Coast, Napa Valley), Muscat Blanc (North Coast, Central Coast), Nebbiolo (Central Coast), Pinot Grigio (Central Coast, Napa Valley, North Coast), Sangiovese (Central Coast, Napa Valley, North Coast).

Dedicated to Italian varietals, this Mondavi brand is housed in the old Vichon winery in Oakville and has grown to 40,000 cases, with all wines carrying the California appellation. The wines are pleasant and simple but not particularly distinctive. Barbera, as typified by the 1996 (86 points), tends to be crisp and firm with cherry, spice and herb flavors. Sangiovese, too, tends toward the lean side; the 1996 (85) had pleasant cherry and herb flavors and moderate body. Whites are typically light and refreshing, as was the 1996 Pinot Grigio (85), which showed generous pear and almond flavors on a silky frame. Worth watching if only to see if quality improves.

LA JOTA VINEYARD CO. (★★★–★★★★)

Howell Mountain, Napa Valley
Founded: 1982. **Owner:** Bill & Joan Smith.
Winemaker: Bill Smith.

MAJOR WINES: PRICE, CASES, RATING

Cabernet Franc Howell Mountain
  ($36, 500)   ★★★
Cabernet Sauvignon Howell Mountain
  ($28, 1,400)   ★★★
Cabernet Sauvignon Howell Mountain
  Anniversary Release
  ($48, 1,000)   ★★★★
Petite Sirah Howell Mountain
  ($28, 500)   ★★★
Viognier Howell Mountain Barrel Fermented
  ($28, 500)   ★★★
Viognier Howell Mountain Cold Fermented
  ($28, 500)   ★★★

WINERY DATA

Case Production: 4,000. **Acres Owned:** 28 acres on Howell Mountain. **Varietals by Acre:** Cabernet Sauvignon (18 acres), Cabernet Franc (4), Merlot (3), Viognier (3). **Varietals Purchased:** Petite Sirah (Howell Mountain).

Oilman and home-winemaker Bill Smith came to Napa Valley to find vineyard land for a development investment. After accomplishing that goal, he and his wife, Joan, decided that a combination weekend retreat and vineyard sounded even better. While scouting around Howell Mountain, Smith discovered a rustic stone winery built in 1895 by Frederick Hess. By 1982, the Smiths had found themselves a winemaker, neighbor Randy Dunn, and their first La Jota Cabernet was released, followed by Zinfandel; later came Cabernet Franc, Viognier, Petite Syrah, Marsanne, and Roussanne.

There's no disputing that La Jota Cabernets are distinctive, intense, sometimes rustic, concentrated and tannic. But my many experiences with the wines show that they often dry out, turning ponderous and tannic before evolving into the more complex and intricate wines they promise to become in their youth. Looking back over years of my notes, I've always liked the Cabernets far more as barrel samples and upon release than after they've been cellared.

In 1991, the winery split its Cabernet production, focusing on its estate Howell Mountain Anniversary Series bottling and a lower-priced Howell Mountain selection. Petite Sirah is also worth the search. Sonoma Coast Pinot Noir is made under a separate brand called W.H. Smith.

TASTING NOTES

CABERNET FRANC HOWELL MOUNTAIN (★★★): Lighter than the Cabernet Sauvignon, with appealing flavors; recent vintages have been more supple and flavorful than earlier ones.

1996: Spicy, complex, concentrated and aromatic, with pretty blackberry, spice, mineral, tobacco, sage and cedar flavors, turning smooth and polished. **91**

1995: Ruggedly tannic and earthy, with a coarse texture and a stalky tobacco, oak and currant range of flavors and a hint of prune. **84**

1994: This wine has an intriguing spicy edge to the meaty currant, cedar, anise, cedar and leathery tree bark edge that gives way to hints of sassafras and mineral. **88**

CABERNET SAUVIGNON HOWELL MOUNTAIN (★★★): Solid, intense and recently more polished. The compact fruit flavors work against significant tannins and buttery oak for a real mouthful of wine. Early vintages have aged well, but not outstandingly.

1996: Ruggedly tannic, with an earthy streak running through the complex core of currant, mineral and cocoa notes, finishing with a rich, tannic aftertaste. **91**

1995: Tight, tannic and leathery, with a tobacco and cedary edge to the core of earthy currant. Well balanced and in need of short-term cellaring. **86**

1994: Rich and exotic, with layers of ripe currant, plum, anise, cedar and mineral flavors, picking up a trace of tobacco and toast on the finish. The texture is smooth and supple for a young Howell Mountain. **90**

1993: Tight and a touch earthy, sporting cedar, currant, cherry and pepper notes. Chewy, chalky tannins on the finish. **87**

1992: Solid with a chunky core of earthy currant and tobacco, turning supple in texture but with ample tannins for short-term cellaring. **88**

1990: Firm and supple, with intense currant, anise and herb notes that turn smooth and fleshy on the finish despite ample tannins. **86**

1989: An appealing 1989 with earthy currant and cherry notes that turn oaky. **83**

1988: Ripe, chunky and balanced, with smoky, earthy notes of currant, mineral, herb and tobacco flavors. **87**

1987: Austere, dry and oaky, with a narrow band of cedary earth and currant notes that dry up on the finish. Unimpressive in my last tasting. **82**

1986: A solid wine with cedar, oak and currant notes, developing a supple, silky texture despite ample tannins and a good dose of oak. It's doubtful that it will live up to earlier expectations. **85**

1985: Still austere, with tightly wound tobacco and currant notes, and I wonder whether it will evolve into a more complex and compelling wine with further cellaring. **83**

CABERNET SAUVIGNON HOWELL MOUNTAIN ANNIVERSARY RELEASE (★★★★)

15th Anniversary Release 1996: A dark, rich, plush, concentrated Cabernet, with layers of currant, spice, anise, sage, cedar, tar and mineral flavors and a long, rich aftertaste. **93**

14th Anniversary Release 1995: A dark, intense wine with a solid core of currant, black cherry and anise-laced Cabernet fruit; lots of oak as well. **89**

13th Anniversary Release 1994: Bold, ripe, rich and concentrated; packed with thick, complex flavors of currant, black cherry, anise and cedar. **93**

12th Anniversary Release 1993: Well-oaked, with plenty of toasty, smoky flavors, currant, cherry and mineral notes and plush tannins. **91**

11th Anniversary Release 1992: Ripe, intense, rich and complex, with layers of currant, anise, mineral and cedary oak flavors and dry tannins. **89**

10th Anniversary Release 1991: Big, rich, chewy and tannic, packed with cedar, currant, earth and oak flavors. Deeply colored and firmly structured, this brawny wine needs time to soften. **87**

PETITE SIRAH HOWELL MOUNTAIN (★★★): Can be quite dense and dramatic, with earthy currant, anise and mineral notes.

1995: A ruggedly tannic style; some floral plum and berry notes, but at this stage the flavors are buried beneath the tannins. **85**

1994: Dense and earthy, but once you push past the tannins there's a core of spicy currant and peppery fruit flavors. **88**

VIOGNIER HOWELL MOUNTAIN VARIOUS BOTTLINGS (★★★): Intense and spicy; true to the variety, showing complexity and finesse.

LA SIRENA WINES (★★★)
Napa Valley
Founded: 1994. **Owner:** Heidi Peterson Barrett.
Winemaker: Heidi Peterson Barrett.

MAJOR WINES: PRICE, CASES, RATING
Sangiovese Napa Valley
($25, 300) ★★★

ALSO PRODUCED
Cabernet Sauvignon Napa Valley ($NA, 225).

WINERY DATA
Case Production: 500. **Acres Owned:** 14 acres in Napa Valley.
Varietals by Acre: Cabernet Sauvignon (12 acres), Sangiovese
(2). **Vineyard Designations:** Juliana Vineyard (Sangiovese)
Varietals Purchased: Cabernet Sauvignon (Napa Valley),
Sangiovese (Napa Valley).

Heidi Peterson Barrett is the daughter of long-time
winemaker/consultant Richard Peterson (see Folie à
Deux) and wife of Chateau Montelena winemaker Bo
Barrett. Many wine drinkers know her through her
clients, which include some of the best wineries in Napa
Valley—Barbour, Grace Family, Oakford, Paradigm and
Screaming Eagle among them. The La Sirena ("mer-
maid" in Spanish and Italian) wines haven't yet reached
the levels of Barrett's clients' wines, but Sangiovese is a
difficult medium. While the 1995 Sangiovese (86 points)
was smooth and polished with strawberry and plum flavors, the 1996 (82) was dry and earthy with modest cherry notes. Barrett's first La Sirena Cabernet, a 1996,
should allow her to show her talent. Currently Barrett
sells the Cabernet and Sangiovese from her estate vineyard and buys grapes for La Sirena.

LA TERRE see SEBASTIANI SONOMA CASK CELLARS

LAETITIA VINEYARD & WINERY (★★★)
San Luis Obispo County
Founded: 1995. **Owner:** Bilo Zarif & Selim Zilkha.
Winemaker: Jonathan Avila.

MAJOR WINES: PRICE, CASES, RATING
Brut San Luis Obispo County Select
($14, 2,000) ★★

Chardonnay San Luis Obispo County
Laetitia Vineyard
($25, 215) ★★★★
Chardonnay San Luis Obispo County
Reserve
($17, 440) ★★★
Crémant de Noirs San Luis Obispo County
($14, 2,000) ★★★
Pinot Blanc San Luis Obispo County
La Colline Vineyard
($25, 100) ★★
Pinot Blanc San Luis Obispo County
Reserve
($17, 430) ★★
Pinot Noir San Luis Obispo County
Laetitia Vineyard
($29, 200) ★★★
Pinot Noir San Luis Obispo County
Reserve ($19, 1,300) ★★★
Sparkling San Luis Obispo County
Elegance Reserve
($23, 2,000) ★★★
Sparkling San Luis Obispo County
Elegance Rosé Reserve
($23, 1,000) ★★★

WINERY DATA
Case Production: 15,000. **Acres Owned:** 189 acres in San Luis
Obispo. **Varietals by Acre:** Chardonnay (74 acres), Pinot Blanc
(50), Pinot Noir (65). **Vineyard Designations:** Laetitia Vineyard
(Chardonnay, Pinot Blanc, Pinot Noir), La Colline Vineyard
(Chardonnay, Pinot Blanc, Pinot Noir). **Varietals Purchased:**
Viognier (Santa Barbara County).

Laetitia Vineyard and Winery was founded in 1991 by
Frenchman Jean Claude Tardivat, Deutz Champagne of
France and Beringer Wine Estates. Initially a sparkling
wine producer called Maison Deutz, the winery shifted
to still wines in the mid-1990s and changed its name to
Laetitia in 1997, after Deutz-Roederer and Beringer
Wine Estates sold their shares to Tardivat. Winery owner-
ship switched again in 1998 when Tardivat sold to
Barnwood Vineyards of Santa Barbara County.
Single-vineyard Chardonnays, Pinot Blancs and Pinot
Noirs have been very good—particularly the
Chardonnays from La Colline Vineyard and Laetitia
Vineyard, which in 1996 (90 and 91 points respectively)

were ripe and creamy with pear and melon flavors framed by toasted oak. The Pinot Noirs showed a bit more intensity in 1995, but the 1996 Laetitia (86) and Les Galets (86) were complex and flavorful, with the Laetitia showing fresh cherry and berry notes while the Les Galets was more earthy with dried fruit flavors. Sparkling wines are good but not noteworthy.

Future quality under new owners and a new wine-maker remains to be seen. This is a winery to watch.

LAIL VINEYARDS (★★★)
Napa Valley
Founded: 1995. **Owner:** Robin Lail. **Winemaker:** Philippe Melka.

MAJOR WINES: PRICE, CASES, RATING
Red Napa Valley
  ($60, 1,000)   ★★★

WINERY DATA
Case Production: 1,000. **Acres Owned:** 5 acres in Napa Valley. **Varietals by Acre:** Cabernet Sauvignon (3 acres), Merlot (2).

This is a new winery founded by Robin Lail, the daughter of John Daniel Jr., who owned Inglenook winery from 1939 to 1964. Daniel's great-uncle was Gustav Niebaum, who founded Inglenook in 1879. Lail had been a co-owner of Dominus Estate and Merryvale Vineyards but sold her shares of both, including the 122-acre Napanook Vineyard (now owned by Dominus) which was the source of Inglenook's great Cabernets in the first half of the 1900s.

Now, Lail and husband Jon make wine from their 2.09-acre Totem Vineyard, once part of the original Napanook Vineyard, and the 2.9-acre Mole Hill vineyard on Howell Mountain. Frenchman Philippe Melka, who worked briefly at Dominus, is making the wines. The 1995 Lail (88 points), a blend of Cabernet and Merlot, was austere with currant, anise and sage flavors. This is a winery to watch.

LAMBERT BRIDGE WINERY (★★★)
Dry Creek Valley, Sonoma County
Founded: 1975. **Owner:** Patti Chambers. **Winemaker:** Julia Iantosca.

MAJOR WINES: PRICE, CASES, RATING
Chardonnay Sonoma County
  ($17, 6,000) ★★★
Crane Creek Cuvée Red
  Dry Creek Valley
  ($30, 500) ★★★
Merlot Dry Creek Valley
  (Discontinued) ★★
Merlot Sonoma County
  ($20, 11,500) ★★★
Petite Sirah Dry Creek Valley
  ($22, 300) ★★★
Sauvignon Blanc Dry Creek
  ($12, 1,500) ★★★
Viognier Dry Creek Valley
  ($18, 300) ★★★
Zinfandel Dry Creek Valley
  ($20, 500) ★★★

WINERY DATA
Case Production: 20,000. **Acres Owned:** 5.5 in Dry Creek Valley. **Varietals by Acre:** Petite Sirah (2 acres), Zinfandel (3.5). **Varietals Purchased:** Cabernet Franc (Dry Creek Valley), Cabernet Sauvignon (Dry Creek Valley), Carignane (Dry Creek Valley), Chardonnay (Sonoma Valley, Russian River, Dry Creek Valley), Merlot (Sonoma Valley, Dry Creek Valley), Petite Sirah (Dry Creek Valley), Sauvignon Blanc (Dry Creek Valley), Sémillon (Dry Creek Valley), Viognier (Dry Creek Valley), Zinfandel (Dry Creek Valley).

Jerry Lambert founded this Dry Creek winery in 1975, six years after buying a 120-acre site. The early product mix included Cabernet, Chardonnay and Merlot. By the end of the 1980s, case production had grown to 25,000 cases.

A protracted legal dispute with its distributors, however, drained Lambert Bridge financially, forcing it to close in 1992. It reopened a year later under new ownership, with Merry Edwards having been hired as a consultant. Julia Iantosca is now in charge of winemaking, and there has been a noticeable improvement in quality. The Crane Creek Cuvée, Chardonnay and Zinfandel have been the best wines of late.

TASTING NOTES

CHARDONNAY SONOMA COUNTY (★★★): The 1996 (88 points) was overshadowed by the 1995 (90), but both were well made and fun to drink.

CRANE CREEK CUVÉE RED DRY CREEK VALLEY (★★★): This wine hit 91 points with the 1994, which was rich, elegant, firm, dark and intense. Could be worth watching.

MERLOT DRY CREEK VALLEY (★★): This is Merlot up to its usual tricks. Tempting, often shy at mid-palate, with just enough flavors to tease.

ZINFANDEL DRY CREEK VALLEY (★★★): The 1995 (90 points) showed what is possible with this wine: a supple, elegant texture with many attractive flavors. The 1996 (87) was not far off the mark.

LAMBORN FAMILY VINEYARDS (★★★)
Howell Mountain, Napa Valley
Founded: 1982. **Owner:** Mike, Terry, Bob and Janet Lamborn. **Winemaker:** Heidi Peterson Barrett.

MAJOR WINES: PRICE, CASES, RATING
Zinfandel Howell Mountain
  Lamborn Family Vineyards
  ($22, 1,000)   ★★★

ALSO PRODUCED
Zinfandel Port Howell Mountain Lamborn Family Vineyards ($25, 600).

WINERY DATA
Case Production: 1,600. **Acres Owned:** 5 acres in Howell Mountain. **Varietals by Acre:** Zinfandel (5 acres). **Vineyard Designations:** Lamborn Family Vineyards. **Varietals Purchased:** Zinfandel (Howell Mountain).

Private investigator Bob Lamborn, who worked on the Patty Hearst kidnapping case, bought a vineyard on Howell Mountain in 1972, and in 1982 started selling wine under the Lamborn Family Vineyards label. His neighbor, Randy Dunn, helped with the first few vintages.

In 1998, Lamborn sold his home, winery and 9-acre vineyard to the Pringle family, who are launching their own label. The Lamborn Family wines are now being made at the Napa Wine Company by Heidi Peterson Barrett, with grapes from a 5-acre Howell Mountain vineyard owned by Lamborn's son, Mike. Production will soon expand, with Mike Lamborn adding 4 acres to his vineyard. With Barrett making the wines, the Lamborn Zins are in good hands.

TASTING NOTES

ZINFANDEL HOWELL MOUNTAIN LAMBORN FAMILY VINEYARDS (★★★): While inconsistent in quality, this wine almost always offers personality. Typically austere, with dusty berry and peppery notes and firm tannins. The 1995 (90 points) was zesty, with cherry, berry and raspberry fruit. The 1996 (82) had rugged tannins, and more herb and mint than ripe fruit. The 1993 The Hang Time Vintage (89) showed what can happen when the grapes get that extra time on the vine.

LANCASTER (★★)
Alexander Valley, Sonoma County
Founded: 1995. **Owner:** Ted Simpkins. **Winemaker:** David Elliott.

MAJOR WINES: PRICE, CASES
Red Alexander Valley
  ($55, 700)   ★★

WINERY DATA
Case Production: 2,500. **Acres Owned:** 55 acres in Alexander Valley. **Varietals by Acre:** Cabernet Franc (3 acres), Cabernet Sauvignon (34), Malbec (3), Merlot (15).

This new winery was founded by Ted Simpkins, president of Southern Wine & Spirits. There are 55 acres in vines planted to Bordeaux varieties. The debut 1995 vintage (84 points) was lean and marked by a green, stalky edge. The 1996 was much better. May be worth watching.

LANDMARK VINEYARDS
(★★★★–★★★★★)

Sonoma Valley
Founded: 1990. **Owner:** Mike & Mary Colhoun, Damaris Ethridge. **Winemaker:** Eric Stern. **Second Label:** Adobe Canyon Cellars.

MAJOR WINES: PRICE, CASES, RATING

Chardonnay Russian River
  Lorenzo Vineyard
  ($36, 300)   ★★★★★
Chardonnay Sonoma-Santa Barbara
  Monterey Counties Damaris Reserve
  ($30, 4,000)   ★★★★★
Chardonnay Sonoma-Santa Barbara-
  Monterey Counties Overlook
  ($21, 12,500)   ★★★★
Pinot Noir Sonoma Mountain
  Van der Kamp Vineyards Grand Detour
  ($34, 980)   ★★★★

ALSO PRODUCED

Pinot Noir Sonoma Coast Kastania ($45, 120).

WINERY DATA

Case Production: 20,000. **Acres Owned:** 15 acres in Sonoma Valley. **Varietals by Acre:** Chardonnay (15 acres). **Vineyard Designations:** Lorenzo Vineyard (Chardonnay), Van der Kamp (Pinot Noir) **Varietals Purchased:** Chardonnay (Russian River), Pinot Noir (Sonoma Mountain).

This winery would certainly get a few votes for the best turnaround of the 1990s. It is making some absolutely delicious Chardonnays, with the Pinot Noirs following close behind in quality. Bill Mabry and his family founded Landmark in Windsor in 1974, producing several popular varietals. Urban encroachment eventually forced the winery out of Windsor, however, and it moved to a new home in Kenwood in the Sonoma Valley in 1990. The move coincided with the winery's acquisition by Damaris Deere W. Ethridge, with Mabry remaining to oversee operations. Mabry left soon after, and Michael and Mary Colhoun took over day-to-day management.

The focus in the 1990s has been on Chardonnay and Pinot Noir, including vineyard-designated versions of both. At one point, Helen Turley (of Marcassin) signed on as a consultant, but now the wines are in the very competent hands of Eric Stern. The winery owns 15 acres of Chardonnay, with production leveling off at 20,000 cases. These wines should be on everyone's shopping list.

TASTING NOTES

CHARDONNAY RUSSIAN RIVER LORENZO VINEYARD (★★★★★): Uniformly very rich and concentrated; made in a delicious style that packs in fruit and finesses it with oak.
1997: Rich, creamy and loaded with complex flavors, it serves up concentrated pear, fig, tangerine, anise, butter and butterscotch flavors that zoom on and on. Delicious. **94**
1996: Delicious, ripe rich, full-bodied and loaded with complex pear, fig, citrus and honey notes. Finishing with a broad, rich aftertaste. **93**

CHARDONNAY SONOMA-SANTA BARBARA-MONTEREY COUNTIES DAMARIS RESERVE (★★★★★): The appellation underwent a change in 1997; earlier vintages were all Sonoma. This wine is delicious, with lots of richness and layers of flavor.
1997: Smooth, creamy, elegant and polished, with a subtle array of peach, pear, fig, nectarine and honey flavors, finishing with a delicious aftertaste that echos fruit. **93**
1996: Tasty, ripe, rich and complex, with layers of pear, vanilla, honey and citrus flavors and a creamy, smooth texture. **92**
1995: Serves up lots of complex, buttery pear, honey, butterscotch and spicy flavors and a smooth, polished texture. **92**
1994: Rich and creamy, with a good dose of toasty, buttery oak and just the right amount of spicy pear and honey notes. **89**

CHARDONNAY SONOMA-SANTA BARBARA-MONTEREY COUNTIES OVERLOOK (★★★★★): The Overlook has changed appellation too (from Sonoma County), starting with the '97 vintage. This is a wonderfully flavorful wine.
1997: Ripe, smooth, rich and creamy, with layers of pear, vanilla, anise and fig flavors that are deep, complex and concentrated; finishing with a long, delicious aftertaste. **92**
1996: Very spicy, rich and complex, with concentrated tiers of pear, fig, apple, melon and spice flavors. **92**
1995: Remarkably elegant; serves up lots of ripe, complex fruit flavors, with notes of pear, apple, spice and cedar. **91**
1994: Well-oaked, rich and creamy, with a pretty core of melon, fig, honey and pear flavors that linger on through the finish. **91**

PINOT NOIR SONOMA MOUNTAIN VAN DER KAMP VINEYARDS GRAND DETOUR (★★★★): This wine has shown steady signs of improvement, with the 1997 vintage sure to raise it a notch. Worth collecting.
1995: Smooth and silky, with a lovely texture and a pretty array of black cherry, anise, wild berry, plum and cedar notes. **90**
1994: Ripe, intense and complex, with rich plum, cherry and currant flavors and peppery, floral overtones. **90**

LANG & REED WINE CO. (★★★)
Napa Valley
Founded: 1996. **Owner:** Tracey & John Skupny.
Winemaker: John Skupny.

MAJOR WINES: PRICE, CASES, RATING

Cabernet Franc Napa Valley	
($18, 2,000)	★★★
Cabernet Franc Napa Valley	
Premiere Étage	
($30, 1,000)	★★★

WINERY DATA
Case Production: 3,000. **Varietals Purchased:** Cabernet Franc (Atlas Peak, Calistoga, Rutherford, St. Helena).

Lang & Reed is dedicated to exploring the nuances and versatility of Cabernet Franc, which has a mixed but improving reputation in California. The winery's name is derived from the middle names of John and Tracey Skupny's sons, John Reed Skupny and Jerzy Lang

Skupny. John Skupny has been working in the wine business for more than 20 years, starting in the restaurant trade, and then working in marketing positions at Caymus, Clos Du Val and Niebaum-Coppola Estate.

The winery's focus is on two styles of Cabernet Franc: a medium-weight Chinon style, and a sturdier version—the Premiere Étage—meant for aging. The goal of the lighter style is to be more like Pinot Noir than Cabernet Sauvignon; the Premiere Étage is richer, with a stronger tannic backbone. A small amount of rosé is made on the side. All of the grapes are purchased. Worth watching, especially as new styles of Cabernet Franc emerge.

TASTING NOTES

CABERNET FRANC NAPA VALLEY (★★★): Succeeds in giving the wine a ripe, supple, polished texture. All three vintages—1993 (88 points), 1996 (87) and 1997 (88)—were complex.

CABERNET FRANC NAPA VALLEY PREMIERE ÉTAGE (★★★): A touch stalky in 1996 (87 points), but the currant and wild berry flavors were appealing.

LANGTRY see GUENOC WINERY

LAUREL GLEN VINEYARD (★★★–★★★★)
Sonoma Mountain
Founded: 1978. **Owner:** Patrick Campbell.
Winemaker: Patrick Campbell, Ray Kaufman. **Second Label:** Counterpoint, Terra Rosa.

MAJOR WINES: PRICE, CASES, RATING

Counterpoint Red Sonoma Mountain	
($22, 2,000)	★★★
Cabernet Sauvignon Sonoma Mountain	
($35, 1,500)	★★★★
Red California	
($7, 31,500)	★★

WINERY DATA

Case Production: 65,000. **Acres Owned:** 40 acres in Sonoma Mountain. **Varietals by Acre:** Cabernet Sauvignon (40 acres). **Varietals Purchased:** Cabernet Sauvignon (California), Rhône Varietals (California).

Patrick Campbell earned a master's degree in the philosophy of religion from Harvard's Divinity School before choosing grape-growing as his calling. After selling his Sonoma Mountain Cabernet grapes to Chateau St. Jean, Kenwood and others, Campbell made experimental wines at home in 1978 and 1979—two of the best Cabernets from that era that I've ever tasted. Both wines are remarkably dark in color and rich in flavor.

In 1981, Campbell began bottling his own wine made from this gently sloping vineyard on Sonoma Mountain. With the exception of a poor 1983 vintage, the Laurel Glen Cabernets are very soundly made, though the past few vintages have been less impressive. All of Laurel Glen's 40 acres are devoted to Cabernet. Terra Rosa and Counterpoint are second labels; Terra Rosa carries a North Coast appellation.

TASTING NOTES

CABERNET SAUVIGNON SONOMA MOUNTAIN (★★★★): Can be brilliant, complex, supple, rich in fruit flavors and distinctively elegant, but it's also variable on occasion, when the tannins gain the upper hand. The 1993, 1994 and 1995 vintages were less impressive than many vintages from the 1980s.
1995: Well crafted, if austere, it's focused on the currant and black cherry fruit, with notes of light toast and cedary oak. **89**
1994: Tight, lean and ruggedly tannic, with a green, stalky edge to the moderately ripe cherry and currant flavors. **86**
1993: Firm and intense, with chewy tannins and a slight green tea edge to the cherry and currant flavors. **85**
1992: Dense and tannic; an austere style with modest plum, cherry and currant notes that wrestle with the tannins. **85**
1991: Dense and concentrated, earthy and leathery, but it opens up to reveal spicy currant and black cherry flavors that turn elegant on the finish despite ample tannins. **89**
1990: Firm and flavorful, its spicy plum and berry aromas and flavors fan across the palate, hinting at bell pepper and herbs on the finish. **90**

Reserve 1990: Firm in texture, with tightly wound berry, plum, cedar and tobacco flavors that wrestle with the tannins. **88**
1989: Deeply concentrated, with minty, cedary aromas and deep cherry and currant flavors accented by the spice and vanilla of oak. Chewy tannins. **88**
1988: Solid, with ripe, rich, concentrated currant, anise, mineral, sage and berry notes that turn tannic on the finish. **88**
1987: Dark, ripe, intense and concentrated; packed with rich, vibrant currant, mineral, spice, cedar and berry flavors. **93**
1986: Strong, complex, firm and tannic, with young, vibrant currant, cherry and mineral flavors. **91**
1985: Ripe, smooth, supple and elegant, with vibrant black cherry, currant and plum flavors that finish with round, smooth tannins and toasty oak shadings. **91**
1984: Tart, with focused, complex cherry and plum flavors in an elegant style. It has medium intensity and depth of flavor, yet the flavors linger. **87**
1983: Lean and vinegary, with spicy plum and pruny notes. A difficult wine to warm up to, although it does not show the musty character that was so prevalent in earlier tastings. **83**
1982: Lean and tart, with an earthy, cedary quality on top of the ripe black cherry flavor. **79**
1981: This remains a magnificent wine with beautifully focused black cherry, currant, plum and cedar flavors that are smooth and supple, with fine, integrated tannins. **88**

LAZY CREEK VINEYARDS (★★)
Anderson Valley, Mendocino County
Founded: 1973. **Owner:** Johann & Theresia Kobler. **Winemaker:** Johann Kobler.

MAJOR WINES: PRICE, CASES, RATING

Chardonnay Anderson Valley ($14, 1,300)	★★
Gewürztraminer Anderson Valley ($9, 1,400)	★★
Pinot Noir Anderson Valley ($14, 1,300)	★★

WINERY DATA
Case Production: 4,000. **Acres Owned:** 20 acres in Anderson Valley. **Varietals by Acre:** Chardonnay (6 acres), Gewürztraminer (4), Pinot Noir (10).

Former restaurateur Johann Kobler and his wife, Theresia, own this 20-acre vineyard estate in Anderson Valley, from which they produce 4,000 cases of Chardonnay, Gewürztraminer and Pinot Noir. All three wines are steady ★★ performers.

LE CLOS see CLOS DU VAL

LE DUCQ (★★★)
Napa Valley
Founded: 1989. **Owner:** Jean Le Ducq. **Winemaker:** Jacques Boissenot. **Second Label:** Sylviane.

MAJOR WINES: PRICE, CASES, RATING
Le Ducq Meritage Napa Valley ($65, 300)	★★★
Sylviane Cabernet Sauvignon Napa Valley ($30, 600)	★★★
Sylviane Merlot Napa Valley ($30, 450)	★★

WINERY DATA
Case Production: 2,000. **Acres Owned:** 35 acres in Napa Valley. **Varietals by Acre:** Cabernet Franc (5 acres), Cabernet Sauvignon (20), Merlot (10), Petit Verdot (less than 1 acre).

Le Ducq is owned by Frenchman Jean Le Ducq, who is also the proprietor of Prince Michel Vineyards in Virginia. After purchasing property and planting a vineyard in Napa in 1989, Le Ducq waited until 1997 to release his first wines. Jacques Boissenot—known for his work at some of Bordeaux's top estates, including Lafite Rothschild and Leoville-Barton—is the consulting enologist.

The Meritage, a blend of Cabernet, Cabernet Franc, Merlot and Petit Verdot, tends to be an elegant, trim wine featuring cedar, currant and spice flavors and firm tannins. The second-label, single-varietal Sylviane wines share the austerity of the Le Ducq; the Sylviane Merlot has shown unripe flavors in the past.

TASTING NOTES

LE DUCQ MERITAGE NAPA VALLEY (★★★)
1995: Well balanced, if a bit lean and trim, with dusty cedar, chocolate and wild berry notes and firm, dry tannins. Turns complex, but needs time to soften. **89**

LEAPING LIZARD see ADLER FELS ESTATE

LEDSON WINERY & VINEYARDS (★★★)
Oakville, Napa Valley
Founded: 1993 **Owner:** Steve Ledson. **Winemaker:** Jack Ryno.

MAJOR WINES: PRICE, CASES, RATING
Chardonnay Carneros Reserve ($35, 200)	★★★★
Merlot Sonoma Valley ($25, 2,000)	★★★
Merlot Sonoma Valley Reserve ($45, 150)	★★★
Sauvignon Blanc Napa Valley ($18, 200)	★★★

ALSO PRODUCED
Chardonnay Sonoma County ($20, 1,000); Johannisberg Riesling Monterey ($14, 750); Michele's Cuvée Sonoma County ($15, 750); Orange Muscat Monterey ($18, 500).

WINERY DATA
Case Production: 5,000 **Acres Owned:** 19 acres in Sonoma Valley. **Varietals by Acre:** Merlot (14 acres), Zinfandel (5). **Varietals Purchased:** Chardonnay (Sonoma County, Carneros), Orange Muscat (Monterey County), Riesling (Monterey), Sauvignon Blanc (Napa Valley).

Steve Ledson, owner of the Sonoma-based Ledson Construction Co., planted a 19-acre vineyard in Sonoma Valley off of Highway 12 in 1989. The large, castle-like, Gothic stone house which adorns the winery's label was meant to be the Ledson family home, but is now a special events and tasting facility. There are plans to build a winery and plant 40 additional acres of vineyards. (The initial wines were made in Oakville.)

The wines, flavorful and lavishly oaked, have shown early promise. The 1996 Reserve Chardonnay (90 points) showed complex flavors of pear, anise and hazelnut. Both the 1995 Reserve Merlot (87) and the 1995 regular bottling (87) featured black fruit flavors and traces of herbal notes. A 1997 Sauvignon Blanc (85) was bright and refreshing, with fig and melon flavors. A winery to watch.

LEEWARD WINERY (★–★★)
Central Coast, Monterey County
Founded: 1979. **Owner:** Chuck Brigham & Chuck Gardner. **Winemaker:** Michael Meagher.

MAJOR WINES: PRICE, CASES, RATING
Chardonnay Central Coast	
($11, 6,500)	★★
Chardonnay Edna Valley Reserve	
($18, 500)	★★
Merlot Napa Valley	
($20, 1,000)	★
Pinot Noir Santa Barbara	
Bien Nacido Vineyard	
($20, 1,000)	★
Pinot Noir Santa Barbara	
Bien Nacido Vineyard Reserve	
($30, 100)	★

ALSO PRODUCED
Cabernet Sauvignon Napa Valley ($20, 1,000).

WINERY DATA
Case Production: 10,000. **Varietals Purchased:** Cabernet Sauvignon (Napa Valley), Chardonnay (Edna Valley, Ysidro), Merlot (Napa Valley), Pinot Noir (Santa Barbara).

Based in Ventura county, this winery focuses on Central Coast Chardonnay and Pinot Noir, along with Cabernet and Merlot from Napa Valley. The red wines are often tough, tannic, and characterized by odd flavors, even when Napa Valley grapes are used. The Chardonnays, on the other hand—the 1996 Central Coast (85 points), for example—can be crisp and fresh tasting.

LEWELLING VINEYARDS (★★★)
Napa Valley
Founded: 1992. **Owner:** Russel & Janice Wight, Alan, Douglas & David Wight. **Winemaker:** David Wight.

MAJOR WINES: PRICE, CASES, RATING
Cabernet Sauvignon Napa Valley	
Lewelling Vineyards	
($32, 300)	★★★

WINERY DATA
Case Production: 300. **Acres Owned:** 30 acres in Napa Valley, St. Helena. **Varietals by Acre:** Cabernet Sauvignon (27 acres), Merlot (3). **Vineyard Designations:** Lewelling Vineyards.

Brothers Douglas and David Wight divide the responsibilities for this family-owned brand: Douglas Wight manages the family's 30-acre vineyard in St. Helena, while David Wight produces the well-focused, flavorful Cabernet at Monticello Cellars. The 1993 Cabernet (88 points), Lewelling's debut vintage, showed an openly fruity style, with black cherry, wild berry and cassis notes, turning tannic on the finish. Could be worth watching.

LEWIS CELLARS (★★★★–★★★★★)
Oakville, Napa Valley
Founded: 1992. **Owner:** Debbie & Randy Lewis. **Winemaker:** Paul Hobbs.

MAJOR WINES: PRICE, CASES, RATING
Cabernet Sauvignon Napa Valley	
Oakville Ranch	
(Discontinued)	★★★★
Cabernet Sauvignon Napa Valley	
Reserve	
($40, 1,800)	★★★★★
Chardonnay Napa Valley Reserve	
($32, 2,100)	★★★★★
Merlot Napa Valley Oakville Ranch	
(Discontinued)	★★★
Merlot Napa Valley Reserve	
($45, 150)	★★★★★
Merlot Sonoma County	
($36, 700)	★★★★
Syrah Napa County	
($36, 250)	★★★★

Winery Data

Case Production: 5,000. **Varietals Purchased:** Cabernet Franc (Napa Valley), Cabernet Sauvignon (Napa Valley), Chardonnay (Carneros, Napa Valley, Sonoma County), Merlot (Napa Valley), Syrah (Carneros).

Former Oakville Ranch partners Randy and Debbie Lewis formed their own winery in 1995, following the death of Bob Miner, who had owned the vineyard for their Oakville Ranch wines. The Lewises went on to hire Paul Hobbs as winemaker, and have created a string of truly exciting wines, including ripe, oaky, polished Cabernets; equally well-oaked, ripe Chardonnays; and Merlots and Syrahs, all of which are of unusually high quality. Each of these wines is worth buying, collecting and cellaring; they should be at or near the top of your shopping list.

Tasting Notes

Cabernet Sauvignon Napa Valley Oakville Ranch (★★★★)

1993: Vibrant cedar, currant and spice flavors that add to the bright cherry nuances, turning tannic on the finish. **88**
1992: Shows wonderful harmony and finesse, with tiers of currant, plum, cherry, light oak and tobacco flavors and supple tannins. **94**

Cabernet Sauvignon Napa Valley Reserve (★★★★★)

1996: Rich and polished, with pretty toasty oak flavors leading to a supple texture and layers of black cherry, currant, coffee, berry and spice, finishing with smooth tannins. **92**
1995: Intense and concentrated, with supple currant, sage, spice, cedar and coffee notes that are rich and complex. **93**
1994: Dramatic, rich and explosive, with layers of bold, ripe currant, black cherry, anise, plum, spice and buttery oak flavors. **94**

Chardonnay Napa Valley Reserve (★★★★★):

Shares the Cabernet's bold, ripe, up-front fruitiness, with pretty oak shadings, too.
1997: Lots of rich fig, citrus, melon, pear, hazelnut and pretty oak flavors; toasty and buttery, leaving a bold, complex aftertaste. **92**
1996: A rich, earthy style, with pronounced ripe fruit, spicy aromatics and lots of complex pear, fig, melon and buttery oak flavors. **93**
1995: Smooth, ripe and juicy, with spicy pear, apple, fig and melon notes, turning supple and elegant on the finish. **93**

1994: Big, ripe, complex pear, apple, fig and melon notes accompany a medley of pretty, smoky, toasty oak flavors. **90**

Merlot Napa Valley Oakville Ranch (★★★)

1993: Firm and compact, with a tight core of black cherry and currant fruit flavors and hints of herb and spice. **88**

Merlot Napa Valley Reserve (★★★★★)

Consistently rich, ripe, and complex.
1996: Features a core of ripe, juicy cherry currant and berryish flavors, framed by spicy, toasty oak. Finishes with a complex aftertaste. **92**
1995: Complex and inviting, with supple, integrated plum, currant, anise, cedar and tobacco, turning tannic on the finish. **91**
1994: Intense and vibrant, with a rich, complex core of plum, black cherry, anise and cedary oak and a tannic, sophisticated finish. **93**

Merlot Sonoma County (★★★★): New with the 1996,

it's unclear whether the Lewises will be committing to Sonoma County Merlot, but the first effort was impressive.
1996: Ripe, with complex spice, plum, herb, cedar and blackberry flavors; sharply focused and supple in texture. **90**

Syrah Napa County (★★★★)

1996: Dark, ripe and intense, with spicy, minty notes leading to a core of chewy plum and wild berry flavors; finishes with a twinge of earthiness from the tannins and some pretty oak. **89**

Limerick Lane Cellars (★★★★)
Russian River Valley, Sonoma County
Founded: 1986. **Owner:** Michael Collins & Ted Markoczy. **Winemaker:** Michael Collins & Ted Markoczy.

Major Wines: Price, Cases, Rating

Zinfandel Russian River Valley Collins
  Vineyard
  ($19, 3,360)   ★★★★

Also Produced

Furmint Russian River Valley Collins Vineyard
($11, 400).

Winery Data

Case Production: 5,000. **Acres Owned:** 30 acres in Russian River Valley. **Varietals by Acre:** Furmint (3 acres), Syrah (2), Zinfandel (25). **Vineyard Designations:** Collins Vineyard (Zinfandel).

Limerick Lane specializes in Russian River-grown Zinfandel from Collins Vineyard, producing several thousand cases a year at its Limerick Lane address in Healdsburg. The wine had been highly variable, but now seems to be settled into a fine groove; both 1994 and 1995 were excellent vintages. Syrah is slated to join the mix in 2000.

TASTING NOTES

ZINFANDEL RUSSIAN RIVER VALLEY COLLINS VINEYARD (★★★★): Quality was once variable, but this wine is now both more consistent and tastier, with lots of zesty Zinfandel fruit flavors. Worth drinking.
1996: Crisp and firm, with earthy raspberry, cherry, cedar and spice; the tannins turn especially firm on finish. **87**
1995: Effusively fruity, with an exotic range of bright blueberry, black cherry and wild berry flavors, turning smooth and polished on the finish. **91**
1994: An elegant and lively Zin from California that showcases lots of rich, complex cherry, berry and raspberry flavors, which persist through the long, fruity finish, with just the right dose of tannin. **90**

LINCOURT VINEYARDS (★★★)
Santa Barbara County
Founded: 1997. **Owner:** William P. Foley. **Winemaker:** Alan Phillips.

MAJOR WINES: PRICE, CASES, RATING
Pinot Noir Santa Maria Valley	
Santa Maria Hills	
($25, 625)	★★★
Chardonnay Santa Barbara	
($16, 2,643)	★★★★
Sauvignon Blanc Santa Barbara County	
($14, 688)	★★★

ALSO PRODUCED
Cabernet Sauvignon Santa Ynez Valley Santa Barbara La Cuesta Vineyard ($25, 900); Merlot Santa Ynez Valley Santa Barbara La Cuesta Vineyard ($20, 223); Chardonnay Santa Maria Valley Bien Nacido Vineyard ($20, 386).

WINERY DATA
Case Production: 40,000. **Acres Owned:** 68 acres in Santa Maria Valley. **Varietals by Acre:** Pinot Noir (68 acres).
Varietals Purchased: Chardonnay (Santa Maria Valley), Pinot Noir (Santa Maria Valley), Syrah (Santa Barbara County).

Businessman Bill Foley purchased Santa Ynez Winery in 1997, re-naming it LinCourt Vineyards after his daughters Lindsay and Courtney. Alan Phillips, formerly of Byington Winery, is making the wines for LinCourt and Foley's other winery, Foley Estate (see entry). Foley is currently planting 220 acres in the Santa Rita Valley section of Santa Ynez Valley near Sanford and Benedict Vineyard. The first wines are expected to be released in 1999. There are plans are to build the brand to 50,000 cases—split among Chardonnay, Pinot Noir and Syrah—once the new vineyard property begins to produce grapes.

LIPARITA CELLARS (★★★)
Napa Valley
Founded: 1989. **Owner:** Bob Burrows. **Winemaker:** Merry Edwards.

MAJOR WINES: PRICE, CASES, RATING
Cabernet Sauvignon Howell Mountain	
($32, 1,900)	★★★
Chardonnay Howell Mountain	
($24, 1,400)	★★★
Merlot Howell Mountain	
($30, 1,500)	★★★

WINERY DATA
Case Production: 9,500. **Varietals Purchased:** Cabernet Sauvignon (Howell Mountain, Napa Valley, Spring Mountain), Chardonnay (Carneros, Dry Creek), Merlot (Carneros, Napa Valley, Sonoma Valley).

San Franciscan Robert Burrows revived this 80-acre vineyard and old winery on Howell Mountain, selling part of his crop to Chateau Montelena, Peter Michael and others over the years. Beginning in 1987, he began making small lots of Chardonnay, followed a few years later by Cabernet and Merlot, but after the 1996 harvest he sold the property to Kendall-Jackson, which uses the grapes for its vineyard-designated wines under the Lokoya label. Overall, the Liparita wines have been both distinctive and well made, with character, depth and complexity. Without a vineyard to rely on, though, changes appear imminent.

TASTING NOTES

CABERNET SAUVIGNON HOWELL MOUNTAIN (★★★): True-to-form Howell Mountain Cabernet, with its density and chewy tannins, but also some polish and finesse.
1995: Tight, with a firm cedary edge to the ripe plum and berry-laced fruit, turning elegant and rich on the finish. **88**
1994: Tightly wound, with an austere, earthy band of currant, spice, cedar, coffee, sage and wild berry flavors, turning deep and complex on the finish. **93**
1993: Vibrant, with rich, earthy currant, tar and cedary oak flavors; a touch of green olive weaves itself into the tannic finish. **88**
1992: Earthy, with a wild berry- and cherry-flavored edge to the firm tannins. **84**
1991: Compact and a bit rustic, with an earthy, leathery edge to the tannic currant and mineral flavors. **86**
1990: Smooth and flavorful, a dense, chewy wine that's packed with currant, anise and black cherry flavors. **88**

CHARDONNAY HOWELL MOUNTAIN (★★★): Improving; there were some impressive wines in 1993 and 1994 as well.
1996: Perfumed and floral, with flinty mint and mineral notes, hints of pear, and grapefruit and citrus flavors that linger on the finish. **88**
1995: A touch earthy, with a flinty, mineral and anise edge to the pear and apple notes. This tightly-wound young wine could stand some short-term cellaring to soften it up a bit. **89**

MERLOT HOWELL MOUNTAIN (★★★): Very good. Typically crisp and fruity, with austere but well mannered tannins.
1995: Crisp and lean, with spicy, cedary oak and hints of currant, anise, plum and berry flavors that linger on the finish. **88**
1994: Tight and focused, with a complex core of black cherry, currant, anise, cedar and spice flavors, turning tannic and offering notes of coffee on the finish. **90**
1993: Serves up an elegant, pretty core of ripe cherry, berry and spice flavors. **88**

LITTLE BILLY see **W.H. SMITH WINES**

LITTORAI (★★★–★★★★)
St. Helena, Napa Valley
Founded: 1993. **Owner:** Heidi & Ted Lemon. **Winemaker:** Ted Lemon.

MAJOR WINES: PRICE, CASES, RATING

Chardonnay Russian River Mays Canyon ($34, 350)	★★★★
Chardonnay Sonoma Coast Occidental ($34, 300)	★★★★
Pinot Noir Anderson Valley One Acre ($34, 350)	★★★
Pinot Noir Anderson Valley Savoy Vineyard ($34, 200)	★★★
Pinot Noir Sonoma Coast Hirsch Vineyard ($34, 350)	★★★

WINERY DATA
Case Production: 1,600. **Vineyard Designations:** Hirsch Vineyard (Pinot Noir), Savoy Vineyard (Pinot Noir). **Varietals Purchased:** Chardonnay (Russian River Valley, Sonoma Coast), Pinot Noir (Sonoma Coast, Anderson Valley).

After earning an enology degree from the University of Dijon, Ted Lemon went to work for a number of domaines in Burgundy, among them Domaine Dujac and Domaine Guy Roulot; while at the latter, he became the first American to manage an estate. He returned to the U.S. in 1992, and signed on to work with several wineries, including Robert Pecota and Chateau Woltner, both as a consultant and as a hands-on winemaker.

In 1993, Ted and his wife, Heidi, founded Littorai with a focus on coastal vineyards planted to Chardonnay and Pinot Noir. Since starting their winery, the Lemons have added various properties to their lineup, including land in Anderson Valley and Sonoma County. At this stage, both of the wines are very well made, with Chardonnay holding a quality edge over Pinot Noir, though both should be on your shopping list.

TASTING NOTES

CHARDONNAY RUSSIAN RIVER MAYS CANYON (★★★★): Lots of ripe, bold, creamy flavors.
1995: Rich and creamy with layers of fig, pear, vanilla, and hazelnut. Finishes complex and concentrated. **91**

CHARDONNAY SONOMA COAST OCCIDENTAL (★★★)
1995: Complex, with a range of ripe pear, citrus, fig and melon and pretty notes of spicy, toasty oak. **90**
1994: Lots of ripe, juicy Chardonnay flavors, with tiers of honey, pear, spice and citrus framed by toasty oak. **92**

PINOT NOIR SONOMA COAST HIRSCH VINEYARD (★★★): Its lean and earthy qualities are typical of what this vineyard sometimes yields.
1995: Tart, lean and earthy, this wine struggles to find a focus; finishes with stemmy, coarse, tealike tannins. **83**
1994: Lean and earthy, with a tightly wound, trim band of dried cherry, wild berry, spice and sage. Finishes with crisp, firm tannins. Shows more depth and concentration with aeration. **88**

PINOT NOIR VARIOUS BOTTLINGS (★★★): The 1995 Anderson Valley One Acre (87 points) was simple, with pleasant dried cherry, herb and berry flavors. The 1995 Anderson Valley Savoy Vineyard (87) leaned toward tart cherry and berry flavors.

LIVINGSTON VINEYARDS (★★★★)
Rutherford, Napa Valley
Founded: 1984. **Owner:** John & Diane Livingston.
Winemaker: John Kongsgaard. **Second Label:** H.W. Helms.

MAJOR WINES: PRICE, CASES, RATING

Cabernet Sauvignon Napa Valley	
Stanley's Selection	
($24, 2,000)	★★
Cabernet Sauvignon Rutherford	
Moffett Vineyard	
($40, 1,400)	★★★★
Chardonnay Napa Valley	
($40, 500)	★★★★
Sangiovese Sonoma County	
($20, 300)	★★★

ALSO PRODUCED
Gemstone Vineyard Napa Valley ($36, 1,000); Syrah Napa Valley Mitchell Vineyard ($20, 800.

WINERY DATA
Case Production: 6,000. **Acres Owned:** 10 acres in Rutherford. **Varietals by Acre:** Cabernet Franc (1.5 acres), Cabernet Sauvignon (8), Sangiovese (0.5). **Vineyard Designations:** Moffett Vineyard (Cabernet Sauvignon), Gemstone Vineyard

(Cabernet Sauvignon), Mitchell Vineyard (Syrah). **Varietals Purchased:** Cabernet Franc (Napa Valley), Cabernet Sauvignon (Napa Valley), Chardonnay (Napa Valley), Merlot (Napa Valley), Pinot Noir (Napa Valley), Syrah (Napa Valley).

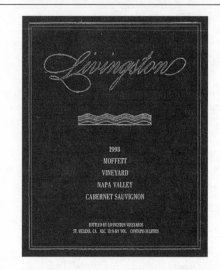

John and Diane Livingston own the 10-acre Moffett Vineyard in West Rutherford, from which they produce their Livingston Cabernet from vines originally planted in 1969. A second Cabernet called Stanley's Selection comes from purchased grapes grown throughout the valley. The winery has branched out to produce Chardonnay, Sangiovese and Syrah, and has hired John Kongsgaard as winemaker, a move that should raise the already high level of quality another notch. Worth buying and collecting.

TASTING NOTES

CABERNET SAUVIGNON RUTHERFORD MOFFETT VINEYARD (★★★★): Dark, ripe and intense, with loads of flavor and full-bodied tannins. Can be dramatic, as it was in 1994, or slightly off the pace. Worth collecting, as it ages well.
1995: Crisp and austere, with bright, ripe black cherry, plum and currant notes that slowly fan out along with the tannins on the finish. **89**
1994: Serves up a wonderful core of deep, concentrated, earthy currant, plum and cherry flavors that turn smooth and silky on the finish. **94**
1993: Firm, compact and tightly wound; cedar, anise and tar accents join cherry and currant flavors and beefy tannins. **89**
1992: Marked by strong, toasty oak flavors and hard tannins with a tight core of spicy currant flavors. **89**
1991: Very ripe and decadent, with earthy black cherry

and currant flavors. Finishes with gritty tannins and a mineral edge. **90**

1990: Ripe, supple and elegant, with layers of complex, concentrated cedar, black cherry, currant and plum flavors. Has a wonderful sense of harmony and finesse, finishing with chewy tannins and a mineral edge. **92**

1989: Despite an earthy edge it's elegant, with cedar, anise and spice notes adding complexity. Firmly tannic. **87**

1988: Nicely focused around ripe cherry, plum, currant, anise, sage and cedar notes. It's mild, supple and well balanced. **88**

1987: Dark, ripe, complex and concentrated, with a solid core of minty currant, anise, cedar and spice flavors and chewy tannins. **94**

1986: Tight, firm and intense; lean and tannic, but the earthy currant and oak flavors are deftly balanced, with fine depth and an elegant aftertaste. **89**

1985: A good but not exceptional 1985, with subdued currant and black cherry notes that have a cedary edge, but it lacks focus. **85**

1984: This remains a wonderfully ripe, fleshy and supple wine with bright, rich black cherry and currant flavors that are youthful and vibrant. The tannins are supple yet firm. **92**

CABERNET SAUVIGNON NAPA VALLEY STANLEY'S SELECTION (★★): Usually young and hard-edged, though the 1995 (88 points) was well crafted, with ripe plum- cherry- and berry-laced flavors. Has room for improvement.

CHARDONNAY NAPA VALLEY (★★★★): New winemaker Kongsgaard excels with this variety, and the 1996 (92 points) was rich and flavorful. Worth watching.

LOCKWOOD VINEYARD (★★★)
Monterey County
Founded: 1981. **Owner:** R. Paul Toeppen, Phil Johnson, Butch Lindley, John Handel, Steve Pessagno. **Winemaker:** Stephen L. Pessagno. **Second Label:** Shale Ridge.

MAJOR WINES: PRICE, CASES, RATING
Cabernet Sauvignon Monterey
($16, 11,637) ★★★
Cabernet Sauvignon Monterey
Partners' Reserve
($22, 234) ★★★
Chardonnay Monterey
($16, 18,293) ★★★
Chardonnay Monterey Partners'
Reserve
($21, 1993) ★★★
Merlot Monterey
($17, 15,000) ★★★
Merlot Monterey Partners' Reserve
($25, 330) ★★★
Pinot Blanc Monterey
($12, 2,500) ★★★
Sangiovese Monterey
($16, 2,300) ★★
Sauvignon Blanc Monterey
($10, 7,202) ★★★
Syrah Monterey
($16, 1,650) ★★★

WINERY DATA
Case Production: 85,000. **Acres Owned:** 1,656 acres in Monterey County. **Varietals by Acre:** Cabernet Franc (47 acres), Cabernet Sauvignon (498), Chardonnay (700), Merlot (247), Pinot Blanc (48), Refosco (27), Sangiovese (12), Sauvignon Blanc (60), Syrah (17). **Varietals Purchased:** Cabernet Franc (Monterey County).

Since the mid-1980's, Lockwood has been a consistent producer of well-made, moderately priced, (usually) well-oaked wines, sourced from its 1,656-acre vineyard in Monterey County. The Cabernet and the Merlot are typically rich, ripe, smooth, well-oaked and full of fruit flavors. The 1995 Cabernet Partners' Reserve hit 90 points, with supple tannins and lots of pretty fruit flavors. Chardonnay also carries rich oak flavors, along with full-bodied apricot, honey and pineapple notes, while the Chardonnay Partners' Reserve shows that this grape can excel in this area. Syrah is a promising addition; like the other reds, it features smooth, oak-laced flavors of plum and wild berry. A floral, herb and citrus-tinged Sauvignon Blanc, a crisp minerally Pinot Blanc, and a Sangiovese (which has yet to prove itself) complete the portfolio.

TASTING NOTES

CABERNET SAUVIGNON MONTEREY PARTNERS' RESERVE (★★★): Can hit the high notes, as it did with the 1994 (88 points) and 1995 (90), but it also struggles to ripen in cooler years.

CHARDONNAY MONTEREY PARTNERS' RESERVE (★★★): Steadily improving; well oaked, with two 90-point wines in 1994 and 1995, both of which featured bold, full-blown Chardonnay flavors.

LOGAN see ROBERT TALBOTT VINEYARDS

J. LOHR WINERY (★★–★★★)
Santa Clara County
Founded: 1974. **Owner:** Jerry Lohr. **Winemaker:** Jeff Meier. **Second Label:** Cypress.

MAJOR WINES: PRICE, CASES, RATING

Cabernet Sauvignon Paso Robles	
Seven Oaks	
($15, 50,000)	★★
Chardonnay Monterey County Riverstone	
($14, 50,000)	★★★★
Pinot Blanc Monterey County	
October Night	
($14, 3,000)	★★★
Syrah Paso Paso Robles Southridge	
($14, 4,000)	★★★
Valdiguié Monterey County Wild Flower	
($9, 13,000)	★★★
White Riesling Monterey County	
Bay Mist	
($9, 18,000)	★★★
Cypress Cabernet Sauvignon Central Coast	
($11, 40,000)	★★
Cypress Chardonnay California	
($10, 40,000)	★★

ALSO PRODUCED
Cabernet Sauvignon Paso Robles Hilltop Vineyard ($30, 3,000); Chardonnay Arroyo Seco Arroyo Vista Vineyard ($23, 3,000); Merlot Paso Robles Los Osos ($10, 40,000).

WINERY DATA
Case Production: 350,000. **Acres Owned:** 1,231 acres (536 in Arroyo Seco, 34 in Napa Valley, 661 in Paso Robles). **Varietals by Acre:** Cabernet Franc (15 acres), Cabernet Sauvignon (514), Chardonnay (409), Merlot (118), Petit Verdot (5), Pinot Blanc (47), Sangiovese (10), Syrah (32), Valdiguié (30), White Riesling (50). **Varietals Purchased:** Cabernet Sauvignon (Paso Robles), Merlot (Paso Robles), Zinfandel (Lodi).

Jerry Lohr had a successful career in construction and development before turning to grape growing and winemaking in Monterey. After planting a 280-acre vineyard in the Greenfield area, he and his then-partner, Bernie Turgeon, purchased an old brewery in San Jose, which they converted for winemaking purposes. After a spotty first decade, the winery has expanded its vineyard holdings to 1,231 acres, with a full offering of most major varietals. The Riverstone Chardonnay is the winery's best effort.

TASTING NOTES

CHARDONNAY MONTEREY COUNTY RIVERSTONE (★★★★): Typically displays wonderful fruit and balance. **1996:** Shows off toasty, smoky aromas and flavors, with fresh, ripe pear, peach, nectarine and tangerine flavors. Elegant and flavorful. **88**
1995: A wonderful balancing act, with a core of juicy pear, apple, pineapple and citrus with toasty vanilla oak shadings that keeps the flavors fresh and lively. **90**
1994: Complex, with a pretty array of elegant pear, spice, honey and hazelnut, picking up a pretty smoky, toasted oak edge on the finish. Combines richness with depth, concentration and finesse. **90**

LOKOYA (★★★–★★★★★)
Oakville, Napa Valley
Founded: 1995. **Owner:** Jess Jackson. **Winemaker:** Marco DiGiulio.

MAJOR WINES: PRICE, CASES, RATING

Cabernet Sauvignon Diamond Mountain	
($100, 350)	★★★
Cabernet Sauvignon Howell Mountain	
($60, 25)	★★★
Cabernet Sauvignon Mount Veeder	
($100, 1,500)	★★★★
Cabernet Sauvignon Rutherford	
($100, 350)	★★★★★

WINERY DATA
Case Production: 2,200. **Acres Owned:** 137 acres (68 on Howell Mountain, 69 on Mount Veeder). **Varietals by Acre:** Cabernet Sauvignon (91 acres), Chardonnay (8), Merlot (38). **Varietals Purchased:** Cabernet Sauvignon (Atlas Peak, Diamond Mountain, Oakville, Rutherford), Merlot (Diamond Mountain, Howell Mountain).

This is one of Jess Jackson's Artisan & Estates brands that was launched in the mid-1990s, focusing in this case on vineyard- and/or appellation-oriented Cabernet Sauvignons and Merlots. Greg Upton was the original winemaker here, but after his his untimely death in 1997, Marco DiGiulio stepped into this position. Also involved with this winery is Charles Thomas, a former winemaker at Robert Mondavi who has been instrumental in working with Kendall-Jackson's specialty brands.

The winery's aim is to make great wines from either winery-owned or purchased grapes. So far, this goal has been realized: the initial wines—three Cabernets, one each from Mount Veeder, Rutherford and Howell Mountain—were all excellent. There is also now a Diamond Mountain Cabernet, and there are plans to add Merlot when quality merits individual bottling.

Lokoya owns 137 acres in Napa Valley, 68 acres on Howell Mountain (the vineyard formerly known as Liparita Vineyard) and 69 acres on Mount Veeder (formerly known as Veeder Peak Vineyard, once owned by William Hill). The Rutherford grapes are purchased from Andy Beckstoffer, and grown on the east side of the valley near Caymus. Lokoya also buys grapes from Norm Kiken of Reverie on Diamond Mountain. Definitely worth watching, though prices were very high for the first releases.

TASTING NOTES

CABERNET SAUVIGNON DIAMOND MOUNTAIN (★★★): Another very intense and tightly framed Cabernet; the 1995 (87 points) may just need some time in the bottle to show more complexity. From Norm Kiken's Reverie Vineyard.

CABERNET SAUVIGNON HOWELL MOUNTAIN (★★★): From the vineyard formerly known as Liparita comes this tightly wound 1995 (88 points); firmly tannic but quite an expressive Cabernet. Worth watching.

CABERNET SAUVIGNON MOUNT VEEDER (★★★): Tamed the tannins quite nicely in the first wine; in the 1995 (92 points), the chunky, chewy style of this appellation was unmistakable. Worth collecting.

CABERNET SAUVIGNON RUTHERFORD (★★★★★): The debut from 1995 (97 points) was among the best of the vintage: broad, ripe and juicy, with lush currant, black cherry, wild berry and plummy Cabernet flavors. Worth watching, to see if it gets even better. Made from the original Veeder Peak property, an early source of William Hill's best Cabernets from the late 1970 and early 1980s.

LOLONIS (★★★)
Redwood Valley, Mendocino County
Founded: 1982. **Owner:** Lolonis Family. **Winemaker:** John Clews.

MAJOR WINES: PRICE, CASES, RATING

Cabernet Sauvignon Redwood Valley ($15, 2,500)	★★
Cabernet Sauvignon Redwood Valley Private Reserve ($24, 2,000)	★★★
Chardonnay Redwood Valley Private Reserve ($23, 900)	★★★
Fumé Blanc Redwood Valley ($11, 6,000)	★★★
Merlot Mendocino County ($22, 2,000)	★★★
Petite Sirah Mendocino County Orpheus ($18, 900)	★★★
Zinfandel Redwood Valley ($14, 3,000)	★★★
Zinfandel Redwood Valley Private Reserve ($19, 1,000)	★★★

ALSO PRODUCED
Chardonnay Redwood Valley ($14, 5,000).

WINERY DATA
Case Production: 25,000. **Acres Owned:** 320 acres in Redwood Valley. **Varietals by Acre:** Cabernet Sauvignon, Chardonnay, Merlot, Petite Sirah, Pinot Gris, Sauvignon Blanc, Valdiguié, Viognier, Zinfandel.

The Lolonis family has been growing grapes in Mendocino since 1920, selling to customers such as Fetzer, Parducci and now Steele Wines. Lolonis produces 25,000 cases a year, focusing on Cabernet, Chardonnay, Petite Sirah and Zinfandel. The 1996 Private Reserve Chardonnay (89 points) was an appealing wine with ripe citrus, pear, and apple flavors. The Zinfandels are usually full of raspberry and plum nuances in high-octane style. Quality has consistently been good, due in part to consulting enologist Jed Steele.

TASTING NOTES

ZINFANDEL REDWOOD VALLEY PRIVATE RESERVE (★★★): Inconsistent, but can hit the mark with its pepper and raspberry flavors.
1996: Lots of ripe, spicy cherry, wild berry, plum, sage, tar and anise. It's elegant, complex, and rich in flavor without being heavy. 88
1995: Shows off a range of ripe Zinfandel flavors, with tar, earth and sage flavors built around the core of ripe plum and wild berry flavors. Finishes with a good length. 87
1994: Dark, ripe, rich and spicy, this is a high octane style with layers of juicy plum, black cherry, raspberry, a hint of port and lots of sage and spice. Finishes off with a burst of fruit and just the right amount of tannin. 92
1993: Funky, with earthy flavors and a spicy cedary edge, picking up some odd nuances on the finish. 79
1992: Appealing for its ripe, bright cherry and berry flavors, hints of anise and spice enhancing the fruit. Finishes with firm tannins. 88
1990: Intense and focused, with bright pepper, plum and raspberry aromas and flavors that capture the essence of Zinfandel. 89

LONETREE (★★★)
Mendocino County
Founded: 1994. **Owner:** John Scharffenberger & Casey Hartlip. **Winemaker:** Casey Hartlip.

MAJOR WINES: PRICE, CASES, RATING
Sangiovese Mendocino
($15, 650) ★★★
Syrah Mendocino
($14, 650) ★★★
Zinfandel Mendocino
($15, 650) ★★★

WINERY DATA
Case Production: 3,000. **Acres Owned:** 75 acres in Mendocino. **Varietals by Acre:** Cabernet Sauvignon (16 acres), Chardonnay (4), Petite Syrah (15), Sangiovese (8), Syrah (12), Zinfandel (20).

John Scharffenberger started sparkling wine producer Scharffenberger Cellars (re-named Pacific Echo and now owned by LVMH of France), before branching out to start the Lonetree label in 1994 with partner-winemaker Casey Hartlip. Syrah, Sangiovese and Zinfandel are made from grapes grown on the partners' 75-acre Eaglepoint Ranch vineyard in Mendocino County, which Scharffenberger has been farming since 1974. While most of their grapes are sold to other wineries, including Fetzer and Hidden Cellars, Hartlip and Scharffenberger plan to keep enough to produce 3,000 cases a year.

All of the wines are well made, but Syrah and Zinfandel have been the most successful. The 1996 Zinfandel (88 points) was marked by spicy currant, blackberry and anise flavors, while the plush, rich 1996 Syrah (90) showed earthy cherry, blackberry and herb notes. Worth watching.

LONG VINEYARDS (★★★–★★★★★)
Napa Valley
Founded: 1977. **Owner:** Bob & Zelma Long. **Winemaker:** Sandi Belcher.

MAJOR WINES: PRICE, CASES, RATING
Cabernet Sauvignon Napa Valley
($40, 400) ★★★
Chardonnay Napa Valley
($30, 2,000) ★★★★★
Johannisberg Riesling Late Harvest
Napa Valley Botrytis
($20, 400) ★★★★

Pinot Grigio Sonoma & Napa Valleys
   ($15, 100) ★★★

Sangiovese Sonoma County
   Seghesio Vineyard
   ($20, 400) ★★★

Sauvignon Blanc Sonoma & Napa Valleys
   ($15, 800) ★★★

WINERY DATA

Case Production: 5,000. **Acres Owned:** 17 acres in Napa Valley. **Varietals by Acre:** Cabernet (2 acres), Chardonnay (12), Riesling (3). **Vineyard Designations:** Seghesio Vineyard (Sangiovese). **Varietals Purchased:** Pinot Grigio (Carneros), Sangiovese (Sonoma County), Sauvignon Blanc (Napa Valley, Sonoma County).

Bob and Zelma Long founded this winery in the hills east of Napa, with Long's parents as financial backers. The two later divorced, but they have remained partners, producing 5,000 cases of wine each year. The lineup consists of Cabernet, Chardonnay, Late Harvest Johannisberg Riesling, a clean, crisp Sauvignon Blanc from Carneros, a lovely Pinot Grigio made from purchased grapes, and a Sangiovese hailing from Sonoma County's Seghesio Vineyard. Long Vineyards is located on Pritchard Hill near Chappellet. Their Cabernet grapes come from a tiny 30-year-old experimental vineyard in Oakville near Robert Mondavi and Martha's Vineyard. Credit long-time winemaker Sandi Belcher with the high quality and deliberate styles of these wines.

TASTING NOTES

CABERNET SAUVIGNON NAPA VALLEY (★★★): Elegant and supple; very complex and fruity upon release, with mild tannins. Early vintages have not aged that well, though, so it's best to drink them early on.
1995: A complex interplay of toasty, cedary oak and ripe cherry, currant and plum flavors, with an especially supple, silky texture. **90**
1994: Serves up an appealing band of ripe cherry, earth, coffee, chocolate and wild berry flavors and smooth tannins. **90**
1993: A tannic wine with strong wood flavors, but the raisin and plum notes are hot and unbalanced. **84**
1990: Thick, dense and tannic, with rich currant, chocolate, mint and berry flavors that spread out on the palate. A big, ripe, opulent wine. **89**

1986: Mature; losing its once delicious core of cherry and currant flavors. **86**

CHARDONNAY NAPA VALLEY (★★★★): Usually sleek, elegant and polished, with a creamy texture. Remarkably fine and consistent.
1996: Crisp and flinty, with fresh, lively pear, melon and apple fruit and a hint of citrus that lingers on the finish. **91**
1995: Bright and lively, with a distinct hazelnut edge to the ripe, complex pear-, fig- and apricot-laced flavors, turning elegant on the finish. **91**
1994: Clean, ripe and refreshing, with a lively, elegant core of ripe apple, pear, spice and honey notes. **91**

JOHANNISBERG RIESLING NAPA VALLEY BOTRYTIS (★★★★): Deliciously fruity, sweet and rich; the 1996 (92 points) was another winner.

RICHARD LONGORIA WINES (★★★)
Santa Ynez Valley, Santa Barbara County
Founded: 1982. **Owner:** Rick & Diana Longoria.
Winemaker: Rick Longoria.

MAJOR WINES: PRICE, CASES, RATING

Cabernet Franc Santa Ynez Valley
   Blues Cuvée
   ($21, 450) ★★

Chardonnay Santa Ynez Valley
   Santa Rita Cuvée
   ($25, 900) ★★★

Merlot Santa Ynez Valley
   ($23, 650) ★★★

Pinot Noir Santa Maria Valley
   Bien NacidoVineyard
   ($32, 470) ★★★

WINERY DATA

Case Production: 2,700. **Acres Owned:** 7.75 acres in Santa Ynez Valley. **Varietals by Acre:** Pinot Noir (7.75 acres). **Vineyard Designations:** Bien Nacido Vineyard (Pinot Noir). **Varietals Purchased:** Cabernet Franc (Santa Ynez Valley), Chardonnay (Santa Ynez Valley), Merlot (Santa Ynez Valley), Pinot Noir (Santa Maria Valley), Syrah (Paso Robles, Santa Barbara County).

Richard Longoria has a long track record with Santa Barbara winegrowing, having done stints at J. Carey and Gainey Vineyard through 1997. Longoria and his wife, Diana, make about 2,700 cases a year of Cabernet Franc, Chardonnay, Merlot and Pinot Noir on their own. Most of their wines are made from purchased grapes, virtually all of which come from the Santa Ynez Valley, with exception of the Pinot Noir, which comes from Bien Nacido and occasionally Sanford & Benedict.

The Longorias just planted a small Pinot Noir vineyard, and have plans to add a Spanish-inspired red in the future. While Longoria on his own has yet to make better wines than he did at Gainey, in time he should be able to match that excellence. Worth watching and buying.

TASTING NOTES

CHARDONNAY SANTA YNEZ VALLEY SANTA RITA CUVÉE (★★★): The 1996 (91 points) is the best yet from this vineyard; ripe, tight and complex, its flavors include green apple, pear, melon and spice. Worth watching.

MERLOT SANTA YNEZ VALLEY (★★★): One of the better reds from this area, which typically yields overly vegetal wines. The 1995 (87 points) and 1994 (88) were both very well made.

PINOT NOIR SANTA MARIA VALLEY BIEN NACIDO VINEYARD (★★★): Usually smooths out the rougher edges sometimes found in wines from this vineyard, and can sometimes show the racier style of this grape.
1996: Smooth and polished, with a splash of vegetal flavor joining the plum and black cherry fruit. **87**
1995: Shows off flashes of pepper and spice, with an earthy, yet elegant core of beefy herb and plum flavors. **88**
1994: Smooth and harmonious, with smoky, toasty oak flavors leading to a trim band of currant and berry notes. **86**

LORENZA-LAKE (★★★)
Napa Valley
Founded: 1992. **Owner:** Michael Ouellette. **Winemaker:** Mitch Cosentino.

MAJOR WINES: PRICE, CASES, RATING
Petite Sirah Napa Valley
  ($25, 120)   ★★★

Zinfandel Napa Valley
  ($17, 590)   ★★★

ALSO PRODUCED
Sauvignon Blanc Napa Valley ($15, 600); Zinfandel California ($12, 240).

WINERY DATA
Case Production: 1,600. **Varietals Purchased:** Petite Sirah (St. Helena), Zinfandel (St. Helena).

Restaurateur Michael Ouellette manages Mustard's Grill in Yountville north of Dominus. He started his winery in 1992, calling it Blockheadia Ringnosii, but dropped that name in favor of Lorenza-Lake. Ouellette makes some tasty old-vine Petite Sirah and Zinfandel from grapes grown in St. Helena; the quality of both has been high. Sauvignon Blanc and a California appellation Zinfandel are new to the lineup.

TASTING NOTES

PETITE SIRAH NAPA VALLEY (★★★): New for 1996 (88 points); dark, dense and chewy, with glimpses of wild berry and raspberry.

ZINFANDEL NAPA VALLEY (★★★): Limited production; once from Niebaum-Coppola, but now from St. Helena. The 1996 (88 points) was ripe, with complex blackberry and raspberry flavors.

LUNA VINEYARDS (★★★)
Napa Valley
Founded: 1995. **Owner:** George Vare & Mike Moone. **Winemaker:** John Kongsgaard.

MAJOR WINES: PRICE, CASES, RATING
Merlot Napa Valley
  ($28, 800)   ★★★
Sangiovese Napa Valley
  ($18, 1,600)   ★★★

ALSO PRODUCED
Pinot Grigio Napa Valley ($18, 1,700).

WINERY DATA

Case Production: 20,000. **Acres Owned:** 62 acres in Napa Valley. **Varietals by Acre:** Merlot (20 acres), Pinot Grigio (42). **Varietals Purchased:** Merlot (Napa Valley), Pinot Grigio (Napa Valley), Sangiovese (Napa Valley).

This venture brings together a group of long-time winemakers. George Vare and Mike Moone have nearly 50 years of wine industry experience between them; Vare was formerly a consultant, and Moone used to head Beringer Wine Estates. Yet another vet, winemaker John Kongsgaard—a Napa native and former winemaker for Newton—heads this winery, which is housed in the former St. Andrews Winery building on Silverado Trail north of the city of Napa.

Even though Chardonnay is Kongsgaard's specialty (see Kongsgaard entry), this winery is aiming at alternative styles with its Pinot Grigio, Sangiovese and Merlot. So far, Merlot and Sangiovese have hit the market, with the 1996 Sangiovese (87 points) offering bright cherry, berry and strawberry flavors. Worth watching.

LYETH (★★)

California
Founded: 1993. **Owner:** Boisset Wines U.S.A. **Winemaker:** William Arbios.

MAJOR WINES: PRICE, CASES, RATING

Cabernet Sauvignon California	
($14, 10,000)	★★
Chardonnay North Coast	
($14, 6,000)	★★
Meritage Red Napa Valley	
($14, 12,000)	★★
Meritage Red Napa Valley Reserve	
($14, 1,000)	★★
Meritage White Sonoma County	
($10, 12,000)	★★

WINERY DATA

Case Production: 40,000. **Varietals Purchased:** Cabernet Franc (Napa Valley, North Coast), Cabernet Sauvignon (Napa Valley, North Coast), Chardonnay (North Coast), Merlot (North Coast), Sauvignon Blanc (North Coast), Sémillon (North Coast).

Founder Munro "Chip" Lyeth advocated Bordeaux blends for his red and white table wines and enjoyed a string of successful vintages before he died in a tragic plane crash. After that the winery struggled, first being acquired by Vintech, which failed financially. The vineyards in Alexander Valley were then sold to Gallo, the winery went to Silver Oak and the brand was sold to Jean-Claude Boisset, who is making Cabernet and Chardonnay under the Lyeth label at another location. Boisset has held the quality of the Lyeth brand above the other negociant-style brands in his portfolio, but recent tastings suggest that it may now be slipping. The 1995 Cabernet Sauvignon California (78 points) was awkward and simple with woody flavors. Not much to look forward to.

LYNMAR (★★★)

Russian River Valley, Sonoma County
Founded: 1980. **Owner:** Lynn & Mara Fritz. **Winemaker:** Daniel Moore.

MAJOR WINES: PRICE, CASES, RATING

Chardonnay Russian River Valley Estate	
Quail Hill Vineyard	
($24, 800)	★★★
Pinot Noir Russian River Valley Estate	
Quail Hill Vineyard	
($30, 2,500)	★★★
Pinot Noir Russian River Valley Estate	
Quail Hill Vineyard Reserve	
($45, 400)	★★★

ALSO PRODUCED

Chardonnay Russian River Valley Estate Quail Hill Vineyard Reserve ($35, 200); Pinot Noir Russian River Valley Estate ($20, 1,000); Pinot Noir Russian River Valley Estate Five Sisters ($70, 100).

WINERY DATA

Case Production: 5,000. **Acres Owned:** 45 acres in Russian River Valley. **Varietals by Acre:** Chardonnay (25 acres), Pinot Noir (20). **Vineyard Designations:** Quail Hill Vineyard (Chardonnay, Pinot Noir).

In recent years Lynmar has distinguished itself with some good-to-very-good—occasionally outstanding—Chardonnays and Pinot Noirs. While the wines have not yet established a solid track record or consistent style, they have improved under new winemaker Daniel Moore. Tending toward a well-oaked style, the Chardonnays are best when focused on pear, apple and melon flavors, as was the case with the 1996 Chardonnay (90 points); however, they are occasionally mired in intensely spicy flavors and bitter notes. The Pinot Noirs are often smooth and rich with plum, cherry and mushroom flavors, but they can also be lean, with a narrow range of flavor. The 1996 Pinot Noir (85) was trim, with dried cherry and leathery nuances, while the 1996 Reserve (87) was more generous, with supple cherry, cola and tea flavors. The 1994 Reserve (91) remains the benchmark for quality, with its smooth, polished core of flavors. A winery to watch.

MacRostie Wines (★★★–★★★★)

Carneros
Founded: 1987. **Owner:** Steven & Thale MacRostie.
Winemaker: Steven MacRostie. **Second Label:** Keltie Brook.

MAJOR WINES: PRICE, CASES, RATING

Chardonnay Carneros ($18, 9,000)	★★★★
Chardonnay Carneros Reserve ($27, 600)	★★★★
Merlot Carneros ($22, 2,000)	★★
Pinot Noir Carneros ($19, 2,000)	★★
Pinot Noir Carneros Reserve ($27, 400)	★★★

WINERY DATA
Case Production: 14,000. **Acres Owned:** 22 acres in Carneros. **Varietals by Acre:** Chardonnay (8 acres), Pinot Noir (11), Syrah (3). **Varietals Purchased:** Cabernet Franc (Carneros), Chardonnay (Carneros), Merlot (Carneros), Pinot Noir (Carneros).

Steve MacRostie spent the first decade of his career as winemaker at Hacienda, where he made some wonderful Chardonnays. In 1987, he started his own his winery. He owns 22 acres in Carneros, and purchases Cabernet Franc, Merlot, Chardonnay and Pinot Noir. His best wines are his Chardonnays, of which he makes a regular

and a reserve bottling. The Merlot and Pinot Noir are both sound, well-made wines.

TASTING NOTES

CHARDONNAY CARNEROS & RESERVE (★★★★): Both the 1995 (91 points) and 1995 Reserve (90) were generous in flavor, with the Reserve a shade more mature tasting.

MERLOT CARNEROS (★★): The 1995 (87 points) offered ripe cherry, tobacco, cedar and spice flavors.

PINOT NOIR CARNEROS (★★) & RESERVE (★★★): Steadily improving, with early vintages a touch earthy. The 1996 (86 points) was crisp, with firm tannins, while the 1995 Reserve (88) was supple and silky, with pretty dried cherry, herb and sage flavors.

MADAME PINOT see MOUNT EDEN VINEYARDS

MADIGAN see WHITE ROCK VINEYARDS

MARCASSIN (★★★★★)

Russian River Valley, Sonoma County
Founded: 1990. **Owner:** Helen Turley & John Wetlaufer.
Winemaker: Helen Turley & John Wetlaufer.

MAJOR WINES: PRICE, CASES, RATING

Chardonnay Alexander Valley Gauer Vineyard Upper Barn ($50, 200)	★★★★★
Chardonnay Carneros Hudson Vineyard E Block ($50, 200)	★★★★★
Chardonnay Sonoma Coast Lorenzo Vineyard ($50, 200)	★★★★★

ALSO PRODUCED
Chardonnay Sonoma Coast Marcassin Vineyard ($NA, 300); Pinot Noir Sonoma Coast Blue Slide Ranch ($NA, 400); Pinot Noir Sonoma Coast Marcassin Vineyard ($NA, 600); Pinot Noir Sonoma Coast Three Sisters Meadow ($NA, 200).

WINERY DATA
Case Production: 2,000. **Acres Owned:** 9 acres in Sonoma Coast. **Varietals by Acre:** Chardonnay (3 acres), Pinot Noir (6). **Vineyard Designations:** Blue Slide Ranch (Pinot Noir), Gauer Vineyard (Chardonnay), Lorenzo Vineyard (Chardonnay), Hudson Vineyard (Chardonnay), Marcassin (Chardonnay, Pinot Noir), Three Sisters (Pinot Noir). **Varietals Purchased:** Chardonnay (Alexander Valley, Carneros, Sonoma Coast), Pinot Noir (Sonoma Coast).

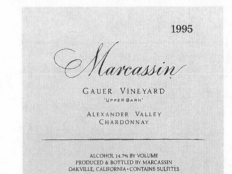

1995

Marcassin

GAUER VINEYARD
'UPPER BARN'

ALEXANDER VALLEY
CHARDONNAY

ALCOHOL 14.7% BY VOLUME
PRODUCED & BOTTLED BY MARCASSIN
OAKVILLE, CALIFORNIA · CONTAINS SULFITES

Helen Turley likes to joke that she's suddenly become an "overnight sensation" after 20 years in the business, but there is indeed some truth to the quip. She began her career as a "cellar rat" for Stonegate. Soon thereafter, she began making some excellent wines for B.R. Cohn and Peter Michael. Turley founded her own brand, Marcassin (which means little wild boar), with her husband, John Wetlaufer, in 1990. The two have since planted a 9-acre vineyard to Chardonnay and Pinot Noir on the Sonoma coast near Fort Ross. Turley is still a busy consultant, counting Bryant Family Vineyard, Martinelli and Pahlmeyer among her current clients.

Turley's formula for success is straightforward: she seeks vineyards that hold crop loads to two tons per acre, cool climates for Chardonnay and Pinot Noir, natural yeast fermentations, judicious use of oak, and minimal handling, including avoiding filtration. Her early success with Chardonnay from Gauer's Upper Barn vineyard and Lorenzo Vineyard near Occidental put her out in front of the pack. She then added Hudson Vineyard in Carneros, which she has since dropped. Her Chardonnays are ultra-rich, ripe and creamy, loaded with deep, complex flavors. Marcassin's case production will never amount to much, even when her densely-spaced vineyard comes into full production. But the quality is very high, and her wines and those of her clients are definitely worth buying.

TASTING NOTES

CHARDONNAY ALEXANDER VALLEY GAUER VINEYARD UPPER BARN (★★★★★): Showcases the exotic, ripe fruitiness of Alexander Valley Chardonnay, adding on layers of flavors.

1996: Enormously complex, rich and elegant, with smoky fig, guava, pineapple, pear and nutmeg scents. A bold, concentrated, long and delicious wine. **96**

1995: Truly exotic; ripe, rich and flavorful, packed with complex, concentrated notes of pear, fig, citrus, anise and spicy oak. **94**

1994: Bold, ripe, ultra-rich and creamy; loaded with tiers of pear, fig and melon flavors, along with echoes of anise and spice. **94**

1993: Ultra-rich and toasty, with bold, complex pear, pineapple, spice, honey and hazelnut flavors that are intense and complex, gaining nuance on the finish. Succeeds with uncommon complexity and depth for the vintage. **92**

1992: Very rich, ripe and creamy, with complex toast, pear, spice and honey notes that are mouth-filling. A no-holds-barred wine that packs in lots of flavor, with a long, full finish. **94**

CHARDONNAY CARNEROS HUDSON VINEYARD E BLOCK (★★★★★): Features the racy, spicy pineapple-tinged flavors of Carneros, plus more layers of complexity.

1996: Smooth, rich and intensely flavored, with a smoky, earthy edge to the ripe pear, flinty mineral and spicy nuances. **94**

1995: Impeccably balanced; smooth, rich and buttery, with a generous core of ripe pear, citrus, tart pineapple and spicy flavors. **93**

1994: A mouthful of ripe pear, grapefruit and lemon flavors framed by toasty, smoky oak and a silky texture. **93**

1993: Smoky and perfumed, with polished honey, pear and butterscotch notes that gain complexity and depth on the finish. Has a sense of harmony and finesse. **92**

CHARDONNAY SONOMA COAST LORENZO VINEYARD (★★★★★): Another tremendous effort, full of ripe, rich, concentrated fruit flavors.

1996: Ultra-rich—the richest of the three Marcassins. Loaded with complex, concentrated pear, fig, anise, toasty oak and spicy flavors; bold and delicious. **96**

1995: A bold, ripe and flavorful style; loaded with spicy anise, creamy pear and vanilla-tinged fruit, turning complex on the finish. **92**

1993: Well oaked, with bold, rich and concentrated tiers of honey, pear and toasty oak flavors that are ripe and well focused, finishing with a long complex aftertaste. **91**
1992: Extremely rich and creamy, with layers of complex pear, spice, honey and butterscotch flavors on a long, full finish. For all its richness, it's wonderfully elegant. **93**

MARIETTA CELLARS (★★)
Geyserville, Sonoma County
Founded: 1980. **Owner:** Chris Bilbro. **Winemaker:** Chris Bilbro.

MAJOR WINES: PRICE, CASES, RATING
Old Vine Red California ($10, 30,000)	★★
Syrah California ($15, 1,900)	★★★
Zinfandel Sonoma County ($15, 6,000)	★★

ALSO PRODUCED
Cabernet Sonoma County ($17, 2,500); Cuvée Alexander Valley Angel ($20, 1,800).

WINERY DATA
Case Production: 40,000. **Acres Owned:** 35 in Alexander Valley. **Varietals by Acre:** Cabernet Sauvignon (10 acres), Merlot (5), Petite Sirah (2), Sangiovese (3), Syrah (4), Zinfandel (11). **Varietals Purchased:** Cabernet Sauvignon (Sonoma), Carignane (California), Gamay (Sonoma), Grenache (Mendocino), Petite Sirah (Sonoma), Syrah (California), Zinfandel (Sonoma).

Chris Bilbro produces well-priced, rustic, flavorful red wines from his 35-acre vineyard in Alexander Valley, with Syrah and Zinfandel the quality leaders. The winery has expanded in recent years, adding 20 acres of vines and doubling its case production, most of which (30,000 cases) goes into the Old Vine Red, a Zinfandel-dominated blend.

MARK WEST (★★–★★★)
Russian River Valley, Sonoma County
Founded: 1974. **Owner:** Dick & Rickie Godwin. **Winemaker:** Kerry Damskey. **Second Label:** Godwin.

MAJOR WINES: PRICE, CASES, RATING
Chardonnay Russian River Valley ($12, 17,000)	★★
Gewürztraminer Russian River Valley ($11, 2,700)	★★
Pinot Noir Russian River Valley ($14, 4,200)	★★
Sauvignon Blanc Russian River Valley ($10, 900)	★★
Godwin Chardonnay Russian River Valley Reserve ($20, 5,000)	★★★

ALSO PRODUCED
Godwin Merlot Alexander Valley Reserve ($20, 5,000).

WINERY DATA
Case Production: 30,000. **Acres Owned:** 199 acres (33 in Alexander Valley, 166 in Russian River Valley). **Varietals by Acre:** Chardonnay (135 acres), Gewürztraminer (13), Merlot (36), Pinot Noir (15). **Varietals Purchased:** Sauvignon Blanc (Russian River Valley).

Bob and Joan Ellis founded this winery and vineyard in 1976 near Mark West Creek, focusing on Chardonnay, Gewürztraminer, Riesling and Pinot Noir, with production peaking at 30,000 cases. The quality of both the Chardonnay and Pinot Noir has ranged from fair to good, although the most recent Chardonnay is more impressive.

The winery has undergone several ownership changes, the most recent taking place in 1994 when it was acquired by the Associated Vintners Group. Plans call for the winery to focus on Chardonnay, Gewürztraminer, Pinot Noir and Sauvignon Blanc, all of which earn a ★★ rating, with the exception of the Godwin Chardonnay Reserve, which rises to the ★★★ mark.

MARKHAM VINEYARDS (★★★–★★★★)
St. Helena, Napa Valley
Founded: 1978. **Owner:** Mercian Corp. **Winemaker:** Michael Beaulac. **Second Label:** Glass Mountain Quarry.

MAJOR WINES: PRICE, CASES, RATING

Cabernet Sauvignon Napa Valley
($20, 15,000) ★★★

Chardonnay Napa Valley
($17, 35,000) ★★★

Chardonnay Napa Valley Reserve
($29, 2,000) ★★★★

Merlot Napa Valley
($19, 50,000) ★★★★

Merlot Napa Valley Reserve
($38, 2,500) ★★★★

Petite Sirah Napa Valley
($18, 2,500) ★★★★

Sauvignon Blanc Napa Valley
($12, 30,000) ★★★

Zinfandel Napa Valley
($18, 2,500) ★★★

WINERY DATA
Case Production: 300,000. **Acres Owned:** 225 acres in Napa Valley. **Varietals by Acre:** Cabernet Franc (10 acres), Cabernet Sauvignon (61), Chardonnay (45), Merlot (80), Muscat Blanc (11), Sauvignon Blanc (15), Sémillon (3). **Varietals Purchased:** Cabernet Franc (Napa), Cabernet Sauvignon (Napa, St. Helena), Chardonnay (Napa, Rutherford), Merlot (Carneros, Napa, Oakville, St. Helena), Petite Sirah (St. Helena), Sauvignon Blanc (Napa, Rutherford, St. Helena), Sauvignon Musque (St. Helena), Sémillon (Napa), Zinfandel (Napa, Rutherford, St. Helena).

In terms of solid winemaking, excellent quality and great value in vineyard-driven wines, Markham is one of California's treasures. Bruce Markham founded this winery in 1977, hiring Bryan del Bondio to run it, and despite an ownership change, del Bondio remains in charge. Markham's old stone winery north of St. Helena was built in 1876 and remodeled in time for the 1978 vintage. In 1988 Markham tired of the wine business and sold it to Sanraku (now Mercian Corp.), Japan's largest winemaker, which proceeded with an extensive remodeling of the facility.

Bruce Markham's legacy lies in the vineyards he acquired, including 61 acres of Cabernet in Yountville next to Napanook and Dominus Estate. Today the winery's vineyard holdings total 225 acres, spread out from Yountville to Calistoga, with the Napa Ranch, near Oak Knoll, devoted primarily to Chardonnay, and both the Calistoga and Yountville ranches planted to Bordeaux varieties. Each of the main wines is produced in significant lots. The reserve wines contribute extra richness to the lineup, and there are some gems, such as Petite Sirah, which add a dimension of intrigue.

TASTING NOTES

CABERNET SAUVIGNON NAPA VALLEY (★★★): Bold, ripe and fruity, with supple currant and black cherry flavors and mild tannins. A few vintages have been sweet beyond ripeness, but the 1994 was wonderful. Hard to beat.
1995: Ripe, with medium-weight currant, black cherry, anise, cedar and spice flavors, finishing with firm, dry tannins. **88**
1994: A wonderful core of ripe, rich currant and black cherry fruit and a supple, polished texture. **92**
1993: Clean and well balanced; a touch simple, with modest cherry and berry flavors that linger on the finish. **86**
1992: Ripe, fruity, supple black cherry, spice and berry notes, picking up a dash of oak and turning complex on the finish. **88**
1991: Spicy, with pretty currant, plum and cherry notes that add complexity and depth. Firmly tannic. **88**
1990: Ripe in flavor and firmly tannic; an opulent wine with spicy, chocolaty plum, berry and currant flavors pushing through the tannins on the finish. **90**
1987: A lighter style, with clean, simple notes of cherry, cedar and berry. **86**
1986: Mature, with a solid frame of ripe, juicy plum and cherry flavors. **87**

CHARDONNAY NAPA VALLEY (★★★): Appealing for early drinking, with a broad range of apple, spice, pear and vanilla flavors. The 1996 (87 points) was smooth and ripe.

CHARDONNAY NAPA VALLEY RESERVE (★★★★): Displays a similar range of flavors similar to those of the standard bottling, but with more concentration.
1995: Smooth, ripe, rich and creamy, with layers of pear, vanilla, fig and melon flavors and a long, rich aftertaste. **92**

MERLOT NAPA VALLEY & RESERVE (★★★★): Among the best: bold, ripe and complex, with supple tannins. Ages well.

1996: Tight and complex, with cherry and wild berry flavors that turn elegant and spicy, finishing with supple tannins. **88**

1995: Lively, ripe up-front fruit flavors, featuring notes of cherry, plum and blackberry; not as complex as previous vintages. **87**

1994: Supple and well balanced, with a zesty, tightly wound core of currant, anise and cedary oak flavors. **88**

Reserve 1994: Rich and flavorful, with tiers of ripe, spicy black cherry, currant, plum and mineral flavors, turning elegant and complex on the finish. **91**

1993: Supple, harmonious and smooth, showing pretty black cherry, plum and currant notes and fleshy tannins. **89**

1992: Ripe and chewy, with chunky black cherry, currant and mineral flavors, finishing with firm tannins and fine length. **88**

1991: Supple and refined, with complex and compact coffee, currant and cedar notes that turn smooth and fan out on the finish. **87**

1990: Bold, ripe and opulent, brimming with rich, complex currant and black cherry flavors that turn smooth and polished. **92**

PETITE SIRAH NAPA VALLEY (★★★★): A welcome addition. From old vines near St. Helena, this is a uniformly ripe and very complex wine. An exceptional value that is worth hunting for.

1995: Floral, with ripe, spicy plum, black cherry, pepper and raspberry, turning smooth and rich on the finish, even with its firm tannins. **92**

1994: Inky dark and spicy, with intense, tannic, tightly wound plummy fruit flavors hung on a very tannic framework. **88**

1993: Dark, firm, rich and tannic, with a spicy mineral edge to the plum and currant flavors. A big, hearty, chewy style that packs in lots of flavor. **90**

SAUVIGNON BLANC NAPA VALLEY (★★★): Usually among the best, with a complex range of citrus, herb, pear and spicy nuances. The 1996 (90 points) showed more richness than the 1997 (88) which was tasted just after bottling. Worth buying.

ZINFANDEL NAPA VALLEY (★★★): New to the mix, but very complex, supple and balanced. Shows this winery knows its vineyard sources.

MARTINELLI VINEYARD (★★★–★★★★★)

Russian River Valley, Sonoma County
Founded: 1987. **Owner:** Lee & Carolyn Martinelli. **Winemaker:** Helen Turley.

MAJOR WINES: PRICE, CASES, RATING

Chardonnay Russian River Valley Gold Ridge ($25, 700)	★★★★★
Chardonnay Sonoma Coast Charles Ranch ($30, 700)	★★★★
Gewürztraminer Russian River Valley Martinelli Vineyard ($14, 500)	★★★
Gewürztraminer Russian River Valley Martinelli Vineyard Dry Select ($18, 100)	★★★
Pinot Noir Russian River Valley Martinelli Vineyard ($30, 500)	★★★
Pinot Noir Russian River Valley Reserve ($38, 400)	★★★
Sauvignon Blanc Russian River Valley Martinelli Vineyard ($14, 700)	★★★
Zinfandel Russian River Valley Jackass Hill ($45, 200)	★★★★
Zinfandel Russian River Valley Jackass Vineyard ($30, 600)	★★★★

ALSO PRODUCED

Muscat Alexandria Russian River Valley Martinelli Vineyard Jackass Hill ($18, 100); Pinot Noir Sonoma Coast Blue Slide Ranch ($45, 75); Zinfandel Russian River Valley Louisa y Giuseppe ($25, 75).

WINERY DATA

Case Production: 6,000. **Acres Owned:** 206 acres in Russian River Valley and Sonoma Coast. **Varietals by Acre:** Chardonnay (115 acres), Gewürztraminer (15), Muscat Alexandria (1), Pinot Noir (35), Sauvignon Blanc (14), Syrah (4), Zinfandel (22). **Vineyard Designations:** Blue Slide Ranch (Pinot Noir), Charles Ranch (Chardonnay), Jackass Vineyard (Zinfandel), Martinelli Vineyard (Gewürztraminer, Pinot Noir, Sauvignon Blanc).

The Martinellis have been grapegrowers in Russian River since 1905. They preside over 206 acres of vines, composed mostly of Chardonnay (115 acres), with smaller parcels of Pinot Noir (35 acres), Gewürztraminer, Sauvignon Blanc and Zinfandel. The property is best known for its Zinfandel; Williams & Selyem Winery produced a hearty Zinfandel from these vineyards for a decade. In 1987, the winery began making small lots of Zinfandel from the Jackass Vineyard (and now Jackass Hill—a small section of Jackass Vineyard—as well), along with Chardonnay and Sauvignon Blanc. Helen Turley (of Marcassin) is consulting, and the wines have been riper, richer and fuller-bodied in recent vintages. This is definitely a work in progress. Worth watching and buying.

TASTING NOTES

CHARDONNAY RUSSIAN RIVER VALLEY GOLD RIDGE (★★★★★): A pure, delicious, bold, ripe Chardonnay. A major turnaround.
1995: Smooth, ripe, complex and harmonious, with layers of fig, melon, apricot and pear, turning spicy and oaky on the finish. **93**
1994: Very ripe, rich and full-bodied, with tiers of pear, fig, honey and melon flavors that linger on the finish. **92**

CHARDONNAY SONOMA COAST CHARLES RANCH (★★★★)
1995: Complex, with ripe, intense, concentrated pear, spice, melon and fig flavors, turning elegant and seamless on the finish, where a hint of tangerine adds dimension. **91**

GEWÜRZTRAMINER RUSSIAN RIVER VALLEY MARTINELLI VINEYARD (★★★): Can be dry or slightly sweet; the 1995 (90 points) offered zesty ripe pear and grapefruit flavors.

PINOT NOIR RUSSIAN RIVER VALLEY MARTINELLI VINEYARD (★★★): Not in the same class as the Chardonnay—yet.
1996: Lean and a bit tart, with dark berry, cherry and spice flavors; notes of oak add dimension. **84**
1995: Mature earth and cola flavors, with hints of cherry and berry fruit joining notes of spicy oak on the finish. **87**
1994: Delicate, ripe, smooth and elegant, with complex cherry, berry and spice flavors and a creamy texture. **88**

PINOT NOIR RUSSIAN RIVER VALLEY MARTINELLI VINEYARD RESERVE (★★★): Shows some finesse, with tea, herb and currant flavors, but doesn't stand out from the standard bottling yet.
1996: Simple and earthy, with flavors of tea, dried cherry, herb and spice; offers delicacy and finesse. **84**
1995: Marked by a smoky, meaty edge; cola and wild berry flavors fold in with woody notes and tannins. **87**
1994: Dark, ripe and intense, with an elegant core of complex and plush cherry, plum, currant and berry flavors and a tarry, spicy aftertaste. **92**

ZINFANDEL RUSSIAN RIVER VALLEY JACKASS HILL (★★★★)
1994: Dark, ripe and intense. Delivers an elegant core of complex, rich, plush plum, cherry, currant and berry flavors, with a tarry, spicy aftertaste. Delicious now and worthy of short-term cellaring. **92**

ZINFANDEL RUSSIAN RIVER VALLEY JACKASS VINEYARD (★★★★): This vineyard is capable of producing ripe, intense, potent Zinfandel (see notes from Williams & Selyem) and now it's under the Martinelli brand. Can be high in alcohol. The name comes from the quip, "Only a jackass would grow grapes on that hill."
1996 Big, potent, and high in extract, with chewy, earthy black cherry, mineral, sage and spice flavors, finishing with notes of cedary oak. **89**
1995 Smooth, ripe and smoky, with lots of black cherry, wild berry, cola and plummy flavors that pick up a complex earthy, spicy edge. **91**
1992: Intense and lively, with earthy, tarry raspberry and cherry flavors that are ripe and focused. Firmly tannic. **88**
1990: A big, jammy style that holds its balance with ripe, almost raisiny flavors of tar and spice, turning tannic on the finish. **91**

MARTINI & PRATI WINES (★–★★)
Russian River Valley, Sonoma County
Founded: 1881. **Owner:** Martini & Godwin Families.
Winemaker: Dennis Hill.

MAJOR WINES: PRICE, CASES, RATING	
Barbera California	
($12, 680)	★
Muscat Canelli California	
($10, 711)	★★
Pinot Bianco Monterey	
($12, 800)	★★

Sangiovese California
($12, 1,500)   ★

White California Vino Grigio
($12, 1,500)   ★★

Zinfandel California
($15, 2,400)   ★★

Zinfandel Russian River Valley Reserve
($18, 400)   ★★

WINERY DATA
Case Production: 8,000. **Varietals Purchased:** Barbera (Sierra Foothills), Muscat Canelli (Paso Robles), Pinot Blanc (Monterey County), Sangiovese (Sierra Foothills), Trousseau Gris (Russian River Valley), Zinfandel (Lodi, Russian River Valley).

While Martini & Prati's winery facility, which dates back to 1881, is owned by the Martini family, the Godwin family owns the majority of the brand. Throughout most of the winery's history, it has produced bulk wines for sale to larger wineries.

LOUIS M. MARTINI WINERY (★★–★★★)
St. Helena, Napa Valley
Founded: 1922. **Owner:** The Martini Family.
Winemaker: Michael Martini.

MAJOR WINES: PRICE, CASES, RATING
Barbera Lake County Heritage Collection
($12, 6,000)   ★★

Cabernet Sauvignon Napa Valley Reserve
($18, 6,000)   ★★

Cabernet Sauvignon North Coast
($10, 35,000)   ★★

Cabernet Sauvignon Sonoma Valley
Monte Rosso Vineyard
($35, 1,500)   ★★★

Chardonnay California
($10, 30,000)   ★★

Chardonnay Russian River Valley Reserve
($18, 5,000)   ★★★

Folle Blanche Sonoma Valley Heritage
Collection
($12, 250)   ★★

Gewürztraminer Russian River Valley
Heritage Collection
($12, 3,000)   ★★★

Merlot California
($10, 62,000)   ★★

Merlot Russian River Valley Reserve
($18, 6,000)   ★★

Sauvignon Blanc Napa Valley
($9, 4,000)   ★★★

Zinfandel Sonoma Valley
Monte Rosso Vineyard Gnarly Vine
($30, 250)   ★★

Zinfandel Sonoma Valley Heritage
Collection
($12, 7,000)   ★★

ALSO PRODUCED
Los Niños Red Sonoma Valley Monte Rosso Vineyard ($50, 250); Sherry California Heritage Collection Cream ($12, 500); Sherry California Heritage Collection Dry ($12, 500).

WINERY DATA
Case Production: 170,000. **Acres Owned:** 711 acres (61 in Lake County, 230 in Napa Valley, 170 in Russian River Valley, 250 in Sonoma Valley). **Varietals by Acre:** Barbera (16 acres), Cabernet Franc (14), Cabernet Sauvignon (161), Carmine (2), Chardonnay (22), Folle Blanche (6), Gewürztraminer (9), Johannisberg Riesling (11), Malbec (1), Merlot (171), Muscat (6), Petite Sirah (10), Petit Verdot (7), Sémillon (13), Zinfandel (88), replantings (174). **Vineyard Designations:** Monte Rosso Vineyard. **Varietals Purchased:** Cabernet Franc (Amador County), Cabernet Sauvignon (Amador County, Dunnigan Hills, Napa Valley), Chardonnay (Amador County, Dunnigan Hills, Lodi, Napa Valley), Dolcetto (Napa Valley), Merlot (Lodi, Marin County, Napa Valley), Nebbiolo (Napa Valley), Sangiovese (Dunnigan Hills, Napa Valley), Sauvignon Blanc (Lodi, Napa Valley), Zinfandel (Lodi, Napa Valley).

Louis M. Martini and his son, Louis P. Martini, were two of the best winemakers in California history. Louis M. moved this family-owned and operated winery from the Central Valley town of Kingsburg to St. Helena in 1934, and quickly established a reputation for savvy winemaking. From the outset, the Martini winery was a no-frills, low-key, quality-oriented operation that relied on keen winemaking and precision farming.

Martini has its roots in a number of excellent vineyards, the most famous being the Monte Rosso Vineyard in the eastern hills of Sonoma Valley at the 1,000-foot elevation, acquired in 1938. It is planted primarily to Cabernet and Zinfandel, and the winery uses it for vineyard-designated wines. Also acquired in 1962 was Los Vinedos del Rio Vineyard in Russian River Valley, which is planted to several varieties, but is best known for the winery's vineyard-designated Merlot. Today, the Martinis own a total of 711 acres, situated in Napa, Sonoma and the Lake counties.

Long-time drinkers of old Martini wines—Barberas, Cabernets, Zinfandels, Pinot Noirs, even Rieslings and Gewürztraminers—know full well how excellent and well crafted these wines were. The best Cabernets from the 1940s, 1950s and 1960s have all aged exceptionally well. Today, the winery makes good-to-very-good wines, and occasionally an exceptional one. Quality to my taste remains about the same, perhaps at times inconsistent and less complex or concentrated than the best cutting-edge wines made today. Still, the winery remains a source of good value, with varietally true wines across the board.

MASON (★★★)
Napa Valley
Founded: 1993. **Owner:** Randy & Megan Mason.
Winemaker: Randy Mason.

MAJOR WINES: PRICE, CASES, RATING
Merlot Napa Valley
($20, 2,000)   ★★★
Sauvignon Blanc Napa Valley
($14, 4,000)   ★★★★

WINERY DATA
Case Production: 7,000. **Varietals Purchased:** Merlot (Napa Valley), Sauvignon Blanc (Napa Valley).

Randy Mason, the CEO of Napa Wine Co., makes elegant, full-flavored Sauvignon Blanc and trim, balanced Merlots from purchased Napa Valley grapes under his Mason label. The Sauvignon Blancs are among the best in California; the 1997 (90 points) was a complex blend of rich melon, fig, grapefruit and herb flavors. The 1995 Merlot (87) was tightly structured, with clean, currant- and cedar-laced flavors.

MATANZAS CREEK WINERY (★★★★–★★★★★)
Sonoma Valley
Founded: 1977. **Owner:** Bill & Sandra MacIver.
Winemaker: Bill Parker & Susan Reed.

MAJOR WINES: PRICE, CASES, RATING
Chardonnay Sonoma Valley
($30, 20,000)   ★★★★★
Chardonnay Sonoma Valley Journey
($80, 300)   ★★★★★
Merlot Sonoma Valley
($45, 9,000)   ★★★★★
Merlot Sonoma Valley Estate
($75, 250)   ★★★★
Merlot Sonoma Valley Journey
($155, 200)   ★★★★★
Sauvignon Blanc Sonoma County
($18, 10,000)   ★★★

ALSO PRODUCED
Syrah Sonoma Valley ($30, 1,000).

WINERY DATA
Case Production: 40,000. **Acres Owned:** 69 acres in Sonoma Valley. **Varietals by Acre:** Cabernet Sauvignon (1 acre), Chardonnay (30), Merlot (31), Sauvignon Blanc (2), Syrah (5). **Varietals Purchased:** Chardonnay (Russian River, Sonoma Valley), Merlot (Sonoma Valley), Sauvignon Blanc (Dry Creek, Mendocino County, Redwood Valley, Russian River), Sémillon (Dry Creek, Carneros), Syrah (Sonoma Valley).

Matanzas Creek has been a steady, reliable producer of high quality wines since its founding. Owners Sandra and Bill MacIver opened this Bennett Valley winery in 1978, with a product mix that included Cabernet, Chardonnay, Merlot, Pinot Noir and Sauvignon Blanc. After only average results with Cabernet and disappointing results with Pinot Noir, however, the MacIvers decided to narrow their focus to the three wines at which they excel: Chardonnay, including a luxury-priced bottling called Journey ($80); Merlot, including a Merlot Journey bottling ($155); and Sauvignon Blanc. While all these wines are among the best of their kind, the MacIvers' success with Merlot stands out because of the challenges involved in its growth and vinification. Syrah has just joined the lineup.

TASTING NOTES

CHARDONNAY SONOMA VALLEY (★★★★★): Starts out tight and flinty, but opens up to reveal a tight and concentrated core of complex flavors. Packs in lots of intensity with a deft hand, and the oak is well balanced. Best early on, but can stand short-term cellaring.
1996: Distinct for its spicy apple, melon and green pear notes, turning elegant on the finish, with spice and light oak shadings. **90**
1995: Remarkably elegant and sophisticated, with a pretty core of spicy citrus, pear, fig and melon; an amazingly detailed wine. **94**
1994: Openly fruity, with appealing floral aromas; hints of apple, pear and spice and subtle oak appear. **90**
1992: Austere and flinty, with bright green apple and spicy pear notes that are complex and vibrant. **89**
1991: Rich, ripe and generous, with honey, pear and vanilla aromas and flavors, remaining flavorful and concentrated through the solid finish. **90**
1990: Wonderfully rich and elegant fig, cream and spice flavors are sharply focused, with pretty, toasty oak shadings. **92**
1988: Attractive, with ripe tropical fruit, apple, pineapple, peach and pear flavors that are sharply focused, finishing with honey and vanilla notes. **91**

CHARDONNAY SONOMA VALLEY JOURNEY (★★★★★): Expensive, super-rich, ripe and oaky, but it all works to produce a wonderfully complex and concentrated wine.
1995: Ripe and flavorful, with a band of tasty pear, apple, lemon and spice flavors. The texture is smooth and polished in this elegant, complex, concentrated wine; echoes notes of spice and hazelnut on the finish. **94**
1993: Enormously complex and concentrated, with ripe, intense layers of honey, pear, peach and nectarine flavors that fan out on the finish. **95**
1992: Well-oaked, rich and complex, with toasty, buttery notes adding to the creamy layers of pear, honey and spice flavors. **91**
1990: Deeply concentrated, with tiers of pear, citrus, buttery oak and spice notes that are intense and lively, but what's most impressive is the remarkable complexity and length of the finish. **94**

MERLOT SONOMA VALLEY (★★★★★): Impeccably balanced, ripe, rich, lush, complex and well-oaked. Has small portions of Cabernet Sauvignon and Cabernet Franc. Ages well, but reaches a pleasant drinking peak early, too.

1995: Supple, with herb, currant and berry notes, finishing with clay, spice and cedary oak flavors. **87**
1994: Tight and focused, with a brilliant core of cedar-tinged currant and black cherry, turning floral, spicy and supple on the finish. **92**
1993: Smooth and polished, with appealing ripe plum, cherry, cedar and spice flavors, picking up a trace of earthiness on the finish. **88**
1992: Dark in color, with lots of rich currant, herb, tobacco and buttery oak, but given its weight and flavor it retains a sense of elegance. **91**
1991: A rich, tight and compact Merlot that displays lots of ripe currant, cherry, herb and vanilla notes from oak aging. Picks up a pretty coffee and cola edge on the finish. **89**
1990: Rich, young and concentrated, with tiers of currant, cherry and plum flavors that pick up coffee and cedar. Firm and tannic. **92**
1989: Ripe and generous, with tiers of complex, smoky currant, plum and cherry flavors and tannins that are fine and polished. **90**
1988: Effusively fruity, with ripe berry, cherry and currant flavors and hints of tar and spice. Firmly tannic. **88**
1987: Smooth, supple and generous, with buttery oak, ripe currant, cherry and plum flavors and very fine, integrated tannins. The finish is long, full, rich and complex. **93**
1986: Tight and tannic, with a seam of elegance and finesse, and finely integrated currant, spice and plum flavors that gain on the finish. **88**

MERLOT SONOMA VALLEY ESTATE (★★★★)
1993: Complex and concentrated, with deep layers of currant, sage, tea, herb, coffee and spice flavors. **90**

MERLOT SONOMA VALLEY JOURNEY (★★★★★): An exaggerated, full-blown style, with intricate spicy aromatics and enormously concentrated fruit flavors. There is no track record for aging, however, and the 1994 proved enormously tannic. Expensive.
1994: Dark and sharply focused, with dense, chewy plum, currant and blackberry flavors, finishing with supple tannins and a cedary edge. Quite tannic. **88**
1992: Dark, dense, ripe and intense, with tiers of rich berry, black cherry, anise and spice flavors that are amazingly complex and firmly tannic. **94**

SAUVIGNON BLANC SONOMA COUNTY (★★★): Typically bright, clean and refreshing, with citrus, mineral and herb flavors.

MAYACAMAS VINEYARDS (★★★)
Mount Veeder, Napa Valley
Founded: 1889. **Owner:** Bob & Nonie Travers.
Winemaker: Bob Travers.

MAJOR WINES: PRICE, CASES, RATING
Cabernet Sauvignon Napa Valley
   ($35, 2,000)   ★★★
Chardonnay Napa Valley
   ($28, 2,000)   ★★★★
Pinot Noir Napa Valley
   ($16, 200)   ★
Sauvignon Blanc Napa Valley
   ($16, 600)   ★★★

ALSO PRODUCED
Merlot Napa Valley ($28, 200).

WINERY DATA
Case Production: 5,000. **Acres Owned:** 52 acres in Mount Veeder. **Varietals by Acre:** Cabernet Franc (1 acre), Cabernet Sauvignon (14), Chardonnay (26), Merlot (5), Pinot Noir (3), Sauvignon Blanc (3).

Mayacamas Vineyards is one of California's original boutique wineries, and for many years, it was one of its top Cabernet producers. Today, the winery's flinty, age-worthy Chardonnay is its top wine. The stone winery was built in 1889—in a remote location, some 2,000 feet up on Mount Veeder—and experienced a rejuvenation in 1941, under Jack and Mary Taylor. Then, in 1968, former stockbroker Robert Travers and his wife, Nonie, bought the winery and vineyard. It was during their tenure that Mayacamas became famous for its intensely flavored and often firmly tannic mountain-grown Cabernets.

The wines from the late 1960s to the mid-1980s are widely admired for their authenticity, rustic personalities, rich fruit concentration and ageworthiness. Vintages such as 1968, 1969, 1970, 1973, 1974, 1977, 1978 and 1979 rank among the best from California. Quality dipped in the 1980s, however, as the wines became lighter, more herbaceous, and less focused and concentrated. The Cabernets since then have remained rustic, but are seemingly even less concentrated and rich in fruit flavors.

Mayacamas has an impressive track record with Chardonnay. It is one of the few Chardonnays still made in the traditional California style, with no malolactic fermentation and minimal oak flavoring. It too ages well,

starting out lean and trim but gaining depth, earthy nuances and complexity with age. For years Mayacamas produced a Zinfandel, often in a late-harvest style, but now the winery focuses on the two main varieties, together with Sauvignon Blanc and a very light, herbal style of Pinot Noir. All of the wines are made with grapes that come from its 52 acres of estate vineyards.

TASTING NOTES
CABERNET SAUVIGNON NAPA VALLEY (★★★): Older vintages are well worth the search for their sheer expression of the Mount Veeder appellation, but the most recent vintages are lighter and less compelling.

1993: Smells and tastes like a mature Cabernet, with earthy, cedary flavors and hints of currant, anise and tar that turn tart on the finish, along with firm tannins. **86**

1992: Tightly wound, with crisp, firm tannins and a narrow, complex band of mineral, herb, currant and cherry flavors. **87**

1980: Rich, smoky and gamy, loaded with currant, anise and earth flavors. Finishes with firm tannins. **89**

1979: Dark, immense and detailed, with rich, earthy currant and black cherry, mineral, anise, sage and cedary flavors, holding its flavor and focus. Could go another 10 years. **91**

1978: Mature, still with chalky tannins, but an immense, complex core of earthy, currant, plum, pepper and mineral. Impeccably balanced. **92**

1977: Dark and inky, packed with plush black cherry, currant, mineral and cedary oak flavors. A big, dramatic, complex and deeply concentrated wine that still has a long life ahead of it. May be the best of the 1977s. **95**

1974: It's holding its deep color, but the aromas of earthy currant, berry and spice turn drier on the palate and the finish is short. It's still a tight and concentrated wine. **88**

1973: Mature, with a smooth texture, but the currant and herb flavors are taking on an earthier profile. May always have a deep color. **88**

1970: Still inky dark and tightly wound, with layers of ripe currant, mineral, anise and spice flavors, picking up a cedary edge on the finish, where the tannins are still evident. This massive, concentrated wine shows little sign of age or of losing its wealth of flavor. **97**

1969: Mature, with an earthy, leathery streak to the dusty Cabernet flavors, picking up complex tar, spice and currant notes that linger on the finish. **89**

1968: Wonderful aromas of ripe, mature Cabernet. On the palate it is smooth and supple, with pretty currant, dried black cherry and anise flavors that linger on the finish. **90**

CHARDONNAY NAPA VALLEY (★★★★): Starts out tight and flinty, but give it some time and it will blossom, turning earthy and complex. Ages very well.

1995: Tart, with green, ripe fig, apple and pear flavors, a hint of mineral and spice on the finish. **88**

1993: Marked by citrus and grapefruit character, this emphasizes the flinty, grassy side of Chardonnay, turning crisp and lemony on the finish. **88**

1992: Crisp and flinty, with pleasant, earthy pear and spice notes. **88**

1990: Ripe and fruity, with pear, nectarine and spice characteristics, but without the heavy hand of oak. **89**

1989: Fresh and vibrant, with elegant nectarine, pear and apple notes that turn complex, gaining an earthy edge. **88**

1987: Has loads of pear, lemon and apple flavors, but it's bound by plenty of acidity and a spicy note on the finish. **86**

1986: Shows the benefits of cellaring, with mature flavors of anise, pear and spice, but also shows signs of maturity, with almond and caramel notes. **86**

1985: Beautifully balanced and tightly wound, with complex apple, peach, honey and toast flavors that unfold. **90**

PINOT NOIR NAPA VALLEY (★): Light and thin, often overly tannic for the fruit, marked by tea and herb flavors. Good only occasionally.

SAUVIGNON BLANC NAPA VALLEY (★★★): Intense and flinty, with tart citrus and spice notes. The 1994 (86 points) was bright, with citrus, herb and vanilla flavors.

MAYO (★★–★★★)
Sonoma Valley
Founded: 1993. **Owner:** Henry & Diane Mayo.
Winemaker: Chris Stanton.

MAJOR WINES: PRICE, CASES, RATING

Cabernet Sauvignon Sonoma Valley Los Chamizal Vineyard ($25, 325)	★★
Chardonnay Sonoma Valley Estate Bottled Laurel Hill Vineyard ($18, 1,500)	★★★
Chardonnay Sonoma Valley Estate Bottled Laurel Hill Vineyard Barrel Select ($23, 500)	★★★
Merlot Sonoma Valley ($20, 200)	★
Pinot Noir Carneros Sangiacomo Vineyard ($22, 150)	★★
Zinfandel Russian River Valley Estate Bottled Ricci Vineyard ($18, 1,300)	★★

WINERY DATA
Case Production: 4,000. **Acres Owned:** 17 acres (10 in Russian River Valley, 7 in Sonoma Valley). **Varietals by Acre:** Chardonnay (7 acres), Zinfandel (10). **Vineyard Designations:** Laurel Hill Vineyard (Chardonnay), Los Chamizal Vineyard (Cabernet Sauvignon), Sangiacomo Vineyard (Pinot Noir), Ricci Vineyard (Zinfandel). **Varietals Purchased:** Cabernet Sauvignon (Sonoma Valley), Merlot (Sonoma Valley), Pinot Noir (Carneros).

A Sonoma Valley-based, family-owned winery, Mayo is still in its infancy. The first wines—Cabernet, Chardonnay, Merlot, Pinot Noir and Zinfandel—have been good, but inconsistent. Estate-bottled Chardonnays have been the best wines; the 1997 Sonoma Valley Chardonnay (87 points) and the 1997 Barrel Select (86) were both tight and concentrated.

MAZZOCCO VINEYARDS (★★)
Dry Creek Valley, Sonoma County
Founded: 1985. **Owner:** Tom & Yvonne Mazzocco.
Winemaker: Phyllis Zouzounis.

MAJOR WINES: PRICE, CASES, RATING

Cabernet Sauvignon Sonoma County ($18, 3,200)	★★
Chardonnay Sonoma County River Lane ($15, 6,600)	★★
Chardonnay Sonoma County Winemaker's Select ($18, 200)	★★
Matrix Dry Creek Valley Meritage ($28, 500)	★★
Merlot Dry Creek Valley ($18, 750)	★★
Petite Sirah Dry Creek Valley ($21, 157)	★★★
Viognier Dry Creek Valley ($25, 115)	★★
Zinfandel Alexander Valley ($22, 400)	★★

Zinfandel Dry Creek Valley
  Cuneo & Saini
  ($22, 400)   ★★
Zinfandel Dry Creek Valley
  Quinn Vineyard
  ($22, 400)   ★★

WINERY DATA
Case Production: 18,000. **Acres Owned:** 46 acres (28 in Dry
Creek Valley, 18 in Alexander Valley). **Varietals by Acre:**
Chardonnay (33), Cabernet Sauvignon/Malbec/Merlot/Petit
Verdot (13). **Vineyard Designations:** Cuneo & Saini
(Zinfandel), Quinn Vineyard (Zinfandel). **Varietals Purchased:**
Cabernet Sauvignon (Alexander Valley), Zinfandel (Alexander
Valley, Dry Creek), Viognier (Dry Creek Valley).

Thomas Mazzocco is a famous eye surgeon who fell in love
with winegrowing. His 18,000-case winery in Alexander
Valley uses both estate-grown grapes from its 46 acres of vineyards and purchased grapes. In the late 1980s, when the winery's production was headed toward 30,000 cases, Mazzocco
sold the winery to Vintech, an investment group that went out
of business a year later. Mazzocco then re-acquired his winery.

Wine quality has fluctuated but is typically good to very
good, with the Chardonnays the most consistent. A 1993
Cabernet blend called Matrix (83 points) and the 1994
Cabernet Sauvignon (85) both showed soft, supple currant,
cedar, olive, and sage flavors of modest depth. The River Lane
Chardonnay is consistently very good, elegant and delicate,
with flavors of pear, fig and spice, as typified by the 1997 bottling (87). Also refined and elegant, the Chardonnay
Winemaker's Select is best when the oak flavors are kept in
check; the 1996 (90) had complex pear, apple and spicy flavors
with light oak shadings. Mazzocco's Dry Creek Valley
Merlots, like the 1995 (87), typically manage to be smooth and
ripe with plum and black currant flavors. The Petite Sirah can
be excellent, as was the 1993 (90) which had all the floral, ripe
plum and black cherry flavors of this varietal but uncommonly
soft, rich tannins.

Mazzocco seems to want to make a statement with its Dry
Creek Zinfandels, producing two vineyard designated and one
general bottling, but the wines haven't held up to their peers.
Generally clean and crisp with a modest range of flavors (like
the 1996 Dry Creek Valley, 83 points), they occasionally
impress with ripe, concentrated fruit flavors (like the 1994
Cuneo & Saini, 89), but can also be thin and coarse-textured
(as was the 1995 Quinn Vineyard, 79).

PETER McCOY VINEYARDS (★★)
Knights Valley, Sonoma County
Founded: 1981. **Owner:** Peter McCoy. **Winemaker:**
Peter McCoy.

MAJOR WINES: PRICE, CASES, RATING
Chardonnay Knights Valley
  Clos des Pierres
  ($25, 900)   ★★

WINERY DATA
Case Production: 2,000. **Acres Owned:** 15 acres in Knights
Valley. **Varietals by Acre:** Chardonnay (15 acres). **Vineyard
Designations:** Clos des Pierres (Chardonnay).

This 2,000-case winery focuses on Knights Valley-grown
Chardonnay from a 15-acre estate vineyard called Clos des
Pierres. Quality is good, but distribution is limited.

McCRAY RIDGE WINERY (★★★)
Dry Creek Valley, Sonoma County
Founded: 1996. **Owner:** Stan & Julie Simpson.
Winemaker: Phyllis Zouzounis & Stan Simpson.

MAJOR WINES: PRICE, CASES, RATING
Merlot Dry Creek Valley
  Two Moon Vineyard
  ($35, 650)   ★★★

WINERY DATA
Case Production: 1,000. **Acres Owned:** 10 acres in Dry Creek
Valley. **Varietals by Acre:** Cabernet Sauvignon (6 acres), Merlot
(4). **Vineyard Designations:** Two Moon Vineyard (Merlot).

Stan Simpson used part of his pension to buy a vineyard in the remote western reaches of Sonoma County,
where the Dry Creek and Russian River appellations
come together. A self-trained "vineyardist" and do-it-
yourself kind of guy, he has spent years tending his
vines, releasing his first wine at the age of 65.

The debut McCray Ridge 1996 Merlot (89 points),
offered an elegant core of spicy cherry and berry flavors
that gushes forth with firm but polished tannins. He's
since added six acres of Cabernet, which may be used
separately or in a blend with Merlot. Worth watching.

McDOWELL VALLEY VINEYARDS (★★★)
McDowell Valley, Mendocino County
Founded: 1979. **Owner:** William Crawford.
Winemaker: William Crawford.

MAJOR WINES: PRICE, CASES, RATING
Marsanne Mendocino
($16, 500)   ★★
Syrah Mendocino
($11, 12,000)   ★★★
Syrah Mendocino McDowell Valley Estate
($16, 600)   ★★★
Viognier Mendocino
($16, 2,400)   ★★★

ALSO PRODUCED
Le Tresor Red Mendocino ($16, 500).

WINERY DATA
Case Production: 23,000. **Acres Owned:** 254 acres in
McDowell Valley. **Varietals by Acre:** Cabernet Sauvignon (32
acres), Chardonnay (50), Grenache (22), Petite Sirah (28),
Sauvignon Blanc (37), Syrah (55), Viognier (10), Zinfandel
(20). **Varietals Purchased:** Marsanne (Mendocino), Roussanne
(Mendocino), Syrah (Mendocino), Viognier (Mendocino).

In 1970, Richard and Karen Keehn purchased a large
ranch east of Hopland with the intention of growing
grapes and selling them. As often happens, they soon
realized that it made greater financial sense to make wine
as well, and began doing so in 1979. Today, the 23,000-
case winery, now owned by William Crawford, has 254
acres, and its own American Viticultural Appellation. A
large portion of the grapes are planted to the Rhône varietals Syrah, Grenache and Viognier, since the winery has
enjoyed better success with these grapes than it has with
such California standards as Cabernet and Chardonnay.

McILROY CELLARS (★★–★★★)
Russian River Valley, Sonoma County
Founded: 1991. **Owner:** Will & Merry McIlroy.
Winemaker: Will McIlroy.

MAJOR WINES: PRICE, CASES, RATING
Chardonnay Russian River Valley
Aquarius Ranch
($20, 1,000)   ★★★
Pinot Noir Russian River Valley
($20, 600)   ★★
Zinfandel Russian River Valley
Porter Bass Vineyard
($20, 600)   ★★★

ALSO PRODUCED
Merlot Russian River Valley ($20, 500); Syrah Sonoma
Country ($20, 400).

WINERY DATA
Case Production: 2,500. **Acres Owned:** 43 acres in Russian
River Valley. **Varietals by Acre:** Chardonnay (31 acres),
Gewürztraminer (4), Merlot (3), Pinot Noir (5). **Vineyard
Designations:** Aquarius Ranch (Chardonnay), Porter Bass
Vineyard (Zinfandel). **Varietals Purchased:** Merlot (Russian
River Valley), Zinfandel (Russian River Valley).

This small new Russian River Valley producer has had
some success with Chardonnay from its Aquarius Ranch
vineyard and with Zinfandel made of grapes purchased from
Porter Bass Vineyard. The 1996 Chardonnay (90 points) was
smooth and complex, with hazelnut, pear and spice flavors,
while the 1996 Zinfandel (86) showed raspberry, pepper and
anise flavors with powdery tannins. McIlroy's Pinot Noir was
light in 1996 (80), with herb and cherry nuances.

MEADOW GLEN see RABBIT RIDGE VINEYARDS

THE MEEKER VINEYARD (★★★)
Dry Creek Valley, Sonoma County
Founded: 1984. **Owner:** Charles & Molly Meeker.
Winemaker: John Quinous.

MAJOR WINES: PRICE, CASES, RATING
Cabernet Sauvignon Dry Creek Valley
Gold Leaf Cuvée
($18, 1,000)   ★★★
Four Kings Red Dry Creek Valley
($24, 900)   ★★★
Red Table Wine Sonoma County
Rack Series
($12, 2,000)   ★★
Zinfandel Dry Creek Valley
Gold Leaf Cuvée
($16, 1,400)   ★★★

ALSO PRODUCED
Merlot Dry Creek Valley Winemaker's Handprint ($25, 400).

WINERY DATA
Case Production: 10,000. **Varietals Purchased:** Cabernet Sauvignon (Dry Creek Valley), Carignane (Napa, Sonoma Coast), Merlot (Dry Creek Valley), Petite Sirah (Napa, Sonoma Coast), Petit Verdot (Dry Creek Valley), Zinfandel (Dry Creek Valley, Russian River Valley, Anderson Valley).

Charles Meeker founded his 10,000-case winery in Dry Creek Valley in 1984. In 1997, he sold the winery and acreage but retained the brand, with plans to move to a new property on Dry Creek Road in 2000.

All of the wines are made from purchased grapes. There are plans to increase production to 20,000 in the future. Quality is average, but the Gold Leaf wines—particularly the Cabernet, Petite Sirah and Zinfandel—can be very good.

MENDELSON VINEYARD (★★★★)
Napa Valley
Founded: 1994. **Owner:** Richard & Marilyn Mendelson. **Winemaker:** Charles Hendricks.

MAJOR WINES: PRICE, CASES, RATING
Pinot Gris Dessert Napa Valley
($35, 340) ★★★★

ALSO PRODUCED
Muscat Canelli Napa Valley ($35, NA).

WINERY DATA
Case Production: 1,000. **Acres Owned:** 1.5 acres in Oak Knoll District. **Varietals by Acre:** Pinot Gris (1.5 acres). **Varietals Purchased:** Muscat Canelli (Napa Valley), Pinot Gris (Napa Valley).

On a trip to the former Soviet Union, Napa attorney Richard Mendelson discovered and then became inspired by "white Ports" while touring the cellars of Massandra. His grapes—Pinot Gris from a small family vineyard north of Napa—are picked ripe, at roughly 28 to 30 Brix and fermented in French oak barrels. During fermentation, the wine is fortified with alambic pot-distilled brandy. The 1996 (95 points) was delicious, very ripe, rich and creamy, with pretty peach and floral notes, turning smooth and sweet on the finish, with fig, melon and apricot flavors. Muscat Canelli is a new addition.

MER SOLEIL (★★★★★)
Santa Lucia Highlands, Monterey County
Founded: 1992. **Owner:** Chuck Wagner. **Winemaker:** Chuck Wagner.

MAJOR WINES: PRICE, CASES, RATING
Chardonnay Central Coast
($36, 9,000) ★★★★★

WINERY DATA
Case Production: 9,000 cases. **Acres Owned:** 390 acres in Santa Lucia Highlands. **Varietals by Acre:** Chardonnay (320 acres), Marsanne (18), Roussanne (8), Sangiovese (7), Viognier (37).

Caymus owner and winemaker Chuck Wagner branched out from Napa Valley in 1992 with the purchase of land in Monterey County. He now owns several hundred acres in vines, as well as this new winery, literally named for the "sea and the sun." At Mer Soleil, the focus is on barrel-fermented, Burgundian-style Chardonnay. Wagner had toyed with Chardonnay at Caymus for years, with mixed results; in Monterey, Wagner finds that it excels. "In my eyes, it's an area of California that's never been dealt with properly," he says. His interest is in matching soil and microclimate with the right grape varieties.

Mer Soleil's vineyard is dominated by Chardonnay (320 acres), followed by smaller acreage of Viognier, Roussanne, Marsanne, and Sangiovese, all of which Wagner intends to vinify experimentally. He has indicated, however, that it is likely that he will make only one or two wines commercially besides Chardonnay, focusing on the grapes he believes have the most potential and selling the remaining grape production to others. The initial production of 1,100 cases has risen to 9,000 cases.

TASTING NOTES

CHARDONNAY CENTRAL COAST (★★★★★): Showcases the ripe, opulent character of Santa Lucia Chardonnay, with its dark gold color and very rich, bold flavors.
1996: A touch earthy up-front, with a range of tangerine, nectarine and spicy fruit flavors; keeps its focus and gains complexity on the long, lingering aftertaste. **91**
1995: Compact, with toasty, cedary oak and a rich core of pear, fig and citrus. Turns complex and sophisticated, with a long, lingering aftertaste. **91**

1994: Bold, ripe, rich and full-bodied; laces the honey, pear and pineapple flavors with nice spicy, toasty shadings. Concentrated and delicious, with a long, lingering aftertaste. **93**

1993: Well oaked, showing toasty, buttery nuances, but it's also richly fruity, with exotic pear, tropical fruit, honey and spice flavors. Packs lots of complexity into a bold style. **91**

MERIDIAN VINEYARDS (★★★–★★★★)
Paso Robles, San Luis Obispo
Founded: 1988. **Owner:** Beringer Wine Estates.
Winemaker: Charles Ortman.

MAJOR WINES: PRICE, CASES, RATING

Cabernet Sauvignon California ($11, 30,000)	★★
Chardonnay Edna Valley Coastal Reserve ($15, 15,000)	★★★★
Chardonnay Santa Barbara County ($11, 100,000)	★★★
Chardonnay Santa Barbara County Limited Release ($25, 1,000)	★★★★
Merlot California ($11, 30,000)	★★
Pinot Noir Santa Barbara County ($14, 10,000)	★★★
Pinot Noir Santa Barbara & San Luis Obispo Counties Reserve ($20, 1,000)	★★★
Sauvignon Blanc California ($9, 50,000)	★★★
Syrah Paso Robles ($14, 1,000)	★★★

ALSO PRODUCED
Cabernet Blanc Paso Robles ($6, NA); Cabernet Sauvignon California Reserve ($20, NA); Zinfandel Paso Robles ($14, NA).

WINE DATA
Case Production: 325,000. **Acres Owned:** 4,116 acres (94 in Edna Valley, 473 in Paso Robles, 185 in San Luis Obispo County, 3,364 in Santa Barbara County). **Varietals by Acre:** Cabernet Franc (5 acres), Cabernet Sauvignon (440), Chardonnay (2,504), Chenin Blanc (328), Gamay Noir (6), Gewürztraminer (195), Johannisberg Riesling (206), Merlot (219), Pinot Gris (15), Pinot Noir (130), Sangiovese (2), Sauvignon Blanc (33), Syrah (33). **Varietals**

Purchased: Cabernet Franc (Paso Robles, San Benito County), Cabernet Sauvignon (Paso Robles, San Benito, Santa Barbara), Chardonnay (Monterey County, San Benito County, Santa Barbara), Merlot (Paso Robles, San Benito County), Petite Syrah (Paso Robles), Pinot Noir (Monterey County, San Benito County, Santa Barbara), Sangiovese (Paso Robles), Sauvignon Blanc (Paso Robles), Syrah (Paso Robles), Zinfandel (Paso Robles).

Winemaker Chuck Ortman, who had a hand in making wines at Spring Mountain, Far Niente and others as a consultant, started this brand in 1984. He then sold the name to Wine World Estates (now Beringer Wine Estates, owner of Beringer, Chateau Souverain, Napa Ridge and Chateau St. Jean). Wine World bought the old Estrella River Winery, and retooled it for the Meridian brand.

Meridian owns 4,116 acres in vines, making it one of the state's largest vineyard owners. The biggest planting is a staggering 2,504 acres of Chardonnay, most of which is in Santa Barbara County. Overall, these wines are very good values.

TASTING NOTES

CHARDONNAY EDNA VALLEY COASTAL RESERVE (★★★★)
1997: Clean and crisp, with a tangy edge to the ripe pear and peachy notes, it fans out to fold in creamy, smoky oak nuances. **88**
1996: Beautifully crafted, rich, complex, concentrated and sharply focused, with layers of ripe pear, fig, peach and honeydew melon. Turns elegant and spicy on a long, lingering finish that echoes fruit and vanilla. **92**

CHARDONNAY SANTA BARBARA COUNTY (★★★): Usually very good; bright, flavorful, fruity and elegant. The 1997 (87 points) was right on target. Very good value.

CHARDONNAY SANTA BARBARA COUNTY LIMITED RELEASE (★★★★): Not made every year. Very complex and elegant, avoiding some of the heavier flavors found in Chardonnays from this area.

1995: Marked by a spicy, Muscat-like quality, the ripe, juicy Chardonnay flavors fold in, with ripe pear, fig and citrus adding dimension to the light toasty oak shadings. Complex and long on the finish. **91**

PINOT NOIR VARIOUS BOTTLINGS (★★★): Some clear successes with this varietal; quality should continue to rise as the winery commits to fine-tuning its vineyards and wines. The 1995 Santa Barbara & San Luis Obispo Counties Reserve (91 points) was rich, supple and very complex with loads of flavor. Worth watching.

SYRAH PASO ROBLES (★★★): This too could well become a star, as the variety does very well in this area. The 1996 (88 points) was ripe and spicy, with peppery, meaty Syrah flavors. Worth watching.

MERRYVALE VINEYARDS
(★★–★★★★★)
Napa Valley
Founded: 1983. **Owner:** Schlatter Family. **Winemaker:** Stephen Test.

MAJOR WINES: PRICE, CASES, RATING

Cabernet Sauvignon Napa Valley Hillside ($18, 5,000)	★★★
Cabernet Sauvignon Napa Valley Reserve ($30, 2,500)	★★★★
Chardonnay Napa Valley Reserve ($30, 3,000)	★★★★★
Chardonnay Napa Valley Starmont ($18, 12,000)	★★★★
Merlot Napa Valley Reserve ($32, 4,000)	★★★
Profile Red Napa Valley ($55, 3,000)	★★★★
Sauvignon Blanc Napa Valley ($17, 3,000)	★★
Vignette White Napa Valley ($22, 1,000)	★★

WINERY DATA
Case Production: 40,000. **Acres Owned:** 25 acres in Napa Valley. **Varietals by Acre:** Cabernet Franc (0.2 acres), Cabernet Sauvignon (21.5), Merlot (3), Petit Verdot (0.3). **Varietals Purchased:** Cabernet Franc (Napa Valley), Cabernet Sauvignon (Napa Valley), Chardonnay (Napa Valley), Merlot (Napa Valley), Sauvignon Blanc (Napa Valley), Sémillon (Napa Valley), Syrah (Napa Valley).

This partnership brought together real estate developers Bill Harlan (Harlan Estate), Peter Stocker, John Montgomery and Robin Lail (John Daniel's daughter and a former partner at Dominus Estate, now owner of Lail Vineyards). Merryvale, named after the Merryvale building in San Francisco, introduced a Bordeaux-style red made from purchased grapes with the 1983 vintage; later came Chardonnay, Merlot and a white Meritage. Ric Forman oversaw winemaking early on, followed by Robert Levy. In 1998, Stephen Test, former winemaker at Stonestreet, came on board. While the red table wine now called Profile held an early lead in quality, it has since been surpassed by the Chardonnay—the Reserve is among the state's richest and most complex.

TASTING NOTES

CABERNET SAUVIGNON NAPA VALLEY HILLSIDE (★★★)
1996: Packs in lots of flavors, with tiers of currant, black cherry, plum and wild berry, holding its focus on a long, complex aftertaste. **90**

CABERNET SAUVIGNON NAPA VALLEY RESERVE (★★★★)
1995: Smooth, ripe and polished, with tiers of plum, black cherry, currant and berry flavors, it's rich, focused, long and complex. **91**

CHARDONNAY NAPA VALLEY RESERVE (★★★★★): A steady performer now, with lots of rich, complex, creamy fruit flavors.
1996: Serves up lots of ripe, creamy pear, hazelnut, fig and toasty oak flavors, turning delicate and complex on the finish. **92**
1995: Bold and flavorful, with tiers of ripe pear, apple, spice and light oak, turning elegant and displaying a smoky nectarine aftertaste. **93**

CHARDONNAY NAPA VALLEY STARMONT (★★★★): Often rivals the Reserve in quality, with a similar style, texture and range of flavors.

1996: Smooth, ripe, rich and creamy, with layers of complex pear, fig and hazelnut flavors. **91**

1995: Remarkably complex, with tiers of ripe pear, fig, apple and vanilla, the texture is smooth and creamy. **93**

MERLOT NAPA VALLEY & RESERVE (★★★): Struggles for consistency—as Merlot often does—but the 1994 (87 points) showed cedar, spice and currant flavors. The 1995 Reserve (88) offered juicy plum, currant and black cherry notes.

PROFILE RED NAPA VALLEY (★★★★): Ripe and complex, with supple tannins and lots of appealing fruit flavors.

1995: Vibrant, with ripe, rich currant, plum, anise, sage and cedary notes and supple tannins that turn complex on the finish. **91**

1994: Tight and concentrated, with complex currant, black cherry, sage, mineral and cedary oak flavors and firm tannins. **91**

1992: Smooth and supple, with a rich core of currant, anise, mint and cherry flavors that fan out nicely on the finish. **88**

1991: Smooth and polished, with supple currant, coffee, mineral and spice flavors followed by firm, dry tannins. **90**

SAUVIGNON BLANC NAPA VALLEY (★★): Typically bright and clean, the 1996 (85 points) offered lemon and grapefruit notes.

PETER MICHAEL WINERY (★★★★★)
Sonoma County
Founded: 1987. **Owner:** Peter Michael. **Winemaker:** Vanessa Wong.

MAJOR WINES: PRICE, CASES, RATING

Chardonnay Napa County Clos du Ciel ($38, 1,500)	★★★★★
Chardonnay Sonoma County Belle Côte ($42, 2,000)	★★★★★
Chardonnay Sonoma County Cuvée Indigène ($55, 500)	★★★★★
Chardonnay Sonoma County Mon Plaisir ($45, 2,500)	★★★★★
Les Pavots Red Knights Valley ($42, 3,000)	★★★★★
Sauvignon Blanc Napa County L'Après-Midi ($28, 700)	★★★★

ALSO PRODUCED
Chardonnay Sonoma County Point Rouge ($85, 150); Pinot Noir Santa Lucia Highlands Pisoni Vineyard ($NA, NA).

WINERY DATA
Case Production: 15,000. **Acres Owned:** 137 acres in Sonoma County (87 in Knights Valley, 50 on Sonoma Coast). **Varietals by Acre:** Cabernet Sauvignon (50 acres), Chardonnay (57), Pinot Noir (20), Sauvignon Blanc (10). **Vineyard Designations:** Belle Côte (Chardonnay), Cuvée Indigène (Chardonnay), L'Après-Midi (Sauvignon Blanc), La Carriere (Chardonnay), Les Pavots (Cabernet Franc, Cabernet Sauvignon, Merlot), Mon Plaisir (Chardonnay), Pisoni Vineyard (Pinot Noir). **Varietals Purchased:** Chardonnay (Sonoma County), Pinot Noir (Santa Lucia Highlands, Sonoma Coast).

Peter Michael Winery has become one of California's consistent high achievers, making dramatic, complex, soulful wines. Based in Sonoma County's Knights Valley, the beautiful winery building is situated at the foot of a steep grade leading to the vineyards, and offers a lovely view of Mount St. Helena. Owner Peter Michael is a London-born computer engineer who bought the 600-acre estate as a vacation retreat, and spends about a month there each year. Early on, with the help of Helen Turley, Michael would purchase Chardonnay grapes from Gauer Estate in Alexander Valley and Howell Mountain in Napa, but he has since planted 137 acres, including 87 at the winery and another 50 along the Sonoma Coast. Winemaker Mark Aubert left to make wines for Colgin Cellars in 1999, and Vanessa Wong, previously the assistant winemaker, was promoted to winemaker.

The Cabernet, Les Pavots ("the poppies"), is a Bordeaux-style red from Michael's own vineyard. The Chardonnays are rich and distinctive; all three share a full-throttle Burgundian character, with rich, creamy textures, hazelnut and spice notes and deep, complex flavors. The Sauvignon Blanc is also exceptional in quality. Worth collecting.

TASTING NOTES
CHARDONNAY NAPA COUNTY CLOS DU CIEL (★★★★): Serves up a wide range of complex flavors with a silky texture and lots of finesse.

1996: Distinct, with rich, creamy tangerine, pear, fig and citrus flavors that are intense and deeply concentrated, yet elegant. **93**

1995: Opens with spicy, toasty oak and concentrated pear, fig and citrus flavors that turn complex and linger on the finish. **94**

1992: Smooth, elegant and polished, with pretty pear, honey, hazelnut and floral notes that are rich and focused, finishing with a pretty aftertaste. **91**

1991: Smooth and polished, with appealing honey, butterscotch and apple flavors. **88**

CHARDONNAY SONOMA COUNTY BELLE CÔTE (★★★★)
1996: Elegant and understated; builds complexity with delicate pear, fig, tangerine, hazelnut, citrus and vanilla flavors. **93**

CHARDONNAY SONOMA COUNTY CUVÉE INDIGENE
(★★★★★): Can be stunning; at its best, it's enormously complex and deeply flavored. (Carried a Napa Valley appellation prior to 1994.)

1994: Enormously rich and complex, with tiers of ripe pear, fig, butterscotch and honey flavors that combine intensity with finesse. **95**

1992: Bold, ripe and concentrated; a seamless wine with layers of honey, pear, toast and hazelnut flavors that turn rich and complex on a long full finish. **93**

1990: Absolutely delicious, ripe, smooth and creamy, with rich pear, nutmeg and fig flavors and subtle oak and earth shadings. Wonderful harmony and finesse, depth and length. **94**

CHARDONNAY SONOMA COUNTY MON PLAISIR (★★★★):
Similar in style to the other Chardonnays; very deep, rich, complex and polished. From Gauer Ranch.

1994: Combines a rich, complex core of ripe pear, honey, peach and hazelnut flavors with a dash of light, toasty oak. **94**

1993: Beautifully crafted, with ripe, rich pear, peach, honey and hazelnut flavors, gaining complexity towards the finish. **93**

1992: Firm and compact, with a trim band of spice, pear, hazelnut and vanilla-laced oak flavors, finishing with a rich, complex aftertaste. **92**

LES PAVOTS RED KNIGHTS VALLEY (★★★★★): Variable early on, but of late very complex, rich, plush and concentrated, ranking amongst the state's finest.

1995: Enormous intensity, concentration and complexity, with firm currant, spice, cedar, tar and wild berry flavors and supple tannins. **93**

1994: Wonderful complexity, depth and concentration, with layers of ripe, juicy plum, currant and black cherry framed by toasty, buttery oak flavors. **94**

1993: Tight and complex, with a cedary grace note to the ripe cherry, currant, anise and spice flavors, finishing with firm tannins. **90**

1992: An elegant, finely balanced wine with pretty currant and cherry flavors; turns creamy and offers supple tannins on the finish. **90**

1991: Turns earthy and leathery, with a gamy streak, but there's enough currant and cherry fruit to maintain a delicate balance. **87**

1990: Smoky, earthy and gamy, with a meaty edge to the flavors, this is a tough, tannic, hard-edged wine whose future is questionable. Needs cellaring in hopes the tannins will soften, but don't bet on that. **80**

1988: Rich and full-bodied, showing layers of plum, currant, coffee and cedar flavors before the tannins clamp down on the finish. **88**

SAUVIGNON BLANC NAPA COUNTY L'APRÈS-MIDI (★★★★)
1996: Quite lemony, with a silky texture, the wine also shows a blend of melon, fig and grapefruit flavors. This is a polished effort, with plenty of oak and lots of finesse. **90**

1995: A tangy, citrus-like wine that packs a punch; finishes with bright lemon-orange flavors. **88**

MICHEL-SCHLUMBERGER (★★)
Dry Creek Valley, Sonoma County
Founded: 1979. **Owner:** Jacques Schlumberger, Jean-Jacques Michel. **Winemaker:** Fred Payne. **Second Label:** Domaine Michel.

MAJOR WINES: PRICE, CASES, RATING

Cabernet Sauvignon Dry Creek Valley ($20, 3,000)	★★
Chardonnay Dry Creek Valley ($20, 2,500)	★★

ALSO PRODUCED
Cabernet Sauvignon Dry Creek Valley Reserve ($35, 400); Merlot Dry Creek Valley ($20, 1,000); Syrah North Coast ($18, 1,400).

WINERY DATA
Case Production: 14,000. **Acres Owned:** 50 acres in Dry Creek Valley. **Varietals by Acre:** Cabernet Franc (3 acres), Cabernet Sauvignon (15), Chardonnay (27), Merlot (5). **Varietals Purchased:** Cabernet Sauvignon (Dry Creek Valley), Syrah (Mendocino), Zinfandel (Dry Creek Valley).

Swiss investment banker Jean-Jacques Michel founded this Dry Creek Winery in 1987 after admiring the success of his close friend Tom Jordan of Jordan Vineyard and Winery. In 1993, Jacques Schlumberger, whose family produces wine in Alsace, France, became majority owner and managing partner.

The winery is beautiful, but the wines have never really inspired me, though recent vintages have been better than earlier efforts. Both the Cabernet and Chardonnay have been underachievers, often showing bland, simple flavors despite repeated efforts to upgrade quality. The winery owns 50 acres in Sonoma, dominated by Chardonnay (27 acres); this will change as new property is planted, pushing the total acreage to 82 acres, including small amounts of Pinot Blanc, Viognier, Pinot Noir and larger blocks of Syrah, Cabernet and other Bordeaux varietals. Chardonnay will be reduced to about 8 acres. Merlot, Syrah and a Cabernet Reserve are new additions to the lineup.

TASTING NOTES

CABERNET SAUVIGNON DRY CREEK VALLEY (★★): Consistently gets mid-80s ratings, which is rather ordinary considering the high overall quality of recent vintages. The 1994 (87 points) showed black cherry, currant and cassis notes, while the 1995 (85) was tight, with a bitter edge.

CHARDONNAY DRY CREEK VALLEY (★★): Fares about as well as most Chardonnays from Dry Creek, which is why few wineries there specialize in it. The 1996 (87 points) was flinty, with a lemony edge.

MIDNIGHT CELLARS (★★)
Paso Robles, San Luis Obispo County
Founded: 1995. **Owner:** Hartenberger Family. **Winemaker:** Rich Hartenberger.

MAJOR WINES: PRICE, CASES, RATING
Cabernet Franc Paso Robles
($15, 270)   ★★
Cabernet Sauvignon Paso Robles
($16, 1,700)   ★★
Chardonnay Central Coast
($16, 1,000)   ★★

Merlot Paso Robles
($19, 250)   ★★
Sauvignon Blanc Paso Robles
($10, 680)   ★★
Zinfandel Paso Robles Dusi Ranch
($17, 200)   ★★

ALSO PRODUCED
White Zinfandel Paso Robles ($7, 400).

WINERY DATA
Case Production: 4,500. **Acres Owned:** 22 acres in Paso Robles. **Varietals by Acre:** Cabernet Sauvignon (6 acres), Chardonnay (4), Merlot (6), Zinfandel (6). **Vineyard Designations:** Dusi Ranch (Zinfandel). **Varietals Purchased:** Cabernet Franc (Paso Robles), Cabernet Sauvignon (Paso Robles), Chardonnay (Paso Robles, Santa Barbara County), Merlot (Paso Robles), Sauvignon Blanc (Paso Robles), Zinfandel (Paso Robles).

This family-owned winery uses estate and purchased grapes for its wines, with Cabernet Sauvignon, Cabernet Franc and Chardonnay the early quality leaders. The winery expects to add some 40 acres in vines by early 2000, and will include Syrah.

MIETZ CELLARS (★★)
Russian River Valley, Sonoma County
Founded: 1989. **Owner:** Keith & Nancy Mietz. **Winemaker:** Keith Mietz.

MAJOR WINES: PRICE, CASES, RATING
Merlot Sonoma County
($21, 2,250)   ★★
Zinfandel Sonoma County
($18, 750)   ★★

WINERY DATA
Case Production: 3,000. **Acres Owned:** 15 acres (3 in Dry Creek Valley, 12 in Russian River Valley). **Varietals by Acre:** Cabernet Sauvignon (3 acres), Merlot (12). **Varietals Purchased:** Zinfandel (Dry Creek Valley, Russian River).

Santa Rosa fireman Keith Mietz and his family specialize in Sonoma County Merlot, a portion of which is grown on their 15 acres of vines in Russian River and Dry Creek. Production is 3,000 cases. The 1989 was a solid debut wine, but the bottlings have been less impressive since. The Zinfandel is on a par with the Merlot.

TASTING NOTES

MERLOT SONOMA COUNTY (★★): Too often this wine has been green and simple, though the 1995 (87 points) worked its way past earthy, leathery notes into some purer Merlot flavors.

MILAGRO see PALOMA WINERY

MILL CREEK VINEYARDS (★★)
Dry Creek Valley, Sonoma County
Founded: 1974. **Owner:** Bill Kreck. **Winemaker:** Hank Skewis.

MAJOR WINES: PRICE, CASES, RATING

Cabernet Sauvignon Sonoma County ($19, 950)	★★
Chardonnay Dry Creek Valley ($13, 2,000)	★★
Gewürztraminer Dry Creek Valley ($10, 1,000)	★★
Merlot Estate Dry Creek Valley ($18, 5,000)	★★
Sauvignon Blanc Dry Creek Valley ($10, 2,000)	★★
Zinfandel Dry Creek Valley ($10, 1,500)	★★

WINERY DATA
Case Production: 15,000. **Acres Owned:** 81 acres (14 in Alexander Valley, 67 in Dry Creek Valley). **Varietals by Acre:** Cabernet Franc (1), Cabernet Sauvignon (21), Chardonnay (9), Gewürztraminer (3), Merlot (36), Sauvignon Blanc (10), Sémillon (1).

In 1965 the Kreck family started planting what is now an 80-acre vineyard in southern Dry Creek Valley, selling part of the crop but keeping enough to produce 15,000 cases a year of Cabernet, Chardonnay, Gewürztraminer, Merlot, and Sauvignon Blanc—with Merlot the volume leader at 5,000 cases. The wines range in quality from ordinary to good and are generally inexpensive. For a period in the 1980s Mill Creek was among California's Merlot pioneers. Quality then tapered off, but some recent wines have shown a slight improvement; the 1997 Chardonnay (88 points) showed a more supple texture than previous years, with focused lemon, green apple, pear, and toasted oak notes. A new addition, the 1997 Zinfandel (87) was soft and ripe with smoky vanilla, chocolate and light cherry flavors. The 1997 Sauvignon Blanc (82) showed straightforward citrus and herb flavors while the 1995 Cabernet (83) and 1995 Merlot (85) were pleasant for their soft tannins and modest range of currant, blackberry and herb flavors.

MINER FAMILY VINEYARDS (★★★★)
Oakville, Napa Valley
Founded: 1998 **Owner:** Dave and Emily Miner, Norma and Ed Miner. **Winemaker:** Gary Brookman.

MAJOR WINES: PRICE, CASES, RATING

Cabernet Sauvignon Napa Valley Oakville ($50, 1,500)	★★★★
Chardonnay Napa Valley Oakville Ranch ($35, 600)	★★★★
Chardonnay Napa Valley Wild Yeast ($45, 207)	★★★★
Chardonnay Napa Valley ($26, 1,500)	★★★★
Merlot Napa Valley Oakville Ranch ($50, 180)	★★★

ALSO PRODUCED
Pinot Noir Monterey County Pisoni Vineyard ($45, 600); Sangiovese Mendocino County ($20, 1,200); Viognier California ($18, 834); Zinfandel Napa Valley ($20, 1,600).

WINERY DATA:
Case Production: 2,000. **Vineyard Designations:** Oakville Ranch Vineyard (Cabernet Sauvignon, Chardonnay, Merlot), Pisoni (Pinot Noir). **Varietals Purchased:** Cabernet Franc (Oakville), Cabernet Sauvignon (Oakville), Chardonnay (Oakville, Napa Valley), Merlot (Oakville), Pinot Noir (Santa Lucia Highlands), Sangiovese (Mendocino), Viognier (Madera County), Zinfandel (Oakville).

Dave Miner, along with his parents and wife Emily, launched Miner Family Vineyards in 1998. The majority of Miner Family's wines are made from grapes grown on Oakville Ranch, which is owned and operated by Dave's aunt, Mary Miner. Dave was president of Oakville Ranch Vineyards (see entry) for five years before purchasing the Oakville Ranch winery facility and starting his own label.

The first wines have been outstanding, with rich complex flavors and lots of depth. Three 1997 Chardonnays—a Chardonnay Napa Valley (94 points), Chardonnay Napa Valley Wild Yeast (93) and Chardonnay Napa Valley Oakville Ranch (93 points)—were silky, concentrated and layered with flavor. A dense flavorful, 1996 Cabernet Sauvignon Napa Valley (93) and a dark, chewy, currant and mineral flavored 1996 Merlot Napa Valley Oakville Ranch (88 points) were also impressive. The winery is also producing Pinot Noir, Sangiovese, Viognier and Zinfandel from purchased grapes. Considering Miner's experience with Oakville Ranch winery and the quality of the Oakville Ranch grapes, these are wines worth buying and collecting.

MIRABELLE see SCHRAMSBERG VINEYARDS

MIRAGE VINEYARDS see CHATEAU JULIEN

MIRASSOU VINEYARDS (★★–★★★★)
Santa Clara County
Founded: 1854. **Owner:** Daniel, Jim, Peter Mirassou. **Winemaker:** Tom Stutz.

MAJOR WINES: PRICE, CASES, RATING

Cabernet Sauvignon California Family Selection ($12, 8,500)	★★
Cabernet Sauvignon Napa Valley Harvest Reserve ($18, 2,400)	★★
Cabernet Sauvignon Stags Leap District Showcase Selection ($30, 400)	★★
Chardonnay Monterey County Family Selection ($11, 19,500)	★★★
Chardonnay Monterey County Harvest Reserve ($16, 5,500)	★★★★
Chardonnay Monterey County Mission Ranch Vineyard Reserve ($18, 500)	★★★
Chardonnay Monterey County San Vicente Vineyard Reserve ($18, 500)	★★★
Chardonnay Monterey County Showcase Selection ($28, 800)	★★★★
Merlot California Family Selection ($13, 16,000)	★★
Merlot Monterey County Harvest Reserve ($18, 6,000)	★★
Petite Sirah Monterey County Family Selection ($12, 3,200)	★★
Pinot Blanc Monterey County Family Selection ($11, 21,000)	★★
Pinot Blanc Monterey County Harvest Reserve ($16, 1,900)	★★
Pinot Noir Monterey County Family Selection ($12, 13,600)	★★
Pinot Noir Monterey County Harvest Reserve ($16, 5,700)	★★
Riesling Monterey County ($9, 17,900)	★
Zinfandel Central Coast Family Selection ($11, 5,900)	★★
Zinfandel Santa Clara Harvest Reserve ($16, 873)	★★

WINERY DATA
Case Production: 105,000. **Acres Owned:** 485 acres (465 in Monterey County, 20 in Santa Clara County). **Varietals by Acre:** Cabernet Sauvignon (10 acres), Chardonnay (140), Gamay (40), Merlot (30), Petite Sirah (40), Pinot Blanc (60), Pinot Noir (75), White Riesling (50), Zinfandel (40). **Vineyard Designations:** Mission Ranch Vineyard (Chardonnay), San Vicente Vineyard (Chardonnay). **Varietals Purchased:** Cabernet Sauvignon (Napa Valley), Merlot (California), Pinot Noir (Central Coast).

Mirassou Vineyards, located in Santa Clara, can trace its origins back to 1854. It is now run by the fifth generation of winemakers, making the Mirassous one of the oldest winemaking families in California. The family played an important role in bringing vine cuttings to California, but it wasn't until the 1940s that the winery began to shift production from bulk wines to better wines, with the Mirassou name attached. The wines of the 1970s and early 1980s were often marked by herbaceous flavors, but the family has persisted in its efforts to raise quality, with some success: the wines presently on the market are better than any it has produced in the past 40 years.

Production is 105,000 cases, most of it good, simple wine from the winery's considerable vineyard holdings. Most of the wines earn ★★ ratings, but the Chardonnay has been excellent of late, particularly the Monterey County bottlings, with the 1995 and 1996 vintages earning outstanding marks. The labels must be read carefully, though, since there are several Chardonnays, and the designations differ from year to year. The best wines appear under the Showcase Selection and Harvest Reserve designations.

TASTING NOTES

CHARDONNAY MONTEREY COUNTY SHOWCASE SELECTION & HARVEST RESERVE (★★★★): Steady work has paid off, as this is now an excellent wine. It is consistently outstanding, with the 1995 (91 points) rich with pear, spice, nectarine and citrus notes. The 1996 Harvest Reserve (91) was smooth, rich and creamy.

CHARLES B. MITCHELL VINEYARD (★–★★)
El Dorado County
Founded: 1994. **Owner:** Charles B. Mitchell.
Winemaker: Charles B. Mitchell.

MAJOR WINES: PRICE, CASES, RATING
Cabernet Franc El Dorado ($14, 500)	★★
Cabernet Sauvignon El Dorado Grand Reserve ($28, 500)	★★
Cabernet Sauvignon El Dorado Reserve ($16, 500)	★★
Cabernet Sauvignon El Dorado Vintner's Cuvée ($11, 1,000)	★★
Chardonnay El Dorado ($10, 1,000)	★★
Côtes du Cosumnes Red El Dorado ($9, 500)	★★
Johannisberg Riesling El Dorado ($8, 500)	★
Merlot El Dorado ($10, 2,000)	★
Port California ($20, 500)	★
Sauvignon Blanc El Dorado ($9, 1,500)	★★
Sauvignon Blanc-Sémillon El Dorado Euphoria ($11, 500)	★★
Zinfandel El Dorado Special Selection ($15, 500)	★★
Zinfandel El Dorado Vintner's Cuvée ($10, 1,000)	★★

ALSO PRODUCED
Monsieur Omo's Red Sunshine El Dorado ($8, 500); Muscat of Alexandria El Dorado ($9, 500); Petite Sirah El Dorado ($18, 500); Pinot Noir El Dorado ($18, 500).

WINERY DATA
Case Production: 12,000. **Acres Owned:** 20 acres in El Dorado. **Varietals by Acre:** Cabernet Franc, Cabernet Sauvignon, Merlot, Petite Sirah, Sauvignon Blanc, Sémillon, Zinfandel.

Founded in 1994 by Charlie Mitchell, this winery produces 12,000 cases of El Dorado-grown wines of very ordinary quality, the best rising to minimal ★★ ratings.

ROBERT MONDAVI COASTAL (★★)
North and Central Coast, California
Founded: 1994 **Owner:** Robert Mondavi Corp.
Winemaker: Ken Shyvers.

MAJOR WINES: PRICE, CASES, RATING
Cabernet Sauvignon North Coast ($10, 225,000)	★★
Chardonnay Central Coast ($10, 250,000)	★★
Johannisberg Riesling Central Coast ($8, 100,000)	★★
Merlot Central Coast ($10, 200,000)	★★
Pinot Noir Central Coast ($8, 35,000)	★★

Sauvignon Blanc North Coast
($8, 47,000) ★★
Zinfandel North Coast
($8, 50,000) ★★

WINERY DATA

Case Production: 800,000. **Acres Owned:** 626 acres (45 acres in Mendocino, 121 acres in Monterey, 460 acres in Santa Barbara). **Varietals by Acre:** Carignane (30 acres), Chardonnay (351), Pinot Noir (199), Sauvignon Blanc (31), Zinfandel (15). **Varietals Purchased:** Cabernet Sauvignon (North Coast, Central Coast), Chardonnay (Central Coast), Johannisberg Riesling (Central Coast), Merlot (Central Coast), Pinot Noir (Central Coast), Sauvignon Blanc (Norh Coast), Zinfandel (North Coast).

Robert Mondavi's Coastal brand is a step up from Woodbridge, focusing on grapes grown in Mendocino, Monterey and Santa Barbara Counties. New vineyard developments in those regions will expand the brand's acreage to 2,242 acres by the year 2000, ensuring more control over grape sources and the ability to increase production dramatically. Plans are to eventually build a winery in Monterey.

The Coastal wines are value-oriented. As such, they rarely excite, but they do usually deliver modest depth and straightforward varietal character. The 1997 Central Coast Chardonnay (83 points) was crisp and leafy with apple and toast flavors, while the 1997 Central Coast Merlot (82) was impressive for the richness of its black cherry flavors. The 1997 Pinot Noir (81) showed a shade less flavor than previous vintages, but was easy to drink, with its light cherry notes. Cabernet, Riesling and Zinfandel are also well made, and are designed for immediate consumption.

ROBERT MONDAVI WINERY (★★★–★★★★★)

Oakville, Napa Valley
Founded: 1966. **Owner:** Robert Mondavi Corp. **Winemaker:** Tim Mondavi, Genevieve Janssens. **Second Label:** La Famiglia di Robert Mondavi, Woodbridge, Robert Mondavi Coastal.

MAJOR WINES: PRICE, CASES, RATING

Cabernet Sauvignon Napa Valley
($22, 100,000) ★★★★
Cabernet Sauvignon Napa Valley
Oakville District
($35, 10,000) ★★★

Cabernet Sauvignon Napa Valley Reserve
($75, 20,000) ★★★★★
Cabernet Sauvignon Stags Leap District
($35, 10,000) ★★★
Chardonnay Carneros
($23, 20,000) ★★★★
Chardonnay Napa Valley
($19, 100,000) ★★★★
Chardonnay Napa Valley Reserve
($34, 15,000) ★★★★★
Fumé Blanc Napa Valley
($12, 100,000) ★★★
Fumé Blanc Napa Valley
To-Kalon Vineyard Reserve
($28, 10,000) ★★★★
Fumé Blanc Napa Valley
To-Kalon Vineyard I-Block
($50, 300) ★★★★
Merlot Napa Valley
($22, 20,000) ★★★
Pinot Noir Carneros
($26, 20,000) ★★★
Pinot Noir Napa Valley
($19, 35,000) ★★★
Pinot Noir Napa Valley Reserve
($34, 8,000) ★★★★
Sauvignon Blanc Stags Leap District
($16, 5,000) ★★★
Zinfandel Napa Valley
($18, 8,000) ★★★★

ALSO PRODUCED

Sauvignon Napa Valley Blanc Botrytis ($50, NA).

WINERY DATA

Case Production: 400,000. **Acres Owned:** 747 acres (227 in Napa Carneros, 115 in Sonoma Carneros, 22 in Napa, 262 in Oakville, 121 in Stag's Leap). **Varietals by Acre:** Cabernet Franc (19 acres), Cabernet Sauvignon (133), Chardonnay (191), Malbec (12), Merlot (72), Muscat Canelli (42), Petit Verdot (2), Pinot Noir (113), Sauvignon Blanc (120), Sauvignon Musque (3), Sémillon (25), Zinfandel (15). **Vineyard Designations:** To-Kalon Estate (Sauvignon Blanc). **Varietals Purchased:** Cabernet Sauvignon (Napa Valley, Oakville, Stags Leap), Chardonnay (Carneros), Merlot (Carneros, Napa Valley), Muscat (Napa Valley), Pinot Noir (Carneros), Sauvignon Blanc (Napa Valley, Oakville, Stags Leap), Zinfandel (Napa Valley).

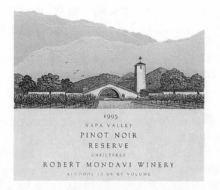

Robert Mondavi remains the single greatest influence on modern California wine. Through his energy, vision, innovation and determination, Mondavi set California wine on the path to greatness when the industry was struggling to regain its momentum after Prohibition, the Great Depression and World War II. Mondavi's roots run deep in Napa Valley, but since 1993 the winery has been a publicly traded firm, and while the quality of some of his wines remains at the highest levels, others have been less compelling of late.

In the 1940s, Mondavi convinced his parents, then living in the Central Valley, that Napa Valley wine had a future, and in 1943, the family purchased the Charles Krug Winery in St. Helena. For the next two decades, Mondavi, his father Cesare and his younger brother Peter overhauled Krug and turned it into one of the valley's most prominent wineries. By the 1960s, however, brothers Robert and Peter were at odds over winery business decisions and strategies, and in 1965, Robert was ousted from Krug.

A year later, in 1966, Robert went on to found his own winery in Oakville with the help of his eldest son, Michael, and Rainier Brewing Co. There, he resumed his efforts to refine and polish his wines through innovative techniques aimed at raising quality. The early Mondavi wines reflected the experimental state of California wine, with Gamay, Petite Sirah, Riesling and Zinfandel all part of the lineup. By the early 1970s, the winery had narrowed its focus, emphasizing Cabernet and Chardonnay, and by the 1980s, Fumé Blanc and Pinot Noir had been added.

One key to the winery's success is that Mondavi emerged from Krug with choice vineyard sites, and continued to acquire the best vineyards and secure long-term contracts with growers willing to follow his directives. The most important vineyard among the winery's acreage is the To-Kalon vineyard, situated around the southern boundaries of the Oakville winery, which is comprised mostly of Cabernet. The winery also has substantial plantings in the Stags Leap District and in Carneros, the latter devoted primarily to Chardonnay and Pinot Noir.

Mondavi's accomplishments are many, and include superb Cabernets, particularly the Reserve. He has also had great success with Chardonnay and Sauvignon Blanc, which he renamed Fumé Blanc when sales were sagging. Recent vintages of Fumé Blanc and Pinot Noir have been less impressive, however. Merlot and Zinfandel are also part of the main product mix, and they're very good—occasionally outstanding—though not among the state's best. In 1995, the winery introduced its first Italian-style wines—Barbera, Malvasia Bianca, Sangiovese and Tocai—under the name La Famiglia di Robert Mondavi.

Robert's son Tim has overseen winemaking since the late 1970s, and deserves credit for many of the advancements, but perhaps for some of the complacency as well. All things considered, this winery, which now makes 400,000 cases of Napa Valley and Carneros wines, offers an impressive lineup, including many cutting-edge wines. Still, there's room for improvement with some of the winery's pet projects, namely Fumé Blanc and Pinot Noir.

Mondavi Corp. also owns Byron Vineyards in Santa Maria Valley; Woodbridge by Robert Mondavi, a multimillion case brand which uses mostly Central Valley grapes; Robert Mondavi Coastal, which uses Coastal Area grapes; and a half interest in Opus One in Napa Valley. It is also involved in joint ventures in Chile with Caliterra—and the Frescobaldi family of Tuscany—where a wine called Luce is made.

TASTING NOTES

CABERNET SAUVIGNON NAPA VALLEY (★ ★ ★ ★): Typically supple and elegant, with ripe, sharply focused currant, black cherry, mint and spice flavors. Showy on release, and should be enjoyed early on.
1995: Dense and well oaked, with plenty of anise, currant, chocolate, cedar and berry flavors to sustain it, turning complex on the finish. **90**
1994: A touch earthy, with a slight leathery edge, it slowly works its way into more complex herb, currant and black cherry flavors. **90**

1993: Ripe, and a touch earthy, with hints of herb and anise and a slight leathery edge to the currant and plum notes. **88**
1992: Smooth and elegant, with a rich, supple core of currant, black cherry and cedary oak, all beautifully proportioned with mild tannins. **91**
1991: A racy wine with lots of ripe, juicy currant, plum and black cherry flavors, picking up toasty oak notes on the finish. **90**
1990: Dark, dense and tannic, but remarkably supple for such a big wine, offering lots of currant, cherry and bitter almond flavors and ample tannins. **90**
1987: Youthful and vibrant, with a firm, tannic dimension to the earthy currant, sage, spice and cedar flavors. **90**

CABERNET SAUVIGNON NAPA VALLEY OAKVILLE DISTRICT (★★★)
1994: Smooth and supple, with a spicy edge to the medium-weight currant, plum and cherry notes. **88**
1993: Complex, with intense plum, cherry and wild berry flavors and nice dashes of spice, cedar and leather. **88**

CABERNET SAUVIGNON NAPA VALLEY RESERVE (★★★★★): Richer and fuller than the Napa bottling; marked by polish and finesse. Drinks well within a year or two of release, and ages well up to the 8 to 15 year mark—sometimes longer. The To-Kalon Vineyard in Oakville is the primary grape source for the Reserve.
1995: Ripe, dark, dense and earthy, with a rich core of currant, mineral and spice, showing off its elegance and finesse. **94**
1994: Supple, complex and harmonious, with a broad range of currant, anise, coffee, cedar and spice flavors, along with notes of toasty oak and supple tannins. **94**
1993: Dark, ripe and intense, with a tight core of currant, mineral, earth and spice flavors, turning dry, tannic and austere on the finish. **90**
1992: Dense and compact, with a tightly wound, rich core of earthy currant, cedar, spice and cherry flavors and chewy tannins. **91**
1991: Dense, compact and firmly tannic, with a beam of mint, currant and chocolate flavors. This is a big, rough-and-tumble wine with high extract. **90**
1990: Herb, olive and currant flavors begin to open up on the finish, where they fold together nicely and pick up a spicy anise accent. **92**
1989: Ripe and firm, with intense, chewy currant and plum flavors, but also has a good dose of tannin and oak. **85**

1988: Chunky and firmly tannic, but well focused for the vintage, with earthy, leathery currant, cedar, mint and spice flavors. **88**
1987: Dark, ripe and intense, with a rich, integrated core of cedar, currant, anise and spice, finishing with a firm, tannic edge. **93**
1986: Elegant and complex, with a gamy currant and mint edge to the earthy Cabernet flavors. Well crafted, but it loses its zest on the finish. **90**
1985: Unfolds slowly, with a grapey accent to the currant and cherry flavors, it turns elegant and delicate, with supple tannins coming through on the finish. **93**
1984: Ripe and firm, with supple black cherry, currant, anise and oak flavors. Balanced and complex. **90**
1983: Austere like the '82, with more tannins than fruit. **82**
1982: A hard-edged, tannic wine with minty currant flavors that turn thin. **82**
1981: Austere and devoid of most its fruit. A weak Reserve that has peaked. **83**
1980: Tastes thin and stripped, with a hint of mint and currant. **80**
1979: Tight, firm and concentrated, showing more spine than the '78 but not the breadth of flavor. A different style, but very impressive. **91**
1978: Ripe, smooth and polished, with complex currant, anise and oak flavors that finish with fleshy tannins. **91**
1977: Still showing plenty of ripe, elegant currant, cedar and spice flavors **87**
1976: It has ripe currant and plum aromas, but it tastes dry and tannic. A drought-year wine that's fairly typical of the vintage. **84**
1975: The 1975 was always elegant and delicate, but its best years are past, leaving it with a leathery currant edge that's drying. **86**
1974: Mature and elegant, with ripe currant, coffee and cedar flavors and a smooth, plush texture. **87**
1973: Most impressive the last time I tried it; ripe and concentrated, with complex cassis, currant and anise notes flanked by firm tannins. **88**
1972: Never a vintage to get excited about, it's a pleasant, earthy wine. **78**
1971: Firm and concentrated, with high extract and currant and spice flavors. A muscular wine that's sturdy and complex. **89**
1970: Long one of my favorites, this is a great wine from a great vintage, packed with ripe currant, herb, olive,

spice and cherry flavors that linger. **90**

1969: Elegant and stylish, with pretty currant and spice flavors. Still showing ample oak and tannin. **88**

1968: From a ripe, rich vintage, it's packed with complex flavors of currant, cedar, spice and mint. **88**

CHARDONNAY CARNEROS (★★★): Steadily improving; distinctive for its bracing acidity and tightly-woven flavors.

1995: Tight, firm and compact, with a rich core of spicy citrus, pear and light oak shadings. **92**

1994: Smells fresh and ripe, with a tart, citrus edge to the pear and apple notes, turning smooth and spicy on the finish. **89**

CHARDONNAY NAPA VALLEY (★★★): A touch leaner than the Reserve, it can nonetheless impress with its vibrant fruit flavors.

CHARDONNAY NAPA VALLEY RESERVE (★★★★★): Combines richness with elegant flavor and complexity, showing beautiful fruit and pretty oak—overall, lots to like. Occasionally has up to 15 percent Santa Barbara County grapes blended in.

1996: Ripe, with complex pear, fig and pineapple flavors that are smooth and polished; gains nuance and elegance on the finish, where the flavors fan out. **90**

1995: Smooth, ripe and creamy, with hints of pear, lemon, light oak and spice, turning elegant and delicate on the finish. **90**

1994: A fantastic Reserve. Starts out tight and trim, then builds tremendous complexity, with notes of ripe pear, apple and citrus, turning elegant and polished on the finish. **95**

1993: Elegant and refined, with a tantalizing array of ripe pear and smoky, toasty oak flavors, together with hints of vanilla and nutmeg. **91**

1992: Remarkably elegant and complex, with tiers of ripe, polished pear, peach, nectarine and honey flavors framed by toasty vanilla and oak. **92**

1991: Tight and complex, with a core of pretty, spicy honey, pear and vanilla flavors that are smooth and elegant, providing a nice blend of fruit and oak. **90**

1990: Bold, rich and striking for its complexity and depth, with lots of smoky oak, pear, fig and melon flavors, finishing with a creamy texture and fine length. Beautifully balanced, long and delicious. **92**

1988: Aging exceptionally well, with youthful, vibrant, complex Chardonnay flavors that echo peach, pear, spice and nutmeg. **91**

1986: Elegant and delicate, with subtle pear, melon, smoke and spicy citrus notes that are complex and long on the finish. A deliberately elegant and restrained wine that follows the 1985 in reshaping the Reserve style. **89**

1985: A distinctively elegant and subtle wine that offers attractive, ripe, well balanced pear, earth and lemon notes that are gentle and enticing, finishing with a touch of smokiness. **88**

FUMÉ BLANC/SAUVIGNON BLANC VARIOUS BOTTLINGS (★★★): Steady, though at times it can be quite tight and lean. The best are the Fumé Blanc Napa Valley To-Kalon Vineyard Reserve and the To-Kalon Vineyard I-Block bottlings. The Reserve relies on the subtlety more than full-bodied flavors, and the 1995 I-Block (89 points) is rich and exotic in flavor, though at $50, it's quite expensive. The 1995 Sauvignon Blanc Stags Leap District (87) offers bright acidity, subtle oak and crisp lemon-lime flavors.

MERLOT NAPA VALLEY (★★★): Steadily improving since its introduction in 1989; marked by complex herb and current flavors. Hit a high note with the 1994 vintage.

1995: Complex, with a spicy, minty dimension, and supple plum, cherry and currant notes. **88**

1994: Distinct for its herb and tarry notes, a touch of bitterness gives way to smoky, toasty oak, plush currant, tea, sage and mineral flavors. **90**

1991: Complex, vibrant and focused, with cherry, currant and spicy oak flavors that pick up chocolate and toasty oak notes on the finish. Firmly tannic. **89**

1990: Tight and firm, with a meaty, leathery edge to the plum and currant aromas and flavors. **86**

PINOT NOIR CARNEROS (★★★)

1996: Complex, with a range of herb, brown sugar, and dried cherry flavors, it turns stemmy, austere, dry, and tannic on the finish. **87**

1995: Earthy and quite tannic, with a stemmy, tealike edge, it takes some time to work into the core of cherry and wild berry flavors. **87**

1994: Elegant, with supple earth and black cherry flavors and a pretty dash of smoky oak. **87**

PINOT NOIR NAPA VALLEY RESERVE (★★★★): This remains a very good, occasionally outstanding wine marked by herb, tea and black cherry flavors, with judicious oak and attractive earthy nuances. In some years, however, it's on the lean side. Best to drink early on.

1996: Strikes a nice balance between its moderately ripe, complex herb, cherry, berry and spicy flavors. **87**

1995: Marked by mint and sage notes, the core of cherry and plum is intense and concentrated, with firm tannins. **91**

1994: Lean and trim, with a smoky, meaty edge to the cherry and berry notes, the flavors slowly build and fan out on the finish. **89**

1993: A touch earthy, but enough plum and cherry flavors emerge to keep it elegant. **89**

1992: Unfiltered; tight and firm, with a crisp band of tart black cherry and spice notes. Finishes with a short aftertaste; short-term cellaring may help. **87**

1991: Smooth, ripe and polished, with a supple texture and mature sage, wild berry, plum and black cherry flavors. **91**

1990: Smooth, elegant and fully mature; marked by dried cherry, herb, sage, tea, anise and spice flavors. **89**

Zinfandel Napa Valley (★★★★): Better of late, with a supple, polished style that mirrors that of Mondavi's other red wines.

1996: Smooth, ripe and supple, with pretty plum, cherry and wild berry flavors and hints of jam and supple tannins. **87**

1995: Bright, ripe and juicy, with a pretty core of cherry, wild berry, plum and currant notes, turning supple and elegant on the finish. **92**

Monte Volpe see Domaine Saint Gregory

The Monterey Vineyard (★–★★)
Monterey County
Founded: 1973. **Owner:** Seagram Chateau & Estate Wines Co. **Winemaker:** Ken Greene.

Major Wines: Price, Cases, Rating

Wine	Rating
Cabernet Sauvignon Monterey County ($7, 130,000)	★
Chardonnay Monterey County ($7, 275,000)	★★
Merlot Monterey-San Joaquin-Stanislaus Counties ($7, 110,000)	★
Pinot Noir Monterey County ($7, 38,000)	★
Sauvignon Blanc Monterey County ($6, 12,500)	★
White Zinfandel Lodi-Monterey ($6, 65,000)	★

Winery Data
Case Production: 650,000. **Acres Owned:** 1,198 acres in Monterey County. **Varietals by Acre:** Cabernet Sauvignon (470 acres), Chardonnay (345), Merlot (281), Pinot Gris (6), Sangiovese (31), Sauvignon Blanc (50), Syrah (15). **Varietals Purchased:** Cabernet Franc (Monterey County), Chardonnay (Monterey County, San Joaquin County), Merlot (Stanislaus County), Pinot Noir (Monterey County), Zinfandel (Monterey County, San Joaquin County).

This winery began as an ambitious venture aimed at capitalizing on the widespread vineyard plantings in Monterey, and the belief that the right grapes were being matched with the proper *terroir* in this region. Hindsight showed, however, that this optimism was premature. The winery struggled, especially with herbal and vegetal reds. Richard Peterson, a one-time winemaker at Beaulieu (now at Folie à Deux, see listing), and wine writer Gerald Asher, then a wine importer, were formerly affiliated with the brand. In 1977, the winery was sold to Coca Cola, and in 1983 it was acquired by Seagram.

Monteviña Wines (★★)
Shenandoah Valley, Amador County
Founded: 1970. **Owner:** Trinchero Family. **Winemaker:** Jeff Meyers. **Second Label:** Terra d' Oro.

Major Wines: Price, Cases, Rating

Wine	Rating
Barbera Amador County ($12, 20,000)	★★
Fumé Blanc California ($7, 7,000)	★★
Nebbiolo Rosato Amador County ($8, 2,000)	★
Refosco Amador County ($10, 1,000)	★★
Sangiovese Amador County ($12, 7,000)	★★
Zinfandel Amador County ($10, 25,000)	★★
Zinfandel Amador County Brioso ($7, 10,000)	★★

Terra d' Oro Barbera Amador County
  ($18, 3,000)   ★★
Terra d' Oro Sangiovese Amador County
  ($16, 2,000)   ★★
Terra d' Oro Zinfandel Amador County
  ($16, 5,000)   ★★★

ALSO PRODUCED
Aglianico Amador County ($12, 300); Aleatico Amador
County ($7, 1,200); Cucina Mista Amador County
($12, 700); Syrah Amador County ($15, 900); White
Zinfandel Amador County ($7, 50,000).

WINERY DATA
Case Production: 130,000. **Acres Owned:** 401 acres in
Amador County. **Varietals by Acre:** Aglianico (4 acres),
Aleatico (3), Barbera (86), Fresia (5), Greco (20), Nebbiolo (6),
Refosco (2), Sangiovese (80), Syrah (30), Teroldego (5),
Zinfandel (160). **Varietals Purchased:** Sangiovese (Amador
County), Zinfandel (Amador County).

In 1988 the Trinchero family, owners of Sutter Home,
purchased Monteviña Wines. Under founder Cary Gott,
Monteviña had played a leading role in developing
Amador County wine styles in the 1970s. Since the
Trinchero takeover, quality has risen, and hopes are high
for richer, more complex wines. The winery owns 401
acres in vines, dominated by Barbera, Sangiovese and
Zinfandel, with the focus on those three wines. The
Zinfandel is made in both a traditional style and a lighter
style, the latter is called Brioso.

MONTHAVEN see EDGEWOOD

MONTICELLO CELLARS (★★)
Napa Valley
Founded: 1980. **Owner:** Jay Corley. **Winemaker:** John
McKay.

MAJOR WINES: PRICE, CASES, RATING
Cabernet Napa Valley Corley Reserve
  ($35, 500)   ★★
Cabernet Napa Valley Jefferson Cuvée
  ($22, 3,500)   ★★

Chardonnay Oak Knoll Napa Valley
  Corley Reserve
  ($26, 1,500)   ★★
Chardonnay Oak Knoll Napa Valley
  Estate
  ($18, 4,000)   ★★
Merlot Oak Knoll Napa Valley
  Corley Reserve
  ($30, 2,000)   ★★
Merlot Oak Knoll Napa Valley
  Estate
  ($22, 2,000)   ★★
Pinot Noir Napa Valley Corley Reserve
  ($32, 300)   ★★
Pinot Noir Oak Knoll Napa Valley
  Estate
  ($22, 2,000)   ★★

ALSO PRODUCED
Sparkling Oak Knoll Napa Valley Domaine Montreaux
Vintage Brut ($26, 2,000); Sémillon-Sauvignon Blanc
Oak Knoll Napa Valley Chateau M Botrytis ($35, 2,200).

WINERY DATA
Case Production: 20,000. **Acres Owned:** 99 acres (67 in Oak
Knoll, 7 in Rutherford, 25 in Yountville). **Varietals by Acre:**
Cabernet Franc (6), Cabernet Sauvignon (32), Chardonnay (27),
Merlot (20), Pinot Noir (14).

Jay Corley began as a grape grower. He founded this
winery in 1980, and produces Cabernet, Chardonnay,
Merlot and Pinot Noir. In an era of great vintages, the
quality of Monticello's wines has declined overall.

The wines, made primarily from grapes grown on the
property, are of good quality, though well shy of outstanding. Both the Corley Reserve and Jefferson Cuvée
Cabernets tend to be austere and tannic, with cedar, currant and black cherry flavors, though the less expensive
Jefferson Cuvée is often more approachable and pleasant
than the Reserve. Merlot, too, is typically tight and tannic; the 1995 Merlot Corley Reserve (82 points) had firm
tannins, but it also had a green side, with herb, sage and
tea notes. Chardonnay has been consistently good; the
1995 Corley Reserve (88) was lean with a complex range
of pear, cedar, apricot and spice flavors. Pinot Noir has
also had some success, generally featuring elegant, well-
balanced cherry, tea and spice flavors, though some
recent bottlings have been leathery, dry and tannic. The

1995 Pinot Noir Corley Reserve (88) was complex and supple with cherry and wild berry flavors, while the 1995 Estate (82) was slightly earthy, with smoke, leather and dried cherry flavors.

In the early 1980s, Corley put together a business group that started Domaine Montreaux, a *méthode champenoise* sparkling wine producer near Monticello. But when its style failed to catch on due to wild stylistic swings, the winery was sold, and the Domaine Montreaux brand moved to Monticello. John McKay, late of Vichon and Merlion, signed on as winemaker in 1994. The winery doubles as a custom crush facility where many other wine brands are made. There is also a hospitality center at the winery, which is a replica of Monticello, Thomas Jefferson's Virginia home.

MORAGA (★★★★)
Bel Air, Los Angeles County
Founded: 1982. **Owner:** Tom & Ruth Jones **Winemaker:** Scott Rich.

MAJOR WINES: PRICE, CASES, RATING
Red Bel Air
  ($55, 600)   ★★★★

WINERY DATA
Case Production: 600. **Acres Owned:** 8 acres in Los Angeles County. **Varietals by Acre:** Cabernet Sauvignon (5 acres), Merlot (1.5), Sauvignon Blanc (1.5).

Aeronautical engineer Tom Jones headed Northrop Aviation and helped develop the B-2 stealth bomber while creating a unique vineyard in the fashionable Los Angeles suburb of Bel Air. In 1978, Jones began planting what is undoubtedly one of the state's most expensive vineyards in shale and calcareous soils that were once part of the ocean bottom. In 1982 the vineyard was attacked by Pierce's disease, requiring total replanting. The vineyard now measures 8 acres and is devoted to red Bordeaux varieties, planted in an extremely dense spacing of 1,600 vines per acre. Tony Soter of Étude made the wines early on. So far, Moraga's wines have been excellent. Too bad there aren't more vineyards like this in Los Angeles.

TASTING NOTES

RED BEL AIR (★★★★): A steady style; more supple and showing added depth and richness in recent vintages. Rich with earth and mineral flavors adding dimension to the supple currant and cherry notes.
1994: Wonderfully complex, with ripe, rich, vibrant flavors and supple notes of currant, tobacco, cedar and spice. **90**
1993: Smooth, rich and supple, with delicious, spicy currant, plum and wild berry flavors, turning silky and complex on the finish. **91**
1991: Well crafted and flavorful, with a supple texture and broad, complex currant and black cherry flavors and mild tannins. **89**
1990: Has worked its way out of its youthful oaky edge, showing more currant and anise flavors. **84**
1989: Deep and ripe, with generous black cherry, plum and anise flavors, finishing with an earthy, tannic edge. **87**

MORGAN WINERY (★★★–★★★★)
Monterey County
Founded: 1982. **Owner:** Dan & Donna Lee. **Winemaker:** Dean DeKarth, Dan Lee.

MAJOR WINES: PRICE, CASES, RATING
Chardonnay Monterey
  ($18, 13,000)   ★★★★
Chardonnay Monterey Reserve
  ($26, 1,500)   ★★★★
Malvasia Bianca Monterey
  ($14, 500)   ★★★
Pinot Noir Monterey
  ($20, 6,500)   ★★★
Pinot Noir Monterey Reserve
  ($30, 500)   ★★★
Sauvignon Blanc Sonoma & Monterey Counties
  ($12, 10,000)   ★★★★
Syrah Monterey
  ($20, 500)   ★★★
Zinfandel Dry Creek Valley
  ($16, 2,500)   ★★

WINERY DATA
Case Production: 35,000. **Acres Owned:** 65 acres in Santa Lucia Highlands. **Varietals by Acre:** Chardonnay (30 acres), Pinot Noir (35). **Varietals Purchased:** Pinot Noir (Santa Lucia Highlands), Zinfandel (Dry Creek Valley).

Dan Lee made wine for both Jekel Vineyards and Durney Vineyards before he and his family founded Morgan in 1982. Lee's experience with Monterey vineyards led to early successes with a Chardonnay and a Reserve, and he has since shown a deft hand with Carmel Valley Cabernet, Monterey- and Carneros-grown Pinot Noir, Dry Creek Valley Viognier and Zinfandel, and with Sauvignon Blanc. Production has steadily risen to 35,000 cases, with a mixture of winery-grown and purchased grapes. All of the wines are well made, balanced, and complex, though Chardonnay gets the highest marks in my tastings, followed closely by Pinot Noir from Monterey and Sauvignon Blanc from Sonoma County. Worth buying and drinking.

TASTING NOTES

CHARDONNAY MONTEREY (★★★★): Consistently well made, smooth, ripe, rich and creamy. I often find the regular bottling superior to the Reserve, which may need more time to develop.
1997: Focused and elegant, with a complex core of detailed citrus, pear, honey, toasted oak and spice flavors which remain concentrated enough on the long, refreshing finish. **91**
1996: Smooth, ripe, rich and creamy, with well-focused pear, vanilla, nutmeg and spice flavors. Holds its focus through the finish, where it turns even more complex. **90**
1995: Opens on an earthy note and then picks up some exotic citrus and tart pineapple flavors. Crisp and earthy on the finish. **90**

CHARDONNAY MONTEREY RESERVE (★★★★): Typically tightly wound, with earthy pear, citrus and tropical fruit flavors.
1996: Intense, even racy, with complex pear, fig, citrus and vanilla notes that turn elegant and supple on the finish. **91**
1995: Complex, with deep, earthy pear, pineapple and citrus flavor and a dash of hazelnut and nectarine. **89**
1994: Rich and full-bodied, with a juicy core of ripe pear and pineapple flavors, a lively aftertaste and a kiss of spicy oak. **89**

MALVASIA BIANCA MONTEREY (★★★): One of the few successes with this grape in California, it's fresh, delicate and complex—a nice alternative. The 1995 and 1996 (both 86 points) were tasty.

PINOT NOIR MONTEREY RESERVE (★★★): Smooth and complex with delicate flavors of cherry, spice, cola and tea.
1996: Smooth and spicy, with a core of ripe black cherry and a touch of vanilla, picking up hints of nutmeg, spice and cola that build on the finish, echoing fruit on the long, creamy aftertaste. **88**
1995: Starts out with a complex smoky, meaty, fruity greeting and shows a fine concentration of cherry, berry, mushroom and spice flavors, building to a rich, well focused aftertaste with mild tannins. **90**
1994: Tastes mature, with pleasant, earthy mushroom flavors and hints of currant and berry, showing lots of polish and delicate notes on the finish. Impressive for it balance and finesse. **89**

SAUVIGNON BLANC VARIOUS BOTTLINGS (★★★★): Has carried several appellations, including Sonoma County and a combined Sonoma-Monterey effort. The Sonoma County 1995 (90 points) was among the best in the state.

ZINFANDEL DRY CREEK VALLEY (★★): Tends to be austere and rustic. The 1995 (84 points) was dry, with cherry and cedary notes.

MOSHIN VINEYARDS (★★–★★★)
Russian River Valley, Sonoma County
Founded: 1989. **Owner:** Rick Moshin. **Winemaker:** Rick Moshin.

MAJOR WINES: PRICE, CASES
Pinot Noir Russian River Valley Moshin Vineyard ($18, 583)	★★
Pinot Noir Russian River Valley Proprietor's Select ($24, 515)	★★

ALSO PRODUCED
Merlot Dry Creek Valley Molinari ($18, 675); Pinot Noir Blanc Russian River Valley Moshin Vineyard ($8, 75)

WINERY DATA
Case Production: 1,500. **Acres Owned:** 10 acres in Russian River. **Varietals by Acre:** Pinot Noir (10 acres). **Vineyard Designations:** Molinari (Pinot Noir). **Varietals Purchased:** Merlot (Dry Creek Valley).

Richard Moshin sold Pinot Noir to Davis Bynum for years before starting his own winery, using grapes from his 10-acre Russian River vineyard. The focus is on Pinot Noir, which is made in two distinct styles: a standard bottling, and a Proprietor's Select bottling. Moshin has also added a Dry Creek Merlot, made from purchased grapes. The Pinot Noirs, typically spicy, with tea and strawberry flavors, have fluctuated from very good to average. While both the 1995 Pinot Noir (87 points) and 1995 Proprietor's Select (88) had complex fruit flavors, the 1996 (78) was light, bitter and tannic.

MOUNT EDEN VINEYARDS
(★★★–★★★★★)
Santa Cruz Mountains
Founded: 1972. **Owner:** Mount Eden Vineyards Corp. **Winemaker:** Jeffrey Patterson. **Second Label:** Madame Pinot.

MAJOR WINES: PRICE, CASES, RATING

Cabernet Sauvignon Santa Cruz Mountains ($23, 1,900)	★★★
Cabernet Sauvignon Santa Cruz Mountains Old Vine Reserve ($36, 450)	★★★
Chardonnay Edna Valley MacGregor Vineyard ($16, 10,500)	★★★★
Chardonnay Santa Cruz Mountains ($38, 1,500)	★★★★★
Pinot Noir Santa Cruz Mountains ($35, 400)	★★★

WINERY DATA
Case Production: 15,000. **Acres Owned:** 47 acres in Santa Cruz Mountains. **Varietals by Acre:** Cabernet Sauvignon (16 acres), Chardonnay (23), Pinot Noir (8). **Vineyard Designations:** MacGregor Vineyard (Chardonnay). **Varietals Purchased:** Chardonnay (Edna Valley).

Mount Eden Vineyards is the former Martin Ray Winery, which Ray founded in the Santa Cruz Mountains in the early 1940s. After protracted legal battles amongst the investors, the property was split. Martin Ray and his family took the

lower half of the property, maintaining the name. (As a footnote, the Martin Ray brand has been recently revived by new owners—see listing). The remaining investors took over the winery facility and renamed it Mount Eden.

The winery produces some 15,000 cases a year from its estate vineyards, which are divided among Cabernet, Chardonnay and Pinot Noir, each yielding wines that are intense and complex. In 1985, the winery began making a MacGregor Vineyard Edna Valley Chardonnay. In 1990, an Old Vine Reserve Cabernet was added. Each of the wines can be outstanding, but vintage variations are significant, as the cool climate can affect the Cabernet and Pinot Noir adversely.

TASTING NOTES

CABERNET SAUVIGNON SANTA CRUZ MOUNTAINS (★★★)
1994: Tart and a touch earthy, it works its way into more interesting flavors, eventually showing hints of currant, anise and chocolate; turns tannic on the finish. **88**
1993: Marked by strong oak and chewy tannins; dense and backward, tasting more like a barrel sample. **84**

CABERNET SAUVIGNON SANTA CRUZ MOUNTAINS OLD VINE RESERVE (★★★): Classic mountain Cabernet in its intensity, structure and tannic strength, it almost always needs time in the bottle for the components to mesh together. Quality swings reflect climatic conditions, as cool years render harder, greener wines. Worth cellaring in warmer vintages, but this microclimate often varies significantly from other areas.
1995: Tough and tannic, with earthy, herbal, mushroomy, earthen-floor nuances dominating the core of currant, coffee and cedary flavors. Definitely needs patience. **88**
1994: Earthy and oaky, but problematic with its strong, raw, cedary character and a dense, unyielding core of currant, blackberry and anise. **84**
1993: Big and rustic, with notes of mineral, currant, oak and cedar, finishing with chewy tannins. **88**
1992: Dark, ripe, and intense; marked by plum, prune, cherry, currant and mineral notes, turning firmly tannic on the finish. **90**

CHARDONNAY EDNA VALLEY MACGREGOR VINEYARD (★★★★): Can rival or even surpass the estate Chardonnay; made in a ripe, full-bodied, opulent style.
1996: Rich and elegant, with ripe pear, spice, melon and fig flavors, turning creamy and complex. **91**

1995: Initially earthy, but it works its way into more complex pear and pineapple flavors, and turns smooth and silky on the finish. **89**

CHARDONNAY SANTA CRUZ MOUNTAINS (★★★★): This wine can be awesome; it is enormously rich and complex, with intense fruit, mineral and spicy flavors. Ages well.

1996: Tight and concentrated, with peach and citrus notes and a complex band of mineral, anise and spice flavors. Slowly unfolds to reveal more elegance and complexity on the finish. **91**

1995: Marked by a snappy acidity, the earthy mineral and light oak shadings add dimension to the pear and melon notes. **91**

1994: Bold, ripe and intense; loaded with rich pear and hazelnut flavors, turning smoky and toasty on the finish. **92**

1988: Firm and slightly tannic, but the smoky pear and nutmeg aromas and flavors are beautifully focused and linger enticingly on the finish. A sturdy wine. **88**

1987: Lavishly oak-aged, with butterscotch, pear and spicy flavors that are woody, but it has a smooth texture and good length on the finish. The smoky aftertaste is pretty. **88**

1986: A shade richer and more complex than the 1985, it is also very elegant and subtle, with pear, lemon, honey and spicy oak adding delicate flavor notes that linger on the palate. **88**

1985: Elegant, refined and impeccably balanced, with pretty pear, lemon, honey and subtle toast notes, this is a youthful wine that, while drinking well, now can still age. Finish is elegant and delicate. **87**

PINOT NOIR SANTA CRUZ MOUNTAINS (★★★): Ranges from stunning, rich and complex when ripe to tannic and green in cold years. A pure reflection of *terroir* in a rustic mode.

1996: Light in color, with a rhubarb edge to the modestly ripe plum and cherry flavors; somewhat lacking in concentration. **86**

1995: Starts out earthy and gamey before working its way into more interesting dried fruit flavors. **87**

1994: Remarkably complex, with a ripe core of currant, coffee, wild berry and cedar; the finish is tight. **90**

1991: Walks the tightrope between exotic and funky, with its span of earthy mushroom and mineral notes and ripe, almost jammy Pinot Noir flavors. **88**

1990: Dark and plummy in color and flavor, turning crisp and tannic. **86**

MOUNT MAROMA see ST. SUPÉRY VINEYARD & WINERY

MOUNT VEEDER WINERY (★★★)
Mount Veeder, Napa Valley
Founded: 1972. **Owner:** Canandaigua Wine Co.
Winemaker: Larry Levin.

MAJOR WINES: PRICE, CASES, RATING

Cabernet Sauvignon Napa Valley ($30, 7,500)	★★★
Red Napa Valley Reserve ($40, 2,500)	★★★
Zinfandel Napa Valley ($25, 750)	★★

WINERY DATA
Case Production: 10,000. **Acres Owned:** 31 acres on Mount Veeder. **Varietals by Acre:** Cabernet Franc (4 acres), Cabernet Sauvignon (15), Malbec (2), Merlot (6), Petit Verdot (1), Zinfandel (3).

Michael and Arlene Bernstein founded this winery in 1972, making a series of good, often tannic, rustic mountain-grown Cabernets and Zinfandels. In 1982, the Bernsteins sold the winery to Henry and Lisele Matheson, who expanded operations to nearly 5,000 cases. In time, the Mathesons found the wine business to be a financial drain, and in 1989, they sold it to the Eckes family, the owners of Franciscan Vineyards. The thread of consistency at the winery for a number of years was winemaker Peter Franus (of Franus, see listing). Franus departed in 1993, however, after starting his own small Zinfandel-focused brand. In 1999, Canandaigua Wines acquired Mount Veeder Winery in a deal which included Franciscan Oakville Estate and Estancia.

The modern Mount Veeder produces 10,000 cases—mostly Cabernet-based reds. As of late, the brand appears to be in limbo, and in need of re-direction.

TASTING NOTES

CABERNET SAUVIGNON NAPA VALLEY (★★★): Showing more harmony and finesse recently, especially the brilliant 1990 and 1995 vintages.

1995: Complex and intense, with a pretty assortment of toasty oak, elegant plum and black cherry flavors and supple tannins. **90**

1994: Clean, ripe and flavorful, with a pretty core of black cherry, herb, plum and berry notes, holding its flavor through the finish, where the flavors linger on. **88**

1993: Firm and compact, with a nice core of ripe cherry, plum and cedary oak flavors that linger on the finish. Mild tannins. **87**

1992: Intense and tannic, with a tightly wound core of currant, cherry, anise and berry flavors, but in the end it's the tannins that stand out in this wine, giving it a hard, biting edge. **87**

1991: Serves up ripe currant and black cherry flavors, picking up a cedar and spice edge on the finish, but it's tough and chewy. **86**

1990: Opulent and chewy, with rich, pretty black cherry, currant and plum flavors, finishing with a delicious encore of fruit and oak. Wonderful depth. **92**

1989: Firm and tight, with ripe plum and currant flavors and a crisp texture. **82**

1987: Tart and firmly tannic, with earthy notes and green wild berry flavors. **87**

1986: A big, blunt wine with very ripe flavors of raisin and currant, finishing with strong tannins. **83**

1984: Shows rich and supple tar, tobacco, plum, currant and spicy flavors, finishing with firm tannins. **83**

1978: Distinct for its earthy, rustic, mushroomy flavors, the core of spicy currant, anise and sage is intense and firmly tannic. **88**

1974: Still sturdy, with strong, dry oak flavors. There are ripe, lean, earthy currant and cedar notes, but it's drying on the finish. **85**

RED NAPA VALLEY RESERVE (★★★): Variable; lighter than the Cabernet; the 1990 is superb.

1993: Tight and tannic, with a core of currant, plum and wild berry flavors, turning austere and firm on the finish. **90**

1992: Tightly wound currant, cherry and berry flavors merge with lively tannins on the finish. **88**

1991: Elegant in style, with attractive earth, anise and currant flavors, but on the palate it turns crisp and lean,

with a beet and cedar edge. **84**

1990: Elegant and supple, with a blend of rich, spicy currant, berry and buttery oak flavors. **92**

1989: Elegant, with toasty oak shadings which add complexity to the cherry and currant flavors. **86**

1988: Firm in texture, with crisp plum and berry flavors emerging through the strong tannins. **83**

ROBERT MUELLER CELLARS (★★★★)
Russian River Valley, Sonoma County
Founded: 1991. **Owner:** Robert & Lori Mueller.
Winemaker: Robert Mueller.

MAJOR WINES: PRICE, CASES, RATING

Wine	Rating
Chardonnay Alexander Valley Gauer Ranch ($20, 300)	★★★★
Chardonnay Russian River Valley ($18, 300)	★★★★
Chardonnay Russian River Valley LB ($20, 1,000)	★★★★
Chardonnay Russian River Valley Oak Meadow ($20, 500)	★★★★
Pinot Noir Russian River Valley Emily's Cuvée ($28, 500)	★★★★
Pinot Noir Russian River Valley Ranch 23 ($28, 500)	★★★

ALSO PRODUCED
Pinot Noir Russian River Valley ($23, 500); Pinot Noir Sonoma Coast Pearlessence ($28, 100); Pinot Noir Sonoma Coast Summa Vineyard ($NA, 100).

WINERY DATA
Case Production: 4,000. **Vineyard Designations:** Gauer Ranch (Chardonnay), Oak Meadow (Chardonnay), Pearlessence (Pinot Noir), Ranch 23 (Pinot Noir), Summa Vineyard (Pinot Noir). **Varietals Purchased:** Chardonnay (Alexander Valley, Russian River Valley), Pinot Noir (Russian River Valley, Sonoma Coast).

Using purchased grapes from Alexander Valley, Russian River and Sonoma Coast, Robert Mueller has quickly established himself as one of the most exciting producers of Chardonnay and Pinot Noir in Sonoma County. Every one of the Mueller wines ranges from very good to outstanding, all showing rich, concentrated flavors with great complexity and finesse. Mueller plans to plant 20 acres of Pinot Noir in Russian River Valley. Summa Vineyard Pinot Noir, once a William Selyem exclusive, will be added to the lineup, starting with the 1998 vintage.

TASTING NOTES

CHARDONNAY ALEXANDER VALLEY GAUER RANCH (★★★★): Features complex, rich, spicy apple, pear and fig flavors.
1996: A ripe, complex and smoky style; loaded with fig, pear, apple, spice and toasty oak flavors. **92**
1995: Ripe, rich and full-bodied, with pretty pear, peach, spice and nectarine notes, turning spicy on the finish. **90**
1994: Begins with spicy, toasty oak and turns toward lean citrus and pear flavors. **89**

CHARDONNAY RUSSIAN RIVER VALLEY (★★★★): Bold, ripe and rich, with a thick texture some years, and elegance and subtlety in others. Always lots of flavor.
1995: Ultra-rich and complex; a big, bold, ripe and buttery style loaded with fresh pear, anise, fig and spice flavors that linger on the finish. **92**
1994: Clean and lively, with an attractive band of citrus, apple, pear and spice flavors, finishing in a subtle nutmeg and honey aftertaste. **90**

CHARDONNAY RUSSIAN RIVER VALLEY LB (★★★★)
1996: Complex, with ripe fruit, creamy nuances, and lots of pear, earth and spice flavors, finishing with hints of citrus and light oak. **90**

CHARDONNAY RUSSIAN RIVER VALLEY OAK MEADOW (★★★★):
1996: Subtle and complex, packing in lots of ripe, intense flavors and a pretty array of rich pear, toasty oak, spice, mineral and citrus notes. **90**

PINOT NOIR RUSSIAN RIVER VALLEY EMILY'S CUVÉE (★★★★): Complex, with a supple texture and dark, concentrated fruit flavors. Named after the Muellers' daughter, Emily.
1996: A touch austere at first, but it opens to reveal a trim band of earthy cherry, spice and vanilla flavors, along with a touch of blackberry and mild, well integrated tannins. **89**
1995: Smooth, supple and polished, with a creamy texture and lots of ripe plum and black cherry flavors, turning silky on the finish. **91**

1994: Serves up a complex, elegant array of ripe, juicy Pinot Noir flavors with tiers of cherry, spice, herb and pretty, buttery oak accents. **91**

PINOT NOIR RUSSIAN RIVER VALLEY RANCH 23 (★★★)
1996: Of medium weight, with earthy cherry and wild berry flavors. Finishes with firm, dry tannins. **87**

MUMM CUVÉE NAPA (★★★)
Rutherford, Napa Valley
Founded: 1986. **Owner:** Seagram Chateau & Estate Wines Co. **Winemaker:** Rob McNeill.

MAJOR WINES: PRICE, CASES, RATING
Blanc de Blancs Napa Valley ($19, 5,000)	★★★
Blanc de Noirs Napa Valley ($15, 55,000)	★★★
Brut Prestige Napa Valley ($15, 150,000)	★★★
DVX Napa Valley ($40, 4,000)	★★★★

WINERY DATA
Case Production: 200,000. **Acres Owned:** 112 acres in Carneros. **Varietals by Acre:** Chardonnay (31 acres), Pinot Gris (5), Pinot Meunier (10), Pinot Noir (66). **Varietals Purchased:** Chardonnay (Carneros, Mendocino County, Napa Valley, Sonoma County), Pinot Gris (Napa Valley, Mendocino County), Pinot Meunier (Napa Valley), Pinot Noir (Carneros, Mendocino County, Napa Valley, Sonoma County).

This winery began as a joint venture between Mumm of Champagne, France, and Seagram Classics Wine Co., the California wine branch of spirits giant Seagram. Plans began in 1984, with the first *méthode champenoise* sparkling wine appearing in 1986. A winery on Silverado Trail was completed in 1987, in time to meet growing expansion that now has the winery producing 200,000 cases of uniformly high-quality sparkling wines.

The winery owns 112 acres in Carneros. The estate-grown grapes are supplemented with purchased grapes, giving the winemaker considerable flexibility and contributing to the wines' complexity. The product mix ranges from Blanc de Blancs (Chardonnay and Pinot Gris) and Blanc de Noirs (mostly Pinot Noir) to Brut Prestige (mostly Pinot Noir), to DVX (a Tête de Cuvée—

named after Guy Devaux, the founding winemaker and former chairman—which is 50% Chardonnay and 50% Pinot Noir). The DVX is intense and complex, and ranks among the state's best.

MURPHY-GOODE ESTATE WINERY (★★★–★★★★)

Alexander Valley, Sonoma County
Founded: 1985. **Owner:** Tim Murphy, Dale Goode, Dave Ready. **Winemaker:** Christina Benz.

MAJOR WINES: PRICE, CASES, RATING

Cabernet Sauvignon Alexander Valley ($19, 5,800)	★★★
Cabernet Sauvignon Alexander Valley Brenda Block Reserve ($24, 1,700)	★★★
Chardonnay Alexander Valley Island Block Reserve ($24, 4,100)	★★★★
Chardonnay Russian River Valley J&K Murphy Vineyard Reserve ($24, 2,400)	★★★
Chardonnay Sonoma County ($15, 42,000)	★★
Fumé Blanc Sonoma County ($12, 39,000)	★★★
Merlot Alexander Valley Murphy Ranch ($18, 6,200)	★★★
Pinot Blanc Sonoma County ($14, 2,900)	★★
Sauvignon Blanc Alexander Valley Fumé II The Deuce ($24, 1,800)	★★★
Sauvignon Blanc Alexander Valley Reserve Fumé ($17, 14,000)	★★★
Zinfandel Sonoma County ($16, 5,000)	★★★

WINERY DATA

Case Production: 90,000. **Acres Owned:** 350 acres (335 in Alexander Valley, 15 in Russian River). **Varietals by Acre:** Cabernet Sauvignon (50 acres), Chardonnay (120), Gewürztraminer (12), Merlot (35), Pinot Noir (12), Petit Verdot (10), Sauvignon Blanc (84), Sauvignon Musque (15), Zinfandel (12). **Vineyard Designations:** J&K Vineyard (Chardonnay),

Brenda Block (Cabernet Sauvignon), Island Block (Chardonnay). **Varietals Purchased:** Cabernet Sauvignon (Alexander Valley), Chardonnay (Alexander Valley, Russian River), Pinot Blanc (Russian River), Sauvignon Blanc (Alexander Valley, Russian River), Zinfandel (Dry Creek).

This partnership includes Dale Goode, Tim Murphy and Dave Ready. Goode and Murphy had been grape growers in Alexander Valley before they founded Murphy-Goode in 1985. The winery has substantial vineyard holdings, with 350 acres in vines led by Chardonnay and Sauvignon Blanc. With Christina Benz as winemaker, the style has evolved into a very attractive line of well-oaked and flavorful wines, including Cabernet, Chardonnay, Merlot, Pinot Blanc and Sauvignon Blanc, with Reserve bottlings appearing on occasion. The house style runs toward ripe, fruity wines and pretty oak nuances. Made to drink on release.

TASTING NOTES

CABERNET SAUVIGNON ALEXANDER VALLEY BRENDA BLOCK RESERVE (★★★): This wine has emerged as the winery's best, and is pushing ★★★★.
1995: Impressive for its up-front fruitiness and complexity, with ripe, spicy cherry, plum and berry flavors, toasty vanilla-scented oak and a long, complex aftertaste. Wonderfully balanced; of medium-weight, with fine tannins. **90**
1994: Firm, tight and tannic, with a rich, concentrated core of currant, plum, anise and tobacco and a light toasty oak finish. Finishes with a smooth aftertaste. **89**

CHARDONNAY ALEXANDER VALLEY ISLAND BLOCK RESERVE (★★★★) AND J & K MURPHY VINEYARD RESERVE (★★★): The Island Block Reserve and J & K Murphy Vineyard Reserve are the top Chardonnays. Both feature ripe flavors and creamy textures.

MERLOT ALEXANDER VALLEY MURPHY RANCH (★★★): Light and supple, with appealing fruit flavors. The 1996 (85 points) has spicy cherry and berry flavors and mild tannins.

SAUVIGNON BLANC ALEXANDER VALLEY FUMÉ II THE DEUCE (★★★): The 1996 (90 points) featured layers of complex herb, grapefruit and hazelnut flavors.

SAUVIGNON BLANC ALEXANDER VALLEY RESERVE FUMÉ (★★★): Very consistent. The 1996 (88 points) was well oaked, with grassy herb and sweet pea flavors.

ZINFANDEL VARIOUS BOTTLINGS (★★★): This wine has carried several appellations and has been very tasty, with the 1995 Dry Creek and Alexander Valleys bottling (88 points) showing silky cherry and berry flavors, while the 1996 Sonoma County (also 88) showed more pepper and wild berry flavors.

ANDREW MURRAY VINEYARDS (★★★)
Santa Ynez Valley, Santa Barbara County
Founded: 1990. **Owner:** Murray Family. **Winemaker:** Andrew Murray.

MAJOR WINES: PRICE, CASES, RATING
Espérance Red Santa Ynez Valley
($18, 1,500)   ★★
Roussanne Santa Ynez Valley
($25, 600)   ★★
Syrah Santa Ynez Valley Hillside Reserve
($25, 400)   ★★★
Viognier Santa Ynez Valley
($25, 1,000)   ★★

ALSO PRODUCED
Syrah Santa Ynez Valley Les Coteaux ($18, 2,000).

WINERY DATA
Case Production: 5,500. **Acres Owned:** 35 acres in Santa Ynez Valley. **Varietals by Acre:** Grenache (3 acres), Mourvèdre (3), Roussanne (6), Syrah (15), Viognier (9).

Andrew Murray established his winery and vineyard in 1990 with the financial aid of his parents, and was twenty-four years old at the time of his first release. The winery sits on property near Zaca Mesa's vineyards in Santa Ynez Valley. Murray and his wife, Kristen, make and sell the wines themselves.

The winery's focus is on Rhône varietals from Murray's 35-acre vineyard, much of which is on a hillside. The early reds, like the 1994 Syrah (84 points) and the 1996 Espérance (86), a Grenache blend, tended to be austere and tannic, with a modest range of herb and spice flavors. The 1996 Syrah Hillside Reserve (90), however, was dense and deeply concentrated, with complex flavors of mineral, black cherry and plum. Whites have also been good, but just short of exciting; the 1996 Viognier (84) and the 1996 Roussanne (86) shared similar profiles: traces of bitterness along with pear, apple and spice notes. This is a winery to watch.

MURRIETA'S WELL (★★–★★★)
Livermore Valley, Alameda County
Founded: 1989. **Owner:** Sergio & Pablo Traverso and the Wente Family. **Winemaker:** Sergio Traverso.

MAJOR WINES: PRICE, CASES, RATING
Vendimia Red Livermore Valley
($30, 5,000)   ★★
Vendimia White Livermore Valley
($22, 2,000)   ★★
Zinfandel Livermore Valley
Raboli Vineyard
($28, 1,100)   ★★★

WINERY DATA
Case Production: 7,000. **Acres Owned:** 90 acres in Livermore Valley. **Varietals by Acre:** Cabernet Franc, Cabernet Sauvignon, Merlot, Sauvignon Blanc, Sémillon, Zinfandel. **Vineyard Designations:** Raboli Vineyard (Zinfandel).

This is a partnership between veteran California winemakers Sergio Traverso (formerly of Sterling and Concannon) and Philip Wente (of Wente Bros.). The focus is on Livermore Valley wines, with 7,000 cases of two upscale Bordeaux-style blends (a red and a white) and a Zinfandel. The grapes come from the historic Louis Mel Vineyard, a 90-acre vineyard that dates back to the 1880s.

The three wines are all very well made, usually scoring in the very good range. The Vendimia Red, a blend of Cabernet Sauvignon, Cabernet Franc, Merlot and Zinfandel, is usually smooth and complex, with currant and plum flavors. The 1995 (86 points) vintage took a slight dip, showing dry tannins and racy, berryish notes with bell pepper and green bean nuances. The 1997 Vendimia White (85), a blend of Sauvignon Blanc, Sémillon and Muscat, was refreshing, with melon, peach and mineral flavors, though it was not up to its usual standards. Zinfandel tends to be complex, ripe and spicy. The 1994 (90) was one of the best wines to come out of this area.

MYSTIC CLIFFS WINE CELLARS (★)
Monterey County
Founded: 1998. **Owner:** Riverland Vineyards, Canandaigua Wine Co. **Winemaker:** Ed Filice.

MAJOR WINES: PRICE, CASES, RATING

Cabernet Sauvignon California	
($8, 125,000)	★
Chardonnay California	
($8, 250,000)	★
Merlot California	
($8, 125,000)	★

WINERY DATA
Case Production: 500,000. **Acres Owned:** 1,500 acres in Monterey County. **Varietals by Acre:** Cabernet Franc (10 acres), Cabernet Sauvignon (530), Chardonnay (495), Malbec (10), Merlot (360), Petit Verdot (10), Pinot Noir (55), Syrah (30). **Varietals Purchased:** Cabernet Sauvignon (California), Chardonnay (California), Merlot (California), Pinot Noir (California), Sauvignon Blanc (California), Syrah (California), Zinfandel (California).

Mystic Cliffs is a new brand developed by Canandaigua Wine Co., the second largest wine company in the United States after Gallo. Much of the grapes for Mystic Cliffs come from Canandaigua's large vineyard holdings in Monterey County. The first wines were merely average in quality, with a simple apple-flavored 1997 Chardonnay (80 points), a weedy 1995 Cabernet (78) and a tart, disjointed 1996 Merlot (75).

NALLE WINERY (★★★)
Dry Creek Valley, Sonoma County
Founded: 1984. **Owner:** Doug Nalle. **Winemaker:** Doug Nalle.

MAJOR WINES: PRICE, CASES, RATING

Zinfandel Dry Creek Valley	
($21, 2,200)	★★★

ALSO PRODUCED
Gewürztraminer Anderson Valley ($17, 250); Riesling Mendocino County ($17, 250).

WINERY DATA
Case Production: 2,700. **Varietals Purchased:** Gewürztraminer (Anderson Valley), Riesling (Mendocino County), Zinfandel (Dry Creek Valley).

After working at Jordan, Souverain, Balverne and Quivira, Doug Nalle started making his own wines, zeroing in on Dry Creek Valley Zinfandel as his speciality, beginning with the 1984 vintage. All of the grapes are purchased from old vines, and the wine includes a dash of Petite Sirah. Production has hovered at around 2,700 cases, and quality has been high. A small amount of Cabernet is made occasionally, also from Dry Creek Valley grapes, but it's a shade lighter and less intriguing than the Zinfandel, which is usually the case with these two grapes in Dry Creek. Gewürztraminer and Riesling are also made in small quantities, using Anderson Valley and Mendocino grapes, respectively.

TASTING NOTES

ZINFANDEL DRY CREEK VALLEY (★★★): Combines ripe, intense, well-focused fruit flavors with polish and finesse. Drinks best early on.
1996: Elegant and refined, smooth, ripe and spicy, with pretty black cherry and raspberry flavors and notes of tar and anise. **88**
1993: Supple and elegant, with ripe cherry and raspberry flavors and light oak shadings that linger on the finish. **87**

NAPA RIDGE (★★–★★★)
Alexander Valley, Sonoma County
Founded: 1986. **Owner:** Beringer Wine Estates. **Winemaker:** David Schlottman.

MAJOR WINES: PRICE, CASES, RATING

Cabernet Sauvignon Central Coast	
($10, 70,000)	★★★
Cabernet Sauvignon Napa Valley Reserve	
($15, 200)	★★
Chardonnay Napa Valley Reserve	
($15, 1,000)	★★★
Chardonnay North Coast	
($9, 200,000)	★★
Chardonnay-Sauvignon Blanc-Sémillon North Coast Triad	
($9, 14,500)	★★

Merlot North Coast
   ($10, 200,000)   ★★

Pinot Noir Carneros Reserve
   ($15, 500)   ★★

Pinot Noir North Coast
   ($11, 60,000)   ★★

Zinfandel Central Coast
   ($9, 8,500)   ★★

WINERY DATA

Case Production: 600,000. **Varietals Purchased:** Cabernet Sauvignon (Central Coast, Napa Valley), Chardonnay (Napa Valley, North Coast), Merlot (North Coast), Pinot Noir (Carneros, North Coast), Sauvignon Blanc (North Coast), Sémillon (North Coast), Zinfandel (Central Coast).

There is no geographical feature named Napa Ridge or even a Napa Ridge Winery; the name is a brand started by Wine World Estates (now Beringer Wine Estates)—owner of Beringer, Chateau St. Jean, Chateau Souverain and Meridian—to compete in the fighting-varietal category of budget-priced wines. Napa Ridge has become an enormous success, both as a business venture and in terms of the good value its high-quality, affordable wines offered to the consumer.

Winemaker David Schlottman has a wealth of Beringer Wine Estates vineyards to choose amongst, from Santa Barbara to Sonoma, and that diversity is reflected in the broad Central Coast and North Coast appellations, although more specific appellations are occasionally used as well. (Reading the labels can be tricky, however; the 1995 Napa Valley Chardonnay (91 points), for example, also says Coastal Reserve.) Case volume is 600,000, with a lineup that stretches from Cabernet to Chardonnay to Pinot Noir, made at the old Italian Swiss Colony winery in Asti. The wines are ripe and fruity and are usually very good values. Moreover, they are made in large enough quantities that they're widely available. Credit David Schlottman for sometimes brilliant efforts. Worth shopping for.

NAPA WINE CO. (★★★)
Oakville, Napa Valley
Founded: 1996. **Owner:** Dawne Dickenson, Andrew Hoxsey, David Hoxsey, Marilyn Harris, Jennifer Harris, Rennick Harris. **Winemaker:** Randy Mason.

MAJOR WINES: PRICE, CASES, RATING

Cabernet Sauvignon Napa Valley
   ($28, 725)   ★★★

Sauvignon Blanc Napa Valley
   ($20, 1,500)   ★★★

ALSO PRODUCED

Pinot Blanc Napa Valley ($18, 400).

WINERY DATA

Case Production: 3,000. **Acres Owned:** 600 acres (390 in Yountville, 210 in Oakville). **Varietals by Acre:** Cabernet Franc (17 acres), Cabernet Sauvignon (90), Chardonnay (51), Dolcetto (6), Flora (9), Malbec (2), Merlot (70), Pinot Blanc (22), Pinot Gris (9), Pinot Meunier (42), Pinot Noir (50), Sauvignon Blanc (119), Sémillon (46), Zinfandel (12).

Napa Wine Co., best known as a custom crush, fermentation and barrel aging facility for a number of Napa's great labels (Bryant Family, Colgin, Pahlmeyer, Staglin Family Vineyards), began producing its own wines in 1996, drawing from its considerable vineyard holdings in Oakville and Yountville. Only three wines are produced: Cabernet Sauvignon, Pinot Blanc and Sauvignon Blanc, all from Napa Valley vineyards owned by Napa Wine Co. The soft, rich 1997 Sauvignon Blanc (87 points) showed grassy passionfruit, grapefruit and melon flavors.

Located on Oakville Crossroad adjacent to the Oakville Grocery, the original winery facility dates to the late 1800s, making it one of the oldest wineries in Napa Valley. The current six owners are all decendants of the Pelissa family, who purchased and renovated the old facility in 1993 and have been Napa grape growers since the 1950s. Randy Mason, who has his own line of Mason wines and once made wine for the now defunct Lakespring Winery, is the winemaker. Production is now at 3,000 cases, with plans to grow to 15,000 cases.

NAPA-VILLAGES see NEWLAN VINEYARDS & WINERY

NAPANOOK see **DOMINUS ESTATE**

NATHANSON CREEK see **SEBASTIANI SONOMA CASK CELLARS**

NAVARRO VINEYARDS (★★★)
Anderson Valley, Mendocino County
Founded: 1974. **Owner:** Ted Bennett, Deborah Cahn.
Winemaker: Jim Klein. **Second Label:** Indian Creek.

MAJOR WINES: PRICE, CASES, RATING

Cabernet Sauvignon Mendocino ($20, 800)	★★★
Chardonnay Anderson Valley Première Reserve ($17, 3,500)	★★★
Chardonnay Mendocino ($13, 2,000)	★★★
Gewürztraminer Anderson Valley ($14, 5,000)	★★★
Muscat Blanc Anderson Valley ($14, 800)	★★
Pinot Gris Anderson Valley ($14, 600)	★★
Pinot Noir Anderson Valley Méthode à l'Ancienne ($18, 3,500)	★★★
Pinot Noir Mendocino ($13, 2,500)	★★★
Riesling Anderson Valley ($12, 700)	★★
Riesling Late Harvest Anderson Valley Sweet ($10, 300)	★★★★
Riesling Late Harvest Anderson Valley Very Sweet Cluster Select ($20, 300)	★★★★
Sauvignon Blanc Mendocino Cuvée 128 ($13, 1,000)	★★★★
Zinfandel Mendocino ($15, 1,000)	★★

ALSO PRODUCED
Gewürztraminer Late Harvest Anderson Valley Cluster Select ($25, 200); Gewürztraminer Late Harvest Anderson Valley ($10, 500).

WINERY DATA
Case Production: 25,000. **Acres Owned:** 85 acres in Anderson Valley. **Varietals by Acre:** Chardonnay (18 acres), Gewürztraminer (30), Muscat Blanc (4), Pinot Gris (4), Pinot Noir (25), Riesling (4). **Varietals Purchased:** Cabernet Sauvignon (Mendocino), Chardonnay (Mendocino), Sauvignon Blanc (Mendocino), Zinfandel (Mendocino).

Ted Bennett and Deborah Cahn built their beautiful winery in picturesque Anderson Valley in 1974 after moving from the Bay Area, where Bennett had owned Pacific Stereo, a chain of music stores. They initially focused on Gewürztraminer, but have since added a full lineup that includes Cabernet, Chardonnay, Riesling (made in three styles, from dry to late harvest) and Pinot Noir. All of Navarro's wines are superbly crafted and very consistent from year to year. Bennett and Cahn have high standards, and resist selling inferior wines—a trap too many wineries fall into. Production is 25,000 cases from 85 acres of winery-owned vineyards. Wines such as Cabernet and Zinfandel are made from purchased grapes grown in warmer inland vineyards. Anderson Valley is one of California's coolest climates, ideal for many of the wines Navarro excels at. As good as these wines are, their quality keeps improving. The dessert wines are among the state's best.

TASTING NOTES

CABERNET SAUVIGNON MENDOCINO (★★★): Ripe, supple and balanced, with complex flavors. A very steady, reliable wine that always shows well.
1992: Chunky, with a firm layer of tannins and a core of intense herb and currant flavors. **89**
1991: Offers a nice core of ripe currant, cherry and plum flavors with hints of herb and cedar. **88**
1990: A complete and complex young red; supple and harmonious, showing rich herb, chocolate, cherry and vanilla notes and plush tannins. **88**

CHARDONNAY ANDERSON VALLEY PREMIÈRE RESERVE (★★★): Consistently intense and creamy, with complex, detailed flavors. Ages well.

1996: Ripe and complex, with a nice interplay of spicy pear and apple flavors and light oak shadings. **88**

1995: Starts off earthy, but a core of ripe apple, pear, melon, fig and spice flavors come through and add some dimension. **88**

1994: Bright and lively, with a tight core of delicate pear, peach, honey and nectarine flavors. **89**

GEWÜRZTRAMINER ANDERSON VALLEY (★★★): One of the few true successes with this variety, with classy lichee, citrus, grapefruit and spicy flavors. The 1996 (89 points) was right on target.

PINOT NOIR ANDERSON VALLEY MÉTHODE À L'ANCIENNE (★★★): Elegant, with delicate berry and cherry flavors and light oak in the background.

1995: Lightly fruity, with appealing plum, cherry and raspberry flavors, picking up spice and floral notes. **87**

1994: Openly fruity, ripe and intense; brimming with juicy black cherry, wild berry, currant and spice flavors. **88**

Unfiltered 1994: Tight and tannic, with a tealike edge to the plum and black cherry flavors. **87**

1993: Mature, with a complex array of black cherry, tea, sage, earth and mushroom notes and a dash of tannin. **90**

1992: Marked by pleasant, ripe plum and cherry notes, along with hints of spice and oak. **85**

1991: Aging well, with lots of tasty fruit and upfront spice, plum, black cherry and raspberry flavors. **88**

1990: Understated but complex, with rich cherry, mushroom, earth and spicy flavors, finishing with a soft, fleshy aftertaste. **88**

1986: Aging well; a delicate style with hints of dried cherry, earth, spice, smoke and mushroom. **88**

RIESLING LATE HARVEST ANDERSON VALLEY SWEET (★★★★)

1994: A racy acidity keeps the rich, sweet pineapple, honey and apricot flavors vibrant and luxurious. **93**

RIESLING LATE HARVEST ANDERSON VALLEY VERY SWEET CLUSTER SELECT (★★★★)

1994: Strong, spicy flavors keep the ripe orange and apricot flavors lively, finishing sweet without being cloying. **87**

SAUVIGNON BLANC MENDOCINO CUVÉE 128 (★★★★): This wine has become a huge success, ranking among the state's best. The 1996 (90 points) showed off complex lemon-lime, grapefruit, pear and hazelnut flavors.

NEWLAN VINEYARDS & WINERY (★★)
Napa Valley
Founded: 1980. **Owner:** Bruce M. Newlan. **Winemaker:** Glen R. Newlan. **Second Label:** Napa-Villages.

MAJOR WINES: PRICE, CASES, RATING

Cabernet Sauvignon Napa Valley ($19, 1,600)	★★★
Chardonnay Napa Valley ($16, 1,000)	★★
Pinot Noir Central Coast ($14, 2,000)	★★
Pinot Noir Napa Valley ($19, 1,500)	★★
Pinot Noir Napa Valley Reserve ($25, 200)	★★
Zinfandel California ($14, 2,000)	★★

ALSO PRODUCED
Cabernet Sauvignon California ($14, 2,000); Cabernet Sauvignon Stags Leap District ($25, 800); Merlot Napa Valley Reserve ($25, 700); Zinfandel Alexander Valley Wallstrum Family Vineyard ($18, 600); Zinfandel Napa Valley ($18, 600).

WINERY DATA
Case Production: 15,000. **Acres Owned:** 30 acres in Napa Valley. **Varietals by Acre:** Cabernet Sauvignon (14 acres), Pinot Noir (16). **Vineyard Designations:** Wallstrum Family Vineyard (Zinfandel). **Varietals Purchased:** Cabernet Sauvignon (Stags Leap), Chardonnay (Napa Valley), Merlot (Napa Valley), Zinfandel (Alexander Valley, Lodi, Napa Valley).

Bruce Newlan worked for Lockheed before opting for a winemaking career. He began as a partner in Alatera Vineyards before starting his own winery, situated north of Napa, in 1980. Today, Newlan is a family-run operation, using 30 acres of estate vineyard, including 16 acres of Pinot Noir and 14 acres of Cabernet. Chardonnay, Riesling and Zinfandel are purchased. Quality varies greatly; there's an occasional very good red wine, but often the wines are rustic, dried out and tannic, with only modest flavors.

NEWTON VINEYARD (★★★–★★★★)
Napa Valley
Founded: 1978. **Owner:** Peter & Su Hua Newton.
Winemaker: Su Hua Newton.

MAJOR WINES: PRICE, CASES, RATING

Cabernet Sauvignon Napa Valley ($29, 2,100)	★★★
Chardonnay Napa & Sonoma Counties ($21, 4,500)	★★★★
Chardonnay Napa Valley Unfiltered ($48, 2,800)	★★★★★
Claret Napa Valley ($17, 5,000)	★★★
Merlot Napa Valley Special Cuvée ($21, 3,200)	★★★
Merlot Napa Valley Unfiltered ($29, 2,400)	★★★
Pinot Noir Napa Valley Special Cuvée ($21, 2,800)	★★

ALSO PRODUCED
Chardonnay Napa Valley Special Cuvée ($15, 5,000).

WINERY DATA
Case Production: 28,000. **Acres Owned:** 194 acres in Napa Valley. **Varietals by Acre:** Chardonnay (57 acres), Merlot/Cabernet Sauvignon/Cabernet Franc (total 135), Viognier (2). **Varietals Purchased:** Chardonnay (Napa Valley, Sonoma), Pinot Noir (Napa Valley).

Peter Newton founded Newton Vineyard at the base of Spring Mountain after a successful career as the founding partner of Sterling Vineyards. While Sterling experienced its share of hits and misses, by the time Newton sold it to the Coca-Cola Bottling Co. in 1977, it ranked among the leaders in Cabernet, Merlot and Sauvignon Blanc. After selling Sterling, Newton and Ric Forman (whom Newton had hired as winemaker for Sterling) started a new winery on Spring Mountain, to be called Forman. But at the last minute the two partners had a falling out and Forman departed to start his own winery after making the first few vintages of Newton Cabernet. The winery focuses on estate-grown Cabernet and Merlot, while the Chardonnay includes some purchased grapes from Carneros. Production is about 28,000 cases, and quality is high and consistent across the board. Newton's wife, Su Hua, took over as winemaker following John Kongsgaard's departure in 1996. Even though the winery is best known for its Merlot, Chardonnay is its finest wine.

TASTING NOTES

CABERNET SAUVIGNON NAPA VALLEY (★★★): Usually very good, occasionally outstanding, it's made in a dense, chewy, somewhat tannic style that requires cellaring. Even with time to mature, though, it struggles to keep pace with the best in Napa Valley.
1995: Tight and trim, with spicy cherry and wild berry flavors, this is an austere, complex, concentrated wine that fans out on the finish. Needs short-term cellaring. **89**
1994: Tightly wound, with a firm, tannic wall built around a core of currant, anise, cherry and berry flavors. **89**
1993: A dense, rich and chewy style with a pronounced leathery edge to the core of currant and earthy flavors. **87**
1991: A real mouthful. Smooth, ripe, rich and harmonious, with tiers of currant, black cherry, chocolate, berry, spice and cedar flavors. **93**

CHARDONNAY NAPA & SONOMA COUNTIES (★★★★)
1996: Smooth and creamy, with lots of ripe fig and pear and a dash of hazelnut, finishing with a long, full aftertaste. **91**
1995: Smooth, ripe, rich and creamy, this silky, delightful wine has layers of fig, pear and apricot, with a dash of toasty oak. **93**
1994: Combines ripe fig and pear flavors with light smoky notes from oak, turning complex and creamy on the finish. **90**

CHARDONNAY NAPA VALLEY UNFILTERED (★★★★★): Rich and concentrated, with layers of complex flavors.
1996: Deliciously rich and concentrated, with layers of fruit flavors and lots of finely tuned pear, fig, spice, ginger and hazelnut flavors. **93**
1995: Smooth, rich and spicy; a delicious, fragrant, effusively fruity style that packs in lots of apple, pear, fig and melon flavors. **91**
1994: Complex, with a rich, spicy edge to the ripe pear, melon and apple flavors and pretty oak shadings. **92**

CLARET NAPA VALLEY (★★★): Good to very good; a Bordeaux-style Cabernet blend that scored 87 points in 1995, with a wine that offered appealing cherry, cedar and spicy notes.

MERLOT NAPA VALLEY SPECIAL CUVÉE (★★★): The less expensive of the Merlot bottlings, but in terms of quality, it's about on par with the Napa Valley Unfiltered.
1995: Marked by earthy, cedary flavors, it slowly finds a fruit focus with its clay and currant nuances and dry tannins. **86**

MERLOT NAPA VALLEY UNFILTERED (★★★): Shows Merlot's austere side with a narrow range of flavors and crisp tannins though well balanced.

1996: Built around a core of coffee, currant, sage and mineral flavors, this wine is tight and tannic, turning dry and austere. **87**

1995: Tight and firm, with a narrow band of currant, cedar, oak and spicy nuances. **86**

1994: Ripe, smooth and supple, with a rich core of currant, berry, cherry and cedary oak flavors. **87**

PINOT NOIR NAPA VALLEY SPECIAL CUVÉE (★★): New to the mix and merely good now, the 1995 (86 points) offered pleasant cherry, spice, herb and sage notes.

NEYERS VINEYARDS (★★★–★★★★)

Napa Valley
Founded: 1992. **Owner:** Bruce & Barbara Neyers, Ehren Jordan. **Winemaker:** Ehren Jordan. **Second Label:** Byrd-Cooper.

MAJOR WINES: PRICE, CASES, RATING

Cabernet Sauvignon Napa Valley ($40, 775)	★★★
Chardonnay Carneros ($25, 2,000)	★★★★
Chardonnay Napa Valley ($25, 1,000)	★★★★
Chardonnay Sonoma Coast El Novillero Vineyard ($35, 325)	★★★★
Chardonnay Sonoma Coast Thieriot Vineyard ($35, 350)	★★★★
Merlot Napa Valley ($25, 2,000)	★★★
Merlot Napa Valley Neyers Ranch-Conn Valley ($35, 300)	★★★★
Syrah Napa Valley Hudson Vineyard ($35, 350)	★★★★
Zinfandel Contra Costa County Pato Vineyard ($22, 500)	★★★

WINERY DATA

Case Production: 15,000. **Vineyard Designations:** Thieriot Vineyard (Chardonnay), Neyers Ranch (Merlot), Hudson Vineyard (Syrah), Pato Vineyard (Zinfandel). **Varietals Purchased:** Cabernet Sauvignon (Napa), Chardonnay (Carneros, Napa, Sonoma Coast), Merlot (Napa), Syrah (Napa), Zinfandel (Contra Costa County).

Bruce Neyers worked for wine importer Kermit Lynch after stints at Mayacamas and Joseph Phelps Vineyards before starting his brand on the side, producing some 15,000 cases of Cabernet, Chardonnay and Merlot, all from purchased grapes. Initially, quality was ordinary; the wines were typically on the lean, austere side, lacking richness and generosity. But with the addition of winemaker Ehren Jordan (Turley Wine Cellars), the wines have been impressively bold, ripe and rich—particularly the Chardonnays. Worth buying now.

TASTING NOTES

CABERNET SAUVIGNON NAPA VALLEY (★★★)
1995: Tightly wound, with firm, rich plum, currant, cedar and spice flavors that have a hard, tannic edge. **88**

CHARDONNAY CARNEROS (★★★★): An almost unbelieveable turnabout in style and quality. Now very full-bodied and displaying tiers of flavors.

1997: Ripe and complex, with lots of peach, pear, fig and nectarine flavors that are smooth and plush, turning elegant and creamy. **92**

1996: Starting off flinty, with a dash of lemon and spice, it slowly unfolds to reveal pretty flavors of ripe pear, fig and smoky oak. **92**

1995: Ripe, rich and creamy, with tiers of spicy pear, honey, apricot and light oak flavors, turning complex on the finish. **90**

1994: Bold, ripe and exotic; loaded with rich pear, nectarine, honey and hazelnut flavors. **91**

CHARDONNAY NAPA VALLEY (★★★★): Just as impressive as the Carneros; made in a similar full-blown, richly-flavored style.

1997: Bold, ripe and distinctive, with layers of plush, creamy, smoky pear, fig, apricot and melon flavors; holds its focus on the finish. **93**

1996: Elegant and complex, with ripe pear, spice, apple and citrus flavors and a pretty overlay of smoky, toasty oak. **91**

CHARDONNAY SONOMA COAST EL NOVILLERO VINEYARD (★★★★)
1997: Intense and tightly wound, with a complex array of pear, peach, anise and spice flavors, finishing with a burst of fruit flavors and some pretty, toasty oak. **92**

CHARDONNAY SONOMA COAST THIERIOT VINEYARD (★★★★): New with the 1995 vintage, but it is similar in style to the other Chardonnay bottlings.
1996: Intense and lively, with a complex, concentrated core of ripe fig, peach, pear and melon flavors and a sophisticated finish. **93**
1995: Impressive, bold and complex; packed with ripe pear, apple, pineapple and spice, with a dash of oak thrown in. **90**

MERLOT NAPA VALLEY (★★★): Has had its moments, with dark, immense wines. It can also be rather tannic and extracted.

MERLOT NAPA VALLEY NEYERS RANCH-CONN VALLEY (★★★★): Much like the Napa Valley bottling, this can be either rich, supple and well-oaked or dry and tannic.
1996: Spicy, with currant, sage, tar and cedary oak flavors; turns dry, austere and tannic on the finish. **86**
1995: Well-oaked, with pretty spice and toasty flavors and a supple, rich and complex center of ripe plum and currant flavors. **91**

SYRAH NAPA VALLEY HUDSON VINEYARD (★★★★): The 1996 (89 points) showed great potential; it's a very rich, detailed wine with lots of complex plum, spice, mineral and berry flavors. Worth watching.

ZINFANDEL CONTRA COSTA COUNTY PATO VINEYARD (★★★): Two vintages have rendered ripe, opulent wines, with high alcohol levels.
1996: A big, ripe, intense and juicy style, with a slight vinegary edge to the jammy cherry and wild berry flavors. **87**
1995: Exotic, rich and flavorful; well-oaked, with juicy plum, wild berry, cherry and vanilla flavors that pick up meaty, smoky-anise nuances. **92**

NICHOLS WINERY (★★★–★★★★)
Arroyo Grande Valley, San Luis Obispo County
Founded: 1991. **Owner:** Keith Nichols. **Winemaker:** Keith Nichols.

MAJOR WINES: PRICE, CASES, RATING

Chardonnay Arroyo Grande Valley Talley Vineyards ($28, 639)	★★★★
Chardonnay Central Coast Blend ($30, 230)	★★★
Chardonnay Central Coast Reserve ($33, 265)	★★★
Chardonnay Edna Valley Paragon ($28, 290)	★★★
Chardonnay Santa Barbara County Cottonwood Canyon ($30, 260)	★★★
Chardonnay Santa Barbara County Bien Nacido Vineyard ($28, 340)	★★★
Pinot Blanc Arroyo Grande Valley La Colline ($21, 195)	★★★
Pinot Noir Arroyo Grande Valley La Colline ($33, 105)	★★★
Pinot Noir Central Coast Blend ($36, 190)	★★★
Pinot Noir Central Coast Reserve ($45, 265)	★★★
Pinot Noir Edna Valley Paragon Vineyard ($28, 150)	★★★
Pinot Noir Monterey County Pisoni Vineyard ($42, 420)	★★★
Pinot Noir Santa Barbara County Cottonwood Canyon ($33, 645)	★★★
Pinot Noir Santa Barbara County Sierra Madre Vineyard (Discontinued)	★★★

ALSO PRODUCED
Cabernet Sauvignon Paso Robles Vinas del Sol ($NA, 800); Zinfandel Central Coast Cienega Valley ($24, 375).

WINERY DATA

Case Production: 5,000. **Vineyard Designations:** Bien Nacido (Chardonnay), Cottonwood Canyon (Chardonnay, Pinot Noir), La Colline (Pinot Blanc, Pinot Noir), Paragon (Chardonnay, Pinot Noir), Pisoni (Pinot Noir), Talley (Chardonnay). **Varietals Purchased:** Cabernet Sauvignon (Paso Robles), Chardonnay (Arroyo Grande Valley, Edna Valley, Santa Barbara County), Pinot Blanc (Arroyo Grande Valley), Pinot Noir (Arroyo Grande Valley, Edna Valley, Monterey County, Santa Barbara County), Zinfandel (Central Coast).

Keith Nichols is the owner-winemaker; the focus is on vineyard-designated Chardonnays, Pinot Blanc and Pinot Noir from some choice spots, including Talley Vineyards, Bien Nacido and Cottonwood Canyon. Early results show he has the upper hand with Chardonnay, and is getting close with Pinot Noir. Worth watching and buying.

TASTING NOTES

CHARDONNAY ARROYO GRANDE VALLEY TALLEY VINEYARDS (★★★★): Two excellent vintages in 1994 and 1995, but a shade leaner in 1996.

1996: On the tart side, with a crisp lemon-lime streak; well-made, with a lean and flinty style. **88**

1995: Ripe and spicy; a complex and beautifully crafted wine that deftly balances its pear, melon and apple flavors and light oak shadings. **92**

1994: Bold, ripe and juicy notes of rich pear, honey, peach and nectarine pick up flavors of toasty, smoky oak. **92**

CHARDONNAY CENTRAL COAST RESERVE (★★★)

1996: Lean and tight, with a crisp band of citrus, pear, mineral and lemon flavors; unfolds to reveal depth and complexity. **92**

CHARDONNAYS VARIOUS BOTTLINGS (★★★): The 1996 Edna Valley Paragon Vineyard (87 points) was tight, with citrus and guava notes. The 1996 Santa Barbara County Cottonwood Canyon Vineyard (91) showed off bright acidity and flavors. The 1996 Bien Nacido Vineyard (87) was lean, with citrus, pear and earthy notes.

PINOT NOIR SANTA BARBARA COUNTY SIERRA MADRE VINEYARD (★★★): Solid, with tight, complex berry flavors and a touch of herb.

1995: Dark, ripe, rich and exotic, with a tightly focused core of tart berry and cherry flavors, finishing with a spice and cedar aftertaste. **87**

1994: Complex, with tart cherry and berry flavors and spicy, earthy nuances that add dimension and depth, turning herbaceous on the finish. **89**

1993: Smooth and elegant, with supple black cherry, wild berry and spice flavors and pretty toasty oak shadings. **91**

PINOT NOIR VARIOUS BOTTLINGS (★★★): Nichols released several 1996 bottlings, many of which were quite impressive. A Central Coast Blend in 1996 (88 points) was smooth, with earthy cherry and spice; a Central Coast Reserve 1996 (89) showed a smoky, meaty edge, with depth and berry flavors; an Edna Valley Paragon Vineyard 1996 (89) offered lots of spicy cherry and berry flavors; a Monterey County Pisoni Vineyards 1996 (89), was dark and rich, with complex cherry and currant flavors; and a Santa Barbara County Cottonwood Canyon 1996 (87) was a bit vegetal.

NIEBAUM-COPPOLA ESTATE WINERY (★★★–★★★★)

Rutherford, Napa Valley
Founded: 1879. **Owner:** Francis & Eleanor Coppola.
Winemaker: Scott McLeod. **Second Label:** Francis Coppola Presents, Francis Coppola Diamond Series.

MAJOR WINES: PRICE, CASES, RATING

Cabernet Franc Rutherford
Francis Coppola Family Wines
($26, 1,000) ★★★
Chardonnay Napa Valley Francis
Coppola Family Wines
($20, 5,200) ★★★
Merlot Rutherford
Francis Coppola Family Wines
($32, 2,000) ★★★
Rubicon Rutherford
($65, 3,000) ★★★★
Zinfandel Rutherford Edizione Pennino
($26, 2,000) ★★★★

ALSO PRODUCED

Cabernet Sauvignon Rutherford Cask ($45, 1,000).

WINERY DATA

Case Production: 110,000 **Acres Owned:** 190 acres in Rutherford. **Varietals by Acre:** Cabernet Franc (13 acres), Cabernet Sauvignon (92), Chardonnay (4), Dolcetto (2), Marsanne (1), Merlot (38), Roussanne (2), Syrah (2), Viognier

(1), Zinfandel (29), other (6). **Varietals Purchased:** Cabernet Sauvignon (Monterey, Paso Robles), Chardonnay (Monterey), Merlot (Monterey, Paso Robles), Sangiovese (Monterey, Lodi), Syrah (Monterey, Lodi), Zinfandel (Lodi, Paso Robles).

Filmmaker Francis Ford Coppola and his wife, Eleanor, purchased the old home of Inglenook founder Gustave Niebaum in 1975, and began making wine from the old Inglenook vineyard shortly thereafter. The goal remains to create long-lived wines in the mold of the great Inglenook Cask Cabernets of the Niebaum and John Daniel eras. Having enjoyed Inglenook wines that dated to the turn of the century, Coppola focused on a style of wine that would age well over the long term.

In 1995, Coppola bought the old Inglenook chateau and 80 acres of vineyard, effectively reuniting most of Gustave Niebaum's old estate. The Coppolas now own 190 acres in vines, and sell a portion of their grape crop to various wineries.

The winery's production, once around 5,000 cases, now tops 110,000, although only about 12 percent of the output is in estate wines; the rest is bottled under Niebaum-Coppola's second labels. The quality leader is the proprietary red table wine called Rubicon, followed by Cabernet Franc and Zinfandel; the latter is bottled under the Edizione Pennino label and is named after Coppola's maternal grandfather. Merlot joined the lineup in 1991. A Cask series, featuring wines aged in large American oak casks, is a new addition.

TASTING NOTES

CABERNET FRANC RUTHERFORD FRANCIS COPPOLA FAMILY WINES (★★★): Solid; the 1996 (87 points) was cedary, with cherry and herb notes.

CHARDONNAY NAPA VALLEY FRANCIS COPPOLA FAMILY WINES (★★★): Shows signs of improvement, with the 1997 (88 points) made in a flinty citrus and tart apple style.

MERLOT RUTHERFORD FRANCIS COPPOLA FAMILY WINES (★★★): Improving, showing refinements in texture and brighter flavors.
1996: Oozing with ripe, rich black cherry, blackberry, plum and jammy notes; turning elegant, polished and sophisticated, with a cedary note adding complexity on the finish. **90**
1995: Rich and concentrated, with crisp black cherry and

blackberry flavors, a touch of mineral and spice and firm tannins. **88**
1994: Remarkably supple and elegant, with a juicy core of ripe black cherry, plum and currant flavors, picking up a dash of spice and herb on the finish. **92**
1993: Complex and supple, with smoky oak, herb, black cherry and currant flavors, turning elegant on the finish. **89**

RUBICON RUTHERFORD (★★★★): Originally a somewhat uneven performer, this wine has become steadier of late. It can be very dense, tannic, chewy, even rustic, and struggles to evolve. Recent vintages have aimed for more polish and supple tannins. Made from the key vineyards that made many long-lived Inglenook Cabernets. Worth collecting.
1995: Classy, with rich, complex, earthy berry, cherry, cedar and spice, gaining complexity and finesse, with supple, polished tannins. **92**
1994: Firm and tightly tannic, with a sharply focused, deeply concentrated core of currant, black cherry, cedar, toast and spice. **92**
1993: Distinct for its minty, herbaceous and earthy flavors and immense tannins; works its way into more interesting currant and cedary oak notes. **90**
1992: Distinctly minty, firm and austere, it slowly evolves into a more supple and flavorful wine, with a core of currant and berry flavors. **92**
1991: Firm and focused, with a dense, tannic core of smoky currant, plum, black cherry, anise and tar flavors. **91**
1990: Bold, ripe and fleshy, with deep, concentrated plum, currant, anise and tar notes, framed by light oak shadings. **90**
1989: Tough and chewy, with hard-core tannins that override the smoky herb and currant flavors. **87**
1988: Herb and mint aromas give way to a core of taut, chewy currant and cherry flavors; the finish is austere and tannic. **86**
1987: Smooth, mature and chewy, with robust cherry, anise and leather flavors that meld nicely. **88**
1986: Mature, with a complex, earthy currant edge to the flavors that adds to the menthol and mint notes. Tannic and oaky. **85**
1985: Tannic and concentrated, with earthy, spicy aromas and ripe plum and anise flavors that pick up a mineral edge. **87**
1984: Gaining richness and depth with age, with layers of chewy currant and black cherry flavors and earthy, tarry notes. **86**

1982: Earthy and tannic, with ripe, mature currant and cherry flavors that are still tightly wound. **82**

1981: Ripe, forward and supple, with plum, cherry and currant flavors that are mature, turning dry and earthy. **84**

1980: Big, intense and tannic, with drying cedar, plum and black cherry flavors. **83**

1979: Deeply colored, with rustic, potent herb and currant flavors that turn earthy and gamy. **80**

1978: Mature, with complex currant, earth and cedar flavors that turn supple on the finish. **85**

ZINFANDEL RUTHERFORD EDIZIONE PENNINO (★★★★): Impressive for its intensity and earthy raspberry flavors. Tilts toward the tannic side, though it's been better balanced of late.

1995: Elegant and refined; ripe and polished, with just the right amount of black cherry, plum and blackberry flavors and spicy, minty nuances. **91**

1993: Intense and austere; the lean, spicy cherry and raspberry flavors expand on the finish. **87**

NOEL VINEYARDS see HARMONY CELLARS

NOVELLO see PAOLETTI VINEYARDS

OAK VINEYARDS see DOMAINE ST. GEORGE

OAKFORD VINEYARDS (★★★–★★★★)
Oakville, Napa Valley
Founded: 1987. **Owner:** Floyd & Carol Wilson. **Winemaker:** Heidi Peterson Barrett.

MAJOR WINES: PRICE, CASES, RATING
Cabernet Sauvignon Oakville
($45, 1,000) ★★★★

WINERY DATA
Case Production: 1,000. **Acres Owned:** 11 acres in Oakville. **Varietals by Acre:** Cabernet Sauvignon (11 acres).

Charles and Catherine Ball established Oakford (the name is a combination of Oakville and Rutherford) in 1987. Situated in the hills above Oakville, this 11-acre,

1,000-case winery focuses on Cabernet Sauvignon. In 1998, Floyd & Carol Wilson purchased the vineyard and brand. Heidi Peterson Barrett remains in charge of winemaking, as she has been since 1994. Quality continues to improve.

TASTING NOTES

CABERNET SAUVIGNON OAKVILLE (★★★★): Supple and well balanced; leaning toward elegance, with spicy currant flavors and mild tannins. Steady progress in quality.

1995: Ripe and juicy, with bright, supple black cherry, currant, and anise flavors that turn elegant and complex. **90**

1994: The best yet. Smooth, ripe and polished, with a pretty array of well integrated plum, black cherry, wild berry, anise and spice flavors. **91**

1993: Dryness is a concern here; there's a slightly bitter edge to the plum and cherry flavors, and it turns tannic on the finish. **86**

1992: Complex aromas; an array of cherry, currant, anise and earthy notes and firm, crisp tannins. **89**

1991: Intense and spicy, with a lively core of currant, plum and berry notes, picking up a nice trace of spicy oak on the finish. **88**

1990: Solid and chunky, with pretty currant, spice and mineral flavors and light oak shadings. Firmly tannic. **88**

1988: Lean, with crisp, firm tannins and an attractive core of currant, tobacco, herb and spice flavors. **86**

OAKVILLE RANCH VINEYARDS (★★★–★★★★)
Oakville, Napa Valley
Founded: 1989. **Owner:** Mary Miner & Family. **Winemaker:** Gary Brookman.

MAJOR WINES: PRICE, CASES, RATING

Cabernet Sauvignon Napa Valley ($35, 1,700)	★★★★
Chardonnay Napa Valley ORV ($32, 600)	★★★★
Chardonnay Napa Valley Vista Vineyard ($26, 440)	★★★★
Merlot Napa Valley ($35, 270)	★★★
Robert's Blend Red Napa Valley ($45, 160)	★★★

ALSO PRODUCED

Zinfandel Napa Valley ($20, 600).

WINERY DATA

Case Production: 4,500. **Acres Owned:** 67 acres in Oakville.
Varietals by Acre: Cabernet Franc (5 acres), Cabernet
Sauvignon (35), Chardonnay (15), Merlot (10), Zinfandel (2).
Vineyard Designations: Vista Vineyard (Chardonnay).

This winery began as a merger of high-tech and high
speed. The late Bob Miner, founder of Oracle Systems
Corp., the computer software giant, together with his
wife, Mary, established the winery's Cabernet and
Chardonnay vineyard in the hills east of Oakville, where
they own a 334-acre ranch. Also partners in the winery
were Debbie and Randy Lewis, the latter a former race
car driver who once finished 14th in the Indianapolis 500.

Quality of both the Cabernets and Chardonnays has been
exceptional. In 1994, Miner's death led to a breakup of the
partnership with the Lewises, who formed their own wine
brand, Lewis Cellars. Oakville Ranch remains worth buying.

TASTING NOTES

CABERNET SAUVIGNON NAPA VALLEY (★★★): Dark,
rich, plush and concentrated. Off to a strong start; should
age well.
1995: Lots of ripe, juicy, elegant black cherry, plum, currant and spice flavors, turning long, complex and tannic
on the finish. **92**
1994: Attractive, with juicy currant- and plum-laced flavors
and pretty oak shadings, turning complex on the finish. **88**
1993: Young and spicy, with a pleasing, tight core of
cherry, currant, herb and anise flavors. **88**
1992: Austere and tightly wound, with a firm band of currant and black cherry flavors and significant tannins. **90**
1991: Serves up rich, supple, complex, ripe currant,
cherry, plum and chocolate flavors, finishing with a good
dose of oak. **90**
RESERVE 1991: Packs in lots of black cherry, currant, mineral and spice flavors, turning smooth and supple on the palate,
finishing with a long, rich, concentrated aftertaste. **92**
1990: Smooth, complex and stylish, with a strong, spicy
streak of cedar, currant and plum aromas and flavors; the
finish is silky and elegant. **93**
1989: Dark, rich and potent, with intense, deeply concentrated currant, plum and berry flavors, spicy vanilla and

oak shadings and fine tannins. **88**

CHARDONNAY NAPA VALLEY ORV (★★★): Impressive,
with complex, rich flavors.
1996: Distinct for its butterscotch flavors; ripe, rich and
focused, with hints of pear, apricot, butter and smoky,
toasty oak. **92**
1995: Tight and concentrated, with a pretty core of spice,
apple, pear and peach flavors, turning complex on the
finish. **91**
1994: Young and tight, with citrus, pear and toasty
vanilla flavors and a long, complex aftertaste. **89**

CHARDONNAY NAPA VALLEY VISTA VINEYARD (★★★):
Steady quality gains make this a wine poised for a
★★★★★ rating.
1997: Ripe, clean and spicy, with pear, nectarine, tangerine, apple and melon fruit; turning a bit crisp and astringent on the finish, but nothing that short-term cellaring
won't soften. **90**
1996: A rich, spicy style, backed by notes of ripe pear
and fig; gains a smoky nuance and turns complex on the
finish. **90**
1995: Beautifully crafted, rich and complex, with a wonderful core of ripe pear, fig, melon and peach flavors. **93**
1994: Slightly awkward, with ripe, complex pear, pineapple and spice flavors that are a bit on the woody side. **88**
1993: Elegant and understated, with ripe pear and melon
notes that turn smooth and polished on the finish. **90**
1992: A big, ripe, buttery wine with spicy pear, nectarine
and vanilla flavors, picking up smoky notes on the finish. **87**
1991: Tight and firm, offering lemon, pear and grapefruit
flavors that are lean and crisp. **88**

MERLOT NAPA VALLEY (★★★): Not yet in the same
league as the Cabernet, but the 1994 (92 points) showed
how plush and complex it can be. The 1995 (86) turned
out tighter and more tannic. Still, it's worth watching.

ROBERT'S BLEND RED NAPA VALLEY (★★★): The latest
vintage, 1995 (89 points), was mostly Cabernet Franc;
tilting toward the tart side, but complex, with layers of
berry flavors.

THE OJAI VINEYARD (★★★)
Ventura County
Founded: 1983. **Owner:** Adam & Helen Tolmach.
Winemaker: Adam Tolmach.

MAJOR WINES: PRICE, CASES, RATING
Chardonnay Arroyo Grande Valley
  Talley Vineyard
  ($19, 1,100)   ★★★
Chardonnay Arroyo Grande Valley
  Talley Vineyard Reserve
  ($25, 380)   ★★★
Chardonnay Santa Barbara County
  Bien Nacido Vineyard
  ($20, 600)   ★★★
Chardonnay Santa Ynez Valley
  Sanford & Benedict Vineyard
  ($25, 300)   ★★★
Pinot Noir Santa Barbara County
  Bien Nacido Vineyard
  ($25, 600)   ★★★
Pinot Noir Santa Lucia Highlands
  Pisoni Vineyard
  ($40, 280)   ★★★
Sauvignon Blanc-Sémillon
  Santa Barbara County
  ($14, 600)   ★★★
Syrah California
  ($18, 1,050)   ★★★
Syrah California Roll Ranch Vineyard
  ($25, 320)   ★★★
Syrah Santa Barbara County
  Bien Nacido Vineyard
  ($28, 730)   ★★★
Syrah Santa Barbara County
  Stolpman Vineyard
  ($23, 125)   ★★★
Viognier California Roll
  Ranch Vineyard
  ($20, 250)   ★★

ALSO PRODUCED
Vin Gris California ($11, 200).

WINERY DATA
Case Production: 6,000. **Vineyard Designations:** Bien Nacido Vineyard (Chardonnay, Pinot Noir, Syrah), Pisoni Vineyard (Pinot Noir), Roll Ranch Vineyard (Syrah, Viognier), Sanford & Benedict Vineyard (Chardonnay), Stolpman Vineyard (Syrah), Talley Vineyard (Chardonnay). **Varietals Purchased:** Chardonnay (Arroyo Grande, Santa Barbara, Santa Ynez Valley), Pinot Noir (Santa Barbara County, Santa Lucia Highlands), Sauvignon Blanc (Santa Barbara County), Sémillon (Santa Barbara County), Syrah (California, Santa Barbara), Viognier (California).

Adam and Helen Tolmach founded Ojai in 1983, but they didn't give the winery their full attention until 1991, when Adam dissolved his partnership with Jim Clendenen at Au Bon Climat. Since then, the Ojai wines have been more consistent and better tasting.

The Tolmachs ran into some bad luck, however, when the winery's vineyard in Ventura County was decimated by Pierce's disease. Following the 1995 harvest, the Tolmachs gave up the battle and pulled out the vines. Grapes for vineyard-designated Chardonnays, Pinot Noirs and Syrahs now come from a number of Central and South Coast growers.

Ojai is best known for its dark, rich Syrahs, which are very good but usually shy of outstanding. Pinot Noirs from the Bien Nacido and Pisoni vineyards are also dark and rich, with elegant, complex flavors of spice, leather and black cherry. The Chardonnays tend toward a restrained, elegant style, with flinty, earthy nuances to the fruit flavors.

TASTING NOTES

PINOT NOIR SANTA BARBARA COUNTY BIEN NACIDO VINEYARD (★★★)
1996: A touch earthy and leathery, with subtle notes of cherry and raspberry woven in. **86**
1995: Dark, ripe, intense and flavorful, with lots of rich, racy black cherry, cola, spice and wild berry flavors. **91**

PINOT NOIR SANTA LUCIA HIGHLANDS PISONI VINEYARD (★★★)
1996: Elegant, spicy, complex and concentrated, with pretty, earthy, leathery nuances, and black cherry, wild berry and mineral flavors. **88**

SYRAH CALIFORNIA ROLL RANCH VINEYARD (★★★):
From a vineyard in Ventura County.
1996: Very dark, rich and textured, with juicy plum and wild berry fruit flavors and hints of spice, leather and mineral flavors. **89**

SYRAH SANTA BARBARA COUNTY BIEN NACIDO VINEYARD (★★★) Dark and concentrated, with rich fruit, leather and mineral flavors.

1996: Dark, but not as concentrated as the color suggests, with stewed plum, cherry and beefy notes and a flash of mineral. **87**

1995: Dark, ripe, rich and concentrated, with intense meaty, smoky, currant, mineral, spice and leathery notes, turning tannic on the finish. **91**

SYRAH SANTA BARBARA COUNTY STOLPMAN VINEYARD (★★★)

1996: Intense, with spicy mineral, wild berry and black cherry flavors, it holds its focus, turning beefy and spicy. **87**

OPTIMA WINE CELLARS (★★★)
Healdsburg, Napa Valley
Founded: 1984. **Owner:** Greg Smith & Mike Duffy. **Winemaker:** Greg Smith & Mike Duffy.

MAJOR WINES: PRICE, CASES, RATING

Cabernet Sauvignon Alexander Valley ($30, 2,400)	★★★
Chardonnay Carneros ($30, 1,000)	★★★
Pinot Noir Russian River Valley ($40, 600)	★★

WINERY DATA
Case Production: 4,000. **Varietals Purchased:** Cabernet Sauvignon (Alexander Valley), Chardonnay (Carneros), Pinot Noir (Russian River Valley).

This partnership between Mike Duffy, winemaker at Field Stone, and Greg Smith, who now owns Fitch Mountain Winery, started like gangbusters, but has since slipped back into the pack. The brand began as a Cabernet-only venture, reliant on purchased grapes from Field Stone's vineyards in Alexander Valley, even though the label has shown both Sonoma County and Alexander Valley appellations. Chardonnay from Carneros joined the lineup in 1989, followed more recently by Pinot Noir. Quality was high early on, with the Cabernets particularly ripe and well oaked, but a tasting of older vintages has shown that they have not aged very well.

OPUS ONE (★★★★★)
Oakville, Napa Valley
Founded: 1979. **Owner:** Robert Mondavi & Baroness Philippine de Rothschild. **Winemakers:** Tim Mondavi & Patrick Léon.

WINE RATINGS.
Red Napa Valley
($120, 30,000)   ★★★★★

WINERY DATA
Case Production: 30,000. **Acres Owned:** 109 acres in Oakville. **Varietals by Acre:** Cabernet Franc (5 acres), Cabernet Sauvignon (89), Malbec (3), Merlot (7), Petit Verdot (2), Sauvignon Blanc (2), Sémillon (1). **Varietals Purchased:** Cabernet Franc (Oakville), Cabernet Sauvignon (Oakville).

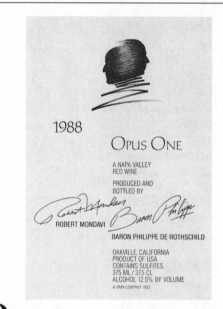

Opus One is the celebrated joint venture between Robert Mondavi Winery in Napa Valley and the late Baron Philippe de Rothschild of Château Mouton-Rothschild in Pauillac, France, who died in 1987. It is the marriage of two great winemaking families as well as two fortunes: the winery cost roughly $20 million, and the families own 109 acres of expensive vineyard land in the Oakville area.

With the first vintage in 1979, Opus One set out to downplay Cabernet's aggressive flavors, aiming for more elegance and finesse. The style that has since evolved features not only more classic Napa Valley Cabernet flavors and expansive oak shadings, but also a core of rich, complex fruit flavors. Production has risen to 30,000 cases. At $120 a bottle, Opus One remains one of California's most expensive wines. Quality is uniformly very high, though the wines are best early on, and, overall, haven't improved much with cellaring.

TASTING NOTES

RED NAPA VALLEY (★★★★): Increasingly reliant on estate-grown Cabernet (now 95 percent of the blend), it features bold, ripe, rich and complex flavors and generally supple tannins, although the winery seems intent on building more longevity into the wine.

1995: Weaves together a complex array of currant, plum, leather, spice and mineral flavors; seamless in texture, with lush tannins. **93**

1994: Earthy, with backward currant, dried cherry, sage and cedar flavors that slowly reveal their elegance and finesse. **94**

1993: Big, ripe and intense, with a rich band of currant, anise, mineral and spice flavors and notes of anise, cedar and blackberry. **91**

1992: Vibrant, with ripe, rich black cherry, currant and cedar flavors that are dense and backward; somewhat unevolved. **91**

1991: Rich and tannic, this is a potent wine that shows dense currant, anise and black cherry flavors before picking up a chalky, chocolate edge on the finish. **93**

1990: A chunky, chewy, sturdy wine that shows perfumed currant and berry flavors, all wrapped in several layers of fine tannins. Complex and concentrated. **94**

1989: Firm and flavorful, with generous, ripe currant, blackberry and cherry flavors shaded by spicy oak and a touch of earth. Firmly tannic. **89**

1988: Solid, with firm, chunky, currant, anise, wild berry and leathery notes, it gains complexity on the finish. **88**

1987: Supple, complex and harmonious, with a range of herb, tea, sage, anise, currant and berry flavors and an excellent length. **94**

1986: The earthy currant, leather and spice notes seem wrapped in a veil of tannin, rendering the finish short and tight. **88**

1985: The best of the early Opus Ones, it's fully mature and complex, with rich, ripe supple currant, anise and black cherry flavors, finishing with soft tannins. **90**

1984: Mature, with the rich, complex currant, black cherry, cedar and anise flavors turning a touch earthy. Tannins are smooth and polished. **92**

1983: Fully mature and declining, this is still a fine bottle of wine, but drink soon because the ripe fruit is fading. **86**

1982: Mature and taking on an earthy currant and anise edge. Drinking well now, but the tannins are drying. **85**

1981: Has peaked, with dry, earthy, complex currant and berry flavors, it has shed its youthful charm and should be consumed soon. **86**

1980: Still big and ripe but softening, allowing the currant, anise, cedar and spice flavors to flow. Mature. **87**

1979: Showing its age, with the earthy side of the currant and cherry flavors. Mature and a shade past its prime. **88**

PACIFIC ECHO SEE SCHARFFENBERGER

PAHLMEYER (★★★★★)
Napa Valley
Founded: 1985. **Owner:** Jayson Pahlmeyer.
Winemaker: Helen Turley. **Second Label:** Jayson.

MAJOR WINES: PRICE, CASES, RATING

Chardonnay Napa Valley ($50, 1,500)	★★★★★
Merlot Napa Valley ($50, 1,500)	★★★★★
Red Napa Valley ($50, 1,500)	★★★★★

WINERY DATA
Case Production: 4,500. **Acres Owned:** 50 acres in Atlas Peak. **Varietals by Acre:** Cabernet Franc, Cabernet Sauvignon, Malbec, Merlot, Petit Verdot. **Varietals Purchased:** Cabernet Franc (Napa Valley), Cabernet Sauvignon (Howell Mountain, Soda Canyon, Spring Mountain, Wooden Valley), Chardonnay (Coombsville), Malbec (Napa Valley), Merlot (Carneros, Soda Canyon, Spring Mountain), Petit Verdot (Napa Valley).

Attorney Jayson Pahlmeyer found he was reading more wine journals than law books, so he decided to change careers in 1985, teaming up first with vineyard owner John Caldwell and then Randy Dunn, who oversaw winemaking through the 1992 vintage. In 1993, Helen Turley became winemaker, and Pahlmeyer stopped buying Caldwell Vineyard Cabernet and signed on with several new vineyards, including Dominus. Pahlmeyer has also purchased land near Atlas Peak, where some 50 acres are planted to Bordeaux varieties, along with another 70-acre parcel in the Sonoma Coast appellation, destined to produce Chardonnay and Pinot Noir.

TASTING NOTES

CHARDONNAY NAPA VALLEY (★★★★★): Packs in lots of rich, ripe, complex flavors, aided by a measure of finesse and polish. From Berhenbach Vineyard.

1996: Rich and smoky, with complex fig, melon, toast and anise flavors that are still a bit disjointed, but all the ingredients are there. A bit more time in the bottle should smooth things out. **95**

1995: Earthy and leesy, this is an elegant, richly flavored, deeply complex wine with a core of grapefruit, citrus and pear flavors. **92**

1994: Starts with a smoky, toasty oak aroma and follows up with elegant, spicy pear, honey and butterscotch flavors. **96**

MERLOT NAPA VALLEY (★★★★★): Steadily improving, with a distinctive style that features lots of flavor and a supple texture.

1996: Impeccably balanced, remarkably complex and concentrated, with layers of currant, cedar, plum and blackberry flavors, turning plush and chocolatey on the long finish. **93**

1995: Well focused, with ripe black cherry, plum and wild berry flavors, a hint of cedar and spice and mild but firm tannins on the finish. **90**

1994: Young and fleshy in texture, with a mere hint of herb accenting the currant, spice and cedar notes; the fruit flavors fan out on the finish. Needs time to soften and evolve. **93**

RED NAPA VALLEY (★★★★★): This Cabernet Blend is uniformly high in quality; intense, complex and concentrated, with firm tannins and an austere edge to the flavors. Ages well, but the track record is limited. Has carried several designations over the years.

1995: Lots of ripe, juicy plum and black cherry flavors up front, with hints of anise, sage and mineral. Finishes with well integrated tannins and a touch of tobacco and creamy oak. **95**

1994: Ripe, complex and full-bodied, with pretty currant, black cherry, spice and cedary oak flavors that continue to develop far into the finish. The tannins are a little rough around the edges, but they're not out of line for a wine this age. **94**

1993: Ripe, rich and full-bodied, with tiers of cherry, currant, anise and spice, finishing with thick, polished tannins and a rich aftertaste. Impressive for its depth and concentration. **92**

1992: Supple and fleshy, displaying ripe, spicy currant and berry flavors, with tobacco and leather accents. Finishes with smooth tannins. **89**

1991: Dense and compact, firmly tannic and hard-edged, with just a glimpse of currant and cherry pushing through on the finish. Needs time, but may always be dry and tannic. **84**

1990: Ripe and intense, with pretty herb, mint, spice and currant flavors, picking up tobacco and cherry notes on a tannic finish. **90**

Minty Cuvée 1990: Potently minty, a flavor that overrides all else, with just a hint of currant and cedar emerging on the finish. For fans of mint-dominated Cabernet. **82**

1989: Deeply colored, austere and complex, with rich, intense currant, spice, mineral and oak shadings. **88**

1988: Firm, tight and tannic, with a leathery streak running through the chewy currant, sage and mineral notes. **87**

1987: Austere, dry and tannic, with firm mint, cedar and currant flavors. **86**

1986: Elegant and refined, with a distinctly minty edge to the sweet, ripe cherry and currant flavors. Finishes with a complex array of flavors and ripe, sweet tannins. **89**

PALOMA WINERY (★★★)
Spring Mountain District, Napa Valley
Founded: 1994. **Owner:** Barbara & Jim Richards.
Winemaker: Bob Foley. **Second Label:** Milagro.

MAJOR WINES: PRICE, CASES, RATING

Merlot Napa Valley Spring
  Mountain District
  ($30, 892)   ★★★★

Milagro Syrah Spring Mountain District
  ($30, 142)   ★★★

WINERY DATA
Case Production: 1,022 **Acres Owned:** 16 acres in Spring Mountain District. **Varietals by Acre:** Cabernet Sauvignon (2 acres), Merlot (14), Syrah (less than 1).

Owners Jim and Barbara Richards manage their 15-acre vineyard at the top of Spring Mountain on their own. Now in their mid-sixties, the couple produced their first wine in 1994 after selling grapes for years. Bob Foley, winemaker for neighboring Pride Mountain Vineyards, makes the wines. The first Merlots have been exciting, dense, minerally reds with wonderful fruit concentration. The Syrah, made under the second label Milagro, is also tasty, showing firm, ripe plum and wild berry flavors. The goal is to reach 3,000 cases. Worth watching.

TASTING NOTES

MERLOT NAPA SPRING MOUNTAIN DISTRICT (★★★): Although carrying the Napa Valley appellation, all the grapes come from Paloma's Spring Mountain Vineyard. Rich, firm and concentrated, these wines have a promising future.
1996: A lot of stuffing, with concentrated currant, plum, mineral and black cherry flavors and pretty oak shadings. **91**
1995: Appealing for its currant, cedar, spice and tobacco flavors, turning rich and complex on the finish. **90**

MILAGRO SYRAH SPRING MOUNTAIN DISTRICT (★★★)
1996: Throws out lots of ripe, spicy plum, mint and wild berry flavors, turning firmly tannic on the finish. **88**

PAOLETTI VINEYARDS (★★★)
Napa Valley
Founded: 1994. **Owner:** John Paoletti. **Winemaker:** Charles Hendricks. **Second Label:** Novello.

MAJOR WINES: PRICE, CASES, RATING
Cabernet Sauvignon Napa Valley	
($30, 650)	★★★
La Forza Red Napa Valley	
($28, 200)	★★★
Merlot Napa Valley	
($28, 150)	★★★

ALSO PRODUCED
Chardonnay Napa Valley Brix Vineyard ($15, 950).

WINERY DATA
Case Production: 2000. **Acres Owned:** 30 acres in Napa. **Varietals by Acre:** Cabernet (8 acres), Malbec (1), Merlot (20), Sangiovese (1). **Vineyard Designations:** Brix Vineyard (Chardonnay). **Varietals Purchased:** Chardonnay (Napa).

Venice-born John Paoletti is chef and owner of West Los Angeles's Ristorante Pepponi (A *Wine Spectator* Grand Award Winner). He first purchased a 10-acre vineyard on Napa Valley's Silverado Trail in 1989, and now owns a total of 30 acres. His wines are full of dark, intense ripe flavors and substantial tannins that suggest aging ability. The 1995 La Forza, a Sangiovese-Cabernet Blend (85 points), is full of ripe plum and black cherry flavors with chewy tannins. The 1994 Cabernet (87) and 1995 Cabernet (87) both displayed a good balance of fruit, earth and herb flavors. The 1995 Merlot (86) was dark, dense and tannic with ripe cherry and currant flavors.

PARADIGM (★★★★)
Oakville, Napa Valley
Founded: 1990. **Owner:** Ren & Marilyn Harris. **Winemaker:** Heidi Peterson Barrett.

MAJOR WINES: PRICE, CASES, RATING
Cabernet Sauvignon Napa Valley	
Oakville	
($40, 2,500)	★★★★
Merlot Oakville	
($32, 500)	★★★★
Zinfandel Oakville	
($22, 70)	★★★★

WINERY DATA
Case Production: 3,500. **Acres Owned:** 50.5 acres in Oakville. **Varietals by Acre:** Cabernet Franc (1 acre), Cabernet Sauvignon (31), Merlot (18), Zinfandel (0.5).

This vineyard was originally planted in 1975. In 1991, Ren and Marilyn Harris bought the property and established the Paradigm label for limited-production Cabernet Sauvignon, Merlot and Zinfandel. Located in Oakville, the vineyard has 50.5 acres in vines; most of the grapes are sold to other wineries. Heidi Peterson Barrett (Screaming Eagle, Grace Family Vineyard, Oakford, La Sirena) is winemaker here, and Cabernet production is in the 2,500-case range. Quality has been increasingly high. Worth collecting.

TASTING NOTES

CABERNET SAUVIGNON NAPA VALLEY OAKVILLE (★★★★): Poised to join the elite. Sharply focused, with broad, rich, complex flavors. Prior to 1994, the appellation was Napa Valley.
1995: Beautifully orchestrated, with a wonderful sense of finesse; ripe, textured currant, black cherry, anise, sage and cedar flavors. **93**
1994: Intense, with a lively core of wild berry, plum and blackberry flavors that pick up a nice spicy edge; tannins are firm. **92**
1993: Smooth and harmonious, with plenty of rich plum, currant and anise flavors that turn plush; the tannins are supple. **89**
1992: Dark and intense, with a hard tannic and oaky edge; the currant and berry flavors struggle with the tannins. **87**
1991: Firm, supple and complex, with pretty anise, currant and cherry flavors framed by toasty, smoky oak. Impressive for its richness and depth. **90**

MERLOT OAKVILLE (★★★★): Quickly becoming a star, with juicy fruit flavors that are complex and textured.
1996: Bold, ripe and juicy; a distinctive style, with a leathery, sandalwood edge to the core of currant, plum and blackberry flavors; turning spicy, with supple tannins and a long finish. **93**
1995: Earthy and focused, firm and tannic, even a bit chunky, but the flavors are rich and supple, with tar, spice, currant and meaty nuances. **91**
1994: Ripe and flavorful, with a rich, complex core of currant, black cherry, plum and anise, finishing with plush, supple tannins. **92**

ZINFANDEL OAKVILLE (★★★★): Not far off the Cabernet and Merlot's pace. It's packed with flavors.
1995: Ripe, intense, well focused and rich in wild berry, cherry, anise, sage and mineral flavors; supple tannins. **89**

PARADUXX see **DUCKHORN VINEYARDS**

PARAISO SPRINGS VINEYARDS (★★)
Santa Lucia Highlands, Monterey County
Founded: 1988. **Owner:** Rich & Claudia Smith.
Winemaker: Philip Zorn. **Second Label:** Cobblestone.

MAJOR WINES: PRICE, CASES, RATING
Wine	Rating
Chardonnay Santa Lucia Highlands ($16, 2,000)	★★
Johannisberg Riesling Santa Lucia Highlands ($9, 2,300)	★★
Pinot Blanc Santa Lucia Highlands ($13, 1,985)	★★★
Pinot Blanc Santa Lucia Highlands Reserve ($23, 1,000)	★★★
Pinot Noir Santa Lucia Highlands ($23, 3,500)	★

ALSO PRODUCED
Gewürztraminer Santa Lucia Highlands ($9, 600); Johannisberg Riesling Late Harvest Santa Lucia Highlands ($25, 500); Pinot Noir Late Harvest Santa Lucia Highlands ($25, 250); Port Souzao Santa Lucia Highlands ($25, 300); Syrah Santa Lucia Highlands ($23, 300).

WINERY DATA
Case Production: 20,000. **Acres Owned:** 125 acres in Santa Lucia Highlands. **Varietals by Acre:** Chardonnay (60 acres), Gewürztraminer (15), Johannisberg Riesling (49), Pinot Blanc (10), Pinot Noir (33), Syrah (8).

Richard and Claudia Smith grew grapes for 15 years before founding Paraiso Springs in 1988. Their 125-acre vineyard is planted primarily to white wine varieties, led by Chardonnay (60 acres) and Johannisberg Riesling (49 acres), but it also contains 33 acres of Pinot Noir and 8 acres of Syrah. Pinot Blanc leads in quality, though it varies stylistically from bright and floral to rich, ripe and oak-driven. The 1996 Pinot Blanc (88 points) was buttery, with toast and melon flavors, while the 1996 Reserve (88) showed fresh apricot and citrus nuances. The Pinot Noir can be ripe and flavorful, as it was in 1995 (85), but unfortunately it is often lightweight and herbal, as was the 1996 (78). The Chardonnay usually displays melon and citrus flavors; the 1996 (84) lacked focus, but was full of pleasant flavors.

PARDUCCI WINE CELLARS (★★)
Mendocino County
Founded: 1932. **Owner:** Carl Thoma. **Winemaker:** Bob Swain, Jim Kakacek. **Second Label:** Big Horn, Van Duzer.

MAJOR WINES: PRICE, CASES, RATING
Cabernet Sauvignon North Coast
($11, 45,000) ★★
Chardonnay Mendocino
($10, 40,000) ★★
Merlot Mendocino
($10, 45,000) ★★
Petite Sirah California
($10, 20,000) ★★★
Pinot Noir Mendocino
($10, 17,000) ★★
Syrah Coastal Mendocino
($11, 2,000) ★★
Zinfandel Mendocino
($10, 10,000) ★

ALSO PRODUCED
Cabernet Sauvignon Napa Valley Big Horn ($20, 5,000); Chardonnay Carneros Big Horn ($20, 10,000); Chenin Blanc Mendocino ($7, 2,000); Red California ($5, 35,000); Sangiovese Mendocino ($10, 3,000); White North Coast ($5, 25,000); White Zinfandel California ($5, 20,000).

WINERY DATA
Case Production: 300,000. **Acres Owned:** 511 acres (36 in Lake, 305 in Mendocino, 105 in Napa, 65 in Oregon). **Varietals by Acre:** Cabernet Sauvignon (59 acres), Carignane (11), Chardonnay (237), Chenin Blanc (9), Flora (10), French Colombard (7), Merlot (80), Petite Sirah (17), Pinot Noir (30), Sauvignon Blanc (17), Sémillon (12), Souzao (7), Zinfandel (15). **Varietals Purchased:** Barbera (Mendocino), Cabernet Franc (Lake County, Mendocino), Cabernet Sauvignon (Lake County, Mendocino, Napa), Charbono (Mendocino), Chardonnay (Lake County, Mendocino, Napa), Carignane (Mendocino), Chenin Blanc (Lake County, Mendocino), French Colombard (Mendocino), Flora (Mendocino), Grenache (Mendocino), Merlot (Lake County, Mendocino), Muscat (Lake County, Mendocino), Gamay (Lake County, Mendocino), Petite Sirah (Lodi, Mendocino), Pinot Noir (Mendocino), Sangiovese (Mendocino), Sauvignon Blanc (Lake County, Mendocino), Sémillon (Lake County), Syrah (Mendocino), Zinfandel (Lake County, Mendocino).

The Parducci family settled in wooded Mendocino County at the turn of the century, pioneering grape-growing and winemaking in most of the appellations that are now associated with Mendocino wines. They started their winery in 1933, buying and growing grapes for a wide variety of wines. By the 1970s, John Parducci had tested, proved and disproved many theories about wine-growing in Mendocino, laying the foundation for modern-day knowledge about what grapes grow best where. He was also a leader in using new techniques such as barrel fermentation, *sur lie* aging, and blending Merlot with Cabernet. The winery excelled at red wines, finding Petite Sirah, Cabernet Sauvignon and Zinfandel ideally suited for many areas in Mendocino, but found itself suddenly unfashionable in the early 1970s when the white wine boom hit.

By 1972, the Parducci family needed cash, and sold the winery to Teachers Management & Investment. TMI retained the Parduccis to run the winery, but a long-running management dispute led to John Parducci's departure in 1994 and a subsequent battle for control of the winery, which Parducci lost in 1995. New owner Carl Thoma is striving to keep Parducci's reputation for good value wines, and has succeeded thus far.

FESS PARKER (★★★)
Santa Ynez Valley, Santa Barbara County
Founded: 1989. **Owner:** Fess Parker. **Winemaker:** Eli Parker.

MAJOR WINES: PRICE, CASES, RATING
Chardonnay Santa Barbara County
($18, 12,000) ★★★
Chardonnay Santa Barbara County
American Tradition Reserve
($22, 2,000) ★★★
Chardonnay Santa Barbara County Marcella
Vineyard American Tradition Reserve
($24, 1,000) ★★★
Merlot Santa Barbara County
($18, 2,000) ★★★
Pinot Noir Santa Barbara County
($18, 3,000) ★★

Pinot Noir Santa Barbara County
    American Tradition Reserve
    ($30, 1,000)   ★★
Syrah Santa Barbara County
    ($18, 4,000)   ★★★
Syrah Santa Barbara County
    American Tradition Reserve
    ($32, 1,000)   ★★★
Viognier Santa Barbara County
    ($22, 1,000)   ★★★

ALSO PRODUCED

Cabernet Franc Santa Barbara County ($18, 500); Chenin Blanc Santa Barbara County ($16, 500); Johannisberg Riesling Santa Barbara County ($10, 2,000); Melange du Rhône Red Santa Barbara County ($22, 500); Meritage American Tradition Reserve Santa Barbara County ($22, 400); Muscat Canelli Central Coast ($10, 1,000); Pinot Blanc Santa Barbara County ($16, 500); Sauvignon Blanc Santa Barbara County ($8, 1,000).

WINERY DATA

Case Production: 35,400. **Acres Owned:** 171 (98 in Santa Barbara County, 73 in Santa Maria Valley). **Varietals by Acre:** Cabernet Franc (5 acres), Chardonnay (74), Grenache (5), Johannisberg Riesling (5), Marsanne (1), Merlot (1), Pinot Noir (15), Roussanne (11), Syrah (38), Viognier (16). **Vineyard Designations:** Marcella Vineyards (Chardonnay). **Varietals Purchased:** Cabernet Franc (Santa Ynez Valley), Cabernet Sauvignon (Santa Ynez Valley), Chardonnay (Santa Maria Valley), Chenin Blanc (Santa Maria Valley), Johannisberg Riesling (Santa Ynez Valley), Merlot (Santa Maria Valley), Muscat Canelli (San Luis Obispo County), Pinot Blanc (Santa Maria Valley), Pinot Noir (Santa Maria Valley), Sauvignon Blanc (Santa Maria Valley, Santa Ynez Valley).

Retired actor Fess Parker, famous for his roles as Davy Crockett and Daniel Boone, produces wine from a mixture of estate-grown and purchased grapes from the Central Coast and Santa Barbara County appellations. Parker's son, Eli, is the winemaker, and was coached by consultant Jed Steele (Steele Wines). The product mix includes Chardonnay, a Muscat Canelli dessert wine, Merlot, Pinot Noir, Riesling and Syrah, with reserve-style wines carrying the American Tradition designation. The majority of the wines fit into the ★★ to ★★★ range, with Chardonnay at times outstanding, and Syrah taking a slight quality lead amongst the reds, over the moderately fruity Pinot Noirs.

TASTING NOTES

SYRAH SANTA BARBARA COUNTY (★★★)
1994: Rich and exotic aromas and a complex core of meaty currant, plum, mineral, leather and smoky flavors. **90**

SYRAH SANTA BARBARA COUNTY AMERICAN TRADITION RESERVE (★★★)
1995: A decidedly spicy, herbal style with a twinge of tomato and anise, along with hints of stewed plum and berry. **87**
1993: Smooth and polished, with an appealing core of anise, plum, celery and spice flavors. **87**

PATZ & HALL WINE CO.
(★★★–★★★★★)
Napa Valley
Founded: 1988. **Owner:** Donald & Heather Patz, Anne Moses, James Hall. **Winemaker:** James Hall.

MAJOR WINES: PRICE, CASES, RATING

Chardonnay Carneros Hyde Vineyard
    ($37, 750)   ★★★★★
Chardonnay Mendocino Alder
    Springs Vineyard
    ($50, 48)   ★★★★
Chardonnay Mount Veeder
    Carr Vineyard
    ($45, 750)   ★★★★★
Chardonnay Napa Valley
    ($30, 2,500)   ★★★★★
Chardonnay Russian River Valley
    ($30, 250)   ★★★★★
Pinot Noir Carneros Hyde Vineyard
    ($37, 150)   ★★★
Pinot Noir Mendocino Alder
    Springs Vineyard
    ($50, 48)   ★★★
Pinot Noir Russian River Valley
    ($30, 750)   ★★★

ALSO PRODUCED

Pinot Noir Santa Lucia Highlands Pisoni Vineyard ($NA).

WINERY DATA

Case Production: 6,000. **Vineyard Designations:** Alder Springs Vineyard (Chardonnay, Pinot Noir), Carr Vineyard (Chardonnay), Hyde Vineyard (Chardonnay, Pinot Noir), Pisoni

Vineyard (Pinot Noir). **Varietals Purchased:** Chardonnay (Carneros, Mendocino County, Mount Veeder, Napa, Russian River Valley, Sonoma Coast), Pinot Noir (Carneros, Mendocino County, Russian River Valley, Santa Lucia Highlands).

Donald Patz and James Hall are two wine industry veterans who met while working at Flora Springs Winery. In 1988, they pooled $5,000 each in capital and started their own brand, aiming for a distinctive Burgundian style of Chardonnay. They have since added several different Chardonnay bottlings, expanding beyond Napa and Carneros into Russian River Valley. They have also ventured into Pinot Noir.

The Chardonnays are simply delicious; they are very rich and creamy, and all are worthy of outstanding ratings. Pinot Noir hasn't been as easy, however; the owners are still trying to find the kinds of grapes that lead to the style of wine they like. Mendocino and Santa Lucia Highlands bottlings of Pinot Noir are in the works as well. Worth buying.

TASTING NOTES

CHARDONNAY CARNEROS HYDE VINEYARD (★★★★★): A terrific wine, very complex and flavorful.
1997: Wonderful complexity and finesse, with rich, supple pear, fig, hazelnut, citrus and spicy flavors built on a smooth, creamy texture. **93**
1996: Distinct for its rich, spicy accents and subtle oak shadings; a complex core of ripe pear, apple and melon flavors. **93**

CHARDONNAY MOUNT VEEDER CARR VINEYARD (★★★★★): Has risen to the top ranks; very complex and concentrated.
1996: An elegant, refined style, with pretty floral and spicy aromas and a silky texture that lets the pear, melon and fig flavors glide. **93**
1995: Delivers a complex array of ripe, well-oaked pear, apple, hazelnut and toasty oak flavors that fold together beautifully. **94**
1994: Bold, delicious, ultra-rich and complex, with tiers of concentrated pear, spice, honey and hazelnut flavors. **94**

CHARDONNAY NAPA VALLEY (★★★★★): Full-blown Burgundian techniques and toasty, buttery oak add texture and flavor dimensions to the ripe and succulent fruit flavors.

1996: Wonderfully ripe and complex, with a pretty core of rich pear, fig and apple flavors and notes of hazelnut; smooth and silky in texture. **94**
1995: Bold, rich and fruity, with an amazing core of fresh, ripe pear, apple, fig and melon flavors and pretty oak shadings. **93**
1994: A rich, elegant white brimming with complex flavors of pear, spice, vanilla and hazelnut and a lovely length. **91**
1993: Delivers a mouthful of ripe pear, peach, honey and hazelnut flavors, turning rich and elegant on the finish where the flavors persist. Beautifully crafted. **91**
1992: Spicy, rich and generous, with complex and distinctive nectarine, vanilla and spice aromas and flavors. **91**
1991: Wonderfully complex, with bold, ripe, concentrated pear, fig, citrus and vanilla flavors that are deep and intense. A real mouthful. **92**

CHARDONNAY RUSSIAN RIVER VALLEY (★★★★★): Very intense, rich and flavorful; true to the house style.
1996: Intense and lively, with a smoky oak edge to the core of ripe apple, pear, fig and melon notes, picking up a dash of nutmeg towards the finish. **93**
1995: Smooth and creamy, with subtle pear, fig, melon and spice notes and light, smoky oak shadings. **91**

PINOT NOIR CARNEROS HYDE VINEYARD (★★★)
1996: Tight and compact, with pretty dark berry, black cherry and light oaky flavors and firm tannins. **88**

PINOT NOIR RUSSIAN RIVER VALLEY (★★★): Lean one year, smoother the next. Still on the learning curve with this grape.
1996: Lean and earthy, the tea, sage, berry and cherry flavors are moderately ripe but not yet especially complex. **86**
1995: Smooth, supple, intense and lively, with a spicy, complex core of zesty cherry and wild berry flavors. **89**

PAVONA (★★)
Monterey County
Founded: 1995. **Owner:** Richard Kanakaris.
Winemaker: Aaron Mosley.

MAJOR WINES: PRICE, CASES, RATING
Pinot Blanc Monterey County
  Paraiso Springs Vineyard
  ($15, 500) ★★
Pinot Noir Monterey County
  ($18, 1,300) ★★
Zinfandel Paso Robles Twin Hills
  ($18, 500) ★★

ALSO PRODUCED
Pinot Noir Monterey County Reserve ($24, 500); Pinot
Noir Rosé Monterey County Camillia ($9, 200);
Zinfandel Napa Valley ($18, 500).

WINERY DATA
Case Production: 3,500. **Vineyard Designations:** Paraiso
Springs Vineyard. **Varietals Purchased:** Pinot Blanc (Monterey
County, Santa Lucia Highlands), Pinot Noir (Monterey County,
Santa Lucia Highlands), Zinfandel (Napa Valley, Paso Robles).

Pavona makes Pinot Blanc, Pinot Noir and Zinfandel
from purchased Monterey County grapes. Quality has
been fair, but none of the wines have really distinguished
themselves.

PEACHY CANYON WINERY (★★–★★★)
Paso Robles, San Luis Obispo County
Founded: 1988. **Owner:** Douglas Beckett. **Winemaker:**
Thomas Westberg.

MAJOR WINES: PRICE, CASES, RATING
Cabernet Sauvignon Paso Robles
  ($20, 1,000) ★★
Merlot Paso Robles
  ($23, 1,000) ★★
Para Siempre Red Paso Robles
  ($28, 800) ★★
Zinfandel California Incredible Red
  ($11, 10,000) ★★
Zinfandel Paso Robles Dusi Ranch
  ($23, 1,500) ★★★

Zinfandel Paso Robles Eastside
  ($15, 1,000) ★★
Zinfandel Paso Robles Westside
  ($19, 5,000) ★★

ALSO PRODUCED
Chardonnay Paso Robles ($18, 1,200); Zinfandel Paso
Robles Especial Reserve Blend ($25, 900); Zinfandel
Paso Robles ($30, 1000).

WINERY DATA
Case Production: 22,000. **Acres Owned:** 60 acres in Paso
Robles. **Varietals by Acre:** Cabernet Sauvignon (15 acres),
Chardonnay (10), Zinfandel (35). **Varietals Purchased:**
Cabernet Sauvignon (Paso Robles), Merlot (Paso Robles),
Zinfandel (Paso Robles).

Doug Beckett owned a chain of liquor stores before he
turned to winemaking, first buying land in Paso Robles,
and a then taking a stab at home winemaking. In 1987,
Peachy Canyon released its first wines, with Beckett
focusing on old-vine Cabernet Sauvignon and Zinfandel,
including a vineyard-designated bottling from Dusi
Ranch, long a source of excellent Zinfandel for Ridge
Vineyards. Merlot was added in 1992, but Zinfandel is
still the specialty. Quality is variable, with wines that
sometimes feature bold, bright, ripe and juicy flavors that
earn solid ★★-★★★ ratings. Other times they're less
complete, so shopping by vintage pays off.

TASTING NOTES

ZINFANDEL PASO ROBLES DUSI RANCH (★★★): Variable
in quality, but often quite ripe and pleasing.
1995: Ripe, with a core of jammy cherry and wild berry
that's supple and complex, finishing with a tar and vanilla edge and a hint of coffee. **87**

ZINFANDEL PASO ROBLES WESTSIDE (★★): Not as
impressive of late, sharing the inconsistency of other
bottlings.
1995: Ripe and juicy with jammy plum and raspberry
flavors picking up an earthy mushroom note on the
finish. **86**

ROBERT PECOTA WINERY (★★★)
Calistoga, Napa Valley
Founded: 1978. **Owner:** Robert Pecota. **Winemaker:** Robert Pecota.

MAJOR WINES: PRICE, CASES, RATING
Cabernet Sauvignon Napa Valley
  Kara's Vineyard
  ($25, 2,500)   ★★★
Merlot Napa Valley Steven André Vineyard
  ($25, 3,000)   ★★★
Muscat Canelli Napa Valley
  Moscato d'Andrea
  ($9, 2,500)   ★★
Sauvignon Blanc California
  ($11, 4,000)   ★★

ALSO PRODUCED
Chenin Blanc Monterey County ($11, 2,000).

WINERY DATA
Case Production: 16,000. **Acres Owned:** 38 acres in Napa Valley. **Varietals by Acre:** Cabernet Sauvignon (12 acres), Merlot (18), Syrah (8). **Vineyard Designations:** Kara's Vineyard (Cabernet Sauvignon), Steven André Vineyard (Merlot). **Varietals Purchased:** Muscat Canelli (Napa Valley), Sauvignon Blanc (Monterey County).

Robert Pecota worked for Beringer Vineyards before starting his winery in 1978. He focused initially on Chardonnay, Muscat Canelli, and Cabernet Sauvignon, including the 10-acre vineyard-designated Kara's Vineyard, named after his daughter. In 1989, Pecota added Steven André Merlot, named after his son. The two reds are the best wines, with both earning ★★★ ratings but edging closer to ★★★★.

TASTING NOTES
CABERNET SAUVIGNON NAPA VALLEY KARA'S VINEYARD (★★★): Ripe, supple and polished; occasionally excellent.
1995: Bright and elegant, even sleek, with juicy wild berry, black cherry, plum and spice flavors, finishing with crisp tannins. **90**
1994: Complex and tightly wound, with a green olive accent to the currant and berry flavors. **88**
1993: Offers a decent core of ripe plum and currant flavors, along with a spicy edge, finishing with mild tannins. **86**
1988: Pleasant, with ripe, spicy black cherry, wild berry

and currant notes, turning earthy on the finish. **86**
MERLOT NAPA VALLEY STEVEN ANDRÉ VINEYARD (★★★): Steadily improving, with more richness and depth.
1996: Tight and oaky, with firm tannins, but it also has a wonderful core of intensely flavored Merlot, with tiers of plum, currant and berry flavors. **91**
1995: Intense and tannic, with a core of earthy currant, coffee, cedar and spice flavors, finishing with a rather hard edge. **87**
1994: Tight and intense; a compact young wine with rich cherry, currant, anise and cedary flavors. **88**
1993: Serves up a decent core of ripe cherry and wild berry flavors, turning crisp and simple on the finish. **85**

PEDRONCELLI WINERY (★★)
Dry Creek Valley, Sonoma County
Founded: 1927. **Owner:** John & Jim Pedroncelli. **Winemaker:** Gary Martin.

MAJOR WINES: PRICE, CASES, RATING
Cabernet Sauvignon Alexander Valley
  Vineyard Selection Morris Fay Vineyard
  ($13, 2,000)   ★★
Cabernet Sauvignon Dry Creek Valley
  Vineyard Selection
  ($10, 8,000)   ★★
Cabernet Sauvignon Dry Creek Valley
  Vineyard Selection Raymond Burr Vineyard
  ($20, 1,000)   ★★
Cabernet Sauvignon Dry Creek Valley
  Vineyard Selection Three Vineyards
  ($13, 8,000)   ★★
Chardonnay Dry Creek Valley
  Vineyard Selection F. Johnson Vineyard
  ($12, 4,000)   ★
Chardonnay Dry Creek Valley
  Vintage Selection
  ($10, 10,000)   ★★
Fumé Blanc Dry Creek Valley
  Vintage Selection
  ($9, 5,000)   ★★
Merlot Dry Creek Valley Vineyard
  Selection Bench Vineyard
  ($13, 10,000)   ★

Pinot Noir Dry Creek Valley Vineyard
  Selection F. Johnson Vineyard
  ($13, 5,000)   ★★
Zinfandel Dry Creek Valley Vineyard
  Selection Mother Clone
  ($12, 9,000)   ★★
Zinfandel Dry Creek Valley Vineyard
  Selection Pedroni-Bushnell Vineyard
  ($13, 2,000)   ★★
Zinfandel Dry Creek Valley
  Vintage Selection
  ($9, 9,000)   ★★
Zinfandel Rosé Sonoma County
  Vintage Selection
  ($8, 3,000)   ★

ALSO PRODUCED
Port Dry Creek Valley Vineyard Selection Burr-Beneyides
Vineyard ($14, 300); Sangiovese Dry Creek Valley
Vintage Selection ($13, 1,000); White Zinfandel
California Vintage Selection ($6, 8,500).

WINERY DATA
Case Production: 90,000. **Acres Owned:** 120 in Dry Creek
Valley. **Varietals by Acre:** Cabernet Franc (6 acres), Cabernet
Sauvignon (25), Merlot (22), Petite Sirah (8), Sangiovese (8),
Sauvignon Blanc (8), Souzao (1), Tinta Madera (1), Tinta Cao
(1), Touriga (1), Zinfandel (40). **Vineyard Designations:**
Bench Vineyard (Merlot), Burr-Beneyides Vineyard (Port
Varietals), F. Johnson Vineyard (Chardonnay, Pinot Noir),
Morris Fay Vineyard (Cabernet Sauvignon), Pedroni-Bushnell
Vineyard (Zinfandel), Raymond Burr Vineyard (Cabernet
Sauvignon). **Varietals Purchased:** Cabernet Franc (Dry Creek
Valley), Cabernet Sauvignon (Alexander Valley, Dry Creek
Valley), Chardonnay (Dry Creek Valley), Merlot (Dry Creek
Valley), Petite Sirah (Dry Creek Valley), Pinot Noir (Dry Creek
Valley), Sauvignon Blanc (Dry Creek Valley), Zinfandel (Dry
Creek Valley).

Pedroncelli Winery dates back to 1904. Throughout its
history, the winery's philosophy has been to make affordable, well balanced, easy-to-drink wines. Brothers John
and Jim Pedroncelli have overseen operations for the past
three decades, with John as winemaker and Jim in charge
of sales and marketing. The winery owns 120 acres of
vineyard in Dry Creek Valley, from which, along with
purchased grapes, it makes a wide range of wines,
including Cabernet, Chardonnay, Chenin Blanc, Gamay,
Merlot, Pinot Noir, Sauvignon Blanc, white Zinfandel

and Zinfandel. The house style through the lineup features simple but pleasant varietal flavors and minimal
oak influence.

PEJU PROVINCE WINERY (★★–★★★★)
Rutherford, Napa Valley
Founded: 1983. **Owner:** Anthony & Herta Peju.
Winemaker: Anthony Peju.

WINE RATINGS
Cabernet Franc Napa Valley
  ($25, 700)   ★★★
Cabernet Sauvignon Napa Valley
  ($28, 2,800)   ★★
Cabernet Sauvignon Napa Valley Estate
  ($28, 1,000)   ★★
Cabernet Sauvignon Napa Valley
  H.B. Vineyard
  ($65, 1,000)   ★★★★
Chardonnay Napa Valley
  ($18, 2,100)   ★★★
Chardonnay Napa Valley H.B. Vineyard
  ($26, 800)   ★★
Merlot Estate Napa Valley
  ($35, 500)   ★★
Provence Red California
  Rhône-Style
  ($17, 2,500)   ★★

ALSO PRODUCED
Chardonnay Napa Valley Estate ($18, 1,000); French
Colombard California Carnival ($10, 2,500);
Chardonnay Late Harvest Napa Valley Estate ($35, 300).

WINERY DATA
Case Production: 15,000. **Acres Owned:** 150 acres (23 in Napa
Valley, 127 in Pope Valley). **Varietals by Acre:** Cabernet Franc
(10 acres), Cabernet Sauvignon (55), Chardonnay (15), Malbec
(3), Merlot (41), Sauvignon Blanc (7), Syrah (7), Zinfandel (12).
Vineyard Designations: H.B. Vineyard (Cabernet Sauvignon,
Chardonnay). **Varietals Purchased:** Cabernet Franc (Napa
Valley), Cabernet Sauvignon (Napa Valley), Chardonnay (Napa
Valley), French Colombard (California, North Coast).

Tony Peju ran a nursery in Los Angeles before deciding to start a winery in Napa Valley, purchasing a vineyard in Rutherford that now measures 23 acres. After a
long battle with the county regarding the winery's design,

Peju Province was completed in 1989. The winery's strength is the Cabernet from its H.B. Vineyard (named for Herta Behensky Peju), but it was uprooted for replanting in 1995, a victim of phylloxera. A large new piece of property in Pope Valley was recently planted, and will start bearing grapes in 2000.

TASTING NOTES

CABERNET SAUVIGNON NAPA VALLEY H.B. VINEYARD (★★★★): This vineyard has turned into a solid performer, consistently yielding rich, complex, flavorful wines.

CHARDONNAY NAPA VALLEY (★★★): Improving, with the 1995 (90 points) showing more complex fruit than the H.B. Chardonnay bottling.

ROBERT PEPI WINERY (★★)
Oakville, Napa Valley
Founded: 1981. **Owner:** Jess Jackson. **Winemaker:** Marco DiGiulio.

MAJOR WINES: PRICE, CASES, RATING

Cabernet Sauvignon-Sangiovese
Napa Valley Due Baci
($25, NA) ★★
Sangiovese California
Two-Heart Canopy
($18, 8,000) ★★
Sangiovese Napa Valley
Colline di Sassi
($25, 2,200) ★★★
Sauvignon Blanc Napa Valley Reserve
($20, NA) ★★
Sauvignon Blanc Napa Valley
Two-Heart Canopy
($14, 11,000) ★★
Tocai Friulano Central Coast
($19, NA) ★★

ALSO PRODUCED
Arneis Central Coast ($19, NA); Barbera Sonoma Valley ($19, NA); Malvasia Bianca Central Coast ($19, NA); Pinot Grigio Central Coast ($19, NA).

WINERY DATA
Case Production: 25,000. **Acres Owned:** (See Cardinale entry).

San Francisco fur dresser Robert Pepi built this winery in Oakville after buying a partially planted 70-acre property north of Yountville. The winery initially made Chardonnay, Sauvignon Blanc and Cabernet Sauvignon from Vine Hill Ranch, located west of the winery, with a Sangiovese blend called Colline di Sassi added later. In 1994, the winery was sold to Jess Jackson, head of the Kendall-Jackson family of wineries. While the winery and brand remain, the property also became home in 1998 to K-J's Lokoya and Cardinale brands; a new winery building for these two was completed in 1999. Today, the Pepi line is undergoing a transformation, adding such wines as Barbera from Sonoma Valley and Arneis from the Central Coast. As of now, the wines are steady ★★ performers, but they may be worth watching to see what develops.

PEPPERWOOD GROVE see CECCHETTI
SEBASTIANI CELLAR AND QUATRO

PER SEMPRE (★★)
Napa Valley
Founded: 1991. **Owner:** David Di Loreto. **Winemaker:** David Di Loreto.

MAJOR WINES: PRICE, CASES, RATING
Cabernet Sauvignon Napa Valley
($35, 1,000) ★★
Cabernet Sauvignon Napa Valley
Select Reserve
($43, 200) ★★

ALSO PRODUCED
Chardonnay Napa Valley ($NA, 300); Dolcetto North Coast ($20, 350); Merlot Sonoma County ($NA, 400); Sangiovese Napa Valley ($29, 500); Shiraz Napa Valley ($40, 400).

WINERY DATA
Case Production: 3,000. **Acres Owned:** 23 acres (10 in Dry Creek Valley, 13 on Mount Veeder). **Varietals by Acre:** Chardonnay (5 acres), Sangiovese (5), Shiraz (6), Zinfandel (9). **Varietals Purchased:** Cabernet Sauvignon (Napa Valley), Dolcetto (Sonoma County), Merlot (Sonoma County).

David Di Loreto makes dense, earthy Napa Valley
Cabernets from purchased grapes. His winemaking style
appeals to some, but the wines tilt heavily to the tannic,
leathery side and can be cumbersome. Two Cabernets, a
Napa Valley and a Napa Valley Select Reserve are produced; new additions include Shiraz, Zinfandel, Merlot
and Chardonnay. Di Loreto's 1994 Cabernets were tough,
backward wines; the Napa Valley (87 points) showed currant, tar and wood flavors along with leathery earthy
notes, while the Napa Valley Select Reserve (86) had a
shade less depth to the fruit flavors but all the chewy tannins and earthy flavors of the former.

MARIO PERELLI-MINETTI (★★★)
Rutherford, Napa Valley
Founded: 1979. **Owner:** Mario Perelli-Minetti.
Winemaker: Gary Galleron.

MAJOR WINES: PRICE, CASES, RATING
Cabernet Sauvignon Napa Valley
  ($18, 3,000)   ★★

WINERY DATA
Case Production: 7,000. **Acres Owned:** 7 acres in Rutherford.
Varietals by Acre: Cabernet Franc (3 acres), Cabernet
Sauvignon (4), Merlot (less than 1 acre). **Varietals Purchased:**
Cabernet Sauvignon (Napa), Chardonnay (Napa).

Mario Perelli-Minetti managed his family's once
giant winery in the Central Valley before setting up a
small winery in Napa Valley in 1977. In 1988, a winery
was built in Rutherford on the Silverado Trail.

The Cabernet has been good; the 1994 (85 points) was
dense, with mint and berry flavors, but was short on finesse.
Winemaker Gary Galleron, previously of Whitehall Lane
and Grace Family (where he made some tremendous wines)
was hired in 1998, and should help raise quality to a new
level. Worth watching to see what develops.

PETERSON WINERY (★★)
Healdsburg, Sonoma County
Founded: 1995. **Owner:** Fred Peterson. **Winemaker:**
Fred Peterson.

MAJOR WINES: PRICE, CASES, RATING
Cabernet Sauvignon Dry Creek Valley
  Bradford Mountain Vineyard
  ($24, 500)   ★★
Zinfandel Dry Creek Valley
  ($16, 1,500)   ★★
Zinfandel Dry Creek Valley
  Bradford Mountain Vineyard
  ($18, 400)   ★★★
Zinfandel Dry Creek Valley Tradizionale
  ($18, 250)   ★★

ALSO PRODUCED
Barbera Dry Creek Valley ($14, 200); Carignane Dry
Creek Valley ($13, 150); Chardonnay Anderson Valley
Floodgate Vineyard ($15, 300); Merlot Dry Creek Valley
($23, 400); Pinot Noir Anderson Valley Floodgate
Vineyard ($18, 350); Sangiovese Dry Creek Valley
Norton Ranch ($13, 400).

WINERY DATA
Case Production: 4,200. **Acres Owned:** 10 acres in Dry Creek
Valley. **Varietals by Acre:** Cabernet Sauvignon (9 acres), Petit
Verdot (1). **Vineyard Designations:** Floodgate Vineyard
(Chardonnay, Pinot Noir), Norton Ranch (Sangiovese).
Varietals Purchased: Barbera (Dry Creek Valley), Cabernet
Sauvignon (Dry Creek Valley), Chardonnay (Anderson Valley),
Merlot (Dry Creek Valley), Pinot Noir (Anderson Valley),
Sangiovese (Dry Creek Valley), Zinfandel (Dry Creek Valley).

Peterson Winery is owned by Fred Peterson, with Bill
Hambrecht as a silent partner. Much of the winery's
grapes are purchased from Hambrecht's considerable
vineyard holdings in Sonoma County. A variety of wines
are produced, with Dry Creek Valley Zinfandel and
Cabernet as the primary focus. The Bradford Mountain
Zinfandel, usually the most complex and flavorful wine
in the portfolio, faltered in 1995 (78 points), showing
green flavors and an austere structure. The 1996 Dry
Creek Valley Zinfandel (82) and the 1996 Dry Creek
Valley Zinfandel Tradizionale (82) were both simple,
with smoky plum and berry flavors.

PEZZI KING (★★★)
Dry Creek Valley, Sonoma County
Founded: 1993. **Owner:** Jim & Jane Rowe and Jim Rowe, Jr. **Winemaker:** Paul Brasset.

MAJOR WINES: PRICE, CASES, RATING
Cabernet Sauvignon Dry Creek Valley
($23, 5,000) ★★★
Chardonnay Sonoma County
($20, 4,000) ★★★
Fumé Blanc Sonoma County
($15, 3,000) ★★
Zinfandel Dry Creek Valley
($25, 1,500) ★★★

ALSO PRODUCED
Merlot Dry Creek Valley Susie's Reserve ($23, 1,000); Syrah Dry Creek Valley Olson Vineyard ($24, 500).

WINERY DATA
Case Production: 15,000. **Acres Owned:** 46 acres in Dry Creek Valley. **Varietals by Acre:** Cabernet Sauvignon (18 acres), Merlot (5), Zinfandel (23). **Vineyard Designations:** Olson Vineyard (Syrah). **Varietals Purchased:** Chardonnay (Dry Creek Valley, Russian River), Fumé Blanc (Alexander Valley, Dry Creek Valley), Merlot (Dry Creek Valley), Syrah (Dry Creek Valley), Zinfandel (Dry Creek Valley).

The Rowe family purchased the old William Wheeler property in Dry Creek Valley in 1993 from Boisset USA. Before the Rowes came on board, much of the hillside Zinfandel and Cabernet vineyard on the property had been poorly maintained for many years, having been used primarily for bulk wines and white Zinfandel. The Rowes have invested heavily in the vineyard, and with the help of consultant Phil Cotturi, have nourished it and replanted and terraced some of its sections. The wines have been very good, particularly the Cabernet, Chardonnay and Zinfandel, and are occasionally outstanding. The Fumé Blanc is refreshing, clean and correct, as was seen in the 1997 vintage (85 points). Estate-grown Merlot and Syrah made from purchased grapes have now been added to the lineup.

TASTING NOTES
CABERNET SAUVIGNON DRY CREEK VALLEY (★★★): Consistently rich and supple, with complex plum, cherry, herb and spice flavors. Drinks well early on.

1996: Dark-hued, with layers of black cherry, plum, herb and anise. The flavors are framed in assertive, smoky, charry oak, all blending together harmoniously. A bit tart on the finish, with firm tannins. **90**
1995: Dry, earthy and tannic, but the blackberry, cherry and currant flavors move steadily to the forefront. **88**
1994: Smooth, ripe, supple and well proportioned, with hints of plum and cherry; turning complex on the finish. **89**

CHARDONNAY SONOMA COUNTY (★★★): Smooth and elegant, with focused citrus, pear, mineral and spice flavors. The 1995 (90 points), 1996 (89) and 1997 (88) share subtle, sophisticated flavors.

ZINFANDEL DRY CREEK VALLEY (★★★): Typically ripe and plush, with cherry, currant, raspberry and cracked pepper notes. The 1996 Zinfandel showed less intensity and richness than the excellent 1995, which was rich, plush and densely fruity.
1996: Lightly fruity, with modest cherry and strawberry flavors that expand on the finish. **86**
1995: Remarkably rich, with a ripe, plush core of raspberry, cherry, currant and plum flavors and lots of spice and pepper notes. **92**
1994: Shows ripe, juicy cherry, currant, plum and berry flavors, finishing with touches of herb and spice and a complex aftertaste. **89**

JOSEPH PHELPS VINEYARDS (★★★–★★★★★)
St. Helena, Napa Valley
Founded: 1973. **Owner:** Joseph Phelps. **Winemaker:** Craig Williams.

MAJOR WINES: PRICE, CASES, RATING
Cabernet Sauvignon Napa Valley
($30, 15,000) ★★★★
Cabernet Sauvignon Napa Valley
Backus Vineyard
($70, 600) ★★★★
Cabernet Sauvignon Napa Valley
Eisele Vineyard
(Discontinued) ★★★★★
Chardonnay Carneros
($20, 9,500) ★★★★

Chardonnay Napa Valley Ovation
($40, 1,000)   ★★★★
Gewürztraminer Anderson Valley
($15, 900)   ★★
Grenache California Vin du Mistral
($13, 8,000)   ★★
Grenache Rosé California Vin du Mistral
($12, 2,938)   ★★
Insignia Red Napa Valley
($75, 10,000)   ★★★★★
Marsanne Napa Valley Vin du Mistral
($20, 250)   ★★★
Merlot Napa Valley
($27, 5,000)   ★★★
Sauvignon Blanc Napa Valley
($14, 7,500)   ★★★
Syrah Napa Valley Vin du Mistral
($26, 500)   ★★★★
Viognier Napa Valley Vin du Mistral
($26, 2,400)   ★★★

WINERY DATA

Case Production: 90,000. **Acres Owned:** 351 acres (43 in Carneros, 55 in Monterey, 158 in Napa Valley, 16 in Oakville, 28 in Rutherford, 51 in Stags Leap). **Varietals by Acre:** Cabernet Sauvignon (100 acres), Chardonnay (56), Grenache (30), Malbec (4), Marsanne (5), Merlot (32), Mourvèdre (9), Petit Verdot (12), Sauvignon Blanc (19), Scheurebe (5), Sémillon (5), Syrah (40), Viognier (34).

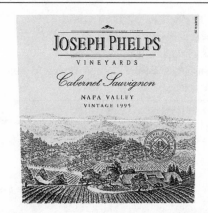

Joseph Phelps Vineyards has become one of the biggest success stories in California. Phelps, a building contractor, came to California from Colorado in the early 1970s and built Souverain (now Rutherford Hill Winery) in Napa, followed by another Souverain in Sonoma County (now Chateau Souverain) before deciding that winemaking was right for him. By 1973 he had built his winery in a narrow fold of hills east of Napa Valley off Taplin Road. With 361 acres in vines, Phelps is among the largest vineyard owners in Napa. The vineyards are well dispersed throughout the Valley, and are dominated by Cabernet (100 acres) and Chardonnay (56), with plantings in Stags Leap, Rutherford and Carneros.

Phelps has also been a low-key but influential leader, pioneering vineyard-designated wines (Eisele and Backus Cabernets and Sangiacomo Chardonnay), a Bordeaux-inspired red blend (Insignia), richly flavored dessert wines (Riesling, Scheurebe and Gewürztraminer) and a line of Rhône-inspired wines bottled under the Vin du Mistral label. Craig Williams has been winemaker since 1983, having replaced Walter Schug, who helped get Phelps off to a great start. To his credit, Williams's wines have surpassed Schug's greatest efforts. Worth collecting.

TASTING NOTES

CABERNET SAUVIGNON NAPA VALLEY (★★★★): This has become a very solid performer; dark, complex and concentrated, and a very good value.
1996: Serves up lots of juicy, ripe fruit, with layers of cherry, currant, blackberry and anise flavors; turning supple and concentrated, with a rich aftertaste that keeps pumping out the flavors. **92**
1995: Tightly wound; a touch earthy and leathery, but shows a rich core of currant, berry, cherry and spicy flavors. **91**
1994: Big, ripe, bold and intense, with concentrated currant, plum, raspberry, cedar and spice flavors and firm tannins. **89**
1993: Dry and a bit rustic, with flavors of currant and cedar marked by an earthy accent. **86**

CABERNET SAUVIGNON NAPA VALLEY BACKUS VINEYARD (★★★★): Steadily improving, dark, intense and well focused. Increasingly reliant on Cabernet for the entire blend; ages well.
1995: Rich and polished for such a young wine. Minty, with sage notes leading to a supple, complex band of currant, coffee, cedar, olive and tar, finishing with mild tannins. **91**
1994: Marked by dense, earthy, chewy tannins and a strong minty edge, which together overshadow the currant and berry flavors. **89**

1992: Ripe, smooth and harmonious, with complex plum, cherry and wild berry flavors, turning tannic on the finish. **89**

1991: Hard-edged, dark and inky; packed with chewy, tannic plum and cherry flavors, this is a big, powerful wine. **90**

1989: Rich and minty, with currant and spice flavors that are concentrated and vibrant, finishing with tight tannins and pretty oak shadings. **88**

1988: Medium-bodied, with rich, earthy mineral, leather and currant flavors; turns supple on the finish. **88**

1987: An elegant wine with ripe, supple plum, mint, herb and currant flavors that are framed by toasty oak and dry, rounded tannins. **88**

1986: Deep, concentrated and intense, with thick currant, plum and spicy mint flavors that are firm and elegant, wrapped in thick tannins. **89**

1985: A rich, sleek, distinctive wine with spice, mint and chocolate flavors and bright cherry and plum notes that stand up to the firm tannins. **90**

1984: Ripe and mature, with spicy cherry, plum and mineral flavors that are lean and crisp. **86**

1983: Tight, lean and crisp, with ripe, mature cherry, chocolate and mint flavors. **85**

1981: Mature but appealing, with lush, ripe cherry, currant, plum and spicy mineral flavors that are very seductive. The tannins are soft and smooth but still potent. **91**

1978: Firm and tense, with rich earth, mineral and currant flavors, hints of anise and cedar and a long, full, complex aftertaste. **92**

1977: Fully mature now, with smooth, rich, supple chocolate, plum, spice and toast flavors. **86**

CABERNET SAUVIGNON NAPA VALLEY EISELE VINEYARD (★★★★★): Some of Napa's most dramatic, rich, plush and deeply concentrated wines have appeared under this designation. Uncommonly thick and complex, with grand aging potential. Capable of lasting 25 to 30 years. 1991 was the last bottling, as Eisele Vineyard is now owned by Araujo Estate.

1991: Shows spicy black cherry and currant flavors before the chewy tannins creep in, turning intense and tannic on the finish. **89**

1989: Lean and crisp, with a leathery edge to the classic currant, mineral and earth flavors that are characteristic of this vineyard. Firmly tannic. **87**

1987: Rich and focused, with a leathery edge to the complex currant and mineral flavors. Focused and balanced, with fine but ample tannins. **88**

1986: A pungently earthy wine with barnyard and leather notes overriding the ripe currant and cherry flavors. **77**

1985: Bold and rich, with concentrated currant, plum, toast, cinnamon and anise flavors that are deep, intense and lively, finishing with firm yet integrated tannins. **94**

1984: A firmly structured wine with a tight core of rich currant and spicy mineral flavors. Mature but still tannic. **87**

1983: Still quite tannic, with tightly knit cedar, currant and plum flavors masked by rough-hewn tannins that are chewy on the finish. **86**

1982: Mature but still taut, with modest earthy mineral and currant flavors. **84**

1981: Wonderfully rich and complex, loaded with currant, herb, anise and mineral flavors that turn deep and concentrated. **93**

1979: Rich and concentrated, with currant, plum, cedar, earth and mineral flavors that are thick and deeply concentrated. **92**

1978: Extraordinary; ripe, rich, deep and complex, with currant, anise, mint and mineral flavors and uncommon depth and polish. **94**

1977: Ripe and mature, with plum and black cherry flavors that are thick, lean and rich. **85**

1975: Deep, rich and enticingly complex, with dense cedar, cigar box, black currant and chocolate notes that unfold on the palate, turning thick, rich and unctuous on the finish. **97**

CHARDONNAY CARNEROS (★★★★): After some struggles with this variety, Phelps is now on top of it; very ripe, complex and polished.

1997: Sleek and elegant, with a spicy edge to the pear, citrus and nectarine flavors, finishing with a touch of oak and fig. **88**

CHARDONNAY NAPA VALLEY OVATION (★★★★): A dramatic, complex, concentrated style.

1996: Lots of ripe, juicy, spicy pear, apple, fig and melon flavors that are rich, concentrated and sharply focused. **93**

1994: Ripe and intense, with a rich core of pear, pineapple and spice flavors and pretty notes of buttery oak, turning elegant on the finish. **92**

INSIGNIA RED NAPA VALLEY (★★★★★): Uncommon depth, concentration and complexity makes this wine built for aging. Drinks well at age 5, but can hold to 15 years.

1995: Dark and concentrated, with ripe, rich, exotic, earthy notes of currant, black cherry, wild berry and plum. **93**

1994: Remarkably elegant and supple, with a silky smooth texture and a wonderful array of ripe currant, plum, cedar, coffee and vanilla flavors. **96**

1993: Shows a nice balance of ripe, spicy currant, cedar, anise and tobacco flavors and a supple texture. **90**

1992: Well-oaked, with pretty currant and cherry flavors that turn supple, polished and complex on the finish. **90**

1991: Dark and intense, with pretty aromas and tight, dense currant, mineral, tar and cedary oak that's a touch astringent. **90**

1990: Firm and compact, with herb and currant flavors that turn lean and tannic on the finish. **88**

1989: Smooth and polished, with a beam of bright raspberry, cherry and currant flavors shining through the firm texture, hinting at leather and mint on the finish. **87**

1988: Medium-bodied and a bit tart, with a green edge to the currant, herb, sage, tea and olive flavors. **87**

1987: Magnificent, dark, ripe, dense, chewy and enormously concentrated; packed with rich currant, mineral, earth, cedar, spice, anise and coffee flavors. **96**

1986: Distinctive for its ripe wild berry, cherry, earth and mint flavors, this wine is complex, elegant, intense and focused. **92**

1985: Amazingly complex and concentrated, with layers of ripe black cherry, currant and mint flavors that are sharply focused, beautifully proportioned and supple. Distinctive for its elegance and complexity. **96**

1984: Firm, tight and compact, with a tough edge to the black currant and mint flavors, finishing with crisp, lean tannins. **89**

1983: Intense and concentrated, packed with rich berry, mint, currant and cedar notes that are now mature. Still firmly tannic. **89**

1982: Developing nicely, with a smooth texture, rounded tannins and a woody, earthy edge to the currant and berry flavors. **85**

1981: Sleek and elegant, brimming with fresh, ripe currant, cherry and plum flavors that are bright and lively. Supple and mature. **92**

1980: Lean but very concentrated, with ripe plum, currant, spice and mineral flavors that are tight and tannic. **90**

1979: A sleek, seductive, beautifully focused wine that's fully mature now, with rich, ripe, supple black cherry, currant, anise and mint flavors, turning smooth and supple. **90**

1978: Complex, with an intriguing array of rich stewed plum, herb, sage, tobacco, cedar and spice flavors, turning elegant and supple on the finish. **93**

1977: Smooth and elegant, with mature earth, herb and cedar complexities that add to the ripe black cherry and plum flavors. **91**

1976: Bold, supple and very ripe, smooth and satiny, with black cherry, currant, anise, mint and oak flavors that are concentrated and powerful. **93**

1975: A Merlot-dominated Insignia that is decidedly herbal and minty, yet elegant and concentrated. **85**

1974: Aging well, with a tight, compact core of spice, mineral and racy fruit flavors, finishing with rich, chewy tannins and a coffee and cedar aftertaste. **88**

Merlot Napa Valley (★★★): Has shown steady improvement, and is now quite complex.

1996: Firm, tight and concentrated, with a compact core of earthy plum, blueberry, sage, toast and spice flavors, finishing with a spicy aftertaste. **88**

1995: Intense and lively, even a touch leathery, with a smoky, meaty accent to the black cherry, currant and herbal flavors. **91**

1994: Complex, with ripe currant, plum and berry flavors, spicy, toasty oak and firm tannins. **89**

Sauvignon Blanc Napa Valley (★★★): Usually solid, with the 1997 (88 points) marked by complex citrus, pepper and earthy-oaky notes.

Syrah Napa Valley Vin du Mistral (★★★★): Variable, but ripe and complex, with plum and mineral notes at its best; can be rich and meaty.

1995: Racy, with a meaty, spicy edge to the dried cherry, sage and wild berry flavors. Finishes with a slightly vegetal edge and firm tannins. **87**

1994: Big, ripe, dark and meaty, with a rich, concentrated core of plum, meat, mineral, herb and cedar notes and plush tannins. **92**

1993: Dark, ripe and intense; a full-throttle style that shows ripe currant, mineral, smoke and anise flavors and firm tannins. **89**

1992: Intense and tight, with a ripe, complex core of pepper and currant flavors, turning oaky, leathery and tannic on the finish. **92**

1991: Firm and chewy, loaded with bright blackberry and black pepper flavors that poke through the tannic finish. **88**

1990: Elegant and polished, with spicy berry flavors that are pure and appealing. **84**

VIOGNIER NAPA VALLEY VIN DU MISTRAL (★★★): Among the best, with spicy peach and nectarine flavors in 1995 (87 points).

THE R.H. PHILLIPS VINEYARD (★★–★★★)
Dunnigan Hills, Yolo County
Founded: 1983. **Owner:** R.H. Phillips Vineyard Inc. **Winemaker:** Barry Bergman. **Second Label:** Chateau St. Nicholas.

MAJOR WINES: PRICE, CASES, RATING

Cabernet Sauvignon-Syrah California Toasted Head ($15, 2,000)	★★
Chardonnay Dunnigan Hills Barrel Cuvée ($8, 200,000)	★★
Chardonnay Dunnigan Hills Toasted Head ($12, 12,000)	★★★
Mistura California Night Harvest ($6, 18,000)	★★
Sauvignon Blanc Dunnigan Hills Night Harvest ($6, 60,000)	★★
Syrah Dunnigan Hills EXP ($12, 8,000)	★★★
Viognier Dunnigan Hills EXP ($12, 12,000)	★★

ALSO PRODUCED
Cabernet Sauvignon California Night Harvest ($8, 45,000); White Zinfandel California Night Harvest ($6, 68,000).

WINERY DATA
Case Production: 435,000. **Acres Owned:** 1,546 acres in Dunnigan Hills. **Varietals by Acre:** Alicante Bouchet (5 acres), Cabernet Sauvignon (117), Chardonnay (600), Malbec (10), Merlot (66), Mourvèdre (5), Petite Sirah (48), Petit Verdot (9), Sauvignon Blanc (185), Sémillon (25), Symphony (2), Syrah (233), Tempranillo (39), Viognier (103), Zinfandel (99). **Varietals Purchased:** Cabernet Sauvignon (Mendocino), Grenache (Cucamonga), Mourvèdre (Cucamonga), Zinfandel (Cucamonga).

Esparto-based R.H. Phillips, which owns 1,546 acres in vines and produces 435,000 cases a year, makes a strong case for the high quality of winegrowing in Yolo County, situated due east of Napa Valley and northwest of Sacramento. All of the wines are well crafted, and carry the California or Dunnigan Hills appellations. The Syrah EXP stands out for its opulence and pure varietal character; the Mourvèdre is also worth seeking out. All of the wines represent good value.

PHOENIX VINEYARDS (★★)
Napa Valley
Founded: 1992. **Owner:** The Bader Family. **Winemaker:** Aaron D. Bader.

MAJOR WINES: PRICE, CASES, RATING

Cabernet Sauvignon Napa Valley ($17, 400)	★★
Zinfandel Napa Valley ($15, 150)	★★★

ALSO PRODUCED
Chardonnay Napa Valley ($12, 300); Meritage Napa Valley Vindicator ($12, 200); Merlot Napa Valley Little Blackbird ($15, 225); Sangiovese Napa Valley Blood of Jupiter ($17, 200).

WINERY DATA
Case Production: 2,000. **Acres Owned:** 13.5 acres in Napa Valley. **Varietals by Acre:** Cabernet Franc (1 acre), Cabernet Sauvignon (6), Chardonnay (2.25), Merlot (2.5), Pinotage (0.25), Sangiovese (0.75), Zinfandel (0.75). **Varietals Purchased:** Cabernet Sauvignon (Napa Valley), Pinotage (Napa Valley), Syrah (Napa Valley), Zinfandel (Napa Valley).

A small, family-owned winery producing rustic, flavorful wines. The 1994 Cabernet (84 points) was ripe and supple, with earthy mineral and black cherry flavors; the 1996 Zinfandel (87), while a bit rough, showed earthy wild berry and sage notes.

Pine Ridge Winery (★★★–★★★★★)
Stags Leap District, Napa Valley
Founded: 1978. **Owner:** Leucadia Cellars Ltd.
Winemaker: Gary Andrus, Stacy Clark.

Major Wines: Price, Cases, Rating

Andrus Reserve Red Napa Valley ($85, 2,000)	★★★★
Cabernet Sauvignon Howell Mountain ($38, 1,500)	★★★
Cabernet Sauvignon Rutherford ($24, 12,000)	★★★
Cabernet Sauvignon Stags Leap District ($38, 3,000)	★★★★
Chardonnay Napa Valley Carneros Dijon Clones ($22, 10,000)	★★★★
Chardonnay Stags Leap District ($34, 3,000)	★★★★★
Chardonnay Stags Leap District Dijon Clones ($34, 1,650)	★★★★
Chenin Blanc-Viognier California ($10, 15,000)	★★★
Merlot Napa Valley Carneros ($22, 10,000)	★★★
Merlot Napa Valley Crimson Creek ($24, 12,000)	★★★

Also Produced
Port Napa Valley Black Diamond ($21, 294).

Winery Data
Case Production: 85,000. **Acres Owned:** 310 acres (69 in Carneros, 15 in Oak Knoll, 28 in Oakville, 121 acres in Rutherford, 77 in Stags Leap District). **Varietals by Acre:** Cabernet Franc (19 acres), Cabernet Sauvignon (89), Chardonnay (71), Chenin Blanc (6), Malbec (10), Merlot (101), Petit Verdot (8), Tannat (1), Viognier (4). **Varietals Purchased:** Chenin Blanc (Clarksburg), Viognier (Napa).

This winery is a candidate for having made the most dramatic turnabout in recent years. Quality had dipped in two difficult vintages, 1988 and 1989. Since then, however, the winery has regained its focus and has made a strong comeback, with many impressive, dramatic wines; recent vintages have shown greater depth and better balance. To Gary Andrus's credit, he declassified the wines in the lesser years, owning up to their shortcomings.

Gary and Nancy Andrus founded the winery in 1978, and decided to focus on vineyard and/or appellation-oriented wines (Rutherford and Stags Leap), using grapes from their vineyards and buying grapes from Diamond Mountain and Howell Mountain as well. Quality across the board is very good; both Chardonnay and Cabernet are occasionally outstanding. Leucadia International became the majority shareholder in the early 1990s, providing a needed cash infusion to expand operations and production, which now hovers around 85,000 cases.

Tasting Notes

Andrus Reserve Red Napa Valley (★★★★): Continues to improve, with intense, complex flavors. Ages well.
1995: Offers intense, complex flavors with tiers of cherry, currant, berry and spice, finishing with a dash of cedary oak and firm, polished tannins. **92**
1994: A big, ripe, rich and flavorful wine loaded with tiers of currant, anise, black cherry and spice, picking up pretty, toasty oak flavors. **93**
1986: Earthy, with a tart, sour cherry note and not a whole lot more in the way of fruit flavor. Turns mildly tannic on the finish. **80**

Cabernet Sauvignon Howell Mountain (★★★): Can be characteristically earthy and austere, though Pine Ridge builds in more suppleness than most from this appellation.
1996: Dark, tight, dense and chewy, with layers of mineral, currant, leather, blackberry and cedary oak flavors that are rich and concentrated; has a long, lingering aftertaste and firm, detailed tannins. **93**
1995: Remarkably supple and refined for Howell Mountain, with spicy currant, herb, sage and mineral flavors, finishing with a dash of tar and cedar. **88**
1994: Broad-shouldered, dense and tannic, but loaded with concentrated anise, cherry, currant and earthy nuances. **90**

1993: Well-oaked, with a smoky edge to the currant and berry flavors, turning tight and firm on the finish. **88**

CABERNET SAUVIGNON RUTHERFORD (★★★): Has become a steady high-80s performer.

1996: The tight, cedary oak leads to a core of plum and cherry flavors of moderate richness, depth and complexity. **88**

1995: A supple band of cherry, currant, cedar and spice flavors, finishing with fleshy tannins and a good length. **89**

1994: Smooth and polished, with a pretty interplay of ripe cherry, currant and spicy, toasty oak flavors. **89**

1992: Smooth and elegant, with a supple core of currant, coffee, toasty oak and spice flavors. **91**

1978: Drinking exceptionally well. Elegant in structure and texture, this complex wine is laden with lively currant, tea, sage, mushroom and spicy nuances. **88**

CABERNET SAUVIGNON STAGS LEAP DISTRICT (★★★★): Supple, showing elegant and rich fruit.

1996: Remarkably plush, rich and concentrated, with layers of ripe plum and black cherry that are sharply focused and intricate, turning long and supple on the finish. **92**

1995: Tight, rich and concentrated, with a complex array of currant, anise, cedar and spice flavors, turning plush on the finish. **90**

1994: Dense and concentrated, with a ripe, rich core of currant, anise, plum and spice, it fills out the palate with heaps of fruit and tannins. **92**

1992: Ripe and complex, with rich tiers of currant, coffee, cedar and black cherry and a sense of finesse. **90**

1991: Combines ripe, intense currant, cherry and spice flavors with cedary oak, finishing with elegant, firm tannins. **89**

CHARDONNAY NAPA VALLEY CARNEROS DIJON CLONES (★★★★): A success at understated elegance, with balance and flavor.

1997: Smooth, rich and complex, with layers of ripe fig, melon, pear, anise and spice flavors; gains nuance from the light, toasty oak. **91**

1996: Tightly wound, but displays attractive flavors; the core of citrus, pear, apple and melon is rich and concentrated. **90**

CHARDONNAY STAGS LEAP DISTRICT (★★★★★): Shows beautifully orchestrated and detailed fruit flavors and a creamy texture.

1995: Understated and elegant; rich in flavor and deceptively concentrated, with lively pear, citrus and hazelnut flavors. **92**

1994: Ripe, rich and complex, with lots of juicy pear, apricot, fig and spicy flavors, finishing with a dash of toasty oak. **92**

CHARDONNAY STAGS LEAP DISTRICT DIJON CLONES (★★★★)

1996: Remarkably complex, deep and rich, with tiers of peach, pear, spice and toasty oak flavors. **91**

MERLOT NAPA VALLEY CARNEROS (★★★)

1996: Elegant and complex, with a supple band of cedar, currant and black cherry, picking up black olive, sage and briary notes; the tannins are ripe and polished. **90**

1995: Rich, with currant, coffee and cherry notes. **90**

MERLOT NAPA VALLEY CRIMSON CREEK (★★★)

1996: Smooth and supple, with ripe, earthy plum, wild berry and black cherry flavors that fold together nicely. Finishes with a complex interplay of flavors and mild, well-integrated tannins. **90**

PLUMPJACK (★★★)
Oakville, Napa Valley
Founded: 1995. **Owner:** Gavin Newsom. **Winemaker:** Nils Venge.

MAJOR WINES: PRICE, CASES, RATING

Cabernet Sauvignon Napa Valley ($32, 1,000)	★★★
Cabernet Sauvignon Napa Valley Reserve ($65, 500)	★★★
Chardonnay Napa Valley Reserve ($28, 540)	★★★

WINERY DATA
Case Production: 7,500. **Varietals Purchased:** Cabernet Sauvignon (Oakville), Chardonnay (Napa Valley).

PlumpJack has essentially moved into the former Villa Mt. Eden Winery in Oakville, using grapes grown in the Mt. Eden vineyard and hiring Villa Mt. Eden's former winemaker, Nils Venge. Gavin Newsom, a San Francisco entrepreneur and member of the city's board of supervisors, is the owner. Quality has been very high, with both the Cabernet and Cabernet Reserve earning ratings of 92 points in 1995, their first year. Chardonnay is the newcomer. Given Venge's knowledge of the vineyard, his success with Cabernet at Saddleback, his own winery, and his tenure at Groth, this is definitely a winery worth watching.

TASTING NOTES

CABERNET SAUVIGNON NAPA VALLEY (★★★):
1995: Supple, fruity, and well-oaked, with toasty, spicy flavors and an elegant band of spice and currant flavors. **92**

CABERNET SAUVIGNON NAPA VALLEY RESERVE (★★★)
1995: Intense, complex and concentrated, with a firm band of cedar, spice, earth, mineral and currant flavors. **92**

PORTER CREEK VINEYARDS (★–★★)
Russian River Valley, Sonoma County
Founded: 1978. **Owner:** George R. Davis. **Winemaker:** Alex Davis.

MAJOR WINES: PRICE, CASES, RATING

Pinot Noir Russian River Valley Creekside Vineyard ($18, 1,200)	★★
Pinot Noir Russian River Valley Hillside Vineyard ($18, 400)	★

ALSO PRODUCED
Chardonnay Russian River Valley ($16, 900).

WINERY DATA
Case Production: 2,500. **Acres Owned:** 20 acres in Russian River Valley. **Varietals by Acre:** Chardonnay (9 acres), Pinot Noir (11). **Vineyard Designations:** Creekside Vineyard (Pinot Noir), Hillside Vineyard (Pinot Noir).

Porter Creek Vineyards is a small, family-owned Russian River Valley winery focusing on Chardonnay and Pinot Noir. Recent wines were of average quality.

The 1996 Pinot Noir Creekside Vineyard (83 points) was light-bodied, with spice, herb and cherry notes, while the 1996 Pinot Noir Hillside Vineyard (78) was coarse, with black cherry and olive flavors.

PORTOLA HILLS see CRONIN VINEYARDS

PRESTON VINEYARDS (★★–★★★)
Dry Creek Valley, Sonoma County
Founded: 1973. **Owner:** Lou & Susan Preston. **Winemaker:** Kevin Hamel.

MAJOR WINES: PRICE, CASES, RATING

Faux Red Dry Creek Valley ($11, 4,000)	★★
Gamay Dry Creek Valley Beaujolais ($10, 2,400)	★★
Le Petit Faux Rosé Dry Creek Valley ($10, 500)	★★
Marsanne Dry Creek Valley ($18, 1,000)	★★
Sauvignon Blanc Dry Creek Valley Cuvée De Fumé ($12, 4,000)	★★
Syrah Dry Creek Valley ($18, 1,340)	★★★
Syrah Dry Creek Valley Vineyard Select ($22, 1,000)	★★
Viognier Dry Creek Valley ($20, 1,000)	★★★
Zinfandel Dry Creek Valley ($18, 2,600)	★★★
Zinfandel Dry Creek Valley Old Vines Old Clones ($18, 2,655)	★★★

ALSO PRODUCED
Barbera Dry Creek Valley ($22, 1,000); Mourvèdre Dry Creek Valley Vineyard Select ($20, NA); Muscat Canelli Dry Creek Valley Moscato Curioso ($15, NA); Petite Sirah Dry Creek Valley ($24, NA); Sémillon Dry Creek Valley ($13, NA); Sangiovese Dry Creek Valley ($28, NA).

WINERY DATA
Case Production: 22,000. **Acres Owned:** 113 acres in Dry Creek Valley. **Varietals by Acre:** Barbera (8 acres), Cabernet Sauvignon (8), Carignane (3), Cinsault (3), Grenache (4), Marsanne (5.5), Mourvèdre (5), Muscat Canelli (3), Napa Gamay (4.5), Petite Sirah (2.5), Sangiovese (3), Sauvignon Blanc (22.5), Sémillon (5), Syrah (9.5), Viognier (9), Zinfandel (18).

Preston Vineyards in Dry Creek Valley is a family-run operation that switched from grape-growing to winemaking. With 113 acres in vines, the Prestons have a wide variety of grapes to choose from, with Sauvignon Blanc, Barbera, Carignane, Grenache, Syrah, Sangiovese and Mourvèdre included in the mix. The wines are good to very good, and are consistent in both style and weight, a testimony to the Prestons' viticultural and enological capabilities. While all of the wines are well made, the winery has taken a fancy to Rhône varietals, including Marsanne and Viognier. The winery also produces a pair of Rhône blends called Faux and Le Petit Faux. Chardonnay is conspicuous by its absence. Interestingly, none of the wines undergoes malolactic fermentation, and all of the reds are styled for immediate consumption.

TASTING NOTES

SYRAH DRY CREEK VALLEY (★★★)
1994: A medium-weighted style of Syrah, with a spicy, meaty edge to the plum and berry notes. Finishes on the short side. **87**
1993: Ripe and lively, with a well focused, if tannic, core of wild berry and cherry flavors, finishing with a complex aftertaste that picks up an anise edge. **88**
1992: Dark in color, with an alluring core of earthy currant, cedar and spice flavors that are tightly wound, finishing with rich tannins. **88**
1991: Dark in color, with a core of rich, earthy, concentrated currant, spice and mineral flavors. **87**

VIOGNIER DRY CREEK VALLEY (★★★): Steadily improving, with pretty honey and spice flavors.
1997: A silky textured wine sporting mandarine orange, lemon, lime and mineral flavors. Finishes long and clean. **87**
1996: Tart, with an ever so slightly bitter edge; enough spicy pear and green fig flavors fold in to hold your interest. **85**

ZINFANDEL DRY CREEK VALLEY (★★★): Of medium weight and intensity, but has attractive fruit flavors and mild tannins.

ZINFANDEL DRY CREEK VALLEY OLD VINES OLD CLONES (★★★)
1996: Shows off a ripe, perfumed, plummy aroma, turning elegant and supple. The black cherry and raspberry flavors are ripe and rich, and stay with you through the long, full finish. **88**
1995: Appealing for its up-front juicy cherry and wild berry flavors. Picks up spice, sage and raspberry notes along the way, and retains its fruitiness on the finish. **87**

PRIDE MOUNTAIN VINEYARDS (★★★–★★★★★)
Spring Mountain District, Napa Valley
Founded: 1991. **Owner:** Jim & Carolyn Pride.
Winemaker: Bob Foley.

MAJOR WINES: PRICE, CASES, RATING

Cabernet Franc Sonoma County ($28, 700)	★★★
Cabernet Sauvignon Napa Valley ($28, 5,000)	★★★★
Cabernet Sauvignon Napa Valley Reserve ($65, 300)	★★★★★
Chardonnay Napa Valley ($20, 1,000)	★★★★
Merlot Napa Valley ($28, 8,000)	★★★★
Reserve Claret Napa Valley ($65, 200)	★★★★
Viognier Sonoma County ($28, 650)	★★★

WINERY DATA
Case Production: 15,000. **Acres Owned:** 65 acres (54 in Napa, 11 in Sonoma). **Varietals by Acre:** Cabernet Franc (7 acres), Cabernet Sauvignon (32), Merlot (20), Petit Verdot (1), Syrah (2), Viognier (5). **Varietals Purchased:** Chardonnay (Napa).

This winery is one of Napa Valley's up-and-coming stars; the wines have steadily improved with recent vintages. Pride Mountain Vineyards was once known as Summit Winery; its first vines were planted in 1968. In 1989, Jim and Carolyn Pride bought 170 acres of volcanic earth on Spring Mountain, 2,000 feet above the valley floor, sitting on the Napa-Sonoma county line. Starting slowly with Cabernet, Cabernet Franc, Chardonnay and Merlot, production from their 65 acres in vines (and some purchased grapes) now approaches 15,000 cases. Winemaker Bob Foley, formerly at Markham, definitely has a touch with both Cabernet and Merlot. Overall, this is a very promising estate making tremendous wines. Worth collecting.

TASTING NOTES

CABERNET FRANC SONOMA COUNTY (★★★): Avoids the herbal notes typically found in Cabernet Franc. The 1995 (85 points) was firmly tannic but showed a core of berry and currant flavors. These grapes come from the Sonoma side of the property.

CABERNET SAUVIGNON NAPA VALLEY (★★★★): Impressive, with ripe, rich, lush and complex flavors, supported by smooth but firm tannins and just the right dose of oak.
1995: Dark, ripe and high in extract, the young currant, anise, plum and spicy flavors burst forth. **92**
1994: Big, ripe and concentrated; dense and chewy, with lots of earthy leather, currant and berry flavors. **92**
1993: A complex interplay of ripe cherry, currant and spicy, toasty oak flavors that offer depth and concentration. **90**
1992: A touch earthy, with leather, currant and mineral flavors that are pleasantly balanced. **87**
1991: Ripe, smooth and polished, with plush cherry, currant and toasty oak flavors, finishing with richness, depth and concentration and supple tannins. **92**

CABERNET SAUVIGNON NAPA VALLEY RESERVE (★★★★★): Very dark, ripe, rich and plush, with big, polished tannins. Impressive.
1995: Firm and tannic, with ripe, dense, compact black cherry, currant and blackberry flavors that are deeply concentrated. **93**
1994: Dark in color; sharply focused on the core of currant, wild berry and black cherry flavors; plush tannins. **92**

CHARDONNAY NAPA VALLEY (★★★★): Builds in intensity and flavor, with flinty, crisp mineral and tart fruit nuances.

MERLOT NAPA VALLEY (★★★★): Shows ripe, complex flavors and good balance. Tannins are polished.
1996: Complex, with a lively range of vanilla, berry, cherry, plum and currant flavors; turning smooth and

polished on the finish. **90**
1995: Lean and trim, with a narrow band of spicy blackberry and currant flavors, slowly revealing depth and complexity. **89**
1994: Smooth, rich and flavorful, with lots of currant, wild berry, cherry and pretty oak shadings that fan out and expand on the finish. **91**
1993: The smooth, supple, ripe and polished cherry, currant and anise flavors turn elegant and complex on the finish; the tannins are plush. **89**
1992: An herbal wine, but the black cherry and cedar flavors show through the supple tannins. **85**
1991: Smooth and spicy, with cedary plum, anise and currant aromas and flavors. Supple tannins. **88**

RESERVE CLARET NAPA VALLEY (★★★★): Offers dramatic quality, richness, depth and polish. Should age well.
1995: Tight, with a firm band of currant, chocolate, herb and coffee flavors and chewy tannins, framed by notes of pretty, toasty oak. **91**
1994: Dark, rich, complex and concentrated; loaded with plush currant, black cherry, plum, mineral, spice and cedary oak flavors. **92**
1993: Impressive for its core of ripe, spicy currant, plum and wild berry flavors, its subtle notes of oak, and its full, lingering aftertaste. **90**

VIOGNIER SONOMA COUNTY (★★★): Complex, with tangerine and nectarine flavors.

PROSPERITY see **FIRESTONE VINEYARD**

QUADY WINERY (★★★)
Madera County
Founded: 1977. **Owner:** Andrew Quady. **Winemaker:** Michael Blaylock.

MAJOR WINES: PRICE, CASES, RATING
Black Muscat California Elysium ($16, 7,000)	★★★
Orange Muscat California Electra ($9, 7,000)	★★★
Orange Muscat California Essensia ($16, 9,000)	★★★

Port California Starboard Batch 88
($16, 1,000) ★★★
Port California Starboard Frank's Vineyard
($24, 200) ★★★

ALSO PRODUCED
Spirit of Elysium ($28, 200); VYA Extra Dry Vermouth
($18, 700); VYA Sweet Vermouth ($18, 700).

WINERY DATA
Case Production: 22,000. **Acres Owned:** 13 acres in Madera
County. **Varietals by Acre:** Orange Muscat (10 acres), Touriga
(3). **Varietals Purchased:** Black Muscat (California), Tinta
Amarela (Amador County), Tinta Cão (Amador County), Tinta
Roriz (California), Touriga Francesa (Amador County),
Orange Muscat (California).

Andrew Quady has focused on Port-style wines for
years now, beginning with Amador County Zinfandel,
and followed by a string of uniquely styled dessert wines
made from Muscat varieties. Elysium is made from
Black Muscat, Essensia is made from Orange Muscat,
and Electra is a low-alcohol Orange Muscat; all are
exceptionally well made. The Port is called "Starboard",
a play on the nautical opposite of Port. Grapes for the
Port come from Frank's Vineyard, which is planted to traditional Port varieties, including Tinta Cão, Tinta
Amerela, Valdepeñas and Bastardo. Vermouth was added
to the lineup in 1998.

QUATRO (★★)
Sonoma County
Founded: 1996. **Owner:** Roy Cecchetti, Don Sebastiani.
Winemaker: Bob Broman. **Affiliated Brands:**
Pepperwood Grove, Cecchetti Sebastiani.

MAJOR WINES: PRICE, CASES, RATING
Cabernet Sauvignon Sonoma County
($12, 2,500) ★★
Chardonnay Sonoma County
($10, 2,500) ★★
Merlot Sonoma County
($12, 1,500) ★★
Pinot Noir Sonoma County
($12, 2,000) ★★

WINERY DATA
Case Production: 12,000. **Varietals Purchased**: Cabernet
Sauvignon (Sonoma County), Chardonnay (Sonoma County),
Merlot (Sonoma County), Pinot Noir (Sonoma County).

This a new line of Sonoma County appellation wines
made by Sebastiani Vineyards chairman Don Sebastiani
and his brother in law, Roy Cecchetti. The two are
founders of the Cecchetti Sebastiani and Pepperwood
brands. The focus is on value.

QUINTESSA (★★★★)
Rutherford, Napa Valley
Founded: 1990. **Owner:** The Eckes Family and Agustin
Huneeus. **Winemaker:** Larry Levin

MAJOR WINES: PRICE, CASES, RATING
Red Rutherford
($75, 2,000) ★★★★

WINERY DATA
Case Production: 2,000 cases. **Acres Owned:** 180 acres in
Rutherford. **Varietals by Acre:** Cabernet Franc (18 acres),
Cabernet Sauvignon (108), Merlot (54).

In 1990, the Eckes family, together with Agustin
Huneeus, purchased this property in Rutherford, north of
Conn Creek Winery. There are now 180 acres planted:
108 in Cabernet, 54 in Merlot and 18 Cabernet Franc.
Plans are to build production to 20,000 cases, focusing
on a Meritage red, Cabernet, Cabernet Franc and Merlot,
each from the best single block on the property.

TASTING NOTES

RED RUTHERFORD (★★★★): Impressive, with ripe, polished flavors. Worth watching.
1995: Complex, elegant and polished, with a neat seam
of currant, black cherry and spice flavors and some light,
toasty oak; turns long and rich on the finish. **92**
1994: Rich, supple and forward, with tasty currant, anise,
cedar, vanilla and spice flavors and polished tannins. **91**

QUIVIRA VINEYARDS (★★–★★★)
Dry Creek Valley, Sonoma County
Founded: 1981. **Owner:** Holly & Henry Wendt.
Winemaker: Grady Wann.

MAJOR WINES: PRICE, CASES, RATING

Cuvée Dry Creek Valley
($13, 2,000) ★★
Sauvignon Blanc Dry Creek Valley
($10, 5,845) ★★
Sauvignon Blanc Dry Creek Valley
Reserve
($16, 2,018) ★★
Zinfandel Dry Creek Valley
($17, 4,875) ★★★

WINERY DATA
Case Production: 20,000. **Acres Owned:** 75 acres owned and 11 acres leased in Dry Creek Valley. **Varietals by Acre:** Grenache (10 acres), Mourvèdre (4), Petite Sirah (6), Sauvignon Blanc (22), Sémillon (4), Syrah (4), Zinfandel (36).

Holly and Henry Wendt founded Quivira in Dry Creek Valley in 1981 as a country retreat where they could ease into retirement. The Wendts spend time at their estate whenever their schedule permits, as Henry is chairman of SmithKline Beecham, a global multi-billion dollar pharmaceutical giant. The Wendts' focus is on Sauvignon Blanc and Zinfandel, though they have also added Cabernet and a red table wine blending Grenache, Syrah and Zinfandel to the mix. Production is now at 20,000 cases, all of it estate-bottled.

TASTING NOTES

ZINFANDEL DRY CREEK VALLEY (★★★): Very consistent, with impeccable balance and just the right mix of berry and pepper flavors. Mild tannins. Drinks best on release.
1996: Of medium weight, with moderately ripe plum and wild berry flavors. It's good, but fails to excite. **85**
1995: Ripe, with a jammy edge to the red cherry, raspberry and plummy notes. **87**
1994: Pleasing for its ripe, pure cherry, currant and berry flavors, with notes of light oak and hints of herb and cedar. **88**
1993: Supple, with a pleasant, earthy edge to the cherry and wild berry flavors and mild tannins. **87**
1992: Smooth, rich and complex, with ripe, concentrated

wild berry, raspberry and spice notes that finish with toasty oak shadings. **89**
1991: Complex, full-bodied and stylish, with toasty, earthy, spicy notes accenting the solid berry and cherry flavors. **90**
1990: Complex and elegant, with a distinct core of red currant and cherry flavors, turning supple on the finish. **88**
1989: Lively and focused, with wild berry and plum flavors and a hint of earthiness. **84**
1988: The appealing ripe plum, black pepper and wild berry flavors are seductive, finishing with firm tannins. **88**
1987: Effusively fruity, teeming with pepper, raspberry, spice and jam notes framed by tannins and a touch of wood. **88**
1986: Effusively fruity, with supple strawberry notes, but firmly wrapped in just enough tannins. **88**
1984: Mature now, but still offering earthy raspberry flavors. **88**

QUPÉ (★★★–★★★★)
Santa Maria Valley, Santa Barbara County
Founded: 1982. **Owner:** Bob Lindquist. **Winemaker:** Bob Lindquist & Jim Adelman.

MAJOR WINES: PRICE, CASES, RATING

Chardonnay Santa Barbara County
Bien Nacido Vineyard
($18, 3,500) ★★★
Chardonnay Santa Barbara County
Bien Nacido Vineyard Reserve
($25, 1,000) ★★★★
Chardonnay Santa Barbara County
Sierra Madre Vineyard
(Discontinued) ★★★
Chardonnay-Viognier Santa Barbara
County Bien Nacido Cuvée
($16, 2,100) ★★★
Los Olivos Cuvée Santa Barbara County
($18, 600) ★★★
Marsanne Santa Barbara County
Ibarra-Young Vineyard
($13, 1,400) ★★
Roussanne Central Coast
($18, 300) ★★★
Roussanne Edna Valley Alban Vineyard
($25, 200) ★★★

Syrah Central Coast
  ($14, 8,000)   ★★★
Syrah Santa Barbara County Bien Nacido
  Hillside Estate
  ($35, 700)   ★★★★
Syrah Santa Barbara County Bien Nacido
  Reserve
  ($25, 2,500)   ★★★★
Viognier Santa Barbara County
  Ibarra-Young Vineyard
  ($25, 500)   ★★

WINERY DATA

Case Production: 20,000. **Acres Owned:** 12 acres in Santa Barbara County. **Varietals by Acre:** Albarino (2 acres), Marsanne (4), Mourvèdre (1), Syrah (3), Viognier (2). **Vineyard Designations:** Alban Vineyard (Roussanne), Bien Nacido Vineyard (Chardonnay, Syrah), Ibarra-Young Vineyard (Marsanne, Viognier). **Varietals Purchased:** Chardonnay (Santa Barbara County), Grenache (Central Coast), Roussanne (Central Coast, Edna Valley), Syrah (Central Coast, Santa Barbara County).

After leaving Zaca Mesa Winery, where he worked with Ken Brown (Byron Vineyards) and Jim Clendenen (Au Bon Climat), Bob Lindquist decided to focus on Rhône-style reds, taking an interest in Syrah, Marsanne and Viognier. But he also kept a hand in Chardonnay, which he makes in a rich and dramatic style. Lindquist owns 12 acres in vines, planted to Rhône varieties. He also purchases grapes from Bien Nacido (Chardonnay and Syrah). His Syrah Bien Nacido Reserve and Syrah Bien Nacido Hillside Estate are among California's best, most consistent Syrahs. The Central Coast Syrah, which is often a blend of Monterey, Paso Robles and Santa Barbara grapes is the winery's volume leader at 8,000 cases.

TASTING NOTES

CHARDONNAY SANTA BARBARA COUNTY BIEN NACIDO VINEYARD (★★★), RESERVE (★★★★): Bold, ripe and concentrated, with citrus and tropical fruit flavors.

SYRAH CENTRAL COAST (★★★): A leading example of this grape; uniformly ripe, complex and deep in fruit concentration. Ages well.
1997: Smooth and complex, with layers of black cherry, stewed plum and spice flavors, picking up notes of anise, sage and cedar. **89**
1991: Ripe, fleshy, and brimming with generous, complex black cherry, raspberry and currant flavors and earthy oak shadings. **90**

SYRAH SANTA BARBARA COUNTY BIEN NACIDO HILLSIDE ESTATE (★★★★): This is the winery's best effort. Concentrated and elegant.
1996: Marked by a meaty, beefy edge, it works in some cherry-berry notes, but then turns dry and tannic. **87**
1995: Peppery and spicy, with a slightly vegetal note, the beefy, stewed plum and berry flavors give this wine character. **90**
1994: Spicy and meaty, with a strong vegetal accent; but it straightens out, showing notes of toast, plum, currant and anise. **90**

SYRAH SANTA BARBARA COUNTY BIEN NACIDO RESERVE (★★★★): Very dense, earthy and complex; distinctive.
1996: A real beauty. Ripe, supple and complex, with a fleshy array of meaty plum, spice, oak and cedar flavors. **90**
1995: Dense and chewy, with a pretty array of meaty plum, cherry and herbal notes that reveal depth and concentration. **91**
1994: Dark, ripe, and concentrated, with a tannic core of cherry and leather Syrah flavors, ending with a mineral note. **88**
1993: Ripe and plummy, with spicy, peppery notes that are deep and concentrated; long on finesse and polish. **91**
1990: Wonderful depth, richness and complexity, with spicy cherry, pepper and currant flavors that are intense and concentrated. **92**
1989: Powerful and spicy, with a cedar, toast and pepper edge to the central core of plum and cherry flavors. **89**
1987: Distinctive, robust and ripe. Extremely dark in color, and peppery and gamy in flavor, with smoke, anise and black cherry notes. **83**

RABBIT RIDGE VINEYARDS
(★★–★★★★)
Russian River Valley, Sonoma County
Founded: 1985. **Owner:** Erich Russell. **Winemaker:**
Erich Russell. **Second Label:** Meadow Glen.

MAJOR WINES: PRICE, CASES, RATING
Allure Red California
($7, 25,000) ★★
Aventura Red Sonoma County
Migliore di Vigneto Reserve
($30, 740) ★★★
Cabernet Sauvignon Russian River Valley
Winemaker's Grand Reserve
($40, 410) ★★★
Carignane Russian River Valley
Hedin Vineyard
($11, 1,800) ★★★
Chardonnay Russian River Valley
Rabbit Ridge Ranch Estate Reserve
($18, 1,750) ★★★
Chardonnay Sonoma County
($12, 12,000) ★★★
Chardonnay Sonoma County Winemaker's
Grand Reserve
($30, 740) ★★★★
Dolcetto Napa Valley
($12, 740) ★★
Merlot California Barrel Cuvée
($9, 30,000) ★★
Merlot Carneros Sangiacomo Vineyard
Reserve
($23, 2,800) ★★★★
Merlot Sonoma County Winemaker's
Grand Reserve
($30, 4,000) ★★★
Nebbiolo California
($18, 780) ★★
Sangiovese Sonoma County
Coniglio Selezione Reserve
($14, 5,200) ★★★
Sauvignon Blanc Russian River Valley
($10, 8,000) ★★★
Syrah Sonoma County Reserve
($20, 840) ★★★

Viognier Sonoma County Heartbreak Hill
($15, 2,500) ★★
Zinfandel Amador County
($12, 3,200) ★★★
Zinfandel California Barrel Cuvée
($9, 40,000) ★★
Zinfandel Dry Creek Valley Olson
Vineyard Reserve
($23, 840) ★★★
Zinfandel Paso Robles Westside Vines
($14, 6,150) ★★
Zinfandel Russian River Valley Hedin
Vineyard Reserve
($23, 1,275) ★★★
Zinfandel Russian River Valley Rabbit
Ridge Ranch Estate Reserve
($30, 740) ★★★
Zinfandel Sonoma County OVZ Reserve
($30, 1,850) ★★★★
Zinfandel Sonoma County San Lorenzo
Reserve
(Discontinued) ★★★★
Zinfandel Sonoma County Winemaker's
Grand Reserve
($32, 740) ★★★★

ALSO PRODUCED
Barbera California ($18, 2,200); Cabernet Sauvignon Sonoma
County ($15, 5,000); Gewürztraminer Russian River Valley
Frank Johnson Vineyard Sweet Susie ($15, 340); Merlot
North Coast ($18, 11,000); Mystique White Sonoma County
Meritage ($7, 7,000); Pinot Noir Russian River Valley Frank
Johnson Vineyard ($18, 2,500); Sauvignon Blanc Late
Harvest Russian River Frank Johnson Vineyard ($18, 400);
Zinfandel Late Harvest Russian River Valley ($20, 110).

WINERY DATA
Case Production: 117,000. **Acres Owned:** 129 acres (35 in
Russian River Valley, 94 in Paso Robles). **Varietals by Acre:**
Barbera (4 acres), Cabernet Franc (7), Cabernet Sauvignon (12),
Chardonnay (10), Dolcetto (1), Malbec (1), Nebbiolo (6), Petite
Sirah (7), Petit Verdot (2), Primitivo (20), Refosco (1), Sangiovese
(10), Sauvignon Blanc (4), Syrah (10), Viognier (5), Zinfandel
(29). **Vineyard Designations:** Frank Johnson Vineyard
(Gewürztraminer, Pinot Noir, Sauvignon Blanc), Hedin Vineyard
(Carignane, Zinfandel), Olson Vineyard (Zinfandel), Rabbit Ridge
Ranch (Chardonnay, Zinfandel), Sangiacomo Vineyard (Merlot).
Varietals Purchased: Barbera (Alexander Valley, Lodi), Cabernet
Sauvignon (Alexander Valley, Napa), Chardonnay (Alexander
Valley, Carneros, Russian River Valley), Merlot (Alexander Valley,

Carneros, Dry Creek Valley), Pinot Noir (Russian River Valley), Sangiovese (Alexander Valley, Dry Creek), Sauvignon Blanc (Alexander Valley, Russian River Valley), Syrah (Alexander Valley, Dry Creek), Zinfandel (Alexander Valley, Amador, Dry Creek, Lodi, Mendocino, Paso Robles, Russian River Valley).

Erich Russell began developing his 40-acre Russian River vineyard in 1985. Today, the winery is producing 117,000 cases, using both estate-grown and purchased grapes, and Russell is devoting himself full-time to the winery after a stint as winemaker at Belvedere. The line-up includes a varied mix of most of the major varietals. Quality is usually high, though there's been a slight dropoff as production has gone from 30,000 cases in 1995 to its current level of 117,000 cases. Chardonnay and Zinfandel remain the stars, and Sangiovese is a success as well. The Paso Robles acreage now totals 94 acres, with a focus on Italian varietals and Zinfandel.

TASTING NOTES

CHARDONNAY RUSSIAN RIVER VALLEY RABBIT RIDGE RANCH ESTATE RESERVE (★★★)
1997: Rich and toasty, with a complex array of pear, fig, melon, smoke and citrus flavors, turning smooth and polished. **91**

CHARDONNAY SONOMA COUNTY WINEMAKER'S GRAND RESERVE (★★★★): Made in a deliberate style; smooth, rich and creamy.
1996: Smooth, ripe, and creamy, with subtle pear, honey, vanilla, hazelnut and creamy notes; long and rich on the finish, where the toasty oak and rich Chardonnay flavors fold together nicely. **91**
1995: Another winner from Rabbit Ridge. This one's rich, elegant and creamy, with complex pear, vanilla, spice and anise flavors, picking up an earthy quality on the aftertaste. **91**

MERLOT CARNEROS SANGIACOMO VINEYARD RESERVE (★★★★)
1995: Intense and complex, with a nice interplay between the herb and currant flavors and the spicy, cedary oak. **89**
1994: Supple and spicy, with pretty Merlot flavors that echo plum and berry and have a soft, fleshy texture. Smells and tastes complex, with a nice integration of fruit and oak. Shows a lot of finesse on the finish, where

the flavors fan out nicely. **91**

MERLOT SONOMA COUNTY WINEMAKER'S GRAND RESERVE (★★★)
1994: Smooth, supple and elegant, with a pretty dash of spicy, toasty oak and just the right amount of ripe plum and cherry flavors that gently unfold. Has a long, complex aftertaste. **90**

ZINFANDEL DRY CREEK VALLEY OLSON VINEYARD RESERVE (★★★): Another terrific vineyard-driven wine; very ripe, with concentrated, broad flavors.
1997: Effusively fruity, ripe, rich and complex, with tiers of sweet-tasting black cherry, wild berry, plum and spicy flavors, all folding together into a tight, complex package, with pretty toasty oak on the aftertaste. Be forewarned, though: this one is almost over-the-top with its sweet, ripe fruit. **91**
1996: Complex and fruity, with ripe plum, berry, cherry and spicy nuances that linger. Turns smooth and supple on the finish. **88**
1995: A yummy wine; ripe and complex, with a minty, spicy edge to the rich plum and wild berry flavors. **88**

ZINFANDEL RUSSIAN RIVER VALLEY HEDIN VINEYARD RESERVE (★★★)
1997: An earthy style that's smooth, ripe and supple, with pretty blackberry, black cherry, cedar and spicy flavors that are detailed with anise, sage and sandlewood notes. **91**

ZINFANDEL RUSSIAN RIVER VALLEY RABBIT RIDGE RANCH ESTATE RESERVE (★★★)
1997: Complex, with a tasty array of ripe plum, black cherry, wild berry and spice flavors. Turns tight and tannic on the finish, but with short-term cellaring it should blossom. **89**
1996: Smooth and supple, with ripe plum, cherry, raspberry and spice flavors. An elegant, tasty Zin that's ideal for drinking now. Turns complex on the finish. **87**
1995: Ripe and racy, with a dense, jammy edge to the plum and wild berry flavors. Fills out the palate, picking up a cedary oak edge on the tannic finish. **90**

ZINFANDEL SONOMA COUNTY OVZ RESERVE (★★★★): From low-yield, old vines grown in Alexander Valley and Russian River Valley, this wine has a dark, rich and dramatic style, and is packed with juicy berry and mineral flavors. This bottling used to carry the San Lorenzo Reserve designation.
1997: Firm, dense and chewy, with a complex wall of

tannins and flavors, offering layers of plum, black cherry, raspberry and wild berry and finishing with a tight, tannic aftertaste. **92**

1996: A broad shouldered wine. A touch earthy and racy, with murky wild berry, cherry and spice flavors, turning firmly tannic and tarry on the finish. **86**

1995: Lovely Zinfandel, ripe, smooth and fleshy, with a creamy edge to the black cherry, plum and wild berry flavors. Finishes with a long, fruity aftertaste. **92**

1994: A touch earthy and waxy, but still serving up lots of flavor and finesse, with hints of wild berry, cherry and hazelnut. Finishes with a cedary edge and crisp tannins. **91**

ZINFANDEL SONOMA COUNTY WINEMAKER'S GRAND RESERVE (★★★★): The richest, most concentrated and lavishly oaked of the bunch.

1997: A sophisticated style; elegant and complex, with a pretty array of toasty, cedary oak accents overriding the concentrated core of raspberry, blackberry, and wild berry flavors. Neatly tapered on the finish. **91**

1996: Strikes a nice balance between spicy, creamy, vanilla-laced oak and a solid core of blackberry, wild berry and cherry flavors. The texture is smooth and polished, finishing with supple tannins and a fine length. **90**

1995: Rich, smooth, ripe and polished, with a supple core of wild berry, black cherry, raspberry and spicy flavors framed by creamy vanilla oak. Turns complex on the finish, where the flavors fan out. **91**

A. RAFANELLI WINERY (★★★★)

Dry Creek Valley, Sonoma County
Founded: 1973. **Owner:** Dave & Patty Rafanelli.
Winemaker: Dave & Shelly Rafanelli.

MAJOR WINES: PRICE, CASES, RATING

Cabernet Sauvignon Dry Creek Valley	
($18, 3,000)	★★★★
Zinfandel Dry Creek Valley	
($18, 6,000)	★★★★

WINERY DATA

Case Production: 10,000. **Acres Owned:** 65 acres in Dry Creek Valley. **Varietals by Acre:** Cabernet Sauvignon (15 acres), Chardonnay (12), Merlot (15), Zinfandel (23). **Varietals Purchased:** Zinfandel (Dry Creek Valley).

The Rafanelli family has been growing grapes in Dry Creek Valley since the 1950s, when Americo and Alberto Rafanelli purchased a large property in Dry Creek planted to various varieties, which they sold to Sonoma wineries. In 1974, the family began making small lots of wine. Today, production is still on a small scale, with 10,000 cases being made, roughly comprised of two-thirds Zinfandel and one-third Cabernet. Both the Cabernet and Zinfandel come from old vines, and share a pure, if not rustic, quality that emphasizes the ripeness, depth and concentration of the fruit. These are formidable wines, and are very consistent from year to year; they drink exceptionally well and represent excellent value.

TASTING NOTES

CABERNET SAUVIGNON DRY CREEK VALLEY (★★★★): Dark, ripe and concentrated with early tannins; ages well.

1995: Tight, firm, and a touch green, it evolves into a core of plum, black cherry and currant flavors before the tannins take over. **88**

1994: Complex and balanced, showing black cherry, plum anise and cedary notes and mild tannins. **88**

1993: Rustic and tannic, but well balanced with currant, black cherry, cedar and spice flavors. **85**

1992: Beautifully focused, rich and complex, layering currant, black cherry and cedar flavors over firm tannins. **92**

1991: Firm and intense, with ripe, juicy currant, black cherry and spicy oak flavors that turn rustic and chunky, but run deep and rich. **91**

1990: Intense, spicy and elegant, a lavish wine that delivers a broad array of berry, currant and nutmeg flavors, hinting at vanilla and coffee on the finish. **90**

1988: Tight, with earthy currant, mineral, leather and herbal flavors, but lacks extra dimensions; finishes with chunky tannins. **87**

1987: Lean and earthy, but shows a range of complex currant, leather, anise and cedar flavors. **91**

1986: Complex and concentrated with a core of earthy mineral, currant and wild berry flavors, finishing firmly tannic. **92**

1985: Dense and concentrated, a rustic style with some odd flavors and hard, tannic fruit notes. **78**

ZINFANDEL DRY CREEK VALLEY (★★★★): Classy, spicy, intense and complex.

1996: Smooth, with ripe plum, black cherry, raspberry and spice flavors that linger on the focused, tannic finish. **88**

1995: A complex array of wild berry, raspberry, cherry and spicy nuances; finishes with firm, dry tannins and lots of depth. **90**

1994: Continues to evolve, showing a core of spicy anise, raspberry and cherry flavors and a supple finish. **90**

1993: Smooth, elegant and supple, with a core of cherry and wild berry flavors and a clean, fruity finish. **88**

1992: Intense and tannic, with pretty, toasty oak and concentrated blackberry and cherry flavors that linger on the finish. **89**

1991: A formidable wine; dense, tannic and concentrated, with a core of earthy, cherry and raspberry flavors. **88**

1990: Aging well, with complex meaty, smoky, earthy flavors showing cherry and berry fruit on the finish. **89**

1989: Aromatic, with a firm, crisp texture and plenty of plum and blackberry flavors to ride the solid stream of fine tannins. **85**

1988: Massively proportioned, with elegant, ripe raspberry, plum and cherry flavors that turn complex and concentrated, seasoned by spicy dill and oak notes. **90**

1987: Offers juicy raspberry and berry flavors that pick up a touch of gaminess on the finish. **84**

1986: Firm and concentrated, layered with blackberry, cassis and plum flavors, cedary overtones from spicy oak and a bracing touch of acidity and tannin to wrap it up. **91**

RAINFOREST see **WILD HORSE WINERY & VINEYARDS**

RAMEY WINE CELLARS (★★★★★)
Napa Valley
Founded: 1996. **Owner:** David & Carla Ramey. **Winemaker:** David Ramey.

MAJOR WINES: PRICE, CASES, RATING
Chardonnay Napa Valley Carneros
  Hyde Vineyard
  ($45, 1,400)   ★★★★★

ALSO PRODUCED
Chardonnay Napa Valley Carneros Hudson Vineyard ($50, 1,100).

WINERY DATA
Case Production: 2,500. **Vineyard Designations:** Hudson Vineyard (Chardonnay), Hyde Vineyard (Chardonnay). **Varietals Purchased:** Chardonnay (Napa, Carneros).

After a distinguished 20-year career making wine at places such as Chalk Hill, Matanzas Creek and Dominus, David Ramey launched his own brand, using purchased grapes. Now general manager and winemaker at Rudd Estate, (formerly Girard Winery), Ramey is using his talents on vineyard-designated Chardonnays from Hudson and Hyde vineyards in Carneros. The debut 1996 Hyde (94 points) was extra rich and deeply flavored, so early expectations were met. Worth buying.

TASTING NOTES

CHARDONNAY NAPA VALLEY CARNEROS HYDE VINEYARD (★★★★)
1996: Ripe and bold, this wine displays juicy pear, citrus, honey and hazelnut flavors, along with smooth, well integrated oak nuances and a silky finish. **94**

RAMSAY see **KENT RASMUSSEN WINERY**

RANCHO SISQUOC WINERY (★★)
Santa Maria Valley, Santa Barbara County
Founded: 1972. **Owner:** Flood Ranch Co. **Winemaker:** Carol Botwright.

MAJOR WINES: PRICE, CASES, RATING
Cabernet Sauvignon Santa Maria Valley
  ($20, 1,200)   ★★
Chardonnay Santa Maria Valley
  ($15, 1,300)   ★★
Merlot Santa Maria Valley
  ($18, 2,400)   ★★
Riesling Santa Maria Valley
  ($10, 500)   ★
Sauvignon Blanc Santa Maria Valley
  ($12, 700)   ★★
Sylvaner Santa Maria Valley
  ($10, 1,000)   ★

ALSO PRODUCED

Cellar Select Red Santa Maria Valley ($30, 150);
Chardonnay Santa Maria Valley Reserve ($30, 150).

WINERY DATA

Case Production: 10,000. **Acres Owned:** 318 acres in Santa Maria Valley. **Varietals by Acre:** Cabernet Franc (6 acres), Cabernet Sauvignon (125), Chardonnay (35), Malbec (4), Merlot (59), Mourvèdre (0.5), Nebbiolo (1.5), Petit Verdot (2), Pinot Noir (7), Riesling (21), Sangiovese (2), Sauvignon Blanc (25), Sylvaner (9), Syrah (22).

Rancho Sisquoc Winery is part of the sprawling 38,000-acre Flood Ranch, a diversified agricultural concern that grows a variety of crops. The oldest part of this 318-acre Santa Maria Valley vineyard was planted in 1968, making it one of the oldest in Santa Barbara County. As such, it has sold grapes to many area wineries. The acreage leader is, perhaps surprisingly, Cabernet (125 acres), with which the winery excels. Farming is still the main endeavor at the ranch; only 10,000 cases of the wine are made.

RANCHO ZABACO see GALLO OF SONOMA
WINERY AND ZABACO

RANDOM RIDGE (★★)
Mount Veeder, Napa Valley
Founded: 1982. **Owner:** William Hawley **Winemaker:** William Hawley.

WINES PRODUCED: PRICE, CASES

Cabernet Sauvignon-Cabernet Franc Mount Veeder Cabernets ($23, 300); Cabernet Sauvignon-Cabernet Franc Mount Veeder Windfall ($12, 100); Sangiovese Mount Veeder Fortunata ($30, 25); Sémillon Sonoma Valley Cloud Break ($12, 300); Zinfandel Sonoma Valley Olas ($14, 200); Zinfandel Sonoma Valley Old Wave ($17, 200).

WINERY DATA

Case Production: 1,200. **Acres Owned:** 10 acres in Mount Veeder. **Varietals by Acre:** Cabernet Franc (3 acres), Cabernet Sauvignon (6), Sangiovese (1). **Varietals Purchased:** Sémillon (Sonoma Valley), Zinfandel (Sonoma Valley).

In 1982, inveterate surfer William Hawley cleared the land on his Mount Veeder property with the help of family and friends, and started a winery. The bottles are adorned with quirky hand-made labels that depict Hawley's sense of humor and love of surfing. Early wines were well-balanced and flavorful; more recent vintages haven't yet been tasted.

KENT RASMUSSEN WINERY (★★★)
St. Helena, Napa Valley
Founded: 1986. **Owner:** Kent A. Rasmussen & Celia E. Ramsay. **Winemaker:** Kent Rasmussen. **Second Label:** Ramsay.

MAJOR WINES: PRICE, CASES, RATING

Chardonnay Napa Valley ($25, 2,500)	★★★
Pinot Noir Carneros ($30, 2,500)	★★

ALSO PRODUCED

Chardonnay Napa Valley Reserve ($45, 300); Dolcetto Napa Valley ($20, 300); Pinot Noir Carneros Reserve ($50, 400).

WINERY DATA

Case Production: 15,000. **Acres Owned:** 14 acres in Carneros, Napa Valley. **Varietals by Acre:** 14 acres of Pinot Noir. **Varietals Purchased:** Alicante Bouchet (Green Valley-Solano County), Chardonnay (Napa Valley), Petite Sirah (Napa Valley), Pinot Noir (Carneros, Napa), Syrah (Napa Valley).

Kent Rasmussen's winemaking credentials include stints in South Africa and Australia, but most of his experience is with Napa Valley- and Carneros-grown grapes. In 1986 he purchased a small vineyard that now measures 14 acres in vines, all devoted to Pinot Noir, but his wine portfolio includes Chardonnay, Dolcetto, Sangiovese, Syrah and Alicante Bouschet made from purchased grapes. Sangiovese, Merlot and Pinot Noir have appeared under the Ramsey label.

TASTING NOTES

CHARDONNAY NAPA VALLEY (★★★): Can be intense and lively, well oaked and complex. The 1995 (92 points) was the best ever, with ripe, delicate fruit upfront, building complexity on the finish.

PINOT NOIR CARNEROS (★★): Solid and well made but shy of outstanding, marked by moderately complex fruit flavors in the best years.

RAVENSWOOD (★★–★★★★)
Sonoma Valley
Founded: 1976. **Owner:** Ravenswood Winery Inc.
Winemaker: Joel Peterson.

MAJOR WINES: PRICE, CASES, RATING

Cabernet Sauvignon Sonoma County
  ($16, 5,481) ★★★
Cabernet Sauvignon Sonoma Valley
  Gregory Vineyard
  ($21, 866) ★★★
Chardonnay California Vintners Blend
  ($10, 16,000) ★★
Chardonnay Sonoma Valley Sangiacomo
  ($20, 1,733) ★★★
Icon Red Sonoma County
  ($20, 2,043) ★★★
Merlot Sonoma County
  ($19, 6,947) ★★★
Merlot Sonoma Valley Donnell Ranch
  ($21, 209) ★★★
Merlot Sonoma Valley Sangiacomo
  Vineyard
  ($21, 2,162) ★★★
Pickberry Vineyard Red Sonoma Mountain
  ($32, 720) ★★★
Rancho Salina Vineyards Red Sonoma Valley
  ($25, 1,628) ★★★
Zinfandel Alexander Valley
  ($14, 1,430) ★★★
Zinfandel Napa Valley Dickerson
  Vineyard
  ($22, 955) ★★★★
Zinfandel Russian River Valley
  Wood Road/Belloni
  ($22, 3,072) ★★★
Zinfandel Sonoma County
  ($16, 11,673) ★★★
Zinfandel Sonoma Valley Cooke
  ($22, 420) ★★★★
Zinfandel Sonoma Valley Monte Rosso
  ($22, 1,696) ★★★★

Zinfandel Sonoma Valley Old Hill
  Vineyard Limited Edition
  ($24, 861) ★★★★

ALSO PRODUCED
Cabernet Franc Sonoma Valley ($14, 688); Chardonnay Sonoma Valley Estate ($12, 336); French Colombard Sonoma County ($8, 469); Gewürztraminer Early Harvest Sonoma Valley ($12, 280); Gewürztraminer Late Harvest Sonoma Valley ($18, 250); Merlot California Vintners Blend ($12, 12,225); Merlot Napa Valley ($19, 749); Merlot Sonoma Valley Estate ($21, 305); Moscato Sonoma Valley ($9, 641); Pentimento Sonoma Valley ($21, 218); Petite Sirah Sonoma County ($14, 893); Zinfandel Alexander Valley Beaterra ($20, 419); Zinfandel Amador County ($14, 4,400); Zinfandel California Vintners Blend ($10, 75,000); Zinfandel Late Harvest Dry Creek Valley McGill Ranch ($24, 79); Zinfandel Lodi ($12, 4,500); Zinfandel Napa Valley ($13, 14,232); Zinfandel Sonoma Valley Kunde Ranch ($20, 216).

WINERY DATA
Case Production: 200,000. **Acres Owned:** 15 acres in Sonoma Valley. **Varietals by Acre:** Merlot (7 acres), Zinfandel (8). **Vineyard Designations:** Beaterra (Zinfandel), Belloni (Zinfandel), Cooke (Zinfandel), Dickerson (Zinfandel), Donnell Ranch (Merlot), Gregory (Cabernet Blend), Kunde Ranch (Zinfandel), McGill Ranch (Zinfandel), Monte Rosso (Zinfandel), Old Hill Ranch (Zinfandel), Rancho Salina (Cabernet Sauvignon), Sangiacomo (Chardonnay, Merlot), Wood Road (Zinfandel). **Varietals Purchased:** Alicante Bouschet (Lodi), Cabernet Franc (Napa Valley, Sonoma Valley), Cabernet Sauvignon (Alexander Valley, Dry Creek Valley, Napa Valley, Sonoma Mountain, Sonoma Valley, Spring Mountain), Carignane (Dry Creek Valley), Chardonnay (Sonoma Valley), French Colombard (Dry Creek Valley), Gewürztraminer (Sonoma Valley), Grenache (Dry Creek Valley, Sonoma Valley), Merlot (Alexander Valley, Lodi, Napa Valley, Sonoma Mountain, Sonoma Valley, Suisun Valley), Mourvèdre (Knights Valley), Muscat Cannelli (Russian River, Sonoma Valley), Nebbiolo (Dry Creek Valley), Petite Sirah (Dry Creek Valley, Sonoma Valley), Pinot Noir (Carneros), Ruby Cabernet (Napa Valley), Zinfandel (Alexander Valley, Dry Creek Valley, Knights Valley, Lodi, Mendocino, Napa Valley, Sonoma Valley, Suisun Valley).

Joel Peterson, winemaker and co-founder of Ravenswood, grew up with wine-loving parents, and developed a keen palate at a young age. His fascination with wine led to his going to work for Joseph Swan in the early 1970s, before he started Ravenswood in 1976.

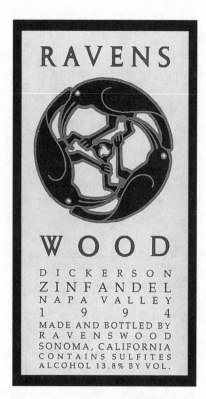

In 1981, Reed Foster joined on at Ravenswood, providing the financial backing necessary to expand operations.

Most of Ravenswood's wines are made from purchased grapes. The winery's strength is ripe, full-throttle Zinfandel made from a series of mostly old-vine, dry-farmed vineyards, the majority of which are in Sonoma Valley (making a strong case for Sonoma Valley Zinfandel). When it comes to understanding how and where Zinfandel grows best, and recognizing the wine's strengths and limitations, Peterson has few peers. He is so in tune with his Zinfandel vineyards and the resultant wines that they routinely overshadow his other fine wines, none of which rises to the heights of the Belloni (Sonoma Valley), Cooke (Sonoma Valley), Dickerson (Napa Valley) or Old Hill Vineyard (Sonoma Valley) Zinfandels.

It appears that Peterson tries to cull as much character from Cabernet, Chardonnay and Merlot as from his Zinfandels, but he somehow comes up just short. Ravenswood's finest Cabernet-style wine is a proprietary blend that includes Merlot and Cabernet Franc from Pickberry Vineyard on Sonoma Mountain. Chardonnay comes from several sources; the Sangiacomo bottling is often excellent. In 1991, Ravenswood moved into the old Haywood winery, and production is now at 200,000 cases. A portion of the winery was offered for sale with an initial public offering in 1999.

TASTING NOTES

CABERNET SAUVIGNON SONOMA VALLEY GREGORY VINEYARD (★★★): Tight and lean; marked by herbal notes.
1994: Firm and tight, with a slight camphor edge to the cherry and currant flavors, along with firm tannins. **88**
1993: Marked by notes of mint, sage and herb, with a good dose of currant and cherry flavors working their way to the forefront; the tannins are supple. **89**
1990: Definitely herbal, with strong mint, sage and tarragon aromas and flavors; the finish is more soft and minty than fruity. **84**
1989: Aromatically pleasing, with minty currant notes, but lean and shy on the palate. **85**
1988: Tough and oaky, with decent cherry and plum flavors accented by cedar and vanilla notes. **80**

MERLOT SONOMA VALLEY SANGIACOMO VINEYARD (★★★): This Sangiacomo bottling packs in lots of flavors and is nearing the class of Ravenswood's Zinfandels. Worth watching.

PICKBERRY VINEYARD RED SONOMA MOUNTAIN (★★★): Shares the same intensity and range of flavors as Ravenswood's Zinfandels, but often to its detriment, as it comes across as a Zinfandel-style Cabernet with wild flavors and brambly tannins.
1994: Tight and restrained, with a band of earth, tar, currant and berry flavors and supple, complex tannins. **90**
1992: Dense, dark and chewy, with a tight core of tannins submerging the earthy currant and berry flavors. **86**
1991: The pretty berry, spice, currant and tobacco flavors are soft, rich and fleshy, with modest tannins. **83**
1990: Ripe, smooth and polished, a supple wine with prune, chocolate and cola aromas and flavors, echoing a hint of cherry on the finish. **86**
1987: Good intensity, even if the cedar, plum and berry flavors lack focus. Tannins are supple. **87**

1986: Mature, but holding, with spicy cherry, herb, anise and currant flavors. **87**

RED RANCHO SALINA VINEYARDS SONOMA VALLEY (★★★)
1995: The earthy currant, leather, spice and cedary oak flavors are elegant and refined; the tannins are firm and supple. **89**
1994: Firm, tight and tannic; marked by minty, leathery flavors, but notes of currant and cherry soon fold in. **87**

ZINFANDEL NAPA VALLEY DICKERSON VINEYARD (★★★★): This Napa vineyard consistently yields a rich, supple, minty, currant core of Zinfandel flavors. Ages well.
1996: Marked by ripe cherry, blackberry, spice and sage, it's an elegant wine with a minty edge and firm, dry tannins on the finish. **88**
1995: Appealing for its jammy, ripe cherry, raspberry and wild berry flavors, finishing with chewy tannins. **89**
1994: Marked by minty sage notes, the core of plum and wild berry flavors folds together nicely; the tannins are firm. **89**
1993: Effusively fruity, ripe and complex, offering pretty black cherry, plum and raspberry jam notes and mild tannins. **89**
1992: Firm, tight, crisp and tannic, with spicy raspberry, wild berry and black cherry flavors that are intense and sharply focused, gaining a minty edge on the finish. **91**
1991: Distinctively minty and spicy, showing ripe raspberry and cherry flavors, but the mint flavors dominate. The tannins are polished. **87**
1990: Sleek, detailed and elegant, with a pretty, minty edge to the sage, tea, spice and berry flavors. **91**
1989: Spicy, oaky notes lead to ripe, intense raspberry flavors and firm tannins. **87**
1988: Marked by strong eucalyptus and menthol flavors, with chunky red cherry and raspberry flavors that persist on the finish. **84**
1987: Tart, intense and tannic, with ripe, powerful plum, blueberry and cherry flavors that are sharply focused. **86**
1986: Tight and tannic, with ripe raspberry and cherry flavors and a touch of vanilla on the finish. **88**
1983: Tight and sharply focused, with ripe plum and spice notes and a smoky, cedary edge. **87**
1981: Mature but holding, with intense plum, raisin and spice flavors that turn tannic. **85**

ZINFANDEL RUSSIAN RIVER VALLEY WOOD ROAD/ BELLONI (★★★): Very ripe and dense; packed with rich fruit flavors that fan out.

1996: Smooth, with rich, tarry wild berry, cola, and earthy notes, it turns complex with supple tannins. **88**
1995: Lots of black cherry and plum flavors, with lively acidity and floral notes that linger along with the tannins on the finish. **88**
1994: Ripe, with pretty cherry and wild berry flavors and a spicy, minty accent. **88**
1993: Rambunctious; marked by chewy tannins, with tight plum and wild berry flavors. **87**
1992: Big, rich, intense and tannic, packing in loads of black cherry, wild berry, spice and floral flavors. **89**
1991: Ripe, jammy and enormously fruity, with mature, rich berry, cherry, raspberry, blackberry and spice flavors. **90**

ZINFANDEL SONOMA COUNTY (★★★★): In the years it's made, this Zinfandel, blended from all the Sonoma Vineyards, can be excellent, supple and complex.
1992: Bright and lively, with spicy cherry, raspberry, plum and currant flavors, turning elegant, with a supple texture and light, toasty oak shadings. **91**
1990: A mouthful of fruit and tannin, offering rich, intense plum and blackberry flavors framed by toasty, buttery oak notes. **89**
1989: Solid and chewy, with a firm texture and ample plum and berry flavors. **82**
1988: Firm and tannic, with tart, well-defined plum and berry flavors that linger. **86**
1987: Despite the tannins, this has attractive raspberry flavors that are spicy, peppery and well balanced. **88**
1986: Massive and fruity, deep and rich, with raspberry and plum flavors and a tannic, powerful finish. **88**
1985: Mature, with earthy, anise and berry notes, fading on the finish. **80**

ZINFANDEL SONOMA VALLEY COOKE (★★★★): Big, ripe, deep and concentrated; loaded with fruit and character.
1996: Lean and tart, with a narrow band of sage and berry flavors, it unfolds to reveal more intensity, but it's best to cellar short term. **88**
1995: Ripe, rich and complex, with a spicy, peppery edge to the cherry and wild berry flavors and firm tannins. **91**
1994: A rustic style, marked by spicy, peppery wild berry and cherry flavors, turning firmly tannic on the finish. **88**
1993: Austere, but very compact and concentrated, featuring crisp cherry and wild berry notes and firm, dry tannins. **89**

1992: Tight and compact, with a firm, tannic edge to the ripe cherry, raspberry and spice flavors that are rich and focused. **91**
1991: Big, deep, rich and concentrated, with ripe, intense tar, cherry, raspberry and spice flavors wrapped firmly in tannins. **88**
1990: Rich, dark, complex and smoky, with black cherry, plum and currant flavors, a lush texture and a long, deep aftertaste. **92**
1987: An intense, lively wine that's dense, deep, rich and concentrated, with pretty raspberry and pepper notes on the finish. **88**

ZINFANDEL SONOMA VALLEY MONTE ROSSO (★★★★)
1996: Serves up ripe cherry, raspberry and strawberry flavors, with firm tannins and sage, tar and herbal notes. **88**
1995: A heady wine, with lots of fruit and tannin; chewy plum and wild berry flavors abound, with dashes of sage and spice showing through on the finish. **89**
1994: Well focused, with bright, ripe and lively currant, cherry and wild berry flavors and touches of cedar and spice. **90**
1993: A compact, supple core of cherry and raspberry flavors picks up notes of spice and anise, adding firm, elegant tannins on the finish. **88**

ZINFANDEL SONOMA VALLEY OLD HILL VINEYARD LIMITED EDITION (★★★★): Serves up lots of bold, ripe, aromatic flavors, with great intensity. Usually quite tannic.
1996: Tight, firmly tannic, with an austere band of spicy wild berry, sage and cherry, it opens up on the finish, so short-term cellaring is advised. **88**
1995: A delicious surge of ripe, juicy black cherry, raspberry and wild berry flavors, turning firmly tannic on the finish. **92**
1994: Tightly wound, the leathery currant and cherry flavors are cloaked in firm tannins. **87**
1993: Ripe and well proportioned, with a rich core of black cherry, wild berry, tar and spice flavors. **90**
1992: Perfumed and floral, with bright, ripe cherry and raspberry jam flavors that border on the exotic. Finishes with crisp tannins. **92**
1991: Tight and firm, with plenty of raspberry and cherry flavors peeking through the cedary, spicy oak and chewy tannins. **87**
1990: A ripe, potent Zinfandel loaded with blackberry, black cherry, spice, floral and earth flavors. **89**

1987: Intensely tannic and packed with ripe raspberry, cherry, plum and spice flavors that are powerful and enduring. **87**
1986: Very rich and concentrated, blanketed by soft tannins, and the blueberry and raspberry flavors are complemented by black pepper and toasty oak shadings. **92**

MARTIN RAY (★★★–★★★★)
Sonoma County
Founded: 1937. **Owner:** Courtney & Derek Benham.
Winemaker: Greg Graziano.

MAJOR WINES: PRICE, CASES, RATING
Cabernet Sauvignon California Saratoga Cuvée ($24, 2,000)	★★★
Cabernet Sauvignon Napa Valley Diamond Mountain ($45, 400)	★★★★
Cabernet Sauvignon Santa Cruz Mountains ($45, 400)	★★★★
Chardonnay California Mariage ($20, 5,000)	★★★★

ALSO PRODUCED
Pinot Noir California La Montana ($20, 1,000); Pinot Noir Sonoma County ($20, 1,000).

WINERY DATA
Case Production: 10,000. **Varietals Purchased:** Cabernet Sauvignon (Napa Valley, Santa Cruz, Sonoma County), Chardonnay (Monterey, Sonoma County), Pinot Noir (Monterey, Sonoma County).

After a long absence, the Martin Ray brand has been revitalized, with some showy wines. After owning the Paul Masson Winery from 1936 to 1943, Martin Ray established a winery and vineyard in the Santa Cruz Mountains, where he produced a number of important (indeed, legendary in some quarters) Cabernets, Chardonnays and Pinot Noirs, both from his property and from purchased grapes. In 1972, a dispute among investors led to the property being divided, with the former Martin Ray Winery facility being renamed Mount Eden, and Ray moving to a separate facility at a lower elevation. After Ray died, in 1976, the brand withered.

In 1991, Courtney Benham received permission from Ray's estate to use his name, and the brand was revived. Production has since grown to 10,000 cases, all from purchased grapes, but the winery knows how to pick its vineyards, and many of the wines are dazzling. The first wines were made at Mendocino's Domaine Saint Gregory winery, but Benham hopes to relocate the winery to Santa Clara. The Cabernet comes from single vineyard sources, while Chardonnay carries the California appellation.

CABERNET SAUVIGNON CALIFORNIA SARATOGA CUVÉE (★★★): Tightly wound on release, with currant, berry, herb and mineral flavors.
1995: Firmly tannic and distinctly herbal, with mint, currant, herb and mineral flavors, picking up hints of mineral and spice. Needs time in the cellar. **88**
1994: Tight and intense, with a range of herb, currant, black cherry and spice, finishing with cedary oak and chewy tannins. **88**
1993: Ripe cherry and currant flavors are generous—avoiding the hollow middle found in so many 1993 Cabernets. Finishes with a fruity aftertaste and crisp tannins. **86**
1992: A backward, restrained style, boasting wild berry, cherry and currant notes with good depth and proportion. **89**

CABERNET SAUVIGNON NAPA VALLEY DIAMOND MOUNTAIN (★★★★): With the 1995, the Diamond Mountain Vineyard is the source of grapes for this stunning wine. Worth buying.
1995: Dark, ripe, rich and plush, with dense, chewy, complex notes of currant, anise, mineral, cedar and spice, turning elegant on the finish. **95**

CABERNET SAUVIGNON SANTA CRUZ MOUNTAINS (★★★★)
1995: Racy and a touch earthy, with a range of herb, currant, pepper, sage and leathery flavors that are intense and concentrated. **91**

CHARDONNAY CALIFORNIA MARIAGE (★★★★): Has been at or close to outstanding since its inception; a highly successful blend of grapes.
1997: Complex in its interplay of smoky, toasty, spicy oak and vibrant pear, nectarine, pineapple, apple and nutmeg notes, finishing long and lively. **90**

RAYMOND VINEYARD & CELLAR (★★–★★★★)
Napa Valley
Founded: 1971. **Owner:** Kirin Brewing Co. and The Raymond Family. **Winemaker:** Walter Raymond, Kenn Vigoda, Kathy George.

MAJOR WINES: PRICE, CASES, RATING
Cabernet Sauvignon California Amberhill ($13, 25,000) ★★
Cabernet Sauvignon Napa Valley Generations ($40, 3,500) ★★★
Cabernet Sauvignon Napa Valley Raymond Estates ($13, 10,000) ★★
Cabernet Sauvignon Napa Valley Raymond Estates Reserve ($20, 35,000) ★★★
Chardonnay California Amberhill ($10, 90,000) ★
Chardonnay Monterey County Raymond Estates ($13, 15,000) ★★★
Chardonnay Napa Valley Generations ($28, 3,500) ★★★★
Chardonnay Napa Valley Raymond Estates Reserve ($15, 40,000) ★★★
Meritage Red Napa Valley Private Reserve (Discontinued) ★★★
Merlot California Amberhill ($13, 10,000) ★★
Merlot Napa Valley Raymond Estates Reserve ($20, 12,000) ★★
Pinot Noir Napa Valley Raymond Estates Reserve ($19, 1,500) ★★
Sauvignon Blanc California Amberhill ($10, 10,000) ★★
Sauvignon Blanc Napa Valley Raymond Estates Reserve ($11, 14,000) ★★

WINERY DATA
Case Production: 250,000. **Acres Owned:** 555 acres (300 in Monterey County, 255 in Napa Valley). **Varietals by Acre:** Cabernet Sauvignon (50 acres), Chardonnay (460), Merlot (23), Pinot Noir (12), Sauvignon Blanc (10). **Varietals Purchased:** Cabernet Sauvignon (Napa Valley), Chardonnay (Napa Valley, California), Merlot (California), Sauvignon Blanc (Napa Valley).

The Raymonds are one of the oldest winemaking families in Napa Valley. They owned Beringer Vineyards until 1971, when they sold it to Nestlé and the Labruyere family of France. With money from the winery sale, Roy Raymond Sr. bought a 90-acre parcel of land on Zinfandel Lane, where he and his sons Roy Jr. and Walt founded this winery. In 1988, a partial interest in the winery was sold to Kirin Brewing Co. of Japan, with the Raymonds remaining in control of management and production. Since then, production has risen substantially to 250,000 cases.

The winery owns 555 acres of vineyard, including 300 acres in Monterey, which fuel the Raymonds' California-appellation Chardonnay and the Amberhill line. The Napa Valley wines—both the Napa Valley and Reserve bottlings—are very well crafted, although in recent vintages there has been less distance between the two lines than was evident in the mid-1980s.

TASTING NOTES

CABERNET SAUVIGNON NAPA VALLEY GENERATIONS (★★★★): A new addition to the portfolio, which raises the overall quality of the Cabernets. Complex, well balanced, and can be quite concentrated.
1995: Complex, with a strong oak presence overriding the pretty band of berry, black cherry and plum flavors, detracting from its intensity. **88**
1994: Dense and chewy, with a slightly rustic, earthy side to the substantial currant, black cherry, cedar and spice flavors. **93**

CABERNET SAUVIGNON NAPA VALLEY RAYMOND ESTATES RESERVE (★★★): The Reserve (called Private Reserve prior to 1993) bottling is a shade less intense and concentrated than the Generations line.
1996: Ripe in flavor and silky in texture, with pretty black cherry, vanilla, chocolate and spice flavors that linger on the finish. **87**
1994: Marked by notes of herb and dill, with a slightly

green edge, there's enough cherry and currant flavors to give it dimension and breadth. **89**
1993: Smooth and harmonious, featuring a supple core of cherry, currant and berry notes, turning complex and spicy on the finish. **90**
1992: Marked by a complex interplay of ripe cherry, currant and anise flavors and notes of buttery, toasty oak. **90**
1991: Clean and correct, with a modest band of currant and cherry flavors, but it lacks the usual additional dimensions. **84**
1990: Supple, with well-integrated herb, currant and spicy, buttery oak flavors and fleshy tannins. **88**
1988: Supple and complex, with spicy currant, herb, anise and cedary oak flavors. **88**
1987: Plenty of depth, complexity and finesse, with a pretty core of ripe black cherry, herb, anise, sage, berry, coffee and vanilla flavors. **90**
1986: Marked by its woody character, with a waxy aroma and dryness in the mouth; showing just a hint of currant and spice. **82**
1985: Smooth and elegant, with well defined currant, plum, herb, cedar and smoky oak flavors that finish with plush tannins. **88**
1984: Ripe and supple, with generous cherry, plum, cedar, anise and olive flavors. **88**
1983: Mature and retaining its tannic edge, with herb, currant and plum flavors emerging on the finish. **84**
1982: Mature, with smoky, herbal berry flavors that finish with smooth tannins. **86**
1981: At its peak, serving up fresh herb, currant and anise flavors. **87**
1980: An herbaceous wine laced with herb, tea, spice and cherry flavors that are elegant and graceful. **85**

CHARDONNAY NAPA VALLEY GENERATIONS (★★★): The Raymonds have always excelled with this ripe, juicy, opulent style of wine.
1996: Slowly unfolds to reveal complex pear, spice, honey and vanilla flavors, with a dash of hazelnut and smoke. **91**
1995: Elegant; packs in lots of flavor, with hints of pear, hazelnut, fig and spice, finishing with a toasty oak flavor. **91**

MERITAGE RED NAPA VALLEY PRIVATE RESERVE (★★★)
1991: Ripe and jammy, with wild berry, cherry and raspberry flavors, picking up a touch of spicy oak on the finish. Overall, clean and well balanced, with a sense of elegance and finesse. **87**

RENAISSANCE VINEYARD & WINERY (★★–★★★)
North Yuba, Yuba County
Founded: 1978. **Owner:** Fellowship of Friends.
Winemaker: Gideon Feinstock. **Second Label:** Da Vinci.

MAJOR WINES: PRICE, CASES, RATING
Cabernet Sauvignon North Yuba	
($12, 16,000)	★★
Chardonnay North Yuba	
($14, 3,500)	★★
Chardonnay North Yuba Reserve	
($27, 250)	★★
Merlot North Yuba	
($15, 4,000)	★
Red North Yuba Reserve	
($20, 2,000)	★★★
Riesling Late Harvest North Yuba	
($20, 500)	★★★
Sauvignon Blanc North Yuba	
($10, 2,500)	★★★
Sauvignon Blanc North Yuba Barrel Select	
($12, 500)	★★★

ALSO PRODUCED
Pinot Noir North Yuba ($18, 1,500); Riesling North Yuba Demi-Sec ($14, 1,000); Riesling North Yuba Dry ($12, 500); Sauvignon Blanc Late Harvest North Yuba ($20, 300-500); Viognier North Yuba ($18, 2,500); Zinfandel North Yuba ($14, 2,500).

WINERY DATA
Case Production: 40,000. **Acres Owned:** 365 acres in North Yuba. **Varietals by Acre:** Cabernet Franc (11 acres), Cabernet Sauvignon (166), Chardonnay (19), Merlot (53), Pinot Noir (12), Riesling (15), Sangiovese (11), Sauvignon Blanc (26), Syrah (15), Viognier (15), Zinfandel (15), other (7).

Renaissance Vineyard & Winery is owned by the Fellowship of Friends, a philosophical group based in the San Francisco Bay Area. It farms 365 acres of grapes in the North Yuba foothills. It's a unique setup situated in a unique locale: it is the only vineyard in this remote northern California county. The Fellowship has invested some $16 million in planting vines and building a winery. The winery produces 40,000 cases of wine, including Cabernet (15,000 cases), Chardonnay (2,000 cases), Riesling and Sauvignon Blanc (10,000 cases), along with dessert-style Riesling and Sauvignon Blanc. Optimism is high about the winery's potential, and the wines have impressed some critics. My own notes indicate that they've ranged from bizarre to ordinary to good, but clearly this is a serious endeavor; given time, Renaissance may well produce more compelling wines.

RENWOOD WINERY (★★–★★★)
Amador County
Founded: 1992. **Owner:** Robert Smerling. **Winemaker:** Gordon Binz. **Second Label:** Santino Wines.

MAJOR WINES: PRICE, CASES, RATING
Barbera Amador County	
($17, 1,500)	★★★
Barbera Amador County Linsteadt	
($20, 1,500)	★★★
Nebbiolo Amador County	
($21, 400)	★★
Sangiovese Amador County	
($17, 1,000)	★★
Syrah Amador County	
($20, 1,200)	★★
Viognier Amador County	
($20, 800)	★★
Zinfandel Amador County Ice Dessert Wine	
($20, 1,200)	★★★
Zinfandel Amador County Grandmère Vineyard	
($22, 2,500)	★★★
Zinfandel Amador County Grandpère Vineyard	
($25, 1,200)	★★★
Zinfandel Amador County Fox Creek Vineyard Jack Rabbit Flat	
($24, 1,600)	★★★
Zinfandel Amador County Old Vine	
($16, 8,000)	★★★
Zinfandel Fiddletown	
($22, 1,200)	★★
Zinfandel Fiddletown Eschen Vineyard	
($25, 1,525)	★★★
Zinfandel Fiddletown Old Vine	
(Discontinued)	★★★
Zinfandel Shenandoah Valley D'Agostini Bros.	
($24, 600)	★★★

ALSO PRODUCED
Amador County Orange Muscat ($16, 400); Port Amador County ($24, 1,000).

WINERY DATA
Case Production: 68,000. **Acres Owned:** 200 acres in Shennadoah Valley. **Varietals by Acre:** NA. **Vineyard Designations:** D'Agostini (Zinfandel), Eschen Vineyard (Zinfandel), Fiddletown (Zinfandel), Grandpère (Zinfandel), Jack Rabbit Flat (Zinfandel), Linsteadt (Barbera).

Renwood—formerly known as Santino Winery under winemaker and owner Scott Harvey—produces 68,000 cases, including wines still made under the Santino brand, and is one of the stars among Amador County wines. The wide-ranging lineup includes Barbera, Fumé Blanc, Nebbiolo, Sangiovese, Sémillon, Syrah, and Viognier. There are eight different bottlings of Zinfandel, including a Grandpère Vineyard Zinfandel—which is said to be the oldest Zinfandel vineyard in California. So far, the Barbera and Zinfandels are the most impressive and most widely distributed wines, but clearly there are some other fine offerings in this stable, which makes it worth watching.

TASTING NOTES

BARBERA AMADOR COUNTY (★★★): Two bottlings are made, an Amador County and the Linsteadt (1000 cases). The standard features ripe, tight, sharply focused flavors.

SYRAH AMADOR COUNTY (★★)
1995: Austere and tannic, with a spicy, cedary edge to the ripe plum and cherry notes. **86**

ZINFANDEL AMADOR COUNTY FOX CREEK VINEYARD JACK RABBIT FLAT (★★★)
1996: Smooth and polished, with ripe, rich blackberry, wild berry and creamy vanilla notes that fan out and turn supple. **90**

ZINFANDEL AMADOR COUNTY GRANDMÈRE VINEYARD (★★★)
1996: Ripe and racy, with a jammy, wild berry, tarry edge to the sage, dusty oak, cedar and spice flavors; finishes with gritty tannins. **88**
1994: Ripe, rustic and intense, with a core of chunky cherry, chocolate and cedary oak flavors. **86**

ZINFANDEL AMADOR COUNTY GRANDPÈRE VINEYARD (★★★): The Grandpère Vineyard, with its 125-year-old vines, is the wine to buy, as it is intense and complex.
1996: Ripe, with an array of rustic wild berry, sage, tea, tar, anise and oak; it's intense and tannic, but packed with flavor. **89**
1992: Dark in color, with very ripe jam, raisin, plum and black cherry flavors that are intense and concentrated, finishing with firm tannins. **88**
1991: Intense and firmly tannic, with briary chocolate and wild berry flavors that turn complex if a bit biting on the finish. **86**
1995: Ripe to the point of jamminess, with lots of cherry and wild berry aromas and flavors that linger on the finish. **88**
1994: Supple, complex and elegant, with pretty, ripe cherry, blackberry, spice and cedar notes that are mildly tannic. **88**
1993: Austere and firmly tannic, with wild berry, cherry and spicy notes. **87**

ZINFANDEL AMADOR COUNTY OLD VINE (★★★): Impressive for its array of ripe, complex flavors.
1996: Ripe, with zesty berry, sage, menthol and berryish flavors; it's dry, leathery and tannic on the finish. **87**
1994: Smooth, ripe, rich and exotic, with layers of plum, cherry and berry and big tannins; a fine depth and richness. **90**
1993: Ripe, flavorful and tannic, with a thick, heady dose of jammy berry, pepper and raspberry flavors. **89**

ZINFANDEL FIDDLETOWN (★★)
1996: An earthy, gamy style that struggles to show ripe fruitiness, the results of which are an earthy core of dry, leathery Zinfandel fruit, with hints of ripe berry and spice, but mostly dry, leathery tannins. **83**

ZINFANDEL FIDDLETOWN ESCHEN VINEYARD (★★★)
1994: Austere and still quite tannic, but it shows more finesse than other Zins from this area. The sharply focused cherry, currant and wild berry flavors slowly unfold and gain depth and complexity. **89**

ZINFANDEL FIDDLETOWN OLD VINE (★★★)
1993: Firm, intense, compact and concentrated, but the flavors are a bit murky and unevolved, adding hints of cedar, spice and earthy berry. The finish is more interesting, but it's dense and tannic getting there. **87**

ZINFANDEL SHENANDOAH VALLEY D'AGOSTINI BROS. (★★★)
1996: Serves up a pretty array of ripe, zesty Zinfandel fruit, along with wild berry, sage, cedar and spice flavors; turns complex on the finish. **89**

REVERIE WINERY (★★★★)
Diamond Mountain, Napa Valley
Founded: 1993. **Owner:** Norman & Evelyn Kiken. **Winemaker:** Norman Kiken, Ted Lemon. **Second Label:** Daydream Cellars, A.S. Kiken Winery.

MAJOR WINES: PRICE, CASES, RATING

Cabernet Sauvignon Diamond Mountain ($40, 800)	★★★
Red Diamond Mountain Special Reserve ($30, 200).	★★★★

ALSO PRODUCED
Cabernet Franc Diamond Mountain ($30, 600); Grenache Diamond Mountain ($30, NA); Petit Verdot Diamond Mountain ($30, NA); Red Diamond Mountain A.S. Kiken ($30, 200); Roussanne Diamond Mountain ($NA, NA); Tempranillo Diamond Mountain ($30, 75).

WINERY DATA
Case Production: 2,500. **Acres Owned:** 30 acres on Diamond Mountain. **Varietals by Acre:** Cabernet Sauvignon (12 acres), Cabernet Franc (6), Merlot (6), Barbera, Grenache, Malbec, Petit Verdot, Roussanne and Tempranillo (6).

Norm Kiken released the first wines made from his 30-acre vineyard under the Daydream Cellars label, believing that they weren't at the level he wanted for Reverie. The 1994 Daydream Cabernet (88 points) was complex and well-balanced, with cedar and currant flavors. The Reverie wines have proven to be excellent as well, and with Kiken's Diamond Mountain grapes and Ted Lemon's winemaking expertise, the future is promising.

TASTING NOTES

CABERNET SAUVIGNON DIAMOND MOUNTAIN (★★★)
1995: Tightly wound, with a focused band of cedar, currant, plum and berry, finishing with leathery, oaky flavors and drying tannins. **88**

RED DIAMOND MOUNTAIN SPECIAL RESERVE (★★★★)
1995: Dense, complex, and concentrated, with an earthy band of cedar, currant, tar, tobacco and black cherry. This is a tightly wound, firmly tannic wine that needs short-term cellaring. **92**

RICHARDSON VINEYARDS (★★)
Sonoma Valley
Founded: 1980. **Owner:** Dennis, Carolyn and Evelyn Richardson and Al Wighton Jr. **Winemaker:** Dennis Richardson.

MAJOR WINES: PRICE, CASES, RATING

Cabernet Sauvignon Sonoma Valley Horne ($22, 350)	★★
Merlot Carneros Sangiacomo ($18, 1,200)	★★★
Pinot Noir Carneros Sangiacomo ($19, 900)	★★
Red Sonoma Valley Synergy ($20, 400)	★★

WINERY DATA
Case Production: 3,000. **Acres Owned:** 5 acres in Sonoma Valley, Carneros. **Varietals by Acre:** Pinot Noir (1 acre), Syrah (3), Viognier (1). **Varietals Purchased:** Cabernet Sauvignon (Sonoma Valley), Merlot (Carneros, Sonoma Valley), Pinot Noir (Carneros, Sonoma Valley).

Located on the Sonoma side of Carneros, Richardson produces Cabernet Sauvignon, Merlot and Pinot Noir, all from purchased grapes. The Sangiacomo Vineyard Merlot leads in quality; the 1995 and 1996 (both 88 points) were firm and focused, with blackberry, cedar and earthy flavors. In 1996, the Sangiacomo Vineyard Pinot Noir (84) showed bright cherry, spice and mint notes. Early Cabernet efforts were not very successful, and were often marked by earthy, herbal flavors and firm tannins.

RIDGE VINEYARDS (★★★–★★★★★)
Santa Cruz Mountains
Founded: 1959. **Owner:** Akihiko Otsuka. **Winemaker:** Paul Draper.

MAJOR WINES: PRICE, CASES, RATING

Cabernet Sauvignon Napa County York Creek (Discontinued)	★★
Cabernet Sauvignon Santa Cruz Mountains ($28, 5,000)	★★★
Chardonnay Santa Cruz Mountains ($25, 2,000)	★★★★★
Geyserville Red Sonoma County ($25, 12,400)	★★★★★
Lytton Springs Red Dry Creek Valley ($25, 12,000)	★★★★★
Mataro Contra Costa County Bridgehead ($20, 1,200)	★★★
Merlot Santa Cruz Mountains ($40, 60)	★★★
Monte Bello Red Santa Cruz Mountains ($100, 3,700)	★★★★★
Petite Sirah Spring Mountain York Creek ($20, 2,000)	★★★
Zinfandel Paso Robles Dusi Ranch ($20, 3,400)	★★★★
Zinfandel Sonoma County Sonoma Station ($18, 10,100)	★★★
Zinfandel Sonoma Valley Pagani Ranch ($25, 4,000)	★★★★★
Zinfandel Spring Mountain York Creek ($25, 3,000)	★★

WINERY DATA
Case Production: 65,000. **Acres Owned:** 327 acres (60 in Santa Cruz Mountains, 70 leased; 161 in Dry Creek, 36 in Alexander Valley leased). **Varietals by Acre:** Barbera (2 acres), Cabernet Franc (1), Cabernet Sauvignon (81), Carignane (3), Chardonnay (20), Grenache (8), Mataro (4), Merlot (35), Petite Sirah (19) Petit Verdot (3), Sangiovese (6), Syrah (8), Viognier (1), Zinfandel (136). **Vineyard Designations:** Monte Bello (Cabernet Blend), Lytton Springs (Zinfandel), York Creek (Cabernet Sauvignon, Petite Sirah). **Varietals Purchased:** Carignane (Alexander Valley), Mataro (Contra Costa), Petite Sirah (Alexander Valley, Spring Mountain), Zinfandel (Alexander Valley, Dry Creek, Paso Robles, Russian River, Spring Mountain).

The amazing thing about Ridge Vineyards is that its wines just keep getting better. Ridge not only excels with its estate-grown Monte Bello Cabernet and various vineyard-designated Zinfandels, but each of the wines keeps improving, with small refinements here and there. To top things off, in the 1990s Ridge has been producing some superb Chardonnays.

Ridge began in 1959, when a trio of Stanford Research Institute engineers headed by Dave Bennion bought an abandoned winery and the Monte Bello vineyard, situated high atop the steep Santa Cruz Mountains, above Cupertino. Bennion and his colleagues began tending the vines on weekends, and started making small lots of wine from the Monte Bello vineyard, while also seeking out old Zinfandel, Petite Sirah and other Italian field blend varietals from Amador County, Dry Creek Valley (Lytton Springs), Alexander Valley (Geyserville), Mendocino, Napa Valley (York Creek), Paso Robles (Dusi Ranch), Howell Mountain (Beatty Ranch), and just about anywhere else they could find grapes that suited their style. Employing basic, if not rustic, winemaking techniques, Ridge developed its own style of big, ripe and often tannic wines which quickly won a devout following. By the mid-1960s, the winery was producing a Monte Bello Cabernet along with as many as six or seven other red wines, most of them Zinfandels. The wines were so good—and popular—that the owners began to convert the winery from a hobby to a business. It soon became apparent that running the winery required more than weekend management, and in 1969, Ridge hired the talented Paul Draper as winemaker, putting him in charge of shaping the wine styles, which he has done admirably.

With its rich soils and cool climate, Monte Bello's 2,600-foot elevation is considered an ideal location for Cabernet Sauvignon. Its proximity to the Pacific Ocean, less than 20 miles away, provides for many damp, foggy mornings and brisk, breezy afternoons, which allow the grapes to ripen slowly and evenly. Only rarely is it too cool for the grapes to ripen. Draper credits the wine's quality to the vineyard's maturity (most of the vines are 40 years old or older), the wild, natural yeasts which provide fermentation, and the fact that Ridge does little in the way of filtration to manipulate its wines.

Through the years, Ridge has stayed its course, gradually adding Cabernet and Petite Sirah from York Creek (Spring Mountain, Napa Valley), Merlot from Bradford

Mountain (Sonoma), Chardonnay (Howell Mountain and Santa Cruz Mountains), Mataro (Bridgehead, Contra Costa County) and another Zinfandel (Pagani Ranch, Sonoma). In 1986, Ridge's partners decided to sell the winery to Otsuka, a large diversified firm based in Japan.

Today, the winery owns 327 acres in vines, with 60 acres in the Santa Cruz Mountains, including Monte Bello. It also bought the Lytton Springs Winery and vineyard (45 acres) in 1991, maintaining its long, successful association with that winery by keeping the vineyard and brand name alive. The lineup is still heavily weighted toward reds, most of which are at the top of their class.

TASTING NOTES

CABERNET SAUVIGNON NAPA COUNTY YORK CREEK (★★): Disappointing in its later vintages, after a run of good-to-very good wines dating to the 1970s; has lacked the richness of fruit and complexity to measure up to the wood and hard tannins. Both the 1988 and the 1989 were mediocre.
1991: Youthful and tight, with smoke and currant flavors that are plush but tannic. **84**
1990: Solid and chunky in texture, with a green, herbal edge to the prune and berry flavors. **88**
1987: Firm and chunky, with smoky, woody notes to the ripe plum and currant flavors. **85**
1986: Has a pleasing, if rustic, core of black currant, cedar and spicy cherry flavors. **88**
1985: Mature and losing its fruit, turning earthy and dry. Drink it before the cherry and currant flavors dry out. **86**
1984: Ripe and fruity, with layers of ripe, supple black cherry, currant, floral and spice flavors. **85**
1980: Ripe and jammy, packed with earthy currant, black cherry and plum flavors, supported by firm tannins. Mature. **85**
1979: Extremely ripe and mature, almost raisiny, with drying tannins. **86**
1978: Elegant, with cedary tobacco and currant flavors, but it turns blunt and tannic. **87**
1977: A very pleasant 1977 with ripe plum, cherry and spicy currant flavors. **88**
1975: Extremely ripe, with earthy plum, currant and black cherry flavors. **87**
1974: Smooth and mature, with supple currant, cherry and spicy oak flavors. **85**

CABERNET SAUVIGNON SANTA CRUZ MOUNTAINS (★★★): The Santa Cruz bottling, which includes Jimsomare Vineyard (once a vineyard-designated wine) has been green, tannic and funky on occasion, but is now steadily improving. Recent bottlings feature ripe, focused fruit flavors and supple tannins.
1992: Intense and focused, with supple, elegant currant, earth and black cherry flavors framed by toasty, cedary oak. **89**
1991: A tough, chewy, earthy wine that packs in lots of flavor, with layers of currant, chocolate, mineral and tar. **89**
1990: Dense and earthy, with a nice layer of focused currant and blackberry flavors to go with the toasty, gamy overtones. **85**

CHARDONNAY SANTA CRUZ MOUNTAINS (★★★★★): Increasingly impressive for its bold, ripe, complex fruit flavors and deft oak shadings. Poised to join the top echelons.
1996: Elegant and complex, with pretty peach, pear, spice and mineral flavors, picking up a hint of anise and toasty oak on the finish. **92**
1995: Starts out with a wonderful earthy aroma, gaining complexity as the layers of pear, spice, hazelnut and light oak flavors begin to emerge. **93**
1994: Complex, featuring creamy pear, fig and vanilla notes, it's elegant and refined, with vibrant, concentrated flavors. **90**

GEYSERVILLE RED SONOMA COUNTY (★★★★): Steady, ranging from very good to excellent, with rich, complex fruit flavors. A blend of Zinfandel, Carignane and Petite Sirah.
1996: Supple and harmonious, with pretty, toasty oak flavors leading to a core of spicy wild berry, cherry jam, plum and raspberry fruit, keeping a sharp focus on the long, lively finish. **93**
1995: Smooth and polished, with a perfumed edge to the ripe plum and black cherry fruit, turning supple and fleshy on the finish. **89**
1994: Some rich, complex cedar, coffee and currant flavors in this ripe, elegant Zin. **91**
1993: Well oaked, with a complex band of flavors; a hint of dill accompanies the ripe plum and cherry notes, turning supple on the finish. **91**
1992: A controversial style with its lush, ripe fruit and earthy, leathery flavors, finishing with a horsey barnyard edge that detracts. **86**
1991: Ripe, rich and concentrated, with complex black cherry, wild berry, raspberry and plum flavors. **91**

1990: Softening; a bit gamy with a pleasant core of earthy cherry and currant notes. **87**

1989: Full-bodied, flavorful and velvety in texture, with straightforward blueberry and blackberry flavors. **84**

1988: Spicy vanilla nuances add grace and complexity to this distinctive wine that's oozing with blackberry and boysenberry flavors. **90**

1987: Intense and well focused, mature now with a complex array of wild berry, spice, cedar and tarry notes, and a long finish. **88**

1986: Lean and firm, with plenty of berry aromas and flavors and plenty of oak too. **79**

1985: A rich, intense, tannic Zin that's loaded with berry and pepper flavors. **83**

LYTTON SPRINGS RED DRY CREEK VALLEY (★★★★★): A great vineyard and wine capable of achieving uncommon depth, richness and complexity. Big, ripe and flavorful, it showcases what Zinfandel can achieve, and it does so often. Includes up to 20 percent Petite Sirah and Carignane.

1996: Well integrated, with complex spicy, plum and wild berry flavors and notes of toasty, cedary oak; turning hot on the finish. **88**

1995: Pleasing with its complex array of earthy wild berry, plum and anise flavors that fan out, showing great concentration. **92**

1994: Tarry and a bit leathery, with dry berry and cherry flavors and spice and cedar notes emerging on the finish. **87**

1993: Deliciously ripe, rich and supple, offering cherry, plum, tar and spice flavors, along with a plush aftertaste. **91**

1992: Bright, lush and rich, brimming with ripe, juicy wild berry, jam and pepper flavors, this wine hangs together extremely well. **91**

1991: Impressive for its distinctive flavors, balance, suppleness and grace; shows a complex core of plum, raspberry, black cherry and spice. **92**

1990: A sturdy, solid, old-style Zin that's bursting with jammy, peppery raspberry and plum flavors. Weaves in a nice touch of oak on the finish. **89**

1989: Firm and tannic, with a delicate balance between the distinctive oak and barnyard flavors. **82**

1988: Tart and fruity, with berry and plum flavors that turn a bit sour on the finish. **82**

1987: Ultra-ripe and complex, teeming with jammy, spicy, peppery flavors and finishing with richness and finesse. **91**

1986: Firm and ripe, with enough supple smoothness to

let the raspberry and plum flavors show through; displays a touch of buttery toast on the finish. **88**

1985: Big, rich and tasty, with ripe berry flavors and spicy, oaky nuances that are well integrated in a thick, full-bodied style. **83**

1974: Mature but holding, with spicy, leathery, smoky fruit flavors. **83**

MERLOT SANTA CRUZ MOUNTAINS (★★★)

1995: Austere and well crafted, with a tight range of currant, cedar and tobacco flavors and mild, well integrated tannins. **88**

1994: Young, firm, tight and peppery, with an earthy, cedary edge to the spicy currant and cherry notes. **89**

1993: Rich and full-bodied, with dark, dense currant, mineral, anise and cedary oak flavors. **88**

1992: Leans toward the earthy, decadent side of Merlot, with its dried fruit, leather, anise and toasty oak flavors. **91**

MONTE BELLO RED SANTA CRUZ MOUNTAINS (★★★★★): Among California's elite. Very consistently dark, concentrated and flavorful, with complex currant, earth and mushroom flavors that develop nicely over time. Moderately tannic, it ages exceptionally well, reaching a peak at about 6 to 7 years after the vintage date, and is capable of aging 20 to 25 years. Contains about 15 percent Merlot.

1995: Shows wonderful focus, if a bit tight; the core of smoky currant, black cherry and blackberry fruit and cedary, toasty oak flavors is impressive, as is the seamless texture. **92**

1994: Tightly wound and a touch earthy, with its tart currant and wild berry fruit becoming concentrated, revealing an even deeper fruit core. **93**

1993: Elegant and understated, with a core of fruit built around ripe cherry and plummy flavors, finishing with supple tannins and a dash of cedar. **89**

1992: Dark, young and tight, it's firmly tannic, but has just enough black cherry, currant and smoky oak flavors. **91**

1990: Distinctive for its elegance and suppleness, with a pleasing array of herb, olive and currant flavors. **91**

1991: Complex and inviting, with a pleasant range of currant, vanilla and herb flavors that fold together nicely, finishing with depth, richness and concentration. **93**

1989: Ripe, rich, smooth and complex, with currant, plum and black cherry flavors and chocolate, vanilla and spice notes, finishing with fine tannins. **90**

1988: Starts out earthy, with gamy, leathery flavors, but then turns supple, with complex anise, currant, berry, mushroom and cedary notes. **88**

1987: Powerful and complex but marked by earth, mushroom and leather overtones to the deep, concentrated currant flavor. **88**

1986: The oak has folded into the black cherry and currant flavors, giving it a greater sense of balance and elegance. **85**

1985: Ripe, supple and fruity, with rich, complex currant, herb, cherry and cedar flavors that are deep and concentrated, turning tarry on the finish. **93**

1984: Mature now, with a supple earthiness joining the ripe currant, black cherry, vanilla and spice flavors. **88**

1982: Tough and tannic, a victim of harvest rains. **75**

1981: Elegant and complex, with firm, compact black currant, plum and cherry aromas and flavors that are well proportioned. **89**

1980: Still lacks focus, and the oak and moderately ripe fruit flavors lack harmony. **80**

1978: Packed with rich, complex, concentrated currant, plum, mushroom, tar and spice flavors that are intense and vibrant. **92**

1977: A shade past its peak, it is very deep and concentrated, with cedar, black currant and cherry flavors that are complex and firmly tannic. **92**

1976: Ripe and raisiny, with drying tannins; past its peak. **83**

1975: Supple and lively, with ripe, complex fruit flavors that are mature and complex. **88**

1974: Deep ruby, with ripe, spicy currant and anise flavors that are fresh, rich and focused, turning smooth and elegant on the finish. There's a wonderful sense of harmony and proportion and the tannins are mild. **94**

1973: Lively, elegant and complex, with mint, cedar, sweet black cherry and anise flavors. **87**

1972: Past its prime, with earthy mushroom aromas, but there are pretty fruit flavors and a touch of bell pepper on the finish. **82**

1971: Fully mature and at its peak, offering prune, plum, cedar and tobacco flavors. **85**

1970: The Monte Bello of the decade; a supple, complex, harmonious wine with layers of currant, anise, cedary oak and earthy mineral flavors. **96**

1969: Amazingly elegant and youthful, with bright, complex spice, plum, black cherry and floral flavors that echo on the finish. **92**

1968: Mature and drying, but there's still a pleasant core of chocolate, cedar and oak flavors. **87**

1965: Complex and elegant, past its prime but holding, with classic cigar box aromas and mature cherry and bell pepper flavors. **86**

1964: Beautifully crafted, smooth and mellow, with complex, well focused Cabernet flavors, cigar box aromas and fine length. **90**

PETITE SIRAH SPRING MOUNTAIN YORK CREEK (★★★): Can be ruggedly tannic, with the peppery fruit struggling to compete.

1991: Dark and tannic, with intense ripe plum, pepper and spice notes that linger. **87**

ZINFANDEL PASO ROBLES DUSI RANCH (★★★★): Can be variable, as Zinfandel often is, but at its best it is brilliant, with bright, ripe, lush, complex fruit.

1996: Supple and elegant, with a fleshy texture and ripe plum, cherry and wild berry flavors that are complex and well focused. **89**

1995: Serves up lots of ripe, complex cherry, plum and wild berry flavors, picking up a nice meaty, nutty edge that turns complex. **91**

1994: Impressive for its polish and finesse, it serves up tasty cherry, berry and spice flavors and avoids excessive tannins. **90**

1993: Smooth and elegant, showing a pleasant band of cherry and spice and picking up an anise and raspberry edge. **86**

1992: Bold and jammy, this is a super-ripe wine with lush black cherry and plum flavors. **90**

1991: Deep in color, with ripe, spicy, jammy berry, cherry, raspberry and plum flavors that turn earthy and complex on the finish. **90**

1990: Smooth and gentle, with pleasant cherry and spice flavors. **84**

1989: There are spicy oak and modest barnyard overtones to the ripe raspberry and plum flavors. **84**

1987: Earthy and gamy, with attractive wild berry and spice notes that give it complexity. **85**

1986: An old-fashioned wine with jammy raspberry flavors and a woody, tannic edge. **81**

ZINFANDEL SONOMA COUNTY SONOMA STATION (★★★): This wine used to be bottled under the brand name Lytton Springs Winery, the name of the small Sonoma County winery which owned the Lytton Springs Vineyard. After acquiring the Lytton Springs Winery, Ridge kept the Lytton Springs designation on the vineyard-designated bottlings, putting the rest of the Lytton estate fruit into the Sonoma Station bottling.

1997: Lots of fresh, lively plum and blueberry fruit leads to a crisp, tightly wound core of spice, cedar, earth and wild berry flavors, finishing with firm tannins. **88**

1996: Well balanced and proportioned, with appealing, ripe berry, cherry, plum and anise flavors, turning complex on the finish. **88**

1995: Curious at first, with an odd, earthy flavor, but possesses enough ripe berry, cherry and plummy notes to fill in the gaps. **88**

1994: Solid, with a core of ripe cherry and wild berry flavors, along with an accent of light, toasty oak and hints of herb and spice. **87**

ZINFANDEL SONOMA VALLEY PAGANI RANCH (★★★★★): Bold and jammy, it's typically very ripe and carries a Late Picked designation at times.

1996: Ripe, earthy and a touch funky, with a twinge of dill adding to the rich and concentrated raisiny fruit flavors, turning tannic. **88**

1995: A wine of harmony and finesse, with smooth, ripe, fruity flavors, offering lovely cherry, jam, wild berry and strawberry notes. **92**

1994: Firm and intense, with a tight core of leathery currant, herb and cedary oak flavors and firm tannins. **90**

1993: Pleasantly balanced, with ripe plum, raspberry and cherry flavors, turning smooth and showing rich tannins. **90**

1992: Packs in lots of ripe, jammy flavors yet maintains its elegance and finesse. The black cherry, wild berry and currant notes are intense and concentrated. **93**

1991: Beautiful, dark, ripe, spicy plum, cherry and raspberry flavors turn dense and chewy, picking up a tarry edge, with smooth but substantial tannins. **89**

ZINFANDEL SPRING MOUNTAIN YORK CREEK (★★): Typically more austere and tannic, as mountain-grown Zin tends to be.

1996: Tight, with a tarry edge to the smoky wild berry, waxy and sage-laced flavors, it firms up and turns tannic on the finish. **87**

1991: Ripe, spicy and opulent, a juicy wine with cherry and raspberry flavors and a good dose of tannins. **88**

RIO SECO VINEYARD (★★)
Paso Robles, San Luis Obispo County
Founded: 1996. **Owner:** Tom & Carol Hinkle.
Winemaker: John Munch.

MAJOR WINES: PRICE, CASES, RATING
Pinot Blanc Monterey San Bernable
  Vineyard
  ($15, 195) ★★
Zinfandel Paso Robles Cherry Vineyard
  ($22, 185) ★★

ALSO PRODUCED
Cabernet Sauvignon Paso Robles Cougar Ridge Vineyard ($20, 125); Zinfandel Central Coast Vineyard Blend ($20, 200).

WINERY DATA
Case Production: 1,300. **Acres Owned:** 31 acres in Paso Robles. **Varietals by Acre:** Cabernet Franc (4 acres), Cabernet Sauvignon (9), Merlot (1), Roussanne (4), Syrah (4), Viognier (1), Zinfandel (9). **Vineyard Designations:** Cougar Ridge Vineyard (Cabernet Sauvignon), San Bernable Vineyard (Pinot Blanc), Cherry Vineyard (Zinfandel). **Varietals Purchased:** Orange Muscat (Hames Valley), Petite Sirah (Monterey), Pinot Noir (Monterey), Viognier (Hames Valley), Zinfandel (Hames Valley, Monterey).

Carol Hinkle, a professional dance teacher, and husband Tom, a baseball scout for the Toronto Blue Jays, purchased their property in Paso Robles in 1996. Early wines were made from purchased grapes at Wild Horse winery; they included ripe, racy 1996 Zinfandel (87 points) and a flinty, 1997 Pinot Blanc (85) with mandarine orange and peach notes. The first wines from the Hinkels' 31-acre vineyard came from the 1998 harvest. In 1999, they completed a winery facility on their property.

RISTOW (★★★★)
Napa Valley
Founded: 1995. **Owner:** Brunno & Urannia Ristow.
Winemaker: Pam Starr.

MAJOR WINES: PRICE, CASES, RATING
Cabernet Sauvignon Napa Valley
  Quinta de Pedras
  ($40, 2,000) ★★★★

WINERY DATA
Case Production: 2,000. **Acres Owned:** 25 acres in Napa Valley. **Varietals by Acre:** Cabernet (23 acres), Merlot (1), Petit Verdot (1). **Vineyard Designations:** Quinta de Pedras.

Plastic surgeon Brunno Ristow and wife Urannia purchased 25 acres in Napa Valley in 1973, and started planting Cabernet in 1982. Chris Phelps made the 1995 Cabernet (89 points), an elegant, polished wine with a range of spicy black cherry, currant, olive and cedar notes. Pam Starr took over as winemaker in 1996. Worth watching given the unique setting of the vineyard, and the fact that the owners are determined to make great wine.

TASTING NOTES

CABERNET SAUVIGNON NAPA VALLEY QUINTA DE PEDRAS VINEYARD (★★★): Impressive for its elegance and range of spicy black cherry, currant, olive and cedary notes. Finishes with ripe, smooth, polished tannins and fine length. **89**

RIVER BEND see **DAVIS BYNUM WINERY**

RIVERSIDE FARMS see **FOPPIANO VINEYARDS**

J. ROCHIOLI VINEYARDS (★★★–★★★★★)
Russian River Valley, Sonoma County
Founded: 1982. **Owner:** Tom & Joe Rochioli. **Winemaker:** Tom Rochioli.

MAJOR WINES: PRICE, CASES, RATING

Cabernet Sauvignon Russian River Valley Neoma's Vineyard (Discontinued)	★★★
Chardonnay Russian River Valley Allen Vineyard ($38, 100)	★★★★★
Chardonnay Russian River Valley Estate ($20, 2,000)	★★★★
Chardonnay Russian River Valley Estate Cuvée Reserve (Discontinued)	★★★★★
Chardonnay Russian River Valley Estate River Block ($32, 150)	★★★★★
Chardonnay Russian River Valley Estate South River Vineyard ($40, 100)	★★★★★
Chardonnay Russian River Valley Reserve (Discontinued)	★★★★★
Pinot Noir Russian River Valley East Block ($65, 100)	★★★★★
Pinot Noir Russian River Valley Estate ($25, 3,000)	★★★★
Pinot Noir Russian River Valley Estate Little Hill ($40, 250)	★★★★
Pinot Noir Russian River Valley Estate Three Corner ($40, 150)	★★★★★
Pinot Noir Russian River Valley Estate West Block ($50, 350)	★★★★★
Pinot Noir Russian River Valley Reserve (Discontinued)	★★★★★
Sauvignon Blanc Russian River Valley Estate ($14, 2,900)	★★★★
Sauvignon Blanc Russian River Valley Estate Old Vines ($22, 300)	★★★★★
Zinfandel Russian River Valley Sodini Vineyard ($20, 500)	★★★★

WINERY DATA
Case Production: 10,000. **Acres Owned:** 118 acres in Russian River Valley. **Varietals by Acre:** Cabernet Sauvignon (2 acres), Chardonnay (32), Gamay (15), Pinot Noir (50), Sauvignon Blanc (13), other (6). **Vineyard Designations:** Allen Vineyard (Chardonnay), Sodini Vineyard (Zinfandel), South River Vineyard (Chardonnay). **Varietals Purchased:** Zinfandel (Russian River Valley).

After years of supplying area wineries with wonderful grapes, J. Rochioli Vineyards has begun to receive the recognition it richly deserves. The wines from this Russian River Valley estate have steadily gained in quality, so much so that the current offerings, from

Chardonnay to Pinot Noir to Sauvignon Blanc to Zinfandel, are now among California's pace-setters.

The Rochioli family are first and foremost farmers, with excellent land. Add to this precision farming, where the right grapes, clones and rootstock are rooted in the proper soils, and you have a recipe for superb grapes and richly flavored wines.

Joe Rochioli began planting vineyards in 1959, on family-owned property dating back to 1938. Early on, he became convinced that this was the place for Pinot Noir, Chardonnay and Sauvignon Blanc, and was well ahead of his time in planting these varieties. Today, Joe Rochioli, who oversees the vineyards, and his son Tom, the wine-maker, farm a total of 118 acres. The plantings are led by Pinot Noir (50 acres) and Chardonnay (32 acres), the winery's top two wines. Cabernet and Zinfandel are planted on the higher slopes of the vineyard. Two versions each of the Chardonnay, Pinot Noir and Sauvignon Blanc are offered: an estate bottling, and a more expensive reserve-type vineyard-designated bottling. Both lines are superb. Cabernet was dropped from the lineup in 1997.

Since the Rochiolis sell much of their crop, production is in the 10,000-case range, but that could easily double. One wonders whether they will expand the Pinot Noir production, given the uniquely high quality of the grapes. Williams & Selyem buy and bottle a Rochioli Vineyard Pinot Noir, and Gary Farrell and Davis Bynum also buy Rochioli grapes.

TASTING NOTES

CABERNET SAUVIGNON RUSSIAN RIVER VALLEY NEOMA'S VINEYARD (★★★): Showed steady improvement. Earlier vintages were hard, tight and austere, but recent offerings were riper, as the winery began to pay more attention to this wine. In 1997, however, the wine was discontinued.
1993: Attractive for its bright, tart cherry, currant and raspberry flavors, it's both intense and balanced. **86**
1991: Firm and chunky, with ripe plum and cherry fruit and a dry oak and tannic aftertaste, picking up a trace of herb and chocolate. **87**
1990: Shows a complexity and finesse missing in earlier vintages, with spicy, buttery, ripe cherry, currant and plum flavors. **87**
1989: Elegant, with spicy currant and plum flavors. **84**

1988: Simple, with spicy plum and currant flavors, but like most 1988s it becomes hollow after the mid-palate, turning tannic. **81**
1987: Tightly knit, with compact currant, berry, oak and spice flavors. **84**
1986: Lean and austere, with firm tannins and meaty, spicy, hard-edged currant and berry flavors. **83**
1985: Tight and firm, with currant and cedar flavors that turn hard on the finish. **83**
1983: Mature, with dried prune and plum aromas, but it's one-dimensional and firmly tannic. **82**
1982: Mature and past its prime, with earthy cedar and tar flavors that turn dry and tannic. **80**

CHARDONNAY RUSSIAN RIVER VALLEY ALLEN VINEYARD (★★★★): Sleek, intense, and tightly wound, showing depth, complexity and sophistication. Ages well.
1996: A wonderful orchestration of fruit and oak, with a ripe, rich, tightly focused core of spicy pear, apple and hazelnut flavors and notes of pretty, smoky, toasty oak. **94**
1995: Elegant and refined, with a supple, complex core of ripe pear, anise, apricot and fig, gaining momentum and length. **94**

CHARDONNAY RUSSIAN RIVER VALLEY ESTATE (★★★★): This bottling is ripe, bold and juicy, with loads of rich fruit and ample oak.
1996: Tightly focused and elegant; rich, with complex pear, citrus, tangerine and smoky, toasty oak notes, it turns smooth and polished on the finish, where the flavors fan out and linger. **91**
1995: Young and tight, with a spicy, flinty edge to the pear and vanilla notes. Clean and refreshing. **88**

CHARDONNAY RUSSIAN RIVER VALLEY ESTATE CUVÉE RESERVE (★★★★★)
1995: Elegant and complex, with subtle ripe pear, apricot, melon and fig notes that slowly unfold to pretty, toasty oak notes. **93**

CHARDONNAY RUSSIAN RIVER VALLEY ESTATE RIVER BLOCK (★★★★★): Another tremendous wine; very deep and complex.
1996: Elegant and understated, with complex pear, hazelnut, honey and anise flavors that show depth and concentration. **93**

CHARDONNAY RUSSIAN RIVER VALLEY ESTATE SOUTH RIVER VINEYARD (★★★★★): Enormous complexity, finesse and flavor.

1996: Greets you with spicy, toasty oak; the core of ripe, rich apple, pear, fig and melon flavors are sharply focused, complex and concentrated, gaining length and depth on the finish. **92**

1995: Big, rich and concentrated, with complex layers of ripe fig, pear and melon and hints of cedar and vanilla. **94**

CHARDONNAY RUSSIAN RIVER VALLEY RESERVE (★★★★★)

1994: Amazingly ripe, rich and complex, with tiers of concentrated pear, hazelnut, honey and toasty oak flavors all folding together wonderfully. **95**

PINOT NOIR RUSSIAN RIVER VALLEY EAST BLOCK (★★★★★)

1994: Tightly wound, with a rich, complex, deeply concentrated core of anise, black cherry, oak and mineral flavors that gush through on the finish. **95**

PINOT NOIR RUSSIAN RIVER VALLEY ESTATE (★★★★): This regular bottling is riper, fuller and fruitier than the vineyard-designated Pinot Noirs, while still complex and concentrated. Great value.

1996: Well proportioned, with a core of plum, cherry and berry flavors, picking up some spicy, toasty oak and a hint of cola. **87**

1995: A wonderful sense of harmony and finesse, with a pretty, fleshy core of plum, cherry, wild berry and spice flavors. **92**

1994: Smooth, rich and complex, with a nice integration of cherry, berry and currant flavors and light toasty oak shadings. **91**

1991: Bright, ripe and spicy, with pretty floral, cherry, raspberry and anise flavors that are rich and concentrated. Picks up hints of cola and vanilla on the finish. **90**

1991: Ripe and complex, with supple plum, black cherry and minty notes, this wine is a shade past its prime. **88**

1990: Broad, ripe and complex, with spicy plum, cherry and raspberry flavors that turn tight and firm. Picks up tea and herb notes on the finish. **88**

PINOT NOIR RUSSIAN RIVER VALLEY ESTATE LITTLE HILL (★★★★): New, from a select hillside site, it's more supple and less concentrated than other parts of the vineyard, but still worth watching.

1995: Tightly wound, with a core of cherry- and berry-laced Pinot Noir fruit. **89**

PINOT NOIR RUSSIAN RIVER VALLEY RESERVE (★★★★★): Rich, plush and concentrated, with uncommon depth and finesse. Smaller lots carry designations from within the vineyard, such as Western and Eastern Block. No longer produced.

1992: Deep in color, with a core of rich, ripe black cherry, currant, anise and spicy oak shadings that run long on the finish. **92**

1991: Aging beautifully. Dark, with lots of ripe, youthful plum, cherry, wild berry and spice flavors and just the right touch of oak. **92**

1990: A tremendously rich, complex and concentrated wine with tiers of black cherry, vanilla, bacon and smoke flavors that are intense and focused. **92**

1989: Shows depth and concentration, with ripe cherry, raspberry, nutmeg and toasty, spicy oak flavors, finishing with a long, crisp aftertaste. **88**

1988: Broad, ripe, rich and complex, with deep cherry, plum and currant notes, finishing with meaty, smoky, toasty oak flavors. **90**

1986: Tightly wound, firm and intense, with concentrated spice, cherry and raspberry flavors. Tannins and oak clamp down on the finish. **85**

PINOT NOIR RUSSIAN RIVER VALLEY ESTATE THREE CORNER (★★★★): Wonderful flavors, complexity and depth.

1996: Moderately ripe plum and cherry fruit flavors combine with spicy vanilla oak nuances, forming a clean, complex finish. **87**

1995: Smooth, ripe and elegant, with a pretty array of earthy cherry and currant flavors, picking up a flash of tar and tea. **89**

1994: Delicious, serving up lots of complex layers of ripe cherry, plum and raspberry flavors, finishing with hints of tea, anise and spice, along with polished tannins. **94**

PINOT NOIR RUSSIAN RIVER VALLEY ESTATE WEST BLOCK (★★★★★): Might be the best of the Pinot Noir vineyard designations. Capable of yielding uncommonly rich and complex wines. Worth collecting.

1996: Marked by bright black cherry, olive, coffee and toasty oak flavors and a complex aftertaste. **88**

1995: Delivers ripe plum- and cherry-laced flavors; a touch of earthy mushroom and spice add dimension. **89**

1994: Stunning, offering an amazing core of ripe, rich, complex and concentrated fruit, with glowing tiers of brilliant black cherry, plum, currant and raspberry flavors. **96**
1993: Pretty aromatics and well defined cherry, plum, mineral and spice flavors fold together nicely, turning complex on the finish. **89**

Sauvignon Blanc Russian River Valley Estate (★★★★): Fruitier and more forward than the Reserve.

Sauvignon Blanc Russian River Valley Estate Old Vines (★★★★★): Crisp, flinty, tightly wound, enormously complex and concentrated. The best in California.
1997: Effusively fragrant, with rich honeysuckle, fig, mint and herb notes. On the palate, it sings with grapefruit, melon, lemon/lime, bright herbal notes and a long finish. It's sleek, firm and elegant. **93**
1996: Strikes a fine balance between ripe pear, tangy grapefruit and fresh melon flavors; wonderfully crisp and vibrant. **90**
1995: Bright and brilliant; generous grapefruit, pear, herb and spice flavors are held tightly in focus by the crisp, lively acidity. **91**
1994: Elegant, lively and balanced, weaving its spice, herb and pear flavors, turning rich and creamy. **91**

Zinfandel Russian River Valley Sodini Vineyard (★★★★): New at Rochioli, but shows the winery's fine winemaking craftsmanship; a beautifully balanced, rich and fruity wine.
1994: Impressive for its ripe, bright, complex cherry, berry, currant and spice flavors. **89**
1993: Well oaked, with toasty vanilla and cedar accents, the wild berry and cherry flavors adding balance and depth. **88**
1992: Smooth, ripe and polished, with bright, lively cherry, raspberry and currant flavors that turn elegant and refined on the finish. **91**

Rocking Horse (★★★)
Rutherford, Napa Valley
Founded: 1989. **Owner:** Jeff Doran, Brian Zealear.
Winemaker: Jim Moore.

Major Wines: Price, Cases, Rating

Cabernet Sauvignon Rutherford Garvey Family Vineyard ($24, 1,500)	★★★
Cabernet Sauvignon Stags Leap District Robinson Vineyard ($32, 300)	★★★
Zinfandel Howell Mountain (Discontinued)	★★★
Zinfandel Howell Mountain Lamborn Family Vineyard ($18, 2,500)	★★★

Winery Data
Case Production: 4,000. **Vineyard Designations:** Garvey Family Vineyard (Cabernet Sauvignon), Lamborn Family Vineyard (Zinfandel), Robinson Vineyard (Cabernet Sauvignon). **Varietals Purchased:** Cabernet Sauvignon (Rutherford, Stags Leap), Zinfandel (Howell Mountain).

Jeff Doran and his partner Brian Zealear were home-winemakers for years before turning commercial in 1989, making small lots of vineyard-designated wines from Lamborn Family Vineyard (Howell Mountain Zinfandel), Garvey Family Vineyard (Rutherford Cabernet) and Robinson Vineyard (Stags Leap Cabernet). The quality has been very good; the wines reflect their varietal characters as well as the areas in which they're grown. Production is 4,000 cases, with all grapes purchased.

Tasting Notes

Cabernet Sauvignon Rutherford Garvey Family Vineyard (★★★): Improving, with the 1994 the best effort yet.
1994: Firmly tannic, with a core of plum, currant and black cherry fruit that's deep, rich and supple. **90**
1993: Earthy and leathery, but the Cabernet fruit rises, giving it a sense of balance and finesse. **87**
1992: Firm and focused, with a band of oaky currant and plum flavors. **86**

CABERNET SAUVIGNON STAGS LEAP DISTRICT ROBINSON VINEYARD (★★★): Shows off the elegance and finesse of the vineyard. Quality varies, however.

1993: Appealing, fruity flavors that turn spicy and simple at mid-palate. **83**

1992: Tight and firm, with a narrow band of focused currant, black cherry and mineral flavors, finishing with crisp tannins. **85**

1991: Smooth and stylish, offering generous plum, berry, chocolate, vanilla and spice aromas and flavors, and the finish is silky and seductive. **90**

1990: Firm, tight, youthful and flavorful, with focused plum and currant flavors that are fleshy and balanced, finishing with fine tannins. **91**

1986: Straightforward, with pleasant currant and berry flavors and mild tannins. **84**

ZINFANDEL HOWELL MOUNTAIN (★★★)

1994: Pure Zinfandel, with zesty pepper, spice and wild berry flavors that turn smooth and supple. **88**

ZINFANDEL HOWELL MOUNTAIN LAMBORN FAMILY VINEYARD (★★★): Reflects the vineyard's earthy, peppery qualities.

1996: Tight, with lots of spicy, peppery, wild berry flavors; turning tannic, with a mushroom note creeping in. **87**

1995: Serves up spicy, peppery wild berry and plummy flavors, but then starts to turn earthy. **85**

1993: Intense, earthy, rich and peppery, sporting spicy wild berry flavors, firm tannins and a supple texture. **89**

1991: Aging well, with complex, earthy plum, wild berry, raspberry and spice flavors, finishing long and complex. **88**

1990: A rich, earthy, mulchy and peppery wine that's distinctive, finishing with soft tannins. **84**

1989: A racy wine with blueberry and spice flavors that hit the mark for Zin. **84**

ROCKLAND ROAD CELLARS
(★★★–★★★★)
Napa Valley
Founded: 1989. **Owner:** Richard & Alice Aubert. **Winemaker:** Richard L. Aubert.

MAJOR WINES: PRICE, CASES, RATING
Cabernet Sauvignon Napa Valley	
($39, 100)	★★★★
Petite Sirah Napa Valley	
($22, 400)	★★★

WINERY DATA
Case Production: 500. **Acres Owned:** 2 acres in Napa Valley. **Varietals by Acre:** Cabernet Sauvignon (2 acres). **Varietals Purchased:** Petite Sirah (Napa Valley).

This is a tiny operation with a 500-case output, but both the Cabernet Sauvignon and Petite Sirah are delicious wines and well worth the search. Owners Richard and Alice Aubert are the parents of Mark Aubert, winemaker at Colgin Cellars.

TASTING NOTES

CABERNET SAUVIGNON NAPA VALLEY (★★★): Offers ripe, complex, detailed flavors.

1994: Truly exotic, rich and complex. Lots of currant, anise, smoke, mineral and berry flavors that fold together quite nicely and turn even more complex on the finish where they show more depth and nuance. **93**

1993: Smooth, ripe and polished, marked by spicy plum, currant and cherry notes and finishing with soft, fleshy tannins and a touch of cedar. Well balanced. **89**

PETITE SIRAH NAPA VALLEY (★★★): Tilts toward the tannic side, but has wonderful flavors to match.

1996: Massive, dense and earthy, with lots of tannin, wild berry, earth, sage, mineral and spice, finishing with a chewy aftertaste. Needs time, though. **91**

1995: Ruggedly tannic, with a ripe, sturdy, rustic style; hints of berry and cherry peek through. **85**

ROEDERER ESTATE (★★★★–★★★★★)
Anderson Valley, Mendocino County
Founded: 1986. **Owner:** Champagne Louis Roederer.
Winemaker: Michel J. Salgues.

MAJOR WINES: PRICE, CASES, RATING
Brut Anderson Valley NV
($18, 55,000) ★★★★
Brut Rosé Anderson Valley NV
($22, 4,000) ★★★
L' Ermitage Anderson Valley
($36, 5,000) ★★★★★

WINERY DATA
Case Production: 65,000. **Acres Owned:** 324 acres in
Anderson Valley. **Varietals by Acre:** Chardonnay (194 acres),
Pinot Noir (130).

Roederer, the French Champagne producer, zeroed in
on the cool Anderson Valley climate for its sparkling
wines. That decision has proven fortuitous, as these
estate-grown wines show remarkable depth, richness and
complexity. In fact, Roederer is the only French
Champagne house in California to grow all its own
grapes. The grapes are rooted in diverse soils covering
324 acres in vines; Chardonnay covers 194 acres, and
Pinot Noir comprises the rest. The winemaker is Michel
Salgues, a Ph.D in enology from Montpellier, France.

The combination of a cool climate, intensely flavored
grapes and deft winemaking (along with the use of oak
barrels for aging young cuvées) has moved Roederer to
the head of the class in California. The non-vintage Brut is
rich and toasty, with complex flavors and excellent depth.
The L'Ermitage Prestige Cuvée is vintage-dated, and possesses richness, depth and finesse. To my taste, it's the
finest sparkling wine in California. Given its rapid ascent,
it will be interesting to see how much better this wine can
become as the vineyards mature and the winemakers
become more familiar with their grapes.

TASTING NOTES

BRUT ANDERSON VALLEY NV (★★★★): Intense and
concentrated, with tiers of honey, pear and hazelnut fla-
vors-the result of a blend that is 70 percent Chardonnay.
A remarkable value that shows complexity and finesse.

L'ERMITAGE ANDERSON VALLEY (★★★★★): Rich and
creamy, with toasty pear, spice, hazelnut and honeyed
notes, amazingly long and complex on the finish. Setting
the pace in California.

ROMBAUER VINEYARDS (★★★)
Napa Valley
Founded: 1980. **Owner:** Koerner & Joan Rombauer.
Winemaker: Gregory Graham.

MAJOR WINES: PRICE, CASES, RATING
Cabernet Sauvignon Napa Valley
($28, 2,000) ★★★
Cabernet Sauvignon Napa Valley
Diamond Mountain Selection
($50, 1,200) ★★★
Chardonnay Carneros
($26, 15,500) ★★★★
Le Meilleur Du Chai Red Napa Valley
($50, 200) ★★★
Merlot Napa Valley
($25, 6,000) ★★★
Zinfandel Napa Valley
($20, 1,500) ★★★

WINERY DATA
Case Production: 30,000. **Acres Owned:** 10 acres in Napa
Valley. **Varietals by Acre:** Zinfandel (10 acres).

Former commercial airline pilot Koerner Rombauer
and his wife Joan were investors in Conn Creek Winery
before building their own facility on Silverado Trail
north of St. Helena. They produce 30,000 cases under the
Rombauer label, and run a diversified custom-crush and
barrel aging facility. Their Carneros Chardonnay is the
star of the portfolio—consistently outstanding, ripe and
rich with focused flavors—but all the wines are flavorful
and well made.

TASTING NOTES

CABERNET SAUVIGNON NAPA VALLEY (★★★): Past vintages have been earthy, rustic and tannic, with a green
edge to the cherry and currant flavors. The 1995 (88
points) was a major improvement, with ripe fruit and
supple tannins.

CABERNET SAUVIGNON NAPA VALLEY DIAMOND MOUNTAIN SELECTION (★★★): A new addition, the 1994 (90 points) was complex, with a dense core of currant, wild berry, cedar and spice.

CHARDONNAY CARNEROS (★★★★): This wine has hit its stride. Typically rich, creamy and focused with good fruit flavors.
1997: Smooth, ripe and creamy, with a pretty array of pear, peach, vanilla, hazelnut and spicy nuances that are bright, rich and focused. **92**
1996: Smooth, spicy and elegant, with lots of attractive fruit flavors, including ripe pear, fig, apricot and melon, and framed by pretty, toasty oak. **91**
1995: Serves up lots of ripe, juicy, complex flavors, with hints of pear, apple, pineapple and guava fruit, turning elegant on the finish. **91**
1994: Ripe and creamy, with silky fig, pear, spice and hazelnut flavors that are smooth, opulent, rich and complex. **93**

LE MEILLEUR DU CHAI RED NAPA VALLEY (★★★): Like the Napa Valley Cabernet, this blend of Cabernet Sauvignon, Cabernet Franc and Merlot tends to be austere, with earthy flavors. Can be rich and elegant in the best years.
1992: Big and earthy, with spicy anise, currant and berry flavors that are somewhat disjointed and lacking in focus. **87**
1989: Mature, with a medium-weight range of pleasant currant and plum flavors. **84**
1987: Starts out nicely, with ripe plum and currant flavors, but it turns austere on the finish and the tannins dominate. **83**
1986: This wine has dried up and has turned overly tannic, showing faded currant and cherry notes. **83**
1985: Lean and austere, with a distinctive minty component along with cedar and black cherry flavors that turn crisp. **89**
1984: Distinctive for its richness and elegance, with supple cedar, black cherry, spice and anise flavors. **88**
1983: A big, thick, muscular and tannic wine with layers of cedar, currant, mint and chocolate flavors. **85**

MERLOT NAPA VALLEY (★★★): Ripe and complex. Typically more supple and generous than the Cabernets.
1995: Weaves together plenty of attractive flavors, with a range of currant, black cherry, plum and spice nuances. **88**
1994: Complex with its array of currant, herb, olive, dill and cedar notes, turning smooth and polished on the finish. **88**
1993: Ripe and complex, with lots of deep, heady plum, cherry and berry flavors. **88**

ZINFANDEL NAPA VALLEY (★★★): Big, ripe and concentrated with peppery blackberry and raspberry flavors.
1996: Ripe, with rich, jammy wild berry and black cherry flavors and plummy, minty notes, it turns rustic and tannic on the finish. **86**
1995: Ripe, complex, and concentrated, with rich, juicy, bright plum, wild berry, black cherry fruit and spicy, peppery notes. **90**
1994: Well crafted in a big, ripe, robust style, with a rich core of pepper and wild berry, raspberry and cedar, framed by pretty oak. **89**
1993: Combines toasty, buttery oak with zesty Zinfandel flavors, picking up lots of spice, earth and raspberry notes. **88**

ROSENBLUM CELLARS (★★★)
Alameda County
Founded: 1978. **Owner:** Rosenblum family.
Winemaker: Kent Rosenblum.

MAJOR WINES: PRICE, CASES, RATING

Black Muscat California ($10, 2,400)	★★
Cabernet Sauvignon Napa Valley Holbrook Mitchell Vineyard ($32, 550)	★★★
Cabernet Sauvignon Napa Valley Hendry Vineyard Reserve ($40, 450)	★★★
Carignane Napa Valley Kenefick Ranch ($16, 325)	★★★
Chardonnay Edna Valley ($23, 1,500)	★★★
Gewürztraminer Sonoma County Sparkling ($15, 500)	★★
Merlot Russian River Valley Lone Oak Vineyard ($21, 1,650)	★★
Mourvèdre Contra Costa County Chateau La Paws ($13, 2,000)	★★★
Petite Sirah Napa Valley Kenefick Ranch ($18, 400)	★★★
Port Sonoma County ($12, 120)	★★★

Red Napa Valley Holbrook Mitchell Trio
   ($35, 900) ★★★

Sémillon Sonoma Valley
   ($15, 100) ★★

White California
   ($10, 3,000) ★★

Zinfandel Alexander Valley Harris Kratka
   Vineyard
   ($22, 750) ★★★

Zinfandel California Vintners Cuvée
   ($10, 6,000) ★★

Zinfandel Contra Costa County
   ($15, 3,000) ★★★

Zinfandel Contra Costa County Continente
   Vineyard Old-Old Vines
   ($20, 250) ★★

Zinfandel Contra Costa County Pato
   Vineyard Reserve
   ($19, 250) ★★★

Zinfandel Mount Veeder Brandlin Ranch
   ($23, 350) ★★★★

Zinfandel Napa Valley Ballentine Vineyard
   ($19, 3,000) ★★

Zinfandel Napa Valley Hendry Vineyard
   Reserve
   ($26, 740) ★★★★

Zinfandel Napa Valley White Cottage
   Vineyard
   ($21, 200) ★★★

Zinfandel Paso Robles Richard Sauret
   Vineyard
   ($17, 2,200) ★★★

Zinfandel Redwood Valley Rhodes
   Vineyard Annette's Reserve
   ($22, 1,450) ★★★

Zinfandel Sonoma County
   (Discontinued) ★★★

Zinfandel Sonoma County Cullinane
   Vineyard
   ($23, 250) ★★★

Zinfandel Sonoma County St. Peter's
   Church
   ($20, 100) ★★★

Zinfandel Sonoma Valley Samsel Vineyard
   Maggie's Reserve
   ($28, 600) ★★★★

Also Produced

Carignane Contra Costa County Chateau La Paws ($11, 3,000); Sémillon Livermore Valley Reserve ($15, 2,500); Viognier Santa Barbara County ($15, 800); Zinfandel Late Harvest Contra Costa County ($16, 100); Zinfandel Sonoma County Rockpile Vineyard ($18, 1,000).

Winery Data
Case Production: 50,000. **Vineyard Designations:** Holbrook Mitchell Vineyard (Cabernet Sauvignon), Kenefick Ranch (Carignane, Petite Sirah), Lone Oak Vineyard (Merlot), Hendry Vineyard, Chateau La Paws (Carignane), Continente Vineyard, Pato Vineyard, Brandlin Ranch, Ballentine Vineyard, White Cottage Vineyard, Richard Sauret Vineyard, Rhodes Vineyard, Cullinane Vineyard, Rockpile Vineyard, St. Peter's Church, Samsel Vineyard (Zinfandel). **Varietals Purchased:** Black Muscat (California), Cabernet Sauvignon (Napa Valley), Carignane (Contra Costa County, Napa Valley), Chardonnay (Edna Valley), Gewürztraminer (Sonoma County), Merlot (Russian River Valley), Mourvèdre (Contra Costa County), Petite Sirah (Napa Valley), Sémillon (Livermore Valley, Sonoma Valley), Viognier (Santa Barbara County), Zinfandel (Alexander Valley, Contra Costa County, Mount Veeder, Napa Valley, Paso Robles, Redwood Valley, Sonoma County, Sonoma Valley).

Veterinarian Kent Rosenblum's wines have multiplied like cats and dogs. The impressive lineup is led by a series of vineyard-designated and appellation-oriented Zinfandels. At last count, he was producing up to 17 different bottlings from Napa Valley, Sonoma Valley, Alexander Valley, Contra Costa, Mount Veeder, and Paso Robles. The individual Zinfandels are distinctive, and two in particular stand out for their high quality: the

Napa Valley Hendry Vineyard Reserve and the Sonoma Valley Samsel Vineyard Maggie's Reserve. The 50,000-case lineup also includes Black Muscat, several Cabernet Sauvignons, Carignane, Chardonnay, Sparkling Gewürztraminer, Merlot, Mourvèdre, Petite Sirah, Sémillon and Viognier—just about everything except Pinot Noir. Worth buying, if you can find them.

TASTING NOTES

CABERNET SAUVIGNON NAPA VALLEY HOLBROOK MITCHELL VINEYARD (★★★)
1996: Lean in structure, with earthy, spicy, herbal notes and modest blackberry and currant flavors. **85**
1995: Elegant, flavorful and well proportioned, with dashes of herb, currant, spice, berry and cherry flavors, turning complex on the finish. **89**

CABERNET SAUVIGNON NAPA VALLEY HENDRY VINEYARD RESERVE (★★★)
1995: Firmly tannic, but the core of plum, currant and wild berry fruit is lively, with good intensity and nice cedary notes. **88**

PETITE SIRAH NAPA VALLEY KENEFICK RANCH (★★★)
1996: Supple and complex, with bright, chewy plum, wild berry, black cherry and strawberry fruit flavors. **90**
1995: Dark, dense and chewy, with a firm, earthy, tannic edge to the ripe plum and wild berry flavors. **88**

RED NAPA VALLEY HOLBROOK MITCHELL TRIO (★★★):
This Cabernet blend can be ripe and berryish, with spicy flavors and mild tannins.
1996: Crisp and austere, with tight acidity and tannins and a narrow beam of cherry- and berry-laced fruit. Turns simple on the finish. **85**
1995: Firm and tight, with compact currant, plum, black cherry and cedary oak flavors. **88**
1994: Well balanced, with a complex band of currant, cedar, leather and spice flavors that fan out on the finish. **88**
1993: Simple, with light spice and berry notes of modest proportion and a trace of herb on the finish. **80**
1991: Ripe and intense, with a firm band of raspberry, cherry and currant flavors, turning tannic. **88**

ZINFANDEL ALEXANDER VALLEY HARRIS KRATKA VINEYARD (★★★): Can be very juicy.
1997: Smooth, ripe and rich in flavor, with a complex array of black cherry, plum, wild berry and spice, finish-

ing with a cascade of flavors. **91**
1996: Ripe and spicy, with jammy plum and black cherry flavors and hints of spice and sage, finishing with firm, chewy tannins. **88**
1995: Beautifully focused, with a pretty array of ripe plum, black cherry, wild berry and strawberry flavors, turning elegant and supple on the finish. **92**
1994: Lively, with compact cherry, wild berry, spice and anise flavors; the addition of 22 percent Carignane lends elegance to this wine. **87**
1993: Rustic, earthy, woody and tannic, with wild berry flavors; this wine is pleasant, but lacks finesse. **83**

ZINFANDEL CONTRA COSTA COUNTY (★★★): A tarry, earthy style.
1996: A ripe, full-bodied but not especially varietal wine, with plummy and tarry notes. **83**
1995: Ripe, brimming with spice, sage and wild berry flavors, it unfolds to reveal lovely cherry, plum and raspberry fruit. **89**
1994: Appealing for its ripe, forward fruitiness and layers of cherry, plum and berry flavors, turning mildly tannic on the finish. **89**
1993: Displays firm, compact and earthy cherry and wild berry flavors and domineering tannins. **86**
1992: Lean, earthy and gamy, with hints of fruit coming through on the finish. **83**
1991: Effusively fruity, with pretty jam, black cherry, plum, pepper and floral flavors that turn rich and firm on the finish. **90**
1990: Bright and concentrated, with focused, jammy raspberry and blackberry aromas and flavors and hints of toast and tobacco. **87**

ZINFANDEL MOUNT VEEDER BRANDLIN RANCH (★★★★): Big, ripe and complex.
1996: Complex, with ripe, rich, plush layers of blackberry, cherry, wild berry and spice, turning bold and elegant on the finish. **91**
1995: Complex, with a spicy, peppery edge to the wild berry and black cherry flavors, finishing with elegant, if leathery, tannins. **89**
1994: A wine of harmony and finesse, the texture is fleshy and polished, with complex tiers of plum, wild berry, cherry and currant that linger on the finish. **92**
1993: Firm and tight, showing off earthy wild berry and raspberry flavors, slowly revealing more fruit and depth. **87**

1992: Tight and firm, with a core of chewy plum and wild berry flavors, turning austere and tannic. **86**

1991: A big, ripe Zin packed with firm tannins and supple currant and berry flavors. **88**

ZINFANDEL NAPA VALLEY HENDRY VINEYARD RESERVE (★★★★): Usually big and ripe, but can be smooth and polished at the same time.

1996: Smooth, ripe and elegant, with a pretty core of plum- and blackberry-laced fruit, turning floral and tannic on the finish. **88**

1995: Big, ripe, robust and tannic, with a good dose of toasty oak and a solid core of rich plum, black cherry and wild berry fruit, together with spicy, peppery flavors. **90**

1994: Smooth, ripe and polished, with a pretty core of plum, wild berry, cherry and anise flavors, finishing with a broad, rich aftertaste. **89**

1993: Displays smooth, plush, ripe plum and black cherry flavors that are well focused and complex, picking up a spicy anise edge. **90**

1992: Ripe and fruity up front, with spicy, supple cherry, raspberry and buttery oak flavors. **86**

1991: Dry and tannic, with the ripe plum and blackberry fruit drying out on the finish. **87**

1990: Smooth, rich and complex, with deep raspberry, loganberry and currant notes, framed by spicy, cedary oak and a tarry edge. **89**

ZINFANDEL PASO ROBLES RICHARD SAURET VINEYARD (★★★): Consistently ripe and fleshy.

1996: Ripe and fruity, with jammy plum, blackberry, cherry and wild berry fruit, turning supple and elegant on the finish. **88**

1995: Racy, with ripe cherry, plum and berry notes, picking up pretty pepper and spice flavors and finishing with firm, dry tannins. **88**

1994: Tightly wound, with intense cherry, plum and berry flavors and a crisp, firmly tannic finish. **87**

1993: Marked by well defined cherry and plum notes that pick up a jammy edge on the finish, where the tannins are smooth. **88**

1992: Lays out ripe, supple, focused black cherry and raspberry flavors that are fresh and lively, finishing with firm tannins. **87**

1991: Bright raspberry flavors and a touch of oak give this wine complexity and finesse. **88**

1990: Firm and ripe, with generous black cherry and plum flavors and well integrated tannins. **87**

ZINFANDEL REDWOOD VALLEY RHODES VINEYARD ANNETTE'S RESERVE (★★★)

1996: Clean, ripe and spicy, with attractive, well focused cherry, wild berry, raspberry and plum notes. **89**

1995: Lean, ripe and spicy, with crushed berry and cherry fruit that finishes with a trace of astringency. **84**

ZINFANDEL SONOMA COUNTY (★★★)

1992: Firm and compact, with a narrow band of currant and earth flavors that turn tannic. **84**

1991: Rich, fruity, fresh and almost jammy, with raspberry, cherry and plum flavors. **86**

1990: Ripe and fleshy, with rich raspberry and wild berry flavors that are complex and concentrated. **88**

ZINFANDEL SONOMA COUNTY

1995: Distinctly peppery, with lots of berry and cherry flavors that fold in nicely, turning mildly tannic. **89**

1994: Smooth and polished, with a ripe core of cherry and wild berry flavors, picking up notes of leather and spice. **88**

1993: Ripe and juicy, its pretty plum, cherry and berry notes turning smooth and supple on the finish. **88**

ZINFANDEL SONOMA VALLEY SAMSEL VINEYARD MAGGIE'S RESERVE (★★★★): One of the state's best. Usually quite ripe, smooth and bright in flavor.

1996: Floral, with ripe, spicy berry and cherry fruit, turning supple and elegant on the finish. **88**

1995: Smooth and supple, with lots of ripe, juicy cherry, raspberry and wild berry flavors and a pretty dash of spice and oak. **92**

1993: Tart and intense, sporting bright cherry, raspberry and anise notes that are ripe and elegant. **89**

1992: A sumptuous Zin with layers of ripe cherry, berry, raspberry and plum flavors that turn spicy on the finish. **89**

1991: Great, bright, vibrant fruit flavors fill out this exuberant Zinfandel. It shows concentrated cherry, plum and raspberry flavors that are simply delicious, fine balance and lots of body. **91**

1990: Ripe, rich and fruity, with intense raspberry, tar, anise, pepper and spice flavors that are concentrated and lively, finishing with polished tannins. **90**

ROSENTHAL—THE MALIBU ESTATE (★★★)

Malibu-Newton Canyon, Los Angeles County
Founded: 1991. **Owner:** George Rosenthal.
Winemaker: Christian Roguenant.

MAJOR WINES: PRICE, CASES, RATING

Cabernet Sauvignon Malibu–Newton
  Canyon ($28, 1,300)   ★★★
Chardonnay Malibu–Newton Canyon
  ($20, 500)   ★★★

ALSO PRODUCED

Merlot Malibu-Newton Canyon ($28, 250).

WINERY DATA

Case Production: 1,700. **Acres Owned:** 21 acres in Malibu-Newton Canyon. **Varietals by Acre:** Cabernet Franc (1 acre), Cabernet Sauvignon (9), Chardonnay (3), Merlot (8).

Rosenthal—The Malibu Estate and Moraga in Bel Air are Southern California's two leading fine wine estates. Real estate investor George Rosenthal planted his 21-acre vineyard, situated in Malibu Canyon, in 1987, initially focusing on Cabernet (beginning with the 1991 vintage), and later adding Chardonnay (1994) and Merlot (1995). The Cabernet was originally made by Bruno D'Alfonso of Sanford winery. Christian Roguenant, formerly of Maison Deutz, is the winemaker.

TASTING NOTES

CABERNET SAUVIGNON MALIBU-NEWTON CANYON (★★★): Well focused and flavorful, if variable in quality. Still worth watching, as this remains a distinctive wine from an unlikely source.
1994: Rich, ripe, intense and focused, with loads of complex currant, spice, dill and cedar flavors. **90**
1993: Marked by strong, pungent menthol notes that dominate the tart cherry and wild berry flavors. **84**
1991: Elegant and concentrated, combining tart, ripe, spicy fruit flavors with toasty, buttery oak. Finishes with lots of flavor and finesse and a good dose of tannins. **91**

STEPHEN ROSS (★★★)

Edna Valley, San Luis Obispo County
Founded: 1994. **Owner:** Stephen & Paula Dooley.
Winemaker: Stephen R. Dooley.

MAJOR WINES: PRICE, CASES, RATING

Chardonnay Edna Valley Edna Ranch
  ($18, 200)   ★★★
Chardonnay Edna Valley Linda's Vineyard
  ($18, 200)   ★★★
Chardonnay Santa Maria Valley
  Bien Nacido Vineyard
  ($18, 200)   ★★★
Pinot Noir Edna Valley Edna Ranch
  ($22, 600)   ★★★
Pinot Noir Santa Maria Valley
  Bien Nacido Vineyard
  ($24, 200)   ★★★

ALSO PRODUCED

Zinfandel Sonoma Valley Monte Rosso Vineyard ($22, 200).

WINERY DATA

Case Production: 1,400. **Vineyard Designations:** Bien Nacido Vineyard (Chardonnay, Pinot Noir), Edna Ranch (Chardonnay, Pinot Noir), Linda's Vineyard (Chardonnay), Monte Rosso Vineyard (Zinfandel). **Varietals Purchased:** Chardonnay (Santa Barbara County), Pinot Noir (Santa Barbara County), Zinfandel (Sonoma County).

Stephen Ross Dooley was president and winemaker for Edna Valley Vineyards before he started his own label in 1994. Dooley's focus has been on vineyard-designated Central Coast Chardonnay and Pinot Noir, though a Monte Rosso Vineyard Zinfandel from Sonoma Valley was added in 1999. The Chardonnays and Pinot Noirs have proven complex and flavorful.

TASTING NOTES

CHARDONNAY VARIOUS BOTTLINGS (★★★): These tend to be elegant and focused. The 1996 Edna Ranch (89 points) was tightly wound, with a core of citrus, pear and guava flavors. The 1996 Linda's Vineyard (87) showed a shade less intensity than the Edna Ranch, with pleasant spicy pear and apple notes.

PINOT NOIR EDNA VALLEY EDNA RANCH (★★★): The style has varied, but these are flavorful, well made wines. **1996:** Tight and crisp, with a well focused core of black cherry, wild berry, plum and spice flavors. **87**
1995: Dark, ripe, rich and concentrated, with well integrated black cherry, spice, cedar and anise flavors and polished tannins. **91**

PINOT NOIR SANTA MARIA VALLEY BIEN NACIDO VINEYARD (★★★)
1997: Ripe, smoky and flavorful, showing a tight range of tea, cherry and herb flavors that linger on the firm finish. **87**
1996: Smooth and polished, with a supple texture and ripe cherry, plum and berry notes and a pretty, spicy oak aftertaste. **88**

ROUND HILL VINEYARDS (★★)
Rutherford, Napa Valley
Founded: 1977. **Owner:** Ernie & Virginia Van Asperen. **Winemaker:** Mark Swain. **Affiliated Brands:** Rutherford Ranch, Van Asperen.

MAJOR WINES: PRICE, CASES, RATING
Cabernet California
($8, 54,000)   ★★
Chardonnay California
($8, 125,000)   ★★
Merlot California
($9, 50,000)   ★★

ALSO PRODUCED
White Zinfandel California ($6, 25,000).

WINERY DATA
Case Production: 400,000. **Acres Owned:** 37 acres in St. Helena. **Varietals by Acre:** Cabernet Sauvignon (37 acres). **Varietals Purchased:** Cabernet Sauvignon (Napa Valley), Chardonnay (California), Merlot (California, Napa Valley), Sauvignon Blanc (Napa Valley), Zinfandel (California, Napa Valley).

Round Hill evolved out of Ernie and Virginia Van Asperen's chain of Ernie's wine and spirits stores, where they bought bulk wines and bottled them under the Ernie's label. The Ernie's chain proved so successful that they sold it and expanded Round Hill; they even built a winery on Silverado Trail.

The key to operating a successful negociant brand is the ability to tap into high quality bulk wines that either

aren't wanted by other wineries or that don't fit into their main blends. Round Hill did this better than most, providing not only a consistent line of popular varietals (Cabernets and Chardonnays), but also such wines as Gewürztraminer and Petite Sirah.

By the mid-1980s, many less renowned wineries zeroed in on what became known as fighting (i.e. inexpensive) varietals, which involved not only the purchase of bulk wines, but also some in-house crushing and vinification of purchased grapes. Today, Round Hill is a diversified winery, crushing and vinifying its own grapes, buying bulk wines and offering a custom label business that services restaurants, hotels and resorts. The winery focuses on Cabernet, Chardonnay, Merlot, Sauvignon Blanc and Zinfandel. The best wines formerly appeared under a Reserve designation, but were recently given a separate brand identity, Van Asperen.

RUBISSOW-SARGENT (★★)
Mount Veeder, Napa Valley
Founded: 1988. **Owner:** Tony Sargent, George Rubissow. **Winemaker:** Tony Sargent.

MAJOR WINES: PRICE, CASES, RATING
Cabernet Sauvignon Mount Veeder
($19, 2,000)   ★★
Les Trompettes Red Mount Veeder
($22, 500)   ★★
Merlot Mount Veeder
($21, 2,000)   ★★

WINERY DATA
Case Production: 5000. **Acres Owned:** 19 acres in Mount Veeder, Napa Valley. **Varietals by Acre:** Cabernet Franc (2 acres), Cabernet Sauvignon (7), Merlot (10).

George Rubissow and Tony Sargent own 19 acres on Mount Veeder planted to Bordeaux varieties, from which they produce some 5,000 cases. While well-made and distinctive, the wines are typically austere, earthy and tannic, as were the 1993 Les Trompettes (82 points), 1994 Cabernet (86) and 1994 Merlot (86).

RUDD ESTATE (★★★★)
Oakville, Napa Valley
Founded: 1980. **Owner:** Leslie Rudd. **Winemaker:** David Ramey. **Second Label:** Girard.

MAJOR WINES: PRICE, CASES, RATING
Girard Cabernet Sauvignon Napa Valley
($35, 6,000)   ★★★
Girard Cabernet Sauvignon Napa Valley
Reserve
($70, 1,200)   ★★★★
Girard Chardonnay Napa Valley
($26, 8,500)   ★★★★

WINERY DATA
Case Production: 15,700. **Acres Owned:** 46 acres in Oakville. **Varietals by Acre:** Cabernet Franc (3.5 acres), Cabernet Sauvignon (37.5), Carmenière (0.5), Malbec (1), Merlot (2.5), Petit Verdot (1). **Varietals Purchased:** Chardonnay (North Coast, Sonoma Coast), Cabernet Sauvignon (Napa Valley).

Formerly the Girard Winery, this facility was purchased by Leslie Rudd in 1996. Rudd has plans for his own high-end brand, and has made Girard in effect a secondary or separate brand. The Girard wines will slowly be phased out, however, as various Rudd Estate Cabernet blends and Chardonnays are introduced. The first Rudd Estate wine, a Cabernet Blend from the 1998 vintage, will not be available until late 2000 or early 2001.

With David Ramey (Matanzas Creek, Chalk Hill, Dominus and Ramey) in charge, the quality should be outstanding. The 46-acre vineyard in Oakville has been planted to six Bordeaux varietals, and the winery has undergone a major remodeling, resulting in a gravity-flow production facility. Rudd Estate wines are 100 percent estate-bottled. Worth watching.

TASTING NOTES

GIRARD CABERNET SAUVIGNON NAPA VALLEY RESERVE (★★★)
1994: Wonderfully elegant, with a complex orchestration of currant, spice, vanilla, cedar and herb notes, turning supple and delicate. **93**
1993: Young, tight and tannic. Reveals ripe cherry, plum, anise and berry flavors, but the tannins are tough. **88**
1992: Austere, with a tight band of currant, earth and cherry flavors, picking up subtle herbal notes. **88**

GIRARD CHARDONNAY NAPA VALLEY (★★★)
1995: Rich and flavorful, with lots of ripe pear, fig and melon flavors, picking up pretty toasty oak flavors. **91**
1994: Harmonious, with ripe pear, honey and butterscotch flavors and a smooth, polished texture. **91**

GIRARD CHARDONNAY NAPA VALLEY RESERVE (★★★★)
1995: Bold, ripe and generous, with a complex interplay of rich fig, vanilla, pear and spice flavors. **91**
1994: Dramatic, with lots of dimensions to the bold, ripe, rich pear, spice, honey, toast and pineapple flavors. **93**

RUSSIAN RIVER VINEYARDS see TOPOLOS AT RUSSIAN RIVER VINEYARDS

RUTHERFORD HILL WINERY (★★★)
Rutherford, Napa Valley
Founded: 1976. **Owner:** Anthony, William and John Terlato. **Winemaker:** Kevin Robinson and Kent Barthman. **Second Label:** Hunter Ashby.

MAJOR WINES: PRICE, CASES, RATING
Chardonnay Napa Valley Reserve
($32, 1,100)   ★★★
Merlot Napa Valley
($19, 65,000)   ★★
Merlot Napa Valley Reserve
($40, 500)   ★★★

ALSO PRODUCED
Cabernet Sauvignon Napa Valley ($18, 8,000); Cabernet Sauvignon Napa Valley Reserve ($23, 500); Chardonnay Napa Valley ($17, 10,000); Gewürztraminer Potter Valley ($14, 1,000); Port Napa Valley Zinfandel ($20, 500); Sangiovese Napa Valley ($29, 300).

WINERY DATA
Case Production: 100,000. **Acres Owned:** 75 acres in Oak Knoll. **Varietals by Acre:** Cabernet Franc (15 acres), Merlot (60). **Varietals Purchased:** Cabernet Franc (Napa Valley, Rutherford), Cabernet Sauvignon (Napa Valley, Rutherford), Chardonnay (Carneros, Napa Valley), Merlot (Napa Valley, Mount Veeder, Oak Knoll, Oakville, Rutherford), Sangiovese (Napa Valley), Sauvignon Blanc (Napa Valley), Zinfandel (Atlas Peak).

Anthony Terlato, head of Paterno Imports, a leading importer of European wines, and his sons, William and John, purchased this winery in 1996, following a phase during which quality had been in sharp decline. The original Rutherford Hill was founded by Bill Jaeger and Chuck Carpy, and had close ties to Freemark Abbey It operates out of the old Souverain Winery, situated in the hills east of Napa near Round Hill.

The Terlatos will continue to focus on Merlot, Rutherford Hill's initial source of success, and will also add Cabernet and Chardonnay to the lineup. The 1995 Merlot Reserve (89 points) was very tasty. Worth watching.

RUTHERFORD RANCH see ROUND HILL VINEYARDS

RUTZ CELLARS (★★–★★★)
Russian River Valley, Sonoma County
Founded: 1992. **Owner:** Keith Rutz. **Winemaker:** David Vergari.

MAJOR WINES: PRICE, CASES, RATING

Cabernet Sauvignon Napa Valley ($28, NA)	★★★
Chardonnay Russian River Valley ($20, NA)	★★
Chardonnay Russian River Valley Dutton Ranch ($30, 900)	★★★
Chardonnay Russian River Valley Maison Grand Cru ($25, 700)	★★
Pinot Noir Mendocino Weir Vineyard ($30, 300)	★★
Pinot Noir Monterey Sleepy Hollow ($28, 1,200)	★★★
Pinot Noir Russian River Valley ($20, 1,300)	★★
Pinot Noir Russian River Valley Dutton Ranch ($30, 500)	★★

ALSO PRODUCED
Chardonnay Russian River Valley Buena Tierra Vineyard ($28, NA); Chardonnay Russian River Valley Quail Hill Vineyard ($28, NA); Pinot Noir California Maison Grand Cru ($25, NA); Pinot Noir Russian River Valley Martinelli ($28, NA).

WINERY DATA
Case Production: 10,000. **Vineyard Designations:** Buena Tierra Vineyard (Chardonnay), Dutton Ranch (Chardonnay, Pinot Noir), Martinelli (Pinot Noir), Quail Hill Vineyard (Chardonnay), Sleepy Hollow (Pinot Noir), Weir Vineyard (Pinot Noir). **Varietals Purchased:** Cabernet Sauvignon (Napa Valley), Chardonnay (Russian River Valley), Pinot Noir (Mendocino County, Monterey County, Russian River Valley).

Established by Keith Rutz in Russian River Valley, Rutz Cellars focuses on vineyard-designated Chardonnay and Pinot Noir from Mendocino, Monterey County and Russian River Valley. A Napa Valley Cabernet is also produced. Rutz also imports his own negociant label, Rutz Lebegue, made from wines purchased from growers in Burgundy.

The Rutz Pinot Noirs and Chardonnays have improved in recent years, with the 1996 Russian River Chardonnay (88 points), 1996 Dutton Ranch Chardonnay (89) and 1996 Chardonnay Maison Grand Cru (86) all showing crisp, elegant, earthy fig and pear flavors. The 1996 Pinot Noir Maison Grand Cru (83) was complex, with dried cherry and spice notes, but leathery flavors detracted from the fruit. The 1996 Pinot Noir Monterey County Sleepy Hollow (88) was smooth and creamy, showing coffee, plum, vanilla and black cherry flavors. A general 1996 Russian River Pinot Noir bottling (83) also showed the earthy, leathery qualities of the 1996 Maison Grand Cru.

SADDLEBACK CELLARS (★★★–★★★★)
Oakville, Napa Valley
Founded: 1988. **Owner:** Nils Venge. **Winemaker:** Nils Venge. **Second Label:** Venge.

MAJOR WINES: PRICE, CASES, RATING

Cabernet Sauvignon Napa Valley ($32, 1,200)	★★★★
Chardonnay Napa Valley ($20, 1,000)	★★★
Pinot Blanc Napa Valley ($15, 1,000)	★★
Venge Cabernet Sauvignon Napa Valley Reserve ($50, 280)	★★★
Venge Merlot Napa Valley Reserve ($35, 280)	★★★

ALSO PRODUCED

Sangiovese Oakville Estate Penny Lane Vineyard Venge ($22, 280); Sauvignon Blanc Napa Valley ($14, 80); Sauvignon Blanc Late Harvest Napa Valley ($14, 80); Zinfandel Napa Valley ($27, 310); Zinfandel/Sangiovese Napa Valley Scout's Honor Venge ($25, 250).

WINERY DATA

Case Production: 3,100. **Acres Owned:** 16 acres in Oakville. **Varietals by Acre:** Cabernet Sauvignon (9.5 acres), Chardonnay (2.5), Merlot (2), Pinot Blanc (1), Pinot Gris (0.5), Zinfandel (0.5). **Varietals Purchased:** Cabernet Sauvignon (Rutherford), Chardonnay (Oakville), Merlot (Oakville), Sangiovese (Oakville), Viognier (San Joaquin), Zinfandel (Calistoga, Sonoma, St. Helena).

Nils Venge continues to amaze. He excelled as winemaker at both Villa Mt. Eden (1974-1982) and Groth Vineyards (1982-1994). While still at Groth, he started Saddleback, moving there full-time in 1994 while starting a consulting business (working for PlumpJack, Del Dotto and Robert Keenan) and expanding this winery. Quality has been been on a steady rise, with uniformly rich, complex and plush-textured wines. Pinot Blanc is very good, crisp and tightly wound. Venge is the label used for the reserve wines. New to the mix are Sangiovese and Zinfandel. Worth buying.

TASTING NOTES

CABERNET SAUVIGNON NAPA VALLEY (★★★★): Improving with each vintage; dark, rich, plush and bold in flavor. An outstanding value.
1995: Packs in lots of flavor, with a range of currant, mineral, earth, sage, coffee and spice notes that are rich and concentrated. **91**
1994: Rich and complex, with a core of plum, currant and red cherry fruit that's deep and concentrated. **91**
1993: Dark, ripe, plush and concentrated, with layers of currant, plum, black cherry and mineral flavors, turning complex on the finish. **92**
1992: Just the right amount of currant and cherry fruit to offset the olive and vegetal flavors. **87**

VENGE CABERNET NAPA VALLEY SAUVIGNON RESERVE (★★★)
1993: Dark and ripe, with a pruney edge to the opulent plum and black cherry flavors. Finishes with smooth, polished tannins. This is a big but graceful wine. **89**

1992: Dark, tight and intense, with a rich core of currant and cherry, finishing with firm tannins and a touch of heat. **88**

VENGE MERLOT NAPA VALLEY RESERVE (★★★)
1995: Tough and chewy, with leathery tannins that dominate the plum, currant and wild berry flavors underneath. **88**

ST. CLEMENT VINEYARDS
(★★★–★★★★★)
St. Helena, Napa Valley
Founded: 1975. **Owner:** Sapporo, USA. **Winemaker:** Bill Ballentine.

MAJOR WINES: PRICE, CASES, RATING

Cabernet Sauvignon Howell Mountain ($45, 260)	★★★★
Cabernet Sauvignon Napa Valley ($26, 3,000)	★★★★
Chardonnay Napa Valley Carneros Abbott's Vineyard ($20, 3,000)	★★★★
Merlot Napa Valley ($24, 3,000)	★★★
Oroppas Red Napa Valley ($35, 1,600)	★★★★★
Sauvignon Blanc Napa Valley ($13, 3,000)	★★★

WINERY DATA

Case Production: 20,000. **Acres Owned:** 22 acres (21 in Carneros, 1 in St. Helena). **Varietals by Acre:** Cabernet Sauvignon (1 acre), Chardonnay (15), Merlot (6). **Vineyard Designations:** Abbott's Vineyard (Chardonnay). **Varietals Purchased:** Cabernet Franc (Napa Valley), Cabernet Sauvignon (Howell Mountain, Napa Valley), Merlot (Carneros, Napa), Sauvignon Blanc (Napa).

Eye surgeon William Casey founded St. Clement in 1975 and developed this small winery around Cabernet, Chardonnay and Merlot. Casey owned the winery until 1987, when Japanese brewer Sapporo USA purchased it, later adding vineyards (Abbott's Vineyard in Carneros) and a Cabernet blend called Oroppas (Sapporo spelled backwards). Quality across the board has been consistently high with all varietals, a tribute to the winemaking skills of Dennis Johns, who joined St. Clement in 1979, but left in 1999 to focus on his own brand, White Cottage

Ranch. Each of the wines shares a house style that features intense, tightly wound fruit flavors, deft balance and light oak shadings. Worth buying.

TASTING NOTES

CABERNET SAUVIGNON HOWELL MOUNTAIN (★★★★): Shows off the earthy, rustic tendencies of the appellation, yet the texture and tannins are polished.
1995: Features floral aromas and currant, mineral, spice and sage flavors, along with a complex aftertaste. 90
1994: Rustic, with an earthy, tarry edge, but turns complex as ripe plum, cherry and wild berry flavors and firm tannins show through. 92
1993: Supple and harmonious, with lots of ripe red cherry, currant, anise and cedary oak flavors. 90

CABERNET SAUVIGNON NAPA VALLEY (★★★★): With top-flight vineyards to draw upon, quality is very high; these well-focused wines feature rich, complex flavors. Reducing the tannin levels makes current offerings even more supple and appealing. Older vintages have aged well.
1995: Complex, with a ripe, supple core of plum, black cherry, currant and wild berry flavors, finishing with a burst of fruit. 90
1994: Well-oaked, with lots of complex cherry, currant, berry and spicy flavors, it turns supple and elegant on the finish. 91
1992: Pleasantly balanced between ripe plum and cherry flavors, light oak shadings and supple tannins. 90
1991: Tight and compact but well focused, with intense, spicy currant, black cherry and anise notes that turn elegant and supple. 90
1990: Firm and chunky, with a full complement of currant, berry and spice aromas and flavors, picking up hints of herb and toast on the finish. 90
1989: Crisp and tannic, but with enough currant and spicy fruit to enjoy. 84
1988: Ripe and balanced, with a crisp band of plum, black cherry, spice and cedary notes. 87
1987: Offers a pretty display of ripe, rich currant, plum and blackberry flavors, with subtle oak shadings in the background. 90
1986: Elegant and refined, offering a core of ripe cherry, currant and plum flavors, with a nice earthy touch. 87
1985: Firm, round and elegant, with complex, polished cherry and currant flavors balanced against smoky, toasty

oak. 90
1984: Mature, but still delivering ripe cherry and currant flavors that turn spicy. 87
1983: Has turned dry and tannic, with mature, earthy currant and spice notes. 85
1982: Mature, with tight, tannic, earthy currant and berry flavors. 87
1981: Austere and tannic, with earthy, spicy plum and currant notes. 85
1980: A thin, lean wine with modest currant and plum flavors. 82
1979: Mature and drying, with a firm core of earthy, spicy currant and cherry notes. 87
1978: Earthy and mature, with ripe but drying cherry, currant, mineral and plum flavors. 88
1977: Past its peak, turning dry and oaky, with most of the fruit turning earthy. 85
NV: A blend of two vintages, 1975 and 1976, it leans toward the 1976 in character with its drying Cabernet flavors. 84

CHARDONNAY NAPA VALLEY CARNEROS ABBOTT'S VINEYARD (★★★★): Bright, complex and well focused, with the emphasis on ripe fruit flavors and just the right touch of toasty, smoky oak.
1996: Ripe and creamy, with well focused pear, hazelnut, spice and toasty oak flavors, turning complex on the finish. 89
1995: Smooth, ripe, creamy and elegant, with hints of pear, citrus, melon and spice, turning rich and complex on the finish. 90

MERLOT NAPA VALLEY (★★★): Usually well balanced and focused, though it can be austere; drinks well early.
1996: Tight, with a firm, cedary edge to the supple core of currant, black cherry, sage, olive and toasty oak flavors. 88

OROPPAS RED NAPA VALLEY (★★★★★): A deliciously complex Cabernet blend, offering bold, ripe, deep and complex fruit flavors.
1996: Elegant and refined, with a pretty core of spicy plum, black cherry and currant fruit, picking up smoky, toasty oak nuances on the finish. 89
1995: Wonderfully rich, supple, complex and harmonious, with elegant layers of ripe cherry, plum, currant and coffee nuances. 93
1994: Smooth, supple and harmonious, with tiers of anise and black cherry and spicy, cedary oak flavors. 91
1993: A nice balance between the toasty, buttery oak and

ripe, juicy plum and currant flavors, turning elegant on the finish. **92**

1992: A terrific wine with a rich core of ripe plum, black cherry, currant and new oak flavors, all of which are bright and well focused, finishing with a long, full aftertaste. **95**

1991: Bold, ripe, rich and generous, with tiers of supple black cherry, currant, spice and anise flavors, all sharply focused and picking up pretty toasty oak and coffee notes on a long finish. **94**

Sauvignon Blanc Napa Valley (★★★): Distinct and complex; a spicy oak and herb blend with pear, spice and flinty notes.

St. Francis Winery (★★★–★★★★★)
Sonoma Valley
Founded: 1979. **Owner:** Joe Martin, Lloyd Canton, Kobrand Corp. **Winemaker:** Tom Mackey.

Major Wines: Price, Cases, Rating

Cabernet Sauvignon Sonoma County
($12, 50,000) ★★★
Cabernet Sauvignon Sonoma Valley Reserve
($30, 5,000) ★★★★★
Chardonnay Sonoma County
($12, 80,000) ★★
Chardonnay Sonoma County Reserve
($22, 5,000) ★★★★
Merlot Sonoma County
($20, 40,000) ★★★
Merlot Sonoma Valley Reserve
($30, 6,000) ★★★★★
Zinfandel Sonoma County Old Vines
($20, 7,500) ★★★
Zinfandel Sonoma Valley Pagani Vineyard Reserve
($28, 900) ★★★★★

Also Produced
Cabernet Sauvignon Sonoma County King Ridge ($75,200); Merlot Sonoma Valley Nun's Canyon ($NA, 1,900).

Winery Data
Case Production: 200,000. **Acres Owned:** 447 acres in Sonoma County. **Varietals by Acre:** Cabernet Sauvignon (132 acres), Chardonnay (136), Merlot (158), Sangiovese (3), Zinfandel (18). **Varietals Purchased:** Cabernet Sauvignon (Dry Creek Valley,

Mendocino, Sonoma Valley), Chardonnay (Carneros, Russian River Valley, Sonoma), Merlot (Alexander Valley, Sonoma Valley), Zinfandel (Russian River Valley, Sonoma Valley).

Joe Martin set up St. Francis Winery across the highway from Chateau St. Jean. He has steadily built production to 200,000 cases, using some 447 acres of winery-owned vineyard plus purchased grapes. Reserve-style wines are made for each variety. Each of Tom Mackey's wines is marked by smoky, toasty, buttery American oak, but they're all well balanced, with rich fruit to stand up to the oak. Only the Chardonnay Reserve is aged in French wood.

Tasting Notes

Cabernet Sauvignon Sonoma County (★★★): Well-oaked and usually ripe and flavorful, but it can have a strong herb and bell pepper edge; drinks well early.

Cabernet Sauvignon Sonoma Valley Reserve (★★★★★): Typically dark, rich and complex, with full-bodied, polished tannins; ages well.

1995: Dark, packed with dense, ripe, rich and chewy plum, black cherry, chocolate and currant flavors and smooth tannins. **92**
1994: Tight, with firm tannins and a good dose of spicy currant, plum and cherry flavors that work their way through the tannic veil. **93**
1993: Distinctive, with minty, wild berry, plum and cherry flavors, finishing with a complex array of fruit, and well-toned, smoky oak. **90**
1992: Deep, dark and gushing with flavor; a complex core of currant, chocolate, black cherry and toasty oak. **92**
1989: Shows depth, intensity and complexity, with pretty currant, cherry, earth and tar notes and pretty oak shadings. **89**
1988: Complex and supple; marked by polished tannins and lots of herb, cherry, currant, coffee and sage notes. **88**
1986: Opulent currant and cedar flavors permeate this harmonious, seamless wine that's smooth and supple. **94**

Chardonnay Sonoma County (★★): Shows the strains of growth, with 28,000 cases, but features ripe pear, apple and cedary oak flavors.

Chardonnay Sonoma Valley Reserve (★★★★): Made in a deliberate style, with very ripe grapes and lots of toasty oak.

1996: Offers a core of smoky, toasty oak and intense pear- and citrus-laced Chardonnay flavors. **90**
1995: Spicy, with toasty vanilla bean notes and lots of ripe pear- and apple-laced fruit. **88**

MERLOT SONOMA COUNTY (★★★): Well oaked and regaining its stature after a rough patch in the late 1980s.
1996: Smooth and herbal, with coffee, cedar and hints of dried plum flavors; it turns smoky, with a slightly charred edge. **86**

MERLOT SONOMA VALLEY RESERVE (★★★★★): Remarkably complex, accentuating the herbal, spice and chocolate flavors of Merlot; well-oaked, with mild tannins.
1995: Well oaked and concentrated, with toasty vanilla flavors standing out alongside cherry, plum and berry notes. **91**
1994: Rich, smooth, complex and harmonious, with layers of well oaked plum, wild berry, cherry and spice flavors. **92**
1993: Smooth and supple, with ripe cherry, currant and berry notes, finishing with a hint of sweet, toasty oak. **88**
1992: Rich, smooth and polished, with a supple core of currant, herb, oak and black cherry flavors; a wonderfully complex and focused wine. **93**
1991: An herbal wine that turns richly fruity, showing currant and cherry notes, lavish oak and a smooth texture. **89**
1990: Ripe, round and spicy, with generous plum, chocolate, currant and vanilla flavors and a plush, velvety finish. **91**
1989: Exotic, with plenty of expensive oak accents over an exuberant base of blueberry and herb flavor, turning supple. **90**
1988: Weedy herb and black cherry flavors turn medicinal on the aftertaste. **82**
1986: Marked by rich, opulent plum, cherry, herb and vanilla flavors, magnificent depth and concentration. **91**

ZINFANDEL SONOMA COUNTY OLD VINES (★★★): The old vines include some from the Pagani Vineyard. It is gaining in quality, striking a fine balance between ripe, complex fruit and St. Francis's signature of toasty oak.
1996: Tight and backward, with band of plum, blackberry, wild berry and spice flavors along with earthy, meaty, leathery nuances. **88**
1995: Rustic, with its forest floor and mushroomy edge, it works its way into more complex wild berry and cherry flavors. **88**
1994: Elegant, with a sense of finesse; a pretty core of cherry and wild berry flavors fanning out nicely on the finish. **89**

1993: Complex, with minty, spicy notes followed by pretty cherry and raspberry flavors, turning smooth and complex on the finish. **91**
1992: Spicy and aromatic, with bay leaf and dill notes, but a gamy, ripe berry edge emerges. **87**
1990: Complex and well integrated, with ripe, rich blueberry, plum and cherry aromas and flavors and pretty, toasty, buttery oak. **88**
1989: Elegant and spicy, with focused, generous black cherry, blackberry, vanilla and nutmeg flavors. **85**

ZINFANDEL SONOMA VALLEY PAGANI VINEYARD RESERVE (★★★★★): This wine continues to impress with its bold, ripe, well oaked flavors.
1996: Big, ripe, oaky and tannic, it packs in lots of rich, concentrated black cherry and blackberry fruit. **90**
1995: Ripe and juicy, with a pretty array of plum, strawberry, currant and raspberry flavors of uncommon richness. **92**
1994: Seductive, ripe and juicy; brimming with rich, complex currant, black cherry, plum and raspberry flavors. **92**

ST. SUPÉRY VINEYARD & WINERY (★★–★★★)
Rutherford, Napa Valley
Founded: 1989. **Owner:** Groupe Skalli, France. **Winemaker:** Michael Scholz. **Second Label:** Bonverre, Mount Maroma.

MAJOR WINES: PRICE, CASES, RATING

Cabernet Sauvignon Napa Valley Dollarhide Ranch ($16, NA)	★★★
Chardonnay Napa Valley Dollarhide Ranch ($13, NA)	★★
Meritage Red Napa Valley Dollarhide Ranch ($40, NA)	★★★
Meritage White Napa Valley Dollarhide Ranch ($20, NA)	★★★
Merlot Napa Valley Dollarhide Ranch ($17, NA)	★★
Sauvignon Blanc Napa Valley Dollarhide Ranch ($10, 15,000)	★★★

ALSO PRODUCED

Moscato Napa Valley Dollarhide Ranch ($14, NA).

WINERY DATA

Case Production: 100,000. **Acres Owned:** 195 acres in Napa Valley. **Varietals by Acre:** Cabernet Franc, Cabernet Sauvignon, Chardonnay, Merlot, Muscat, Petit Verdot, Sauvignon Blanc, Sémillon, Zinfandel. **Vineyard Designations:** Dollarhide Ranch (Cabernet Sauvignon, Chardonnay, Merlot, Sauvignon Blanc).

The Skalli family of France, owners of a giant, diversified food and wine company, began this winery with the purchase of a vineyard property in Pope Valley, northeast of Napa Valley. The vineyard, named Dollarhide Ranch, covers nearly 200 acres and is planted to a wide variety of grapes. St. Supéry takes its name from French winemaker Edward St. Supéry who in 1899 made wine on the property in Rutherford on Highway 29, where the modern winery sits today. The goal here is not to make Napa's greatest wines—merely good ones that sell for reasonable prices. The lineup is targeted toward the most popular varietals: Cabernet, Chardonnay, Merlot and Sauvignon Blanc. All of the wines carry the broader Napa Valley appellation, but also indicate the more specific designation—Dollarhide Ranch. Bonverre and Mount Madrona are second labels.

TASTING NOTES

CABERNET SAUVIGNON NAPA VALLEY DOLLARHIDE RANCH (★★★): Consistent, with supple, well balanced cherry, herb and currant flavors with mild tannins; ready on release.

CHARDONNAY NAPA VALLEY DOLLARHIDE RANCH (★★): Emphasizes the fruit, with ripe, uncomplicated flavors, but good balance and minimal oak influence.

MERLOT NAPA VALLEY DOLLARHIDE RANCH (★★): Well balanced, with pleasantly ripe fruit flavors and a supple texture.

SAUVIGNON BLANC NAPA VALLEY DOLLARHIDE RANCH (★★★): In 1997 (88) and 1998 (91) the Sauvignon Blanc showed much fresher, livelier fruit flavors than in the past. If quality holds this will merit ★★★★.

SAINTSBURY (★★★–★★★★★)

Carneros
Founded: 1981. **Owner:** Richard Ward, David Graves.
Winemaker: Byron Kosuge.

MAJOR WINES: PRICE, CASES, RATING

Chardonnay Carneros ($17, 13,000)	★★★★
Chardonnay Carneros Reserve ($30, 1,800)	★★★★★
Pinot Noir Carneros ($20, 18,000)	★★★
Pinot Noir Carneros Brown Ranch ($75, 300)	★★★★
Pinot Noir Carneros Garnet ($13, 10,000)	★★★
Pinot Noir Carneros Reserve ($35, 2,500)	★★★★★
Vin Gris of Pinot Noir Carneros ($9, 1,200)	★★

WINERY DATA

Case Production: 48,000. **Acres Owned:** 53 acres in Carneros. **Varietals by Acre:** Chardonnay (10 acres), Pinot Noir (43). **Varietals Purchased:** Chardonnay (Carneros), Pinot Noir (Carneros).

Inspired by a love of Burgundy, long-time friends David Graves and Richard Ward formed a partnership in 1981 focusing on Burgundian-style wines, naming their Carneros-based winery after British wine writer George Saintsbury ("Notes on a Cellarbook"). With its beautifully crafted Chardonnays and Pinot Noirs, Saintsbury has been a model of intelligent winemaking on several counts. The winery's style emphasizes ripe fruit flavors and supple textures and the ratio of quality to price is high.

Saintsbury's success is tied to a quartet of Pinot Noirs, ranging from its supple, delicate, easy-drinking Garnet, to its standard Carneros bottling, to its Reserve wine, which features richer fruit and more oak seasoning to its first vineyard-designated Pinot Noir from Brown Ranch. Chardonnay, too, is remarkably well crafted, and is split into two styles: a Carneros and a Reserve bottling.

Saintsbury purchases most of its grapes, which gives it a diverse mix of clones, soil and climatic differences. With that diversity, the wines are very consistent from year to year, even given vintage vagaries. The winery has been able to increase volume, and the reserve wines in particular have taken a leap in quality. Worth collecting.

TASTING NOTES

CHARDONNAY CARNEROS (★★★): Rich and complex; well oaked, with lots of tropical fruit flavors.

1996: Well focused, with a snappy edge to the peach, pear and apple flavors. Clean and refreshing. **88**

1995: Smooth and creamy, with an elegant band of ripe fig, apple, pear and spice, finishing with a spicy aftertaste and a silky texture. **92**

CHARDONNAY CARNEROS RESERVE (★★★★★): Has joined the elite; very rich, intense and concentrated, with bold oak and fruit flavors, but best of all, lots of finesse.

1995: Crisp and lively, with a core of grapefruit and citrus flavors that slowly unfold to reveal more depth and elegance, and a green pear and tropical fruit edge. **93**

1994: Beautifully crafted, bold, ripe, smooth and creamy; a real mouthful, with layers of ripe pear, fig and honey flavors framed by smoky, toasty oak. **95**

1993: Intense and spicy, with ripe pear, apple and butterscotch flavors that turn complex and smoky on the finish. **89**

1992: Tight and focused, with a rich core of pear, pineapple and citrus notes that turn spicy and complex, with light oak shadings. **91**

1991: Complex and classy, with layers of ripe pear, honey, spice and subtle earth notes framed by pretty, toasty, smoky oak. **92**

PINOT NOIR CARNEROS (★★★): Complex and concentrated, always bordering on outstanding. Ages well, turning earthy and complex.

1997: Smooth and supple, with ripe plum, tea, tar and spicy notes, finishing with a clean cherry flavor. **88**

1996: Crisp and spicy, with a band of cola, black cherry, spice and cedar. Shows lots of richness and depth on the finish. **88**

1995: Elegant, with spicy cherry and earthy nuances, hints of plum and strawberry and a complex aftertaste. **88**

1992: Delicate, with fresh, crisp cherry, strawberry and spice flavors, picking up a pleasant earthy edge on the finish. **85**

1991: Complex, with smoke, anise, cherry and berry flavors, it turns delicate and elegant on the finish. **88**

1990: Ripe, rich and complex, with sharply focused cherry, earth, cola and rhubarb flavors that are tightly knit, finishing with firm tannins. **89**

1989: Crisp and focused, with ripe black cherry, plum and toast flavors that linger. **85**

1988: Elegant, with spicy raspberry and cherry flavors that turn supple and earthy, and a complex aftertaste. **87**

1987: Firm, with pretty cherry, earth, strawberry and toasty oak flavors. **85**

1986: Mature, rich and tasty, with a decadent edge to the ripe strawberry, cherry, spice and oak flavors. **88**

1985: At its peak, it has taken on a decadent, earthy, tarry edge that adds flavor and complexity to the spicy cherry and wild berry flavors. **87**

PINOT NOIR CARNEROS BROWN RANCH (★★★★): The winery's first single vineyard wine. The 1996 ranked among the best—very harmonious, with pretty cherry and berry flavors.

1996: Ripe, supple, and harmonious, with rich black cherry, plum and berry flavors and smooth, polished tannins. **91**

PINOT NOIR CARNEROS GARNET (★★★): Very appealing for early drinking; light in color, yet flavorful, with spicy strawberry and cherry notes.

1997: Clean, ripe and spicy, with black cherry, wild berry, strawberry and tea; delightful to drink now. **87**

PINOT NOIR CARNEROS RESERVE (★★★★★): Deep, rich and concentrated, with an earthy streak to the ripe cherry and plum fruit. Well oaked, with toasty, spicy flavors. Showing more polish and finesse of late.

1996: A complex and sophisticated wine that combines pretty ripe cherry, plum and currant fruit flavors with notes of spicy, toasty oak. **90**

1995: Smooth and silky; an elegant style with dense, rich, black cherry, plum, leather, earth and beefy flavors and notes of pretty, toasty oak. **93**

1994: Clean and compact, with a complex band of spicy cherry and plum flavors supported by light, toasty oak. **92**

1993: Smells more complex than it tastes with its ripe cherry and oaky nuances, but it is focused and intense. **88**

1992: Complex and flavorful, with ripe, spicy black cherry, herb, cedar and earth nuances. **89**

1991: At its peak, with mature, earthy, ripe cherry, plum and wild berry flavors, turning supple and complex on the finish. **90**

1990: Complex, with ripe, rich and concentrated plum, spice and buttery oak flavors that fan out, adding depth. **92**

SALVESTRIN WINE CO. (★★)
St. Helena, Napa Valley
Founded: 1994. **Owner:** Richard & Shannon Salvestrin, Edward & Susanne Salvestrin. **Winemaker:** Gregory Graham.

MAJOR WINES: PRICE, CASES, RATING
Cabernet Sauvignon Napa Valley
   ($31, 410)   ★★

WINERY DATA
Case Production: 500. **Acres Owned:** 40 acres in Napa Valley. **Varietals by Acre:** Cabernet Sauvignon (17 acres), Merlot (6), Petite Sirah (1), Sangiovese (0.5), Sauvignon Blanc (9), Zinfandel (6).

Long-time grape growers, the Salvestrins have been farming their Napa Valley property since the 1930s. Most of their grapes are sold to other wineries, but a small amount of Cabernet Sauvignon has been made since 1994. Both the 1994 (83 points) and the 1995 (87) were a bit rustic, with earthy, oaky flavors, along with cherry and currant notes.

SANFORD WINERY (★★★–★★★★★)
Santa Barbara County
Founded: 1981. **Owner:** Richard and Thekla Sanford. **Winemaker:** Bruno D'Alfonso.

MAJOR WINES: PRICE, CASES, RATING
Chardonnay Santa Barbara County
   ($18, 20,000)   ★★★★
Chardonnay Santa Barbara County
  Barrel Select
   ($30, 2,000)   ★★★★★
Chardonnay Santa Barbara County
  Sanford & Benedict Vineyard
   ($27, 1,700)   ★★★★
Chardonnay Santa Ynez Valley
  Estate Bottled
   ($26, 685)   ★★★★
Pinot Noir Santa Barbara County
   ($22, 10,000)   ★★★★
Pinot Noir Santa Barbara County Sanford
  & Benedict Vineyard Barrel Select
   ($34, 2,000)   ★★★★★
Pinot Noir Santa Barbara County Vin Gris
   ($14, 1,300)   ★★
Sauvignon Blanc Central Coast
   ($14, 7,000)   ★★★

WINERY DATA
Case Production: 44,000. **Acres Owned:** 6 acres in Santa Barbara County. **Varietals by Acre:** Chardonnay (3 acres), Pinot Noir (3). **Vineyard Designations:** Sanford & Benedict Vineyard (Chardonnay, Pinot Noir). **Varietals Purchased:** Chardonnay (Santa Barbara County), Pinot Noir (Santa Barbara County), Sauvignon Blanc (Central Coast).

Sanford Winery began in the early 1970s, when Richard Sanford and Michael Benedict parlayed their wine interests into the establishment of the 112-acre Sanford & Benedict Vineyard in Santa Ynez Valley, where they believed the soil and climate would be ideal for their passion, Pinot Noir. At the time it looked like a long shot, but after the first few wines were made from their grapes, it became apparent that they were right on target with their vineyard site. In 1980, the partnership dissolved over differences in style and the winery's direction, and Sanford formed his own winery, eventually settling in a warehouse in Buellton. Benedict managed the vineyard for several years before selling it to Robert and Janice Atkins of London, who in turn hired Sanford to manage it, thereby reuniting him with his original vineyard in time for the 1990 vintage.

Using mostly purchased grapes from the best vineyards in the area (Bien Nacido, Sierra Madre, Cottonwood Canyon), winemaker Bruno D'Alfonso has developed a remarkably distinctive (and consistent) house style. Each of the winery's specialties—Chardonnay (three wines including a new Sanford & Benedict Vineyard bottling), Pinot Noir (two wines) and Sauvignon Blanc—features a bold and exotic range of flavors, intensely varietal and marked by rich, smooth textures. Even the Pinot Noir Vin Gris is fresh and snappy. There are plans to build a winery and add vineyard acreage near the original vineyard site. Considering that most of the grapes are purchased, winemaker Bruno D'Alfonso deserves credit for much of the care that goes into these wines. Worth buying.

TASTING NOTES

CHARDONNAY SANTA BARBARA COUNTY (★★★★): Consistently delivers rich, creamy, complex tropical fruit flavors.
1997: There is a hint of botrytis to the ripe pear, fig, apricot and tangerine flavors; complex and concentrated, lingering on the finish. **90**
1996: Tight and flinty, with crisp citrus, pear and earthy flavors; it's not flashy, but has lots of flavor and richness. **88**
1995: Distinct for its ripe, clean, zingy fruit and hints of peach, fig, pear and melon, with flavors that fan out on the finish. **91**
1994: Elegant and complex, with flavors of ripe pear, hints of vanilla, pineapple and citrus and light oak shadings. **90**

CHARDONNAY SANTA BARBARA COUNTY BARREL SELECT (★★★★★): The Barrel Select raises the ante, displaying even more fruit and oak with uncommon depth and finesse. Ages well.
1996: Ripe, smooth and creamy, with well integrated fruit flavors; hints of pear, melon, apple, spice, and silky oak come through nicely. **92**
1995: Intense and complex, with a tightly wound core of pear, peach and tropical fruit flavors that carry through on the finish. **91**
1994: Ripe and flavorful, with bold pear, honey, fig and butterscotch flavors that are complex and concentrated. **92**
1992: Well crafted, with a nice marriage of honey, pear, citrus and spicy, toasty oak, all folding together neatly on the finish, where the flavors echo. **90**
1991: Complex, with spice, pear, pineapple and honey notes that gain a toasty, buttery edge from oak, turning smooth and elegant. **91**

CHARDONNAY SANTA YNEZ VALLEY ESTATE BOTTLED (★★★★)
1996: Elegant and sophisticated, with hints of green apple, pear, citrus and spice; tightly focused, with lively mineral notes. **91**
1994: A brilliant Chardonnay, with an amazing core of ripe pear, vanilla, hazelnut, anise and citrus flavors, picking up pretty oak nuances. **94**

PINOT NOIR SANTA BARBARA COUNTY (★★★★): While early vintages were often variable, the most recent efforts have yielded ripe, well focused wines marked by herb, black cherry, earth and cola flavors.
1996: Gamy, with an earthy, murky, leathery streak that runs through the herb, dried cherry and stewed plumlike flavors. **87**
1995: Well focused, with a supple, elegant core of spicy cherry, wild berry and light, toasty oak shadings. **90**
1994: Shows off some pretty, ripe Pinot Noir fruit with hints of cherry, cola, herb and spice, finishing with a nice touch of oak. **88**
1992: Strikes a fine balance between spicy herb and ripe black cherry flavors, picking up an earthy anise note on the supple finish. **88**
1991: Supple, elegant and fruity, with ripe cherry, cola, earth, sage and spice flavors, finishing with gentle tannins. **88**
1990: Bold, ripe, rich and lush, with tiers of pretty black cherry, raspberry, spice and toast flavors that are sharply focused, firm tannins and great complexity. **89**

PINOT NOIR SANTA BARBARA COUNTY SANFORD & BENEDICT VINEYARD BARREL SELECT (★★★★★): The Barrel Select can be absolutely stunning—well dressed in toasty, smoky oak, but usually with sufficient fruit to measure up to it. Ages exceptionally well, with vintages dating back to the mid-1970's still fascinating to drink.
1996: Tightly wound and firmly tannic, but it has substantial depth and substance. Offers a solid core of black cherry, cola, berry and spice flavors. **88**
1995: Smooth, rich and complex, with appealing wild berry, cherry, tea and spice flavors, turning smooth and polished on the finish. **91**
1994: Smooth and polished, with rich cherry, herb, spice and dried berry flavors, turning complex and elegant on the finish. **91**
1993: Tight and compact, with a trim band of black cherry, herb, anise and spice notes, showing a pleasing sense of harmony. **88**
1992: Firm and tight, with a narrow beam of herb, spice and dried cherry flavors, finishing with crisp tannins. **88**
1991: Supple and elegant, with focused cherry, herb, cola and berry flavors that are rich and polished. **88**
1990: Mature, with complex cherry, earth, tar and anise flavors that are beautifully proportioned, rich and concentrated. **92**

1989: Simply wonderful. Ripe, smooth and creamy, it's a classic Sanford Pinot, with broad, rich, complex raspberry, plum, cherry, earth and spice notes. Soft tannins give it a supple texture. **95**

1986: Bold, ripe, rich and intense, packed with spicy black cherry, herb, tea and mint flavors, this is a wonderfully complex and elegant wine with a long, lingering finish and soft tannins. **92**

1985: Starts out elegant and spicy, with earthy black cherry flavors, but it dries out. **79**

1984: Mature but firm and intense, with pretty smoky, meaty, orange rind, cherry and earth notes. A complex wine with polish and finesse. **92**

SAUVIGNON BLANC CENTRAL COAST (★★★): Intensely varietal, with pungent herb, citrus and grassy flavors, but serves up so much flavor it's delicious. The 1996 (89 points) offered spicy honeydew melon, fig and citrus flavors.

SANTA BARBARA WINERY (★★–★★★)
Santa Ynez Valley, Santa Barbara County
Founded: 1962. **Owner:** Pierre Lafond. **Winemaker:** Bruce McGuire.

MAJOR WINES: PRICE, CASES, RATING
Cabernet Sauvignon Santa Ynez Valley
  ($15, 1,000) ★★★
Chardonnay Santa Barbara County
  ($15, 6,000) ★★
Chardonnay Santa Ynez Valley Lafond
  Vineyard
  ($30, 200) ★★★
Chardonnay Santa Ynez Valley Reserve
  ($24, 2,000) ★★★
Pinot Noir Santa Barbara County
  ($20, 3,000) ★★
Pinot Noir Santa Barbara County Reserve
  ($40, 500) ★★★
Sauvignon Blanc Santa Ynez Valley
  ($11, 2,000) ★★
Syrah Santa Barbara County
  ($21, 1,200) ★★★
Zinfandel Santa Ynez Valley
  ($18, 600) ★★★

ALSO PRODUCED
Zinfandel Santa Ynez Valley Beaujour ($10, 1,200).

WINERY DATA
Case Production: 25,000. **Acres Owned:** 97 acres in Santa Ynez Valley. **Varietals by Acre:** Cabernet Franc (2 acres), Cabernet Sauvignon (7), Chardonnay (23), Pinot Noir (30), Sauvignon Blanc (8), Syrah (18), Zinfandel (9). **Vineyard Designations:** Lafond Vineyard (Chardonnay).

Santa Barbara Winery dates back to 1962, when architect Pierre Lafond decided to build a winery, thus launching the first winemaking in the county since Prohibition. Santa Barbara began making dessert wines which were sold locally, but by 1972 it had expanded operations and now it produces 25,000 cases. Much of its fruit is grown in its 97-acre vineyard in Santa Ynez Valley, which is dominated by Chardonnay and Pinot Noir. Chardonnay is the quality leader, but like the other wines, it is prone to stylistic swings. The wines can be excellent, as was the 1996 Chardonnay Santa Ynez Valley Reserve (90 points), which featured smooth, ripe and elegant flavors of pear and spice; or they can be disappointing, like the 1995 Pinot Noir Reserve (85), which was rich and concentrated, but at $40 should have shown more elegance and less tannin-dominated herbal and vegetal flavors.

SANTA CRUZ MOUNTAIN VINEYARD (★★★–★★★★)
Santa Cruz Mountains
Founded: 1974. **Owner:** Ken Burnap. **Winemaker:** Jeff Emery.

MAJOR WINES: PRICE, CASES, RATING
Cabernet Sauvignon Santa Cruz Mountains
  Bates Ranch
  ($20, 400) ★★★
Chardonnay Santa Cruz Mountains
  S. Miller
  ($19, 200) ★★★
Merlot San Ysidro
  ($19, 1,300) ★★
Pinot Noir Santa Cruz Mountains
  ($25, 250) ★★★★
Pinot Noir Santa Cruz Mountains Ciaradella
  Vineyard
  ($25, 400) ★★★

Pinot Noir Santa Cruz Mountains
  Matteson Vineyard
  ($18,145)   ★★★

ALSO PRODUCED
Duriff San Luis Obispo County ($18, 300); Syrah San
Luis Obispo County Meeker Vineyard ($18, 500).

WINERY DATA
Case Production: 3,500. **Acres Owned:** 14 acres in the Santa
Cruz Mountains. **Varietals by Acre:** Pinot Noir (14 acres).
Vineyard Designations: Ciaradella Vineyard (Pinot Noir),
Matteson Vineyards (Pinot Noir), Meeker Vineyard (Syrah),
Bates Ranch (Cabernet Sauvignon). **Varietals Purchased:**
Cabernet Sauvignon (Santa Cruz Mountains), Chardonnay
(Santa Cruz Mountains), Merlot (San Ysidro), Pinot Noir (Santa
Cruz Mountains), Syrah (San Luis Obispo County).

Ken Burnap's quest for the perfect vineyard led him
to the rugged Santa Cruz Mountains, where the former
restaurateur (The Hobbit in Orange County) owns 14
acres of Pinot Noir (his passion) and a 3,500-case winery. He makes Cabernet, Chardonnay, Merlot, Petite
Sirah (he calls it Duriff) and two bottlings of Pinot Noir.
Each of Burnap's wines shows a rustic, even rugged, personality, which renders reds earthy and ultra-ripe,
intensely tannic and in need of cellaring (if only for a few
years). Few California Cabernets can match the sheer
concentration and tannic intensity of Burnap's Bates
Ranch bottling. The Pinot Noirs, while well out of the
mainstream, age and gain flavor better than most,
although they are difficult and tannic early on.

TASTING NOTES

**CABERNET SAUVIGNON SANTA CRUZ MOUNTAINS BATES
RANCH (★★★):** Typically dark, intense, earthy and
packed with fruit and tannins, their wine is almost always
in need of short-term cellaring. Ages well, while retaining its rustic qualities.
1991: Serves up currant and berry flavors that are supple
in texture, but finishes dry and bitter. **86**
1990: Tannins hold the upper hand in this earthy, currant-
and berry-laced wine; showing off intense mineral and
leathery notes. **85**
1989: Marked by dense, tannic, earthy flavors, tilting
more toward cedar, bark and earthen floor nuances than
ripe Cabernet fruit. Finishes with murky, somewhat muddled mushroomy flavors. This is a highly stylized wine

that's worth holding onto if it's in your cellar. Far from
great, it still needs time. **86**
1988: Appealing for its ripe, jammy cherry and currant
flavors and intensity, finishing with herb notes and firm
tannins. **87**
1987: Big, ripe, dense and chewy; loaded with thick,
earthy currant, sage, cherry and spice flavors and substantial tannins. **89**
1986: Thick and rich, with a marvelous density of currant, plum and cedar flavors and hints of herbs on the
finish. Firmly tannic. **89**
1985: Firm, tight and austere, with layers of rich, ripe,
lean black cherry, herb, spice and cedar flavors and firm
tannins. **92**
1984: Ripe, lean and focused, with attractive black cherry, currant, spice and cedar notes and crisp, firm tannins. **87**
1983: Crisp, lean and austere, with a tight core of tannic,
earthy currant flavors. **84**
1982: From a rainy vintage, it is earthy and woody, with
barely ripe fruit. **75**
1981: Heavily oaked, with a dry, woody flavor that dominates the fruit. **80**
1980: Extremely ripe, with heady black cherry and currant flavors that are supple and concentrated, supported
by firm tannins. **86**
1979: Tough, dry and earthy, with hints of cedar and
black currant. **81**
1978: Big, ripe, dense and chewy; packed with rich,
earthy currant, mineral, sage and leathery aromas and
flavors. **91**

MERLOT SAN YSIDRO (★★): Maintains the winery's
style of intense character despite the California appellation. The 1996 (81 points) was weighted in favor of
herbal flavors.

PINOT NOIR SANTA CRUZ MOUNTAINS (★★★★):
Intense and potent, very ripe and concentrated, often
earthy, occasionally funky, but usually consistent and
capable of aging 10 to 15 years.
1991: Sturdy, with intense, complex earthy, wild berry,
black cherry, anise and mineral notes, finishing with
firm, crisp tannins. **88**
1990: Earthy and decadent, with black cherry and spicy
oak flavors struggling to work through the funkiness. **81**
1989: Intense, ripe and powerful, with lively raspberry,
black cherry, spice and toast aromas and flavors. **90**

1988: Rich, ripe and opulent, with intense cherry, currant and gamy Pinot Noir flavors framed by spicy, toasty oak. Firmly tannic. **92**
1987: This is a tight, firm, focused and concentrated wine with rich, spicy currant, herb, oak and earth notes. **90**
1985: Deep and dark, with a rich concentration of deeply scented black cherry, plum and spice flavors and a thick dose of tannin. **89**

PINOT NOIR SANTA CRUZ MOUNTAINS MATTESON VINEYARD (★★★): Can vary in quality and style, but such is Pinot Noir. Bottom line is this is usually a pretty tasty wine.
1996: Distinctive and flavorful, ripe and earthy; concentrated, with a dill edge to the mineral, black cherry and mushroom flavors. Finishes long, smooth and rich. **88**
1995: Bold, ripe and racy, with hints of plum, wild berry, cherry and spice, turning complex and leathery on the finish. **89**
1993: Earthy and leathery, with hints of herb and wild berry, its range of complex coffee, tar and cedar flavors slowly grows on you. **88**
1992: Smells of beguiling, ripe cherry and berry aromas, leading to complex flavors of truffle, earth and cedar. **89**
1991: Mature, offering a soft core of earth and mushroom and hints of cherry and pepper on the finish. **88**
1990: Ripe and generous, with a juniper berry, smoke and toffee edge that overrides the black cherry and currant flavors. **87**
1989: Rich, smooth and complex, with spicy currant, herb, anise and nutmeg flavors and a velvety texture. **87**

SANTA LUCIA see **WILD HORSE WINERY & VINEYARDS**

SANTINO WINES see **RENWOOD WINERY INC.**

SAPPHIRE HILL VINEYARD (★★★)
Russian River Valley, Sonoma County
Founded: 1989. **Owner:** Tim Meinken, Anne Giere, John Hall, Denice Engstrom **Winemaker:** Mike Scholz.

MAJOR WINES: PRICE, CASES, RATING
Chardonnay Russian River Valley
($20, 3,000)   ★★★

ALSO PRODUCED
Pinot Noir Russian River Valley ($30, 200); Syrah Dry Creek ($25, 200); Syrah Russian River Valley ($30, 100).

WINERY DATA
Case Production: 3,500. **Acres Owned:** 28 acres in Russian River Valley. **Varietals by Acre:** Chardonnay (20 acres), Pinot Noir (5), Syrah (3). **Varietals Purchased:** Syrah (Dry Creek).

The Sapphire Hill partners developed a 28-acre vineyard in Russian River Valley in 1989, selling grapes to Sonoma-Cutrer, Kendall-Jackson and others before making their first wine in 1996. Husband-and-wife team Tim Meinken and Anne Giere are doing most of the work themselves, with winemaking help from Mike Scholz of St. Supéry. The 1997 Chardonnay (87 points) was smooth and complex, with subtle layers of toast, fig, pear and spice.

V. SATTUI WINERY (★★★)
St. Helena, Napa Valley
Founded: 1885. **Owner:** Daryl Sattui. **Winemaker:** Rick Rosenbrand.

MAJOR WINES: PRICE, CASES, RATING
Cabernet Sauvignon Rutherford
  Morisoli Vineyard
  ($25, 600)   ★★★
Chardonnay Yountville Carsi Vineyard
  ($20, 1,100)   ★★★
Zinfandel Howell Mountain
  ($18, 250)   ★★★
Zinfandel St. Helena Suzanne's Vineyard
  ($17, 1,300)   ★★★

ALSO PRODUCED
Cabernet Sauvignon Napa Valley ($18, 2,200); Cabernet Sauvignon Napa Valley Reserve ($65, 250); Cabernet Sauvignon Rutherford Preston Vineyard ($27, 850); Cabernet Sauvignon St. Helena Suzanne's Vineyard ($23, 1,300); Chardonnay Napa Valley ($17, 1,800); Gamay Rouge Napa ($13, 4,500); Johannisberg Riesling California ($13, 6,200); Johannisberg Riesling California Dry ($13, 4,700); Madera California ($22, 1,500); Merlot Napa Valley ($25, 800); Muscat California ($14, 2,100); Sauvignon Blanc St. Helena Suzanne's Vineyard ($13, 1,600); White Zinfandel ($9, 5,200).

WINERY DATA

Case Production: 40,000. **Acres Owned:** 158 acres (100 in Carneros, 30 in St. Helena, 28 in Yountville). **Varietals by Acre:** Cabernet Sauvignon (17.5 acres), Chardonnay (39), Cortese (10), Johannisberg Riesling (37.5), Merlot (15), Pinot Noir (18.5), Sangiovese (8), Sauvignon Blanc (6), Zinfandel (6.5). **Vineyard Designations:** Carsi Vineyard (Chardonnay), Morisoli Vineyard (Cabernet Sauvignon), Preston Vineyard (Cabernet Sauvignon), Suzanne's Vineyard (Cabernet Sauvignon, Sauvignon Blanc, Zinfandel). **Varietals Purchased:** Cabernet Franc (St. Helena), Cabernet Sauvignon (Rutherford), Merlot (Napa), Zinfandel (Howell Mountain).

Sattui Winery is among Napa Valley's most profitable enterprises. Tourists know it as a one-stop winery-deli-picnic destination on Highway 29 south of St. Helena, where Darryl Sattui plays host to tens of thousands of visitors each year. Those who've visited the winery and tasted the wines can attest to the quality and diversity of his products. The winery owns 158 acres of vineyard and produces 40,000 cases, most of which is sold directly to tourists at the highest profit margins. The lineup ranges from Cabernet (four bottlings) and Chardonnay to Madeira, Johannisberg Riesling, Muscat, Sauvignon Blanc and Zinfandel (two bottlings). Quality across the board is high, with Cabernet holding an edge. Because of the clientele, the wines are styled for immediate consumption.

SAUCELITO CANYON VINEYARD (★★★★)

Arroyo Grande Valley, San Luis Obispo County
Founded: 1982. **Owner:** William Greenough.
Winemaker: William Greenough.

MAJOR WINES: PRICE, CASES, RATING

Zinfandel Arroyo Grande Valley
  ($19, 2,000)   ★★★★

ALSO PRODUCED

Cabernet Sauvignon Arroyo Grande Valley ($17, 300); Zinfandel Late Harvest Arroyo Grande Valley ($16, 75).

WINERY DATA

Case Production: 2,000. **Acres Owned:** 9 acres in Arroyo Grande Valley. **Varietals by Acre:** Cabernet Sauvignon (1 acre), Zinfandel (8).

Upon buying a remote 100-acre ranch in Arroyo Grande Valley in 1974, Bill Greenough discovered the remnants of an old winery and an even older and much neglected Zinfandel vineyard, dating back to 1880. Greenough revived the Zinfandel vines and planted more of them; he also planted one acre of Cabernet. The winery's focus is on Zinfandel, with production at 2,000 cases. Quality has been uniformly high.

TASTING NOTES

ZINFANDEL ARROYO GRANDE VALLEY (★★★★): Elegant, flavorful, ripe and polished, with supple cherry and berry flavors and smooth tannins.
1996: Lots of spice, earth, mineral and leather nuances appear before the raspberry, rhubarb and berry flavors fold in. **87**
1995: Ripe, complex plum, wild berry, black cherry and spicy qualities add many dimensions to this wine. **92**
1993: Ripe and refreshing, offering pretty floral notes and strawberry jam, cherry and wild berry flavors, turning elegant on the finish. **91**

SAUSAL WINERY (★★★)

Alexander Valley, Sonoma County
Founded: 1973. **Owner:** David & Edward Demonstene, Roselee Dunlavy, Lucinda Martin. **Winemaker:** David Demostene.

MAJOR WINES: PRICE, CASES, RATING

Cabernet Sauvignon Alexander Valley ($20, 500)	★★
Sogno Della Famiglia Red Alexander Valley ($25,180)	★★★
Zinfandel Alexander Valley ($10, 10,000)	★★★
Zinfandel Alexander Valley Century Vines ($18, 500)	★★★
Zinfandel Alexander Valley Private Reserve ($16, 2,000)	★★★

ALSO PRODUCED

Sangiovese Alexander Valley ($14, 1,000).

WINERY DATA

Case Production: 14,000. **Acres Owned:** 84 acres in Alexander Valley. **Varietals by Acre:** Cabernet Franc (2 acres), Cabernet Sauvignon (10), Chardonnay (8), Malbec (3), Sangiovese (5), Zinfandel (55), other (1).

In 1953, Leo Demostene purchased the Sausal Ranch in Alexander Valley, expanding a vineyard that dated to the mid-1920s. The winery started commercial winemaking in 1974, a year after Demostene died. Grgich Hills and Joseph Phelps purchased the Zinfandel grapes for several years. Production has gradually expanded to 14,000 cases, featuring Cabernet and three bottlings of Zinfandel; the latter is the winery's strength.

TASTING NOTES

CABERNET SAUVIGNON ALEXANDER VALLEY (★★): Medium-weight with modest flavors. Ordinary, especially when compared with the Zinfandels.

SOGNO DELLA FAMIGLIA RED ALEXANDER VALLEY (★★★)
1996: This Zinfandel blend is elegant with spicy cherry and berry fruit and a touch of wild berry, cedar and light oak flavoring; turns complex on the finish. **88**

ZINFANDEL ALEXANDER VALLEY (★★★): Very consistent, with ripe, supple flavors and fine balance.
1996: Ripe raspberry, black cherry and lightly smoky, earthy flavors come together on a soft frame with mild tannins. **88**
1995: Marked by a tarry edge, the plum and cherry flavors are supple up until the finish, where the tannins are chewy. **84**
1994: Intense, with earthy berry and spice flavors, turning tannic on the finish. **84**
1993: Firm and intense, with a well focused core of earthy plum, cherry and raspberry fruit that's rich and concentrated. Packs in lots of intensity and flavor. **88**
1992: Big, ripe and smooth, with pretty plum and blackberry flavors and a satiny texture. **89**
1990: Ripe, fruity and elegant, with spicy, peppery raspberry and cherry aromas and flavors. Mild tannins. **85**

ZINFANDEL ALEXANDER VALLEY CENTURY VINES (★★★): Typically on par with the Private Reserve, though usually softer and fleshier.

1996: A touch nutty, with a stewed plum and loganberry flavor, it's tight, compact and worthy of short-term cellaring. **88**
1995: Supple and harmonious; a claret style that features ripe, fleshy plum, cherry and blackberry fruit. **88**
1993: Solid, chunky flavors of cherry and currant; picks up notes of anise and leather on the finish. **84**

ZINFANDEL ALEXANDER VALLEY PRIVATE RESERVE (★★★): Very consistent, with ripe, supple flavors and fine balance.
1996: Crisp, with tight black cherry and blackberry fruit that's elegant and fun to drink, finishing with firm tannins. **88**
1995: Tight, with a firm edge to the wild berry- and blackberry-laced Zinfandel, but the core of fruit is focused and tannic. **88**
1994: A touch earthy, but the core of fruit is appealing, with hints of sage, plum, berry and pepper. **89**
1992: Ripe and round, packed with vanilla-scented plum and berry flavors. **87**
1991: Spicy and peppery, with elegant cherry and raspberry flavors and fine tannins. **87**

SCHARFFENBERGER (★★★)
Anderson Valley, Mendocino County
Founded: 1981. **Owner:** Louis Vuitton Moët Hennessy. **Winemaker:** Willis "Tex" Sawyer.

MAJOR WINES: PRICE, CASES, RATING

Blanc de Blancs Anderson Valley ($24, NA)	★★★
Brut Mendocino County ($19, NA)	★★★
Brut Mendocino County Private Reserve ($30, NA)	★★★★
Brut Rosé Mendocino County ($24, NA)	★★★

ALSO PRODUCED
Crémant Anderson Valley ($19, NA).

WINERY DATA
Case Production: 40,000. **Acres Owned:** 97 acres in Anderson Valley. **Varietals by Acre:** Chardonnay (27 acres), Pinot Noir (70). **Varietals Purchased:** Chardonnay (Anderson Valley), Pinot Noir (Anderson Valley).

John Scharffenberger—who has since created Lonetree, a Mendocino table wine brand—established this sparkling wine company in 1981, but sold the company eight years later to French luxury goods group Louis Vuitton Moët Hennessey. The winery produces five wines, all well made, with the Brut Private Reserve leading in quality followed by the Blanc de Blancs, and the standard Brut bottling. Hoping to be more clearly identified as a California sparkling wine, Scharffenberger has rebranded its wines Pacific Echo, so while the winery name remains the same, consumers will have to look for the Pacific Echo label on retail shelves.

SCHEID (★★)
Monterey County
Founded: 1989. **Owner:** Scheid Vineyards.
Winemaker: Steve Storrs.

MAJOR WINES: PRICE, CASES, RATING
Cabernet Sauvignon Monterey
($20, 300) ★★
Chardonnay Monterey
($20, 500) ★★
Merlot Monterey
($22, 300) ★

ALSO PRODUCED
Gewürztraminer Monterey Viento Vineyard ($12, 200); Riesling Monterey ($9, 200).

WINERY DATA
Case Production: 5,000. **Acres Owned:** 5,667 in Monterey (4,080 owned; 1,587 managed). **Varietals by Acre:** Cabernet Franc (21 acres), Cabernet Sauvignon (1,013), Chardonnay (1,607), Gewürztraminer (82), Grenache (13), Malbec (15), Merlot (770), Mourvèdre (6), Napa Gamay (20), Petite Sirah (6), Petit Verdot (19), Pinot Noir (294), Sangiovese (5), Sauvignon Blanc (239), Sémillon (3), Souzao (11), Syrah (91), White Riesling (58), Zinfandel (86), not yet determined (1,308). **Vineyard Designations:** Viento Vineyard.

Scheid is primarily a grape grower—indeed, it's the largest independent grape grower in Monterey County—selling to large producers including Canandaigua and Heublien; only a small amount of wine is made here. Early wines have been average to good; the 1995 Chardonnay (85 points) featured nutty citrus flavors

while the 1994 Cabernet (83) offered modest smoky, berry flavors with a slightly herbal note. The 1995 Merlot (79) was marked by herbal coffee flavors and a bitter finish.

In 1997, the company went public. Production will increase slightly in the future.

F. SCHERRER VINEYARD (★★★)
Russian River Valley, Sonoma County
Founded: 1991. **Owner:** Fred & Judith Scherrer.
Winemaker: Fred Scherrer.

MAJOR WINES: PRICE, CASES, RATING
Zinfandel Alexander Valley Old &
Mature Vines
($23, 1,600) ★★★
Zinfandel Alexander Valley The Shale Terrace
($20, 400) ★★★

ALSO PRODUCED
Cabernet Sauvignon Alexander Valley ($NA, 200); Chardonnay Alexander Valley ($22, 200); Zinfandel Vin Gris Alexander Valley Dry Rosé ($16, 23).

WINERY DATA
Case Production: 2,400. **Acres Owned:** 28 acres in Alexander Valley. **Varietals by Acre:** Cabernet Sauvignon (7 acres), Chardonnay (4), Zinfandel (17). **Vineyard Designations:** Scherrer Vineyard.

This family-owned vineyard holds 28 acres in Alexander Valley, divided up among Cabernet, Chardonnay and Zinfandel; the latter is the focus and the best-made wine. The winery offers two main Zin bottlings, The Shale Terrace and the Old and Mature Vines, which are both worth buying. A small portion of the Zinfandel grapes are sold to Greenwood Ridge. Owner/winemaker Fred Scherrer worked previously at Dehlinger.

TASTING NOTES

ZINFANDEL ALEXANDER VALLEY OLD & MATURE VINES (★★★): Deftly crafted wines; well-focused, bright and lively, with supple tannins.
1996: Smooth, ripe and polished, with black cherry, wild berry, strawberry and spice flavors, turning elegant and supple on the finish. **89**

1995: Complex, with a tight core of juicy plum and cherry flavors, picking up a dash of sage and spice, with firm tannins. **89**

1994: Smooth and polished, striking a nice balance between ripe cherry, plum and berry flavors, with spicy vanilla and oak notes. **86**

1993: Tight and compact, with a dense, earthy character to the black cherry and raspberry flavors, turning tannic on the finish. **87**

1992: Firm and fleshy, with a core of ripe, supple black cherry, plum and spice flavors. **90**

1991: Smooth and polished, with bright raspberry and blackberry flavors that pick up hints of vanilla and black pepper on the finish. **87**

ZINFANDEL ALEXANDER VALLEY THE SHALE TERRACE (★★★): The first bottling in 1996 was impressive, as the winery has identified a part of its vineyard that yields a distinctive wine. Worth watching.

1996: Serves up a tight range of ripe, juicy plum, cherry and blackberry fruit, picking up notes of mint, sage and spice. **89**

SCHRAMSBERG VINEYARDS
(★★★–★★★★)
Napa Valley
Founded: 1965. **Owner:** Jamie Davies. **Winemaker:** Mike Reynolds. **Second Label:** Mirabelle.

MAJOR WINES: PRICE, CASES, RATING

Blanc de Blancs Napa Valley ($26, 13,000)	★★★
Blanc de Noir Napa Valley ($25, 7,000)	★★★
Brut Napa Valley (Discontinued)	★★★
Brut Reserve Napa Valley ($150, 1,400)	★★★
Brut Rosé Napa Valley ($27, 2,500)	★★★
Crémant Demi-Sec Napa Valley ($27, 2,500)	★★★
J. Schram Sparkling Napa Valley ($65, 1,500)	★★★★

WINERY DATA
Case Production: 40,000. **Acres Owned:** 50 acres in Napa Valley. **Varietals by Acre:** Chardonnay (25 acres), Pinot Noir (25). **Varietals Purchased:** Chardonnay (Mendocino, Monterey, Napa, Sonoma), Pinot Blanc (Napa), Pinot Meunier (Napa), Pinot Noir (Mendocino, Napa, Sonoma), Flora (Napa).

Jack and Jamie Davies revived the historic Jacob Schram property midway between St. Helena and Calistoga in 1965, naming their winery after the pioneer who first made wine there in 1862 and whose wines were praised by Robert Louis Stevenson. The couple came to Napa knowing little about winemaking, but with a desire to succeed and a sense of style and commitment. The early Schramsberg Champagnes (as they're called) set new quality standards in California.

Since Jack Davies's death in 1998, Jamie and Hugh Davies continue to lead the winery. Production is now 40,000 cases, part of which comes from 50 acres of estate-grown grapes. Quality is high across the board; the new prestige cuvée, J. Schram, was introduced with the 1987 vintage.

TASTING NOTES

BRUT NAPA VALLEY (★★★): Offers the most complexity and finesse, with rich flavors and an elegant texture.

BRUT ROSÉ NAPA VALLEY (★★★): Variable, often showing mature flavors, but it can be complex and flavorful.

CRÉMANT DEMI-SEC NAPA VALLEY (★★★): Off-dry, with spicy fig and honey notes.

J. SCHRAM SPARKLING NAPA VALLEY (★★★★): Easily the best of Schram's wines, offering uncommon richness, depth and concentration; complex and well focused. A blend of Chardonnay and Pinot Noir.

SCHUG CARNEROS ESTATE WINERY (★★–★★★)

Carneros
Founded: 1980. **Owner:** Walter & Gertrud Schug.
Winemaker: Michael Cox. **Second Label:** L 'Etage.

MAJOR WINES: PRICE, CASES, RATING

Cabernet Sauvignon Sonoma Valley ($18, 1,000)	★★
Cabernet Sauvignon Sonoma Valley Heritage Reserve ($40, 500)	★★★
Chardonnay Carneros Barrel Fermented ($18, 4,000)	★★★
Chardonnay Carneros Heritage Reserve ($25, 500)	★★★
Chardonnay Sonoma Valley ($14, 2,500)	★★
Merlot Carneros ($20, 500)	★★
Pinot Noir Carneros ($18, 5,000)	★★
Pinot Noir Carneros Heritage Reserve ($30, 500)	★★
Pinot Noir North Coast ($14, 4,000)	★★
Sauvignon Blanc North Coast ($12, 1,200)	★★
Sparkling Pinot Noir Rouge de Noir Carneros ($25, 300)	★★

WINERY DATA

Case Production: 20,000. **Acres Owned:** 40 acres in Carneros.
Varietals by Acre: Chardonnay (23 acres), Pinot Noir (17).
Varietals Purchased: Cabernet Franc (Amador County), Cabernet Sauvignon (Sonoma Valley), Chardonnay (Sonoma Valley), Merlot (Carneros), Pinot Noir (Carneros), Sauvignon Blanc (Carneros, Mendocino County).

After a remarkable decade as winemaker for Joseph Phelps, where he produced a number of quintessential California wines (Eisele Vineyard Cabernet, Insignia and amazingly complex dessert-style wines), Walter Schug stepped out on his own with the 1980 vintage, aiming for a different style of wines. The focus is primarily on Carneros-grown Chardonnay and Pinot Noir, and the style is much leaner and earthier, with a narrower range of flavors. Schug's wines are far less interesting than those he crafted at Phelps, although recent vintages have shown improved quality.

TASTING NOTES

CABERNET SAUVIGNON SONOMA VALLEY HERITAGE RESERVE (★★★): Cabernet has emerged as the most distinctive wine, perhaps not surprisingly, given Schug's past success with this wine.
1995: Pleasant cherry, berry and plummy Cabernet flavors work their way into more complex smoky, toasty currant flavors, picking up a touch of mineral and sage. **88**
1994: Intense and concentrated, with firm, raw tannins and a band of spice, currant, cherry and wild berry fruit that's dense and chewy. **89**

CHARDONNAY VARIOUS BOTTLINGS (★★): Quality is highly variable, with wines that are often short on fruit and frankly bland. Recent vintages are still variable.

PINOT NOIR VARIOUS BOTTLINGS (★★): Lean, earthy and ultimately simple, lacking the richness and depth found in so many Carneros Pinot Noirs.

SCREAMING EAGLE (★★★★★)

Oakville, Napa Valley
Founded: 1989. **Owner:** Jean Phillips. **Winemaker:** Heidi Peterson Barrett.

MAJOR WINES: PRICE, CASES, RATING

Cabernet Sauvignon Napa Valley ($75, 500)	★★★★★

WINERY DATA

Case Production: 500 cases. **Acres Owned:** 59 acres in Oakville. **Varietals by Acre:** Cabernet Franc (2 acres), Cabernet Sauvignon (36), Merlot (21).

A great success story of the 1990s, Jean Phillips has managed to capture the essence of one great Cabernet site in Oakville. Though she owns 59 acres—and sells most of her grapes—she has tapped into a small acre-plus portion of her vineyard to make this deliciously complex, intricate and deeply flavored Cabernet. The emergence of Screaming Eagle ranks as one of the highlights of the decade. Worth buying and collecting if you can find it. The wine has sold for up to 10 times its release price.

TASTING NOTES

CABERNET SAUVIGNON NAPA VALLEY (★★★★★):
Uniformly dark, intense, deeply concentrated and loaded
with complex flavors. A real treat to drink. Should age
well.
1995: Deliciously complex, brimming with ripe, juicy
flavors that echo black cherry, currant, berry and spice
and rich tannins. **96**
1994: Broad, smooth, ripe and harmonious, with a supple
texture and a wonderful core of plush currant, black cherry, anise and cedary oak flavors. **95**
1993: Dark, ripe, intense and concentrated, with lots of
currant, earth, leather and anise flavors, turning dry and
tannic on the finish. **93**
1992: Dark, intense and concentrated, with a rich, earthy
core of mint, currant and leathery flavors, turning complex and polished on the finish. **94**

SEAN H. THACKREY & CO. (★★★–★★★★)
Marin County
Founded: 1980. **Owner:** Sean Thackrey. **Winemaker:**
Sean Thackrey.

MAJOR WINES: PRICE, CASES, RATING
Orion Red California Old Vines Rossi Vineyards
  ($60, 400)   ★★★★
Pleiades Red California Old Vines
  ($18, 1,400)   ★★★

WINERY DATA
Case Production: 2,000. **Varietals Purchased:** Carignane
(California), Grenache (California), Mourvèdre (California),
Nebbiolo (California), Petite Sirah (Napa Valley), Syrah
(California, Napa Valley), Zinfandel (California).

Art dealer Sean Thackrey pursued winemaking as a
creative outlet, starting out with small lots of wine, then
gradually focusing on what he calls "native American
varietals"—mostly old vine-Mourvèdre, Petite Sirah and
Syrah, all from purchased grapes. For years, his key
Syrah vineyard was Schmidt Vineyard in Yountville, but
it has since been purchased by Swanson. A second key
vineyard source, Marston Vineyard on Spring Mountain,
provided Petite Sirah, but it has since been leased to
Beringer, and has been replanted to other varietals.
Thackrey is now focusing on Rossi Vineyard near

Spottswoode in St. Helena for his Orion Syrah. These
vines, planted in 1905, yield a half-ton per acre. Pleiades
is a blend of lesser wines, and is designed for immediate
consumption.

TASTING NOTES

ORION RED CALIFORNIA OLD VINES ROSSI VINEYARDS
(★★★★): Despite changing vineyard sources, the style
of this Syrah blend remains ripe, high-extract and well-
oaked with big, but polished, tannins; ages well.
1996: Openly ripe and grapey; dark, rich and concentrated,
with hints of currant, anise, sage and spice. Packs in lots of
flavor, a wall of tannins and a long, rich aftertaste. **91**
1990: Big, rich, dark and chewy, with potent plum, cherry and leather flavors that pick up an earthy, peppery
edge. **83**
1989: Intense, ripe, deep and rich, with tiers of plum,
cherry and chocolate flavors, finishing with lavish oak
and firm tannins. **90**
1988: Ripe, rich and generous, glowing with meaty berry
and pepper flavors that are smooth, polished and tannic. **89**
1987: Dark, dense and remarkably supple, with layers of
plum and cherry flavors graced with hints of mint and
spice, rounded out with delicious oak. **92**
1986: Deep, dense and dark, with mint and pepper overtones to the plum and cherry flavors. **89**

SEAVEY VINEYARD (★★★–★★★★)
Napa Valley
Founded: 1990. **Owner:** William & Mary Seavey.
Winemaker: Philippe Melka.

MAJOR WINES: PRICE, CASES, RATING
Cabernet Sauvignon Napa Valley
  ($30, 1,300)   ★★★★
Chardonnay Napa Valley
  ($18, 500)   ★★★
Merlot Napa Valley
  ($24, 200)   ★★★★

WINERY DATA
Case Production: 2,000. **Acres Owned:** 38 acres in Napa
Valley. **Varietals by Acre:** Cabernet Franc (1 acre), Cabernet
Sauvignon (25), Chardonnay (6), Merlot (4), Petit Verdot (2).

In 1979, San Francisco attorney Bill Seavey bought an old 143-acre ranch in Conn Valley that was once the Franco-Swiss Cellar, built around 1881. In 1981, Seavey restored the old stone cellar and planted a 33-acre vineyard, dividing it nearly equally between Cabernet and Chardonnay. The first commercial release was the 1990 vintage, with Gary Galleron (formerly of Grace Family Vineyard and Whitehall Lane, now at Mario Perelli-Minetti) overseeing winemaking. The Cabernet has been impressive for its rich, complex core of fruit and mineral flavors. Production is expected to grow to 4,000 cases, with Seavey continuing to sell a portion of his grapes. Worth watching.

TASTING NOTES

CABERNET SAUVIGNON NAPA VALLEY (★★★★): Dark, rich and complex, with well focused cherry, currant, mineral and spice notes. Has the power and finesse to age.
1995: Ripe, rich and concentrated, with a dense, complex core of currant, anise, black cherry and spice flavors. **92**
1994: Tough and chewy, with an earthy edge to the currant, herb and tobacco flavors; gaining complexity on the finish. **89**
1993: A fine balance between ripe, complex cherry and plum flavors, turning smooth and polished on the finish. **88**
1992: Tightly wound, with pleasant herb, olive, cedar, currant and spice flavors and a pretty aftertaste. **88**
1991: Tight and compact; firmly tannic and earthy, with currant, cherry, berry and cedar flavors leading to a complex finish. **89**
1990: Dark, rich, chewy and supple, with layers of currant, anise, cherry and cedary oak flavors, finishing with supple tannins. **89**

CHARDONNAY NAPA VALLEY (★★★)
1997: Tight and flinty; with earthy grapefruit and pear-laced fruit flavors, it's racy and complex. **88**

MERLOT NAPA VALLEY (★★★★): Impressive. The 1994 (91 points) was smooth, with currant, cedary oak and spicy notes.

SEBASTIANI SONOMA CASK CELLARS (★★★)
Sonoma Valley
Founded: 1904. **Owner:** Sebastiani & Cuneo Families. **Winemaker:** Mary Sullivan & Mark Lyon. **Second Label:** Vendange, Talus, Nathanson Creek, Heritage, La Terre.

MAJOR WINES: PRICE, CASES, RATING

Barbera Sonoma County ($20, 1,500)	★★
Cabernet Sauvignon Sonoma County ($15, 40,000)	★★★
Cabernet Sauvignon Sonoma Valley Cherryblock Old Vines ($50, 1,200)	★★★
Chardonnay Russian River Valley Dutton Ranch ($30, 2,000)	★★★★
Chardonnay Sonoma County ($12, 65,000)	★★★
Merlot Sonoma County ($16, 45,000)	★★★
Merlot Sonoma County Town ($30, 1,000)	★★★
Mourvèdre Sonoma County ($15, 600)	★★
Zinfandel Sonoma County Old Vines ($20, 2,000)	★★
Zinfandel Sonoma Valley Domenici ($24, 1,000)	★★★

WINERY DATA
Case Production: Sebastiani 160,000; second labels 7 million. **Acres Owned:** 320 acres in Sonoma. **Varietals by Acre:** Cabernet Sauvignon (14 acres), Chardonnay (150), Merlot (156). **Vineyard Designations:** Domenici (Zinfandel), Dutton Ranch (Chardonnay). **Varietals Purchased:** Barbera (Sonoma County), Cabernet Sauvignon (Sonoma County), Chardonnay (Russian River Valley, Sonoma County), Merlot (Sonoma County), Mourvèdre (Sonoma Valley), Zinfandel (Sonoma County, Sonoma Valley).

Sebastiani Vineyards dates to 1904, when Italian immigrant Samuele Sebastiani purchased a small winery in Sonoma. There, he produced wines by buying both grapes and bulk wines, selling them in San Francisco. In 1944, his son, August, took charge and began slowly building volume, so that by the 1960s and 1970s,

Sebastiani Vineyards was one of the largest wine producers in the state. A shrewd businessman, August Sebastiani succeeded with mass marketing programs for his bulk wines. As the market began to shift in the 1970s—moving away from sweet wines and red wines to drier wines—Sebastiani found itself out of style and behind the times. Technology and innovation were replacing traditional techniques, as wineries moved away from redwood tanks and rustic red wines (blends of Zinfandel, Petite Sirah, Gamay and others) to temperature-controlled stainless steel fermenters, small French oak barrels and varietals such as Cabernet and Chardonnay. Sebastiani continued to sell large volumes of wine, but struggled to keep pace as consumers began drinking less wine overall, instead focusing on better quality wines at higher prices.

At the time of August's death in 1980, Sebastiani Vineyards was in need of a major overhaul. His son, Sam, gradually reduced the winery's volume from 2.4 million cases and slowly raised quality, with vineyard-designated Cabernets (Eagle Vineyard), and a greater emphasis on quality varietals (Chardonnay, Sauvignon Blanc). Shrinking case volume and strong disagreements from within the family led to Sam's ouster in 1986. He departed with his wife Vicki to found Viansa (on the Carneros Highway in Southern Sonoma), and August's youngest son, Don, took over.

Under Don's direction, the winery has pursued the best of both worlds. Quality has continued to improve, and Sebastiani winery has grown in volume, reaching 7 million cases in 1999. The winery buys most of its grapes, and owns a winemaking facility in Lodi where the Vendange and August Sebastiani lines are produced under a California appellation. It owns 320 acres in vines, dominated by Chardonnay (150 acres) and Merlot (156 acres.) The best wines are bottled under the Sebastiani Vineyards Sonoma Series label and carry either the Sonoma Valley or Sonoma County appellations. The wines include Barbera, Cabernet, Chardonnay, Merlot and Zinfandel, with some vineyard designated bottlings. Richard Cuneo Sparkling Wine appeared in the mid-1980s, when Sebastiani bought finished cuvées from Sonoma-Cutrer, that winery having decided not to pursue sparkling wine.

TASTING NOTES

CABERNET SAUVIGNON SONOMA VALLEY CHERRYBLOCK OLD VINES (★★★)

1994: Dark, rich and complex, capturing ripe, elegant black cherry, wild berry, anise, currant, spice and cedary notes, turning supple on the finish. **90**
1992: Complex, with mature currant, cherry, bell pepper and cedary oak flavors. **89**
1991: Firm and intense, with moderately rich and concentrated cherry, spice and currant flavors and chunky tannins. **88**
1989: Tough, with coarse tannins and modest currant and plum flavors that turn a bit raisiny. **82**
1987: Firmly tannic, with coffee, cedar, currant and olive flavors that are distinctive and focused. **84**

CHARDONNAY RUSSIAN RIVER VALLEY DUTTON RANCH (★★★★)

1996: Delicate and understated, with lovely floral fruit, light oak flavors and notes of ripe pear, fig, apple and melon. **91**
1995: Ripe and complex, with well proportioned layers of pear, fig, toasty oak and citrus flavors. **90**
1994: Clean, bright and refreshing, with a rich, complex core of pear, spice and apricot and a hint of vanilla. **92**
1993: Complex, with bold, ripe, creamy pear, hazelnut and spicy nuances, turning elegant and rich on the finish. **90**

SEBASTOPOL VINEYARDS (★★★)
Russian River Valley, Sonoma County
Founded: 1995. **Owner:** Joe & Tracy Dutton. **Winemaker:** Joe Dutton.

MAJOR WINES: PRICE, CASES, RATING

Chardonnay Russian River Valley
  Dutton Ranch
  ($24, 700) ★★★
Pinot Noir Russian River Valley
  Dutton Ranch
  ($26, 300) ★★★

WINERY DATA
Case Production: 1,400. **Acres Owned:** 30 acres in Russian River Valley. **Varietals by Acre:** Chardonnay (30 acres). **Varietals Purchased:** Pinot Noir (Russian River Valley).

The Dutton Ranch has provided Kistler and Sebastiani with high quality Russian River Valley Chardonnay for years. Now, some of the Duttons are taking a stab at winemaking themselves. Husband and wife team Joe and Tracy Dutton's 1995 Chardonnay (90 points) was crisp and clean with ripe apple, fig and citrus flavors, but the 1996 Chardonnay (87) was slightly less successful, while still displaying ripe pear, fig and apple. The 1995 Pinot Noir (86) and the 1996 Pinot Noir (84) both show wild berry flavors along with spice and sage notes. Worth watching.

SEGHESIO WINERY (★★–★★★★)
Dry Creek Valley, Sonoma County
Founded: 1985. **Owner:** The Seghesio Family.
Winemaker: Ted Seghesio. **Second Label:** Keyhole Ranch.

MAJOR WINES: PRICE, CASES, RATING
Arneis California
  ($14, 400) ★★
Barbera California
  ($14, 300) ★★
Chardonnay Sonoma County
  (Discontinued) ★★
Omaggio Red Sonoma County
  ($30, 400) ★★★
Sangiovese Alexander Valley Nonno's
  Clones
  ($14, 2,000) ★★
Sangiovese Alexander Valley Vitigno Toscano
  ($15, 1,800) ★★
Sauvignon Blanc Sonoma County
  ($9, 6,500) ★★
Zinfandel Alexander Valley Home Ranch
  ($20, 200) ★★★
Zinfandel Alexander Valley San Lorenzo
  ($20, 200) ★★★
Zinfandel Sonoma County Old Vine
  ($20, 1,800) ★★★★
Zinfandel Sonoma County Sonoma
  ($12, 20,000) ★★★

Keyhole Ranch Pinot Noir
  Russian River Valley
  ($20, 1,700) ★★★

ALSO PRODUCED
Muscat Canelli California ($14, 100); Nonna Rosa Sonoma County ($15, 600); Pinot Grigio Russian River Valley ($14, 600).

WINERY DATA
Case Production: 40,000. **Acres Owned:** 253 acres (in Alexander Valley, Dry Creek Valley and Russian River Valley). **Varietals by Acre:** Arneis (8 acres), Barbera (10), Cabernet (43), Pinot Grigio (14), Pinot Noir (29), Sangiovese (20), Zinfandel (129). **Varietals Purchased:** Arneis (California), Barbera (California), Zinfandel (Alexander Valley, Dry Creek Valley).

This is another old-time Sonoma winery, dating back to 1902. For most of its history it sold finished wines to others for bottling or blending. In 1985, the family turned to commercial winemaking using its own name, and quality has steadily risen, thanks to extensive vineyard holdings in Alexander, Dry Creek and Russian River valleys. The 253 acres under vine are still dominated by reds, with Zinfandel the leader, followed by Cabernet. Sauvignon Blanc and white Zinfandel are also part of the 40,000-case mix. Currently most of these wines offer simple styles at honest prices. Given the vineyard resources, a little fine-tuning of the winemaking could work wonders. The Old Vine Zinfandel, carrying a Sonoma County appellation, is the best wine, with 90-point ratings in both 1995 and 1996, and is worth buying.

TASTING NOTES

PINOT NOIR VARIOUS BOTTLINGS (★★): Light and often on the green side with tart cherry and strawberry notes, but it's easy to drink.

SANGIOVESE ALEXANDER VALLEY NONNO'S CLONES (★★), VITIGNO TOSCANO (★★): The former includes a dose of Cabernet Sauvignon, while the latter is 100 percent Sangiovese from old vines. Medium-bodied and well proportioned.

SAUVIGNON BLANC SONOMA COUNTY (★★): Intense, with earthy pear and grassy notes.

ZINFANDEL ALEXANDER VALLEY SAN LORENZO 1995: Starts ripe, smooth and spicy before tannins wrap themselves around the core of mint, berry, sage and spice flavors. **88**

ZINFANDEL SONOMA COUNTY OLD VINE (★★★★): This wine has emerged as the best at Seghesio, offering lots of flavor.

1996: Smooth, ripe, rich and concentrated, with broad black cherry, plum and wild berry fruit and a touch of cedar and spice. **90**

ZINFANDEL VARIOUS BOTTLINGS (★★★): Improving, but mostly medium-bodied styles with pleasant cherry and raspberry flavors.

SELBY WINERY (★★★)
Russian River Valley, Sonoma County
Founded: 1992. **Owner:** Susie Selby. **Winemaker:** Susie Selby.

MAJOR WINES: PRICE, CASES, RATING

Chardonnay Sonoma County
  ($22, 1,000)   ★★★
Merlot Sonoma County
  ($25, 800)   ★★★
Pinot Noir Russian River Valley
  ($20, 600)   ★★
Syrah Sonoma County
  ($20, 600)   ★★★
Zinfandel Sonoma County Old Vines
  ($20, 800)   ★★★

WINERY DATA
Case Production: 4,300. **Acres Owned:** 80 acres in Paso Robles. **Varietals by Acre:** Not yet planted. **Varietals Purchased:** Chardonnay (Sonoma County), Pinot Noir (Russian River).

Suzie Selby left a marketing job in Texas to come and work with her former fiancée, Erich Russell of Rabbit Ridge, in the Russian River Valley. Initially, Selby was helping to market the Rabbit Ridge wines, but she soon discovered that she felt more at home at the winery. While Selby and Russell are now just friends, she continues to help him make the Rabbit Ridge wines, and has since started her own label.

Selby's wines are very good, polished and concentrated. A 1995 Zinfandel (85 points) was balanced and focused, but less intense and flavorful than Selby's 1996 (91), which showed lots of flavor and finesse. The 1994 Syrah (88) was supple, with flavors of smoke, meat, cur-

rant and spice flavors. The 1996 Chardonnay (90) was silky, with rich, concentrated fig, spice and melon flavors. Less impressive was the 1995 Merlot (86), which was tough and austere, hiding its currant and berry core. An 80-acre property was recently purchased in Paso Robles to be planted to Zinfandel and Syrah.

SELENE WINES (★★★–★★★★)
Napa Valley
Founded: 1991. **Owner:** Mia Klein & Ed Powers.
Winemaker: Mia Klein.

MAJOR WINES: PRICE, CASES, RATING

Merlot Napa Valley
  ($28, 700)   ★★★
Sauvignon Blanc Carneros Hyde Vineyards
  ($20, 1,000)   ★★★★

ALSO PRODUCED
Merlot Carneros Hyde Vineyards ($25, 300).

WINERY DATA
Case Production: 2,000. **Vineyard Designations:** Hyde Vineyards (Merlot, Sauvignon Blanc). **Varietals Purchased:** Merlot (Carneros, Calistoga, Coombsville, St. Helena), Sauvignon Blanc (Carneros).

Mia Klein, along with her former partner Tony Soter, is responsible for crafting some of the very greatest wines produced in California, at Araujo and Dalla Valle. Klein's focus is on Merlot and Sauvignon Blanc, which she buys from Hyde Vineyards. So far, the Sauvignon Blanc, holds a slight quality edge.

TASTING NOTES

MERLOT NAPA VALLEY (★★★): Some vintages have been ripe, rich and complex while others have been modest in body and flavor.

1996: Smooth and complex, with ripe plum and black cherry fruit and pretty, smoky oak flavors, turning perfumed and supple. **88**

SAUVIGNON BLANC CARNEROS HYDE VINEYARDS (★★★★): Consistently crisp and flavorful, with citrus, mineral, fig and melon flavors. The 1997 (90 points), Klein's best yet, was rich in flavor and texture while remaining elegant, with citrus, herb and sweet pea flavors.

SEQUOIA GROVE VINEYARDS (★★★)
Rutherford, Napa Valley
Founded: 1980. **Owner:** Allen Family & Kobrand Corp.
Winemaker: James W. Allen & Michael Trujillo.
Second Label: Allen Family.

MAJOR WINES: PRICE, CASES, RATING

Cabernet Sauvignon Napa Valley ($22, 11,916)	★★★
Cabernet Sauvignon Rutherford Estate Reserve ($35, 1,300)	★★★
Chardonnay Carneros ($18, 7,677)	★★
Chardonnay Rutherford Estate Reserve ($25, 1,113)	★★★

WINERY DATA
Case Production: 25,000. **Acres Owned:** 17 acres in Rutherford. **Varietals by Acre:** Cabernet Franc (1.25 acres), Cabernet Sauvignon (10.91), Chardonnay (4), Malbec (0.3), Merlot (0.63), Petit Verdot (0.21). **Varietals Purchased:** Cabernet Sauvignon (Napa Valley, Oakville, Rutherford), Chardonnay (Carneros, Napa Valley), Gewürztraminer (Rutherford).

Brothers Jim and Steve Allen toyed with home wine-making for years before buying a property in Rutherford where they established Sequoia Grove, named after a cluster of towering sequoias on the property. The focus from the start has been on Cabernet and Chardonnay, with early vintages carrying different appellations (Napa Valley and Alexander Valley for Cabernet) along with different lot numbers. In 1985 the focus narrowed to two Cabernets (Estate Reserve, which took the Rutherford appellation in 1993, and Napa Valley) and two Chardonnays (Napa Valley and Carneros). The Carneros Chardonnay comes from a vineyard the Allens purchased in conjunction with a partnership that evolved into the Taittinger Domaine Carneros sparkling wine venture.

Production is 25,000 cases, evenly divided between the two grapes. Quality remains good to very good, but the winery has not kept pace with Napa Valley in the 1990s; given all the great wines being made, Sequoia Grove's efforts have paled by comparison.

TASTING NOTES

CABERNET SAUVIGNON NAPA VALLEY (★★★)
1995: Opens with earthy, leathery flavors, fleshing out with notes of ripe plum, cherry, blackberry, spice and cedary oak. **88**
1992: Deep, intense fruit and lively acidity, with a rich core of earthy currant, chocolate, cedar and vanilla flavors, turning tannic on the finish. **90**

CABERNET SAUVIGNON RUTHERFORD ESTATE RESERVE (★★★): Capable of achieving uncommon suppleness and complexity, yet recent vintages have been less inspiring.
1995: Tightly wound, with firm, gripping tannins that wrap around the core of the currant, black cherry, plum and berry flavors. **89**
1994: Awkward, with a slight sawdust edge that detracts from the currant and berry flavors. **83**
1993: Combines ripe, complex currant, cedar, tobacco and spice flavors, turning supple and graceful on the finish. **88**
1992: Serves up a complex range of flavors, with tiers of currant, coffee, cedar and toasty oak, all well focused, finishing with firm tannins and a leathery edge. **89**
1991: Ripe, firm and focused, with a core of intense currant, cherry, plum and spice flavors, turning supple and smoky. **91**
1990: Smooth and supple, a very soft-textured wine with a nice array of spice, chocolate, currant and prune flavors that turn supple and complex. **91**
1989: Seductive, ripe, round and generous, with a nice tension between the supple plum, black cherry and currant flavors and the spicy oak finish. **87**

SEQUOIA RIDGE see DANIEL LAWRENCE

SEVEN PEAKS (★★–★★★)
Central Coast, Contra Costa County
Founded: 1996. **Owner:** Independence Wine Company.
Winemaker: Ian Shepherd.

MAJOR WINES: PRICE, CASES, RATING

Cabernet Sauvignon Central Coast ($12, 8,200)	★★
Cabernet-Shiraz Central Coast ($16, 1,780)	★★

Chardonnay Central Coast
($12, 30,500) ★★
Chardonnay Edna Valley Reserve
($18, 6,800) ★★
Shiraz Paso Robles
($16, 3,400) ★★

WINERY DATA
Acres Owned: 400 acres in Paso Robles. **Varietals by Acre:** Not yet planted. **Varietals Purchased:** Cabernet Sauvignon (Central Coast), Chardonnay (Central Coast, Edna Valley), Shiraz (Central Coast, Paso Robles).

Seven Peaks was launched in 1996 by Southcorp, Australia's largest winery company, in partnership with Paragon Vineyard Co. The majority of the grapes come from Paragon's 1,000 acres of Central Coast vineyards, but Southcorp also plans to plant a 400-acre Cabernet and Syrah vineyard on property it owns in Paso Robles.

The wines at Seven Peaks are well-priced, supple and flavorful. The 1996 Cabernet-Shiraz (87 points) displayed smooth cassis, blackberry, herb and mineral flavors, while the 1996 Cabernet (84) had a similar flavor profile but less richness and complexity. Both the 1996 Chardonnay (87) and the 1996 Chardonnay Reserve (88) featured silky textures and melon flavors, but the Reserve displayed extra layers of fruit, spice and vanilla. The 1996 Shiraz (85) was ripe and lively, with flavors of chocolate, plum and toasted oak.

SHAFER VINEYARDS (★★★–★★★★★)
Stags Leap District, Napa Valley
Founded: 1979. **Owner:** The Shafer Family. **Winemaker:** Elias Fernandez.

MAJOR WINES: PRICE, CASES, RATING
Cabernet Sauvignon Napa Valley
($30, 7,500) ★★★★
Cabernet Sauvignon Stags Leap District
Hillside Select
($85, 2,500) ★★★★★
Chardonnay Napa Valley Carneros
Red Shoulder Ranch
($30, 8,000) ★★★★★
Firebreak Red Napa Valley
($27, 2,000) ★★★

Merlot Napa Valley
($28, 10,000) ★★★★

WINERY DATA
Case Production: 30,000. **Acres Owned:** 146 acres (68 in Carneros, 25 in Oak Knoll, 53 in Stags Leap District). **Varietals by Acre:** Cabernet Franc (2 acres), Cabernet Sauvignon (49), Chardonnay (38), Merlot (41), Sangiovese (16).

John Shafer left a 23-year career in book publishing in Chicago for a back-to-the-land lifestyle, buying vineyard land in the Stags Leap District. Concentrating his plantings on Cabernet Sauvignon and Merlot, Shafer released his first Cabernet with the 1978 vintage; in a 1998 tasting, this wine had just reached an amazingly complex peak. The early lineup also included Zinfandel, but by the mid-1980s the winery had narrowed its focus to estate-grown Cabernet (Hillside Select and Stags Leap District bottlings), Merlot, Chardonnay and a Sangiovese blend called Firebreak. Production is at 30,000 cases, drawing from the winery's 146 acres of vineyard, including 38 acres of Carneros Chardonnay. Quality across the board is very high, and continues to improve. Even Chardonnay, which lagged early on, is now excellent. Credit winemaker Elias Fernandez with some of the fine tuning in wine quality.

TASTING NOTES

CABERNET SAUVIGNON NAPA VALLEY (★★★★): More forward and polished than the Hillside Select, but it's just as complex and satisfying. Matures earlier; very drinkable up on release and in its first few years.
1995: Firm, focused, intense and concentrated, with notes of ripe cherry, currant, plum and berry, finishing with rich, complex flavors. **93**
1994: Clean, ripe and supple, marked by cherry, currant and anise notes, leading to earthy, leathery tannins. **88**
1993: Smooth and supple, with a pleasant band of ripe cherry, plum and currant flavors. **86**
1992: Ripe and fruity, with attractive plum and cherry notes that turn smooth and harmonious on the finish. **91**
1991: Rich and supple, with focused earth, tobacco and currant flavors that pick up a cedary oak edge and mineral notes. **90**
1990: Ripe and generous, with plum, blackberry, prune and chocolate flavors that turn supple and delicate. **90**

1989: Polished cherry and currant flavors that turn elegant and full-bodied, accented by vanilla and cedar from oak. **86**

1988: Crisp and lively, with pleasant plum, berry and coffee aromas and flavors, hinting at cedar on the finish. **87**

1987: Supple and complex, with ripe currant and cherry flavors framed by toasty, spicy oak that turns chocolaty. Hints of vanilla and berry come through on the finish. **90**

1986: Elegant and polished, with plenty of tannin to carry the cedar, tobacco, currant and plum flavors through to a long finish. **89**

1985: Delivers sharply defined ripe cherry, cassis, currant and spice flavors that have a gentle underlying intensity. **88**

1984: Offers harmony and finesse, with beautifully integrated, smooth, ripe, fleshy cherry, currant, vanilla and spice flavors and supple tannins. **88**

1983: Lean, concentrated, elegant and well focused, with rich, ripe black cherry, currant, herb and mint flavors. **87**

1982: Tight and concentrated, with a firm structure and plenty of herb, cherry and cassis flavors. **88**

1980: A herbaceous wine in which the bell pepper and herbs override the cherry and currant flavors. **82**

1979: Ripe, opulent and flavorful, with cherry and currant flavors that are drying out. **88**

1978: A real mouthful, with rich currant, cherry, anise, sage and cedary flavors and firm, rustic tannins that sustain the flavors. **92**

CABERNET SAUVIGNON STAGS LEAP DISTRICT HILLSIDE SELECT (★★★★★): Ripe, intense, complex and well-focused, brimming with rich fruit and just the right touch of oak. Grapes come from the sloping hillside vineyard that surrounds the winery. Ages well, peaking at five to seven years of age, but is capable of lasting 15 years or more. It's among the best in Stags Leap and Napa Valley.

1995: Ripe and plump, with a rich, supple core of plum and black cherry; anise and wild berry flavors add dimension. **94**

1994: Deliciously complex and concentrated, with a wide array of earthy currant and black cherry flavors tinged with dusty sage and cedary oak. **95**

1993: Big, broad and lushly flavored; packed with rich currant, leather, earth, tar, cedar, anise, mint and smoky nuances. **94**

1992: Richly flavored, complex and focused with concentrated cherry, currant, mineral and spice flavors and deep, plush tannins. **93**

1991: Rich, thick and plush, with a tight core of currant, mineral, cedar and black cherry fruit that's complex and deeply concentrated. **93**

1990: A wine with harmony, finesse, excellent depth and richness; the supple, complex, toasty oak, currant, herb, spice and mineral flavors finish with firm, plush tannins. **94**

1989: Solid and well crafted, with ripe, pretty currant, mineral, spice, tar and earth notes, turning firmly tannic on the finish. **88**

1988: Deep, rich and complex, with a supple array of spicy black cherry, plum and wild berry fruit and smooth tannins. **89**

1987: Serves up layers of ripe, rich currant, cherry, chocolate, spice, anise and vanilla flavors that are plush, supple and deeply concentrated. **96**

1986: Dark, ripe, rich and intense, with a core of currant, mineral, cherry, coffee and herb flavors that are supple and polished. **90**

1985: A seamless wine that displays tremendous harmony and finesse, with supple, bright, complex and opulent currant, anise, spice and cedary oak flavors. **94**

1984: Complex and concentrated, with plush black cherry and currant flavors that are silky and polished, finishing with spicy anise notes. **90**

1983: Austere, with firm tannins holding an edge over the currant, cherry and herb notes. **86**

CHARDONNAY NAPA VALLEY CARNEROS RED SHOULDER RANCH (★★★★★): Has moved to the forefront; very ripe, complex and detailed.

1997: Rich and racy, with lots of distinctive peach, citrus, grapefruit and pear flavors; fairly lean and a touch coarse now, but very tasty; finishes with intriguing flavors. **93**

1996: Elegant and refined, with subtle, creamy pear, vanilla, citrus and apple notes that are well focused; long and lively on the finish. **92**

1995: Spicy and perfumed, with elegant pear, melon and apple flavors that are rich and complex. **91**

1994: Big, ripe, intense and juicy; loaded with rich, complex pear, anise, fig and spice flavors; remarkably elegant. **93**

FIREBREAK RED NAPA VALLEY (★★★): This style showcases the spice and anise notes of Sangiovese, and includes varying amounts of Cabernet for color and backbone.

1995: Firm, tight and concentrated, with a complex core of currant, berry, cherry and spice flavors. Gets a bit of backbone from its 12% of Cabernet; finishes with a good length. **87**

1994: Young, tight and tannic, offering lots of flavor, with currant, anise, mineral and spicy nuances and a long, full finish. **88**

MERLOT NAPA VALLEY (★★★★): Forward, supple and polished. Very appealing to drink on release as it serves up lots of ripe, juicy fruit and is not weighted down with tannins.
1996: Tight, with attractive plum, currant, berry and herbal notes, fanning out on the complex and tannic finish. **88**
1995: Smooth, ripe and supple, with a pleasant band of currant, herb and sage notes, finishing with tender tannins. **86**
1994: Lean and leathery, with a narrow band of cherry- and plum-laced Merlot fruit. **85**
1993: Of medium weight, supple and flavorful, featuring currant, cherry, herb and berry notes and mild tannins. **88**
1992: A smooth and elegant wine with cedary oak and currant flavors that are well integrated, finishing with a pretty berry aftertaste. **88**
1991: Supple, ripe and generous, with rich, fleshy currant, anise, herb and cherry aromas and flavors that are focused and lively. **89**
1990: Full, rich and generous, with complex currant, chocolate and herb aromas and flavors shaded by sweet oak. **91**
1989: Offers pretty, ripe black cherry, currant, spice and cedar flavors that are elegant and polished. **87**
1988: Elegant, with pretty plum, currant and olive notes and a coarse finish. **83**
1987: Lavishly oaked, with rich, supple, concentrated currant, spice and plum flavors that linger on the finish. **90**
1986: Fine concentration and depth, with ripe plum and raspberry notes adding to the toasty, chocolaty flavors. **88**

SHALE RIDGE see LOCKWOOD VINEYARD

SHENANDOAH VINEYARDS (★★–★★★)
Shenandoah Valley, Amador County
Founded: 1977. **Owner:** Leon & Shirley Sobon.
Winemaker: Leon Sobon.

MAJOR WINES: PRICE, CASES, RATING
Barbera Amador County
  ($15, 1,000)   ★★
Cabernet Sauvignon Amador County
  ($13, 2,000)   ★★★

Cabernet-Shiraz Amador County
  ($12, 800)   ★★
Sangiovese Amador County
  ($13, 1,000)   ★★
Sauvignon Blanc Amador County
  ($8, 4,800)   ★★★
Zinfandel Amador County Special Reserve
  ($9, 5,700)   ★★★
Zinfandel Amador County Vintners Selection
  ($15, 1,200)   ★★★
Zingiovese Amador County
  ($12, 800)   ★★

ALSO PRODUCED
Black Muscat Amador County ($13, 1,000); Orange Muscat Amador County ($13, 600); White Zinfandel Amador County ($6, 1,800).

WINERY DATA
Case Production: 20,700. **Acres Owned:** 37 acres in Amador County and Shenandoah Valley. **Varietals by Acre:** Cabernet Franc (3 acres), Cabernet Sauvignon (5.5), Grenache (3), Mourvèdre (1), Muscat Hamburg (3.5), Orange Muscat (1), Roussanne (3), Sauvignon Blanc (5), Syrah (5), Viognier (7). **Varietals Purchased:** Barbera (Amador County), Sangiovese (Amador County), Sauvignon Blanc (Amador County), Zinfandel (Amador County).

After a career as a Silicon Valley research scientist, Leon Sobon shifted gears first to home winemaking, and later to being commercial vintner. His focus (and strength) at Shenandoah has always been Amador-grown Zinfandel, although Cabernet and Sauvignon Blanc are also well-made and well-priced. New additions to the portfolio include Barbera, Sangiovese, and Cabernet-Shiraz and Sangiovese-Zinfandel blends.

The 1996 Barbera (84 points) was light-bodied, with plum and anise flavors, while the 1996 Cabernet Sauvignon (87) showed more depth and structure with herb, cassis and leathery flavors. Typically citrusy, the 1997 Sauvignon Blanc (87) also featured fig and sweet pea notes. The 1996 Zinfandel Special Reserve (85) was softer in texture than in previous years, with pleasant blueberry and smoke flavors. The 1995 Zinfandel Vintners Selection (86), also smooth and soft, displayed raspberry, tar and spicy notes. The blends haven't quite hit their stride yet; the 1996 Zingiovese (85) had the crisp, hard-edged qualities of Sangiovese and the ripe blackberry and spice flavors of Zinfandel, but the 1996 Cabernet-Shiraz (82) favored earthy, mineral-like flavors over fruit.

In 1989, the Sobons purchased the old D'Agostini Winery and renamed it Sobon Estate.

SHOOTING STAR see STEELE WINES

SHV see STONY HILL VINEYARD

SIDURI CELLARS (★★★)
Russian River Valley
Founded: 1994. **Owner:** Adam & Dianna Lee. **Winemaker:** Adam & Dianna Lee.

MAJOR WINES: PRICE, CASES, RATING
Pinot Noir Anderson Valley Rose Vineyard
  (Discontinued) ★★★★
Pinot Noir Oregon
  ($28, 550) ★★★
Pinot Noir Santa Lucia Highlands
  Pisoni Vineyard
  ($45, 270) ★★★
Pinot Noir Sonoma Coast Hirsch Vineyard
  ($45, 250) ★★★
Pinot Noir Sonoma Mountain
  Van Der Kamp Vineyard Old Vines
  ($45, 150) ★★★

ALSO PRODUCED
Pinot Noir Oregon Archery Summit Estate Vineyard ($48, 95); Pinot Noir Oregon Muirfield Vineyard ($45, 240); Pinot Noir Sonoma Coast Coastlands Vineyard ($48, 20).

WINERY DATA
Case Production: 1,800. **Vineyard Designations:** Archery Summit Estate Vineyard (Pinot Noir), Pisoni Vineyard (Pinot Noir), Hirsch Vineyard (Pinot Noir), Van Der Kamp Vineyard (Pinot Noir). **Varietals Purchased:** Pinot Noir (Anderson Valley, Oregon, Santa Lucia Highlands, Sonoma Coast, Sonoma Mountain).

This young husband-and-wife team moved to California in 1993 with the firm intention of making wine. One year later, they started Siduri, making their wine with grapes purchased from Anderson Valley. Their

first Pinot Noirs, the 1994 Anderson Valley Rose Vineyard (95 points) and the 1995 Rose Vineyard (92) were dark, rich concentrated wines with wild berry, plum and spice flavors. In 1995, the couple produced their first Hirsch Vineyard Pinot Noir (88), a complex wine with earthy, tea, cola and spice notes. Recent efforts from the 1996 and 1997 vintages have all been less dark and intense than the earlier vintages. 1995 was the last vintage of Rosé Vineyard for Siduri, as those grapes are now sold exclusively to Kendall-Jackson. The Lees are now making wines in their own facility based in Santa Rosa, and are producing a number of vineyard-designated Pinot Noirs from Oregon and California. Given the individuality of each wine, this is a winery worth watching, and its wines are worth buying.

TASTING NOTES

PINOT NOIR ANDERSON VALLEY ROSE VINEYARD (★★★★)
1995: Smooth, ripe and generous, with pretty, complex plum, cherry, berry and vanilla shadings that are sharply focused. **92**
1994: Enormously rich and complex, offering layers of plush dark cherry, wild berry, plum and spice flavors, along with pretty, toasty oak. **95**

PINOT NOIR SANTA LUCIA HIGHLANDS PISONI VINEYARD (★★★)
1997: Ripe, smooth and polished, with a slight earthy edge to the black cherry, plum and raspberry flavors. **88**

PINOT NOIR SONOMA COAST HIRSCH VINEYARD (★★★): Shows attractive flavors on a supple frame, but comes up short on concentration.
1997: Medium weight, ripe and spicy, with good intensity and hints of plum and berry, turning herbal and stemmy. **85**
1996: Strives for complexity with appealing up-front toasty oak, berry and cherry fruit, but simply lacks concentration. **86**
1995: Marked by spicy cola and earthy berry flavors; evolves into a more complex wine. **88**

PINOT NOIR SONOMA MOUNTAIN VAN DER KAMP VINEYARD OLD VINES (★★★): Has delicate plum, cherry and raspberry flavors, but is light in color and intensity.

1997: Almost light enough in color for a rosé of Pinot, it nonetheless is appealing for its snappy wild berry, watermelon and raspberry flavors. Finishes with firm tannins. **87**
1996: Upfront plum and cherry flavors are appealing in a light, elegant manner, but it loses its modest level of intensity and turns simpler on the finish. **86**

SIERRA see STEVENOT WINERY

SIERRA VISTA WINERY (★★)
El Dorado County
Founded: 1971. **Owner:** MacCready Family.
Winemaker: John MacCready.

MAJOR WINES: PRICE, CASES, RATING
Chardonnay El Dorado Barrel Fermented ($16, 500)	★★
Fleur de Montage Red El Dorado ($14, 500)	★★
Syrah El Dorado Red Rock Ridge ($17, 700)	★★
Viognier El Dorado Estate Bottled ($20, 400)	★★
Zinfandel El Dorado ($13, 900)	★★
Zinfandel El Dorado Herbert Vineyard ($15, 900)	★★
Zinfandel El Dorado Reeves Vineyard ($15, 500)	★★★

ALSO PRODUCED
Cabernet Sauvignon El Dorado ($14, 500); Fumé Blanc El Dorado ($9, 900); Merlot El Dorado ($15, 500); Syrah El Dorado ($10, 1,500).

WINERY DATA
Case Production: 8,000. **Acres Owned:** 44 acres in El Dorado.
Varietals by Acre: Cabernet Sauvignon (5), Chardonnay (4), Cinsault (1), Grenache (3), Merlot (4), Roussanne (1), Sauvignon Blanc (4), Syrah (8), Viognier (3), Zinfandel (11).
Vineyard Designations: Herbert Vineyard (Zinfandel), Reeves Vineyard (Zinfandel).

Beginning in 1972, John and Barbara MacCready began planting their 44-acre vineyard in El Dorado County; commercial winemaking commenced in 1974.

The MacCreadys produce a wide range of wines, but Rhône varietals and Zinfandel are their best. Fleur de Montage is a pleasant Syrah-based Rhône blend; the 1997 (86 points) brought together cherry, raspberry and herb flavors. The 1991 Syrah Red Rock Ridge (81) was slightly dry, with a core of blackberry and currant, but also some distracting herbal, tarry notes. The MacCreadys' Zinfandels share peppery black cherry, plum and leather characters; in 1996 the Reeves Vineyard bottling (88) was the most balanced and generous.

SIGNORELLO VINEYARDS (★★★–★★★★★)
Napa Valley
Founded: 1985. **Owner:** Ray Signorello, Jr.
Winemaker: Ray Signorello, Jr.

MAJOR WINES: PRICE, CASES, RATING
Cabernet Sauvignon Napa Valley ($35, 2,500)	★★★
Cabernet Sauvignon Napa Valley Founder's Reserve ($55, 400)	★★★★
Chardonnay Napa Valley ($30, 1,800)	★★★★
Chardonnay Napa Valley Founder's Reserve ($30, 1,000)	★★★★★
Chardonnay Napa Valley Hope's Cuvée ($60, 44)	★★★★★
Petite Sirah Napa Valley ($25, 1,250)	★★★
Pinot Noir Carneros Las Amigas Vineyard ($48, 400)	★★★
Pinot Noir North Coast Founder's Reserve ($NA, NA)	★★★
Pinot Noir Russian River Martinelli Vineyard ($48, 400)	★★★
Sauvignon Blanc Napa Valley (Discontinued)	★★★
Sémillon Napa Valley ($22, 600)	★★★
Syrah Napa Valley ($30, 100)	★★★

Zinfandel Napa Valley
($25, 100) ★★★

ALSO PRODUCED
Viognier Napa Valley Estate ($30, 50).

WINERY DATA
Case Production: 8,000. **Acres Owned:** 42 acres in Oak Knoll District, Napa Valley. **Varietals by Acre:** Cabernet Franc (3 acres), Cabernet Sauvignon (13), Chardonnay (14.5), Merlot (6), Sauvignon Blanc (1), Sémillon (2), Syrah (2), Viognier (0.5). **Vineyard Designations:** Las Amigas Vineyard (Pinot Noir), Martinelli Vineyard (Pinot Noir). **Varietals Purchased:** Pinot Noir (Carneros, Russian River Valley), Zinfandel (Napa Valley).

Ray Signorello Sr. founded this vineyard and winery on a 100-acre property in the Oak Knoll area of Napa south of the Stags Leap District. He farmed grapes there for nearly a decade before starting a winery with his son, Ray Jr. The Signorellos still sell grapes, but since 1985 the winery has been producing wines from both its own and purchased grapes. Production has slowly grown to 8,000 cases, with a diversified mix that includes two Cabernets (including a Founder's Reserve), two Chardonnays (another Founder's Reserve), along with Petite Sirah, Pinot Noir (Carneros and Russian River), Sauvignon Blanc, Sémillon and Zinfandel. Recent vintages of all the wines have stepped up in quality, so this winery merits even closer attention. Worth buying.

TASTING NOTES

CABERNET SAUVIGNON NAPA VALLEY (★★★): Steadily improving, with dark, ripe, opulent flavors. Worth watching and buying.
1995: Dark, ripe and intense, with spicy currant, plum and blackberry fruit, picking up pretty, spicy oak, anise and tobacco notes on the finish. **93**
1994: A well proportioned, medium-bodied style with attractive green olive, currant and cherry-laced fruit. **88**
1991: Supple, with ripe plum, currant and spicy oak flavors that finish with mild tannins and an earthy note. **87**
1990: Beautifully crafted, with a core of rich, elegant, spicy cherry, currant, anise and buttery oak flavors, turning supple and silky. **90**

CABERNET SAUVIGNON NAPA VALLEY FOUNDER'S RESERVE (★★★★): Shows a deft house-style with bold,

ripe, seductive fruit flavors that are well-oaked, keeping the tannins in check. Impressive.
1995: Ripe and plummy, with a firm tannic backbone and plenty of black cherry, smoky, toasty oak, anise, earth and tar nuances. **93**
1994: Distinctive for its earthy, mineral, currant and wild berry flavors, it's deeply concentrated and firmly tannic. **90**
1993: Ripe and fruity, with complex black cherry, currant, anise and light oak shadings, turning tannic on the finish. **88**
1992: Smooth and polished for such a young wine, with an appealing array of black cherry, currant, plum and spice, finishing with light oak and firm tannins. **90**
1991: Rich and chewy, packed with currant, mineral, herb and tobacco flavors that open up, leading to a firm tannic edge and pretty oak shadings. **90**
1990: Ripe, round and chewy, a complex wine with brilliantly focused currant, chocolate and buttery oak flavors that linger. **92**
1989: Ripe and chewy, with powerful currant, plum and cherry aromas and flavors framed by spicy vanilla and oak. **85**
1988: Ripe and complex, with deep, tannic, peppery berry flavors, smoky chocolate nuances and a deep plush texture. Superb for the vintage. **90**

CHARDONNAY NAPA VALLEY (★★★★): Bigger, bolder, riper and more complex of late; poised to join the elite.
1996: Sharply focused, ripe, rich and lively, with complex, concentrated pear, apple, spice and peach flavors. **92**
1995: Bold, ripe, rich and complex, with layers of fig, pear and apple fruit and pretty, toasty oak shadings. **92**
1994: Elegant, with ripe fig, pear and melon flavors shaded by toasty oak, turning complex on the finish. **87**

CHARDONNAY NAPA VALLEY FOUNDER'S RESERVE (★★★★★): Well-oaked, with prominent vanilla and toasty, buttery notes, but also a rich, high-extract core of fruit. Delicious.
1996: Intense, supple and complex, with a creamy texture and ripe, rich pear, fig, melon and apricot flavors. **93**
1995: Ripe, elegant and complex, with a wonderful array of pear, apple, citrus and hazelnut flavors. **92**
1994: Bold, ripe, rich and complex, offering tiers of fig, pear, apple and honeysuckle notes and toasty hazelnut flavors. **92**

CHARDONNAY NAPA VALLEY HOPE'S CUVÉE (★★★★★)
1996: A complex mouthful of Chardonnay, with toasty fig, pear, melon, apricot and hazelnut flavors that fan out

and gain nuance and depth on the finish. **92**

1995: Bold, concentrated, and brimming with layers of ripe, rich fig, pear, citrus and buttery hazelnut flavors. **93**

PETITE SIRAH NAPA VALLEY (★★★): Packed with rich, supple fruit in a style that's most appealing. The 1996 (88 points) was dark, dense and chewy; from 110-year-old vines.

PINOT NOIR CARNEROS LAS AMIGAS VINEYARD (★★★): Improving, showing more depth and polish.

1996: Smooth, ripe, rich and complex, with plush black cherry, wild berry and vanilla nuances. This wine is impressive for its focused, bright flavors. **89**

1995: Serves up ripe cherry, strawberry, earth, tea and spice, along with some firm, chewy tannins. **88**

1994: Ripe, bright and lively, with attractive plum, cherry and wild berry notes that turn simple on the finish. **85**

1991: Has pungent, spicy aromas and delivers ripe fruit flavors that pick up vanilla from oak, turning complex. **87**

1990: Pungent minty flavors dominate the light, spicy plum notes. **82**

1989: Mint, dill and pickle flavors overshadow the plum and cherry notes. Has lots of oak and tannin, too, making for a heavy-handed, rustic wine. **78**

1988: A ripe, stylish wine that emphasizes spicy vanilla flavors from aging in new oak barrels. **85**

SAUVIGNON BLANC NAPA VALLEY (★★★): Oak again plays a prominent role, giving a buttery edge to the herb and grassy varietal notes.

SÉMILLON NAPA VALLEY (★★★): Very consistent and well made in a full-blown, oaky style.

SYRAH NAPA VALLEY (★★★)

1996: A solid, beefy style, with ripe, stewed plum, sage, anise and berry notes; finishes with firm, dry tannins and a good length. **88**

ZINFANDEL NAPA VALLEY (★★★): The 1990 was lean and austere, lacking the supple character of the other reds.

SILVER OAK CELLARS (★★★★)
Napa Valley & Alexander Valley
Founded: 1972. **Owner:** Justin Meyer & Ray Duncan.
Winemaker: Daniel Baron.

MAJOR WINES: PRICE, CASES, RATING

Cabernet Sauvignon Alexander Valley ($45, 39,000)	★★★★
Cabernet Sauvignon Napa Valley ($50, 11,000)	★★★★
Cabernet Sauvignon Napa Valley Bonny's Vineyard (Discontinued)	★★★★★

WINERY DATA
Case Production: 50,000. **Acres Owned:** 215 acres (200 in Alexander Valley, 15 in Napa Valley). **Varietals by Acre:** Cabernet Sauvignon (215 acres). **Varietals Purchased:** Cabernet Sauvignon (Napa Valley).

When Justin Meyer and Raymond Duncan founded Silver Oak Cellars in 1972, few would have predicted it would become one of California's most successful—and probably most profitable—wineries. Meyer, a former member of the Christian Brothers order, and Duncan, a Colorado oilman, focused solely on 100 percent Cabernet Sauvignon, and initially used only Alexander Valley grapes despite being based in Oakville, Napa Valley since 1982. By 1979, Silver Oak had added two more Cabernets, one a Napa Valley bottling, primarily from Calistoga-area grapes, and a second from Meyer's own vineyard, Bonny's in Oakville, which was named after his wife; it has since been discontinued. Total production is 50,000 cases from 215 winery-owned acres. Despite that the winery holds onto its wines for five years, they sell out almost instantly at high prices.

Meyer's philosophy is simple: his wines should be ready to drink and enjoy on release, so he polishes the tannins with extended barrel aging (mostly American oak at a fraction of the cost for French) and ages the wines in the bottle as well. The Alexander Valley Cabernet is laced with herb and cedary oak flavors, and showcases that appellation's smooth tannins. The Napa Valley Cabernet is round and harmonious, often a shade richer and more structured. Because of their distinctive features, Silver Oak wines have their critics, but consumers speak loud and clear that this is a wine style they love. What's surprising is that for all Silver Oak's success, few wineries have tried to mirror its style. The winery is experimenting with French oak, and adding small portions of Merlot and Cabernet Franc to its Cabernets, a good sign that no one is complacent or unwilling to try new tricks.

TASTING NOTES

CABERNET SAUVIGNON ALEXANDER VALLEY (★★★★): Supple, complex and well-oaked, with strong cedar, vanilla and herbal streaks, but also a wealth of rich, polished currant-laced fruit and supple tannins. Drinks well on release and ages nicely up to 10 years and beyond. Among best and most consistent Alexander Valley Cabernets.

1994: Combines ripe, rich complex anise, currant, sage and cedary notes that are both supple and harmonious. **89**

1993: Complex, with ripe currant, plum and cedary oak flavors that are somewhat chunky and drying. **90**

1992: Smooth and polished, with well focused cherry, plum and currant flavors wrapped in a firm dose of dill-scented oak. **90**

1991: Lavishly oaked, rich and harmonious, with an herb and dill edge to the currant and berry fruit. **91**

1990: An herbal wine with a peppery dill edge, turning smooth and supple and finishing with plum and cherry notes and soft tannins. **89**

1989: Soft and fleshy, with herb, currant, plum and earth notes on the finish. **82**

1988: Stylish, rich and complex, with classy, smoky oak notes adding to the dense, chewy core of currant and herb flavors. **88**

1987: Intense and concentrated, with notes of exotic, spicy cedar and sage paired with currant, vanilla, berry, anise and tar flavors. **91**

1986: Smooth and supple, with spicy mineral, currant, anise and cedar flavors and a long, plummy aftertaste. **92**

1985: Enormously rich, complex and concentrated, with layers of ripe, fleshy, intense plum, currant, cedar and anise flavors that are lively and elegant. **91**

1984: Complex and supple, with cedar, vanilla, cherry and plum flavors that are fresh and lively. **89**

1983: Rich, supple and tannic, with earthy currant and cedar flavors. **85**

1982: Still tight, lean and tannic, with a cedary edge to the plum and currant notes. **88**

1981: A ripe, supple, complex 1981 with distinctive green olive and ripe plum flavors, turning mature. **86**

1980: Very ripe, almost jammy and Port-like in aroma, this is a deeply concentrated wine packed with mature, earthy plum, currant and spicy jam notes that are full-bodied. **88**

1979: Elegant and complex, with tart black cherry, currant and cedar flavors that are backed by fine, firm tannins. **85**

1978: Fading, with just a glimmer of herb, cherry and currant notes; nuances of spicy American oak appear on the finish. **86**

1977: Ripe, rich and supple, with complex plum, currant and cedary oak flavors that are bright and lively. **88**

1976: Has peaked, with deep, rich and drying cherry, chocolate and earth notes. **84**

1975: Mature but still elegant and refined, with spicy cherry and plum flavors that turn supple and a touch earthy. **88**

1974: Fully mature and light in color, with smoky currant and stewed plum flavors that turn smooth and soft on the finish. **84**

1973: Still quite oaky, with the mature Cabernet flavors fading. **80**

1972: Still impressive, with earthy, mature cherry, cedar and smoky anise flavors. **83**

CABERNET SAUVIGNON NAPA VALLEY (★★★★): Similar in style to the Alexander Valley bottling, but shows Napa's structure and deeper tannic strength. Complex and ageworthy.

1994: Complex and sophisticated, with layers of concentrated currant, herb, coffee, sage, mineral and spice flavors. **91**

1993: Starts out woody, but there are chewy currant and plummy flavors that fill in the gaps and give this wine dimension. **88**

1992: Big, ripe and oaky, with rich flavors to match.

Loaded with currant, plum and wild berry flavors and framed by notes of smoky, toasty oak. **93**

1991: Big, ripe, dark and intense, with complex, ripe cherry, currant and meaty notes and a hint of dusty oak. **90**

1990: A complex marriage of cedar and dill flavors with accents of tart cherry, berry and tar. **89**

1989: Complex and supple, with ripe prune and chocolate flavors that turn to herb and spice. **86**

1988: Round in texture, with tightly wrapped cherry, tobacco and anise flavors extending into a long finish, hinting at toast and spice. **88**

1987: Starts out earthy, with hints of currant and berry and a metallic edge to the tannins. **87**

1986: Beautifully crafted, firm and rich, with complex currant and dill flavors that are rich, powerful and long on the finish. **92**

1985: Tight, firm and tannic, with an accent of herb and dill and a richly focused core of currant, cherry and berry flavors. **88**

1984: Rich, with a core of black cherry, herb, dill and spice flavors that turn supple and complex. **87**

1983: Lean and light, with a vegetal edge to the currant flavors, turning tannic. **74**

1982: Mature now but still impressive for its cherry and currant flavors accented by spicy oak notes. **86**

1981: Lavishly oaked, perhaps to a fault. The fruit struggles to compete. **79**

1980: Marked by tar and vegetal flavors of modest appeal. **73**

1979: Still hard and drying, with the plum and herb flavors turning earthy. **81**

CABERNET SAUVIGNON NAPA VALLEY BONNY'S VINEYARD (★★★★★): Dropped after the 1991 vintage, which is too bad; it had really come into its own.

1991: Dark, rich and complex, with tiers of polished currant, cherry, herb, dill and tea flavors that are well integrated. **93**

1990: Exotic oak, mineral and Cabernet flavors are expanded by dill, ripe plum, cherry and herbal nuances. **91**

1987: Shows a wonderful complexity and density of flavor, with layers of smoky currant, coffee, plum, cherry, cedar, dill and oak flavors. **95**

1986: A delicious treat. Ripe, rich and complex, with tiers of smoke, toasty oak, ripe plum, cherry and berry flavors, turning exotic and spicy on the finish. **94**

1985: Showing tremendous improvement, having evolved into a richer, fuller, fruitier wine with plush, racy

black cherry, currant and anise flavors. **90**

1984: Marked by supple, complex green olive, plum and spicy tobacco notes along with bell pepper flavors that are deep and long. **84**

1983: A lighter wine that's mature, with the signature herb, dill and currant notes. **82**

1981: Mature and fading, with a decadent edge to the cherry and spice flavors. **77**

1980: Marked by pungent vegetal, pickle and green chili pepper flavors. **73**

1979: Potent pickle, chili pepper and vegetable flavors fail to make it into the fruit zone. **72**

SILVERADO CELLARS see CHATEAU MONTELENA WINERY

SILVERADO VINEYARDS (★★★–★★★★★)
Stags Leap District, Napa Valley
Founded: 1981. **Owner:** Ron & Diane Miller. **Winemaker:** John Stuart.

MAJOR WINES: PRICE, CASES, RATING

Cabernet Sauvignon Napa Valley ($25, 12,500)	★★★
Cabernet Sauvignon Napa Valley Limited Reserve ($65, NA)	★★★★★
Chardonnay Napa Valley ($19, 32,000)	★★★
Chardonnay Napa Valley Limited Reserve ($36, NA)	★★★★
Merlot Napa Valley ($23, 12,000)	★★★
Sangiovese Napa Valley ($20, 4,000)	★★
Sauvignon Blanc Napa Valley ($12, 24,000)	★★★

WINERY DATA
Case Production: 85,000. **Acres Owned:** 345 acres in the Napa Valley. **Varietals by Acre:** Cabernet Franc (9 acres), Cabernet Sauvignon (107), Chardonnay (105), Merlot (60), Sangiovese (18), Sauvignon Blanc (40), Sémillion (2), Zinfandel (4).

Silverado Vineyards is owned by the family of the late Walt Disney. After purchasing this large property on Silverado Trail in the Stags Leap District in 1976, Lillian Disney and her family planted grapes and began winemaking in 1981, and have been producing excellent wines ever since. The winery owns 345 acres, dominated by Cabernet and Chardonnay, from which it produces 85,000 cases. Chardonnay is the volume leader, followed by Sauvignon Blanc, Cabernet and Merlot, all modestly priced given their quality. John Stuart has been winemaker since the start, and has steadily improved the wines' quality, as well as achieving new heights with the Limited Reserve Cabernet and Chardonnay, both of which are extraordinary. While all the wines are well made, the reds hold a slight edge in quality. The Sangiovese bottling is the only wine that seems to lack focus.

TASTING NOTES

CABERNET SAUVIGNON NAPA VALLEY (★★★): Bright, lively and well focused, with complex cherry, currant and olive notes and supple tannins. A shade less complex and compelling of late.

1995: Despite a hint of green bean, there's enough cherry, plum and berry fruit to sustain this one. **87**

1993: Well crafted, with attractive herb, cherry and currant flavors and firm tannins. **87**

1992: Firm and rich, with complex cherry, anise, currant and cedary oak flavors. Young, intense and tannic, but in need of short-term cellaring. **90**

1991: Bright and lively, ripe and richly concentrated, with focused cherry, berry and currant flavors, finishing with firm tannins. **93**

1990: Smooth, polished and elegant, offering complex plum, currant, spice and vanilla aromas and flavors that are smoothly blended, ending with supple tannins. **90**

1989: Soft and simple, with a stalky edge to the modest currant and chocolate flavors. **81**

1988: Ripe and full-bodied, with a slightly weedy edge to the plum, black cherry and blackberry fruit. **87**

1987: Ripe, round and lively, brimming with spicy strawberry and currant flavors, turning smooth, elegant and complex. **90**

1986: Nicely balanced, with complex, youthful currant, anise and cherry flavors and supple tannins. **88**

1985: Beautifully styled, elegant and supple, with rich currant, black cherry, raspberry and vanilla flavors and buttery nuances on the finish. **89**

1984: Mature, with an earthy, decadent edge to the currant, plum and cherry flavors, but it delivers a lot of flavor. **88**

1983: This wine has peaked. It remains tannic, but still delivers lots of flavor, with a core of chunky cassis, currant and black cherry flavors. **85**

1982: Fully mature and a shade past its prime, with earthy cherry, oak, chocolate and mint flavors that turn decadent on the finish. **84**

1981: Past its peak now but still pleasing, with a complex array of mature Cabernet flavors. **84**

CABERNET SAUVIGNON NAPA VALLEY LIMITED RESERVE (★★★★★): Uncommon richness, depth and concentration; lavishly oaked but beautifully proportioned. Drinks well early and has a sense of harmony. Ages well. No 1992 was produced.

1995: A bold, dramatic wine, packed with rich, complex nuances of currant, black cherry, plum, anise and spice, and hints of tar, cedar, sage and vanilla. **95**

1994: Dramatic, bold, ripe, rich and concentrated; gushing with minty currant, black cherry, plum and wild berry flavors. **93**

1993: Offers a tight band of herb, currant and cherry flavors and a dash of toasty oak; turns tannic and complex on the finish. **90**

1991: Another stunner; dark, ripe, rich and complex with a wide range of black cherry, plum and currant flavors, framed by toasty, buttery oak and a long complex finish. **95**

1990: Beautifully crafted, ripe, rich and complex, with currant, black cherry, cedar, vanilla and spice flavors that unfold to reveal wonderful depth and uncommon complexities. **97**

1987: Exotic and rich in flavor, texture and body, with layered notes of ripe currant, black cherry, anise, mint, sage and tea. **96**

1986: Plush and generous, with rich, sharply focused, delicious cherry, plum, currant, oak and spice flavors that are tight and concentrated. **96**

CHARDONNAY NAPA VALLEY (★★★): Features lots of ripe fruit flavors and pretty oak shadings.

CHARDONNAY NAPA VALLEY LIMITED RESERVE (★★★★): Enormously complex and concentrated, with lots of rich fruit and oak in a dramatic style, though it's inconsistent and at times too lean.

1996: Distinct for its clean, tangy core of pineapple, apple and spicy citrus notes, but it's not as bold as past efforts have shown. **88**

1995: Elegant and complex, with a band of smoky oak, ripe pear, fig and melon and lots of spicy nuances. **88**
1994: Smooth, rich and harmonious, with layers of ripe fig, melon, pear and toasty oak, turning elegant and complex on the finish. **93**

MERLOT NAPA VALLEY (★★★): Typically firm and well focused, with attractive fruit flavors, mild tannins and early drinking appeal.

MERLOT NAPA VALLEY LIMITED RESERVE
1992: Supple and fruity, with bright, lively, juicy cherry and currant fruit, picking up a trace of herb and chocolate on the finish. **89**

SAUVIGNON BLANC NAPA VALLEY (★★★): Strikes a fine balance between herb, fruit and light oak shadings. The 1997 (87 points) was right on target with its passion fruit and citrus flavors.

SIMI WINERY (★★★–★★★★)
Alexander Valley, Sonoma County
Founded: 1876. **Owner:** Canandaigua Wines **Winemaker:** Nick Goldschmidt.

MAJOR WINES: PRICE, CASES, RATING

Cabernet Sauvignon Alexander Valley ($22, 35,000)	★★★
Cabernet Sauvignon Alexander Valley Reserve ($40, 4,000)	★★★★
Chardonnay Carneros ($21, 6,000)	★★★★
Chardonnay Sonoma County ($18, 80,000)	★★★
Chardonnay Sonoma County Reserve ($29, 3,500)	★★★★
Pinot Noir Carneros ($18, 700)	★★
Sauvignon Blanc Sonoma County ($12, 20,000)	★★★
Sendal White Sonoma County ($16, 1,100)	★★★
Shiraz Alexander Valley ($17, 300)	★★★

WINERY DATA
Case Production: 175,000. **Acres Owned:** 227 acres (127 in Alexander Valley, 100 in Russian River Valley). **Varietals by Acre:** Cabernet Franc (17 acres), Cabernet Sauvignon (99), Chardonnay (95), Merlot (13), Petit Verdot (3). **Varietals Purchased:** Cabernet Franc (Alexander Valley, Sonoma Mountain), Cabernet Sauvignon (Alexander Valley, Sonoma Mountain), Chardonnay (Carneros, Mendocino, Russian River Valley), Merlot (Alexander Valley, Dry Creek), Muscat Canelli (Dry Creek), Petite Sirah (Alexander Valley, Clarksburg), Pinot Noir (Carneros, Russian River Valley), Sauvignon Blanc (Alexander Valley, Carneros, Dry Creek, Knights Valley, Russian River Valley), Sémillon (Russian River Valley, Sonoma Valley), Syrah (Alexander Valley).

Simi was founded by the Simi family in 1876, and remained family-owned until 1969, when they were forced to sell. A series of ownership changes followed. In 1999, in an attempt to diversify their largely low-end bulk brand portfolio, Canandaigua Wines purchased Simi from Louis Vuitton Moët Hennessy for $55 million.

Simi draws on its 227 acres of estate vineyards, including 100 acres in Russian River Valley and 127 acres in Alexander Valley, but it also relies on purchased grapes. Cabernet (35,000 cases) and Chardonnay (80,000 cases) are the volume leaders, with smaller lots of Reserve wines for both. Quality has been high, as have expectations—many of which have been realized, especially for the Reserve Chardonnay, which is remarkably complex and ageworthy. The Cabernets of the 1990s have also begun to meet expectations; the Reserve bottling is particularly inspiring. The winery's newly planted Cabernet vineyard is now in production, and winemaker Nick Goldschmidt clearly has a handle on quality and style. Some new varieties have been introduced, including Pinot Noir, Shiraz and Zinfandel. Many wines are worth buying; others are worth watching.

TASTING NOTES

CABERNET SAUVIGNON ALEXANDER VALLEY (★★★): No longer so variable; usually very good, bordering on outstanding. It is elegant and complex, well proportioned and built for mid-range cellaring of between four and six years.
1995: Smooth, ripe and polished, with lots of pretty plum, currant, black cherry and spicy flavors, turning supple on the finish. **89**
1994: Tight and tannic, with a core of currant, herb, tea and leather flavors working its way to the forefront. **88**

1993: Smooth and polished, this wine is appealing for its ripe plum and cherry flavors and supple tannins. **88**

1992: Ripe and plush, with rich, supple, earthy currant and cherry flavors and firm, chewy tannins. **89**

1989: Tough and tannic, with earthy barnyard and leather flavors that override the modest berry notes. **77**

1988: Firm and focused, with a nice core of currant and berry flavors. **84**

1987: Rich, complex and enticing, with intense, well integrated cherry, toast, currant, plum and chocolate flavors. **89**

1986: This compact and concentrated wine delivers ripe currant and black cherry flavors. **85**

1985: Elegantly crafted, with sharply focused currant, cherry, herb and oak flavors folding together. **91**

1984: Smooth and supple, with bright cherry, cranberry and raspberry flavors and an elegant style. **86**

CABERNET SAUVIGNON ALEXANDER VALLEY RESERVE (★★★★): Now ranks as among Sonoma's best; consistently outstanding, with rich, polished flavors.

1994: Brilliant, ripe and complex, with earthy currant, herb, coffee, black cherry and spicy flavors and rich tannins. **93**

1992: Remarkably complex and concentrated, serving up lots of fresh cherry, currant, plum and berry flavors. **93**

1991: Supple and harmonious, with well focused cherry, currant, mineral and spice notes leading to firm tannins. **92**

1990: Centennial Edition: An earthy wine with just enough supple plum and cherry flavors to fight off the earthiness. **84**

1988: Clean, ripe and focused, with currant, black cherry, wild berry and cedary flavors. **87**

1987: Dark, ripe, rich and intense, with a solid core of currant, anise, berry and spice flavors; picks up a trace of cedary oak on the finish. **92**

1986: Supple and harmonious, with a complex range of herb, currant and berry flavors giving this wine finesse. **91**

1985: Dense, rich and complex, offering coffee, cherry, nutmeg, plum, herb and currant flavors, finishing with plush tannins. **90**

1984: Brimming with ripe currant, plum and spice flavors that turn supple, with modest tannins. **88**

1982: Lean and concentrated, with a tannic edge to the anise and plum flavors. **85**

1981: Smells and tastes mature, turning smoky and spicy on the finish. Drying up. **86**

1980: Oaky and tannic, very tight and backward, in danger of drying up. **80**

1979: Firm, oaky and still tannic, with mature, earthy berry, plum and spice components. **84**

Special Reserve 1974: Distinctive for its weedy, herbal edge, it is well past its peak, finishing on a spicy, tarry note. **82**

CHARDONNAY SONOMA COUNTY (★★★): Elegant and fruity; the complex oak adds dimension, but the fruit is the main focus.

CHARDONNAY SONOMA COUNTY RESERVE (★★★★): Among the state's elite, combining deep, ripe, rich and complex fruit flavors with pretty oak shadings. Ages exceptionally well. The winery holds the wine for two years for additional bottle age. Increasingly reliant on Russian River grapes.

1995: Smooth, ripe, rich and creamy, with pretty pear, vanilla, tangerine and spicy flavors that turn silky and complex on the finish. **93**

1994: Exotic for its range of fig, tropical fruit, melon, grapefruit and spice, showing elegance and finesse. **91**

SAUVIGNON BLANC SONOMA COUNTY (★★★): Strikes a nice balance between herb, citrus and pear-laced fruit and light oak notes.

SENDAL WHITE SONOMA COUNTY (★★★): Combines Sauvignon Blanc with a smaller dose of Sémillon, rendering a complex and understated wine.

SINE QUA NON (★★★)
Los Angeles County
Founded: 1994. **Owner:** Elaine & Manfred Krankl. **Winemaker:** Manfred Krankl.

MAJOR WINES: PRICE, CASES, RATING

Red Central Coast ($31, 700) ★★★★

White Central Coast Alban Vineyard ($31, 600) ★★★

ALSO PRODUCED
Pinot Noir Oregon Shea Vineyard ($31, 1000); Red Central Coast Rosé ($18, 100).

WINERY DATA
Case Production: 1,500. **Vineyard Designations:** Shea Vineyard, Alban Vineyard. **Varietals Purchased:** Chardonnay (Central Coast), Grenache (Santa Barbara), Pinot Noir (Oregon), Roussanne (Central Coast), Syrah (Central Coast, Santa Barbara).

Los Angeles restaurateur Manfred Krankl—a co-owner of Campanile and La Brea Bakery—and his wife, Elaine, started Sine Qua Non in 1994, making their wine from purchased grapes. Today, Krankl continues to purchase all of his grapes from a variety of ever-changing sources, but has found a comfortable focus on Central Coast Rhône varietals. Taking an irreverent approach to marketing his wines, Krankl gives every wine a new name upon release, creates all of the labels himself, and bottles the wines in absurdly heavy, oddly shaped bottles.

The wines are as distinctive and impressive as the packaging: dense and rich, with complex varietal flavors and lots of oak. His first release, a 1994 Syrah Queen of Spades (92 points), featured deep, dark, ripe fruit flavors, while remaining elegant and supple. The 1995 Chardonnay-Roussanne blend called The Bride (92) was exotic, with bright passion fruit, citrus, fig and melon flavors. A 1995 Grenache, Syrah and Mourvèdre blend called Red Handed showed rich, concentrated flavors of wild berry, plum and mineral. Thus far, the only stumble was the 1995 Syrah called The Other Hand (84), which showed meaty, earthy flavors and excessive oak.

ROBERT SINSKEY VINEYARDS
(★★–★★★)
Stags Leap District, Napa Valley
Founded: 1986. **Owner:** Robert Sinskey. **Winemaker:** Jeff Virnig. **Second Label:** Aries, Solstice, Zinskey.

MAJOR WINES: PRICE, CASES, RATING
Chardonnay Carneros
($24, 1,000) ★★★
Claret Stags Leap District
($33, 1,200) ★★★
Merlot Carneros
($22, 3,500) ★★★
Merlot Carneros Reserve
($33, 1,500) ★★★
Pinot Noir Carneros
($24, 6,100) ★★
Pinot Noir Carneros Reserve
($40, 1,000) ★★

ALSO PRODUCED
Cabernet Franc Carneros ($20, 500); Vin Gris Carneros ($16, 500); Zinfandel Carneros ($22, 100).

WINERY DATA
Case Production: 20,000. **Acres Owned:** 147 acres (142 in Carneros, 5 in Stags Leap District). **Varietals by Acre:** Cabernet Franc (6 acres), Cabernet Sauvignon (15), Chardonnay (10), Merlot (53), Pinot Blanc (3.5), Pinot Noir (59), Zinfandel (0.4).

Eye surgeon Robert Sinskey was a founding partner at Acacia and acquired a 35-acre Carneros vineyard before Acacia was sold to the Chalone Wine Group. After the sale, Sinskey purchased the property on the Silverado Trail where the current Sinskey winery stands. The winery owns 142 acres in Carneros, dominated by Pinot Noir and Merlot, along with five acres in Stags Leap; Cabernet Sauvignon and Pinot Blanc are among the most recent additions to the vineyards. The goal is to be an all-estate-bottled winery. Aries, the winery's second label, offers good value in Merlot and Pinot Noir.

TASTING NOTES

CHARDONNAY CARNEROS (★★★): Made in a tart, tight style, with crisp, intense fruit that's typical of Carneros.

CLARET STAGS LEAP DISTRICT (★★★): Occasionally shows signs it's getting closer to outstanding, but it still doesn't measure up to the valley's best.
1994: Dense, with earthy, chewy currant, mineral and leathery flavors and tarry, smoky notes. **88**
1993: A tight, crisp, firm young wine, with a solid core of spicy currant, anise, sage and herb flavors, turning tannic on the finish. **89**
1990: Tight, firm and focused, with cedar, ripe cherry, plum and wild berry flavors that turn supple on the finish. **87**
1989: Tight and intense, with deep, focused currant and spice flavors held in check by firm tannins and crisp acidity. **88**
1988: Tight and firm, with hard-edged currant and oak flavors. It's 59 percent Cabernet Sauvignon, 22 percent Merlot and 19 percent Cabernet Franc. **83**

MERLOT CARNEROS RESERVE (★★★): Less variable of late, and while it can be elegant and harmonious it lacks extra elements of depth and complexity.

PINOT NOIR CARNEROS RESERVE (★★): Variable, lacking the extra facets found in many of the best Carneros Pinots.

SKEWIS WINES (★★)
Sonoma County
Founded: 1994. **Owner:** Hank Skewis. **Winemaker:** Hank Skewis.

MAJOR WINES: PRICE, CASES, RATING
Pinot Noir Anderson Valley
  Floodgate Vineyard
  ($29, 240)   ★★

ALSO PRODUCED
Pinot Noir Russian River Valley Montgomery Vineyard ($31, 100).

WINERY DATA
Case Production: 500. **Vineyard Designations:** Floodgate Vineyard, Montgomery Vineyard. **Varietals Purchased:** Pinot Noir (Anderson Valley, Russian River Valley), Syrah (Russian River Valley).

Hank Skewis, winemaker for Mill Creek (see entry) started his eponymous winery in 1994 with Sonoma County Pinot Noir. Syrah and two new Pinot Noirs have been added to the portfolio. The 1996 Pinot Noir Floodgate Vineyard (87 points) showed smooth, ripe cherry and mushroom flavors, turning tart and focused on the finish.

SMITH & HOOK (★★)
Monterey County
Founded: 1974. **Owner:** Nicky and Gaby Hahn. **Winemaker:** Art Nathan. **Second Label:** Hahn Estates.

MAJOR WINES: PRICE, CASES, RATING
Cabernet Sauvignon Santa Lucia Highlands
  ($18, 8,000)   ★★
Cabernet Sauvignon Santa Lucia Highlands
  Masterpiece Edition
  ($40, 850)   ★★

Merlot Santa Lucia Highlands
  ($19, 10,000)   ★★
Viognier Arroyo Seco
  ($18, 850)   ★★

ALSO PRODUCED
Chardonnay Arroyo Seco Masterpiece Edition ($25, 850).

WINERY DATA
Case Production: 20,000. **Acres Owned:** 936 acres (293 in Arroyo Seco, 643 in Santa Lucia Highlands). **Varietals by Acre:** Cabernet Franc (75 acres), Cabernet Sauvignon (170), Chardonnay (310), Malbec (3), Merlot (280), Viognier (21), other (77).

Smith and Hook, the marriage of two large vineyards, owns 936 acres of grapevines, including a beautifully terraced 250-acre parcel west of Highway 101 near Soledad. The winery's focus is on Bordeaux-style reds based on Cabernet and Merlot. The reds tend to be rustic and austerely structured, with earthy plum, cherry and herbal flavors. The 1994 Cabernet (85 points) had unusual but pleasant smoky, bacon-like flavors as well as mint, anise and black currant. The 1995 Merlot (83) showed tart cranberry and raspberry flavors.

The second label, Hahn Estates, is a 100,000-case brand under which owners Nicky and Gaby Hahn also produce Cabernet, Merlot and Chardonnay, which are of average quality.

W.H. SMITH WINES (★★–★★★)
Sonoma Coast
Founded: 1992. **Owner:** Bill and Joan Smith. **Winemaker:** Bill Smith. **Second Label:** Little Billy.

MAJOR WINES: PRICE, CASES, RATING
Pinot Noir Sonoma Coast
  ($26, 600)   ★★
Pinot Noir Sonoma Coast Hellenthal
  Vineyard
  ($36, 600)   ★★★

ALSO PRODUCED
Pinot Noir Sonoma Coast Little Billy ($18, 300).

WINERY DATA
Case Production: 1,200. **Vineyard Designations:** Hellenthal
Vineyard (Pinot Noir). **Varietals Purchased:** Pinot Noir
(Sonoma Coast).

La Jota founders Bill and Joan Smith own 360 acres
in the Sonoma Coast appellation, where they plan to
begin planting a small, densely-spaced vineyard focusing
on Pinot Noir. To date, their W.H. Smith Pinot from the
Hellenthal Vineyard has been variable, with one terrific
effort in 1995.

TASTING NOTES

PINOT NOIR SONOMA COAST (★★)
1997: Light in color and weight, with herbal cherry, wild
berry and simple spicy notes, finishing with tame tannins. **85**
1996: Light and uncomplicated, with modest tea and
wild berry flavors. **79**

**PINOT NOIR SONOMA COAST HELLENTHAL VINEYARD
(★★★):** Highly variable: dark and plush one year, very
light the next.
1997: Firm, with cedary oak flavors overriding the core
of herb-laced black cherry and forest floor-type flavors,
turning tannic. **86**
1996: Light in color, with plum and berry notes of modest concentration and complexity. Turns simple on the
finish. **84**
1995: Smooth, ripe, rich and flavorful, with a supple,
elegant core of ripe cherry, plum, wild berry and nutmeg
flavors, finishing with a cola and chocolate aftertaste. **93**

SNOWDEN (★★★★)
Rutherford, Napa Valley
Founded: 1993. **Owner:** Snowden Family. **Winemaker:**
John Gibson.

MAJOR WINES: PRICE, CASES, RATING
Cabernet Sauvignon Napa Valley
($35, 385)   ★★★★

WINERY DATA
Case Production: 1,200. **Acres Owned:** 22 acres in
Rutherford. **Varietals by Acre:** Cabernet Franc (0.75 acres),
Cabernet Sauvignon (18), Merlot (3), Petit Verdot (0.25).

The Snowden family bought and planted this hillside
property east of Napa Valley proper behind the Joseph
Phelps Vineyards winery in the 1950s. For years the
grapes were sold to Caymus, Stag's Leap Wine Cellars,
Kendall-Jackson and Silver Oak. The winery is now
owned by Scott Snowden, a Napa County Superior Court
judge, his wife, Joann Ortega of Ortega Design in St.
Helena (who has designed wine labels for Guenoc, Simi,
Forman and Marilyn Merlot, among others), and
Snowden's brother Randy and his wife Janet.

Snowden Vineyards is planted primarily to Cabernet
Sauvignon, but also has a few acres of Merlot, Cabernet
Franc and Petit Verdot, and there are plans to add another
seven acres of Cabernet. Initial releases were very impressive, making this a winery worthy of collecting.

TASTING NOTES

CABERNET SAUVIGNON NAPA VALLEY (★★★★): These
are immensely concentrated, structured wines that will
need several years to show their full potential. Still, the
raw ingredients are there for greatness, and it may only
be a matter of time before these wines merit a five-star
rating.
1994: Tough, tight and austere, with concentrated plum
and cherry flavors that are submerged in tannin. **91**
1993: Deep, rich and concentrated, with layers of earthy
currant, spice, cedar and berry flavors and notes of
smoky oak. **92**

SOBON ESTATE (★★)
Shenandoah Valley, El Dorado County
Founded: 1856. **Owner:** Leon & Shirley Sobon.
Winemaker: Leon Sobon.

MAJOR WINES: PRICE, CASES, RATING
Roussanne California Shenandoah Valley
($15, 600)   ★★★
Syrah California Shenandoah Valley
($12, 1,000)   ★★
Zinfandel California Shenandoah Valley
Cougar Hill
($15, 1,000)   ★★

Zinfandel California Shenandoah Valley
Rocky Top
($15, 1,500) ★★
Zinfandel Fiddletown Lubenko Vineyard
($15, 1,000) ★★

ALSO PRODUCED
Rosé California Shenandoah Valley ($9, 500); Viognier
California Shenandoah Valley ($15, 1,400).

WINERY DATA
Case Production: 7,200. **Acres Owned:** 87 acres in
Shenandoah Valley. **Varietals by Acre:** Barbera (10 acres),
Carignane (2 acres), Primitivo (8.5), Roussanne (2.5)
Sangiovese (4), Syrah (2.5), Zinfandel (57.5). **Vineyard
Designations:** Lubenko Vineyard (Zinfandel).

In 1989, Leon and Shirley Sobon bought the old, run-
down D'Agostini Winery (founded in 1856) in the
Shenandoah Valley and began replanting the vineyards
and restoring the winery, which they renamed Sobon
Estate. Zinfandel and Rhône varietals are the focus here.
While the wines are often very good, they are just as
likely to be lower than average in quality. Recent vintages of Syrah have varied from the funky 1995 (80
points) to the complex 1996 (87), which featured ripe
blackberry, anise and herb flavors. Zinfandel makes wild
swings too, from the 1995 Fiddletown (88), which was
concentrated and tarry with raspberry, earth and mineral
flavors, to the 1996 Fiddletown (78), with its austere,
unripe fruit flavors. The 1996 Zinfandel Shenandoah
Valley Cougar Hill (78) was another weak effort, showing a modest core of fruit flavors, but turning dry and
tannic, while the 1996 Zinfandel Rocky Top (88) was
balanced and concentrated, with wild berry, sage and
mineral flavors and tarry, smoky nuances.

SOLSTICE see **ROBERT SINSKEY VINEYARDS**

SONOMA-CUTRER VINEYARDS (★★★)
Sonoma Coast
Founded: 1973. **Owner:** Brown-Forman Corp.
Winemaker: Terry Adams.

MAJOR WINES: PRICE, CASES, RATING
Chardonnay Sonoma Coast Les Pierres
($29, 5,000) ★★★
Chardonnay Sonoma Coast Russian River
Ranches
($17, 75,000) ★★★
Chardonnay Sonoma Coast The Cutrer
Vineyard
($29, 7,000) ★★★★

ALSO PRODUCED
Chardonnay Sonoma Coast Founders Reserve ($69, 164).

WINERY DATA
Case Production: 150,000. **Acres Owned:** 1,000 acres in
Sonoma Coast. **Varietals by Acre:** Chardonnay (1,000 acres).

Sonoma-Cutrer Vineyards began in 1973 as a grape-
growing business, but by the early 1980s operations had
shifted to winemaking, with the highly regarded Bill
Bonetti overseeing production of three different
Chardonnay bottlings designed for long-term aging. The
winery has stuck with Chardonnay, and owns some 1,000
acres in vines, ranging from Russian River Valley to
Carneros (Les Pierres).

Sonoma-Cutrer is known for its ultra-modern, state-
of-the-art winemaking facility. Despite early successes in
the mid-1980s, quality has tapered off in recent vintages
as production has risen to 150,000 cases. Given all that is
done to achieve perfection, complexity and ageworthiness, Sonoma-Cutrer's Chardonnays age only moderately
well. By the early 1990s, the winery had re-evaluated its
entire philosophy, from vineyard to barrel. Having taken
a much closer look at what's done in Burgundy—and
why—they've concluded that the winery's style, which
involves no malolactic fermentation, needs an overhaul,
or at the least a retooling.

In 1999, Brown-Forman, the global drinks firm that
owns Jack Daniel's and Fetzer Vineyards, among others,
bought a controlling interest in the winery.

TASTING NOTES

CHARDONNAY SONOMA COAST LES PIERRES (★★★): A star in the 1980s, but a victim of phylloxera after 1988. Les Pierres, "the stones" in French, is a single vineyard wine that takes its name from the stony, rocky soil that usually shows up in the wines as a stony, flinty, mineral character. The vineyard was replanted in the early 1990s.
1996: Intense, ripe and concentrated, with a flinty, earthy edge to the core of pear, anise and mineral notes, turning elegant. **89**
1995: Crisp and intense, with a flinty band of pear, hazelnut, light oak and spice flavors, gaining complexity on the finish. **89**
1994: Elegant and refined, with a flinty citrus edge to the tart pear and light spicy notes, turning delicate on the finish. **88**
1991: A subtle, flinty style with mature pear, spice, honey and light toast shadings that pick up a citrus edge. **88**
1990: Crisp and flinty, with spicy pear, apple and nutmeg flavors that offer a hint of maturity. Stays lean and focused through the finish. **87**

CHARDONNAY SONOMA COAST RUSSIAN RIVER RANCHES (★★★): This wine comes from a trio of winery-owned vineyards. It's usually ripe and fruity, with light oak shadings. A good value.
1997: Tight and crisp, with a flinty edge to the narrow band of pear, spice and apricot flavors, it slowly unfolds to reveal more nuance and complexity. **90**
1996: Intense and spicy, with a core of fruit built around racy citrus and pineapple flavors. **89**
1995: Bright, fresh and lively, with a pretty interplay of ripe pear, citrus, melon and spicy notes and light, toasty oak. **90**

CHARDONNAY SONOMA COAST THE CUTRER VINEYARD (★★★★): The steadiest performer of late, it is ripe and intense, with crisp pear and peach-laced fruit.
1995: Intense, lively, rich and concentrated, with shadings of anise, pear, hazelnut and light vanilla. **90**
1994: Smooth, ripe, rich and creamy; loaded with fig, pear, melon and butterscotch notes, gaining complexity on the finish. **92**

SONOMA-LOEB (★★★★)
Sonoma County
Founded: 1990. **Owner:** John L. Loeb Jr. **Winemaker:** Philip Titus.

MAJOR WINES: PRICE, CASES, RATING
Chardonnay Sonoma County
  ($20, 3,200) ★★★★
Chardonnay Sonoma County Private Reserve
  ($35, 800) ★★★★

WINERY DATA
Case Production: 5,000. **Acres Owned:** 116 acres (47 in Alexander Valley, 69 in Russian River Valley). **Varietals by Acre:** Cabernet Sauvignon, Chardonnay, Pinot Noir. **Varietals Purchased:** Chardonnay (Sonoma).

John Loeb, Jr., a former U.S. ambassador to Denmark, bought land in Sonoma County as a tax shelter in the 1970s. He picked good Chardonnay turf, settling next to Robert Young Vineyards in Alexander Valley; he also owns another vineyard in the Russian River Valley near Davis Bynum Winery. Loeb sold his grapes to Fetzer, Clos du Bois and Piper-Sonoma before turning to winemaking himself, encouraged by Seagram Classics' Sam Bronfman II. The goal is to make Burgundian-style Chardonnays, and early results are encouraging.

TASTING NOTES

CHARDONNAY SONOMA COUNTY PRIVATE RESERVE (★★★★): Comes from vineyards in Alexander Valley and Russian River. The early wines were well oaked and richly fruity, with polished textures.
1996: Notes of toasty oak lead to a core of ripe pear, apple, fig and melon flavors that are elegant and deeply concentrated. **93**
1995: Smooth and spicy, with a silky texture and lots of pretty pear, spice, apricot and honey flavors that turn elegant on the finish. **92**

SOQUEL VINEYARDS (★★)

Santa Cruz Mountains
Founded: 1987. **Owner:** Peter & Paul Bargetto and Jon Morgan. **Winemaker:** Paul Bargetto and Jon Morgan.

MAJOR WINES: PRICE, CASES, RATING

Cabernet Sauvignon Santa Cruz Mountains Partners' Reserve ($40, 325)	★★
Chardonnay Santa Cruz Mountains ($20, 750)	★★★
Merlot Santa Cruz Mountains Partners' Reserve ($30, 275)	★★

ALSO PRODUCED
Syrah-Mataro Santa Cruz Mountains ($25, 51).

WINERY DATA
Case Production: 2,000. **Varietals Purchased:** Cabernet Sauvignon (Santa Cruz Mountains), Chardonnay (Santa Cruz Mountains), Merlot (Santa Cruz Mountains).

Paul and Peter Bargetto make Santa Cruz Mountains-appellation wines under their Soquel label. The wines are average in quality, with flavorful, firm, chewy but coarse Cabernets and Merlots, and ripe, tangy Chardonnays. The 1995 Cabernet Partners' Reserve (85 points) was tightly structured, with pleasant cherry cedar and spice flavors; the 1996 Merlot Partners' Reserve (87) displayed young, rustic flavors of tar, herb and ripe black cherry. The 1996 Chardonnay (89) was just short of outstanding, with rich butterscotch, peach, pear and honey flavors framed by refreshing citrus notes.

SPENKER WINERY (★★)

Lodi, Sacramento County
Founded: 1994. **Owner:** Charles & Bettyann Spenker. **Winemaker:** Bettyann Spenker.

MAJOR WINES PRODUCED:
Zinfandel Lodi ($15, 1,100).

WINERY DATA
Case Production: 1,100. **Acres Owned:** 60 acres in Lodi. **Varietals by Acre:** Zinfandel (60 acres).

The Spenkers have been home winemakers and grape-growers in the Lodi area for many years. Their 1995 Zinfandel (90 points), featuring plump cherry, blackberry and smoky cola flavors, was a pleasant surprise from this underrated region. Perhaps due to inexperience, the 1996 Zinfandel (60) was badly spoiled by bacteria and should not have been released. Still, the 1995 Zinfandel is an indication that both Spenker and Lodi have potential. Keep watching.

SPOTTSWOODE VINEYARD & WINERY (★★★–★★★★★)

St. Helena, Napa Valley
Founded: 1982. **Owner:** Mary Weber Novak. **Winemaker:** Rosemary Cakebread.

MAJOR WINES: PRICE, CASES, RATING

Cabernet Sauvignon Napa Valley ($55, 5,000)	★★★★★
Sauvignon Blanc Napa Valley ($18, 3,500)	★★★

WINERY DATA
Case Production: 8,500. **Acres Owned:** 35.5 acres in St. Helena, Napa Valley. **Varietals by Acre:** Cabernet Franc (2 acres), Cabernet Sauvignon (31), Sauvignon Blanc (1.5), Zinfandel (1). **Varietals Purchased:** Sauvignon Blanc (Napa Valley), Sémillon (Napa Valley).

Spottswoode continues to produce beautifully crafted Cabernets from its vineyard in St. Helena and this wine ranks among the most consistent in California. The vineyard is the key, as the soils and climate combine to yield wines that are consistently excellent, rich and deeply concentrated with suitably thick but polished tannins.

Owner-founder Mary Novak and her late husband Jack moved to Napa Valley in the early 1970s to ease into a country lifestyle, and ended up purchasing one of the valley's great vineyards. Mary Novak still oversees operations, having had the wisdom (and good fortune) to hire Tony Soter early on as winemaker; he had a hand in shaping and refining the style. Rosemary Cakebread was hired as winemaker in 1997. Most of the vineyard on the western outskirts of St. Helena is planted to Cabernet (31 acres) and Cabernet Franc (2). Winery production is

8,500 cases, led by Cabernet (5,000 cases). The Sauvignon Blanc is a blend of estate and purchased grapes. A new winery was completed in 1996.

TASTING NOTES

CABERNET SAUVIGNON NAPA VALLEY (★★★★★): Uniformly rich and well focused, with deep, complex and concentrated currant, black cherry, and spicy flavors. Well oaked but not overdone. Tannins are thick but polished and well integrated. Ages well up to 10-12 years, as the wines from the early and mid-1980s are holding up well.
1995: Ripe, with supple, polished tannins and a wonderful core of currant, black cherry, berry and spice flavors, turning plush on the finish. **93**
1994: Supple and harmonious, with a ripe, complex core of cherry, plum and wild berry flavors that fan out nicely on the finish. **92**
1993: Supple and elegant, with tiers of currant, cherry and spice flavors, turning smooth and complex on the finish. **90**
1992: Tightly wound; dark and plummy, with rich, well focused currant and black cherry flavors coupled with notes of pepper and mineral. **90**
1991: Ripe, smooth and polished, packing in pretty currant, black cherry and anise flavors that are rich, focused, complex and concentrated, finishing with plush tannins. **93**
1990: Big and classy, with loads of rich, silky tannins and berry, currant, tobacco and mint aromas and flavors. **93**
1989: Smooth and polished, this is a pretty wine with black cherry and spice flavors and integrated tannins that turn supple. **89**
1988: Supple and balanced, with a tightly focused band of currant, black cherry, anise, tar and cedar flavors. **88**
1987: Ripe, smooth, rich and plush, with loads of currant, black cherry and wild berry fruit, spicy anise flavors and soft tannins. **93**
1986: Youthful, vibrant, and remarkably complex, with elegant, well preserved black cherry and currant flavors. **92**
1985: Tight and tart, with crisp black cherry, currant, and spice flavors that turn elegant and supple on the finish. **89**
1984: Ripe, supple and harmonious, with pretty, toasty oak, and ripe plum, cassis and currant flavors that are rich and generous. Mature. **90**
1983: Impressive for its structure and firm tannins, which allow the cassis, currant, plum and mint flavors to emerge. Complex and mature. **88**

1982: Firm and deeply concentrated, with tight, thick tannins wrapped around an abundance of ripe plum, cherry and cassis flavors. **88**

SAUVIGNON BLANC NAPA VALLEY (★★★): Shares the Cabernet's sense of balance and proportion, with complex flavors.

SPRING MOUNTAIN (★★★)
Spring Mountain District, Napa Valley
Founded: 1968. **Owner:** Jacob Safra, Tom Ferrell. **Winemaker:** Tom Ferrell.

MAJOR WINES: PRICE, CASES, RATING

Red Spring Mountain	
District Miravalle-Alba-Chevalier	
($36, 5,000)	★★★
White Spring Mountain District	
Miravalle-La Perla-Chevalier	
($20, 900)	★★★

WINERY DATA
Case Production: 5,000. **Acres Owned:** 220 acres in Spring Mountain District, Napa Valley. **Varietals by Acre:** Cabernet Franc (4 acres), Cabernet Sauvignon (140), Merlot (40), Muscat (3), Petit Verdot (8), Pinot Noir (1), Sauvignon Blanc & Sémillon (10), Syrah (9), Viognier (5).

Jacob Safra has revived Spring Mountain, hiring Tom Ferrell as winemaker and adding new vineyards, now totaling 220 acres in the Spring Mountain District of Napa Valley. Original owner Mike Robbins put the winery up for sale in the late 1980s and kept dropping the price until a group of investors, headed by Safra, took control in 1990, paying $4 million. Shortly thereafter, the group acquired two other out-of-business wineries nearby, Chateau Chevalier and Streblow. By 1994, Safra's Good Wine Co. had acquired nearly 400 acres on Spring Mountain, 100 of them in vines.

TASTING NOTES

RED SPRING MOUNTAIN DISTRICT MIRAVALLE-ALBA-CHEVALIER (★★★): Showing improvement, with firmly tannic, concentrated wines. Worth watching.

1995: Tight, with an earthy side to the currant and cherry flavors and herb and cedary notes; it is rich and concentrated. **89**

1994: Shows restraint while delivering the goods, with tightly reined in currant, black cherry, cedar, anise and plum, fanning out on the finish where it holds its focus and flavors. **90**

Lot H 68-69 NV: A blend of wines from the 1968 and 1969 vintages that includes Heitz Martha's 1969; it's mature and cedary now. **83**

Staglin Family Vineyard (★★★–★★★★)
Rutherford, Napa Valley
Founded: 1985. **Owner:** The Staglin Family. **Winemaker:** Celia Masyczek.

Major Wines: Price, Cases, Rating
Cabernet Sauvignon Rutherford ($43, 5,000)	★★★★
Chardonnay Rutherford ($40, 1,500)	★★★
Sangiovese Rutherford Stagliano ($40, 200)	★★★

Winery Data
Case Production: 6,700. **Acres Owned:** 50 acres in Rutherford. **Varietals by Acre:** Cabernet Franc (0.5 acres), Cabernet Sauvignon (37.5), Chardonnay (10), Sangiovese (2).

This 50-acre estate is dominated by Cabernet (37.5 acres), with smaller parcels of Chardonnay (10), Cabernet Franc (0.5) and Sangiovese (2). Cathy Corison had a hand in the early wines, which were made in very small quantities. The Cabernets have shown steady improvement, and are reflective of the Rutherford appellation, with their plush fruit flavors and fine tannins. A portion of the Cabernet crop is sold to Corison and St. Clement. Worth watching.

Tasting Notes
Cabernet Sauvignon Rutherford (★★★★): Keeps improving, with well focused and complex fruit flavors and mild, supple tannins. I still expect great Cabernet from this estate.

1995: Elegant and supple, with a pretty array of currant, blackberry, cherry, toasty oak and spice flavors, with smooth tannins. **92**

1994: Firm, tight and tannic, with a chewy edge to the earthy currant and black cherry flavors and notes of coffee and cedar. **90**

1992: Tightly wound and a touch austere, with tiers of fleshy plum and black cherry flavors, finishing with firm tannins. **91**

1991: Intense, lively and tightly wound, with lovely, supple plum and currant flavors that pick up a spicy, cedary edge. **88**

1990: Tight, firm and oaky, with vanilla and chocolate notes showing through and black cherry and currant flavors underneath. **88**

1989: Smooth and supple, with artful oak and spice shadings to the ripe plum and blackberry flavors. **87**

Chardonnay Rutherford (★★★): New to the mix; made in a non-malolactic style.

1997: Tight, crisp and concentrated, with spicy pear, hints of peach, vanilla and mineral, finishing clean. **88**

Sangiovese Rutherford Stagliano (★★★): A pleasant, well-balanced wine, made using Sangiovese and a small percentage of Cabernet. The 1996 (87 points) was filled with spicy cherry and plummy flavors.

Stag's Leap Wine Cellars (★★★–★★★★★)
Stags Leap District, Napa Valley
Founded: 1972. **Owner:** Warren & Barbara Winiarski. **Winemaker:** Michael Silacci. **Second Label:** Hawk Crest.

Major Wines: Price, Cases, Rating
Cabernet Sauvignon Napa Valley ($26, 15,000)	★★★
Cabernet Sauvignon Napa Valley Fay Vineyard ($50, 5,000)	★★★★
Cabernet Sauvignon Napa Valley S.L.V. ($50, 4,000)	★★★★★
Cask 23 Red Napa Valley ($100, 2,000)	★★★★★
Chardonnay Napa Valley ($24, 15,000)	★★★

Chardonnay Napa Valley Beckstoffer
Ranch
($28, 800) ★★★★

Chardonnay Napa Valley Reserve
($37, 1,000) ★★★★

Merlot Napa Valley
($26, 4,000) ★★★

Petite Sirah Napa Valley
($22, 800) ★★

Sauvignon Blanc Napa Valley
($15, 5,000) ★★★

ALSO PRODUCED

White Riesling Napa Valley ($15, 2,500).

WINERY DATA

Case Production: 150,000. **Acres Owned:** 170 acres (69 in
Napa Valley, 101 in Stags Leap District). **Varietals by Acre:**
Cabernet Sauvignon (103 acres), Chardonnay (29), Merlot (16),
Pinot Noir (15), Sauvignon Blanc (6). **Vineyard Designations:**
Beckstoffer Ranch (Chardonnay), Fay Vineyard (Cabernet
Sauvignon), Stag's Leap Vineyard (Cabernet Sauvignon).
Varietals Purchased: Cabernet Sauvignon, Chardonnay, Merlot,
Petite Sirah, Sauvignon Blanc, White Riesling (Napa Valley).

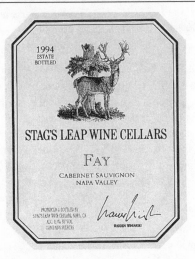

Stag's Leap Wine Cellars is the winery that vaulted to
international fame with its second vintage, when its 1973
Cabernet placed first in the famous Paris Tasting of
1976. Founders Warren and Barbara Winiarski had left
Chicago in the 1960s, with Warren, a former lecturer in
Greek classics at the University of Chicago, abandoning
his academic career for winemaking. Once in Napa, he
worked for Lee Stewart at the old Souverain Winery and
later joined Robert Mondavi Winery before putting
together a group of investors to start his own winery.

The initial focus was on Cabernet, made from a 45-
acre vineyard near the winery. Later, the winery made
headlines during a protracted legal battle with Stags'
Leap Winery over who owned the Stag's Leap name
(irrespective of spelling). The outcome of the battle was
that both wineries were allowed to use the name, having
started at about the same time.

Production is currently 150,000 cases, with a series of
Cabernets (Cask 23, SLV, and Fay Vineyard bottlings) still
the stars; Chardonnay, Merlot, Petite Sirah, Riesling and
Sauvignon Blanc are also made. A large number of the
wines here are bottled under the Hawk Crest label. Even
though Stag's Leap remains best known for its rich and
distinctive Cabernets, the Chardonnay Reserve has been
remarkably well crafted since the mid-1980s. The winery
owns 170 acres, including the famous Fay Vineyard,
which it acquired in 1986 and replanted. Worth collecting.

TASTING NOTES

CABERNET SAUVIGNON NAPA VALLEY (★★★): Steadily
improving as the winery builds more depth and richness
into the wines, which have been medium-bodied and
somewhat simple.

1995: Appealing for its ripe, supple plum and wild berry
flavors; it's well focused, moderately rich and tannic. **87**

1994: Shows earthy, spicy Cabernet flavors, with hints of
wild berry, cherry, sage and cedar, finishing with firm
tannins and good length. **88**

1993: Of medium weight, with spicy currant, light oak,
cherry and cedar nuances. Gains complexity and finesse
on the finish, where the texture is smooth, and shows a
fine interplay of flavors. **88**

1991: Firm, focused and supple, with herb and leather
aromas and berry and currant flavors, finishing with a
bite of tannin and a hint of vanilla. **87**

1990: Sleek and flavorful, with pretty mint and currant
aromas, a smooth texture and supple tannins. **89**

1989: Crisp and distinctive, with mint and bay leaf flavors and firm tannins. **83**

1988: Ripe and generous, with berry and currant aromas
and flavors that turn complex. **87**

Cabernet Sauvignon Napa Valley Fay Vineyard (★★★★): Capable of uncommon richness, harmony and finesse; can rival the Cask 23 for complexity.

1995: Lots of up-front cedar, coffee and toasty oak notes, but then the currant, plum, black cherry and meaty flavors unfold, adding depth. **93**

1994: Concentrated, with a rich center of currant, anise, cedar, sage and black olive flavors; the tannins are firm, yet supple. **92**

1993: Seductive, with ripe, rich, sweet fruit that unfolds to a core of cherry, currant, plum, wild berry, herb, cedar and coffee notes. **91**

1992: Supple and polished, with an herbal, leathery edge to the ripe, rich currant and black cherry flavors. **91**

1991: Rich and intense, with an earthy edge to the currant and cherry flavors, picking up tobacco and herb notes. **88**

1990: A firm, weighty wine with rich, spicy currant and sandalwood notes, finishing with firm, complex tannins. **90**

1989: Marked by an oaky, herbaceous edge to the currant and plum aromas and flavors, finishing with light tannins. **84**

1989 SLV/Fay Vineyard Blend: A crisp, thin wine with tight currant, earth and cedar flavors of modest depth. **80**

Cabernet Sauvignon Napa Valley SLV (★★★★★): Rivals Cask 23 in the best years; offers distinctive flavors, complexity and finesse.

1995: Decidedly supple and elegant, with ripe, rich, smooth and polished layers of currant, black cherry, vanilla, herb, anise and spice flavors. **93**

1994: Lovely fruit, with tiers of spicy currant, black cherry, olive, sage and tar flavors and a remarkably supple and fleshy texture. **91**

1993: Ripe and flavorful, with a nice band of earthy cherry, currant and plum flavors, picking up hints of coffee, herb and anise. **90**

1992: Austere, but quite concentrated, with tightly wound herb, currant and anise flavors leading to a firmly tannic finish. **88**

1990: Smooth, supple and complex, with rich, intense herb, currant, olive, coffee and cedar flavors that fan out, finishing with fine tannins and excellent depth. **90**

1988: Smooth and polished, with complex currant, coffee, cedar and herbal notes and well integrated tannins. **88**

1987: Decidedly herbal, earthy and ripe, with rich plum, cherry, dill and pickle flavors that turn dry and bitter. **77**

1986: A ripe, supple, rich and complex wine, with layers of currant, cherry, coffee, cedar and spice flavors. **91**

1985: Ripe and concentrated, brimming with currant, cherry, spice and cedar flavors that turn supple, with well integrated tannins. **94**

1984: Very ripe and flavorful, loaded with supple cherry, cedar, currant and anise flavors that are broad and lush, with smooth, supple tannins. **89**

1981: Attractive, with ripe currant, cedar and cherry flavors and a nice touch of toasty vanilla oak. **88**

1978: Rich, smooth and concentrated, delicately balanced, with spice, cedar and cherry flavors. **89**

1978 Lot 2: Minty herbal notes add complexity to the fleshy, forward Cabernet flavors. **88**

1977: Ripe and earthy yet elegant and harmonious, with mature, complex cherry, cedar and currant flavors. **85**

1977 Lot 2: Similar to Lot 1, with cedar and chocolate flavors that are rich and satisfying on the finish. **88**

1974: Plenty of fruit, harmony, elegance and grace. At its peak now, it should be consumed while the fruit is still fresh, concentrated and lively on the palate. **87**

1973: The famous Paris Tasting winner showed very well the last time I tried it, with complex aromas and spicy cherry, cedar, toast and chocolate flavors. **86**

1972: The first vintage is old and fading. **70**

Cask 23 Red Napa Valley (★★★★★): A blend of Fay Vineyard and SLV (Stag's Leap Vineyard). This wine is variable: At its best it is among the most complex and distinctive of California Cabernets, capable of amazing intricacy and ageworthiness, and marked by plush herb, olive, currant, coffee and spicy flavors with smooth polished tannins. It can also be pungently earthy, with a mulchy, weedy, tobacco edge. Ages very well. Produced only in exceptional years.

1995: Tremendous. Ultra-rich, supple, complex and concentrated, it delivers a wave of plush currant, black cherry, black olive, sage and spice flavors. **94**

1994: Intense and concentrated, with a rich, supple texture and loads of currant, anise, black cherry, plum and berry notes woven together. **93**

1992: Elegant and refined, with well focused, complex currant, cherry, spice and earth flavors, picking up supple anise and leathery notes on the finish. **94**

1991: Tightly wound and tannic, but loaded with currant, coffee, herb and anise flavors that run rich, deep and long. Complex and concentrated. **92**

1990: Deliciously complex and sophisticated, with lots

of exotic spice, currant, mineral and herbal scents and an array of flavors to match. **95**

1987: Delivers a modest band of cedar, herb, currant and spice flavors, with soft, fleshy tannins. **87**

1986: Mature, with a complex array of herb, cedar, anise, leaf, mineral, currant and slightly pruny flavors and supple tannins. **88**

1985: An amazing range of complex flavors, with notes of plush, supple bell pepper, green olive, currant, black cherry and black olive. **98**

1984: Mature, with lush, expansive herb, currant, anise and herb flavors that turn supple. **89**

1983: Remarkably well balanced and concentrated, with intense, spicy cherry flavors that stand up to the firm tannins. **86**

1979: Soft, supple and harmonious, with black cherry and herb flavors that are rich, complex and persistent. **88**

1978: Mature and drying, but complex, with supple, fleshy, elegant plum, currant, herb and berry flavors. **88**

1977: Fully mature, with complex cedar, herb, cherry and spice notes that turn supple. **89**

1974: Rich and supple, vibrant and complex, with currant, tar, tobacco and spice notes that turn smooth and polished, silky and elegant. **94**

CHARDONNAY NAPA VALLEY (★★★): Steadily improving, with ripe fruit flavors and a smooth, silky texture. Best on release.

CHARDONNAY NAPA VALLEY BECKSTOFFER RANCH (★★★★): Combines elegance and finesse with bright, rich and complex flavors.

1996: Sleek and elegant, with pretty pear, spice, nutmeg and hazelnut flavors, turning long and complex on the finish. **91**

1995: Deliciously fruity and complex, brimming with bright, ripe pear, apple, citrus, spice and melon flavors. **92**

CHARDONNAY NAPA VALLEY RESERVE (★★★★)

1995: Lots of complexity, with ripe pear, fig, apple, citrus and light oak shadings, turning richer and more sophisticated on the finish. **93**

1994: Smooth, ripe and creamy, with pretty pear, apple, melon and spicy nutmeg flavors, turning elegant and complex on the finish. **91**

MERLOT NAPA VALLEY (★★★): Variable as Merlot goes, ranging from light and simple to ripe and plush.

PETITE SIRAH NAPA VALLEY (★★)

1992: Chewy, earthy, spicy and distinctive with leathery, peppery notes. This is a small-scale wine with possibilities. **93**

STAGS' LEAP WINERY (★★–★★★★)
Stags Leap District, Napa Valley
Founded: 1893. **Owner:** Beringer Wine Estates.
Winemaker: Robert Brittan.

MAJOR WINES: PRICE, CASES, RATING

Cabernet Sauvignon Napa Valley ($30, 23,800)	★★
Merlot Napa Valley ($28, 13,690)	★★
Petite Sirah Napa Valley ($25, 10,000)	★★★★
Petite Sirah Napa Valley Reserve ($45, 200)	★★★★

ALSO PRODUCED
Chardonnay Napa Valley ($21, 9,800).

WINERY DATA
Case Production: 60,000. **Acres Owned:** 90 acres in Stags Leap District. **Varietals By Acre:** Cabernet Franc (1 acre), Cabernet Sauvignon (40), Merlot (29), Petite Sirah (20). **Varietals Purchased:** Cabernet (Napa Valley), Chardonnay (Napa Valley), Merlot (Napa Valley), Petite Sirah (Napa Valley), Viognier (Napa Valley).

Stags' Leap Winery is the lesser known of the two Stags Leap wineries, but its history dates to 1893 when it was named Stags' Leap Manor. When Carl Doumani bought it in 1972 he decided to focus on his favorite (and best) wine, Petite Sirah, and his version is among the finest in the state. The winery owns 121 acres at the base of the Stags Leap rock outcropping, dominated by Cabernet (58 acres) and Merlot (42), with 19 acres of old vine Petite Sirah. The 60,000-case output is led by Merlot, Cabernet and Chardonnay, but Petite Sirah is still the most distinctive wine. Beringer Wine Estates bought the winery in 1997.

TASTING NOTES

CABERNET SAUVIGNON NAPA VALLEY (★★): Steadily improving as the winery builds more depth and richness into the wines, which have been medium-bodied and somewhat simple.

Merlot Napa Valley (★★): Variable as Merlot goes, ranging from light and simple to ripe and plush.

Petite Sirah Napa Valley (★★★★): Can be enormously bold, rich, dense and peppery with firm tannins. Capable of aging for 10 to 15 years in the best vintages. A Reserve bottling appears occasionally.

Reserve 1993: Dense and chewy, packed with rugged tannins, which only allows a glimpse of the ripe plum and spicy berry fruit flavors, which are pretty. Finishes with a dash of spice, but tannins remain formidable. **88**

1990: Bold, ripe and richly fruity, with layers of fresh, spicy cherry, plum, anise and tar notes. It has wonderful balance and a sense of harmony and finesse. **91**

1989: A light (for Stags' Leap) vintage with moderate depth and intensity to the cherry and plum flavors. **84**

1988: Ripe, supple and fruity, with toasty plum and cherry flavors that are elegant. **86**

Reserve 1988: Firm and austere, with ample tannins, yet the texture at mid-palate is smooth, with floral, plum and cherry notes. **86**

1987: Extremely oaky, with charred, buttery oak flavors that overpower the cherry and plum notes. **83**

Petite Syrah 1987: Firm, tannic and flavorful, with generous blackberry, black cherry and smoke flavors. **82**

1986: Supple and elegant, with ripe black cherry, earth, tar and spice notes. **87**

1985: Simple and lightly fruity, with cherry and plum flavors that are pleasant and of modest concentration. **84**

1984: Marked by a wild, earthy, leathery edge, with spicy cherry and plum flavors and a slightly horsey edge. **85**

1983: Austere, dry and tannic, with fruit that's dropping out. **82**

1982: Earthy and austere, with a tight, tannic core of cherry, pepper and spice flavors. **86**

1981: Its modest flavors taste stripped. **80**

1980: An earthy, tarry wine with fruit that's dropping out. **80**

1979: Lean, austere and unripe, with earthy cherry notes. **79**

1978: Big, ripe and chewy, with rich, dark currant and black cherry flavors that pick up a nice, earthy mineral edge on the finish. **89**

1977: Dry and lean, with tannic cherry and plum aromas that turn dry on the palate. **83**

1976: Rich, ripe, intense and tannic, with ripe plum and raisin flavors that have a coarse texture. **89**

1975: Austere and tight, with a narrow band of spice and fruit flavors. **84**

1974: A big, ripe, slightly alcoholic wine, almost a caricature of Petite Sirah with its intense, rich pepper and plum flavors. Lacks finesse and finishes with an earthy mineral edge. **87**

1973: Smooth in texture, it is not quite as complex as the 1972 but offers ripe, spicy plum and cherry flavors. **88**

1972: Deep in color, with delicious, ripe black cherry and plum flavors and peppery, spicy mineral aromas that turn to anise and cedar on the palate. **91**

STEELE WINES (★★★–★★★★★)
Lake County
Founded: 1991. **Owner:** Jedediah & Marie Steele. **Winemaker:** Jedediah T. Steele. **Second Label:** Shooting Star.

Major Wines: Price, Cases, Rating

Cabernet Sauvignon Anderson Valley ($26, 550)	★★★★
Chardonnay California Steele Cuveé ($18, 10,000)	★★★★
Chardonnay Carneros Durell Vineyard ($25, 600)	★★★★★
Chardonnay Carneros Sangiacomo Vineyard ($24, 800)	★★★★★
Chardonnay Mendocino Dennison Vineyard ($22, 250)	★★★★
Chardonnay Mendocino DuPratt Vineyard ($28, 600)	★★★★
Chardonnay Mendocino Lolonis Vineyard ($28, 800)	★★★★★
Chardonnay Santa Barbara County Bien Nacido Vineyard ($25, 700)	★★★★★
Chardonnay Santa Barbara County Goodchild Vineyard ($26, 700)	★★★★★
Chardonnay Sonoma Valley Parmelee Hill Vineyard ($26, 500)	★★★★

Pinot Blanc Santa Barbara County
Bien Nacido Vineyard
($15, 2,000) ★★★★
Pinot Noir Anderson Valley
($22, 500) ★★★
Pinot Noir Carneros
($18, 5,000) ★★★★
Pinot Noir Carneros Durell Vineyard
($26, 400) ★★★
Pinot Noir Carneros Sangiacomo
Vineyard ($25, 800) ★★★★
Pinot Noir Mendocino DuPratt Vineyard
($28, 100) ★★★
Pinot Noir Santa Barbara County
Bien Nacido Vineyard
($25, 800) ★★★
Syrah Clear Lake
($15, 500) ★★★★
Zinfandel Clear Lake Catfish Vineyard
($16, 700) ★★★★
Zinfandel Mendocino DuPratt Vineyard
($18, 1,200) ★★★★
Zinfandel Mendocino Pacini Vineyard
($15, 3,000) ★★★

WINERY DATA

Case Production: 32,000. **Acres Owned:** 65 acres (35 in Lake County, 30 in Mendocino). **Varietals by Acre:** Grenache/ Marsanne/ Roussanne/Syrah/Viognier (35 acres), Zinfandel (30). **Vineyard Designations:** Bien Nacido Vineyard (Chardonnay, Pinot Blanc, Pinot Noir), Catfish Vineyard (Zinfandel), DuPratt Vineyard (Chardonnay, Pinot Noir, Zinfandel), Durell Vineyard (Chardonnay, Pinot Noir), Goodchild Vineyard (Chardonnay), Lolonis Vineyard (Chardonnay), Parmelee Hill Vineyard (Chardonnay), Sangiacomo Vineyard (Chardonnay, Pinot Noir), Pacini Vineyard (Zinfandel). **Varietals Purchased:** Cabernet Sauvignon (Anderson Valley), Chardonnay (Carneros, Mendocino County, Santa Barbara County, Sonoma County), Syrah (Lake County), Pinot Blanc (Santa Barbara County, Pinot Noir (Carneros, Santa Barbara County), Zinfandel (Lake County, Mendocino).

Jed Steele has been around long enough to know that it's possible to make great wine without owning vineyards. (The secret is to buy grapes from great vineyards). His career has included a stint at the old Edmeades Winery in Anderson Valley, followed by a period at Kendall-Jackson as chief winemaker from 1982 to 1989, when production topped 1 million cases. While the Steele label (including the second label, Shooting Star) is now at 32,000 cases, Steele still consults on and helps to shape the wines from Villa Mt. Eden, Conn Creek and Fess Parker.

Among Steele's talents are an ability to tap into superb vineyards (Bien Nacido in Santa Barbara, Dennison in Mendocino, DuPratt in Mendocino, Durell in Sonoma Valley, Lolonis in Mendocino and Sangiacomo in Carneros), and to make harmonious wines that are complex and easy to drink. Steele Wines focuses on Chardonnay, Pinot Blanc, Pinot Noir and Zinfandel, with smaller lots of Shooting Star Cabernet Franc, Chardonnay and Merlot. Even as quality has risen and held at a high level, prices for these wines remain very reasonable. More importantly, they're fun to drink. Worth buying.

TASTING NOTES

CABERNET SAUVIGNON ANDERSON VALLEY (★★★)
1995: Dark, ripe and deeply flavored, with a complex array of currant, cedar, spice and cherry, finishing with a complex aftertaste. **90**

CHARDONNAY VARIOUS BOTTLINGS (★★★★–★★★★★):
The thread that runs through all of Steele's Chardonnays is their emphasis on ripe, clean, juicy fruit and a judicious use of oak.

CHARDONNAY CALIFORNIA STEELE CUVÉE (★★★★)
1997: Lots of up-front fruit; spicy, with tiers of fig, pear, melon, apricot and nutmeg, finishing with a long, intricate aftertaste. **91**

CHARDONNAY CARNEROS DURRELL VINEYARD (★★★★)
1997: Perfumed, with an array of pear, fig, spice, vanilla and melon notes that turn elegant and delicate on the finish. **92**
1996: Thick and concentrated, with an earthy streak that runs through the core of pear, spice and vanilla flavors. **93**
1995: Ripe, rich and full-bodied, with a complex core of spice, pear, apple and honey notes, turning silky and polished on the finish. **92**

Chardonnay Carneros Sangiacomo Vineyard (★★★★★)

1997: Lots of rich, smooth, creamy pear, fig and vanilla flavors combine to lend this wine depth and distinction; finishes with a complex, spicy aftertaste. **90**

1996: An ultra-rich, almost cloying style, with ripe, sweet-tasting fig, pear and honey flavors. **90**

1995: Smooth, ripe, rich and creamy, with layers of fig, pear, melon and apricot flavors, turning elegant and silky on the finish. **93**

Chardonnay Mendocino Dennison Vineyard (★★★★)

1995: Smooth and creamy, with a pretty core of pear- and peach-laced Chardonnay fruit, finishing with a spicy edge. **90**

Chardonnay Mendocino DuPratt Vineyard (★★★★)

1996: Rich and focused, with a complex core of pear, fig, apple, spice and mineral flavors and hints of nutmeg tinged oak. **92**

1995: Smooth, rich and concentrated, this is a bold, complex young wine oozing with juicy pear, melon, apricot and hazelnut flavors. **92**

Chardonnay Mendocino Lolonis Vineyard (★★★★★)

1997: Smooth, ripe and rich; loaded with complex pear, fig, melon, spice and pretty oak shadings. Finishes with a long, complex aftertaste that weaves the flavors together nicely. **91**

1996: Starts out earthy, then offers more appealing flavors, with notes of pear, apple, butterscotch and citrus fruit. **93**

1995: Serves up lots of ripe, creamy pear, fig, apricot and peach flavors, turning smooth and elegant on the finish. **91**

Chardonnay Santa Barbara County Bien Nacido Vineyard (★★★★★)

1996: Rich, with lots of finesse and a creamy texture; notes of ripe pear, tropical fruit, guava and fig come through, turning elegant on the finish. **92**

1995: Bold, ripe and complex, with a rich core of tropical fruit and hints of pear, pineapple and guava, turning elegant on the finish. **92**

Chardonnay Santa Barbara County Goodchild Vineyard (★★★★★)

1996: Smooth, rich and creamy, with sharply focused tropical fruit flavors, showing hints of pear, guava, spice and nectarine. **92**

1995: Ripe and full-bodied, with an earthy side to the pear, fig and spicy flavors and a most impressive finish. **92**

Chardonnay Sonoma Valley Parmelee Hill Vineyard (★★★★)

1996: Bright and lively, with well focused anise, pear and spicy nuances, turning tight and focused on the finish. **90**

Pinot Blanc Santa Barbara County Bien Nacido Vineyard (★★★★)

1996: Simply delicious, with lots of complexity and finesse; bursting with rich pear, fig, melon, vanilla and hazelnut flavors. **92**

1995: Tight but complex, with hints of peach, pear and spice that fold together nicely. **88**

Pinot Noir various bottlings (★★★–★★★★): Like the Chardonnays, the focus is always aimed at ripe, berryish fruit and silky, polished tannins. The use of toasty oak adds a pleasant dimension.

Pinot Noir Anderson Valley (★★★★)

1996: Ripe and plush, with complex layers of rich plum, cherry, light vanilla-scented oak, herb and spice, turning supple. **89**

1995: Distinct for its smoky cola and raspberry notes, it's tight and firmly tannic. **88**

1994: Tight, offering a hint of plum and berry, showing more spice and oak as it opens up. **88**

Pinot Noir Carneros (★★★★)

1996: An earthy, funky and complex style, with notes of mushroom, dried cherry and leather. **87**

1995: Ripe and polished, with a rich band of smoky, tarry plum and cherry flavors and nuances of sage, tea and anise. **90**

1991: Openly fruity and youthful, with lovely cherry, plum and wild berry flavors and ripe, supple tannins. **91**

Pinot Noir Carneros Durell Vineyard (★★★)

1996: Intensely varietal, with flavors that border on stewed plum and tomato. It features lots of anise and spice, but there are also some off-beat, meaty flavors; it straightens out, however, on the finish. **87**

1995: Elegant, with tea, herb, sage and dried cherry fruit, turning dry on the finish. **88**

PINOT NOIR CARNEROS SANGIACOMO VINEYARD (★★★★)

1996: Supple, complex and harmonious, with pretty, toasty oak and plenty of ripe cherry, strawberry and spicy nuances. **89**

1995: Smooth, ripe and juicy, with a pretty array of plum, cherry, sage, tea and spice flavors, turning elegant on the finish. **90**

1994: A wonderful integration of flavors, with layers of black cherry, cola, earth and light, spicy oak, turning complex on the finish. **91**

PINOT NOIR MENDOCINO DUPRATT VINEYARD (★★★)

1996: Smooth and spicy, with an elegant band of earthy cherry, wild berry, raspberry and perfumed aromas. Needs some time. **89**

1995: Firmly tannic, with a wonderful core of plum, wild berry and blueberry fruit flavors, picking up tasty notes of cedary oak, anise and tar. **92**

1994: Complex, with its ripe plum, cherry, berry and cedary oak flavors, it shows elegance and finesse and turns delicate on the finish. **91**

PINOT NOIR SANTA BARBARA COUNTY BIEN NACIDO VINEYARD (★★★)

1996: Ripe, smooth and polished, this is a lovely wine with earthy cola, black cherry, herb and sage notes. **88**

1995: Displays a wonderful fruit intensity and a sharp focus, with bright, lively wild berry, cherry, spice and earthy raspberry flavors. **93**

SYRAH CLEAR LAKE (★★★★)

1996: Firm and beefy, with stewed plum and wild berry flavors; turning leathery and chunky, with big tannins. **87**

ZINFANDEL VARIOUS BOTTLINGS (★★★★):

Well-oaked, but have the rich fruit to stand up to the oak flavors; captures the essence of Zinfandel with berryish fruit and polished tannins.

ZINFANDEL CLEAR LAKE CATFISH VINEYARD (★★★★)

1996: Intense and concentrated; marked by spice, mint and wild berry flavors. **87**

1994: Serves up lots of complex flavors, with tiers of spice, raspberry, earth, cherry and wild berry. **91**

1993: A complex balance between spicy, toasty oak and ripe cherry and raspberry flavors. **89**

ZINFANDEL MENDOCINO DUPRATT VINEYARD (★★★★)

1996: Firm and chunky, with earthy wild berry, raspberry and cherry-laced flavors that turns rustic, minty and tannic. **87**

1995: Big, ripe, rich and tannic; a blockbuster style that packs in lots of exotic mineral and wild berry flavors. **89**

1994: Big, ripe and intense, with rich, plush and juicy wild berry, cherry, anise and raspberry fruit. **93**

ZINFANDEL MENDOCINO PACINI VINEYARD (★★★)

1996: Features bright, spicy and juicy cherry, wild berry, plum and cedar flavors, finishing with ripe, firm tannins. **90**

1995: Bold and ripe, with Port-like aromas and flavors, it's a big, assertive, chewy wine that stretches the boundaries for a Zinfandel. **88**

1993: Tight, firm and well-oaked, with toasty, buttery flavors paired with a substantial core of wild berry and cherry notes, turning tannic on the finish. **87**

STELTZNER VINEYARDS (★★–★★★)
Stags Leap District, Napa Valley
Founded: 1983. **Owner:** Richard Steltzner. **Winemaker:** Charles Hendricks.

MAJOR WINES: PRICE, CASES, RATING

Cabernet Sauvignon Stag's Leap District ($24, 2,500)	★★★
Cabernet Sauvignon Stag's Leap District Barrel Select ($35, 500)	★★
Claret Stag's Leap District ($14, 3,000)	★★
Merlot Stag's Leap District ($22, 2,500)	★★
Sauvignon Blanc Oak Knoll ($10, 3,000)	★★

ALSO PRODUCED

Chardonnay Oak Knoll ($18, 3,000); Pinotage Stag's Leap District ($18, 700); Sangiovese Stag's Leap District ($18, 700).

WINERY DATA

Case Production: 12,500. **Acres Owned:** 73 acres (18 in Oak Knoll District, 55 in Stags Leap District). **Varietals by Acre:** Cabernet Franc (3 acres), Cabernet Sauvignon (31), Chardonnay (10), Merlot (15), miscellaneous red (2), Pinotage (2), Sangiovese (2), Sauvignon Blanc (8).

Richard Steltzner grew grapes—and planted and managed other people's vineyards, including Diamond Creek and Spring Mountain—for more than a decade before easing into winemaking. The 1973 Conn Creek Cabernet is a memorable bottling from his vineyard's grapes, and his 1978 showed exceptionally well in a 20-year retrospective from that vintage. In 1977, he started producing Cabernet from his Stags Leap vineyard; since then he's added claret, Merlot and Sauvignon Blanc to his lineup. Quality across the board is usually very good, but occasionally suffers from what appears to be bad winemaking, with too many off-aromas. The reds share a chunky, rustic edge, especially when compared with other Stags Leap District offerings, but they hold up well. Production is 12,500 cases and headed upward, with a new winery and caves having been completed in 1995.

TASTING NOTES

CABERNET SAUVIGNON STAG'S LEAP DISTRICT (★★★): Variable, but ripe, intense, openly fruity and firmly tannic at its best. Makes no pretense at finesse, but packs in lots of chewy flavors. Ages well up to 10 years.
1994: Roughly hewn, the dusty, cedary oak flavors override the modest core of plum and berry. **83**
1991: Earthy and tannic, with a leathery edge to the currant and cherry flavors. It opens up with aeration. **85**
1990: Firm and compact, with focused currant, cherry and spice flavors that finish with crisp tannins. **87**
1988: Light and simple, with currant aromas and flavors tinged with a touch of earthiness and gaminess. **82**
1987: Offers herb, currant, cherry and spice flavors that hang together nicely, but it's tight. **85**
1986: Mature, with strikingly firm tannins and a sharp acidity which enlivens the herb, black cherry and spice nuances. **87**
1985: Firm and tight, with a gamy edge to the black cherry, raspberry, currant and plum flavors. **88**
1984: Turning tannic and austere, with cherry, berry and anise flavors that finish with gripping tannins. **87**
1983: Crisp and austere, with firm tannins now overshadowing the earthy fruit flavors. **83**
1981: Mature, with an earthy, dry edge to the plum and currant flavors. **84**
1980: Tart, compact and mature, with an earthy edge to the currant flavors. **85**

1978: Ripe and plush, with complex currant, plum and cherry aromas and flavors and smooth tannins on the finish. **88**
1977: Pleasant but past its prime, with drying Cabernet flavors. **82**

CLARET STAG'S LEAP DISTRICT (★★): Lean and earthy, with decent flavor, but less interesting of late.
1992: Tight, with hard currant, cedary oak and earth notes. **84**
1991: A lean and earthy wine with some pretty, ripe, juicy cherry and berry flavors. **84**
1990: Ripe and juicy, with intense plum and black cherry flavors that are lively and supple. **87**

MERLOT STAG'S LEAP DISTRICT (★★): Lacks the depth and intensity of the Cabernet, but is pleasant enough, with its herb and cherry notes.

STERLING VINEYARDS (★★–★★★★)
Calistoga, Napa Valley
Founded: 1964. **Owner:** Seagram Chateau & Estate Wines Co. **Winemaker:** Rob Hunter.

MAJOR WINES: PRICE, CASES, RATING
Cabernet Sauvignon Napa Valley	
($14, 76,000)	★★
Cabernet Sauvignon Napa Valley Diamond Mountain Ranch Vineyard	
($18, 6,400)	★★
Chardonnay Napa Valley	
($15, 65,000)	★★★
Chardonnay Napa Valley Carneros Winery Lake Vineyard	
($20, 4,000)	★★
Merlot Napa Valley	
($14, 85,000)	★★
Merlot Napa Valley Carneros Winery Lake Vineyard	
($35, 1,000)	★★★
Merlot Napa Valley Diamond Mountain Ranch	
($35, 800)	★★★
Merlot Napa Valley Three Palms Vineyard	
($25, 2,500)	★★★

Pinot Noir Napa Valley Carneros Winery
Lake Vineyard
($16, 7,750)   ★★
Red Napa Valley Reserve
($50, 6,400)   ★★★★
Red Napa Valley Three Palms Vineyard
(Discontinued)   ★★★
Sauvignon Blanc North Coast
($12, 81,000)   ★★

WINERY DATA

Case Production: 350,000. **Acres Owned:** 733 acres in Napa Valley & Carneros. **Varietals by Acre:** Cabernet Franc (50 acres), Cabernet Sauvignon (239), Chardonnay (130), Malbec (9), Merlot (109), Petit Verdot (9), Pinot Noir (64), Sangiovese (5), Sauvignon Blanc (93) Sémillon (25). **Vineyard Designations:** Diamond Mountain Ranch Vineyard (Cabernet Sauvignon, Merlot), Winery Lake Vineyard (Chardonnay, Merlot, Pinot Noir), Three Palms Vineyard (Merlot). **Varietals Purchased:** Cabernet Franc (Napa Valley), Cabernet Sauvignon (Howell Mountain, Mendocino, Napa Valley, Sonoma), Charbono (Napa Valley), Chardonnay (Napa Valley, Sonoma), Malvasia Bianca (Central Coast), Merlot (Howell Mountain, Napa Valley, Sonoma), Muscat Canelli (Napa Valley), Pinot Gris (Napa Valley, Sonoma), Sangiovese (Napa Valley, Sonoma), Sauvignon Blanc (Howell Mountain, Napa Valley, Mendocino, Sonoma), Sauvignon Musque (Napa Valley), Sémillion (Napa Valley), Syrah (Sonoma), Viognier (Sonoma), Zinfandel (Napa Valley, Sonoma).

In the early 1960s, a group of Sterling International Paper Co. executives headed by Peter Newton founded Sterling Vineyards, building the white, monastic-looking winery on a hill south of Calistoga with the goal of creating a tourist destination, complete with a tram ride to the top of the hill. Sterling hired Ric Forman as winemaker for the 1969 vintage, focusing on Bordeaux-style wines (red and white) and on Chardonnay. In 1977, Sterling's owners decided to sell to the Coca-Cola Bottling Co. of Atlanta. (Newton and Forman left to start a winery together, then went their separate ways, each emerging with his own winery.) Sterling was sold to Seagram in 1983.

Throughout the early years, quality—especially that of the Cabernet, Sauvignon Blanc and Merlot—was usually very good. In the early 1980s, Sterling's Diamond Mountain Ranch vineyard began producing grapes for two lines of vineyard-designated wines, Cabernet and Chardonnay. Sterling acquired Winery Lake Vineyard in Carneros in 1986, and began producing vineyard-designated Chardonnay and Pinot Noir. As volume has increased, how-ever, quality has slipped across the board; the Cabernet, Chardonnay, Merlot and Sauvignon Blanc have all become lighter and simpler. Moreover, the vineyard-designated wines—most notably Winery Lake Chardonnay and Pinot Noir—have at times been disappointing.

Sterling has considerable vineyard holdings to draw upon, with 733 acres in vines, led by Cabernet (239 acres), Chardonnay (130), Merlot (109) and Sauvignon Blanc (93). The standard bottlings of these four varietals are each made in the 65,000–80,000-case range, and the winery plans to further increase production. Bill Dyer, an employee since 1977, was winemaker from 1985 to 1996, enjoying his greatest success with the often brilliant Sterling Reserve, a Cabernet-based red that is often among the state's best. Rob Hunter has now replaced him, moving to Sterling from Markham, and Greg Fowler of Mumm is also involved in the winemaking. I expect quality to improve, making this winery worth watching.

TASTING NOTES

CABERNET SAUVIGNON NAPA VALLEY (★★): Has declined in quality. Often lean and herbal with earthy flavors, though when it has riper flavors it offers good value.
1995: Lean and trim, with a tight, narrow band of currant, cedar, earth and clay-like flavors. Finishes with firm tannins. **88**
1994: Solid, with a band of leathery currant, cherry and cedary oak flavors and a finish marked by firm tannins. **84**
1993: Shows herb and cedary notes laced with just enough cherry and berry flavors to keep it interesting. Turns simple on the finish. **84**
1992: Austere and tannic, adding a spicy, minty edge to the currant and berry flavor. Could use some more finesse and generosity. **85**

CABERNET SAUVIGNON NAPA VALLEY DIAMOND MOUNTAIN RANCH VINEYARD (★★): Less complex and focused of late, it comes across as simple, earthy and tannic. Older vintages haven't aged well.
1995: Tight and smoky, with firm, earthy tannins and notes of mineral, currant, sage and cedary; turns complex and leathery on the finish. **88**
1994: Ruggedly tannic, with a strong leathery edge, it takes a while for the earthy currant notes to fight through the tannins. **85**
1993: Tight and tannic, with a pleasant array of earthy

currant, mineral, smoky oak and herbal flavors and substantial tannins. **88**

1992: Ripe, harmonious, supple currant, black cherry, anise and cedary notes finish with crisp acidity and firm tannins. **88**

CHARDONNAY NAPA VALLEY (★★★): While this wine was once quite lean and hard-edged, recent vintages have been more appealing. The 1997 (88 points) was refreshingly fruity.

CHARDONNAY NAPA VALLEY CARNEROS WINERY LAKE VINEYARD (★★): Declined sharply in quality, hitting bottom in 1992 with an earthy, metallic wine. The 1995 (88 points) was better, focusing on ripe pear and citrus flavors.

MERLOT NAPA VALLEY (★★): Has declined in quality, with modest fruit flavors.

MERLOT NAPA VALLEY CARNEROS WINERY LAKE VINEYARD (★★★)
1995: Packs in plenty of flavors, with ripe plum, currant, sage and spice, picking up anise and coffee notes along with a pleasant earthiness on the finish. **87**

MERLOT NAPA VALLEY DIAMOND MOUNTAIN RANCH (★★★): Seemingly more supple and polished than the Cabernet.
1995: Shows a measure of polish and finesse, with the spicy, toasty oak flavors integrated into the core of coffee, currant and dried cherry. Holds its focus and it's well balanced with ripe tannins. **87**
1994: Supple and harmonious, with a dense core of earthy currant, spice and herbal notes and a pretty overlay of buttery oak. Firm tannins. **88**

MERLOT NAPA VALLEY THREE PALMS VINEYARD (★★★)
1995: Tough, tight and tannic; just a glimmer of currant and cherry fruit peeks through. Finishes with tobacco, tar, coffee and cedary notes, turning dry on the finish. 86
1994: Dense and chewy, with firm, earthy tannins and a slight leathery edge to the currant and plum. **85**

PINOT NOIR NAPA VALLEY CARNEROS WINERY LAKE VINEYARD (★★): After an impressive debut wine in 1986, these wines became increasingly light and simple. Though recent efforts have had more appeal, they're still off the pace of the best from Carneros.

RED NAPA VALLEY RESERVE (★★★★): Sterling's best wine; typically dark, ripe, rich, complex and well-oaked, with smooth, polished tannins. Ages well, peaking at about five to eight years.

1995: Deliciously complex, with a pretty array of ripe currant, black cherry, sage, cedar and spice, gaining depth and nuance on the long, intricate aftertaste that keeps pumping out the flavor. **94**
1994: Firm and well oaked, with a hard edge to the cedar, currant and tobacco flavors; it lacks additional dimensions, however. **88**
1993: Pleasant, with its spicy currant and plum flavors; finishes with a sense of elegance and finesse. **88**
1992: Well oaked, with firm, dry tannins, cherry and currant fruit, light oak and chewy tannins. **87**
1991: Firm, dark and intense, with complex currant, black cherry, cedar and spice flavors, showing the most depth and finesse of any Sterling Cabernet since 1986. **91**
1990: Elegant, with spicy oak and vanilla notes and supple currant and black cherry flavors. **87**
1989: Delivers ripe currant, black cherry, anise and spice flavors, then frames them with toasty, buttery, smoky oak notes. **88**
1988: Modestly flavorful, with drying, tough tannins dominating the tart cherry and herb flavors. **85**
1987: Round, smooth and supple, with an elegant core of earthy currant, tar, black cherry, sage and herb flavors. **90**
1986: Elegant and complex, offering ripe cherry, currant, anise, smoke and meat flavors and fine tannins. **90**
1985: A supple, elegant and complex wine packed into a firm package, it's powerful, smooth, supple and finely focused, glowing with plum, cherry and cassis flavors that are deep and concentrated. **96**
1984: Beautifully defined, rich, supple and concentrated, with layers of ripe plum, currant, mint and spice flavors that are intense, yet fine. **90**
1983: Extremely dry and tannic, very austere and concentrated, with lean mint, currant and berry flavors. **82**
1982: Marked by weedy, mulchy and herbal flavors. **75**
1981: Austere and tannic, with a drying edge to the modest currant, cherry and oak flavors. **83**
1980: Mature, with rich, earthy plum, black cherry and smoky oak flavors. It has peaked. **88**
1979: A dry, dusty oakiness overrides the currant and spice flavors. **77**
1978: Smooth, polished, fully mature and showing well,

with intense currant, herb and olive flavors that are complex and lingering. **90**

1974: Along with an earthy tannic streak, this wine offers complex spice, tart black cherry and mature currant flavors that turn dry on the finish. **83**

1973: Mature, with a core of hearty, earthy currant and spicy wood flavors. **85**

RED NAPA VALLEY THREE PALMS VINEYARD (★★★): More tannic and austere than the Reserve. This vineyard south of the winery yields more austere wines, as evidenced by Duckhorn's bottling, which is similar in texture and weight to Sterling's.

1991: Tight, youthful and chewy, packing in ripe berry and currant flavors and ample tannins. **86**

1988: Tight and firm, with attractive plum, currant, spice and tobacco flavors. **85**

1987: Big and tannic, with a core of currant and black cherry flavors, but the tannins really box it in. **87**

1986: Rich, supple, tannic and flavorful, with decent depth and ripe currant and plum notes. **85**

1985: Graced with ripe currant, black cherry and plum flavors along with buttery oak, offering depth and complexity. **89**

SAUVIGNON BLANC NORTH COAST (★★): Once a leader, but the most recent bottlings have been light and thin, marked by herbal flavors. The 1997 (82 points) offered moderate fruit flavors.

STEVENOT WINERY (★★)
Sierra Foothills, Calaveras County
Founded: 1978. **Owner:** Barden Stevenot. **Winemaker:** Chuck Hovey. **Second Label:** Sierra.

MAJOR WINES: PRICE, CASES, RATING
Barbera Sierra Foothills
  ($18, 500)   ★★
Cabernet Sauvignon Sierra Foothills
  ($14, 4,000)   ★★
Chardonnay Calaveras County Shaw Ranch
  ($18, 1,000)   ★★
Chardonnay Sierra Foothills
  ($8, 2,000)   ★★
Chardonnay Sierra Foothills Reserve
  ($12, 10,000)   ★★
Merlot Sierra Foothills
  ($12, 10,000)   ★★
Sangiovese Sierra Foothills
  ($18, 500)   ★★
Sauvignon Blanc Sierra Foothills
  ($12, 2,400)   ★★
Syrah Sierra Foothills
  ($18, 500)   ★★
Zinfandel Sierra Foothills
  ($10, NA)   ★★

ALSO PRODUCED
White Zinfandel Amador County ($8, 4,000).

WINERY DATA
Case Production: 40,000. **Acres Owned:** 25 acres in Calaveras County. **Varietals by Acre:** Cabernet Sauvignon (5 acres), Chardonnay (15), Merlot (1), Zinfandel (4). **Varietals Purchased:** Barbera (Sierra Foothills), Cabernet Franc (Sierra Foothills), Cabernet Sauvignon (Sierra Foothills), Chardonnay (Sierra Foothills), Merlot (Sierra Foothills), Sangiovese (Sierra Foothills), Sauvignon Blanc (Sierra Foothills), Sémillion (Sierra Foothills), Syrah (Sierra Foothills), Zinfandel (Sierra Foothills).

Barden Stevenot bought an old cattle ranch in 1969 and planted a 25-acre vineyard on it. He opened his winery in 1978, and has built a brand that now produces 40,000 cases. The focus is on Cabernet, Chardonnay, Merlot and Zinfandel. There is not much consistency in style, though the wines are generally fair to good, with Chardonnay and Sauvignon Blanc the best of the bunch in recent years. The 1996 Chardonnay (88 points) was smoky and rich with tropical fruit flavors, while the 1996 Chardonnay Shaw Ranch (85) was smooth, with notes of mineral and citrus. The 1996 Sauvignon Blanc (88) was bright and tangy with mineral-laced lime and grapefruit flavors. Recent reds such as the 1996 Syrah (80), 1996 Barbera (82) and 1996 Zinfandel (82) all displayed simple berry flavors, marked by earthy or slightly bitter streaks. The 1996 Sangiovese (85) was an exception, showing generous berry and plum flavors on a polished frame.

STONEGATE WINERY (★★)
Calistoga, Napa Valley
Founded: 1973. **Owner:** California Wine Co.
Winemaker: Andy Schweiger.

MAJOR WINES: PRICE, CASES, RATING
Cabernet Sauvignon Blend Napa Valley
($14, 2,500) ★★
Chardonnay Sonoma County
($15, 750) ★★★

ALSO PRODUCED
Cabernet Franc Blend Napa Valley ($18, 281); Merlot Blend Napa Valley ($20, 1,400); Sauvignon Blanc Late Harvest Napa Valley ($15, 200); Sauvignon Blanc Napa Valley ($10, 186).

WINERY DATA
Case Production: 15,000. **Acres Owned:** 210 acres in Napa Valley. **Varietals by Acre:** Cabernet Franc (10 acres), Cabernet Sauvignon (100), Malbec (5), Merlot (75), Petit Verdot (5), Sauvignon Blanc (15). **Varietals Purchased:** Cabernet Sauvignon (Napa), Chardonnay (Sonoma), Merlot (Napa).

In 1969, Jim Spaulding, a journalism professor, moved his family to Napa Valley, and purchased mountain property for vineyards. In 1973, he established Stonegate off of Highway 29, south of Calistoga, near Sterling Vineyards. The winery focuses on a Cabernet Blend, Cabernet Franc (Pershing Hills Vineyard), Chardonnay (Bella Vista Vineyard, Sonoma) and Sauvignon Blanc. Quality has been highly variable, but recent vintages have shown more polish and fruit flavors. In 1997, the winery was sold to the California Wine Co., owner of Bandiera Winery.

STONESTREET (★★★–★★★★)
Alexander Valley, Sonoma County
Founded: 1989. **Owner:** Jess Jackson. **Winemaker:** Mike Westrick.

MAJOR WINES: PRICE, CASES, RATING
Cabernet Sauvignon Alexander Valley
($36, 10,000) ★★★
Cabernet Sauvignon Alexander Valley
Alexander Mountain Estate
($42, 500) ★★★★
Cabernet Sauvignon Alexander Valley
Three Block Alexander Mountain Estate
($60, NA) ★★★★
Chardonnay Alexander Valley Alexander
Mountain Estate Upper Barn
($34, 500) ★★★★
Chardonnay Sonoma County
($24, 30,000) ★★★★
Gewürztraminer Anderson Valley Mendocino
($18, 500) ★★★
Legacy Red Alexander Valley
($65, 3,500) ★★★★
Merlot Alexander Valley
($36, 14,000) ★★★
Pinot Noir Russian River Valley
($30, 2,500) ★★★
Sauvignon Blanc Alexander Mountain Estate
($20, 500) ★★★

WINERY DATA
Case Production: 62,000. **Acres Owned:** 1,225 acres in Alexander Valley. **Varietals by Acre:** Cabernet Franc (20 acres), Cabernet Sauvignon (650), Chardonnay (280), Merlot (240), Sauvignon Blanc (35).

Stonestreet, another one of Jess "Stonestreet" Jackson's (Kendall-Jackson) properties, was established in the former Stephen Zellerbach winery in 1989. The winery now has 1,225 acres in Alexander Valley, tilted heavily toward Cabernet Sauvignon, but there is also a large number of acres dedicated to Chardonnay and Merlot. The winery plans to move into a new home near Jimtown in Alexander Valley by the year 2000.

Under the direction first of Stephen Test and now of Mike Westrick, the quality of the wines has been very good and steadily improving, with Cabernet Sauvignon, Meritage red (Legacy), Chardonnay, Gewürztraminer, Merlot, Pinot Noir and Sauvignon Blanc, each impressive for their distinctive styles. Worth buying and collecting.

TASTING NOTES

CABERNET SAUVIGNON ALEXANDER VALLEY (★★★★): Steadily improving, with riper, richer, more complex flavors. **1995:** Complex, intense and well integrated, with ripe, rich fruit and lots of currant, anise, earth, mineral and spice flavors, turning leathery on the finish. **91**

1994: Well balanced, with supple coffee, herb, currant and cedary oak flavors, it turns smooth and polished on the finish. **91**

1993: Displays a pleasant band of cedar, spice and currant flavors, but it lacks richness and loses concentration on the finish. **84**

1992: Tight and compact, with complex, concentrated, well focused cherry, currant and cedar flavors. **91**

1991: Smooth and elegant, with appealing cherry, currant and cedary notes, finishing with good length and crisp tannins. **87**

1989: Has ripe currant and spicy oak flavors with a strong herbal, floral edge and a note of green bean and bell pepper. **82**

1988: Crisp and fruity, with modestly intense currant, plum and smoke aromas and flavors laced with an herbal, woody overtone. **82**

CABERNET SAUVIGNON ALEXANDER VALLEY THREE BLOCK ALEXANDER MOUNTAIN ESTATE (★★★★): The first bottling from the 1995 vintage was impressive.

1995: Elegant and complex, with layers of cedar, black cherry, wild berry and spicy nuances, turning sleek and earthy on the finish, where the tannins are mild but firm. **92**

CHARDONNAY ALEXANDER VALLEY ALEXANDER MOUNTAIN ESTATE UPPER BARN (★★★★): Rich, creamy and well-oaked, but packs lots of complex flavors. From a site that has served Helen Turley of Marcassin quite well.

1996: Elegant, with flavors of spicy, toasty oak, picking up complex pear, tart apple and citrus fruit, along with subtle, earthy nuances. **92**

1995: Smooth, ripe and creamy, with rich apple, pear, citrus and spice flavors and a touch of stalkiness around the edges. **88**

CHARDONNAY SONOMA COUNTY (★★★★)

1995: A big, ripe and intense style, with layers of rich fig, melon, apple, pear and apricot, finishing with a smoky oak edge. **91**

LEGACY RED ALEXANDER VALLEY (★★★★): Rich, complex and well-oaked, with tannins in check; now a consistently strong performer.

1995: Tight, rich and concentrated, with tiers of coffee, currant, anise, sage and berry, it slowly unfolds to reveal its wonderful flavors. **91**

1994: Smooth, supple and deeply concentrated, with a

rich, detailed core of mineral, coffee, currant, cherry and sage and a long, complex finish. **93**

1992: Supple, complex and harmonious, with layers of smoky oak, currant, cherry and spice and smooth, thick tannins. **92**

1991: Smooth, plush and elegant, with a core of rich, focused plum and currant flavors, turning mildly tannic. **91**

1990: Crisp and spicy, with a chocolate edge to the core of modest berry and currant flavors. **86**

MERLOT ALEXANDER VALLEY (★★★): Rich and complex, with a nice balance between ripe fruit and spicy oak seasonings.

1995: The flavor core is built around dry coffee, herb and currant flavors, turning austere and tannic on the finish. **86**

1994: Tight, with a pretty core of currant, chocolate, berry and spice flavors, finishing with firm tannins and a good length. **88**

PINOT NOIR RUSSIAN RIVER VALLEY (★★★): Improving, with elegant herb and cherry-laced fruit.

1995: Ripe and spicy; an elegant style with pretty plum, wild berry, tea, herb and cherry flavors. **89**

1994: Complex, with earthy, ripe plum and cherry flavors, turning toasty and tannic on the finish. **87**

SAUVIGNON BLANC ALEXANDER MOUNTAIN ESTATE (★★★): Very distinctive, rich and textured.

STONY HILL VINEYARD (★★★★)
St. Helena, Napa Valley
Founded: 1952. **Owner:** Peter and Willinda McCrea. **Winemaker:** Michael Chelini. **Second Label:** SHV.

MAJOR WINES: PRICE, CASES, RATING
Chardonnay Napa Valley
($21, 3,000)   ★★★★

ALSO PRODUCED
Gewürztraminer Napa Valley ($12, 250); Sémillon Napa Valley Sémillon de Soleil ($12, 150); White Riesling Napa Valley ($12, 550).

WINERY DATA
Case Production: 5,000. **Acres Owned:** 38 acres in Napa Valley. **Varietals by Acre:** Chardonnay (28 acres), Gewürztraminer (3), Sémillon (1), White Riesling (6).

Stony Hill is one of Napa Valley's legendary wineries because of its long-lived Chardonnays, but it's been a long time since this winery has really produced anything of note. Fred and Eleanor McCrea bought the property as a weekend retreat in 1943. Situated north of St. Helena in the western hills near Napa Valley-Bothe State Park, Stony Hill took its name from the rugged terrain. In 1946, the McCreas began planting their vineyard at one to two acres a year, focussing initially on Chardonnay, and later adding Riesling, Gewürztraminer and Sémillon. They started producing wine commercially in 1952.

Although the winery had the size and appearance of a hobby, the McCreas took winemaking seriously, slowly building production, and always paying the greatest attention to quality and detail. The Stony Hill Chardonnay style emphasized tight, tart, flinty green apple and pear notes early on, but what really set these wines apart from others was their ability to age and develop for years.

Only in the late 1980s and early 1990s did the wines take a dip in quality. Much of the 38-acre vineyard has been replanted, a victim of Pierce's disease, and grapes have been bought from Howell Mountain, both for the SHV bottling and now for part of the main Stony Hill line. While the most recent vintages have seemed simpler and fruitier that those of yesteryear, it remains to be seen how wines from the new plantings will evolve. Most of the Chardonnay, Riesling and Gewürztraminer are sold via mailing list.

TASTING NOTES

CHARDONNAY NAPA VALLEY (★★★★): Even though the most recent vintages have lacked the depth and focus of the glory years, this remains a great estate based on its amazing track record for superb wines, dating back to the 1950s. These wines do not undergo malolactic fermentation, are not *sur lie* aged, nor do they see the insides of toasty French oak barrels. As such, they are often lean, floral, tart and subtle wines that need time in the bottle.

1992: Austere and earthy, with a metallic edge to the pineapple and citrus flavors. **83**

1991: Elegant and vibrant, with pretty peach, nectarine and spice nuances. **88**

1990: Firm, tight and spicy, with compact pear, apple and light citrus notes that come through on the finish. **88**

1988: Wonderfully complex and elegant, with tiers of pure pear, honey and melon flavors and a charming touch of spicy nutmeg and oak seasoning. **90**

1986: Ripe, rich and full of fresh pear, honey, nutmeg and oak flavors, this is a very youthful wine that needs time to fill out. The flavors are focused and well balanced, with all the ingredients to move up a notch or two. **87**

1985: Ripe and rich, with intense, sharply focused pear, honey, toast, melon and nutmeg flavors that are remarkably elegant and smooth. **92**

1984: Very ripe and forward, with generous pear, melon, spice flavors and subtle pine and oak shadings. **90**

1982: Quite successful for this troubled vintage, it has with age become more pleasing, with elegant, delicate, creamy pear and melon flavors and fine balance, finishing with good length. At its peak. **85**

1981: Typical of the vintage; very ripe, rich and forward, big and full, with spice, honey, pear, vanilla and nutmeg flavors that glide across the palate with a creamy, smooth texture. At its peak. **86**

1980: Aging gracefully; rich, full-bodied and ripe, with intense honey, pear, spice and vanilla flavors all neatly knit and balanced. This wine is ready to drink, although it has the depth and richness to gain for a few more years. **86**

1979: Deep, mature color, with toasty hazelnut, spice and fig flavors, but in decline and beginning to lose its fruit. Drink soon. **81**

1978: Fully mature, yellow-gold, a bit alcoholic but holding up well, with rich, ripe pear, lemon, honey, spice and cocoa flavors and a soft, smooth texture. Not likely to improve; drink soon. **85**

1977: Almost opposite in style from the 1976, this wine is high in acidity and austere in character, with fresh, vibrant pear, citrus and melon notes that are clean and refreshing. Delicate, with excellent balance, it still has years of life ahead. **91**

1976: Very rich, bold and ripe, with layers of honey, pear, toast and butter flavors that offer excellent depth. With aeration it develops further complexities and subtleties. One of the few successes of the 1976 vintage. **88**

1975: A sulfuric quality is evident in this wine; a strong flavor and aroma and a coarseness on the palate. It has a charm of its own, but some may not be able to look past the sulfur. **75**

1974: Appears to have more oak and sulfur than fruit, giving it a slight rubbery flavor. It's pleasant, but those especially sensitive to sulfur may find that quality distracting. **73**

1973: Fading now, but early on it was quite lovely.

Delicate, with pretty pear and melon flavors. **79**

1972: Elegant and delicate, with pear, anise and spice notes that are a bit blunt, it's a very good wine from a difficult vintage. **83**

1971: Fresh and open when first poured, but not quite as full in the glass, where the ginger, pear and vanilla flavors are delicate and light. Past its prime but still enjoyable. **80**

1970: Ripe, rich, smooth and complex, in peak condition, with distinctive vanilla flavors, a creamy texture and hints of pear, spice and honey. **92**

1968: A wine of great concentration and depth that may still be a few years from peaking. It offers intense honey, pear, spice and vanilla flavors that are rich, elegant and very sharply focused. **93**

1965: Forward and fruity, with a silky smooth texture and honey, pear, melon and spice nuances that are amazingly persistent, elegant and impeccably balanced. Acidity carries the flavors on and on. **90**

1964: The greatest Stony Hill ever produced and the finest California Chardonnay I've ever tasted, the 1964 opens up to reveal rich, intense, deeply concentrated fruit flavors that echo earth, mushroom, honey, toast and pear notes before developing a creamy butterscotch aftertaste. **98**

1962: Absolutely wonderful, complex and elegant, with subtlety and finesse and sharply focused pear, honey, butterscotch and nutmeg flavors that fan out on the palate. **96**

1960: Remarkably youthful and lively for a 30-something Chardonnay, still quite rich, with delicate pear, pineapple and spice flavors, deftly balanced, with a creamy vanilla texture and a long, lingering finish. **88**

STORYBOOK MOUNTAIN VINEYARDS (★★★)

Calistoga, Napa Valley
Founded: 1976. **Owner:** Jerry & Sigrid Seps.
Winemaker: Jerry Seps.

MAJOR WINES: PRICE, CASES, RATING
Zinfandel Howell Mountain
($19, 800) ★★★
Zinfandel Napa Valley Estate Eastern Exposures
($21, 800) ★★★
Zinfandel Napa Valley Estate Mayacamas Range
($19, 5,000) ★★★
Zinfandel Napa Valley Estate Reserve
($29, 800) ★★★

WINERY DATA
Case Production: 7,000. **Acres Owned:** 40 acres in Napa Valley. **Varietals by Acre:** Zinfandel (40 acres). **Varietals Purchased:** Zinfandel (Howell Mountain).

Jerry Seps taught history at Stanford University before turning to wine, initially as an apprentice for Joseph Swan in Sonoma. He started his winery in 1976, purchasing the old Grimm Brothers Winery (founded 1882) north of Calistoga, which was planted to Zinfandel. Zinfandel quickly became Storybook Mountain's specialty. Seps's goals are twofold: to craft long-lived and age-worthy Zinfandels (which he does), and to raise the grape's image among wine lovers. (He's done that too, having helped found ZAP, Zinfandel Advocates and Producers). His 40-acre vineyard yields wines of distinctive character; the Reserve wines in particular are big, ripe, intense and earthy—traits many feel make Storybook's the quintessential mountain-grown Zinfandel, despite its heavy-handedness. Production is 7,000 cases, including a new bottling from purchased Howell Mountain grapes. Most recently the style has shifted to somewhat fruitier wines.

TASTING NOTES

ZINFANDEL HOWELL MOUNTAIN (★★★): Can be brilliant, with classic pepper and berry flavors, but it can also be ruggedly earthy, tannic and disjointed, depending on the year.

ZINFANDEL NAPA VALLEY ESTATE EASTERN EXPOSURES (★★★): Tends to be austere and lean, though consistent.
1995: Austere, even tart, with a mix of sage, berry, mineral and spice flavors and firm tannins. **87**
1994: Tight, tart and mildly tannic, with a pretty core of black cherry, wild berry, earth, anise and spice flavors. **88**
1992: Warm, ripe, supple and harmonious, the pretty plum and black cherry flavors turn smooth on the finish. **89**

ZINFANDEL NAPA VALLEY ESTATE MAYACAMAS RANGE (★★★): Shows more ripe, juicy flavors, and a polished texture.
1996: Appealing for its ripe fruitiness, with plum, floral and wild berry flavors, turning tannic on the finish. **88**
1994: Ripe and juicy, with layers of plum, black cherry,

spice and cedar, it's vibrant and zesty. **90**

ZINFANDEL NAPA VALLEY ESTATE RESERVE (★★★): Similar to the regular bottling in its inconsistency and earthy tannins, but the early 1980s vintages have aged well, surrendering their fresh raspberry fruit to earthy, anise and tarry notes, but softening nonetheless. Recent vintages appear more variable and may show better with short-term cellaring.
1991: Tightly wound, with austere berry, pepper and sage notes, turning tannic on the finish. **86**
1989: Dense, oaky and earthy, this is tough and chewy, with its fruit submerged beneath the oak and earth. **71**
1988: Powerful, full-bodied and tannic, with peppery aromas and ample blackberry, tart cherry and spice flavors. **86**
1987: Amazingly ripe and powerful, with deep, rich, complex berry, cherry, pepper and spice flavors, turning very tannic. **89**
1986: Spicy, firm in texture and fragrant, with black pepper and raspberry aromas and flavors. **82**
1985: Extremely concentrated and tannic, with ripe, jammy plum and berry flavors, finishing with pepper and spice. **88**
1984: Ripe, concentrated and tannic, brimming with cherry, raspberry and plum flavors and a touch of mint. **88**

RODNEY STRONG VINEYARDS (★★–★★★)
Russian River Valley, Sonoma County
Founded: 1959. **Owner:** Tom Klein. **Winemaker:** Rick Sayre.

MAJOR WINES: PRICE, CASES, RATING

Cabernet Sauvignon Northern Sonoma Alexander's Crown Vineyard ($23, 2,000)	★★★
Cabernet Sauvignon Northern Sonoma Reserve ($35, 2,000)	★★★
Cabernet Sauvignon Sonoma County ($13, 10,000)	★★
Chardonnay Chalk Hill Estate ($16, 3,000)	★★
Chardonnay Sonoma County ($12, 10,000)	★★
Merlot Sonoma County ($16, 10,000)	★★
Pinot Noir Russian River Valley Estate Vineyard ($17, 3,000)	★★
Sauvignon Blanc Northern Sonoma Charlotte's Home Estate ($10, 2,000)	★★★
Zinfandel Northern Sonoma Old Vines ($16, 3,000)	★★★

WINERY DATA
Case Production: 300,000. **Acres Owned:** 543 acres (193 in Alexander Valley, 145 in Chalk Hill, 205 in Russian River Valley). **Varietals by Acre:** Cabernet Franc (6 acres), Cabernet Sauvignon (85), Chardonnay (257), Merlot (32), Pinot Noir (75), Sauvignon Blanc (59), Zinfandel (24). **Vineyard Designations:** Alexander's Crown Vineyard (Cabernet Sauvignon), Charlotte's Home Estate (Sauvignon Blanc). **Varietals Purchased:** Cabernet Sauvignon (Alexander Valley, Dry Creek, Russian River Valley), Chardonnay (Chalk Hill, Russian River), Merlot (Alexander Valley, Dry Creek, Russian River Valley), Zinfandel (Alexander Valley).

Rodney Strong Vineyards has gone through more changes than most wineries. It began in 1959 as Tiburon Vintners, then became Windsor Vineyards, a wine mail-order business. In 1970, it was renamed Sonoma Vineyards before shifting gears again, becoming Rodney Strong Vineyards. Through it all, Rodney Strong oversaw winemaking and management before easing into semi-retirement in 1995. The winery has generally produced good to very good wines, its star being the Alexander's Crown Cabernet from Alexander Valley, which dates back to 1974. Production is 300,000 cases under the Strong label, drawing from 543 acres of vineyard.

TASTING NOTES

CABERNET SAUVIGNON NORTHERN SONOMA ALEXANDER'S CROWN VINEYARD (★★★): Can be rich and complex, but has been variable of late, with more medium-bodied flavors than rich, concentrated fruit. Older bottlings carry the Sonoma Vineyards label.
1995: Strong cedary oak flavors override the mature, ripe plum and currant flavors that diffuse on the finish. **82**
1994: Clean and ripe, with appealing black cherry, currant, herb, earth and spice, firming up on the finish, where the tannins kick in. **86**
1993: Elegant, with a supple, well balanced core of currant, plum and wild berry, finishing with firm tannins and good length. Moderate richness and concentration. **88**

1992: Smooth and polished, with a focused, deftly balanced core of currant, plum and cherry flavors. Finishes with mild, smooth tannins and good length. **87**
1991: Light and spicy, with a fine thread of bright berry flavors to keep it lively. **86**

CABERNET SAUVIGNON NORTHERN SONOMA RESERVE (★★★): Of variable quality; not much of an improvement over the Alexander's Crown Vineyard bottling.
1994: A bit a raw and astringent, with firm, chewy tannins, it struggles to find a focus. Perhaps with time in the bottle the core of currant and cherry-laced fruit will become more harmonious. **86**
1993: Lean and trim, with a spicy band of black cherry, plum and berry notes. **87**
1992: Ripe, smooth and harmonious. Shows a supple core of plum, cherry, currant and mineral flavors, finishing with a touch of spice, herb and cedar. Plenty of tannins show up on the finish, but they're smooth and round. **89**
1991: Intense, if a bit murky in its focus, with spicy, toasty oak and a range of cherry and currant fruit underneath. Hangs together where the finish picks up a spicy edge. **86**

CHARDONNAY CHALK HILL ESTATE (★★): Quality was variable in 1991 and 1992; lacks the extra dimensions the best Sonoma Chardonnays display.

CHARDONNAY SONOMA COUNTY (★★): Medium-weight, with ripe fruit and light oak shadings.

MERLOT SONOMA COUNTY (★★): New to the lineup; light- to medium-bodied.

PINOT NOIR RUSSIAN RIVER VALLEY RIVER ESTATE VINEYARD (★★): Light in color, body and texture, but with attractive tea, herb and cherry notes. Best to drink early on.

SAUVIGNON BLANC NORTHERN SONOMA CHARLOTTE'S HOME ESTATE (★★★): Offers good intensity and lots of ripe fruit flavors.

ZINFANDEL NORTHERN SONOMA OLD VINES (★★★): This is an elegant wine, well oaked, with peppery berry notes.

STUHLMULLER VINEYARDS (★★★)
Alexander Valley, Sonoma County
Founded: 1996. **Owner:** Fritz Stuhlmuller. **Winemaker:** Kerry Damskey.

MAJOR WINES: PRICE, CASES, RATING
Chardonnay Alexander Valley
   ($21, 1,300)   ★★★

ALSO PRODUCED
Cabernet Sauvignon Alexander Valley ($35, 400).

WINERY DATA
Case Production: 2,000. **Acres Owned:** 140 acres in Alexander Valley. **Varietals by Acre:** Cabernet Sauvignon (65 acres), Chardonnay (75).

Fritz Stuhlmuller owns the Stuhlmuller brand, and his parents own the 140-acre vineyard in Alexander Valley which supplies the grapes. The Stuhlmullers sell most of their Cabernet and Chardonnay grapes, a portion of which has appeared in Cronin's wines. The 1996 Chardonnay (90 points) displays complex flavors of concentrated spicy apple, pear, citrus and melon. One to watch.

SULLIVAN VINEYARDS WINERY (★★)
Rutherford, Napa Valley
Founded: 1978. **Owner:** Jim Sullivan. **Winemaker:** Jim Sullivan.

MAJOR WINES: PRICE, CASES, RATING
Cabernet Sauvignon Rutherford
   ($32, 1,400)   ★★
Coeur de Vigne Red Rutherford
   ($60, 300)   ★★
Merlot Rutherford
   ($20, 1,000)   ★

ALSO PRODUCED
Chardonnay Rutherford ($20, 1,000).

WINERY DATA
Case Production: 4,000. **Acres Owned:** 22 acres in Rutherford. **Varietals by Acre:** Cabernet Sauvignon (11 acres), Merlot (11).

Graphic designer Jim Sullivan made the transition from home to commercial winemaking in 1979, buying the first four acres of what is now a 22-acre vineyard in Rutherford, east of Franciscan Vineyards. The red wines are made in a dense, rustic, often tannic style and require several years of aging to soften. The 1993 Coeur de Vigne Red (88 points) and the 1993 Cabernet Sauvignon (86) had tough, astringent tannins, along with ripe fruit flavors. The 1994 Merlot (77) was less successful, with coarse tannins and a vinegary edge.

SUMMERS (★★)
Napa Valley
Founded: 1992. **Owner:** James P. Summers. **Winemaker:** Corey Beck. **Second Label:** Villa Andriana.

MAJOR WINES: PRICE, CASES, RATING
Chardonnay Napa Valley
  ($20, 800)   ★★
Merlot Knights Valley Summers Ranch
  ($24, 2,000)   ★★★
Villa Andriana Bianco di Palisides
  ($9, 500)   ★★
Villa Andriana Charbono Napa Valley
  Vineyard
  ($18, 1,200)   ★★

ALSO PRODUCED
Rosso di Palisides Villa Andriana ($8, 100); Zinfandel Napa Valley Villa Andriana Vineyard ($16, 1,500).

WINERY DATA
Case Production: 7,000. **Acres Owned:** 50 acres (28 in Knights Valley, 22 in Napa Valley). **Varietals by Acre:** Cabernet Sauvignon (7 acres), Charbono (5), Merlot (33), Zinfandel (5). **Varietals Purchased:** Chardonnay (Napa Valley).

James Summers purchased the old San Pietro Vara winery on Tubbs Lane in Calistoga in 1996, moving the production of his Knights Valley Merlot and Napa Valley Charbono there. Zinfandel, Cabernet and Chardonnay have also been added to the portfolio. The 1995 Merlot (88 points) was smooth and polished, with ripe plum, currant and sage flavors. The Charbono tends to be rich, generous and fun to drink, with ripe blackberry, plum and spice flavors; the 1997 vintage (84) was supple, with grape flavors.

SUNSTONE VINEYARDS & WINERY (★★–★★★)
Santa Barbara County
Founded: 1989. **Owner:** The Rice Family. **Winemaker:** Fred Rice.

MAJOR WINES: PRICE, CASES, RATING
Cabernet Sauvignon Santa Barbara
  County
  ($18, 300)   ★
Chardonnay Santa Barbara County
  Marcellas Vineyards
  ($18, 2,200)   ★★★
Meritage Red Santa Barbara County Estate
  ($28, 1,250)   ★★
Merlot Santa Barbara County Estate
  ($20, 4,657)   ★★
Syrah Santa Barbara County
  ($24, 583)   ★★★

ALSO PRODUCED
Muscat Canelli Central Coast ($12, 240); Red Santa Barbara County ($22, 298); Viognier Santa Barbara County ($24, 272); White Santa Barbara County ($22, 292).

WINERY DATA
Case Production: 10,000. **Acres Owned:** 54 acres (26 in Santa Ynez Valley owned, 28 in Santa Ynez Valley leased). **Varietals by Acre:** Cabernet Franc (6 acres), Cabernet Sauvignon (3), Merlot (33), Syrah (11), Viognier (1). **Vineyard Designations:** Marcellas Vineyards (Chardonnay). **Varietals Purchased:** Chardonnay (Santa Barbara County), Marsanne (Santa Barbara County), Muscat Canelli (Central Coast), Viognier (Santa Barbara County).

This family-owned winery in Santa Ynez Valley had been focusing on Cabernet, Merlot, a Cabernet blend and Chardonnay with mixed results. Rhône varietals, particularly Syrah, have performed well here, and a push has been made to increase Syrah production with a combination of 29 new acres on two Santa Barbara County sites. Plantings of Cabernet Franc and Merlot, which have also done well, will likewise be increased.

While most of Sunstone's reds carry some earthy qualities, the Cabernet struggles to escape green, vegetal flavors. The Merlot, however, has improved since earlier vintages, and is now showing black cherry, cassis and licorice notes, as was seen in the 1996 (85 points). The

1995 Syrah (87) wrapped its meaty, herbal notes in plush anise and plum flavors. Chardonnay, showing hints of earth and mineral, can also be very good; the 1996 (87) showed firm citrus, nectarine, pea and mineral notes.

SUTTER HOME WINERY (★★)
Napa Valley
Founded: 1874. **Owner:** Trinchero Family. **Winemaker:** Steve Bertolucci.

MAJOR WINES: PRICE, CASES, RATING
Cabernet Sauvignon California
  ($6, 600,000) ★★
Chardonnay California
  ($6, 1,500,000) ★★
Merlot California
  ($6, 500,000) ★★
Sauvignon Blanc California
  ($5, 200,000) ★★
Zinfandel California
  ($5, 200,000) ★★

ALSO PRODUCED
Chenin Blanc California ($5, 50,000); Gewürztraminer California ($6, 75,000); Merlot Rosé California ($6, 125,000); Moscato California ($6, 80,000); Red Soleo California ($5, 150,000); White Soleo California ($5, 150,000); White Zinfandel California ($5, 4,000,000).

WINERY DATA
Case Production: 10,000,000. **Acres Owned:** 4,222 acres.
Varietals by Acre: Barbera (324 acres), Cabernet (222), Chardonnay (939), Chenin Blanc (250), Merlot (79), Sauvignon Blanc (250), Zinfandel (2,078), others (80).

The original Sutter Home Winery dates back to 1874. The Trinchero family bought the winery in 1947, bottling a wide assortment of wines. In 1968, Louis "Bob" Trinchero launched Amador County Zinfandel, which the winery produced through the 1970s. In 1972, Sutter Home experimented with a Blanc de Noirs, pressing Zinfandel grapes and leaving just a pink tinge and hint of sweetness; it was labeled white Zinfandel. That and other so-called "blush" wines triggered an explosion of similarly styled wines, but Sutter Home's proved the most successful, and its name became synonymous with white Zinfandel.

The success of white Zinfandel propelled Sutter Home to great financial heights. The winery has since added other varietals, including Cabernet, Chardonnay, Merlot, Sauvignon Blanc and Zinfandel, all made in a light- to medium-bodied, easy-to-drink style. Production now tops 10 million cases. The winery has vast vineyard resources, measuring 4,222 acres in vines (mostly in the Sacramento Valley), led by 2,078 acres of Zinfandel.

Amador Zin is still part of the product mix, albeit a small part. The winery has now extended its holdings in Amador, buying the Montevina Winery. It has also resumed producing Napa Valley appellation wines, led by a Cabernet and Chardonnay under the M. Trinchero label, both of which are very good.

TASTING NOTES

CABERNET SAUVIGNON VARIOUS BOTTLINGS (★★): Good, but the early tries were unexceptional.

CHARDONNAY CALIFORNIA (★★): Simple and lightly fruity, but a decent value.

MERLOT CALIFORNIA (★★): Light and simple too, with modest herbal flavors.

SAUVIGNON BLANC CALIFORNIA (★★): Simple, with a citrus edge to the flavors.

ZINFANDEL VARIOUS BOTTLINGS (★★): Well balanced, with tarry berry and earth notes.

JOSEPH SWAN VINEYARDS (★★★)
Russian River Valley, Sonoma County
Founded: 1969. **Owner:** Rod & Lynn Berglund. **Winemaker:** Rod Berglund.

MAJOR WINES: PRICE, CASES, RATING
Chardonnay Russian River Valley Estate
  ($20, 120) ★★★
Pinot Gris Russian River Valley
  Saralee's Vineyard
  ($15, 75) ★★★
Pinot Noir Russian River Valley
  ($10, 300) ★★★

Pinot Noir Russian River Valley Estate
($30, 250) ★★★
Pinot Noir Russian River Valley
Lone Redwood Ranch
($12, 200) ★★★
Pinot Noir Russian River Valley
Saralee's Vineyard
($15, 75) ★★★
Pinot Noir Sonoma Mountain Steiner
Vineyard
($22, 350) ★★★
Pinot Noir Sonoma Mountain Wolfspierre
Vineyard
($16, 75) ★★★
Zinfandel Russian River Valley Frati
Ranch
($24, 200) ★★★
Zinfindel Russian River Valley V.H.S.R.
Vineyard
(Discontinued) ★★★
Zinfandel Russian River Valley Zeigler
Vineyard
($20, 300) ★★★
Zinfandel Sonoma Valley Stellwagen
Vineyard
($20, 300) ★★★

ALSO PRODUCED
Cabernet Sauvignon Russian River Valley Estate ($25, 50);
Cabernet Sauvignon Sonoma Mountain Steiner Vineyard
($20, 125); Cotes du Rosa Russian River Valley ($12,
250); Mourvèdre Russian River Valley ($16, 90);
Zinfandel Russian River Valley Lone Redwood Ranch
($20, 600); Zinfandel Russian River Valley Mancini
Ranch ($1,000, NA).

WINERY DATA
Case Production: 5,000. **Acres Owned:** 10 acres in Russian
River Valley. **Varietals by Acre:** Cabernet Sauvignon (1 acre),
Chardonnay (1), Pinot Noir (7), Syrah/Viognier (1). **Vineyard
Designations:** Steiner Vineyard (Cabernet Sauvignon, Pinot Noir),
Saralee's Vineyard (Pinot Noir), Lone Redwood Ranch (Pinot
Noir, Zinfandel), Wolfspierre Vineyard (Pinot Noir), Stellwagen
Vineyard (Zinfandel), Frati Ranch (Zinfandel), Mancini Ranch
(Zinfandel), Zeigler Vineyard (Zinfandel). **Varietals Purchased:**
Cabernet Sauvignon (Sonoma Mountain), Pinot Gris (Russian
River Valley), Pinot Noir (Russian River Valley, Sonoma
Mountain), Zinfandel (Russian River Valley, Sonoma Valley).

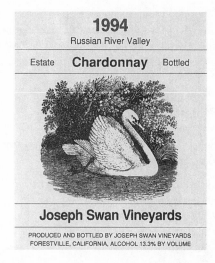

Over the years, Joseph Swan has become something of a
Zinfandel legend, but the winery also excels with Pinot Noir.
Among his many admirers and pupils were Joel Peterson
(Ravenswood) and Jerry Seps (Storybook Mountain), both
of whom credit Swan's passion for and success with
Zinfandel for their pursuit of that wine. For many, Swan
Zinfandels typified the big, bold, ripe, high-extract style of
the 1970s; many of them have aged well, further encourag-
ing the use of this style, however exaggerated.

In the 1980s, Swan lost some of his key vineyards,
and quality dipped, with Pinot Noir emerging as his best
wine. After Swan's death in 1988, son-in-law Rod
Berglund became winemaker. The most recent
Zinfandels are very well crafted, with vineyard-designated wines forming part of the mix. Production hovers at
around 5,000 cases. The winery owns a total of 10 acres
of vines, planted mostly to Pinot Noir.

TASTING NOTES

PINOT NOIR RUSSIAN RIVER VALLEY (★★★): Marked
by earthy flavors and tannin.
1993: Austere and tannic for the level of fruit; crisp with
a band of citrus and tart berry. **82**
1992: Mature, with supple black cherry, plum and spice
notes, finishing with a complex aftertaste. **87**
1991: Elegant, with racy cherry and wild berry flavors,
firm tannins and hints of anise and sage. **86**

PINOT NOIR RUSSIAN RIVER VALLEY ESTATE (★★★):

Ages well, showing rich, concentrated cherry, wild berry and earthy herb-tinged flavors.

1996: A touch earthy and crisp but has wonderful richness to the plum, wildberry and anise flavors. **90**

1995: Tough, with dry, earthy and leathery tannins, it slowly reveals a core of cherry and berry fruit. **87**

1994: The ripe cherry, plum and berry flavors are appealing, but the texture is tough and coarse. **88**

1991: Elegant, with racy cherry and wild berry flavors. Drinking well now, with light tannins and a hint of anise and sage on the finish. Good, but not especially complex, though more supple than it was on release. **86**

1990: Delicious Pinot Noir, pure and simple, with a juicy core of ripe, rich raspberry, black cherry, anise and plum flavors that are deep, complex and concentrated. Finishes with a long fruity aftertaste that keeps pumping out the flavors. **94**

PINOT NOIR SONOMA MOUNTAIN STEINER VINEYARD (★★★)

1996: Tight and firmly tannic, with a green tea-like edge to the barely ripe Pinot Noir fruit flavors. **84**

1995: A touch earthy and herbal, with cedar, tar and spicy berry flavors, finishing with chewy tannins. **87**

PINOT NOIR SONOMA MOUNTAIN WOLFSPIERRE VINEYARD (★★★)

1996: Elegant, ripe and spicy, with pretty black cherry and strawberry fruit and hints of sage, mineral and vanilla. **86**

1995: Decidedly minty, with a bay leaf and sage edge to the dried cherry flavors, turning crisp and tannic on the finish. **88**

ZINFANDEL RUSSIAN RIVER VALLEY FRATI RANCH

(★★★★): Decidedly improved since the 1980s, showing more depth, flavor and consistency.

1996: A touch earthy, with a mushroomy edge, it works its way into dried fruit flavors, with hints of plum, raspberry, spice and cedar that linger. **88**

1995: Ripe, juicy, rich and flavorful; brimming with black cherry, wild berry, plum and raspberry fruit and complex, detailed tannins. **91**

1993: Dark, ripe and rich, with complex cherry, plum, spice and raspberry flavors, turning tannic and showing notes of herb and spice. **90**

1992: Very dark and jammy, with layers of ripe wild berry, black cherry and plum flavors. **92**

ZINFANDEL RUSSIAN RIVER VALLEY V.H.S.R. VINEYARD

(★★★): Rivaled the Frati Ranch for richness and complexity in 1992.

1992: Dark, rich and chocolaty, with intense, focused wild berry and black cherry flavors that are ripe and lively. **92**

ZINFANDEL SONOMA COUNTY ZEIGLER VINEYARD

(★★★): Ripe, with pretty cherry, spice and pepper notes.

1996: Smooth, ripe and spicy, with a pretty array of black cherry, raspberry, tar, anise and cedar flavors, firming up on the finish. **88**

1995: Tight but focused, with a core of peppery cherry- and raspberry-scented fruit that's elegant and refined. **90**

1993: Medium-bodied, with some light, simple, earthy berry flavors. **81**

1987: Very ripe, with cherry and raspberry notes and pepper seasoning. **86**

ZINFANDEL SONOMA VALLEY STELLWAGEN VINEYARD

(★★★): Has improved considerably, with lots of classy Zinfandel flavors.

1995: Lots of ripe, spicy cherry, wild berry, raspberry and anise notes, turning rich and elegant on the finish. **90**

1993: Classy, with smooth, ripe, peppery flavors; lush, with cherry and raspberry fruit; shows an overall sense of harmony. **88**

1992: Dill, oregano and bay leaf aromas and flavors render it one-dimensional. **77**

1989: An offbeat wine with tart cranberry and menthol flavors that miss the mark. **80**

1987: Firm and tannic, with pepper, cherry, raspberry and jam flavors seasoned by nutmeg and spice. **86**

SWANSON VINEYARDS (★★★★)
Rutherford, Napa Valley
Founded: 1985. **Owner:** Clark Swanson, Jr. **Winemaker:** Marco S. Cappelli.

MAJOR WINES: PRICE, CASES, RATING

Alexis Red Napa Valley	
($40, 2,000)	★★★★
Cabernet Sauvignon Napa Valley	
($26, 1,000)	★★★★
Chardonnay Napa Valley Carneros	
($26, 2,000)	★★★

Merlot Napa Valley
  ($24, 9,000)   ★★★
Sangiovese Napa Valley
  ($24, 2,500)   ★★★
Sangiovese Napa Valley Rosato di Sangiovese
  ($14, 1,100)   ★★
Sémillon Late Harvest Napa Valley
  ($30, 100)   ★★★★
Syrah Napa Valley
  ($40, 500)   ★★★★

ALSO PRODUCED
Pinot Grigio Napa Valley ($18, 300).

WINERY DATA
Case Production: 22,000. **Acres Owned:** 112 acres in
Oakville, Napa Valley. **Varietals by Acre:** Cabernet Franc (3
acres), Cabernet Sauvignon (9), Chardonnay (16), Merlot (51),
Petite Sirah (2.5), Pinot Grigio (8), Sangiovese (9),
Sémillon/Sauvignon Blanc (1), Syrah (12), Tempranillo (0.5).

Swanson Foods heir and newspaper publisher Clarke
Swanson Jr. purchased a large vineyard in Oakville in 1985.
He then bought the former Cassayre-Forni winery in
Rutherford, where his 22,000-case winery operates today.
Swanson has expanded his vineyards to 112 acres in vines,
led by Merlot—his primary focus—(51), Chardonnay (16)
and a prized Syrah vineyard in Yountville (2) that for years
was the source of grapes for Sean Thackrey's Orion Syrah
bottlings. Under the winemaking direction of Marco
Capelli, quality across the board has been high. Alexis, a
proprietary blend named after his daughter, is the best wine.

TASTING NOTES

ALEXIS RED NAPA VALLEY (★★★★): A unique and distinctive blend of Cabernet Sauvignon, Cabernet Franc,
and Syrah that's elegant and complex.
1996: Remarkably complex, with an intriguing array of
cedary oak, tar, berry, currant and cherry fruit, gaining
depth and finesse on the finish. **92**
1995: Smooth, ripe, rich and harmonious, with lots of
complex spice, cherry, currant and chocolate flavors. **92**
1994: Ripe, rich and complex, with a sense of elegance
and finesse; shows tiers of plum, black cherry, currant
and wild berry flavors. **91**

CABERNET SAUVIGNON NAPA VALLEY (★★★): Poised for
greatness. Recent vintages have been right on the mark,

with bold, ripe, supple and complex wines made in the
best years. Worth watching.
1995: Complex, with a pretty interplay of earthy, ripe cherry and plummy fruit and a touch of mineral and mint. **91**
1994: Smooth, ripe and supple, with a pretty core of
chocolate, vanilla, black cherry and currant flavors, turning complex on the finish. **91**
1993: Firmly tannic, with dusty berry, cherry and spicy
flavors and an impressive length. **88**
1992: Dark, ripe and intense, with well focused currant,
black cherry, spice and mineral flavors framed by toasty,
spicy oak. **90**
1991: Supple, complex, rich and flavorful; laced with
buttery oak and full of ripe cherry, currant and spice flavors, turning tannic. **90**
1990: Deep, dense and elegant, its ripe berry, cherry and
currant flavors are wrapped in a tight blanket of fine tannin, echoing toast and spice on the finish. **89**
1988: Hard and chewy, but the ripe currant, earth and
oak flavors are appealing, if a bit hollow. **82**
1987: Still quite tannic, with a hollowness to the core of
earthy currant, anise, sage, cedar and spice flavors. **88**

CHARDONNAY NAPA VALLEY CARNEROS (★★★): Firm and
well-focused, with a nice balance between ripe fruit and oak.
1996: Good intensity, with notes of ripe pear, spice,
vanilla, anise and smoke. **88**
1995: Complex, with its band of earthy citrus, pear and
pineapple flavors, fanning out and turning creamy on the
finish. **89**

MERLOT NAPA VALLEY (★★★): Even though this was
once the winery's main goal, it's currently the least interesting of the reds, yet it can be close to outstanding.
1996: Lean, yet smooth, with herb, chocolate, dill, currant and berry notes and leathery tannins. **86**
1995: Marked by a racy, oaky edge; the core of fruit is
deep and intense, showing blackberry, spice, herb and
spicy oak flavors. **89**
1994: Starts out earthy, but soon complex currant, chocolate and cedar flavors emerge, finishing with a nice dash
of spice. **89**
1993: Young and intense, with firm tannins, crisp acidity
and tight, earthy currant and berry flavors. **85**
1992: Marked by cedary oak and a leathery edge, the
wild berry and cherry flavors battle the tannins right up
to the finish. Needs time. **86**

1991: Ripe and supple, with smooth, rich plum, herb and spicy pepper notes that are intense and concentrated. **89**

1990: Hard and tannic, this is a medium-weight wine with modest fruit flavors and a strong leafy, woody component. **82**

SANGIOVESE NAPA VALLEY (★★★): Combines ripe, complex fruit with a sense of elegance and finesse.

SÉMILLON LATE HARVEST NAPA VALLEY (★★★★): Can be quite stunningly rich and honeyed, as the brilliant 1992 was.

1992: Rich, sweet and unctuous, offering a cascade of spicy, cinnamon-nutmeg-scented, toasty almond, pear, honey and apricot flavors. **97**

1991: Sweet and silky, unfolding its delicious fig, tobacco and honey flavors nicely. Gets a little sugary on the finish, though. **88**

1988: Distinctive almond, toast, fig and honey aromas and flavors come off sweet and a little sticky, but it would be pleasant to drink with or after dessert. **80**

SYRAH NAPA VALLEY (★★★★): Recently replanted, the Schmidt Vineyard that produces this wine has been a great source for many vintners, including Sean Thackery (Orion). It yields rich, meaty, sometimes quite tannic wines.

1996: A well-oaked style, with vanilla and toasty notes leading to supple, spicy, wild berry, blackberry, anise and sage notes that are complex and lingering. **90**

1995: Lots of exotic, spicy flavors, followed by a core of dark wild berry and blackberry fruit and firm tannins. **88**

1994: Big, ripe, rich and concentrated, with lots of chewy currant, anise, leather, plum and spicy qualities, turning meaty on the finish. **93**

1993: Dark in color and substantial in tannic strength, this wine packs in lots of flavor, with notes of earthy currant, mint and herbs. **89**

1992: Dark and inky, with a tight band of spice, prune, currant and meaty Syrah flavors. The tannins coat the mouth and win hands down. **89**

SYLVIANE see **LE DUCQ**

TABLAS CREEK (★★)
Paso Robles, San Luis Obispo County
Founded: 1990. **Owner:** Jean Pierre Perrin, Francois Perrin, Robert Haas. **Winemaker:** The Perrins, Robert Haas, Neil Collins. **Second Label:** Tablas Hills.

MAJOR WINES: PRICE, CASES, RATING

Paso Robles Blanc ($28, 1,000 - 4,000)	★★
Tablas Hills Paso Robles Blanc ($19, 200 - 600)	★★
Tablas Hills Paso Robles Rouge ($19, 2,000)	★★

ALSO PRODUCED
Paso Robles Rouge ($45, 3,000 - 16,000).

WINERY DATA
Case Production: 4,000 +. **Acres Owned:** 50 acres in Paso Robles. **Varietals by Acre:** Counoise (4 acres), Grenache Blanc (1), Grenache Noir (8), Marsanne (2), Mourvèdre (9), Roussanne (10), Syrah (8), Viognier (8).

Tablas Creek is a partnership linking the Perrin family, owners of Château de Beaucastel of Chateauneuf-du-Pape in the Rhône Valley, and Robert Haas, owner of Vineyard Brands, a wine importer and wholesaler. The goal is to create Rhône-style wines from the winery's estate vineyard that will approach the quality of the Perrin family's French efforts. Other than the initial 10 acres of vines on the 120-acre estate, all other plantings come from vine cuttings imported from France and quarantined at Tablas Creek's nursery in Paso Robles. The vineyard is being planted slowly, with the ultimate goal of having nearly the entire 120 acres planted by 2001. Syrah, Grenache, Mourvèdre and Roussanne will make up the majority of acreage, with 25 acres each of the reds, and about 22 acres of Roussanne.

Only two wines will be produced: a red Rhône-style blend of Counoise, Grenache, Mourvèdre and Syrah, and a white blend of Grenache Blanc, Marsanne, Roussanne and Viognier. Earlier blends that didn't meet the quality demands for the Tablas Creek label were bottled under the Tablas Hills brand. The first Tablas Creek wine, the 1997 Blanc (89 points), was silky, with well-integrated flavors of mineral-tinged apricot, citrus and hazelnut. The first Tablas Creek Rouge, a 1997 vintage, is being released in the fall of 1999. The Tablas Hills wines have not been as interesting; the 1995 and 1996 Rouge (82 and 83 points respectively) showed only modest varietal flavors. The 1996 Tablas Hill Blanc (87) was quite good, however, with pear, apple, orange and mineral notes. Initial production levels have been low, but with new plantings, plans are to produce 25,000 cases by 2002.

TAFT STREET WINERY (★★)
Russian River Valley, Sonoma County
Founded: 1982. **Owner:** Taft Street Inc. **Winemaker:** John Tierney.

MAJOR WINES: PRICE, CASES, RATING
Cabernet Sauvignon California ($13, 5,000)	★★
Chardonnay Sonoma County ($10, 22,000)	★★
Merlot Sonoma County ($14, 5,000)	★
Sauvignon Blanc Russian River Valley ($9, 2,800)	★★
Zinfandel Sonoma County ($12, 4,200)	★★

WINERY DATA
Case Production: 40,000. **Varietals Purchased:** Cabernet Sauvignon (Alexander Valley, Dry Creek, Monterey County, San Luis Obispo County), Chardonnay (Alexander Valley, Monterey County, Russian River Valley), Merlot (Dry Creek Valley, Monterey County, Russian River Valley), Pinot Noir (Russian River Valley), Sauvignon Blanc (Russian River Valley), Zinfandel (Alexander Valley, Dry Creek).

Taft Street is a 40,000-case operation producing Sonoma County Chardonnay, Merlot and Sauvignon Blanc, with Chardonnay the volume leader at 22,000 cases. The brand is known for good values; quality falls in the fair-to-good range. The 1995 Cabernet (84 points) had moderate cedar, spice and blackberry flavors, while the 1995 Merlot (77) was marked by weedy, oaky flavors. Chardonnay and Sauvignon Blanc tend to be clean and crisp; the 1996 Chardonnay (86) was light and refreshing, with pear and mineral flavors, and the 1997 Sauvignon Blanc (85) showed hints of herb, pear and citrus flavors.

ROBERT TALBOTT VINEYARDS (★★★★)
Monterey County
Founded: 1982. **Owner:** Robert Talbott. **Winemaker:** Sam Balderas. **Second Label:** Logan, Case.

MAJOR WINES: PRICE, CASES, RATING
Chardonnay Monterey Cuvée Cynthia ($45, 500)	★★★★★
Chardonnay Monterey Diamond T Estate ($50, 1,500)	★★★★★
Chardonnay Monterey Sleepy Hollow Vineyard ($30, 7,000)	★★★★★

WINERY DATA
Case Production: 20,000. **Acres Owned:** 549 acres in Monterey. **Varietals by Acre:** Chardonnay (339 acres), Gewürztraminer (30), Pinot Noir (100), Riesling (80). **Vineyard Designations:** Diamond T Estate (Chardonnay), Sleepy Hollow Vineyard (Chardonnay).

The Talbott family of necktie fame founded this Carmel Valley winery in 1982. The focus is on Chardonnay from Diamond T Estate and Sleepy Hollow Vineyard, as well as a new bottling called Cuvée Cynthia, all of which are ripe, full-bodied, well-oaked wines that are consistently excellent; they are among the best not only from Monterey, but from all of California. The winery owns 549 acres of vines, with 339 acres planted to Chardonnay. There are also 100 acres planted to Pinot Noir, indicating that Pinot Noir may eventually be added to the product list. Worth buying and collecting.

TASTING NOTES

CHARDONNAY MONTEREY CUVÉE CYNTHIA (★★★★★): Combines bold, ripe, juicy fruit with toasty, smoky oak, rendering rich and complex wines with deep, full-bodied flavors. **1996:** Ripe, lush and concentrated, with a leafy, celery edge to the spicy pear, toasty oak and nutmeg-scented flavors. **92**
1995: Ripe, rich and buttery, with a creamy texture and intense pear, spice, pineapple and citrus notes. Long and lingering on the finish. **92**
1994: Marked by exotic tropical fruit flavors, with tiers of pineapple, pear, guava and spice. Well oaked, too, but the fruit more than stands up to it. Finishes with a lively aftertaste with hints of citrus and grapefruit. **91**

CHARDONNAY MONTEREY DIAMOND T ESTATE
(★★★★★): Bold, ripe and delicious.

1995: Ripe, complex and exotic, with tropical fruit notes, pineapple, citrus and grapefruit notes. Intense and lively; long and lingering on the finish. **91**

1994: Smells complex with its spice, nectarine and light oak shadings, it turns elegant and picks up a tropical fruit flavor. **90**

1992: A bold, rich and earthy style, loaded with complex pear, honey and toasty, buttery oak flavors. **91**

1991: Rich, complex and lively, with pretty spice, pear, apple and melon notes that are bright and elegant. **90**

CHARDONNAY MONTEREY SLEEPY HOLLOW VINEYARD
(★★★★★): Ripe, rich and creamy; very intense and flavorful.

1996: Impresses with its rich, complex array of pear, peach, spice and nectarine flavors, gaining intensity and richness before finishing with a flinty mineral aftertaste. **92**

1995: Ripe, rich and creamy, with layers of pear, pineapple, fig and spice, and a pretty dose of smoky, toasty oak folding in on the finish, which is long and luxurious. **93**

1994: A subtle, well integrated, flavorful wine that manages to maintain its sense of elegance even with its rich core of honey, pear, pineapple, vanilla and butterscotch flavors. Finishes with a long, complex aftertaste. **90**

1993: Distinctive for its overt fruitiness, with complex, earthy fig, pear, honey and apricot flavors. A bold and ripe California Chardonnay with rich, complex flavors. **91**

TALLEY VINEYARDS (★★★–★★★★★)
Arroyo Grande Valley, San Luis Obispo County
Founded: 1986. **Owner:** The Talley Family. **Winemaker:** Steve Rasmussen.

MAJOR WINES: PRICE, CASES, RATING
Chardonnay Arroyo Grande Valley
($20, 6,700) ★★★★★
Chardonnay Arroyo Grande Valley
Rincon Vineyard
($30, 250) ★★★★★
Chardonnay Arroyo Grande Valley
Rosemary's Vineyard
($30, 250) ★★★★★
Chardonnay Edna Valley Oliver's Vineyard
($18, 1,500) ★★★★

Pinot Noir Arroyo Grande Valley
($25, 1,000) ★★★
Pinot Noir Arroyo Grande Valley
Rincon Vineyard
($32, 300) ★★★★
Pinot Noir Arroyo Grande Valley
Rosemary's Vineyard
($36, 200) ★★★★★

ALSO PRODUCED
Sauvignon Blanc Arroyo Grande Valley ($11, 800); White Riesling Arroyo Grande Valley ($9, 200).

WINERY DATA
Case Production: 12,000. **Acres Owned:** 106 acres (90 in Arroyo Grande Valley, 16 in Edna Valley). **Varietals by Acre:** Chardonnay (78 acres), Pinot Noir (20), various varieties (8). **Vineyard Designations:** Rincon Vineyard (Chardonnay, Pinot Noir), Rosemary's Vineyard (Chardonnay, Pinot Noir), Oliver's Vineyard (Chardonnay).

Long-time farmers in Arroyo Grande Valley, the Talley family turned to planting vineyards in 1982. They began to make their own wine in 1986, while still selling a portion of their 106 acres in grapes to customers such as Au Bon Climat. They've slowly built production to 12,000 cases. Chardonnay and Pinot Noir are the main wines; there are several bottlings of each. Quality has risen to impressive heights, making this one of the more exciting brands to develop and evolve in the 1990s. Worth buying.

TASTING NOTES

CHARDONNAY ARROYO GRANDE VALLEY (★★★★): Shows nice body and texture, and the flavors are delicious.

1996: Supple and creamy, with rich, attractive pear, vanilla, spice and citrus, turning elegant and delicate on the finish, where the flavors linger on. **90**

1995: Crisp, lean and flinty, with a tart core of pear, nectarine and spice flavors that fan out and linger on the palate, finishing with a clean aftertaste and hints of fruit and spice. **91**

CHARDONNAY ARROYO GRANDE VALLEY RINCON VINEYARD (★★★★★): Shows signs of being a great site for Chardonnay.

1996: Aromatically complex, with yeast, oak and earthy Chardonnay aromas, and a supple, elegant, concentrated center of ripe pear, fig and melon, weaving the flavors together on the finish. **93**

Chardonnay Arroyo Grande Valley Rosemary's Vineyard (★★★★★): Impressive for its brilliant flavors and polished texture.

1996: Smooth, ripe, rich and creamy, with pretty pear, nectarine, peach, fig and melon flavors, all sharply focused and deeply concentrated. Wonderful texture, balance and finesse. **93**

1995: Intense and tightly wound, with a rich, complex core of pear, nectarine, citrus and light oak, this is a remarkably deep and concentrated wine. The finish is long and sophisticated, with lots of flavor. **93**

Chardonnay Edna Valley Oliver's Vineyard (★★★★): New with the 1996 vintage, but shows the same high quality as the other bottlings.

1997: Smooth, rich and creamy, with polished pear, citrus, fig, melon and apricot flavors that fan out, gaining complexity and nuance. **91**

1996: Intense and spicy, rich and concentrated, this is a well focused, complex wine with layers of buttery pear, honey, hazelnut and spice notes. Finishes with a pretty, fruity aftertaste. **92**

Pinot Noir Arroyo Grande Valley (★★★): Solid, even complex and fruity, though lacking the extra dimensions of the other Pinots.

1996: Austere, with a tight ring of tannin wrapped around the core of earthy, slightly stemmy wild berry and black cherry-laced fruit, it slowly unfolds to reveal a solid core of intense, concentrated fruit. **87**

1994: An elegant, delicate style that captures ripe black cherry, spice and a hint of plum flavors. Well focused, with supple tannins and fine length. **88**

Pinot Noir Arroyo Grande Valley Rincon Vineyard (★★★★): Capable of rendering ultra-rich and complex Pinots. Poised to join the state's elite.

1996: Tightly wound, with firm, intense, currant, plum and black cherry flavors. Definitely needs time in the bottle to soften, but it has a lot going for it. **88**

1995: Deeply flavored, rich and complex, with concentrated cherry, currant, wild berry and a dash of raspberry. The flavors are beautifully integrated and they hold their focus through a long, lively and flavorful aftertaste. **92**

1994: Deliciously complex, with layers of ripe plum, cherry, wild berry and spicy, toasty oak. Elegant and classy Pinot Noir that delivers lots of flavor, yet no single facet dominates. Impressive for its texture. **91**

1993: Well oaked, tight and tannic, with a trim band of spicy cherry and subtle earthy notes. **85**

Pinot Noir Arroyo Grande Valley Rosemary's Vineyard (★★★★★): Consistently outstanding, distinctive, flavorful wines with uncommon complexity.

1996: Ultra-rich and concentrated, packed with ripe, rich, supple plum, black cherry, currant and berry flavors, rounded out with spice and pretty, toasty oak. **92**

1995: Dark, rich and complex, with deep currant, wild berry, black cherry, plum and spicy flavors, all folding together in a harmonious style, finishing with hints of smoke, toasty oak and spice. **93**

1994: A delicious mouthful of Pinot Noir. Captures perfectly ripe, complex fruit, with layers of black cherry, plum, anise, smoke and light oak. Wonderfully balanced. **93**

1993: Ripe, rich and intense, with a measure of finesse and elegance, showcasing the pretty black cherry, sage, spice and wild berry notes. Finishes with thick, firm tannins. **90**

Talus see **Sebastiani Sonoma Cask Cellars**

Iván Tamás Cellars (★★)
Livermore Valley, Alameda County
Founded: 1984. **Owner:** Iván Tamás LLC. **Winemaker:** Steve Mirassou.

Major Wines: Price, Cases, Rating

Cabernet Sauvignon Livermore Valley ($9, 4,000)	★
Cabernet Sauvignon Livermore Valley Reserve ($15, 1,000)	★
Chardonnay Central Coast ($9, 10,000)	★★
Chardonnay Central Coast Reserve ($15, 1,000)	★★
Pinot Grigio Central Coast ($9, 8,000)	★★
Sangiovese Livermore Valley ($15, 1,000)	★★
Trebbiano Livermore Valley ($10, 2,000)	★★
Zinfandel Livermore Valley ($9, 1,000)	★★

Also Produced
White Zinfandel Central Coast ($6, 4,000).

Winery Data
Case Production: 55,000. **Acres Owned:** 6 acres in Livermore Valley. **Varietals by Acre:** Cabernet Sauvignon (3 acres), Sangiovese (3). **Varietals Purchased:** Cabernet Sauvignon (Livermore), Chardonnay (Livermore, Monterey), Pinot Grigio (Monterey), Sangiovese (Livermore), Trebbiano (Livermore), Zinfandel (Central Coast, Livermore).

This negociant brand owned by Iván Tamás Fuezy (with Steve Mirassou as a partner) has grown to 55,000 cases, featuring Cabernet, Chardonnay, Trebbiano, Sangiovese, Pinot Grigio and Zinfandel. Chardonnay is the volume leader at 11,000 cases, though Pinot Grigio (8,000 cases) is not far behind. Quality is usually fair, but occasionally good. Cabernet tends to be soft and herbal, as was the 1994 Reserve (80 points). Light, simple Chardonnays such as the 1996 Livermore Valley (82) are the norm, but the 1995 Reserve (88) showed a surprising amount of flavor and richness. Sangiovese, Pinot Grigio, Trebbiano and Zinfandel are all typically light, with a very modest amount of varietal flavor.

Lane Tanner Winery (★★★)
Santa Barbara County
Founded: 1989. **Owner:** Lane Tanner. **Winemaker:** Lane Tanner.

Major Wines: Price, Cases, Rating
Pinot Noir Santa Barbara County
($20, 600) ★★★
Pinot Noir Santa Maria Valley
Bien Nacido Vineyard
($25, 700) ★★★
Pinot Noir Santa Maria Valley Julia's
Vineyard
($25, 300) ★★★
Pinot Noir Santa Maria Valley
Sierra Madre
(Discontinued) ★★★

Also Produced
Syrah Santa Ynez Valley J.K. Vineyard ($25, 250).

Winery Data
Case Production: 1,850. **Vineyard Designations:** Bien Nacido Vineyard (Pinot Noir), J.K. Vineyard (Syrah), Julia's Vineyard (Pinot Noir). **Varietals Purchased:** Pinot Noir (Santa Maria Valley), Syrah (Santa Ynez Valley).

Lane Tanner worked for Mount Konocti, Zaca Mesa, Firestone and Hitching Post wineries before starting her own Pinot Noir brand using grapes bought from Bien Nacido. For years she also bottled a Sierra Madre Pinot Noir, but the vineyard was purchased by Robert Mondavi Winery in 1996, and Tanner lost her source. Quality has been uniformly very good, with a style that's distinctive. Syrah is new to the lineup.

Tasting Notes

Pinot Noir Santa Maria Valley Bien Nacido Vineyard (★★★): True to Tanner's style, this is an austere, trim wine that's well-structured and built to age a few years.
1996: Lean and spicy, with notes of rhubarb, black cherry, spice and berry and hints of mineral, sage and cedary oak. **87**
1995: A lean style that's a touch earthy, with a green, slightly stemmy edge to the tart cherry and wild berry flavors. **85**
1994: Trim and tart, sporting ripe, spicy cherry, berry and earthy flavors that are vibrant and lively. **86**
1993: Serves up a beam of ripe black cherry and wild berry fruit and holds its focus, even if it is a bit one-dimensional. **84**

Pinot Noir Santa Maria Valley Sierra Madre (★★★)
1996: Clean, crisp and spicy, with tart black cherry and tea flavors, it slowly evolves into a more supple, textured wine. **88**
1995: Tart, with a sour cherry edge to the plum and wild berry fruit, it turns racy on the finish. **82**
1994: Good intensity, but also possesses earthy and tannic qualities which dominate the cherry and berry flavors, turning complex on the finish. **88**

Tay see **Cornerstone Cellars**

TERRA D'ORO see MONTEVIÑA WINES

TERRA ROSA see LAUREL GLEN VINEYARD

TERRA VIN see VIGIL VINEYARD

THE TERRACES (★★★★)
Rutherford, Napa Valley
Founded: 1982. **Owner:** Wayne Hogue. **Winemaker:** Wayne Hogue.

MAJOR WINES: PRICE, CASES, RATING
Cabernet Sauvignon Rutherford
($45, 350)   ★★★★
Zinfandel Rutherford
($25, 400)   ★★★★

WINERY DATA
Case Production: 750. **Acres Owned:** 8 acres in Rutherford.
Varietals by Acre: Cabernet Sauvignon (3 acres), Zinfandel (5).

Personal investment counselor Wayne Hogue was born and raised on a farm in Riverside in Southern California. In 1977, he bought his Napa Valley vineyard, situated off of the Silverado Trail. Hogue's 8-acre vineyard is planted to Cabernet Sauvignon and Zinfandel. Winemaking was originally handled by Chuck Wagner of Caymus Vineyards, and both wines reflect Wagner's efforts to stretch the band of flavors and frame them with toasty oak. The Cabernet spends 36 months in oak, almost a year longer than most Napa Valley Cabernets. Production and distribution are limited. It is best to write to the winery in Rutherford in order to obtain the wines.

TASTING NOTES

CABERNET SAUVIGNON RUTHERFORD (★★★★): This wine has returned to the success of its early brilliant vintages after a slight dip in quality. The wines drink well on release, and age for up to 10 years.
1995: Smooth and creamy, with a core of firm tannins, it works its way into an appealing array of vanilla, currant, plum, anise, sage and cedary notes, whereupon the tannins weigh in strongly once again. **92**

1994: Starts with a strong dill, cedar and anise flavor before the currant and black cherry flavors start to show, revealing more depth, richness and complexity. Could go on for a decade. **91**
1993: Complex, with a nice interplay of spicy, toasty oak and rich currant. Turns smooth and polished on the finish, where it picks up coffee and herb notes. **91**
1992: Complex and well balanced, striking a nice balance between ripe cherry, plum and wild berry flavors and a dash of anise and oak. **88**
1991: Tight and austere, offering a trim band of currant, spice, cedar and berry, hints of prune and anise and a firmly tannic finish. **88**
1990: The extremely leathery and tannic notes override the cedar, black currant and plum flavors that lurk beneath. **86**
1989: Dark, rich and supple, it offers currant, herb and anise flavors that are polished and fleshy, with shades of light vanilla oak. **88**
1988: Firm and lean, with a tight range of currant, cedar and anise flavors and oaky vanilla nuances. **88**
1987: Mature and in fine drinking shape, as the currant, black cherry, anise and earthy flavors are round and supple, turning smooth and polished on the finish. **90**
1986: Complex plum, herb and cherry flavors and a pruny accent still hold the fort, but it's starting to dry out. Mature. **89**

ZINFANDEL RUTHERFORD (★★★★): Shares the Cabernet's intensity and range of flavors, with fine balance and pretty oak shadings. Steadily improving.
1995: Well oaked, but there's plenty of fruit to match it, with lots of spice, tart raspberry, black cherry and wild berry flavors that fan out on the finish, picking up all kinds of nuances. **92**
1994: Well crafted, striking a nice balance between the spicy currant, wild berry and cherry notes and light, toasty oak shadings. Finishes with a zingy, fruity aftertaste. **90**
1993: Smooth and spicy, with a nice dash of smoky, toasty oak to complement the spicy cherry and berry flavors as they fan out. **87**

TESSERA (★)
Monterey County
Founded: 1996. **Owner:** Seagram Chateau & Estate Wines Co. **Winemaker:** Phil Franscioni.

MAJOR WINES: PRICE, CASES, RATING
Cabernet Sauvignon California
  ($10, 65,000) ★
Chardonnay California
  ($10, 40,000) ★
Merlot California
  ($10, 75,000) ★
Zinfandel California
  ($10, 8,000) ★

WINERY DATA
Case Production: 200,000 +. **Varietals Purchased:** Cabernet Sauvignon (California), Chardonnay (California), Merlot (California), Zinfandel (California).

This new brand was launched in 1996 by Seagram Chateau & Estate, the wine and spirits division of the Seagram empire. The focus here is on large-production, value-oriented, California appellation wines. The wines are made at Seagram's Monterey Vineyard winery, and have been of average quality. The 1996 Chardonnay (81 points), Merlot (80) and Zinfandel (78) showed simple, clean, compact flavors.

TESTAROSSA VINEYARD (★★★–★★★★)
Santa Cruz Mountains
Founded: 1993. **Owner:** Rob & Diana Jensen. **Winemaker:** George Troquato.

MAJOR WINES: PRICE, CASES, RATING
Chardonnay California George Troquato
  Signature Reserve
  ($39, 200) ★★★★
Chardonnay Chalone
  ($28, 500) ★★★★
Chardonnay Chalone Michaud Vineyard
  ($39, 200) ★★★
Chardonnay Santa Maria Valley
  ($26, 500) ★★★★
Chardonnay Santa Maria Valley
  Bien Nacido Vineyard
  ($32, 400) ★★★★
Pinot Blanc Chalone
  ($21, 250) ★★★
Viognier Chalone
  ($28, 200) ★★★

ALSO PRODUCED
Chardonnay Santa Cruz Ashley Hill Vineyard ($28, 125); Chardonnay Santa Lucia Highlands Pisoni Vineyard ($32, 500); Chardonnay Santa Lucia Highlands Sleepy Hollow Vineyard ($32, 500); Pinot Noir Chalone ($26, 350); Pinot Noir Santa Lucia Highlands Cuvée Niclaire Reserve ($45, 150); Pinot Noir Santa Lucia Highlands Pisoni Vineyard ($39, 250); Pinot Noir Santa Lucia Highlands Sleepy Hollow Vineyard ($35, 400); Pinot Noir Santa Maria Valley ($26, 250).

WINERY DATA
Case Production: 4,500. **Vineyard Designations:** Ashley Hill Vineyard (Chardonnay), Bien Nacido Vineyard (Chardonnay), Michaud Vineyard (Chardonnay), Pisoni Vineyard (Chardonnay, Pinot Noir), Sleepy Hollow Vineyard (Pinot Noir). **Varietals Purchased:** Chardonnay (Chalone, Santa Cruz Mountains, Santa Lucia Highlands, Santa Maria Valley), Pinot Blanc (Chalone), Pinot Noir (Santa Cruz Mountains, Santa Lucia Highlands, Santa Maria Valley), Viognier (Chalone).

Computer software salesman Rob Jensen and his wife, Diana, make a range of outstanding, rich, complex Chardonnays, Pinot Blancs and a Viognier with the help of George Troquatro (the winemaker at Cinnabar Vineyards)—all from purchased grapes. They will also be adding Pinot Noirs from Chalone, Santa Lucia Highlands and Santa Maria Valley, along with a Santa Lucia Highlands Syrah and some new vineyard-designated Chardonnays. The Jensens plan to plant 27 acres, to be divided amongst Pinot Noir, Syrah and Chardonnay, on property they own in the Santa Cruz Mountains. Production is slowly increasing. Worth buying.

TASTING NOTES

CHARDONNAY CHALONE (★★★★): Complex and elegant, with great concentration of flavors.
1996: A wine of elegance and finesse, with ripe, spicy pear, fig and toasty oak flavors, picking up a twinge of earthy mushroom on the aftertaste, where it gains nuance

and dimension. **90**

1995: Complex and richly flavored, with elegant, sharply focused, creamy pear, vanilla, spice, nutmeg and anise notes that fold together nicely. **91**

1994: Ripe and complex, its juicy pear, apple, melon and fig flavors turn rich and concentrated, revealing their depth on the finish, where they pick up a smoky, toasty oak accent. **91**

CHARDONNAY SANTA MARIA VALLEY (★★★★):

1996: Deliciously rich and smoky with a smooth creamy texture and lots of fig, vanilla, apricot and a hint of anise and citrus on the finish. **92**

CHARDONNAY SANTA MARIA VALLEY BIEN NACIDO VINEYARD (★★★★): Ripe and rich with lots of smoky oak and concentrated fruit flavors.

1996: A tremendous wine; ripe, complex, concentrated and sharply focused, brimming with pear, fig, apricot and spicy fruit flavors. The finish goes on and on. **93**

1995: Ultra-rich and concentrated, with ripe pear, fig, melon and spice and lots of pretty smoky, toasty oak flavors. Finishes with subtle, complex notes. **92**

PINOT BLANC CHALONE (★★★): Tight and flinty, with minerally fruit flavors; quite distinctive.

1996: Tight, tart and flinty, with a rich, complex core of pear, peach and hazelnut, picking up a slight nutty edge on the finish. **88**

1995: A touch earthy, with a slight musty edge; enough ripe pear, mineral and spice flavors work their way to the forefront to capture your interest. **86**

VIOGNIER CHALONE (★★★): The 1996 (89 points) was impressive, with a pleasing earthy edge to the creamy pear, fig and melon flavors.

THE YOUNTVILLE WINERY see COSENTINO WINERY

THORNTON (★★)

Temecula, South Coast
Founded: 1981. **Owner:** John & Sally B. Thornton.
Winemaker: Jon McPherson.

MAJOR WINES: PRICE, CASES, RATING

Brut Reserve California	
($21, 5,000)	★★
Cabernet-Merlot South Coast	
($14, 675)	★
Côte Red South Coast	
($15, 900)	★★
Zinfandel Cucamonga Valley Old Vine	
($13, 250)	★★

ALSO PRODUCED

Aleatico Cucamonga Valley ($13, 250); Blanc de Noir California ($12, 3,000); Brut California Culbertson ($12, 5,000); Chardonnay Santa Barbara County ($8, 3,000); Cuvée de Frontignan ($12, 900); Cuvée Rouge California ($12, 1,200); Moscato South Coast ($8, 850); Pinot Blanc South Coast ($10, 2,600); Syrah South Coast ($15, 275).

WINERY DATA

Case Production: 45,000. **Acres Owned:** 6 acres in Temecula. **Varietals by Acre:** Aleatico (1.5 acres), Viognier (4.5). **Varietals Purchased:** Barbera (South Coast), Cabernet Sauvignon (South Coast), Cinsault (Cucamonga), Chardonnay (Santa Barbara), Grenache (Cucamonga), Merlot (South Coast), Mourvèdre (Cucamonga, South Coast), Muscat of Alexandria (South Coast), Muscat Canelli (South Coast), Nebbiolo (South Coast), Pinot Blanc (South Coast), Roussanne (Temecula), Terret Noir (Temecula), Syrah (Temecula), Viognier (South Coast), Zinfandel (Cucamonga).

Thornton (originally called Culbertson) was founded by John Culbertson. After engaging in home winemaking for a time, he purchased an avocado ranch in northern San Diego County and began making commercial wines. He started *méthode champenoise* sparkling wine production in 1981, and in 1988, he built a winery in Temecula, near Callaway Vineyard and Winery. In 1991, John and Sally Thornton took over ownership from Culbertson.

Quality has swung erratically, with the Rhône varietals making a much better show than the others. A 1996 Côte Red Rhône blend (86 points) had interesting earthy, plum and cherry flavors. Sparkling wines under the Culbertson label can be decent, but they don't reach the quality level of their Northern California peers. The 1992

Brut Reserve (82) showed modest floral and honey flavors, but carried a $25 price tag.

THUNDER MOUNTAIN (★★–★★★★)
Santa Cruz Mountains
Founded: 1995. **Owner:** Milan Maximovich, Scott Sterling. **Winemaker:** Milan Maximovich.

MAJOR WINES: PRICE, CASES, RATING
Cabernet Sauvignon Santa Cruz Mountains
  Beauregard Ranch
  ($45, 600) ★★
Chardonnay Santa Cruz Mountains
  Bald Mountain
  ($29, 500) ★★★★
Chardonnay Santa Cruz Mountains
  Matteson Vineyard
  ($29, 100) ★★★★

ALSO PRODUCED
Cabernet Sauvignon San Benito Doc's Vineyard ($49, 700); Pinot Noir Santa Cruz Mountains Ciardella Vineyard ($30, 300); Star Ruby Santa Cruz Mountains ($49, 250).

WINERY DATA
Case Production: 2,500. **Varietals Purchased:** Cabernet Sauvignon (Santa Cruz Mountains), Chardonnay (Santa Cruz Mountains), Pinot Noir (Santa Cruz Mountains). **Vineyard Designations:** Beauregard Ranch (Cabernet Sauvignon), Doc's Vineyard (Cabernet Sauvignon), Matteson Vineyard (Chardonnay), Ciardella Vineyard (Pinot Noir).

Retired aerospace engineer Milan Maximovich has only a few vintages behind him, but his Santa Cruz Mountains Chardonnays and Cabernets have been distinctive. Two of the 1996 Chardonnays—the Matteson Vineyard (92 points) and the Bald Mountain Vineyard (91)—were both ultra-rich, bold wines with nutty, butterscotch, melon, pear and vanilla flavors. The Cabernets—1995 Beauregard Ranch (83) and 1995 Bates Ranch (85)—were less inspiring, but were interesting for their herb- and olive-tinged blackberry and cherry fruit. More vineyard-designated wines, including a Pinot Noir, have been added. Worth watching.

TITUS (★★)
Napa Valley
Founded: 1990. **Owner:** The Titus Family. **Winemaker:** Phillip Corallo-Titus.

MAJOR WINES: PRICE, CASES, RATING
Cabernet Sauvignon St. Helena
  ($24, 900) ★★
Zinfandel St. Helena
  ($17, 1,800) ★★

ALSO PRODUCED
Cabernet Franc St. Helena ($22, 300).

WINERY DATA
Case Production: 3,000. **Acres Owned:** 44 acres in St. Helena. **Varietals by Acre:** Cabernet Franc (4 acres), Cabernet Sauvignon (17), Chardonnay (6), Malbec (1), Merlot (4), Petit Verdot (1), Zinfandel (11). **Varietals Purchased:** Petite Sirah (Calistoga).

The Titus family sold grapes to local wineries for many years before starting their own label. The wines have been good overall; the Cabernets tend to be big and rustic, with currant and cedar notes, as was the case with the 1994 vintage (87 points), while the Zinfandel—the 1995 (83), for example—is of medium weight, with berry flavors.

TIVOLI see S. ANDERSON VINEYARD

PHILIP TOGNI VINEYARD (★★★★–★★★★★)
Spring Mountain District, Napa Valley
Founded: 1983. **Owner:** Togni Family. **Winemaker:** Philip Togni.

MAJOR WINES: PRICE, CASES, RATING
Cabernet Sauvignon Napa Valley
  ($53, 1,100) ★★★★★
Black Muscat Dessert Napa Valley Ca' Togni
  ($32, 50) ★★★★

WINERY DATA
Case Production: 1,200. **Acres Owned:** 10.5 acres on Spring Mountain. **Varietals by Acre:** Black Hamburg (0.3 acres), Cabernet Franc (0.2), Cabernet Sauvignon (8.8), Merlot (1.1), Petit Verdot (0.1).

Philip Togni's wine resumé is impressive, but he's done his best work at this winery estate on Spring Mountain. A graduate of the University of Bordeaux, where he studied under the great enologist Emile Peynaud, he began making wine in 1954 at Château Lascombes in Margaux. In 1958, he worked at Mayacamas, followed by stints at Chalone (where he was the first winemaker), E. & J. Gallo, Chappellet and Cuvaison.

In 1983, he and his wife Brigitta founded their estate winery on a steep slope on Spring Mountain. Production remains small at 1,200 cases, with Cabernet Sauvignon the volume leader, followed by a tiny amount of Ca' Togni Black Muscat, a dessert wine. Quality is high across the board, with wines of enormous varietal intensity.

TASTING NOTES

CABERNET SAUVIGNON NAPA VALLEY (★★★★): Ultra-ripe, high extract, dense and chewy. Packed with flavor and substantial tannins, yet well balanced, and the early wines are aging well.
1996: Distinctive for its coffee bean, herbal and complex berry flavors, this wine is intense, with a chewy core of currant- and blackberry-laced flavors. Best to cellar short-term, although it is less rustic and backward at this stage than previous vintages have been. **93**
1994: Ripe and toasty, with buttery oak, ripe cherry and plum flavors and a good dose of elegant, spicy fruit. **90**
1992: Deep, dark and tannic, this one packs a wallop of fruit and tannin, but there's a solid core of earthy currant, tar and spice flavors. **91**
1991: Rich and complex, with lovely herb and mineral notes adding complexity to the mouth-filling currant and berry flavors. **90**
1990: Plush and flavorful, with deep, concentrated plum, currant, blackberry, pepper and anise flavors that extend onto a smooth, supple finish. **92**
1989: Tough and tannic, with herbal, tarry, gamy notes around a core of ripe, jammy currant and berry flavors. **84**
1988: Serves up a wide range of chunky, exotic currant, wild berry, herb and olive flavors, along with a touch of green bean. **90**
1987: Big, ripe, bountiful and dazzling, with loads of exotic plum and wild berry fruit and enough chewy, supple tannins for aging. **93**
1986: Dark and intense, with a ripe, exotic core of anise, plum and mineral flavors, showing signs of dryness on the finish. **89**
1985: Lavishly oaked, with a spicy cedar note that overrides the thick, austere, concentrated black currant, plum and cherry flavors. Firmly tannic. **89**
1984: Cedary oak notes overshadow the ripe, earthy plum and currant flavors. **85**
1983: Still hard, tight and tannic, with a core of weedy black currant flavors framed by spicy, cedary oak. **84**

TOPOLOS AT RUSSIAN RIVER VINEYARDS (★★)
Russian River Valley, Sonoma County
Founded: 1978. **Owner:** Michael & Jerry Topolos. **Winemaker:** Jac Jacobs. **Second Label:** Russian River Vineyards.

MAJOR WINES: PRICE, CASES, RATING

Zinfandel Russian River Valley Piner Heights ($17, 4,000)	★★
Zinfandel Sonoma Mountain Ultimo ($36, 350)	★★
Zinfandel Sonoma Valley Pagani ($35, 250)	★★
Zinfandel Sonoma Valley Rossi ($25, 1,200)	★★

ALSO PRODUCED
Alicante Bouschet Sonoma Valley Rossi/Pagani ($18, 1,200); Charbono Napa ($12, 1,000); Chardonnay Russian River Valley ($18, 600); Petite Sirah Sonoma ($18, 500); Pinot Noir Russian River Valley ($18, 400); Sauvignon Blanc Russian River Valley Organic ($10, 1,200); Zinfandel California ($10, 3,500).

WINERY DATA
Case Production: 20,000. **Acres Owned:** 31 acres (10 on Sonoma Mountain, 21 in Russian River Valley). **Varietals by Acre:** Chardonnay (10 acres), Merlot (3), Pinot Noir (8), Zinfandel (10). **Varietals Purchased:** Alicante Bouchet (Sonoma Valley), Sauvignon Blanc (Russian River Valley), Zinfandel (Sonoma Mountain, Sonoma Valley, Russian River Valley).

Red-wine-oriented Topolos has now added Chardonnay to its lineup, but Alicante Bouschet, Petite Sirah and

Zinfandel (Rossi Ranch) are the wines for which it is best known (although Cabernet and Pinot Noir are also part of the product mix). The Topolos family has owned this winery since 1978, and have 31 acres in vines. The quality of their wines is generally in the fair-to-good range.

MARIMAR TORRES ESTATE
(★★★–★★★★)
Green Valley, Sonoma County
Founded: 1989. **Owner:** Torres Family. **Winemaker:** Marimar Torres.

MAJOR WINES: PRICE, CASES, RATING
Chardonnay Russian River Valley Don
  Miguel Vineyard
  ($22, 9,192) ★★★★
Pinot Noir Russian River Valley Don
  Miguel Vineyard
  ($25, 3,656) ★★★

WINERY DATA
Case Production: 15,000. **Acres Owned:** 55 acres in Russian River Valley Green Valley. **Varietals by Acre:** Chardonnay (30 acres), Pinot Noir (25). **Vineyard Designations:** Don Miguel Vineyard (Chardonnay, Pinot Noir).

Marimar Torres is a member of the well-known Torres wine family of Spain. In 1983, Torres and her father, Miguel, ended their search for prime California vineyard property in Sonoma's Green Valley. She now presides over the 55-acre Don Miguel Vineyard, which is planted to Chardonnay (30 acres) and Pinot Noir (25 acres).

TASTING NOTES

CHARDONNAY RUSSIAN RIVER GREEN VALLEY DON MIGUEL VINEYARD (★★★★): Beautifully crafted, ripe, rich, smooth and polished, with intense fruit flavors and lots of oak.
1996: Sleek and elegant, with ripe, complex, creamy pear, vanilla, apple, and honey notes, holding its focus through the finish. **90**
1995: Ripe and fruity, with lots of rich tangerine, pear, melon and spicy flavors and a long, lingering aftertaste. **90**

PINOT NOIR RUSSIAN RIVER VALLEY DON MIGUEL VINEYARD (★★★): Improving, with herb and cherry-laced fruit and deft oak shadings.
1996: The bottles I've tasted have varied. The best ones display nuances of smoky oak, earthiness and a slightly funky streak to match the blackberry and cherry flavors. Others, unfortunately, are more vegetal. **87**
1995: Tasty, with ripe, rich, supple black cherry, wild berry, plum and spice flavors that are well focused, deep and lively. **89**
1994: Young, firm and tannic, with a slightly green edge to its cherry, tea, leather and spice flavors; the tannins emerge on the finish. **87**
1993: Medium-bodied, with pleasant cola, berry, light oak and spice notes of modest depth. **84**
1992: Ripe and supple, with a trim band of plum, herb and cherry flavors. **86**

TREANA WINERY (★★★)
Paso Robles, San Luis Obispo County
Founded: 1996. **Owner:** The Hope Family. **Winemaker:** Chris Phelps, Austin Hope.

MAJOR WINES: PRICE, CASES, RATING
Red Paso Robles
  ($32, 11,000) ★★★

ALSO PRODUCED
White Monterey County Mer Soleil Vineyard (6,000).

WINERY DATA
Case Production: 17,000. **Acres Owned:** 17 acres in Paso Robles. **Varietals by Acre:** Cabernet Sauvignon (7 acres), Merlot (5), Syrah (5). **Vineyard Designations:** Mer Soleil Vineyard (White Rhône Blend). **Varietals Purchased:** Cabernet Sauvignon (Paso Robles), Grenache (Paso Robles), Marsanne (Monterey County), Merlot (Paso Robles), Mourvèdre (Paso Robles), Petite Sirah (Paso Robles), Roussanne (Monterey County), Sangiovese (Paso Robles), Syrah (Paso Robles), Viognier (Monterey County).

Treana is a new brand, bringing together the Hope family—long-time Paso Robles grape growers—with Chris Phelps, the former winemaker for Dominus Estate, and Chuck Wagner of Caymus.

    Two wines are made here: a blend of Cabernet, Syrah, Merlot, Sangiovese and Petite Sirah from the Hopes' Paso Robles vineyards, and a blend of Marsanne, Roussanne and Viognier from grapes grown on Wagner's Mer Soleil Vineyard in Monterey. Given the combination of talent and grapes, Treana should be well worth watching.

TASTING NOTES

RED PASO ROBLES (★★★)
1996: This blend is smooth and polished, with a green tea like edge to the dried cherry, plum, sage, herb and wild berry flavors, finishing with mild tannins. **88**

TREFETHEN VINEYARDS (★★)
Napa Valley
Founded: 1973. **Owner:** Janet & John Trefethen. **Winemaker:** David Whitehouse. **Second Label:** Eshcol.

MAJOR WINES: PRICE, CASES, RATING
Cabernet Sauvignon Napa Valley ($20, 16,000)	★★★
Cabernet Sauvignon Napa Valley Reserve ($50, 1,100)	★★★
Chardonnay Napa Valley ($21, 23,000)	★★
Merlot Napa Valley ($24, 3,500)	★★
Riesling Napa Valley Dry ($12, 3,100)	★★

ALSO PRODUCED
Cabernet Sauvignon Napa Valley Library Selection ($40, NA); Chardonnay Napa Valley Library Selection ($35, 1,000).

WINERY DATA
Case Production: 120,000. **Acres Owned:** 565 acres in Napa Valley. **Varietals by Acre:** Cabernet Franc (5 acres), Cabernet Sauvignon (135), Chardonnay (185), Merlot (50), Pinot Noir (170), White Riesling (20).

In 1968, former Kaiser Industries executive Gene Trefethen and his wife Katie purchased the old Eschol estate north of Napa. In 1973, their son, John, and his wife, Janet, founded Trefethen Vineyards. The family owns a large vineyard (565 acres) dominated by Chardonnay (185), Pinot Noir (170) and Cabernet (135). The winery's strength is its Chardonnay, although the Cabernet is well balanced, and has been particularly notable in the warmer years. A new Reserve Cabernet comprised of hillside grapes has shown more intensity.

Given all the vines that Trefethen owns, and given how many great vintages have occurred in Napa Valley, however, its been a long time since anything truly distinctive or exciting was released from this winery. Even efforts to hold back older vintages of some wines for the library selection program have turned out to be disappointing.

TASTING NOTES

CABERNET SAUVIGNON NAPA VALLEY (★★★): Medium-bodied and well balanced, with herb and cherry notes and mild tannins.

CABERNET SAUVIGNON NAPA VALLEY RESERVE (★★★): Shows more depth, intensity and complexity. Aged in the bottle at the winery for a later release.

CHARDONNAY NAPA VALLEY (★★): Once among Napa's best, it is now merely ordinary. The style remains the same, but the resulting wines come across as simple and fruity. There is no malolactic barrel fermentation nor *sur lie* aging, and little new oak. Can age well, but often older vintages that are held back for longer aging are tired on release.

TRENTADUE WINERY (★)
Alexander Valley, Sonoma County
Founded: 1969. **Owner:** Leo & Evelyn Trentadue. **Winemaker:** Chris Gebhardt.

MAJOR WINES: PRICE, CASES, RATING
Merlot Alexander Valley ($18, 800)	★
Old Patch Red Rhône Blend Sonoma County ($14, 3,000)	★
Petite Sirah Sonoma County ($16, 700)	★
Sangiovese Alexander Valley ($18, 1,000)	★
Zinfandel Sonoma County ($14, 1,100)	★

ALSO PRODUCED

Cabernet Sauvignon Dry Creek Valley ($22, 750); Merlot Port Alexander Valley ($20, 310); Petite Sirah Port Alexander Valley ($20, 300).

WINERY DATA
Case Production: 8,000. **Acres Owned:** 98 acres (90 in Alexander Valley, 8 in Dry Creek) **Varietals by Acre:** Cabernet Sauvignon (8 acres), Carignane (15), Chardonnay (16), Merlot (29), Petite Sirah (9), Sangiovese (6), Zinfandel (16). **Varietals Purchased:** Carignane (Dry Creek), Zinfandel (Dry Creek).

Simple, rustic reds are still the main focus at Trentadue Winery, situated off of Highway 101 east of Chateau Souverain, near Geyserville. The family owns 98 acres in vines, the majority in red varieties. Case production is 8,000, with quality in the fair-to-good range. The 1994 Old Patch Red (79 points) had modest tart cherry and chocolate flavors and firm tannins. The 1994 Sangiovese (86) had crisp blackberry and tar flavors, and the 1995 Merlot (80) showed bright cherry and berry flavors with hints of tea and a bitter finish.

TRIA (★★–★★★)
Napa Valley
Founded: 1993. **Owner:** William Knuttel, Philip Zorn. **Winemaker:** William Knuttel, Philip Zorn.

MAJOR WINES: PRICE, CASES, RATING
Labyrinth Red California ($18, 500)	★★★
Pinot Noir Carneros ($22, 2,000)	★★
Pinot Noir Monterey ($20, 1000)	★★
Port Monterey Souzao ($16, 500)	★★
Syrah Sonoma ($20, 750)	★★
Zinfandel Dry Creek Valley ($18, 1,000)	★★★
Zinfandel Napa Valley ($16, 1,000)	★★★

ALSO PRODUCED
Syrah Monterey ($20, 750); Viognier California ($18, 500).

WINERY DATA
Case Production: 8,000. **Varietals Purchased:** Cabernet Franc (Sonoma County), Cabernet Sauvignon (Sonoma County, Napa Valley), Johannisberg Riesling (Monterey), Malbec (Sonoma County), Petit Verdot (Sonoma County), Pinot Blanc (Monterey), Pinot Noir (Carneros, Monterey County), Souzao, Syrah (Alexander Valley, Dry Creek Valley, Knights Valley, Monterey County), Viognier (Napa Valley), Zinfandel (Dry Creek Valley, Howell Mountain, Napa Valley).

William Knuttel made excellent wines at Saintsbury, and still makes wines at Chalk Hill. His partner, Philip Zorn, winemaker for Paraiso Springs, has had a lot of experience with Monterey County grapes, from which Tria makes Pinot Noir, Syrah and Port. Considering Knuttel and Zorn's combined experience and backgrounds, the Tria wines have not met expectations. Many of the reds, including Pinot Noir and the Cabernet blend Labryinth, have been dry and earthy with leathery flavors. The Syrah can be tough and tannic, as was the 1996 (83 points), which had a narrow range of flavors. Zinfandel, in particular the Dry Creek Valley bottling, has been the most consistently flavorful and supple; the 1997 (88) was smooth, with wild berry, black cherry and spicy nuances, finishing with firm, crisp tannins.

M. TRINCHERO (★★★)
Napa Valley
Founded: 1998. **Owner:** Bob, Roger & Vera Trinchero. **Winemaker:** Derek Holstein.

MAJOR WINES: PRICE, CASES, RATING
Cabernet Sauvignon Napa Valley Founder's Estate ($35, 3,000)	★★★
Chardonnay Napa Valley Founder's Estate ($25, 4,000)	★★★

ALSO PRODUCED
Cabernet Sauvignon California Founder's Selection ($13, 15,000); Chardonnay California Founder's Selection ($13, 50,000); Merlot California Founder's Selection ($13, 50,000).

WINERY DATA
Case Production: 150,000. **Acres Owned:** 589 acres (394 in Los Alamos, 195 in Napa Valley). **Varietals by Acre:** Cabernet Franc (3 acres), Cabernet Sauvignon (42), Chardonnay (465),

Merlot (9), Petit Verdot (3), Pinot Noir (54), Sauvignon Blanc (6), Sauvignon Musque (6), Sémillon (1). **Varietals Purchased:** Cabernet Sauvignon (Monterey, Napa Valley, Santa Barbara), Chardonnay (Monterey, Napa Valley, Santa Barbara), Merlot (Monterey, Napa Valley, Santa Barbara).

This is a new brand from the Trinchero family of Sutter Home, and shows the quality the Trincheros can pull together from their extensive vineyard holdings and grape contracts. Production is substantial, at 150,000 cases. The label takes its name from Mario Trinchero, who, along with his brother John Trinchero, renovated the abandoned Sutter Home winery in the 1940s.

Initial releases have been very good; the 1996 Chardonnay Founder's Estate (88 points) was elegant and delicate with pretty toasty oak, lemon, pear and spice flavors. The 1995 Cabernet Sauvignon Founder's Estate (88) was heavily oaked, but also had lots of plum and currant flavors with cedar, anise and sage nuances.

Two proprietary blends are planned, one composed of red Bordeaux varietals and one of white Bordeaux varietals.

TRUCHARD VINEYARD
(★★★★–★★★★★)
Carneros
Founded: 1990. **Owner:** Tony and Jo Ann Truchard.
Winemaker: Sal DeIanni.

MAJOR WINES: PRICE, CASES, RATING

Cabernet Sauvignon Carneros ($24, 1,700)	★★★★
Cabernet Sauvignon Carneros Reserve ($48, 200)	★★★★
Chardonnay Carneros ($24, 1,300)	★★★★★
Merlot Carneros ($24, 2,800)	★★★★
Pinot Noir Carneros ($25, 1,700)	★★★★
Syrah Carneros ($27, 1,300)	★★★★
Zinfandel Carneros ($18, 600)	★★★★

WINERY DATA
Case Production: 10,000. **Acres Owned:** 170 acres in Carneros. **Varietals by Acre:** Cabernet Franc (15 acres),

Cabernet Sauvignon (40), Chardonnay (40), Merlot (45), Pinot Noir (25), Syrah (4), Zinfandel (1).

When Tony and Jo Ann Truchard decided to buy land and plant grapes in 1973, they chose Carneros, where the land was far less expensive than in Napa, and the potential for winegrowing largely unknown. It proved to be a brilliant move, and the Truchards have now assembled some 170 acres in vineyards, situated on a sloping grade that extends to the northern boundary of Carneros, west of the city of Napa. Truchard has turned out to be a great vineyard for all its wines. The winery's focus is on Chardonnay, Merlot, Pinot Noir and Syrah, the latter showing tremendous potential on the steep, rocky soils at the top of the Truchard hillside.

Now retired from his medical practice, Tony Truchard oversees the vineyard. The winery's goal is to isolate the best sections of the vineyard for its own wines, but to continue to sell grapes at the same time. The Truchards' Chardonnay, Merlot and Pinot Noir grapes are popular among area wineries; Acacia and Duckhorn are among the dozens who have purchased them. Production is at 10,000 cases, but is headed upward, with quality remaining high across the board. Worth watching.

TASTING NOTES

CABERNET SAUVIGNON CARNEROS (★★★★): Typically smooth and polished, with supple currant, spice and chocolate notes. Drinks well early and might age well, but it's probably best to enjoy these wines early on. Has steadily improved.
1995: A delicious, complex, youthful Cabernet with currant, black cherry, coffee, cedar, anise and blackberry flavors and mild, supple tannins. **91**
1994: Marked by earthy, leathery shadings up-front, the core of currant, herb and spicy flavors works its way to the forefront, where it picks up a peppery, dill-like coffee edge on the finish. **91**
1993: Supple and harmonious, with a nice toasty, buttery oak accent to the ripe currant and plummy flavors. Avoids being overly tannic or hard and finishes with hints of sweet fruit. **90**
1991: Supple and compact, this is a well proportioned Cabernet, with currant and cherry flavors that turn tannic. **87**
1990: Ripe and spicy, with pepper and currant notes that pick up pretty toast and buttery oak flavors. **86**
1989: Smooth and buttery, with a chocolaty, spicy vanilla

streak running through the prune and black cherry flavors. **85**

CABERNET SAUVIGNON CARNEROS RESERVE (★★★★)
1994: Rich, complex and flavorful, with tiers of currant, sage, mineral, anise and cherry flavors that slowly unfold to reveal even more depth and concentration. The finish goes on and on. The first reserve wine from Truchard. **91**

CHARDONNAY CARNEROS (★★★★★): Ripe, with deft balance between the rich, tropical fruit and pretty oak shadings. Steady improvement, too.
1997: Smooth, ripe, rich and concentrated, with tiers of fig, pear, melon, apple and hazelnut flavors; turning creamy and rich on the finish, with an aftertaste that goes on and on. **94**
1996: Smooth, ripe, rich and creamy, with lots of complex pear, anise, fig, hazelnut and earthy nuances. The texture is silky smooth, and the finish echoes fruit, spice and light oak. **92**
1995: Young and a touch on the austere side, with flavors built around a core of grapefruit, citrus and green pear. Well focused and well made. **91**

MERLOT CARNEROS (★★★★): Solid in a medium-bodied style, with attractive herb, currant and anise notes. Recent vintages have shown more depth and complexity.
1995: Complex, with rich, spicy, exotic currant, berry and plummy fruit. Turns elegant and supple on the finish, with delicate tannins and fine length. **91**
1994: A well oaked and concentrated style, with a rich core of currant, spice, pepper and cedary oak, and finishing with firm, earthy tannins. **89**

PINOT NOIR CARNEROS (★★★★): More delicate early on, but now showing greater depth and complexity.
1996: Smooth, ripe and polished, a well made '96 with cola, berry, cherry and spice, showing off a nice dose of oak, but best of all, well balanced. Turns complex on the finish. **87**
1995: Serves up lots of juicy plum, strawberry and black cherry flavors with decided earth and herbal notes, finishing with firm tea-like tannins. **91**
1994: Takes a while to unfold, but as it does, the cherry, spice, herb, and berry notes are ripe, rich and well focused, finishing with a long, full aftertaste. **91**
1993: Elegant, well focused cherry, plum and berry notes acquire a light oaky edge on aftertaste. Medium in body, smooth-textured and polished, leading to a subtle finish. **88**

SYRAH CARNEROS (★★★★): May well end up being the star, as the best vintages show tremendous richness, depth and character, and intensity without weight. Shows classic Syrah flavors with finesse.
1996: Ripe and plump, with juicy cherry, plum and wild berry flavors, along with rich, supple tannins, finishing with complex, meaty, leathery notes. **89**
1995: Dense and earthy, with a smoky, meaty, leathery edge to the ripe currant and berry flavors. Finishes with a chewy tannic aftertaste. **90**
1994: Remarkably concentrated and distinctive. Displays ripe, complex tiers of currant flavors with smoky meaty nuances and just enough oak. Finishes with a long, full aftertaste. **91**

ZINFANDEL CARNEROS (★★★★): Another sleeper from this producer, with two back-to-back successes in 1995 and 1996.
1996: Dark, rich and structured, with thick, opulent black cherry, berry, pepper, sage and spice, turning minty on the aftertaste. Amazing depth, richness and concentration for Carneros Zinfandel—a tribute to the diversity and excellence of this vineyard. **91**
1995: Rich with deep, complex, exotic spicy qualities to the equally exotic fruit flavors, with tiers of black cherry, raspberry, blackberry and logan berry flavors. For all its flavor, it is supple and harmonious. **91**

TUDAL WINERY (★★)
St. Helena, Napa Valley
Founded: 1979. **Owner:** Arnold & Alma Tudal. **Winemaker:** Arnold Tudal.

MAJOR WINES: PRICE, CASES, RATING
Cabernet Sauvignon Napa Valley
    ($25, 2,000)   ★★

WINERY DATA
Case Production: 2,000. **Acres Owned:** 7 acres in Napa Valley.
Varietals by Acre: Cabernet Sauvignon (7 acres).

Replacing an old walnut grove with vines, Arnold Tudal founded this small vineyard and winery north of St. Helena in 1979. The 7-acre Cabernet vineyard produces about 2,000 cases a year. The wines are consistently good, but quality can vary.

TASTING NOTES

CABERNET SAUVIGNON NAPA VALLEY (★★): Fluctuates from vintage to vintage, dipping dramatically in tough vintages, resurfacing again in good ones.

1992: Distinct vegetal, dill notes, but enough currant and cherry fruit to keep it interesting. Flavors are complex and concentrated. **83**

1990: Smooth, supple and stylish, a spicy wine with ripe currant and chocolate flavors extending onto a generous finish. **88**

TULOCAY WINERY (★★–★★★)
Napa Valley
Founded: 1975. **Owner:** William Cadman. **Winemaker:** William Cadman.

MAJOR WINES: PRICE, CASES, RATING

Cabernet Sauvignon Napa Valley Cliff Vineyard ($18, 400)	★★
Cabernet Sauvignon Napa Valley DeCelles Vineyard ($18, 120)	★★

ALSO PRODUCED
Chardonnay Napa Valley ($16, 500); Pinot Noir Napa Valley Haynes Vineyard ($16, 500); Zinfandel Napa Valley Casanova Vineyard ($21, 250).

WINERY DATA
Case Production: 2,000. **Vineyard Designations:** Cliff Vineyard (Cabernet Sauvignon), DeCelles Vineyard (Cabernet Sauvignon), Haynes Vineyard (Pinot Noir), Casanova Vineyard (Zinfandel). **Varietals Purchased:** Cabernet Sauvignon (Napa Valley), Chardonnay (Napa Valley), Pinot Noir (Napa Valley), Zinfandel (Napa Valley).

Former stockbroker William Cadman has worked at several Napa wineries, and on the side makes 2,000 cases of Cabernet, Chardonnay, Pinot Noir and Zinfandel, all from purchased grapes. The wines are often lean and earthy, a bit simple by Napa standards, but occasionally they receive good marks. Older vintages of Cabernet have aged well, softening a bit but still holding on to the tight tannins which typify these wines. Each wine carries a vineyard designation.

TURLEY WINE CELLARS (★★★★–★★★★★)
St. Helena, Napa Valley
Founded: 1993. **Owner:** Larry & Suzanne Turley. **Winemaker:** Ehren Jordan.

MAJOR WINES: PRICE, CASES, RATING

Petite Sirah Napa Valley Aïda Vineyard (Discontinued)	★★★★★
Petite Sirah Napa Valley Hayne Vineyard ($38, 500)	★★★★★
Petite Sirah Napa Valley Rattlesnake Acres ($30, 400)	★★★★
Zinfandel Alexander Valley Vineyard 101 ($35, 200)	★★★★
Zinfandel California Old Vines ($22, 1,200)	★★★★
Zinfandel Contra Costa County Duarte Vineyard ($22, 600)	★★★★
Zinfandel Dry Creek Valley Grist Vineyard ($32, 300)	★★★★
Zinfandel Howell Mountain Black-Sears Vineyard ($26, 700)	★★★★★
Zinfandel Lodi Spenker Vineyard ($24, 127)	★★★
Zinfandel Napa Valley Aïda Vineyard (Discontinued)	★★★★★
Zinfandel Napa Valley Hayne Vineyard ($40, 500)	★★★★★
Zinfandel Napa Valley Moore Earthquake Vineyard ($30, 500)	★★★★
Zinfandel Napa Valley Tofanelli Vineyard ($28, 600)	★★★★
Zinfandel Napa Valley Whitney Tennessee Vineyard (Discontinued)	★★★★

ALSO PRODUCED
Viognier Napa Valley Estate ($35, 100).

WINERY DATA

Case Production: 5,000. **Acres Owned:** 15.5 acres (2 in Alexander Valley, 12 in Howell Mountain, 3.5 in Napa Valley). **Varietals by Acre:** Petite Syrah (3 acres), Viognier (0.5), Zinfandel (12). **Vineyard Designations:** Aïda Vineyard (Petite Sirah, Zinfandel), Black-Sears Vineyard (Zinfandel), Duarte Vineyard (Zinfandel), Hayne Vineyard (Petite Sirah, Zinfandel), Grist Vineyard (Zinfandel), Moore "Earthquake" Vineyard (Zinfandel), Rattlesnake Acres (Zinfandel), Tofanelli Vineyard (Zinfandel), Vineyard 101 (Zinfandel).

Larry Turley was a co-founder and partner at Frog's Leap before selling his interest there and focusing on small-case production of vineyard-designated Zinfandels from his property, the original Frog Farm north of St. Helena (after which Frog's Leap was named). Other vineyards have since been added, with a total of 15 different wines made in 1997, mostly Zinfandels but also Petite Sirahs; the lineup was trimmed back to 12 wines for the 1998 vintage. The wines are uniformly delicious across the spectrum; very ripe, intense and fruity, often high in alcohol (14-plus readings are not unusual) but very tasty, distinctive, and considering the ultra-ripe style, among the very finest made in California. Turley is currently planting some 20 acres, mostly of Zinfandel, on Howell Mountain near Black-Sears Vineyard. Worth going out of your way to buy.

TASTING NOTES

PETITE SIRAH NAPA VALLEY AÏDA VINEYARD (★★★★★): About all you could ask for from Petite Sirah: richly flavored, textured, dark and flavorful. A powerful 1997 was the last year for this vineyard.

1996: Young and grapey, with a deep, saturated color and appealing ripe berry and cherry flavors. **90**
1995: Inky dark, dense and chewy, this is a potent Petite Sirah, with a peppery edge to the plum and currant notes and a dash of black cherry. Will need time to show its best. **88**
1993: Dark and immensely concentrated; packed with rich berry and peppery flavors and the requisite tannins. Big in every way, yet beautiful in its own way. **90**

PETITE SIRAH NAPA VALLEY HAYNE VINEYARD (★★★★★): Dark and immense; loaded with rich, berryish and peppery flavors.
1996: Ultra-dark in color, packed with rich, deep, dense currant, plum and wild berry flavors; turning plush and

concentrated on the finish. **92**
1995: Big, ripe, dark and richly flavored, with a tight core of juicy plum, currant and black cherry, finishing with a mouthful of chewy tannins and a spicy aftertaste. **91**
1994: Dark, rich and intense, loaded with chocolate, cherry, wild berry and spice flavors, accented by a wonderful dose of smoky, toasty oak. **96**

ZINFANDEL ALEXANDER VALLEY VINEYARD 101 (★★★)
1997: Lots of ripe, juicy, cherry, berry, plum and jammy notes, turning plush and fleshy on the finish. **91**
1996: Ripe and complex, with spicy, toasty oak and a pretty core of juicy plum, blackberry, cherry and spice. Deliciously fruity and complex on the finish. Mildly tannic. **91**

ZINFANDEL CALIFORNIA OLD VINES (★★★)
1997: Effusively fruity, with juicy cherry, plum and wild berry flavors that are very ripe and plush, finishing with firm tannins. **91**
1996: A ripe, jammy style, with lots of fresh strawberry, black cherry and raspberry flavors that are rich, supple and focused. Finishes with a long, fruity aftertaste and hints of anise and sage. **90**

ZINFANDEL CONTRA COSTA COUNTY DUARTE VINEYARD (★★★)
1997: Very ripe and jammy, with layers of ripe plum, black cherry, wild berry and spice, turning tannic. **89**
1996: Ripe, almost sweet, with a range of plum, sage and blackberry, turning earthy and dry on the aftertaste. **86**
1995: Smooth, ripe, rich and harmonious, with a wonderful integration of ripe, spicy cherry, currant and wild berry fruit with a pretty overlay of toasty oak. Finishes with an amazingly long and full-bodied finish. **95**

ZINFANDEL DRY CREEK VALLEY GRIST VINEYARD (★★★)
1997: Smooth, ripe and jammy, with layers of ripe plum, cherry, wild berry and blackberry flavors, finishing with firm, dry tannins. **91**
1996: Ripe, pushing raisiny, with dry, earthy, sage, wild berry and black cherry flavors. It's a mouthful of Zin, with a wide range of flavors. Finishes with firm tannins. **89**
1995: Smooth, ripe and juicy, this is a late harvest style that serves up lots of juicy black cherry, blackberry, currant and plum flavors. Impressive balance, even with its high (17.3 percent) alcohol level and one percent residual sugar. **93**

ZINFANDEL HOWELL MOUNTAIN BLACK-SEARS VINEYARD (★★★★★)
1996: Marked by distinctive spice, mint and peppery flavors built around a core of plum and blackberry. Finishes with a long, lingering aftertaste and remarkably plush, polished tannins. **91**
1995: Intense and deeply concentrated, with a distinct pepper and herbaceous edge, showing off complex cherry, berry and plummy flavors, and finishing with a long, lingering aftertaste. **95**
1994: A wonderful array of spicy blackberry and wild berry flavors with substantial finesse, depth and concentration. **93**

ZINFANDEL LODI SPENKER VINEYARD (★★★)
1997: Very ripe, with jammy, tarry, earthy, cedary flavors that are rich and intense, finishing with a complex array of flavors. **89**

ZINFANDEL NAPA VALLEY AÏDA VINEYARD (★★★★★):
Can be massive yet elegant, packed with rich fruit flavors and full of finesse. Grapes from this vineyard are no longer sold to Turley; the last vintage was 1997.
1997: Very ripe and earthy, with complex berry, cherry and plummy notes, finishing with a tannic edge. **90**
1996: A big, ripe, massive style that packs in lots of flavor, with tiers of mineral, spice, blackberry, black cherry and currant, finishing with firm but supple tannins and a long, full, lingering aftertaste. **94**
1995: Smooth, dark, rich and polished, with a supple core of coffee, spicy oak, currant and wild berry, finishing with an unusual dried-fruit flavor that gives it a pruney edge. **90**
1994: Pretty plum, sage, cedar and spice notes and firm but not overpowering flavors. **90**
1993: Dark, rich and intense, with potent wild berry, chocolate, cherry and buttery oak with full-blown but polished tannins. **93**

ZINFANDEL NAPA VALLEY HAYNE VINEYARD (★★★★★):
Planted in 1908, this vineyard yields the most distinctive Zinfandel in California: very ripe, ultra-rich layers of flavor and texture, and sometimes 17 percent alcohol.
1996: Dense, chewy and jam packed with rich, concentrated plum, black cherry, blackberry and spice. **95**
1995: A dark, ripe, rich and expansive wine loaded with smoky currant, plum, black cherry and blackberry notes, it oozes with flavor, finishing with dry tannins. **94**

1993: Enormously complex and concentrated, with well focused wild berry, black cherry and currant flavors, finishing with buttery oak and supple tannins. **95**

ZINFANDEL NAPA VALLEY MOORE EARTHQUAKE VINEYARD (★★★★): Serves up lots of complex fruit flavors and exotic spicy nuances.
1996: Spot-on Napa Zinfandel, with lots of cherry, blackberry and pepper oak spice notes. Tightly focused, finely balanced and quite pleasurable to drink. **91**
1995: A sweet, late-harvest style—so be forewarned—it is ripe and juicy, brimming with cherry, wild berry, plum and coffee notes, it picks up a hint of caramel. **93**
1994: Dense and tannic; delivers a wallop of anise, black cherry, wild berry and spicy nuances. **94**
1993: Tight and intense, well focused and compact, offering lively wild berry, spice and raspberry flavors. **90**

ZINFANDEL NAPA VALLEY TOFANELLI VINEYARD (★★★★)
1997: Juicy, with ripe plum, cherry, wild berry and spicy flavors, finishing with a long, lingering aftertaste that keeps pumping out the juicy berry flavors. **90**
1996: A potent, powerful wine that has some rough edges, it nonetheless delivers a ripe, juicy, tannic core of black cherry, wild berry, plum and cedar flavors. **92**

ZINFANDEL NAPA VALLEY WHITNEY TENNESSEE VINEYARD (★★★★)
1996: Hits the right notes, with pretty blackberry, black cherry, pepper and spice notes, the flavors zoom along the palate. The last Whitney Tennessee bottling for Turley. **92**
1995: Young and tight, with a rich, complex core of blueberry, blackberry and cherry flavors, turning smooth and polished on the finish. **90**
1994: Displays tiers of smoky, meaty, currant, wild berry, plum and cherry flavors; very complex finish. **91**

TURNBULL WINE CELLARS (★★★)
Oakville, Napa Valley
Founded: 1993. **Owner:** Patrick O'Dell. **Winemaker:** Jon Engelskirger.

MAJOR WINES: PRICE, CASES, RATING
Cabernet Sauvignon Napa Valley Oakville
($22, 6,000) ★★★

Syrah Napa Valley Oakville
($25, 500)   ★★★

Also Produced
Merlot Napa Valley Oakville ($22, 1,000); Sangiovese
Napa Valley Oakville ($20, 1,000); Sauvignon Blanc
Napa Valley Oakville ($12, 2,000); Zinfandel Napa
Valley Oakville ($18, 500).

Winery Data
Case Production: 11,000. **Acres Owned:** 148 acres in
Oakville. **Varietals by Acre:** Cabernet Sauvignon (56 acres),
Merlot (33), Sangiovese (12), Sauvignon Blanc (10), Sauvignon
Musque (11), Syrah (4), other Bordeaux (11), other Italian (4),
other (7).

Attorney Reverdy Johnson and architect William
Turnbull founded Johnson Turnbull and produced their first
Cabernet in 1979, having decided that their vineyard produced exceptional grapes and that owning a weekend
retreat vineyard involved more work than they imagined.
With some 20 acres of Cabernet Sauvignon and Cabernet
Franc in Oakville, Johnson Turnbull had built production to
5,000 cases by the mid-1980s. The style of wine was characterized by a strong mint, bay leaf and oregano character
so pronounced that the partners began producing two
Cabernets in 1986: Vineyard Selection 67 emphasizing the
oregano quality, and Vineyard Selection 82 showcasing
brilliant currant and cherry notes. By the late 1980s, their
vineyard fell victim to phylloxera and needed to be replanted. In 1993, the winery was sold to Patrick O'Dell, who
changed the name to Turnbull Wine Cellars and added land
that now totals 148 acres. The grape mix includes Merlot,
Sangiovese, Syrah and Zinfandel. Worth watching.

Tasting Notes

Cabernet Sauvignon Napa Valley Oakville
(★★★): While quality varied under the old regime, it
remains to be seen how the new wines will fare.
1994: Young, tight and tannic, with a leathery, earthy
edge to the currant, plum and berry notes. **87**
1991: Shows the classic mint and bay leaf aromas of this
vineyard, and it also delivers juicy currant and cherry
flavors. **88**
Vineyard Selection 67 1987: Minty menthol aromas give
way to ripe, rich black cherry, plum and currant flavors. **88**

Vineyard Selection 82 1986: Intense and concentrated,
with tart black cherry, currant, spice and cedar flavors
that are sharply focused and framed by firm tannins and
toasty oak. **89**

Turning Leaf see **Gallo of Sonoma Winery**

Unalii (★★★)
Sonoma County
Founded: 1995. **Owner:** Bev Salinger & Diane Harder.
Winemaker: Bev Salinger.

Major Wines: Price, Cases, Rating
Chardonnay Sonoma County
($15, 1,500)   ★★★
Syrah Mendocino
($16, 550)   ★★★

Also Produced
Merlot Napa Valley ($25, 75); Sémillon Napa Valley
Block House ($11, 340); Zinfandel Lodi ($15, 580).

Winery Data
Case Production: 3,000. **Varietals Purchased:** Chardonnay
(Sonoma County), Merlot (Napa Valley), Sémillon (Napa
Valley), Syrah (Mendocino), Zinfandel (Lodi).

Bev Salinger and Diane Harder are making accessible,
affordable wines from purchased grapes. The 1997
Sonoma County Chardonnay (88 points) was well
focused, with pretty flavors of citrus and fig and elegant
pineapple notes woven together with a light spiciness.
The 1996 Syrah (87) is both meaty and earthy as well as
rich in cassis and blackberry flavors.

Valley of the Moon Winery (★★)
Sonoma Valley
Founded: 1863. **Owner:** Gary Heck. **Winemaker:** Pat
Henderson.

Major Wines: Price, Cases, Rating
Chardonnay Sonoma County
($20, 10,000)   ★★
Pinot Blanc Sonoma County
($20, 4,000)   ★★

Syrah Sonoma County ($25, 3,000) ★★
Zinfandel Sonoma Valley ($25, 5,000) ★★

ALSO PRODUCED
Cuvée De La Luna Red Sonoma County ($25, 8,000); Sangiovese Sonoma County ($25, 4,000).

WINERY DATA
Case Production: 35,000. Acres Owned: 60 acres in Sonoma Valley. Varietals by Acre: Barbera (6 acres), Petite Sirah (5), Pinot Blanc (10), Sangiovese (7), Zinfandel (25). Varietals Purchased: Cabernet Sauvignon (Sonoma Valley), Chardonnay (Russian River, Sonoma Valley), Merlot (Alexander Valley, Sonoma Valley), Pinot Blanc (Russian River), Sangiovese (Alexander Valley), Zinfandel (Sonoma Valley).

Valley of the Moon Winery dates to 1857. After years of producing ordinary wines, the winery was purchased in 1997 by Gary Heck, owner of Korbel and Kenwood Vineyards, and $13 million was spent restoring the old stone winery and updating equipment, with the intent of making first-class wines.

The first releases have been good, if somewhat restrained wines of modest depth and flavor. The 1997 Chardonnay (85 points) was delicate, with tangerine, tropical fruit and spice flavors; the 1996 Pinot Blanc (87) was firm, with apple, pear and hazelnut notes. The 1995 Syrah (87) showed black cherry and cassis flavors, with hints of herb and spice. The 1996 Zinfandel (86) was a bit rustic, with firm tannins, a good dose of oak flavors, and pleasant, ripe cherry notes.

VAN ASPEREN (★★★)
Rutherford, Napa Valley
Founded: 1997. Owner: Ernie & Virginia Van Asperen. Winemaker: Mark Swain. Affiliated Brands: Round Hill, Rutherford Ranch.

MAJOR WINES: PRICE, CASES, RATING
Cabernet Sauvignon Napa Valley
  Signature Reserve ($24, 400) ★★★
Zinfandel Napa Valley ($10, 1,600) ★★

ALSO PRODUCED
Cabernet Sauvignon Napa Valley ($15, 7,200); Chardonnay Napa Valley ($11, 5,000); Merlot Napa Valley ($15, 8,800); Sauvignon Blanc Napa Valley ($10, 1,200).

WINERY DATA
Case Production: 24,000. Acres Owned: 370 acres in Napa Valley. Varietals by Acre: Cabernet Sauvignon (37 acres). Varietals Purchased: Chardonnay (Napa Valley), Merlot (Napa Valley), Sauvignon Blanc (Napa Valley), (Zinfandel (Napa Valley).

This is the reserve line from Round Hill owners Ernie and Virginia Van Asperen. So far, both the Cabernet and Zinfandel have been good, but not among Napa's best—at least not yet.

VAN DUZER see PARDUCCI WINE CELLARS

VENDANGE see SEBASTIANI SONOMA CASK CELLARS

VENEZIA see GEYSER PEAK WINERY

VENGE see SADDLEBACK CELLARS

VENTANA VINEYARDS (★★)
Monterey County
Founded: 1978. Owner: Doug Meador. Winemaker: Doug Meador.

MAJOR WINES: PRICE, CASES, RATING
Chardonnay Monterey Gold Stripe ($12, 18,000) ★★
Merlot Monterey ($12, 2,200) ★
Riesling Monterey Dry ($10, 1,400) ★★
Sauvignon Blanc Monterey ($10, 5,100) ★★

ALSO PRODUCED

Cabernet Sauvignon Monterey ($12, 3,000);
Gewürztraminer Monterey ($10, 2,100); Orange Muscat
Monterey ($10, 700); Riesling Monterey ($8, 1,500);
Syrah Monterey ($14, 300).

WINERY DATA

Case Production: 40,000. **Acres Owned:** 300 acres in
Monterey. **Varietals by Acre:** Cabernet Sauvignon (15 acres),
Chardonnay (130), Chenin Blanc (6), Gewürztraminer (16),
Merlot (15), Orange Muscat (10), Riesling (36), Sauvignon
Blanc (34), Syrah (15), other (23).

Douglas Meador's Ventana Vineyard has experienced a
checkered financial past, but Meador persists with a
wide range of vineyard research; the 300-acre vineyard is
a source of grapes to many wineries. Production has
grown to 40,000 cases, led by the Gold Stripe
Chardonnay (18,000 cases), which continues to improve
after a serious dip in quality in the mid-1980s when the
winery and vineyard underwent a costly financial reorganization. Chenin Blanc, Johannisberg Riesling, Merlot,
Pinot Blanc, Sauvignon Blanc and Syrah are also produced in smaller case quantities. The wines are of average quality overall, though the Chardonnay can a be
good value. The 1996 Gold Stripe Chardonnay (86
points) featured youthful flavors of orange and pear.

VIADER VINEYARDS & WINERY (★★★★)
Napa Valley
Founded: 1987. **Owner:** Delia Viader. **Winemaker:**
Amy Aiken.

MAJOR WINES: PRICE, CASES, RATING

Viader Red Napa Valley
  ($35, 4,000)   ★★★★

WINERY DATA

Case Production: 4,000. **Acres Owned:** 23 acres in Napa
Valley. **Varietals by Acre:** Cabernet Franc (8 acres), Cabernet
Sauvignon (12), Petit Verdot (0.5), Syrah (2.5). **Varietals
Purchased:** Cabernet Franc (Napa Valley), Cabernet Sauvignon
(Napa Valley).

Argentina-born Delia Viader owns a steep, densely
planted 23-acre Cabernet Sauvignon and Cabernet Franc

vineyard on Howell Mountain (but below the appellation
elevation altitude), where she produces 4,000 cases of
wine, with a St. Emilion-style blend in mind. Quality is
very high; the wine is distinctive, complex and elegant.
Worth buying and collecting. Winemaker Amy Aiken,
wife of Beaulieu's Joel Aiken, joined Viader in 1999.

TASTING NOTES

VIADER RED NAPA VALLEY (★★★★): Very impressive
in the first vintages, as it uniformly offers ripe, complex
and fleshy currant, earth, anise and smoky oak flavors,
with supple tannins. A blend of 60 percent Cabernet
Sauvignon and 40 percent Cabernet Franc. The wines
have the depth and balance to improve with cellaring.
1996: Tightly wound, with an earthy green olive edge to
the spicy plum and currant notes; complex, elegant, spicy
and balanced. **89**
1995: Ripe and complex, with pretty plum, black cherry and
wild berry flavors, a smooth texture and supple tannins. **92**
1994: Smooth, ripe, rich and smoky, with a plush, elegant
core of currant, plum, cherry, sage and mineral flavors. **93**
1992: Well-oaked, with strong vanilla and chocolate
notes balanced by rich currant and cherry flavors. **88**
1991: Supple and generous, with layers of ripe plum,
currant, anise and smoke flavors, finishing with rich,
plush tannins. **91**
1990: Ripe, complex and concentrated, with a core of
rich currant, earth and berry flavors, finishing with
toasty oak and supple tannins. **91**
1989: Smooth and polished, with complex cedar, spice,
chocolate and cherry flavors that turn supple on the finish. **87**

CONRAD VIANO WINERY (★★–★★★)
Contra Costa County
Founded: 1946. **Owner:** The Viano Family.
Winemaker: The Viano Family.

MAJOR WINES: PRICE, CASES, RATING

Cabernet Sauvignon Contra Costa County
  ($12, 200)   ★★
Zinfandel Contra Costa County
  Sand Rock Hill Reserve Selection
  ($12, 800)   ★★★

WINERY DATA
Case Production: 2,000. **Acres Owned:** 60 acres in Contra Costa County. **Varietals by Acre:** Cabernet Sauvignon (10), Chardonnay (9), Sangiovese (1), Zinfandel (25), others (15).

The Viano family founded this winery in Martinez in 1946, and owns 60 acres of vineyards from which come about 2,000 cases of Cabernet, Chardonnay, dessert wine and Zinfandel. At 800 cases, Zinfandel is the volume leader. All the wines carry a Contra Costa County appellation. Distribution is very limited.

TASTING NOTES

ZINFANDEL CONTRA COSTA COUNTY SAND ROCK HILL RESERVE SELECTION (★★★): Steadily improving; very ripe and flavorful. From an area that increasingly merits more attention.
1995: Packs sweet oak, black cherry and ripe plum flavors together into a well-balanced, harmonious blend. Elegant and full-bodied, yet delicate. **89**
1994: A complex, seductive style, with ripe plum, blueberry and currant flavors swirling through a rich, plush texture. **90**
1993: Dark, ripe, rich and plush; a real mouthful of berry, cherry, plum and smoke, picking up a meaty aftertaste. **90**
1992: Intense, spicy and packed with well focused black cherry, currant and plum notes, turning tannic on the finish. **89**

VIANSA WINERY (★★–★★★★)
Carneros
Founded: 1988. **Owner:** Sam & Vicki Sebastiani. **Winemaker:** Michael Sebastiani.

MAJOR WINES: PRICE, CASES, RATING	
Cabernet Sauvignon-Cabernet Franc	
Napa Valley Ossidiana	
($75, 250)	★★★
Cabernet Sauvignon	
Napa & Sonoma Counties	
($19, 2,000)	★★★
Primitivo-Zinfandel Sonoma Prindelo	
($28, 2,000)	★★★★
Sangiovese North Coast Piccolo	
($18, 2,000)	★★

ALSO PRODUCED
Aleatico Sonoma Di Pacomio ($17, 1,000); Arneis North Coast ($25, 2,000); Barbera Sonoma Augusto ($45, 250); Chardonnay Sonoma Carneros Cento Per Cento ($35, 2,000); Dolcetto Northern California Athena ($19, 2,500); Freisa North Coast ($27, 750); Nebbiolo North Coast ($17, 2,000); Pinot Grigio Sonoma Vitoria ($19, 2,500); Sangiovese Sonoma Thalia ($35, 1,000); Tocai Friulano North Coast Frescolina ($28, 1,500); Trebbiano California Riserva Anatra Bianco ($15, 1,500); Vernaccia Sonoma Di Pierina ($24, 1,500); Zinfandel Sonoma ($18, 750).

WINERY DATA
Case Production: 20,000. **Acres Owned:** 88 acres in Carneros, Sonoma. **Varietals by Acre:** Pinot Grigio, Primitivo, Sangiovese, Vernaccia.

After working for and leading Sebastiani Vineyards from the 1970s to the mid-1980s, Sam Sebastiani was ousted as president of the historic Sonoma winery in 1986 after a family dispute about the winery's future. He and his wife, Vicki, promptly started Sam J. Sebastiani Vineyards, but due to market confusion with Sebastiani Vineyards, changed the winery's name to Viansa (short for Vicki and Sam). They later built an attractive Italian villa-style winery on Highway 121 in Carneros, where they cater to tourists.

Their 20,000 cases of wine are made mostly from purchased grapes. The long-term plan is to focus on native Italian varietals such as Sangiovese and Nebbiolo. Quality ranges from good to very good. The wines are mostly sold at the winery, and are worth a stop to sample.

VIGIL VINEYARD (★★)
Napa Valley
Founded: 1992. **Owner:** James Pawlak. **Winemaker:** Mike Loftus. **Second Label:** Terra Vin.

MAJOR WINES: PRICE, CASES, RATING	
Vigilante Red California	
($9, 2,200)	★★
Zinfandel California Tres Condados	
($12, 2,200)	★★
Zinfandel Lodi Mohr-Fry Ranch Old Vines	
($16, 1,200)	★★

Zinfandel-Carignane California Napa Valley
 Terra Vin
 ($10, 3,400)   ★★
Zinfandel-Carignane Napa Valley
 Terra Vin Reserve
 ($22, 400)   ★★★

ALSO PRODUCED
Cabernet Franc Napa Valley Solari Vineyard ($22, 500); Chardonnay Russian River Valley Windsor Criks Vineyard ($16, 1,000); Meritage Red Napa Valley ($20, 1,600); Zinfandel Howell Mountain Beatty Vineyard ($22, 400).

WINERY DATA
Case Production: 13,000 **Acres Owned:** 5 acres in Napa Valley. **Vineyard Designations:** Beatty Vineyard (Zinfandel), Criks Vineyard (Chardonnay), Solari Vineyard (Cabernet Franc). **Varietals Purchased:** Cabernet Sauvignon (Napa Valley), Chardonnay (Russian River Valley), Zinfandel (Howell Mountain, Lodi).

James Pawlak purchases grapes from a number of California appellations, including Lodi Zinfandel, Russian River Chardonnay and Napa Valley Cabernet. The red wines are variable: occasionally rustic and earthy, and at other times soft and light. The 1996 Zinfandel-Carignane Terra Vin Reserve (87 points) was smoky and ripe, with anise, prune and spice flavors on a soft frame.

VILLA ANDRIANA see SUMMERS

VILLA MT. EDEN (★★–★★★★)
St. Helena, Napa Valley
Founded: 1969. **Owner:** Stimson Lane Vineyards & Estates. **Winemaker:** Mike McGrath.

MAJOR WINES: PRICE, CASES, RATING
Cabernet Sauvignon California
 ($12, 35,000)   ★★
Cabernet Sauvignon Mendocino
 Signature Series
 ($45, 750)   ★★★★
Cabernet Sauvignon Napa Valley
 Grand Reserve
 ($20, 3,000)   ★★★

Chardonnay Santa Maria Valley Bien
 Nacido Vineyard Grand Reserve
 ($20, 10,000)   ★★★★
Chardonnay Santa Maria Valley Bien
 Nacido Vineyard Signature Series
 ($35, 750)   ★★★★★
Merlot California
 ($20, 800)   ★★★
Pinot Blanc Santa Maria Valley Bien
 Nacido Vineyard Grand Reserve
 ($20, 1,300)   ★★★
Pinot Noir California
 ($12, 9,000)   ★★
Pinot Noir Santa Maria Valley
 Bien Nacido Vineyard Grand Reserve
 ($20, 2,000)   ★★★
Zinfandel California
 ($12, 9,000)   ★★
Zinfandel Sonoma Valley Monte Rosso
 Vineyard Grand Reserve
 ($20, 1,200)   ★★★

ALSO PRODUCED
Cabernet Franc Indian Springs Vineyard Nevada County ($15, 1,100); Chardonnay California ($12, 80,000); Syrah California Grand Reserve ($20, 1,300).

WINERY DATA
Case Production: 135,000. **Acres Owned:** 429 acres (194 in Monterey, 235 in Napa Valley). **Varietals by Acre:** Cabernet Franc (6 acres), Cabernet Sauvignon (132), Chardonnay (102), Malbec (20), Merlot (44), Petit Verdot (2), Pinot Blanc (20), Pinot Gris (10), Pinot Noir (79), Primitivo (0.5), Sauvignon Blanc (1), Syrah (13). **Vineyard Designations:** Bien Nacido Vineyard (Chardonnay, Pinot Blanc, Pinot Noir), Monte Rosso Vineyard (Zinfandel). **Varietals Purchased:** Chardonnay (Carneros, Santa Maria), Pinot Blanc (Santa Maria), Pinot Noir (Carneros, Santa Maria), Syrah (Nevada County), Zinfandel (Sonoma).

Dating back to 1881, this winery was rejuvenated in 1970 by James and Anne McWilliams, the latter the granddaughter of A.P. Giannini, founder of the Bank of America. After early success, including fine 1974 and 1978 Cabernets made by Nils Venge, quality declined, and in 1982 Venge departed to Groth Vineyards. In 1986 the McWilliamses sold the winery to Stimson Lane, the owner of Chateau Ste. Michelle in Washington.

Since the takeover, the focus has been on building volume, with a full array of wines now drawing from 429 acres in vines, including 235 in Napa Valley and another 194 in Monterey. Quality ranges from good to sensational, with the Cabernet Mendocino Signature Series and Chardonnay Santa Maria Valley Bien Nacido Signature Series the two standouts. Worth buying.

TASTING NOTES

CABERNET SAUVIGNON MENDOCINO SIGNATURE SERIES (★★★★): Perhaps the greatest Cabernet coming from Mendocino; very ripe, rich and polished, with pretty oak and firm tannins.
1995: Dense, chewy, complex and concentrated; brimming with currant, black cherry, herb, mineral and sage flavors framed by nuances of toasty oak. **94**
1994: Big, ripe and plush, showing off its earthy, leathery tannins and a center of ripe currant and cherry flavors. **92**
1993: Trim and well focused, with supple cherry, plum and currant flavors of moderate depth and richness. **88**
1992: Firm and chunky, with a tight, concentrated beam of cherry and currant fruit, finishing with firm tannins and a long toasty aftertaste. **92**

CABERNET SAUVIGNON NAPA VALLEY GRAND RESERVE (★★★)
1995: Supple and elegant, with pleasing coffee, cedar, currant and spicy berry flavors that are woven together. Turns firm and tart on the finish, with sharp acidity. **87**
1993: Dry, tannic and austere, with a leathery quality that overshadows the ripe plum and cherry flavors. **82**
1992: Tight and firmly tannic. Minty currant and berry flavors fight through, but on the finish the tannins show their raw side. **88**
1991: Tight and a touch green, with firm tannins and just enough ripe currant and berry flavors. **83**
1990: The best Villa Mt. Eden Cabernet in years, this is an elegant and flavorful wine with currant and cherry notes framed by light, toasty oak. Drink it now or cellar it through the decade. **87**
1989: Simple, with currant and black cherry flavors and fine tannins. **84**
1988: Ripe and generous, with a soft, creamy texture and lively currant, plum and berry flavors. **86**

CHARDONNAY SANTA MARIA VALLEY BIEN NACIDO VINEYARD GRAND RESERVE (★★★★): Bright, lively, intense and well focused, with pretty oak shadings.
1996: Smooth, ripe, creamy and complex, with tiers of toasty, spicy oak and hints of pear, nectarine and peach. **91**

CHARDONNAY SANTA MARIA VALLEY BIEN NACIDO VINEYARD SIGNATURE SERIES (★★★★★): Ripe and opulent, yet elegant and detailed.
1996: A wonderful sense of harmony and finesse, balancing ripe, complex tiers of peach, pear and nectarine flavors with a silky texture. **95**
1995: Bold, ripe and intense, with rich, spicy pear, fig, melon and apple flavors and a creamy finish. **92**

MERLOT NAPA VALLEY GRAND RESERVE (★★★): Strikes a nice balance between herbs and cherry-laced fruit, with light oak notes.

PINOT BLANC SANTA MARIA VALLEY BIEN NACIDO VINEYARD GRAND RESERVE (★★★): Impressive for its bright, rich, complex flavors and deft oak shadings.

PINOT NOIR SANTA MARIA VALLEY BIEN NACIDO VINEYARD GRAND RESERVE (★★★)
1996: Serves up an appealing range of ripe plum, wild berry, cherry and earthy flavors, turning smooth and polished on the finish. **88**
1995: Marked by strong earth flavors and a mushroom edge; shows just enough ripe cherry and berry fruit, turning elegant and supple on the finish. **89**
1994: Good intensity, with nice, ripe flavors, showing hints of cherry, raspberry and spice. **86**

ZINFANDEL SONOMA VALLEY MONTE ROSSO VINEYARD GRAND RESERVE (★★★)
1995: Dry and earthy, with only modest fruit flavors peeking through the dry tannins. **84**
1994: Ripe and zesty, with rich pepper, wild berry fruit and lots of spicy nuances; a big but well mannered wine that's fairly tannic. **88**
1993: Bold, ripe, complex and flavorful, offering rich, concentrated notes of wild berry, plum, cherry and mint. **88**

VINE CLIFF CELLARS (★★★–★★★★★)
Oakville, Napa Valley
Founded: 1989. **Owner:** Nell & Charles Sweeney. **Winemaker:** Rolando Herrera.

MAJOR WINES: PRICE, CASES, RATING

Cabernet Sauvignon Napa Valley
Oakville Estate
($36, 2,000)   ★★★★
Chardonnay Napa Valley
($25, 2,000)   ★★★★★
Chardonnay Napa Valley
Proprietress Reserve
($34, 500)   ★★★★
Merlot Napa Valley
($27, 2,000)   ★★★

WINERY DATA

Case Production: 6,500. **Acres Owned:** 26 acres in Napa
Valley (6 in Calistoga, 20 in Oakville). **Varietals by Acre:**
Cabernet Franc (1 acre), Cabernet Sauvignon (23), Merlot (2).
Varietals Purchased: Chardonnay (Carneros, Napa Valley),
Merlot (Napa Valley).

Crown Sterling Suites president Charles Sweeney and
his wife Nell revived an old winery built on their property
back in 1871, planting 25 acres of terraced vineyard to
Bordeaux varieties for their Vine Cliff Cellars winery on
Silverado Trail in Oakville. Production is 6,500 cases,
including a Proprietress Reserve Chardonnay made from
purchased grapes. Quality remains very high. Worth buying.

TASTING NOTES

CABERNET SAUVIGNON NAPA VALLEY OAKVILLE ESTATE
(★★★★): Continues to improve, with elegant, well-
focused, deftly balanced wines that are structured for
aging.
1995: A classy style, with ripe, complex, concentrated
cherry, plum and berry fruit flavors and pretty, toasty oak
shadings. **92**
1994: Dense and chewy, with a ripe, tight, well focused
core of earthy currant, black cherry and wild berry flavors, turning tannic on the finish. **90**
1993: Firm, ripe and intense, with a complex band of
currant, plum, cherry and anise flavors that fan out and
linger on the finish. **90**
1991: Elegant, with cedar, tobacco and currant flavors
that fold together nicely. **88**
1990: Tight and firm, with chewy cherry and herb flavors that finish with mild tannins. **87**

CHARDONNAY NAPA VALLEY (★★★★★)
1996: Impeccably balanced, long and rich, with generous, supple, up-front fruitiness, offering seamless pear,
apple, apricot and melon flavors. **93**
1995: Very complete and harmonious, with a complex
array of ripe pear, melon, hazelnut and spicy flavors,
turning elegant on the finish. **93**

CHARDONNAY NAPA VALLEY PROPRIETRESS RESERVE
(★★★★): Packs in lots of rich, complex flavors and is
well-oaked, yet balanced.
1995: Elegant and understated, with attractive lemon, citrus, pear and honey flavors that pick up nuances of pretty, smoky oak. **92**
1994: A tight, complex, well focused, flinty style with
lots of depth and richness; laden with apple, pear and
melon flavors. **91**

MERLOT NAPA VALLEY (★★★)
1995: Tough and chewy, but the core of flavors is appealing, built around ripe cherry and currant, sage and mineral
notes. Turns complex on the finish, with firm tannins. **88**

VINELAND see **ARCIERO WINERY**

VINEYARD 29 (★★★)

Napa Valley
Founded: 1992. **Owner:** Tom Paine & Theresa Norton
Winemaker: Heidi Peterson Barrett.

MAJOR WINES: PRICE, CASES, RATING

Cabernet Sauvignon Napa Valley
($55, 500)   ★★★

WINERY DATA

Case Production: 500. **Acres Owned:** 3.5 acres in Napa Valley.
Varietals by Acre: Cabernet Sauvignon (3.5 acres).

Tom Paine and Theresa Norton began planting their
3.5-acre vineyard in 1988 and produced their first wine
in 1992. Just one wine is made, a Cabernet Sauvignon,
which is sold through the Grace Family Vineyards mailing list. Current production is just over 500 cases, but
plans to increase acreage by 2 to 3 acres could double
production by 2005.

TASTING NOTES

CABERNET SAUVIGNON NAPA VALLEY

1994: Marked by spice, cedar and dill notes, with just enough ripe cherry and currant flavors to fill in the gaps, gaining complexity on the finish. **90**

1992: Smooth and supple, with a band of cedar, spice, dried cherry and plum flavors and fleshy tannins. **86**

VINEYARD DRIVE see TABLAS CREEK

VINO NOCETO (★★)

Shenandoah Valley, Amador County
Founded: 1990. **Owner:** Suzy & Jim Gullett.
Winemaker: Scott Harvey.

MAJOR WINES: PRICE, CASES, RATING

Sangiovese Shenandoah Valley
($12, 2,350)   ★★

ALSO PRODUCED

Sangiovese Shenandoah Valley Riserva ($20, 214).

WINERY DATA

Case Production: 2,550. **Acres Owned:** 12.5 acres in Shenandoah Valley. **Varietals by Acre:** Sangiovese (12.5 acres). **Varietals Purchased:** Sangiovese (Shenandoah Valley).

Vino Noceto, dedicated solely to Sangiovese, was started by Suzy and Jim Gullet in 1990. The wines are elegant and balanced, with black cherry, anise and herb flavors. The 1995 (84 points) was unusual, with earthy, coffee flavors, but some richness as well.

VON STRASSER (★★★–★★★★)

Diamond Mountain, Napa Valley
Founded: 1990. **Owner:** Rudy & Rita von Strasser.
Winemaker: Rudy von Strasser. **Second Label:** Freestone.

MAJOR WINES: PRICE, CASES, RATING

Cabernet Sauvignon Diamond Mountain
($36, 1,500)   ★★★★
Chardonnay Napa Valley
($30, 500)   ★★★

ALSO PRODUCED

Cabernet Sauvignon Meritage Blend Reserve ($75, 100).

WINERY DATA

Case Production: 10,000. **Acres Owned:** 15 acres in Diamond Mountain. **Varietals by Acre:** Cabernet Sauvignon (13 acres), Merlot (1), Petit Verdot (1). **Varietals Purchased:** Cabernet Sauvignon (Napa Valley), Merlot (Napa Valley), Sauvignon Blanc (Napa Valley).

Rudy and Rita von Strasser bought the former Roddis Vineyard on Diamond Mountain in 1990, using the Cabernet Sauvignon estate vineyard for their wine. Close to the dusty Volcanic Hill Vineyard at Diamond Creek, the vineyard has begun to produce some distinctive, classy wines. Chardonnay comes from purchased grapes. Production has climbed from 1,500 cases to 10,000, with Freestone as a second label.

TASTING NOTES

CABERNET SAUVIGNON DIAMOND MOUNTAIN (★★★★):

Consistently well made and focused, with appealing currant, herb and pretty oak shadings. Time will tell how the wines age, but they're well balanced and reflect the appellation. Worth buying.

1995: A delicious Cabernet, with ripe, plummy, complex cedar, black cherry, spice and herbal menthol notes, it zooms along, turning supple on the finish. **93**

1994: Lots of complex coffee, currant, cherry and tea-like notes; smoothly textured, with considerable finesse and chewy tannins. **92**

1992: Tough, chewy and tannic, with a core of muscular, earthy currant and cherry flavors submerged beneath the tannins. **88**

1991: Ripe and chewy, youthful and tannic, with currant, plum and mint flavors emerging on the finish. **88**

1990: Tight and firm, with herb, anise and currant flavors that turn supple and elegant on the finish. Tannins are fine and soft at this stage. **89**

CHARDONNAY NAPA VALLEY (★★★)

1996: Lots of ripe, fresh, up-front fruitiness, with gentle peach, apricot, fig and pear flavors that linger on. Impressive for its elegance and balance. **90**

1995: A spicy style with a twinge of bitterness on the finish. The core of pear and apple-scented fruit is a bit out of focus, but perhaps short-term cellaring will bring it into balance. **87**

VOSS VINEYARDS (★★★)
Napa Valley
Founded: 1991. **Owner:** Robert Hill Smith.
Winemaker: Alan Hoey.

MAJOR WINES: PRICE, CASES, RATING
Merlot Napa Valley
   ($18, 2,310)   ★★★
Sauvignon Blanc Napa Valley
   ($13, 4,013)   ★★★
Sauvignon Blanc Napa Valley Botrytis
   ($19, NA)   ★★
Shiraz Napa Valley
   ($22, 262)   ★★★

WINERY DATA
Case Production: 8,000. **Acres Owned:** 41 acres in Napa Valley. **Varietals by Acre:** Merlot (14 acres), Sauvignon Blanc (12), Sémillon (3), Shiraz (12). **Varietals Purchased:** Merlot (Napa Valley), Shiraz (Napa Valley).

Australian Robert Hill Smith, whose family owns several wineries, including Yalumba, owns this brand; its 8,000 cases of Merlot, Sauvignon Blanc and Shiraz are made from both estate and purchased grapes grown in Napa Valley. Quality has been good, particularly the Sauvignon Blanc. Shiraz, too, looks promising. Worth buying.

TASTING NOTES

MERLOT NAPA VALLEY (★★★)
1996: Lean and tannic, with a core of clayish cherry and berry fruit, turning dry and tannic on the finish. **81**
1995: An elegant, understated style with a pretty interplay of ripe plum and cherry fruit and spicy, cedary, toasty oak. Turns complex on the finish, where the flavors fold together quite nicely. **88**
1994: Wonderful aromas; young, tight and tannic, but the core of fruit is well focused and concentrated, with a band of currant, earth, herb and cedar. **88**

SAUVIGNON BLANC NAPA VALLEY (★★★)
1997: Vibrant gooseberry and passion flavors that are complex, with layers of grapefruit, lemon and lime. **91**
1996: Features melon, grass, herbs, celery, honey and citrus flavors that are bright and lively. **87**
1995: Smooth, polished and vibrant, with sweet pea, pear and ever-so-slightly gamy flavors. Has real complexity and depth. **90**

SHIRAZ NAPA VALLEY (★★★)
1995: Dark and chewy, with an earthy, leathery edge to the plum and mineral flavors. Turns complex and fans out on the finish, but needs time to shed tannins. **89**

WASHINGTON STREET CELLARS see BELL WINE CELLARS

WATTLE CREEK WINERY (★★–★★★)
Alexander Valley, Sonoma County
Founded: 1994. **Owner:** Chris & Kristine Williams.
Winemaker: Tony Jordan.

MAJOR WINES: PRICE, CASES, RATING
Cabernet Sauvignon Alexander Valley
   ($30, 2,000)   ★★
Chardonnay Alexander Valley
   ($18, 1,000)   ★★
Sauvignon Blanc Alexander Valley
   ($14, 1,000)   ★★★
Shiraz Alexander Valley
   ($24, 2,000)   ★★

WINERY DATA
Case Production: 6,000. **Acres Owned:** 40 acres in Alexander Valley. **Varietals by Acre:** Cabernet Sauvignon (8 acres), Malbec (3), Merlot (6), Shiraz (20), Viognier (3). **Varietals Purchased:** Chardonnay (Alexander Valley), Sauvignon Blanc (Alexander Valley).

Seeking vineyard property in a region similar to the Barossa Valley in Australia, Australians Chris and Kristine Williams settled on Alexander Valley. In addition to their 40-acre estate, they recently purchased 600 acres in Mendocino, of which 160 will be planted in 1999–2000. The wines are typically well made, restrained and tightly wound; the 1995 Cabernet (87 points) features layers of black currant, anise, plum, leather and smoke flavors and powdery tannins. The 1996 Chardonnay (86) has smooth, delicate pear and citrus flavors. Sauvignon Blanc has been just short of outstanding; the 1997 (89) showed tropical fruit, melon and citrus flavors on a refreshing, full-bodied frame. Typically Aussie with its American oak accents, the 1995

Shiraz (87) was also firmly structured, with cherry, strawberry and herb flavors.

WEINSTOCK see BARON HERZOG

WELLINGTON VINEYARDS (★★)
Sonoma Valley
Founded: 1986. **Owner:** John & Peter Wellington.
Winemaker: Peter Wellington.

MAJOR WINES: PRICE, CASES, RATING

Cabernet Sauvignon Mount Veeder District
  Random Ridge
  ($18, 400) ★★
Cabernet Sauvignon Sonoma County
  Mohrhardt Ridge Vineyard
  ($15, 500) ★★
Chardonnay Sonoma County
  ($14, 1,000) ★★
Merlot Sonoma Valley
  ($16, 1,200) ★★
Syrah Russian River Valley Alegría Vineyard
  ($17, 450) ★★★
Victory Red Sonoma County Reserve
  ($24, 220) ★★
Viognier Russian River Valley
  ($16, 200) ★★
Zinfandel Russian River Valley
  ($14, 1,100) ★★
Zinfandel Sonoma Valley Estate
  100-Year-Old Vines
  ($20, 150) ★★

ALSO PRODUCED
Alicante Bouschet Sonoma Valley Noir de Noirs ($18, 300);
Port Sonoma Valley Estate Old Vines ($14, 600).

WINERY DATA
Case Production: 6,000. **Acres Owned:** 24 acres in Sonoma Valley.
Varietals by Acre: Cabernet Sauvignon (2 acres), Chardonnay (3), Merlot (6), Syrah (1), Zinfandel (3), Also: Alicante Bouschet, Cabernet Franc, Carignan, Criolla, Grand Noir, Grenache, Lenoir, Marsanne, Palomino, Petite Bouschet, Petite Sirah, Roussanne, Sémillon, Valdepenas. **Vineyard Designations:** Random Ridge (Cabernet Sauvignon), Mohrhardt Ridge Vineyard (Cabernet Sauvignon). **Varietals Purchased:** Alicante Bouschet (Sonoma Valley), Cabernet Franc (Mount Veeder), Cabernet Sauvignon

(Mount Veeder, Sonoma Coast, Sonoma Valley), Chardonnay (Russian River Valley, Sonoma Mountain, Sonoma Valley), Syrah (Russian River Valley), Zinfandel (Russian River Valley).

The Wellington family founded this 6,000-case winery in 1986. It includes an old vineyard which has been expanded to 24 acres and is now used as a part of Wellington's diverse mix of Cabernet, Chardonnay, Merlot, red table wine and Zinfandel. The rustic Cabernet, Syrah and Zinfandel bottlings are best. The 1995 Cabernet Mohrhardt Ridge Vineyard (85 points) showed rich, concentrated mineral and iodine notes and black cherry, currant and anise flavors on a plush, ripe frame. The 1996 Alegría Vineyard Syrah (86) was austere, with blackberry, blueberry and herb flavors and firm tannins. The 1995 Zinfandel 100-Year-Old Vines (87) was packed with plum, anise and blackberry flavors, but lacked finesse.

WENTE VINEYARDS (★–★★★)
Livermore Valley, Alameda County
Founded: 1883. **Owner:** Wente Family. **Winemaker:** Willy Joslin.

MAJOR WINES: PRICE, CASES, RATING

Cabernet Sauvignon Livermore Valley
  ($10, 75,000) ★
Cabernet Sauvignon Livermore Valley
  Charles Wetmore
  ($24, 1,000) ★
Chardonnay Central Coast
  ($10, 175,000) ★★
Chardonnay Livermore Valley
  Herman Wente Vineyard Reserve
  ($20, 2,500) ★★★
Merlot Livermore Valley Crane Ridge
  ($14, 10,000) ★★
Pinot Noir Arroyo Seco Monterey
  Reliz Creek
  ($14, 2,500) ★
Sauvignon Blanc Livermore Valley
  ($8, 5,000) ★★★

ALSO PRODUCED
Chardonnay Arroyo Seco Monterey ($14, 5,000); Chenin Blanc Central Coast Le Blanc du Blanc ($7, 10,000); Johannisberg Riesling Central Coast ($7, 10,000); Riesling

Late Harvest Arroyo Seco ($20, 1,000); Brut Reserve Arroyo Seco ($14, 5,000).

WINERY DATA
Case Production: 300,000. **Acres Owned:** 2,075 acres (701 in Arroyo Seco, 1,374 in Livermore Valley). **Varietals by Acre:** Cabernet Franc (13 acres), Cabernet Sauvignon (286), Chardonnay (1,047), Chenin Blanc (29), Counoise (7), French Colombard (36), Gewürztraminer (30), Grenache Noir (5), Grey Riesling (16), Merlot (167), Muscat Canelli (2), Orange Muscat (4), Petite Sirah (21), Petit Verdot (10), Pinot Blanc (64), Pinot Gris (15), Pinot Noir (77), Roussanne (5), Sangiovese (13), Sauvignon Blanc (46), Sémillion (57), Syrah (16), Trebbiano (14), Viognier (3), White Riesling (43), Zinfandel (49).

One of California's true wine dynasties, Wente Vineyards. dates back to 1883, and is now run by the family's fourth generation of winemakers. From its base in Livermore Valley, Wente has enjoyed success with white wines both before and after Prohibition, planting many of the old-world varieties (which it sold as bulk wines) during its early years and refining many varietals—including Sémillon, Sauvignon Blanc, Grey Riesling, Pinot Blanc and Chardonnay—after Repeal. In 1981, Wente purchased the old Cresta Blanca winery site and replanted the vineyard, calling it the Charles Wetmore Vineyard. In 1992 Philip Wente joined forces with Sergio Traverso, forming Murrieta's Well, and in 1992 the winery bought Concannon Vineyards.

Today the winery makes 300,000 cases, and owns 2,075 acres in vines (1,047 of that Chardonnay). Central Coast Chardonnay is the volume leader at 175,000 cases, followed by California Cabernet (75,000 cases). The Herman Wente Reserve and Riva Ranch Chardonnays, along with the Sauvignon Blanc lead in quality. The 1996 Riva Ranch (85 points) was flavorful but lacked elegance, and showed tangerine, peach and toast flavors. The 1995 Herman Wente Reserve (89) was ripe and complex, with lots of smoky vanilla flavors and focused fruit notes. Typical of Sauvignon Blanc, the 1997 (87) featured grass, herb, grapefruit and melon flavors with a refreshing finish.

TASTING NOTES

CHARDONNAY LIVERMORE VALLEY HERMAN WENTE VINEYARD RESERVE (★★★): Shows more depth, intensity and complexity than the other bottlings.

MERLOT LIVERMORE VALLEY CRANE RIDGE (★★): Good and well balanced, but lacks extra dimensions.

WILLIAM WHEELER WINERY (★)
Sonoma County
Founded: 1970. **Owner:** Jean Claude Boisset Wines. **Winemaker:** William Arbios.

MAJOR WINES: PRICE, CASES, RATING
Cabernet Sauvignon California
($14, 1,050)   ★
Malbec California
($12, 180)   ★
Viognier California
($12, 750)   ★

WINERY DATA
Case Production: 2,000. **Varietals Purchased:** Cabernet Sauvignon (California), Malbec (California), Viognier (California).

Boisset purchased the William Wheeler Winery and Vineyard in 1992, and later sold the 30-acre Dry Creek Vineyard to Pezzi King, retaining only the brand name. Made from purchased grapes and bulk wines, the Wheeler wines were fairly good value in past years, but Boisset almost always runs his brands into the ground with wines aimed at the lowest common denominator.

WHITCRAFT WINERY (★★★)
Santa Barbara County
Founded: 1985. **Owner:** Christopher Whitcraft. **Winemaker:** Christopher Whitcraft.

MAJOR WINES: PRICE, CASES, RATING
Chardonnay Santa Maria Valley
Bien Nacido
($25, 1,000)   ★★★
Chardonnay Santa Ynez Valley
Sanford & Benedict
($35, 150)   ★★★
Pinot Noir Santa Maria Valley
Bien Nacido
($35, 300)   ★★★

Pinot Noir Santa Maria Valley
  Bien Nacido N Block
  ($40, 300) ★★
Pinot Noir Santa Maria Valley
  Bien Nacido Q Block
  ($40, 300) ★★★
Pinot Noir Sonoma Coast
  Hirsch Vineyard
  ($40, 150) ★★

WINERY DATA
Case Production: 2,100. **Vineyard Designations:** Bien Nacido (Chardonnay, Pinot Noir), Hirsch Vineyard (Pinot Noir), Sanford & Benedict (Chardonnay). **Varietals Purchased:** Chardonnay (Santa Maria Valley, Santa Ynez Valley), Pinot Noir (Santa Maria Valley, Sonoma Coast).

Former wine retailer and wholesaler Chris Whitcraft owns this small brand, which purchases Chardonnay and Pinot Noir primarily from Santa Barbara County but also from the Sonoma Coast region. The Pinot Noirs are distinctive, dark, rich wines with complex fruit flavors and a smoky leather and game edge, but can stray into strange and racy territory with vegetal flavors. It is unclear how these wines will age; the 1994 Bien Nacido Pinot Noir, initially an outstanding wine, became decadent and gamy with short-term cellaring. The Chardonnays have been very good, although they have yet to find a stylistic focus; they're often crisp and citrusy with complex flavors, but occasionally smooth, rich and creamy. Consistency is clearly an issue.

TASTING NOTES

PINOT NOIR SANTA MARIA VALLEY BIEN NACIDO (★★★)
1996: A racy style, with peppery wild berry and black cherry flavors that are supple and elegant and a spicy finish. **88**
1995: Ripe and zesty; an exotic style, with tart, meaty, sour cherry and wild berry flavors that push the outer limits for Pinot Noir. **88**
1994: Dark, rich and intense, with wonderful tiers of black cherry, mineral and leather flavors, accented by a meaty, smoky edge. **89**

PINOT NOIR SANTA MARIA VALLEY BIEN NACIDO N BLOCK (★★)
1996: Strays out of bounds for Pinot Noir, with intense spicy, racy, vegetal flavors coupled with wild berry,

tomato and minty notes. **79**
1993: A touch earthy and gamy, with a nuance of smoked bacon and leathery tannins, picking up hints of plum and cherry flavors. **87**

PINOT NOIR SANTA MARIA VALLEY BIEN NACIDO Q BLOCK (★★★)
1996: Dark, ripe, rich and complex, with black cherry, herb, tea and spicy flavors that turn smooth and supple on the finish. **88**
1995: Tart, tight and exotic, with lots of spice, wild berry, black cherry and spicy oak flavors. **88**
1994: Austere, but flavorful, with a tightly reined-in style that shows off notes of black cherry, herb and mint, finishing on the tannic side. **88**

PINOT NOIR SONOMA COAST HIRSCH VINEYARD (★★)
1996: Intense and tannic, with racy blackberry, wild berry and cherry flavors that are vibrant, but a bit funky. **82**
1995: A Rhône-like style of Pinot. Truly exotic in its spicy profile, with a tart, tightly wound core of wild blackberry fruit and hints of clove. **87**

WHITE COTTAGE (★★★★)
Howell Mountain, Napa Valley
Founded: 1994. **Owner:** Adele and Dennis Johns. **Winemaker:** Dennis Johns.

MAJOR WINES: PRICE, CASES, RATING
Cabernet Sauvignon Howell Mountain
  ($40, 200) ★★★★

ALSO PRODUCED
Merlot Howell Mountain ($33, 90); Red Howell Mountain ($22, 90); Sangiovese Howell Mountain ($30, 90).

WINERY DATA
Case Production: 500. **Acres Owned:** 20 acres on Howell Mountain. **Varietals by Acre:** Cabernet Franc (2 acres), Cabernet Sauvignon (12), Merlot (2), Sangiovese (2), Syrah (1), Zinfandel (1).

Dennis Johns, previously the winemaker for St. Clement, started his own brand in 1994 from grapes grown on his 20-acre vineyard. All the wines are made in tiny quantities, and are sold through a mailing list, but the outstanding Cabernet Sauvignon can also be found in some shops and restaurants.

WHITE ROCK VINEYARDS **535**

TASTING NOTES

CABERNET SAUVIGNON HOWELL MOUNTAIN (★★★★):
Rich, complex and concentrated, with mineral, currant
and herb notes. The 1995 was less tight and focused than
the 1994.
1995: Elegant, with ripe, complex currant, black cherry,
mineral, sage and cedary oak flavors, picking up a touch
of clay and toasty oak. **90**
1994: Tight and sharply focused, with a wonderful core
of currant, wild berry, mineral and spicy flavors, turning
rich and complex on the finish. **93**

WHITE OAK VINEYARDS & WINERY (★★)

Alexander Valley, Sonoma County
Founded: 1981. **Owner:** William E. Myers. **Winemaker:**
Stephen Ryan.

MAJOR WINES: PRICE, CASES, RATING

Chardonnay Russian River Valley Poplar
  Vineyard
  ($20, 500) ★★
Chardonnay Sonoma County
  ($13, 5,000) ★★
Chardonnay Sonoma County Myers
  Limited Reserve
  ($18, 500) ★★
Zinfandel Alexander Valley Estate
  Old Vines
  ($15, 2,000) ★★★

ALSO PRODUCED

Cabernet Franc Alexander Valley ($15, 500); Meritage
Sonoma County ($25, 200); Merlot Sonoma County
($21, 1,000); Zinfandel Dry Creek Valley Saunders
($17, 200).

WINERY DATA

Case Production: 15,000. **Acres Owned:** 11 acres in Alexander
Valley. **Varietals by Acre:** Chardonnay (3 acres), Merlot (5),
Zinfandel (3). **Vineyard Designations:** Poplar Vineyard
(Chardonnay). **Varietals Purchased:** Cabernet Franc
(Alexander Valley), Cabernet Sauvignon (Napa), Chardonnay
(Russian River Valley, Sonoma County), Merlot (Alexander
Valley), Sauvignon Blanc (Napa), Zinfandel (Dry Creek,
Sonoma County).

Bill Myers founded this 15,000-case winery in 1981.
He offers a complete lineup of popular varietals, from
Cabernet to Zinfandel. Chardonnay is the volume leader
at more than 5,000 cases, and one of the two best wines;
Zinfandel is the other quality leader. Syrah and Pinot
Noir will be added in the future. The most recently tasted
wine was the 1996 Chardonnay Myers Limited Reserve
(87 points) which was soft-textured with apple, pear and
spice flavors.

WHITE ROCK VINEYARDS (★★★)

Napa Valley
Founded: 1979. **Owner:** Claire & Henri Vandendriessche.
Winemaker: Douglas Danielak **Second Label:** Madigan.

MAJOR WINES: PRICE, CASES, RATING

Chardonnay Napa Valley
  ($20, 1,100) ★★★
Claret Napa Valley
  ($28, 1,100) ★★★

WINERY DATA

Case Production: 3,000. **Acres Owned:** 36 acres in Napa
Valley. **Varietals by Acre:** Cabernet Franc (2 acres), Cabernet
Sauvignon (16), Chardonnay (15), Merlot (2), Petit Verdot (1).

Henry and Claire Vandendriessche were looking for a
home in the country in 1977, when they came across the
Pettingill estate, a winery and vineyard dating to 1970
that is tucked away in a narrow fold of hills behind
the Stags Leap rock outcropping. In 1979 the
Vandendriessches bought the property and began planting 36 acres in vines, producing their first wines in 1986.
They call their Bordeaux-style red "claret," as it is a
blend of the classic varieties and made in a tight, austere
style. The Chardonnay is crisp and flinty. Winemaker
Douglas Danielak also makes the wine for Jade
Mountain.

TASTING NOTES

CHARDONNAY NAPA VALLEY (★★★): Consistently well
made in a delicate, understated style, but with plenty of
flavor and finesse.
1997: Perfumed, with ripe fruit flavors, nutmeg, cinnamon, pear, fig and melon, it's complex and elegant, with

a long, spicy finish. **89**

1996: Light and simple, with cedary oak flavors and ripe, spicy pear and appley flavors. Turns elegant on the finish, where the fruit comes through. **87**

CLARET NAPA VALLEY (★★★): Improving, has softened slightly, becoming more generous. Earlier vintages were austere, with a tight, narrow but focused band of currant, cedar and currant flavors.

1995: Complex, with dusty, cedary oak and ripe plum, tobacco, mineral and sage notes, finishing with firm but gentle tannins. **87**

1994: Ripe and generous; not a big wine, with nicely modulated berry and leather flavors that keep swirling through the polished finish. **87**

1992: Firm and tannic, with a mint and anise edge to the currant and berry flavors, a strong eucalyptus edge on the finish and leathery tannins. **87**

1991: Marked by a stalky, slightly green edge, it walks a tightrope between oak and tannins, with a cedary edge to the currant fruit. **85**

1990: Tight and firm, with a narrow band of spice, cedary oak and plum flavors, turning tannic. **88**

WHITEHALL LANE WINERY
(★★★–★★★★)
Rutherford, Napa Valley
Founded: 1979. **Owner:** Thomas Leonardini.
Winemaker: Dean Sylvester.

MAJOR WINES: PRICE, CASES, RATING

Cabernet Sauvignon Napa Valley	
($22, 7,000)	★★★
Cabernet Sauvignon Napa Valley Gallerón	
(Discontinued)	★★★★
Cabernet Sauvignon Napa Valley Leonardini Vineyard	
($50, 500)	★★★★
Cabernet Sauvignon Rutherford Morisoli Vineyard	
($36, 2,000)	★★★★
Cabernet Sauvignon Napa Valley Reserve	
($38, 2,000)	★★★★
Chardonnay Napa Valley	
($15, 6,000)	★★★
Merlot Napa Valley	
($22, 7,000)	★★★
Merlot Napa Valley Leonardini Vineyard	
($38, 500)	★★★★
Sauvignon Blanc Rutherford	
($13, 4,000)	★★
Zinfandel Napa Valley	
($22, 200)	★★★

ALSO PRODUCED
Merlot Knights Valley ($22, 2,500).

WINERY DATA
Case Production: 30,000. **Acres Owned:** 62 acres (46 in Rutherford, 16 in St. Helena). **Varietals by Acre:** Cabernet Sauvignon (11.5 acres), Chardonnay (7), Chenin Blanc (12), Merlot (16.5), Sauvignon Blanc (14), Zinfandel (1). **Vineyard Designations:** Leonardini Vineyard (Cabernet Sauvignon, Merlot), Morisoli Vineyard (Cabernet Sauvignon). **Varietals Purchased:** Cabernet Sauvignon (Knights Valley, Oakville, Rutherford), Chardonnay (Carneros, Napa Valley), Merlot (Knights Valley, Napa Valley, Rutherford).

Brothers Art Finkelstein and Alan Steen founded this winery in Rutherford in 1979, one year after buying a vineyard which they replanted. In the interim, most of the grapes for their wines were purchased in Napa and Knights valleys, with production in the 10,000-case range. In 1988, the winery was sold to Hideaki Ando of Japan, who owned it until financial constraints forced him to sell to entrepreneur Tom Leonardini, owner of the Napa Valley Winery Exchange, a wine shop in San Francisco.

In 1994, the winery began upgrading its wines, and Gary Galleron (formerly of Grace Family Vineyard) was hired as winemaker. Production is at 30,000 cases now, including wines to be sold under a second label. The winery owns 62 acres, 46 in Rutherford and 16 in St. Helena, and buys grapes from Morisoli Vineyard in Rutherford for a vineyard-designated Cabernet. Grapes for Merlot are sourced from Leonardini's Leonardini Vineyard. The reds have improved significantly with the past few vintages, and while winemaker Gary Galleron, the man responsible for many of the improvements, has moved on, this is a winery to keep watching.

TASTING NOTES

CABERNET SAUVIGNON NAPA VALLEY (★★★)
A well focused, smooth textured wine with currant and cherry flavors.

CABERNET SAUVIGNON NAPA VALLEY GALLERÓN (★★★★)
1994: Smooth, ripe and juicy, with lots of rich currant, plum and wild berry flavors, turning plush and complex. **91**

CABERNET SAUVIGNON NAPA VALLEY LEONARDINI VINEYARD (★★★★): This is an excellent vineyard for both Cabernet and Merlot, so watch for this wine to get even better.
1995: Ultra-rich and deeply concentrated; loaded with complex currant, spice and black cherry flavors, along with hints of plum and toasty oak. **92**

CABERNET SAUVIGNON NAPA VALLEY RESERVE (★★★★): Has really stepped up with the 1995 vintage; it remains a wine to watch.
1995: Big and ripe, with a wonderfully supple and seductive style, offering layers of juicy plum, black cherry, currant and blackberry flavors that linger nicely on the finish. **95**
1992: Firm, tightly wound and beautifully focused, with a dense, complex core of currant, anise, cedar and spice flavors. **92**
1991: Provides a nice core of currant, cherry and berry fruit that's framed by toast and supported by firm tannins. **89**
1990: Firm, intense and spicy, with a tight band of currant, cherry, anise and cedary oak flavors. **89**
1989: Distinctive for its minty, herbal edge, it's also complex and concentrated, with layers of currant and berry underneath. **87**
1988: Marked by spicy, minty aromas, it has a core of ripe plum and currant flavors, turning smooth and fleshy. **87**
1987: Tight and focused, with spice, mint and oak nuances, but there are also ripe, concentrated cherry, currant and raspberry flavors that turn silky. **90**

CABERNET SAUVIGNON RUTHERFORD MORISOLI VINEYARD (★★★★): The other wine to watch, as this vineyard yields excellent grapes for several Napa wines.
1994: Young, dark and concentrated, with sharply focused currant, black cherry, plum and spice flavors and a long, rich aftertaste. **92**
1993: Intense and well focused, with a spicy, minty band

of cherry and currant flavors, gaining some complex nuances and finesse on the finish. **91**
1992: Remarkably complex and concentrated, with an appealing core of currant, black cherry, vanilla and spice flavors. **93**
1991: Well constructed, with ripe plum, currant and cherry fruit and a sense of elegance and finesse. **88**
1990: Tight and intense, with a green edge to the currant and cherry notes, finishing with firm tannins. **87**

MERLOT NAPA VALLEY (★★★): Typically smooth, ripe and polished; a good value.
1996: Smooth and polished, with a complex array of ripe plum, herb, and chocolate flavors. Firms up on the finish, where the tannins are ripe and well integrated. **89**

MERLOT NAPA VALLEY LEONARDINI VINEYARD (★★★★): Poised for greatness; it can be dark, intense and concentrated.
1996: Complex, with ripe, rich plum, black cherry, currant and spice flavors, finishing with smooth, polished tannins. **89**
1995: Dark, ripe, intense, concentrated and well-oaked, with the cherry, chocolate and wild berry flavors adding dimension. **90**
1993: Features dark, intense black cherry, plum and berry notes, finishing with austere tannins and a dash of oak. **88**

ZINFANDEL NAPA VALLEY (★★★): New to the mix, but impressive in its first two vintages.
1995: Austere, with crisp tannins, firm acidity and a well focused core of cherry and wild berry flavors. **89**
1994: The wild berry, cherry and raspberry flavors reign here, despite the tannins and a slightly waxy, green olive accent. **89**

WILD HORSE WINERY & VINEYARDS (★★–★★★)
Paso Robles, San Luis Obispo County
Founded: 1982. **Owner:** The Volk Family/Ken Volk.
Winemaker: Jon Priest. **Second Label:** Aqua Pumpkin Canyon, Rainforest, Santa Lucia.

MAJOR WINES: PRICE, CASES, RATING
Cabernet Sauvignon Paso Robles
($16, 5,000)   ★★

Chardonnay Central Coast
($14, 20,000) ★★
Malvasia Monterey
($13, 3,500) ★★
Merlot Paso Robles
($16, 2,500) ★★
Pinot Blanc Monterey
($13, 6,000) ★★
Pinot Noir Central Coast
($18, 14,000) ★★
Pinot Noir Central Coast
Cheval Sauvage
($NA, NA) ★★★

ALSO PRODUCED
Merlot Central Coast ($16); Pinot Grigio Monterey ($13); Roussanne Paso Robles ($18, 500); Trousseau Central Coast ($13); Trousseau Gris Central Coast ($13); Valdiguié Paso Robles ($13); Viognier Paso Robles ($24, 300); Zinfandel Paso Robles ($13, 3,000).

WINERY DATA
Case Production: 100,000. **Acres Owned:** 47 acres in Paso Robles. **Varietals by Acre:** Blaufrankisch (2 acres), Chardonnay (17.5), Merlot (7), Pinot Gris (4), Pinot Noir (7), Roussanne (3.5), Sangiovese (0.5), Tocai Friulano (0.5), Verdelho (2), Vermentino (1), Viognier (1.5). **Vineyard Designations:** James Berry Vineyard (Mourvèdre, Syrah). **Varietals Purchased:** Cabernet Sauvignon (Paso Robles), Chardonnay (Monterey), Malvasia (Monterey), Merlot (Paso Robles), Mourvèdre (Paso Robles), Pinot Blanc (Monterey), Pinot Noir (Santa Maria), Roussanne (Paso Robles), Syrah (Monterey, Paso Robles), Trousseau (Central Coast), Valdiguié (San Luis Obispo), Viognier (Paso Robles).

Ken Volk founded Wild Horse Winery in 1982 with the idea of planting a vineyard and then reselling it, but changing directions, he soon decided to make wine. The winery's strengths are Chardonnay, Pinot Blanc and Pinot Noir; these wines also make up the bulk of the production. Pinot Noir dominates with 14,000 cases; the 1996 (86 points) featured spicy cherry, herb and wild berry flavors. Chardonnay production doubled from 1996 to 1997, growing to 20,000 cases; however, the quality of the 1997 Chardonnay (83), which was clean, with citrus flavors and moderate depth, did not compare to the 1996 (88). The Pinot Blanc (6,000 cases) has also doubled its production; the 1997 (87) was crisp, clean and delicate, with citrus and mineral flavors. Cabernet is often good,

as was the supple 1996 (88), which showed layers of coffee, spice, plum, currant and herb flavors.

Central Coast and Paso Robles Syrahs and a Paso Robles Mourvèdre have now been added, and may help elevate the quality of the red wine portfolio further. A number of other white wines, including Malvasia, Pinot Grigio, Roussanne, Trousseau and Viognier, are also being produced.

TASTING NOTES

PINOT NOIR VARIOUS BOTTLINGS (★★★): Can be enormously rich and complex, but usually strikes a fine balance between spicy cherry, herb, cola and earthy nuances. Ages well, particularly the Cheval Sauvage, which is only produced in exceptional vintages.

PINOT NOIR CENTRAL COAST CHEVAL SAUVAGE (★★★)
1994: Elegant and lively, with a pretty, spicy edge to the tea leaf, plum and cherry flavors, finishing with notes of strawberry and tea. **88**
1993: Mature, with a complex, elegant array of ripe plum, black cherry, wild berry, spice and toasty oak flavors. **92**

WILDHURST VINEYARDS (★–★★)
Lake County
Founded: 1991. **Owner:** Myron and Marilyn Holdenried. **Winemaker:** Mark S. Burch.

MAJOR WINES: PRICE, CASES, RATING
Cabernet Sauvignon Clear Lake
($14, 1,200) ★★
Chardonnay Clear Lake
($11, 2,100) ★
Merlot Clear Lake
($14, 9,000) ★
Sauvignon Blanc Clear Lake
($9, 1,800) ★★
Zinfandel Clear Lake
($14, 1,200) ★

ALSO PRODUCED
Cabernet Franc Clear Lake ($13, 1,200); Chardonnay Sonoma County Reserve ($18, 500); Mackinaw California Red ($10, 700); Mackinaw California White ($10, 1,000).

WINERY DATA
Case Production: 19,000. **Acres Owned:** 310 acres in Clear Lake. **Varietals by Acre:** Cabernet Sauvignon (55 acres),

WILLIAMS SELYEM WINERY   **539**

Chardonnay (75), Johannisberg Riesling (10), Merlot (60), Petite Sirah (10), Sauvignon Blanc (50), Zinfandel (50). **Varietals Purchased:** Cabernet Franc (Clear Lake), Chardonnay (Sonoma County).

Wildhurst farms 310 acres in Clear Lake, selling much of its grapes to other wineries. So far, the wines from their estate grapes have been variable, simple and rustic. A 1996 Zinfandel (80 points) was straightforward, with strawberry and spice flavors.

WILLIAMS SELYEM WINERY (★★★★–★★★★★)
Russian River Valley, Sonoma County
Founded: 1981. **Owner:** John Dyson. **Winemaker:** Burt Williams, Bob Cabral.

MAJOR WINES: PRICE, CASES, RATING

Wine	Rating
Chardonnay Russian River Valley Allen Vineyard ($75, 120)	★★★★★
Chardonnay Sonoma Coast Hirsch Vineyard ($75, 90)	★★★★
Pinot Noir Anderson Valley Ferrington Vineyard ($50, 160)	★★★★
Pinot Noir Russian River Valley ($40, 500)	★★★★
Pinot Noir Russian River Valley Allen Vineyard ($55, 1,200)	★★★★★
Pinot Noir Russian River Valley Olivet Lane Vineyard ($45, 1,400)	★★★★
Pinot Noir Russian River Valley Riverblock Vineyard ($45, 900)	★★★★
Pinot Noir Russian River Valley Rochioli Vineyard ($78, 250)	★★★★★
Pinot Noir Sonoma Coast ($45, 390)	★★★★
Pinot Noir Sonoma Coast Coastlands Vineyard ($45, 650)	★★★★
Pinot Noir Sonoma Coast Hirsch Vineyard ($45, 1,800)	★★★★
Pinot Noir Sonoma County ($30, 1,000)	★★★
Zinfandel Russian River Valley Leno Martinelli Vineyard (Discontinued)	★★★★★

ALSO PRODUCED
Pinot Noir Sonoma Coast Precious Mountain Vineyard ($65, 220).

WINERY DATA
Case Production: 7,000. **Vineyard Designations:** Allen Vineyard (Pinot Noir, Chardonnay), Ferrington Vineyard (Pinot Noir), Hirsch Vineyard (Pinot Noir), Olivet Lane Vineyard (Pinot Noir), Precious Mountain Vineyard (Pinot Noir), Riverblock Vineyard (Pinot Noir), Rochioli Vineyard (Pinot Noir). **Varietals Purchased:** Chardonnay (Russian River Valley, Sonoma Coast), Pinot Noir (Russian River Valley, Sonoma Coast, Mendocino County).

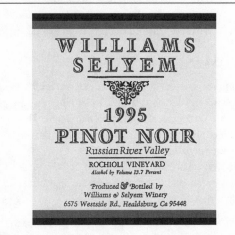

The emergence of Williams & Selyem as California's Pinot Noir leader is an improbable success story. Founders Burt Williams and Ed Selyem started making wine under the Hacienda del Rio Winery label in a garage in Fulton. Their first wine was a 1981 Zinfandel, but by 1982 they began their quest for great Pinot Noir. By the late 1980s, Williams had retired as a typesetter and Selyem had left his job as a wine retailer, and they devoted themselves full-time to winemaking.

With no vineyards of its own, Williams & Selyem is fortunate to have secured long-term contracts to buy some of Sonoma's best Pinot Noir from Rochioli, Allen, Olivet Lane and Summa vineyards. Ferrington Vineyard in Anderson Valley (Mendocino) impressed in its 1992 debut, and Cohn Vineyard, another Russian River vineyard, appeared with the 1993 vintage. A barrel or two of Allen Vineyard Chardonnay comprise the rest of the winery's 7,000-case production.

Quality across the board is exceptionally high, with a first decade that included many exciting wines, most notably the Pinot Noirs. There are no secrets to Williams & Selyem's success: they seek low-yield, fully ripened grapes from superb vineyard sources. The wines are well oaked, achieving extra flavor dimensions, yet preserving the integrity of the fruit. In 1990, Williams & Selyem moved into a small facility near their key vineyard sources. The wines are sold mainly through a mailing list that is increasingly difficult to get onto. In 1997, John Dyson bought the winery and has plans to plant a 20-acre Russian River vineyard and gradually expand production. Burt Williams indicated he would continue to make wine into 2000, after which Bob Cabral, formerly of Alderbrook and Hartford Court, will take over.

TASTING NOTES

CHARDONNAY RUSSIAN RIVER VALLEY ALLEN VINEYARD (★★★★★): Very hard to get, as production in some years is only 25 cases; 200 is the maximum. This is an ultra-ripe, high-alcohol (14.5%), intensely flavored and well-oaked style of wine. Ages well.
1995: Deliciously rich in flavor and body, with a silky, smooth texture and a load of spicy pear, apple, peach and hazelnut flavors. **95**

PINOT NOIR ANDERSON VALLEY FERRINGTON VINEYARD (★★★★): Tight, somewhat austere for Williams Selyem, but not shy on flavor or complexity.
1996: Dark, ripe and brimming with complex plum, black cherry and raspberry fruit that's rich and sharply focused. **91**
1995: Tight, young and tannic, with concentrated floral, berry and dried cherry flavors, it still needs a bit of time. **90**
1994: Ripe and juicy; brimming with dense, focused black cherry, earth, mushroom and berry flavors. **91**
1993: Well focused, plush and concentrated, this wine is impressive for its color and for the depth of its plum and

cherry flavors. **91**
1992: Combines ripe black cherry, spice and currant notes with cedary oak flavors, all folded together nicely, finishing with a complex aftertaste and firm tannins. **92**

PINOT NOIR RUSSIAN RIVER VALLEY (★★★★): The Russian River bottling can claim similar attributes to those of the Anderson Valley Ferrington Vineyard, even though the appellation extends farther east. A Sonoma County bottling appears occasionally.
1995: Ripe and flavorful, with layers of plum, cherry and wild berry flavors that are still tight, with firm tannins. **90**
1994: Serves up lots of ripe cherry, plum and berry fruit, turning smooth and elegant on the finish. **89**
1993: Light and elegant, with a slight tea and herbal edge to the modest cherry flavors. **85**
1992: A touch coarse and tannic, but the core of plum and cherry flavors is solid and complex. **89**
1991: Ripe, rich, smooth, supple and very complete, with lots of berry flavors, a soft, silky texture and a long finish. **93**
1990: Complex and lively, serving up lots of ripe, rich, concentrated black cherry, wild berry, plum and spice flavors. **91**
1989: Ripe and complex, with a smoky, meaty flavor that adds to the youthful cherry and wild berry fruit. **89**
1988: Dark, ripe and intense, with a citrus edge to the racy blackberry flavor, turning complex on the finish. **90**

PINOT NOIR RUSSIAN RIVER VALLEY ALLEN VINEYARD (★★★★★): The Allen Vineyard borders the Rochioli Vineyard and rivals it in quality. It is capable of rendering enormously complex, rich and concentrated wines, loaded with flavor and finesse; ages well.
1996: Ripe and rich, with creamy oak and lots of plum, blackberry and cherry fruit, turning tannic and sophisticated. **90**
1995: Quite seductive, with supple oak, cherry, wild berry and spicy nuances, it's impressive for its delicacy and finesse. **93**
1994: Smooth, polished, supple and harmonious, with young, vibrant cherry and wild berry flavors. **92**
1993: Crisp, complete and complex, with pretty cherry and strawberry notes that linger on the finish. **88**
1992: Smooth, ripe, rich and polished; loaded with tightly-wound, ripe plum and cherry flavors. **93**
1991: Delicious, deep, rich and concentrated, with layers of

mint, plum and raspberry flavors and a mile-long finish. **95**
1989: Complex, with mature, ripe dried cherry and strawberry fruit, turning supple and elegant on the finish. **89**
1988: Ripe and forward, with rich, complex, juicy plum and cherry flavors. **91**
1987: Smoky and tarry, with a strong anise and herbal edge to the ripe cherry flavors. **90**

PINOT NOIR RUSSIAN RIVER VALLEY COHN VINEYARD
1993: Tight, focused and complex, yet unevolved; offers a tasty core of spice and raspberry flavors. **88**

PINOT NOIR RUSSIAN RIVER VALLEY OLIVET LANE VINEYARD (★★★★): Impressive, with bold, ripe, juicy Pinot Noir flavors that are complex and silky; usually lighter in color and tannins.
1995: Smooth, rich and polished, with a broad, ripe core of supple black cherry, plum and berry notes, turning complex on the finish. **93**
1994: Lean for this vintage, with an herb and tea edge to the lightly scented cherry and berry fruit. **88**
1993: Austere, with firm tannins, crisp acidity and spicy cherry notes, it fans out nicely on the finish. **88**
1992: Well focused, with a complex core of spicy cherry and berry flavors, finishing with crisp acidity. **88**
1991: Juicy, with pretty, supple plum and black cherry fruit and a dash of cola; impressive for its texture and finesse. **92**
1990: A high-acidity style; lean and trim, with a tart band of spicy cherry flavor. **87**
1989: Lightly aromatic, but builds depth and complexity on the palate, where the ripe plum and cherry flavors fill in the gaps. **89**

PINOT NOIR RUSSIAN RIVER VALLEY RIVERBLOCK VINEYARD (★★★★)
1995: Unfolds to reveal a core of cherry, berry and spice flavors, with hints of tea, cedar and anise. **90**

PINOT NOIR RUSSIAN RIVER VALLEY ROCHIOLI VINEYARD (★★★★★): Rochioli is among the finest, if not the finest, Pinot Noir vineyard in California. Consistently yields wines of amazing depth, richness, concentration and flavor, with tiers of ripe cherry, plum, currant and wild berry. Ages well for up to a decade.
1996: A complex, intriguing array of ripe plum, cherry, cola, spice and anise flavors; not especially dense, but distinctive and elegant and long on the finish. **90**

1995: A wine of great subtlety and finesse, with slowly unfolding black cherry, berry, vanilla and spice flavors that are smooth and polished. **94**
1994: A beauty. Dark, ripe, rich and remarkably concentrated, with tiers of plum, black cherry, wild berry and spice flavors. **94**
1993: Ripe and very complete, yet somewhat unevolved, with plum, cherry and wild berry flavors. **88**
1992: This wine has it all. It shows a striking combination of richness, power, finesse, depth and concentration, and is packed with ripe, juicy plum and black cherry fruit, along with spicy, toasty oak flavors. **97**
1991: Shows tremendous complexity, with a pretty interplay of vanilla-tinged oak and lots of currant- and black cherry-laced fruit. **95**
1989: Rich, supple and polished, with lots of ripe plum and wild berry fruit and a gentle, supple texture. **92**
1988: Amazingly elegant, complex and delicate, with deliciously, ripe, smooth and juicy tiers of plum, black cherry, anise and spice. **95**
1987: Distinct for its spicy raspberry flavors and firm tannins, it's aging well, with no signs of fatigue. **88**
1986: Still deep in color and rich in flavor, with lots of complex, lively cherry, currant and plum flavors. **92**
1985: Mature, but complex, with a tarry, herb and earthy edge to the currant and plum flavors. **90**

PINOT NOIR SONOMA COAST (★★★★): From the coolest, most westerly vineyards in Sonoma County. This wine is not produced every year, but when it is made it shares the winery's house style of ultra-ripe and complex flavors.
1995: Elegant and understated, with a pretty array of ripe, supple cherry, plum and wild berry flavors, picking up hints of anise, cedar and spice. **90**
1994: Smooth and polished, with herb, smoky oak, cherry and berry fruit, gaining focus on the finish. **89**
1993: Finely knit and supple in texture, with elegant, understated cherry and wild berry fruit flavors that unfold gently. **91**
1991: Smooth and harmonious, with a pretty tea and sage edge to the spice and cherry flavors. **90**
1990: Lean and trim, with notes of herb, tart cherry, spice and anise. **87**
1989: Marked by smoky, tarry nuances, the ripe, tart cherry notes fill in the gaps nicely. **87**
1988: Remarkable for its rich, deep, complex chocolate, cherry, toast and vanilla flavors that are smooth and concen-

trated, backed with toasty oak and firm, supple tannins. **92**

1986: Lots of pretty aromas of fruit, toast and cherries, followed by rich, ripe, spicy coffee, strawberry and black cherry flavors. **91**

1985: Light in color, turning pale garnet, with earthy, tarry herb and dried cherry flavors. An elegant wine that's fully mature. **84**

1982: Bottled under the Hacienda del Rio label. Mature and aging very well, with tea, herb and dried cherry flavors that turn delicate and floral notes on the finish. **89**

Pinot Noir Sonoma Coast Coastlands Vineyard (★★★★)

1995: Ripe, smooth and polished, with a silky texture and lots of pretty plum, black cherry, spice and berry flavors. **92**

1994: Smooth, rich and smoky, with a pretty, toasty oak edge to the plum and cherry fruit, turning elegant. **92**

Pinot Noir Sonoma Coast Hirsch Vineyard (★★★★)

1996: Firm, with chewy tannins, the core of flavors are built around wild berry, black cherry, sage, mineral and spice. **88**

1995: Remarkably complex and flavorful; rich, supple, concentrated and loaded with plum, cherry and wild berry fruit. **94**

1994: Displays lots of wild berry and cherry flavors, picking up an exotic toasty oak edge and finishing with a long, full aftertaste. **92**

Pinot Noir Sonoma Coast Precious Mountain Vineyard

1996: Elegant, with delicate, complex strawberry, plum, raspberry and vanilla shadings, and modest tea- like tannins. **89**

Pinot Noir Sonoma Coast Summa & Coastlands Vineyards

1993: Smells more attractive than it tastes; the plum, cherry and berry notes are rather austere, with a touch of tea and herb. **85**

Pinot Noir Sonoma Coast Summa Vineyard (★★★★): This is a rare bottling, produced in extremely small quantities. Ultra-concentrated and detailed.

1991: Amazing depth and finesse; dark, ripe, rich and potent, with a distinctly spicy edge to its blackberry and black cherry flavors. **96**

1988: Lean, with a smoky orange rind and tea leaf edge

to the barely ripe fruit flavors. **86**

Pinot Noir Sonoma County (★★★)

1994: Complete on its own terms, but lacking the depth and complexity of the best wines from this year. **87**

1987: Mature, with a pleasant core of spicy cherry and wild berry flavors. **88**

1986: There is an earthy dryness to the mature Pinot Noir flavors. Fading. **82**

1985: A light, mature style with an elegant, spicy rhubarb edge. **87**

1984: Muddled and murky, with mature ripe fruit of modest proportions. **82**

1983: Stalky, with a green bean edge to the barely ripe cherry and berry fruit. **85**

1982: A touch waxy, with dried cherry, spice and earthy notes, but finishes with a long aftertaste. **90**

1981: Fading, with a floral, wilted strawberry edge, and finishing with a subtle, elegant aftertaste. **88**

Zinfandel Mendocino County

1994: Supple and elegant; marked by cherry and berry flavors, it picks up a trace of tar and spice on the finish. **88**

Zinfandel Russian River Valley

1992: Ultra-dark and rich, with a big, ripe, intense style that doesn't hide its alcohol and dried cherry and wild berry flavors. **89**

Zinfandel Russian River Valley Leno Martinelli Vineyard (★★★★★): From 1981 to 1992, this Russian River vineyard was the source for a string of excellent Zinfandels, made in a very ripe, high-extract, intense Williams Selyem style with firm tannins, marked by wild berry, raspberry, anise and tarry flavors. Since 1992, Martinelli Winery has been bottling its own wine from this vineyard. Ages well.

1992: Packs in lots of juicy, ripe Zin flavors, with rich plum, cherry and raspberry notes that are firm and concentrated. **91**

1991: A beautifully crafted Zin with layers of bright, ripe, spicy raspberry, cherry and vanilla flavors. Intense and lively, with a long, full, lingering aftertaste. **92**

1990: Combines all the ripe, rich, intense flavors of this old vineyard with a sense of balance and finesse, showing tiers of spicy, peppery black cherry and raspberry nuances. **92**

1989: Crisp, elegant, supple and balanced, with black

cherry, raspberry and anise flavors that linger long on the palate. **89**

1988: Stretches the ripeness to the edge of late harvest. This is a ripe, intense, jammy wine with elegant raspberry, black cherry and plum flavors that turn spicy on the finish. **89**

1987: Broad, ripe, rich and lush, with jammy, concentrated raspberry, plum and currant flavors that are polished and seductive, finishing with firm tannins. **90**

1986: Austere, tight, firm and focused, packing in lots of compact raspberry, anise and plum flavors that are bright and lively, finishing with a good dose of tannin. **88**

1985: Tight and lean but focused, with anise, black cherry, spice and raspberry flavors that are still firmly wound. **87**

1984: Intense and jammy, with raisin and Port-like flavors, but the richness, concentration, depth and alcohol stay in balance. Raspberry, anise and tar notes linger on a long, hot finish. **88**

1983: Tight, crisp and tannic, with plum and raspberry aromas and flavors that are still tightly tannic. **86**

1982: Sonoma County; Very ripe and jammy, with a funky, earthy edge, but it's big and concentrated. **84**

1981: Sonoma County; Bottled under the Hacienda del Rio label. Still youthful and vibrant, with tart, earthy plum and raspberry flavors that pick up a touch of anise and spice on the finish. **88**

WINDWARD VINEYARD (★★)
Paso Robles, San Luis Obispo County
Founded: 1990. **Owner:** Marc Goldberg. **Winemaker:** Ken Volk.

MAJOR WINES: PRICE, CASES, RATING
Pinot Noir Paso Robles Monopole
($25, 1,200) ★★

WINERY DATA
Case Production: 1,200. **Acres Owned:** 10 acres in Paso Robles. **Varietals by Acre:** Pinot Noir (10 acres).

This small producer in Paso Robles makes Pinot Noir from grapes grown on its 10-acre vineyard. There are plans to add 8 acres to the existing vineyard in 1999. The 1996 (83 points) was well balanced, with pleasant plum, strawberry and herb flavors.

WOODBRIDGE (★)
Lodi
Founded: Owner: Robert Mondavi Corp. **Winemaker:** David Akiyoshi.

MAJOR WINES: PRICE, CASES, RATING
Cabernet Sauvignon California
($6, NA) ★
Cabernet Sauvignon California Twin Oaks
($10, NA) ★
Chardonnay California
($6, NA) ★
Chardonnay California Twin Oaks
($10, NA) ★
Sauvignon Blanc California
($5, NA) ★
Viognier California Twin Oaks
($10, NA) ★
Zinfandel White California
($4, NA) ★

WINERY DATA
Case Production: 5 million. **Acres Owned:** 501 acres (68 in Lodi, 433 in San Luis Obispo). **Varietals by Acre:** Cabernet Sauvignon (91 acres), Chardonnay (5), Muscat (72), Port varieties (2), Sauvignon Blanc (155), Zinfandel (140). **Varietals Purchased:** Cabernet Sauvignon (Central Coast, North Coast, Lodi), Chardonnay (Central Coast, North Coast, Lodi), Merlot (Central Coast, Lodi), Port varieties (Lodi), Sauvignon Blanc, (Central Coast, Lodi), Zinfandel (Central Coast, Lodi).

Robert Mondavi Corp.'s Woodbridge brand is one of the ten largest wine brands in the United States with 5 million cases produced annually. Located in Lodi in the Central Valley, Woodbridge is also Mondavi's greatest source of revenue. The wines are of average quality, and at best are pleasant and simple, though they can be awkward and tough. The Twin Oaks wines are moderately more expensive than the general bottlings, and show a touch more character. The 1996 Cabernet Sauvignon (74 points) was an odd combination of smoky, rubbery, herbal flavors. The 1995 Cabernet Sauvignon Twin Oaks (80) also showed some funky flavors, but was smooth, with blackberry notes as well. Chardonnays, like the 1997 (80), have been more reliable, with light citrus and toast flavors. Zinfandel is erratic: sometimes tasting candied, sometimes rich and plummy, and occasionally, like the 1996 (74), tart and tannic. A Merlot will be added to the portfolio in the future.

Zabaco (★★)

Sonoma County
Founded: 1996. **Owner:** E&J Gallo Winery. **Winemaker:**
Marcello Monticelli and Gina Gallo. **Second Label:**
Rancho Zabaco.

Major Wines: Price, Cases, Rating

Chardonnay Russian River Valley
($14, 15,000)   ★★
Zinfandel Dry Creek Valley
($14, 10,000)   ★★
Zinfandel Sonoma County
($10, 20,000)   ★★

Winery Data
Case Production: 45,000. **Varietals Purchased:** Chardonnay
(Russian River Valley), Zinfandel (Dry Creek Valley, Sonoma
County).

Gallo's new Zabaco brand focuses on Chardonnay and
Zinfandel purchased in Sonoma County. The wines have
been generally good, with modest flavor and depth,
though some, like the bold, ripe and complex 1996
Russian River Valley Chardonnay (88 points), have been
very impressive. The 1996 Zinfandel Dry Creek Valley
(84) and the 1995 Sonoma County Zinfandel (85) were
medium-bodied, with firm tannins and flavors of pepper,
black cherry and herbs.

Eventually, the Zabaco Sonoma County wines will be
phased out as the Rancho Zabaco brand of more specific
Russian River Valley and Dry Creek Valley appellations
is established.

Zaca Mesa Winery (★★★)

Santa Ynez Valley, Santa Barbara County
Founded: 1972. **Owner:** John C. Cushman III & Louis
B. Cushman. **Winemaker:** Kathy Joseph.

Major Wines: Price, Cases, Rating

Chardonnay Santa Barbara County
Zaca Vineyards
($14, 22,000)   ★★★
Roussanne Santa Barbara County
Zaca Vineyards
($15, 3,900)   ★★★

Syrah Santa Barbara County
($18, 7,400)   ★★★
Z Cuvée Santa Barbara County
($15, 7,000)   ★★★

Also Produced
Viognier Late Harvest Santa Barbara County ($18, 550);
Z Gris Rosé Santa Barbara County ($9, 3,900).

Winery Data
Case Production: 45,000. **Acres Owned:** 268 acres in Santa
Barbara County. **Varietals by Acre:** Chardonnay (109 acres),
Cinsault (3), Counoise (3), Grenache Noir (38), Johannisberg
Riesling (2), Mourvèdre (10), Roussanne (20), Syrah (56),
Viognier (27). **Vineyard Designations:** Zaca Vineyards
(Chardonnay, Roussanne, Syrah).

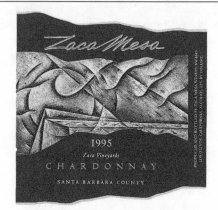

In the early 1970s, oil executive Louis Ream mapped
out a plan for Zaca Mesa Winery involving some 340
acres in vines; at its peak point production reached
100,000 cases. Ken Brown (now at Byron) oversaw
winemaking, and a succession of now well-known winemakers—among them Jim Clendenen (Au Bon Climat,
Vita Nova), Adam Tolmach (Ojai) and Bob Lindquist
(Qupe)—assisted. Zaca Mesa experimented with a range
of wines, including a Cabernet, which tended to be overly
herbaceous.

The focus now is on the winery's 268 acres in vines
with Chardonnay (109 acres) the acreage leader. Case
volume has climbed to 45,000 as the winery moves to
improve quality and focus. Each of the wines is well
made, with the Syrah probably the best and Roussanne
showing more potential here than in most other areas.

TASTING NOTES

CHARDONNAY SANTA BARBARA COUNTY ZACA VINEYARDS (★★★): Made in a bright, crisp, lively style.

1996: Bright and lively, with a distinct spicy tangerine, nectarine and peach flavors that are smooth and concentrated, finishing with a long, spicy aftertaste. **89**

1995: Clean and refreshing, with a slight celery edge to the ripe pear and spicy citrus flavors. Finishes with a bright aftertaste. **87**

ROUSSANNE SANTA BARBARA COUNTY ZACA VINEYARDS (★★★): Very successful and consistent, with distinct tropical fruit flavors.

1997: Bright peach, apple and citrus flavors are supported by tangy acidity. A very fruity wine, with a silky, velvety finish. **87**

1996: A blend of tropical fruit brings to mind papaya, mango, bright colored oranges and lemons. It lingers nicely on the finish with tangy acidity. **88**

SYRAH SANTA BARBARA COUNTY ZACA VINEYARDS (★★★): Increasingly consistent and impressive for its weight, array of flavors and complexity. The 1993 was a stunner.

1995: Clean, ripe and juicy, with a core of beefy, meaty currant and blackberry flavors, turning elegant and supple on the finish. **88**

1994: Dark and spicy, with an earthy edge to the wild berry and cherry notes, turning leathery and tannic on the finish. **89**

1993: Rich and fruity, with gobs of ripe cherry, wild berry, currant and raspberry flavors. It gradually picks up anise, cedar and spice notes, and then turns smooth and complex on the finish. **94**

Z CUVÉE SANTA BARBARA COUNTY (★★★)

1996: Young and grapey, with snappy wild berry and raspberry-laced fruit that's clean and refreshing. **86**

1995: Ripe, rich and exotic, with layers of ripe plum, cherry, anise and spice, finishing with a slightly meaty edge. **88**

ZAHARIAH see **JUDD'S HILL**

ZD WINES (★★–★★★★)

Rutherford, Napa Valley
Founded: 1969. **Owner:** The de Luze Family.
Winemaker: Robert de Luze.

MAJOR WINES: PRICE, CASES, RATING

Cabernet Sauvignon Napa Valley ($32, 3,000)	★★★★
Cabernet Sauvignon Napa Valley Reserve ($60, 1,000)	★★★★
Chardonnay California ($25, 20,000)	★★★
Pinot Noir Carneros ($27, 3,000)	★★

ALSO PRODUCED
Pinot Noir Carneros Rosa Lee ($17, 500).

WINERY DATA
Case Production: 27,500. **Acres Owned:** 36 acres (32 in Carneros, 4 in Rutherford). **Varietals by Acre:** Cabernet Sauvignon (4 acres), Chardonnay (25), Pinot Noir (7). **Varietals Purchased:** Chardonnay (Carneros, Monterey, Santa Maria), Pinot Noir (Carneros).

Aerospace engineers Gino Zepponi and Norman de Leuze founded ZD, starting in Sonoma but later relocating to a site on Silverado Trail in Rutherford. The winery was expanded in 1990 to its current 27,500-case production. California-appellation Chardonnay remains the focal point, using grapes from Carneros, Napa, Monterey, Santa Barbara and Santa Maria; the wines have a rich, earthy, distinctly Burgundian touch to them. Cabernet (from Napa Valley, including an occasional Reserve) and Pinot Noir (from Carneros) are also part of the mix; about 3,000 cases of each are made. Quality across the board is very good to outstanding, with each of the wines showing an exotic edge. The winery is owned entirely by the de Leuze family.

TASTING NOTES

CABERNET SAUVIGNON NAPA VALLEY (★★★★): Typically firm and high in extract. There are dense, earthy tannins, but usually with enough ripe cherry and currant flavors to keep them in balance.

1995: Dark, ripe, rich and chocolatey, with a slightly leathery edge to the dense currant and plum fruit and spicy herbal flavors. **91**

1994: Firm, with crisp tannins, the currant and cherry fruit is tightly wound, picking up an earthy, leathery edge. **88**

1990: A tight, austere wine that's showing more oak and tannin than fruit at this stage, but it has an appealing core of weedy black currant and spice flavors. **88**

1989: Walks a tightrope between earthy, barnyardy notes and modest fruit flavors. **78**

1988: Supple, with spicy oak notes, moderate cherry and plum flavors and firm tannins. **86**

1987: Smooth, rich and complex, packing in deep currant, plum, anise and oak flavors. **88**

1986: Tight, firm and tannic; a backward wine that needs time for the spicy currant flavors to emerge. **85**

1985: Ripe, supple and complex, with nicely integrated currant, spice, anise and buttery oak flavors. **87**

1984: Tough, oaky and tannic, a blockbuster that's just beginning to reveal its ripe currant flavor. Turns dry and tannic. **85**

CABERNET SAUVIGNON NAPA VALLEY RESERVE (★★★★)

1995: Smooth, ripe, rich and polished, with currant, cherry, coffee, prune and tobacco flavors, turning silky and supple on the long, rich aftertaste. **92**

1994: Tightly wound, muscular and compact, with ripe, rich floral, plum and berry flavors and nuances of mineral and spice. **90**

1993: Just shy of outstanding, this elegant wine offers a range of spicy currant, cherry and berry flavors and light oak shadings. **88**

1987: Tough and earthy, with a powerful structure and broad, juicy black cherry and tobacco flavors. **89**

CHARDONNAY CALIFORNIA (★★★): Not quite as complex of late, but intense and concentrated.

1997: Racy, with a citrus and grapefruit edge to the core of pear and sweet pea flavors, it turns diffuse on the finish but holds its flavors. A bit of light oak shows up in the background. **89**

1996: Crisp, with a core of citrus, pear, nectarine, herb and spice. The texture is a bit raw, but the wine is concentrated. **88**

ZEBRA ZIN see **HARRISON WINERY & VINEYARDS**

ZINSKEY see **ROBERT SINSKEY VINEYARDS**

ZOOM VINEYARDS (★★)
Alameda County
Founded: 1996. **Owner:** John Eppler, Jerry Martin, Brad Waggener. **Winemaker:** John Eppler.

MAJOR WINES: PRICE, CASES, RATING
Zinfandel Contra Costa County
  Continente Vineyard
  ($23, 360)   ★★★

ALSO PRODUCED
Zinfandel Paso Robles ($22, 250).

WINERY DATA
Case Production: 650. **Vineyard Designations:** Continente Vineyard (Zinfandel). **Varietals Purchased:** Zinfandel (Contra Costa County, Paso Robles).

Winemaker John Eppler works in marketing at Rosenblum Cellars, where he also produces his own label. The 1996 Zinfandel (88 points) was riper and richer than many others from the same vintage, with plum, cherry, wild berry and spicy raspberry fruit and supple tannins.

WINERY DIRECTORY

❖

The wineries below are listed in the same order as in Chapter 7 of this book. That is, a winery named for a person will be alphabetized under the person's last name. Example: Robert Mondavi Winery is alphabetized under M.

Please keep in mind that while the following information was checked as close to press time as possible, phone and fax numbers change frequently, especially as new area codes are added in many areas.

Abreu Vineyards
Fax: 707 963-5104

Acacia Winery
2750 Las Amigas Rd.
Napa 94559
Phone: 707 226-9991
Fax: 707 226-1685

Adelaida Cellars
5805 Adelaida Rd.
Paso Robles 93446
Phone: 805 239-8980
Fax: 805 239-4671
Email: adelaidac@aol.com

Adler Fels Estate
5325 Corrick Lane
Santa Rosa 95409
Phone: 707 539-3123
Fax: 707 539-3128
Email: adlerfel@pacbell.net

Alban Vineyards
8575 Orcutt Rd.
Arroyo Grande 93420
Phone: 805 546-0305
Fax: 805 546-9879

Albini Family Vineyards
886 Jensen Lane
Windsor 95492
Phone: 707 838-9249

Alderbrook Vineyards & Winery
2306 Magnolia Dr.
Healdsburg 95448
Phone: 707 433-5987
Fax: 707 433-0165
Email: office@alderbrook.com
Web: www.alderbrook.com

Alexander Valley Vineyards
8644 Highway 128
Healdsburg 95448
Phone: 707 433-7209
Fax: 707 433-9408
Email: avv@avvwine.com

Altamura Vineyards & Winery
P.O. Box 3209
Napa 94558
Phone: 707 253-2000
Fax: 707 255-3937

Amador Foothill Winery
12500 Steiner Rd.
Plymouth 95669
Phone: 209 245-6307
Fax: 209 245-3580
Email:
  winenerd@amadorfoothill.com
Web: www.amadorfoothill.com

Ancien Wines
P.O. Box 10667
Napa 94581
Phone: 707 255-3908
Fax: 707 255-6104

S. Anderson Vineyard
1473 Yountville Cross Rd.
Yountville 94599
Phone: 707 944-8642
Fax: 707 944-8020
Email: savwines@4bubbly.com
Web: www.4bubbly.com

Anderson's Conn Valley Vineyards
680 Rossi Rd.
St. Helena   94574
Phone: 707 963-8600
Fax: 707 963-7818

Araujo Estate Wines
2155 Pickett Rd.
Calistoga   94515
Phone: 707 942-6061
Fax: 707 942-6471
Email: wine@araujoestate.com

Arbios
4145 Shadow Lane #426
Santa Rosa   95405
Phone: 707 539-5641
Fax: 707 539-5641
Email: wynguy@msn.com

Arcadian
P.O. Box 891
Santa Ynez   93460
Phone: 805 688-1149
Fax: 805 686-5501

Arciero Winery
P.O. Box 1287
Paso Robles   93447
Phone: 805 239-2562
Fax: 805 239-2317
Web: www.arcierowinery.com

Armida Winery
2201 Westside Rd.
Healdsburg   95448
Phone: 707 433-2222
Fax: 707 433-2202

Arns
P.O. Box 652
St. Helena   94574
Phone: 707 963-3429
Fax: 707 963-5780

Arrowood Vineyards & Winery
P.O. Box 1240
Glen Ellen   95442
Phone: 707 938-5170
Fax: 707 938-1543

Atlas Peak Vineyards
P.O. Box 948
Healdsburg   94558
Phone: 707 226-1094
Fax: 707 226-2306
Web: www.atlaspeak.com

Au Bon Climat
P.O. Box 113
Santa Barbara   93441
Phone: 805 937-9801
Fax: 805 937-2539

Azalea Springs Cellars
P.O. Box 1089
Calistoga   94515
Phone: 415 346-3300
Fax: 415 567-2677
Email: 2790bway@
  compuserve.com

Babcock Vineyards
5175 E. Highway 246
Lompoc   93436
Phone: 805 736-1455
Fax: 805 736-3886
Email: babcock@silcom.com
Web: www.wineaccess.com/
  babcock

Bacio Divino
P.O. Box 432
Rutherford   94573
Phone: 707 942-8101
Fax: 707 942-8101
Email: cloudy@baciodivino.com
Web: www.baciodivino.com

Baileyana Vineyards
5880 Edna Rd.
San Luis Obispo   93401
Phone: 805 544-9080
Fax: 805 546-0413

Bannister Vineyards
1139 Sunnyside Dr.
Healdsburg   95448
Phone: 707 433-2606
Email: bannwine@aol.com

Barbour Vineyards
975 Vintage Ave.
St. Helena   94574
Phone: 707 963-0540
Fax: 707 963-1465
Email: barbourvyds@aol.com

Lawrence J. Bargetto Winery
3535 North Main St.
Soquel   95073
Phone: 408 475-2258
Fax: 408 475-2664
Web: www.bargetto.com

Barnett Vineyards
4070 Spring Mountain
St. Helena   94574
Phone: 707 963-7075
Fax: 707 963-3724
Email: barnettv@napanet.com

Barnwood
453 Deutz Dr.
Arroyo Grande   93420
Phone: 888 809-VINE
Fax: 310 275-9890

Baron Herzog
12378 Saratoga/Sunnyvale Rd.
  Suite 10
Saratoga   95070
Phone: 408 252-2526
Fax: 408 996-9232

Bartholomew Park Winery
1000 Vineyard Lane
Sonoma 95476
Phone: 707 935-9511
Fax: 707 935-0549
Email: wines@bartholomewpark
  winery.com
Web: www.bartholomewpark
  winery.com

Bayliss & Fortune
20 Ragsdale Dr. Suite 240
Monterey 93940
Phone: 831 375-7100
Fax: 831 375-3626
Web: www.worldwidewines.com

Bayview Cellars
1150 Bayview Ave.
Napa 94559
Phone: 707 255-8544
Fax: 707 226-2069

Beaucanon Winery
1695 St. Helena Highway
St. Helena 94574
Phone: 707 967-3520
Fax: 707 967-3527

Beaulieu Vineyard
P.O. Box 219
Rutherford 94573
Phone: 707 967-5200
Fax: 707 963-5920
Web: www.bv-wine.com

Beckmen Vineyards
P.O. Box 542
Los Olivos 93441
Phone: 805 688-8664
Fax: 805 688-9983

Bedford Thompson
P.O. Box 507
Los Alamos 93440
Phone: 805 344-2107
Fax: 805 344-2047

Behrens & Hitchcock
1421 Second St.
Calistoga 94515
Phone: 707 942-4433

Bell Wine Cellars
6200 Washington St.
Yountville 94599
Phone: 707 944-1673
Fax: 707 944-1674
Email: bellcab@aol.com
Web: www.bellwine.com

Belvedere Winery
4035 Westside Rd.
Healdsburg 95448
Phone: 707 433-8236
Fax: 707 431-0826
Web: www.belvedere-wines.com

Benessere
1010 Big Tree Rd.
St. Helena 94574
Phone: 707 963-5853
Fax: 707 963-9546
Email: bnsrevyd@aol.com

Benziger Family Winery
1883 London Ranch Rd.
Glen Ellen 95442
Phone: 707 935-3000
Fax: 707 935-3018
Email: benziger@wco.com
Web: www.benziger.com

Beringer Vineyards
P.O. Box 111
St. Helena 94574
Phone: 707 963-7115
Fax: 707 963-1735
Web: www.beringer.com

Bernardus Winery
P.O. Box 1800
Carmel Valley 93924
Phone: 408 659-1900
Fax: 408 659-1676

Robert Biale Vineyards
2040 Brown St.
Napa 94559
Phone: 707 257-7555
Fax: 707 257-0105
Email: bialezin@aol.com

Black Sears Winery
2615 Summit Lake Dr.
Angwin 94508
Phone: 707 963-1334
Fax: 707 963-3920

Boeger Winery Inc.
1709 Causon Rd.
Placerville 95667
Phone: 530 622-8094
Fax: 530 622-8112
Email: sboeger@ns.net
Web: www.boegerwinery.com

Bogle Vineyards
37783 County Rd. 144
Clarkburg 95612
Phone: 916 744-1139
Fax: 916 744-1187
Email: info@boglewinery.com
Web: www.boglewinery.com

Bonny Doon Vineyard
P.O. Box 8376
Santa Cruz 95061
Phone: 408 425-3625
Fax: 415 425-3856

Bouchaine Vineyards
1075 Buchli Station Rd.
Napa 94559
Phone: 707 252-9065
Fax: 707 252-0401

The Brander Vineyard
P.O. Box 92
Los Olivos 93441
Phone: 805 688-2455
Fax: 805 688-8010
Web: www.brander.com

August Briggs
1911 Emerald Dr.
Calistoga   94515
Phone: 707 942-4912
Fax: 707 942-4912

Brophy Clark Cellars
P.O. Box 955
Nipomo   93444
Phone: 805 929-4830
Fax: 805 929-8301
Email: coastvines@utech.net

David Bruce Winery
21439 Bear Creek Rd.
Los Gatos   95033
Phone: 408 354-4214
Fax: 408 395-5478
Web: www.davidbrucewinery.com

Brutocao Cellars
P.O. Box 780
Hopland   95449
Phone: 707 744-1066
Fax: 707 744-1046
Web: www.brutocaocellars.com

Bryant Family Vineyard
701 Market St. Suite 1200
St. Louis, MO   63101
Phone: 314 613-3640
Fax: 314 231-4859

Buehler Vineyards
820 Greenfield Rd.
St. Helena   94574
Phone: 707 963-2155
Fax: 707 963-3747
Web: www.buehlervineyards.com

Buena Vista Winery
P.O. Box 182
Sonoma   95476
Phone: 707 252-7117
Fax: 707 252-0392

Burgess Cellars
P.O. Box 282
St. Helena   94574
Phone: 707 963-4766
Fax: 707 963-8774

Byington Winery
21850 Bear Creek Rd.
Los Gatos   95033
Phone: 408 354-1111
Fax: 408 354-2782
Email: accounting@byington.com
Web: www.byington.com

Davis Bynum Winery
8075 Westside Rd.
Healdsburg   95448
Phone: 707 433-5852
Fax: 707 433-4309
Email: info@davisbynum.com
Web: www.davisbynum.com

Byron Vineyards & Winery
5230 Tepusquet Rd.
Santa Maria   93454
Phone: 805 937-7288
Fax: 805 937-1246
Email: info@byronwinery.com

Cafaro Cellars
1591 Dean York Lane
St. Helena   94574
Phone: 707 963-7181

Cain Vineyard & Winery
3800 Langtry Rd.
St. Helena   94574
Phone: 707 963-1616
Fax: 707 963-7952
Email: winery@cainfive.com
Web: www.cainfive.com

Cakebread Cellars
P.O. Box 216
Rutherford   94573
Phone: 707 963-5221
Fax: 707 963-1067
Email: cellars@cakebread.com
Web: www.cakebread.com

Oliver Caldwell Cellars
P.O. Box 808
St. Helena   94574
Phone: 707 963-2037
Fax: 707 963-2057

Cale Family Wines
16060 Sonoma Hwy.
Sonoma   95476
Phone: 707 939-8363
Fax: 707 939-8363
Email: calewines@aol.com

Calera Wine Co.
11300 Cienega Rd.
Hollister   95023
Phone: 408 637-9170
Fax: 408 637-9070

Callaway Vineyard & Winery
P.O. Box 9014
Temecula   92589-9014
Phone: 909 676-4001
Fax: 909 676-5209
Web: www.callawaywine.com

Cambria Winery & Vineyard
5475 Chardonnay Lane
Santa Maria   93454
Phone: 805 937-8091
Fax: 805 934-3589
Email: info@coolwines.com
Web: www.cambriawine.com

Canepa Cellars
511 Lowell Ave.
Mill Valley 94941
Phone: 415 388-3222
Fax: 415 388-8824

Cardinale
P.O. Box 328
Oakville 94562
Phone: 707 944-2807
Fax: 707 944-5628

Carmenet Winery
1700 Moon Mountain Dr.
Sonoma 95476
Phone: 707 996-5870
Fax: 707 996-5302
Email: pr@carmenetwinery.com
Web: www.carmenetwinery.com

Carneros Creek Winery
1285 Dealy Lane
Napa 94559
Phone: 707 253-9464
Fax: 707 253-9465
Web: www.carneroscreek.com

Castalia
1207 South Fitch Mountain Rd.
Healdsburg 95448
Phone: 707 433-6602
Fax: 707 433-6602
Email: castalia@sonic.net

Caymus Vineyards
8700 Conn Creek Rd.
Rutherford 94573
Phone: 707 963-4204
Fax: 707 963-5958

Cecchetti Sebastiani Cellar
P.O. Box 1607
Sonoma 95476
Phone: 707 996-8463
Fax: 707 996-0424

Chalk Hill Winery
10300 Chalk Hill Rd.
Healdsburg 95448
Phone: 707 838-4306
Fax: 707 838-1907

Chalone Vineyard
P.O. Box 518
Soledad 93960
Phone: 408 678-1717
Fax: 408 678-2742

Chappellet Vineyard
1581 Sage Canyon Rd.
St. Helena 94574
Phone: 800 494-6370
Fax: 707 963-7445
Email: winery@chappellet.com
Web: www.chappellet.com

Chateau Julien
P.O. Box 221775
Carmel 93922
Phone: 831 624-2600
Fax: 831 624-6138
Web: www.chateaujulien.com

Chateau Montelena Winery
1429 Tubbs Lane
Calistoga 94515
Phone: 707 942-5105
Fax: 707 942-4221
Web: www.montelena.com

Chateau Potelle
3875 Mt. Veeder Rd.
Napa 94558
Phone: 707 255-9440
Fax: 707 255-9444
Email: potellevgs@aol.com
Web: www.virtualcities.com/ca/
chateaupotelle

Chateau Souverain
P.O. Box 528
Geyserville 95441
Phone: 707 433-8281
Fax: 707 433-5174
Email: chatsouv@aol.com
Web: www.chateausouverain.com

Chateau St. Jean
P.O. Box 293
Kenwood 95452
Phone: 707 833-4134
Fax: 707 833-4200
Web: www.chateaustjean.com

Chateau Woltner
3500 Silverado Trail
St. Helena 94574
Phone: 707 963-1744
Fax: 707 963-8135

Chauffe-Eau Cellars
P.O. Box 47
Geyserville 95441
Phone: 707 857-3722

Chimney Rock Winery
5350 Silverado Trail
Napa 94558
Phone: 707 257-2641
Fax: 707 257-2036
Web: www.chimneyrock.com

Christophe Vineyards
650 Fifth St., Suite 403
San Francisco   94107
Phone: 415 979-0630

Christopher Creek Winery
P.O. Box 842
Healdsburg   95448
Phone: 707 433-2001
Fax: 707 431-0183

Cinnabar Vineyards
P.O. Box 245
Saratoga   95071
Phone: 408 741-5858
Fax: 408 745-5860

Claiborne & Churchill Vintners
2649 Carpenter Canyon Rd.
San Luis Obispo   93401
Phone: 805 544-4066
Fax: 805 544-7012

Clark-Claudon Vineyards
P.O. Box 15
St. Helena   94574
Phone: 707 965-9393
Fax: 707 965-1135
Email: ccvin@napanet.net

Claudia Springs Winery
P.O. Box 348
Philo   95466
Phone: 707 895-3926

Cline Cellars
24737 Arnold Dr.
Sonoma   95476
Phone: 707 935-4310
Fax: 707 935-4319
Web: www.clinecellars.com

Clos du Bois Winery
19410 Geyserville Ave.
Geyserville   95441
Phone: 707 857-1651
Fax: 707 857-1667
Web: www.closdubois.com

Clos Du Val Wine Co.
5330 Silverado Trail
Napa   94558
Phone: 707 259-2200
Fax: 707 252-6125
Web: www.closduval.com

Clos LaChance Wines
21511 Saratoga Heights Dr.
Saratoga   95070
Phone: 408 741-2920
Fax: 408 741-2921
Email: wjmurphy@aol.com
Web: www.clos.com

Clos Pegase
1060 Dunaweal Lane
Calistoga   94515
Phone: 707 942-4981
Fax: 707 942-4993
Email: clospegase@aol.com
Web: www.clospegase.com

Codorniu Napa
1345 Henry Rd.
Napa   94559
Phone: 707 224-1668
Fax: 707 224-1672

David Coffaro Vineyard & Winery
7485 Dry Creek Rd.
Geyserville   95441
Phone: 707 433-9715
Fax: 707 433-6008
Email: david@coffaro.com
Web: www.coffaro.com

B.R. Cohn
15140 Sonoma Hwy.
Glen Ellen   95442
Phone: 707 938-4064
Fax: 707 938-4585
Web: www.brcohn.com

Cold Heaven
P.O. Box 717
Solvang   93464
Phone: 805 688-8630
Fax: 805 688-3593
Email: morganch@utech.net

Colgin
3029 St. Helena Hwy. North
St. Helena   94574
Phone: 707 963-0999

Collier Falls
9931 West Dry Creek Rd.
Healdsburg   95448
Phone: 707 433-7373
Fax: 707 433-7878

Concannon Vineyard
4590 Tesla Rd.
Livermore   94550
Phone: 925 456-2500
Fax: 925 456-2501
Web: www.livermore.com/
   wine.html

Conn Creek Winery
8711 Silverado Trail
St. Helena   94574
Phone: 707 963-9100
Fax: 707 963-7840

Constant
P.O. Box 440-B
St. Helena   94574
Phone: 707 963-9661
Fax: 707 963-8566

Cooper-Garrod Vineyards
22600 Mt. Eden Rd.
Saratoga 95070
Phone: 408 741-8094
Fax: 408 741-1169

Corbett Canyon Vineyards
2195 Corbett Canyon Rd.
San Luis Obispo 93403
Phone: 805 544-5800
Fax: 805 544-7205

Corison Wines
P.O. Box 427
St. Helena 94574
Phone: 707 963-0826
Fax: 707 963-4906

Cornerstone Cellars
P.O. Box 10767
Napa 94581
Phone: 707 255-6884
Fax: 707 255-4324
Email: bscotland@aol.com

Cosentino Winery
P.O. Box 2818
Yountville 94599
Phone: 707 944-1220
Fax: 707 944-1254

H. Coturri & Sons Ltd.
P.O. Box 396
Glen Ellen 95442
Phone: 707 525-9126
Fax: 707 525-8039
Web: www.coturriwinery.com

Robert Craig
830 School St., Suite 14
Napa 94559
Phone: 707 252-2250
Fax: 707 252-2639

Creston Manor Vineyards & Winery
P.O. Box 577
Templeton 93465
Phone: 805 434-1399
Fax: 805 434-2426

Crichton Hall
1150 Darms Lane
Napa 94558
Phone: 707 224-4200
Fax: 707 224-224-4218

Cronin Vineyards
11 Old La Honda Rd.
Woodside 94062
Phone: 650 851-1452
Fax: 650 851-5696

Cuvaison
P.O. Box 384
Calistoga 94515
Phone: 707 942-6266
Fax: 707 942-5732
Email: info@cuvaison
Web: www.cuvaison.com

Dalla Valle Vineyards
P.O. Box 329
Oakville 94562
Phone: 707 944-2676
Fax: 707 944-8411

Daniel Lawrence
520 Mendocino Ave., Suite 330
Santa Rosa 95401
Phone: 800 204-2640
Fax: 707 935-1262
Web: www.daniellawrence.com

Dark Star Cellars
2985 Anderson Rd.
Paso Robles 93446
Phone: 805 237-2389
Fax: 805 237-2589
Email: darkstarcellars@msn.com
Web: www.darkstarcellars.com

Dashe Cellars
1080 Dolores St.
San Francisco 94110
Phone: 415 642-1169
Fax: 415 642-1602
Email: zinner@aol.com
Web: www.dashecellars.com

David Arthur Vineyards
1521 Sage Canyon Rd.
St. Helena 94574
Phone: 707 963-5190
Fax: 707 963-3711
Email: davwine@aol.com

D-Cubed Cellars
P.O. Box 771
Angwin 94508
Phone: 707 965-1003
Fax: 707 965-1337
Email: ddappen@napanet.net

De Loach Vineyards
1791 Olivet Rd.
Santa Rosa 95401
Phone: 707 526-9111
Fax: 707 526-4151
Email: deloachvyd@aol.com
Web: www.deloachvineyards.com

de Lorimier Winery
P.O. Box 487
Geyserville 95441
Phone: 800 546-7718
Fax: 707 857-3262
Email: discover@delorimier winery.com
Web: www.delorimierwinery.com

Dehlinger Winery
6300 Guerneville Rd.
Sebastopol 95472
Phone: 707 823-2378
Fax: 707 823-0918

Del Dotto
P.O. Box 2692
Yountville   94574
Phone: 707 963-2134
Fax: 707 963-3531
Web: www.ddvwine.com

Delectus
918 Enterprise Way
Napa   94558
Phone: 707 255-1252
Fax: 707 226-5412

Deux Amis
P.O. Box 831
Sebastopol   95473
Phone: 707 431-7945
Fax: 707 433-3753

Di Bruno
3630 Montebello St.
Santa Ynez   93460
Phone: 805 688-8792
Fax: 805 688-7381

Diamond Creek Vineyards
1500 Diamond Mountain Rd.
Calistoga   94515
Phone: 707 942-6926
Fax: 707 942-6936

Dickerson Vineyard
21 Tamal Vista, Suite 212
Corte Madera   94925
Phone: 415 924-7711
Fax: 415 435-7619

Domaine Carneros
P.O. Box 5420
Napa   94581
Phone: 707 257-0101
Fax: 707 257-3020

Domaine Chandon
One California Dr.
Yountville   94599
Phone: 707 944-8844
Fax: 707 944-1123
Email: dchandon@napanet.net
Web: www.dchandon.com

Domaine de la Terre Rouge
P.O. Box 41
Fiddletown   95629-0041
Phone: 209 245-3117
Fax: 209 245-5415
Email: terouge@volcano.net

Domaine St. George
350 Sansome St. Suite 1010
San Francisco   94104
Phone: 415 394-6454
Fax: 415 394-7005

Domaine Saint Gregory
1170 Bel Arbres Rd.
Redwood Valley   95470
Phone: 707 463-1532
Fax: 707 485-9742

Dominus Estate
P.O. Box 3327
Yountville   94599
Phone: 707 944-8954
Fax: 707 944-0547
Email: dominus@napanet.net
Web: www.dominusestate.com

Dover Canyon Winery
RT. 2 Box 40 Bethel Rd.
Templeton   93465
Phone: 805 434-0319
Fax: 805 434-0509
Email: dovercanyon@tcsn.net
Web: www.dovercanyon.com

Draxton
P.O. Box 789
Geyserville   95441
Phone: 707 857-3594
Fax: 707 857-3822

Dreyer Sonoma Winery
P.O. Box 484
Graton   95444
Phone: 650 851-9448
Fax: 650 851-3268

Dry Creek Vineyard
3770 Lambert Bridge Rd.
Healdsburg   95448
Phone: 707 433-1000
Fax: 707 433-5329
Web: www.drycreekvineyard.com

Duckhorn Vineyards
1000 Lodi Lane
St. Helena   94574
Phone: 800 354-8885
Fax: 707 963-7595
Email:
   info@duckhornvineyards.com

Duncan Peak Vineyards
P.O. Box 358
Hopland   95449
Phone: 925 283-3632
Fax: 925 283-3632
Email: wine@duncanpeak.com
Web: www.duncanpeak.com

Dunn Vineyards
P.O. Box 886
Angwin   94508
Phone: 707 965-3642
Fax: 707 965-3805

Dunnewood Vineyards & Winery
2399 North State St.
  P.O. Box 268
Ukiah   95482
Phone: 707 462-2985
Fax: 707 462-0323

Dunning Vineyards
1953 Niderer Rd.
Paso Robles   93446
Phone: 805 238-4763

Durney Vineyards
P.O. Box 999
Carmel   93924
Phone: 408 659-6220
Fax: 408 659-6226
Email: durney@redshift.com
Web: www.usawines.com/durney

Eberle Winery
P.O. Box 2459
Paso Robles   93447
Phone: 805 238-9607
Fax: 805 237-0344

Echelon Vineyards
621 Airpark Rd.
Napa   94558
Phone: 707 254-4200
Fax: 707 254-4204

Tom Eddy
P.O. Box 10468
Napa   94581
Phone: 707 257-1153
Fax: 707 257-1637

Edgewood
401 St. Helena Hwy. South
St. Helena   94574
Phone: 800 707-5345
Fax: 707 963-0745

Edmeades Vineyards
421 Aviation Blvd.
Santa Rosa   95403
Phone: 707 895-3232
Fax: 707 895-3232

Edmunds St. John
1331 Walnut St.
Berkeley   94709
Phone: 510 654-1230
Fax: 510 654-8314

Edna Valley Vineyard
2585 Biddle Ranch Rd.
San Luis Obispo   93401
Phone: 805 544-5855
Fax: 805 544-0112

Merry Edwards
8132 Speer Ranch Rd.
Forestville   95436
Phone: 707 887-8644
Fax: 707 887-0322

Ehlers Grove
P.O. Box 452
St. Helena   94574
Phone: 707 963-3200
Fax: 707 963-5910
Email: ehlers@napanet.net
Web: www.cartlidgebrowne.com

Volker Eisele
3080 Lowe Chiles Valley Rd.
St. Helena   94574
Phone: 707 965-2260
Fax: 707 965-9609

El Molino Winery
P.O. Box 306
St. Helena   94574
Phone: 707 963-3632
Fax: 707 963-1647

Elan
575 Lincoln Ave., #300 C
Napa   94558
Phone: 707 252-3339
Fax: 707 252-4996

Elyse Wines
2100 Hoffman Lane
Napa   94558
Phone: 707 944-2900
Fax: 707 945-0301

Emmolo
P.O. Box 7
Rutherford   94573
Phone: 707 963-6075
Fax: 707 963-6075

Eric Ross
P.O. Box 2156
San Anselmo   94979
Phone: 707 874-3046
Fax: 415 332-7141
Email: jstory@ericross.com
Web: www.ericross.com

Estancia Estates
P.O. Box 407
Rutherford   94573
Phone: 707 963-7112
Fax: 707 963-7867
Web: www.franciscan.com

Etude Wines
P.O. Box 3382
Napa   94558
Phone: 707 257-5300
Fax: 707 257-6022
Web: www.etudewines.com

Fanucchi Vineyards
P.O. Box 159
Fulton   95439
Phone: 707 545-6806
Fax: 707 544-6106

Far Niente Winery
P.O. Box 327
Oakland   94562
Phone: 707 944-2861
Fax: 707 944-2312
Web: www.welcome@farniente.com

Gary Farrell Wines
P.O. Box 342
Forestville   95436
Phone: 707 433-6616
Fax: 707 433-9060
Web: www.wines.com/gary_farrell/
gary.html

Ferrari-Carano Winery
P.O. Box 1549
Healdsburg   95448
Phone: 707 433-6700
Fax: 707 431-1742
Web: ferrari-carano.com

Gloria Ferrer Champagne Caves
P.O. Box 1427
Sonoma   95476
Phone: 707 996-7256
Fax: 707 996-0720

Fetzer Vineyards
P.O. Box 611
Hopeland   95449
Phone: 707 744-7600
Fax: 707 744-7605
Web: www.fetzer.com

Ficklin Vineyards
30246 Ave. 7 1/2
Madera   93637
Phone: 209 674-4598

Fiddlehead Cellars
1667 Oak Ave., Suite B
Davis   95616
Phone: 530 756-4550
Fax: 530 756-4558

Field Stone Winery
10075 Hwy. 128
Healdsburg   95448
Phone: 707 433-7266
Fax: 707 433-2231

Fife Vineyards
P.O. Box 553
St. Helena   94574
Phone: 707 963-1534
Fax: 707 963-8620
Email: fifevyds@aol.com

Firestone Vineyard
P.O. Box 244
Los Olivos   93441
Phone: 805 688-3940
Fax: 805 686-1256
Email: info@firestonevineyard
.com
Web: www.firestonevineyard.com

Fisher Vineyards
6200 St. Helena Rd.
Santa Rosa   95404
Phone: 707 539-7511
Fax: 707 539-3601

Flora Springs Wine Co.
1978 W. Zinfandel Lane
St. Helena   94574
Phone: 707 963-5711
Fax: 707 963-7518
Web: www.florasprings.com

Flowers
28500 Seaview Rd.
Cazadero   95421
Phone: 707 847-3661
Fax: 707 847-3740
Email: flowers@mcn.org

Thomas Fogarty Winery
3270 Alpine Rd.
Portola Valley   94028
Phone: 650 851-6777
Fax: 650 851-5840
Email: tfogarty@aol.com
Web: www.fogartywinery.com

Foley Estate
1711 Alamo Pintado Rd.
Solvang   93463
Phone: 805 688-8554
Fax: 805 688-9327

Folie à Deux Winery
3070 St. Helena Hwy. North
St. Helena   94574
Phone: 707 963-1160
Fax: 707 963-9223
Email: Fantasy@folie_a_deux.com
Web: www.flavorweb.com/
folie.htm

Foppiano Vineyards
P.O. Box 606
Healdsburg   95448
Phone: 707 433-7272
Fax: 707 433-0565
Web: www.foppiano.com

Forman Vineyard
P.O. Box 343
St. Helena   94574
Phone: 707 963-0234
Fax: 707 963-5384

Foxen Vineyard Inc.
7200 Foxen Canyon Rd.
Santa Maria   93454
Phone: 805 937-4251
Fax: 805 937-0415

Franciscan Oakville Estate
P.O. Box 407
Rutherford   94573
Phone: 707 963-7112
Fax: 707 963-7867
Web: www.franciscan.com

Peter Franus Wine Co.
2055 Hoffman Lane
Napa   94558
Phone: 707 945-0542
Fax: 707 945-0931
Email: franuswine@aol.com

Frazier
40 Lupine Hill Rd.
Napa 94558
Phone: 707 255-3444
Fax: 707 252-7573
Email: frazwine@aol.com

Freemark Abbey Winery
P.O. Box 410
St. Helena 94574
Phone: 707 963-9694
Fax: 707 963-0554
Email: wineinfo@freemarkabbey
  .com
Web: www.freemarkabbey.com

Frick Winery
23072 Walling Rd.
Geyserville 95441
Phone: 415 776-7331
Fax: 415 776-7331
Email: frickvin@ix.netcom.com

J. Fritz
2526 California St.
San Francisco 94115
Phone: 415 771-1900
Fax: 415 771-9398

Frog's Leap
P.O. Box 189
Rutherford 94573
Phone: 707 963-4704
Fax: 707 963-0292
Email: ribbitt@frogsleap.com

The Gainey Vineyard
P.O. Box 910
Santa Ynez 93460
Phone: 805 688-0558
Fax: 805 688-5864

Galante Vineyards
3030 Bridgeway, Suite 205
Sausalito 94965
Phone: 415 331-1247
Fax: 415 331-2039
Email: wineline@galante-
  vineyards.com

Gallo of Sonoma Winery
3387 Dry Creek Rd.
Healdsburg 95448
Phone: 707 431-5500
Fax: 707 431-5515

Garretson Wine Co.
1509 Las Brisas Dr.
Paso Robles 93446
Phone: 805 239-1205
Fax: 805 239-1205
Email: mrviognier@aol.com

Daniel Gehrs Wines
77 Ironwood Way
Solvang 93463
Phone: 805 688-0694
Fax: 805 688-6121

Georis Winery
4 Pilot Rd.
Carmel Valley 93924
Phone: 408 659-1050
Fax: 408 659-1050
Email: georiswine@aol.com

Geyser Peak Winery
25 Geyserville Rd.
Geyserville 95441
Phone: 707 857-9420
Fax: 707 857-9401
Web: www.geyserpeakwinery.com

Glen Ellen Winery
P.O Box 219
Rutherford 94573
Phone: 707 939-6277
Fax: 707 938-2592

Grace Family Vineyards
1210 Rockland Rd.
St. Helena 94574
Phone: 707 963-0808
Fax: 707 963-5271

Green & Red Vineyard
3208 Chiles Valley Rd.
St. Helena 94574
Phone: 707 965-2346
Fax: 707 965-1241

Greenwood Ridge Vineyards
5501 Hwy. 128
Philo 95466
Phone: 707 895-2002
Fax: 707 895-2001
Web: www.avwines.com

Gregory Graham
P.O. Box 6916
Napa 94581
Phone: 707 224-3227
Fax: 707 224-3227
Web: www.ggwine.com

Grgich Hills Cellar
P.O. Box 450
Rutherford 94573
Phone: 707 963-2784
Fax: 707 963-8725

Groth Vineyards & Winery
P.O. Box 390
Oakville 94562
Phone: 707 944-0290
Fax: 707 944-8932
Email: grothwines@aol.com

Guenoc Winery
P.O. Box 1146
Middletown 95461
Phone: 707 987-2385
Fax: 707 987-9351
Web: www.guenoc.com

Hamel Wines
P.O. Box 1355
Healdsburg   95448
Phone: 707 433-9055
Fax: 707 433-9055
Email: hamelwines@aol.com

Handley Cellars
P.O. Box 66
Philo   95466
Phone: 707 895-3876
Fax: 707 895-2603
Email: handley@zapcom.net

Hanna Winery Inc.
9280 Hwy 128
Healdsburg   95448
Phone: 707 431-4310
Fax: 707 431-4314
Email: hannawine@pacbell.net

Hanzell Vineyards
18596 Lomita Ave.
Sonoma   95476
Phone: 707 996-3860
Fax: 707 996-3862

Harlan Estate
P.O. Box 352
Oakville   94562
Phone: 707 944-1441
Fax: 707 944-1444
Web: www.harlanestate.com

Harmony Cellars
P.O. Box 2502
Harmony   93435
Phone: 805 927-1625
Fax: 805 434-1035

Harrison Winery & Vineyards
1527 Sage Canyon Rd.
St. Helena   94574
Phone: 707 963-8271
Fax: 707 963-4552

Hartford Court Winery
8075 Martinelli Rd.
Forestville   95436
Phone: 707 887-1756
Fax: 707 887-7158

Hartwell Vineyards
5795 Silverado Trail
Napa   94558
Phone: 707 255-4269
Fax: 707 255-4289

Havens Wine Cellars
2055 Hoffman Lane
Napa   94558
Phone: 707 945-0921
Fax: 707 945-0931
Email: havenswine@earthlink.net

Hawley Wines
P.O. Box 1831
Healdsburg   95448
Phone: 707 431-2705
Fax: 707 431-2705

Haywood Winery
P.O. Box 182
Sonoma   95476
Phone: 707 252-7998
Fax: 707 252-0392

Heitz Wine Cellars
500 Taplin Rd.
St. Helena   94574
Phone: 707 963-3542
Fax: 707 963-7454

Hendry Ranch
3104 Redwood Rd.
Napa   94558
Phone: 707 223-2130
Fax: 707 226-1345

The Hess Collection Winery
P.O. 4140
Napa   94558
Phone: 707 255-1144
Fax: 707 253-1682
Web: www.hesscollection.com

Hidden Cellars Winery
P.O. Box 448
Talmage   95481
Phone: 707 462-0301
Fax: 707 462-8144

William Hill Winery
1761 Atlas Peak Rd.
Napa   94558
Phone: 707 224-5424
Fax: 707 224-4477
Web: www.williamhillwinery.com

Hitching Post
P.O. Box 365
Buellton   93427
Phone: 805 688-7843
Fax: 805 686-1353

Paul Hobbs
707 Hidden Acres Rd.
Healdsburg   95448
Phone: 707 824-9879
Fax: 707 431-0708
Email: phwine@aol.com

Honig Cellars
P.O. Box 406
Rutherford   94573
Phone: 707 963-5618
Fax: 707 963-5639
Web: www.honigwine.com

Hop Kiln Winery
6050 Westside Rd.
Healdsburg   95448
Phone: 707 433-6491
Fax: 707 433-8162

Howell Mountain Vineyards
P.O. Box 521
St. Helena 94574
Phone: 707 963-2915
Fax: 707 963-3920
Web: www.howellmountain.com

Robert Hunter Winery
15655 Arnold Dr.
Sonoma 95476
Phone: 707 996-3056
Fax: 707 996-3065

Husch
P.O. Box 189
Talmage 95481
Phone: 707 462-5370
Fax: 707 462-5374
Email: sales@huschvineyards.com
Web: www.huschvineyards.com

Iron Horse Vineyards
9786 Ross Station Rd.
Sebastopol 95472
Phone: 707 887-1507
Fax: 707 887-1337
Web: www.ironhorsevineyards.com

Ironstone
1894 Six Mile Rd.
Murphy 95247
Phone: 209 728-1251
Fax: 209 728-1275
Email: kautz@goldrush.com
Web: www.ironstonevineyard.com

J Wine Co.
P.O. Box 6009
Healdsburg 95448
Phone: 707 431-5400
Fax: 707 431-5410
Web: www.jwine.com

Jade Mountain
2340 Mt. Veeder Rd.
Napa 94559
Phone: 415 921-8667
Fax: 415 921-6937

Jaffurs
P.O. Box 1452
Summerland 93067
Phone: 805 962-7003
Fax: 805 962-7003
Web: www.jaffurswine.com

Tobin James Cellars
8950 Union Rd.
Paso Robles 93446
Phone: 805 239-2204
Fax: 805 239-4471

Jarvis
2970 Monticello Rd.
Napa 94558
Phone: 707 255-5280
Fax: 707 255-5282
Email: wines@jarvisnapa.com
Web: www.jarvisnapa.com

JC Cellars
2220 Santa Clara Avenue
Alameda 94501
Phone: 510 749-9463
Fax: 510 749-9463
Email: jccellars@earthlink.com

Jekel Vineyards
P.O. Box 336
Greenfield 93927
Phone: 831 674-5522
Fax: 831 674-3767

Jepson Vineyards Ltd.
10400 South Hwy. 101
  Ukiah 95482
Phone: 707 468-8936
Fax: 707 468-0362

Jordan Vineyard & Winery
P.O. Box 878
Healdsburg 95448
Phone: 707 431-5250
Fax: 707 431-5262

Joullian Vineyards
P.O. Box 1400
Carmel Valley 93924
Phone: 408 659-2800
Fax: 408 659-2802

Judd's Hill
P.O. Box 415
St. Helena 94574
Phone: 707 963-9093
Fax: 707 963-1147

Justin Vineyards & Winery
11680 Chimney Rock Rd.
Paso Robles 93446
Phone: 805 238-6932
Fax: 805 238-7328
Email: justinewine@aol.com
Web: www.justinwine.com

Karl Lawrence
P.O. Box 3598
Napa 94558
Phone: 707 255-2843
Fax: 707 255-5245
Email: klcellar@napanet.net
Web: www.karllawrence.com

Karly Wines
P.O. Box 729
Plymouth 95669
Phone: 209 245-3922
Fax: 209 245-4874
Email: karly@volcano.net

Keegan Cellars
P.O. Box 5150
Napa 94581
Phone: 707 257-6966
Fax: 707 253-0554
Email: ekcellars@aol.com

Robert Keenan Winery
P.O. Box 142
St. Helena 94574
Phone: 707 963-9177
Fax: 707 963-8209
Web: www.keenanwinery.com

Kendall-Jackson Winery
421 Aviation Blvd.
Santa Rosa 95403
Phone: 707 544-4000
Fax: 707 544-4013
Email: kjwines@kj.com
Web: www.kj.com

Kathryn Kennedy Winery
13180 Pierce Rd.
Saratoga 95070
Phone: 408 867-4170
Fax: 408 867-9463
Web: www.kathrynkennedywinery
.com

Kenwood Vineyards
P.O. Box 447
Kenwood 95452
Phone: 707 833-5891
Fax: 707 833-6572
Email: kenwine@pacbell.net
Web: www.kenwoodvineyards.com

Kistler Vineyards
4707 Vine Hill Rd.
Sebastopol 95472
Phone: 707 823-5603
Fax: 707 823-6709

Kongsgaard Wines
P.O. Box 349
Oakville 94562
Phone: 415 885-8050
Fax: 415 292-5935

F. Korbel and Bros.
13250 River Rd.
Guerneville 95446
Phone: 707 824-7000
Fax: 707 869-2981
Email: info@korbel.com
Web: www.korbel.com

Kristone Champagne Cellars
5475 Chardonnay Lane
Santa Maria Valley 93454
Phone: 805 937-8091
Fax: 805 934-3589
Email: info@coolwines.com
Web: www.cambriawine.com

Charles Krug Winery
P.O. Box 191
St. Helena 94574
Phone: 707 967-2200
Fax: 707 967-2291
Email: charleskrug@pmondavi
.com

Kunde Estate Winery
P.O. Box 639
Kenwood 95452
Phone: 707 833-5501
Fax: 707 833-2204
Email: wineinfo@kunde.com
Web: www.kunde.com

Kynsi
P.O. Box 356
San Luis Obispo 93406
Phone: 805 544-6181
Fax: 805 544-6181
Email: kynsi@thegrid.net
Web: www.kynsi.com

La Crema
3690 Laughlin Rd.
Windsor 95492
Phone: 707 571-1504
Fax: 707 571-1448
Email: mail@lacrema.com
Web: www.lacrema.com

La Famiglia di Robert Mondavi
P.O. Box 106
Oakville 94562
Phone: 707 226-1395
Fax: 707 251-4386
Email: info@robertmondavi.com
Web: www.robertmondavi.com

La Jota Vineyard Co.
1102 Las Posadas Rd.
Angwin 94508
Phone: 707 965-3020
Fax: 707 965-0324

La Sirena Wines
P.O. Box 441
Calistoga 94515
Phone: 707 942-1105
Fax: 707 942-9390

Laetitia Vineyard & Winery
453 Deutz Dr.
Arroyo Grande 93420
Phone: 805 481-1772
Fax: 805 481-6920
Web: www.laetitia@thegrid.net

Lail Vineyards
P.O. Box 249
Rutherford 94573
Phone: 707 963-3329
Fax: 707 963-7519

Lambert Bridge Winery
4085 West Dry Creek Rd.
  Healdsburg 95448
Phone: 707 431-9600
Fax: 707 433-3215
Email: wines@lambertbridge.com
Web: www.lambertbridge.com

Lamborn Family Vineyards
120 Village Square, #13
Orinda 94563
Phone: 925 254-0511
Fax: 925 254-4531
Email: lambornwine@
  earthlink.net
Web: www.lamborn.com

Lancaster
15001 Chalk Hill Rd.
Healdsburg 95448
Phone: 707 433-8178
Fax: 707 433-2169

Landmark Vineyards
101 Adobe Canyon Rd.
Kenwood 95452
Phone: 707 833-0053
Fax: 707 833-1164
Email: wine@landmarkwine.com
Web: www.landmarkwine.com

Lang & Reed Wine Co.
P.O. Box 662
St. Helena 94574
Phone: 707 963-7547
Fax: 707 963-7333
Email: langreed@napanet.net

Laurel Glen Vineyard
P.O. Box 1419
Glen Ellen 95442
Phone: 707 526-3914
Fax: 707 526-9801
Web: www.wineaccess.com/
  laurelglen

Lazy Creek Vineyards
4610 Hwy 128
Philo 95466
Phone: 707 895-3623

Le Ducq
3120 St. Helena Hwy. North
St. Helena 94574
Phone: 888 819-9463
Fax: 888 811-9463

Ledson Winery & Vineyards
P.O. Box 653
Kenwood 95452
Phone: 707 833-2330
Fax: 707 996-6996

Leeward Winery
2784 Johnson Dr.
Ventura 93003
Phone: 805 656-5054

Lewelling Vineyards
1951 Olive Ave.
St. Helena 94574
Phone: 707 963-1685
Fax: 707 963-1685
Email: lewvyds@napanet.net
Web: www.lewellingvineyards.com

Lewis Cellars
524 El Cerrito Ave.
Hillsborough 94010
Phone: 650 342-8017
Fax: 650 342-8018
Web: www.lewiscellars.com

Limerick Lane Cellars
1023 Limerick Lane
Healdsburg 95448
Phone: 707 433-9211
Fax: 707 433-1652
Email: limerick@monitor.net
Web: www.wines.com/limericklane

LinCourt Vineyards
343 North Refugio Rd.
Santa Ynez 93460
Phone: 805 688-8381
Fax: 805 688-3764

Liparita Cellars
410 La Fata St., #200
St. Helena 94574
Phone: 707 963-2775
Fax: 707 963-2776
Web: www.liparita.com

Littorai
P.O. Box 180
St. Helena 94574
Phone: 707 963-4762
Fax: 707 963-7332
Email: littorai@aol.com
Web: www.littorai.com

Livingston Vineyards
1895 Cabernet Lane
St. Helena 94574
Phone: 707 963-2120
Fax: 707 963-9385
Email: livcab@aol.com
Web: www.livingston-wines.com

Lockwood Vineyard
24600 Silver Cloud Ct., #104
Monterey 93940
Phone: 800 753-1424
Fax: 831 644-7829
Web: www.lockwood-wine.com

J. Lohr Winery
1000 Lenzen Ave.
San Jose 95126
Phone: 408 288-5057
Fax: 408 993-2276
Web: www.jlohr.com

Lokoya
P.O. Box 328
Oakville 94562
Phone: 707 944-2807
Fax: 707 944-5628
Web: www.lokoya.com

Lolonis
1905 Rd. D
Redwood Valley 95470
Phone: 925 938-8066
Fax: 925 938-8069
Email: lolonis@pacbell.net
Web: www.lolonis.com

Lonetree
P.O. Box 401
Philo 95466
Phone: 888 686-9463
Fax: 888 686-9463
Email: chzin@aol.com
Web: www.lonetreewine.com

Long Vineyards
P.O. Box 50
St. Helena 94574
Phone: 707 963-2496
Fax: 707 963-2907
Email: longvine@ix.netcom.com

Richard Longoria Wines
P.O. Box 186
Los Olivos 93441
Phone: 805 688-0305
Fax: 805 688-2676
Email: rlongoria@thegrid.net

Lorenza-Lake
1764 Scott St.
St. Helena 94574
Phone: 707 963-8593
Fax: 707 967-9548
Email: lorenza176@aol.com

Luna Vineyards
2921 Silverado Trail
Napa 94558
Phone: 707 255-5862
Fax: 707 255-6385
Email: luna@hooked.net

Lyeth
650 Fifth St., Suite 403
San Francisco 94107
Phone: 415 979-0630
Fax: 415 979-0305

Lynmar
P.O. Box 742
Sebastopol 95473
Phone: 707 829-3374
Fax: 707 829-0902
Email: info@lynmarwinery.com
Web: www.lynmarwinery.com

MacRostie Wines
P.O. Box 340
Sonoma 95476
Phone: 707 996-4480
Fax: 707 996-3726
Email: macrostie@aol.com

Marcassin
P.O. Box 332
Calistoga 94515
Phone: 707 258-3608
Fax: 707 942-5633

Marietta Cellars
P.O. Box 1436
Healdsburg 95448
Phone: 707 433-2747
Fax: 707 857-4910

Mark West
7010 Trenton-Healdsburg Rd.
Forestville 95436
Phone: 707 836-9647
Fax: 707 836-0147
Email: markwest@sonic.net

Markham Vineyards
P.O. Box 636
St. Helena 94574
Phone: 707 963-5292
Fax: 707 963-4616
Web: www.markhamvineyards.com

Martinelli Vineyard
3360 River Rd.
Windsor 95492
Phone: 707 525-0570
Fax: 707 525-9463

Martini & Prati Wines
2191 Laguna Rd.
Santa Rosa 95401
Phone: 707 823-2404
Fax: 707 829-6151
Web: www.martini-prati.com

Louis M. Martini Winery
P.O. Box 112
St. Helena 94574
Phone: 707 963-2736
Fax: 707 963-8750
Web: www.louismartini.com

Mason
7830-40 St. Helena Hwy.
Oakville 94562
Phone: 707 944-9159
Fax: 707 944-9159
Web: www.napawineco.com

Matanzas Creek Winery
6097 Bennett Valley Rd.
Santa Rosa 95404
Phone: 707 528-6464
Fax: 707 571-0156
Email: matcrkwine@aol.com
Web: www.matanzascreek.com

Mayacamas Vineyards
1155 Lokoya Rd.
Napa 94558
Phone: 707 224-4030
Fax: 707 224-3979
Email: mayacama@napanet.net
Web: www.mayacamas.com

Mayo
9200 Sonoma Highway
Kenwood 95452
Phone: 707 833-3300
Fax: 707 833-2883
Email: jeffmayo@aol.com
Web: www.mayofamilywinery.com

Mazzocco Vineyards
P.O. Box 486
Healdsburg 95448
Phone: 707 433-9035
Fax: 707 431-2369
Email: vino@mazzocco.com
Web: www.mazzocco.com

Peter McCoy Vineyards
17050 Hwy. 128
Calistoga 94515
Phone: 415 461-6047
Fax: 415 461-8249

McCray Ridge
P.O. Box 1402
Healdsburg 95448
Phone: 707 433-2932
Fax: 707 433-3753
Email: simpson@mccrayridge.com

McDowell Valley Vineyards
P.O. Box 449
Hopland 95449
Phone: 707 744-1053
Fax: 707 744-1826
Email: mcdowell@
 mcdowellsyrah.com
Web: www.mcdowellsyrah.com

McIlroy Cellars
P.O. Box 1387
Forestville 95436
Phone: 707 576-1716
Fax: 707 576-1716

The Meeker Vineyard
5377 Dry Creek Rd.
Healdsburg 95448
Phone: 707 431-2148
Fax: 707 431-2549

Mendelson Vineyard
1226 Third St.
Napa 94559
Phone: 707 255-7825
Fax: 707 255-6876
Web: www.mendelsonvineyard
 .com

Mer Soleil
P.O. Box 35
Rutherford 94573
Phone: 831 675-7919
Fax: 707 963-5958

Meridian Vineyards
P.O. Box 3289
Paso Robles 93447
Phone: 805 237-6000
Fax: 805 239-5715
Web: www.meridianvineyards.com

Merryvale Vineyards
1000 Main St.
St. Helena 94574
Phone: 707 963-2225
Fax: 707 963-1949
Web: www.merryvale.com

Peter Michael Winery
12400 Ida Clayton Rd.
Calistoga 94515
Phone: 707 942-4459
Fax: 707 942-0209
Web: www.petermichael.com

Michel-Schlumberger
4155 Wine Creek Rd.
Healdsburg 95448
Phone: 707 433-7427
Fax: 707 433-0444
Email: winebench@aol.com
Web: www.michelschlumberger
 .com

Midnight Cellars
2867 Township Rd.
Paso Robles 93446
Phone: 805 239-8904
Fax: 805 237-0383
Email: midcellars@aol.com

Mietz Cellars
1345 West Dry Creek Rd.
Healdsburg 95448
Phone: 707 431-7671
Fax: 707 433-8578
Email: mietzwine@aol.com

Mill Creek Vineyards
P.O. Box 758
Healdsburg 95448
Phone: 707 431-2121
Fax: 707 431-1714
Email: brian@mcvonline.com
Web: www.mcvonline.com

Miner Family Vineyards
P.O. Box 367
Oakville 94562
Phone: 707 945-1260
Fax: 707 945-1280

Mirassou Vineyards
3000 Aborn Rd.
San Jose 95135
Phone: 408 274-4000
Fax: 408 270-5716
Email: email@mirassou.com
Web: www.mirassou.com

Charles B. Mitchell Vineyard
8221 Stoney Creek Rd.
Fairplay 95684
Phone: 530 620-3467
Fax: 530 620-1005
Email: cbmvwine@inform.net

Robert Mondavi Winery
P.O. Box 106
Oakville 94562
Phone: 707 226-1395
Fax: 707 251-4386
Email: info@robertmondavi.com
Web: www.robertmondavi.com

The Monterey Vineyard
1200 Jefferson St.
Napa 94559
Phone: 707 255-7667
Fax: 707 255-1119
Email: balzaccom@aol.com
Web: www.balzac.com

Monteviña Wines
P.O. Box 100
Plymouth 95669
Phone: 209 245-6942
Fax: 209 245-6617
Email: q&a@montevina.com
Web: www.montevina.com

Monticello Cellars
4242 Big Ranch Rd.
Napa 94558
Phone: 707 253-2802
Fax: 707 253-1019
Email: wine@monticellovineyards
  .com

Moraga
650 North Sepulveda Blvd.
Los Angeles 90049
Phone: 310 471-8560
Fax: 310 471-6435

Morgan Winery
590 Brunken Ave.
Salinas 93901
Phone: 831 751-7777
Fax: 831 751-7780
Email: mrgnwine@ix.netcom.com

Moshin Vineyards
P.O. Box 66176
Scotts Valley 95067
Phone: 831 438-0235
Fax: 831 438-0235
Email: moshin@cruzio.com
Web: www2.cruzio.com/~moshin

Mount Eden Vineyards
22020 Mt. Eden Rd.
Saratoga 95070
Phone: 408 867-5832
Fax: 408 867-4329
Email: wine@mounteden.com
Web: www.mounteden.com

Mount Veeder Winery
P.O. Box 407
Rutherford 94573
Phone: 707 963-7112
Fax: 707 963-7867
Web: www.franciscan.com

Robert Mueller Cellars
P.O. Box 1392
Healdsburg 95448
Phone: 707 431-1353
Fax: 707 431-8365
Email: rrpinot@muellerwine.com
Web: www.muellerwine.com

Mumm Cuvée Napa
P.O. Drawer 500
Rutherford 94573
Phone: 707 942-3400
Fax: 707 942-3469
Email: concierge@sparkling.com
Web: www.mumm.com

Murphy-Goode Estate Winery
P.O. Box 158
Geyserville 95441
Phone: 707 431-7644
Fax: 707 431-8640
Email: general@murphygoode
  winery.com

Andrew Murray Vineyards
P.O. Box 718
Los Olivos 93441
Phone: 805 686-9604
Fax: 805 686-9704

Murrieta's Well
5565 Tesla Rd.
Livermore 94550
Phone: 925 456-2390
Fax: 925 447-4837
Web: www.murrietaswell.com

Mystic Cliffs Wine Cellars
P.O. Box 780
Gonzales 93926
Phone: 831 675-8838
Fax: 831 675-2611

Nalle Winery
P.O. Box 454
Healdsburg 95448
Phone: 707 433-1040
Fax: 707 433-6062

Napa Ridge
P.O. Box 530
Geyserville 95441
Phone: 707 857-4459
Fax: 707 433-5174

Napa Wine Co.
7830-40 St. Helena Hwy.
Oakville 94562
Phone: 707 944-8669
Fax: 707 944-9749
Email: info@napawineco.com
Web: www.napawineco.com

Navarro Vineyards
P.O. Box 47
Philo 95466
Phone: 800 537-9463
Fax: 707 895-3647
Email: sales@navarrowine.com
Web: www.navarrowine.com

Newlan Vineyards & Winery
5225 Solano Ave.
Napa 94558
Phone: 707 257-2399
Fax: 707 252-6510
Email: napawine@wine.com
Web: www.wine.com/nvw

Newton Vineyard
2555 Madrona Ave.
St. Helena 94574
Phone: 707 963-9000
Fax: 707 963-5408

Neyers Vineyards
P.O. Box 1028
St. Helena 94574
Phone: 707 963-8840
Fax: 707 963-8894

Nichols Winery
8180 Manitoba St., #356
Playa Del Rey 90293
Phone: 310 305-0397
Fax: 310 305-0397

Niebaum-Coppola
P.O Box 208
Rutherford 94573
Phone: 707 968-1100
Fax: 707 963-9084
Web: www.niebaum-coppola.com

Oakford Vineyards
P.O. Box 410
Oakville 94562
Phone: 707 945-0445
Fax: 707 945-0140
Email: oakfordv@pacbell.net

Oakville Ranch Vineyards
P.O. Box 367
Oakville 94562
Phone: 707 944-9500
Fax: 707 945-1280

The Ojai Vineyard
P.O. Box 952
Oak View 93022
Phone: 805 649-1674
Fax: 805 649-4651

Optima Wine Cellars
P.O. Box 1691
Healdsburg 95448
Phone: 707 431-8222
Fax: 707 433-5844

Opus One
P.O. Box 106
Oakville 94562
Phone: 707 226-1395
Fax: 707 251-4386
Email: info@robertmondavi.com
Web: www.robertmondavi.com

Pahlmeyer
P.O. Box 2410
Napa 94558
Phone: 707 255-2321
Fax: 707 255-6786
Email: directsales@
 pahlmeyer.com
Web: www.pahlmeyer.com

Paloma Winery
4013 Spring Mountain Rd.
St. Helena 94574
Phone: 707 963-7504
Fax: 707 963-7504
Email: palomawine@aol.com

Paoletti Vineyards
11590 Sunset Blvd.
West Los Angeles 90049
Phone: 707 942-0689
Fax: 310 472-9688

Paradigm
P.O. Box 323
Oakville 94562
Phone: 707 944-1683
Fax: 707 944-9328
Email: info@paradigmwinery.com
Web: www.paradigmwinery.com

Paraiso Springs Vineyards
38060 Paraiso Springs Rd.
Soledad 93960
Phone: 831 678-0300
Fax: 831 678-2584
Email: psvwines@aol.com
Web: www.usawines.com/Paraiso

Parducci Wine Cellars
501 Parducci Rd.
Ukiah 95482
Phone: 707 463-5350
Fax: 707 462-7260
Web: www.parducci.com

Fess Parker
P.O. Box 908
Los Olivos 93441
Phone: 805 688-1545
Fax: 805 686-1130
Email: fparker@ibm.net
Web: www.fessparker.com

Patz & Hall Wine Co.
P.O. Box 518
Rutherford 94573
Phone: 707 963-4142
Fax: 707 963-9713
Email: mail@patzhall.com

Pavona
P.O. Box 5664
Monterey 93944
Phone: 831 646-1506
Fax: 831 649-8919

Peachy Canyon Winery
2025 Nacimiento Lake Dr.
Paso Robles 93446
Phone: 805 237-1577
Fax: 805 237-2248
Email: peachy@tcsn.net
Web: www.peachycanyon
  winery.com

Robert Pecota Winery
P.O. Box 303
Calistoga 94515
Phone: 707 942-6625
Fax: 707 942-6671
Email: rpecota@aol.com
Web: www.robertpecotawinery
  .com

Pedroncelli Winery
1220 Canyon Rd.
Geyserville 95441
Phone: 707 857-3531
Fax: 707 857-3812
Email: jpedwine@sonic.net
Web: www.pedroncelli.com

Peju Province Winery
P.O. Box 478
Rutherford 94573
Phone: 707 963-3600
Fax: 707 963-8680
Web: www.peju.com

Robert Pepi Winery
P.O. Box 328
Oakville 94562
Phone: 707 944-2807
Fax: 707 944-5628

Per Sempre
1112 Rahara Dr.
Lafayette 94549
Phone: 925 299-0976
Fax: 925 299-0671

Mario Perelli-Minetti
P.O. Box 1635
Burlingame 94011
Phone: 650 344-3721
Fax: 650 347-5706

Peterson Winery
P.O. Box 1374
Healdsburg 95448
Phone: 707 431-7568
Fax: 707 431-1112
Email: petersonwinery@juno.com

Pezzi King
3510 Unocal Place, Suite 208
Santa Rosa 95403
Phone: 707 569-1400
Fax: 707 569-1402
Web: www.pezziking.com

Joseph Phelps Vineyards
P.O. Box 1031
St. Helena 94574
Phone: 707 963-2745
Fax: 707 963-4831
Email: jpvwines@aol.com
Web: www.jpvwines.com

The R.H. Phillips Vineyard
26836 County Rd. 12 A
Esparto 95627
Phone: 530 662-3215
Fax: 530 662-2880
Email: rhp@rhphillips.com
Web: www.rhphillips.com

Phoenix Vineyards
3175 Dry Creek Rd.
Napa 94558
Phone: 707 252-8381
Fax: 707 255-1971
Email: phoenix@fcs.net
Web: www.members.tripod.com/
  ~Phoenixwine/

Pine Ridge Winery
5901 Silverado Trail
Napa 94558
Phone: 707 253-7500
Fax: 707 253-1493
Email: info@pineridgewine.com
Web: www.pineridgewinery.com

PlumpJack
620 Oakville Crossrd.
Napa 94558
Phone: 707 945-1220
Fax: 707 944-0744
Email: plumpjck@napanet.net

Porter Creek Vineyards
8735 Westside Rd.
Healdsburg 95448
Phone: 707 433-6321
Fax: 707 433-4245
Email: dijon1@sonic.net

Preston Vineyards
9282 West Dry Creek Rd.
Healdsburg 95448
Phone: 707 433-3372
Fax: 707 433-5307
Email: mail@prestonvineyards
  .com
Web: www.prestonvineyards.com

Pride Mountain Vineyards
4026 Spring Mountain Rd.
St. Helena 94574
Phone: 707 963-4949
Fax: 707 963-4848
Web: www.pridewines.com

Quady Winery
P.O. Box 728
Madera 93639
Phone: 559 673-8068
Fax: 559 673-0744
Email: quadywinery@
  lightspeed.net
Web: www.quadywinery.com

Quatro
P.O. Box 1607
Sonoma   95476
Phone: 707 996-8463
Fax: 707 996-0424

Quintessa
P.O. Box 407
Rutherford   94573
Phone: 707 963-7112
Fax: 707 963-7867
Email: winemaker@franciscan
  .com
Web: www.franciscan.com

Quivira Vineyards
4900 W. Dry Creek Rd.
Healdsburg   95448
Phone: 707 431-8333
Fax: 707 431-1664
Email: quivira@quivirawine.com
Web: www.quivirawine.com

Qupé
P.O. Box 440
Los Olivos   93441
Phone: 805 688-2477
Fax: 805 686-4470

Rabbit Ridge Vineyards
3291 Westside Rd.
Healdsburg   95448
Phone: 707 431-7128
Fax: 707 431-8018

A. Rafanelli Winery
4685 West Dry Creek Rd.
Healdsburg   95448
Phone: 707 433-1385
Fax: 707 433-3836

Ramey Wine Cellars
1784 Warm Springs Rd.
Glen Ellen   95442
Fax: 707 833-5620

Rancho Sisquoc Winery
6600 Foxen Canyon Rd.
Santa Maria   93454
Phone: 805 934-4332
Fax: 805 937-6601
Email: sisquoc@fix.net
Web: www.ranchosisquoc.com

Random Ridge
P.O. Box 691
Glen Ellen   95442
Phone: 707 938-9085
Fax: 707 576-0175
Email: info@randomridge.com
Web: www.randomridge.com

Kent Rasmussen Winery
1001 Silverado Trail
St. Helena   94574
Phone: 707 963-5667
Fax: 707 963-5664
Email: krwine@aol.com

Ravenswood
18701 Gehricke Rd.
Sonoma   95476
Phone: 888 669-4679
Fax: 707 938-9459
Email: rwwine@ravenswood-
  wine.com
Web: www.ravenswood-wine.com

Martin Ray
9060 Graton Rd.
Graton   95444
Phone: 707 824-2585
Fax: 707 824-2592

Raymond Vineyard & Cellar
849 Zinfandel Lane
St. Helena   94574
Phone: 800 525-2659
Fax: 707 963-8498
Email: director@raymondwine
  .com
Web: www.raymondwine.com

Renaissance Vineyard & Winery
P.O. Box 1000
Oregon House   95962
Phone: 800 655-3277
Fax: 530 692-2497
Web: www.renaissancewinery.com

Renwood Winery
12225 Steiner Rd.
Plymouth   95669
Phone: 209 245-6979
Fax: 209 245-3732
Email: ljm@renwood.com
Web: www.renwood.com

Reverie Winery
1520 Diamond Mtn. Rd.
Calistoga   94515
Phone: 707 942-6800
Fax: 707 942-6803
Email: reverie@sonic.net
Web: www.sonic.net/~reverie

Richardson Vineyards
2711 Knob Hill Rd.
Sonoma   95476
Phone: 707 938-2610

Ridge Vineyards
P.O. Box 1810
Cupertino   95015
Phone: 408 867-3233
Fax: 408 868-1350
Web: www.ridgewine.com

Rio Seco Vineyard
8375 San Marcos Rd.
Atascadero   93422
Phone: 805 460-9463
Fax: 805 460-9463
Email: rioseco@thegrid.net

Ristow
5040 Silverado Trail
Napa   94558
Phone: 877 747-8693
Fax: 415 674-4987
Email: email@ristowestate.com
Web: www.ristowestate.com

J. Rochioli Vineyards
6192 Westside Rd.
Healdsburg   95448
Phone: 707 433-2305
Fax: 707 433-2358

Rocking Horse
P.O. Box 5868
Napa   94581
Phone: 707 226-5555
Fax: 707 255-1506

Rockland Road Cellars
1291 Rockland Dr.
St. Helena   94574
Phone: 707 963-7439
Fax: 707 942-0248
Email: rockland@webtv.net

Roederer Estate
P.O. Box 67
Philo   95466
Phone: 707 895-2288
Fax: 707 895-2120
Email: info@roedererestate.net
Web: www.avwines.com

Rombauer Vineyards
3522 Silverado Trail
St. Helena   94574
Phone: 707 963-5170
Fax: 707 963-5752
Web: www.rombauervineyards
.com

Rosenblum Cellars
2900 Main St.
Alameda   94501
Phone: 510 865-7007
Fax: 510 865-9225
Email: drzin@rosenblumcellars
.com
Web: www.rosenblumcellars.com

Rosenthal—The Malibu Estate
100 Wilshire Blvd.
Santa Monica   90401
Phone: 310 899-8900
Fax: 310 899-8910

Stephen Ross
2330 Johnson Ave.
San Luis Obispo   93401
Phone: 805 594-1318
Fax: 805 594-0178
Email: sdooley@aol.com

Round Hill Vineyards
1680 Silverado Trail
St. Helena   94574
Phone: 707 963-5251
Fax: 707 963-0834

Rubissow-Sargent
2413 4th St.
Berkeley   94710
Phone: 510 841-9463
Fax: 510 848-7792

Rudd Estate
P.O. Box 105
Oakville   94562
Phone: 707 944-8577
Fax: 707 944-2823

Rutherford Hill Winery
P.O Box 427
Rutherford   94573
Phone: 707 963-1871
Fax: 707 963-1878
Email: info@rutherhill.com
Web: www.rutherfordhill.com

Rutz Cellars
540 9th St.
San Francisco   94103
Phone: 415 252-0215
Fax: 415 252-0293

Saddleback Cellars
P.O. Box 141
Oakville   94562
Phone: 707 944-1305
Fax: 707 944-1325
Web: www.saddlebackcellars.com

St. Clement Vineyards
2867 St. Helena Hwy.
St. Helena   94574
Phone: 800 331-8266
Fax: 707 963-1412
Email: info@stclement.com
Web: www.stclement.com

St. Francis Winery
8450 Sonoma Hwy.
Kenwood   95452
Phone: 707 833-4666
Fax: 707 833-6534
Email: stfranciswine@msn.com
Web: www.stfranciswine.com

St. Supéry Vineyard & Winery
P.O. Box 38
Rutherford   94573
Phone: 707 963-4507
Fax: 707 963-4526
Email: divinecab@stsupery.com
Web: www.stsupery.com

Saintsbury
1500 Los Carneros Ave.
Napa   94559
Phone: 707 252-0592
Fax: 707 252-0595

Salvestrin Wine Co.
397 Main St.
St. Helena   94574
Phone: 707 963-5105
Fax: 707 963-5105

Sanford Winery
7250 Santa Rosa Rd.
Buelton   93427
Phone: 805 688-3300
Fax: 805 688-7381

Santa Barbara Winery
202 Anacapa St.
Santa Barbara   93101
Phone: 805 963-3633
Fax: 805 962-4981
Email: wine@sbwinery.com
Web: www.sbwinery.com

Santa Cruz Mountain Vineyard
2300 Jarvis Rd.
Santa Cruz   95065
Phone: 831 426-6209
Fax: 831 426-6209
Web: www.webwinery.com

Sapphire Hill Vineyard
150 Old Vine Lane
Windsor   95492
Phone: 707 838-3245
Fax: 707 838-3245
Web: www.sapphirehill.com

V. Sattui Winery
1111 White Lane
St. Helena   94574
Phone: 707 963-7774
Fax: 707 963-4324
Web: www.vsattui.com

Saucelito Canyon Vineyard
3180 Biddle Ranch Rd.
San Luis Obispo   93401
Phone: 805 489-8762
Fax: 805 534-2111
Email: saucelitocanyon@thegrid.net

Sausal Winery
7370 Hwy. 128
Healdsburg   95448
Phone: 707 433-2285
Fax: 707 433-5136
Email: zinfanz@metro.net
Web: www.sausalwinery.com

Scharffenberger
P.O. Box 365
Philo   95466
Phone: 800 824-7754
Fax: 707 895-2758
Web: www.pacific-echo.com

Scheid
1972 Hobson Ave.
Greenfield   93927
Phone: 831 385-4801
Fax: 831 385-0136

F. Scherrer Vineyard
966 Tiller Lane
Sebastopol   95472
Phone: 707 823-8980
Fax: 707 823-8980

Schramsberg Vineyards
1400 Schramsberg Rd.
Calistoga   94515
Phone: 707 942-4558
Fax: 707 942-5943
Email: schramsbrg@aol.com
Web: www.schramsberg.com

Schug Carneros Estate Winery
602 Bonneau Rd.
Sonoma   95476
Phone: 800 966-9365
Fax: 707 939-9364
Email: schug@schugwinery.com
Web: www.schugwinery.com

Screaming Eagle
P.O. Box 134
Oakville   94562
Phone: 707 944-0749
Fax: 707 944-9271

Sean H. Thackrey & Co.
P.O. Box 58
Bolinas   94924
Phone: 415 868-1781
Fax: 415 868-9290

Seavey Vineyard
1310 Conn Valley Rd.
St. Helena   94574
Phone: 707 963-8339
Fax: 707 963-0232
Email: seaveyvineyard@msn.com

Sebastiani Sonoma Cask Cellars
P.O. Box AA
Sonoma   95476
Phone: 800 888-5532
Fax: 707 933-3370
Web: www.sebastiani.com

Sebastopol Vineyards
8757 Green Valley Rd.
Sebastopol   95472
Phone: 707 829-9463
Fax: 707 829-5368
Email: info@sebastopolvineyards
.com
Web: www.sebastopolvineyards
.com

Seghesio Winery
14730 Grove St.
Healdsburg   95448
Phone: 707 433-3579
Fax: 707 433-0545
Email: seghesio@seghesio.com
Web: www.seghesio.com

Selby Winery
5 Fitch St.
Healdsburg 95448
Phone: 707 431-1703
Fax: 707 431-0439
Web: www.selbywinery.com

Selene Wines
P.O. Box 3131
Napa 94558
Phone: 707 258-8119
Fax: 707 258-8132
Web: www.selenewines.com

Sequoia Grove Vineyards
8338 St. Helena Highway
Napa 94558
Phone: 707 944-2945
Fax: 707 963-9411
Email: info@sequoiagrove.com
Web: www.sequoiagrove.com

Seven Peaks
60 Garden Court, Suite 220
Monterey 93940
Phone: 831 655-4848
Fax: 831 655-0904
Web: www.7peaks.com

Shafer Vineyards
6154 Silverado Trail
Napa 94558
Phone: 707 944-2877
Fax: 707 944-9454
Email: shafer@shafervineyards
  .com
Web: www.shafervineyards.com

Shenandoah Vineyards
12300 Steiner Rd.
Plymouth 95669
Phone: 209 245-4455
Fax: 209 245-5156
Email: info@sobonwine.com
Web: www.sobonwine.com

Siduri Cellars
980 Airway Ct., Suite C
Santa Rosa 95403
Phone: 707 578-3882
Fax: 707 578-3884
Email: pinot@siduri.com
Web: www.siduri.com

Sierra Vista Winery
4560 Cabernet Way
Placerville 95667
Phone: 530 622-7221
Fax: 530 622-2413
Email: syrah@innercite.com
Web: www.sierravistawinery.com

Signorello Vineyards
4500 Silverado Trail
Napa 94558
Phone: 707 255-5990
Fax: 707 255-5999
Email: resig@aol.com
Web: www.signorellovineyards
  .com

Silver Oak Cellars
P.O. Box 414
Oakville 94562
Phone: 707 944-8808
Fax: 707 944-2817
Web: www.silveroak.com

Silverado Vineyards
6121 Silverado Trail
Napa 94558
Phone: 707 257-1770
Fax: 707 257-1538
Web: www.silveradovineyards.com

Simi Winery
16275 Healdsburg Ave.
Healdsburg 95448
Phone: 707 433-6981
Fax: 707 433-6253
Email: simiwine@simiwinery.com
Web: www.simiwinery.com

Sine Qua Non
918 El Toro Rd.
Ojai 93023
Phone: 805 640-0997
Fax: 805 640-1230

Robert Sinskey Vineyards
6320 Silverado Trail
Napa 94558
Phone: 707 944-9090
Fax: 707 944-9092
Web: www.robertsinskey.com

Skewis Wines
16109A Healdsburg Ave.
Healdsburg 95448
Phone: 707 431-2160
Fax: 707 431-2160

Smith & Hook
Drawer C
Soledad 93960
Phone: 831 678-2132
Fax: 831 678-2005
Web: www.hahnestates.com

W.H. Smith Wines
1102 Las Posadas Rd.
Angwin 94508
Phone: 707 965-3020
Fax: 707 965-0324
Email: lajota@scs.net

Snowden
P.O. Box 84
St. Helena 94574
Phone: 707 963-4292
Fax: 707 963-9534

Sobon Estate
12300 Steiner Rd.
Plymouth 95669
Phone: 209 245-4455
Fax: 209 245-5156
Email: info@sobonwine.com
Web: www.sobonwine.com

Sonoma-Cutrer Vineyards
4401 Slusser Rd.
Windsor 95492
Phone: 707 528-1181
Fax: 707 528-1561
Email: info@sonomacutrer.com
Web: www.sonomacutrer.com

Sonoma-Loeb
50 Broad St., Suite 1137
New York 10004
Phone: 800 989-2440
Fax: 212 509-0255
Web: www.sonoma-loeb.com

Soquel Vineyards
P.O. Box 1555
Soquel 95073
Phone: 831 462-9045
Fax: 831 429-8680

Spenker Winery
17303 North DeVries Rd.
Lodi 95242
Phone: 209 367-0467
Fax: 209 368-5746

Spottswoode Vineyard & Winery
1902 Madrona Ave.
St. Helena 94574
Phone: 707 963-0134
Fax: 707 963-2886
Email: spottswde@aol.com
Web: www.spottswoode.com

Spring Mountain
P.O. Box 991
St. Helena 94574
Phone: 707 967-4188
Fax: 707 963-2753

Staglin Family Vineyard
P.O. Box 680
Rutherford 94573
Phone: 707 963-1749
Fax: 707 963-8784
Email: info@staglinfamily.com
Web: www.staglinfamily.com

Stag's Leap Wine Cellars
5766 Silverado Trail
Napa 94558
Phone: 707 944-2020
Fax: 707 257-7501

Stags' Leap Winery
6150 Silverado Trail
Napa 94558
Phone: 800 640-LEAP
Fax: 707 944-9433
Web: www.stagsleapwinery.com

Steele Wines
P.O. Box 190
Kelseyville 95451
Phone: 707 279-9475
Fax: 707 279-9633

Steltzner Vineyards
5998 Silverado Trail
Napa 94558
Phone: 707 252-7272
Fax: 707 252-2079
Email: wine@steltzner.com
Web: www.steltzner.com

Sterling Vineyards
1111 Dunaweal Lane
Calistoga 94515
Phone: 707 942-3300
Fax: 707 942-3469
Web: www.sterlingvineyards.com

Stevenot Winery
2690 San Domingo Rd.
Murphys 95247
Phone: 209 728-3436
Fax: 209 728-3710
Web: www.stevenotwinery.com

Stonegate Winery
1183 Dunaweal Lane
Calistoga 94515
Phone: 707 942-6500
Fax: 707 942-9721

Stonestreet
4611 Thomas Rd.
Healdsburg 95448
Phone: 707 433-9000
Fax: 707 433-9469

Stony Hill Vineyard
P.O. Box 308
St. Helena 94574
Phone: 707 963-2636
Fax: 707 963-1831
Email: stony-hill-
vineyard@worldnet.att.net

Storybook Mountain Vineyards
3835 Hwy. 128
Calistoga 94515
Phone: 707 942-5310
Fax: 707 942-5334
Email: sigstory@aol.com
Web: www.storybookwines.com

Rodney Strong Vineyards
P.O. Box 368
Windsor 95492
Phone: 707 433-6521
Fax: 707 433-0939
Email: info@rodneystrong.com
Web: www.rodneystrong.com

Stuhlmuller Vineyards
World Trade Center, Suite #222
San Francisco 94111
Phone: 415 291-0766
Fax: 415 291-9280
Email: stuhlie@earthlink.net

Sullivan Vineyards Winery
P.O. Box G
Rutherford 94573
Phone: 707 963-9646
Fax: 707 963-0377
Email: info@sullivanwine.com
Web: www.sullivanwine.com

Summers
P.O. Box 496
Calistoga 94515
Phone: 707 942-5508
Fax: 707 942-4039
Email: sumranch@aol.com
Web: www.sumwines.com

Sunstone Vineyards & Winery
P.O. Box 1747
Santa Ynez 93460
Phone: 805 688-9463
Fax: 805 688-8133
Web: www.sunstonewinery.com

Sutter Home Winery
P.O. Box 248
St. Helena 94574
Phone: 707 963-3104
Fax: 707 963-2381
Email: info@sutterhome.com
Web: www.sutterhome.com

Joseph Swan Vineyards
2916 Laguna Rd.
Forestville 95436
Phone: 707 573-3747
Fax: 707 575-1605
Email: swanwinery@compuserve
  .com

Swanson Vineyards
P.O. Box 459
Rutherford 94573
Phone: 707 944-0905
Fax: 707 944-0955
Email: swansonmlu@aol.com

Tablas Creek
9339 Adeladia Rd.
Paso Robles 93446
Phone: 805 237-1231
Fax: 805 237-1314
Email: tablascreek@tcsn.net
Web: www.vineyardbrands.com

Taft St. Winery
2030 Barlow Lane
Sebastopol 95472
Phone: 707 823-2049
Fax: 707 823-8622
Email: taftst@sonic.net

Robert Talbott Vineyards
P.O. Box 776
Gonzales 93926
Phone: 831 675-3000
Fax: 831 675-3120
Email: rtvino@rtvino.com

Talley Vineyards
3031 Lopez Dr.
Arroyo Grande 93420
Phone: 805 489-0446
Fax: 805 489-0996
Email: tvynds@aol.com
Web: www.talleyvineyards.com

Iván Tamás Cellars
5443 Tesla Rd.
Livermore 94550
Phone: 925 456-2380
Fax: 925 456-2381
Web: www.ivantamas.com

Lane Tanner Winery
P.O. Box 286
Santa Maria 93456
Phone: 805 929-1826
Fax: 805 929-1826
Web: www.sbwines.com

The Terraces
P.O. Box 511
Rutherford 94573
Phone: 707 963-1707

Tessera
P.O. Drawer 500
Rutherford 94573
Phone: 707 942-3787
Fax: 707 942-3469
Web: www.tesserawines.com

Testarossa Vineyard
300 College Ave.
Los Gatos 95030
Phone: 408 354-6150
Fax: 408 354-8250
Email: wine@testarossa.com
Web: www.testarossa.com

Thornton
P.O. Box 9008
Temecula 92589
Phone: 909 699-0099
Fax: 909 699-5536
Email: gr8wine@ix.netcom.com
Web: www.wines.com/thornton

Thunder Mountain
P.O. Box 3969
Santa Cruz 95063
Phone: 831 439-8716
Fax: 831 439-9710
Email: tm@winemaker.com
Web: www.winemaker.com

Titus
3264 Ehlers Lane
St. Helena 94574
Phone: 707 963-3235
Fax: 707 963-3257
Email: titer@napanet.net

Philip Togni Vineyard
P.O. Box 81
St. Helena 94574
Phone: 707 963-3731
Fax: 707 963-9186

**Topolos at Russian River
  Vineyards**
5700 Gravenstein Hwy. North
Forestville 95436
Phone: 800 867-6567
Fax: 707 887-1399
Email: topolos@topolos.com
Web: www.topolos.com

Marimar Torres Estate
11400 Graton Rd.
Sebastopol 95472
Phone: 707 823-4365
Fax: 707 823-4496

Treana Winery
P.O. Box 3260
Paso Robles 93447
Phone: 805 238-6979
Fax: 805 238-4063

Trefethen Vineyards
P.O. Box 2460
Napa 94558
Phone: 707 255-7700
Fax: 707 255-0793
Email: winery@trefethen.com
Web: www.trefethen.com

Trentadue
19170 Geyserville Ave.
Geyserville 95441
Phone: 707 433-3104
Fax: 707 433-5825
Email: info@trentadue.com
Web: www.trentadue.com

Tria
P.O. Box 10787
Napa 94581
Phone: 707 253-2292
Email: triawine@aol.com

M. Trinchero
100 St. Helena Hwy. South
St. Helena 94574
Phone: 707 963-3104
Fax: 707 963-2381
Web: www.mtrinchero.com

Truchard Vineyard
3234 Old Sonoma Rd.
Napa 94559
Phone: 707 253-7153
Fax: 707 253-7234

Tudal Winery
1015 Big Tree Rd.
St. Helena 94574
Phone: 707 963-3947
Fax: 707 963-9288

Tulocay Winery
1426 Coombsville Rd.
Napa 94558
Phone: 707 255-4064
Fax: 707 255-4064
Email: tulocay@aol.com

Turley Wine Cellars
3358 St. Helena Hwy.
St. Helena 94574
Phone: 707 963-0940
Fax: 707 963-8683
Web: www.turleywinecellars.com

Turnbull Wine Cellars
P.O. Box 29
Oakville 94562
Phone: 707 963-5839
Fax: 707 963-4407
Email: turnbull@humbolt1.com
Web: www.humbolt1.com/
  ~turnbull

Unalii
660 Staton
St. Helena 94574
Phone: 707 524-9375
Fax: 707 963-9620
Email: tsalinger@aol.com

Valley of the Moon Winery
P.O. Box 1951
Glen Ellen 95442
Phone: 707 996-6941
Fax: 707 996-5809
Email: luna@vomwinery.com
Web: www.valleyofthemoonwinery
  .com

Van Asperen
1680 Silverado Trail
St. Helena 94574
Phone: 707 963-9503
Fax: 707 963-0834
Email: wineclub@napanet.net

Ventana Vineyards
2999 Monterey/Salinas Hwy.
Monterey   93940
Phone: 831 372-7415
Fax: 831 655-1855
Email: ventanawines@
redshift.com
Web: www.ventana.wines.com

Viader Vineyards & Winery
P.O. Box 280
Deer Park   94576
Phone: 707 963-3816
Fax: 707 963-3817
Web: www.viader.com

Conrad Viano Winery
150 Morello Ave.
Martinez   94553
Phone: 925 228-6465
Fax: 925 228-0288

Viansa Winery
25200 Arnold Dr.
Sonoma   95476
Phone: 707 935-4700
Fax: 707 996-4632
Web: www.viansa.com

Vigil Vineyard
3340 Highway 128
Calistoga   94515
Phone: 707 942-2900
Fax: 707 942-2902
Email: vigilwine@aol.com

Villa Mt. Eden
8711 Silverado Trail
St. Helena   94574
Phone: 707 963-9100
Fax: 707 963-7840

Vine Cliff Cellars
7400 Silverado Trail
Napa   94558
Phone: 707 944-1364
Fax: 707 944-1252
Email: vineclif@pacbell.net
Web: www.vineycliff.com

Vineyard 29
1210 Rockland Rd.
St. Helena   94574
Phone: 707 963-0808
Fax: 707 963-5271

Vino Noceto
11011 Shenandoah Rd.
Plymouth   95669
Phone: 209 245-6556
Fax: 209 245-3446
Email: vinnoce@cdepot.net

von Strasser
1510 Diamond Mountain Rd.
Calistoga   94515
Phone: 707 942-0930
Fax: 707 942-0454
Email: winemaker@vonstrasser
.com
Web: www.vonstrasser.com

Voss Vineyards
1862 El Centro Ave.
Napa   94558
Phone: 707 259-0993
Fax: 707 259-1510
Email: negusa@negociants.com

Wattle Creek Winery
25510 River Rd.
Cloverdale   95425
Phone: 707 894-5166
Fax: 707 894-2982

Wellington Vineyards
P.O. Box 568
Glen Ellen   95442
Phone: 707 939-0708
Fax: 707 939-0378
Email: wv@wellingtonvineyards
.com
Web: www.wellingtonvineyards
.com

Wente Vineyards
5565 Tesla Rd.
Livermore   94550
Phone: 925 456-2300
Fax: 925 456-2301
Web: www.wentevineyards.com

William Wheeler Winery
650 Fifth St., Suite 403
San Francisco   94107
Phone: 415 979-0630
Fax: 415 979-0305
Web: www.boissetusa.com

Whitcraft Winery
1637 Shoreline Dr.
Santa Barbara   93109
Phone: 805 965-0956
Fax: 805 962-5655

White Cottage
1217 Edwards St.
St. Helena   94574
Phone: 707 965-0516
Fax: 707 967-0262
Email: wineinfo@whitecottage
ranch.com

White Oak Vineyards & Winery
7505 Hwy. 128
Healdsburg   95448
Phone: 707 433-8429
Fax: 707 433-8446
Web: www.whiteoakwines.com

White Rock Vineyards
1115 Loma Vista Dr.
Napa   94558
Phone: 707 257-7922
Fax: 707 257-7922

Whitehall Lane Winery
1563 St. Helena Hwy.
St. Helena   94574
Phone: 707 963-9454
Fax: 707 963-7035
Email: whthal@aol.com

Wild Horse Winery & Vineyards
P.O. Box 910
Templeton   93465
Phone: 805 434-2541
Fax: 805 434-3516
Email: mrviognier@aol.com
Web: www.wildhorsewinery.com

Wildhurst Vineyards
P.O. Box 1223
Kelseyville   95451
Phone: 800 595-9463
Fax: 707 279-4875
Email: info@wildhurst.com
Web: www.wildhurst.com

Williams Selyem Winery
6575 Westside Rd.
Healdsburg   95448
Phone: 707 433-6425
Fax: 707 433-6546

Windward Vineyard
1380 Live Oak Rd.
Paso Robles   93446
Phone: 805 239-2565
Fax: 805 239-4005
Web: www.windwardvineyard.com

Woodbridge
P.O. Box 106
Oakville   94562
Phone: 707 226-1395
Fax: 707 251-4386
Email: info@robertmondavi.com
Web: www.robertmondavi.com

Zabaco
3387 Dry Creek Rd.
Healdsburg   95448
Phone: 707 431-5606
Fax: 707 431-5607

Zaca Mesa Winery
P.O. Box 899
Los Olivos   93441
Phone: 805 688-9339
Fax: 805 688-8796
Email: zacamesa@zacamesa.com
Web: www.zacamesa.com

ZD Wines
8383 Silverado Trail
Napa   94558
Phone: 707 963-5188
Fax: 707 963-2640
Email: info@zdwines.com
Web: www.zdwines.com

Zoom Vineyards
2900 Main St.
Alameda   94501
Phone: 510 769-6367
Fax: 510 865-9225

APPENDIX 2
WINERY STAR RATINGS

❖

5-STAR WINERIES (★★★★★)

Abreu Vineyards
Araujo Estate Wines
Arrowood Vineyards & Winery
Bryant Family Vineyard
Caymus Vineyards
Colgin
Robert Craig
Dalla Valle Vineyards
Diamond Creek Vineyards
Dominus Estate
Dunn Vineyards
Etude Wines
Forman Vineyard
Grace Family Vineyards
Harlan Estate
Kistler Vineyards
Kongsgaard Wines
Marcassin
Mer Soleil
Peter Michael Winery
Opus One
Pahlmeyer
Ramey Wine Cellars
Screaming Eagle
Robert Talbott Vineyards

4 TO 5-STAR WINERIES (★★★★−★★★★★)

Dehlinger Winery
Far Niente Winery
Landmark Vineyards
Lewis Cellars
Matanzas Creek Winery
Roederer Estate
Philip Togni Vineyard
Truchard Vineyard
Turley Wine Cellars
Williams Selyem Winery

4-STAR WINERIES (★★★★)

Altamura Vineyards & Winery
S. Anderson Vineyard
Anderson's Conn Valley Vineyards
Arns
Au Bon Climat
Barbour Vineyards
Beaulieu Vineyard
Bernardus Winery
Robert Biale Vineyards
Byington Winery
Byron Vineyards & Winery
Calera Wine Co.
Cardinale
Chalk Hill Winery
David Coffaro Vineyard & Winery

Constant
Cornerstone Cellars
David Arthur Vineyards
Del Dotto
Tom Eddy
El Molino Winery
Fife Vineyards
Flowers
Groth Vineyards & Winery
Hartwell Vineyards
Howell Mountain Vineyards
Limerick Lane Cellars
Livingston Vineyards
Mendelson Vineyard
Miner Family Vineyards
Moraga
Robert Mueller Cellars
Paradigm
Quintessa
A. Rafanelli Winery
Reverie Winery
Rudd Estate
Saucelito Canyon Vineyard
Silver Oak Cellars
Snowden
Sonoma-Loeb
Stony Hill Vineyard
Swanson Vineyards
The Terraces
Viader Vineyards & Winery
White Cottage

576

3 TO 5-STAR WINERIES (★★★−★★★★★)

Beringer Vineyards
Chalone Vineyard
Chateau St. Jean
Gary Farrell Wines
Ferrari-Carano Winery
Flora Springs Wine Co.
Gallo of Sonoma Winery
Grgich Hills Cellar
Hanzell Vineyards
Lokoya
Long Vineyards
Martinelli Vineyard
Robert Mondavi Winery
Mount Eden Vineyards
Patz & Hall Wine Co.
Joseph Phelps Vineyards
Pine Ridge Winery
Pride Mountain Vineyards
Ridge Vineyards
J. Rochioli Vineyards
St. Clement Vineyards
St. Francis Winery
Saintsbury
Sanford Winery
Seavey Vineyard
Shafer Vineyards
Signorello Vineyards
Silverado Vineyards
Spottswoode Vineyard & Winery
Stag's Leap Wine Cellars
Steele Wines
Talley Vineyards
Vine Cliff Cellars

3 TO 4-STAR WINERIES (★★★−★★★★)

Acacia Winery
Behrens & Hitchcock
David Bruce Winery
Chateau Potelle
Chateau Souverain
Cuvaison
Duckhorn Vineyards
Gloria Ferrer Champagne Caves
Franciscan Oakville Estate
Greenwood Ridge Vineyards
Harrison Winery & Vineyards
The Hess Collection Winery
Paul Hobbs
Laurel Glen Vineyard
Littorai
MacRostie Wines
Markham Vineyards
Meridian Vineyards
Morgan Winery
Murphy-Goode Estate Winery
Newton Vineyard
Neyers Vineyards
Nichols Winery
Niebaum-Coppola Estate Winery
Oakford Vineyards
Oakville Ranch Vineyards
Qupé Vineyards
Martin Ray
Ristow
Rockland Road Cellars
Saddleback Cellars
Santa Cruz Mountain Vineyard
Schramsberg Vineyards
Sean H. Thackrey & Co.
Seavey Vineyard
Selene Wines

Simi Winery
Staglin Family Vineyard
Stonestreet
Testarossa Vineyard
Marimar Torres Estate
von Strasser
Whitehall Lane Winery

3-STAR WINERIES (★★★)

Alban Vineyards
Alderbrook Vineyards & Winery
Ancien Wines
Arbios
Arcadian
Azalea Springs Cellars
Babcock Vineyards
Bacio Divino
Bannister
Barnett Vineyards
Beckmen Vineyards
Benessere
Benziger Family Winery
Bonny Doon Vineyard
August Briggs
Brophy Clark Cellars
Buehler Vineyards
Burgess Cellars
Cafaro Cellars
Cain Vineyard & Winery
Cakebread Cellars
Oliver Caldwell Cellars
Cambria Winery & Vineyard
Canepa Cellars
Carmenet Winery
Castalia
Chauffe-Eau Cellars
Chimney Rock Winery

Cinnabar Vineyards

Clark-Claudon Vineyards

Clos LaChance

Codorniu Napa

Collier Falls

Corison Wines

Cosentino Winery

H. Coturri & Sons Ltd.

Cronin Vineyards

Dashe Cellars

Delectus

Di Bruno

Domaine Carneros

Domaine Chandon

Domaine de la Terre Rouge

Dry Creek Vineyard

Eberle Winery

Edmeades Vineyards

Edmunds St. John

Edna Valley Vineyard

Merry Edwards

Volker Eisele

Elan

Elyse Wines

Ficklin Vineyards

Firestone Vineyard

Fisher Vineyards

Thomas Fogarty Winery

Foley Estate

Foxen Vineyard

Peter Franus Wine Co.

Frazier

J. Fritz

Frog's Leap

The Gainey Vineyard

Galante Vineyards

Garretson Wine Co.

Daniel Gehrs Wines

Geyser Peak Winery

Green & Red Vineyard

Gregory Graham

Hamel Wines

Hartford Court Winery

Havens Wine Cellars

Hendry Ranch

Hidden Cellars Winery

Hitching Post

Robert Hunter Winery

Iron Horse Vineyards

Jaffurs

Jarvis

JC Cellars

Jepson Vineyards

Jordan Vineyard & Winery

Judd's Hill

Justin Vineyards & Winery

Karl Lawrence

Kristone Champagne Cellars

Kunde Estate Winery

Kynsi

La Crema

La Sirena Wines

Laetitia Vineyard & Winery

Lail Vineyards

Lambert Bridge Winery

Lamborn Family Vineyards

Lang & Reed Wine Co.

Le Ducq

Ledson Winery & Vineyard

Lewelling Vineyards

LinCourt Vineyards

Liparita Cellars

Lockwood Vineyard

Lolonis

Lonetree

Richard Longoria Wines

Lorenza-Lake

Luna Vineyards

Lynmar

Mason

Mayacamas Vineyards

McCray Ridge

McDowell Valley Vineyards

The Meeker Vineyard

Meridian Vineyards

Mount Veeder Winery

Mumm Cuvée Napa

Andrew Murray Vineyards

Nalle Winery

Napa Wine Co.

Navarro Vineyards

The Ojai Vineyard

Optima Wine Cellars

Paloma Winery

Paoletti Vineyards

Fess Parker

Peachy Canyon Winery

Robert Pecota Winery

Mario Perelli-Minetti

Pezzi King

PlumpJack

Quady Winery

Kent Rasmussen Winery

Rocking Horse

Rombauer Vineyards

Rosenblum Cellars

Rosenthal—The Malibu Estate

Steven Ross

Rubissow-Sargent

Rutherford Hill Winery

Sapphire Hill Vineyard

V. Sattui Winery

Sausal Winery

Scharffenberger

F. Scherrer Vineyard

Sebastiani Sonoma Cask Cellars

Sebastopol Vineyards

Selby Winery

Sequoia Grove Vineyards

Siduri Cellars

Sine Qua Non
Sonoma-Cutrer Vineyards
Spring Mountain
Storybook Mountain Vineyards
Stuhlmuller Vineyards
Joseph Swan Vineyards
Lane Tanner Winery
Treana Winery
M. Trinchero
Turnbull Wine Cellars
Unalii
Van Asperen
Vineyard 29
Voss Vineyards
Whitcraft Winery
White Rock Vineyards
Zaca Mesa Winery

2 TO 5-STAR WINERIES (★★—★★★★★)

Chateau Montelena Winery
Guenoc Winery
Heitz Wine Cellars
Kenwood Vineyards
Merryvale Vineyards

2 TO 4-STAR WINERIES (★★—★★★★)

Clos du Bois
Clos Du Val Wine Co.
B. R. Cohn
Conn Creek Winery
De Loach Vineyards
Estancia Estates
Freemark Abbey Winery
J Wine Co.
Kendall-Jackson Winery
Kathryn Kennedy Winery
Mirassou Vineyards
Peju Province Winery
Rabbit Ridge Vineyards
Ravenswood
Raymond Vineyard & Cellar
Seghesio Winery
Stags' Leap Winery
Sterling Vineyards
Thunder Mountain
Viansa Winery
Villa Mt. Eden
ZD Wines

WINE STAR RATINGS

❖

This is a listing of the wines with three-star or higher ratings in each of the major varietal categories. The category listed as White Blend includes Meritage-style and other blends.

BARBERA

★★★   Renwood Amador County

★★★   Renwood Amador County Linsteadt

CABERNET BLEND

★★★★★ Dalla Valle Vineyards Maya Napa Valley

★★★★★ Dominus Estate Dominus Estate Yountville

★★★★★ Harlan Estate Napa Valley

★★★★★ Opus One Napa Valley

★★★★★ Pahlmeyer Napa Valley

★★★★★ Peter Michael Winery Les Pavots Knights Valley

★★★★★ Joseph Phelps Vineyards Insignia Napa Valley

★★★★★ St. Clement Vineyards Oroppas Napa Valley

★★★★★ Stag's Leap Wine Cellars Cask 23 Napa Valley

★★★★ Beaulieu Vineyard Tapestry Napa Valley Reserve

★★★★ Cardinale Napa & Alexander Valleys

★★★★ Conn Creek Winery Anthology Napa Valley

★★★★ Constant Diamond Mountain Vineyard Napa Valley

★★★★ David Coffaro Vineyard & Winery Estate Cuvée Dry Creek Valley Coffaro Estate Vineyard

★★★★ Robert Craig Affinity Napa Valley

★★★★ Del Dotto Giovanni's Tuscan Reserve Napa Valley

★★★★ Ferrari-Carano Winery Trésor Sonoma County Reserve

★★★★ Flora Springs Wine Co. Trilogy Napa Valley

★★★★ Franciscan Oakville Estate Magnificat Napa Valley Oakville Estate

★★★★ Geyser Peak Alexandre Alexander Valley Reserve

★★★★ Jarvis Lake William Napa Valley

★★★★ Merryvale Vineyards Profile Napa Valley

★★★★ Moraga Bel Air

★★★★ Niebaum-Coppola Estate Winery Rubicon Rutherford

★★★★ Pine Ridge Winery Andrus Reserve Napa Valley

★★★★ Pride Mountain Vineyards Reserve Claret Napa Valley

★★★★ Quintessa Rutherford

★★★★ Sterling Vineyards Napa Valley Reserve

★★★★ Stonestreet Legacy Alexander Valley

★★★★ Swanson Vineyards Alexis Napa Valley

★★★★ Viader Vineyards & Winery Napa Valley

★★★ Adelaida Cellars Calitage Paso Robles

★★★ Anderson's Conn Valley Vineyards Éloge Napa Valley

★★★ Bacio Divino Napa Valley

★★★ Benziger Family Winery Estate Tribute Sonoma Mountain

★★★ Beringer Vineyards Alluvium Knights Valley

★★★ Bernardus Winery Marinus Carmel Valley

★★★ Clos du Bois Winery Marlstone Vineyard Alexander Valley

★★★ Cosentino Winery M. Coz Napa Valley Meritage

★★★ Cosentino Winery The Poet Napa Valley Meritage

★★★ Cain Vineyard & Winery Cain Five Napa Valley

★★★ Chimney Rock Winery Élevage Stags Leap District

★★★ Cosentino Winery Chiaretto California

★★★ Cronin Vineyards Concerto Stags Leap District Robinson Vineyard

★★★ David Arthur Vineyards Meritaggio Napa Valley

★★★ Estancia Estates Duo Alexander Valley

★★★ Fisher Vineyards Coach Insignia Napa Valley

★★★ Havens Wine Cellars Bourriquot Napa Valley

★★★ Justin Vineyards & Winery Isosceles Paso Robles

★★★ Charles Krug Winery Napa Valley Generations

★★★ Lail Vineyards Napa Valley

★★★ Lambert Bridge Winery Crane Creek Cuvée Dry Creek Valley

★★★ Laurel Glen Vineyard Counterpoint Sonoma Mountain

★★★ The Meeker Vineyard Four Kings Dry Creek Valley

★★★ Mount Veeder Winery Napa Valley Reserve

★★★ Newton Vineyard Claret Napa Valley

★★★ Oakville Ranch Vineyards Robert's Blend Napa Valley

★★★ Paoletti Vineyards La Forza Napa Valley

★★★ Renaissance Vineyard & Winery North Yuba Reserve

★★★ Ravenswood Pickberry Vineyard Sonoma Mountain

★★★ Ravenswood Rancho Salina Vineyards Sonoma Valley

★★★ Rosenblum Cellars Napa Valley Holbrook Mitchell Trio

★★★ Rombauer Vineyards Le Meilleur Du Chai Napa Valley

★★★ Sausal Winery Sogno Della Famigilia Alexander Valley

★★★ Seghesio Winery Omaggio Sonoma County

★★★ Shafer Vineyards Firebreak Napa Valley

★★★ Robert Sinskey Vineyards Claret Stags Leap District

★★★ Spring Mountain Spring Mountain District Miravalle-Alba-Chevalier

★★★ Sterling Vineyards Napa Valley Three Palms Vineyard

★★★ Tria Labyrinth California

★★★ Viansa Winery Ossidiana Napa Valley

★★★ White Rock Vineyards Claret Napa Valley

CABERNET FRANC

★★★ Foxen Vineyard Santa Maria Valley Tinaquaic Vineyard

★★★ Jarvis Napa Valley

★★★ Justin Vineyards & Winery Paso Robles

★★★ L'Ecosse Napa Valley Cuvée Homage de Jeanne d'Arc

★★★ La Jota Vineyard Co. Howell Mountain

★★★ Lang & Reed Wine Co. Napa Valley

★★★ Lang & Reed Wine Co. Napa Valley Premiere Etage

★★★ Niebaum-Coppola Estate Winery Rutherford Francis Coppola Family Wines

★★★ Peju Province Winery Napa Valley

★★★ Pride Mountain Vineyards Sonoma County

CABERNET SAUVIGNON

★★★★★ Abreu Vineyards Napa Valley Madrona Ranch

★★★★★ Araujo Estate Wines Napa Valley Eisele Vineyard

★★★★★ Arrowood Vineyards & Winery Sonoma County Réserve Spéciale

★★★★★ Beaulieu Vineyard Napa Valley George de Latour Private Reserve

★★★★★ Beaulieu Vineyard Rutherford Clone 4/Clone 6 Signet Selection

★★★★★ Beringer Vineyards Howell Mountain Bancroft Vineyard

★★★★★ Beringer Vineyards Napa Valley Chabot Vineyard

★★★★★ Beringer Vineyards Napa Valley Marston Vineyard

★★★★★ Beringer Vineyards Napa Valley Private Reserve

★★★★★ Beringer Vineyards Napa Valley State Lane Vineyard

★★★★★ Bryant Family Vineyard Napa Valley

★★★★★ Caymus Vineyards Napa Valley

★★★★★ Caymus Vineyards Napa Valley Special Selection

★★★★★ Chateau Montelena Winery Napa Valley The Montelena Estate

★★★★★ Chateau St. Jean Sonoma County Reserve

★★★★★ Colgin Napa Valley Herb Lamb Vineyard

★★★★★ Robert Craig Howell Mountain

★★★★★ Robert Craig Mount Veeder

★★★★★ Dalla Valle Vineyards Napa Valley

★★★★★ Diamond Creek Vineyards Napa Valley Gravelly Meadow

★★★★★ Diamond Creek Vineyards Napa Valley Lake Vineyard

★★★★★ Diamond Creek Vineyards Napa Valley Red Rock Terrace

★★★★★ Diamond Creek Vineyards Napa Valley Volcanic Hill

★★★★★ Dunn Vineyards Howell Mountain

★★★★★ Etude Wines Napa Valley

★★★★★ Flora Springs Wine Co. Rutherford Hillside Reserve

★★★★★ Forman Vineyard Napa Valley

★★★★★ Freemark Abbey Winery Napa Valley Bosché Vineyard

★★★★★ Gallo of Sonoma Winery Northern Sonoma Estate Bottled

★★★★★ Grace Family Vineyards Napa Valley

★★★★★ Groth Vineyards & Winery Napa Valley Reserve

★★★★★ Heitz Wine Cellars Napa Valley Martha's Vineyard

★★★★★ Kenwood Vineyards Sonoma Valley Artist Series

★★★★★ Lewis Cellars Napa Valley Reserve

★★★★★ Lokoya Rutherford

★★★★★ Robert Mondavi Winery Napa Valley Reserve

★★★★★ Joseph Phelps Vineyards Napa Valley Eisele Vineyard

★★★★★ Pride Mountain Vineyards Napa Valley Reserve

★★★★★ Ridge Vineyards Monte Bello Santa Cruz Mountains

★★★★★ St. Francis Winery Sonoma Valley Reserve

★★★★★ Screaming Eagle Napa Valley

★★★★★ Shafer Vineyards Stags Leap District Hillside Select

★★★★★ Silver Oak Cellars Napa Valley Bonny's Vineyard

★★★★★ Silverado Vineyards Napa Valley Limited Reserve

★★★★★ Spottswoode Vineyard & Winery Napa Valley

★★★★★ Stag's Leap Wine Cellars Napa Valley S.L.V.

★★★★★ Philip Togni Vineyard Napa Valley

★★★★ Altamura Vineyards & Winery Napa Valley

★★★★ S. Anderson Vineyard Stags Leap District Richard Chambers Vineyard

★★★★ Anderson's Conn Valley Vineyards Napa Valley Estate Reserve

★★★★ Arns Napa Valley

★★★★ Arrowood Vineyards & Winery Sonoma County

★★★★ Barbour Vineyards Napa Valley Barbour Vineyards

★★★★ Barnett Vineyards Spring Mountain District Rattlesnake Hill

★★★★ Baron Herzog Alexander Valley Special Edition

★★★★ Baron Herzog Alexander Valley Special Reserve

★★★★ Baron Herzog Napa Valley Special Reserve

★★★★ Behrens & Hitchcock Napa Valley Kenefick Ranch Vineyard

★★★★ Chateau Potelle Mount Veeder V.G.S.

★★★★ Chateau St. Jean Sonoma County Cinq Cépages

★★★★ Chateau Souverain Alexander Valley Library Reserve

★★★★ Chateau Souverain Alexander Valley Winemaker's Reserve

★★★★ Chimney Rock Winery Stags Leap District

★★★★ Chimney Rock Winery Stags Leap District Reserve

★★★★ Clos du Bois Winery Alexander Valley Winemaker's Reserve

★★★★ Clos Du Val Napa Valley Reserve

★★★★ B. R. Cohn Sonoma Valley Olive Hill Estate Vineyard

★★★★ B. R. Cohn Sonoma Valley Olive Hill Estate Vineyard Special Selection

★★★★ Cornerstone Cellars Howell Mountain Beatty Ranch

★★★★ Cosentino Winery Napa Valley Reserve

★★★★ Cuvaison Napa Valley ATS

★★★★ David Arthur Vineyards Napa Valley

★★★★ David Arthur Vineyards Napa Valley Elevation 1147

★★★★ Del Dotto Napa Valley

★★★★ Dehlinger Winery Russian River Valley

★★★★ Duckhorn Vineyards Napa Valley

★★★★ Dunn Vineyards Napa Valley

★★★★ Tom Eddy Napa Valley

★★★★ Far Niente Winery Napa Valley

★★★★ Fisher Vineyards Napa Valley Lamb Vineyard

★★★★ Freemark Abbey Winery Napa Valley Sycamore Vineyards

★★★★ Grgich Hills Cellar Napa Valley

★★★★ Grgich Hills Cellar Napa Valley Yountville Selection

★★★★ Groth Vineyards & Winery Napa Valley

★★★★ Guenoc Winery Napa Valley Beckstoffer Vineyard Reserve

★★★★ Guenoc Winery Napa Valley Bella Vista Vineyard Reserve

★★★★ Harrison Winery & Vineyards Napa Valley

★★★★ Hartwell Vineyards Stags Leap District Grace

★★★★ Hartwell Vineyards Stags Leap District Sunshine Vineyard

★★★★ Heitz Wine Cellars Rutherford Trailside Vineyard

★★★★ The Hess Collection Winery Mount Veeder Napa Valley

★★★★ The Hess Collection Winery Mount Veeder Napa Valley Reserve

★★★★ Paul Hobbs Napa Valley Carneros Hyde Vineyard

★★★★ Kathryn Kennedy Winery Santa Cruz Mountains Estate

★★★★ Kendall-Jackson Winery California Grand Reserve

★★★★ La Jota Vineyard Co. Howell Mountain Anniversary Release

★★★★ Laurel Glen Vineyard Sonoma Mountain

★★★★ Lewis Cellars Napa Valley Oakville Ranch

★★★★ Livingston Vineyards Rutherford Moffett Vineyard

★★★★ Lokoya Mount Veeder

★★★★ Merryvale Vineyards Napa Valley Reserve

★★★★ Miner Family Vineyards Napa Valley Oakville

★★★★ Robert Mondavi Winery Napa Valley

★★★★ Oakford Vineyards Oakville

★★★★ Oakville Ranch Vineyards Napa Valley

★★★★ Paradigm Napa Valley Oakville

★★★★ Peju Province Winery Napa Valley H.B. Vineyard

★★★★ Joseph Phelps Vineyards Napa Valley

★★★★ Joseph Phelps Vineyards Napa Valley Backus Vineyard

★★★★ Pine Ridge Winery Stags Leap District

★★★★ Pride Mountain Vineyards Napa Valley

★★★★ A. Rafanelli Winery Dry Creek Valley

★★★★ Martin Ray Napa Valley Diamond Mountain

★★★★ Martin Ray Santa Cruz Mountains

★★★★ Ristow Napa Valley Quinta de Pedras

★★★★ Rockland Road Cellars Napa Valley

★★★★ Rudd Estate Napa Valley Reserve

★★★★ Saddleback Cellars Napa Valley

★★★★ St. Clement Vineyards Howell Mountain

★★★★   St. Clement Vineyards Napa Valley

★★★★   Seavey Vineyard Napa Valley

★★★★   Shafer Vineyards Napa Valley

★★★★   Signorello Vineyards Napa Valley Founder's Reserve

★★★★   Silver Oak Cellars Alexander Valley

★★★★   Silver Oak Cellars Napa Valley

★★★★   Simi Winery Alexander Valley Reserve

★★★★   Snowden Napa Valley

★★★★   Stag's Leap Wine Cellars Napa Valley Fay Vineyard

★★★★   Staglin Family Vineyard Rutherford

★★★★   Steele Wines Anderson Valley

★★★★   Stonestreet Alexander Valley Alexander Mountain Estate

★★★★   Swanson Vineyards Napa Valley

★★★★   Tay Napa Valley

★★★★   The Terraces Rutherford

★★★★   Truchard Vineyard Carneros

★★★★   Truchard Vineyard Carneros Reserve

★★★★   Villa Mt. Eden Mendocino Signature Series

★★★★   Vine Cliff Cellars Napa Valley Oakville Estate

★★★★   von Strasser Diamond Mountain

★★★★   White Cottage Howell Mountain

★★★★   Whitehall Lane Winery Napa Valley Gallerón

★★★★   Whitehall Lane Winery Napa Valley Leonardini Vineyard

★★★★   Whitehall Lane Winery Napa Valley Reserve

★★★★   Whitehall Lane Winery Rutherford Morisoli Vineyard

★★★★   ZD Wines Napa Valley

★★★★   ZD Wines Napa Valley Reserve

★★★   Adelaida Cellars Paso Robles

★★★   S. Anderson Vineyard Stag Leap District

★★★   Arbios Alexander Valley

★★★   Barnett Vineyards Spring Mountain District

★★★   Beaulieu Vineyard Napa Valley Rutherford

★★★   Beckmen Vineyards Santa Barbara County

★★★   Behrens & Hitchcock Napa Valley Inkgrade Vineyard

★★★   Benziger Family Winery Sonoma County

★★★   Benziger Family Winery Sonoma Mountain Reserve

★★★   Beringer Vineyards Knights Valley

★★★   August Briggs Napa Valley

★★★   Buehler Vineyards Napa Valley

★★★   Buehler Vineyards Napa Valley Estate

★★★   Buena Vista Winery Carneros Grand Reserve

★★★   Burgess Cellars Napa Valley Vintage Selection

★★★   Cafaro Cellars Napa Valley

★★★   Cafaro Cellars Napa Valley Reserva

★★★   Cakebread Cellars Napa Valley

★★★   Cakebread Cellars Napa Valley Benchland Select

★★★   Cakebread Cellars Napa Valley Rutherford Reserve

★★★   Cakebread Cellars Napa Valley Three Sisters

★★★   Oliver Caldwell Cellars Napa Valley Aïda Vineyard

★★★   Chalk Hill Winery Chalk Hill

★★★   Chappellet Vineyard Napa Valley Signature

★★★   Chateau Montelena Winery Calistoga Cuvée Napa Valley

★★★   Chateau Souverain Alexander Valley

★★★   Chauffe-Eau Cellars Alexander Valley Smith-Reichel Vineyard

★★★   Cinnabar Vineyards Santa Cruz Mountains Saratoga Vineyard

★★★   Clark-Claudon Vineyards Napa Valley

★★★   Clos du Bois Winery Alexander Valley Briarcrest Vineyard

★★★   Clos Pegase Napa Valley

★★★   Clos Pegase Napa Valley Hommage Artist Series Reserve

★★★   David Coffaro Vineyard & Winery Dry Creek Valley Coffaro Estate Vineyard

★★★   Corison Wines Napa Valley

★★★   Cosentino Winery Napa Valley

★★★   Cronin Vineyards Santa Cruz Mountains

★★★   Cuvaison Napa Valley

★★★   De Loach Vineyards Russian River Valley O.F.S.

★★★   Delectus Napa Valley

★★★ Domaine Grand Archer Sonoma County

★★★ Dry Creek Vineyard Dry Creek Valley

★★★ Dry Creek Vineyard Dry Creek Valley Reserve

★★★ Dry Creek Vineyard Sonoma County

★★★ Ehlers Grove Napa Valley Winery Reserve

★★★ Volker Eisele Napa Valley Chiles Valley District

★★★ Elan Atlas Peak

★★★ Elyse Wines Napa Valley Morisoli Vineyard

★★★ Gary Farrell Wines Sonoma County Hillside Selection

★★★ Gary Farrell Wines Sonoma County Ladi's Vineyard

★★★ Ferrari-Carano Winery Sonoma County

★★★ Fetzer Vineyards Napa Valley Reserve

★★★ Field Stone Winery Alexander Valley Staten Family Reserve

★★★ Fife Vineyards Spring Mountain District Reserve

★★★ Fisher Vineyards Sonoma County Wedding Vineyard

★★★ Flora Springs Wine Co. Napa Valley

★★★ Flora Springs Wine Co. Pope Valley Cypress Ranch

★★★ Thomas Fogarty Winery Napa Valley

★★★ Foxen Vineyard Santa Barbara County

★★★ Franciscan Oakville Estate Napa Valley

★★★ Peter Franus Wine Co. Napa Valley

★★★ Frazier Napa Valley Lupine Hill Vineyard

★★★ Freemark Abbey Winery Napa Valley

★★★ Frick Winery Dry Creek Valley

★★★ Frog's Leap Napa Valley

★★★ Galante Vineyards Carmel Valley Estate Blackjack Pasture

★★★ Galante Vineyards Carmel Valley Estate Red Rose Hill

★★★ Gallo of Sonoma Winery Dry Creek Valley Frei Ranch Vineyard

★★★ Gallo of Sonoma Winery Dry Creek Valley Stefani Vineyard

★★★ Geyser Peak Alexander Valley Reserve

★★★ Geyser Peak Sonoma County

★★★ Greenwood Ridge Vineyards Mendocino Ridge

★★★ Harrison Winery & Vineyards Napa Valley Reserve

★★★ Heitz Wine Cellars Napa Valley

★★★ Heitz Wine Cellars Napa Valley Bella Oaks Vineyard

★★★ Hendry Ranch Napa Valley Block 8

★★★ Paul Hobbs Howell Mountain Liparita Vineyard

★★★ Honig Cellars Napa Valley

★★★ Husch Mendocino La Ribera Vineyards

★★★ Jarvis Napa Valley

★★★ Jarvis Napa Valley Lot 4

★★★ Jordan Vineyard & Winery Alexander Valley

★★★ Judd's Hill Napa Valley

★★★ Justin Vineyards & Winery Paso Robles

★★★ Justin Vineyards & Winery San Luis Obispo County Reserve

★★★ Karl Lawrence Howell Mountain

★★★ Kendall-Jackson Winery Alexander Valley Buckeye Vineyard Single Vineyard Series

★★★ Kenwood Vineyards Sonoma Valley Jack London Vineyard

★★★ Charles Krug Winery Napa Valley Vintage Selection

★★★ La Jota Vineyard Co. Howell Mountain

★★★ Lewelling VineyardsNapa Valley Lewelling Vineyards

★★★ Liparita Cellars Howell Mountain

★★★ Lockwood Vineyard Monterey

★★★ Lockwood Vineyard Monterey Partners' Reserve

★★★ Lokoya Diamond Mountain

★★★ Lokoya Howell Mountain

★★★ Lolonis Redwood Valley Private Reserve

★★★ Long Vineyards Napa Valley

★★★ Markham Vineyards Napa Valley

★★★ Louis M. Martini Winery Sonoma Valley Monte Rosso Vineyard

★★★ Mayacamas Vineyards Napa Valley

★★★ The Meeker Vineyard Dry Creek Valley Gold Leaf Cuvée

★★★ Merryvale Vineyards Napa Valley Hillside

★★★ Robert Mondavi Winery Napa Valley Oakville District

★★★ Robert Mondavi Winery Stags Leap District

★★★ Mount Eden Vineyards Santa Cruz Mountains

★★★ Mount Eden Vineyards Santa Cruz Mountains Old Vine Reserve

★★★ Mount Veeder Winery Napa Valley

★★★ Murphy-Goode Estate Winery Alexander Valley

★★★ Murphy-Goode Estate Winery Alexander Valley Brenda Block Reserve

★★★ Napa Ridge Central Coast

★★★ Napa Wine Co. Napa Valley

★★★ Navarro Vineyards Mendocino

★★★ Newlan Vineyards & Winery Napa Valley

★★★ Newton Vineyard Napa Valley

★★★ Neyers Vineyards Napa Valley

★★★ Optima Wine Cellars Alexander Valley

★★★ Paoletti Vineyards Napa Valley

★★★ Robert Pecota Winery Napa Valley Kara's Vineyard

★★★ Pezzi King Dry Creek Valley

★★★ Pine Ridge Winery Howell Mountain

★★★ Pine Ridge Winery Rutherford

★★★ PlumpJack Napa Valley

★★★ PlumpJack Napa Valley Reserve

★★★ Rabbit Ridge Vineyards Russian River Valley Winemaker's Grand Reserve

★★★ Martin Ray California Saratoga Cuvée

★★★ Ravenswood Sonoma County

★★★ Ravenswood Sonoma Valley Gregory Vineyard

★★★ Raymond Vineyard & Cellar Napa Valley Generations

★★★ Raymond Vineyard & Cellar Napa Valley Raymond Estates Reserve

★★★ Ridge Vineyards Santa Cruz Mountains

★★★ J. Rochioli Vineyards Russian River Valley Neoma's Vineyard

★★★ Rocking Horse Rutherford Garvey Family Vineyard

★★★ Rocking Horse Stags Leap District Robinson Vineyard

★★★ Rombauer Vineyards Napa Valley

★★★ Rombauer Vineyards Napa Valley Diamond Mountain Selection

★★★ Rosenblum Cellars Napa Valley Hendry Vineyard Reserve

★★★ Rosenblum Cellars Napa Valley Holbrook Mitchell Vineyard

★★★ Rosenthal—The Malibu Estate Malibu-Newton Canyon

★★★ Rudd Estate Napa Valley

★★★ Rutz Cellars Napa Valley

★★★ St. Francis Winery Sonoma County

★★★ St. Supéry Vineyard & Winery Napa Valley Dollarhide Ranch

★★★ Santa Barbara Winery Santa Ynez Valley

★★★ Santa Cruz Mountain Vineyard Santa Cruz Mountains Bates Ranch

★★★ V. Sattui WineryRutherford Morisoli Vineyard

★★★ Schug Carneros Estate Winery Sonoma Valley Heritage Reserve

★★★ Sebastiani Sonoma Cask Cellars Sonoma County

★★★ Sebastiani Sonoma Cask Cellars Sonoma Valley Cherryblock Old Vines

★★★ Sequoia Grove Vineyards Napa Valley

★★★ Sequoia Grove Vineyards Rutherford Estate Reserve

★★★ Shenandoah Vineyards Amador County

★★★ Signorello Vineyards Napa Valley

★★★ Silverado Vineyards Napa Valley

★★★ Simi Winery Alexander Valley

★★★ Stag's Leap Wine Cellars Napa Valley

★★★ Steltzner Vineyards Stag's Leap District

★★★ Stonestreet Alexander Valley

★★★ Rodney Strong Vineyards Northern Sonoma Alexander's Crown Vineyard

★★★ Rodney Strong Vineyards Northern Sonoma Reserve

★★★ Sylviane Napa Valley

★★★ Trefethen Vineyards Napa Valley

★★★ Trefethen Vineyards Napa Valley Reserve

★★★ M. Trinchero Napa Valley Founder's Estate

★★★ Turnbull Wine Cellars Napa Valley Oakville

★★★ Van Asperen Napa Valley Signature Reserve

★★★ Venezia Alexander Valley

★★★ Venge Napa Valley Reserve

★★★ Viansa Winery Napa & Sonoma Counties

★★★ Villa Mt. Eden Napa Valley Grand Reserve

★★★ Vineyard 29 Napa Valley

★★★ Whitehall Lane Winery Napa Valley

CARIGNANE

★★★ Hidden Cellars Winery Mendocino Hillside

★★★ David Coffaro Vineyard & Winery Dry Creek Valley

★★★ Rabbit Ridge Vineyards Russian River Valley Hedin Vineyard

★★★ Rosenblum Cellars Napa Valley Kenefick Ranch

CHARDONNAY

★★★★★ Arrowood Vineyards & Winery Sonoma County Cuvée Michel Berthoud Réserve Spéciale

★★★★★ Beringer Vineyards Napa Valley Private Reserve

★★★★★ Beringer Vineyards Napa Valley Sbragia Limited Release

★★★★★ Byron Vineyards & Winery Santa Maria Valley Estate

★★★★★ Byron Vineyards & Winery Santa Maria Valley Reserve

★★★★★ Chalk Hill Winery Chalk Hill

★★★★★ Chalk Hill Winery Chalk Hill Estate Vineyard Selection

★★★★★ Chalone Vineyard Chalone

★★★★★ Chalone Vineyard Chalone Reserve

★★★★★ Chateau St. Jean Alexander Valley Robert Young Vineyard

★★★★★ Chateau St. Jean Alexander Valley Robert Young Vineyard Reserve

★★★★★ De Loach Vineyards Russian River Valley O.F.S.

★★★★★ Gary Farrell Wines Russian River Valley Allen Vineyard

★★★★★ Ferrari-Carano Winery Alexander Valley

★★★★★ Ferrari-Carano Winery Alexander Valley TreMonte

★★★★★ Ferrari-Carano Winery Napa-Sonoma Counties Reserve

★★★★★ Flora Springs Wine Co. Napa Valley Reserve

★★★★★ Forman Vineyard Napa Valley

★★★★★ Gallo of Sonoma Winery Northern Sonoma Estate Bottled

★★★★★ Grgich Hills Cellar Napa Valley

★★★★★ Guenoc Winery Guenoc Valley Genevieve Magoon Vineyard Estate Reserve

★★★★★ Guenoc Winery Guenoc Valley Genevieve Magoon Vineyard Unfiltered Estate Reserve

★★★★★ Hanzell Vineyards Sonoma Valley

★★★★★ Kistler Vineyards Carneros Hudson Vineyard

★★★★★ Kistler Vineyards Carneros Hyde Vineyard

★★★★★ Kistler Vineyards Russian River Valley Dutton Ranch

★★★★★ Kistler Vineyards Russian River Valley Vine Hill Road Vineyard

★★★★★ Kistler Vineyards Sonoma Coast

★★★★★ Kistler Vineyards Sonoma Coast Camp Meeting Ridge

★★★★★ Kistler Vineyards Sonoma County Cuvée Cathleen

★★★★★ Kistler Vineyards Sonoma Mountain McCrea Vineyard

★★★★★ Kistler Vineyards Sonoma Valley Durell Vineyard

★★★★★ Kistler Vineyards Sonoma Valley Kistler Estate Vineyard

★★★★★ Kongsgaard Wines Napa Valley

★★★★★ Landmark Vineyards Russian River Lorenzo Vineyard

★★★★★ Landmark Vineyards Sonoma-Santa Barbara-Monterey Counties Damaris Reserve

★★★★★ Lewis Cellars Napa Valley Reserve

★★★★★ Long Vineyards Napa Valley

★★★★★ Marcassin Alexander Valley Gauer Vineyard Upper Barn

★★★★★ Marcassin Carneros Hudson Vineyard E Block

★★★★★ Marcassin Sonoma Coast Lorenzo Vineyard

★★★★★ Martinelli Vineyard Russian River Valley Gold Ridge

★★★★★ Matanzas Creek Winery Sonoma Valley

★★★★★ Matanzas Creek Winery Sonoma Valley Journey

★★★★★ Mer Soleil Central Coast

★★★★★ Merryvale Vineyards Napa Valley Reserve

★★★★★ Peter Michael Winery Napa County Clos du Ciel

★★★★★ Peter Michael Winery Sonoma County Belle Côte

★★★★★ Peter Michael Winery Sonoma County Cuvée Indigène

★★★★★ Peter Michael Winery Sonoma County Mon Plaisir

★★★★★ Robert Mondavi Winery Napa Valley Reserve

★★★★★ Mount Eden Vineyards Santa Cruz Mountains

★★★★★ Newton Vineyard Napa Valley Unfiltered

★★★★★ Pahlmeyer Napa Valley

★★★★★ Patz & Hall Wine Co. Carneros Hyde Vineyard

★★★★★ Patz & Hall Wine Co. Mount Veeder Carr Vineyard

★★★★★ Patz & Hall Wine Co. Napa Valley

★★★★★ Patz & Hall Wine Co. Russian River Valley

★★★★★ Pine Ridge Winery Stags Leap District

★★★★★ Ramey Wine Cellars Napa Valley Carneros Hyde Vineyard

★★★★★ Ridge Vineyards Santa Cruz Mountains

★★★★★ J. Rochioli Vineyards Russian River Valley Allen Vineyard

★★★★★ J. Rochioli Vineyards Russian River Valley Estate Cuvée Reserve

★★★★★ J. Rochioli Vineyards Russian River Valley Estate River Block

★★★★★ J. Rochioli Vineyards Russian River Valley Estate South River Vineyard

★★★★★ J. Rochioli Vineyards Russian River Valley Reserve

★★★★★ Saintsbury Carneros Reserve

★★★★★ Sanford Winery Santa Barbara County Barrel Select

★★★★★ Shafer Vineyards Napa Valley Carneros Red Shoulder Ranch

★★★★★ Signorello Vineyards Napa Valley Founder's Reserve

★★★★★ Signorello Vineyards Napa Valley Hope's Cuvée

★★★★★ Steele Wines Carneros Durell Vineyard

★★★★★ Steele Wines Carneros Sangiacomo Vineyard

★★★★★ Steele Wines Mendocino Lolonis Vineyard

★★★★★ Steele Wines Santa Barbara County Bien Nacido Vineyard

★★★★★ Steele Wines Santa Barbara County Goodchild Vineyard

★★★★★ Talley Vineyards Arroyo Grande Valley

★★★★★ Talley Vineyards Arroyo Grande Valley Rincon Vineyard

★★★★★ Talley Vineyards Arroyo Grande Valley Rosemary's Vineyard

★★★★★ Robert Talbott Vineyards Monterey Cuvée Cynthia

★★★★★ Robert Talbott Vineyards Monterey Diamond T Estate

★★★★★ Robert Talbott Vineyards Monterey Sleepy Hollow Vineyard

★★★★★ Truchard Vineyard Carneros

★★★★★ Villa Mt. Eden Santa Maria Valley Bien Nacido Vineyard Signature Series

★★★★★ Vine Cliff Cellars Napa Valley

★★★★★ Williams Selyem Winery Russian River Valley Allen Vineyard

★★★★ Acacia Winery Carneros Reserve

★★★★ S. Anderson Vineyard Napa Valley Proprietor's Reserve

★★★★ Arrowood Vineyards & Winery Sonoma County

★★★★ Au Bon Climat Arroyo Grande Valley Talley Reserve

★★★★ Au Bon Climat Edna Valley Alban Vineyard

★★★★ Au Bon Climat Santa Barbara County

★★★★ Au Bon Climat Santa Barbara County Le Bouge D'à Côté

★★★★ Au Bon Climat Santa Barbara County Nuits-Blanches

★★★★ Au Bon Climat Santa Ynez Valley Sanford and Benedict Reserve

★★★★ Babcock Vineyards Santa Ynez Valley Grand Cuvee

★★★★ Beaulieu Vineyard Carneros Reserve

★★★★ Benziger Family Winery Carneros Yamakawa Vineyards Reserve

★★★★ Bernardus Winery Monterey County

★★★★ Byington Winery Santa Cruz Dirk Vineyard

★★★★ Byington Winery Santa Cruz Mountains

★★★★ Byington Winery Santa Cruz Mountains Bald Mountain Vineyard

★★★★ Calera Wine Co. Central Coast

★★★★ Calera Wine Co. Mount Harlan

★★★★ Cambria Winery & Vineyard Santa Maria Valley Katherine's Vineyard

★★★★ Chateau Montelena Winery Napa Valley

★★★★ Chateau Potelle Mount Veeder V.G.S.

★★★★ Chateau St. Jean Alexander Valley Belle Terre Vineyard

★★★★ Chateau St. Jean Carneros Durell Vineyard

★★★★ Chateau Souverain Russian River Valley Winemaker's Reserve

★★★★ Cronin Vineyards Santa Cruz Mountains Nancy's Cuvée

★★★★ Cuvaison Napa Valley Carneros ATS

★★★★ Cuvaison Napa Valley Carneros Reserve

★★★★ Dehlinger Winery Russian River Valley

★★★★ El Molino Winery Napa Valley

★★★★ Estancia Estates Monterey County Reserve

★★★★ Far Niente Winery Napa Valley

★★★★ Gary Farrell Wines Russian River Valley Rochioli Vineyard

★★★★ Gary Farrell Wines Santa Barbara County Bien Nacido Vineyard

★★★★ Gloria Ferrer Champagne Caves Carneros

★★★★ Flora Springs Wine Co. Carneros Napa Valley Lavender Hill Vineyard

★★★★ Flora Springs Wine Co. Napa Valley

★★★★ Flowers Sonoma Coast

★★★★ Flowers Sonoma Coast Camp Meeting Ridge

★★★★ Flowers Sonoma County Porter-Bass Vineyards

★★★★ Thomas Fogarty Winery Santa Cruz Mountains

★★★★ Thomas Fogarty Winery Santa Cruz Mountains Estate Reserve

★★★★ Franciscan Oakville Estate Napa Valley

★★★★ Franciscan Oakville Estate Napa Valley Cuvée Sauvage

★★★★ Freemark Abbey Winery Napa Valley Carpy Ranch

★★★★ J. Fritz Russian River Valley Dutton Ranch

★★★★ J. Fritz Russian River Valley Dutton Vineyard Shop Block

★★★★ The Gainey Vineyard Santa Barbara County Limited Selection

★★★★ Gallo of Sonoma Winery Dry Creek Valley Stefani Vineyard

★★★★ Gallo of Sonoma Winery Russian River Valley Laguna Ranch

★★★★ Greenwood Ridge Vineyards Mendocino Ridge Du Pratt Vineyard

★★★★ Harrison Winery & Vineyards Napa Valley

★★★★ Hartwell Vineyards Stags Leap District

★★★★ The Hess Collection Winery Napa Valley

★★★★ Paul Hobbs Russian River Valley Walker Station Vineyard

★★★★ Paul Hobbs Sonoma Mountain Dinner Vinyard Cuvée Augustina

★★★★ Paul Hobbs Sonoma Mountain Richard Dinner Vineyard

★★★★ Paul Hobbs Sonoma Valley Kunde Vineyard

★★★★ Kendall-Jackson Winery California Grand Reserve

★★★★ Kendall-Jackson Winery Santa Maria Valley Camelot Vineyard Single Vineyard Series

★★★★ Kenwood Vineyards Sonoma-Santa Maria Reserve

★★★★ Laetitia Vineyard & Winery San Luis Obispo County Laetitia Vineyard

★★★★ Landmark Vineyards Sonoma-Santa Barbara-Monterey Counties Overlook

★★★★ Ledson Winery & Vineyards Carneros Reserve

★★★★ LinCourt Vineyards Santa Barbara

★★★★ Littorai Russian River Mays Canyon

★★★★ Littorai Sonoma Coast Occidental

★★★★ Livingston Vineyards Napa Valley

★★★★ J. Lohr Winery Monterey County Riverstone

★★★★ MacRostie Wines Carneros

★★★★ MacRostie Wines Carneros Reserve

★★★★ Markham Vineyards Napa Valley Reserve

★★★★ Martinelli Vineyard Sonoma Coast Charles Ranch

★★★★ Mayacamas Vineyards Napa Valley

★★★★ Meridian Vineyards Edna Valley Coastal Reserve

★★★★ Meridian Vineyards Santa Barbara County Limited Release

★★★★ Merryvale Vineyards Napa Valley Starmont

★★★★ Miner Family Vineyards Napa Valley

★★★★ Miner Family Vineyards Napa Valley Oakville Ranch

★★★★ Miner Family Vineyards Napa Valley Wild Yeast

★★★★ Mirassou Vineyards Monterey County Harvest Reserve

★★★★ Mirassou Vineyards Monterey County Showcase Selection

★★★★ Robert Mondavi Winery Carneros

★★★★ Robert Mondavi Winery Napa Valley

★★★★ Morgan Winery Monterey

★★★★ Morgan Winery Monterey Reserve

★★★★ Mount Eden Vineyards Edna Valley MacGregor Vineyard

★★★★ Robert Mueller Cellars Alexander Valley Gauer Ranch

★★★★ Robert Mueller Cellars Russian River Valley

★★★★ Robert Mueller Cellars Russian River Valley LB

★★★★ Robert Mueller Cellars Russian River Valley Oak Meadow

★★★★ Murphy-Goode Estate Winery Alexander Valley Island Block Reserve

★★★★ Newton Vineyard Napa & Sonoma Counties

★★★★ Neyers Vineyards Carneros

★★★★ Neyers Vineyards Napa Valley

★★★★ Neyers Vineyards Sonoma Coast El Novillero Vineyard

★★★★ Neyers Vineyards Sonoma Coast Thieriot Vineyard

★★★★ Nichols Winery Arroyo Grande Valley Talley Vineyards

★★★★ Oakville Ranch Vineyards Napa Valley ORV

★★★★ Oakville Ranch Vineyards Napa Valley Vista Vineyard

★★★★ Patz & Hall Wine Co. Mendocino Alder Springs Vineyard

★★★★ Joseph Phelps Vineyards Carneros

★★★★ Joseph Phelps Vineyards Napa Valley Ovation

★★★★ Pine Ridge Winery Napa Valley Carneros Dijon Clones

★★★★ Pine Ridge Winery Stags Leap District Dijon Clones

★★★★ Pride Mountain Vineyards Napa Valley

★★★★ Qupé Santa Barbara County Bien Nacido Vineyard Reserve

★★★★ Rabbit Ridge Vineyards Sonoma County Winemaker's Grand Reserve

★★★★ Martin Ray California Mariage

★★★★ Raymond Vineyard & Cellar Napa Valley Generations

★★★★ J. Rochioli Vineyards Russian River Valley Estate

★★★★ Rombauer Vineyards Carneros

★★★★ Rudd Estate Napa Valley

★★★★ St. Clement Vineyards Napa Valley Carneros Abbott's Vineyard

★★★★ St. Francis Winery Sonoma County Reserve

★★★★ Saintsbury Carneros

★★★★ Sanford Winery Santa Barbara County

★★★★ Sanford Winery Santa Barbara County Sanford & Benedict Vineyard

★★★★ Sanford Winery Santa Ynez Valley Estate Bottled

★★★★ Sebastiani Sonoma Cask Cellars Russian River Valley Dutton Ranch

★★★★ Signorello Vineyards Napa Valley

★★★★ Silverado Vineyards Napa Valley Limited Reserve

★★★★ Simi Winery Carneros

★★★★ Simi Winery Sonoma County Reserve

★★★★ Sonoma-Cutrer Vineyards Sonoma Coast Cutrer Vineyard

★★★★ Sonoma-Loeb Sonoma

★★★★ Sonoma-Loeb Sonoma County Private Reserve

★★★★ Stag's Leap Wine Cellars Napa Valley Beckstoffer Ranch

★★★★ Stag's Leap Wine Cellars Napa Valley Reserve

★★★★ Steele Wines California Steele Cuveé

★★★★ Steele Wines Mendocino Dennison Vineyard

★★★★ Steele Wines Mendocino DuPratt Vineyard

★★★★ Steele Wines Sonoma Valley Parmelee Hill Vineyard

★★★★ Stonestreet Alexander Valley Alexander Mountain Estate Upper Barn

★★★★ Stonestreet Sonoma County

★★★★ Stony Hill Vineyard Napa Valley

★★★★ Talley Vineyards Edna Valley Oliver's Vineyard

★★★★ Testarossa Vineyard California George Troquato Signature Reserve

★★★★ Testarossa Vineyard Chalone

★★★★ Testarossa Vineyard Santa Maria Valley

★★★★ Testarossa Vineyard Santa Maria Valley Bien Nacido Vineyard

★★★★ Thunder Mountain Santa Cruz Mountains Bald Mountain

★★★★ Thunder Mountain Santa Cruz Mountains Matteson Vineyard

★★★★ Marimar Torres Estate Russian River Valley Don Miguel Vineyard

★★★★ Villa Mt. Eden Santa Maria Valley Bien Nacido Vineyard Grand Reserve

★★★★ Vine Cliff Cellars Napa Valley Proprietress Reserve

★★★★ Williams Selyem Winery Sonoma Coast Hirsch Vineyard

★★★ Acacia Winery Carneros

★★★ Alderbrook Vineyards & Winery Dry Creek Valley

★★★ Alderbrook Vineyards & Winery Dry Creek Valley Dorothy's Vineyard

★★★ Ancien Wines Carneros

★★★ S. Anderson Vineyard Napa Valley Carneros

★★★ S. Anderson Vineyard Stags Leap District

★★★ Anderson's Conn Valley Vineyards Carneros Fournier Vineyard

★★★ Arcadian Santa Maria Valley Bien Nacido Vineyard

★★★ Babcock Vineyards Santa Ynez Valley Mt. Carmel Vineyard

★★★ Bannister Vineyards Russian River Valley Allen Vineyard

★★★ Bannister Vineyards Russian River Valley Porter-Bass Vineyard

★★★ Baron Herzog Wine Cellars Co. Alexander Valley Special Reserve

★★★ Baron Herzog Wine Cellars Co. Russian River Valley Special Reserve

★★★ Beaulieu Vineyard Carneros

★★★ Beckmen Vineyards Santa Barbara County

★★★ Belvedere Winery Russian River Valley

★★★ Belvedere Winery Sonoma County Preferred Stock

★★★ Benziger Family Winery Carneros Reserve

★★★ Benziger Family Winery Sonoma County

★★★ Beringer Vineyards Napa Valley

★★★ Bonterra Mendocino County

★★★ August Briggs Carneros Leveroni Vineyards

★★★ August Briggs Russian River Valley

★★★ Brutocao Cellars Mendocino County Bliss Vineyard

★★★ Buehler Vineyards Russian River Valley Reserve

★★★ Buena Vista Winery Carneros Grand Reserve

★★★ Burgess Cellars Napa Valley

★★★ Burgess Cellars Napa Valley Triere Vineyard Reserve

★★★ Byington Winery Napa Valley Twin Mountains

★★★ Davis Bynum Winery Russian River Valley Allen & McIlroy Vineyards Limited Edition

★★★ Byron Vineyards & Winery Santa Maria Valley

★★★ Cakebread Cellars Napa Valley

★★★ Cakebread Cellars Napa Valley Reserve

★★★ Cale Family Wines Carneros Sangiacomo Vineyard

★★★ Cambria Winery & Vineyard Santa Maria Valley Reserve

★★★ Canepa Cellars Alexander Valley Gauer Vineyard Adobe III

★★★ Carmenet Winery Sonoma Valley Carneros Sangiacomo Vineyard

★★★ Chappellet Vineyard Napa Valley Signature

★★★ Chateau Julien Monterey County Grand Reserve

★★★ Chateau St. Jean Sonoma County

★★★ Chateau Souverain Sonoma County

★★★ Chateau Woltner Howell Mountain Frederique Vineyard

★★★ Chateau Woltner Howell Mountain St. Thomas Vineyard

★★★ Chateau Woltner Howell Mountain Titus Vineyard

★★★ Chauffe-Eau Cellars Carneros Sangiacomo Vineyard

★★★ Christopher Creek Winery Santa Cruz Mountains

★★★ Claiborne & Churchill Vintners Edna Valley MacGregor Vineyard

★★★ Clos du Bois Winery Alexander Valley Calcaire Vineyard

★★★ Clos du Bois Winery Dry Creek Valley Flintwood Vineyard

★★★ Clos Du Val Wine Co. Napa Valley Carneros Estate Reserve

★★★ Clos Du Val Wine Co. Napa Valley Carneros Reserve

★★★ Clos LaChance Wines Santa Cruz Mountains

★★★ Clos LaChance Wines Santa Cruz Mountains Vintner's Reserve

★★★ Clos Pegase Carneros Mitsuko's Vineyard

★★★ B. R. Cohn Carneros Joseph Herman Vineyard Reserve

★★★ B. R. Cohn Sonoma Valley

★★★ Cosentino Winery Napa County

★★★ Cosentino Winery Napa Valley The Sculptor Reserve

★★★ Cronin Vineyards Alexander Valley Stuhlmuller Vineyard

★★★ Cronin Vineyards Santa Cruz Mountains

★★★ Cuvaison Napa Valley Carneros

★★★ De Loach Vineyards Russian River Valley

★★★ De Loach Vineyards Sonoma Cuvée

★★★ Domaine Grand Archer Sonoma County

★★★ Dry Creek Vineyard Sonoma County

★★★ Dry Creek Vineyard Sonoma County Reserve

★★★ Edmeades Vineyards Anderson Valley

★★★ Edna Valley Vineyard Edna Valley Paragon Vineyard

★★★ Ehlers Grove Napa Valley Winery Reserve

★★★ Fetzer Vineyards Mendocino County Barrel Select

★★★ Fetzer Vineyards Mendocino County Reserve

★★★ Field Stone Winery Sonoma County

★★★ Firestone Vineyard Santa Ynez Valley

★★★ Fisher Vineyards Sonoma County Coach Insignia

★★★ Fisher Vineyards Sonoma County Whitney's Vineyard

★★★ Freemark Abbey Winery Napa Valley

★★★ J. Fritz Russian River Valley Dutton Vineyard Ruxton Ranch

★★★ J. Fritz Russian River Valley Poplar Vineyard

★★★ Frog's Leap Carneros

★★★ Geyser Peak Alexander Valley Reserve

★★★ Geyser Peak Sonoma County

★★★ Godwin Russian River Valley Reserve

★★★ Groth Vineyards & Winery Napa Valley

★★★ Guenoc Winery North Coast

★★★ Handley Cellars Dry Creek Valley Handley Vineyard

★★★ Hartford Court Winery Russian River Valley Seascape Vineyard

★★★ Hendry Ranch Napa Valley Block 9

★★★ William Hill Winery Napa Valley

★★★ William Hill Winery Napa Valley Reserve

★★★ Iron Horse Vineyards Sonoma Green Valley

★★★ Jarvis Napa Valley

★★★ Jepson Vineyards Ltd. Mendocino County

★★★ Jordan Vineyard & Winery Sonoma County

★★★ Justin Vineyards & Winery Paso Robles

★★★ Kendall-Jackson Winery Arroyo Seco Monterey Paradise Vineyard Single Vineyard Series

★★★ Kendall-Jackson Winery California Vintner's Reserve

★★★ Kenwood Vineyards Sonoma County

★★★ Kunde Estate Winery Sonoma Valley

★★★ Kunde Estate Winery Sonoma Valley Kinneybrook

★★★ Kunde Estate Winery Sonoma Valley Reserve

★★★ Kunde Estate Winery Sonoma Valley Wildwood

★★★ La Crema Sonoma Coast

★★★ La Crema Sonoma Coast Reserve

★★★ Laetitia Vineyard & Winery San Luis Obispo County Reserve

★★★ Lambert Bridge Winery Sonoma County

★★★ Liparita Cellars Howell Mountain

★★★ Lockwood Vineyard Monterey

★★★ Lockwood Vineyard Monterey Partners' Reserve

★★★ Lolonis Redwood Valley Private Reserve

★★★ Richard Longoria Wines Santa Ynez Valley Santa Rita Cuvée

★★★ Lynmar Russian River Valley Estate Quail Hill Vineyard

★★★ Markham Vineyards Napa Valley

★★★ Louis M. Martini Winery Russian River Valley Reserve

★★★ Mayo Sonoma Valley Estate Bottled Laurel Hill Vineyard

★★★ Mayo Sonoma Valley Estate Bottled Laurel Hill Vineyard Barrel Select

★★★ McIlroy Cellars Russian River Valley Aquarius Ranch

★★★ Meridian Vineyards Santa Barbara County

★★★ Mirassou Vineyards Monterey County Family Selection

★★★ Mirassou Vineyards Monterey County Mission Ranch Vineyard Reserve

★★★ Mirassou Vineyards Monterey County San Vicente Vineyard Reserve

★★★ Murphy-Goode Estate Winery Russian River Valley J&K Murphy Vineyard Reserve

★★★ Napa Ridge Napa Valley Reserve

★★★ Navarro Vineyards Anderson Valley Première Reserve

★★★ Navarro Vineyards Mendocino

★★★ Nichols Winery Central Coast Blend

★★★ Nichols Winery Central Coast Reserve

★★★ Nichols Winery Edna Valley Paragon

★★★ Nichols Winery Santa Barbara County Bien Nacido Vineyard

★★★ Nichols Winery Santa Barbara County Cottonwood Canyon

★★★ Niebaum-Coppola Estate Winery Napa Valley Francis Coppola Family Wines

★★★ The Ojai Vineyard Arroyo Grande Valley Talley Vineyard

★★★ The Ojai Vineyard Arroyo Grande Valley Talley Vineyard Reserve

★★★ The Ojai Vineyard Santa Barbara County Bien Nacido Vineyard

★★★ The Ojai Vineyard Santa Ynez Valley Sanford & Benedict Vineyard

★★★ Optima Wine Cellars Carneros

★★★ Fess Parker Santa Barbara County

★★★ Fess Parker Santa Barbara County American Tradition Reserve

★★★ Fess Parker Santa Barbara County Marcella Vineyard American Tradition Reserve

★★★ Peju Province Winery Napa Valley

★★★ Pezzi King Sonoma County

★★★ The R.H. Phillips Vineyard Dunnigan Hills Toasted Head

★★★ PlumpJack Napa Valley Reserve

★★★ Qupé Santa Barbara County Bien Nacido Vineyard

★★★ Qupé Santa Barbara County Sierra Madre Vineyard

★★★ Rabbit Ridge Vineyards Russian River Valley Rabbit Ridge Ranch Estate Reserve

★★★ Rabbit Ridge Vineyards Sonoma County

★★★ Kent Rasmussen Winery Napa Valley

★★★ Ravenswood Sonoma Valley Sangiacomo

★★★ Raymond Vineyard & Cellar Monterey County Raymond Estates

★★★ Raymond Vineyard & Cellar Napa Valley Raymond Estates Reserve

★★★ Rosenblum Cellars Edna Valley

★★★ Rosenthal—The Mailbu Estate Malibu-Newton Canyon

★★★ Stephen Ross Edna Valley Edna Ranch

★★★ Stephen Ross Edna Valley Linda's Vineyard

★★★ Stephen Ross Santa Maria Valley Bien Nacido Vineyard

★★★ Rutherford Hill Winery Napa Valley Reserve

★★★ Rutz Cellars Russian River Valley Dutton Ranch

★★★ Saddleback Cellars Napa Valley

★★★ Santa Barbara Winery Santa Ynez Valley Lafond Vineyard

★★★ Santa Barbara Winery Santa Ynez Valley Reserve

★★★ Santa Cruz Mountain Vineyard Santa Cruz Mountains S. Miller

★★★ Sapphire Hill Vineyard Russian River

★★★ V. Sattui Winery Yountville Carsi Vineyard

★★★ Schug Carneros Estate Winery Carneros Barrel Fermented

★★★ Schug Carneros Estate Winery Carneros Heritage Reserve

★★★ Seavey Vineyard Napa Valley

★★★ Sebastiani Sonoma Cask Cellars Sonoma County

★★★ Sebastopol Vineyards Russian River Valley Dutton Ranch

★★★ Selby Winery Sonoma County

★★★ Sequoia Grove Vineyards Rutherford Estate Reserve

★★★ Silverado Vineyards Napa Valley

★★★ Simi Winery Sonoma County

★★★ Robert Sinskey Vineyards Carneros

★★★ Sonoma-Cutrer Vineyards Sonoma Coast Les Pierres

★★★ Sonoma-Cutrer Vineyards Sonoma Coast Russian River Ranches

★★★ Soquel Vineyards Santa Cruz Mountains

★★★ Stag's Leap Wine Cellars Napa Valley

★★★ Staglin Family Vineyard Rutherford

★★★ Sterling Vineyards Napa Valley

★★★ Stonegate Winery Sonoma County

★★★ Stuhlmuller Vineyards Alexander Valley

★★★ Sunstone Vineyards & Winery Santa Barbara County Marcellas Vineyards

★★★ Joseph Swan Vineyards Russian River Valley Estate

★★★ Swanson Vineyards Napa Valley Carneros

★★★ Testarossa Vineyard Chalone Michaud Vineyard

★★★ M. Trinchero Napa Valley Founder's Estate

★★★ Unalii Sonoma County

★★★ Venezia Alexander Valley

★★★ Venezia Napa Valley

★★★ von Strasser Napa Valley

★★★ Wente Vineyards Livermore Valley Herman Wente Vineyard Reserve

★★★ Whitcraft Winery Santa Maria Valley Bien Nacido

★★★ Whitcraft Winery Santa Ynez Valley Sanford & Benedict

★★★ White Rock Vineyards Napa Valley

★★★ Whitehall Lane Winery Napa Valley

★★★ Zaca Mesa Winery Santa Barbara County Zaca Vineyards

★★★ ZD Wines California

CHENIN BLANC

★★★★ Chalone Vineyard Chalone

★★★ Chappellet Vineyard Napa Valley Dry

★★★ Chappellet Vineyard Napa Valley Moelleux

★★★ Chappellet Vineyard Napa Valley Old Vine Cuvée

★★★ Daniel Gehrs Wines Monterey Carmel Vineyard Le Cheniére

DESSERT/LATE HARVEST

★★★★★ Arrowood Vineyards & Winery White Riesling Late Harvest Russian River Valley Oak Meadow Vineyard Select

★★★★★ Arrowood Vineyards & Winery White Riesling Late Harvest Russian River Valley Preston Ranch Select

★★★★★ Beringer Vineyards Nightingale Napa Valley

★★★★★ Bonny Doon Vineyard Muscat Canelli Monterey County Vin de Glaciere

★★★★★ Dolce Sémillon-Sauvignon Blanc Blend Late Harvest Napa Valley

★★★★★ Grgich Hills Cellar Violetta Late Harvest Napa Valley

★★★★ David Coffaro Vineyard & Winery Sauvignon Blanc Late Harvest Dry Creek Valley

★★★★ Ferrari-Carano Winery Eldorado Gold Late Harvest Dry Creek Valley

★★★★ Freemark Abbey Winery Johannisberg Riesling Late Harvest Napa Valley Edelwein Gold

★★★★ Greenwood Ridge Vineyards White Riesling Late Harvest Mendocino Ridge

★★★★ Long Vineyards Johannisberg Riesling Late Havest Napa Valley Botrytis

★★★★ Mendelson Vineyard Pinot Gris Dessert Napa Valley

★★★★ Navarro Vineyards Riesling Late Harvest Anderson Valley Sweet

★★★★ Navarro Vineyards Riesling Late Harvest Anderson Valley Very Sweet Cluster Select

★★★★ Swanson Vineyards Sémillon Late Harvest Napa Valley

★★★★ Philip Togni Black Muscat Napa Valley Ca' Togni

★★★ Arrowood Vineyards & Winery Viognier Late Harvest Russian River Valley Saralee's Vineyard Select

★★★ Cline Cellars Muscat Canelli Sonoma Valley

★★★ Jekel Vineyards Johannisberg Riesling Late Harvest Monterey

★★★ Quady Black Muscat California Elysium

★★★ Quady Winery Orange Muscat California Electra

★★★ Quady Winery Orange Muscat California Essensia

★★★ Renaissance Vineyard & Winery Riesling Late Harvest North Yuba

GEWÜRZTRAMINER

★★★ Babcock Vineyards Santa Ynez Valley Estate Grown

★★★ Edmeades Vineyards Anderson Valley

★★★ Thomas Fogarty Winery Monterey County

★★★ Martinelli Vineyard Russian River Valley Martinelli Vineyard

★★★ Martinelli Vineyard Russian River Valley Martinelli Vineyard Dry Select

★★★ Louis M. Martini Winery Russian River Valley Heritage Collection

★★★ Navarro Vineyards Anderson Valley

★★★ Stonestreet Anderson Valley Mendocino

GRENACHE

★★★ Alban Vineyards Edna Valley Alban Vineyard

★★★ Jaffurs Santa Barbara County Stolpman Vineyard

MARSANNE

★★★ Karly Wines Amador County

★★★ Joseph Phelps Vineyards Napa Valley Vin du Mistral

MERLOT

★★★★★ Beringer Vineyards Howell Mountain Bancroft Ranch

★★★★★ Lewis Cellars Napa Valley Reserve

★★★★★ Matanzas Creek Winery Sonoma Valley

★★★★★ Matanzas Creek Winery Sonoma Valley Journey

★★★★★ Pahlmeyer Napa Valley

★★★★★ St. Francis Winery Sonoma Valley Reserve

★★★★ Arrowood Vineyards & Winery Sonoma County

★★★★ Chateau St. Jean Sonoma County Reserve

★★★★ Cuvaison Napa Valley ATS

★★★★ Duckhorn Vineyards Napa Valley

★★★★ Duckhorn Vineyards Napa Valley Estate Grown

★★★★ Duckhorn Vineyards Napa Valley Howell Mountain

★★★★ Lewis Cellars Sonoma County

★★★★ Markham Vineyards Napa Valley

★★★★ Markham Vineyards Napa Valley Reserve

★★★★ Matanzas Creek Winery Sonoma Valley Estate

★★★★ Neyers Vineyards Napa Valley Neyers Ranch-Conn Valley

★★★★ Paloma Winery Napa Valley Spring Mountain District

★★★★ Paradigm Oakville

★★★★ Pride Mountain Vineyards Napa Valley

★★★★ Seavey Vineyard Napa Valley

★★★★ Shafer Vineyards Napa Valley

★★★★ Truchard Vineyard Carneros

★★★★ Whitehall Lane Winery Napa Valley Leonardini Vineyard

★★★ S. Anderson Vineyard Stags Leap District Reserve

★★★ Azalea Springs Cellars Napa Valley

★★★ Behrens & Hitchcock Oakville

★★★ Belvedere Winery Dry Creek Valley Preferred Stock

★★★ Cafaro Cellars Napa Valley

★★★ Cakebread Cellars Napa Valley

★★★ Chalk Hill Winery Chalk Hill

★★★ Chateau St. Jean Sonoma County

★★★ Chateau Souverain Alexander Valley

★★★ Clos du Bois Winery Alexander Valley Alexander Valley Selection

★★★ B. R. Cohn Sonoma Valley Olive Hill Estate Vineyard

★★★ Cosentino Winery Napa Valley Oakville Estate

★★★ Cosentino Winery Napa Valley Reserve

★★★ Cosentino Winery North Coast

★★★ Cuvaison Napa Valley Carneros

★★★ Delectus Oakville Stanton Vineyard

★★★ Dry Creek Vineyard Dry Creek Valley Reserve

★★★ Duckhorn Vineyards Napa Valley Three Palms Vineyard

★★★ Emmolo Rutherford

★★★ Gary Farrell Wines Russian River Valley

★★★ Gary Farrell Wines Sonoma County Ladi's Vineyard

★★★ Ferrari-Carano Winery Sonoma County

★★★ Fife Vineyards Napa Valley

★★★ Fisher Vineyards Napa Valley RCF Vineyard

★★★ Flora Springs Wine Co. Napa Valley

★★★ Flora Springs Wine Co. Rutherford Windfall Vineyard

★★★ Forman Vineyard Napa Valley

★★★ Frazier Napa Valley Lupine Hill Vineyard

★★★ Freemark Abbey Winery Napa Valley

★★★ Frog's Leap Napa Valley

★★★ Galante Vineyards Carmel Valley Estate

★★★ Gallo of Sonoma Winery Northern Sonoma

★★★ Gallo of Sonoma Winery Sonoma County

★★★ Geyser Peak Alexander Valley Reserve

★★★ Geyser Peak Sonoma County

★★★ Greenwood Ridge Vineyards Mendocino Ridge

★★★ Groth Vineyards & Winery Napa Valley

★★★ Harrison Winery & Vineyards Napa Valley

★★★ Havens Wine Cellars Carneros Reserve

★★★ Havens Wine Cellars Napa Valley

★★★ The Hess Collection Winery Mount Veeder Napa Valley

★★★ Jarvis Napa Valley

★★★ Judd's Hill Napa Valley Juliana Vineyards

★★★ Justin Vineyards & Winery Paso Robles

★★★ Kendall-Jackson Winery California Grand Reserve

★★★ Lambert Bridge Winery Sonoma County

★★★ Ledson Winery & Vineyards Sonoma Valley

★★★ Ledson Winery & Vineyards Sonoma Valley Reserve

★★★ Lewis Cellars Napa Valley Oakville Ranch

★★★ Liparita Cellars Howell Mountain

★★★ Lockwood Vineyard Monterey

★★★ Lockwood Vineyard Monterey Partners' Reserve

★★★ Lolonis Mendocino County

★★★ Richard Longoria Wines Santa Ynez Valley

★★★ Luna Vineyards Napa Valley

★★★ Mason Napa Valley

★★★ McCray Ridge Winery Dry Creek Valley Two Moon Vineyard

★★★ Merryvale Vineyards Napa Valley Reserve

★★★ Miner Family Vineyards Napa Valley Oakville Ranch

★★★ Robert Mondavi Winery Napa Valley

★★★ Murphy-Goode Estate Winery Alexander Valley Murphy Ranch

★★★ Newton Vineyard Napa Valley Special Cuvée

★★★ Newton Vineyard Napa Valley Unfiltered

★★★ Neyers Vineyards Napa Valley

★★★ Niebaum-Coppola Estate Winery Rutherford Francis Coppola Family Wines

★★★ Oakville Ranch Vineyards Napa Valley

★★★ Paoletti Vineyards Napa Valley

★★★ Fess Parker Santa Barbara County

★★★ Robert Pecota Winery Napa Valley Steven André Vineyard

★★★ Joseph Phelps Vineyards Napa Valley

★★★ Pine Ridge Winery Napa Valley Carneros

★★★ Pine Ridge Winery Napa Valley Crimson Creek

★★★ Rabbit Ridge Vineyards Carneros Sangiacomo Vineyard Reserve

★★★ Rabbit Ridge Vineyards Sonoma County Winemaker's Grand Reserve

★★★ Ravenswood Sonoma County

★★★ Ravenswood Sonoma Valley Donnell Ranch

★★★ Ravenswood Sonoma Valley Sangiacomo Vineyard

★★★ Richardson Vineyards Carneros Sangiacomo

★★★ Ridge Vineyards Santa Cruz Mountains

★★★ Rombauer Vineyards Napa Valley

★★★ Rutherford Hill Winery Napa Valley Reserve

★★★ St. Clement Vineyards Napa Valley

★★★ St. Francis Winery Sonoma County

★★★ Sebastiani Sonoma Cask Cellars Sonoma County

★★★ Sebastiani Sonoma Cask Cellars Sonoma County Town

★★★ Selby Winery Sonoma County

★★★ Selene Wines Napa Valley

★★★ Silverado Vineyards Napa Valley

★★★ Robert Sinskey Vineyards Carneros

★★★ Robert Sinskey Vineyards Carneros Reserve

★★★ Stag's Leap Wine Cellars Napa Valley

★★★ Sterling Vineyards Napa Valley Carneros Winery Lake Vineyard

★★★ Sterling Vineyards Napa Valley Diamond Mountain Ranch

★★★ Sterling Vineyards Napa Valley Three Palms Vineyard

★★★ Stonestreet Alexander Valley

★★★ Summers Knights Valley Summers Ranch

★★★ Swanson Vineyards Napa Valley

★★★ Venge Napa Valley Reserve

★★★ Villa Mt. Eden California

★★★ Vine Cliff Cellars Napa Valley

★★★ Voss Vineyards Napa Valley

★★★ Whitehall Lane Winery Napa Valley

MOURVÈDRE

★★★ Bonny Doon Vineyard California Old Telegram

★★★ Cline Cellars Contra Costa County

★★★ Rosenblum Cellars Contra Costa County Chateau La Paws

PETITE SIRAH

★★★★★ Turley Wine Cellars Napa Valley Aïda Vineyard

★★★★★ Turley Wine Cellars Napa Valley Hayne Vineyard

★★★★ David Bruce Winery Paso Robles Ranchita Canyon Vineyard

★★★★ David Bruce Winery Paso Robles Shell Creek Vineyard

★★★★ David Coffaro Vineyard & Winery Dry Creek Valley

★★★★ Hidden Cellars Winery Mendocino Eaglepoint Ranch

★★★★ Markham Vineyards Napa Valley

★★★★ Stag's Leap Wine Cellars Napa Valley

★★★★ Stags' Leap Winery Napa Valley

★★★★ Stags' Leap Winery Napa Valley Reserve

★★★★ Turley Wine Cellars Napa Valley Rattlesnake Acres

★★★ Beaulieu Vineyard Napa Valley Signet Collection

★★★ Bogle Vineyards California

★★★ David Bruce Winery Central Coast

★★★ Oliver Caldwell Cellars Napa Valley Aïda Vineyard

★★★ Fife Vineyards Redwood Valley Redhead Vineyard

★★★ Foppiano Vineyards Russian River Valley

★★★ Guenoc Winery California

★★★ Hidden Cellars Winery Mendocino

★★★ JC Cellars St. Helena Napa Valley St. George Vineyard

★★★ La Jota Vineyard Co. Howell Mountain

★★★ Lambert Bridge Winery Dry Creek Valley

★★★ Lolonis Mendocino County Orpheus

★★★ Lorenza-Lake Napa Valley

★★★ Mazzocco Vineyards Dry Creek Valley

★★★ Parducci Wine Cellars California

★★★ Ridge Vineyards Spring Mountain York Creek

★★★ Rockland Road Cellars Napa Valley

★★★ Rosenblum Cellars Napa Valley Kenefick Ranch

★★★ Signorello Vineyards Napa Valley

PINOT BLANC

★★★★★ Chalone Vineyard Chalone Reserve

★★★★ Arrowood Vineyards & Winery Russian River Valley Saralee's Vineyard

★★★★ Chalone Vineyard Chalone

★★★★ Steele Wines Santa Barbara County Bien Nacido Vineyard

★★★ Au Bon Climat Santa Barbara County Bien Nacido Reserve

★★★ Benziger Family Winery North Coast Imagery

★★★ Byron Vineyards & Winery Santa Maria Valley Estate

★★★ Etude Wines Carneros

★★★ J. Lohr Winery Monterey County October Night

★★★ Lockwood Vineyard Monterey

★★★ Nichols Winery Arroyo Grande Valley La Colline

★★★ Paraiso Springs Vineyards Santa Lucia Highlands

★★★ Paraiso Springs Vineyards Santa Lucia Highlands Reserve

★★★ Testarossa Vineyard Chalone

★★★ Villa Mt. Eden Santa Maria Valley Bien Nacido Vineyard Grand Reserve

PINOT GRIGIO/PINOT GRIS

★★★ Byron Vineyards & Winery Santa Maria Valley Estate

★★★ Chalk Hill Winery Chalk Hill Estate Vineyard Selection

★★★ Di Bruno Santa Ynez Valley Sanford & Benedict Vineyard

★★★ Long Vineyards Sonoma & Napa Valleys

★★★ Joseph Swan Vineyards Russian River Valley Saralee's Vineyard

PINOT NOIR

★★★★★ Au Bon Climat Arroyo Grande Valley Rosemary's Talley Vineyard

★★★★★ Dehlinger Winery Russian River Valley

★★★★★ Dehlinger Winery Russian River Valley Goldridge Vineyard

★★★★★ Dehlinger Winery Russian River Valley Octagon Vineyard

★★★★★ Dehlinger Winery Russian River Valley Reserve

★★★★★ Gary Farrell Wines Russian River Valley Allen Vineyard

★★★★★ Gary Farrell Wines Russian River Valley Rochioli Vineyard

★★★★★ Kistler Vineyards Russian River Valley Kistler Vineyard

★★★★★ Kistler Vineyards Sonoma Coast Camp Meeting Ridge

★★★★★ Kistler Vineyards Sonoma Coast Cuvée Catherine

★★★★★ Kistler Vineyards Sonoma Coast Hirsch Vineyard

★★★★★ J. Rochioli Vineyards Russian River Valley East Block

★★★★★ J. Rochioli Vineyards Russian River Valley Estate Three-Corner

★★★★★ J. Rochioli Vineyards Russian River Valley Estate West Block

★★★★★ J. Rochioli Vineyards Russian River Valley Reserve

★★★★★ Saintsbury Carneros Reserve

★★★★★ Sanford Winery Santa Barbara County Sanford & Benedict Vineyard Barrel Select

★★★★★ Talley Vineyards Arroyo Grande Valley Rosemary's Vineyard

★★★★★ Williams Selyem Winery Russian River Valley Allen Vineyard

★★★★★ Williams Selyem Winery Russian River Valley Rochioli Vineyard

★★★★ Acacia Winery Carneros Beckstoffer Vineyard Reserve

★★★★ Au Bon Climat Arroyo Grande Valley Rincon and Rosemary's

★★★★ Au Bon Climat California Isabelle

★★★★ Au Bon Climat Santa Barbara County La Bauge Au-dessus

★★★★ David Bruce Winery Santa Cruz Mountains

★★★★ David Bruce Winery Santa Cruz Mountains Estate Reserve

★★★★ Calera Wine Co. Mount Harlan Jensen

★★★★ Calera Wine Co. Mount Harlan Mills

★★★★ Flowers Sonoma Coast Camp Meeting Ridge

★★★★ Flowers Sonoma Coast Camp Meeting Ridge Moon Select

★★★★ Hitching Post Santa Ynez Valley Sanford & Benedict Vineyard

★★★★ Landmark Vineyards Sonoma County Grand Detour

★★★★ Landmark Vineyards Sonoma Mountain Van der Kamp Vinyards

★★★★ Robert Mondavi Winery Napa Valley Reserve

★★★★ Robert Mueller Cellars Russian River Valley Emily's Cuvée

★★★★ J. Rochioli Vineyards Russian River Valley Estate

★★★★ J. Rochioli Vineyards Russian River Valley Estate Little Hill

★★★★ Saintsbury Carneros Brown Ranch

★★★★ Sanford Winery Santa Barbara County

★★★★ Santa Cruz Mountain Vineyard Santa Cruz Mountains

★★★★ Siduri Cellars Anderson Valley Rose Vineyard

★★★★ Steele Wines Carneros

★★★★ Steele Wines Carneros Sangiacomo Vineyard

★★★★ Talley Vineyards Arroyo Grande Valley Rincon Vineyard

★★★★ Truchard Vineyard Carneros

★★★★ Williams Selyem Winery Anderson Valley Ferrington Vineyard

★★★★ Williams Selyem Winery Russian River Valley

★★★★ Williams Selyem Winery Russian River Valley Olivet Lane Vineyard

★★★★ Williams Selyem Winery Russian River Valley Riverblock Vineyard

★★★★ Williams Selyem Winery Sonoma Coast

★★★★ Williams Selyem Winery Sonoma Coast Coastlands Vineyard

★★★★ Williams Selyem Winery Sonoma Coast Hirsch Vineyard

★★★ Acacia Winery Carneros

★★★ Acacia Winery Carneros Reserve

★★★ Acacia Winery Carneros St. Clair Vineyard Reserve

★★★ Ancien Wines Carneros

★★★ Au Bon Climat Arroyo Grande Valley Piccho and Rincon

★★★ Au Bon Climat Santa Maria Valley

★★★ Au Bon Climat Santa Ynez Valley Sanford & Benedict Reserve

★★★ Au Bon Climat Santa Ynez Valley Sanford & Benedict Vineyard

★★★ Babcock Vineyards Santa Barbara County

★★★ Babcock Vineyards Santa Ynez Valley Grand Cuvee

★★★ Bannister Vineyards Anderson Valley Floodgate Vineyard

★★★ Beaulieu Vineyard Carneros

★★★ Beaulieu Vineyard Carneros Reserve

★★★ Beringer Vineyards Carneros Stanly Ranch

★★★ Bernardus Winery Santa Maria Valley Bien Nacido Vineyard

★★★ Brophy Clark Cellars Arroyo Grande Valley

★★★ David Bruce Winery Central Coast

★★★ David Bruce Winery Chalone

★★★ David Bruce Winery Russian River Valley

★★★ David Bruce Winery Russian River Valley Reserve

★★★ Byron Vineyards & Winery Santa Maria Valley

★★★ Byron Vineyards & Winery Santa Maria Valley Reserve

★★★ Cakebread Cellars Napa Valley Carneros

★★★ Calera Wine Co. Central Coast

★★★ Calera Wine Co. Mount Harlan Reed

★★★ Calera Wine Co. Mount Harlan Selleck

★★★ Cambria Winery & Vineyard Santa Maria Valley Julia's Vineyard

★★★ Cambria Winery & Vineyard Santa Maria Valley Reserve

★★★ Carneros Creek Winery Carneros

★★★ Carneros Creek Winery Carneros Signature Reserve

★★★ Castalia Russian River Valley Rochioli Vineyard

★★★ Chalone Vineyard Chalone

★★★ Chalone Vineyard Chalone Reserve

★★★ Chateau St. Jean Carneros Durell Vineyard

★★★ Cosentino Winery Napa Valley

★★★ Cosentino Winery Russian River Valley

★★★ Cuvaison Napa Valley Carneros

★★★ Cuvaison Napa Valley Carneros Eris

★★★ De Loach Vineyards Russian River Valley

★★★ De Loach Vineyards Russian River Valley O.F.S.

★★★ Domaine Carneros Carneros

★★★ Domaine Carneros Carneros The Famous Gate

★★★ Edmeades Vineyards Anderson Valley

★★★ El Molino Winery Napa Valley

★★★ Estancia Estates Monterey Reserve

★★★ Etude Wines Carneros

★★★ Etude Wines Rosé American

★★★ Gary Farrell Wines Russian River Valley

★★★ Gary Farrell Wines Santa Barbara County Bien Nacido Vineyard

★★★ Fiddlehead Cellars Santa Maria Valley

★★★ Flora Springs Wine Co. Carneros Lavender Hill Vineyard

★★★ Flowers Carneros

★★★ Flowers Sonoma Coast Hirsch

★★★ Thomas Fogarty Winery Santa Cruz Mountains Estate

★★★ Thomas Fogarty Winery Santa Cruz Mountains Estate Reserve

★★★ Foxen Vineyard Santa Maria Valley

★★★ Foxen Vineyard Santa Maria Valley Bien Nacido Vineyard

★★★ Foxen Vineyard Santa Maria Valley Julia's Vineyard

★★★ Foxen Vineyard Santa Ynez Valley Sanford & Benedict

★★★ The Gainey Vineyard Santa Maria Valley Limited Selection

★★★ Greenwood Ridge Vineyards Anderson Valley

★★★ Hanzell Vineyards Sonoma Valley

★★★ Hartford Court Winery Russian River Valley Arrendell Vineyard

★★★ Hartford Court Winery Russian River Valley Dutton Ranch Sanchietti Vineyard

★★★ Hartford Court Winery Sonoma Coast

★★★ Hitching Post Santa Maria Valley

★★★ Hitching Post Santa Maria Valley Bien Nacido Vineyard

★★★ Kynsi Edna Valley

★★★ La Crema Sonoma Coast

★★★ La Crema Sonoma Coast Reserve

★★★ Laetitia Vineyard & Winery San Luis Obispo County Laetitia Vineyard

★★★ Laetitia Vineyard & Winery San Luis Obispo County Reserve

★★★ LinCourt Vineyards Santa Maria Valley Santa Maria Hills

★★★ Littorai Anderson Valley One Acre

★★★ Littorai Anderson Valley Savoy Vineyard

★★★ Littorai Sonoma Coast Hirsch Vineyard

★★★ Richard Longoria Wines Santa Maria Valley Bien Nacido Vineyard

★★★ Lynmar Russian River Valley Estate Quail Hill Vineyard

★★★ Lynmar Russian River Valley Estate Quail Hill Vineyard Reserve

★★★ MacRostie Wines Carneros Reserve

★★★ Martinelli Vineyard Russian River Valley Martinelli Vineyard

★★★ Martinelli Vineyard Russian River Valley Reserve

★★★ Meridian Vineyards Santa Barbara County

★★★ Meridian Vineyards Santa Barbara & San Luis Obispo Counties Reserve

★★★ Robert Mondavi Winery Carneros

★★★ Robert Mondavi Winery Napa Valley

★★★ Morgan Winery Monterey

★★★ Morgan Winery Monterey Reserve

★★★ Mount Eden Vineyards Santa Cruz Mountains

★★★ Robert Mueller Cellars Russian River Valley Ranch 23

★★★ Navarro Vineyards Anderson Valley Méthode à l'Ancienne

★★★ Navarro Vineyards Mendocino

★★★ Nichols Winery Arroyo Grande Valley La Colline

★★★ Nichols Winery Central Coast Blend

★★★ Nichols Winery Central Coast Reserve

★★★ Nichols Winery Edna Valley Paragon Vineyard

★★★ Nichols Winery Monterey County Pisoni Vineyard

★★★ Nichols Winery Santa Barbara County Cottonwood Canyon

★★★ Nichols Winery Santa Barbara County Sierra Madre Vineyard

★★★ The Ojai Vineyard Santa Barbara County Bien Nacido Vineyard

★★★ The Ojai Vineyard Santa Lucia Highlands Pisoni Vineyard

★★★ Patz & Hall Wine Co. Carneros Hyde Vineyard

★★★ Patz & Hall Wine Co. Mendocino Alder Springs Vineyard

★★★ Patz & Hall Wine Co. Russian River Valley

★★★ Rutz Cellars Monterey Sleepy Hollow

★★★ Saintsbury Carneros

★★★ Saintsbury Carneros Garnet

★★★ Santa Barbara Winery Santa Barbara County Reserve

★★★ Santa Cruz Mountain Vineyard Santa Cruz Mountains Ciaradella Vineyard

★★★ Santa Cruz Mountain Vineyard Santa Cruz Mountains Matteson Vineyard

★★★ Sebastopol Vineyards Russian River Valley Dutton Ranch

★★★ Siduri Cellars Oregon

★★★ Siduri Cellars Santa Lucia Highlands Pisoni Vineyard

★★★ Siduri Cellars Sonoma Coast Hirsch Vineyard

★★★ Siduri Cellars Sonoma Mountain Van Der Kamp Vineyard Old Vines

★★★ Signorello Vineyards Carneros Las Amigas Vineyard

★★★ Signorello Vineyards North Coast Founders Reserve

★★★ Signorello Vineyards Russian River Martinelli Vineyard

★★★ W.H. Smith Wines Sonoma Coast Hellenthal Vineyard

★★★ Steele Wines Anderson Valley

★★★ Steele Wines Carneros Durell Vineyard

★★★ Steele Wines Mendocino DuPratt Vineyard

★★★ Steele Wines Santa Barbara County Bien Nacido Vineyard

★★★ Stephen Ross Edna Valley Edna Ranch

★★★ Stephen Ross Santa Maria Valley Bien Nacido Vineyard

★★★ Stonestreet Russian River Valley

★★★ Joseph Swan Vineyards Russian River Valley

★★★ Joseph Swan Vineyards Russian River Valley Estate

★★★ Joseph Swan Vineyards Russian River Valley Lone Redwood Ranch

★★★ Joseph Swan Vineyards Russian River Valley Saralee's Vineyard

★★★ Joseph Swan Vineyards Sonoma Mountain Steiner Vineyard

★★★ Joseph Swan Vineyards Sonoma Mountain Wolfspierre Vineyard

★★★ Talley Vineyards Arroyo Grande Valley

★★★ Lane Tanner Winery Santa Barbara County

★★★ Lane Tanner Winery Santa Maria Valley Bien Nacido Vineyard

★★★ Lane Tanner Winery Santa Maria Valley Julia's Vineyard

★★★ Lane Tanner Winery Santa Maria Valley Sierra Madre

★★★ Marimar Torres Estate Russian River Valley Don Miguel Vineyard

★★★ Villa Mt. Eden Santa Maria Valley Bien Nacido Vineyard Grand Reserve

★★★ Whitcraft Winery Santa Maria Valley Bien Nacido

★★★ Whitcraft Winery Santa Maria Valley Bien Nacido Q Block

★★★ Wild Horse Winery & Vineyards Central Coast Cheval Sauvage

★★★ Williams Selyem Winery Sonoma County

PORT

★★★ Ficklin Vineyards California Special Bottling

★★★ Ficklin Vineyards California Ten-Year-Old Tawny

★★★ Guenoc Winery California

★★★ Quady Winery California Starboard Batch 88

★★★ Quady Winery California Starboard Frank's Vineyard

★★★ Rosenblum Cellars Sonoma County

RIESLING

★★★ Chateau St. Jean Johannisberg Riesling Sonoma County Riesling

★★★ Firestone Vineyard Johannisberg Riesling Santa Barbara County Selected Harvest

★★★ Greenwood Ridge Vineyards White Riesling Mendocino Ridge

★★★ J. Lohr Winery White Riesling Monterey County Bay Mist

ROUSSANNE

★★★ Qupé Central Coast

★★★ Qupé Edna Valley Alban Vineyard

★★★ Sobon Estate California Shenandoah Valley

★★★ Zaca Mesa Winery Santa Barbara County Zaca Vineyards

SANGIOVESE

★★★★ Altamura Vineyards & Winery Napa Valley

★★★ Beaulieu Vineyard Napa Valley

★★★ Benessere Napa Valley

★★★ Cambria Winery & Vineyard Santa Maria Valley Tepusquet Vineyard

★★★ Flora Springs Wine Co. Napa Valley

★★★ Thomas Fogarty Winery Santa Cruz Mountains Estate Reserve

★★★ Iron Horse Vineyards Alexander Valley T-T Vineyards

★★★ La Sirena Wines Napa Valley

★★★ Livingston Vineyards Sonoma County

★★★ Lonetree Mendocino

★★★ Long Vineyards Sonoma Seghesio Vineyard

★★★ Luna Vineyards Napa Valley

★★★ Robert Pepi Winery Napa Valley Colline di Sassi

★★★ Rabbit Ridge Vineyards Sonoma County Coniglio Selezione

★★★ Staglin Family Vineyard Rutherford Stagliano

★★★ Swanson Vineyards Napa Valley

★★★ Venezia Mendocino County Eagle Point Ranch

★★★ Venezia Russian River Valley Alegria Vineyard

SANGIOVESE BLEND

★★★★ Ferrari-Carano Winery Siena Sonoma County

★★★ Rabbit Ridge Vineyards Aventura Sonoma County Migliore de Vigneto Reserve

SAUVIGNON BLANC/FUMÉ BLANC

★★★★★ J. Rochioli Vineyards Russian River Valley Estate Old Vines

★★★★ Babcock Vineyards Santa Barbara County Eleven Oaks

★★★★ Bernardus Winery Monterey County

★★★★ Caymus Vineyards Napa Valley

★★★★ Chalk Hill Winery Chalk Hill

★★★★ Grgich Hills Cellar Fumé Blanc Napa Valley

★★★★ Mason Napa Valley

★★★★ Peter Michael Winery Sonoma County L' Après-Midi

★★★★ Robert Mondavi Winery Fumé Blanc Napa Valley To-Kalon Vineyard I-Block

★★★★ Robert Mondavi Winery Fumé Blanc Napa Valley To-Kalon Vineyard Reserve

★★★★ Morgan Winery Sonoma & Monterey Counties

★★★★ Navarro Vineyards Mendocino Cuvée 128

★★★★ J. Rochioli Vineyards Russian River Valley Estate

★★★★ Selene Wines Carneros Hyde Vineyard

★★★ Araujo Estate Wines Napa Valley Eisele Vineyard

★★★ Beckmen Vineyards Santa Barbara County

★★★ Beringer Vineyards Napa Valley

★★★ Boeger Winery, Inc. El Dorado

★★★ Bogle Vineyards California

★★★ The Brander Vineyard Santa Ynez Valley

★★★ The Brander Vineyard Santa Ynez Valley Au Naturel

★★★ Brophy Clark CellarsSanta Barbara & San Luis Obispo Counties

★★★ Cain Vineyard & Winery Monterey Ventana Vineyards Musqué

★★★ Cakebread Cellars Napa Valley

★★★ Chateau Potelle Napa Valley

★★★ Chateau St. Jean Fumé Blanc Russian River Valley La Petite Etoile Vineyard

★★★ Chateau Souverain Alexander Valley

★★★ De Loach Vineyards Fumé Blanc Russian River Valley

★★★ de Lorimier Winery Alexander Valley

★★★ Dry Creek Vineyard Fumé Blanc Dry Creek Valley Reserve

★★★ Dry Creek Vineyard Fumé Blanc Sonoma County

★★★ Duckhorn Vineyards Napa Valley

★★★ Ehlers Grove Napa Valley Winery Reserve

★★★ Estancia Estates Fumé Blanc Monterey Pinnacles

★★★ Ferrari-Carano Winery Fumé Blanc Sonoma County

★★★ Ferrari-Carano Winery Fumé Blanc Sonoma County Reserve

★★★ Firestone Vineyard Santa Ynez Valley

★★★ Flora Springs Wine Co. Napa Valley

★★★ Flora Springs Wine Co. Napa Valley Soliloquy

★★★ Foley Estate Santa Barbara County

★★★ J. Fritz Dry Creek Valley Jenner Vineyard

★★★ J. Fritz Russian River Valley Poplar Vineyard

★★★ Daniel Gehrs Wines Monterey Carmel Vineyard

★★★ Geyser Peak Sonoma County

★★★ Greenwood Ridge Vineyards Mendocino Ridge

★★★ Groth Vineyards & Winery Napa Valley

★★★ Handley Cellars Dry Creek Valley Handley Vineyard

★★★ Iron Horse Vineyards Fumé Blanc Alexander Valley T-T Vineyards

★★★ Jepson Vineyards Mendocino County

★★★   Joseph Phelps Vineyards Napa Valley

★★★   Joullian Vineyards Carmel Valley Family Reserve

★★★   Karly Wines Amador County

★★★   Kenwood Vineyards Sonoma County

★★★   Kenwood Vineyards Sonoma Valley Reserve

★★★   Lambert Bridge Winery Dry Creek Valley

★★★   Ledson Winery & Vineyards Napa Valley

★★★   LinCourt Vineyards Santa Barbara County

★★★   Lockwood Vineyard Monterey

★★★   Lolonis Fumé Blanc Redwood Valley

★★★   Long Vineyards Sonoma & Napa Valleys

★★★   Markham Vineyards Napa Valley

★★★   Martinelli Vineyard Russian River Valley Martinelli Vineyard

★★★   Louis M. Martini WineryNapa Valley

★★★   Matanzas Creek Winery Sonoma County

★★★   Mayacamas Vineyards Napa Valley

★★★   Meridian Vineyards California

★★★   Robert Mondavi Winery Fumé Blanc Napa Valley

★★★   Robert Mondavi Winery Stags Leap District

★★★   Murphy-Goode Estate Winery Fumé Blanc Alexander Valley Fumé The Deuce

★★★   Murphy-Goode Estate Winery Fumé Blanc Alexander Valley Reserve Fumé

★★★   Murphy-Goode Estate Winery Fumé Blanc Sonoma County

★★★   Napa Wine Company Napa Valley

★★★   Rabbit Ridge Vineyards Russian River Valley

★★★   Renaissance Vineyard & Winery North Yuba

★★★   Renaissance Vineyard & Winery North Yuba Barrel Select

★★★   St. Clement Vineyards Napa Valley

★★★   St. Supéry Vineyard & Winery Napa Valley Dollarhide Ranch

★★★   Sanford Winery Central Coast

★★★   Shenandoah Vineyards Amador County

★★★   Signorello Vineyards Napa Valley

★★★   Silverado Vineyards Napa Valley

★★★   Simi Winery Sonoma County

★★★   Spottswoode Vineyard & Winery Napa Valley

★★★   Stag's Leap Wine Cellars Napa Valley

★★★   Stonestreet Alexander Valley Alexander Mountain Estate

★★★   Rodney Strong Vineyards Northern Sonoma Charlotte's Home Estate

★★★   Voss Vineyards Napa Valley

★★★   Wattle Creek Winery Alexander Valley

★★★   Wente Vineyards Livermore Valley

SÉMILLON

★★★★★ Chalk Hill Winery Chalk Hill Botrytised Estate Vineyard Selection

★★★   Clos Du Val Stags Leap District

★★★   Signorello Vineyards Napa Valley

SHIRAZ

★★★   Geyser Peak Sonoma County

★★★   Geyser Peak Sonoma County Reserve

★★★   Simi Winery Alexander Valley

★★★   Voss Vineyards Napa Valley

SPARKLING

★★★★★ Roederer Estate L' Ermitage Anderson Valley

★★★★   S. Anderson Vineyard Blanc de Blancs Napa Valley

★★★★   S. Anderson Vineyard Blanc de Noirs Napa Valley

★★★★   S. Anderson Vineyard Brut Napa Valley

★★★★   S. Anderson Vineyard Brut Napa Valley Reserve

★★★★   S. Anderson Vineyard Diva Napa Valley

★★★★   Domaine Carneros Le Reve Blanc de Blancs Carneros

★★★★   Gloria Ferrer Champagne Caves Brut Carneros Cuvée Late Disgorged

★★★★   Iron Horse Vineyards Blanc de Blancs Sonoma Green Valley LD

★★★★   J Wine Co. Sonoma County

★★★★   Mumm DVX Napa Valley

★★★★   Roederer Estate Brut Anderson Valley NV

★★★★   Scharffenberger Brut Mendocino County Private Reserve

★★★★ Schramsberg Vineyards J. Schram Napa Valley

★★★ S. Anderson Vineyard Rosé Napa Valley

★★★ Codorniu Napa Blanc de Blancs Napa Valley

★★★ Codorniu Napa Brut Napa Valley

★★★ Codorniu Napa Reserve Napa Valley

★★★ Codorniu Napa Rosé Napa Valley

★★★ Domaine Carneros Brut Carneros

★★★ Domaine Chandon Blanc de Noirs Carneros

★★★ Domaine Chandon Brut Sonoma-Napa Counties

★★★ Domaine Chandon Étoile Napa Valley

★★★ Domaine Chandon Étoile Rosé Napa Valley

★★★ Domaine Chandon Reserve Cuvée Napa County

★★★ Gloria Ferrer Champagne Caves Blanc de Noirs Carneros

★★★ Gloria Ferrer Champagne Caves Brut Sonoma

★★★ Gloria Ferrer Champagne Caves Brut Rosé Carneros

★★★ Handley Cellars Brut Anderson Valley

★★★ Handley Cellars Brut Rosé Anderson Valley

★★★ Robert Hunter Winery Brut de Noirs Sonoma Valley Extended Tirage

★★★ Iron Horse Vineyards Brut Sonoma Green Valley Classic Vintage

★★★ Iron Horse Vineyards Brut Sonoma Green Valley LD

★★★ Iron Horse Vineyards Brut Rosé Sonoma Green Valley

★★★ Iron Horse Vineyards Sonoma Green Valley Russian Cuvée

★★★ Iron Horse Vineyards Sonoma Green Valley Vrais Amis

★★★ Iron Horse Vineyards Sonoma Green Valley Wedding Cuvée

★★★ Jepson Vineyards Ltd. Blanc de Blancs Mendocino County Burnee Hill Vineyard

★★★ Kristone Champagne Cellars Blanc de Blancs California

★★★ Kristone Champagne Cellars Blanc de Noirs California

★★★ Kristone Champagne Cellars Brut Rosé California

★★★ Laetitia Vineyard & Winery Crémant de Noirs San Luis Obispo County

★★★ Laetitia Vineyard & WinerySan Luis Obispo County Elegance Reserve

★★★ Laetitia Vineyard & WinerySan Luis Obispo County Elegance Rosé Reserve

★★★ Mumm Blanc de Noirs Napa Valley

★★★ Mumm Brut Prestige Napa Valley

★★★ Mumm Cuvée Napa Blanc de Blancs Napa Valley

★★★ Roederer Estate Brut Rosé Anderson Valley NV

★★★ Scharffenberger Blanc de Blancs Anderson Valley

★★★ Scharffenberger Brut Mendocino County

★★★ Scharffenberger Brut Rosé Mendocino County

★★★ Schramsberg Vineyards Blanc de Blancs Napa Valley

★★★ Schramsberg Vineyards Blanc de Noirs Napa Valley

★★★ Schramsberg Vineyards Brut Napa Valley

★★★ Schramsberg Vineyards Brut Reserve Napa Valley

★★★ Schramsberg Vineyards Brut Rosé Napa Valley

★★★ Schramsberg Vineyards Crémant Demi-Sec Napa Valley

SYRAH

★★★★★ Araujo Estate Wines Napa Valley Eisele Vineyard

★★★★★ Dehlinger Winery Russian River Valley

★★★★ Arrowood Vineyards & Winery Russian River Valley Saralee's Vineyard

★★★★ Dehlinger Winery Russian River Valley Goldridge Vineyard

★★★★ Hidden Cellars Winery Mendocino

★★★★ Jaffurs Santa Barbara County Thompson Vineyard

★★★★ Kathryn Kennedy Winery Santa Cruz Mountains Maridon Vineyard

★★★★ Lewis Cellars Napa County

★★★★ Neyers Vineyards Napa Valley Hudson Vineyard

★★★★ Joseph Phelps Vineyards Napa Valley Vin du Mistral

★★★★ Qupé Santa Barbara County Bien Nacido Hillside Estate

★★★★ Qupé Santa Barbara County Bien Nacido Reserve

★★★★ Steele Wines Clear Lake

★★★★ Swanson Vineyards Napa Valley

★★★★ Truchard Vineyard Carneros

★★★ Alban Vineyards Edna Valley Alban Estate Reva

★★★ Beaulieu Vineyard Dry Creek Valley Signet Collection

★★★ Beckmen Vineyards Santa Barbara County

★★★ Bedford Thompson Winery & Vineyard Santa Barbara County

★★★ Bonterra Mendocino County

★★★ Cambria Winery & Vineyard Santa Maria Valley Tepusquet Vineyard

★★★ Domaine de la Terre Rouge Shenandoah Valley Sentinel Oak Vineyard

★★★ Domaine de la Terre Rouge Sierra Foothills

★★★ Eberle Winery Paso Robles Fralich

★★★ Eberle Winery Paso Robles Steinbeck

★★★ Edmunds St. John Sonoma County Fenaughty Vineyard

★★★ Edmunds St. John Sonoma Valley Durell Vineyard

★★★ Foxen Vineyard Santa Ynez Valley Morehouse Vineyard

★★★ Daniel Gehrs Wines Paso Robles

★★★ Hamel WinesRussian River Valley

★★★ Havens Wine Cellars Carneros

★★★ Hitching Post Santa Ynez Valley Fess Parker Vineyard

★★★ Jaffurs Santa Barbara County

★★★ Jaffurs Santa Barbara County Bien Nacido Vineyard

★★★ JC Cellars Santa Barbara Mesa Vineyard

★★★ Tobin James Cellars Paso Robles

★★★ Karly Wines Amador County

★★★ Kendall-Jackson Winery California Vintner's Reserve

★★★ Kunde Estate Winery Sonoma Valley

★★★ Kynsi San Luis Obispo County

★★★ Lockwood Vineyard Monterey

★★★ J. Lohr Winery Paso Robles Southridge

★★★ Lonetree Mendocino

★★★ Marietta Cellars California

★★★ McDowell Valley Vineyards Mendocino

★★★ McDowell Valley Vineyards Mendocino McDowell Valley Estate

★★★ Meridian Vineyards Paso Robles

★★★ Milagro Spring Mountain District

★★★ Morgan Winery Monterey

★★★ Andrew Murray Vineyards Santa Ynez Valley Hillside Reserve

★★★ The Ojai Vineyard California

★★★ The Ojai Vineyard California Roll Ranch Vineyard

★★★ The Ojai Vineyard Santa Barbara County Bien Nacido Vineyard

★★★ The Ojai Vineyard Santa Barbara County Stolpman Vineyard

★★★ Fess Parker Santa Barbara County

★★★ Fess Parker Santa Barbara County American Tradition Reserve

★★★ The R.H. Phillips Vineyard Dunnigan Hills EXP

★★★ Preston Vineyards Dry Creek Valley

★★★ Qupé Central Coast

★★★ Rabbit Ridge Vineyards Sonoma County

★★★ Santa Barbara Winery Santa Barbara County

★★★ Selby Winery Sonoma County

★★★ Signorello Vineyards Napa Valley

★★★ Sunstone Vineyards & Winery Santa Barbara County

★★★ Turnbull Wine Cellars Napa Valley Oakville

★★★ Unalii Mendocino

★★★ Wellington Vineyards Russian River Valley Alegria Vineyard

★★★ Zaca Mesa Winery Santa Barbara County

SYRAH BLEND

★★★★ Fife Vineyards Napa Valley Max Cuvée

★★★★ Sine Qua Non Central Coast

★★★★ Sean H. Thackrey & Co. Orion California Old Vines Rossi Vineyards

★★★ Bonny Doon Vineyard Le Cigare Volant California

★★★ Domaine de la Terre Rouge Noir Sierra Foothills

★★★ Domaine de la Terre Rouge Noir Sierra Foothills Grande Année

★★★ Edmunds St. John Les Côtes Sauvages Sonoma/Mendocino

★★★ Jaffurs Cuvée Santa Barbara County

★★★ Qupé Los Olivos Cuvée Santa Barbara County

★★★ Ravenswood Icon Sonoma County

★★★ Treana Winery Paso Robles

★★★ Sean H. Thackrey & Co. Pleiades California Old Vines

★★★ Zaca Mesa Winery Z Cuvée Santa Barbara County

VIOGNIER

★★★★ Gregory Graham Knights Valley

★★★ Beaulieu Vineyard Napa Valley Signet Collection

★★★ Beringer Vineyards Napa Valley

★★★ Bonterra Mendocino County

★★★ Calera Wine Co. Mount Harlan

★★★ Cambria Winery & Vineyard Santa Maria Valley Tepusquet Vineyard

★★★ Domaine de la Terre Rouge Shenandoah Valley

★★★ Foxen Vineyard Santa Ynez Valley Rothberg Vineyard

★★★ Daniel Gehrs Wines Santa Barbara County

★★★ Gregory Graham Napa Valley

★★★ Iron Horse Vineyards Alexander Valley T-T

★★★ Jaffurs Santa Barbara County

★★★ Kunde Estate Winery Sonoma Valley

★★★ La Jota Vineyard Co. Howell Mountain Barrel Fermented

★★★ La Jota Vineyard Co. Howell Mountain Cold Fermented

★★★ Lambert Bridge Winery Dry Creek Valley

★★★ McDowell Valley Vineyards Mendocino

★★★ Fess Parker Santa Barbara County

★★★ Joseph Phelps Vineyards Napa Valley Vin du Mistral

★★★ Preston Vineyards Dry Creek Valley

★★★ Pride Mountain Vineyards Sonoma County

★★★ Testarossa Vineyard Chalone

WHITE BLEND

★★★★★ Caymus Vineyards Conundrum California

★★★ Benziger Family Winery Estate Tribute Sonoma Mountain

★★★ Beringer Vineyards Alluvium Blanc Knights Valley

★★★ The Brander Vineyard Cuvée Natalie Santa Ynez Valley

★★★ The Brander Vineyard Cuvée Nicolas Santa Ynez Valley

★★★ Cosentino Winery The Novelist California Meritage

★★★ de Lorimier Winery Spectrum Meritage Alexander Valley

★★★ Domaine de la Terre Rouge Enigma Sierra Foothills

★★★ Guenoc Winery Meritage Guenoc Valley Langtry

★★★ The Ojai Vineyard Sauvignon Blanc-Sémillon Santa Barbara County

★★★ Pine Ridge Winery Chenin Blanc-Viognier California

★★★ Qupé Chardonnay-Viognier Santa Barbara County Bien Nacido Cuvée

★★★ St. Supéry Vineyard & Winery Meritage Napa Valley Dollarhide Ranch

★★★ Simi Winery Sendal Sonoma County

★★★ Sine Qua Non Central Coast Alban Vineyard

★★★ Spring Mountain Spring Mountain District Miravalle-La Perla-Chevalier

ZINFANDEL

★★★★★ Ridge Vineyards Sonoma Valley Pagani Ranch

★★★★★ J. Rochioli Vineyards Russian River Valley Sodini Vineyard

★★★★★ St. Francis Winery Sonoma Valley Pagani Vineyard Reserve

★★★★★ Turley Wine Cellars Howell Mountain Black-Sears Vineyard

★★★★★ Turley Wine Cellars Napa Valley Aïda Vineyard

★★★★★ Turley Wine Cellars Napa Valley Hayne Vineyard

★★★★★ Williams Selyem Winery Russian River Valley Leno Martinelli Vineyard

★★★★ Alderbrook Vineyards & Winery Russian River Valley Gamba Vineyard

★★★★ Alderbrook Vineyards & Winery Sonoma County George's Vineyards

★★★★ Beaulieu Vineyard Napa Valley Signet Collection

★★★★ Robert Biale Vineyards Napa Valley Aldo's Vineyard

★★★★ Robert Biale Vineyards Sonoma Valley Monte Rosso Vineyard

★★★★ Chateau Potelle Mount Veeder V.G.S.

★★★★ David Coffaro Vineyard & Winery Dry Creek Valley Coffaro Estate Vineyard

★★★★ De Loach Vineyards Russian River Valley O.F.S.

★★★★ Green & Vineyard Napa Valley Chiles Mill Vineyard

★★★★ Greenwood Ridge Vineyards Sonoma County Scherrer Vineyard

★★★★ Haywood Winery Sonoma Valley Los Chamizal Vineyard Rocky Terrace

★★★★ Hidden Cellars Winery Mendocino Eaglepoint Ranch

★★★★ Howell Mountain Vineyards Howell Mountain Beatty Ranch

★★★★ Howell Mountain Vineyards Howell Mountain Black Sears Vineyard

★★★★ Howell Mountain Vineyards Howell Mountain Old Vine

★★★★ JC Cellars Redwood Valley Mendocino Rhodes Vineyard

★★★★ Kunde Estate Winery Sonoma Valley Robusto

★★★★ Limerick Lane CellarsRussian River Valley Collins Vineyard

★★★★ Martinelli Vineyard Russian River Valley Jackass Hill

★★★★ Martinelli Vineyard Russian River Valley Jackass Vineyard

★★★★ Robert Mondavi Winery Napa Valley

★★★★ Niebaum-Coppola Estate Winery Rutherford Edizione Pennino

★★★★ Paradigm Oakville

★★★★ Rabbit Ridge Vineyards Sonoma County OVZ Reserve

★★★★ Rabbit Ridge Vineyards Sonoma County San Lorenzo Reserve

★★★★ Rabbit Ridge Vineyards Sonoma County Winemaker's Grand Reserve

★★★★ A. Rafanelli Winery Dry Creek Valley

★★★★ Ravenswood Napa Valley Dickerson Vineyard

★★★★ Ravenswood Sonoma Valley Cooke

★★★★ Ravenswood Sonoma Valley Monte Rosso

★★★★ Ravenswood Sonoma Valley Old Hill Vineyard Limited Edition

★★★★ Ridge Vineyards Paso Robles Dusi Ranch

★★★★ Rosenblum Cellars Mount Veeder Brandlin Ranch

★★★★ Rosenblum Cellars Napa Valley Hendry Vineyard Reserve

★★★★ Rosenblum Cellars Sonoma Valley Samsel Vineyard Maggie's Reserve

★★★★ Saucelito Canyon Vineyard Arroyo Grande Valley

★★★★ Seghesio Winery Sonoma County Old Vine

★★★★ Steele Wines Clear Lake Catfish Vineyard

★★★★ Steele Wines Mendocino DuPratt Vineyard

★★★★ The Terraces Rutherford

★★★★ Truchard Vineyard Carneros

★★★★ Turley Wine Cellars Alexander Valley Vineyard 101

★★★★ Turley Wine Cellars California Old Vines

★★★★ Turley Wine Cellars Contra Costa Duarte Vineyard

★★★★ Turley Wine Cellars Dry Creek Grist Vineyard

★★★★ Turley Wine Cellars Lodi Spenker Vineyard

★★★★ Turley Wine Cellars Napa Valley Moore Earthquake Vineyard

★★★★ Turley Wine Cellars Napa Valley Tofanelli Vineyard

★★★★ Turley Wine Cellars Napa Valley Whitney Tennessee Vineyard

★★★ Alderbrook Vineyards & Winery Sonoma County OVOC

★★★ Bannister Vineyards Russian River Valley Rochioli Vineyard

★★★ Beaulieu Vineyard Napa Valley

★★★ Behrens & Hitchcock Napa Valley

★★★ Robert Biale Vineyards Napa Valley Falleri Vineyard

★★★ Robert Biale Vineyards Napa Valley Old Crane Ranch

★★★ Robert Biale Vineyards Sonoma Valley Valsecchi Vineyard

★★★ Boeger Winery, Inc. El Dorado Walker Vineyard

★★★ August Briggs Napa Valley

★★★ David Bruce Winery Paso Robles Ranchita Canyon Vineyard

★★★ Buehler Vineyards Napa Valley Estate

★★★ Burgess Cellars Napa Valley

★★★ Cakebread Cellars Howell Mountain

★★★ Oliver Caldwell Cellars Napa Valley Aïda Vineyard

★★★ Chateau Souverain Dry Creek Valley

★★★ Cline Cellars Contra Costa County Ancient Vines

★★★ Cline Cellars Contra Costa County Big Break

★★★ Cline Cellars Contra Costa County Bridgehead

★★★ Cline Cellars Contra Costa County Live Oak

★★★ Cline Cellars Contra Costa County Reserve

★★★ Collier Falls Dry Creek Valley

★★★ Cornerstone Cellars Howell Mountain Beatty Ranch

★★★ Cosentino Winery California CigarZin

★★★ Cosentino Winery California The Zin

★★★ D-Cubed Cellars Howell Mountain

★★★ Dashe Cellars Dry Creek Valley

★★★ De Loach Vineyards Russian River Valley Barbieri Ranch

★★★ De Loach Vineyards Russian River Valley Gambogi Ranch

★★★ De Loach Vineyards Russian River Valley Papera Ranch

★★★ De Loach Vineyards Russian River Valley Pelletti Ranch

★★★ De Loach Vineyards Russian River Valley Saitone Ranch

★★★ De Loach Vineyards Russian River Valley Estate

★★★ Deux Amis Dry Creek Valley Rued Vineyard

★★★ Dickerson Vineyard Napa Valley Limited Reserve

★★★ Dry Creek Vineyard Sonoma County Old Vines

★★★ Dry Creek Vineyard Sonoma County Reserve

★★★ Easton Fiddletown

★★★ Easton Shenandoah Valley

★★★ Eberle Winery Paso Robles Sauret

★★★ Edmeades Vineyards Mendocino

★★★ Edmeades Vineyards Mendocino Ciapusci

★★★ Edmeades Vineyards Mendocino Zeni

★★★ Edmeades Vineyards Russian River Valley Hartford Court

★★★ Edmunds St. John Amador County

★★★ Elyse Wines Howell Mountain

★★★ Elyse Wines Napa Valley Coeur du Val

★★★ Elyse Wines Napa Valley Morisoli Vineyard

★★★ Fanucchi Vineyards Russian River Valley Fanucchi Wood Road Vineyard Old Vine

★★★ Gary Farrell Wines Russian River Valley

★★★ Gary Farrell Wines Russian River Valley Collins Vineyard

★★★ Gary Farrell Wines Sonoma County Old Vine Selection

★★★ Ferrari-Carano Winery Sonoma County

★★★ Fife Vineyards Mendocino

★★★ Fife Vineyards Napa Valley Old Vines

★★★ Fife Vineyards Redwood Valley Redhead Vineyard

★★★ Franciscan Oakville Estate Napa Valley

★★★ Peter Franus Wine Co. Contra Costa County Planchon Vineyard

★★★ Peter Franus Wine Co. Mount Veeder Brandlin Ranch

★★★ Peter Franus Wine Co. Napa Valley Hendry Vineyard

★★★ J. Fritz Dry Creek Valley Old Vine

★★★ J. Fritz Dry Creek Valley Rogers Reserve Eighty-Year-Old Vines

★★★ Frog's Leap Napa Valley

★★★ Gallo of Sonoma Winery Alexander Valley Barrelli Creek Vineyard

★★★ Gallo of Sonoma Winery Dry Creek Valley Chiotti Vineyard

★★★ Gallo of Sonoma Winery Dry Creek Valley Frei Ranch Vineyard

★★★ Gallo of Sonoma Dry Creek Valley Stefani Vineyard

★★★ Gallo of Sonoma Winery Sonoma County

★★★ Green & Vineyard Napa Valley Chiles Valley Vineyard

★★★ Greenwood Ridge Vineyards Mendocino Ridge

★★★ Grgich Hills Cellar Sonoma County

★★★ Hanna Winery Inc. Alexander Valley Pourroy Vineyard Reserve

★★★ Hartford Court Winery Russian River Valley Fanucchi Vineyard

★★★ Hartford Court Winery Russian River Valley Hartford Vineyard

★★★ Haywood Winery Sonoma Valley Los Chamizal Vineyard

★★★ Hendry Ranch Napa Valley Block 7

★★★ The Hess Collection Winery Napa Valley

★★★ Hidden Cellars Winery Mendocino Ford-Hitzman

★★★ Hidden Cellars Winery Mendocino Old Vine

★★★ Hop Kiln Winery Sonoma County

★★★ Hop Kiln Winery Sonoma County Primitivo

★★★ Howell Mountain Vineyards Howell Mountain

★★★ Tobin James Cellars Paso Robles James Gang Reserve

★★★ JC Cellars Russian River Valley Sonoma Alegria Vineyard

★★★ JC Cellars St. Helena Napa Valley Balduc Vineyard

★★★ Karly Wines Amador County Warrior Fires

★★★ Kendall-Jackson Winery California Grand Reserve

★★★ Kenwood Vineyards Geyserville Mazzoni

★★★ Kenwood Vineyards Sonoma Valley

★★★ Kenwood Vineyards Sonoma Valley Nuns Canyon

★★★ La Crema Sonoma Coast Reserve

★★★ Lambert Bridge Winery Dry Creek Valley

★★★ Lamborn Family Vineyards Howell Mountain Lamborn Family Vineyards

★★★ Lolonis Redwood Valley

★★★ Lolonis Redwood Valley Private Reserve

★★★ Lonetree Mendocino

★★★ Lorenza-Lake Napa Valley

★★★ Markham Vineyards Napa Valley

★★★ McIlroy Cellars Russian River Valley Porter Bass Vineyard

★★★ The Meeker Vineyard Dry Creek Valley Gold Leaf Cuvée

★★★ Murphy-Goode Estate WinerySonoma County

★★★ Murrieta's Well Livermore Valley Raboli Vineyard

★★★ Nalle Winery Dry Creek Valley

★★★ Neyers Vineyards Contra Costa County Pato Vineyard

★★★ Peachy Canyon Winery Paso Robles Dusi Ranch

★★★ Peterson Winery Dry Creek Bradford Mountain

★★★ Pezzi King Dry Creek Valley

★★★ Phoenix VineyardsNapa Valley

★★★ Preston Vineyards Dry Creek Valley

★★★ Preston Vineyards Dry Creek Valley Old Vines Old Clones

★★★ Quivira Vineyards Dry Creek Valley

★★★ Rabbit Ridge Vineyards Amador County

★★★ Rabbit Ridge Vineyards Dry Creek Valley Olson Vineyard Reserve

★★★ Rabbit Ridge Vineyards Russian River Valley Hedin Vineyard Reserve

★★★ Rabbit Ridge Vineyards Russian River Valley Rabbit Ridge Ranch Estate Reserve

★★★ Ravenswood Alexander Valley

★★★ Ravenswood Russian River Valley Wood Road Belloni

★★★ Ravenswood Sonoma County

★★★ Renwood Winery Amador County Fox Creek Vineyard Jack Rabbit Flat

★★★ Renwood Winery Amador County Grandmère Vineyard

★★★ Renwood Winery Amador County Grandpère Vineyard

★★★ Renwood Winery Amador County Ice Dessert Wine

★★★ Renwood Winery Amador County Old Vine

★★★ Renwood Winery Fiddletown Eschen Vineyard

★★★ Renwood Winery Fiddletown Old Vine

★★★ Renwood Winery Shenandoah Valley D'Agostini Bros.

★★★ Ridge Vineyards Sonoma County Sonoma Station

★★★ Rocking Horse Howell Mountain

★★★ Rocking Horse Howell Mountain Lamborn Family Vineyard

★★★ Rodney Strong Vineyards Northern Sonoma Old Vines

★★★ Rombauer Vineyards Napa Valley

★★★ Rosenblum Cellars Alexander Valley Harris Kratka Vineyard

★★★ Rosenblum Cellars Contra Costa County

★★★ Rosenblum Cellars Contra Costa County Pato Vineyard Reserve

★★★ Rosenblum Cellars Napa Valley White Cottage Vineyard

★★★ Rosenblum Cellars Paso Robles Richard Sauret Vineyard

★★★ Rosenblum Cellars Redwood Valley Rhodes Vineyard Annette's Reserve

★★★ Rosenblum Cellars Sonoma County

★★★ Rosenblum Cellars Sonoma County Cullinane Vineyard

★★★ Rosenblum Cellars Sonoma County St. Peter's Church

★★★ St. Francis Winery Sonoma County Old Vines

★★★ Santa Barbara Winery Santa Ynez Valley

★★★ V. Sattui Winery Howell Mountain

★★★ V. Sattui Winery St. Helena Suzanne's Vineyard

★★★ Sausal Winery Alexander Valley

★★★ Sausal Winery Alexander Valley Century Vines

★★★ Sausal Winery Alexander Valley Private Reserve

★★★ F. Scherrer Vineyard Alexander Valley Old & Mature Vines

★★★ F. Scherrer Vineyard Alexander Valley The Shale Terrace

★★★ Sebastiani Sonoma Cask CellarsSonoma Valley Domenici

★★★ Seghesio Winery Alexander Valley Home Ranch

★★★ Seghesio Winery Alexander Valley San Lorenzo

★★★ Seghesio Winery Sonoma County Sonoma

★★★ Selby Winery Sonoma County Old Vines

★★★ Shenandoah Vineyards Amador County Special Reserve

★★★ Shenandoah Vineyards Amador County Vintners Selection

★★★ Sierra Vista Winery El Dorado Reeves Vineyard

★★★ Signorello Vineyards Napa Valley

★★★ Steele Wines Mendocino Pacini Vineyard

★★★ Storybook Mountain Vineyards Howell Mountain

★★★ Storybook Mountain Vineyards Napa Valley Estate Eastern Exposures

★★★ Storybook Mountain Vineyards Napa Valley Estate Mayacamas Range

★★★ Storybook Mountain Vineyards Napa Valley Estate Reserve

★★★ Joseph Swan Vineyards Russian River Valley Frati Ranch

★★★ Joseph Swan Vineyards Russian River Valley V.H.S.R. Vineyard

★★★ Joseph Swan Vineyards Russian River Valley Zeigler Vineyard

★★★   Joseph Swan Vineyards Sonoma Valley Stellwagen Vineyard

★★★   Terra d' Oro Amador County

★★★   Tria Dry Creek Valley

★★★   Tria Napa Valley

★★★   Conrad Viano Winery Contra Costa County Sand Rock Hill Reserve Selection

★★★   Villa Mt. Eden Sonoma Valley Monte Rosso Vineyard Grand Reserve

★★★   White Oak Vineyards & Winery Alexander Valley Estate Old Vines

★★★   Whitehall Lane Winery Napa Valley

★★★   Zoom VineyardsContra Costa County Continente Vineyard

ZINFANDEL BLEND

★★★★★ Ridge Vineyards Geyserville Sonoma County

★★★★★ Ridge Vineyards Lytton Springs Dry Creek Valley

★★★★ Viansa Winery Primitivo-Zinfandel Sonoma Valley Prindelo

★★★   Hidden Cellars Winery Sorcery Mendocino

★★★   Vigil Vineyard Zinfandel-Carignane Napa Valley Terra Vin Reserve

OTHER

★★★★ Malbec: Arrowood Vineyards & Winery Sonoma County

★★★   Malvasia Bianca: Morgan Winery Monterey

★★★   Mataro: Ridge Vineyards Contra Costa Bridgehead

★★★   Valdiguié: J. Lohr Winery Monterey County Wild Flower

CALIFORNIA VINTAGE CHART: 1933 TO 1998

1. RECENT VINTAGES

VINTAGE	OVERALL	CABERNET SAUVIGNON	CHARDONNAY	MERLOT	PINOT NOIR	ZINFANDEL
1998	★★★–★★★★	★★★★	★★★★	★★★	★★★	★★★
1997	★★★★★	★★★★★	★★★★★	★★★	★★★	★★★★★
1996	★★★	★★★★	★★★★★	★★★	★★★	★★★
1995	★★★★★	★★★★★	★★★★★	★★★	★★★★★	★★★★★
1994	★★★★★	★★★★★	★★★★★	★★★★	★★★★★	★★★★★
1993	★★★	★★★★	★★★★	★★	★★★	★★★
1992	★★★★	★★★★★	★★★★★	★★★★	★★★★	★★★★
1991	★★★★★	★★★★★	★★★★★	★★★★	★★★★	★★★★★
1990	★★★★★	★★★★★	★★★★★	★★★★	★★★★★	★★★★★
1989	★★	★★★	★★★	★★★	★★	★★
1988	★★	★★	★★★★	★★	★★	★★
1987	★★★★	★★★★★	★★★★	★★★★	★★	★★★★
1986	★★★★	★★★★★	★★★★★	★★★	★★★★	★★★★
1985	★★★★★	★★★★★	★★★★★	★★★★	★★★★	★★★★★
1984	★★★★	★★★★★	★★★★	★★★	★★★★	★★★★
1983	★★	★★	★★	★★★★	★★	★★★
1982	★★	★★	★★	★★★	★★	★★★
1981	★★★	★★★	★★★★	★★★	★★★	★★
1980	★★	★★	★★★	★★	★★★	★★

KEY:

★★★★★ Outstanding ★★★★ Excellent ★★★ Good to Very Good ★★ Average ★ Poor

2. OLDER VINTAGES

1970s

VINTAGE	OVERALL
1979	★★★★
1978	★★★★★
1977	★★★
1976	★★
1975	★★★★
1974	★★★★★
1973	★★★
1972	★
1971	★
1970	★★★★★

1960s

VINTAGE	OVERALL
1969	★★★★
1968	★★★★★
1967	★★
1966	★★★★
1965	★★★
1964	★★★★
1963	★
1962	★
1961	★★
1960	★★★

1950s

VINTAGE	OVERALL
1959	★★★
1958	★★★★★
1957	★★
1956	★★★
1955	★★★
1954	★★★
1953	★
1952	★★★
1951	★★★★★
1950	★★★★

1940s

VINTAGE	OVERALL
1949	★★★
1948	★
1947	★★★
1946	★★★★
1945	★★★★
1944	★★
1943	★★
1942	★★★
1941	★★★★
1940	★★★★

1930s

VINTAGE	OVERALL
1939	★★★
1938	★★
1937	★★★
1936	★★★★
1935	★★
1934	★★★
1933	★★★

KEY:

★★★★★ Outstanding   ★★★★ Excellent   ★★★ Good to Very Good   ★★ Average   ★ Poor

VINEYARD DIRECTORY

❖

This is a listing of the major vineyards in which vineyard-designated wines are grown. It does not include vineyards whose wines are estate grown and bottled (such as Chateau Montelena), unless a separate vineyard designation is used (as in Diamond Creek Gravelly Meadow). The vineyards in this chart typically yield wines that earn a three-star rating or higher.

Key: ★★★★★ Outstanding   ★★★★ Excellent   ★★★ Good to Very Good

RATING	VINEYARD	APPELLATION	ACRES	MAJOR VARIETALS GROWN	WINERIES USED BY
★★★★★	Aïda	Napa Valley	17	Cabernet Sauvignon, Petite Sirah, Zinfandel	Oliver Caldwell Cellars, Turley Wine Cellars
★★★	Alban	Edna Valley	60	Chardonnay, Grenache, Marsanne, Roussanne, Syrah, Viognier	Au Bon Climat, Alban, Cold Heaven, Qupé, Sine Qua Non
★★★★	Aldo's	Napa Valley	9	Zinfandel	Robert Biale Vineyards
★★★★	Alexander Mountain Estate (Gauer Ranch)	Alexander Valley	1,100	Cabernet Franc, Cabernet Sauvignon, Chardonnay, Merlot, Sauvignon Blanc	Canepa, Marcassin, Peter Michael Winery, Mueller, Stonestreet
★★★★★	Allen	Russian River Valley	35	Chardonnay, Pinot Noir	Bannister Winery, Davis Bynum, Gary Farrell Wines, Rochioli, Williams & Selyem Winery
★★★★	Backus	Napa Valley	6.6	Cabernet Sauvignon	Joseph Phelps Vineyards
★★★★★	Bancroft Ranch	Howell Mountain	90	Cabernet Sauvignon, Cabernet Franc, Merlot	Beringer Vineyard
★★★	Barbieri Ranch	Russian River Valley	20	Zinfandel	De Loach Vineyards
★★★	Barrelli Creek	Alexander Valley	610	Barbera, Cabernet Sauvignon, Merlot, Sauvignon Blanc, Zinfandel	Gallo of Sonoma
★★★	Bates Ranch	Santa Cruz Mountains	28	Cabernet Sauvignon, Cabernet Franc, Merlot	Byington, Thunder Mountain, Santa Cruz Mountain
★★★★	Beatty Ranch	Howell Mountain	45	Cabernet Sauvignon, Zinfandel	Cornerstone, Howell Mountain, Vigil
★★★	Bella Oaks	Napa Valley	17	Cabernet Sauvignon	Heitz Wine Cellars
★★★★	Belle Terre	Alexander Valley	110	Cabernet Franc, Cabernet Sauvignon, Chardonnay	Chateau St. Jean
★★★	Belloni	Russian River Valley	10	Zinfandel	Ravenswood Winery
★★★★	Bien Nacido	Santa Maria Valley	826	Barbera, Cabernet Sauvignon, Chardonnay, Merlot, Pinot Blanc, Pinot Gris, Pinot Noir, Syrah	Au Bon Climat, Babcock, Bernardus, Cold Heaven, Gary Farrell, Fetzer Vineyards, Foley, Foxen, Hitching Post, Jaffurs, Longoria, The Ojai Vineyard, Qupé, Stephen Ross, Steele Wines, Lane Tanner, Testarossa, Villa Mt. Eden, Whitcraft
★★★★	Black Sears	Howell Mountain	25	Cabernet Sauvignon, Zinfandel	Cornerstone, Howell Mountain, Turley Wine Cellars
★★★★★	Bosché	Napa Valley	23	Cabernet Sauvignon, Merlot	Freemark Abbey Winery
★★★	Brandlin Ranch	Mount Veeder	12	Zinfandel, Mourvèdre, Charbono, Carignane	Peter Franus
★★★	Briarcrest	Alexander Valley	20	Cabernet Sauvignon	Clos du Bois
★★★★	Brown	Carneros		Pinot Noir	Saintsbury

RATING	VINEYARD	APPELLATION	ACRES	VARIETALS	USED BY
★★★	Calcaire	Alexander Valley	40	Chardonnay	Clos du Bois
★★★★★	Camp Meeting Ridge	Sonoma Coast	23	Chardonnay, Pinot Noir	Flowers, Kistler Vineyards
★★★	Carpy Ranch	Napa Valley	80	Cabernet Sauvignon, Chardonnay, Merlot, Sangiovese, Viognier	Freemark Abbey Winery
★★★★★	Carr	Mount Veeder	16	Chardonnay	Patz & Hall Wine Co.
★★★	Catfish	Clear Lake	12	Zinfandel	Steele Wines
★★★★★	Chabot	Napa Valley	33	Cabernet Sauvignon	Beringer Vineyard
★★★★	Chambers, Richard	Stags Leap District	20	Cabernet Sauvignon, Cabernet Franc, Merlot, Petit Verdot	S. Anderson Vineyard
★★★★	Charles Ranch	Sonoma Coast	20	Chardonnay	Martinelli
★★★	Cherryblock	Sonoma Valley	26	Cabernet Sauvignon	Sebastiani Vineyards
★★★	Chiles Mill	Napa Valley	30	Zinfandel, Petite Sirah, Syrah, Barbera	Green and Red Vineyard
★★★	Ciapusci	Anderson Valley	12	Zinfandel	Edmeades Winery
★★★★	Coastlands	Sonoma Coast	6	Pinot Noir	Williams Selyem
★★★	Collins	Russian River Valley	30	Furmint, Syrah, Zinfandel	Gary Farrell Wines, Limerick Lane
★★★★	Cooke	Sonoma Valley	12	Zinfandel	Ravenswood Winery
★★★★	Cutrer	Sonoma Coast	230	Chardonnay	Sonoma-Cutrer Vineyards
★★★	Diamond Mountain	Napa Valley	123	Cabernet Franc, Cabernet Sauvignon, Merlot	Sterling Vineyards
★★★★★	Diamond T Estate	Monterey County	24	Chardonnay	Robert Talbott Vineyards
★★★★	Dickerson	Napa Valley	18	Cabernet Franc, Cabernet Sauvignon, Merlot, Ruby Cabernet, Zinfandel	Ravenswood Winery
★★★★	Duarte	Contra Costa County		Zinfandel	Turley Wine Cellars
★★★★	DuPratt	Anderson Valley	6	Zinfandel	Greenwood Ridge Vineyards, Steele Wines
★★★★	Durell	Carneros	115	Cabernet Sauvignon, Chardonnay, Merlot, Pinot Noir, Syrah	Chateau St. Jean, Edmunds St. John, Kendall-Jackson, Kistler Vineyards, Steele Wines
★★★★	Dusi Ranch	Paso Robles	40	Zinfandel	Peachy Canyon Winery, Ridge
★★★★★	Dutton Ranch	Russian River Valley	800	Chardonnay, Pinot Noir, Merlot, French Columbard, Syrah, Pinot Gris, Zinfandel	Anderson's Conn Valley, Fritz, Hartford Court, Kistler Vineyards, Merryvale, Rutz, Sebastiani, Sebastopol,
★★★	Eaglepoint	Mendocino	75	Cabernet Sauvignon, Chardonnay, Petite Sirah, Sangiovese, Syrah, Zinfandel	Lonetree, Hidden Cellars, JC Cellars, Fetzer
★★★★★	Eisele	Napa Valley	41	Cabernet Franc, Cabernet Sauvignon, Petite Sirah, Sauvignon Blanc, Syrah, Viognier	Araujo Estate Wines
★★★	Eschen	Fiddletown	35	Zinfandel	Amador Foothill Winery, Renwood
★★★★	Fay	Stags Leap District	66	Cabernet Sauvignon, Merlot, Petit Verdot	Stag's Leap Wine Cellars
★★★★	Ferrington	Anderson Valley	75	Sauvignon Blanc, Pinot Noir	Williams & Selyem Winery
★★★★★	Flowers Ranch	Sonoma Coast	27	Chardonnay, Pinot Noir	Flowers
★★★★	Frei Ranch	Dry Creek Valley	710	Cabernet Sauvignon, Merlot, Zinfandel	Gallo
★★★	Gambogi Ranch	Russian River Valley	12	Zinfandel	De Loach Vineyards
★★★★★	Geyserville	Alexander Valley	36	Carignane, Mataro, Petite Sirah, Zinfandel	Ridge Vineyards
★★★★★	Goldridge	Russian River Valley	7	Pinot Noir	Dehlinger
★★★★	Grandpère	Shenandoah Valley	10	Barbera, Zinfandel	Folie à Deux, Renwood
★★★★★	Gravelly Meadow	Napa Valley	5	Cabernet Sauvignon	Diamond Creek Vineyards
★★★	Gregory	Carneros	15	Cabernet Sauvignon, Merlot	Ravenswood Winery
★★★★	Grist	Dry Creek Valley	70	Zinfandel	Morgan, Turley Wine Cellars
★★★★★	Hayne	Napa Valley	60	Cabernet Sauvignon, Zinfandel, Petite Sirah	Turley Wine Cellars
★★★	Hendry	Napa Valley	118	Cabernet Franc, Cabernet Sauvignon, Chardonnay, Malbec, Merlot, Petit Verdot, Pinot Gris, Pinot Noir, Sauvignon Blanc, Zinfandel	Hendry, Rosenblum Cellars
★★★★★	Herb Lamb	Napa Valley	5	Cabernet Sauvignon	Colgin, Karl Lawrence

RATING	VINEYARD	APPELLATION	ACRES	VARIETALS	USED BY
★★★★	Hirsch	Sonoma Coast	47	Chardonnay, Pinot Noir	Flowers, Kistler Vineyards, Littorai, Siduri, Whitcraft, Whitethorn, Williams Selyem
★★★★★	Hudson	Carneros	182	Cabernet Franc, Chardonnay, Grenache, Merlot, Pinot Gris, Pinot Noir, Syrah, Viognier	Havens Wine Cellars, Jade Mountain, Kistler Vineyards, Kongsgaard, Marcassin, Neyers
★★★★	Hyde	Carneros	134	Cabernet Franc, Cabernet Sauvignon, Chardonnay, Merlot, Sauvignon Musque, Sémillon, Pinot Noir	Paul Hobbs Winery, Kistler Vineyards, Patz & Hall, Ramey, Selene Wines, Whitethorn
★★★★	Jackass Vineyard	Russian River Valley	15	Zinfandel	Martinelli
★★★★	Jensen	Mount Harlan	14	Pinot Noir	Calera Wine Co.
★★★	Julia's	Santa Maria Valley	200	Pinot Noir	Cambria Winery & Vineyard, Foxen, Hitching Post, Lane Tanner
★★★★★	Kistler Vineyards	Sonoma Valley	22	Chardonnay	Kistler Vineyards
★★★	Laguna Ranch	Russian River Valley	360	Chardonnay, Pinot Noir	Gallo of Sonoma
★★★★	La Petite Étoile	Russian River Valley	42	Sauvignon Blanc	Chateau St. Jean
★★★	Ladi's	Sonoma County	13	Cabernet Sauvignon, Merlot	Gary Farrell
★★★★★	Lake	Napa Valley	0.75	Cabernet Sauvignon	Diamond Creek Vineyards
★★★★	Lamb	Napa Valley	10	Cabernet Sauvignon	Fisher Vineyards
★★★★	Leonardini	St. Helena	13	Cabernet Sauvignon, Merlot, Zinfandel, Petite Sirah	Whitehall Lane Winery
★★★★★	Les Pavots	Knights Valley	25	Cabernet Sauvignon	Peter Michael Winery
★★★	London Ranch, Jack	Sonoma Valley	125	Cabernet Franc, Cabernet Sauvignon, Merlot, Pinot Noir, Syrah, Zinfandel	Kenwood Vineyards
★★★★★	Lorenzo	Russian River Valley	10	Chardonnay	Landmark, Marcassin
★★★★	Lytton Springs	Dry Creek Valley	45	Zinfandel, Petite Sirah, Grenache	Ridge Vineyards
★★★★	MacGregor	Edna Valley	60	Chardonnay	Claiborne & Churchill, Mount Eden Vineyards
★★★★★	Madrona Ranch	St. Helena	5	Cabernet Sauvignon	Abreu Vineyards
★★★★★	Marcassin	Sonoma Coast	9	Chardonnay, Pinot Noir	Marcassin
★★★	Marlstone	Alexander Valley	45	Cabernet Sauvignon, Cabernet Franc, Merlot, Malbec, Petit Verdot	Clos du Bois
★★★★	Marston	Spring Mountain	33	Cabernet Sauvignon, Merlot, Syrah	Beringer
★★★★★	Martha's	Napa Valley	34	Cabernet Sauvignon	Heitz Wine Cellars
★★★	Martinelli	Russian River Valley	170	Chardonnay, Gewurztraminer, Pinot Noir, Sauvignon Blanc	Martinelli, Signorello
★★★★★	Maya	Oakville	4	Cabernet Franc, Cabernet Sauvignon	Dalle Valle
★★★★★	McCrea	Sonoma Mountain	30	Chardonnay	Kistler Vineyards
★★★★★	Mer Soleil	Monterey	390	Chardonnay, Marsanne, Roussanne, Sangiovese, Viognier	Mer Soleil, Treana
★★★★	Mills	Mount Harlan	12	Pinot Noir	Calera Wine Co.
★★★★	Moffett	Rutherford	8	Cabernet Sauvignon	Livingston Wines
★★★★★	Monte Bello	Santa Cruz Mountains	59	Cabernet Sauvignon, Cabernet Franc, Merlot, Petit Verdot	Ridge Vineyards
★★★★	Monte Rosso	Sonoma Valley	240	Cabernet Sauvignon, Zinfandel, Malbec, Petit Verdot, Cabernet Franc, Sémillon, Folle Blanche, Muscat	Louis M. Martini Winery, Ravenswood Winery, Robert Biale Vineyards
★★★★★	Moore	Napa Valley	6	Zinfandel	Turley Wine Cellars
★★★★	Morisoli	Rutherford	50	Cabernet Sauvignon, Zinfandel	Whitehall Lane Winery, Elyse Vineyards
★★★★★	Oakville Ranch	Oakville	75	Cabernet Franc, Cabernet Sauvignon, Chardonnay, Merlot	Miner Family Vineyards, Oakville Ranch Vineyards
★★★★★	Octagon	Russian River Valley	2	Pinot Noir	Dehlinger

RATING	VINEYARD	APPELLATION	ACRES	VARIETALS	USED BY
★★★★	Old Hill	Sonoma Valley	10	Zinfandel	Ravenswood Winery
★★★★	Olive Hill	Sonoma Valley	61	Cabernet Sauvignon, Chardonnay, Merlot, Pinot Noir	B.R. Cohn Winery
★★★★	Oliver's Vineyard	Edna Valley	16.5	Chardonnay	Talley
★★★★	Olivet Lane	Russian River Valley	65	Chardonnay, Pinot Noir	Merry Edwards, Kenwood, Olivet Lane, Williams & Selyem Winery
★★★★★	Pagani Ranch	Sonoma Valley	38	Petite Sirah, Mourvèdre, Alicante	Ridge Vineyards
★★★★	Papera Ranch	Russian River Valley	17	Zinfandel	De Loach Vineyards
★★★	Paragon	Edna Valley	560	Chardonnay, Pinot Noir, Sémillon	Carmenet Vineyard, Edna Valley, Nichols
★★★★	Pelletti Ranch	Russian River Valley	9	Zinfandel	De Loach Vineyards
★★★★	Pickberry	Sonoma Mountain	18	Cabernet Sauvignon, Cabernet Franc, Merlot	Ravenswood Winery
★★★★	Pisoni	Santa Lucia Highlands	40	Chardonnay, Pinot Noir, Syrah	Flowers, Peter Michael, Miner Family, Nichols, The Ojai Vineyard, Siduri, Testarossa
★★★★	Porter Bass	Russian River Valley	20	Chardonnay, Pinot Noir, Zinfandel	Flowers, Bannister
★★★★	Precious Mountain	Sonoma Coast		Pinot Noir	Williams Selyem
★★★★★★	Red Rock Terrace	Napa Valley	7	Cabernet Sauvignon	Diamond Creek Vineyards
★★★★★★	Redhead Vineyard	Redwood Valley	13	Petite Sirah, Zinfandel	Fife Vineyard
★★★★	Reed	Mount Harlan	5	Pinot Noir	Calera Wine Co.
★★★★	Rincon	Arroyo Grande	66	Chardonnay, Pinot Noir, Riesling, Sauvignon Blanc	Au Bon Climat, Talley
★★★★★★	Riverblock	Russian River Valley		Pinot Noir	Rochioli
★★★★★★	Rochioli	Russian River Valley	118	Cabernet Sauvignon, Chardonnay, Gamay, Pinot Noir, Sauvignon Blanc	Bannister Winery, Davis Bynum, Castalia, Gary Farrell Wines, Williams & Selyem Winery
★★★	Roll Ranch	Ventura County	7	Syrah, Viognier	The Ojai Vineyard
★★★★★★	Rosemary's	Arroyo Grande	23	Chardonnay, Pinot Noir	Talley
★★★★★★	Sanford & Benedict	Santa Ynez Valley	118	Chardonnay, Pinot Noir	Au Bon Climat, Cold Heaven, Di Bruno, Foxen Vineyard, Hitching Post, Kynsi, Sanford Winery, Whitcraft
★★★★	Sangiacomo	Carneros	1,000	Chardonnay, Merlot, Pinot Noir, Sauvignon Blanc	Benziger, Cale Cellars, Carmenet, Chauffe-Eau, Fetzer, Gundlach Bundschu, Mayo, Rabbit Ridge, Ravenswood, Richardson, Steele Wines
★★★★★	Saralee's	Russian River Valley	275	Chardonnay, Gewürztraminer, Pinot Blanc, Pinot Gris, Syrah, Viognier	Arrowood Vineyards & Winery, Joseph Swan
★★★★	Sauret, Richard	Paso Robles		Zinfandel	Eberle Winery, Rosenblum
★★★★	Scherrer	Alexander Valley	28	Cabernet Sauvignon, Chardonnay, Zinfandel	Greenwood Ridge Vineyards
★★★★	Selleck	Mount Harlan	5	Pinot Noir	Calera Wine Co.
★★★★	Sleepy Hollow	Monterey County	410	Riesling, Pinot Noir, Chardonnay	Arcadian, Monterey Peninsula Winery, Rutz, Talbott
★★★★★	S.L.V.	Stags Leap District	44	Cabernet Sauvignon, Merlot	Stag's Leap Wine Cellars
★★★★★★	South River	Russian River Valley		Chardonnay	Rochioli
★★★	Stanly Ranch	Napa Valley	198	Chardonnay, Pinot Noir, Viognier, Merlot	
★★★	Stefani	Dry Creek Valley	200	Chardonnay, Cabernet Sauvignon, Zinfandel	Gallo of Sonoma
★★★	Stolpman	Santa Barbara County	132	Cabernet Franc, Cabernet Sauvignon, Grenache, Malbec, Merlot, Mourvèdre, Nebbiolo, Sangiovese, Petit Verdot, Roussanne, Syrah, Viognier	Jaffurs, The Ojai Vineyard
★★★★	Stuhlmuller	Alexander Valley	140	Cabernet Sauvignon, Chardonnay	Cronin Vineyards, Stuhlmuller
★★★★	Summa	Sonoma Coast	6	Pinot Noir	Mueller, Williams & Selyem Winery
★★★★	Sycamore	Napa Valley	23	Cabernet Franc, Cabernet Sauvignon, Merlot	Freemark Abbey Winery

RATING	VINEYARD	APPELLATION	ACRES	VARIETALS	USED BY
★★★★	Talley	Arroyo Grande	106	Chardonnay, Pinot Noir	Au Bon Climat, Babcock Vineyards, Nichols, The Ojai Vineyard, Talley
★★★★	Three Palms	Napa Valley	74	Cabernet Franc, Cabernet Sauvignon, Malbec, Merlot, Petit Verdot	Duckhorn Vineyards, Sterling Vineyards
★★★★	To-Kalon	Oakville	550	Cabernet Sauvignon, Cabernet Franc, Merlot, Sauvignon Blanc, Sémillon	Robert Mondavi Winery
★★★★	Tofanelli	Napa Valley	25	Charbono, Chardonnay, Sauvignon Blanc, Sémillon, Zinfandel	Turley Wine Cellars
★★★★	Trailside	Napa Valley		Cabernet Sauvignon	Heitz Wine Cellars
★★★	Van der Kamp	Sonoma Mountain	20	Pinot Noir, Chardonnay, Cabernet Sauvignon, Pinot Meunier	Landmark, Siduri
★★★★★	Vine Hill	Russian River Valley	18	Chardonnay, Pinot Noir	Kistler Vineyards
★★★★	Vineyard 101	Geyserville	2.5	Zinfandel	Turley Wine Cellars
★★★★★	Volcanic Hill	Napa Valley	8	Cabernet Sauvignon	Diamond Creek Vineyards
★★★	Wedding	Sonoma Mountain	8	Cabernet Sauvignon	Fisher Vineyards
★★★	Whitney	Sonoma Mountain	4.5	Chardonnay	Fisher Vineyards
★★★	Winery Lake	Carneros	176	Chardonnay, Merlot, Pinot Noir	Mumm Napa Valley, Sterling
★★★	York Creek	Spring Mountain	22.5	Cabernet Sauvignon, Petite Sirah, Zinfandel	Ridge Vineyards
★★★★★	Young, Robert	Alexander Valley	350	Cabernet Sauvignon, Chardonnay, Merlot, Cabernet Franc, Pinot Blanc, Melón, Syrah, Sauvignon Blanc, White Riesling, Sangiovese, Zinfandel, Viognier	Chateau St. Jean
★★★★	Zeni	Anderson Valley	3	Zinfandel	Edmeades Winery

GLOSSARY

ACETIC ACID: All wines contain acetic acid, or vinegar, but usually the amount is quite small—from 0.03% to 0.06%—and not perceptible to smell or taste. Once table wines reach 0.07% or above, a sweet/sour vinegary smell and taste becomes evident. At low levels, acetic acid can enhance the character of a wine, but at higher levels (over 0.1%), it can become the dominant flavor and is considered a major flaw. A related substance, ethyl acetate, contributes a nail polish-like smell.

ACID: A compound present in all grapes and an essential component of wine that preserves it, enlivens and shapes its flavors and helps prolong its aftertaste. There are four major kinds of acids—tartaric, malic, lactic and citric—found in wine. Acid is identifiable by the crisp, sharp character it imparts to a wine.

ACIDIC: Used to describe wines whose total acid is so high that they taste tart or sour and have a sharp edge on the palate.

ACIDITY: The acidity of a balanced dry table wine is in the range of 0.6% to 0.75% of the wine's volume. It is legal in California to correct deficient acidity by adding acid, although this is often overdone, leading to unusually sharp, acidic wines.

ACRID: Describes a harsh or bitter taste or pungent smell that is due to excess sulfur.

AERATION: The process of letting a wine "breathe" in the open air, or swirling wine in a glass. It's debatable whether aerating bottled wines (mostly reds) improves their quality. Aeration can soften young, tannic wines; it can also fatigue older ones.

AFTERTASTE: The taste or flavors that linger in the mouth after the wine is tasted and spit out or swallowed. The aftertaste or "finish" is the most important factor in judging a wine's character and quality. Great wines have rich, long, complex aftertastes.

AGGRESSIVE: Unpleasantly harsh in taste or texture, usually due to a high level of tannin or acid.

ALCOHOL: Ethyl alcohol, a chemical compound formed by the action of natural or added yeast on the sugar content of grapes during fermentation.

ALCOHOL BY VOLUME: As required by law, wineries must state the alcohol level of a wine on its label. This is usually expressed as a numerical percentage of the volume. For table wines the law allows a 1.5% variation above or below the stated percentage as long as the alcohol does not exceed 14%. Thus, wineries may legally avoid revealing the actual alcohol content of their wines by labeling them as "table wine."

ALCOHOLIC: Used to describe a wine that has too much alcohol for its body and weight, making it unbalanced. A wine with too much alcohol will taste uncharacteristically heavy or hot as a result. This quality is noticeable in aroma and aftertaste.

AMERICAN OAK: Increasingly popular as an alternative to French oak for aging barrels, as quality improves and vintners learn how to treat the wood to meet their needs. Marked by strong vanilla, dill and cedary notes, it is used primarily for aging Cabernet, Merlot and Zinfandel, for which it is the preferred oak. It's less desirable, although used occasionally, for Chardonnay or Pinot Noir. Many wineries use American oak, yet claim to use French oak because of its more prestigious image. American oak barrels sell for about half the cost of French barrels.

AMERICAN VITICULTURAL AREA (AVA): A delimited, geographical grape-growing area that has officially been given appellation status by the Bureau of Alcohol, Tobacco and Firearms. Two examples are Napa Valley and Sonoma Valley. See also VITICULTURAL AREA.

AMPELOGRAPHY: The study of grape varieties.

APPEARANCE: Refers to a wine's clarity, not color.

APPELLATION: Defines the area where a wine's grapes were grown, such as Alexander Valley or Russian River Valley. In order to use an appellation on a California wine label, 85% of the grapes used to make the wine must be grown in the specified district.

AROMA: Traditionally defined as the smell that wine acquires from the grapes and from fermentation. Now it more commonly means the wine's total smell, including changes that resulted from oak aging or that occurred in the bottle—good or bad. "Bouquet" has a similar meaning.

ASTRINGENT: Describes a rough, harsh, puckery feel in the mouth, usually from tannin or high acidity, that red wines (and a few whites) have. When the harshness stands out, the wine is astringent.

AUSTERE: Used to describe relatively hard, high acid wines that lack depth and roundness. Usually said of young wines that need time to soften, or wines that lack richness and body.

AWKWARD: Describes a wine that has poor structure, is clumsy or is out of balance.

BACKBONE: A wine that is full-bodied, well-structured and balanced by a desirable level of acidity is said to have backbone.

BACKWARD: Used to describe a young wine that is less developed than others of its type and class from the same vintage.

BALANCE: A wine has balance when its elements are harmonious and no single element dominates.

BARREL FERMENTED: Denotes wine that has been fermented in small casks (usually 55-gallon oak barrels) instead of larger tanks. Advocates believe that barrel fermentation contributes greater harmony between the oak and the wine, increases body and adds complexity, texture and flavor. Its liabilities are that more labor is required and greater risks are involved. It is being used increasingly with California Chardonnay.

BITE: A marked degree of acidity or tannin. An acid grip in the finish should be more like a zestful tang and is tolerable only in a rich, full-bodied wine.

BITTER: Describes one of the four basic tastes (along with sour, salty and sweet). Some grapes—notably Gewürztraminer and Muscat—often have a noticeable bitter edge to their flavors. Another source of bitterness is tannin or stems. If the bitter quality dominates the wine's flavor or aftertaste, it is considered a fault. In sweet wines a trace of bitterness may complement the flavors. In young red wines it can be a warning signal, as bitterness doesn't always dissipate with age. Normally, a fine, mature wine should not be bitter on the palate.

BLANC DE BLANCS: "White of whites," meaning a white wine made of white grapes, such as Champagne made of Chardonnay.

BLANC DE NOIRS: White wine made of red or black grapes. The juice is squeezed from the grapes and fermented without skin contact. The wine may have a pale pink hue.

BLUNT: Strong in flavor and often alcoholic, but lacking in aromatic interest and development on the palate.

BODY: The impression of weight or fullness on the palate; usually the result of a combination of glycerin, alcohol and sugar. Commonly expressed as full-bodied, medium-bodied or medium-weight, or light-bodied.

BOTRYTIS CINEREA: Called the "noble rot." A beneficial and often highly desirable mold or fungus that attacks grapes under certain climatic conditions and causes them to shrivel, deeply concentrating the flavors, sugar and acid.

BOTTLE SICKNESS: A temporary condition characterized by muted or disjointed fruit flavors. It often occurs immediately after bottling or when wines (usually fragile wines) are shaken in travel. Also called bottle shock. A few days of rest is the cure.

BOTTLED BY: Means the wine could have been purchased ready-made and simply bottled by the brand owner, or made under contract by another winery. When the label reads "produced and bottled by" or "made and bottled by" it means the winery produced the wine from start to finish.

BOUQUET: The smell that a wine develops after it has been bottled and aged. Most appropriate for mature wines that have developed complex flavors beyond basic young fruit and oak aromas.

BRAWNY: Used to describe wines that are hard, intense, tannic and that have raw, woody flavors. The opposite of elegant.

BRIARY: Describes young wines with an earthy or stemmy wild berry character.

BRIGHT: Used for fresh, ripe, zesty, lively young wines with vivid, focused flavors.

BRILLIANT: Describes the appearance of very clear wines with absolutely no visible suspended or particulate matter. Not always a plus, as it can indicate a highly filtered wine.

BRIX: A measurement of the sugar content of grapes, must and wine, indicating the degree of the grapes' ripeness (meaning sugar level) at harvest. Most table-wine grapes are harvested at between 21 and 25 Brix. To get an alcohol conversion level, multiply the stated Brix by .55.

BROWNING: Describes a wine's color, and is a sign that a wine is mature and may be faded. A bad sign in young red (or white) wines, but less significant in older wines. Wines 20 to 30 years old may have a brownish edge yet still be enjoyable.

BRUT: A general term used to designate a relatively dry-finished Champagne or sparkling wine, often the driest wine made by the producer.

BURNT: Describes wines that have an overdone, smoky, toasty or singed edge. Also used to describe overripe grapes.

BUTTERY: Indicates the smell of melted butter or toasty oak. Also a reference to texture, as in "a rich, buttery Chardonnay."

CARBONIC MACERATION: Fermentation of whole, uncrushed grapes in a carbon dioxide atmosphere. In practice, the weight of the upper layers of grapes in a vat will break the skins of the lowest layer; the resultant wine is partly a product of carbonic maceration and partly of traditional fermentation of juice.

CASK NUMBER: A meaningless term sometimes used for special wines, as in Stag's Leap Wine Cellars Cask 23, but often applied to ordinary wines.

CEDARY: Denotes the smell of cedar wood associated with mature Cabernet Sauvignon and Cabernet blends aged in French or American oak.

CELLARED BY: Means the wine was not produced at the winery where it was bottled. It usually indicates that the wine was purchased from another source.

CHAPTALIZATION: The addition of sugar to juice before fermentation, used to boost sugar levels in underripe grapes. Illegal in California.

CHARMAT: Mass production method for sparkling wine. Indicates the wines are fermented in large stainless steel tanks and later drawn off into the bottle under pressure. Also known as "bulk process."

CHEWY: Describes rich, heavy, tannic wines that are full-bodied.

CIGAR BOX: Another descriptor for a cedary aroma.

CLEAN: Fresh on the palate and free of any off-taste. Does not necessarily imply good quality.

CLONE: A group of vines originating from a single, individual plant propagated asexually from a single source. Clones are selected for the unique qualities of the grapes and wines they yield, such as flavor, productivity and adaptability to growing conditions.

CLOSED: Describes wines that are concentrated and have character, yet are shy in intensity.

CLOUDINESS: Lack of clarity to the eye. Fine for old wines with sediment, but it can be a warning signal of protein instability, yeast spoilage or re-fermentation in the bottle in younger wines.

CLOYING: Describes ultra-sweet or sugary wines that lack the balance provided by acid, alcohol, bitterness or intense flavor.

COARSE: Usually refers to texture, and in particular, excessive tannin or oak. Also used to describe harsh bubbles in sparkling wines.

COLD STABILIZATION: A clarification technique in which a wine's temperature is lowered to 32°F, causing the tartrates and other insoluble solids to precipitate.

COMPLEXITY: An element in all great wines and many very good ones; a combination of richness, depth, flavor intensity, focus, balance, harmony and finesse.

CORKED: Describes a wine having the off-putting, musty, molding-newspaper flavor and aroma and dry aftertaste caused by a tainted cork.

CRUSH: Harvest season, when the grapes are picked and crushed.

CUVÉE: A blend or special lot of wine.

DECANTING: A process for separating the sediment from a wine before drinking. Accomplished by slowly and carefully pouring the wine from its bottle into another container.

DELICATE: Used to describe light- to medium-weight wines with good flavors. A desirable quality in wines such as Pinot Noir or Riesling.

DEMI-SEC: In the language of Champagne, a term relating to sweetness. It can be misleading; although demi-sec means half-dry, demi-sec sparkling wines are usually slightly sweet to medium sweet.

DENSE: Describes a wine that has concentrated aromas on the nose and palate. A good sign in young wines.

DEPTH: Describes the complexity and concentration of flavors in a wine, as in a wine with excellent or uncommon depth. Opposite of shallow.

DIRTY: Covers any and all foul, rank, off-putting smells that can occur in a wine, including those caused by bad barrels or corks. A sign of poor winemaking.

DOSAGE: In bottle-fermented sparkling wines, a small amount of wine (usually sweet) that is added back to the bottle once the yeast sediment that collects in the neck of the bottle is removed.

DRY: Having no perceptible taste of sugar. Most wine tasters begin to perceive sugar at levels of 0.5% to 0.7%. For my purposes, I describe as dry any wine with residual sugar of 0.5% or less.

DRYING OUT: Losing fruit (or sweetness in sweet wines) to the extent that acid, alcohol or tannin dominate the taste. At this stage the wine will not improve.

DUMB: Describes a phase young wines undergo when their flavors and aromas are undeveloped. A synonym of closed.

EARLY HARVEST: Denotes a wine made from early-harvested grapes, usually lower than average in alcoholic content or sweetness.

EARTHY: Used to describe both positive and negative

attributes in wine. At its best, a pleasant, clean quality that adds complexity to aroma and flavors. The flip side is a funky, barnyard character that borders on or crosses into dirtiness.

ELEGANT: Used to describe wines of grace, balance and beauty.

EMPTY: Similar to hollow; devoid of flavor and interest.

ENOLOGY: The science and study of winemaking. Also spelled *oenology*.

ESTATE BOTTLED: A term once used by producers for those wines made from vineyards that they owned and that were contiguous to the winery "estate." Today it indicates the winery either owns the vineyard or has a long-term lease to purchase the grapes.

ETHYL ACETATE: A sweet, vinegary smell that often accompanies acetic acid. It exists to some extent in all wines and in small doses can be a plus. When it is strong and smells like nail polish, it's a defect.

EXTRA DRY: A common Champagne term not to be taken literally. Most Champagnes so labeled are sweet.

EXTRACT: Richness and depth of concentration of fruit in a wine. Usually a positive quality, although high-extract wine can also be highly tannic.

FADING: Describes a wine that is losing color, fruit or flavor, usually as a result of age.

FAT: Full-bodied, high-alcohol wines low in acidity give a "fat" impression on the palate. Can be a plus with bold, ripe, rich flavors; can also suggest the wine's structure is suspect.

FERMENTATION: The process by which yeast converts sugar into alcohol and carbon dioxide; turns grape juice into wine.

FIELD BLEND: When a vineyard is planted to several different varieties and the grapes are harvested together to produce a single wine, the wine is called a field blend.

FILTERING: The process of removing particles from wine after fermentation. Most wines unless otherwise labeled are filtered for both clarity and stability.

FINING: A technique for clarifying wine using agents such as bentonite (powdered clay), gelatin or egg whites, which combine with sediment particles and cause them to settle to the bottom, where they can be easily removed.

FINISH: The key to judging a wine's quality is finish, also called aftertaste—a measure of the taste or flavors that linger in the mouth after the wine is tasted. Great wines have rich, long, complex finishes.

FLABBY: Soft, feeble, lacking acidity on the palate.

FLAT: Having low acidity; the next stage after flabby. Can also refer to a sparkling wine that has lost its bubbles.

FLESHY: Soft and smooth in texture, with very little tannin.

FLINTY: A descriptor for extremely dry white wines such as Sauvignon Blanc, whose bouquet is reminiscent of flint struck against steel.

FLORAL (also FLOWERY): Literally, having the characteristic aromas of flowers. Mostly associated with white wines.

FORTIFIED: Denotes a wine whose alcohol content has been increased by the addition of brandy or neutral spirits.

FOXY: A term used to describe the unique musky and grapey character of many native American *labrusca* varieties.

FREE-RUN JUICE: The juice that escapes after the grape skins are crushed or squeezed prior to fermentation.

FRESH: Having a lively, clean and fruity character. An essential for young wines.

FRUITY: Having the aroma and taste of fruit or fruits.

GRACEFUL: Describes a wine that is harmonious and pleasing in a subtle way.

GRAPEY: Characterized by simple flavors and aromas associated with fresh table grapes; distinct from the more complex fruit flavors (currant, black cherry, fig or apricot) found in fine wines.

GRASSY: A signature descriptor for Sauvignon Blanc and a pleasant one unless overbearing and pungent.

GREEN: Tasting of unripe fruit. Wines made from unripe grapes will often possess this quality. Pleasant in Riesling and Gewürztraminer.

GRIP: A welcome firmness of texture, usually from tannin, which helps give definition to wines such as Cabernet and Port.

GROWN, PRODUCED AND BOTTLED: Means the winery handled each aspect of wine growing.

HALF-BOTTLE: Holds 375 milliliters or 3/8 liter.

HARD: Firm; a quality that usually results from high acidity or tannins. Often a descriptor for young red wines.

HARMONIOUS: Well balanced, with no component obtrusive or lacking.

HARSH: Used to describe astringent wines that are tannic or high in alcohol.

HAZY: Used to describe a wine that has small amounts of visible matter. A good quality if a wine is unfined and unfiltered.

HEARTY: Used to describe the full, warm, sometimes rustic qualities found in red wines with high alcohol.

HEADY: Describes high-alcohol wines.

HERBACEOUS: Denotes the taste and smell of herbs in a wine. A plus in many wines such as Sauvignon Blanc, and to a lesser extent Merlot and Cabernet. Herbal is a synonym.

HOLLOW: Lacking in flavor. Describes a wine that has a first taste and a short finish, and lacks depth at mid-palate.

HOT: High alcohol, unbalanced wines that tend to burn with "heat" on the finish are called hot. Acceptable in Port-style wines.

IMPERIAL: An oversized bottle holding six liters; the equivalent of eight standard bottles.

LATE HARVEST: On labels, indicates that a wine was made from grapes picked later than normal and at a higher sugar (Brix) level than normal. Usually associated with botrytized and dessert-style wines.

LEAFY: Describes the slightly herbaceous, vegetal quality reminiscent of leaves. Can be a positive or a negative, depending on whether it adds to or detracts from a wine's flavor.

LEAN: A not necessarily critical term used to describe wines made in an austere style. When used as a term of criticism, it indicates a wine is lacking in fruit.

LEES: Sediment remaining in a barrel or tank during and after fermentation. Often used as in *sur lie* aging, which indicates a wine is aged "on its lees."

LEGS: The viscous droplets that form and ease down the sides of the glass when the wine is swirled.

LENGTH: The amount of time the sensations of taste and aroma persist after swallowing. The longer the better.

LIMOUSIN: A type of oak cask from Limoges, France.

LINGERING: Used to describe the flavor and persistence of flavor in a wine after tasting. When the aftertaste remains on the palate for several seconds, it is said to be lingering.

LIVELY: Describes wines that are fresh and fruity, bright and vivacious.

LUSH: Wines that are high in residual sugar and taste soft or viscous are called lush.

MACERATION: During fermentation, the steeping of the grape skins and solids in the wine, where alcohol acts as a solvent to extract color, tannin and aroma from the skins.

MADE AND BOTTLED BY: Indicates only that the winery crushed, fermented and bottled a minimum of 10% of the wine in the bottle. Very misleading.

MADERIZED: Describes the brownish color and slightly sweet, somewhat carmelized and often nutty character found in mature dessert-style wines.

MAGNUM: An oversized bottle that holds 1.5 liters.

MALIC: Describes the green applelike flavor found in young grapes which diminishes as they ripen and mature.

MALOLACTIC FERMENTATION: A secondary fermentation occurring in most wines, this natural process converts malic acid into softer lactic acid and carbon dioxide, thus reducing the wine's total acidity. Adds complexity to whites such as Chardonnay and softens reds such as Cabernet and Merlot.

MATURE: Ready to drink.

MEATY: Describes red wines that show plenty of concentration and a chewy quality. They may even have an aroma of cooked meat.

MERCAPTANS: An unpleasant, rubbery smell of old sulfur; encountered mainly in very old white wines.

MERITAGE: An invented term, used by California wineries, for Bordeaux-style red and white blended wines. Combines "merit" with "heritage." The term arose out of the need to name wines that didn't meet minimal labeling requirements for varietals (i.e., 75% of the named grape variety). For reds, the grapes allowed are Cabernet Sauvignon, Merlot, Cabernet Franc, Petite Verdot and Malbec; for whites, Sauvignon Blanc and Sémillon. Joseph Phelps Insignia and Flora Springs Trilogy are examples of wines whose blends vary each year, with no one grape dominating.

MÉTHODE CHAMPENOISE: The labor-intensive and costly process whereby wine undergoes a secondary fermentation inside the bottle, creating bubbles.

MURKY: More than deeply colored; lacking brightness, turbid and sometimes a bit swampy. Mainly a fault of red wines.

MUST: The unfermented juice of grapes extracted by crushing or pressing; grape juice in the cask or vat before it is converted into wine.

MUSTY: Having an off-putting moldy or mildewy smell. The result of a wine being made from moldy grapes, stored in improperly cleaned tanks and barrels, or contaminated by a poor cork.

NOBLE ROT: See BOTRYTIS CINEREA.

NOSE: The character of a wine as determined by the olfactory sense. Also called aroma; includes bouquet.

NOUVEAU: A style of light, fruity, youthful red wine bottled and sold as soon as possible. Applies mostly to Beaujolais.

NUTTY: Used to describe oxidized wines. Often a flaw, but when it's close to an oaky flavor it can be a plus.

OAKY: Describes the aroma or taste quality imparted to a wine by the oak barrels or casks in which it was aged. Can be either positive or negative. The terms toasty, vanilla, dill, cedary and smoky indicate the desirable qualities of oak; charred, burnt, green cedar, lumber and plywood describe its unpleasant side.

OFF-DRY: Indicates a slightly sweet wine in which the residual sugar is barely perceptible—0.6% to 1.4%.

OXIDIZED: Describes wine that has been exposed too long to air and taken on a brownish color, losing its freshness and perhaps beginning to smell and taste like Sherry or old apples. Oxidized wines are also called maderized or sherrified.

PEAK: The time when a wine tastes its best. A very subjective term.

PERFUMED: Describes the strong, usually sweet and floral aromas of some white wines.

pH: A chemical measurement of acidity/alkalinity; the higher the pH the weaker the acid. Used by some wineries as a measurement of ripeness in relation to acidity. Low pH wines taste tart and crisp; higher pH wines are more susceptible to bacterial growth. A range of 3.0 to 3.4 is desirable for white wines, while 3.3 to 3.6 is best for reds.

PHYLLOXERA: Tiny aphids or root lice that attack *Vitus vinifera* roots. The disease was widespread in both Europe and California during the late 19th century, and returned to California in the 1980s.

POTENT: Intense and powerful.

PRESS WINE (or PRESSING): The juice extracted under pressure after pressing for white wines and after fermentation for reds. Press wine has more flavor and aroma, deeper color and often more tannins than free-run juice. Wineries often blend a portion of press wine back into the main cuvée for added backbone.

PRIVATE RESERVE: This description, along with Reserve, once stood for the best wines a winery produced, but in the absence of a legal definition many wineries use it or a spin-off (Proprietor's Reserve) for rather ordinary wines. Depending upon the producer, it may still signify excellent quality.

PRODUCED AND BOTTLED BY: Indicates that the winery crushed, fermented and bottled at least 75% of the wine in the bottle.

PRUNY: Having the flavor of overripe, dried-out grapes. Can add complexity in the right dose.

PUCKERY: Describes highly tannic and very dry wines.

PUNGENT: Having a powerful, assertive smell linked to a high level of volatile acidity.

RACKING: The practice of moving wine by hose from one container to another, leaving sediment behind. For aeration or clarification.

RAISINY: Having the taste of raisins from ultra-ripe or overripe grapes. Can be pleasant in small doses in some wines.

RAW: Young and undeveloped. A good descriptor of barrel samples of red wine. Raw wines are often tannic and high in alcohol or acidity.

REDUCED: Commonly used to describe a wine that has not been exposed to air.

RESIDUAL SUGAR: Unfermented grape sugar in a finished wine.

RICH: Wines with generous, full, pleasant flavors, usually sweet and round in nature, are described as rich. In dry wines, richness may be supplied by high alcohol and glycerin, by complex flavors and by an oaky vanilla character. Decidedly sweet wines are also described as rich when the sweetness is backed up by fruity, ripe flavors.

ROBUST: Means full-bodied, intense and vigorous, perhaps a bit overblown.

ROUND: Describes a texture that is smooth, not coarse or tannic.

RUSTIC: Describes wines made by old-fashioned methods or tasting like wines made in an earlier era. Can be a positive quality in distinctive wines that require aging. Can also be a negative quality when used to describe a young, earthy wine that should be fresh and fruity.

SMOKY: Usually an oak barrel byproduct, a smoky quality can add flavor and aromatic complexity to wines.

SOFT: Describes wines low in acid or tannin (sometimes both), making for easy drinking. Opposite of hard.

SPICY: A descriptor for many wines, indicating the presence of spice flavors such as anise, cinnamon, cloves, mint and pepper, which are often present in complex wines.

STALE: Wines that have lost their fresh, youthful qualities are called stale. Opposite of fresh.

STALKY: Smells and tastes of grape stems or has leaf- or hay-like aromas.

STEMMY: Wines fermented too long with the grape stems may develop this quality: an unpleasant and often dominant stemmy aroma and green astringency.

STRUCTURE: The interaction of elements such as acid, tannin, glycerin, alcohol and body as it relates to a wine's texture and mouthfeel. Usually preceded by a modifier, as in "firm structure" or "lacking in structure".

SUBTLE: Describes delicate wines with finesse, or flavors that are understated rather than full-blown and overt.

A positive characteristic.

SUPPLE: Describes texture, mostly with reds, as it relates to tannin, body and oak. A positive characteristic.

SUR LIE: Wines aged *sur lie* are kept in contact with the dead yeast cells and are not racked or otherwise filtered. Adds complexity to Chardonnay and Sauvignon Blanc; can occasionally be overdone and lead to a leesy flavor that is off-putting.

TANKY: Describes dull, dank qualities that show up in wines aged too long in tanks.

TANNIN: The mouth-puckering substance—found mostly in red wines—that is derived primarily from grape skins, seeds and stems, but also from oak barrels. Tannin acts as a natural preservative that helps wine age and develop.

TART: Sharp-tasting because of acidity. Occasionally used as a synonym for acidic.

TARTARIC ACID: The principal acid in wine.

TARTRATES: Harmless crystals of potassium bitartrate that may form in cask or bottle (often on the cork) from the tartaric acid naturally present in wine.

THIN: Lacking body and depth.

TIGHT: Describes a wine's structure, concentration and body, as in a "tightly wound" wine. Closed or compact are similar terms.

TINNY: Metallic tasting.

TIRED: Limp, feeble, lackluster.

TOASTY: Describes a flavor derived from the oak barrels in which wines are aged. Also, a character that sometimes develops in sparkling wines.

VEGETAL: Some wines contain elements in their smell and taste which are reminiscent of plants and vegetables. In Cabernet Sauvignon a small amount of this vegetal quality is said to be part of varietal character. But when the vegetal element takes over, or when it shows up in wines in which it does not belong, those wines are considered flawed. Wine scientists have been able to identify the chemical constituent that makes wines smell like asparagus and bell peppers, but are not sure why it occurs more often in Central Coast vineyards than in others.

VELVETY: Having rich flavor and a silky, sumptuous texture.

VINICULTURE: The science or study of grape production for wine and the making of wine.

VINOUS: Literally means "winelike" and is usually applied to dull wines lacking in distinct varietal character.

VINTAGE DATE: Indicates the year that a wine was made. In order to carry a vintage date, a wine must come from grapes that are be at least 95% from the stated calendar year.

VINTED BY: Largely meaningless phrase that means the winery purchased the wine in bulk from another winery and bottled it.

VINTNER: Translates as wine merchant, but generally indicates a wine producer or winery proprietor.

VINTNER-GROWN: Means wine from a winery-owned

vineyard situated outside the winery's delimited viticultural area.

VITICULTURAL AREA: Defines a legal grape-growing area distinguished by geographical features based on climate, soil, elevation, history and other definable boundaries. In the U.S., a wine must be 85% from grapes grown within the viticultural area to carry the appellation name. For varietal bottling, a minimum of 75% of that wine must be made from the designated grape variety.

VITICULTURE: The cultivation, science and study of grapes.

VOLATILE (or VOLATILE ACIDITY): Describes an excessive and undesirable amount of acidity, which gives a wine a slightly sour, vinegary edge. At very low levels (0.1%), it is largely undetectable; at higher levels it is considered a major defect.

YEAST: Micro-organisms that produce the enzymes which convert sugar to alcohol. Necessary for the fermentation of grape juice into wine.

INDEX